Meeting the Needs of Students with Special Physical and Health Care Needs

Jennifer Leigh Hill

University of Victoria
Victoria, British Columbia
Canada

D1445192

Merrill,
an imprint of Prentice Hall
Upper Saddle River, New Jersey   Columbus, Ohio

Library of Congress Cataloging-in-Publication Data

Hill, Jennifer Leigh.
    Meeting the needs of students with special physical
       and health care needs / Jennifer Leigh Hill.
       p.   cm.
    Includes bibliographical references (p.   ) and index.
    ISBN 0-13-262601-2 (hardcover)
     1. Handicapped students—Health and hygiene—
United States—Handbooks, manuals, etc.
    2. Chronically ill children—Medical care—United
States—Handbooks, manuals, etc.   3. Teachers of
handicapped children—United States—Handbooks,
manuals, etc.   4. Medicine, Physical—Handbooks,
manuals, etc.   I. Title.
    LB3409.U5H55   1999
    371.7'1—dc21   98-26893
                                  CIP

Cover photo: © Tom Hogan/Children's Hospital,
   Columbus, Ohio
Editor: Ann Castel Davis
Production Editor: Sheryl Glicker Langner
Production Coordination: Gail Gavin/The Clarinda
   Company
Design Coordinator: Diane C. Lorenzo
Cover Designer: Tanya Burgess
Production Manager: Laura Messerly
Director of Marketing: Kevin Flanagan
Marketing Manager: Suzanne Stanton
Marketing Coordinator: Krista Groshong

This book was set in Galliard by The Clarinda Company
and was printed and bound by R.R. Donnelley & Sons
Company. The cover was printed by Phoenix Color Corp.

Printed in the United States of America

10 9 8 7 6 5 4 3 2 1

ISBN: 0-13-262601-2

Prentice-Hall International (UK) Limited,London
Prentice-Hall of Australia Pty. Limited, Sydney
Prentice-Hall Canada Inc., Toronto
Prentice-Hall Hispanoamericana, S.A., Mexico
Prentice-Hall of India Private Limited, New Delhi
Prentice-Hall of Japan, Inc., Tokyo
Pearson Education Asia Pte. Ltd., Singapore
Editora Prentice-Hall do Brasil, Ltda., Rio de Janeiro

Dedicated to the memory of Dr. Walter Henry Philip Hill,
my mentor and my father

and to Treena, April, and John,
three students whose short lives touched me
in ways I will never forget

Preface

This book has been written with two groups of people in mind. The first group is the teachers of tomorrow: My purpose in writing this book is to provide you with a greater understanding of the unique children who have special physical and health care needs. I hope that in your course of study and during your student teaching assignments, you will have the opportunity of sharing your lives with children such as Amy, Jennifer, and Darren, who are students you will meet in the first chapter. This book is designed not only to give you basic information about the types of chronic physical and health problems that children in our school systems may be facing, but more importantly, to give you an understanding of how their illnesses or disabling conditions affect their everyday lives. I hope that this will be a book that you keep in your professional library, referring to it often as you work with students who have special needs.

The second group that this book is written for is the teachers of today: My purpose in writing this book is to provide you with up-to-date information on the needs of the students in your school who have experienced periods of poor health or physical adversity and who, in returning to your classroom, require specialized services or accommodations that would have, in some cases, been unheard of twenty years ago. This book is designed to not only give you information that might answer some of your questions, but also to be a starting point in obtaining further information. I hope that you will use this as a reference book, turning to it when you have a particular child in mind and you are looking for suggestions on how to better serve him or her in your classroom. I also hope that this will be a book that you, like the new teacher starting out, choose to keep in your professional library, sharing it with your colleagues who may have the same questions and concerns that you have. The teaching tips given are intended to stimulate discussion on how the needs of these students can be best met on entry or reentry into the system.

This book covers many of the topics found in similar books. However, there are a few features that make it unique. In the introductory part, there is considerable discussion on how physical and health problems not only affect a child, but a child's parents, siblings, community members, and friends. Current legislation is reviewed, and a summary is provided of some of the recent court cases that have had an impact on services to children with special needs. In addition, a brief historical overview of services is given and material is presented, both in the first unit and the last, that may be of assistance in developing both policies and service delivery models.

The remainder of the book is divided into eight units, each covering a specific system of the body. In each unit, information is given on the more common conditions, and although some material is devoted to the cause of a condition, its incidence and prevalence, the typical characteristics, and how that condition is treated, the emphasis is on how the condition affects the child's ability to attend school and how we as teachers can best assist the student, given the limitations that the illness or condition may have placed on the child. In addition to the more commonly recognized chronic physical and health care conditions, this book also discusses those that are such everyday occurrences that they tend to be overlooked in other texts. Examples include lead poisoning, eating disorders, communicable diseases, and a plethora of skin conditions, including scabies, lice, and acne. Practical information, such as how to deal with the common bumps and bruises that occur every day on the playground and how to allergy-proof your classroom, is given, as is information on how to use specialized equipment and how to provide specialized health care procedures in a safe manner.

Acknowledgments

Special thanks to the staff at Prentice Hall, in particular my editor, Ann Davis, and her assistant, Pat Grogg; to Sheryl Langner, production editor; to the staff at The Clarinda Company, in particular Gail Gavin and Cindy Miller; to the staff at Academy Artworks; to Cindy Hake, copyeditor; to John Edeen, book designer; to Deborah Cady, proofreader; and to my colleagues and students at the University of Victoria, especially Nancy Steacy and Priya Mani, both of whom were of great assistance in the final months of editing and revising. Additional thanks to the following reviewers for their assistance in shaping the manuscript into the final product that you see before you: Janis Chadsey-Rusch, University of Illinois; Ann Harrell, Radford University (Virginia); Ann L. Lee, Bloomsburg University of Pennsylvania; Ann Riall, University of Wisconsin, Whitewater; and Charlotte Myles-Nixon, University of Central Oklahoma.

Brief Contents

Contents

Children and Young Adults with Special Physical and Health Care Needs:

Unique Students—Unique Challenges

In the accompanying box, you will read about five children—Sheila, Amy, Jason, Darren, and Jennifer. Each child has a potentially serious physical or medical condition. Looking beyond their health problems, they are children who have parents, grandparents, aunts and uncles, siblings, classmates, and girlfriends or boyfriends. They are each a member of a particular culture, ethnic group, and religion and have hobbies, favorite activities, and chores to complete. Like all children, each of them has basic physiologic needs, including proper nutrition, exercise, adequate rest, and sleep. Most importantly, they need the emotional support of those around them who understand their pain, fear, anxiety, frustration, and, in some cases, anger. With adequate assistance from their parents, friends, and professionals, each of these children may develop into a mature, competent adult.

As you read these passages, consider the impact of having a child with special physical or health care needs in your classroom. Like many teachers, your first reaction may be one of fear. It is not uncommon for people to feel helpless, frustrated, and uncomfortable as they face the unknown. In addition, you may feel a sense of incompetence, for most teachers are trained to work with healthy, vigorous children.

Even though the children in these vignettes have some type of physical or health problem in common, their educational needs vary greatly. Both Jason and Darren have experienced or are experiencing a period of poor health; however, their educational needs are not complex, particularly in comparison to those of Sheila, Amy, and Jennifer. Academically, with extra help from hospital and homebound teaching staff, Jason was able to keep up with his classmates, so that when he returned to school, he did not need any remedial assistance. However, Darren, although he will miss only a week or so of classes, may need some assistance from his teacher to ensure that he is not behind in his lessons. It is not anticipated that there will be any long-term academic consequences of Darren's brief illness. Both Darren and Jason are typical of the children one sees everyday in the general education classrooms of our public and private schools—children who, almost as a fact of life, "catch" all the common childhood illnesses or who injure themselves "just being kids."

In contrast to Darren and Jason, the educational programs of Amy, Sheila, and Jennifer have been or will be greatly affected by their health problems. Sheila, the child born prematurely, has long-term health needs that will continue throughout her education. However, with proper equipment and understanding teachers, she should be able to attend school on a regular basis alongside her peer group and participate in all, or nearly all, of the regular activities offered in the school program. In the past, children like Sheila would probably not have been very welcome in the school system because of the complexity of her condition and the amount of physical care that is required each school day.

Amy, the student with cerebral palsy, has been able to keep up with the other children in the class; however, she has also benefited from regular speech therapy and from an adaptive physical education program. Amy is typical of a child who, in the past, would have been described as "handicapped" or "disabled"—a child who, in all likelihood, would have been placed in a "special" class, away from her able-bodied peers. Jennifer has a chronic condition in which flare-ups are common. Although many children with this disease lead a relatively normal life, in Jennifer's case the kidney involvement is of concern, because it is potentially life-threatening. As a result of joint involvement, Jennifer may have to reconsider her plans to pursue a course in physical therapy. However, her most pressing need at this time is ongoing emotional support from her family, friends, and medical professionals. Her parents have arranged for her to obtain counseling to assist her in dealing with depression. Jennifer is a member of a growing population of children who have long-term special health care needs that result from a serious chronic illness. In the past, many children who, like Jennifer, experienced poor health simply stayed at home, missing out on the opportunity of being with their friends and continuing on in their schooling.

❦ Children with Physical and Medical Challenges: Five Vignettes

Sheila, having just turned 6 years of age, is looking forward to going to school in September with her older sister, Jane. Sheila was born prematurely and only after many months in the hospital was she able to go home. However, as a result of extensive damage to her lungs, Sheila requires oxygen on an almost continuous basis. Despite her respiratory problems, Sheila is just like every other girl her age. She has been attending a local preschool program once a week with her mother, and she particularly enjoys listening to stories and has even learned how to read several dozen words. Sheila's parents never thought that the day would come that she would be able to attend her local school—particularly without her mother in attendance—but she has done so well at the preschool that they are optimistic that she will be able to keep up with her peers in the regular school program. Their biggest concern at this point is that Sheila does not develop too many colds, because she is very susceptible to developing infections in her respiratory system. Even though her teacher is worried about having Sheila in her class, over the summer she and the other staff who will be in contact with her have met on a regular basis to discuss her medical needs. All the staff have taken an extensive first-aid course that included certification in cardiopulmonary resuscitation and have met with the respiratory therapist to ensure that they understand how oxygen is to be administered and what to do in the case of an emergency.

Amy has just entered grade 3. She was born with cerebral palsy. Although she is able to walk, her gait is unsteady. To some, her speech is unintelligible; however, her friends and classmates have no difficulty understanding her because she has been in the same class with them since kindergarten. She receives 3 hours of speech therapy per week. She is fully integrated and is able to keep up academically with the other students in the class. She participates in an adaptive physical education program.

Jason, a grade 5 student, recently broke his leg in a skiing accident. He was in the hospital 2 weeks before returning home. While in the hospital he was able to "attend" school. Each day his homeroom teacher wrote a brief summary of the work accomplished that day and faxed it to the hospital, along with cards from his classmates wishing him a speedy recovery. Each morning Jason went to the hospital classroom for 2 hours. During this time, he worked with the hospital teacher to cover the assignments that his class-mates had completed. He was even able to go to the hospital library and start writing a report on orthopedic injuries that he hoped to present upon his return to school during an upcoming health sciences class. After 2 weeks at home, during which the teacher of homebound stu-dents was able to visit twice a week, Jason returned to school. Luckily his school had an elevator, so getting to and from class on crutches was not too much of a problem. His only major limitation was in terms of physical activities; however, his teachers were able to find alterna-tive activities for him, such as keeping score and being in charge of the equipment, so that he felt that he was a part of the school program. After 3 months, the cast was removed, and after several months of physical therapy (scheduled after school hours), Jason was able to resume all his regular activities, including rejoining the school's soccer team. He can't wait to ski next winter.

Darren's mother just received a phone call from his teacher. Darren is complaining of a headache and a general feeling of malaise, and his forehead feels warm to the touch. Even though there is no obvious swelling in his jaw, his teacher suspects mumps, because he is the third child in the grade 7 classroom who has come down with these symptoms this week. After a period of bed rest, with a diet of soft, bland foods and lots of fluids, Darren will be able to return to school when the symptoms subside, probably in 7 to 10 days.

Continued

🍎 Children with Physical and Medical Challenges: Five Vignettes—cont'd

Jennifer hopes to graduate from high school this spring. She is an "A+" student who is interested in a career in a medical field, perhaps physical therapy. Throughout the fall term, and over the Christmas holidays, she has not been feeling all that well, complaining of "achiness" and stiffness in her joints and general fatigue that makes studying for her final exams difficult. Her parents, concerned about her well-being and her noticeable weight loss, have made an appointment with her doctor. After a series of tests, the doctor has informed Jennifer and her parents that she has systemic lupus erythematosus, a chronic inflammatory disease that can affect many systems of the body, including the renal (kidney) system and the circulatory system. The doctor has prescribed a number of drugs to alleviate the pain and swelling in her joints and has suggested that she talk to her school counselor regarding her condition and its impact on future vocational plans. After a recent flare-up of the condition, during which there were signs of kidney involvement, Jennifer is very depressed and is thinking of quitting school.

CHAPTER 1

Children and Young Adults with Special Physical and Health Care Needs:

An Introduction

KEY WORDS_____

Acute illness	Handicap	Physiologic functioning
Adventitious	Health	Predictability
Chronic illness	Illness	Prevalence
Cognitive functioning	Impairment	Remission
Communication skills	Incidence	Sensory functioning
Course of illness	Limitations	Sequela
Disability	Medically fragile children	Survival
Disease	Mobility	Technology-dependent children
Disorder	Morbidity rate	Uncertainty
Duration	Mortality rate	Visibility
Emotional/social functioning	Onset	Wellness
Exacerbation		

All children are unique and have unique needs, but there are certain commonalities in students who are described as having "physical or medical challenges." First, it is important to remember that each boy or girl should be seen as a child first, then as a pupil who happens to have a special health care need (Lehr, 1990; Potter, 1987). While many may view children with long-term needs as being "sick," those working with these students should attempt to recognize them as individuals who may need to use health care support in order to maintain their health (Lehr & McDaid, 1993). The child who requires a respirator should be considered simply as a child who breathes in a different manner than most children; similarly a child who is fed by means of a gastrostomy tube that is surgically implanted in the child's stomach is merely a child who eats in a manner that differs from the norm (Lehr & McDaid).

Second, it is important for teachers to recognize that children with physical or medical problems are, in most cases, more similar to their peers who are experiencing good health than they are different. A 6-year-old child with diabetes is more like his or her friends who are of the same age than a 10-year-old or 15-year-old child with the same condition. It is probable that his or her favorite activities are identical to any other child of the same age and that, like all other 6-year-olds, he or she is excited about starting school, meeting new friends, and learning to read and write.

Third, it is important for educators to focus on the person behind the condition rather than on the condition itself, and in doing so, to treat the child as normally as possible (Potter, 1987). However, the disease or disorder cannot be totally ignored, nor would it be proper to do so. Van Eys (1977), when discussing a child with cancer, made the following observation:

> The child with cancer is just that, nothing more or less. He is not a normal child who has a cancer that can be removed without any trace, nor is he a child who labors under a burden that should be constantly lifted from him as the overwhelming focus of his care. The child should be accepted for what he is, a child with cancer, who would be a different person if the cancer suddenly did not exist or if the memory were suddenly erased. (p.166)

Finally, because of the similarities, children with chronic physical and medical conditions are usually best served in the general education classroom, alongside their friends, as long as their health permits, rather than in a segregated setting with other children who have similar or even different special health care needs. However, for them to succeed in the classroom, certain accommodations may need to be made. For some children with special physical or health care needs, the need may be as simple as having a special standing frame to facilitate working together with their classmates or having medication to be administered on a regular basis; for others, the need may be as complex as having a head pointer to access an adapted computer or a ventilator to assure air movement in and out of their lungs.

Throughout this text all children who have special health care needs will be referred to as children first—children who happen to have a specific disease or disorder. Even though all children with hemophilia have certain characteristics as a result of the condition, each child is different and has different medical, developmental, and educational needs. In this text, the student who has this particular bleeding disorder will not be referred to as "a hemophiliac" or a "bleeder," but rather, as "a child with hemophilia" or "student with hemophilia," putting the individual first and foremost in the reader's mind. In addition, although the impact of a chronic physical or medical condition on a child and the child's family may be considerable, terms that may have a negative connotation, such as "victim" or "sufferer," will not be used to describe children with special health care needs or their families. Similarly, children who use a wheelchair in order to navigate their surroundings will not be described as being "confined to a chair" or "wheelchair-bound" because a wheelchair is, in fact, a device that "liberates" children so that they can explore their environment with children who do not have a motoric problem.

This book focuses on a unique group of children, those with long-term health care needs, which result in most cases from either a permanent physical condition or from a chronic illness, and who are attending school during periods of relatively good health—children like Sheila, Amy, and Jennifer, who, as a result of their needs, require an understanding teacher who is willing to accept the challenge. Unfortunately, many educators often report that they are inadequately trained to meet the needs of these children (Izen & Brown, 1991; Johnson, Lubker, & Fowler, 1988; Lynch, Lewis, & Murphy, 1993; Parette, Bartlett, & Holder-Brown, 1994) and that they are overwhelmed by the knowledge that a child with a chronic condition, having special health care needs, will be part of their classroom, fearing for the safety of the child and their own liability (Caldwell & Sirvis,

1991). The purpose of this book is to provide information on the more common chronic conditions found in students having special physical or medical needs, in an attempt to lessen the fears of those working with these children. Throughout the text, suggestions on how educators can best support the integration of children who have physical and medical challenges are presented. With appropriate accommodations, all children with health care needs should be able to take their rightful place in their school and become fully participating members of their class.

Reverend Robert K. Massie, Jr., a young man who has struggled throughout life with severe hemophilia and persistent arthritis, perhaps best described some of the turmoil experienced by children with chronic conditions in his article entitled "The Constant Shadow: Reflections on the Life of a Chronically Ill Child" (1985). He offered a simple but effective solution to some of the problems these children may face, particularly appropriate for individuals working in educational settings:

> Chronic illness is a constant and sometimes overwhelming companion, a shadow both inseparable and eternal . . . [which] . . . creates a tremendous need in the patient—child or adult—for a group of supportive and caring human beings who show by their words and actions that they will stay with the patient through the physical and emotional roller-coaster ride of disease . . . The greatest burden for a chronically ill child is not the pain, the anguish, or the disappointment; it is the wall of emotional isolation with which we have encircled that child because of our own fears. We must look inside ourselves, face those fears, and despite them, reach out. Only the power of a warm heart can alleviate the deep chill of a child's constant shadow. (pp. 14, 22–23)

In commenting on this excerpt, Jessop and Stein (1989) made the following succinct observation: "It is not enough for individual people to be warm—political, professional, and institutional programs and systems must be more responsive as well" (p. 72). This book is also written for administrators and other support staff who may be in direct contact with children who have a disabling condition.

This chapter introduces the reader to some of the common terminology used to describe the population of children who have physical and medical needs. A noncategorical classification system is discussed and information related to the incidence and prevalence of children with chronic conditions is presented so that readers may develop an understanding of the number of children whose needs must be met within the educational system.

Com[...]
Character[...]

In the medical litera[...] to describe children who [...] condition. Some have a very s[...] are used somewhat interchangeabl[...] few of the more common terms are d[...]

Children who have physical or medical n[...] erally are not experiencing or have not experie[...] good health. **Health** is a state of physical, mental, and social well-being, occurring concomitantly with the absence of disease or any other abnormal condition (*Mosby's*, 1994). Health is often thought of as being on a continuum, with **wellness**, the highest level of optimum health, being at one end, and **illness**, the state of diminished or impaired health, at the other. The term **morbidity** is used to refer to the state of being ill, and the rate at which a sickness occurs is referred to as the **morbidity rate** (*Webster's*, 1996). Morbidity rate should not be confused with **mortality rate**, also known as the **death rate** (i.e., the number of deaths in a given time or place).

Children who have a **chronic illness** have some type of condition that typically (1) interferes with day-to-day functioning for more than 3 months in a year, (2) results in hospitalization for more than 1 month in a year, or (3) at time of diagnosis, is likely to result in either of these states (Perrin, 1985). All children who have a chronic condition either have some type of disease (e.g., rheumatic fever, ringworm, AIDS) or disorder (e.g., hemophilia, cerebral palsy, diabetes) that affects the normal functioning of the body. A **disease** is defined as "an impairment of the normal state of the living body or one of its parts that interrupts or modifies the performance of the vital functions and is a response to environmental factors (as malnutrition), to specific infective agents (as viruses), to inherent defects of the organism (as genetic anomalies), or to combinations of these factors" (*Webster's*, 1996, p. 181). A **disorder** is a more global term, referring to any "abnormal physical or mental condition" (*Webster's*, 1996, p. 182).

The term **impairment** is often used by medical personnel to refer to an abnormality that affects the ability of the individual to participate in activities that are considered "normal" for the individual's particular age group (*Mosby's*, 1994). Used in this manner, an impairment is similar to a disorder; however, some use the term to refer only to those conditions that and Young Adults with Special Physical and Health Care

Chronic vs. Acute Conditions and
...on Definitions and
...tics

...have a number of terms are used
...have a physical or medical
...In this section; others
...In this section a
...fined.
...eds gen-
...ced

...require a
...prevention of
...n the role of the
medi... ...t" children from becoming disa... ...t place (e.g., through the
provision of immu... ...tion programs or by means of
genetic engineering) or to "treat" those who are ill
so that they do not become disabled (e.g., through
the development of new surgical and medical techniques); it is the role of the educational system to
prevent a child who may have a disability from becoming handicapped (e.g., through the provision of
supportive services, such as special education programs and specialized therapies). In many cases, the
handicap results from the actions of others. The role
of society is to ensure that architectural or environmental barriers are removed so that persons with a
disability are able to participate in activities that are
of interest to them. Curb cuts, entrance and exit
ramps, and lift-equipped transportation, for example, are three common methods to ensure that those
who are in a wheelchair have access to their community alongside their able-bodied peers.

Chronic conditions typically require lifelong
follow-up care because they are ever present or may
recur sporadically (Jackson & Saunders, 1993;
Lubkin, 1986; Travis, 1976). Some children are born
with a chronic condition; others may develop the
problem in later life. Typically, children with chronic
illnesses are admitted to the hospital at the time of initial onset of the disease for a diagnosis and initiation
of a treatment plan. With certain chronic conditions,
the child may be readmitted to the hospital periodically if the illness enters an acute stage. The term **exacerbation** is used to refer to the increased seriousness
and intensity of the symptoms of a particular disease
during an acute stage of the condition (*Mosby's,*

Jennifer, who is described in the introductory
...n, has a chronic illness that is marked by acute
...des of the condition, sometimes referred to as
...**s events** or **flare-ups.** If she continues her
...hooling at the post-secondary level, she may need
...ertain accommodations, such as extensions on assignments, to ensure that she gets the necessary bed
rest to regain her strength during exacerbations.

The term **remission** is used to refer to the period
in which the symptoms of a chronic condition have
partially or completely disappeared (*Mosby's,* 1994).
As mentioned previously, chronic conditions are
generally thought to last a lifetime; however, if a
child goes into remission that appears to be permanent (i.e., no sign of the disease for a lengthy period), the child is considered "cured." Unfortunately, for many children with a chronic condition, a
cure, or a state of complete recovery, may not be
possible. For them, the goal of treatment is management and control of the illness (Larson, 1986).
Treatment should lessen symptoms or lengthen periods between exacerbations.

The term **acute** is generally given to a condition in
which change occurs over a short period of time, coming to a peak before it subsides. Included in this category are illnesses that range from common childhood
upsets, such as a cold or the flu, to serious diseases,
such as meningitis or pneumonia. Darren, the child
with mumps described in the introductory section, is
an example of a child with an acute viral infection. The
goal of treatment for an acute illness is the complete
elimination of the symptoms of the disease (Jackson &
Saunders, 1993). In most cases, children who have
had acute illnesses are expected to return to school
with no further health care needs (Kleinberg, 1982).

The term acute is also used to refer to conditions
that may arise as a result of some form of trauma, for
example, the physical injury experienced by Jason
while he was skiing. Some traumatic injuries (e.g.,
closed head injuries resulting from motor vehicle or bicycle accidents) may result in protracted medical problems that affect the child throughout schooling. The
term **sequelae** (pl.; **sequela,** sing.), from the Latin, *se-
qui,* meaning "to follow," is often used to refer to the
aftereffects of a particular disease or injury (e.g., facial
scarring that results from burns to the head) or of some
type of procedure or treatment (e.g., loss of hearing
from administration of quinine) (*Mosby's,* 1994). Sequelae can result from either chronic or acute conditions. There is not necessarily a direct correlation between the severity of illness and the severity of the
sequelae. Some children with a moderately severe

condition may face few consequences, whereas some children with a very limited disability may be severely affected (Perrin & MacLean, 1988). For example, although most people would tend to think of epilepsy as a serious neurologic disorder, many children with this condition in good control have full lives and are able to attend school regularly with few limitations; however, children with asthma, a respiratory condition that can be quite mild, may experience a lifetime of restrictions (e.g., limitations on travel and activities).

🖤 A Classification System for Describing Chronic Conditions: A Noncategorical Approach

It is not uncommon for children with chronic conditions to be "grouped" together into various categories, such as "physically handicapped" or "health impaired," on the basis of the underlying cause of the child's problem. However, Stein and Jessop (1982),

al. (
proach
ical or med
gorical, partial c
method takes into a
shared physiologic and
that may influence the attitu
with the children, the delivery of s
velopment of public policy, as well as
efforts (Perrin et al., 1993). These charact
discussed in greater detail in subsequent chapte
are only briefly mentioned here to introduce concep
and terminology. The characteristics, as shown in Figure 1.1, are often viewed as a series of continua, ranging from mild to profound.

Duration

Most health problems can be divided into two groups: brief and lengthy. In most cases, acute

Figure 1.1
Dimensions for Describing a Child with a Chronic Condition

A. Duration	Brief ←	→ Lengthy
B. Age of onset	Congenital ←	→ Acquired
C. Limitation of age-appropriate activities	None ←	→ Unable to conduct
D. Visibility	Not visible ←	→ Highly visible
E. Expected survival	Usual longevity ←	→ Immediate threat to life
F. Mobility	Not impaired ←	→ Extremely impaired
G. Physiologic functioning	Not impaired ←	→ Extremely impaired
H. Cognition	Normal ←	→ Extremely impaired
I. Emotional/Social	Normal ←	→ Extremely impaired
J. Sensory functioning	Not impaired ←	→ Extremely impaired
K. Communication	Not impaired ←	→ Extremely impaired
L. Course	Stable ←	→ Progressive
M. Uncertainty	Episodic ←	→ Predictable

Source: Perrin, E. C., Newacheck, P., Pless, B., Drotar, D., Gortmaker, S. L., Leventhal, J; Perrin, J. M., Stein, R. E. K., Walker, D. K., & Weitzman, M. (1993). Issues involved in the definition and classification of chronic health conditions. Reproduced by permission of *Pediatrics,* Vol. 91, pages 787-793, 1993.

Pless and Perrin (1985), have promoted the use of a differential, or genetic approach, cant some of the characteristics future research

A **self-limi**... ...s one that resolves without treatment. Typically, the duration is short; however, in some diseases, the symptoms take longer to disappear. An example of a self-limited disease is rubella, or German measles, in which the symptoms last 2 to 3 days and then disappear, regardless of any form of treatment.

Although it should be easy to distinguish between chronic and acute conditions, such is not always the case. In some situations, the time of onset may be unknown; in others, there may be a long period between onset of symptoms and diagnosis of disease. Some conditions are not likely to result in long-term illness, even though the condition may have a protracted course (e.g., traumatic injury to a limb). Certain recurrent acute illnesses are characterized by brief episodes that occur on a frequent basis (e.g., migraine headaches), and some conditions can be corrected surgically but may still require continued follow-up (e.g., heart defects). Perrin and his colleagues (1993) have suggested that by extending the cutoff for a chronic condition from 3 to 12 months, some of the problems outlined above may be eliminated. However, they have also pointed out that such an approach lacks a strong theoretical basis.

Age of Onset

Age of onset or age at acquisition refers to the age at which the child developed the condition. Some conditions, such as sickle cell anemia, are **congenital**

(at birth), whereas others, such as leukemia, **...quired** or are **adventitious** (develop later in ...ome, but by no means all, congenital diseases ...nditions are **genetic disorders** (inherited from ...individual's mother or father or both). Genetic ...orders are also called **hereditary disorders** or **in...erited disorders.**

Some late-onset conditions may, in fact, be inherited disorders. For example, diabetes mellitus, a metabolic disorder that results in high levels of sugar in the bloodstream, has been found to occur in certain families more often than would be expected by chance. Although there has been no solid evidence that diabetes is a genetic disorder, it is often referred to as a **familial condition** (i.e., more likely to be found in one family than another or in more family members than expected).

In acquired conditions, age of onset is compounded by type of onset. In some conditions, the onset is gradual (e.g., a brain tumor that slowly affects motor skills); in others, the onset is sudden (e.g., a child with epilepsy who has the first seizure at age 10).

Limitation of Age-Appropriate Activities

Some children may find that their physical or medical condition imposes few, if any, limits or restrictions on their activities, but others may find that they are unable to participate as fully as they might prefer. For example, those children who tire easily (e.g., children with leukemia) may not be able to enjoy after-school activities, such as "hanging out" at the local mall, and consequently, may feel separated from their peers.

The degree of **severity** is often used to describe the limitation imposed by various illnesses. Often, in describing the impact of illness on children and their lifestyles, the terms "mild," "moderate," "severe," and "profound" are used to rate the degree of restriction of a condition on the life of the child.

Visibility

In some children, chronic conditions are not easily recognized because the problem is **invisible.** Invisible conditions include asthma, cardiac diseases, cystic fibrosis, diabetes, epilepsy, and renal disease. Children with such conditions appear healthy until they start to wheeze or cough, become exceedingly weak, have pain, or have a seizure. In contrast,

visible conditions are easily noticed. Visible conditions include arthritis, burns, cerebral palsy, and spina bifida.

In some cases, the "condition" per se is not visible, but the necessary special orthopedic appliances (e.g., wheelchairs, braces or splints, crutches), special equipment (e.g., adapted tables, modified toilets, respirators), or special devices to decrease injury (e.g., helmets) are obvious to those around the child. For some children, particularly those attending school, the special services that they receive (e.g., therapy sessions for which the child is "pulled out" from the classroom) may attract attention, rather than the physical or medical disorder itself.

Expected Survival

Some conditions, such as certain forms of cancer or brain tumors, are considered to be **life-threatening,** whereas others, such as recurrent otitis media (middle ear infection), are not. Children with **non–life-threatening** illness are generally expected to have a normal life expectancy; however, some conditions, such as asthma and epilepsy, which are considered by many to be primarily non–life-threatening, may result in death (e.g., an acute asthma attack that results in respiratory failure or severe seizure that results in asphyxiation). Consequently, the life span is shorter than originally anticipated.

Great strides recently have been made in treatment of chronic conditions. In fact, it has been estimated that 80% of all children with a chronic illness will survive into their adult years. In commenting on this statistic, Perrin and MacLean (1988, p. 1327) said: "Much (but not all) of the achievable improvement in mortality already has occurred. The clinical corollary is that greater attention must now go to the morbidity of long-term illness."

Mobility

Some conditions have a significant (real or perceived) impact on the student's ability to travel freely in the environment. Illnesses that impair mobility (e.g., cardiac disorders) may prevent children from participating in certain activities, such as sports, normally enjoyed by their peers. Many children with a physical disorder find that their resultant condition severely affects their overall ability to explore and experience their environment.

Physiologic Functioning

Often, chronic conditions are classified according to the organ or the organ system most directly involved (e.g., heart disease or disease of the cardiovascular system). However, this approach is compounded by the fact that many chronic conditions affect more than one organ (e.g., heart problems cause respiratory difficulty; neurologic problems affect the urinary system). In general, if more than one organ system is involved, the effects of the condition on the overall health status and on body function are greater. However, some diseases of a single organ system (e.g., congenital heart problems) may be immediately life-threatening, whereas diseases that involve multiple organ systems (e.g., cystic fibrosis) may result in periods of relative health for many decades.

Cognitive Functioning

Some children with certain chronic conditions may have impaired cognitive (intellectual) functioning. However, most children with chronic physical or medical conditions have normal intelligence. Children who have a chronic health condition *and* a cognitive deficit are often described as having mild, moderate, severe, or profound impairments on the basis of the cumulative impact of the concomitant problems. In school, children who have a chronic physical or medical problem and who are cognitively delayed have different needs than those of normal intelligence.

Emotional/Social Functioning

For children with chronic physical or medical challenges, there may be emotional and social implications to their condition. A child who misses a great deal of school may feel isolated and lonely; a child who is missing a limb may have an altered body image and poor self-esteem. The **self-concept,** i.e., the "composite of ideas, feelings, and attitudes that a person has about his or her own identity, worth, capabilities, and limitations" (*Mosby's,* 1994, p. 1414), of a child who is ill is often affected by the attitudes and opinions held by others.

Sensory Functioning

Children with chronic problems may experience a loss of sensory functioning, e.g., the child who, as a result of chronic ear infections, develops a significant hearing loss, or the child with diabetes in whom diabetic retinopathy develops, which results in a loss of visual acuity. Children who have the combination of a chronic condition *and* a loss of sensory acuity are often also rated as having mild, moderate, severe, or profound impairments on the basis of the cumulative impact of their multiple problems. A child who is blind and has well-controlled diabetes, for example, may be less severely impaired than a child who is both blind and on a ventilator.

Communication Skills

Some children with chronic physical or medical conditions have difficulty in the area of communicating their wants and needs. For example, a child with chronic respiratory problems who requires a tracheostomy to facilitate breathing has difficulty communicating **vocally** (i.e., using the speech mechanisms of the body). As a result of the surgical intervention, he or she may need to learn an alternative form of communication (e.g., sign language) in order to be understood **verbally** (i.e., using words).

Course of Illness

Some conditions are described as being static, others as being dynamic. A **static condition,** or one that remains fairly stable over time, differs markedly from a **dynamic disorder,** in which there is change over time. Dynamic disorders can be further differentiated into three groups: (1) those that improve (e.g., Legg-Calvé-Perthes disease, a disorder that results in the degeneration of the head of the thigh bone in children, which improves over time as the bone regenerates, to the point that there is sometimes full recovery), (2) those that deteriorate (e.g., AIDS, certain forms of cancer), and (3) those that fluctuate (i.e., those that are marked by exacerbations, which result in the child moving from a state of relative health to a state of illness and back again, such as systemic lupus erythematosus). Deteriorating conditions are often referred to as being progressive. One of the more common degenerative diseases of childhood is muscular dystrophy, a neuromotor impairment that is marked by progressive atrophy or weakening of certain groups of skeletal muscles.

Not only does the course of the condition differ from person to person and from disease to disease, the amount of medical supervision and treatment required during the course of the illness also varies greatly. Some conditions require very little intervention, whereas others may require very aggressive and intensive treatment over a short or long period.

Uncertainty or Predictability

Diseases in which symptoms occur on an irregular basis are often referred to as **episodic conditions.** Such conditions differ greatly from those in which symptoms have a more regular occurrence, or are **predictable.** Some conditions, such as asthma and epilepsy, can be both episodic *and* predictable given the nature of the illness and, in some cases, the response to treatment. Some children with asthma have irregular asthma episodes, whereas others may have daily attacks. Similarly, some children with epilepsy may be "seizure-free" for long periods, whereas others may have repeated seizures over a short period.

"Combinations" of Characteristics

The various groupings described above are neither exhaustive nor mutually exclusive (Harkins, 1994; Perrin et al., 1993). A child may have a condition that is invisible *and* life-threatening (e.g., a child with a brain tumor) or a condition that is visible but non–life-threatening (e.g., a child with juvenile rheumatoid arthritis). Additionally, the categories can change over time (Harkins). For example, before the middle of the twentieth century, every child with leukemia was considered to have a life-threatening disease. With the advent of drugs in the 1940s that, in many cases, resulted in the remission of the disease, leukemia no longer always results in death. In fact, 75% of children with acute lymphocytic leukemia, the most common childhood leukemia, survive 5 or more years after initial treatment (Waskerwitz, 1994).

❦ Classification Systems for Describing Chronic Conditions: Educational Terminology

Terms used in medical literature do not always correspond to terms used in educational literature. In this section, some of the more commonly used educational terms are defined. Legal definitions included in U.S. Public Laws 94-142, 101-476, and 105-17 are presented in chapter 2.

Children with chronic illnesses or disabling conditions are frequently referred to in the educational literature in a very general manner. One of the most common terms is **students with special health care needs** (or **SSHCN**). Koenning and her colleagues at Texas Children's Hospital (1995, p. 119) proposed the following operational definition for this group: "SSHCN have a broad range of chronic illnesses which may require adaptation in the regular school environment for daily functioning, prolonged or periodic hospitalizations, and/or the delivery of health services at home and school."

Historically, children with physical disabilities and children with health problems have been grouped together, because both populations have limitations that interfere with school attendance or learning to the point that special services, training, equipment, materials, or facilities may be required (Hallahan & Kauffman, 1994). Until recently, the term **crippled and other health impaired (COHI)** has been used commonly by the educational system to categorize these two groups. While the term "crippled" has been replaced with the more global term "physically disabled" or the more specific term "orthopedically impaired,"[1] the term "other health impaired" (or simply "health impaired") continues to be part of the English lexicon.

The term **medically fragile** is a recent addition to the educational literature on children with health care needs. However, it is a term that has proven difficult to define. For many, the phrase refers to a state, which is often transitory, rather than a specific condition (Caldwell & Sirvis, 1991). Typically included in this diverse group are those children who have a temporary medical crisis, those who are consistently fragile, and those whose health continues to deteriorate to a life-threatening point. These are the children who, in the past, would have most likely spent long periods in the hospital or at home as a result of their complex and extreme health needs.

The Council for Exceptional Children (1988), which prefers the term "students with specialized health care needs" to "medically fragile," offers a broad-based functional definition that refers to these children as requiring "specialized technological health care procedures for life support and/or health support during the school day" (p. 1). In defining this group of children, the term "medically fragile" is used by some to refer to a subset of children who are **technology-dependent** (i.e., children whose conditions require technology to support their lives, such as those who are dependent upon mechanical ventilators for respiration for at least part of each day). However, not all children who may require specialized equipment are in a perilous state, and vice versa. Examples of students who may be considered medically fragile are children with certain types of cancer, some forms of muscular atrophy, and those with inoperable heart conditions. Many of these children would not require any technologic aids to access school programs.

Lehr and McDaid (1993), in a recent article entitled "Opening the Door Further: Integrating Students with Complex Health Care Needs," raise concern over the use of the term "medically fragile":

> The term . . . is one that must be carefully considered because of its power in frightening school personnel. Webster's defines fragile as "easily broken or destroyed." Many, however, who work with students who are [medically fragile] remark about the resilience of these children. Many of these children can be seen as incredibly strong—survivors of many adverse conditions, who in fact are not fragile at all, but remarkably strong to be able to rebound from periods of acute illness. (pp. 6–7)

Lehr and McDaid prefer the term **"students with complex health care needs"** for two reasons: (1) the term reflects that the children are often not ill—in fact, many are quite healthy because of the care that is provided to them; and (2) the term emphasizes the support that the children need rather than their condition. In this text, those students who require specialized assistance in the school system as a result of a specified chronic condition, regardless of its origin (i.e., physical vs. health-related), are referred to as those who have "special physical and health care needs."

❦ Incidence and Prevalence of Chronic Physical and Medical Conditions

There is great variation in the occurrence rates of the various chronic conditions common to children. Some disorders (e.g., asthma) are quite common; others occur less often (e.g., sickle cell anemia); and

---

[1] **Orthopedics** is a branch of medicine concerned with the correction or prevention of deformities that affect the locomotory system (*Mosby's*, 1994). Interestingly, the term *orthopedics* comes from the Greek *orthos*, meaning straight, and *pais*, meaning child. An orthopedist would be involved in the treatment of problems related to the skeleton, muscles, joints, and related tissues.

some are very rare (e.g., phenylketonuria). Interestingly, there are major differences between the types of chronic conditions seen in children and those seen in adults. Typically, children face a large number of rare diseases (e.g., Tay-Sachs disease, hemophilia, cystic fibrosis), whereas adults most often face a much smaller number of common diseases (e.g., arthritis, diabetes, coronary artery disease) (Perrin & MacLean, 1988).

Even though chronic illness is one of the most widespread health care problems affecting children and their families and is one of the leading health problems in the industrialized world, many have reported that demographic data are not widely available (Gortmaker, 1985; Gortmaker & Sappenfield, 1984) and that the rates of occurrence of many chronic illnesses are difficult, if not impossible, to calculate with total accuracy (Harkins, 1994). The difficulties are caused, in part, by the lack of an accepted definition of chronic illness in children, the rarity of children with chronic illnesses, and variations in the methods used for the collection and analysis of data (Gortmaker & Sappenfield; Hymovich & Hagopian, 1992; Newacheck & Taylor, 1992; Perrin et al., 1993).

There are two different types of occurrence rates—incidence and prevalence. **Incidence** is defined as the number of new occurrences of a disease or disorder during a specific period of time. Most often the reported period is one calendar year, for example, January 1, 1998, to December 31, 1998. **Prevalence** refers to the number of persons that

have the condition (i.e., both those who have had the disease for some time and those who have just acquired the disease) at a particular point in time. A particular day, for example January 1, 1999, could be chosen as the reporting date for the prevalence statistic. Incidence is usually reported as either a precise or approximated integer or as a proportion per unit of population. Prevalence can be reported as a number, a percentage, or as a proportion converted into a percentage.

Using diabetes mellitus as an example, various statistics related to the occurrence of this particular disease are shown in Table 1.1 to illustrate the difference between incidence and prevalence rates. As a result of imprecise reporting, the statistics given are, at best, approximations.

For certain conditions (e.g., rare syndromes, infectious diseases), physicians are obligated to report the condition to a regulating body. An example is the Centers for Disease Control and Prevention (CDC), branches of which are located throughout the United States and Canada. Statistical data related to "reportable" conditions generally are more accurate. An example of a specific incidence figure reported in a publication of the CDC can be seen in the April 7, 1995, edition of *Morbidity and Mortality Weekly Report*. Here it was reported that 126 of 188,905 newborns (i.e., an incidence rate of 6.7 per 10,000) were born with fetal alcohol syndrome (FAS) in 1993. This may be compared to the period between 1979 and 1993, when 2,032 of 9,434,560 children were born with FAS (i.e., a rate of 2.2 per

TABLE 1.1

Incidence vs. Prevalence: An Example from the Data on Diabetes

---

INCIDENCE

- Approximately 500,000 to 700,000 new cases of diabetes mellitus (regardless of age) are reported each year [i.e., *overall incidence for the total population*].
- Each year, 11,000 to 12,000 children and teenagers are diagnosed with insulin-dependent diabetes mellitus (IDDM) [i.e., *incidence for particular age groups for a one-year period*].

PREVALENCE

- Approximately 14 million people (regardless of age) in the United States have diabetes mellitus [i.e., *overall prevalence for total population*].
- Compared with non–Hispanic whites, rates for non–insulin-dependent diabetes (NIDDM) are 60% higher in American blacks and 110% to 120% higher in Mexican Americans and Puerto Ricans. In Pima Indians living in the United States, one out of two (50%) of all adults have NIDDM [i.e., *prevalence for particular ethnic groups*].

Source: National Institutes of Health (1994). *Diabetes overview* (NIH Pub.# 94-3235). Washington, DC: Author.

10,000). Of course, some cases do go unreported, even though there is an obligation to notify the CDC, so there may be some error.

While incidence and prevalence statistics may be viewed individually, they are, in fact, very much related. The incidence and prevalence rates of chronic conditions may vary as the result of many factors, singly or in combination, such as the following:

- An increase (or decrease) in the birth rate that would result in a change in the number of children who are born with or who later develop a chronic illness or condition; similarly, an increase (or decrease) in the number of immigrants or emigrants may have an effect on the number of persons in that nation who have a chronic condition, develop a chronic illness, or give birth to offspring who may have or develop a long-term disease
- A decrease (or increase) in mortality rate that would result in a change in the number of children who continue to have a chronic illness for a protracted period of time
- An increase in the number of individuals who develop a condition that has been in existence for some time, caused by factors such as poor sanitation, lack of immunization, or the effects of environmental pollution (i.e., a poor standard of living), or conversely, a decrease in the number of persons who develop a condition that has been occurring for some time, as a result of factors such as better nutrition, improved water supply, or assured access to medical treatment (i.e., a more favorable standard of living)
- An increase in the number of persons in whom a condition develops that was not previously recognized, such as pediatric AIDS, or as a result of epidemics of conditions that normally do not appear in great numbers, such as rubella (i.e., German measles); or conversely, a decrease in the occurrence of new diseases or outbreaks of known diseases (e.g., AIDS or rubella), as a result of new or better treatments becoming available (e.g., development of new vaccines) or increased immunization programs that result in the prevention of the disease
- A decrease in number of individuals born with certain chronic conditions or syndromes commonly associated with chronic illnesses (e.g., Down syndrome), as a result of the selective termination of pregnancies (i.e., abortions) on the basis of prenatal tests, such as amniocentesis, chorionic villus sampling, and alpha-fetoprotein screening

- An increase in the survival rates of children and adults with chronic illnesses, such as renal failure, or traumatic episodes, such as accidents or abuse, as a result of better treatment practices that include new drugs, new surgical procedures, or new advances in technology (e.g., the development of mechanical ventilators); similarly, an increase in the survival rate of at-risk individuals, such as very low birth weight infants, who may not have lived in the past and who are now living longer as a result of dramatic medical advances, but who are experiencing chronic health problems (e.g., children with bronchopulmonary dysplasia who require continual oxygen therapy in order to live)

There may be wide variation in the incidence or prevalence rates for certain conditions that lead to long-term health problems. Geographical irregularities and differences on the basis of gender or ethnic background have been reported.

In terms of geographical differences, occurrence rates of specific diseases can differ (a) throughout the world, (b) within a geographical area, or (c) within a particular country. For example, it is known that (a) the worldwide incidence of insulin-dependent diabetes mellitus is much higher among white individuals than black, (b) on the continent of Africa, less than a quarter of the countries are polio-free, while the others continue to have relatively high rates, and (c) the incidence of lead poisoning is higher in certain areas of the United States and Canada than in others.

In terms of gender or ethnic background, within the population as a whole, there also may be wide variation in the occurrence rate of particular conditions. For example, hemophilia is a disease that primarily affects males and is rarely seen in females, whereas Tay-Sachs disease occurs in the Ashkenazi Jewish population of Eastern European descent with greater frequency than in any other ethnic population.

Over the past few decades, better medical case-finding efforts have resulted in recognition of conditions that may not have been recognized in earlier diagnosis than in the past. This has resulted in an apparent increase in the incidence and prevalence of certain conditions.

Although it is difficult to establish incidence and prevalence statistics with precision as a result of the methodologic problems in data collection and the previously mentioned factors that cause fluctuating demographic data, there have been several attempts to quantify the number of children with physical or medical problems. Reports published between 1967 and 1990 indicated that the proportion of children with chronic illnesses in the United States ranged from less than 5% to more than 30% of the population (Newacheck & Taylor, 1992). Until recently, the statistic most often cited by American researchers was that approximately 10 million children (10% to 15% of all children) had a chronic health condition and that 1 million children (1% to 2% of all children) had a severe form of illness (Gortmaker & Sappenfield, 1984; Haggerty, 1984). However, more recent information has shown that these numbers may not, according to some, give an accurate picture of the enormity of the problem. Based on data from the large population-based sample of children (N = 17,110 individuals) included in the National Health Interview Survey (NHIS) on Child Health, conducted in 1988 by the National Center for Health Statistics (NCHS), Newacheck and

TABLE 1.2

Estimated Prevalence of Specified Chronic Conditions among Children under Age 18 by Age, Gender, and Race, 1988 (in Cases per 1,000)

Condition	Age Under Age 10	Age Ages 10–17	Gender Boys	Gender Girls	Race White	Race Black
ALL CHILDREN WITH CHRONIC CONDITIONS	302.2	315.0	326.2	288.2	324.4	246.5
IMPAIRMENTS						
Musculoskeletal impairments	10.9	20.9	16.7	13.6	15.9	10.5
Deafness/hearing loss	14.1	17.0	18.3	12.3	17.7	6.0
Blindness/visual impairment	10.3	16.0	11.4	14.2	13.9	8.4
Speech defects	31.6	18.9	35.3	16.7	25.9	33.5
Cerebral palsy	2.2	1.2[a]	2.0	1.5[a]	1.9	0.5[a]
DISEASES						
Diabetes	0.6[a]	1.5[a]	1.5	0.5[a]	1.2	0.1
Sickle cell disease	1.3[a]	0.9[a]	0.9[a]	1.4	0.1[a]	6.9
Anemia	11.0	5.8	8.4	9.1	8.6	10.0
Asthma	39.3	46.8	50.7	33.9	41.0	51.4
Respiratory allergies	71.8	130.3	106.5	87.7	106.1	53.2
Eczema & skin allergies	31.1	35.2	30.1	35.8	34.3	22.8
Epilepsy & seizures	1.7[a]	3.3	1.7[a]	3.1	2.5	2.3[a]
Arthritis	1.5[a]	8.7	4.2	4.9	4.5	5.3[a]
Heart disease	13.6	17.4	16.4	13.9	17.3	7.5
Frequent/repeated ear infections	120.6	33.6	88.5	78.1	91.6	53.2
Frequent diarrhea/bowel trouble	22.6	9.6	18.1	15.9	17.8	13.6
Digestive allergies	23.2	21.1	25.6	18.9	24.5	9.7
Frequent/severe headaches	9.9	45.8	22.8	27.9	26.5	21.9
Other	12.1	30.0	19.3	20.3	21.9	9.9

Source: Newacheck, P. W., & Taylor, W. R. (1992). Childhood chronic illness: prevalence, severity, and impact. *American Journal of Public Health, 82,* 364–371. Copyright 1992 by the American Public Health Association. Reprinted by permission.
[a] Standard error exceeds 30% of estimate value.

Taylor estimated that 31% of children under age 18, or almost 20 million children in the United States, had one or more chronic conditions. In discussing these findings, the authors suggested that even this number may be inaccurate because not all childhood chronic conditions—particularly those related to mental health and cancer—were included in the checklist parents were asked to complete. Based on the data obtained related to the "frequency" and "bother" caused by chronic conditions (e.g., days spent ill in bed, days missed from school) and the resultant use of medications, physician services, and health care use patterns, Newacheck and Taylor were able to estimate that children living in the United States who are chronically ill can be divided into three different groups of differing proportions. Specifically, 20% of all children had mild conditions that resulted in little or no bother or activity limitation, 9% had problems of moderate severity, and 2% had a severe condition that impacted greatly on their lives.

While the estimates of the incidence and prevalence rates of chronic conditions are discussed in detail for each condition described in subsequent chapters, the data presented in Table 1.2 show the prevalence of specified chronic conditions, as well as the breakdown by age, gender, and race in the United States in 1988, as reported by Newacheck and Taylor (1992).

In addition to our knowledge about the prevalence of specific chronic conditions, information is emerging regarding the number of children who are assisted by various types of technology. Recently, by examining the data from the state of Massachusetts and applying the prevalence rate of 0.16 for children aged 17 and younger in this state to the rest of the nation (assuming that experiences are comparable across the country), Palfrey and her colleagues (1994) have estimated that there were over 100,000 children dependent on medical technology in the United States alone in 1990. Most of these children would be considered to be a subset of the total number of children with chronic illnesses and consequently should be considered part of the approximately 20 million children mentioned previously.

🐛 Summary

There are many terms that are used to describe children with physical and medical challenges. Some of the terms are primarily medical, others come from

the educational literature. The purpose of this chapter has been to introduce the reader to the myriad of terms in common usage. In addition, incidence and prevalence statistics have been presented to show the enormity of the population. More than 20 million children in the United States alone have one or more chronic conditions. Many of these children are attending neighborhood public school programs alongside their peers. In the next chapter, a brief overview of the historical practices that have resulted in the movement from "segregation" to "inclusion" are presented, along with the applicable current legislation and cases brought to trial that ensure that the needs of children with chronic physical and medical challenges have been met in the school systems of today.

References

Caldwell, T. H., & Sirvis, B. (1991). Students with special health conditions: An emerging population presents new challenges. *Preventing School Failure, 35*(3), 13–18.

Centers for Disease Control (CDC). (1995). Update: Trends in fetal alcohol syndrome—United States, 1979–1993. *Morbidity and Mortality Weekly Report, 44,* 249–251.

Council for Exceptional Children. (1988). *Report of the Council for Exceptional Children's ad hoc committee on medically fragile students.* Reston, VA: Author.

Gortmaker, S. L. (1985). Demography of chronic childhood diseases. In N. Hobbs & J. M. Perrin (Eds.), *Issues in the care of children with chronic illness: A sourcebook on problems, services, and policies* (pp. 135–154). San Francisco: Jossey-Bass.

Gortmaker, S. L., & Sappenfield, W. (1984). Chronic childhood disorders: Prevalence and impact. *Pediatric Clinics of North America, 31*(1), 3–18.

Haggerty, R. J. (1984). Foreword to symposium on chronic disease in children. *Pediatric Clinics of North America, 31*(1), 1–2.

Hallahan, D. P., & Kauffman, J. M. (1994). *Exceptional children: Introduction to special education* (6th ed.). Boston: Allyn & Bacon.

Harkins, A. (1994). Chronic illness. In C. L. Betz, M. M. Hunsberger, & S. Wright (Eds.), *Family-centered nursing care of children* (2nd ed., pp. 651–688). Philadelphia: W. B. Saunders.

Hymovich, D. P., & Hagopian, G. A. (1992). *Chronic illness in children and adults: A psychosocial approach.* Philadelphia: W. B. Saunders.

Izen, C. L., & Brown, F. (1991). Education and treatment needs of students with profound, multiply handicapping, and medically fragile conditions: A survey of teachers' perceptions. *Journal of the Association for Persons with Severe Handicaps, 16,* 94–103.

Jackson, D. B., & Saunders, R. B. (1993). *Child health nursing: A comprehensive approach to the care of children and their families.* Philadelphia: J. B. Lippincott.

Jessop, D. J., & Stein, R. E. K. (1989). Meeting the needs of individuals and families. In R. E. K. Stein (Ed.), *Caring for children with chronic illness: Issues and strategies* (pp. 63–74). New York: Springer.

Johnson, M. P., Lubker, B. B., & Fowler, M. G. (1988). Teacher needs assessment for the educational management of children with chronic illnesses. *Journal of School Health, 58,* 232–235.

Kleinberg., S. B. (1982). *Educating the chronically ill child.* Rockville, MD: Aspen.

Koenning, G. M., Todaro, A. W., Benjamin, J. E., Curry, M. R., Spraul, G. E., & Mayer, M. C. (1995). Health services delivery to students with special health care needs in Texas public schools. *Journal of School Health, 65,* 119–123.

Larson, G. (1986). *Managing the school age child with a chronic health condition.* Wayzata, MN: DCI Publishing.

Lehr, D. H. (1990). Educating students with special health care needs. In E. L. Meyen (Ed.), *Exceptional children in today's schools* (pp. 107–130). Denver: Love Publishing.

Lehr, D. H., & McDaid, P. (1993). Opening the door further: Integrating students with complex health care needs. *Focus on Exceptional Children, 25*(6), 1–7.

Lubkin, I. M. (1986). *Chronic illness: Impact and interventions.* Boston: Jones & Bartlett.

Lynch, E. W., Lewis, R. B., & Murphy, D. S. (1993a). Improving education for children with chronic illnesses. *Principal, 73*(2) 38–40.

Lynch, E. W., Lewis, R. B., & Murphy, D. S. (1993b). Educational services for children with chronic illnesses: Perspectives of educators and families. *Exceptional Children, 59,* 210–220.

Massie, R. K. (1985). The constant shadow: Reflections on the life of a chronically ill child. In N. Hobbs & J. M. Perrin (Eds.), *Issues in the care of children with chronic illness: A sourcebook on problems, services, and policies* (pp. 13–23). San Francisco: Jossey-Bass.

Mosby's medical, nursing, and allied health dictionary (1994) (4th ed.). St. Louis: Mosby.

National Institutes of Health. (1994). *Diabetes overview* (NIH Pub.# 94-3235). Washington, DC: Author.

Newacheck, P. W., & Taylor, W. R. (1992). Childhood chronic illness: Prevalence, severity, and impact. *American Journal of Public Health, 82,* 364–371.

Palfrey, J. S., Haynie, M., Porter, S., Fenton, T., Cooperman-Vincent, P., Shaw, D., Johnson, B., Bierle, T., & Walker, D. K. (1994). Prevalence of medical technology assistance among children in Massachusetts in 1987 and 1990. *Public Health Reports, 109,* 226–233.

Parette, H. P., Bartlett, C. R., & Holder-Brown, L. (1994). The nurse's role in planning for inclusion of medically fragile and technology-dependent children in public school settings. *Issues in Comprehensive Pediatric Nursing, 17*(2), 61–72.

Perrin, J. M., (1985). Introduction. In N. Hobbs & J. M. Perrin (Eds.), *Issues in the care of children with chronic illness: A sourcebook on problems, services, and policies* (pp. 1–10). San Francisco: Jossey-Bass.

Perrin, J. M., & MacLean, W. E. (1988). Children with chronic illness: The prevention of dysfunction. *Pediatric Clinics of North America, 35,* 1325–1337.

Perrin, E. C., Newacheck, P., Pless, B., Drotar, D., Gortmaker, S. L., Leventhal, J., Perrin, J. M., Stein, R. E. K., Walker, D. K., & Weitzman, M. (1993). Issues involved in the definition and classification of chronic health conditions. *Pediatrics, 91,* 787–793.

Pless, I. B., & Perrin, J. M. (1985). Issues common to a variety of illnesses. In N. Hobbs & J. M. Perrin (Eds.), *Issues in the care of children with chronic illness: A sourcebook on problems, services, and policies* (pp. 41–60). San Francisco: Jossey-Bass.

Potter, M. L. (1987). Children and chronic illness. In A. Thomas & J. Grimes (Eds.), *Children's needs: Psychological perspectives* (pp. 96–103). Silver Springs, MD: National Association of School Psychologists. (ERIC Document Reproduction Service No. ED 353 487).

Stein, R. E. K., & Jessop, D. J. (1982). A non-categorical approach to chronic childhood illness. *Public Health Report, 97,* 355–359.

Travis, G. (1976). *Chronic illness in children: Its impact on child and family.* Stanford, CA: Stanford University Press.

van Eys, J. (1977). The outlook for the child with cancer. *Journal of School Health, 47,* 165–169.

Waskerwitz, M. J. (1994). Neoplasms/Cancer. In C. L. Betz, M. M. Hunsberger, & S. Wright (Eds.), *Family-centered nursing care of children* (2nd ed., pp. 1874–1937). Philadelphia: W. B. Saunders.

Webster's new complete medical dictionary (1996). New York: Smithmark.

CHAPTER 2

Serving Children with Special Physical and Health Care Needs in the School System

KEY WORDS

Medical services

Orthopedic impairment

"Other health impaired"

Related services

School health services

Attendance in school was uncommon until the early 1900s for many children with physical and medical challenges. In tracing trends in providing services to these students, Walker and Jacobs (1985) delineated several factors that contributed to children being denied an education. One factor was the high mortality rates that resulted from unsophisticated medical practices of the time. As late as 1890, approximately 20% of children died before reaching the age of 2, and 50% did not live to adulthood (Scipien, 1991). Common causes of death were diseases, such as smallpox, diphtheria, measles, or dysentery, and accidents, particularly those resulting from burns caused by open fireplaces or gun powder. Societal attitudes also tended to ostracize those that were different or disabled, and education was viewed as a privilege rather than a right. However, these trends began to reverse in the late 1800s and early 1900s, and children with chronic illnesses have been slowly entering the school system, forcing "schools into previously uncharted territories" (Walker & Jacobs, pp. 615–616).

❦ Historical Overview of Practices, Legislation, and Litigation

Around the turn of the 20th century, children with physical and health impairments were first educated in local schools, most commonly in special classes for the "crippled" or "delicate" (Connor, Scandary, & Tullock, 1988), which were segregated from those in the "regular" programs. Walker and Jacobs (1985) attributed the movement of these children into the general school system to the serious outbreaks of tuberculosis and polio that occurred in the early 1900s. Although these children survived the epidemics with their cognitive abilities intact, "the illnesses were so widespread that the necessity to accommodate sufferers or survivors could not be ignored by school systems" (p. 618). As a result, classes in hospitals and sanatoriums became common, as did home tutoring and specially paced curricula in segregated classrooms. Unfortunately, efforts to enroll children with obvious disabilities were not always as successful as planned. In Wisconsin in 1919, the court ruled that the attendance of an academically competent child with cerebral palsy should not be allowed: the reason was that the effects on the able-bodied classmates would be "depressing" and "nauseating" (Connor et al., 1988).

Typically at that time, educational placements were decided by medical staff. In describing this period, Connor et al. made the following comments regarding the role of medical professionals in making educational decisions:

> Because physical/medical impairments were the unique, readily identified characteristics of this group of students, medical jurisdiction usually took precedence over education considerations. Frequently it was a medical advisor who prescribed educational placement and programming. Educational decisions to *ignore, isolate,* and *institutionalize* these children were often based on mental incompetence *presumed* because of physical disabilities, especially those involving communication and use of upper extremities. (p. 6, italics added)

Through the early 20th century, more and more children with chronic health problems, considered by today's standards as "mild," were able to return to school because of a number of factors. The primary one was the presence of school nurses who were able to treat minor problems. Increased survival rates resulting from medical advances in treatment and prevention (e.g., the introduction of antibiotics and insulin, improved surgical procedures, and improved prenatal care) resulted in more children attending school. However, until the 1950s, "special" (i.e., separate) classes, separate schools, and homebound or hospital instruction still remained the most common placements or service delivery options.

Major social changes occurred in the United States in the second half of the 20th century, including the civil rights movement, which brought attention to the disenfranchised; the enactment of legislation requiring that buildings be accessible; a proliferation of court cases that challenged the segregation of students with disabilities; the questioning of the efficacy of special education practices such as special class placements; deinstitutionalization and dehospitalization; the return of disabled veterans into the community after World War II; and the development of innovative rehabilitation programs. One would have expected that the unmet educational needs of children with chronic health illnesses would have been thoroughly addressed during these changes. However, such was not always the case. Walker and Jacobs (1985) attributed the situation to three reasons: (a) the relatively small numbers of children with chronic health problems in comparison to other more "established" groups (e.g., children who were mentally retarded); (b) the fracturing of the group into smaller competitive groups organized around discrete conditions or illnesses (e.g., diabetes or epilepsy), which resulted in the members becoming organized around narrowly defined issues rather than the larger more global needs common to all; and (c) the confusion of parents regarding how "special education" applied to their children, who may not necessarily have had the severe cognitive, orthopedic, or communicative difficulties traditionally considered to be educational "problems."

During the period from 1950 to 1970, a few students with more "severe" physical and health problems were enrolled full-time in general classrooms; however, they were the exception. Connor et al. (1988, p. 6) described these children as being "intellectually competent children of assertive parents who worked independently of officially constituted groups." More common was placement of children in a special setting, sponsored by a specific organization, such as the United Cerebral Palsy Association, that provided *both* education *and* therapy. In many jurisdictions, the public school system provided the teacher(s) and the organization provided the therapist(s), who offered therapeutic services (e.g., occupational therapy, physical therapy, speech therapy) to students.

By the 1970s many more children with chronic health care problems, including those with more "moderate" conditions, such as asthma, diabetes, and epilepsy, were beginning to attend public schools. However, in some cases the children did not attend their own neighborhood school but were bused to special schools or center programs that were designed to serve students from a wider geographic area (Connor et al., 1988). In general, necessary treatment was completed at home or in hospital, and schools were *not* considered to be responsible for the provision of any direct physical or medical care (Caldwell & Sirvis, 1991).

Passage of Public Law (P. L.) 94-142, the Education for the Handicapped Act (EHA) in 1975, reauthorized in 1990 under the new title the Individuals with Disabilities Education Act (IDEA) (P. L. 101-476),[1] changed the situation for many children with chronic health problems, particularly those with more "severe" physical and medical needs. P. L. 94-142 mandated that all children ages 3 to 21 receive a free and appropriate education in the least restricted environment. These laws mandated services for many groups of children, including those who were orthopedically impaired and "other health impaired." Public Law 101-476 contains the following definitions:

> **Orthopedic impairment** means a severe orthopedic impairment that adversely affects a child's educational performance. The term includes impairments caused by a congenital anomaly (e.g., club foot, absence of some member, etc.), impairments caused by disease (e.g., poliomyelitis, bone tuberculosis, etc.), and impairments from any other causes (e.g., cerebral palsy, amputations, and fractures or burns which cause contractures).
> **Other health impaired** means having limited strength, vitality, or alertness, due to chronic or acute health problems such as a heart condition, tuberculosis, rheumatic fever, nephritis, asthma, sickle cell anemia, hemophilia, epilepsy, lead poisoning, leukemia, or diabetes that adversely affect a child's educational performance.

P. L. 94-142 and its amendments emphasized the importance of the provision of **related services** to assist in the removal of any potential barriers to the successful inclusion of a child with special health care needs into the general education classroom (Palfrey, 1995). The following related services were included in P. L. 101-476:

> . . . transportation and such developmental, corrective and other supportive services as are required to assist a handicapped child to benefit from special education, and includes speech pathology and audiology, psychological services, physical and occupational therapy, recreation, early identification and assessment of disabilities in children, counseling services, and medical services for diagnostic and evaluation purposes. The term also includes school health services, social work services in schools, and parent counseling and training . . .

In addition, the same educational legislation defined **medical services** as "services provided by a licensed physician to determine a child's medically related disability that results in the child's need for special education and related services" and **school health services** as "services provided by a school nurse or other qualified person." In describing the impact of the IDEA, Palfrey (1995) made the following comment: "Probably more than any other aspect of the law, the related services provision transformed the educational environment and changed schools from solely *scholastic* institutions into *therapeutic* agencies" (p. 265, italics added).

---

[1] Reauthorized again in 1997 as P. L. 105-17 under the same title.

Given the nature of the needs of many of the children with physical and medical conditions, many problems quickly became evident because the legislation did not stipulate what was meant by the term "benefit from special education." Many of the children did not have any cognitive difficulties that would affect their ability to learn; however, in order to attend school, they needed support but not necessarily the "academic" support offered by the "traditional" special education programs. Walker and Jacobs (1985) posed the following questions to illustrate the confusion that abounded in the period subsequent to the passage of P. L. 94-142:

> If a child with diabetes needs to have a gym class at a different time of day from classmates, should scheduling be a concern of special education? Or can it be arranged within the general education framework? Is a child whose leukemia has been in remission for more than a year a special education student because it is still necessary to see a school social worker regularly for supportive counseling? When a child with asthma needs daily medication administered in school, is that a school health or a special education function? (p. 625)

Even so, in the past 20 years there has been a gradual increase in the number of children with complex medical needs who are being integrated into the general public school system. The increase has been due, in large part, to the litigative efforts of the children's parents. For example, in one early case, *Department of Education, State of Hawaii, v. Katherine D.* (1982/1993/1995), it was ruled that a child with multiple health impairments living in the State of Hawaii must be placed in an integrated classroom and be provided with related medical services (in this case, intermittent suctioning of a tracheostomy), because it was deemed that a homebound instructional program did not meet the least restrictive environment standard of the law. Similarly, in *Case No. SE-27-84* (1984) in the State of Illinois, the Board of Education ruled that the school district was responsible for educating a ventilator-dependent student with quadriplegia in a public school classroom rather than in his home, and for providing him with appropriate equipment and emergency medical backup to make the placement safe if the equipment malfunctioned.

Today many children with special health care needs, including those who would be considered by many to have "profound" problems and who in the past would had been cared for in hospitals or other residential institutions, are living at home and being integrated at school with their able-bodied peers. However, many controversial issues have not yet been resolved and continue to be "settled" through ongoing court cases. Many of the difficult questions that have arisen center around the extent of responsibility assumed by teachers and schools in caring for the child's physical and health needs, given the fact that many of the services required by children with chronic health problems, such as administration of medications, catheterization, and gastrostomy feeding, are considered by many to be of a "medical" rather than "educational" nature (Heward & Orlansky, 1992). Concerns regarding the liability of the schools and school personnel have also been voiced, particularly in cases where the child's medical problem may lead to emergency situations (Todaro, Failla, & Caldwell, 1993). During times of fiscal restraint and declining dollars, the costs involved in providing care for these children (e.g., costs of equipment and increased staff) continue to be problematic to school districts in which limited budgets must be used to provide education to all students, including those with disabilities and chronic health problems.

While the litigation involving children with physical and medical needs has increased over time, many inconsistencies in the decisions have resulted from the lack of unity in the circuit court interpretations of IDEA concerning the legal obligation of the public school system (Weiss & Dykes, 1995). Rapport (1996), in reviewing some of the various cases that have been settled over the past 15 years, suggested that "the limited case law available . . . has not provided consistent opinion across all federal circuits—adding to the difficulty of school districts, parents of children with special health care needs, and attorneys in determining the division of financial responsibility and service delivery of these children" (p. 538). Although it would be impossible to review here all the decisions related to educational needs of children with physical and medical needs, some of the most important decisions are discussed briefly. For a more thorough review of legal precedents, the reader is referred to the articles by Rapport (1996) and Weiss and Dykes (1995).

One of the first, and most controversial, cases that dealt with the responsibilities of school-based professionals to provide health care services is *Irving Independent School District v. Tatro* (1984). Originally the case came to the court level in 1980;

however, there was a lengthy appeal process that resulted in a U.S. Supreme Court decision in 1984. In the appeal, the Supreme Court decided that Amber Tatro, a 3½-year-old child with spina bifida who needed clean intermittent catheterization (CIC) every 3 to 4 hours in order to prevent a chronic kidney infection, must be accommodated by the school district, which had previously refused to administer the procedure on the basis that it was a medical, not an educational, service. The school district claimed that CIC could only be performed by a physician or a nurse with a physician in attendance. In its decision, the court ruled that catheterization was a "supportive service" or "related service" that is similar to such services as transportation and counseling, as opposed to a "medical service" under Section 140 (17) of the Education for All Handicapped Children Act. Justice Warren Earl Burger, in his decision, stated that "services like CIC that permit a child to remain at school during the day are no less related to the effort to educate than are services that enable the child to reach, enter, or exist in the school" (p. 7). The ruling also clarified the difference between the school's responsibility for "medical" services and for "school health" services. While it was decided that schools are not responsible for medical services provided by physicians (except those for diagnostic and evaluation purposes), the Supreme Court decreed that they are responsible for some medical services (such as CIC) that can be carried out by a school nurse (or other qualified person) and, as such, could be included as a "related service" in a child's individual educational program. The Court of Appeals developed a tripartite standard that would "limit the types of health care and allay the reverberating fears of school districts nationwide over the potential array of new services never before considered to be the responsibility of schools" (Rapport, 1996). The standards were as follows:

1. A life-support service must be rendered to a child who is handicapped so as to require special education.
2. The life-support service must be necessary to the handicapped child to benefit from special education to be provided.
3. The life-support service must be one which a nurse or other qualified person can perform. (pp. 541–542)

There has been much discussion of this case in the literature. Vitello, in referring to *Tatro,* summarized the pertinent issues by suggesting that "whether a particular medical service is excludable or not is determined by who provides the service, not the type of service *per se*" (1986, p. 355). Martin (1984, cited in Walker, 1991) made the following comments regarding this case: "This ruling greatly expanded the definition and scope of related services. The court rejected the notion that medical needs, excess costs, or staff liability should impede school attendance." Although the *Tatro* case provided some assistance in determining "who" should provide "what," the controversy has not ended; in recent years, it has transcended to a level involving more extensive and invasive health care procedures (Rapport, 1996).

Several recent cases have attempted to resolve the controversy regarding whether it is reasonable for school districts to provide (and to pay for) highly specialized services to children with complex health needs. In *Detsel v. Board of Education of the Auburn Enlarged City School District* (1986/1997), *Bevin H. v. Wright* (1987), *Clovis Unified School District v. California Office of Administrative Hearings* (1990), and *Shannon M. v. Granite School District* (1992), it was decided that health services that are extremely costly and beyond the skills of school personnel were *not* mandated under the existing law. For example, in the first case, Melissa Detsel's parents requested that the school provide a nurse in attendance to constantly monitor her vital signs, to administer medication to her via a tube inserted into her intestinal tract, and to suction the lungs to prevent the accumulation of mucus, among other things. Similarly, in the case of *Bevin H.,* the courts determined that the school board was not responsible for providing intensive nursing services that were needed on a continuous basis (e.g., tracheostomy and gastrostomy care, administration of oxygen, chest therapy, suctioning). In the case of *Clovis,* it was determined that the school board was not required to provide psychiatric services, because school staff were not sufficiently competent to provide such services. In the case of *Shannon M.,* the cost of a one-on-one nurse (approximately $30,000 per school year) was considered to be too excessive for the school district to absorb. However, in a more recent case, *Neely v. Rutherford County Schools* (1994/1995/1996), also involving the need for daily nursing care for a student, Samantha Neely, a child with a respiratory condition that necessitated the use of tracheotomy tube, it was determined by the courts that daily nursing care was a supportive service that should be provided by the school district. This decision was, however, overturned on appeal in 1996.

Rather than deciding what services do not need to be provided, some cases have established what are considered by the court to be allowable school health services (i.e., no exclusion possible). Interestingly, one of the best known cases involved a student with multiple disabilities and complex health needs, known as Joshua S., who, like other children in previously cited cases, required suctioning. Joshua, however, required tracheostomy care not only in school, but also while riding on the school bus on his way to and from school. In this decision, *Macomb County Intermediate School District v. Joshua S.* (1989), contrary to other similar cases, it was decided that "medically-related services short of requiring a licensed physician . . . are the student's right" (p. 826) and that since Joshua was not eligible for homebound education, the service had to be provided. Similarly, in a recent case in the state of Iowa, *Cedar Rapids Community School District v. Garret F.* (1997), it was determined that the school was bound to provide services to a medically fragile student that could be provided by a nurse or qualified layperson (as opposed to a physician). In this particular case the services included, among others, urinary bladder catheterization, tracheostomy suctioning, manual resuscitation, blood pressure monitoring, and help with eating and drinking at lunch. Up until these cases, it would have appeared that "single" procedures, such as tracheostomy suctioning or catheterization, are deemed to be supportive services. However, this case seems to stress that as long as a doctor is not required, any combination of services, regardless of cost, should be the responsibility of the school district. Needless to say, in states where such services can only be provided legally by a registered nurse, this decision has serious ramifications.

Even though court cases continue to attempt to establish which services are allowable or excludable, historically, education laws such as EHA and IDEA have, in effect, limited access to related services to only those children whose educational performance has been "adversely" affected by their health impairment (i.e., students who traditionally would have been referred to as needing "special education"). For those students who are able to perform up to the normal standard in school, but who still need some type of assistance, services have not always

been provided. To remedy this situation, the courts have looked to other legislation, specifically the Rehabilitation Act of 1973 (P. L. 93-112) and the Americans with Disabilities Act (ADA) of 1990 (P. L. 101-336) for direction. Recent cases, citing these two pieces of legislation, have involved children in the general education system who have an autoimmune disease, chronic asthma, severe allergies, arthritis, diabetes, epilepsy, and several different types of infectious diseases, such as AIDS and hepatitis (Martin, 1992; Weber, 1991; Weiss & Dykes, 1995).

Section 504 of the Rehabilitation Act, which states that "no qualified handicapped person shall, on the basis of handicap, be excluded from participation in, be denied the benefits of, or otherwise be subjected to discrimination under any program or activity which receives or benefits from federal financial assistance," is a particularly important piece of legislation because lawyers have interpreted the law to mean that a child who is *not* in special education (i.e., a child with a health problem who is in a general education classroom) is eligible for related services (Porter et al., 1992, p. 43). For example, in *Elizabeth S. v. Gilhool* (1987), the state acknowledged its responsibility under Section 504 to provide insulin injections and snacks to an insulin-dependent diabetic child, as well as its obligation to develop a plan to manage any medical crises that developed. Similarly, in *Martinez v. School Board of Hillsborough County, Florida* (1988/1989), the school was required to place a child with AIDS in a regular school classroom (because the risk of transmission to the other children in the school was deemed to be insignificant) or face charges of discrimination.

The Americans with Disabilities Act of 1990 mandates that all facets of the private sector be accessible to those who have disabling conditions, not just to those that had been previously covered under Section 504 (Oberg, Bryant, & Bach, 1994). In the case of *Thomas v. Davidson Academy* (1994), the parents of a student with idiopathic thrombocytopenic purpura used the ADA to fight the expulsion of their child from a private school. In this particular case, the girl had cut herself accidentally during school hours, and as a result of her disruptive behavior, the school's administrative staff had attempted to have her expelled. The courts determined that she had a disability, and therefore that she was covered not only by IDEA but also by ADA, and that since there had been no previous history of disruptive behavior (just this isolated incidence) the school board did not have grounds to dismiss the student.

As new situations arise, it is inevitable that there will be more court challenges in the future. In an article published in 1988, Osborne, reviewing court cases that involved the need for extensive nursing services (e.g., *Tatro*, *Detsel*, *Bevin H.*), made the following prediction:

> The courts will be called upon again in the future to narrow the gap between required and exempted services even further. In addition to looking at how costly a given service is and how easily it could be provided, they may also have to determine whether the school district is currently providing an adequate level of school health services. A school district should not be expected to provide expensive medically related services to a handicapped student, but it should not be allowed to avoid its obligations under the related services mandate simply because it customarily provides all of its students with a low level of school health services. (p. 940)

Summary

Children with chronic physical and medical conditions are being integrated into general public schools alongside their age- and grade-appropriate peers in far greater numbers than in the past. Some have attributed this change, particularly for students with orthopedic impairments, to the removal of physical barriers in the school environment and to changes in attitudes and beliefs (Sawyer, McLaughlin, & Winglee, 1994). Ensuring that the needs of the children are met adequately requires careful planning involving administrators, teachers, parents, and students. The desired outcome in providing services to children with special health care needs is the promotion of optimal growth and development in a community that is safe, nurturing, and stimulating (Graff & Ault, 1993).

The most recent statistics regarding enrollment of students ages 6 through 21 with one or more physical or medical problems, from the school years 1992–93 and 1993–94, are shown in Table 2.1. The increase in the number of children with "other health impairments" is probably attributable to the identification of more students with Attention and Deficit Disorder in 1993–94 than in the year previously. The figure for orthopedic impairments does not include those children who are multiply disabled (and in many cases have a major physical limitation). In 1993–94 there were 109,746 children with multiple disabilities in comparison to 103,279 in 1992–93, an increase of 6,467 children (6.3%).

Children with chronic illnesses are eager to attend school and to learn (Palfrey et al., 1992). Schools must respond in a positive manner and ensure that each child reaches the fullest potential. Educators must look beyond the health impairment and see the child as a child first, more like his or her peers than different, and having the same needs as all children. The most basic human need is acceptance. Recently, Stein (1989) made the following urgent plea:

> It has been suggested that children are our most precious resources and that a society can be judged in part or in whole by how it treats its most vulnerable members. Children with chronic physical conditions represent a vulnerable population, and the time has come for us to go beyond the recognition of that fact to remedy the problems and address the needs. At present we lag behind many other nations in our

TABLE 2.1

Number and Percentage Change of Selected Students Age 6 Through 21 Served Under Part B and Chapter 1 (SOP): School Years 1992–93 Through 1993–94

Disability	Total		Change	
	1992–1993	1993–1994	Number	Percent
Orthopedic impairments	52,588	56,616	4,028	7.7
Other health impairments	66,063	83,279	17,216	26.1
Traumatic brain injury	3,960	5,295	1,335	33.7
TOTAL	122,611	145,190	22,579	

Source: U. S. Department of Education (1995). *Seventeenth annual report to Congress on the implementation of the Individuals with Disabilities Education Act: To assure the free appropriate public education of all children with disabilities.* Washington, DC: Author.

willingness to assure a wide range of services to children and their families. The challenge for all of us is to continue to make our own individual and collective contributions to caring for children with chronic illness and to assume a leadership role in setting a high standard for the provision of comprehensive and humane services to these children and their families. (p. xxix)

References

Bevin H. v. Wright, 666 F. Supp. 71, 41 Ed. Law 535 (W.D. Pa. 1987).

Caldwell, T. H., & Sirvis, B. (1991). Students with special health conditions: An emerging population presents new challenges. *Preventing School Failure, 35*(3), 13–18.

Case No. SE-27-84, 1984-85 Educ. Handicapped L. Rep. 506: 103 (Ill. State Bd. of Educ. 1984).

Cedar Rapids Community School District v. Garret F., 25 IDELR 439 (8th Cir. 1997).

Clovis Unified School District v. California Office of Administrative Hearings, F. 2d 9th Cir. (1990).

Connor, F. P., Scandary, J., & Tullock, D. (1988). Education of physically handicapped and health impaired individuals: A commitment to the future. *DPH Journal, 10*(1), 5–24.

Department of Education, State of Hawaii, v. Katherine D., 517, 2 Ed. Law 1057 (D. Hawaii 1982), 727 F. 2d 809 (9th Cir. 1983); *certiorari denied,* 471 U. S. 1117 (1985).

Detsel v. Board of Education of the Auburn Enlarged City School District, 637 F. Supp. 1022 (N.D. N.Y. 1986), 33 Ed. Law 726 (N.D. N.Y. 1986); *affirmed* 820 F. 2d 587, 40 Ed. Law 79 (2nd Cir. 1987); *certiorari denied,* 108 S. Ct. 495, 98 L. Ed. 2d 494, 43 Ed. Law 20 (1987).

Elizabeth S. v. Gilhool, F. Supp. (M.D. Pa 1987).

Graff, J. C., & Ault, M. M. (1993). Guidelines for working with students having special health care needs. *Journal of School Health, 63,* 335–338.

Heward, W. L., & Orlansky, M. D. (1992). *Exceptional children: An introductory survey of special education* (4th ed.). New York: Merrill.

Irving Independent School District v. Tatro, 468 U. S. 883, 104 S. Ct. 3371 (1984).

Macomb County Intermediate School District v. Joshua S., 715 F. Supp. 824 (E.D. Mich. 1989).

Martin, D. A. (1992). Ethical and legal issues in child health care. In P. T. Castiglia & R. E. Harbin, *Child health care: Process and practice* (pp. 41–56). Philadelphia: J. B. Lippincott.

Martinez v. School Board of Hillsborough Co. Fla., 861 F 2d 1502 (11th Cir. 1988); *on remand,* 711 F. Supp. 1066 (M.D. Fla. 1989).

Neely v. Rutherford County Schools, 851 F. Supp. 888 (M.D. Tenn. 1994); reversed, 68 F. 3d 965 (6th Cir. 1995); *cert. denied,* 116 S. Ct. 1418 (1996).

Oberg, C. N., Bryant, N. A., & Bach, M. L. (1994). Ethics, values, and policy decisions for children with disabilities: What are the costs of political correctness? *Journal of School Health, 64,* 223–228.

Osborne, A. G. (1988). Extensive nursing services are not required under the EHCA. *West's Education Law Reporter, 45,* 935– 940.

Palfrey, J. S. (1995). Amber, Katie, and Ryan: Lessons from children with complex medical conditions. *Journal of School Health, 65,* 265–267.

Palfrey, J. S., Haynie, M., Porter, S., Bierle, T., Cooperman, P., & Lowcock, J. (1992). Project School Care: Integrating children assisted by medical technology into educational settings. *Journal of School Health, 62,* 50–54.

Porter, S., Burkley, J., Bierle, T., Lowcock J., Haynie, M., & Palfrey, J. S. (1992). *Working toward a balance in our lives: A booklet for families of children with disabilities and special health care needs.* Boston: Harvard U. Press.

Public Law 93-112, *The Rehabilitation Act of 1973,* Section 504; 87 Stat.

Public Law 94-142, *The Education for All Handicapped Children Act of 1975* (EHCA), 20 U.S.C., 1400 *et seq.*

Public Law 100-407, *The Technology-Related Assistance for Individuals with Disabilities Act of 1988,* 29 U.S.C. 2202, Section 3 [1].

Public Law 101-336, *The Americans with Disabilities Act of 1990,* 42 U.S.D.A. §12101 *et seq.*

Public Law 101-476, *The Individuals with Disabilities Education Act of 1990,* U.S.C., Title 20 §1400–1485.

Rapport, M. J. K. (1996). Legal guidelines for the delivery of special health care services in schools. *Exceptional Children, 62,* 537–549.

Sawyer, R. J., McLaughlin, M. J., & Winglee, M. (1994). Is integration of students with disabilities happening? An analysis of national data trends over time. *Remedial and Special Education, 15,* 204–215.

Scipien, G. M. (1991). Basic pediatric nursing care. In B. L. Christensen & E. O. Kockrow (Eds.), *Foundations of nursing* (pp. 1194–1217). St. Louis, MO: Mosby.

Shannon M. v. Granite School District, 787 F. Supp. 1020 (D. Utah 1992).

Stein, R. E. K. (1989). Introduction. In R. E. K. Stein (Ed.), *Caring for children with chronic illness: Issues and strategies* (pp. i–xxx). New York: Springer.

Thomas. v. Davidson Academy, 846 F. Supp. 611 (M.D. Tenn. 1994).

Todaro, A. W., Failla, S., & Caldwell, T. H. (1993). A model for training community-based providers for children with special health care needs. *Journal of School Health, 63,* 262–265.

U.S. Department of Education (1995). *Seventeenth annual report to Congress on the implementation of the Individuals with Disabilities Education Act: To assure the free appropriate public education of all children with disabilities.* Washington, DC: Author.

Vitello, S. J. (1986). The Tatro case: Who gets what and why. *Exceptional Children, 52,* 353–356.

Walker, D. K., & Jacobs, F. H. (1985). Public school programs for chronically ill children. In N. Hobbs & J. M. Perrin (Eds.), *Issues in the care of children with chronic illness: A sourcebook on problems, services, and policies* (pp. 615–656). San Francisco: Jossey-Bass.

Walker, P. (1991). Where there is a way, there is not always a will: Technology, public policy, and the school integration of children who are technology-assisted. *Children's Health Care, 20,* 68–74.

Weber, M. C. (1991). Legal advocacy for medically complex children in foster care. In N. J. Hochstadt & D. M. Yost (Eds.), *The medically complex child: The transition to home care.* Chur, Switzerland: Harwood Academic Publishers.

Weiss, K. E., & Dykes, M. K. (1995). Legal issues in special education: Assistive technology and supportive services. *Physical Disabilities: Education and Related Services, 14*(1), 29–36.

CHAPTER 3

The Entry or Reentry Process: Transition from Home or Hospital to School

KEY WORDS _____

Child/student-specific training

Communication plan

Daily log

Do not resuscitate (DNR) orders

Education coordinator

Emergency care plan

Entry/reentry process

General training/orientation

Health team

Hospital health care coordinator

Individualized Education Plan

Individualized Health Care Plan

Predictable and unforeseen emergencies

School health care coordinator

Training plan

Transportation plan

Treatment plan

The time at which children with chronic physical and medical conditions enter or reenter the educational system marks a critical juncture for both the children and their families. Students whose conditions were present at birth or which arose during the early preschool years *enter* the classroom identified from the onset as children having "special needs." Others who started school as "normal" students and whose conditions developed during their childhood years *reenter* the system, typically after hospitalization, with new needs. In this chapter the entry or reentry process is examined in detail. The major focus of this chapter is on how school staff can prepare for the entry or reentry of a child with special health needs so that the transition is as smooth as possible for the child and family and for the school. The importance of adequate training of staff is also discussed. Much of the literature in this area deals specifically with the reentry of children after hospitalization. Many of the points raised are equally important for children who are either entering a new school for the first time or for children who transfer from one program to another during their school years.

The Entry or Reentry Process

The Need for Advance Planning and Collaboration

Cahners (1979, cited in Sexson & Madan-Swain, 1993), referring specifically to children who have been disfigured in some manner, has suggested that the return to school of a youngster who has developed a chronic condition is as critical for his or her social survival as medical or surgical treatment may be for his or her physical survival. The key to the successful entry or reentry into the school setting and provision of necessary services is systematic planning and collaboration among persons involved in the student's medical care and education.

Sexson and Madan-Swain (1993), in an article that addressed the reintegration needs of children and adolescents who have been out of school for some period of time as a result of a chronic illness, have suggested that although no single intervention plan can be applied to all situations, certain actions may facilitate the process. The plan must, according to these authors, include (a) preparation of the youngster and family, (b) preparation of school personnel, (c) preparation of classmates, and (d) continued follow-up of the student's progress after reentry.

Henning and Fritz (1983) suggest four additional principles referring specifically to the return of children with cancer. They suggest that (a) the efforts on behalf of the child be individualized, (b) the availability of an experienced professional be essential, (c) the activities of medical, educational, and social service professionals be coordinated, and (d) the child be treated with the expectation of success. All of these suggestions are equally appropriate for those entering the school system directly from the community as opposed to the hospital, such as the child born with spina bifida who has not been hospitalized since birth, but who requires catheterization on a regular basis during the school day.

As the youngster moves from the hospital to the home, and from home to school, a shift in delivery system is needed so that there is a continued delivery of health-related services required to support the student (Parette, Bartlett, & Holder-Brown, 1994). The school system must be prepared for this to occur. One of the first steps is to ensure that the school district has developed a set of policies and procedures that address the needs of students with chronic conditions and special health care needs. For example, policies regarding storage and administration of medication are critical, as are policies regarding the training of school personnel to carry out health care procedures. Although it is beyond the scope of the text to address all of these issues, suggested guidelines are presented, specifically in chapter 24, for some of the policy areas that are of primary concern to teachers working with these students. To assist school boards to ensure that they are properly prepared, a checklist of policy issues is shown in Table 3.1.

At the individual school level (as opposed to the district level), a clear step-by-step plan ensures that the transition process from home to school proceeds in an orderly manner. The staff of *Project School Care* at the Children's Hospital in Boston (Haynie, Palfrey, & Porter, 1989; Palfrey et al., 1992; Caldwell et al., 1997) have provided a model that outlines the key components in planning for the provision of services to students who have special health care needs. The model, shown in Figure 3.1, involves several major steps, including referral, creation of the school health team, assessment and planning, development of an individualized health care plan, training of staff and students, placement of the youngster into an appropriate school program, and ongoing follow-up and evaluation. Each of these steps, as described by those involved with the project, is discussed in detail.

TABLE 3.1
Policy Development: A Checklist

DOES YOUR SCHOOL DISTRICT HAVE POLICIES THAT DEAL WITH. . . .

☐ administration of specialized health care procedures, including policies related to liability of personnel?

☐ delivery of educational programming in the event of school absences?

☐ identification and assessment of students with chronic conditions?

☐ maintenance of health records and confidentiality of records?

☐ methods to deal with disagreements between the student's physician and school health personnel?

☐ preparation for natural disasters and the provision of care to students during emergency situations?

☐ prevention of communicable diseases and the management of students with such diseases?

☐ provision of emergency care and the management of "Do Not Resuscitate" (DNR) orders?

☐ provision of medical supplies and maintenance of specialized equipment?

☐ storage and administration of medications, including a policy on self-administration of medication?

☐ supervision of paraprofessionals (i.e., unlicensed assistive personnel) providing health care assistance?

☐ training of school personnel to carry out the health care procedures and to use universal precautions when dealing with body fluids?

The step-wise planning process outlined in this model provides hospitals and schools with guidelines for the safe provision of care that are appropriate for *all* children and young adults with special physical and health care needs and could be readily adapted to the needs of a particular school district. The steps may need to be modified slightly, depending on the individual circumstances of the student, his or her family, and the school. However, in most situations each step is necessary to ensure a smooth transition from home to school.

Referral of the Student to the Education System

Early referral of the youngster to the appropriate school personnel is of primary importance. For the child or young adult who is in the hospital, referral should occur before discharge. For the youngster at home who is just entering school, or for a student who may be transferring between programs, referral should occur as soon as a move is anticipated. Both possibilities are described in greater detail below.

The Reentry Process: Hospital to School   Even though the youngster does not reenter the school system until there has been maximum recovery and physical rehabilitation, early planning is crucial to ensure appropriate transition planning (Parette et al., 1994; Stuart & Goodsitt, 1996). In describing

the reintegration of students with cancer, Katz, Varni, Rubenstein, Blew, and Hubert (1992) have suggested that the return to school should be discussed as soon as possible after the time of diagnosis (i.e., when the youngster's medical condition has stabilized and treatment has begun) and that such discussion should be part of the student's overall medical treatment plan.

To facilitate the reentry process, one health care provider in the hospital (e.g., child life program teacher, nurse, social worker) should be designated as the **hospital health care coordinator** (also referred to in the literature as the **hospital liaison person, hospital discharge planner** or **transition liaison facilitator**) whose first responsibility is to make the initial contacts with the youngster's school. The responsibilities of the coordinator include the following: (a) making the initial contact with the school, (b) providing the school with current medical information on the student, (c) acting as a liaison between the student's health care providers (e.g., physicians, therapists) and school staff, (d) ensuring that all medical orders (e.g., schedule for the administration of a drug or a therapeutic procedure) are obtained in writing and determining the types of related services or assistive devices that are needed to enable the student to attend school, and (e) providing follow-up monitoring of the student's progress after discharge (Prendergast, 1995; Stuart & Goodsitt, 1996).

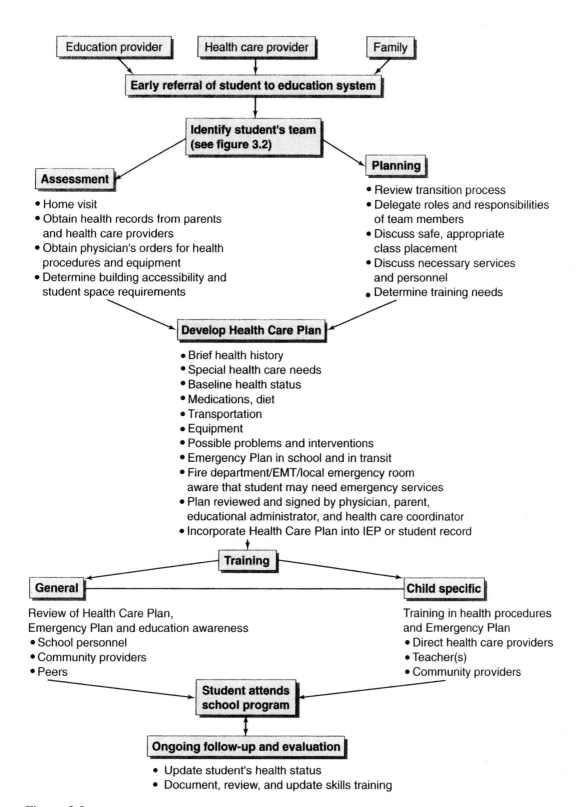

Figure 3.1

Education Entrance Process for Student with Special Health Care Needs

Source: Palfrey, J. S., Haynie, M., Porter, S., Bierle, T., Cooperman, P., & Lowcock, J. (1992). Project School Care: Integrating children assisted by medical technology into educational settings. *Journal of School Health, 62,* 50–54. Copyright 1992 by the American School Health Association, Kent, Ohio. Reprinted by permission.

There must be a key person in the school who is responsible for the transition process. Typically, one person at the school, most often the school nurse, is designated the **school health care coordinator** (also referred to in the literature as the **school health liaison person**). If the school district does not have a nurse, or the nurse has only a limited amount of time available, the school district may opt to contract with county or community nurse services (Utah State Office of Education, 1995). Choosing one person, who has the necessary time and inclination, in the school to coordinate the educational planning is particularly important in situations where the student has more than one teacher who needs current information on the student and the educational implications of the student's special physical or health care needs (Sexson & Madan-Swain, 1993).

The responsibilities of the school coordinator are multifaceted, including the following: (a) obtaining health information from health care providers; (b) determining the relative importance of the information, particularly in light of the educational implications of the student's condition; (c) coordinating and scheduling meetings with the family, the school staff, and the health service providers; (d) serving as a liaison for school, family, and medical team; (e) developing the student's health care plan; and (f) ensuring that all the necessary paperwork (e.g., consent forms) is completed (Utah State Office of Education, 1995). Parette and Bartlett (1996, p. 35) have suggested that the major function of coordinator is to merge the "multidisciplinary medical team with a multidisciplinary educational team to form a collaborative medico-educational team."

The health information that needs to be assembled by the school coordinator varies from student to student. Perry and Flanagan (1986) have suggested that the school should have complete information on: (a) the student's medical condition and treatment; (b) the side effects of all medications; (c) the limitations imposed by the medical condition; (d) the adaptations, both academic and environmental, that the condition necessitates; (e) the level of knowledge of the condition on the part of the youngster and his or her siblings; and (f) how parents want information about their son or daughter discussed with others (e.g., school personnel, classmates). Without this information, the coordinator will have difficulty determining the specific needs of the student and the impact that the student's medical problem will have on his or her ability to return to school and to participate.

In addition to the school health care coordinator, in some schools an educator (e.g., the principal, a special education consultant, a counselor) is assigned to be the **education coordinator,** also referred to as the **educational liaison person.** In many schools, the school health care coordinator serves the dual role of both health coordinator and education coordinator. However, medical personnel, in particular those who work out of a medical facility, may "lack knowledge of what schools can and must provide" (Perry & Flanagan, 1986, p. 337).

The Entry Process: Home to School or School to School Not all youngsters enter or reenter the school system directly from a medical care facility. Consequently, the original referral is *not* always initiated by a medical service provider. For a child who has had special needs since infancy and who has been living at home with his or her parents, the referral may come from an educational provider (e.g., a staff member at a program the child is attending or an itinerant therapist who sees the child in his or her home) or from the parents directly. Similarly, if the youngster has moved into a new school district or changed schools some time after being discharged from the hospital, the initial referral may come from staff at the child's school or from the parents, rather than from health care personnel.

Ideally, the referral for a first-time admission should occur at least 3 to 5 months *before* the youngster is to enter school (Caldwell et al., 1997). Unfortunately, early referral, regardless of the initiator, does not always occur. In many cases, the youngster's medical problems are only identified at the time of enrollment, during review of paperwork completed by the parents at initial registration. Schools should provide opportunities for early registration, and parents should be encouraged to contact the school as early as possible, so that delays do not result in problems with availability of services.

When the referral does not come directly from the hospital, the first step involves gathering current information on the youngster (Prendergast, 1995). Typically, the school nurse is responsible for gathering the necessary information and beginning the planning process as described previously for youngsters reentering the system.

Establishing the Student's Health Team

The next step in the process is the development of the **student's health team** (also referred to, in the literature, as the student's **medico-educational team**). In addition to the liaison persons already described, the team, shown in Figure 3.2, may include some or all of the following: the student's parents or guardians, and if appropriate, the student and his or her sibling(s) or closest friend(s), appropriateness being based on the age and maturity of the student and the degree of involvement of the siblings and friends in the student's day-to-day activities; the various health care providers from the hospital setting (e.g., attending physician, psychologist or psychiatrist, social worker, clinical nurse specialist, child life worker; therapists); other general or special education staff (e.g., homeroom teacher, physical

education teacher); relevant community providers (e.g., public health nurse, members of the emergency medical response system); and related services personnel (e.g., therapists, transportation officer).

The primary role of the health team is to ensure that the educational experiences of the student are enhanced through the creation of a safe environment within the school (Palfrey et al., 1992). To achieve this goal, some of the tasks, described in greater detail later, include: (a) determining the availability of an educational placement that is best able to meet the educational and medical needs of the student; (b) determining the availability of services and equipment and finalizing the necessary arrangements before the student enters or returns to school; (c) determining the availability of staff, their training needs, their comfort with the needs of the student, and their ability to carry out their

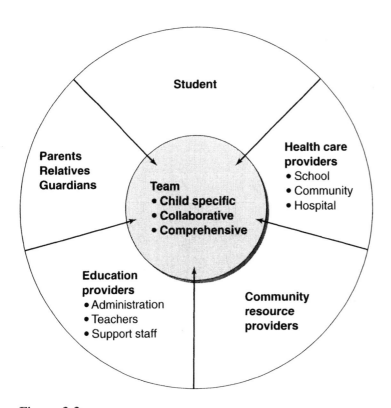

Figure 3.2

Student Team Model

Source: Palfrey, J. S., Haynie, M., Porter, S., Bierle, T., Cooperman, P., & Lowcock, J. (1992). Project School Care: Integrating children assisted by medical technology into educational settings. *Journal of School Health, 62,* 50–54. Copyright 1992 by the American School Health Association, Kent, OH. Reprinted by permission.

responsibilities to the student with special needs and to the other students in the class; (d) determining the degree to which the child's future educational environment is accessible; and (e) if appropriate, providing opportunities for the student's classmates to learn about the health care needs of the student who is returning to school and to voice any concerns that they may have.

One of the first tasks of the team is to determine the most appropriate placement for the youngster, in relationship to his or her educational needs and needs for certain related services, in particular various therapies. Typically, students with special physical or health needs are educated in their neighborhood school with their age and grade peers in a general education classroom, even if an individual caregiver is required to give continuous one-on-one care; however, in some cases, alternative plans must be made (Caldwell & Sirvis, 1991). For example, if the student needs daily scheduled nursing care (e.g., periodic dressing changes), a general education class in a magnet school (e.g., in a neighboring district), which has a school nurse or a nursing assistant on campus or someone who is able to provide services on a regular basis (i.e., an itinerant nurse or nursing assistant), might be most appropriate. Similarly, for a student who may need emergency treatments on a periodic basis (e.g., a child with a bleeding disorder

such as hemophilia), a general education class in a school in close proximity to a hospital or health clinic might be the most justifiable placement.

For a student who is in the general education classroom, the provision of related services is a major concern, in particular the various therapies (i.e., occupational therapy, physical therapy, speech therapy). Orelove and Sobsey (1991), in discussing the needs of those children with multiple needs, directed the following cautionary comments toward the various health team members:

> The challenge for the team is to determine how to work with and around the students' medical and physical needs to provide an appropriate education, rather than turning the school day into an extended therapy session. Therapy and specialized health care procedures should facilitate, not replace, instruction. (pp. 3–4)

To determine whether or not a particular service is a "related" service (a service that must be provided by the school district) or a "medical" service (a service that does not need to be provided by a school system), the health team members may be guided by the questions, adapted from Greismann, listed in Table 3.2.

Scheduling of meetings is often difficult. Typically the team will have one or more meetings before the youngster enters or reenters school. The

TABLE 3.2
Related vs. Medical Service: Factors to Be Considered

1. Is the child disabled under Public Law 101–476, The Individuals with Disabilities Education Act (IDEA)?
2. If so, does the child require a related service(s)?
3. If so, who is to provide the related service(s)?
4. If a school nurse, some other qualified person (e.g., Licensed Practical Nurse, or LPN), or layperson can provide the service, the service is probably a "related service."
5. If a physician is required to perform the service, the service is a "medical service" excluded under IDEA, unless it is for diagnostic or evaluation purposes only.
6. If the service cannot be performed by a school nurse, some other qualified person, or layperson but does not require the services of a physician, the Local Education Authority (LEA) must consider:
   a. What is the extent and complexity of the child's needs and required services?
   b. How frequently must the child be attended to?
   c. Who will be providing the services (e.g., an LPN, or some other professional)?
   d. Are the services beyond the scope of a school nurse?
   e. What skills are required to provide the service? and
   f. What is the cost to the LEA?

Source: Greismann, Z. (1990). Commentary: Medically fragile children. *West's Education Law Reporter, 61,* 403–408. Copyright 1990 by West Group. Reprinted by permission.

initial meeting most likely would not involve all the members of the health team meeting; however, the key members (i.e., the health coordinators, school nurse, homeroom teacher, parent, and student) should meet in order to "ensure the effective bridging of the medical-rehabilitation and educational committees" (Parette et al., 1994, p. 66). Subsequent meetings are held as required, and depending on the agenda of the particular meeting, additional team members may be requested to participate. For example, if the purpose of the meeting is to look at accessibility issues, the student's physical or occupational therapists might be key persons to invite.

While getting the team (or as many people as needed) together is critical, determining the best location and arranging for face-to-face meetings may be challenging. The initial meeting can take place at a variety of sites (Parette et al., 1994). Depending on the geographic constraints, the school, the student's home, or the hospital (if the student is in the hospital) may be suitable. If excessive distances are involved (i.e., the hospital is in another city), a convenient location should be identified.

In many cases, it is difficult to ensure that all health care professionals are able to attend the meetings. Even though they may not be able to participate due to other responsibilities, their reports and recommendations should "be the cornerstone of the information exchange regardless of their attendance at scheduled meetings" (Parette & Bartlett, 1996, p. 37). In some situations, a telephone conference call may be substituted; however, if possible, a face-to-face meeting should occur.

Assessment and Planning

The initial process of gathering information about the family and child and their health care needs during the assessment and planning phase is generally carried out by the hospital health care coordinator, if the child is in the hospital (Palfrey et al., 1992). If the youngster is not in the hospital at time of referral, the initial gathering of health-related information is typically performed by the school health care coordinator. Regardless of *who* obtains the information, once the initial assessment data are obtained, the designated person reports back to the overall team, which meets to decide the best placement in the school and to begin the process of preparing the school for admission.

To determine the educational and health care needs of a particular youngster, various types of information are needed. Of primary importance are the health history, information on physical status (including the ability to see, hear, and communicate), and information on how physical status will affect educational potential or ability to participate fully in the school setting as well as information regarding the cognitive ability, level of adaptive behavior, and level of social and emotional development. Details regarding the youngster's need for specific treatment (i.e., physician's orders for health procedures), related services, and specialized equipment should also be made available. Information on activity restrictions (e.g., contraindications for certain physical activities) and on anticipated absences should also be noted. If the youngster requires specialized equipment, determining space requirements is also critical (e.g., site accessibility, storage facilities).

To determine the student's educational needs, Parette and Bartlett (1996) have advocated the use of an ecological assessment. The primary area of concern would be an assessment of energy and stamina, for such information is "prerequisite to examining the environments and activities in which the child will participate in the school setting" (p. 38). Parette and Bartlett have stressed the importance of examining *all* of the environments that the student will participate in, so that the degree of accessibility, the need for equipment, and the need for specific emergency procedures can be identified, along with the training needs of personnel. They listed the following environments and activities as being essential: (a) transport to and from school; (b) entering and leaving the school building; (c) entering and leaving the school classroom; (d) transit between classrooms; (e) participation in academic classes, physical education, art, and music; (f) eating lunch; (g) using rest rooms; (h) access to drinking water; (i) using the library; (j) participation in assemblies and extracurricular activities; and (k) other activities (p. 39). Additional environments would be student-specific or school-specific (e.g., swimming pool; vocational training areas, such as the home economics kitchen or the shop). To assist school staff in gathering all of the information needed for successful entry or reentry, a checklist is provided in Appendix A. Checklists to determine the degree of accessibility of a school site are also included in Appendix A.

Development of the Health Care Plan

Once the basic information is gathered, the main task of the team is to develop a student-specific **Individualized Health Care Plan** (IHCP or IHP[1]), also referred to by some as a **Health Management Plan** (HMP). If the student is receiving special education programming and has an **Individualized Education Plan** (IEP) in place, the health care plan should be incorporated into the educational plan "as a clearly identified special section of that document" (Weiss, 1997, p. 5)[2]. For those who do not have an IEP (i.e., those who do not fall under IDEA), the health care plan is developed independently. For students whose condition is not life-threatening, the health care plan does not necessarily need to be finalized before entry. However, in such cases, it is recommended that the plan be completed no later than 30 days after the student enters or reenters the school system (Utah State Office of Education, 1995).

Individualized health care plans have been described by Haas (1993, p. 41) as a "variation of the time-honored nursing care plan adapted specifically for the school setting." Poulton (1996) defined an individualized health care plan as follows:

> An IHP is the written, preplanned and ongoing plan of care for students requiring special health services developed by licensed health personnel and the education team. It includes the nursing process of assessment, nursing diagnosis, planning, intervention, and evaluation. It also includes a plan for emergencies. The IHP is updated as needed and annually. (p. 1)

In a document prepared in 1991 by the American School Health Association (ASHA) entitled "Implementation Guide for the Standards of School Nursing Practice," the importance of a health management plan was stressed:

> The HMP contributes to the student's educational achievement and facilitates school attendance. . . . Health management plans assist in the legal

requirement that all students be able to participate in their education in the least restrictive environment. The plan allows the student to travel to off-campus field trips, work and participate in community-based events, and go to school sponsored events beyond the limits of the classroom in as safe a manner as possible. HMP's assure that any student who required medication, therapeutic treatment, specialized health services, or life-sustaining procedures during the school day will receive the service from appropriate school personnel. . . . HMP's not only assure proper services to students, they are an excellent parent public relations tool. Parents of special needs students are appreciative and comforted when a plan for their child is developed and implemented. The principal is always glad for good parent-school relations, and the HMP provides this important link. (p. 79)

Haas (1993) has suggested that not only will a health care plan ensure quality of school nursing service and serve as a means to evaluate the staffing needs of a district (e.g., by documenting the number of hours of service per week, per student), the written document also functions "as a legal protection by showing that proper plans and safeguards were in place even if a bad outcome occurred" (p. 44). Not only should the plan outline what typically occurs from day to day, it also should include backup plans in case of absent staff members (Parette et al., 1994). One of the key purposes of the plan is to "foster consistency for health care across all environments for students," including transit to and from school, in school, on field trips, and for after-school programs (Caldwell et al., 1997, p. 53).

The ASHA has outlined 14 points to writing a successful health plan. They are shown in Table 3.3. A sample Health Care Plan is contained in Appendix B. In the following pages, some of the key subsections of a student's health plan (e.g., emergency plan, transportation plan) are described in greater detail.

Emergency Care Plans   The emergency care plan, typically separate from the health care plan, includes the procedures, developed by the health team (in particular the student's physician), with guidance from the student's parents, school nurse, classroom staff, and community health professionals, that must be followed during a crisis event. For students who have a life-threatening condition, such as a severe allergy to certain food substances, it is critical that student-specific emergency procedures be clearly identified before the youngster returns to school (Graff & Ault, 1993). If contingency procedures

---

[1] Because "health care" is also commonly written as one word (healthcare), two acronyms are given.

[2] It should be noted that the concept of the IHCP is not contained in IDEA. If the IHCP is part of the IEP document, "school employees and parents will be better placed to take advantage of the legal requirement that related services identified in a child's IEP must be provided by the school district" (Weiss, 1997, p. 5). In addition, if the IHCP is part of the IEP, all people working with the child will have a greater understanding of his or her needs.

TABLE 3.3
14 Points to Writing a Successful Health Plan

1. Define the medical condition and formulate the educationally relevant nursing diagnosis.
2. Define the desired outcome or educationally relevant student-centered goals.
3. Describe the symptoms to be observed.
4. Describe the precautions or action to be taken, including time factors, potential risk factors, and safeguards required.
5. Define the course of nursing or health intervention needed and when it is needed, e.g., the plan of action.
6. Identify the school personnel responsible for implementing the plan.
7. Describe the method of recording and reporting the use of the HMP to parent, physician, or others concerned with the care of student when appropriate.
8. Identify when and how the plan will be evaluated for effectiveness or need for revision.
9. Write the plan on a form approved by the school district.
10. Obtain required signatures, e.g., nurse, parent, student if applicable, coordinator, administrator.
11. Identify availability, maintenance and storage requirements of equipment, supplies, apparatus, oxygen, medication, etc., which may be needed. Provision of the preceding is the responsibility of the parent.
12. Complete appropriate authorization forms.
13. Disseminate the completed written plan and necessary recording log to the school health office, each of the student's teachers, parents, student, bus driver, and any other identified school personnel involved with the student. The physician may be interested in receiving a copy.
14. Plan any in-service training or education needed for implementation of the health management plan.

Source: American School Health Association (1993). *Implementation guide for the standards of school nursing practice.* Kent, OH: Author. Copyright 1993 by American School Health Association, Kent, OH. Reprinted by permission.

have not been fully specified, the student should not be allowed to return to school (Utah State Office of Education, 1995). In such situations, the youngster should be provided with homebound services until the plan has been finalized.

Emergency situations can either be predictable or unforeseen (Graff & Ault, 1993). For those that are anticipated, specific steps should be established well before the situation arises, and the steps should be delineated in the health care plan and emergency care plan. For example, if a student who is on oxygen occasionally has periods in which breathing is abnormally slow, staff can be taught to respond by repositioning the student, stimulating the student to increase respiratory response, and increasing the flow of the oxygen. For those crises that are unexpected, training in first aid and cardiopulmonary resuscitation (CPR) is essential. All staff should be encouraged to be certified.

"Predictable" emergencies. The typical components included in a child-specific emergency care plan are shown in Table 3.4. All emergency procedures must be clear and easy to follow, and the plan must be accessible to all personnel working with the student. The clearly delineated steps must be posted next to the telephone in *all* locations where the student might be present. Telephone numbers of emergency response teams, parents, designated alternatives if the parents are unavailable, and physicians also need to be clearly evident. An example of an emergency care plan, with detailed steps to follow if a life-threatening emergency occurs, is shown in Appendix C.

For children who are extremely medically fragile, part of the emergency care plan may be a set of orders, known as **Do Not Resuscitate (DNR) orders,** which apply to that student and that student alone. Such orders request that those in contact with the student refrain from intervening in life-threatening emergency situations, such as cardiac arrest. DNR orders, issued by the student's doctor upon request of the parents or guardians, are written for those students who are known to have a terminal condition and typically include such statements as "Do not call 911," "Do not institute artificial breathing," "Do not clear the airway if blocked," or "Do not perform CPR."

DNR orders in educational settings (as opposed to medical facilities) are controversial. Some believe

TABLE 3.4
Typical Components of an Emergency Care Plan

1. Student-specific medical emergencies (specific signs of distress should be defined)
2. Designated personnel in the community (fire, police, hospitals, ambulance, and any other emergency departments) should be notified/consulted when the student with special health care needs is attending school
3. Designated personnel in the school (school nurse, back-up personnel) who have been trained to deal with the emergency
4. A summary of the student's medical condition and needs which should be on file at the local hospital emergency room, if indicated
5. The preferred hospital emergency room identified in case of the need to transport
6. A written plan with emergency contacts for family, physician and emergency personnel (post telephone numbers in various locations)
7. Provisions for extra medication, backup equipment and generators in case of a natural disaster
8. A formal, documented procedure to review the plan with ALL personnel on a regular basis

Source: Utah State Office of Education (1995). *Utah guidelines for serving students with special health care needs.* Salt Lake City, UT: Author. Copyright 1995 by Utah State Office of Education. Reprinted by permission.

that such requests force educators to make medical judgments that are outside their level of professional competency (Kloppenburg & Dykes, 1995). Others, however, are of the opinion that, at least for the youngster, the best thing that can be "done" in such emergency situations is to hold the youngsters, reassuring them that they are not alone, while another staff person phones the student's parents to notify them of the situation (Rushton, Will, & Murray, 1994). For further discussion of DNR policies, see chapter 24.

"Unforeseen" emergencies. All school staff should also have an emergency care plan in place that is *not* child-specific. To assist in the development of such a plan, the American Academy of Pediatrics Committee on School Health (1990) has provided a series of guidelines that may be invaluable for school staff in dealing with urgent care of students in school, regardless of whether the care is being given to a child with a chronic condition or the emergency involves a student with no known health problem. The guidelines are shown in Table 3.5.

Treatment Plans   If schools are going to agree to administer medications (i.e., physician-prescribed, parent-prescribed, and self-prescribed medications) or carry out prescribed health care procedures (e.g., chest physiotherapy), the district must ensure that adequate safety measures are in place. Policies and guidelines for the safe administration of both long- and short-term medications are given in chapter 24.

Sample permission forms and treatment logs are found in Appendix D.

Transportation Plans   Many youngsters who have chronic physical or medical conditions travel to school by buses provided either by the local school district or by companies hired by the school district to supply transportation services. Although some students with health care needs travel with an aide, many who have chronic conditions travel without any assistance. However, it is these same youngsters who may have a serious asthma attack or a seizure en route to school or home. School districts should ensure that all school buses are equipped with a two-way radio or cellular telephone in case of such emergencies.

Bus drivers and bus attendants (and substitutes) should know health care plan(s) of the student(s) they are transporting and should be encouraged to participate in team planning meetings. The Colorado State Pupil Transportation Association Special Education Committee (1991, pp. 8–9) has delineated two functions of transportation staff persons in their role as members of the health care team. The first function is "to educate the assessment team members regarding the transportation environment (e.g., type and configuration of the vehicle the student would likely be assigned to ride; the probable length of ride; conditions with respect to temperature extremes during loading/unloading and on the bus; the type of device/occupant securement system to be used; the emergency communication system available; degree

TABLE 3.5
Guidelines for Urgent Care in School

1. Every school district should identify individuals who are authorized and trained to make urgent medical care decisions.

2. An emergency care manual and standing orders for first aid should be written and made available to nurses, athletic staff, and faculty volunteers.

3. Procedures should be in place to summon help in catastrophic and urgent care situations from emergency sources within the community, including rescue squads and, where available, the 911 system.[a] Transportation to a hospital or medical facility should be accessible.

4. The school nurse in each building should be the key person to carry out the program as she or he is most familiar with the students' health problems. All nurses should be trained in a program of emergency care developed by physicians, emergency medical technicians, and/or other nurses with special training in emergency care.

5. As school nurses or physicians cannot always be available, two or more regular members of the school staff, depending on school size, should be designated and trained to handle emergencies according to established protocols until the nurse, physician, or other emergency personnel can be reached. Programs should include training in first aid, cardiopulmonary resuscitation, and anaphylaxis recognition[b] and treatment. These programs can be directed by school nurses trained in emergency care with a physician's supervision as described in the preceding paragraph. If this training is not available, the Red Cross or Emergency Medical Technician training may be used. Training should be on a voluntary basis with certificates provided. State certification could be offered, if available. Periodic recertification should be required to ensure competence. Those faculty members who are trained can be used to help nurses train all teachers and students in first aid principles.

6. Legislation should be encouraged in each state, under the "Good Samaritan Act," to provide legal protection for emergency care givers.

7. An emergency medical kit and anaphylaxis kit should be kept with the medications in each school, and the kits should be made available to trained staff volunteers.

8. Emergencies related to participation in athletics may be handled by a trainer or athletic staff member trained in sports medicine and emergency care.

9. Parents must be informed about injuries their children receive at school as quickly as possible. If a parent or legal guardian cannot be reached, the name and telephone number of an individual to be contacted in case of an emergency should be readily available. Description and disposition of illnesses or injuries of a serious nature (those illnesses or injuries in which a student, staff member, or visitor is released from school to see a physician or to be seen at a hospital) should be recorded on an illness and accident form according to predetermined district procedures.[c]

[a] See Appendix C for information on emergency telephone procedures.
[b] See chapter 22.
[c] See Appendix C for a sample Accident Report Form.
Source: American Academy of Pediatrics, Committee on School Health (1990). Guidelines for urgent care in school, *Pediatrics, 86,* 999–1000. Copyright 1990 by The American Academy of Pediatrics. Reprinted by permission.

of training and skills of the driver; the availability of a bus attendant)"; the second function is to "gather information regarding the student's expected transportation needs so as to properly plan for a timely, efficient, and safe initiation of transportation service." Based on the information gained by the transportation staff, a transportation plan can be written. Appendix E shows a sample transportation plan form.

The following skills, along with knowledge of the student's unique health care needs (including the type of emergency the student might have on the bus), basic first aid, and cardiopulmonary resuscitation, are critical for transport staff (Utah State Office of Education, 1995):

- Knowledge of the emergency departments located near the specific bus route
- Knowledge of the shortest route to any emergency hospital from any location on the bus route
- Means to obtain emergency assistance from police, fire, or ambulance services
- Ability to evacuate the bus in an orderly and efficient fashion and to control the students after they have left the bus
- Knowledge of techniques for lifting and carrying students correctly without causing harm to the student or themselves
- Knowledge of specific procedures required if the bus is involved in an accident

Transportation staff should also be trained to carry out universal precautions (see chapters 23 and 24) to ensure that students and staff on the school bus are not unnecessarily exposed to infectious and communicable disease. Transportation staff should receive student-specific training before the students enter or return to school.

Recently, the American Academy of Pediatrics (1994) has issued a set of guidelines for the safe transportation of persons who are in wheelchairs, strollers, or special seating devices or who travel with specialized equipment (e.g., liquid oxygen cylinders). For further information on the transportation of students with special health care needs, the reader is referred to that document and to a survey published by Everly, Bull, Stroup, Goldsmith, Doll, and Russell (1993) that isolated some of the problems that occur when schools, rehabilitation facilities, and community agencies attempt to transport clients with disabilities (e.g., size and weight of student, different types of disabilities, variations between types of vehicles). In this article, and in a recent article by Daley and Larsen (1997), sources for seating and transportation equipment (e.g., car seats, security vests) are provided. The previously mentioned Colorado State Pupil Transportation Association publication may also be of assistance.

Training of Staff and Students

Before the child enters or reenters school, a variety of staff persons need either general or student-specific training, depending on the extent of their contact with the student. One of the primary persons is the youngster's teacher. In discussing the need for teacher training, Stein (1986, p. 72) made the following comments:

> It is quite unrealistic to expect educators to become fully acquainted with every aspect of every condition. On the other hand, it is equally naive to expect educators to have a child in their programs whose medical safety may be jeopardized because the teachers do not understand the child's medical status at all.

- *General training.* Also referred to as **orientation,** general training should be offered to all school personnel who may be in contact with the student. School personnel does not just include teachers and teacher aides. It is critical that nurses and nursing assistants, therapists and therapy aides, bus drivers and bus monitors, playground supervisors,

and, in particular, the school secretary (often the first order helper in times of crisis) be fully aware of the needs of students who are members of the school community. General training may also be appropriate for classmates.

- *Child/student-specific training.* In contrast to general training, student-specific training is offered to all staff who will be providing specialized health care services (e.g., nurses, health aides, teachers, teacher aides) to the pupil while attending school. Before the implementation of the various training sessions and in consultation with the parents, the specific information that is to be shared must be determined, as well as with whom and how it will be shared.

Training Plans   As part of the student's individualized health care plan, a **training plan,** itemizing who should be trained and by whom, should be developed. A sample personnel training plan is shown in Appendix F. Since care-givers may not always be available when needed to perform a particular task, some school districts have implemented a policy that more than one person be trained. For example, Gwinnett County Public Schools, in Georgia, requires that a team of four staff members be trained to perform each and every student-specific procedure (Jordan & Weinroth, 1996). Given the normal turnover of staff, training should be offered on a regular basis. Training is addressed in further detail in the next section.

Providing for Ongoing Communication

The final step before entry or reentry is the identification of a process that will be used to ensure *ongoing* communication about the student's health (Graff & Ault, 1993). Parents will want to communicate regularly with school staff regarding absences, homework, minor illnesses, appointment schedules, updates on the child's progress, and any other problems that might arise at home. Teaching staff will want to inform the parents of any problems that might have occurred during the day at school, as well as request additional supplies or equipment, which the parent provides.

Communication Plans   Ongoing communication is generally best accomplished by maintaining a **daily log** that travels from home to school and back again. Since the information that needs to be shared differs from student to student, and from day to day, it is probably unlikely that one set form will be adopted. Staff should experiment with different forms, but a basic rule of thumb is to keep it easy. The simpler (and less time-consuming) the form is to complete, the more likely staff and parents will use it. A sample daily log form is shown in Appendix G. Blank copies of the form can be placed in a loose-leaf binder and filed at the end of the month.

Follow-up and Evaluation

Once the team feels that an appropriate placement has been determined, school staff are adequately trained, emergency procedures have been developed, a mechanism for ongoing communication is in place, and the necessary staff, supplies, and equipment are available, the team is ready for the youngster to enter or reenter school. At this point, the health care plan is signed by all members of the team. To ensure that all the steps have been followed, the checklist shown in Appendix H may be of assistance.

The work of the student's health care team is *not*, however, completed simply because the student has entered or reentered school. Regular, ongoing follow-up of the student's progress is essential. In the case of a student who has been recently released from hospital, the hospital liaison person should remain in contact with the school (e.g., by means of regular phone calls to the teacher or school liaison person) at least for the first month or two after discharge, in order to monitor any school-related difficulties that may have arisen (Sexson & Madan-Swain, 1993). This support can be slowly withdrawn, particularly if the reintegration process is proceeding smoothly, and especially if responsibility for the educational programming of the student is being fully assumed by the school staff themselves. Members of the school-based team must be encouraged to contact hospital staff at any time, even if it is months after discharge, if questions or concerns arise.

In order to evaluate the outcomes of intervention, Poulton (1996) has listed six critical steps. They are shown in Table 3.6. In addition, Sobsey and Cox (1991) have itemized the following questions that should be asked routinely:

(a) Is the procedure being provided in a safe and effective manner? (b) Is the record-keeping system sufficient without being cumbersome? (c) Are staffing needs adequate? (d) Is the process supportive of the

TABLE 3.6
Steps to Evaluating the Outcomes of an IHP

1. Review predicted student goal or outcome.
2. Collect data as specified in the goals and interventions (i.e., daily log from classroom or student questionnaire).
3. Compare actual outcome to desired outcome/goal.
4. Document the actual student outcome on IHP.
5. Relate interventions to goal achievement.
6. Review and modify plan as necessary.

Source: Poulton, S. (1996). *Guidelines to writing individualized healthcare plans.* Reprinted by permission.

student's education program? (e) Are the parents comfortable with and supportive of the plan? and (f) Is communication between the school and home ongoing and effective? (p. 178)

All follow-up meetings of the health care team should be carefully documented in a health care plan log, and any problems (e.g., excessive absenteeism, poor mental state) should be referred back to the student's attending physician either directly or via the hospital health care coordinator. If the student's doctor changes any treatment procedures or suggests alternative equipment based on evolving needs, this information must also be incorporated into the youngster's health care plan on an ongoing basis (Parette et al., 1994). As part of the monitoring of the student's situation, regular inservice training sessions should be scheduled to update skills of existing staff and new staff.

Ensuring Safe, High-Quality Services: A Training Model

Adequate training is crucial in developing a comprehensive system of care for students with chronic conditions. In many cases, the amount of training required depends on the background qualifications of the persons being trained. Some staff working in schools will have completed some level of medical training (e.g., registered nurses, licensed practical nurses, health aides); others will have specialized training in one therapeutic approach (e.g., occupational, physical, speech, and respiratory therapists). Some (e.g., teachers, child care workers) may be trained to work with students in educational settings; others (e.g., special education teachers) may be trained to work with persons who have physical or medical disabilities. In addition, some staff (e.g., social workers, psychologists, counselors) may be trained in social and emotional development, and finally, some (e.g., secretaries, lunch aides, playground supervisors, bus drivers) may have had little or no training in working specifically with children.

Before implementing a training program, several points must be considered. Each jurisdiction (e.g., state, province) has its own regulations regarding *who* can provide certain services. The school health team must ensure that the person(s) designated to receive instruction have the proper qualifications to avoid conflict with currently mandated professional standards.[2] For example, although a registered nurse may be trained to work with persons dependent on a ventilator and be trained to provide tracheostomy care, that same nurse is not trained as a respiratory therapist and may not be allowed, by legal statute, to adjust the controls of a ventilator. Similarly, even though a licensed practical nurse or a health aide may be trained to feed persons through a nasogastric tube (a tube inserted into the stomach via the nose) if they have adequate supervision from a registered nurse, they may not, in certain states under the Nurse Practice Act (e.g., Illinois, Indiana), be allowed to give medication through the tube (or by any other method, for that matter).

Even though some medically trained staff may be trained, their skills may not be adequate because of lack of practice or changing technologies and techniques, and they may not feel comfortable instructing new workers without updating their skills (Todaro, Failla, & Caldwell, 1993). For example, a school nurse may have received instruction in providing postural drainage, a technique used to drain secretions from the lungs, during initial nursing training and may have considerable experience in carrying out the procedure, but the nurse may not be aware of the correct positions to use with a specific youngster and will need student-specific training before providing the treatment or instructing someone else to carry out the procedure. In this situation, the school nurse should receive upgrading from the respiratory therapist who has worked with the youngster, before the student enters the school system.

Finally, some teachers may feel very uneasy with the prospect of having a particular student with a chronic condition in their classrooms (e.g., a student with a seizure disorder, a youngster dependent on a ventilator) or may not feel comfortable providing certain health-related procedures, even though they may be capable of providing the assistance (e.g., administering oral medications). While there are no easy solutions to this situation, often fears and anxieties can be lessened with adequate training. Youngsters should never be placed in classrooms where they are not welcomed, and if at all possible, alternative arrangements must be made (e.g., another teacher chosen, the child moved to a different school).

Levels of Training

With these initial points in mind, a training model developed by the National Maternal and Child Health Resource Center at Children's Hospital, New Orleans, Louisiana (Caldwell, Todaro & Gates, 1989; Caldwell, Todaro, Gates, Failla, & Kirkhart, 1991; Todaro et al., 1993) will be described. The overall model, shown in Table 3.7, involves 12 steps that must be followed in order to adequately manage the care of students with special health care needs in community settings, such as schools, in an organized manner. In this model there are three different levels of training: orientation or general training, child-specific training, and trainer's training. Each level is described in detail.

Orientation or General Training   This first level of training should be provided to all personnel in contact with the student. Orientation provides staff with a general overview of the student's medical condition and up-to-date information about the illness, its treatment, and related technologic advances. The Center recommends that parents, mental health professionals, physicians, nurses, and others who are experienced in caring for children with chronic illnesses be involved in the orientation sessions.

The goal of the first level of training is to "positively influence attitudes and provide an information base from which providers can design technical

---

[2] For further information regarding the training of school personnel, and specifically educational support personnel, the reader is referred to the comprehensive handbook by Weiss (1997) available online at http://nea.org.

TABLE 3.7
Steps for Managing the Care of Children with Special Health Care Needs

1. Obtain individualized prescriptions and protocols for procedures to be performed.
2. Review protocols approved by the physician with parents, and have them sign a form indicating their agreement with the procedures outlined in the protocol.
3. Include parents/guardians and child in the training.
4. Provide an appropriate level of training for anyone who will be involved in the child's care, including bus drivers, etc.
5. Train at least two individuals about the daily care of a child.
6. Include maintenance and emergency procedures in the training.
7. Document that appropriate training, based on protocols, has occurred. Include person's name, specific procedures demonstrated, and the date of scheduled rechecks.
8. Establish contingency plans. Train other personnel who will take over when the major caretakers are not available and who will be available to assist the major caretaker in an emergency situation.
9. Develop and document plans with physicians and parents for transport to and service in the local emergency room.
10. Provide information to agencies providing services to the school/agency, such as electric and telephone companies, to advise them of the need of priority service reinstatement.
11. Provide information to agencies interacting with the school/agency during natural disasters, such as fire department or Red Cross, to acquaint them with the child's participation in the particular school/agency and the needs that the child will have during an emergency.
12. Document the needs and how they will be met in the Individual Education Plan (IEP), the school health care plan, or other designated forms.

Source: Todaro, A. W., Failla, S., & Caldwell, T. H. (1993). A model for training community-based providers for children with special health care needs. *Journal of School Health, 63,* 262–265. Copyright 1993 by Children's Hospital, National MCH Resource Center, New Orleans, LA. Reprinted by permission.

assistance plans" and is geared toward increasing the knowledge of participants and sensitizing workers to the needs of the child and the family (Todaro et al., 1993, p. 265). In addition, general training helps to "demystify" the youngster's situation and to ensure that basic information, such as who to get further information from and what to do in an emergency situation, is provided (Palfrey et al., 1992). As part of the initial training, it is recommended that all school personnel complete a basic first-aid course, including training in cardiopulmonary resuscitation (CPR), and that regular follow-up inservice training be provided to ensure that CPR certification remains current. General training should also include training on how to minimize the spread of infection through adherence to universal precautions.

Orientation sessions often provide opportunities for discussions of the psychosocial issues related to chronic illness and childhood. Such sessions allow school personnel the opportunity to explore their own conceptions of illness, body changes, handicapping conditions (Perry & Flanagan, 1986), and the inevitability of death. If a school has a student who

has a life-threatening condition, it is appropriate to offer staff training in how to deal with death and dying and how to access resources that may be appropriate and useful with the child's peers, so that they will be as well prepared for the event as possible.

Orientation of the youngster's peers may differ significantly from that offered to adults in contact with the student. In Table 3.8, some guidelines are presented to assist in developing age-appropriate inservice sessions.

Sexson and Madan-Swain (1993) have listed a number of questions that are frequently asked by peers. Persons providing student-specific information should be prepared to answer questions such as those in Table 3.9.

Child/Student-Specific Training The training that is needed to work with a specific student must be provided to those who will be physically caring for the student and to back-up personnel who are required to fill in when the primary care giver is not available. Nurses, nurse aides, health aides, teachers, teacher aides, and bus aides are the primary recipients of this

TABLE 3.8
Orientation of Peers

1. Involve the child with special health needs in decision making and planning.

2. Allow the child to decide whether he/she will participate or whether he/she wants to be identified as the child with the condition being discussed.

3. Keep in mind the age of the child and child's peers when designing interventions. The complexity and type of materials used will vary depending on the age of the children.

4. Use pictures, drawings, and audiovisuals. Whenever possible, provide the opportunity for hands-on experiences.

5. Compare "normal" anatomy so that they can compare special functioning to their functioning, e.g., compare a tracheotomy to a nose.

6. Prepare the child with special health needs ahead of time. Some questions may be difficult to answer. Make sure to include some of the more difficult questions in your preparation, e.g., Will you die soon? Let the child know that he/she may choose to answer or not answer difficult questions.

7. Prepare classmates for the presentation by providing background information and encouraging open communication regarding the health condition.

8. Training plans should include the opportunity for children to gain specific information, to relate the disability to their own experiences, e.g., "My grandmother has arthritis," and to discuss their experiences and feelings about the topic being discussed.

9. Answer questions simply and without a lot of detail. Give simple answers and ask if more clarification is needed.

10. Treat the child and peers with respect and answer questions as openly as possible.

Source: Caldwell, T. H., Todaro, A. W., Gates, A. J., Failla, S., & Kirkhart, K. (Eds.) (1991). *Community provider guide: An information outline for working with children with special health needs: 1991 addendum.* New Orleans: National MCH Resource Center, Children's Hospital. Copyright 1991 by National MCH Resource Center. Reprinted by permission.

type of preparation. Student-specific training is generally given by the staff from the local medical facility, home health care providers, or other community-based health care professionals with specific clinical

TABLE 3.9
Questions Typically Asked by Peers

- Is the disease contagious?
- Will _____ die from it?
- Will he/she lose any more limbs?
- Can _____ still play, visit me at home, drive, date, etc.?
- Should we talk about _____ 's illness or should we ignore it?
- What will other kids think if I'm still friends with _____ ?
- What's wrong with _____ ?
- Will _____ be different (look funny, bleed, faint, cough, vomit) when he/she comes back?

Source: Sexson, S. B., & Madan-Swain, A. (1993). School reentry for the child with chronic illness. *Journal of Learning Disabilities, 26,* 115–125. Copyright 1993 by PRO-ED, Inc. Reprinted by permission.

expertise, such as respiratory therapists, occupational therapists, and physical therapists. While child-specific training is typically thought of as training required to carry out medical procedures, teachers need to know specific information regarding the student with a chronic condition. Weiss (1997) has prepared a typical "curriculum" for training Educational Support Personnel (ESP) (Table 3.10).

The school health coordinator must ensure that staff are adequately trained and that their skills are reviewed routinely, particularly those related to emergency situations that are not often performed. Child-specific training should be repeated on a regular basis. It should be offered (a) at least once a year, (b) after an emergency has occurred, (c) when new staff are employed, and (d) whenever there has been a change in the student's health care status (Utah State Office of Education, 1995).

After completion of the training, personnel are required to demonstrate an adequate level of competency before being allowed to work with the student. The Center has developed a set of guidelines (Table 3.11) that can be used to determine proficiency. Competency levels of staff must be carefully documented by the trainer.

TABLE 3.10
Curriculum for ESP Training

> - The five "rights" of medication administration
>   The right medication
>   The right dose
>   The right time
>   The right student
>   The right route to administer the medication
> - The specific needs of individual students (i.e.,
>   what to do for each student in their care)
> - How to document medication administration or
>   health care procedures.
> - Proper protocol for emergencies
> - How to store medication
> - Information about legal issues affecting ESPs
>   who provide health care. For example:
>   Sexual harassment laws
>   Liability
>   What to do when ordered to perform a ser-
>   vice if it endangers the student
>   Confidentiality
>   Chain of command

Source: Weiss, J. (1997). *Providing safe health care: The role of educational support personnel.* Copyright 1997 by the National Education Association. Adapted by permission.

Persons working with the student must recognize their personal and professional limitations and know who to contact for assistance (Graff & Ault, 1993). Additionally, those without adequate medical training (e.g., teachers, teacher aides, bus aides) must not apply skills which are specific to one student to another, regardless of the similarity of the health problems.

An often forgotten aspect of child-specific training is the preparation of the *child* with the chronic condition. Children with special physical or health care needs who have been in a hospital may have been sheltered from the teasing and the stares of the other children. Similarly, those who are not in a hospital may have been isolated by their parents in their own home and had little contact with able-bodied, healthy peers. As a consequence, these youngsters may not have had to answer questions related to their condition or the treatment of the condition posed by uninformed persons and may need to learn how to answer these questions. Henning and Fritz (1983) have suggested that practice in answering specific questions would be beneficial, along with the opportunity to talk to others who have had similar experiences. Sexson and Madan-Swain (1993) have suggested that students could practice the strategies that they have learned with others, such as classmates at Sunday school, prior to returning to

TABLE 3.11
Competency Guidelines for Child-Specific Training of Nonlicensed Care Providers

> 1. Verbalizes description of child's medical condition and related health maintenance requirements. The description should include knowledge of regular structure and function of health systems.
> 2. Uses a guideline to review the child's health status, including but not limited to mental/emotional, heart, lung, nutritional, skin, neurological, and musculoskeletal status.
> 3. Verbalizes essential steps of prescribed health procedure that fulfills physician, school/agency, and parent requirements.
> 4. Verbalizes warning signs and symptoms and precautions specific to the child's health procedure, abnormal physiological responses, and equipment failure.
> 5. Demonstrates 100% competency in the delivery of procedure in accordance with written guidelines for a minimum number of times.
> 6. Demonstrates ability to troubleshoot, determine problem, initiate and carry out designated emergency procedures in cases of equipment malfunction, and/or abnormal physiological responses of the child.
> 7. Demonstrates clear and concise documentation of child's functioning and responses to care.
> 8. Responds appropriately to "what if . . ." questions posed during training.
> 9. Identifies procedures to request technical assistance from licensed personnel to provide ongoing supervision and rechecks.

Source: Todaro, A. W., Failla, S., & Caldwell, T. H. (1993). A model for training community-based providers for children with special health care needs. *Journal of School Health, 63,* 262–265. Copyright 1993 by Children's Hospital, National MCH Resource Center, New Orleans, LA. Reprinted by permission.

TABLE 3.12
Competency Guidelines for Trainers: Technical Skills

1. Assesses child's health status.
2. Verbalizes description of child's medical condition and related health maintenance requirements. The description should include knowledge of regular structure and function of health systems.
3. Obtains written prescription from the physician for each health maintenance procedure required for a specific child.
4. Uses a guideline to develop a comprehensive health plan including but not limited to mental/emotional, heart, lung, nutritional, skin, neurological, and musculoskeletal status.
5. Individualizes health maintenance procedures for each child in collaboration with the child's parent or legal guardian and obtains signature.
6. Verbalizes essential steps of prescribed health procedure that fulfills physician, school/agency, and parent requirements.
7. Verbalizes and documents warning signs, symptoms, and precautions specific to the child's health procedure, abnormal physiological responses, and equipment failure.
8. Demonstrates procedure in accordance with written guidelines.
9. Develops a written child-specific emergency plan.
10. Demonstrates ability to troubleshoot, determine problem, initiate, and carry-out designated emergency procedures in case of equipment malfunction, and/or abnormal physiological responses of the child.
11. Demonstrates clear and concise documentation of child's functioning and responses to care.
12. Demonstrates training of at least two caregivers who will be working with two different children.
13. Develops system for reviewing and updating the child's health plan with the family and trainee as indicated by school's/agency's policies and procedures and/or indicated by changes in child's health status.

Source: Todaro, A. W., Failla, S., & Caldwell, T. H. (1993). A model for training community-based providers for children with special health care needs. *Journal of School Health, 63,* 262–265. Copyright 1993 by Children's Hospital, National MCH Resource Center, New Orleans, LA. Reprinted by permission.

school. In addition, the youngsters may need the opportunity to express their fears and may need help in dealing with their first peer encounter, in terms of both their peers' anxiety and their own (Kagen-Goodheart, 1977).

Trainer's Training   In many situations, it is common for family members (e.g., parents) or primary caregivers (e.g., foster parents, child care workers) to be directly involved in providing assistance to those with chronic conditions. At the time of initial diagnosis, before the youngster is discharged from the hospital, family members or primary caregivers are trained by hospital staff to carry out the required procedures at home and in many cases have had considerable experience working with the student before the return to school. Even though they may be fully trained and may have mastered the competencies required to carry out the procedures, they may not be sufficiently trained to instruct others in how to carry out the procedures in question. In the final level of training, referred to

as trainer's training, instruction is provided that will make such persons successful in passing on their skills and knowledge to others. Competency guidelines for trainers, in terms of technical skills and teaching skills, are provided in Tables 3.12 and 3.13 respectively.

Since there is the possibility of harm occurring if procedures are not carried out in the prescribed manner, it is better to have staff instructed by medically trained personnel rather than by persons who are not medically trained (Prendergast, 1995). It is the school health care coordinator's duty to ensure that training is provided by competent, adequately trained personnel.

While the model developed by Todaro and her colleagues provides a wealth of information, the issue of the qualifications (i.e., background training in medical and other fields) of the person being trained was not addressed, except as noted in the area of training the trainers. Policies regarding the credentials of those providing health-related services are explored in further detail in chapter 24.

TABLE 3.13
Competency Guidelines for Trainers: Teaching Skills

1. Individualizes methods of training to maximize skills and knowledge of the trainee.
2. Responds appropriately to questions posed during the training sessions.
3. Reviews appropriate documentation related to child's health care.
4. Poses "what if . . ." questions during training to evaluate knowledge and skills of the trainee.
5. Documents trainee's performance of the essential steps of the individualized procedure.
6. Documents strengths and weaknesses of each trainee for each specific health maintenance procedure.
7. Recommends time periods for rechecks of trainee's skills.
8. Provides or designates person for follow-up of trainee's skills.
9. Documents trainee's skills level at each recheck.

Source: Todaro, A. W., Failla, S., & Caldwell, T. H. (1993). A model for training community-based providers for children with special health care needs. *Journal of School Health, 63,* 262–265. Copyright 1993 by Children's Hospital, National MCH Resource Center, New Orleans, LA. Reprinted by permission.

Summary

As the life expectancy of youngsters with chronic conditions increases, and as more and more are able to leave the confines of the hospital and return to the community, schools must be prepared to accept them into the classrooms. However, a new collaborative approach is needed if the reentry process is to be successful. In an article entitled "Stop the World, They Want to Get On," DiCroce (1990) made the following statements about the collected effort required:

> For a child with a hospital-to-home-to-school cycle and a need to master the increasing base of knowledge and treatment technology available, the best chance for success lies in effective coordination and cooperation of various groups of people who share concerns for children and their well-being.
>
> Creative ideas are needed to maximize collective efforts of health care professionals, teachers, community groups like fraternal and school organizations, families, and the children themselves without increasing costs, already prohibitive to many. As long as these groups continue to function in isolation, they will maintain their biases. But by working together, they can pinpoint a common goal and share responsibility to meet the goal. (p. 81–82)

In chapter 4, the impact of chronic health problems on children is discussed. How a specific illness can affect schooling is addressed, and some of the problems related to attendance and school performance are examined in greater detail. In chapter 5 the impact of a child's poor health on family members, school staff, and friends is considered.

References

American Academy of Pediatrics, Committee on Injury and Poison Prevention (1994). School bus transportation of children with special needs. *Pediatrics, 93,* 129–130.

American Academy of Pediatrics, Committee on School Health (1990). Guidelines for urgent care in school, *Pediatrics, 86,* 999–1000.

American School Health Association (1993). *Implementation guide for the standards of school nursing practice.* Kent, OH: Author.

Caldwell, T. H., Janz, J. R., Alcouloumre, D. S., Porter, S., Haynie, M., Palfrey, J. S., Bierle, T., Silva, T., Still, J., Sirvis, B. P., Schwab, N., & Mahony, A. S. (1997). Entrance and planning process for students with special health care needs. In S. Porter, M. Haynie, T. Bierle, T. H. Caldwell, & J. S. Palfrey (1997), *Children and youth assisted by medical technology in educational settings: Guidelines for care* (2nd ed., pp. 41–62). Baltimore: Paul H. Brookes.

Caldwell, T. H., & Sirvis, B. (1991). Students with special health conditions: An emerging population presents new challenges. *Preventing School Failure, 35*(3), 13–18.

Caldwell, T. H., Todaro, A. W., & Gates, A. J. (1989). *Community provider's guide: An information outline for working with children with special health needs.* New Orleans, LA: National MCH Resource Center, Children's Hospital.

Caldwell, T. H., Todaro, A. W., Gates, A. J., Failla, S., & Kirkhart, K. (Eds.) (1991). *Community provider guide: An information outline for working with children with special health needs: 1991 addendum.* New Orleans: National MCH Resource Center, Children's Hospital.

Colorado State Pupil Transportation Association (1991). *Transporting the special needs student.* Denver: Author.

Daley, J. E., & Larsen, S. M. (1997). Transportation of students with special health care needs. In S. Porter, M. Haynie, T. Bierle, T. H. Caldwell, & J. S. Palfrey (1997), *Children and youth assisted by medical technology in educational settings: Guidelines for care* (2nd ed., pp. 63–71). Baltimore: Paul H. Brookes.

DiCroce, H. R. (1990). Stop the world, they want to get on. *Health Progress, 71*(3), 80–82.

Everly, J. S., Bull, M. J., Stroup, K. B., Goldsmith, J. J., Doll, J. P., & Russell, R. (1993). A survey of transportation services for children with disabilities. *The American Journal of Occupational Therapy, 47*, 804–810.

Graff, J. C., & Ault, M. M. (1993). Guidelines for working with students having special health care needs. *Journal of School Health, 63*, 335–338.

Greismann, Z. (1990). Commentary: Medically fragile children. *West's Education Law Reporter, 61*, 403–408.

Haas, M. B. (1993). Individualized healthcare plans. In M. B. Haas (Ed.), *The school nurse's source book of individualized healthcare plans* (pp. 41–45). North Branch, MN: Sunrise River Press.

Haynie, M., Palfrey, J. S., & Porter, S. M. (1989). *Children assisted by medical technology in educational settings: Guidelines for care.* Boston: Project School Care, The Children's Hospital.

Henning, J., & Fritz, G. K. (1983). School reentry in childhood cancer. *Psychosomatics, 24,* 261–264, 269.

Jordan, A., & Weinroth, M. D. (1996). A school system's model for meeting special health care needs. *Physical Disabilities: Education and Related Services, 15*(1), 27–32.

Kagen-Goodheart, L. (1977). Reentry: Living with childhood cancer. *American Journal of Orthopsychiatry, 47,* 651–658.

Katz, E. R., Varni, J. W., Rubenstein, C. L., Blew, A., & Hubert, N. (1992). Teacher, parent, and child evaluative rating of a school reintegration intervention for children with newly diagnosed cancer. *Children's Health Care, 21,* 69–75.

Kloppenburg, D., & Dykes, M. K. (1995, May). Do not resuscitate! The schools' response to DNR orders. *CEC Today, 1*(12), 14.

Orelove, F. P., & Sobsey, D. (1991). *Education children with multiple disabilities: A transdisciplinary approach* (2nd ed.). Baltimore: Paul H. Brookes.

Palfrey, J. S., Haynie, M., Porter, S., Bierle, T., Cooperman, P., & Lowcock, J. (1992). Project School Care: Integrating children assisted by medical technology into educational settings. *Journal of School Health, 62,* 50–54.

Parette, H. P., & Bartlett, C. S. (1996). Collaboration and ecological assessment: Bridging the gap between medical and educational environments for students who are medically fragile. *Physical Disabilities: Education and Related Services, 15*(1), 33–47.

Parette, H. P., Bartlett, C. R., & Holder-Brown, L. (1994). The nurse's role in planning for inclusion of medically fragile and technology-dependent children in public school settings. *Issues in Comprehensive Pediatric Nursing, 17*(2), 61–72.

Perry, J. D., & Flanagan, W. K. (1986). Pediatric psychology: Applications to the schools needs of children with health disorders. *Techniques: A Journal for Remedial Education and Counseling, 2,* 333–340.

Poulton, S. (1996). *Guidelines to writing individualized healthcare plans.* [On-line]. Available http://www.nursing.uiowa.edu/www/ nursing/courses/96-22/students/sp1996/96-222WE/guidelines.htm.

Prendergast, D. E. (1995). Preparing for children who are medically fragile in educational programs. *Teaching Exceptional Children, 27*(2), 37–41.

Rushton, C. H., Will, J. C., & Murray, M. G. (1994). To honor and obey—DNR orders and the school. *Pediatric Nursing, 20,* 581–585.

Sexson, S. B., & Madan-Swain, A. (1993). School reentry for the child with chronic illness. *Journal of Learning Disabilities, 26,* 115–125.

Sobsey, D., & Cox, A. W. (1991). Integrating health care and educational programs. In F. P. Orelove & D. Sobsey, *Educating children with multiple disabilities: A transdisciplinary approach* (2nd ed., pp. 155–185). Baltimore: Paul H. Brookes.

Stein, R. E. K. (1986). Promoting communication between health care providers and educators of chronically ill children. *Topics in Early Childhood Special Education, 5*(4), 70–81.

Stuart, J. L., & Goodsitt, J. L. (1996). From hospital to school: How a transition liaison can help. *Teaching Exceptional Children, 28*(2), 58–62.

Todaro, A. W., Failla, S., & Caldwell, T. H. (1993). A model for training community-based providers for children with special health care needs. *Journal of School Health, 63,* 262–265.

Utah State Office of Education (1995). *Utah guidelines for serving students with special health care needs.* Salt Lake City, UT: Author.

Weiss, J (1997). *Providing safe health care: The role of educational support personnel.* [On-line]. Available http://nea.org.

CHAPTER 4

The Impact of Chronic Health Problems on the Child or Young Adult Who Is Ill

KEY WORDS

Developmental milestone

Developmental task

Normalcy

Self-care

Physical and cognitive development

Psychosocial development

In the following passage, Lynch, Lewis, and Murphy (1993a) underscore the overwhelming impact of chronic illness on early life:

> Childhood is supposed to be a time for fun, a time to grow and learn, to make mistakes while developing the skills of adulthood. With adolescence come opportunities for risk-taking, assertion, rebellion, and self-development. But for young people with chronic illnesses, childhood and adolescence may be radically altered. From the moment of diagnosis, their lives are never quite the same. For some, hospitalizations replace slumber parties and camping trips. For others, fast foods may be off-limits; outdoor activity may be forbidden; or they may be embarrassed by loss of hair or other physical changes. For still others, their illness may be life-threatening and their days of childhood numbered. (p. 38–39)

In this chapter, the effects of a chronic condition on the child and young adult are explored. Although the focus of this chapter is on chronic illness, in most cases, unless otherwise noted, the discussion is equally appropriate for those with a long-term physical disability. Of course, not all chronic illnesses are seriously disabling to the individual and not all disabilities are a result of a chronic illness.

❧ Chronic Illness: The Concept of Normalcy

Fithian (1984), in discussing how children cope with a chronic illness, differentiated between **"a normal child with an illness"** and a **"child with an illness trying to be normal."** Using a child with diabetes as an example, she pointed out some of the dangers in the use of the term "normal":

> Physicians and nurses will often try to comfort parents of a child newly diagnosed with diabetes by telling them that they have a "normal" child with diabetes and stressing the "normal" life that the child can live. This advice, despite being well meaning, has unwanted consequences simply because it is not true and trivializes the experiences related to the disorder.
> It is not normal to have diabetes, just as it is not normal to have lupus erythematosus, cystic fibrosis, or spina bifida. It is not a trivial matter to undergo time-consuming treatments, endure pain and discomfort and sometimes embarrassment, and to have one's hopes for certain goals dashed. Long-term disorders in childhood can significantly and permanently interfere with the child's physical and emotional growth and development. (p. 4)

Fithian, however, proceeded to stress that children with chronic illness should be treated as "normally" as possible (p. 7). For example, in discussion of children who are seriously ill, she made the following observations:

> A serious medical condition does not confer the wings of an angel on a child. Some children use their illness to get out of difficult, tedious, or uninteresting school tasks. . . . Disruptive behavior should not be excused in any child. When it is excused in a child with a serious illness, the child gets the message that the condition is so hopeless that he or she is allowed to act unacceptably to make up for the unfortunate situation. . . . If these children are to take their place in the adult world—and most of them will—they should not be allowed to grow up to be obnoxious, self-centered, and inconsiderate. (p. 7)

Lynch and her colleagues (1993a) have also stressed the importance of normalcy in the child's life, particularly those who are acutely ill:

> Some people may ask why it's important to emphasize learning when a child with chronic illness may have little time or energy for it. Why not let such children do whatever they can while getting the most out of life? While this approach may be appropriate for some children and their families, for most it is not. School is the work of children for six to seven hours a day. Children who are not in school are in a void, and all the trips to Disneyland or other attractions don't make up for the emptiness of a child not being with his or her peers. For many acutely ill children, just knowing that the school hasn't given up on them gives them the motivation to hang on. (p. 40)

Perrin and MacLean (1988) have suggested that children with chronic illnesses best be understood as **"normal children in an abnormal situation."** Their rationale for this stance is twofold. First, this position tends to cast children with chronic illnesses and their families in a "normalizing framework," thereby allowing the use of theories of development in conceptualizing and predicting the difficulties that will be encountered by the children and their families. Second, this particular outlook views illnesses as an atypical situation in which conventional stress and coping paradigms may be used to delineate a set of coping tasks brought about by the illnesses, for it is these coping skills that determine whether or not the children will adjust adequately to their conditions or exhibit some form of dysfunction.

❦ Chronic Illness and Development

Although it is difficult to predict how an illness may interfere with "normal" development, there are a number of factors that may potentially impact on a developing child's overall response to an illness. Harkins (1994) listed the following factors: (a) the nature and course of the illness; (b) the amount of separation that results from the illness or hospitalization; (c) the degree to which the illness affects the child's sensory abilities, physical mobility, and social interaction, especially with the child's peers; (d) the degree of dependency that the child will have on others; (e) the amount of fear that the child develops regarding treatments and procedures and the amount of pain associated with the illness; (f) the child's concerns about death; and (g) the effect of the illness on normal activities enjoyed by all children.

In addition, Silkworth (1993) has suggested that there are a number of factors that are likely to be correlated with the development of secondary problems (e.g., emotional, psychological, social, behavioral, or learning problems). They include the following: (a) the age of onset of the illness; (b) the permanence of the disability; (c) the severity of the condition; (d) the visibility of the disability; and (e) the number of chronic health care problems. Similarly, Whaley and Wong (1995) have suggested that the child's reaction to an illness is mediated by several specific factors, including (a) the child's level of development; (b) the child's temperament; (c) the coping mechanisms that the child has developed; and (d) the reactions of others to the child and the illness. Harkins (1994) has also suggested that the way that individuals manage symptoms of a condition depends on the meaning of the symptoms to and the coping ability of the child and family. Other sociocultural factors that may affect the manner in which a child (and family) copes with a chronic illness include economic status, religious beliefs, cultural background, and community involvement (Potter, 1987).

Patterson and Blum (1996), after reviewing the literature on risk factors, made the following comments on the current understanding of the dynamics between the child and the illness: "Empirical knowledge about variability in child characteristics among those with chronic conditions is *meager* at best and, for the most part, *nonexistent*" (p. 694, italics added). Notwithstanding this comment, the authors proceeded to isolate three child characteristics that they considered to have a major impact on the child's ability to cope with a chronic illness: (a) boys with a chronic illness generally experience more problems than girls; (b) children with an easy, more sociable temperament fare better than other personality types; and (c) uncertainty about the degree of the child's cognitive impairment (that results, for example, in confusion regarding the amount of autonomy to allow) may be a source of confusion for the parents, putting both the child and family at risk for negative developmental outcomes.

The majority of children and young adults with chronic health conditions do *not* have identifiable mental health problems, although behavioral or emotional symptoms can be identified in some (American Academy of Pediatrics, 1993, Silverman & Koretz, 1989). In fact, it has been suggested that those with chronic health impairments may be as much as 1.5 to 3 times more likely to have emotional, behavioral, or educational difficulties (Meyers & Weitzman, 1991) than those who are in good health. Typically the difficulties range from impaired self-image to bouts of depression or anxiety. Taking a broad look at the development of secondary psychosocial problems, Meyers and Weitzman (1991) have suggested that difficulties typically arise from a combination of the child's reaction to a chronic illness and the reaction of parents, peers, professionals, and society as a whole to the child. Specifically, they have suggested the following reasons for the development of psychosocial problems:

> In part, these problems are due to a prolonged experience of the "sick role": the chronically ill child may be bombarded with overt and covert messages that he or she is impaired and that less is expected of him or her than healthy peers. Eventually, the child may internalize this view of himself or herself, leading directly or indirectly to emotional, behavioral, and functional problems. An increased prevalence of secondary psychosocial problems has been documented for children in virtually every category of chronic health impairment investigated, but there is no apparent relationship between the child's specific health problems or its severity and the type, prevalence, or severity of associated mental health problems. Rather, common to all forms of secondary psychosocial difficulty, to a greater or lesser degree, is restriction of activity, deprivation and alteration of social interaction, and the impact of the reaction of others on the child. (p. 171)

Sargent and Liebman (1985, p. 299) have offered the following list of indicators of maladaptation to chronic illness (and the resultant need for therapy): (a) poor compliance with prescribed treatment; (b) repeated hospitalization that results from poor control of the illness; (c) less than the expected degree of physical functioning, despite adequate medical treatment; (d) signs of social withdrawal, depression, or emotional immaturity; (e) level of school performance below expectations; (f) behavior that is reckless or aggressive; (g) signs of family strife that result from difficulty coping with the illness or managing the child's care; and (h) concerns about the child's future (i.e., the ability to mature into adolescence or adulthood).

Regardless of the age or developmental stage of the individual, a chronic illness can be a major disruption in the life of that person. In children who are already trying to master the developmental tasks needed to become self-sufficient adults, an illness may "thwart" progress toward this mastery (Fithian, 1984). Cerreto (1986, p. 25) has suggested that "chronic illness modifies both the maturational processes and the experiences of the child, which in turn affect the achievement of developmental tasks, often making them more difficult to achieve or attainable at a slower rate." For example, as children move from infancy to toddlerhood, they move from a stage in which they are bonding or attaching to their parents during infancy to a stage of development of a sense of individuality and separateness. However, children whose condition affects their ability to explore the environment may develop feelings of shame and doubts about their ability to be independent from the primary caregiver, rather than developing a sense of autonomy. Similarly, the impact of illness on an adolescent who is attempting to develop a sense of identity may be quite different from that experienced by an older adult who is secure in his or her self-knowledge. Some of the potential effects of having a chronic illness on the mastery of specific developmental tasks are shown, by age group, in Tables 4.1 through 4.5.

Of course there are major differences if the individual is born with the chronic condition or it develops in later life. For the child in whom the condition develops at birth or in the first months of life, there is most likely not a need for adjustment to the loss of a particular function or capacity, whereas the

individual in whom the condition develops later in life may have to accept that certain activities can no longer be performed that had been performable for some period of time (Perrin, 1986). Similarly, there are differences depending on the constraints of the illness (Perrin & Gerrity, 1984). The development of a child who has a chronic disability that results in a severe restriction of the ability to access the environment will undoubtedly be more affected than that of a child whose impairment is not as severe.

Falvo (1991), in discussing the impact of chronic illness on development, made the following comments:

> All aspects of development are related. Each life stage must be understood within the context of the individual's past and current experience. Each individual with an illness or disability must be considered in the context of his or her particular point in life and the way in which the changes and limitations associated with the medical condition influence attitudes, perceptions, actions, and behaviors characteristics of the individual's life stage. The stage of life serves not only as a guideline in assessing the individual's functional capacity, but also as a guideline to determine potential stressors and reactions.
>
> Individuals with an illness or disability and those without such conditions have similar age-related problems and stresses as they progress from one life stage to the other. Ideally, those with an illness or disability should be encouraged to progress through each stage of development as normally as possible, despite the illness or disability. Individuals whose emotional, social, educational, or occupational development has been thwarted may be more handicapped by their inability to cope with the subsequent challenges of life than by any limitations experienced because of illness or disability per se. (pp. 11-12)

Children's Concept of Health and Illness

How children or young adults react to the presence of a chronic illness, either in themselves or in friends, is somewhat dependent on their concept of health and illness. Most research has shown that understanding of illness causality follows a developmental progression, similar to that put forth by Piaget in his cognitive-developmental framework, in which there is increased sophistication of thought, moving from circular, egocentric reasoning to more consistent, abstract logical thinking (Kury & Rodrigue, 1995). For example, the young child who does not fully

TABLE 4.1
Effects of Chronic Illness on Developmental Tasks of Infancy: Birth to Age 1

A. PSYCHOSOCIAL DEVELOPMENT

Developmental Tasks	Effects of Chronic Illness
Development of bonding and attachment to parents.	Bonding and attachment to the parents may potentially be delayed as a result of parental grief or anger, guilt, inability to accept the child's condition, and/or embarrassment that may result from the visibility of the child's condition.
	Attachment may be further diminished as a result of the decreased responsiveness of the infant (e.g., the child who is in pain, is cranky, or is listless may not smile when the parent enters the room). Similarly the child may not enjoy being held, fed, or fondled by the parent or caregiver.
Achievement of emotional stability	Prolonged separation, resulting from repeated stays in the hospital, may lead to a decreased interaction between the child and parents. For the child who has not yet developed a sense of object permanence, separation may be particularly traumatic if the child believes that the parents will not return when they leave the room. Fear of abandonment is common in this age group, particularly if the child is in unfamiliar surroundings and is separated from the parent or primary caregiver during treatment.
Acquisition of a sense of trust in self and in the caring adults and a realization of hope	The development of a sense of trust may be delayed because the child's needs may not be met in a consistent manner. If the child is hospitalized, inconsistent nurturing resulting from the presence of multiple caregivers and from repeated separation from parents may lead to a sense of mistrust.
	Infants with a chronic illness who are in contact with a number of strangers in the course of the day may develop severe "stranger anxiety," particularly in the presence of strangers who are wearing uniforms. Able-bodied children who experience stranger anxiety typically cling to their primary caregiver in order to feel safe. In a hospital, the primary caregiver may not be there when needed the most.
	Persons who the child should be able to trust may "hurt" the child in the process of caring for him or her (e.g., give the child an injection, change a dressing). As the disease progresses, the child may have more painful experiences than pleasurable ones.

B. PHYSICAL AND COGNITIVE DEVELOPMENT

Emerging development of eye-hand coordination, sensory discrimination, and object permanence	The infant learns primarily by physical exploration (sucking and mouthing of objects). Limitations such as casts, braces, or forced bed rest may result in restricted mobility and fewer opportunities to explore the immediate environment.
Mastery of rudimentary motor skills by means of repeated sensorimotor experiences	Both gross motor skills (sitting and standing without support, pulling to standing position, walking first steps) and fine motor skills (eye-hand coordination development of a pincer grasp, ability to wave "bye-bye") may be delayed as a result of restrictions or limitations. A sensory deficit (e.g., blindness, deafness) may also contribute to delays in mastering specific developmental milestones (e.g., walking, talking).
	Even if the condition does not limit exploration, the parents may overprotect and prevent the child from experiencing the normal environmental interactions. Opportunities for socializing with peers may also be restricted by the condition or parents.
Emergence of early language skills	Language acquisition may be hampered by lack of experience (lack of language play with caregivers) or from illness (the presence of a cleft palate) or its treatment (a respirator). Typically, an able-bodied child who is age 1 is able to speak as many as five words. The chronically ill or disabled child may show the early signs of a language disorder.

C. SELF-CARE

Progression from fluids to semisolids to solid food	Illness may affect the child's appetite (nausea) or ability to feed (weak suck response). The child may not progress as expected.

TABLE 4.2

Effects of Chronic Illness on Developmental Tasks of Toddlerhood: Ages 1 to 3

A. PSYCHOSOCIAL DEVELOPMENT

Developmental Tasks	Effects of Chronic Illness
Development of a sense of autonomy and individuality	Limitations imposed may continue to affect the child's ability to explore the world. Lack of "worldly" experience and experimentation and dependence on others may result in difficulties in developing a sense of autonomy and separateness. Rather than feeling in control, children at this stage may develop feelings of shame and doubt because they are not in control of themselves or their world.
Development of a sense of separateness from the primary caregiver	Most toddlers go through a period of "separation" anxiety (prolonged agitation and screaming when the primary caregiver leaves the room). Children with chronic illness may have extreme anxiety because of a lack of understanding of when the parents may return and the fear of abandonment. Most toddlers have developed object permanence, but they do not comprehend time. If the parents say they will be back in 5 minutes, in the mind of the toddler 5 minutes could be 5 hours or 5 days.
Development of a realization of will or assertion of independence	The overprotective parent may further impede development of independent behavior by being reluctant to set limits or condoning inappropriate behaviors rather than correcting them. They are not desirable role models for children, who all need guidance as to what is and is not appropriate.

B. PHYSICAL AND COGNITIVE DEVELOPMENT

Continued mastery of gross and fine motor abilities, in particular further elaboration of locomotion	Typically, toddlers become more proficient motorically as a result of increased exploration and experimentation. A typical 3-year-old is able to walk up and down stairs with alternating feet, ride a tricycle, and run with good balance. A child with a chronic illness or disability may show deficits in this area. Similarly, fine motor skills may be disrupted. A typical 3-year-old is able to stack between eight and ten blocks, turn one page in a book at a time, and use a pencil or crayon to draw.
	The child who develops an illness or becomes disabled as a toddler may regress with the onset of the condition (lose the ability to walk or revert to needing diapers). Loss of previously mastered skills can be very upsetting.
Continuing emergence and development of functional communication	Toddlers typically master the ability to make themselves understood by means of speech. By age 3 most children are capable of using complete sentences and all parts of speech. However, the 3-year-old with a chronic illness or disability may, because of limited opportunities, show signs of delay. Certain illnesses or treatment protocols may further hamper the child's ability to develop speech; for the child with good speech skills, regression is possible with the onset of a serious condition.
Refinement of play	The emergence of more sophisticated play skills (such as pretend play) is closely associated with the development of speech and language skills. Toddlers enjoy playing with other children but are egocentric in their play and prefer parallel play and the use of concrete objects. Play skills development may be severely curtailed by a chronic condition and the limitations and restrictions it imposes, in particular the isolation that may result from confinement.

C. SELF-CARE

Mastery of beginning self-help skills: feeding, toileting, bathing	Most toddlers learn to feed and dress themselves independently, and the majority have successfully attained bowel and bladder control, the mastery of which leads to enhanced self-esteem. For the child with a chronic condition, lack of opportunity may hamper the acquisition of some daily living skills. In addition, certain medical conditions (chronic diarrhea) or treatment protocols (a body cast) may make toilet training difficult.

TABLE 4.3
Effects of Chronic Illness on Developmental Tasks of Early Childhood: Ages 3 to 6

A. PSYCHOSOCIAL DEVELOPMENT	
Developmental Tasks	**Effects of Chronic Illness**
Development of a sense of initiative and a realization of purpose	Preschoolers without health problems typically appear to be tireless, and as a result of their increased activity, are capable of learning new skills at a phenomenal rate. Because of their experiences, they develop a sense of initiative (a readiness to engage in new activities and experiences) and a sense of self confidence in their ability. However, it is not uncommon to find "negativism." "No" is a typical response by many children to requests by their parents. For the child with a chronic illness, refusal to eat, take medication, rest, etc., can be stressful to the caregiver who anticipates that the child's behaviors may jeopardize their current health status and future recovery.
	Overprotective parents of children with a chronic illness or disability may discourage the development of initiative and purpose. Restrictions and limitations imposed by the condition may further impede social and emotional growth. Restrictions may severely limit the sense of mastery; consequently a sense of defeat and/or guilt may develop over the inability to progress at a rate comparable to peers.
Development of a sense of body image and of sexual identification	The preschool years are marked by the refinement of the sense of self. Children typically know their gender and the gender of others and are aware of some of the basic cultural differences among individuals. Experimentation with their bodies has led to knowledge of what it looks and feels like and what it can do. Recognition of being "different" can be painful for the child who is ill. Restrictions in activities may hamper development. Children whose bodies are disfigured may develop a distorted body image.

B. PHYSICAL AND COGNITIVE DEVELOPMENT	
Further development of motor skills, language skills, and play skills	The typical youngster can run, hop on one foot, jump several steps, jump rope, skip, and dance. The play of the preschooler is still mostly egocentric; however, most children, if allowed the opportunity (such as in preschool programs), have begun to develop more advanced play skills (cooperating, turn taking, sharing) and have begun to make firm friendships. Many of their preferred play activities reflect the developing language skills of children at this stage. Preschoolers engage in both dramatic and pretend play (dress-up and "house") and many favor rhythmic play (skipping to chants). Being read to is also a very pleasurable activity for the preschooler. Their play also reflects their improved fine muscle control. Preschoolers enjoy activities such as using scissors to cut out pictures, drawing, completing puzzles, and arts and craft activities. A child with a chronic illness may show deficits in the attainment of all these skills.
Development of peer relationships	Many children with a chronic illness or a disability may be perceived by their friends as being "a baby" and may be shunned by their more "sophisticated" peers with better motoric, language, and play skills. Many children have been overprotected by their parents and as a result may be hesitant to interact with children who are the same age, fearing that they will be criticized or ostracized.

C. SELF-CARE	
Continuing independence in activities of daily living.	Preschoolers typically are able to meet most of their self-care needs. Some assistance may be needed in skills that are particularly difficult. In addition, most preschoolers enjoy "helping out" around the house. Illness can affect the child's level of independence and initiative to learn new skills and limit the opportunities to master these skills. For the child who becomes disabled, regression is common.

TABLE 4.4
Effects of Chronic Illness on Developmental Tasks of Middle Childhood: Ages 6 to 12

A. PSYCHOSOCIAL DEVELOPMENT

Developmental Tasks	Effects of Chronic Illness
Acquisition of a sense of industry and the realization of competence	Most school-aged children, as a result of increased opportunities to compete both physically and academically, are proud of their accomplishments. These years are often referred to as the "I can do" years. However, the child with a chronic illness or a disability may lack opportunities to excel (perhaps as a result of excessive school absenteeism) or may not have the strength to compete. As a result, feelings of inferiority ("I can't") to peers can develop. Inferiority may also result from the parents' overprotective attitude ("You can't do that").
Development of sensitivity to societal expectations and recognition of need for strong peer relationships	Friendships are important to children this age. Socialization teaches children to relate to others. At this stage, their primary interest is in others of the same sex. For the child who is ill, there may be fewer opportunities because of the restrictions imposed by the disease or treatment to participate in school events and after-school social opportunities. Caregivers, fearing that the child may fail, may isolate the child unnecessarily in order to prevent possible emotional pain.
	For the child whose condition is visible, feelings of being different may result in the child withdrawing from the peer group and will also foster a negative sense of self, particularly if the child is subject to derision or ridicule. The child with a chronic illness, particularly the child whose physical appearance has been altered, may be rejected by his or her peers. In some cases, the child may reject his or her peers. The student who has an active social life when feeling well may discourage attempts by friends to socialize when not feeling up to such contacts.
	For the child whose condition is not visible, rejection by the peer group may occur as a result of differential treatment of the child with the illness. Children may reject those who are given "special favors" or those who are perceived to be the "teacher's pet" because of special accommodations they may need.

B. PHYSICAL AND COGNITIVE DEVELOPMENT

Continued mastery of gross and fine motor skills and the acquisition of athletic "prowess"	Physically, the normally developing school-aged child continues to show increased gross motor ability and strength. Competitive sports and being part of a "team" are important factors in developing certain skills such as cooperation and socialization. Confidence in ability may be undermined by an illness or a disability. Lack of confidence often leads to feelings of inadequacy and loss of self-esteem.
Mastery of the three "Rs"	Learning to read, write, and do math are major milestones for this age group. For the child who misses a great deal of school or for the child whose treatment protocol may affect the learning process, attainment of new academic skills may be severely hampered.

comprehend the notion of cause and effect may interpret pain as punishment for "being bad." The older child, because of reluctance to ask questions or to talk about irrational fears and reasons for the illness, may assume inappropriate responsibility for his or her own illness (Isaacs & McElroy, 1980).

Bibace and Walsh (1980, 1981) and Perrin and Gerrity (1981) have been instrumental in examining the various stages that children go through in developing their understanding of illness and its causation. Building on the work of these research teams,

Yoos (1987, 1988, 1994) has outlined the various "stages" (which Yoos prefers to describe as developmental "patterns," "steps," or "sequences") seen at different points in the life of the child, described the unique characteristics of each period, and offered a variety of intervention strategies appropriate for caregivers working with children who are chronically ill. Although written for health professionals, this information (Table 4.6) may help teachers develop a better understanding of how children react to being ill.

TABLE 4.5
Effects of Chronic Illness on Developmental Tasks of Adolescence: Ages 12 to 18

A. PSYCHOSOCIAL DEVELOPMENT	
Developmental Tasks	**Effects of Chronic Illness**
Development of a sense of identity	The major task of the adolescent is to become independent, in particular from the family. For the adolescent with a chronic illness or a disability, complete autonomy may be impossible, and the degree of independence that may be achieved, now and in the future, may be restricted by the condition. The teenager with a chronic illness may be overwhelmed by the prospect of poor health and the potential limitations (real or imagined) of his or her condition, which may be personal, sexual, social, emotional, educational, vocational, or financial.
	Relationships with parents or caregivers are often strained during adolescence because the teenager wants to be independent but the illness forces dependence on others. In some cases, the parents force the teenager to remain dependent upon them. Some parents are reluctant to "let go" and fear the consequences of not being there to "save them" if things go wrong.
Development of a realization of fidelity	As teenagers are attempting to become more independent, they are also attempting to develop an identity that is accepted by the peer group. At this stage, conformity that may lead to social acceptance is so critical that it is common to see adolescents dressing, talking, and acting in a similar manner. To the adolescent, being "different" in terms of health status, appearance, abilities, or skills is unacceptable. Feelings of sadness and depression and hostility and anger towards others are common in adolescents who have some type of illness or disability, which in their minds makes them a "freak."
	The teenager's perception of being different, and therefore "unacceptable" to others, may result in risk-taking behaviors and noncompliance with prescribed treatment plans.
Development of a sense of intimacy and solidarity and a realization of love	The adolescent begins to develop an interest in establishing a meaningful relationship with another individual. Developing a sense of intimacy and engaging in a loving relationship with another person may be hampered by a chronic condition or its treatment. Examples include lack of sexual development as a result of kidney disease or alteration of appearance. Embarrassment may lead to social withdrawal.
Development of a degree of comfort for one's body	Loss of self-concept and self-esteem are common to those who are not comfortable with their own body. A major dilemma for teenagers with a chronic illness, particularly an "invisible" one, is whether to tell their friends about it. This dilemma is compounded if the friend is of sexual interest.
Development of a realistic future orientation	The major academic focus for the teenager is on attaining the necessary skills to either continue study or enter the work force. In some, a sense of pessimism may prevail: Teenagers with a chronic illness ask "What's the point?" when they realize that their hopes and dreams may be dashed by their health.
	For the teenager who has just developed a chronic illness, educational goals and vocational plans may suddenly need to be drastically altered. Many adolescents do not have anyone to talk to about their future because few guidance counselors are knowledgeable about the effects of chronic illness on vocation and may have difficulty helping to establish realistic future goals.

TABLE 4.6

Developmental Conceptions of Illness and Intervention Strategies

Developmental Level	Characteristics of Illness Concept	Intervention Strategies
I. Prelogical Thinking (2-6 yrs of age)	Characterized by children's inability to distance themselves from their environment and results in explanations accounting for cause-effect relationships in terms of the immediate spatial or temporal cues that dominate their experience.	
Phenomenism	Illness is defined in terms of a single external symptom—often a sight or a sound that the child has at one time or another associated with the illness. Illness is attributed to an external phenomenon that coincides with the illness but is spatially or temporally remote. ("A heart attack is falling on your back.") The child centers on a single, concrete aspect of his or her own experience to define an illness. Thinking is often magical.	Preschool children may be relatively unaware of the nature of their illness. Body sensations and objective indicators of illness can be pointed out to them. Their ideas about the cause of illness can be discussed. Simple explanations may be offered (Pidgeon, 1985). Information about sensations likely to be experienced may help reduce stress (Collier, 1981).
Contagion	Illness is defined in terms of a single external symptom, such as a physical activity that is usually observed in connection with the illness and is often restricted inappropriately to a single body part. The source of the illness is usually either a person or object spatially near to the ill person or an activity or event temporally prior to the occurrence of the illness. Even though the child still centers on a single concrete aspect of experience, the child can now specify an event that is more relevant to the domain of illness. Children may be preoccupied with "catching" a variety of illnesses from others and overextend the concept of contagion to noncontagious illnesses.	Give reassurance that illness was not caused by something the child did or failed to do. An effective approach to health teaching might involve describing the situation and delineating short-term outcomes (Flaherty, 1986). Be aware of the fear of contagion and offer reassurance. The evidence in the literature is inconclusive as to whether or not pre-operational children's conceptions are sophisticated enough for them to comprehend and benefit from a great deal of information about illnesses (Potter & Roberts, 1984). It may be more appropriate to deal with their immediate sensations, experiences, and feelings.
II. Concrete-Operational Thinking (7-10 yrs)	Although thought remains limited to the child's own concrete experiences, concrete-operational children are able to focus simultaneously on several dimensions of a situation, are sensitive to transformations of perceptual referents, and can reverse the direction of their thinking. Children at this stage can clearly differentiate between themselves and others and have developed the ability to distinguish what phenomena are internal vs. external. They can begin to appreciate the relativity and multiplicity of cause and effect relationships.	
Contamination	Children can now distinguish between the cause of the illness and the manner in which it is effected. The definition of an illness now encompasses multiple symptoms. While the source of illness is still external, children now concretize the causal link between the source and its effect on the body. The cause of illness is most often viewed as a person, object or action external to the child, which has an aspect of quality that is "bad" or "harmful" for the body	The concreteness and specificity of school-aged children's illness concepts need to be taken into consideration in the selection of teaching methods. An illness can be made concrete through the use of models, drawings, or diagrams. Being "concrete" in the explanation of some illnesses that provide few such perceptual cues may require the provision of concrete examples to describe the underlying process, the

(for example, people get colds when they go outside without a hat).

		symptoms, and some sense of causation. Use of metaphors has been suggested to "concretize" teaching about illnesses which are obscure and invisible (Whitt, Dykstra, & Taylor, 1979). These should be used judiciously.
Internalization	Children at this stage of development still consider the cause of illness to be external but now link the external cause of illness to some internal effect on the body. Illness is now located inside the body, while its ultimate cause may be external. The external cause, usually a person or object, is linked to the internal effect of illness through a process of internalization—for example, swallowing or inhaling ("people get colds by breathing in germs"). Although illness is now located within the body, it is described in only vague terms, evidencing confusion about internal organs and functions. The internalization explanations still reflect the child's thinking in terms of concrete operational thinking. While the child is able to mention an internal organ, he or she cannot articulate how it operates physiologically ("the heart is a pump"). Children now see themselves for the first time as able to prevent illness through proper care.	School-aged children are particularly receptive to health teaching (Pidgeon, 1985). They can often describe the symptoms of an illness but may not understand the illness process and the relation of symptoms to it. When they describe the illness process in general terms, it can be made more explicit to the child. Relationships between indicators of illness and the illness process that are essential to the management of a chronic illness should be explained to chronically ill children. Clinicians can help them sort out misinformation.
III. Formal-Logical Thinking (11 yrs and older)	Children at this stage are no longer bound by concrete reality but are now able to include possibilities. Only now do children seem to have a generalized understanding of the principles of infection, health maintenance, and multiple treatments (Kalnis & Love, 1982). They understand that there are many interrelated causes of illness, that the body may respond variably to a combination of agents and that illness can be caused and cured as a result of a complex integration between host and agent factors (Perrin & Gerrity, 1981).	
Physiologic	While the cause of illness may be triggered by external events, the child describes and explains illness in terms of internal organs and functions. Illness is defined in terms of internal physiological structures and functions whose malfunction manifests itself in multiple external symptoms. The cause of illness is now clearly thought to be a malfunctioning of an internal body part or process. The child can describe functions and structure that are not visible and is aware of the gaps in understanding.	Not all adolescents will be reasoning at the formal operational level. Generally their concepts of illness are physiologic and abstract. Chronically ill adolescents can be questioned to determine if they understand the illness process and relation among its different features. Missing information can be given and misconception can be corrected (Pidgeon, 1985).
Psychophysiologic	Illness is described in terms of internal physiological processes, but the child now perceives an additional or alternative cause of illness—psychological cause. The child is aware that a person's thoughts or feelings can affect the way the body functions (for example, "people get heart attacks by being nerve-wracked").	

Continued

TABLE 4.6
Developmental Conceptions of Illness and Intervention Strategies *(Continued)*

Psychophysiologic *(Continued)*	New cognitive abilities attained in adolescence may also exacerbate existing disabilities. With adolescents' newfound capacity to think about other people's thinking, they often assume others are as preoccupied with their appearance and behavior as they are. This produces a heightened self-consciousness, which may be particularly painful to teenagers with handicaps. Another mental construct of adolescents, which Elkind (1985) calls the "personal fable," can contribute to the exacerbations of handicaps. The fable may contribute to a young person's denial of the illness to the point that medication is refused. The belief is that "other diabetics have to take insulin but not me" and this belief in speciality can lead teenagers to deny a chronic illness.	Elkind (1985) suggests that the single most important rule in dealing with these cognitive constructs is not to challenge them directly—to do so only entrenches the adolescent in his or her position. He suggests that clinicians not argue with the young person's reality but neither do we accept it in total. Rather, we recognize the young person's reality, even if it is variance with the reality shared by others. If a teenager believes that he can get along without medication, it will not help either to argue against or to agree with him. We can say "Look, you may be able to get along without the medication; it is not usual, but sometimes it happens, let's try it for a couple of days (hours, weeks, whatever is a safe trial period) and see how it goes." In this way, we do not deny the teenager's reality, but we do assert the claim of our reality as well.

Source: Yoos, L. (1988). Cognitive development and the chronically ill child. Reprinted from *Pediatric Nursing,* 1988, Volume 14, Number 5, pp. 375–378. Reprinted with permission of the publisher, Jannetti Publications, Inc., East Holly Avenue, Box 56, Pitman, NJ 08071-0056; phone (609) 256-2300; FAX (609) 589-7463. For a sample copy of the journal, please contact the publisher.

 ## Chronic Illness and Schooling

Many have stressed the importance of school attendance for children with special health care needs. The following excerpts are representative:

> School is a major part of a normal child's life and the sick child can never approach normality in life style unless he is in school and is productive in the role of learner. This is the best distraction from his condition which the child can have. The quality of his school life is vital to his mental health, which in turn significantly affects his physical health. (Cyphert, 1973, p. 215)

> School is important in the life of every child. In addition to imparting knowledge, school is a proving ground for the exercise of physical abilities, for the development of social skills, and for the display of special talents. For the child with a chronic illness, it can be the place where the limitations of the illness are transcended, where one's identity comes not from a diagnostic label as a diabetic or a hemophiliac but from achievement in schoolwork, in the band, or on the stage. (Hobbs, Perrin, & Ireys, 1985, p. 102)

However, there are a number of problems faced by children with chronic illnesses who attend school alongside their normally developing peers. Hobbs et al. (1985) have eloquently stated some of the pitfalls:

> School can . . . be the place where one's limitations are most acutely felt. The child with asthma who avoids gym, the young adolescent who is physically immature because of an illness, the youngster who never becomes a full member of the class because of frequent absences—all of these children are viewed by their classmates as different, stigmatized in some way. The resulting isolation and sense of rejection can compromise the achievement and self-confidence of even the brightest child. (p. 102)

For the classroom teacher, probably the major concern is how the child's illness influences his or her academic future. While it is not typical for most chronic illnesses to directly affect a student's cognitive ability (the major exception being certain neurologic impairments), the student's capacity to progress academically may be hampered by a number of factors, including (a) the number of days absent from school, (b) the effects of treatment on the child's stamina or ability to concentrate, and (c) the emotional state of the student (Potter, 1985). In addition, the provision of adaptations to compensate for the condition, and the degree to which the adaptations are effective, may affect the student's ability to perform in the classroom (Heller, Alberto, Forney, & Schwartz-man, 1996). Some of the potential physiologic and psychologic/psychosocial effects of chronic illnesses are shown in Tables 4.7 and 4.8, respectively. In these tables some general intervention strategies that might be appropriate in the classroom setting are also presented; however, in the following chapters the educational implications of various illnesses are described in greater detail and specific suggestions are given that are appropriate for each of the various conditions. The intent of including this material at this time is simply to introduce to the reader the notion of some

of the wide-reaching effects of illness on schooling and how teachers can support the student both physically and emotionally in the classroom setting.

School Attendance

School attendance is frequently reported in the literature as a measure of "functioning" in children with chronic illness (Sexson & Madan-Swain, 1993). Citing data from the National Health Interview Survey conducted in 1986, Klerman (1988) reported that as many as 226.4 million days of school are lost per

TABLE 4.7
Potential Physiologic Effects of Illness on Schooling

Potential Effects of Illness (Definition/Description)[a]	Typical Intervention Strategies
Activity intolerance/limited endurance (i.e., a state in which an individual has insufficient physiologic or psychologic energy to endure or complete required or desired daily activities)	Promote the development of an appropriate program of exercise (and rest) and waive requirements for participation in activities that may be too strenuous (e.g., certain scheduled physical education activities).
Fatigue (i.e., an overwhelming sustained sense of exhaustion and decreased capacity for physical and mental work)	If possible, permit students to have periods of "quiet time," in a secluded room (e.g., nurse's station).
Sleep pattern disturbance (i.e., a disruption of sleep time that causes a person discomfort or interferes with the desired lifestyle)	Encourage students to attend school on a part-time basis (e.g., mornings only) so that they can rest (in the afternoon) in order to become refreshed.
Altered growth and development (i.e., the state in which an individual demonstrates deviation in norms from his/her age group)	Structure an individualized educational program so that the student is able to work at his or her own level and pace.
High risk for infection (i.e., the state in which an individual is at increased risk for being invaded by pathogenic organisms)	Encourage all students to practice good hygiene in order to prevent the spread of communicable diseases (e.g., to cover their mouths when coughing, to dispose of used facial tissues carefully). Separate students (e.g., move desks further apart) to ensure minimal contact between a student who is immuno-suppressed and one who has an obvious illness.
Impaired physical mobility (i.e., the state in which the individual experiences a limitation of ability for independent physical movement)	Arrange schedule so that all classes are on the same floor. If there are great distances between rooms, allow the student extra travel time (e.g., let the student start out a few minutes early). Permit the student to use the elevator. Encourage the student to use a wheelchair while on a school outing; arrange for home-school transportation (even if the student lives too close to the school to "qualify").
Pain (i.e., a state in which an individual experiences and reports the presence of severe discomfort or an uncomfortable sensation)	Since distraction is the best nonmedical pain relief measure, a well-balanced school program, one that offers a variety of activities, with the necessary periods of rest, can distract students from focusing on themselves. Recognize that humor is one of the best distractions. Cutaneous stimulation, such as rocking or hugging a student or giving the student a back rub, can be very effective in combating pain.

[a] The Potential Effects of Illness (Definitions/Descriptions) are from the North American Nursing Diagnosis Association's manuscript entitled *NANDA Nursing Diagnoses: Definitions and Classifications* (1994). Reprinted with permission, Nursecom, Inc.

TABLE 4.8
Potential Psychologic/Psychosocial Effects of Illness on Schooling

Potential Effects of Illness (Definition/Description)[a]	Typical Intervention Strategies
Altered family processes (i.e., the state in which a family that normally functions effectively experiences a dysfunction)	Encourage the student and family to become involved in a support group (either disease-specific or one for parents of children with a chronic illness or disability). Provide suggestions to parents on how to talk with their child regarding the impact of chronic illness on the normal developmental stages.
Anxiety (i.e., a vague, uneasy feeling, the source of which is often nonspecific or unknown to the individual) **and/or fear** (i.e., a feeling of dread related to an identifiable source that the person validates)	By understanding some of the anxieties and fears that the student may be facing, a compassionate, caring teacher can be extremely supportive. Encourage the student to talk to his or her physician or counselor regarding specific health concerns (e.g., treatment plan, limitations and restrictions imposed by the condition, prognosis).
Body image disturbance (i.e., a disruption in the way one perceives one's body image)	Discuss with the student ways in which he or she is different from peers and assist the student to develop a realistic body image. Suggest approaches that may make the student more "like the crowd" (e.g., wearing clothing that is in style, using well-applied make-up, having an up-to-date hairstyle). Be alert to any problems that may arise as a result of changes in the student's appearance (e.g., name-calling, teasing).
Hopelessness (i.e., a subjective state in which an individual sees limited or no alternatives or personal choices available and is unable to mobilize energy on own behalf) **and powerlessness** (i.e., a perception that one's own action will not significantly affect an outcome)	Assist the student to recognize things that make him or her feel hopeful and powerful rather than hopeless and powerless. Reinforce the student's actions when he or she uses constructive coping or appropriate decision-making skills and shows interest in taking control of the immediate situation (e.g., responsibility for health care management, schoolwork, chores).
Ineffective individual coping (i.e., an impairment of adaptive behaviors and problem-solving abilities of a person in meeting life's demands and roles)	Assist the student to explore various coping methods (e.g., relaxation techniques, stress-reducing activities). Help the student recognize when he or she is coping ineffectively (e.g., showing signs of destructive behavior) rather than effectively (e.g., using good problem-solving skills).
Noncompliance (i.e., a person's informed decision not to adhere to a therapeutic recommendation)	Maintain a positive attitude toward the student and assist the student to follow the treatment plan (e.g., provide a private room in which therapy can take place, permit the student to leave the room in order to take medication as unobtrusively as possible, discuss the importance of taking "good" [i.e., prescribed] vs. "bad" [i.e., illegal] drugs). Explore the reasons for non-compliance (e.g., not wanting to appear to be different from the "group") and discuss the implications of not following the treatment plan (e.g., the worsening of the condition) in a factual, nonjudgmental manner.
Self-esteem disturbance (i.e., negative self-evaluation and/or feelings about self or self-capabilities, which may be directly or indirectly expressed)	Discuss with the student the possibility of counseling and support the student's decision to seek (or refuse) assistance.
Social isolation (i.e., aloneness experienced by the individual and perceived as imposed by others and as a negative or threatened state)	Ensure that the student remains part of the class regardless of days absent (e.g., send cards home, videotape lessons, maintain computer linkages, encourage classmates to visit hospital or home, if permitted). Explore social activities that the student would like to engage in (both during school hours and after school) and encourage the student to participate.

[a] The Potential Effects of Illness (Definitions/Descriptions) are from the North American Nursing Diagnosis Association's manuscript entitled *NANDA Nursing Diagnoses: Definitions and Classifications* (1994). Reprinted with permission, Nursecom, Inc.

year in the United States (i.e., 5 days' absence per child) alone. These numbers reflect both acute and chronic conditions in children between the ages of 5 and 17. While the rates for females are slightly higher than those for males (5.8 vs. 4.3) and for whites than blacks (4.5 vs. 2.9), most of the lost school days were found to be a result of acute conditions (as opposed to chronic conditions), the most common being respiratory conditions, in particular influenza. Respiratory conditions were followed in frequency of occurrence by infective and parasitic diseases, injuries, digestive system conditions, and finally, ear infections.

A limited number of studies have attempted to examine the attendance patterns in students with chronic illnesses. One of the earlier studies, conducted by Cook, Schaller, and Krischer (1985), involved the examination of the attendance records of 336 chronically ill children residing in a 24-county area of northern Florida. Only 4% of children with chronic illnesses had perfect attendance, while one

in ten (10.4%) missed more than 20% of the school year. On average, in the previous year, the children were absent for 16.9 days (SD = 20.7), and while the exact numbers were not given, several children missed at least half of the school year. The mean percent of days absent was 9.4% (SD = 11.5). Interestingly, in this study, the researchers found that the chronicity of the illness and its impact on the child and family were of more significance than the specific diagnosis. The mean school absences by diagnostic category are shown in Table 4.9.

Even though the means differed quite dramatically (2.0 vs. 26.0 days) in the study by Cook and her colleagues, the relatively large standard deviations (5.6 vs. 35.1 days) show extreme variation within groups. Interestingly, two factors were found to be significant in predicting the number of days missed: (1) students who participated at least sometimes in physical activities were found to miss *less* school, and (2) children of poorly educated caregivers tended to miss *more* school than children

TABLE 4.9
Mean School Absences by Diagnostic Category (N = 336)

Diagnostic Category	n	Mean (# of days)	SD
Infectious disease	6	9.2	5.6
Neoplasms	8	16.9	26.6
Endocrine, nutritional and metabolic diseases and immunity disorders	10	16.1	9.2
Diseases of the blood and blood-forming organs	11	14.2	16.7
Mental disorders	13	8.6	10.4
Diseases of the nervous system and sense organs	86	16.7	20.2
Diseases of the circulatory system	10	17.8	13.4
Diseases of the respiratory system	28	17.4	11.7
Diseases of the digestive system	10	7.8	8.0
Diseases of the genitourinary system	12	13.5	11.6
Diseases of the skin and subcutaneous tissue	1	11.0	—
Diseases of the musculoskeletal system and connective tissue	24	16.1	13.2
Congenital anomalies	39	20.1	27.1
Certain conditions originating in the perinatal period	1	2.0	—
Symptoms, signs and ill defined conditions	62	18.7	25.9
Injury and poisoning	13	23.9	35.1
None (i.e., no reported diagnosis)	2	26.0	11.3

whose caregivers had more education. The authors suggested that the "inability to participate in physical activities most likely indicates a multitude of physical problems," whereas the inverse relationship between days missed and amount of education may reflect the better educated parents' "ability to overcome some problems associated with chronic illness" (p. 267).

Although it is true that those with chronic illnesses are absent from school more than students who are well, illness, chronic or acute, is not the only reason that students miss school. In a review of studies that investigated the causes of school absenteeism, Klerman (1988) suggested that most excessive school absence, particularly in the intermediate and high schools, is more related to chaotic family environments, lack of achievement motivation, understaffed and uninviting schools, and other societal problems (e.g., lowered socioeconomic status [SES], families in which one or both parents are missing), than to poor health.

School Performance

Even in the absence of known cognitive impairments, students with chronic illnesses do not always perform at a level commensurate with their healthy peers. Dworkin (1989), in reviewing a variety of epidemiologic surveys, concluded that as many as one-quarter to one-third of all chronically ill children have problems in the area of academic achievement. Schlieper (1985) and Bloch (1986) have suggested that the number of children encountering difficulties may be higher than that proposed by Dworkin (1989). Both of these authors have suggested that as many as 40% of children with chronic illnesses may be underachieving academically.

Specific School-Related Problems

In a very thorough review of the literature on the academic problems of students with chronic illness, Sexson and Madan-Swain (1993) examined some of the specific aspects of the chronic illness or the treatment regimen that make it difficult for the student to compete with peers. Factors that appear to contribute include (a) the physical state of the student (e.g., lethargy, nausea, weakness, and fatigue all have a negative influence); (b) pain; (c) decreased mobility; (d) effects of medications (e.g., sedation, increased irritability, or decreased attention span);

(e) effects of treatment (e.g., radiation, which may result in the development of learning difficulties); (f) decreased resistance to minor illnesses, which in turn may result in increased absenteeism; and (g) medically necessitated absences (e.g., clinic appointments). Dworkin (1989) listed the following factors that may affect performance: (a) altered expectations of teacher or parents; (b) prejudicial or preferential treatment by teachers or parents; (c) psychosocial maladjustment; and (d) instruction of inferior quality. In the following chapters, some of the school-related problems specific to certain conditions (e.g., learning problems that result from treatment of certain cancers) are examined in greater detail.

Several studies have attempted to examine in detail some of the more common school-related problems encountered by students with chronic illnesses, regardless of the type of illness. Recently Lynch, Lewis, and Murphy (1993b) investigated both the school districts' and the parents' perceptions of the difficulties encountered by children who are chronically ill. The problems most frequently cited by each group are shown in Table 4.10. Interestingly, in this study the most pressing problem, according to school district personnel, was absenteeism, whereas for parents the limitations imposed by the child's illness, such as restrictions on activities, exercise, diet, and mobility, including side effects of treatment, were of utmost concern. In general, as would be expected, school staff highlighted classroom and programming issues, whereas parents focused on issues that reflected the pervasiveness of the illness in their child's life, underscoring the difficulties of "growing up sick."

Parents were also asked by the research team what they believed would be the greatest concern for their child when he or she returned to school. Almost half of the parents (45%) reported that their child was most concerned about being behind their classmates in school, 23% indicated that their child was worried about not being accepted by other children, and 15% thought that their child was concerned about changes in physical appearance. These findings are strikingly similar to those of Chesler and Barbarin (1986) in whose study parents of children with cancer were asked what types of problems their children encountered after they returned to school. Over half of the respondents (51%) indicated that the children did encounter some type of problem, the most often mentioned problems being "teasing by peers" (37%)

TABLE 4.10

Districts' and Families' Perceptions of the Problems Most Frequently Encountered by Children with Chronic Illness (rank ordered)

Districts' Perceptions	Families' Perceptions
Absences (27%)	Other[a] (43%)
Falling behind in school (13%)	Feeling different (31%)
Lack of interaction with peers (13%)	Constant medical procedures (8%)
School can't meet child's needs (12%)	Pain (7%)
Social adjustment (11%)	Facing death (6%)

[a] Perceptions listed by families included restrictions on a child's activities, exercise, diet, and mobility, as well as side effects of treatment.

Source: From "Educational services for children with chronic illnesses: Perspectives of educators and families" by Lynch, E. W., Lewis, R. B., & Murphy, D. S., *Exceptional Children*, Vol. 59, 1993, pp. 210–220. Copyright 1993 by The Council for Exceptional Children. Reprinted with permission.

and "missing much school" (31%). A small proportion of the parents (12%) indicated that the children had problems in their "relations with teachers."

In both of these studies, the respondents were the child's parents. In neither study were students actually asked about their specific concerns. However, in a recent study by Speckhard (1996) student concerns were the major focus. This study involved interviewing 15 school-age students, ages 9 through 15 (mean age, 12 years, 6 months), who were attending grades 4 through 11 (mean grade level, 7th grade), and who, at the time of the study, were hospitalized as a result of illness. Of particular concern to the researcher was the students' apparent "lack of concern" regarding the importance of schoolwork, as evidenced by the time spent watching TV, playing video games, or socializing with patients and staff while in the hospital unit, and the possibility that the students' behaviors were a "manifestation of a state of denial regarding the reality of their situation."

Responses indicated that the students, on the whole, were looking forward to returning to school, not necessarily in order to resume their academic work, but rather because they desired to be with their friends and to participate in specific class events, such as field trips. In terms of actual schoolwork, nearly half of the students reported that they had not kept up with assignments, and over half of the students indicated that it would be impossible to continue their studies as they did not have their school books with them. A majority of the students worried that they would be behind the rest of the class, and almost two-thirds of the students indi-

cated that they "dreaded" going back because they would be behind academically. Finally, the study revealed that the majority of the students had had little contact with home school teachers. Only 2 of the 15 participants indicated that they had spoken with their teacher(s) while they had been in the hospital. Lack of contact with the school was more common with those who had chronic illnesses and multiple hospital admissions than with those who were in the hospital for the first time.

Summary

Although children and young adults with special health care needs are at higher risk for developing academic and psychosocial problems, the impact of a chronic illness on a child is just as child-specific as the illness itself. The child's response to his or her state is dependent on a number of factors that differ significantly from child to child and from family to family. Participation in school is often viewed by a child who has been ill as a return to a life of "normalcy" and, as such, should be an immediate priority. In this chapter the impact of chronic illness has been examined, as well as children's concept of health and illness. In considering the effects of illness on children, the following thoughts should be kept in mind:

Illness is an inescapable childhood event for all children. To the young child, the sense of "aliveness," as well as the characteristics of health and illness are a mystery. The child explores all concepts with the combination of facts and fantasy. The understanding of body integrity and function is limited by experience, anxiety level, and cognitive development.

Chronic illness presents a special challenge to a child's optimal growth and development. In the past, children's response to chronic illness was assessed and treated based on psychoanalytical theory: fear, anger, anxiety, withdrawal, and depression were thought to reflect illness trauma. Intervention included acknowledging and modifying these negative feelings (Bibace & Walsh, 1981). However, recent research supports the hypothesis that children develop an understanding of illness in a systematic and predictable sequence. Thus, cognitive developmental theory can provide a clear framework for understanding the chronically ill child's response to illness. Some of the child's negative feelings about the illness may well be related to the child's understanding (or lack of understanding) of that illness. (Yoos, 1988, p. 375)

In the following chapter, the impact of the illness on others who are in contact with the student who is ill, specifically the student's family and other acquaintances (e.g., teachers and peers) whose lives are touched by the child or young adult in question, is examined in detail.

References

American Academy of Pediatrics, Committee on Children with Disabilities and Committee on Psychosocial Aspects of Child and Family Health (1993). Psychosocial risks of chronic health conditions in childhood and adolescence. *Pediatrics, 92,* 876–878.

Bibace, R., & Walsh, M. E. (1980). Development of children's concepts of illness. *Pediatrics, 66,* 912–917.

Bibace, R., & Walsh, M. E. (1981). Children's conceptions of illness. In R. Bibace & M. E. Walsh (Eds.), *New directions for child development* (pp. 31–38). San Francisco: Jossey-Bass.

Bloch, A. (1986). Chronic illness and its impact on academic achievement. *Pediatrician, 13,* 128–132.

Cerreto, M. C. (1986). Developmental issues in chronic illness: Implications and applications. *Topics in Early Childhood Special Education, 5*(4), 23–35.

Chesler, M. A., & Barbarin, O. A. (1986). Parents' perspectives on the school experiences of children with cancer. *Topics in Early Childhood Special Education, 5*(4) 36–48.

Cook, B. A., Schaller, K., & Krischer, J. P. (1985). School absence among children with chronic illness. *Journal of School Health, 55,* 265–267.

Cyphert, F. R. (1973). Back to school for the child with cancer. *Journal of School Health, 43,* 215–217.

Dworkin, P. H. (1989). School failure. *Pediatrics in Review, 10,* 301–312.

Falvo, D. R. (1991). *Medical and psychosocial aspects of chronic illness and disability.* Gaithersburg, MD: Aspen.

Fithian, J. (1984). General overview. In J. Fithian (Ed.), *Understanding the child with a chronic illness in the classroom* (pp. 1–13). Phoenix: Oryx Press.

Harkins, A. (1994). Chronic illness. From C. L. Betz, M. M. Hunsberger, & S. Wright (Eds.), *Family-centered nursing care of children* (2nd ed., pp. 651–688). Philadelphia: W. B. Saunders.

Heller, K. W., Alberto, P. A., Forney, P. E., & Schwartzman, M. N. (1996). *Understanding physical, sensory, and health impairments: Characteristics and educational implications.* Pacific Grove, CA: Brooks/Cole.

Hobbs, N., Perrin, J. M., & Ireys, H. T. (1985). *Chronically ill children and their families.* San Francisco: Jossey-Bass.

Isaacs, J., & McElroy, M. R. (1980). Psychosocial aspects of chronic illness in children. *Journal of School Health, 50,* 318–321.

Klerman, L. V. (1988). School absence—A health perspective. *Pediatric Clinics of North America, 35,* 1253–1269.

Kury, S. P., & Rodrigue, J. R. (1995). Concepts of illness causality in a pediatric sample: Relationship to illness duration, frequency of hospitalization, and degree of life-threat. *Clinical Pediatrics, 34,* 178–182.

Lynch, E. W., Lewis, R. B., & Murphy, D. S. (1993a). Improving education for children with chronic illnesses. *Principal, 73*(2), 38–40.

Lynch, E. W., Lewis, R. B., & Murphy, D. S. (1993b). Educational services for children with chronic illnesses: Perspectives of educators and families. *Exceptional Children, 59,* 210–220.

Meyers, A., & Weitzman, M. (1991). Pediatric HIV disease: The newest chronic illness of childhood. *Pediatric Clinics of North America, 38,* 169–194.

North American Nursing Diagnoses Association [NANDA] (1994). *NANDA nursing diagnoses: Definitions and classifications.* Philadelphia, PA: Author.

Patterson, J., & Blum, R. W. (1996). Risk and resilience among children and youth with disabilities. *Archives of Pediatric and Adolescent Medicine, 150,* 692–698.

Perrin, E. C., & Gerrity, P. S. (1981). There's a demon in your belly: Children's understanding of illness. *Pediatrics, 67,* 841–849.

Perrin, E. C., & Gerrity, P. S. (1984). Development of children with a chronic illness. *Pediatric Clinics of North America, 31*(1), 19–31.

Perrin, J. M., (1986). Chronically ill children: An overview. *Topics in Early Childhood Special Education, 5*(4) 1–11.

Perrin, J. M., & MacLean, W. E. (1988). Children with chronic illness: The prevention of dysfunction. *Pediatric Clinics of North America, 35,* 1325–1337.

Potter, M. L. (1985). Chronic illness in childhood and adolescence: Considerations for school personnel. In J. Grimes & A. Thomas (Eds.), *Psychological approaches to problems of children and adolescents* (Vol. 2) (pp. 41–82). Des Moines, IA: Department of Public Instruction.

Potter, M. L. (1987). Children and chronic illness. In A. Thomas & J. Grimes (Eds.), *Children's needs: Psychological perspectives* (pp. 96–103). Silver Springs, MD: National Association of School Psychologists. (ERIC Document Reproduction Service No. ED 353 487).

Sargent, J., & Liebman, R. (1985). Childhood chronic illness: Issues for psychotherapists. *Community Mental Health Journal, 21*, 294–311.

Schlieper, A. (1985). Chronic illness and school achievement. *Developmental Medicine and Child Neurology, 27*, 69–79.

Sexson, S. B., & Madan-Swain, A. (1993). School reentry for the child with chronic illness. *Journal of Learning Disabilities, 26*, 115–125, 137.

Silkworth, C. K. (1993). Psychological aspects of chronic health conditions. In M. B. Haas (Ed.), *The school nurse's source book of individualized healthcare plans* (pp. 61–70). North Branch, MN: Sunrise River Press.

Silverman, M. M., & Koretz, D. S. (1989). Preventing mental health problems. In R. E. K. Stein (Ed.), *Caring for children with chronic illness: Issues and strategies* (pp. 213–229). New York: Springer.

Speckhard, N. J. (April, 1996). *A qualitative study: The perceptions of hospitalized school-aged children regarding their return to the classroom.* Paper presented at the Council for Exceptional Children Annual Conference, Orlando, FL.

Whaley, L. F., & Wong, D. L. (1995). *Nursing care of infants and children* (5th ed.). St. Louis: Mosby Year Book.

Yoos, L. (1987). Chronic childhood illnesses: Developmental issues. *Pediatric Nursing, 13*, 25–28.

Yoos, L. (1988). Cognitive development and the chronically ill child. *Pediatric Nursing, 14*, 375–378.

Yoos, L. (1994). Children's illness concepts: Old and new paradigms. *Pediatric Nursing, 20*, 134–140.

CHAPTER 5

The Impact of Chronic Health Problems on Family Members, Community Members, and Friends

KEY WORDS_____

Adaptive tasks

Life cycle stages

Objective Passive/Outcome
Approach

Parental reactions

Parental satisfaction

Stage theories

Subjective Active/Process
Approach

In the previous chapter, the impact of illness on the child or young adult who is ill was examined in detail. However, those who have a chronic condition do not live in a vacuum, and their illnesses have an impact on others around them. In this chapter, issues related to the understanding by family members, community members, and friends regarding the health status of the child or young adult are discussed.

🐾 Impact of Illness on Families

The following two quotations, the first by a professional who works with children who are chronically ill and the second by a parent of a child who has multiple impairments, give the reader an idea of the effect that chronic illness in a child may have on family members:

> Chronic illness in a child affects each family member and the fabric of family life. Childhood chronic illness has been shown to increase stress, disrupt relationships, and interfere with family developmental tasks. Chronic illness in one member may be an underlying cause of a variety of symptoms in other family members. Chronic illness may disrupt communication patterns, impose financial hardships, and bring about changes in housing, careers, and sleep and recreation patterns. Disruptions in roles, resentment among siblings, and feelings of parental guilt, anxiety, helplessness, and despair can all be manifestations of a chronic illness in a family. These effects can be seen, to varying degrees, across the continuum that also includes families who thrive and become more cohesive. (Harkins, 1994, p. 665)

> A child's [disability] attacks the fabric of a marriage in four ways. It excites powerful emotions in both parents. It acts as a dispiriting symbol of shared failure. It reshapes the organization of the family. It creates fertile ground for conflict. (Featherstone, 1980, p. 91)

While this text is primarily concerned with children and youth with chronic illnesses and disabilities in the school system, teachers should have an understanding of how family members may respond to the presence of a chronic illness or disability. Some of the more common concerns of parents are addressed briefly. This section concludes with a set of guidelines that may assist teachers and families to develop a partnership that helps them work cooperatively to meet the needs of the child or teenager with a chronic illness or disability.

Research Approaches: Reactions of Parents to Illness in Their Child

Interest in how families respond to the presence of a chronic illness has grown steadily over the past 20 years to the point that there is a substantial body of research that has attempted to describe the family's response and the variables related to the various patterns of response seen in families of children who have a chronic illness or a disability. However, in describing this "impressive volume" of literature, Knafl and Deatrick (1987) outlined some of the limitations of the research that has been conducted to date:

> Ideally, this body of research should provide a rich data base for practitioners working with families in which there is an ill or disabled child member. In reality, it presents an overwhelming and confusing body of information characterized by competing hypotheses, conflicting findings, and tentative conclusions. Moreover, different studies are predicated on different underlying assumptions regarding the nature of the illness experience and the family's response to it. As a result, the practitioner may find it all but impossible to discern what the knowledge base for practice in this area is. (p. 300)

After reviewing approximately 100 published articles on the topic, the authors were able, however, to isolate two general approaches that conceptualize how a family responds to illness. The first approach, referred to as the **Objective Passive/Outcome Approach (OPOA)**, is one in which researchers "tend to ignore or discount the family's subjective definition of the situation and to conceptualize the family as responding passively to a member's chronic illness or disability" (p. 300).

A major characteristic of OPOA research, according to Knafl and Deatrick, is interest "in measuring what illness *does to family life* as opposed to describing what families *do to manage illness*" (italics added) (p. 301). The major purpose of OPOA research is to determine the variables that are associated with differing family outcomes (i.e., positive or negative outcomes), so that the "studies will provide a sound empirical base for developing interventions which clinicians can use to allay the *deleterious consequences* of chronic illness for family life" (italics added) (p. 302).

Studies such as that conducted by Juanita Fleming and her colleagues (1994), in which four different groups of technology-dependent children were examined in light of the impact that the nature of their illness had on the family, are an example of OPOA research. In this study, parents were asked to rate the impact that bringing their child home has had on the family by responding to *negative* statements, such as "The illness is causing financial problems for the family," "We see family and friends less because of the illness," and "Fatigue is a problem for me because of my child's illness," and *positive* statements, such as "My relatives have been understanding and helpful with my child," "Because of what we have shared, we are a better family," and "Learning to manage my child's illness has made me feel better about myself." Parents were asked to state whether or not they agreed strongly, agreed, disagreed, or disagreed strongly with each of the statements. In a similar manner, the parents were asked to rate how they have felt recently. Using the week before the completion of the survey, parents were asked if they had experienced the feelings rarely, some or little of the time, occasionally or a moderate amount of the time, or most of the time. Statements that indicated negative feelings, such as "I did not feel like eating; my appetite was poor," "I felt depressed," and "I felt lonely" were combined with statements indicating the parents felt more positive, such as "I enjoyed life," "I felt that I was just as good as other people," and "I felt hopeful about the future." Not surprisingly, the researchers found that families with high incomes had fewer symptoms indicative of a depressed state and that parenting a technology-dependent child is difficult when the parents are young, have limited education, and are isolated geographically.

Recently OPOA research has begun to focus on the impact of chronic illness on siblings, an example being the work by Thompson, Curtner, and O'Rear (1994). In this study it was found that the healthy siblings of children who are chronically ill are *not* at greater risk for developing psychosocial adjustment problems than healthy siblings of healthy children. However, in those who do encounter problems, in the main, the problems are related to family structure characteristics (e.g., family income, education of parents), child characteristics (e.g., gender, birth order), or parenting (i.e., differential treatment) rather than attributable to the presence of a child with health concerns in a particular family.

The second approach to conceptualizing family response, referred to as the **Subjective Active/ Process Approach (SAPA),** maintains that "there is no single, objective meaning to chronic illness or disability" (Knafl & Deatrick, 1987, p. 302). This approach focuses on "how families *actively manage* such situations" (italics added) (p. 302). The major purpose of SAPA research is to attempt to understand the process of coping with chronicity rather than simply measuring outcomes. SAPA research "conceptualizes families as *responding actively* to illness situations" (italics added) (p. 302).

Much of the research using the SAPA approach has focused on the family members' perceptions of health care services and needs. An example of SAPA research is the study by Martin, Brady, and Kotarba (1992). After examining how a chronic illness in a young child affects the daily lives of family members, the researchers described the participants, three sets of parents who had chosen to keep and to care for their medically fragile children at home, as "unsinkable" families. Using the analogy of a ship, the authors described the unique situations of the families, in their efforts to cope with the day-to-day conditions, as follows:

> The future and present lives and decisions of the families are dependent on the course of their child's illness. In this way the family may be viewed as a ship in and out of port, all the while making decisions that affect the course of life of all family members. When the decision process is active, the trip is planned and charted ahead, the necessary knowledge is sought out, and the family takes the helm and heads into an unpredictable future. If the decision process is passive, they board the boat that takes them as the tides and the wind will. By weathering the toughest storms, these families are *unsinkable in their refusal to allow the added daily stresses of having a chronically ill child weigh them down or toss them about*. . . . Their children's handicapping conditions were not the only storms through which these families passed. The economic tides, career leaks, and societal currents were constant challenges to these families, although these were secondary to the life and death aspects inherent to chronic illness. (italics added) (pp. 13–14)

At first glance, the reader might have a tendency to select one approach over the other. However, as Knafl and Deatrick (1987) have pointed out, each approach makes a distinct contribution to our understanding of how families adjust to the presence of a chronic illness or disability. The major contribution of the OPOA research has been to assist in the identification of family groups that might be *at risk* for specific negative outcomes and to assist the practitioner to identify potentially problematic situations and to identify services and programs that are needed by the family. The major contribution of the SAPA research has been to alert the reader to the ability of family members to actively define, manage, and accommodate chronic illness and to support the practitioner's belief in working collaboratively with the family in order to shape the specific content of services and programs.

There are several examples of research that combines both the OPOA and SAPA approaches, one of the more recent being the work of Youngblut, Brennan, and Swegart (1994). In this study of families with medically fragile children, not only did the researchers isolate the problems the families were encountering most frequently (i.e., toileting, transportation, sleep/wake patterns, nutrition, and discipline), but they also recognized the major coping strategies the various families used (e.g., sharing difficulties with relatives, seeking information and advice from the family doctor, seeking professional counseling and help, receiving gifts and favors from neighbors, and having faith in God) and isolated the persons who were most helpful in making decisions (i.e., physicians, nurses, relatives, and therapists) and in solving problems (i.e., religious fathers, relatives, teachers, and rehabilitation personnel).

Parental Reactions: Stage Theories of Adaptation and Acceptance

Regardless of the research approach, it is generally accepted that families, in particular parents, go through a grieving process when their child is first recognized as having a chronic illness or disability. However, the reactions of parents may be dependent upon or tempered by one or more influencing factors (Whaley & Wong, 1995). For example, the parent of a child with an illness that is going to result in a shortened life span will react differently than the parent whose child, although being adversely affected by the illness, will probably live a relatively normal life, perhaps with periods in which the illness is exacerbated. Some of the factors that potentially affect a parent's response to chronic illnesses are listed in Table 5.1. As suggested by Silverman and Koretz (1989), when looking at the various factors that affect the family's response to illness, remember the "interactional nature of the family system" and the fact that "the parents and siblings are in [a] constantly evolving relationship

with the chronically ill child, and the child, in turn, may serve as initiator and reactor in the unfolding family dynamics related to the illness" (p. 219).

Much of the literature, particularly that related to the impact of a disability on the family, has been adapted from the work by Elisabeth Kubler-Ross (1969), who in her seminal work *On Death and Dying* outlined the stages of grief that individuals go through in their response to the death of a loved one. Several stage theories have been proposed to describe the parents' journey from a state of "disorganization to one of reintegration" (Chomicki, Sobsey, Sauvageot, & Wilgosh, 1995, p. 18). For example, Freitag-Koontz (1988) described five different stages that parents of children with a severe neurologic impairment or a congenital malformation went through in the process of accepting their children's condition. The stages according to this author included (a) shock; (b) denial, disbelief, and bargaining; (c) sadness, anger, and anxiety; (d) establishing equilibrium; and (e) reorganization.

In a similar manner, Anderegg, Vergason, and Smith (1992) described a model with three distinct phases, each with three distinctive behaviors. The stages were as follows: (a) confronting (shock, denial and blame or guilt); (b) adjusting (traditional responses of depression, anger, and bargaining); and (c) adapting (change of lifestyle, realistic planning, and altered expectations).

Those researchers who have examined the stages that parents go through in the adjustment to chronic illness, as opposed to a disability, have, in some cases, proposed a structure that is dependent on the chronology of the illness (Potter, 1985). For example, McCollum and Gibson (1970), in describing the reactions of families in which a child had cystic fibrosis, outlined a four-stage process. The stages were as follows: (a) the prediagnostic stage (i.e., the period between the recognition that something is wrong and the establishment of a diagnosis); (b) the confrontational stage (i.e., the period of acute stress, typically an anticipatory mourning reaction, associated with the confirmation of the diagnosis); (c) the long-term adaptation stage (i.e., the period in which the parents attempt to maintain a gratifying relationship with their dying child while fulfilling the child's physical and psychological needs; a period often marked by the defense mechanism of denial); and (d) the terminal stage (i.e., the period in which the parents recognize and accept that the child is not

TABLE 5.1
Factors Affecting Parental Reactions and Responses to a Child's Illness

FACTORS RELATED TO ILLNESS OR CONDITION:
- Diagnosis (e.g., negative attitudes towards certain conditions)
- Severity of the illness, likely prognosis, and availability of an effective treatment (i.e., seriousness of the threat to the child)
- Medical procedures involved in diagnosis and treatment (e.g., invasive vs. noninvasive procedures)
- Nature of the illness (e.g., visibility of the condition)
- Effect of the illness (e.g., degree of dysfunction)
- Age of onset (i.e., congenital or acquired)

FACTORS RELATED TO CHILD:
- Developmental level
- Personal ego strength
- The degree to which the child understands the condition
- Coping skills

FACTORS RELATED TO PARENTS:
- Coping skills
- Prior experience with illness or hospitalization
- Personal ego strength

FACTORS RELATED TO PARENTS AND CHILD:
- Quality of parent-child relationship
- Degree of acceptance of the child and his or her illness

FACTORS RELATED TO FAMILY UNIT:
- Family size and structure and stage of family life cycle
- Presence of other affected or nonaffected siblings
- Effects of the home management program on family
- Realignment of family members (e.g., mother bearing the brunt of day-to-day responsibilities; siblings spending more time with father or another adult)
- Restrictions placed on family life (e.g., repeated hospitalizations or surgical procedures)
- Additional stresses on the family system (e.g., preexisting emotional disturbance within family; intrafamilial tension; disruption to work schedules)
- Financial costs to family (e.g., obvious costs, such as having to purchase a wheelchair accessible van; hidden costs, such as lost opportunities, lost work time, lost chances to advance in one's career)
- Support systems and community resources available to family
- Beliefs of family (e.g., cultural and religious beliefs)
- Ability of family members to communicate effectively

Sources: Jessop & Stein, 1989; Silverman & Koretz, 1989; Whaley & Wong, 1995.

going to survive). In a manner similar to McCollum and Gibson, Ross (1978, cited in Potter, 1985) proposed a five-stage process for parents of children with cancer. The stages were as follows: (a) before diagnosis, (b) the diagnostic period, (c) remission, (d) relapse, and (e) death and mourning.

Regardless of the number of stages or phases, or the terms used to describe them, family members, especially parents, typically react in a number of ways before they finally accept the child's condition. Some parents do appear to progress through the various stages as outlined in the literature, but some seem to go through the stages in their own particular order, and some seem to adjust to the circumstances at hand without appearing to pass through any of the phases in the grieving process. Jessop and Stein (1989), in reviewing the psychological costs of chronic illness to families, made the following comments: "Although much clinical literature suggests this sequence of reactions [shock, denial, sadness, anger, reestablishment of equilibrium], there is no solid research evidence for an invariant progression of states in families' reactions. Parents and patients talk more of going back and forth from one reaction to another" (p. 65).

Family members may be at different stages at the same time (e.g., one parent may be still consumed with anger, while the other is starting to adapt to the situation and making appropriate plans), and parents may regress to an earlier stage in the cycle when faced with a particularly trying experience (e.g., entrance into school, change in school placement, move from elementary to secondary school). Finally, teachers must be aware that while much of the literature on family adaptation focuses on the negative consequences of a disability, it has also been pointed out, in a more positive light, that "family adaptation to chronic illness can generate family growth, increased individual and family autonomy, and family mastery of adaptive tasks" (Clawson, 1996, p. 54).

There is very little literature on the impact of illness on grandparents. Harkins (1993) has suggested, however, that, like parents, grandparents may go through a grieving process. The feelings grandparents may experience may be compounded by the fact that their grief is not only for themselves but also for their own child (i.e., the mother or father of the ill child), for their well grandchildren, and for their ill grandchild. Harkins has suggested that grandparents may be particularly important, for they may be able to model the "strength, patience, and faith that the family needs to learn as they adjust to living with chronic illness" (p. 669). There is a body of literature that deals with sibling reactions, some of which is reviewed in a following section.

Life Cycle Stages of Families

Families of children with special needs encounter different problems as they and their child age. Turnbull and Turnbull (1990) have outlined some of the concerns that might be encountered by both parents over time (Table 5.2).

Complete acceptance of the illness or disability of the child may be impossible for some. In the literature, particularly the written material on parental responses to intellectual disability published since the early 1960s, the term "chronic sorrow" has been used extensively. In summarizing some of the published research in this area, Chomicki and her colleagues (1995) have suggested that parents of children with disabling conditions not only "grieve for the 'perfect' child they had hoped for at birth," but also continue to grieve throughout the child's life span, albeit the "intensity of emotion is diminished" over time (p. 19).

Adaptive Tasks of Parents

Family adaptation to a chronic illness or disability in one of the family members requires time, because it is an ongoing process (Clawson, 1996). Patterson (1991, cited in Patterson & Blum, 1996) identified a number of factors that lead to resiliency in families. In order to cope, according to these authors, families must be able to do the following: (a) balance the chronic conditions with other family needs (e.g., by meeting child development needs as well as special needs, by taking time for family needs other than those associated with the chronic condition, and by maintaining family routines and rituals); (b) maintain clear family boundaries so that, for example, there is less likelihood of overinvolvement of one parent with the ill child; (c) develop communication competence (e.g., by developing the ability to solve problems, make decisions, resolve conflicts, and express feelings, even when they are negative and appear unjustified); (d) attribute positive meanings to the situation (e.g., by acknowledging the positive contributions of the child and how their lives have developed more meaning as the result of the child's disability); (e) maintain family flexibility (e.g., by being able to shift gears, change expectations, and alter roles and rules); (f) maintain a commitment to the family (i.e., as evidenced by signs of cohesion and bonds of unity and commitment); (g) engage in active coping efforts (e.g., by actively seeking information and services); (h) maintain social integration (e.g., by maintaining supportive relationships with friends, relatives, and other people in the community, such as other parents of chronically ill children); and (i) develop collaborative relationships with

TABLE 5.2
Possible Issues Encountered by Parents at Life Cycle Stages

EARLY CHILDHOOD, AGES 0–5	• Obtaining an accurate diagnosis • Informing siblings and relatives • Locating services • Seeking to find meaning in the exceptionality • Clarifying a personal ideology to guide decisions • Addressing issues of stigma • Identifying positive contributions of exceptionality • Setting great expectations
ELEMENTARY SCHOOL, AGES 6–12	• Establishing routines to carry out family functions • Adjusting emotionally to educational implications • Clarifying issues of mainstreaming vs. special class placement • Participating in IEP conferences • Locating community resources • Arranging for extracurricular activities
ADOLESCENCE, AGES 12–21	• Adjusting emotionally to possible chronicity of exceptionality • Identifying issues of emerging sexuality • Addressing possible peer isolation and rejection • Planning for career/vocational development • Arranging for leisure time activities • Dealing with physical and emotional change of puberty • Planning for postsecondary education
ADULTHOOD, AGES 21 ON	• Planning for possible need for guardianship • Addressing the need for appropriate adult residence • Adjusting emotionally to any adult implications of dependency • Addressing the need for socialization opportunities outside the family • Initiating career choice or vocational program

Source: Families, professionals, and exceptionality: A special partnership (2nd ed), by Turnbull, A. P., & Turnbull, H. R., III, © 1990. Adapted by permission of Prentice-Hall, Inc., Upper Saddle River, NJ.

professionals (e.g., by sharing information, working together, respecting differences, and avoiding attempts to control).

Canam (1993), in an approach similar to that of Patterson and Blum, also isolated what she perceived to be the common adaptive tasks that face parents as they go through the period of adjustment. The specified tasks are important in accepting the health status of their child and in managing the long-term effects of their child's illness. Interestingly, while both sets of authors have specified a number of areas of concern, the lists are not identical in terms of content or order, even though there is some degree of overlap. The tasks, as outlined by Canam, include: (a) acccepting the child's condition; (b) managing the child's condition on a day-to-day basis; (c) meeting the child's normal developmental needs; (d) meeting the developmental needs of the other family members;

(e) coping with ongoing stress and periodic crises; (f) assisting the various family members in managing their feelings; (g) educating others about the child's condition; and (h) establishing a support system. In discussing the nurse's role, Canam made the following comments, which may also be appropriate to educational support personnel:

> The role of the nurse or other health professional working with the family is to assess whether or not parents are accomplishing each task and, if they are not, to determine what knowledge, skills, or resources they need to enable them to complete the task. The nurse can then assist them in developing the knowledge and skills they need, either directly or through referral to appropriate resources. (p. 51)

Parental Roles in the Education of Children with Chronic Conditions

Parents, in the past, often were not particularly involved in the education of their children. However, today, parents appear to want to be an integral part of the educational team and, in the case of a child with a chronic condition, a vital member of the child's health team. While most schools seem to recognize that the parents are the major providers of child-specific information and, if appropriate, child-specific training, Haynie, Palfrey, and Porter (1989) have suggested that parents have several other roles, including (a) acting as an advocate on behalf of their child; (b) providing school staff with access to health care providers; (c) participating in planning and training meetings held before reentry; (d) giving approval of the Individualized Education Plan, the Health Care Plan, and emergency plans developed to assist their child in times of crisis; and (e) notifying school personnel of any changes to their child's condition and subsequent health-related requirements. To this list, Porter, Haynie, Bierle, Caldwell, and Palfrey (1997) added the roles of maximizing the student's educational and social opportunities and planning transitions.

One of the major roles of the parents is being the "supplier" of child-specific information. In an interesting study, Andrews (1991) attempted to examine the nature of medical information the parents *want* the school to have, *who* the parents believe should provide the information, and *to whom* the information should be given. Overall, parents of children with conditions that might require emergency care,

with poor prognoses, and with visible illnesses were more in favor of disclosing medical information than those whose children were less likely to have emergency problems, whose prognoses were more optimistic, and whose conditions were not visible to those around them. Parents were asked to respond to the following question: "For a child with a chronic illness, should the school know about. . . .?" Items included the following: an impending medical emergency; medicine side effects; seriousness of the illness in general; participation in gym class; and how the child feels about the illness. Parents indicated 65% of school contacts (i.e., teachers, principal, school nurse, and classmates) should be informed about how to recognize the symptoms of the child's illness and the treatment effects, 64% of contacts should be informed about the seriousness of the illness and the need for isolation, 54% of the contacts should be aware of the restrictions that the illness has on the activities of the child. However, only 49% of the contacts need to know about the emotional aspects of the child's illness. When the 16 items were regrouped by individual school contacts (i.e., teachers vs. students, principal vs. school nurse) the parents indicated that teachers needed the most information about children's health problems (85% of the 16 items listed), followed by the principal (66%), the school nurse (64%), and finally, the child's classmates (19%). In terms of who should supply information regarding the child, the parents overwhelmingly reported that it was their responsibility. In response to the question "Who should tell the school about . . . ?", for the 16 items listed, the mean response rate indicating that it was the parents' responsibility was 89%. Doctors were considered the appropriate informant only 54% of the time, nurses, 26%, and the child, 24%.

Parental Satisfaction with the Educational Program of Their Child

Very few studies have specifically looked at parental satisfaction with the educational program of students with special health care needs. One of the most recent studies was conducted by Jones, Clatterbuck, Marquis, Turnbull, and Moberly (1996), who were interested specifically in the types of problems encountered by children who were ventilator-assisted. By having parents complete written questionnaires and participate in in-depth interviews, it was found that parents were generally satisfied with the schools' ability to meet the needs of their children. In particular, the majority of the respondents reported satisfaction with the schools' success in meeting students' academic needs (83%), health care needs (80%), socialization needs (78%), and psychological or emotional needs (70%). While 61% of parents indicated that the schools met the therapy needs of their children, 36% indicated some degree of dissatisfaction (i.e., they wanted more therapy than the schools were able to provide).

In a slightly different type of study, Turner-Henson, Holaday, Corser, Ogletree, and Swan (1994) interviewed parents of 365 children with chronic illnesses, in an attempt to examine what the authors referred to as the "experiences of discrimination." While almost two-thirds of the sample (65.5%) reported that discrimination had not been problematic, the remaining third (34.5%) reported specific incidences of discrimination. Even though the school system was not the focus of this study, surprisingly, most of the problems cited—over one half (55%)—were associated with the school system. The second most common source of discrimination was the child's peers (36%). Other major sources of discrimination (6.5%) included organized groups (e.g., Scouts, Little League), amusement parks or resorts, restaurants, and theaters. The types of problems that the students were reported to have experienced, related to the school system, are shown in Table 5.3.

In a study by Chesler and Barbarin (1986), parents of children with cancer were asked to comment on actions by teachers that were helpful and those that were not. Helpful teachers were characterized as being caring, treating the child as normal, giving the

TABLE 5.3
Types of School-Related Discrimination Reported by Parents

Types	Percent of Parents Reporting (%)
Physical education classes (e.g., teacher overprotective of child, would not let child run; teacher forces child to participate, forced child to run)	19
School personnel unwilling to provide special care (e.g., personnel do not want a child in diapers and resent having to take child to lavatory; do not always follow doctors' recommendations)	9
Exclusion from school activities (e.g., child not allowed to play because of brace; child excluded from parties because of food limitations)	7
Field trips and visits (e.g., school does not want the responsibility of taking child on trips)	7
School officials wanted child to go to another school (e.g., teacher refused to take child into her class because of child's disability and toilet needs)	5
People prevent child from eating or eating certain foods (e.g., child not allowed to have snack in class, so must eat in hallway or go to nurse's office; teacher thinks child is faking low blood sugar)	5
Other verbal attacks by teachers	2
School bus (e.g., driver would not pick child up because child was in a wheelchair)	1

Source: Turner-Henson, A., Holaday, B., Corser, N., Ogletree, G., & Swan, J. H. (1994). The experiences of discrimination: Challenges for chronically ill children. Reprinted from *Pediatric Nursing,* 1994, Volume 20, Number 6, p. 574. Reprinted with permission of the publisher, Jannetti Publications, Inc., East Holly Avenue, Box 56, Pitman, NJ 08071-0056; phone (609) 256-2300; FAX (609) 589-7463. For a sample copy of the journal, please contact the publisher.

child special academic help, and keeping the parents informed. Teachers who were rated as not being helpful were characterized as insensitive or overprotective.

Finally, in the study by Lynch, Lewis, and Murphy (1993), cited in chapter 4, the researchers attempted to delineate some of the potential barriers to providing services to children with special health care problems in the school system. Eighty-eight percent of the parents reported that they were either very satisfied or generally satisfied with the programs offered, 76% reported that they had no difficulty obtaining services, and 70% stated that services had been available "usually" or "most of the time." The respondents did cite two problematic areas: (a) the inability of the teachers to understand the needs of their child, and (b) the misinformation school personnel had regarding the illness of the child. Parents in this study were also asked to identify potential solutions to the barriers that prevented the provision of services. The following suggestions were given by the respondents: (a) improve schools in general; (b) increase and improve communication between home and school, recognize the pressures that children and families experience, and be more sensitive; (c) allocate adequate funds to education of students who are chronically ill; (d) provide a full range of service delivery options, especially home tutoring; (e) make information available and serve as a resource person for parents and children; and (f) consider modifications in grading policies and procedures that are tailored to the needs of children with chronic illnesses (p. 216).

🐾 Impact of Illness on Well Siblings

In the previous section the impact of illness on families, in particular on parents, was discussed. Recently, interest in the response of siblings has been the focus of several research endeavors. The following statement from Potter (1985) highlights some of the difficulties encountered by the brothers and sisters of children who are chronically ill:

> It is easy for siblings to become the forgotten partners in the family's dealings with chronic illness. . . . Yet chronic illness is a major disruptive force within the family, often drastically altering roles, expectations, and lifestyle. Siblings are very much a part of this situation, affecting it and being affected by it. Sibling relationships may vary widely, but they are generally relationships which last a lifetime and which are very special. The siblings of a chronically ill person thus have a definite stake in what is going on, but their ability to cope may be affected by a multitude of factors such as age, maturity, ability to comprehend the situation, their own place and adjustment within the family, and the honesty and appropriateness with which the parents communicated with them about the illness and its ramifications. (p. 59)

As in the case of research on the impact of illness in a child on his or her parents, research on the reactions of well siblings to their brother's or sister's illness has shown contradictory results. Some studies have shown siblings of children with chronic illnesses to be "psychologically disturbed, behaviorally disagreeable, or behaviorally offensive," whereas others have shown that "no significant differences" exist when siblings of children who are ill are contrasted with siblings of healthy children (Harkins, 1994). Negative reactions described in the literature have included poorer academic performance, deprivation of parental attention, increased attention-seeking behavior, and feelings of isolation (Gallo, Breitmayer, Knafl, & Zoeller, 1992). Positive effects have included decreased self-centeredness, along with increased empathy, helpfulness, maturity, and responsibility (Faux, 1993). Table 5.4 shows a list of such responses.

In criticizing the research that has shown that chronic illness has a negative impact on well siblings, Harkins (1994) has suggested that in some cases researchers have actually set out to "demonstrate untoward effects" (p. 667). This has been accomplished, according to this author, by questioning parents (particularly mothers) rather than the siblings themselves. The results of such investigations reflect the parental (maternal) concerns (and guilt) that arise because of "the amount of time, energy, and financial resources that are necessarily focused on the child with the chronic condition" instead of on the siblings (p. 667). While Harkins does agree that siblings may "experience stress or act out frustrations, anger, fear, jealousy, or resentment," such feelings are to be expected when a child is confronted with "such an intense experience" (p. 667). She cautions that the reactions of the siblings must be "placed in context of stage of development of the sibling, family communication and support patterns, and individual personality" (p. 667).

TABLE 5.4

Well Siblings' Negative and Positive Responses to Ill Siblings

NEGATIVE RESPONSES	POSITIVE RESPONSES
• Fear	• Empathy
• Resentment	• Nurturing
• Anger	• Cooperation
• Jealousy	• Sensitivity
• Anxiety	• Compassion
• Poor school achievement	• Maturity
• Sibling rivalry	• Self-esteem
• Attention-seeking behaviors	• Cognitive mastery
• Behavioral problems	• Ability to assume responsibilities
• Development of physical symptoms	• Tolerance
• Withdrawal	• Appreciation of family bonds
• Isolation	• Idealism
• Deprivation	• Sense of family pride
• Inadequate knowledge of illness	• Sense of family loyalty
• Inferiority	• Coping skills
• Prone to failure	• Problem-solving skills
• Increased competition	• Appreciation of own health
• Egocentricity	
• Guilt conflict	
• Self-blame	
• Communication	

Source: Powell, M. L. (1993). Impact of chronic illness on children and families. In D. B. Jackson & R. B. Saunders (Eds.), *Child health nursing: A comprehensive approach to the care of children and their families* (pp. 485–508). Philadelphia: J. B. Lippincott. Copyright 1993 by J. B. Lippincott Co. Reprinted by permission.

While it is generally accepted that most well siblings of chronically ill children do not become disabled themselves, research has shown that there are factors related to the well sibling (e.g., birth order, age, and gender) and to the chronically ill child (e.g., the type and visibility of the disability, the severity of the illness) that may influence the reactions of the siblings. For example, in a recent study of 28 well siblings of children with chronic illnesses (e.g., diabetes, chronic renal failure, juvenile rheumatoid arthritis, asthma) by Gallo et al. (1992), it was found that siblings who were younger than the ill child exhibited more behavior problems than siblings who were older than the ill child. However, a study by Thompson et al. (1994) of 19 well siblings of chronically ill children (i.e., children with a diagnosis of asthma, heart trouble, blood disorder, immune deficiency, or seizures) found that female siblings had a greater tendency to engage in headstrong behaviors than their male counterparts.

Siblings experience stress at different periods in their life cycle. For example, the young child may be concerned about starting school, particularly if his or her disabled sibling is in the same school, whereas the adolescent siblings of a chronically ill child may be apprehensive about bringing their dates home because of embarrassment of having a child with a disability in the home. For adult siblings, concerns about their responsibility towards the affected child, particularly if their parents are unable to care for the child as a result of illness or age, may be paramount. Some of the stressors experienced by siblings throughout the life span are shown in Table 5.5. For a thorough review of the literature on siblings of children with chronic physical and cognitive disabilities, the reader is referred to the

TABLE 5.5
Possible Issues Encountered by Siblings at Life Cycle Stages

EARLY CHILDHOOD, AGES 0–5	• Less parental time and energy for sibling needs • Feelings of jealousy over less attention • Fears associated with misunderstandings of exceptionality
ELEMENTARY SCHOOL, AGES 6–12	• Division of responsibility for any physical care needs • Oldest female sibling may be at risk • Limited family resources for recreation and leisure • Informing friends and teachers • Possible concern over younger sibling surpassing older • Issues of "mainstreaming" into same school • Need for basic information on exceptionality
ADOLESCENCE, AGES 12–21	• Overidentification with sibling • Greater understanding of differences in people • Influence of exceptionality on career choice • Dealing with possible stigma and embarrassment • Participation in sibling training programs • Opportunity for sibling support groups
ADULTHOOD, AGES 21 ON	• Possible issues of responsibility for financial support • Addressing concerns regarding genetic implications • Introducing new in-laws to exceptionality • Need for information on career/living options • Clarify role of sibling advocacy • Possible issues of guardianship

Source: Families, professionals, and exceptionality: A special partnership (2nd ed), by Turnbull, A. P., & Turnbull, H. R., III, © 1990. Adapted by permission of Prentice-Hall, Inc., Upper Saddle River, NJ.

article by Faux (1993) and the text by Stoneman and Berman (1993).

🖤 Impact of Illness on Community Members

Daily, children and young adults with special health care needs interact with others in the community— Girl Scout or Boy Scout leaders, ministers, shop clerks, bus drivers, and teachers—to list a few. Unfortunately, in many cases, the reaction of others will not be positive. Stein (1986), in the following passage, describes the reactions of the public:

Almost everyone who thinks about a chronic or serious ongoing health problem in a young child responds emotionally with a certain amount of recoil. To many of us childhood is synonymous with a sense of future,

health, and optimism. The fact that something could be permanently and seriously wrong with a youngster seems to contradict this idea of childhood. (p. 71)

However, for the child or young adult with a chronic illness and his or her family, members of the community may be a source of considerable assistance. Patterson and Blum (1996) differentiate between the three different types of support that are offered informally to parents by members in the community. The first type is **emotional** support, which includes making the parents feel liked, cared about, and valued by others. The second type is **informational** support, referring to the ideas, resources, facts, advice, and helpful hints that assist in problem-solving and decision-making. Finally, **tangible** support refers to the actions of others that result in concrete assistance to the family. A neighbor who runs an errand for the parents or a friend who offers to baby-sit are both examples of tangible assistance. Unfortunately, the authors report that, based on their own personal experience and the experience of others, "the attitudes and behavior of people in the community are often a greater source of strain for [parents] than having a child with a chronic condition" (p. 695).

As mentioned previously, children who have a chronic illness or a disability are attending regular public schools in greater numbers than ever before. Some of the most important members of the community are the teachers who will be in contact with the children. The importance of teachers in the life of the child with a chronic illness has been described by Potter (1985):

> School is often perceived by the chronically ill student to be a haven of normality and the teacher is a symbol of that normality. By their actions, teachers often will determine how other students will react to a student with medical problems and limitations. Thus the teacher may be influential in determining how well the student copes with the limitations of the illness as well as how well other people cope with it. School staff with their knowledge of normal children and adolescents can be invaluable resources to parents who may no longer have a good sense of what is "normal." (p. 62)

Even though the teacher of a child with a chronic illness has a major impact on that child's life, little is known about how that illness affects the teacher of the child. However, teachers may go through the same stages as parents as they come to grips with the knowledge that one of the students in their class has a serious illness (Potter, 1985).

Since teachers play such a critical role, parents and teachers must work together cooperatively and collaboratively to provide students with educational programs that best meet their needs. Unfortunately, interaction between professionals and parents is often "marked by confusion, dissatisfaction, disappointment, and anger" (Hardman, Drew, Egan, 1996, p. 92). In the study by Lynch and her colleagues (1993), mentioned previously, families of children with chronic illness were asked what they would "like to say if they could give just one piece of advice to teachers." Suggestions given focused on six areas: (a) treating the child normally; (b) being better informed about the illness of the child and the implications of the illness; (c) communicating with parents; (d) remaining hopeful; (e) building confi-

dence and self-esteem in the child; and (f) being sensitive to the needs of the entire family.

In an article by Wadsworth, Knight, and Balser (1993), a set of guidelines was presented to assist parents and teachers of children who are either medically fragile or technology dependent in developing a satisfactory working arrangement between the home and school. While these children have unique needs that are not common to all children who have a chronic illness or a disability, some of the suggestions offered by this team may be useful in establishing "a basic understanding of both the parents' and the educator's points of view" (p. 102):

1. Children come first for both parents and educators, but a teacher's priorities may not be the same as the parents'. The teacher and related service staff must manage and consider all their students' needs and interests simultaneously. Parents should not misinterpret the staff's primary goal of educating the entire class as negligence toward any one child. Parents and school personnel should remember that compromise and flexibility go a long way toward resolving differences and building positive relationships.

2. Families and educators need to establish communication lines and mutual respect from the beginning in order to minimize conflict in handling problems. The teacher or the child's service coordinator is the first person the parents should go to when a problem related to the child and school arises. Likewise, educators should solicit and involve parental expertise in resolving difficulties in the classroom.

3. Educators cannot be expected by families to do all the medical care for a child that is done in the home. Legal constraints (which vary from state to state) require that only specifically trained personnel perform this care at school. Treatments prescribed by the child's physician must be followed exactly, and exclusively, by trained personnel in the schools. Although this may not, and often cannot, be the way the parents are accustomed to doing things at home, only by the parents contacting the child's doctor, and obtaining new written prescriptions, can existing orders be changed or procedures added to the school schedule.

4. Parents and educators need to have empathy for each other. The teacher's career goal is teaching, not nursing. Likewise, parents have not planned to have children who are medically fragile or technology dependent. Teachers may need a little time to develop rapport with the child, to establish a learning environment that minimizes medical treatment distractions, and to organize a class routine that includes all children in daily activities. Communicating confidence and having patience with the

teacher's ability to learn to care for their child is critical for parents.

5. School personnel should acknowledge parental anxiety at placing their medically fragile or technology dependent child in the care of the educational system. Parents will not always be able to remove themselves from the classroom immediately upon placement. From the beginning, school personnel need to assist families in developing a plan for separation and providing opportunities for their child to develop independence and relationships apart from the family.[1]

Finally, teachers may have a vital role (a) in achieving balance in cases where the parents are either overprotective or overpermissive or (b) by acting as a child advocate in cases where the parents are displaying inappropriate responses, such as neglect, rejection of the child, or denial of the severity of the symptoms (Fithian, 1984).

🐾 Impact of Illness on Well Friends and Classmates

In the previous section the impact of illness on community members, especially teachers, was addressed. An often neglected area is the effect of illness on the friends and classmates of the child who is ill. Potter (1985) describes the reactions of peers of children who have a chronic illness or disability:

> Having a close friend who is faced with a debilitating or even potentially terminal disease or a permanent disability due to injury may be almost as traumatic as actually having the disability. Suddenly, perceptions of life and death and plans for the future may be thrown into confusion. . . .
>
> In some cases, peers may automatically rally around their disabled friend; in other cases modeling of acceptance and encouragement of active support may be necessary. Nor should friendship systems be expected to remain the same both before and after the illness/injury. Friendships wax and wane as interests and people change; the young person may need help in sorting out a relationship that continues out of a sense of duty from one that is based on mutual interests and camaraderie. (pp. 60–61)

Peers of the chronically ill child, like siblings, must not be forgotten. There is often an expectation that the friends of the chronically ill child will be accepting and continue to have a relationship with their friend, regardless of the outcome of the illness. However, as Potter asks, "How can we expect adolescents to know how to act around a disabled peer when adults with much more experience in interpersonal relationships often feel uncomfortable and unsure around handicapped people?" (1985, p. 60).

Of particular concern is the reaction of friends and acquaintances to the death of a peer. Schnieders and Ludy (1996), in an article entitled "Grief and Death in the Classroom," differentiate between the symptoms of grief common to children and those common to adults (Table 5.6).

Not all symptoms of grief in children are visible, particularly in cases of death of a close friend. Wharton, Levine, and Jellenick (1993) have offered the following cautionary comments:

> Children and adolescents grieve in a variety of specific ways after loss. When the loss is of a peer rather than a family member, their grieving is often subtle and private, and thus unacknowledged and unattended. This absence of overt mourning should not be misinterpreted as successful coping, since even the most profoundly affected students may grieve in silence. (p. 676)

While it is beyond the extent of this book to fully address the issues related to the grieving process in friends and family of the child who dies, suggestions, specifically written for teachers, culled from the literature on death and dying by Thornton and Krajewski (1993), are provided in Table 5.7.

Children's understanding of death, not unlike children's understanding of illness, develops progressively as aging occurs. Some of the characteristics of children, by age group, are shown in Table 5.8.

For further information on children and death, the reader is referred to the articles and books listed in Table 5.9. Teachers must be prepared to discuss the issues of death and dying with their students, particularly if there is a student in the classroom who may have a shortened life expectancy resulting from some type of chronic illness or disability. The role of the teacher is critical, and with proper training, teachers "can have a positive impact in teaching children healthy emotional responses to one of life's most challenging situations" (Thornton & Krajewski, 1993, p. 34).

---

[1] Wadsworth, D. E., Knight, D., & Balser, V. (1993). Children who are medically fragile or technology dependent: Guidelines. *Intervention in School and Clinic, 29,* 102–104. Copyright 1993 by PRO-ED, Inc. Reprinted by permission.

TABLE 5.6

Symptoms of Grief

Children	Adults
PHYSICAL SYMPTOMS	**PHYSICAL SYMPTOMS**
Somatic distress	Sleep problems
Difficulty swallowing	Physical illness
Difficulty breathing	Tearfulness
Need to sigh	
Lack of appetite	
Exhausted feelings	
Difficulty sleeping	
Lack of muscle power	
Empty feeling in stomach	
Hyperactivity	
Tears	
BEHAVIORAL SYMPTOMS	**PROFESSIONAL SYMPTOMS**
Regression	Professional feelings of ineffectiveness
Assumes mannerisms of deceased	Sense of loss of self-control
Changes in roles	Helplessness
School problems	Unwillingness to make emotional commitments
Delinquency	
Substance abuse	
Gives away possessions	
EMOTIONAL SYMPTOMS	**EMOTIONAL SYMPTOMS**
Hostile reactions toward deceased or others	Mood changes
Replacement	Depression
Idealization of deceased	Irritability
Panic	Sudden outbursts of anger over minor occurrences
Guilt (real and imaginary)	Small problems are seen as insurmountable
Isolation or withdrawal	Relationships with others become difficult
Shock/numbness	Crying for no reason
Anger	General feeling of emptiness
Relief	Poor self-image
Loneliness	Disorganization
Low self-esteem	Overly active
Lack of demonstrated emotion	Mummification

Source: From "Grief and death in the classroom" by Schnieders, C. A., & Ludy, T. J., *Physical Disabilities: Education and Related Services,* Vol. 14, 1996, pp. 61–74. Copyright 1996 by The Council for Exceptional Children. Reprinted with permission.

TABLE 5.7
Guidelines for Helping a Child Deal with Grief

1. Encourage children to express their feelings but don't push for too much or require that they do so.
2. Be honest. Answer questions truthfully and express your own emotions honestly.
3. Keep it simple. Discuss death in terms children can understand. Don't give them more information than they can handle at their developmental level.
4. Relate to children at their developmental level. If you're unsure of their level, ask them for their interpretation of what happened.
5. Be patient. Be aware that children may repeat the same question as they seek reassurance and deal with confusion and fear. Also remember that the length of grieving differs from child to child and may last for some time.
6. Don't preestablish expectations. Each child deals with death differently.
7. Do suggest some ways a child can memorialize the person such as planting a tree in that person's honor, drawing a special picture, or writing something about the person.
8. Accept the child's feelings, perceptions, and reactions. Allow for differences of opinion, doubt, and questions.
9. Refer the child (and perhaps the parents) to other support people or services if necessary.
10. Prepare children for the continuation of their life. Reassure them that they will feel better after a time and that the time differs from person to person. Children should be assured that, in time, they will be able to play and have fun and that doesn't mean they love the person any less.

Source: Thornton, C., & Krajewski, J. (1993). Death education for teachers: A refocused concern relative to medically fragile children. *Intervention in School and Clinic, 29,* 31–35. Copyright 1993 by PRO-ED, Inc. Reprinted by permission.

One of the most instrumental researchers and writers in the field of bereavement and children was Eugenia Waechter, a professor of nursing at the University of California, who died prematurely in a house fire at the age of 57. In a speech presented to medical staff and students at St. Louis University in St. Louis, Missouri, on May 14, 1976, published posthumously in 1987, Dr. Waechter made the following comments, which are equally appropriate for educational personnel:

> The medical team must make a commitment to children while they are here. They must always be considered as living children, though they may be dying. The danger inherent in seeing children as dying is that of

TABLE 5.8
Some Developmental Characteristics of Children's Understanding of Death

Age Level	Reversibility	Fear/Anxiety	Biological Functioning	Basic Understanding
EARLY CHILDHOOD (3–6 years)	Death is gradual, may be reversed	Brief, recurrent fear of abandonment, guilt	Concern about hunger, warmth of dead person	Magical
MIDDLE CHILDHOOD (6–10 years)	Death is final and irreversible	Increase in fear (8–9 years), may personify death	Dead can see, hear, receive messages	Specific and concrete
ADOLESCENCE	Death is final, irreversible and universal	Anxiety and denial about own death, goals interfered with	Cessation of functioning understood	Universal but remote

CHARACTERISTIC OF DEATH CONCEPT

Source: Knowles, D., & Reeves, N. (1981). Understanding children's concerns about death and dying. *B.C. Journal of Special Education, 5*(1), 33–40. Copyright 1981 by B.C. Journal of Special Education. Reprinted by permission.

TABLE 5.9
Printed Materials on Death and Dying: Resources for Teachers

Betz, D. L., & Poster, E. C. (1984). Children's concepts of death: Implications for pediatric practice. *Nursing Clinics of North America, 19,* 341–349.

Bryant, E. H. (1978). Teacher in crisis: A classmate is dying. *Elementary School Journal, 78,* 233–241.

Cassini, K. K., & Rogers, J. L. (1989). *Death and the classroom: A teacher's guide to assist grieving students.* Cincinnati, OH: Griefwork of Cincinnati.

Elbert, A. M. (1982). The forgotten ones: Helping children and adolescents cope with death. From Grimes, J. (Ed.), *Psychological approaches to problems of children and adolescents* (pp. 211–245). Des Moines, IA: Iowa Department of Public Instruction.

Fredlund, D. J. (1977). Children and death from the school setting viewpoint. *Journal of School Health, 47,* 533–537.

Fulton, R. A. B., & Moore, C. M. (1995). Spritual care of the school-age child with a chronic condition. *Journal of Pediatric Nursing, 10,* 224–231.

Gordon, A., & Klass, D. (1979). *They need to know: How to teach children about death.* Englewood Cliffs, NJ: Prentice-Hall.

Krulik, T., Holaday, B., & Marinson, I. M. (Eds.) (1987). *The child and family facing life-threatening illness.* Philadelphia: J. B. Lippincott.

McHutchion, M. E. (1991). Student bereavement: A guide for school personnel. *Journal of School Health, 61,* 363–366.

Postel, C. A. (1985, Winter). Death in my classroom? *Teaching Exceptional Children,* 139–143.

Reeves, N., & Knowles, D. (1981). Helping children deal with death concerns. *B.C. Journal of Special Education, 5*(1), 41–48.

Rudman, M. K., Gagne, K. D., & Bernstein, J. E. (1994). *Books to help children cope with separation and loss: An annotated bibliography* (4th ed.). New Providence, NJ: R. R. Bowker.

Schaefer, D., & Lyons, C. (1988). *How do we tell the children? Helping children understand and cope when someone dies.* New York, NY: New-Market Press.

Schowalter, J. E., Patterson, P. R., Tallmer, M., Kutscher, A. H., Gullo, S. V., & Peretz, D. (1983). *The child and death.* New York, NY: Columbia University Press.

Seibert, D., Drotlet, J. C., & Getro, J. V. (1993). *Are you sad too? Helping children deal with loss and death.* Santa Cruz, CA: ETR Associates.

Walker, C. L. (1993). Sibling bereavement and grief responses. *Journal of Pediatric Nursing, 8,* 325–334.

Webb, N. B. (Ed.) (1993). *Helping the bereaved child.* New York: Guilford Press.

Wilson, P. G. H. (1988). Helping children cope with death. In J. Sandoval (Ed.), *Crisis counseling, intervention, and prevention in the schools* (pp. 131–149). Hillsdale, NJ: Lawrence Erlbaum.

Wrenn, R. L. (1994). A death at school: Issues and interventions. *Counseling and Human Development, 26*(7), 1–8.

freedom for abandonment before their actual death. Their continued development is tremendously important until their last breath, and they must be supported—allowed and encouraged to experience the full range of human emotion, actively engaged in the business of life and kept in contact with other significant people in their world.

It may seem to some that to support the goals of continued growth and life in the midst of disease and death is a paradox. It *is* a fascinating paradox; yet no professional can function adequately and successfully with children or their families if those children are viewed continuously within the context of death. It is an extremely difficult challenge to remain constantly available to the child and yet to let go when the timing is appropriate.

All children deserve and need the support of the professional team to live in dignity; to master difficult situations at the level of which they are capable; to find whatever pleasure is possible in their circumstances; to draw closer to others with the freedom to discuss both life and death; to reach their potentials for living, loving, and sharing of their experiences; and to die with dignity. (pp. 233–234)

❦ Summary

Many people are affected by the presence of a chronic condition in a child—the child, the child's family, and their acquaintances and friends. Working together, all of the people that are in contact with the child can assist the child to remain in school. In this chapter, the response of those in contact with the child or young adult has been explored. The remainder of the book examines the various physical and medical conditions that are typically found in children. The conditions are grouped by the physiologic system of the body that is most affected. Each section begins with a brief description of how the particular body system works and how, in time of illness, the system can break down. The primary focus in every chapter is on how teachers can assist students with chronic conditions to reach their fullest potential.

References

Anderegg, M. L., Vergason, G. A., & Smith, M. C. (1992). A visual representation of the grief cycle for use by teachers with families of children with disabilities. *Remedial and Special Education, 13*(2), 17–23.

Andrews, S. G. (1991). Informing schools about children's chronic illness: Parents' opinions. *Pediatrics, 88,* 306–311.

Canam, C. (1993). Common adaptive tasks facing parents of children with chronic conditions. *Journal of Advanced Nursing, 18,* 46–53.

Chesler, M. A., & Barbarin, O. A. (1986). Parents' perspectives on the school experiences of children with cancer. *Topics in Early Childhood Special Education, 5*(4), 36–48.

Chomicki, S., Sobsey, D., Sauvageot, D., & Wilgosh, L. (1995). Surviving the loss of a child with a disability: Is loss the end of chronic sorrow? Three case studies. *Physical Disabilities: Education and Related Services, 13*(2), 17–30.

Clawson, J. A. (1996). A child with chronic illness and the process of family adaptation. *Journal of Pediatric Nursing, 11,* 52–61.

Faux, S. A. (1993). Siblings of children with chronic physical and cognitive disabilities. *Journal of Pediatric Nursing, 8,* 305–317.

Featherstone, H. (1980). *A difference in the family: Living with a disabled child.* New York: Basic Books.

Fithian, J. (1984). General overview. In J. Fithian (Ed.), *Understanding the child with a chronic illness in the classroom* (pp. 1–13). Phoenix: Oryx Press.

Fleming, J., Challela, M., Eland, J., Hornick, R., Johnson, P., Martinson, I., Nativio, D., Nokes, K., Riddle, I., Steele, N., Sudela, K., Thomas, R., Turner, Q., Wheeler, B., & Young, A. (1994). Impact on the family of children who are technology dependent and cared for in the home. *Pediatric Nursing, 20,* 379–388.

Freitag-Koontz, M. J. (1988). Parents' grief reaction to the diagnosis of their infant's severe neurologic impairment and static encephalopathy. *Journal of Perinatal Neonatal Nursing, 2*(2), 45–57.

Gallo, A. M., Breitmayer, B. J., Knafl, K. A., & Zoeller, L. H. (1992). Well siblings of children with chronic illness: Parents' reports of their psychologic adjustment. *Pediatric Nursing, 18,* 23–27.

Hardman, M. L., Drew, C. J., & Egan, M. W. (1996). *Human exceptionality: Society, school and family* (5th ed.). Boston: Allyn & Bacon.

Harkins, A. (1994). Chronic illness. From C. L. Betz, M. M. Hunsberger, & S. Wright (Eds.). *Family-centered nursing care of children* (2nd ed., pp. 651–688). Philadelphia: W. B. Saunders.

Haynie, M., Palfrey, J. S., & Porter, S. M. (1989). *Children assisted by medical technology in educational settings: Guidelines for care.* Boston: Project School Care, The Children's Hospital.

Jessop, D. J., & Stein, R. E. K. (1989) Meeting the needs of individuals and families. In R. E. K. Stein (Ed.), *Caring for children with chronic illness: Issues and strategies* (pp. 63–74). New York: Springer.

Jones, D. E., Clatterbuck, C. C., Marquis, J., Turnbull, H. R., III, & Moberly, R. L. (1996) Educational placements for children who are ventilator assisted. *Exceptional Children, 63,* 47–57.

Knafl, K. A., & Deatrick, J. A. (1987). Conceptualizing family response to a child's chronic illness or disability. *Family Relations, 36,* 300–304.

Knowles, D., & Reeves, N. (1981). Understanding children's concerns about death and dying. *B.C. Journal of Special Education, 5* (1), 33–40.

Kubler-Ross, E., (1969). *On death and dying.* New York: Macmillan.

Kury, S. P., & Rodrigue, J. R. (1995). Concepts of illness causality in a pediatric sample: Relationship to illness duration, frequency of hospitalization, and degree of life-threat. *Clinical Pediatrics, 34,* 178–182.

Lynch, E. W., Lewis, R. B., & Murphy, D. S. (1993). Educational services for children with chronic illnesses: Perspectives of educators and families. *Exceptional Children, 59,* 210–220.

Martin, S. S., Brady, M. P., & Kotarba, J. A. (1992). Families with chronically ill young children: The unsinkable family. *Remedial and Special Education,* (2), 6–15.

McCollum, A. T., & Gibson, L. E. (1970). Family adaptation to the child with cystic fibrosis. *Journal of Pediatrics, 77,* 571–578.

Patterson, J., & Blum, R. W. (1996). Risk and resilience among children and youth with disabilities. *Archives of Pediatric and Adolescent Medicine, 150,* 692–698.

Porter, S., Burkley, J., Bierle, T., Lowcock J., Haynie, M., & Palfrey, J. S. (1992). *Working toward a balance in our lives: A booklet for families of children with disabilities and special health care needs.* Boston: Harvard U. Press.

Porter, S., Haynie, M., Bierle, R. Caldwell, T. H., & Palfrey, J. S. (1997). *Children and youth assisted by medical technology in educational settings: Guidelines for Care* (2nd ed.). Baltimore: Paul H. Brookes.

Potter, M. L. (1985). Chronic illness in childhood and adolescence: Considerations for school personnel. In J. Grimes & A. Thomas (Eds.), *Psychological approaches to problems of children and adolescents* (Vol. 2) (pp. 41–82). Des Moines, IA: Department of Public Instruction.

Powell, M. L. (1993). Impact of chronic illness on children and families. In D. B. Jackson & R. B. Saunders (Eds.), *Child health nursing: A comprehensive approach to the care of children and their families* (pp. 485–508). Philadelphia: J. B. Lippincott.

Ross, J. (1978). Social work intervention with families of children with cancer: The changing critical phases. *Social Work in Health Care, 3,* 257–272.

Schnieders, C. A., & Ludy, T. J. (1996). Grief and death in the classroom. *Physical Disabilities: Education and Related Services, 14*(2), 61–74.

Silverman, M. M., & Koretz, D. S. (1989). Preventing mental health problems. In R. E. K. Stein (Ed.), *Caring for children with chronic illness: Issues and strategies* (pp. 213–229). New York: Springer.

Stein, R. E. K. (1986). Promoting communication between health care providers and educators of chronically ill children. *Topics in Early Childhood Special Education, 5*(4), 70–81.

Stoneman, Z., & Berman, P. W. (Eds.) (1993). *The effects of mental retardation, disability, and illness on sibling relationships: Research issues and challenges.* Baltimore, MD: Paul H. Brookes.

Thompson, A. B., Curtner, M. E., & O'Rear, M. R. (1994). The psychosocial adjustment of well siblings of chronically ill children. *Children's Health Care, 23,* 211–226.

Thornton, C., & Krajewski, J. (1993). Death education for teachers: A refocused concern relative to medically fragile children. *Intervention in School and Clinic, 29,* 31–35.

Turnbull, A. P., & Turnbull, H. R., III (1990). *Families, professionals, and exceptionality: A special partnership* (2nd ed.). Columbus, OH: Merrill.

Turner-Henson, A., Holaday, B., Corser, N., Ogletree, G., & Swan, J. H. (1994). The experiences of discrimination: Challenges for chronically ill children. *Pediatric Nursing, 20,* 571–577.

Wadsworth, D. E., Knight, D., & Balser, V. (1993). Children who are medically fragile or technology dependent: Guidelines. *Intervention in School and Clinic, 29,* 102–104.

Waechter, E. H. (1987). Outcomes of care. In T. Krulik, B. Holaday, & I. M. Marinson (Eds.), *The child and family facing life-threatening illness* (pp. 232–238). Philadelphia: J. B. Lippincott.

Whaley, L. F., & Wong, D. L. (1995). *Nursing care of infants and children* (5th ed.). St. Louis: Mosby Year Book.

Wharton, R. H., Levine, K., & Jellenick, M. S. (1993). Pediatrician's role after hospital-based death and permanent disability in school-aged children. *Clinical Pediatrics, 32,* 675–680.

Youngblut, J. M., Brennan, P. F., & Swegart, L. A. (1994). Families with medically fragile children: An exploratory study. *Pediatric Nursing, 20,* 463–468.

PART II

Oxygenation:

Children and Young Adults with Altered Respiratory Function

CHAPTER **6**
Asthma

CHAPTER **7**
Other Respiratory Conditions

Breathing is almost an unnoticeable function, but anyone who has experienced panic when choking on a object or inhaling fluid has been reminded that the human body cannot survive if breathing ceases (Wallace, 1991). Individuals cannot do without oxygen for any length of time, even though they may able to do without food or water for a little while without any serious sequelae (Hunsberger & Feenan, 1994). The primary function of the **respiratory system,** working in conjunction with the cardiovascular and the hematologic system, is to provide body cells with the continuous supply of oxygen (O_2) required for them to carry out their specialized metabolic activities and to remove the waste product, carbon dioxide (CO_2), so that it does not accumulate within the cells. If the system fails, the life of the individual may be threatened, as oxygen starvation can result in sudden death, regardless of age.

Respiratory problems are particularly common in infants and young children because the respiratory system continues to develop until approximately age 8 (Jackson & Saunders, 1993). Acute respiratory problems account for approximately 50% of all illness in children between birth and age 5 and 30% of illness in children between ages 5 and 12 (Hunsberger & Feenan, 1994). Most acute respiratory illnesses are caused by viral infections; however, some are caused by bacterial infections. Many respiratory problems are chronic, and as many as one in every ten children may have a chronic respiratory disease (Hunsberger & Feenan, 1994). Chronic conditions can be divided into five categories (Porter, Haynie, Bierle, Caldwell, & Palfrey, 1997). They include those that affect (a) the **stimulus to breathe** (e.g., brain damage that results from near-drowning), (b) the **strength of the respiratory muscles** (e.g., muscular dystrophy or spinal cord injuries), (c) the **upper part of the respiratory system** (e.g., structural abnormalities of the oral cavity, such as cleft palate, or the passageway from the mouth to the lungs, such as a narrowing of the throat), (d) the **lower part of the respiratory system** (e.g., cystic fibrosis, a genetic condition that results in the production of increased amounts of mucus that "plug" the airway), and (e) **disorders of the alveoli,** the air sacs through which O_2 moves into the blood and CO_2 moves out of the blood (e.g., pneumonia, bronchopulmonary dysplasia). In this section, a brief overview of the anatomy and physiology of the respiratory system and an introduction to the mechanics of breathing are presented.

The Respiratory System: Review of Structure and Function

The respiratory system can be divided into two sections. The upper respiratory tract consists of the nose, pharynx, larynx, and the trachea. The lower respiratory tract includes the bronchi, bronchioles, alveolar ducts, and alveoli. The major parts of the upper and lower respiratory tract are shown in Figure II.1.

Upper Respiratory Tract

Air is brought in from the outside environment primarily through the nose or, when the nose is obstructed, through the mouth. The main function of the nose is to condition the air for the lower respiratory tract. This is accomplished by (a) filtering dust, other foreign particles, and infectious organisms; (b) adding moisture; and (c) warming the air as it passes through the nasal cavities. If the air is brought in through the mouth, there is less filtering; however, the air is moistened and warmed as it passes through the oral cavity.

The major function of the **pharynx** (throat) is to conduct the air brought in through the nose or mouth to the **trachea** (windpipe) and to serve as a passageway for food entering the **esophagus** (gullet). The trachea is supported by C-shaped rings of cartilage that keep it from collapsing. **Cartilage** is a "tough" connective tissue that consists of a variety of cells and fibers, including those that contain **collagen,** an insoluble protein arranged in bundles to give strength to the tissues. Cartilage is found primarily in the thorax, body joints, the rigid tubes of

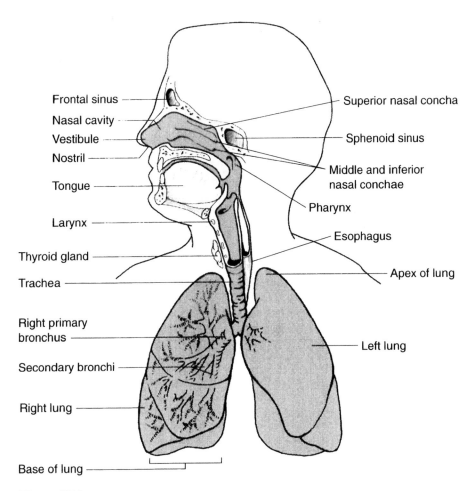

Frontal sinus —
Nasal cavity —
Vestibule —
Nostril —
Tongue —
Larynx —
Thyroid gland —
Trachea —
Right primary bronchus —
Secondary bronchi —
Right lung —
Base of lung —

Superior nasal concha —
Sphenoid sinus —
Middle and inferior nasal conchae —
Pharynx —
Esophagus —
Apex of lung —
Left lung —

Figure II.1
The Respiratory Tract
Source: Adapted from *Mosby's*, 1994, p. A-26.

the respiratory system (e.g., trachea and larynx), and in the ear. Collagenous fibers are also found in other types of connective tissue, such as bone, and in the heart and blood vessels.

The **larynx** (voice box) is supported by nine areas of cartilaginous tissues, the largest being the thyroid cartilage or **Adam's apple,** and it connects the throat to the trachea. The larynx contains the vocal cords, vital for the production of speech, and is protected by the **epiglottis,** an area of thin cartilage that closes during swallowing. The epiglottis also directs the food toward the esophagus to be transported to the stomach for digestion.

The larynx and the trachea are lined with a mucous membrane covered with tiny **cilia** (hair cells) that sweep any dust or debris upward toward the pharynx and the nasal cavity. Large particles entering

the trachea stimulate the **cough reflex,** which assists in the evacuation of foreign material. Overall, the upper respiratory tract functions in the transportation of inhaled air from outside the body to the lower respiratory tract; no gas exchange occurs in this section of the respiratory tract.

Lower Respiratory Tract

The **bronchi** (pl.; sing. **bronchus**) are the two principal branches that lead from the trachea to the lungs. Each bronchus divides and subdivides, forming progressively smaller tubes, referred to as **bronchioles,** each less than 0.04 inch (1 mm) in diameter (Millet, 1992). As the bronchi branch and become smaller, the cartilage disappears. There may be more than one million bronchioles in each lung (Wallace, 1991), all

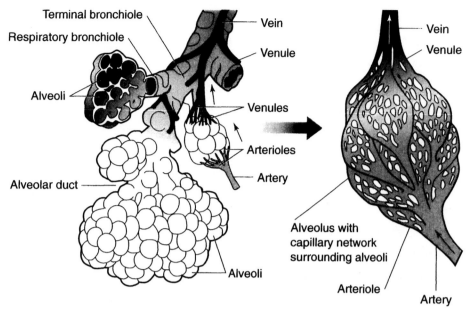

Figure II.2
Gas Exchange in the Alveolar Sac
Source: Adapted from Heller, Alberto, Forney, & Schwartzman, 1996, p. 279.

lined with a ciliated mucous membrane, similar to that found in the upper respiratory tract. The bronchioles continue to divide into smaller, tube-like structures, called **terminal bronchioles** or **alveolar ducts.** At the end of each duct are the **alveoli,** which resemble a cluster of grapes, each a single one-cell thick **alveolus.** Each group of alveoli is contained in a small sac, the **alveolar sac.** Each alveolus is surrounded by a blood capillary through which the diffusion of oxygen (into the arterial blood) and carbon dioxide (from the venous blood) occurs (see Figure II.2). Alveoli give shape and form to the lungs.

The lungs of the newborn infant have about 20 to 30 million alveoli, compared with the 300 to 600 million found in older children or adults (Hunsberger & Feenan, 1994; Sexton, 1990). The alveoli and the alveolar sacs increase the surface area of the lungs and are responsible for approximately 65% of the alveolar gas exchange (Millet, 1992). In an average adult, the surface area of the alveoli is approximately 70 to 80 square meters, depending on the size of the individual (Sexton, 1990).

Mechanics of Breathing

The trachea, bronchi, and lungs are protected by a bony structure that consists of 12 pairs of **ribs** and their cartilages, 12 **vertebrae** and **intervertebral discs,** and the **sternum** (breastbone). The entire structure is referred to as the **thorax** (chest), the **thoracic cavity,** the **bony thorax,** or the **thoracic cage** and is divided into the two spaces, one containing the right lung, the other, the left. Each lung is lined with two thin layers of membranes, referred to as the **pleura.** The inner layer, or the **visceral pleura,** covers the lung, whereas the outer layer, or the **parietal pleura,** lines the bony structures and the diaphragm. In the "potential" space between the two layers of the pleura, a thin layer of **pleural fluid** lubricates the two layers, allowing them to glide over each other, thereby ensuring painless movement as breathing occurs. Normally the space between the layers is not apparent unless the lung collapses, or air or fluid collects between the membranes.

Inspiration

The drawing in of air (or inspiration) is an active process that involves the coordinated movement of the respiratory muscles that surround all but the smallest airways and the **diaphragm,** the dome-shaped sheet of tendon and muscle located at the base of the lungs between the thorax and the abdomen. Somewhat similar to the action of a piston in an engine, the diaphragm moves down or flattens (i.e., contracts) during inspiration. At the same time, the chest muscles expand, displacing the ribs and causing them to flare or swing upward (i.e., increasing the size of thoracic cavity), thereby causing the lungs to expand. These movements create a change in pressure (i.e., the air pressure in the chest cavity becomes lower than that of the air outside the body) that results in the rush of air into the lungs (Sexton, 1990).

Expiration

The action of inspiration has been described as being analogous to pulling an elastic band to its limit (Jackson & Saunders, 1993; Millet, 1992). When the band has been stretched to its maximum, contraction must occur (i.e., it must return it to its resting state) and consequently, during expiration, or the passive process of expelling air from the lungs, the diaphragm relaxes and the respiratory muscles

TABLE II.1
Terms Used to Describe Breathing Patterns

APNEA

Total absence or cessation of breathing or airflow to the lungs for more than 15 to 20 seconds. Periodic breathing, with sporadic brief apneic periods, no longer than 10 to 20 seconds in duration, and with no other alterations in body function, is normal in both children and adults during sleep. Persistent apnea (beyond 2 minutes) is referred to as **respiratory arrest.** Respiratory arrest may result from acute obstruction of the upper airway or depression of the brain's respiratory center (e.g., as a result of head trauma, stroke, or narcotic overdose).

BRADYPNEA

Abnormally slow respirations (under 10 breaths per minute). May be due to brain disorders; administration of a sedative, narcotic, or tranquilizer; metabolic disorders; blood gas disturbances; or overfatigue in the critically ill patient.

DYSPNEA

Labored or difficult breathing. Dyspnea, or **shortness of breath (SOB)**, can occur at rest or upon exertion. Causes include fever; drugs; acid-base imbalance; stiff chest wall or lung; airway obstruction; certain heart conditions; weak muscles; and anxiety.

HYPERPNEA

A normal increased depth of respiration usually occurring with an increased rate of respiration, required to meet an increased metabolic demand (e.g., during exercise).

HYPERVENTILATION

Increase in both rate and depth of respiration, resulting in overventilation (i.e., volume of air greater than metabolic needs of the body). Hyperventilation offsets the oxygen–carbon dioxide balance and can result in dizziness. Common in those with a fever, but can be stress-related.

HYPOVENTILATION

The opposite of hyperventilation is hypoventilation, a pattern of slow, irregular, shallow breaths, which results in underventilation. Commonly due to prolonged depression of the respiratory center (e.g., from drug overdose or anesthesia).

ORTHOPNEA

Discomfort in breathing or the feeling of being short of breath in all positions except erect sitting or standing postures. Occurs in many disorders of the respiratory and cardiac systems, including asthma and emphysema.

TACHYPNEA

Abnormally rapid respirations (i.e., respiratory rate faster than normal) that can be associated with hyperventilation or hypoventilation. In infants, a respiratory rate greater than 60 is considered abnormal; in older children and adults, a rate greater than 20 above baseline is considered problematic. Found commonly in persons with pain, anxiety, fever, and various blood gas disturbances.

---

contract, pulling the ribs downward and inward, causing the thoracic cage to "collapse" around the lungs and to resume its resting dimension. The lungs recoil, primarily due to the contraction of the elastic fibers contained within the organ, resulting in greater pressure in the lungs than in the atmosphere; consequently, the stale air is released to be replaced with fresh air in the next breath. The "in-out" cycle ends when sufficient air has been released so that the pressure in the lungs equals that of the atmosphere.

Rate of Respiration and Breathing Patterns

Once the ventilatory cycle or the inspiration-expiration cycle is established (i.e., at birth), continuous breathing results from the interplay of the respiratory muscles, the alterations in respiratory pressures, and the elasticity or compliance of the lung tissue and thoracic cavity (Jackson & Saunders, 1993). One inspiration and one expiration makes one **respiration,** or **respiratory movement.** The respiratory rate of the newborn is 30 to 60 breaths per minute; for an infant, 20 to 40 breaths; for young children, 15 to 20 breaths; and for adolescents, 10 to 20 (Millet, 1992). Respiratory rates are affected by gender, activity, disease, and body temperature (Wallace, 1991). A variety of terms are used to describe the breathing patterns (both normal and abnormal) of children and adults. They are defined in Table II.1.

The basic rhythm and depth of respirations are controlled primarily at the brain stem level (i.e., involuntarily) by the **respiratory control center,** located in the medulla oblongata and the pons; however, there is some voluntary control that allows alteration of breathing patterns, such as when breath is held for a short period of time. In such situations,

as the carbon dioxide level increases in the blood, the respiratory center is stimulated and a message is sent to the respiratory muscles, causing breathing to resume on an involuntary basis. For this reason, it is impossible to kill oneself by holding one's breath (Wallace, 1991). Additionally, breathing patterns can be altered voluntarily during speaking, singing, crying, laughing, and swallowing.

References

Heller, K. W., Alberto, P. A., Forney, P. E., & Schwartzman, M. N. (1996). *Understanding physical, sensory, and health impairments.* Pacific Grove, CA: Brooks/Cole.

Hunsberger, M., & Feenan, L. (1994). Altered respiratory function. In C. L. Betz, M. M. Hunsberger, & S. Wright, *Family-centered nursing care of children* (2nd ed., pp. 1167–1275). Philadelphia: W. B. Saunders.

Jackson, D. B., & Saunders, R. B. (1993). *Child health nursing: A comprehensive approach to the care of children and their families.* Philadelphia: J. B. Lippincott.

Millet, S. J. S. (1992). Alterations in respiratory function. In P. T. Castiglia & R. E. Harbin, *Child health care: Process and practice* (pp. 515–563). Philadelphia: J. B. Lippincott.

Mosby's medical, nursing, and allied health dictionary. (4th ed.). (1994). St. Louis: Mosby.

Porter, S., Haynie, M., Bierle, T., Caldwell, T. H., & Palfrey, J. S (1997). *Children and youth assisted by medical technology in educational settings: Guidelines for care* (2nd ed.). Baltimore: Paul H. Brookes.

Sexton, D. L. (1990). Anatomy and physiology. In D. L. Sexton (Ed.), *Nursing care of the respiratory patient.* Norwalk, CT: Appleton & Lange.

Wallace, C. M. (1991). Care of the patient with a respiratory disorder. In B. L. Christensen & E. O. Kockrow (Eds.), *Foundations of nursing* (pp. 820–871). St. Louis: Mosby.

CHAPTER 6

Asthma

KEY WORDS

Airway hyperresponsiveness	Bronchodilators	Immunotherapy
Allergen/antigens	Cough variant asthma	Instrinsic asthma
Anti-asthma medications	Environmental control	Irritants/precipitants
Asthma action plan	Exercise-induced asthma	Noctural asthma
Asthma diary	Extrinsic asthma	Obstructive airflow disease

Asthma is characterized by episodes or attacks of wheezing, dyspnea, or both. The term "asthma" comes from the Greek word for "panting." Other symptoms may include tightness in the chest and a wet *or* dry cough (i.e., with or without mucus being coughed up and expectorated through the mouth). Asthma is often referred to as an **obstructive airflow disease.** The "obstruction" is the constriction of the respiratory passages, which results in the typical symptoms (Hill, Szefler, & Larsen, 1992). The term **airway hyperresponsiveness** is often used to refer to the individual's propensity for constriction of the lower respiratory tract. Some asthmatics are symptom-free for long periods of time, only having periodic episodes; others may have a more severe form of the disease in which the symptoms are virtually continuous. Unlike a cold or flu, asthma is not a contagious illness, nor is it associated with other health problems (e.g., cancer, heart disease) in later life (Wilmott, Kolski, & Burg, 1984).

❦ Etiology

It has been hypothesized that asthma is caused by the interactions of hereditary and environmental influences (Isbell & Barber, 1993). While several studies have shown a significant familial component in asthma (cf. Ownby, 1990; Young et al., 1991), the mode of inheritance is not fully understood (Morgan & Martinez, 1992). In many cases, a genetic link may not be evident, and finding out what actually triggers an asthmatic attack is difficult. For some individuals, one specific trigger may result in symptoms; for others, a combination of triggers may be required to bring on an episode (Canny & Levison, 1991). Several factors are known to be associated with the onset of asthma, including viral infections, exercise, allergies and irritants, weather changes, and emotional upset.

Viral Infections

Asthma is often triggered by a viral upper respiratory infection (i.e., a "head cold" or the "flu"). While the exact mechanism is unknown, the infection produces an inflammatory process in the airway (Hill et al., 1992). The asthma sequelae may persist for days or weeks after the infection. In some cases, the individual may have cold symptoms (e.g., stuffy nose) for a day or two before the more typical asthma symptoms

appear (Canny & Levison, 1991). In other cases, full-blown episodes may develop rapidly, and prompt, effective treatment is important to prevent a trip to the emergency department or admission to hospital (Levison, 1991).

Exercise

In many children, the symptoms of asthma are triggered by exercise. This form of asthma is called **exercise-induced asthma** and appears to be related to the temperature or humidity of the inhaled air (Orenstein, 1988) and to the amount of heat or water lost from the airways as a result of the exercise (Hill et al., 1992). The symptoms of exercise-induced asthma usually start 5 to 6 minutes *after* the start of the exercise, are most likely to occur after the individual has been participating in intense exercise, and generally become more severe when the exercise is completed. The episode, on average, lasts for 20 to 30 minutes; occasionally, the attack continues for several hours (Gold & Zimmerman, 1986). Exercise-induced asthma is most likely to occur during cold, dry weather.

Allergies and Irritants

Exposure to various **allergens**[1] can result in airway hyperresponsiveness in children and young adults. Some allergens are inhaled (e.g., dust, pollen); others are ingested (e.g., eggs, peanut butter). Asthma resulting from an allergic response is often referred to as **extrinsic asthma,** and a person with allergies is often referred to as being **atopic.**[2] Once the offending allergens have been identified, the individual with asthma should avoid or limit exposure as much as possible. Research has shown that an allergy to a particular substance may take months or years to develop; consequently, some substances may only result in symptoms later in life. Multiple factors (e.g., the status of the immune system, the dosage of inhalant exposure, and the length of exposure) all play

---

[1] Also known as antigens.

[2] An allergic response is a pathologic reaction (e.g., a hypersensitivity that results in sneezing, itching, or a skin rash) to a substance, situation, or physical state that would not affect the average individual in the same manner (*Webster's,* 1996). For further information on hypersensitivity and allergic responses, see chapter 22.

a major role in the rate at which persons become sensitized to a particular allergen (Duff & Platts-Mills, 1992). In some cases an individual may "outgrow" an allergy and no longer show any reaction to the allergen (Canny & Levison, 1991). The most common source of allergen around the world appears to be the dust mite. For children and young adults attending school, an allergy to chalk dust is often problematic.

Asthma that occurs in individuals not known to have a pathologic allergic response, often referred to as **intrinsic asthma,** may be caused by a vast array of irritants or precipitants (e.g., smoke from wood stoves, cigarettes, cigars, and pipes; smog; certain medications). A list of common allergens and irritants is included in Table 6.1.

Weather Changes

Sudden changes in temperature or general climate (e.g., increasing coldness, sudden rainstorm), wind, and humidity (e.g., too dry, too humid) have been linked to the onset of asthma attacks. High sodium dioxide, nitrogen dioxide, and ozone levels during

TABLE 6.1
Common Allergens

INHALED ALLERGENS	INGESTED ALLERGENS
Household Allergens	**Drugs**
House dust mites	Aspirin
Animals	Nonsteroidal anti-inflammatory drugs that result
Dander from furred or feathered pets (esp. cats)	in β block (e.g., ibuprofen)
Saliva	Alcohol
Urine (e.g. rodent)	**Sulfiting Agents[a]**
Skin fragments	Sulfur dioxide
Cockroach droppings	Potassium metabisulfite
Inert dusts (e.g., cotton, wood)	**Foods**
Molds and bacteria (esp. in humidifiers and air conditioners)	Chocolate
Hair dyes	Nuts (especially peanuts & peanut butter)
Bleaches and detergents	Eggs
Western red cedar	Shellfish
California redwood	Orange juice
Particulates	Milk
Aerosols	**Other**
Glues	Monosodium glutamate
Organic grain dust	Tartrazine[b]
Cleaning agents	
Pollens/Spores	
Trees and shrubs	
Weeds	
Grasses and herbs	
Fumes	
Sulfur dioxide, nitrogen dioxide, and ozone	
Cigarette, cigar, and pipe smoke	
Wood smoke	
Strong perfumes	
Paint	
Cooking fumes	

[a] Chemicals used to preserve foods and drugs.
[b] Chemical dyes in some foods and medicines.

periods of severe air pollution may also contribute to the onset of symptoms (Vedal, 1992). It is difficult to separate the effects of air pollution from the effects of other **aeroallergens** (inhaled allergens) or airborne particles, such as dust and pollen, when they occur concomitantly during periods of poor air quality (Morgan & Martinez, 1992). On particularly cold days or on days with poor air quality, individuals may be more likely to spend time indoors. Pope (1993) has raised concern regarding the increasing indoor pollutant concentrations as a result of reduced ventilation in energy-efficient buildings. Of particular interest to educators is the increased pollution that may be experienced in some of the newer "sealed" airtight schools.

Emotional Factors

Not that long ago, asthma was considered to be a psychosomatic illness. This belief resulted in inappropriate referrals for psychological evaluations and treatment and in parents being blamed for the cause of the illness (Wilmott et al., 1984). Although emotional problems on their own do not cause asthma, anxiety, excitement, and tension can exacerbate an episode (Canny & Levison, 1991). Excessive laughing, yelling, shouting, hard crying, and coughing are known to be triggers of asthma in some cases (Isbell & Barber, 1993; Majer & Joy, 1993; Wilmott et al., 1984). However, it is not the emotional component of these particular activities that is responsible for triggering an attack per se, but rather the deep breathing and other physiologic changes that stimulate the narrowing of the airways (Wilmott et al., 1984).

 ## Incidence and Prevalence

Asthma has been recognized as a potentially fatal disease since the second century (Chan-Yeung, 1992). It occurs worldwide and is considered by many to be the most common pediatric chronic pulmonary disorder and the leading cause of morbidity in childhood. Attempts to determine the incidence and prevalence of asthma have been hampered by lack of consensus regarding the definition of the

TABLE 6.2
Estimated Prevalence of Childhood Asthma for Various Subgroups

Subgroup	% of Population with Asthma	Subgroup	% of Population with Asthma
TOTAL POPULATION	4.3	**GENDER**	
		Female	3.4
AGE, YEARS		Male	5.1
0–4	2.9		
5–11	5.0	**INCOME**	
12–17	4.5	Low	5.4
		Higher	4.1
RACE/ETHNICITY			
White	4.1	**BIRTH WEIGHT, GRAMS**	
Black	5.1	<2500	5.8
Hispanic	3.5	≥2500	4.1
Non–Hispanic	4.3		
		URBANIZATION	
REGION		Urban	4.3
Northeast	4.6	Rural	4.1
North Central	4.3		
South	4.1		
West	4.3		

Source: Weitzman, M., Gortmaker, S. L., Sobol, A. M., & Perrin, J. M. (1992). Recent trends in the prevalence and severity of childhood asthma. *Journal of the American Medical Association, 268,* 2673–2677. Copyright 1992 by the American Medical Association. Reprinted by permission.

disease, lack of uniform diagnostic criteria, and differing methodologic approaches used in data collection (Bloomberg & Strunk, 1992; Chan-Yeung, 1992). It has been estimated that somewhere between 3 million and 8 million school-age youths in the United States have asthma (Zamula, 1990). However, this figure is under dispute (as being too low) because some purport that many children and young adults with asthma have not been recognized as a result of being misdiagnosed as having bronchitis or bronchiolitis (inflammation of the bronchi or bronchioles), viral diseases, or recurrent pneumonia (Zamula, 1990). Approximately 1.1 million Canadians have asthma; about 500,000 children and teenagers are included in that number (Paterson, 1991).

In a study that examined data from a random sample of 17,110 children aged 1 to 17 in the United States in 1988, Weitzman, Gortmaker, Sobol, and Perrin (1992) reported the estimated prevalence of asthma to be 4.3% overall. However, by examining various subgroups, the authors found considerable differences in the prevalence on the basis of several factors (Table 6.2).

Weitzman et al. (1992) also found that the estimated prevalence of asthma among children, when compared with a previous sample of 15,224 children studied in 1981, had increased by almost 40% (i.e., from 3.1% to 4.3%). The increase occurred almost exclusively among white children, even though the prevalence of asthma remained higher in black children than in white over this period. The authors attributed the increase to greater recognition of less severe cases; however, this finding has been challenged by Nordstrom, Rowe, Falk, and Remington (1993). These figures differ significantly from those of Hen (1986), who reported that as many as 11% of all school-age children in the United States were affected with asthma.

For school-age children, asthma is the leading cause of school absenteeism. Although the number of days missed as a result of asthma is unknown, estimates have ranged from 10 *million* (Majer & Joy, 1993) to 130 *million* days per year if data on hay fever and asthma are combined (McLoughlin & Nall, 1994). More school days are lost as a result of asthma than to any other chronic disease common to children (Zamula, 1990). While most children with asthma only miss a day here and there, Weitzman et al.(1992) reported that in 1988, some students with asthma (3.1%) missed more than 30 days per year. However, when comparing rates of school absen-

teeism over time, the researchers found a decrease from a rate of 5.7% reported in 1981. Interestingly, in comparing school attendance in white and black students, the proportion of black children and teenagers missing more than 30 days of school was less than that found for white (i.e., 1.5% vs. 3.5%) in the 1988 data.

Characteristics

As mentioned previously, an individual experiencing an acute asthma episode will often complain of wheezing, shortness of breath, chest tightness, and coughing. There are three events or processes that cause the symptoms. The first is a spasm of the smooth muscle of the bronchi (i.e., **bronchospasm**), which results in a narrowing and blocking of the bronchial tubes (i.e., **reversible bronchial obstruction** (Figure 6.1). Bronchospasm is further complicated by inflammation or swelling of the epithelial lining of bronchial tubes and lungs (i.e., **mucosal edema**) and by the increased production and retention of bronchial and pulmonary mucoid secretions (i.e., **phlegm** or **sputum**), which are thick and tenacious. The term "reversible" is used to describe the possibility of remission of the symptoms and normalization of pulmonary function, which generally results from appropriate treatment. In some cases, however, asthma can result in permanent changes to the respiratory system (i.e., **irreversible obstructive pulmonary disease**).

As the airway becomes blocked, the individual may begin to wheeze. The accompanying high-pitched whistling sound characteristic of a wheeze results from forcing the air out of the narrowed bronchial tubes as exhalation occurs. However, about 5% of people with asthma do not wheeze. For them, the most common symptom is a chronic cough (Levison, 1991), resulting from the bronchial wall spasm and swelling. Many of these individuals, referred to as having **cough variant asthma,** are misdiagnosed as having a cold, bronchitis, or sinusitis (inflammation of the sinus cavities) (Lurye, 1993). For some, coughing and wheezing occurs mainly at night. This type of asthma, referred to as **nocturnal asthma,** is believed to occur as a result of the fall in pulmonary function that occurs during sleep (Hill et al., 1992) and is also thought to be indicative of poor asthma control and inadequate drug treatment (Levison, 1991).

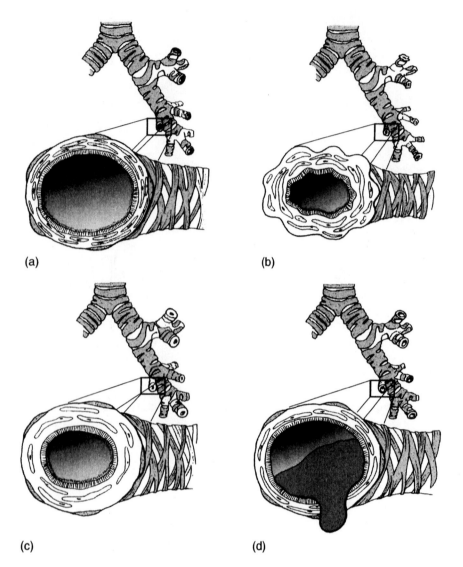

Figure 6.1
Normal Airway vs. Obstructed Airway due to Bronchospasm: (a) normal;
(b) bronchospasm; (c) bronchial edema; (d) increased mucus production.
Source: Adapted from Hagerdorn, 1990, p. 1023.

🐾 Diagnosis and Treatment

In establishing a diagnosis of asthma, the physician relies on three primary sources of information: (a) a comprehensive medical history, (b) a complete physical examination, and (c) the results of laboratory studies that investigate the respiratory system (Haggerty, 1990), which include lung function tests to measure the severity of the bronchial obstruction, allergy tests to determine specific allergens that may trigger a reaction, and chest x-rays to rule out the presence of other causes of wheezing, such as aspira-

tion of a foreign object (Canny & Levison, 1991). Although teachers are not normally involved in the diagnosis of asthma, they should report to the student's parents any information that may assist assessment of the student's level of functioning and any changes in status (e.g., frequency and severity of attacks) that may necessitate a change in treatment.

In the past, the major goals of treatment of individuals with asthma have been (in decreasing order of importance) the "suppression of symptoms to a degree sufficient to avoid death, respiratory failure, hospitalizations, urgent medical visits, days lost from work or school, disturbed sleep, limitations on physical exertions, and the symptoms of asthma"; more recently, the goals have been to prevent the "establishment of chronic asthma" and to "induce complete, durable remission of the underlying disease" (Sullivan, 1992, p. 1363). In other words, in the past asthma was not thought to be a "curable" disease; today, asthma, particularly the mild to moderate forms of the disease, is thought to be "potentially curable" with the judicious use of drugs (i.e., **pharmacotherapy**). **Chrysotherapy,** the use of gold salts to treat illness, and **chemotherapy,** normally used in the treatment of cancer, have been used to induce the remission of asthma with varying degrees of success (Sullivan, 1992). However, the most commonly used classes of drugs are bronchodilators and anti-asthma medications.

Bronchodilators (e.g., beta-adrenergic agents, theophylline products, and anticholinergics) are drugs that serve to relax the bronchial muscles and to relieve some of the airway obstruction; they are often given on an "as needed" basis ("pro re nata," or **PRN**) and are taken by children and teenagers during school hours, most often to alleviate the symptoms of an asthma attack (e.g., given to a student who has begun to wheeze in a science class where there are irritating fumes in the air). Used in this manner, this group of drugs is sometimes referred to as "rescue medication" (Rachelefsky, Fitzgerald, Page, & Santamaria, 1993). When used in this manner they are not treating the underlying inflammation. However, bronchodilators can also be given as a "preventative" measure to thwart an asthma episode (e.g., given to a student allergic to animal dander before a field trip to a zoo; given to a person with exercise-induced asthma a few minutes before exercise). Anti-asthma medications, described below, appear to be more successful in preventing attacks from occurring.

Anti-asthma drugs (e.g., cromolyn, nedocromil, and glucocorticoids) act by reducing the inflammation of the airways and decreasing the amount of phlegm produced, thereby improving pulmonary function and reducing airway hyperresponsiveness; they are considered to be "preventative" drugs. Many anti-asthma medications are given daily, even if there are no signs of an impending asthmatic attack.

The major advantages and disadvantages of each class of medication used to treat asthma are shown in Table 6.3. Although it is beyond the scope of this text to discuss the pharmacology of medications, teachers should have a basic understanding of the

drug the student is taking and be able to recognize any side effects, especially since many of the drugs cause symptoms similar to those of attention-deficit and hyperactivity disorder (ADHD).

In addition to pharmacotherapy, the use of **environmental control** (i.e., eliminating allergens or irritants that cause asthma) has also been shown to be an effective form of treatment (O'Connell & Heilman, 1996) and may, in fact, result in a decreased need for medication. However, it is often difficult or impossible to avoid all possible triggers; consequently, most persons with asthma are prescribed some drugs to decrease the number of attacks or reduce their severity. For some, when the specific allergen is known, the administration of "allergy shots" over an extended period of time **(immunotherapy),** may be beneficial (O'Connell & Heilman, 1996). Immunotherapy has been shown to reduce symptoms in those allergic to cat dander, house dust, ragweed, and grass pollen (Rachelefsky et al., 1993).

Nonpharmacological approaches, such as the use of natural foods, herbal medicines, relaxation therapy, and biofeedback, have also been used in the treatment of asthma; however, in most cases drug therapy has been more successful than alternative methods of treatment (Haggerty, 1990). Many children and young adults undergo **breathing retraining,** which involves practicing breathing exercises, postural relaxation, and effective coughing techniques to develop better abdominal breathing patterns, to increase the mobility of the lower chest, and to correct postural defects (Haggerty, 1990; Kleinberg, 1982; Sexton, 1990).

❦ Administration of Inhalant Medications

Some asthma medications are taken orally (e.g., tablet or liquid). Most are inhaled. Three different devices are used: (a) a metered-dose inhaler, (b) a powdered-dose inhaler, or (c) a nebulizer.

Metered-Dose Inhaler (MDI)

Most individuals who take inhalant medication use an MDI. The term "metered-dose" refers to the fact that each "puff" provides a fixed amount of medication. These devices are often referred to as "puffers" by children and can be used independently by children age 7 and older. Since this device is so common, its use is described in Table 6.4.

TABLE 6.3

Advantages, Disadvantages, and Side Effects of Asthma Medications

---

BRONCHODILATORS

Beta-Adrenergic Agents (or Beta$_2$-agonists)

Advantages: Rapidity with which they act; fewer cardiac side effects in comparison with some of the other available medications; side effects are not considered serious and drugs are not addictive; can be given orally or by inhalation; can be used as a "preventative" measure for exercise-induced asthma and/or before allergen exposure

Possible side effects: Muscle tremor (typically a fine shaking of hands that diminishes over time); slight increase in heart rate; stimulant sensation (e.g., irritability, restlessness)

Theophylline Products

Advantages: Long duration of action (beneficial for nocturnal asthma); can be used in moderate to severe forms of asthma not controlled by other medicines; easy to administer (can be given orally with food, if necessary, to decrease gastrointestinal side effects); side effects typically disappear as the body adjusts to the medication (i.e., after 1–2 weeks); can be given before exercise and allergen exposure

Possible side effects: Flushing, headaches, and dizziness; loss of appetite, upset stomach, heartburn, vomiting, and diarrhea; restlessness, irritability, and hyperactivity; linked to lowered cognitive functioning and poor school performance

Note: Teachers should be aware of warning signs of theophylline toxicity (e.g., behavior changes such as jitteriness, irritability, or nervousness; involuntary discharge of urine; insomnia; anorexia; nausea; vomiting; epigastric pain; dizziness; headaches)

Anticholinergics

Advantages: Used in the treatment of acute asthma, most commonly with adults; few side effects

Disadvantages: Only administered by inhaler; unpleasant taste

Possible side effects: May cause dry mouth or throat

ANTI-ASTHMA MEDICATIONS

Cromolyn

Advantages: Safe drug with few side effects; useful in preventing asthma triggered by exercise, allergy, cold air, and sulfur dioxide

Disadvantages: Must be given daily, even in the absence of symptoms; may need to be taken for 4–6 weeks before benefits are noted; does not control a sudden asthmatic attack

Possible side effects: Coughing, wheezing, hoarseness, nausea and vomiting, dizziness, hives and other skin rashes, pneumonia

Nedocromil

Advantages: Few side effects

Disadvantages: Newer drug used primarily with adults; use in children has not been adequately explored; must be given two to four times daily to inhibit allergen-induced episodes

Possible side effects: Unpleasant taste; headache; nausea

Glucocorticoids (glucocorticosteroids or corticosteroids)

Advantages: Most potent anti-inflammatory agents available; can be given as inhalant, orally, or intravenously

Possible side effects: Oral corticosteroids have the potential of several serious side effects when given in high dosage for a protracted period of time, including stunting of growth, increased appetite or fluid retention resulting in weight gain, heartburn, gastrointestinal bleeding, acne and fullness in face, cataracts and glaucoma, hair growth, back or rib pain, increased blood pressure, increased blood sugar, bone changes, decreased ability to handle physiologic stress and fight off infection, drowsiness, memory deficits, and psychiatric problems that range from mild depressive symptoms (e.g., nervousness, moodiness) to psychosis; when given orally, may result in a yeast infection of the mouth and throat; may cause coughing or wheezing.

TABLE 6.4

Using a Metered-Dose Inhaler

1. Assemble inhaler, if necessary, by inserting the drug canister (with stem down) into canister tube. Remove mouthpiece cap and shake the inhaler about four times. *Note:* If not shaken adequately, sufficient medication will not be released and the student will be inhaling propellant rather than medication.

2. Take in a full breath and then breathe out completely through pursed lips without straining (i.e., to the end of a normal breath).

3. Holding the inhaler with the tube upright (i.e., drug canister upside down) in one hand with thumb under the canister and index finger on top, place the mouthpiece between lips (with the mouthpiece extending beyond the teeth) *or* hold approximately 1½ to 2 inches in front of open mouth. With the other hand, hold the tube attached to the mouthpiece to steady the inhaler. If placed in mouth, close lips tightly over mouthpiece. *Note:* If the inhaler is held with the drug canister stem *up,* the medication will not be released properly.

4. With the head tilted back slightly (a) activate the canister by pressing down on the metal vial to release one puff of medication and at the same time breathing in one slow breath as deeply as possible as if sucking through a straw *or* (b) begin to breathe in slowly and then activate the inhaler by pressing on the button. Ensure that the tongue is down and out of the way. *Note:* Ideally, the breath should last for 2 to 5 seconds. If the student breathes too quickly, the medication will be deposited in the mouth and throat, rather than in the lungs. If the student activates the inhaler at the end of the breath, sufficient medication will not be inhaled.

5. Take the inhaler out of mouth and hold breath for as long as possible—ideally for 10 seconds—minimum of 3–5 seconds for a younger child.

6. Breathe out through nose without straining. If the nose is blocked, breathe out through mouth with lips pursed.

7. Breathe normally for 30 seconds to 1 minute—or longer, if indicated by the physician—taking another puff, if necessary, or if instructed by the physician. *Note:* Student should not take more puffs than ordered.

8. To eliminate any residual medication from mouth, rinse mouth with water (optional). Blow nose to remove residual medication from nasal cavity (optional).

9. On a regular basis, clean the inhaler. Remove the canister from the plastic casing; wash casing in warm, soapy water. Rinse in clean water; leave to dry. When reassembled store in a clean plastic bag or container. Store at room temperature. Do not place close to any source of heat. When empty, discard unit in the garbage. Do not puncture or burn.

10. Periodically check the amount of medication remaining in the canister by floating the device in room-temperature water. If full, the canister will sink to the bottom of a container of water. If half full, the device will float perpendicularly with bottom up. If one-quarter full, it will float with the bottom up, but on an angle. If empty, the device will float on its side.

Very young children, ages 3 to 7, and some older children, may have difficulty breathing in at the same time that the "puff" of medication is being released from the canister. By adding a plastic tube, known as a **"spacer,"** the medication is released into the reservoir, ready to be inhaled when the individual is ready. Commonly available spacers include Ellipse, AeroChamber, Optihaler, Breathancer, Inhal-Aid, and InspirEase. For a very young child, between birth and age 3, a **face mask** can be attached to the spacer to facilitate the inspiration of the medication.

Powder Inhaler

Powder inhalers, often known by their trade names, such as Turbuhaler, Spinhaler, Diskhaler, and Roto-haler, permit the inhalation of a powdered form of medication. The benefit of this type of device is that it is easier to use (i.e., requiring less coordination) than MDIs. The medication, usually in the form of a capsule, is loaded into the inhaler. After the inhaler is activated, the individual breathes in, with the lips tightly closed around the mouthpiece until all the powder is inhaled. Most children over the age of 3 can be instructed to use a powder inhaler independently.

Nebulizer

A nebulizer, also known as nebulizer unit, is an electric compressor that forces air through a liquid medicine, thereby producing a fine mist that can be inhaled by means of a face mask or a mouthpiece. When the nebulizer is turned on, the individual breathes normally until the medication is used up. Often used in hospitals, portable nebulizers may also be used in the school and the home for children who have difficulty using or are too young (as young as 18 months) to use other devices (Ellis, 1988).

Early Recognition and Treatment of Acute Asthma Attacks

Many adults with asthma identify the specific precipitators and early symptoms of an attack easily, but this is not always the case with children (Haggerty, 1990). As a result, children are at higher risk for severe exacerbations that may lead to respiratory distress. To assist teachers in recognizing the early stages of an impending attack, some warning signs are shown in Table 6.5. In some cases, the sign appears singly; in others, signs may appear in a "cluster." In some children, the early signs may appear as much as 6 hours before the attack.

There are several steps that a teacher can undertake to assist the student before and during an attack. They are shown in Table 6.6.

TABLE 6.5
Early Warning Signs of an Asthma Episode

- Abdominal discomfort
- Changes in breathing pattern (e.g., SOB)
- Cough
- Dark circles under the eyes
- Dry mouth
- Fever (low-grade)
- "Odd feeling" in the chest
- Glassy eyes
- Headache
- Itchy chin, neck, or chest
- Itchy throat
- Loss of appetite
- Moodiness, nervousness, anxiety, or irritability
- Paleness
- Runny nose
- Sadness or apathy
- Sleep disturbance and resulting fatigue

Sources: Hagerdorn, 1990; Whaley & Wong, 1995.

Emergency Procedures

Many individuals with asthma live relatively healthy, normal lives and only occasionally have to cope with asthma episodes. In most cases, the child or young adult will respond positively if the steps listed in Table 6.6 are followed. It is important to remember that an asthma episode may appear to be worse than it actually is (Paasche, Gorrill, & Strom, 1990). However, if the student does not respond to treatment as expected, it is important to get emergency help early, before the episode becomes a full-blown attack. The guidelines, shown in Table 6.7, may assist school staff in determining when emergency room/hospital assistance is required. The general rule is "when in doubt, get assistance." An emergency care plan (see Appendix C) *must* be developed for each student who has asthma.

Educational Implications and Teaching Tips

Asthma is a chronic respiratory illness that may greatly affect the lives of students. However, most boys and girls with asthma can attend school and participate in most activities without undue attention (Wilmott et al., 1984). In reviewing the literature on the implications of asthma on students, Celano and Geller (1993, p. 25) found that many writers and researchers have suggested that students with asthma could be at risk for poor performance for a number of reasons, including (a) increased absenteeism; (b) iatrogenic effects of asthma medication (i.e., side effects, such as sleepiness, produced inadvertently by the treatment); (c) teachers' or parents' perception that the student is too vulnerable to participate in school activities; (d) acute exacerbations of symptoms; and (e) stress associated with a chronic illness. The authors cautioned that lack of controlled empirical studies precludes firm conclusions regarding the increased risk for students with asthma when compared to healthy peers. However, for students who have frequent exacerbations, the authors suggested that educators and health professionals do the following: (a) implement self-management programs for the students; (b) monitor adverse effects of asthma medication; (c) adopt a multidisciplinary psychoeducational evaluation for referred children; and (d) institute educational programs to promote age-appropriate

TABLE 6.6
Assisting the Student with Asthma

1. Determine whether the student is beginning to have an attack:
   a. Listen for wheezing, usually most evident when exhaling. However, do *not* judge the severity of the attack by the amount of wheezing. If the airways are extremely blocked, there may not be an audible sound.
   b. Observe the respiratory movements. With asthma, the chest wall may be retracted (i.e., "sucked in" as the student breathes in). Retractions are most obvious below the rib cage, between the ribs, above the sternum (breast bone), and around the collar bone. The neck muscles may appear to be prominent due to the individual using the muscles to assist in breathing; similarly, nasal flaring may be evident as inhaling is attempted.
   c. Observe length of exhalation. During an attack there is difficulty getting air out of the lungs. Usually exhalation is more prolonged or labored.
   d. Observe the breathing rate. During an asthma episode the student may become short of breath. Many have difficulty talking during an episode; at night or nap time, inability to sleep may result from shortness of breath.
   e. If prescribed by the physician, assist the student to measure pulmonary functioning by means of a peak flow meter.
2. If possible, remove the trigger (i.e., allergen or irritant) of the episode or remove the student from the source of the trigger. Treatment is less effective if exposure to the trigger is continued.
3. Assist the student to sit with shoulders relaxed. Be calm and reassuring. To distract the student from breathing difficulties, encourage the student to participate in a quiet task (e.g., listening to music; playing with a puzzle; reading).
4. Help the student take the prescribed medications. If requested by the physician, assist the student to test the peak flow rate 5 to 10 minutes after treatment.
5. Encourage the student to drink clear fluids, which assists in thinning mucus.
6. Maintain a record of the asthma episode. Send home a written report to the parents at the end of the day (see Appendix G).
7. Check that there is sufficient medication for future episodes. Notify the parents if additional supplies are required.

Sources: Canny & Levison, 1991; NIH—National Asthma Education Program, 1994; Silkworth & Jones, 1986.

functioning at home and at school. For an excellent review of the role of self-management programs (i.e., programs designed to help families and children learn to become active partners in disease management), the reader is referred to the article entitled "Patient Education" by Howell, Flaim, and Lung (1992). In addition, the article entitled "Managing Asthma: A Growth and Development Approach" by Ladebauche (1997) will give the reader a greater understanding of the developmental issues facing students with asthma.

In this section, specific suggestions are given to assist teachers who have a student with asthma in their classroom. These teaching tips should lessen the level of discomfort often shown by teachers and administrators. While these suggestions are written for teachers who know that there is a person with asthma in their classroom, teachers play an important role in observing children in general and may be the first to notice that a child is displaying some of the common symptoms. By sharing their concerns with the family or the school nurse, teachers may play a vital role in motivating parents to further investigate an undiagnosed illness (McLoughlin & Nall, 1994).

1 *The most important thing a teacher can do for a student with asthma is to give him or her as normal a classroom experience as possible* (Silkworth & Jones, 1986). Treating the student differently or having different expectations for the student is counterproductive. Those who have had severe asthma attacks in the past may be fearful of future attacks, and consequently may be unwilling to participate fully. Some children and young adults with asthma may become very manipulative and develop behavior problems, particularly if school staff are not consistent in their approach. In most cases, a knowledgeable teacher, who is accepting of the student and understands the nature of the disorder,

TABLE 6.7
Emergency Situations

1. The student has blue-gray lips and/or nail beds, becomes tired from the amount of energy required to breathe, or is not fully alert. These signs indicate severe illness. **Call 911 immediately or take to the emergency room. If the student stops breathing, resuscitative breathing should be started. If the heart stops, CPR should be started.**

2. The student does not respond to the medications given within an appropriate time frame (i.e., wheeze, cough, or shortness of breath gets progressively worse) or there are no medications to give the child.

3. The peak flow rate declines or stays the same after treatment (or drops to 50% or less of the child's normal baseline).

4. The child needs inhaled bronchodilators more often than every four hours.

5. The child is vomiting oral medications.

6. The child is having extreme difficulty speaking, walking, or sleeping because of excessive shortness of breath or wheezing.

7. The child stops playing and cannot start any activity again.

8. Based on previous experience, it appears that the child is having a severe asthma episode.

Sources: Canny & Levison, 1991; NIH—National Asthma Education Program, 1994.

can "nip" any untoward behavior in the "bud." By being supportive, school personnel can encourage the development of a confident, independent attitude in the student. Overprotection does not help the student. "Shielding" the student from stressful situations, such as academic or athletic competitions or musical performances, is seldom appropriate (Wilmott et al., 1984).

2 *Communication between the teacher, the parents, and the health care providers is crucial.* To facilitate open communication, the following suggestions are given:

a. Parents should be encouraged to meet before the beginning of school with the teacher, particularly if the teacher is not familiar with the student's needs, to discuss the condition, any specific concerns regarding the school program (e.g., restrictions in exercise; specific triggers to be avoided),

the treatment regimen and procedures to be followed during asthma episodes, and actions to be taken if the student has a severe attack. The school nurse, the school principal, and the physical education teacher should also attend this meeting.

If there is a need for training of staff (e.g., how to use a nebulizer), arrangements should be undertaken before the beginning of the school year. All staff should be adequately trained in cardiopulmonary resuscitation (CPR) and ensure that their skills are updated on a regular basis.

An **asthma action plan,** which summarizes information regarding the student and actions to take in the event of an asthma episode, should be developed for each student (see Appendix C). School staff must have up-to-date phone numbers of persons to contact during emergencies (e.g., parents, guardians, physicians).

b. Additional meetings should be scheduled as needed, particularly if there are any changes in the student's condition or if there are changes in the treatment or action plan. Ideally the parent and the teacher should meet at the beginning of each term to discuss any concerns, particularly if the teacher changes each term.

c. Teachers should be encouraged to maintain a communication log, also called an **asthma diary,** for recording asthma episodes. For a sample log, modified from Schwartz (1984), see Appendix G.

It is impossible to protect students from "catching" a cold or the flu, but teachers, by means of daily communication, can notify parents that their son or daughter has been exposed to a virus. Some doctors recommend that asthma medications be started at the first sign of a cold (Canny & Levison, 1991).

d. While some students miss days because of asthma episodes, teachers and parents should be alert to unnecessary absences. Teachers should make an effort to encourage students with asthma to attend school and to avoid using their illness as an excuse. Some students have been known to exaggerate their symptoms (i.e., to start wheezing just before the school bus arrives) in order to play "hooky." Unfortunately, some parents are easily manipulated and "give in."

The guidelines developed by Freudenberg et al. (1980) (Table 6.8) may assist parents and teachers to determine whether or not staying at home is necessary. Parents should discuss school attendance

TABLE 6.8
Checklist for Deciding About School Attendance

CLUES FOR SENDING CHILD TO SCHOOL

1. Stuffy nose, but **no** wheezing
2. Mild wheezing, which clears after medicine
3. Good exercise tolerance (able to participate in usual daily activities)
4. No extra effort needed with breathing pattern

CLUES FOR KEEPING CHILD HOME

1. Evidence of infection—red throat, sore throat, or swollen glands
2. Child has fever—over 100°F orally or over 101°F rectally (hot and flushed)
3. Wheezing which continues to increase 1 hour after medicine is taken
4. Child is too weak or tired to take part in routine daily activities
5. Child's breathing pattern is irregular, labored, or rapid (respiratory rate is over 25 breaths per minute while at rest)

Source: Freudenberg, N., Feldman, C. H., Clark, N. M., Millman, E. J., Valle, I., & Wasilewski, Y. (1980). The impact of bronchial asthma on school attendance and performance. *Journal of School Health, 50*(10), 522–526, December 1980. American School Health Association, Kent, Ohio. Reprinted by permission.

with their child's physician, for each child is different, and what might be appropriate for one may not be appropriate for another. If teachers notice that absenteeism is becoming excessive, they (or the school nurse) may want to approach the parents and tactfully discuss the problem. If the student's absence is due to increased medical problems, the parents should be encouraged to seek advice from their child's physician. With a change in treatment, attendance may be improved.

3 *Students who take special medication for asthma should be allowed to take the medication as prescribed, where needed.* They should *not* be required to go to the principal's office or the nurse's station, for a delay in taking the medication can result in a more severe attack.[3] Similarly, if students

---

[3] For a discussion of guidelines for the administration of medications in schools, see chapter 24.

need to get a drink of water, they should be able to do so without asking. Sufficient intake of fluids is necessary to thin the mucus that results from asthma.

For young students, the teacher should be trained to administer or to assist in the administration of the medication; for older students, teachers should be adequately trained to supervise the administration of medications. Responsible students should be allowed to keep their inhalers with them in the classroom and to self-medicate (Bloomberg & Strunk, 1992; Richards, 1992). By having to leave the room, the student may feel more "different" than if the medication was simply taken in the classroom. Teachers who have a student with asthma in their class should be prepared by storing extra medication in their desk.

Teachers should check the expiration date of medications periodically and have the medication replaced before it has run out. Individuals with asthma, particularly those on corticosteroids, should be encouraged to wear a Medic-Alert bracelet or necklace.

Teachers should be alert to medication side effects and report any concerns to the parents. Asthma in itself may cause fatigue, as do some of the medications used to treat the condition. Some medications have the opposite effect, leading to loss of attention, irritability, and restlessness. The problems generally develop slowly over time, and there often is not a radical change in the behavior of the individual (Klein & Timerman, 1994). If the student is particularly lethargic or hyperactive in school, the teacher should inform the parents so that they can contact their pediatrician. Bronchodilators may cause fine muscle tremors and affect the student's fine motor skills. Long-term use of corticosteroids can lead to vision problems. Teachers should be alert to any sign of vision loss.

Teachers should be alert to those students who appear to be overusing their medication and report any suspicions to the parents, who can contact their physician. Teachers should also be alert to those students (particularly teenagers) who appear unwilling to take medication (e.g., perhaps because of embarrassment) and should encourage taking it as needed. In such situations, the student may benefit from being allowed to leave the classroom to take it.

The effects of **theophylline products** used to treat asthma on cognitive functioning and school performance have been of concern to physicians and educators. However, in a recently published article by Lindgren et al. (1992) based on the results of nationally standardized scholastic achievement test scores of 101 children with asthma and their siblings without asthma, the authors found no significant differences between the two groups. They concluded that the academic achievement of the children under investigation (i.e., children whose health status was closely monitored in a structured treatment program) was unaffected by both the condition (asthma) and the treatment (administration of theophylline). Interestingly, in this study 28% of the parents believed that the child's asthma or the medication was, in fact, causing learning problems; however, as the authors cogently point out, the converse (i.e., the attribution of high achievement or good behavior to the effects of asthma or its treatment) is unlikely to be reported.

4   *In general, most students are able to complete a regular school program without any major accommodation.* Teachers should try *not* to limit involvement in the various school activities, because this may encourage a lowered self-concept. In most cases, common sense will dictate what a student can or cannot do, and minor accommodations may need to be implemented. Depending on the student, the following suggestions may be applicable:

a. A student with a known allergy to airborne pollen should not sit beside an open window (unless it is equipped with an air conditioning unit and filter) or under an air vent during the seasons when pollen is circulating freely in the air. If a student is allergic to plant pollen, flowers should not be grown in or brought to the classroom. A botany class may be problematic to a high school student.

If the student is very sensitive to grass pollen, the student should be encouraged to avoid playing on grassy playgrounds; however, if the school grounds have a paved area (e.g., basketball court), being outside for short periods of time (with or without medication) may be tolerated. Those who are allergic to molds may have problems on hikes in the forest or woods, especially near piles of fallen leaves or rotting wood.

b. On very cold, humid, or windy days the student may benefit from staying inside during recess or outdoor gym periods. However, the administration of medication before going outside may lessen

the effects, allowing the student to participate in outdoor activities with peers. On very cold days, the student may benefit from using a scarf over the mouth and nose or from pulling a shirt up over the mouth, to prevent the onset of a wheezing episode. Overheating may also trigger an attack; teachers should monitor the temperature in the classroom as well as the type of clothing the student is wearing (Swanson & Thompson, 1994), particularly after coming in from the cold.

c. Certain field trips (e.g., a trip to a farm or zoo) may not be suitable for a student with a specific allergy (e.g., to animals). In some cases, however, if the family is informed beforehand, the student will be able to take medication before the trip, thereby lessening the effects. In some cases, it may be appropriate for the teacher to substitute an alternative activity for the class. For some students, having various animals come into the school (perhaps into the gym) for a short period may not provoke an attack, particularly if the student observes from a distance and does not touch the animals. There are many films and video tapes that describe the lives of various animals in their natural habitats that can be shown to the class as an alternative activity.

d. Certain fumes in the school may cause a reaction (e.g., chemicals in the laboratory or photography darkroom, paints in the classroom or art studio, solder in shop courses), particularly if the room is not well ventilated. The student may benefit from wearing an air filter mask, available in most hardware stores. In some cases, medication can lessen the effects; however, in extreme cases, alternatives must be planned. All paint cans should be closed when not in use.

e. Some students with asthma have allergies to certain foods and food additives. This may cause a problem if food is brought to the school (e.g., for school parties) or the student goes on outings where food is consumed (e.g., field trip to a dairy). When food is brought in to the school, it is best that the parents of the student with asthma substitute food that has been prepared at home, thereby eliminating any possibility that the student will inadvertently consume something that may cause a reaction. Even though reports of fatal or near-fatal reactions to foods in children are rare, occasionally individuals unknowingly ingest foods that can result in life-threatening situations. Self-injectable epinephrine (EpiPen) or injectable epinephrine (Ana-

Kit and Ana-Guard) should be made available, and all immediate caretakers (e.g., teachers, health aides, bus drivers) must be trained to administer these medications[4] and know how to respond during emergency situations (Sampson, Mendelson, & Rosen, 1992).

f. Counselors at the school should assist the teenager with asthma to explore appropriate career choices. While most types of work would be suitable for persons with asthma, occupations involving extremes of weather or exposure to dust, fumes, or animals generally should be avoided (Canny & Levison, 1991).

5 *Students with asthma should be encouraged to participate in a program of physical exercise according to their capacity.* Some are even capable of engaging in competitive sports with proper medication and education.[5] Orenstein (1988), in an article that addressed exercise tolerance in those with chronic lung disease, is quite emphatic about the need for exercise:

> Many children with asthma have chosen, or have had their parents or teachers choose for them, to omit physical education classes and other opportunities for exercise and are consequently considerably less fit than their peers. Behavior can be altered without limiting physical activity. Swimming or bicycling can be chosen as one's sport, rather than running. Among running events, long slow distance running or short sprints can be chosen in preference to 1-mile and 2-mile races. . . . The benefits of exercise are so important for children and adults, and prevention of EIA [exercise-induced asthma] is so easy for the majority of patients, that physicians should encourage their patients with asthma to be active and should not allow themselves to be enlisted in a conspiracy to avoid physical education classes or other activity. (p. 1046)

Several steps can be taken to lessen the chances for an asthma episode occurring during physical exercise (Table 6.9). For further information on safe participation in physical activities, the reader is referred to the sources cited in the table.

The American Academy of Pediatrics, Committee on Sports Medicine and Fitness (1994) has recently developed a set of recommendations regarding the use of metered-dose inhalers (MDIs) for athletes with exercise-induced asthma who require Beta$_2$-agonists or cromolyn sodium, particularly in light of some of the "restrictive medication and drug policies of school districts, or by individual coaches and teachers."

6 *If a student is unable to participate in a particular activity, staff should attempt to provide suitable alternatives.* Students should never be penalized for not being able to participate in routine activities. For a student who has to miss out on a field trip, it is not appropriate, in most cases, to give an additional assignment that the rest of the students are not required to complete (e.g., a written assignment). Similarly, if a student is unable to play a particular sport, participation in some way (e.g., be the score keeper or time keeper) should be encouraged, rather than being sent to the library to read a book. However, if a student is unable to paint in art class, due to the fumes from the paint, it may be appropriate for the student to sketch with colored pens or pencils. Some felt-tip markers can emit fumes that are irritating to those with asthma. Encourage students to replace the tops on pens and paint pots when not in use.

7 *Schools should attempt to be as "allergy-free" as possible.* Teachers may find this difficult "since the very teaching strategies they employ may include objects and activities that serve as triggers" (Swanson & Thompson, 1994, p. 182). There are a variety of routine procedures that can decrease the number of potential triggers:

a. For students with allergies to animals, certain pets should not be housed in the classroom (especially those with hair, fur, or feathers). However, some animals without dander may not cause any reaction (e.g., snakes, amphibians, insects, fish) and can be substituted. Unfortunately, stuffed animals (and other soft, fluffy toys) can be problematic because they collect dust. However, if they are washed every month, wrapped in a plastic bag, and placed in the freezer overnight, the dust mites will be eliminated or at least lessened (Canny & Levison, 1991).

b. Dust and molds often cause reactions in individuals with asthma. Some areas of the school are particularly problematic (e.g., kitchens, gyms,

---

[4] For further information on the use of these medications, see chapter 22.

[5] Guidelines, published by the American Academy of Pediatrics, regarding participation in athletics are found in Appendix J.

TABLE 6.9
Physical Activity Guidelines for Students with Asthma

1. Medications, if prescribed by the physician, should be taken before the activity occurs (usually 10 to 15 minutes before exercise program).

2. Exercise environment should be warm, mildly to moderately humid, and free of allergens; if the environment is cold and dry, a face mask, scarf, or hand should be use to cover the mouth and nose.

3. If the activity is being held outdoors, pollution or smog may be problematic; a mask may lessen the intake of pollen in the spring and fall; in the summer, high humidity may provoke an attack.

4. Students should be encouraged to breathe through the nose rather than the mouth, so that the air is warmed, filtered, and humidified; if the nose is blocked, an over-the-counter antihistamine might be used before class to open up the passages and ease nasal breathing, if recommended.

5. Warm-up exercises, including breathing exercises, lasting approximately 10 minutes, should be completed before beginning a vigorous workout.

6. Students should measure their peak expiratory flow rate (PEFR) before the class begins, if recommended; in general, if the measurement falls 15% below normal values, they should not exceed an intensity level of 50% to 60% of their maximum heart rate; however, it is important that the student's physician be consulted to ensure that this guideline is acceptable.

7. Teachers and coaches should choose activities that are well tolerated; in general, those that require only short bursts of energy (e.g., Alpine skiing, gymnastics, baseball, tennis) are better than those that involve greater endurance (e.g., long distance running, soccer, basketball); activities that are most likely to result in an episode (in decreasing order) include running, cycling, walking, and swimming.

8. Anaerobic activities (e.g., short games, racket sports, softball) often do not induce asthma symptoms; circuit training and interval training are usually well tolerated, as the student has an opportunity to rest between stations or exercise bouts.

9. Teachers and coaches should carefully examine the "positions" within specific sports to determine the level of activity; those that require less movement (e.g., goalie in hockey; pitcher, catcher, and first baseman positions in softball or baseball) may be appropriate.

10. Activities that encourage thoracic mobility (e.g., ball throwing, archery, karate, swimming) should be included in the exercise program.

11. Programs should gradually be increased as the students' level of fitness improves; at first there should be two to three short aerobic routines, with a 5-minute rest between each workout; the PEFR should be measured between bouts of activity; if it drops more than 15%, the activity should be terminated and a cool down of stretching exercises be undertaken.

12. Students with asthma should not be pushed beyond their limits, but at the same time should not be made to feel inferior because of the limits; students with asthma should not participate in physical activity if they have a cold or virus, or if they are showing the typical symptoms of an asthma episode.

13. Activity period should end with a cool down period of light exercise (e.g., walking, calisthenics, yoga), lasting approximately 10 minutes.

14. Additional medication should be available nearby; either the student should carry an inhaler (or have an inhaler in the locker or gym bag) or the teacher or coach should make sure that one is available (particularly if the student forgets to bring it to class).

15. Students should take fluids regularly while exercising.

Sources: Goldberg, 1990; Klein & Timerman, 1994; Richards, 1992; Rimmer, 1989; Walsh & Ryan-Wenger, 1992.

lockers, auditoriums, libraries, music rooms). Regular cleaning is important. Frequent dusting or damp-mopping of floors, furniture, and book shelves keeps the level of dust down. Forced-air heating ducts should be covered with a dust guard. Shower stalls should be washed with Lysol or bleach at least every one to three months. Shower curtains should be washed on a regular basis. All cleaning supplies should be stored away from classrooms, in sealed containers, labeled with a danger symbol sticker.

The school building should be cleaned after the students have gone home so that they (1) do not inhale the fumes of the cleaning solvents, and (2) are not exposed to dust that becomes airborne as a result of the cleaning process. If at all possible, natural cleaning agents should be used rather than toxic, chemical agents.

c. Smoking should not be permitted within the school. In many schools with a "no smoking" policy, staff and students congregate around the doors during their breaks to have a cigarette; however, it is through these same doors that students (and staff or visitors) with asthma must enter or leave the building. No-smoking policies should indicate explicitly where smoking is and is not permitted. Smoking should not be allowed in any cars or buses that are used to transport students. All teenagers, but particularly those with asthma, should be counseled not to smoke tobacco or marijuana (which may be contaminated with mold, fungi, or other material that can trigger an allergic reaction) (Klein & Timerman, 1994).

d. For some, chalk dust is problematic. The newer "write-on" boards that use nonpermanent felt-tip pens can be substituted for the older "chalk" boards. However, as mentioned previously, some felt-tip pens can precipitate an asthmatic reaction and may not be suitable for the student with asthma to use, even though the rest of the students should be using them instead of chalk to keep the dust level in the classroom as low as possible. Students who experience an allergy to chalk should be seated away from the board and should not be asked to clean the chalk erasers. Ideally the boards should be cleaned while the student with the allergy is not in the classroom. Similarly, pencil sharpener dust can be irritating to some. The sharpener should be cleaned out daily, after the student goes home.

e. Carpeting, drapes, and venetian blinds in schools may cause a problem for some, due to the dust mites that collect in or on them. Stuffed furniture (e.g., easy chairs and couches) also may cause a reaction. Carpets, drapes, and furniture should be vacuumed regularly; however, some vacuum cleaners (i.e., particularly those with poor filters) may worsen the problem by dispersing dust particles in the air. If possible, a classroom without carpeting and drapes should be chosen. If the school is carpeted, ideally the carpets should be steam-cleaned once or twice a year. Rug shampoos do not remove deeply imbedded dust particles (Gold & Zimmerman, 1986). Several commercial products, such as

benzyl benzoate powder or tannic acid, can be used to treat carpets (Swanson & Thompson, 1994). Carpets should be vacuumed weekly.

Young children should not have naps on the floor or on stuffed furniture; a cot or mat may lessen the problem. All bedding should be washed at least once every 10 days (Swanson & Thompson, 1994).

f. In classrooms that are very dry, a humidifier or vaporizer may help to add moisture to the air. However, such devices are "breeding grounds" for molds and fungi and should be cleaned frequently. Ideally, the level of humidity should be less than 50%, because high humidity levels can result in an increase in dust mites.

g. In classrooms that are very humid, a dehumidifier or air conditioner may remove some of the moisture. As in the case of humidifiers and vaporizers, these devices must be cleaned out regularly so that molds and fungi do not grow. Air conditioner vents should be vacuumed regularly and the filter changed routinely.

h. Indoor air cleaners and purifiers fitted with a HEPA (high-efficiency particulate air) filter may reduce exposure to inhalant particles or gases; however, little research has been conducted to evaluate their effectiveness in preventing asthma episodes (Vedal, 1992). They may have some use in certain rooms in the school where polluted air is particularly problematic (e.g., laboratories). Air cleaners and purifiers should be cleaned regularly and the filter changed routinely.

i. Staff should try to avoid wearing (or limit their wearing of) strong perfume; scented soaps, lotions, or talcum powder; hair sprays; or colognes or after-shave lotion.

j. Many students will benefit from being allowed to travel to school by school bus to avoid being exposed to irritants (e.g., pollen) that may trigger an attack. However, school buses are often very dusty and need to be cleaned regularly. In rural schools, it is common, especially in winter, for the school buses to "line up" outside the school with the engines running; while this practice cannot be avoided, the students should remain inside until the bus is about to leave so that they do not breathe in the exhaust fumes.

k. Some schools routinely treat the school grounds with a fertilizer and weed killer in the spring and the fall. If possible, this should be done late on Friday afternoons so that there is sufficient time for the chemicals to dissipate before Monday morning (Rapp, 1990). Parents should be notified when the treatment will occur, particularly if the school grounds are used routinely by the children and teenagers on the weekends.

8 *Students with asthma must deal with the stress of having a chronic illness.* A recent study by Walsh and Ryan-Wenger (1992), involving 84 children with asthma, attempted to examine any other stressors that the children might be encountering. The stressors listed by the participants were ranked in terms of severity (i.e., how bad it would make the child feel) and on frequency (i.e., how often it happened). The top ten stressors were as follows: Being pressured to try something new, like a cigarette, that you really don't want to try; having parents separate; feeling left out of the group; feeling sick; having parents argue in front of you; not spending enough time with Mom or Dad; not getting along with your teacher; not having enough money to spend; moving from one place to another; and not being good enough at sports. In terms of rank order of frequency, the top five stressors were: Feeling sick; not having enough money to spend; having nothing to do; having parents argue in front of you; and not being good enough at sports. Other common stressors involving school included: Feeling left out of the group (6th); not having homework done on time (10th); not getting along with the teacher (12th); feeling pressured to get good grades (13th); being late for school (17th); and changing schools (18th).

In order to deal with stress, teachers can assist students with asthma to develop coping strategies. In a second study, this time involving 78 children with asthma, Ryan-Wenger and Walsh (1994) identified a variety of methods that have been found to be most effective. The methods used by at least 50% of the sample included, in rank order: Trying to relax and staying calm (77%); watching TV or listening to music (70%); praying (69%); saying I'm sorry or telling the truth (68%); doing something about it (68%); talking to someone (58%); walking, running, or riding a bike (57%); drawing, writing, or reading something (57%); and sleeping or taking a nap (56%).

9 *Staff working with students who have asthma must recognize some of the more serious psychological issues they may face.* Falvo (1991), in discussing the functional implications of respiratory conditions in general, described the difficulties that persons who have breathing problems must deal with:

> Prolonged breathing difficulty often causes feelings of helplessness and despair. For those individuals who have been active and self-sufficient, the inability to engage in even simple activities without breathing difficulty can be devastating. Depression is common. Individuals may focus on the activities in which they can no longer participate, at least not as vigorously, rather than attempt to attain their highest level of functional capacity. (p. 60)

Falvo also commented on the response of family members to those who are encountering breathing difficulties. She suggested that it is not common for family members to "unintentionally place an individual with a respiratory condition in an invalid role, reducing their expectations of the family structure or removing responsibility from the individual, even though he or she may be capable of engaging in a number of activities" (p. 61). Teachers not only should be aware of this possibility occurring in the family, but must ensure that they themselves do not do likewise, for "the individual may respond to these reactions by using the breathing difficulty to escape from life's demands, to receive emotional rewards, or to manipulate or control the behavior of others" (p. 61).

Falvo also stresses the importance of parents (and teachers) not reacting in the opposite manner, i.e., underestimating the seriousness of the condition, for such a reaction "may push the individual to go beyond his or her functional capacity or to ignore the physician's specific recommendations for control of the condition" (p. 61).

❧ Summary

In this chapter, the various causes of asthma and its treatment have been explored. The suggestions given should assist teachers to understand this condition. One of the goals of successful treatment is to ensure that the condition does not affect the student's performance from day to day. It is the responsibility of the school system to ensure the converse—

school must not adversely affect the health of the student (Klein & Timerman, 1994). In the following chapter, two less commonly occurring respiratory conditions, bronchopulmonary dysplasia and tuberculosis, are discussed in detail. Guidelines for the safe use of oxygen in schools are also covered.

References

American Academy of Pediatrics, Committee on Sports Medicine and Fitness (1994). Metered-dose inhalers for young athletes with exercise-induced asthma, *Pediatrics, 94,* 129–130.

Bloomberg, G. R., & Strunk, R. C. (1992). Crisis in asthma care. *Pediatric Clinics of North America, 39,* 1225–1241.

Canny, G. J., & Levison, H. (1991). *Childhood asthma: A handbook for parents.* Toronto, ONT: Thompson Canada.

Celano, M. P., & Geller, R. J. (1993). Learning, school performance, and children with asthma: How much at risk? *Journal of Learning Disabilities, 26,* 23–32.

Chan-Yeung, M. (1992). Increasing asthma morbidity and mortality. *British Columbia Medical Journal, 35,* 651–653.

Duff, A. L., & Platts-Mills, T. A. E. (1992). Allergens and asthma. *Pediatric Clinics of North America, 39,* 1277–1291.

Ellis, E. F. (1988). Asthma: Current therapeutic approach. *Pediatric Clinics of North America, 35,* 1041–1052.

Falvo, D. R. (1991). *Medical and psychosocial aspects of chronic illness and disability.* Gaithersburg, MD: Aspen.

Freudenberg, N., Feldman, C. H., Clark, N. M., Millman, E. J., Valle, I., & Wasilewski, Y. (1980). The impact of bronchial asthma on school attendance and performance. *Journal of School Health, 50,* 522–526.

Gold, M., & Zimmerman, B. (1986). *Allergies and children: A handbook for parents from the Hospital for Sick Children.* Toronto, ONT: Kids Can Press.

Goldberg, B. (1990). Children, sports, and chronic disease. *The Physician and Sportsmedicine, 16*(1) 45–50, 53–56.

Hagerdorn, M. (1990). Oxygenation: Implications of abnormalities in structure and function. In S. R. Mott, S. R. James, & A. M. Sperhac, *Nursing care of children and families* (pp. 955–1047). Redwood City, CA: Addison-Wesley.

Haggerty, M. C. (1990). Asthma. In D. L. Sexton (Ed.), *Nursing care of the respiratory patient* (pp. 137–168). Norwalk, CT: Appleton & Lange.

Hen, J. (1986). Office evaluation and management of pediatric asthma. *Pediatric Annals, 15,* 111–123.

Hill, M., Szefler, S. J., & Larsen, G. L. (1992). Asthma pathogenesis and the implications for therapy in children. *Pediatric Clinics of North America, 39,* 1205–1224.

Howell, J. H., Flaim, T., & Lung, C. L. (1992). Patient education. *Pediatric Clinics of North America, 39,* 1343–1361.

Isbell, R. A., & Barber, W. H. (1993). Respiratory disorders: An update and status report for educators. *B. C. Journal of Special Education, 17,* 244–255.

Klein, G. L., & Timerman, V. (1994). *Keys to parenting the asthmatic child.* Hauppauge, NY: Barron's.

Kleinberg, S. B. (1982). *Educating the chronically ill child.* Rockvillle, MD: Aspen.

Ladebauche, P. (1997). Managing asthma: A growth and development approach. *Pediatric Nursing, 23,* 37–44.

Levison, H. (1991). Canadian consensus on the treatment of asthma in children. *Canadian Medical Association Journal, 145,* 1449–1455.

Lindgren, S., Lokshin, B., Stromquist, A., Weinberger, M., Nassif, E., McCubbin, M., & Frasher, R. (1992). Does asthma or treatment with theophylline limit children's academic performance? *New England Journal of Medicine, 32,* 926–930.

Lurye, D. R. (1993). Catch your breath: Asthma's on the rise! *PTA Today, 18*(3), 16–17.

Majer, L. S., & Joy, J. H. (1993). A principal's guide to asthma. *Principal, 73*(2), 42–44.

McLoughlin, J. A., & Nall, M. (1994). Allergies and learning/behavioral disorders. *Intervention in School and Clinic, 29,* 198–207.

Morgan, Q. J., & Martinez, F. D. (1992). Risk factors for developing wheezing and asthma in childhood. *Pediatric Clinics of North America, 39,* 1185–1203.

National Institutes of Health (NIH)—National Asthma Education Program (1994). *Executive summary: Guidelines for the diagnosis and management of asthma.* Bethesda, MD: National Heart, Lung, and Blood Institute, U.S. Department of Health and Human Services. Publication No. 94-3042A.

Nordstrom, D. L., Rowe, M. G., Falk, M. C., & Remington, P. L. (1993). Functional status of children with asthma [letter to the editor]. *Journal of the American Medical Association, 269,* 1941.

O'Connell, E. J., & Heilman, D. K. (1996). Asthma. In F. D. Burg, W. R. Wald, J. R. Inglefinger, & R. A. Polin (Eds.), *Gellis & Kagan's current pediatric therapy* (15th ed., pp. 708–713). Philadelphia: W. B. Saunders.

Orenstein, D. M. (1988). Exercise tolerance and exercise conditioning in children with chronic lung disease. *Journal of Pediatrics, 112,* 1043–1047.

Ownby, D. R. (1990). Environmental factors versus genetic determinants of childhood inhalant allergies. *Journal of Allergy and Clinical Immunology, 86,* 279–287.

Paasche, C. L., Gorrill, L., & Strom, B. (1990). *Children with special needs in early childhood settings.* Menlo Park, CA: Addison-Wesley.

Paterson, J. (1991, May 23). Don't treat just wheeze of asthma: Treat underlying problem—expert. *Victoria Times Colonist*, p. C1.

Pope, A. M. (1993). Indoor allergens—assessing and controlling adverse health effects. *Journal of the American Medical Association, 269,* 2721.

Rachelefsky, G., Fitzgerald, S., Page, D., & Santamaria, B. (1993). An update on the diagnosis and management of pediatric asthma. *Nurse Practitioner, 18*(2), 51–62.

Rapp, D. J. (1990). Allergies: The hidden hazard. *The Principal, 70* (2), 27–28.

Richards, W. (1992). Asthma, allergies, and school. *Pediatric Annals, 21,* 575–585.

Rimmer, J. H. (1989). A vigorous physical education program for children with exercise-induced asthma. *Journal of Physical Education, Recreation and Dance, 60*(6), 90–95.

Ryan-Wenger, N. M., & Walsh, M. (1994). Children's perspectives on coping with asthma. *Pediatric Nursing, 20,* 224–228.

Sampson, H. A., Mendelson, L., & Rosen, J. P. (1992). Fatal and near-fatal anaphylactic reactions to food in children and adolescents. *New England Journal of Medicine, 327,* 380–384.

Schwartz, R. H. (1984). Children with chronic asthma: Care by the generalist and the specialist. *Pediatric Clinics of North America, 31,* 87–105.

Silkworth, C. S., & Jones, D. (1986). Helping the student with asthma. In G. Larson (Ed.), *Managing the school age child with a chronic health condition: A practical guide for schools, families and organizations* (pp. 75–93). Wayzata, MN: DCI Publishing.

Sullivan, T. J. (1992). Is asthma curable? *Pediatric Clinics of North America, 39,* 1363–1382.

Swanson, M. N., & Thompson, P. E. (1994). Managing asthma triggers in school. *Pediatric Nursing, 20,* 181–184.

Vedal, S. (1992). Asthma and air pollution. *B.C. Medical Journal, 35,* 654–656.

Walsh, M., & Ryan-Wenger, N. M. (1992). Sources of stress in children with asthma. *Journal of School Health, 62,* 459–463.

Webster's new complete medical dictionary (1996). New York: Smithmark.

Weitzman, M., Gortmaker, S. L., Sobol, A. M., & Perrin, J. M. (1992). Recent trends in the prevalence and severity of childhood asthma. *Journal of the American Medical Association, 268,* 2673–2677.

Whaley, L. F., & Wong, D. L. (1995). *Nursing care of infants and children* (5th ed.). St. Louis: Mosby.

Wilmott, R., Kolski, G., & Burg, I. (1984). Asthma. In J. Fithian (Ed.), *Understanding the child with a chronic illness in the classroom* (pp. 14–27). Phoenix: Oryx Press.

Young, S., Le Souëf, P. N., Geelhoed, G. C., Stick, S. M., Turner, K. J., & Landau, L. I. (1991). The influence of a family history of asthma and parental smoking on airway responsiveness in early infancy. *New England Journal of Medicine, 324,* 1168–1173.

Zamula, E. (1990) Childhood asthma: More than snuffles. *FDA Consumer, 24*(6), 10–13.

CHAPTER 7

Other Respiratory Conditions

Hypoxemia

Mechanical ventilators (respirators)

Negative and positive pressure machines

Oxygen therapy: intermittent and continuous

Prematurity/preterm

Tracheostomy

Very low birth weight (VLBW)

A number of other chronic respiratory conditions affect children and young adults much less often than asthma. In this chapter, bronchopulmonary dysplasia, a condition found in infants born too small or born too soon, is described, and tuberculosis, a treatable infectious disease, usually considered an acute rather than a chronic disease, is discussed. In most cases, the teaching suggestions given in chapter 6 for children with asthma are appropriate for those with less common problems, as the effects of the conditions (e.g., shortness of breath, coughing, wheezing) are similar, regardless of the underlying cause of the disease. This chapter also includes a discussion of the use of oxygen as therapy, the types of mechanical ventilators (respirators) available, and the needs of students who have a tracheostomy, a surgical opening into the windpipe.

🌱 Bronchopulmonary Dysplasia

Bronchopulmonary dysplasia (BPD),[1] also know as **chronic respirator lung disease,** is a pathologic condition that develops in the lungs of infants, particularly those who have a very low birth weight (VLBW) (i.e., less than 52.5 ounces, or 1,500 grams) or those who are premature (i.e., born before 37 weeks' gestation, regardless of birth weight). It has been estimated that as many as 69% of babies who weigh less than 35 ounces (1,000 grams) and 15% of those who are preterm develop the condition (Gerdes, Abbasi, & Bhutani, 1996). The incidence of BPD is believed to be between 7,000 and 10,000 cases per year, making it the leading cause of chronic lung disease in infants in the United States (Harvey, 1996).

BPD is described as an **iatrogenic chronic lung disease** of infants. An iatrogenic condition, as mentioned previously, is secondary to some type of treatment, in this case the medical intervention at birth in response to the breathing problems experienced by those with immature lungs. The administration of high concentrations of oxygen by means of ventilators that "force" oxygen into the lungs results in cellular changes in the lung tissue, such as thickening of the alveolar ducts and bronchial walls. This damage leads to a reduction in the diameter of the airway

and results in the infant having to work considerably harder than normal to obtain sufficient oxygen (Bernbaum & Batshaw, 1997). Many of the infants that survive require frequent hospitalization as a result of their borderline respiratory reserve, hyperactive airway, and increased susceptibility to respiratory infections (Whaley & Wong, 1995).

BPD is often classified as mild, moderate, or severe. Those that have a mild to moderate condition may require bronchodilator treatment, similar to those who have asthma, and **diuretic** medication, commonly known as "water pills," which increases the excretion of fluid and decreases the accumulation of fluid in the lungs (i.e., **pulmonary edema**). A child with severe BPD may need a tracheostomy and mechanical ventilatory support for prolonged periods of time (Harvey, 1996). In infants who have severe BPD, other disabilities, such as mental retardation, learning disabilities, epilepsy, deafness, blindness, and cerebral palsy, are common. As a result, infants with BPD often need early intervention programs that stress the development of physical and developmental skills (Bernbaum & Batshaw, 1997). Additional disabilities are most likely to be a result of a very low birth weight or prematurity rather than of the pulmonary dysplasia. Approximately 18% of all infants with BPD exhibit a severe form of the disease (Gerdes et al., 1996).

🌱 Educational Implications and Teaching Tips: Students with Bronchopulmonary Dysplasia

Even though the mortality rates for VLBW and preterm children are very high, many children are surviving their early childhood years and entering the general education system. However, even though the effects of BPD on the respiratory system tend to decrease over time, an estimated 70% of adolescents show continued airway obstruction and 52% show some signs of airway hyperreactivity (Harvey, 1996). Some children continue to have serious chronic respiratory difficulties for the rest of their lives, requiring oxygen therapy on a regular basis.

1   *Many children with BPD have a limited tolerance for physical exercise and may need special considerations in school.* Examples are a waiver of physical education or provision of an adaptive physical education program. All children should be en-

---

[1] The term **dysplasia** is used commonly in the medical profession to refer to any abnormal growth or development of cells or organs (*Webster's*, 1996).

couraged to participate in as many physical activities as possible; however, they should never be pushed beyond their limit. Alternative activities that do not require as great an expenditure of energy should be provided.

2 *Children with BPD are prone to respiratory tract infections.* Parents should be informed of any outbreaks of communicable diseases, including respiratory infections, so that preventative measures can be taken, if appropriate. In some cases, students should be kept home to avoid excess exposure. Provisions must be made to ensure that the students do not fall behind in their schoolwork.

In addition, children with BPD often have gastroesophageal reflux disease (GERD), a condition in which the contents of the stomach leak into the esophagus. Reflux can result in an inflammation of the esophagus (esophagitis), which can be quite painful. Nausea and bouts of vomiting are not uncommon. Some students miss school as a result.

3 *Children with BPD typically breathe faster than normal children, thereby expending more effort.* Consequently they require additional supplemental nutrients and high-calorie food. If the child is eating at a school cafeteria, it would be appropriate for the school dietitian to discuss the student's dietary needs with the parents to ensure proper foods are available. Some students bring high-calorie drinks (e.g., Boost, Ensure) to school for consumption during recess or lunch.

If the child is on a diuretic medication, supplemental potassium may be needed to counteract the loss of this mineral in the urine (Jaudes, 1991). As a result of the increased production of urine, the student should be allowed to use the toilet whenever necessary.

4 *Children who required long-term mechanical ventilation during their first years may show signs of language delay and, consequently, may benefit from speech and language therapy.* For children who continue to receive ventilator support, alternative forms of communication may need to be explored if speech is not possible.

Partially as the result of the effects of poor nutritional status, children with BPD often show signs of growth delay. Reduced height and weight are typically evident into the middle childhood and adoles-

cent years (Harvey, 1996). Body image and acceptance by peers may become issues of importance for some of these children when they enter school. Teachers should be alert to signs of teasing and provide counseling.

5 *The child with BPD often needs ongoing therapy (e.g., chest physiotherapy and medication therapy) on a very regular basis.* This also applies to children who have cystic fibrosis.[2] Medical orders must be obtained to ensure that the services are provided and staff are trained (see Appendix D).

6 *Most children with BPD become adults with asthma and, as a result, will need to take their health into consideration when determining their vocational future* (Harvey, 1996). Career options for those with asthma were mentioned in chapter 6.

 ## Tuberculosis

Tuberculosis (TB) is a long-term communicable disease caused by the tubercle bacillus *Mycobacterium tuberculosis.*[3] The primary site of infection is the lungs; however, other parts of the body, such as the kidneys, liver, lymph nodes, bones, and brain, may be involved. Children under the age of 3 are most vulnerable to this particular infection, as are older children (particularly girls) during the years immediately before, during, or after puberty (Feroli, 1994). Most often transmission of the disease is by means of inhalation of the aerosolized sputum from a person with active disease, referred to as the **contact.** The sputum is usually discharged when the individual coughs, sneezes, or laughs.

The normal incubation period for TB is 2 to 10 weeks. Most individuals are asymptomatic during this time and are unaware that they have the disease until a positive diagnosis is made. A significant majority of infected children or young adults do not develop an active case of the disease; however, they will remain at risk of reactivation throughout their lifetimes (Jackson, 1993).

Symptoms of TB include fatigue or malaise, weight loss, anorexia (loss of appetite), night sweats,

---

[2] For further information on CF and its treatment, see chapter 20.

[3] For further discussion of bacterial infections, see chapter 23.

cough, wheeziness, tightness in the chest, and a low-grade fever. Diagnosis is confirmed by means of chest x-ray, tubercular skin test, and a sputum smear analysis. Treatment involves the administration of antituberculosis drugs (e.g., isoniazid and rifampin), which are administered for at least 12 months in children under the age of 2, and 9 months for older children. In some cases anti–TB drugs are given in combination with other medications, such as antibiotics or corticosteroids.

❦ Educational Implications and Teaching Tips: Students with Tuberculosis

For the classroom teacher, several points need to be understood regarding the student with tuberculosis:

1 *Tuberculosis is on the increase* (American Academy of Pediatrics [AAP], 1994; Jacobs & Starke, 1993; Natale, 1992). In 1990 there were 25,701 active cases (children and adults combined) in the United States. This figure represents a 9.4% increase over the previous year and the largest annual increase since 1953, when national figures were first kept. In 1992, the number of cases rose to 26,273, a further increase of 2.2%.

The increase is not exclusive to adults. In the period between 1985 and 1992, there was a 54.5% increase of cases in the 25 to 44 age group, a 36.1% increase in children up to age 4, and a 34.1% increase in children between the ages of 5 and 14. In 1991, in the United States, more than 2,000 children under age 19 developed clinically active TB (Ott, Horn, & McLaughlin, 1995).

Recently, concern has been raised about the possibility of public schools, family day care homes, and nursery schools being sites for transmission of the disease, even though the disease does not spread as easily among young children as it does among older children and adults. Such outbreaks usually result from an adult or older adolescent caregiver with primary TB being the contact (Jacobs & Starke, 1993). In an extreme case, one school in Missouri reported that more than half of the 343 children in the school were infected with TB, with 32 children having full-blown, active disease. In addition, 14 staff members tested positive for the disease, and one staff member had an especially contagious form of the disease. It was this staff member's health that had spurred the original testing of the children and staff (Natale, 1992).

There are several variables that put schools at risk for outbreaks of tuberculosis (Table 7.1). The primary ones, most likely operating in combination with each other, are the school's location and the makeup of its student and staff populations (Natale, 1992).

In terms of location, the greatest overall increase in cases of TB has been reported to be in major urban areas. In some American cities, the rates rival those found in developing countries (Ott et al., 1995). One of the reasons for increased incidence in large cities may be immigration of persons from areas where TB incidence is very high, such as Asia, Africa, the Middle East, Latin America, and the Caribbean (Whaley & Wong, 1995). Schools that have increased numbers of foreign-born children or children whose parents come from countries with a high incidence of TB may be at risk for outbreaks; similarly, schools that employ people from these countries may also be at risk (Natale, 1992).

An additional reason for increased incidence in large urban areas is poverty. Children who live in crowded conditions with poor sanitation, are inadequately nourished, maintain poor hygiene practices, and do not have access to adequate medical services (which include proper immunization) are at risk for many diseases, including TB. One of the groups with the highest incidence rates for TB are homeless persons (Castiglia, 1992).

The final two populations particularly at risk for developing TB are Native Americans and persons with AIDS. In a study conducted in Canada, it was found that the rate of TB was 43 times higher among natives than among non-natives born in the country. The infection rate for native Canadians in 1992 was found to be 81.3 per 100,000 persons compared with a rate of 1.9 per 100,000 for non-native Canadians (Canadian Press, 1994). In the population of persons with AIDS, it has been predicted that as the number of HIV-infected people increases, so will the number of TB cases (Natale, 1992).

2 *While most people fear TB, isolation is rarely necessary in children with the disease.* Many children are treated on an outpatient basis and return immediately to school (Jackson & Saunders,

TABLE 7.1

Infants, Children, and Adolescents at High Risk for Tuberculous Infection

- Contact of adults with infectious tuberculosis
- Those who are from or have parents who are from regions of the world with a high prevalence of tuberculosis
- Those with abnormalities on chest roentgenogram [x-ray] suggestive of tuberculosis
- Those with clinical evidence of tuberculosis
- HIV-seropositive children [i.e., blood tests indicate presence of the human immunodeficiency virus, the virus that is the causative agent of AIDS]
- Those with other medical risk factors: Hodgkin's disease, lymphoma, diabetes mellitus, chronic renal failure, malnutrition
- Incarcerated adolescents
- Children frequently exposed to the following adults: HIV-infected individuals, homeless persons, users of intravenous and other street drugs, poor and medically indigent city dwellers, residents of nursing homes, migrant farm workers

Source: American Academy of Pediatrics, Committee on Infectious Diseases. (1994). Screening for tuberculosis in infants and children. *Pediatrics, 93,* 131–134. Used with permission of the American Academy of Pediatrics.

1993). However, for those whose condition is determined to be communicable (particularly the older child), the student is typically isolated until there is no danger of contagion, usually 2 to 4 weeks after treatment has started. Once students are determined to not be contagious, they may return to school even when continuing to take medications.

3 *Fatigue is a major concern for students with TB, who often require brief rest periods during the day.* They must also be protected from other infections (e.g., influenza, colds). While a child with TB may participate to a limited degree in some sports, competitive sports are discouraged because they may exceed the student's limits (Feroli, 1994). Children with TB need a nutritionally balanced diet, particularly rich in foods supplying protein and calcium. School meal programs are very beneficial to those children who are not receiving adequate nutrition in the home.

4 *Many older students with TB are aware of the stigma associated with the disease and may respond by withdrawing from their friends and the normal activities of their peer group, perhaps out of fear of infecting their friends* (Feroli, 1994). Since TB develops from contact with infected persons, if the contact is a peer, the relationship may be strained. In most cases, the source of infection is a member of the household; however, the contact can be a

baby-sitter, a frequent visitor to the house, or a school employee. Support groups may be of assistance in counseling students to understand the disease and provide an opportunity for them to vent their feelings of anger towards the disease and the limitations it places on their lives.

5 *The "best defense" for schools is knowledge about the disease and how to guard against it* (Natale, 1992). In the past, when TB was considered a major threat, students and staff were required to have TB tests before entering the school. More recently, when it appeared that TB was on the wane, these requirements may have been slackened. The Academy of Pediatrics (1994, pp. 133–134) has recently made a series of recommendations regarding routine testing for children, including:

a. Routine annual skin testing for tuberculosis (Mantoux TB test) in children with no risk factors residing in low-prevalence communities is not indicated. In such settings, positive skin test reactions are most likely to be false-positive reactions.

b. Children at high risk [Table 7.1] should be tested annually using Mantoux tuberculin tests. All results (positive or negative) should be read routinely by qualified medical personnel.

c. Children who have no risk factors but who reside in high-prevalence regions and children whose history for risk factors is incomplete or unreliable may receive periodic Mantoux skin tests, such as at the ages of 1, 4 to 6, and 11 to 16 years. Such a decision should be based on local epidemiology of tuberculosis.

In addition to testing school-age children, administrators should implement a program of testing of new school employees in conjunction with the local public health authority. In areas of high risk, regular testing of both new and returning employees should be implemented.

Oxygen Therapy

Some students with chronic respiratory problems may require the administration of oxygen (O_2) to prevent **hypoxemia** (a deficiency of oxygen in ar-terial blood) that leads to hypoxia (lack of oxygen in the tissues of the body). For some individuals, hypoxemia can occur at rest; for others, it may occur at specific times (e.g., while eating). Other reasons for the administration of oxygen include poor growth rate, poor exercise tolerance, and chronic lethargy (Gerdes, Abbasi, & Bhutani, 1996).

Some individuals require oxygen to be given **intermittently**; others may need oxygen on a **continuous basis.** Those that require intermittent oxygen include children and young adults with congenital heart defects and those with chronic obstructive pulmonary disease, such as emphysema, a condition of overinflation that results in destructive changes to the alveolar walls. Persons who require continuous

TABLE 7.2
Safe Use of Oxygen in Schools

Safety Guidelines	Rationale
Use only the flowmeter setting prescribed by the doctor.	Oxygen is a prescribed drug. The physician will know the correct dose (percentage and flow rate) to be administered based on the student's condition. Too high an oxygen flow may irritate the nose and mouth; too low may result in respiratory distress.
Secure oxygen tank, cylinder, or thermal storage container in an upright position in its stand, especially during transportation. Always make sure the gauge and valve stem are protected from damage. Ensure that the room or vehicle is well-ventilated.	Oxygen tanks and cylinders are highly explosive. If a horizontally positioned tank explodes, the rapid release of oxygen can catapult sections of the tank or cylinder through walls and into people.
Keep oxygen tanks at least 5 feet from heat sources and electrical devices (e.g., space heaters, heating vents or radiators, fireplaces, stoves, radios, vaporizers, humidifiers). Oxygen should be kept away from direct sunlight. Never put anything over the oxygen tank.	Heat can increase pressure inside the tank, causing it to explode.
Ensure that no one smokes in the room or area of the oxygen tank. Post a visible sign indicating that oxygen is in use as well as NO SMOKING signs. Ensure that there are no open flames (e.g., pilot light) near the oxygen source.	Smoking increases the risk of fire, which could cause the tank to explode. Escaped oxygen would feed the fire.
Never permit oil, grease, or highly flammable material to come into contact with oxygen cylinders, liquid oxygen, valves, regulators or fittings. Do not lubricate with oil or other flammable substances, and do not handle equipment with greasy hands or rags.	Flammable materials increase the risk of fire.
Use water-soluble jelly to relieve dryness of the student's mouth. Do not use alcohol- or oil-based substances, such as petroleum jelly, vitamin A and D ointment, or baby oil. Note that lemon-glycerin swabs may increase dryness.	Alcohol and oil are both flammable and increase the risk of fire.

oxygen, often administered by means of a mechanical ventilator, generally fall into one of four categories (O'Donohue et al., 1986): (a) those with **ventilatory muscle dysfunction** (disorders in the functioning of the muscular tissues required to inhale and exhale), including those with muscular dystrophy; (b) those with **central hypoventilation syndromes** (disorders that affect the neurologic control of breathing), such as those who develop hypoventilation as a result of head trauma or neurologic surgery affecting critical areas in the brainstem respiratory centers; (c) those with **restrictive lung diseases** (diseases that are characterized by a restriction in the person's ability to expand the lungs or chest wall), such as those with chronic pulmonary fibrosis; and (d) those with **obstructive lung diseases,** such as children and young adults with asthma or bronchopulmonary dysplasia.

Delivery Systems and Sources of Oxygen

There are three delivery systems by which oxygen can be administered: (a) by means of an **oxygen concentrator,** a piece of equipment that extracts oxygen from room air, which is used primarily when there is a long-term need of low flow oxygen, particularly in rural areas where there is a scarcity of oxygen supply companies (Jaudes, 1991); (b) by means of **liquid oxygen,** a thermal system in which oxygen is kept at $-300°F$ ($148.9°C$) in a liquid state, which is used primarily for those who need intermittent or continuous oxygen at low to moderate flow rates; and (c) by means of **compressed oxygen gas,** in which oxygen is stored under pressure in a tank or cylinder, which is particularly useful when a high flow use of oxygen is required either intermittently or continuously. Each method differs in terms of cost-effectiveness, need for a source of humidity,

TABLE 7.2
Safe Use of Oxygen in Schools *(Continued)*

Safety Guidelines	Rationale
Have the student wear cotton garments.	Silk, wool, and synthetics (e.g., polyester & nylon) can generate static electricity and cause fire.
The local fire department and electrical company should be notified that oxygen is in use in the school. Keep a fire extinguisher readily available. The fire department should be contacted at least once a year to inspect the building to ensure proper procedures and precautions are being followed. If a concentrator, which requires a source of electricity, is used, a back-up emergency oxygen tank must be available in case of a power failure.	In case of fire, emergency personnel must be aware of the potential for explosion. In case of a power outage, the electric company will attempt to restore power as soon as possible if it is made aware of an urgent need.
Turn off both volume regulator and flow regulator when O_2 is not in use.	If the volume regulator is on when oxygen is turned on, the student may receive a rapid, forceful flow of oxygen in the face that could be frightening and uncomfortable. Keeping the source of oxygen sealed when not in use prevents leaking.
Be careful that the oxygen tubing does not become kinked, blocked, or disconnected. Do not run the tubing under furniture, rugs, or clothing.	Oxygen leakage, which might not be detected because oxygen is odorless, can cause fire.
Know the home oxygen supply company contact person; have the phone number posted in an obvious place. Return any defective equipment to the authorized company for replacement.	In case of emergency or defective equipment (e.g., a hissing tank) it is important to have quick access to proper personnel.
Have spare oxygen readily accessible, based on the student's needs. This should be stored safely in a secure place. Extra tubing and tank equipment (wrenches, etc.) must be kept in an easily accessible place.	Ensure there is at least a 2- to 3-day supply to avoid an emergency situation.

Sources: Hagerdorn (1990); Porter et al. (1997).

portability, and space requirements. The student's physician, in consultation with the respiratory therapist or technician and the home oxygen supplier, determines which system is best for the student and which is the best route of administration (e.g., into the nose via nasal prongs, into the mouth by means of a face mask, or into the trachea by means of a tracheostomy collar).

While a classroom teacher is not directly involved in the administration of oxygen, awareness of certain safety precautions that must be undertaken when oxygen is being administered and sufficient training to act in emergency situations are necessary (Table 7.2).

Oxygen should only be administered by a nurse or health care aide who has been properly trained in its use and who can accurately monitor the needs of the student. The steps required in the administration of oxygen by means of **nasal cannula, face mask,** or **tracheostomy collar** are outlined in Table 7.3. All staff in the school who have contact with a student with severe respiratory problems should be trained in CPR.

❧ Long-Term Mechanical Ventilation

In the past, children and young adults who required long-term mechanical ventilation remained in the hospital; however, since many of them did not require any "other" specialized hospital care, their parents pressured the government and the health care system to allow their children to return home and to resume their regular lives, which included, if possible, enrolling in local school programs (Lantos & Kohrman, 1991). In 1987, the number of children and young adults in the United States requiring ventilator assistance was estimated at between 680 and 2,000 (Office of Technology Assessment, 1987). Undoubtedly, by now, this number has increased dramatically. Many of these individuals have bronchopulmonary dysplasia, described previously, secondary to premature birth. Others may have a congenital heart disease, paralysis of the nerve leading to the diaphragm (i.e., the phrenic nerve), a disorder affecting central control of breathing (e.g., head injury), airway anomalies (e.g., tracheoesophageal fistula), spinal cord injury, Arnold-Chiari malformation associated with spina bifida, a degenerative muscular condition (e.g., muscular dystro-

phy, spinal muscular atrophy), or severe curvature of the spine (e.g., kyphoscoliosis).

Types of Mechanical Ventilators

There are two types of mechanical ventilators that can provide students with continuous O_2. In this section, they are discussed briefly to familiarize the reader; however, for more detailed information, the reader should consult O'Donohue et al. (1986) and Connors and Rosental-Dichter (1997).

Negative Pressure Machines   Ventilators that rely on the principle of **"negative" pressure** include (a) the **tank respirator** (commonly referred to as an "iron lung"), (b) **cuirass** (or chest shell), and (c) **body wrap** (or portable pulmowrap). With each of these approaches, the abdomen or chest wall is "pulled out" mechanically, forcing the diaphragm to lower, thereby creating a negative pressure situation (i.e., subatmospheric) in the lungs that results in the inspiration of air (Caldwell, Todaro, Gates, & Pailet, 1991). Because air is drawn in through the mouth and nose, persons with negative pressure ventilators do not have a tracheostomy. These devices are used primarily with individuals who have extreme muscular weakness in the chest wall and have, in general, normal pulmonary functioning (i.e., the lungs are not damaged by injury or disease). They are often used to augment or provide ventilation during the night or to provide periodic muscle rest during the day (O'Donahue et al., 1986).

Positive Pressure Machines   Ventilators that rely on the principle of **"positive" pressure** "inflate" the lungs by increasing airway pressure above atmospheric pressure (i.e., superatmospheric). Positive pressure ventilation can be either noninvasive, i.e., applied to the "natural" airway, or invasive, i.e., delivered via an "artificial opening," the tracheostomy tube (Levy & O'Rourke, 1997). Invasive ventilation is the more common in children.

Positive pressure machines are classified according to the factors that regulate cycling (Whaley & Wong, 1995) and are prescribed on the basis of the person's respiratory conditions and ventilation needs. In a **pressure-cycled ventilator** the inspiratory pressure is preset and the respiratory cycle terminates when the pressure is reached. In a **volume-cycled ventilator** the volume of oxygen is preset and the respiratory cycle terminates when the

TABLE 7.3

Administration of Oxygen

1. Assemble the appropriate equipment (e.g., oxygen or compressed air source; nasal cannula, face mask or collar; tubing; humidification reservoir containing distilled water; heater and proper adapters) as required. Equipment required is determined by route of administration.

2. Check supply of oxygen to ensure sufficient quantity. Place **No Smoking—Oxygen in Use** signs in prominent locations.

3. Wash hands before handling cannula, mask, or tracheostomy collar to prevent contamination.

4. Attach the cannula, mask, or collar to source of oxygen or compressed air by means of tubing. Ensure tubing is not kinked and connections are tight.

5. If student is using nasal prongs, ensure nostrils are patent. Administer nasal spray, if ordered by the physician, to clear nasal passages of mucus.

6. **Before Giving O$_2$ to Student:** Initiate delivery of oxygen or compressed air at the flow rate prescribed. Ensure oxygen is being released (i.e., flush equipment to ensure maximum release of oxygen before placing cannula, mask or collar on the student) by holding cannula, face mask, or collar against hand or cheek. Nasal prongs can be placed in a cup of water to ensure tubing and prongs are patent (i.e., look for bubbles rising).

   Use of Nasal Cannula: Place nasal prongs into child's nose (one prong into each nostril). Place cannula tubing over ears and under neck *or* over ears and around back of head. Adjust to fit comfortably. Secure by sliding clasp until there is not excessive slack in the tubing. Do not overtighten. If necessary, secure tubing to face with non-allergenic tape. Pad pressure areas (especially between tubing and ears), if necessary, with gauze, lamb's wool, or cotton balls under tubing.

   Use of Face Mask: Slip mask over the student's head. Place mask over chin, mouth, and nose (if possible, have student hold the mask while you place your hand over the student's hand). Adjust elastic strap or band so that it lies just above the student's ears and is snug but not tight. Gently pinch metal band on top of mask to fit comfortably over student's nasal bridge. Pad pressure areas, if needed.

   Use of Tracheostomy Collar: If the student has a humidifier device, ensure that a fine mist is coming out of the end of the tubing by holding the collar up to a light source. Place the collar over student's tracheostomy, ensuring that the source of oxygen is over the tracheostomy tube that protrudes from the student's neck. Tighten the straps to ensure a snug, but not too tight, fit.

7. Monitor student's response to therapy (e.g., breathing patterns, skin color, and warmth) after 15 minutes and then on a regular basis (no less than every 30 minutes) throughout period of administration.

8. Monitor equipment function at least every 2 hours (i.e., check flow rate, water level in humidifier, oxygen supply, patency of tubing and nasal cannulae, fit of mask) and make necessary adjustments. If student is mobile (i.e., using a portable system) checks should occur more frequently. Check for pressure points. Check lips and nose for dryness and irritation or breakdown and lubricate with water-based lubricant. Provide sufficient liquids to prevent dehydration. If student is using a mask, remove every one to two hours to clean skin and ensure it is dry.

9. Record procedures and document any problems in daily log (Appendix G).

Sources: Hagerdorn, 1990; Porter et al., 1997; Jamerson, 1991; Wallace, 1991.

correct amount of air is delivered. In a **time-cycled ventilator** the length of time for each breath is preset and the respiratory cycle terminates when the time is completed.

Since the newer portable ventilators only weigh 30 to 40 pounds, they can be transported easily beneath a wheelchair, in a wagon, or on any other type of wheeled device. Some are totally portable, because they are powered by an internal or external 12-volt battery. If the student is stationary at all times, the device can be plugged into the regular electrical current.

🐾 Educational Implications and Teaching Tips: Students Using Mechanical Ventilation

The training needs of caregivers of students who use some form of long-term mechanical ventilation depend on the device being used, the overall medical status of the student, and in some cases, the age of the student. Children, particularly infants and young children, generally require a medically trained caregiver (i.e., nurse or respiratory therapist) in attendance, able to respond immediately to any crisis situation. Some older children and young adults, however, may be managed successfully by a nonmedical attendant under the supervision of a school nurse (e.g., health aide) (O'Donohue et al., 1986). If a trained staff caregiver or a trained back-up caregiver is not available, the student should not attend school unless a family member is able to take over the responsibility for meeting his or her needs (Porter et al., 1997).

All caregivers, including the student's teacher, should be adequately trained to assess the respiratory status of the student (e.g., be able to recognize color changes and signs of respiratory distress) and understand how to initiate the emergency plan that has been established. Children, especially those who are very young, need to be watched more carefully than adults, because they are more prone to respiratory infections; consequently, assessment of the child's status must be continuous.

Although it is unlikely that anything will go wrong, staff should be prepared. A written emergency plan (see Appendix C) that includes detailed instruction in how to respond during emergencies should be developed. The phone numbers of the student's parents and physician must be prominently displayed, along with the phone number of the equipment supplier in case of equipment malfunction. All staff should be trained in CPR.

Even though many teachers and administrators are often hesitant to have a student who depends on technology for survival in their school, the benefits of home care may far outweigh those of hospital care (e.g., more normalized environment that fosters growth and development; increased opportunity for socialization; decreased costs to family and state). With careful attention to detail by medical personnel, family, and school staff, many of these students live productive lives and the potential rewards are great (O'Donohue et al., 1986). The following points highlight some of the special considerations that a student who is on long-term ventilation requires during the school day[4]:

---

[4] For further information on children who use long-term ventilators the reader is referred to Caldwell et al., 1989; Caldwell, Sirvis et al, 1991; Caldwell, Todaro et al., 1991; Carroll, 1987; O'Donohue et al., 1986; Porter et al., 1997; Rovinski & Zastocki, 1989; and White & Perez, 1986. However, such sources of information are *not* sufficient for complete training. Training must be provided by appropriately trained respiratory therapists or technicians, nurses, and physicians.

1 *Portable ventilators are typically powered by a rechargeable external battery capable of operating for 10 to 20 hours.* An internal battery is available for short-term emergency use (approximately 1 hour). Ventilators also can operate on regular household electric current. All electrical outlets in the student's immediate surroundings (e.g., classroom, gym, lunchroom) must be checked to ensure that they are functional, accessible, and properly grounded. An adapter that allows the ventilator to be attached to a vehicle's battery by means of the cigarette lighter is critical for students who are transported to and from school by car or bus.

If the student is on a ventilator on a continuous basis (i.e., is not able to breathe independently), a backup ventilator is required. This equipment should be checked daily to ensure that it is functional, even if it is not used regularly. In case of a power outage, a manual resuscitation bag must be kept with the student at all times. A battery-operated light should be available in order for caregivers to see the equipment and ensure conversion to backup sources of power or resuscitation device.

2 *The electricity company and fire department should be notified that a student using life-sustaining equipment is located in the school.* In the event of power failure, the utility company gives priority restoration service to those on such equipment. Students' names should be registered with the local hospital, so that hospital staff are alert to their needs during emergency situations. If the outage is protracted, the student may have to be hospitalized where there are power generators.

3 *The designated caregiver should check the student's equipment on arrival at school and at least every 2 to 4 hours to ensure the equipment is operational and sufficient supplies are available.* This is particularly important if the student is mobile and moves from room to room within the school setting.

Checks should include a thorough examination of the following: (a) power source(s); (b) oxygen source; (c) humidifier; (d) all tubing and valves (referred to as the circuit) that connect the ventilator to the student; and (d) alarm systems. A detailed checklist (see Appendix G) that documents what the caregiver sees and does should be completed after each check. The list should be kept in a loose-leaf binder attached to the ventilator. In addition to daily checks, the equipment should be checked at least every month by the equipment vendor to ensure proper functioning.

The caregiver should also ensure that there is always a sufficient quantity of oxygen (enough to last at least one day) and notify the supplier if the oxygen needs to be replaced before a scheduled delivery (e.g., in the case of a leak or if the student uses the oxygen faster than anticipated).

4   *Most students using a ventilator have a tracheostomy; therefore, it is crucial that an emergency tracheostomy kit, including a manual resuscitation bag and proper suction equipment, be with the student at all times.* This includes going to and from school, on field trips, in the school auditorium, etc. Further information on tracheostomy care is presented later.

5   *Each ventilator is individual-specific; the student's physician prescribes the proper settings. This includes the concentration of oxygen and the amount of time the student should be on the ventilator. All ventilators should have a lockable Plexiglas covering so that the control dials cannot be manipulated by the student or unauthorized persons.*

Settings should be checked at least every 1 to 2 hours. A laminated safety card that lists the settings should be mounted in a prominent location on the ventilator for quick access. Ventilator settings may need to be changed periodically as the child grows, but such changes must only be made by the attending physician. For children from birth to age two, reevaluation should occur at least once every 3 months; for older children, reassessment should be considered at least every 6 months.

6   *All ventilators are equipped with alarm systems that indicate specific individual-related problems (e.g., pressure alarm that indicates either too high or too low inspiratory pressure) or equipment malfunction.* **The alarm system must never be turned off.** All staff must be trained to be aware of the sounds that the various alarms make (e.g., a continuous alarm indicates a low pressure, typically caused by the accidental disconnection of the tube from the ventilator; an intermittent alarm indicates high pressure, typically the result of something ob-

structing the flow of air, such as a kinked tube or a mucus plug in the student's throat).

If the alarm sounds, the student should be checked immediately. For this reason, there must always be a responsible trained adult in the vicinity of the student to act appropriately and quickly. If the student appears to be all right (e.g., color is good, chest is rising), the ventilator should be checked, because the tubing might be kinked or the exhalation valve may be obstructed. **It is critical to always reassure and stay with the student.** If there are signs of distress, the student should be disconnected from the machine and manually ventilated until the problem is rectified.

7   *All students on a ventilator must have an alarm system that they can activate themselves to summon help if they are unable to call out for help.* A bell attached to the child's wrist is a common device. Some students are hooked up to a buzzer system.

8   *All students on ventilators are prone to infections and common illnesses.* As a preventative measure, there may be times when students should remain home in order to decrease contact with persons who have communicable diseases. Efforts should be made to ensure that the student is able to keep up with schoolwork (e.g., provision of a home tutor).

9   *Special care must be taken in transporting the student who uses a ventilator.* Sudden movements (sharp turns, sudden braking) can result in the student being disconnected from the equipment. The bus driver and bus attendant must be properly trained in the health needs of the student before transporting the student.

Children Who Have a Tracheostomy

A **tracheostomy** is a surgical opening of the trachea, between the second and fourth tracheal rings, below the Adam's apple (Figure 7.1). An indwelling plastic or metal tube, known commonly as the **trach tube,** is inserted into the trachea, and the end of the tube exits through an opening in the skin, known as a

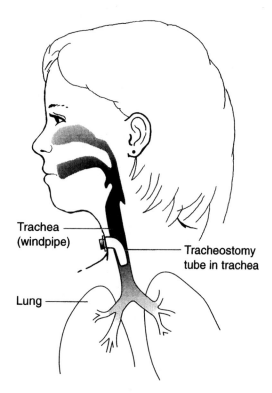

Figure 7.1
A Student with a Tracheostomy Tube

stoma. The trach tube is loosely held in place by padded ties that surround the child's neck. If the student is on a ventilator, the trach tube is attached to the ventilator tube. However, not all children who have a tracheostomy require a ventilator; some are able to breathe independently through the opening in the neck.

For some the trach tube is a temporary measure that is removed when the individual is able to resume mouth or nose breathing. For others the trach tube, along with a ventilator, is a permanent fixture in their lives. In some cases, the student has a tracheostomy solely for the purpose of suctioning secretions from the chest area.

Educational Implications and Teaching Tips: Students with Tracheostomies

Children and young adults who have a tracheostomy require, in most cases, a full time trained health provider (e.g., nurse, licensed practical nurse, certified health aide, respiratory therapist or technician) in the classroom to provide the necessary care. Regular **tracheostomy care** is provided for three primary reasons: (a) to ensure that air moves easily in and out the child's airway; (b) to prevent infection occurring around the trachea or in the lungs; and (c) to prevent irritation around the stoma into the trachea (Graff, Ault, Guess, Taylor, & Thompson, 1990).

Regardless of the presence of a trained person, all school staff in contact with the student should have a basic knowledge regarding the care of persons with tracheostomies and should be sufficiently trained to recognize signs and symptoms of respiratory distress and to respond in crisis situations. **All staff should be trained to provide CPR to individuals with a tracheostomy.**

Many children with tracheostomies attend school without encountering any serious problems. However, given the possible emergency situations that might arise, adequate staff training is crucial before the student returns to school. Procedures not frequently used are easily forgotten. Sherman and Rosen (1990) have suggested that skills of staff that are not routinely providing assistance (e.g., bus drivers) be reviewed on a regular basis and "mock" emergencies be scheduled at least twice a year to ensure that the written emergency plans in place are adequate and strictly implemented.

It is beyond the scope of the present text to outline the nursing intervention required to care for students with a tracheostomy (e.g., tracheal, mouth, or nose suctioning; trach tube changing; using a manual resuscitator), particularly since these specialized procedures, if completed improperly, can result in life-threatening emergencies. The following are some basic pointers that are critical to remember for all staff working with students who have a tracheostomy[5]:

1 *A trach kit, a flashlight, a suction machine, and an oxygen source must be housed in the classroom in a location known by everyone who works with the student.* A trach kit includes a spare tube,

---

[5] For more information on the care needs of those with tracheostomies, the reader is referred to Caldwell et al., 1989; Caldwell et al., 1991; Graff et al., 1990; Hagerdorn, 1990; Holvoet and Helmstetter (1989); Hunsberger, 1989; Lapakko, 1986; Porter et al., 1997 Rovinski & Zastocki, 1989; and Sherman & Rosen, 1990. These sources of information are *not* sufficient for complete training. Training must be provided by respiratory therapists or technicians, nurses, or doctors.

extra tracheostomy ties, gauze pads, swabs, sterile saline solution, round-tipped bandage scissors, an extra suction catheter, and a manual resuscitation bag with adapter. If the student is in more than one place on a regular basis (e.g., library, gym, resource room, school bus), additional kits and sources of oxygen should be located in these spots. If the student is going on a field trip or traveling to an area where an emergency kit is not routinely housed (e.g., to another classroom to watch a film), the kit, easily packed in a backpack or gym bag, must accompany the student.

2 *Regular, routine tracheostomy care is usually provided by the parents in the home; however, if care is needed, clean supplies and necessary equipment must be available in the nurse's station or a private area of the student's classroom.* Caregivers must wash their hands before caring for the student and use aseptic technique in order to lessen the chances of contamination.

All equipment needed for the child, as well as all back-up equipment, should be checked daily by the caregiver to ensure that it is assembled and ready for immediate use. **If any equipment is absent or nonfunctional, the student should be kept home until it is replaced.** There should be enough supplies for 1 week.

For some students, a humidifier may be required to prevent the drying out of secretions in the trachea and lungs. A backup should be readily available in case of malfunction.

3 *Emergency plans for both inside school and outside of school must be developed for each student with a trach (e.g., how to deal with the dislodged trach tube or one plugged with mucus).* **In emergency situations, all personnel should remain calm and reassure the student. A student encountering any type of distress must not be left alone.** If the classrooms in the school do not have an intercom or telephone system, portable walkie-talkies or cellular telephones should be available for emergencies.

All staff should be trained to be alert to the signs that indicate that a student needs suctioning or oxygen. Signs include the following: restlessness or agitation; difficulty breathing or faster breathing; coughing or wheezing; a frightened look; flaring of the student's nostrils; retraction of skin between the ribs or above and below the sternum; pale or bluish color around the mouth, eyes, toenails, or fingernails; bubbles of mucus that are seen or heard at the opening of the tracheostomy tube; sweating; and excessive drowsiness. The tracheostomy ties that hold the trach tube in place should always be secure. If they are too loose, the tube may move up and down as the student breathes and consequently may become dislodged.

4 *Care given to students should be documented and a record sent home to the parents daily.* A sample health care procedure log is contained in Appendix D. The following should be noted: abnormalities in the amount, consistency, color, and odor of secretions removed from the trachea; deterioration in the condition of the skin around the stoma (e.g., redness or crusting); shortness of breath; fever; and change in the color of lips or nails.

5 *It is important that the tracheostomy be protected from objects or small particles entering the tracheostomy.* This includes dust; chalk dust; sand; glitter; lint; animal hair; bugs; toys, especially those with removable parts; fingers; food; and fluids. Irritants (e.g., aerosol sprays such as room deodorizers; powders; perfumes; smoke; cleaning agents with ammonia; and glues) can cause a reaction and should also be avoided. The use of an **artificial nose,** a device that can be attached to the trach tube to filter out airborne particles, may be useful. For very young children, the child's peers must not insert foreign objects into the trach and never touch or pull on the tube.

If a student does aspirate a foreign body, it must be suctioned out before oxygen is administered or a resuscitation bag is used, to prevent the aspirated object from being forced into the lungs.

6 *Clothes that could block the airway, such as turtleneck sweaters or plastic bibs, must be avoided.* Similarly, for the young child, fuzzy clothing and toys or blankets that could be picked up and put in the airway should be avoided.

7 *A student with a tracheostomy should be protected, when outdoors, from cold air and dust.* A scarf or handkerchief loosely tied around the neck or an artificial nose provides some protection. The young child should be supervised when near water and should not be permitted to play in sandboxes or boxes filled with small objects (e.g., pellets of rice).

8 *In the case of a power outage, an alternative method of suctioning not requiring a source of electricity must be available, and staff must be appropriately trained.* Examples are a De Lee suction catheter or a battery-operated suction machine. In cases of power outages, a battery-powered light source must be available.

9 *Because air from the lungs bypasses the vocal cords, a student with a trach is typically not able to speak in a normal manner.* Some individuals who have a trach, but who are not connected full time to a ventilator, are able to learn to communicate by covering the opening with either their hand or a trach cap, or by using a Passey-Muir valve which directs the air through the vocal cords (Jackson & Saunders, 1993). Covering the tube, however, must never be done without the permission of the physician.

The student with a trach may not be able to vocally cry out for help; consequently, a system must be developed to alert help (e.g., a bell worn in the form of a bracelet; a buzzer or a toy clicker attached to the student's desk). A speech and language therapist should be involved to assist in the development of some alternative form of communication (e.g., Blisssymbolics, American Sign Language), particularly if the student is going to have the trach inserted for a long period of time.

10 *Most individuals who have a tracheostomy are able to consume food and fluids in a normal manner.* This is because ingested food travels down the esophagus, bypassing the tracheal opening. However, some children may require modifications to their diet (Porter et al., 1997); others may need to be fed through a gastrostomy tube.[6]

---

[6] See chapter 17.

Summary

In this chapter two less common respiratory conditions, bronchopulmonary dysplasia and tuberculosis, were described. In addition, information was presented on the needs of students who require supplemental oxygen in order to sustain life and the needs of students who depend on ventilators. Practical information on the needs of students who have tracheostomies was also covered. Even though the material on O_2 delivery has been presented in the unit on students who have altered respiratory functioning, some children require oxygen or are dependent on mechanical devices for a source of oxygen even though their primary problem is not related to the respiratory system. Children and young adults with circulatory problems (i.e., altered cardiovascular and hematologic function) and those with innervation problems (i.e., altered neurologic function) often have difficulty maintaining a sufficient level of oxygen in the tissues of their body as a result of an inability of the heart to pump the oxygen-rich blood to the peripheral extremities of the body, the inability of the blood to become sufficiently saturated with oxygen, or as a result of injury to the respiratory center in the brain or injury to the pathway from the brain to the lungs (i.e., the spinal cord). These types of children will be the focus of the next two sections.

References

American Academy of Pediatrics, Committee on Infectious Diseases (1994). Screening for tuberculosis in infants and children. *Pediatrics, 93,* 131–134.

Bernbaum, J. C., & Batshaw, M. L. Batshaw (1997). Born too soon, born too small. In M. L. Batshaw (Ed.), *Children with disabilities* (4th ed., pp. 115–139). Baltimore: Paul H. Brookes.

Caldwell, T. H., Sirvis, B., Todaro, A. W., & Accouloumre, D. S. (1991). *Special health care in the school.* Reston, VA: Council for Exceptional Children.

Caldwell, T. H., Todaro, A. W., Gates, A. J., & Pailet, J. F. (Eds.) (1989). *Community provider's guide: An information outline for working with children with special health needs.* New Orleans, LA: Children's Hospital.

Caldwell, T. H., Todaro, A. W., Gates, A. J., Failla, S., & Kirkhart, K (Eds.) (1991). *Community provider's guide: An information outline for working with children with special health needs: 1991 addendum.* New Orleans, LA: Children's Hospital.

Canadian Press. (1994, December 1). Study: TB in natives tops levels in Africa. *Times Colonist*, p. C8.

Carroll, P. F. (1987). Home care for the ventilator patient: A checklist you can use. *Nursing, 17*(1), 82–83.

Castiglia, P. T. (1992). Caring for children with infectious diseases. In P. T. Castiglia & R. E. Harbin, *Child health care: Process and practice* (pp. 415–437). Philadelphia: J. B. Lippincott.

Connors, C. A., & Rosental-Dichter, C. (1997). Components of breathing: Pediatric ventilatory challenges. *Critical Care Nurse, 17*, 60–70.

Feroli K. L. (1994). Infectious disease. In C. L. Betz, M. M. Hunsberger, S. Wright (Eds.), *Family-centered nursing care of children* (2nd ed., pp. 1678–1716). Philadelphia: W. B. Saunders.

Gerdes, J. S., Abbasi, S., & Bhutani, V. K. (1996). Bronchopulmonary dysplasia. In F. D. Burg, J. R. Ingelfinger, E. R. Ward, & R. A. Polin (Eds.), *Gellis & Kagan's current pediatric therapy* (15th ed., pp. 769–771). Philadelphia: W. B. Saunders.

Graff, J. C., Ault, M. M., Guess, D., Taylor, M., & Thompson, B. (1990). *Health care for students with disabilities: An illustrated medical guide for the classroom*. Baltimore: Paul H. Brookes.

Hagerdorn, M. (1990). Oxygenation: Implications of abnormalities in structure and function. In S. R. Mott, S. R. James, & A. M. Sperhac, *Nursing care of children and families* (pp. 955–1047). Redwood City, CA: Addison-Wesley.

Harvey, K. (1996). Bronchopulmonary dysplasia. In P. L. Jackson & J. A. Vessey (Eds.), *Primary care of the child with a chronic condition* (2nd. ed., pp. 172–192). St. Louis: Mosby.

Holvoet, J. F., & Helmstetter, E. (1989). *Medical problems of students with special needs: A guide for educators*. Boston: College-Hill.

Jackson, D. B., & Saunders, R. B. (1993). *Child health nursing: A comprehensive approach to the care of children and their families*. Philadelphia: J. B. Lippincott.

Jackson, M. M. (1993). Tuberculosis in infants, children, and adolescents: New dilemmas with an old disease. *Pediatric Nursing, 19*, 437–442.

Jacobs, R. F., & Starke, J. R. (1993). Tuberculosis in children. *Medical Clinics of North America, 77*, 1335–1351.

Jamerson, P. A. (1991). Administering and monitoring oxygen. In D. P. Smith (Ed.) *Comprehensive child and family nursing skills* (pp. 568–577). St. Louis: Mosby.

Jaudes, P. K. (1991). The medical care of children with complex health care needs: An overview for caretakers. In N. J. Hochstadt & D. M. Yost (Eds.), *The medically complex child: The transition to home care* (pp. 29–60). Chur, Switzerland: Harwood Academic Publishers.

Lantos, J., & Kohrman, A. F. (1991). Ethical aspects of pediatric home care. In N. J. Hochstadt & D. M. Yost (Eds.), *The medically complex child: The transition to home care* (pp. 245–257). Chur, Switzerland: Harwood Academic Publishers.

Lapakko, S., (1986). Care of the student with a tracheostomy. In G. Larson (Ed.), *Managing the school age child with a chronic health condition* (pp. 223–235). Wayzata, MN: DCI Publishing.

Levine, J. M. (1996). Including children dependent on ventilators in school. *Teaching Exceptional Children, 28*(3), 25–29.

Levy, S. E., & O'Rourke, M. (1997). Technological assistance: Innovations for independence. In M. L. Batshaw (Ed.), *Children with disabilities* (4th ed., pp. 687–708). Baltimore: Paul H. Brookes.

Natale, J. A. (1992). TB is back. *The Education Digest, 58*(2), 58–61.

O'Donohue, W. J., Giovannoni, R. M., Goldberg, A. I., Keens, T. G., Make, B. J., Plummer, A. L., & Prentice, W. S. (1986). *Long-term mechanical ventilation: Guidelines for management in the home and at alternate community sites*. Report of the Ad Hoc Committee, Respiratory Care Section, American College of Chest Physicians. *Chest (July Supplement), 90*(1), 1S–38S.

Office of Technology Assessment (1987). *Technology-dependent children: Hospital vs. home care—A technical memorandum*. (OTA-TM-H-38). Washington, DC: Government Printing Office. (ERIC Document Reproduction Service No. ED 303 949).

Ott, M. J., Horn, M., & McLaughlin, D. (1995). Pediatric TB in the 1990s. *Maternal and Child Nursing, 20*(1), 16–20.

Porter, S., Haynie, M., Bierle, T., Caldwell, T. H., & Palfrey, J. S. (1997). *Children and youth assisted by medical technology in educational settings: Guidelines for care* (2nd ed.). Baltimore: Paul H. Brookes.

Rovinski, C. A., & Zastocki, D. K. (1989). *Home care: A technical manual for the professional nurse*. Philadelphia: W. B. Saunders.

Sherman, L. P., & Rosen, C. D. (1990). Development of a preschool program for tracheostomy dependent children. *Pediatric Nursing, 16*, 357–361.

Wallace, C. M. (1991). Care of the patient with a respiratory disorder. In B. L. Christensen & E. O. Kockrow (Eds.), *Foundations of nursing* (pp. 820–871). St. Louis: Mosby.

Webster's new complete medical dictionary (1996). New York: Smithmark.

Whaley, L. F., & Wong, D. L. (1995). *Nursing care of infants and children* (5th ed.). St. Louis: Mosby.

White, K. D., & Perez, P. W. (1986). Your ventilator patient *can* go home again. *Nursing, 16*(12), 54–56.

PART III

Circulation:

Children and Young Adults with Altered Cardiovascular and Hematologic Function

An estimated 24,000 to 32,000 children are born each year in the United States with some form of cardiovascular disease, i.e., disease affecting the heart or the blood-carrying vessels of the body. Of these children, 85 percent survive their childhood years with medical or surgical intervention (Sparacino, 1994). An unknown number of individuals develop cardiovascular disease during childhood and adolescence. The majority of these also survive the disease condition and enter their adult years with or without major complications. Newacheck and Taylor (1992) estimated that in the United States alone there were, in 1988, approximately 965,000 children under age 18 with some form of heart disease.

The actual number of children with hematologic disorders, i.e., disorders of the blood and blood-forming organs, is unknown. However, most disorders of this type are relatively uncommon compared with other chronic conditions of childhood—the exception being lead poisoning, which occurs in as many as 4% of children in some areas of the world. Other more common conditions involving the blood system include anemia and sickle cell disease, which occur at a rate of 8.8 and 1.2 per 1,000, respectively. In 1988 in the United States alone, an estimated 557,000 children had some form of anemia, and 74,000 children had some form of sickle cell disease (Newacheck & Taylor, 1992). Other less commonly occurring conditions include leukemia, a cancer of the blood-forming organs, and hemophilia, a bleeding disorder found predominantly in males.

The primary function of the respiratory system is to provide the cells and tissues of the body with an adequate supply of oxygen. However, without the assistance of the cardiovascular and the hematologic systems, oxygen and other substances required for the various chemical processes that occur in the human body (i.e., metabolites) could not be transported throughout the body. To understand the nature of the various cardiovascular and hematologic disorders of childhood, basic understanding of the anatomy and physiology of these two systems is necessary. The importance of these systems is illustrated in the following:

> It [the heart] races with fear, hammers in anger, throbs with love. No wonder the ancient Hebrews believed that this one-pound, fist-size organ was the seat of thought and emotion. . . . The heart is the font of life, the cessation of its lub-dub the definition of death. (Dowling, 1997, p. 65).

> In ancient times the blood was referred to as the "river of life," or "fluid of life." Some even believed it had magical properties. All knew it was necessary to maintain life. (Turner, 1991, p. 703).

The Cardiovascular System: Review of Structure and Function

The cardiovascular system, from the Greek *kardia*, meaning heart, and the Latin *vasculum*, meaning little vessel, consists of the **heart** and its various conduits, collectively referred to as the **blood vessels.** The system, also referred to as the **circulatory system,** has two major functions: (a) the transportation of blood, rich in nutrients, to the fluids that surround the cells located throughout the body and (b) the conveyance of waste products from these same cells to the various excretory organs of the body, such as the lungs and kidneys.

Heart

The heart is a hollow, cone-shaped, four-chambered muscular organ, which, at maturity, is approximately the size of a clenched fist. It lies behind and slightly to the left of the sternum, resting above the diaphragm between the lungs, in a space known as the **mediastinum.** The heart can be thought of as a mechanical pump whose purpose is to propel blood in a specified direction. In one day, the mature heart beats approximately 100,000 times, shunting 1,000 gallons of blood through 60,000 miles of blood vessels (Turner, 1991). It has been estimated that in a lifetime, the heart may pump enough blood to fill the fuel tanks of 56 moon rockets (Dowling, 1997).

The heart (Figure III.1) is composed primarily of muscle tissue and a series of one-way openings. On the outside, the heart is encased in the **pericardium,** a loose-fitting, double-layered, fibrous sac. The inner layer of the pericardium that adheres to the heart is known as the **visceral pericardium.** The outer layer that anchors the heart to the chest wall is the **parietal pericardium.** Between the two layers, in the **pericardial space,** there is a small amount of **pericardial fluid,** which allows frictionless, painless movement of the muscle as the heart beats. The primary role of the pericardium is to protect the heart and its delicate membranes. If the pericardium becomes inflamed as a result of injury or illness, the individual is said to have **pericarditis.** One of the first symptoms of this condition is chest pain that radiates from the heart to the shoulder and neck.

The heart is composed of three different layers. The outer layer, or **epicardium,** is composed primarily of elastic connective tissue and fat cells. The middle layer, or **myocardium,** is made up principally of layers and bundles of muscle tissue, interlaced by a network of blood vessels. Tough fibers containing collagen run between the muscle tissues and the blood vessels. The innermost layer, or **endocardium,** consists of a thin layer of endothelial cells that are rich in blood supply, along with a few bundles of smooth muscle. The endocardial layer is continuous with the lining of the blood vessels that enter or exit the heart. If the muscles of the heart become inflamed, the person is diagnosed as having **carditis.** Typically, more than one layer of muscle, such as the endocardium *and* the myocardium, is involved (e.g., endocarditis, myocarditis). Symptoms

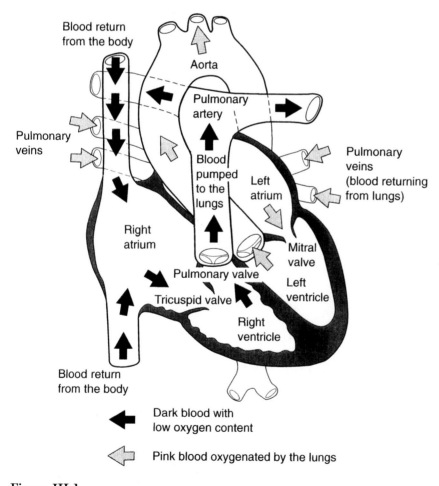

Figure III.1
The Heart: Normal Blood Flow
Source: Adapted from Bricker and McNamara, 1983, p. 223.

131

of carditis include chest pain and irregular heart beat. Without treatment, the muscle tissues may become permanently damaged and the person's health may be severely compromised.

The four chambers of the heart each have a different function. The two upper chambers, the **right** and **left atria** (sing. **atrium**), are often described as the receiving chambers: they receive blood as it comes from the body. The lower chambers, the **right** and **left ventricles,** are the pumping chambers: they pump blood from the heart to the body. The left side of the heart is considerable larger than the right. This disparity is caused primarily by the difference in size of the two pumping chambers. The left ventricle, which pumps blood throughout the whole body, is larger than the right ventricle, which pumps blood to the lungs alone.

The atria and the ventricles are separated from each other by a partition known as a **septum** (pl. **septa**). The **atrial septum** separates the relatively thin walls of the right and left atria; the **ventricular septum** separates the thicker muscular walls of the right and left ventricles. In the healthy heart, there are no openings between the two atria or between the two ventricles. However, on each side of the heart the chambers are "joined" by an opening (i.e., a **valve**) that is constructed to only permit blood to flow in one specific direction.

Blood Vessels

The largest blood vessels of the body can be differentiated into arteries and veins. The major ones are shown in Figure III.2.

Blood that is transported *to* the tissues throughout the body travels through a variety of muscular tubes that compose the **arterial circulatory system.** Typically, **arteries** carry blood rich in oxygen *away* from the heart; however, the pulmonary artery and its branches carry blood that is low in oxygen from the heart to the lungs. Blood that is rich in oxygen is often referred to as **saturated, or oxygenated, blood.**[1] Principle arteries include the **aorta** with its branches that go to the neck and head, the **axillary artery** that provides blood to the chest area and to the upper extremities, the **mesenteric artery** with its branches that go to the major organs (e.g., kidney, stomach, and spleen), the **common iliac artery** that leads into several arteries that travel down the legs to the feet, and the **pulmonary artery.**

Arteries become progressively smaller the further they are from the heart. **Arterioles** are microscopic arteries, and **capillaries,** arising from the arterioles, are the smallest of the blood-carrying vessels. Because of their relatively small size (approximately 0.008 mm in diameter) capillaries are able to branch into the various tissues that are located throughout the body and to exchange oxygen and other essential nutrients that are needed by the cells for waste products, including carbon dioxide, that are produced during metabolism.

The blood vessels in the **venous circulatory system** return the poorly oxygenated blood from body tissues *to* the heart and eventually back out to the lungs where the carbon dioxide is exchanged for oxygen. Typically, veins carry oxygen-depleted blood, but the pulmonary veins carry oxygenated blood from the lungs to the heart. Poorly oxygenated blood is also referred to as **desaturated, unsaturated, deoxygenated,** or **unoxygenated blood.**

Blood from the capillaries begins its route back to the heart via small blood vessels known as **venules,** similar in size to the arterioles. Increasing in size, the venules eventually coalesce into **veins.** The major veins include the **superior vena cava** that returns the blood from the head and arms, the **inferior vena cava** that carries blood from the abdomen and the lower extremities, and the **pulmonary vein** that returns oxygen-rich blood from the lungs. Although the structure of a vein is similar to that of an artery, the walls of a vein are thinner and are less elastic. Most veins lie deep within the body; however, there are several veins, such as those on the back of the hand or in the crook of the elbow joint, that are near the surface of the skin and are easily visible. These veins are used as locations for obtaining blood samples and donations; administering medications or nutrients directly into the bloodstream, i.e., **intravenous (IV) therapy;** and for administering **blood transfusions.**

The arteries, arterioles, capillaries, venules, and veins, collectively, can be further divided into the **systemic circulatory system,** also referred to as the **"greater circulation" system,** and the **pulmonary circulatory system.** The systemic system takes blood to and from the body, and the pulmonary system carries blood to and from the lungs.

---

[1] The term **oxygenation** is used to refer to the process of impregnating, combining, or supplying with oxygen (*Webster's,* 1996). The opposite is **deoxygenation.**

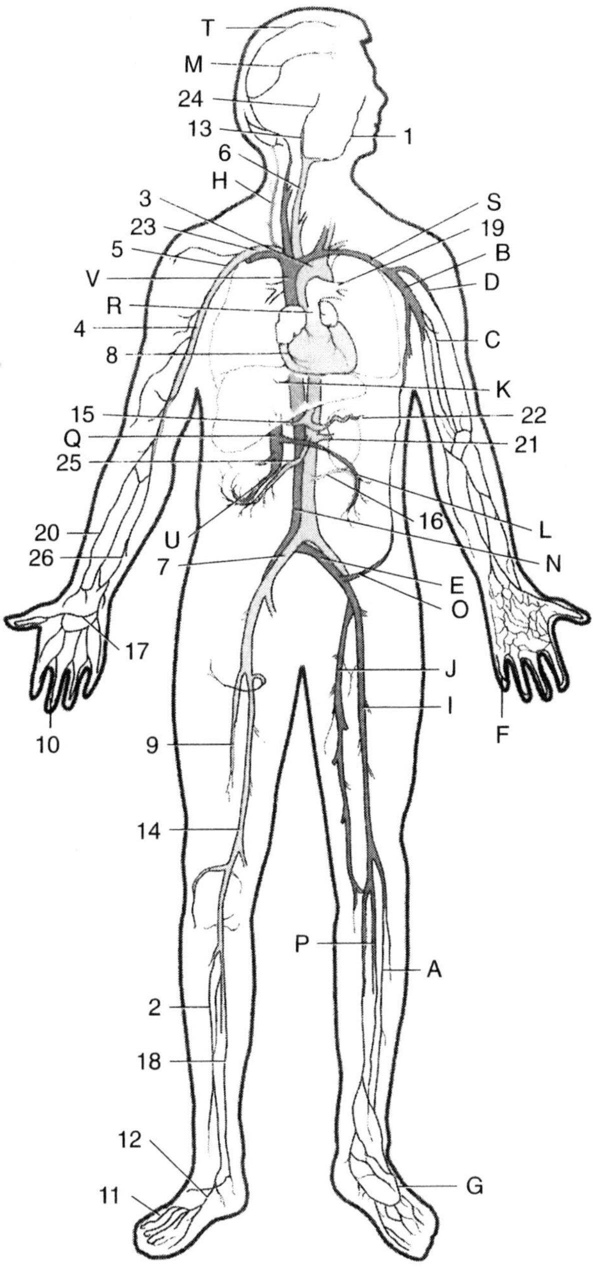

Principal arteries
1. Angular
2. Anterior tibial
3. Aorta
4. Axillary
5. Brachial
6. Common carotid, right
7. Common iliac, right
8. Coronary, left
9. Deep femoral
10. Digital
11. Dorsal metatarsal
12. Dorsalis pedis
13. External carotid
14. Femoral
15. Hepatic
16. Inferior mesenteric
17. Palmar arch, deep
18. Posterior tibial
19. Pulmonary
20. Radial
21. Renal
22. Splenic
23. Subclavian, right
24. Superficial temporal
25. Superior mesenteric
26. Ulnar

Principal veins
A Anterior tibial
B Axillary
C Brachial
D Cephalic
E Common iliac, left
F Digital
G Dorsal venous arch
H External jugular
I Femoral
J Great saphenous
K Hepatic
L Inferior mesenteric
M Inferior sagittal sinus
N Inferior vena cava
O Lateral thoracic
P Peroneal
Q Portal
R Pulmonary
S Subclavian, left
T Superior sagittal sinus
U Superior mesenteric
V Superior vena cava

Figure III.2
The Circulatory System

🫀 Postnatal Circulation

At birth, the circulatory system of the neonate undergoes a series of major changes, primarily as a result of separation from the placenta and the functioning of the infant's lungs to obtain oxygen. Within hours of birth, the circulatory system of the newborn child resembles that of an adult, and the blood travels in a prescribed path. Starting at the right atrium, the route is as follows:

1. Deoxygenated venous blood from the head, neck, arms, and upper trunk enters the right

133

atrium of the heart through the superior vena cava. Deoxygenated blood from the lower body returns via the inferior vena cava. Blood from the heart muscle returns to the general circulatory system via a series of veins that group together to form the **coronary sinus.**[2]

2. The blood from the right atrium flows into the right ventricle, passing through the **tricuspid valve,** so named because of the three flaps or cusps of endocardial tissue that make up the structure.

3. The right ventricle pumps the blood through the **pulmonic valve** to the lungs via the right and left pulmonary arteries. This valve, also known as the **pulmonary semilunar valve,** consists of three cusps and resembles, in shape, a half moon. In the alveolar sacs, located in the bronchioles of the lungs, the carbon dioxide in the capillary blood is exchanged for oxygen.

4. Oxygenated blood returns to the heart by means of four pulmonary veins. The left atrium is the receiving chamber for the oxygen-rich blood.

5. Blood from the left atrium flows into the left ventricle, through the **bicuspid valve,** composed of two flaps or cusps, also referred to as the **mitral valve,** because it is shaped like a miter, the liturgical headdress worn by certain members of the clergy.

6. The left ventricle pumps oxygenated blood through the **semilunar aortic valve** to the aorta, which supplies blood to the body tissues. The heart is supplied with blood by means of coronary arteries that branch off from the aorta just above the aortic valve. Arterial blood carries both oxygen and nutrients to body tissues, and these nutrients are exchanged for waste products (e.g., water, carbon dioxide, sodium chloride, nitrogenous salts).

7. Blood from the body is returned to the heart via the network of veins that lead into the superior and interior vena cavae and from the heart via the coronary sinus; at this point the cycle starts again.

---

[2] From the Latin word *corona,* meaning crown, the adjective **coronary** is used to describe any structure that encircles another. In relationship to the heart, broadly speaking, the adjective "coronary" is used to mean "of or relating to the heart" (*Webster's,* 1996). However, as a noun the word "coronary" is often used, in a nontechnical manner, to refer to a heart attack (i.e., a myocardial infarction).

Cardiac Rates and Rhythm

As stated previously, the main pumping action of the heart occurs in the two ventricles. In order to ensure the proper **rate** (speed) and **rhythm** (regularity) of contractions, the heart has its own electrical system that works in combination with the body's nervous and endocrine systems. Electrical impulses, created by the exchange of specific electrolytes, particularly sodium and potassium, travel through a series of **nodes** (masses of cells) and **tracts** (elongated pathways of cells) in the heart to the muscles located in the ventricles and stimulate them to contract. The major node involved in the production of these impulses is the **sinoatrial (SA) node,** which is located in the right atrial wall near the opening of the superior vena cava and is composed of a cluster of hundreds of cells. Within the cluster are a number of specialized cells, referred to as **pacemakers,** which ensure that the heart beats regularly and independently of stimulation from the central nervous system.

Each time the pacemaker cells in the SA node generate an impulse, the atria contract and an impulse is sent on to the **atrioventricular (AV) node,** a bundle of cells located in the septal wall of the right atrium. When these cells "fire," the impulse contracts to the walls of the ventricles. This muscular action, **myocardial contraction,** forces the blood on its route through the body and lungs.

The rate and rhythm of the myocardial contractions, commonly referred to as the individual's "pulse," can easily be measured by **direct palpitation** with fingers, or by **auscultation** with a stethoscope, on a superficial artery. The carotid artery in the neck and the radial artery in the wrist are two common sites for a pulse assessment. At birth the neonate's heart beats about 120 beats per minute (bpm). By the time the child has entered school the rate has slowed down to 100 bpm. The slowing down is caused primarily by the increased weight of the heart. By adolescence, a pulse rate of 70 to 75 bpm is normal. On average, adolescent girls and women have a rate slightly higher than their male counterparts. Rates can be affected by a number of factors, including vigorous activity (e.g., exercise), emotional reactions (e.g., crying), illness, and injury. In some cases the heart may beat too slowly; in others it may beat too fast. In some cases, the rhythm may be irregular.

The term **bradycardia** refers to a condition in which the heart rhythm is regular but the rate is slower than normal (i.e., less than 90 bpm in infants; less than 60 bpm in children). As bradycardia results in decreased cardiac output (i.e., less blood, therefore less oxygen, traveling throughout the body), faintness, dizziness, and chest pain are typical. The causes of bradycardia include heart disease, brain tumor, and drug overdose.

The opposite of bradycardia is **tachycardia,** in which the rhythm is regular but the rate is too rapid (i.e., more than 100 bpm) and an increased amount of oxygen is transported to the cells of the body. Most hearts can handle such an increase, but damaged hearts may not be able to sustain the increased workload. Tachycardia typically results from fever, increased exercise, or excessive nervous excitement.

Deviations or irregularities in the rhythm, referred to as **arrhythmias** or **dysrhythmias,** may be the result of a heart defect or surgery which damaged the electrical conduction system. One of the more common abnormalities is **atrial fibrillation,** in which the atria of the heart "quiver" rather than contract normally. As a result of the incomplete contraction, the ventricles do not fill with as much blood as normal, and insufficient blood in the ventricles decreases the amount of blood available to the body. Atrial fibrillation is associated with certain congenital and acquired heart disorders, such as mitral stenosis and rheumatic heart disease, respectively. In most cases, the condition can be treated with drugs (e.g., digitalis).

Some children or young adults with an abnormal heart rhythm, e.g., those with significant bradycardia, may need to have an electrical **cardiac pacemaker** implanted to stimulate the heart to beat regularly. Some pacemakers are temporary, in use until surgery can correct the abnormality. However, if the abnormality cannot be corrected, a permanent pacemaker may be required.

Blood Pressure

The pressure of the blood on the walls of the arteries can be easily measured by a **sphygmomanometer,** more often referred to as a **blood pressure monitor.** Typically the measurement is taken on the upper arm; however, blood pressure can also be easily measured in the upper thigh. Blood pressure is recorded as a ratio, e.g., 120/70 mm Hg (millimeters of mercury). The first number, known as the **systole,** is a measurement of the pressure exerted in the large arteries during the contraction phase of the heartbeat;

the second number, known as the **diastole,** is the pressure recorded during the relaxation phase. As children age there is an increase in the blood pressure recording. The increase results from the increase in size and muscle strength of the heart; pressure peaks at adolescence. For school-age children, the normal systolic pressure is between 84 and 120 mm Hg and the normal diastolic pressure is between 54 and 80 mm Hg. Adolescents should have a systolic pressure of between 94 and 140 mm Hg and a diastolic pressure of between 62 and 88 mm Hg.

A blood pressure reading of higher than 126/82 mm Hg for children under age 12; 142/92 mm Hg for adolescents under age 18; and 140/90 to 160/90 mm Hg in adults is considered to be **hypertension.** The opposite, abnormally low blood pressure, is referred to as **hypotension.**

The Hematologic System: Review of Structure and Function

Blood, the viscous liquid that is pumped by the heart through the various blood vessels, consists of two components: **plasma,** the clear liquid portion of the blood, and **formed elements,** the cellular portions that are "floating" in the plasma. Blood cells are produced in **hematopoietic,** or blood-forming, organs, i.e., the red bone marrow and the organs of the lymphatic system (e.g., the lymph nodes, spleen, thymus, tonsils). The process is known as **hematopoiesis.**

Blood, by definition, is an "organ" of the body, composed of several kinds of tissues that are united to form a special function, and the only organ of the body that exists in a fluid state (Turner, 1991). Average blood volume, at adulthood, is between 5 and 6 liters and comprises about 7% to 8% of the total weight of the body. Blood travels at a speed of about 30 centimeters per second, making a complete circuit in about 20 seconds (*Mosby's,* 1994).

Plasma

The composition of plasma is shown in Figure III.3. The major constituent, 92% by volume, is water. The remaining 8% consists of substances including proteins, metabolites, and ions.

Plasma has several main functions, the main one being to contribute to the maintenance of

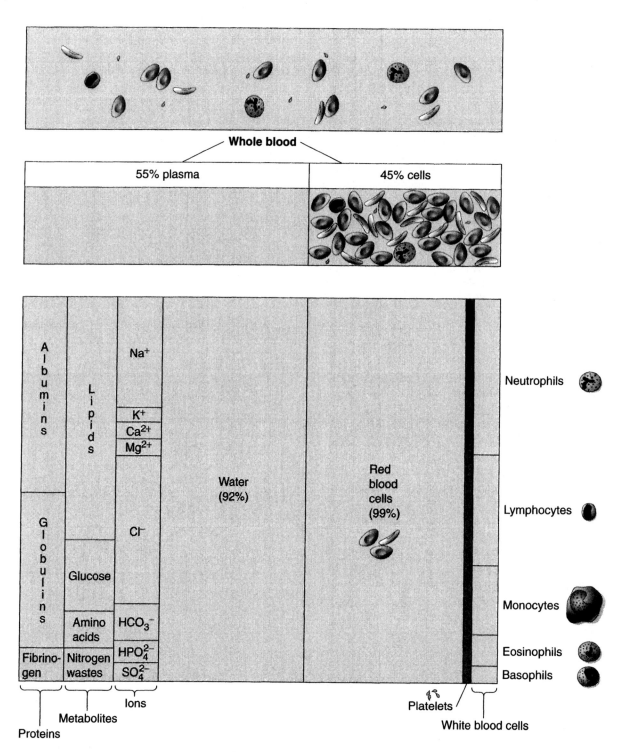

Figure III.3
The Composition of Whole Blood
Source: Adapted from Martini, 1992, p. 607.

homeostasis, the state of relative constancy in the internal environment of the body and its tissues (*Mosby's*, 1994), which is achieved by: (a) conveyance of blood cells through the system; (b) the transport of nutrients required by the cells; (c) maintenance of the acid-base balance of the body; and (d) removal of wastes from cells to excretory organs.

Formed Elements The major cells of the blood are **red blood cells, white blood cells,** and **platelets.** These cells make up 45% to 50% of the blood.

Red blood cells (RBCs). Also known as **erythrocytes,** RBCs are the major cellular element of the blood, making up about 99% of the total cells and giving blood its color. Red blood cells, biconcave or disk-shaped in appearance, function primarily in the transportation of oxygen and carbon dioxide between body tissues and the lungs. The most important component of the erythrocyte is **hemoglobin** (Hb), a compound that is made up of an iron-containing pigment, known as **heme,** and a protein, known as **globin.** Each erythrocyte has between 200 and 300 molecules of hemoglobin within its walls.

In the lungs, where the concentration of oxygen is high, hemoglobin has the capacity to bind with oxygen to form **oxyhemoglobin.** As the blood travels to areas where oxygen is scarce, such as peripheral tissues, the oxygen is released from oxyhemoglobin and is replaced by carbon dioxide, forming **carboxyhemoglobin.** In the lungs, carboxyhemoglobin releases carbon dioxide, picks up more oxygen, and the cycle begins again. Blood that is low in oxygen is dark blue-red, compared with oxygenated blood, which is bright red.

Erythrocytes are produced in the bone marrow of the long bones, by means of a process known as **erythropoiesis.** Each cell lives approximately 120 days before being destroyed, which occurs primarily in the liver and spleen. Approximately 1% of the body's red blood cells are replaced each day. At birth, a full-term infant has between 4.8 and 7.1 million red blood cells per cubic millimeter (mm^3) of blood. By age 6, the average number has dropped slightly to between 3.8 and 5.5 million/mm^3. In adolescence and adulthood, females have fewer red blood cells (4.2 to 5.4 million/mm^3) than males (4.7 to 6.1 million/mm^3). Consequently, women have less hemoglobin in their blood (between 12 and 16 grams per deciliter) compared with men (14

to 18 g/dl). Young children typically have between 11 and 16 g/dl of fluid.

Since the primary role of RBCs is to carry oxygen, persons who live at high altitudes where the amount of atmospheric oxygen is lower than at sea level need to produce more RBCs to compensate. If such individuals do not produce more erythrocytes, they would be susceptible to developing **altitude anoxia,** a condition in which the cells of the body are deprived of oxygen. Some individuals, those who engage in activities at high altitudes, such as mountain climbers or pilots who fly in unpressurized aircraft, can develop a temporary form of altitude anoxia, known as **altitude sickness,** or **acute mountain sickness.** This illness, characterized by dizziness, headache, difficulty breathing, irritability, and in some cases, euphoria, can be serious in older persons, particularly those who have respiratory or cardiac disease. Treatment typically involves the administration of oxygen and the return to a lower altitude. If a person living at high altitude produces too many erythrocytes, the blood can become thick and "sluggish," a condition referred to as **polycythemia vera.** A person with chronic altitude sickness is said to have **Monge's disease.** Polycythemia can also by caused by certain types of lung or heart disease and can result in enlargement of the liver (hepatomegaly) and spleen (splenomegaly).

White blood cells (WBCs). Also known as **leukocytes,** WBCs are a major part of the body's defense against infections. WBCs function primarily as **phagocytes** or "eaters" of microorganisms such as bacteria, fungi, and viruses, as well as other foreign cells, such as the products of cellular breakdown. White blood cells also function in the detoxification of substances that are damaging to the system (i.e., toxic proteins) that result from allergic reactions and injuries of the cellular tissues.

There are five different types of white blood cells, categorized on the basis of whether or not they contain granular substances within the cell structures. **Granulocytes** include **neutrophils, eosinophils,** and **basophils. Agranulocytes,** non-granular WBCs, include **monocytes** and **lymphocytes.** Leukocytes are very small, between 8 and 20 microns (μm), or micrometers,[3] in diameter; consequently, they are able to move readily through intracellular spaces.

---

[3] One micron is one millionth of a meter.

Neutrophils are the most common white blood cell, comprising between 55% and 70% of all white cells in the blood. The second most common WBCs are lymphocytes (20% to 40%). In decreasing order of number are monocytes (2% to 8%), eosinophils (1% to 4%), and basophils (.5% to 1%). White blood cells can live from a few days to several years.

Depending on the type of white blood cell, leukocytes are formed in the lymph nodes, spleen, tonsils, thymus, bone marrow, gastrointestinal tract, or liver. In a newborn, there are between 9,000 and 30,000 white blood cells/mm^3 of blood. This number drops to between 6,000 and 17,000/mm^3 by age 2. For children over age 2, adolescents, and adults the normal count is between 5,000 and 10,000 leukocytes/mm^3. In situations where the body needs more white blood cells, e.g., to fight off an infection, the number can increase substantially.[4]

Platelets. Also known as **thrombocytes,** platelets are the smallest blood cells. Somewhat similar in shape to erythrocytes, platelets differ in that they do not contain any hemoglobin. Platelets have one primary role, to assist in the clotting of blood, a process known as **coagulation.**

In order for bleeding to stop when the wall of a blood vessel is damaged, platelets must release a vasoconstrictive agent, known as **serotonin,** that causes a blood vessel to "shrink" in diameter at the site of the tear or rupture. This process serves to slow the degree of bleeding and ensures that the next two steps can occur. Secondly, the platelets must adhere to the inner surface of the blood vessel at the site of damage, eventually forming a temporary plug, known as a **platelet plug,** that assists in stopping the flow of the blood from the wound. Fi-

nally, the platelets must release some of the plasma proteins, known as **coagulation factors,**[5] which interact with other substances in the platelet plug (e.g., calcium) to form a permanent clot, known as a **fibrin clot.** If any of these processes are abnormal in any manner, the person is said to have a **bleeding disorder,** the most common one being hemophilia. The term **hemorrhage** refers to any major loss of blood that occurs over a relatively short period of time. Persons with bleeding disorders are sometimes referred to as having a **hemorrhagic disorder.** The term **hemostasis** is used to refer to the various processes described above that result in hemorrhage being prevented.

The life span of a platelet is approximately 8 to 10 days. Throughout a person's lifetime, it is normal to have approximately 200,000 to 400,000 platelets per mm^3 of blood, regardless of age.

References

Bricker, J. T., & McNamara, D. G. (1983). Heart disorders. In J. Umbreit (Ed.), *Physical disabilities and health impairments: An introduction* (pp. 222-232). New York: Merrill.

Dowling, C. G. (1997, February). Body voyage. *Life,* 33–81.

Martini, F. (1995). *Fundamentals of anatomy and physiology.* (3rd ed.). Upper Saddle River, NJ: Prentice-Hall.

Mosby's medical, nursing, and allied health dictionary (4th ed.). (1994). St. Louis: Mosby.

Newacheck, P. W., & Taylor, W. R. (1992). Childhood chronic illness: Prevalence, severity, and impact. *American Journal of Public Health, 82,* 364–371.

Sparacino, P. S. A. (1994). Adult congenital heart disease: An emerging population. *Nursing Clinics of North America, 29,* 213–219.

Turner, P. J. (1991). Care of the patient with a cardiovascular or blood disorder. In B. L. Christensen & E. D. Kockrow (Eds.), *Foundations of nursing* (pp. 702–765). St. Louis: Mosby.

Webster's new complete medical dictionary (1996). New York: Smithmark.

---

[4] See part IX for further discussion of the body's immune system and the role of WBCs in fighting infection.

[5] There are 13 coagulation factors, each identified by a Roman numeral (e.g., factor I to factor XIII). All 13 plasma proteins are necessary to ensure that bleeding is not excessive.

Cardiovascular Disorders

Cardiovascular disorders in children and young adults can be divided into two subgroups—congenital and acquired. **Congenital heart disease** (CHD) is defined as any "structural or functional heart disease that is present at birth, even if it is discovered much later" (Hoffman, 1990, p. 25); **acquired heart disorders** (AHD) are "disease processes or abnormalities that occur after birth and can be seen in the normal heart or in the presence of congenital heart defects" (Whaley & Wong, 1995, p. 1494).

While age at onset is the major difference between congenital and acquired conditions, there is often difference in terms of the *type* of abnormality. In CHD, the heart itself is usually damaged, but in acquired cardiac disorders the coronary arteries are typically affected.

Often the first sign of a congenital heart defect is a cardiac **murmur,** an abnormal sound that is detected by auscultatory examination of the heart. Different types of murmurs distinguish one type of defect from another. Further investigation of the condition generally involves diagnostic tests and the measurement of pulse and blood pressure. One of the most common tests, used to diagnose both CHD and AHD, is the **electrocardiogram (ECG),** which measures the electrical activity of the heart and is used to recognize abnormal situations, such as irregularities of rhythm. Other tests commonly used in diagnosis include **echocardiography,** in which ultrasound is used to determine the structure of the cardiac chamber; the **stress test,** a measure of heart functioning during exercise; and **cardiac catheterization,** in which dye is injected into the various chambers of the heart so that the structure can be visible by means of x-ray film.

Incidence and Prevalence

Even though there is an abundance of information on the number of children born with a heart abnormality, the accuracy of the statistics that are commonly cited are often in dispute. Incidence and prevalence figures are difficult to establish for a variety of factors, including the proficiency of physicians who diagnose such conditions, the availability of new diagnostic tools required for an accurate assessment, and the accessibility of trained physicians to the population in question (Hoffman, 1990; Roy et al., 1994). The available figures probably underestimate the numbers of children with CHD, particu-

larly since children who are aborted spontaneously, who are stillborn, or who die within the first week of life as a result of CHD are not routinely reported in the incidence figures (Hoffman, 1990).

In reviewing studies of children born between 1946 and 1983, Hoffman (1990) reported the incidence rates of CHD to be between 4.05 and 10.2 per 1,000 infants born alive. However, the author cautioned that the figures reported may be underestimates of the true incidence, since several of the studies reviewed only reported gross structural malformations in infants and others did not take into account those conditions, even though congenital in nature, that were not detected during the short follow-up period after birth, during which such abnormalities are normally reported. While there are more than 35 well-recognized congenital heart defects, Hoffman found that nine defects accounted for approximately 80% of all congenital heart diseases. Ventricular septal defects, the most commonly occurring lesions, are found in 30% to 40% of all children with CHD. The nine conditions identified by Hoffman are described in greater detail in the following sections. The estimated occurrence for each type of defect is shown in Table 8.1.

While the exact incidence of AHD is unknown, it may occur less than one-tenth as often as CHD (Daberkow, 1989).

TABLE 8.1
Estimated Occurrence of Various Cardiac Defects

Defect	Incidence
Ventricular septal defects	1 in 400 live births
Patent ductus arteriosus	1 in 830 live births
Atrial septal defects	1 in 1,000 live births
Pulmonary valve stenosis	1 in 1,000 live births
Coarctation of the aorta	1 in 1,000 live births
Tetralogy of Fallot	1 in 1,000 live births
Aortic valve stenosis	1 in 2,000 live births
Transportation of the great arteries	1 in 2,000 live births
Atrioventricular septal defects	1 in 2,500 live births

Source: Bricker, J. T., & McNamara, D. G. (1983). Heart disorders. In J. Umbreit (Ed.), *Physical disabilities and health impairments: An introduction* (pp. 222–232). New York: Merrill. Copyright 1983 by Macmillan Publishing Company. Reprinted by permission.

❦ Congenital Heart Disease (CHD)

The birth of a child with heart disease is often devastating to families. Jackson and Saunders (1993) perhaps best expressed the feeling of families faced with the knowledge that their child has a heart problem:

> The inherent symbolism of the heart makes the diagnosis of heart disease in children particularly difficult for families. The heart is seen not only as a pump but also the center of life, love, and feelings. Even a relatively simple, asymptomatic problem may stimulate greater fear and concern than a more life-threatening problem in another part of the body. (p. 1009)

There are many different types of congenital heart defects with a wide range of both *severity* and *prognosis*. The assumption that a child with heart defect always has a poor prognosis (i.e., life-threatening) is a faulty one. Such an assumption can, unfortunately, lead to overprotectiveness by others and may result in the student developing a sense of helplessness (Heller, Alberto, Forney, & Schwartzman, 1996).

Etiology

It has been estimated that 90% of CHD cases are a result of **multifactorial inheritance** (i.e., both genetic and environmental factors are involved). In the case of CHD, during the first 2 months of pregnancy, when the heart and major blood vessels are developing, genetic factors such as CHD in one or both parents interact with one or more **environmental triggers** (Daberkow, 1989) to cause the defect. Known environmental triggers include the following: (a) maternal ingestion of drugs, both therapeutic (e.g., antiepileptic drugs) and recreational (e.g., alcohol); (b) maternal infections during pregnancy, such as German measles or rubella, and cytomegalovirus; and (c) maternal conditions and diseases during pregnancy, such as diabetes, lupus erythematosus, and phenylketonuria. Other possible environmental triggers include radiation, pollution, and pesticides.

Approximately 8% of CHD cases are attributed to **chromosomal abnormalities,** the most common being trisomy 21, the causative factor of Down syndrome. Two percent of CHD cases are caused by environmental factors alone (i.e., without a genetic predisposition).

Classification

Traditionally, CHD has been divided into two main groups on the basis of altered **hemodynamics** (blood flow) *and* the **potential complications** that result from the altered flow. In this system, CHD was divided on the basis of the presence or absence of **cyanosis,** the bluish or purplish discoloration of the skin and mucous membranes that results from the lack of oxygen in the arterial blood (hypoxemia), which in turn, results in inadequate oxygen in the cells (hypoxia). However, characterization of CHD on the basis of presence or absence of cyanosis is problematic, because some children with acyanotic defects (i.e., those without cyanosis) do, in fact, develop cyanosis as a result of their disorder (Whaley & Wong, 1995).

Using hemodynamic characteristics *alone,* a second system, now more commonly used than the first, divides CHD into four groups: (1) conditions that result in increased pulmonary blood flow; (2) those with decreased pulmonary blood flow; (3) those in which there is an obstruction in the flow of blood out of the heart; and (4) those that result in a mixing of oxygenated and deoxygenated blood, known as mixed flow defects.

❦ Defects Characterized by Increased Pulmonary Blood Flow

Congenital heart defects that result in increased pulmonary blood flow also result in a corresponding decreased systemic blood flow, i.e., too much blood travels to the lungs while not enough travels to the body. Typically, an abnormal opening, called a **left-to-right shunt** (i.e., from the left side of the heart to the right side) is the underlying cause of the problem. Because the metabolic demands of the tissues of the body are not met in an individual with this condition, **congestive heart failure (CHF)** often develops, a condition that, if left untreated, as the name suggests, can result in death. The child with CHF usually shows a variety of symptoms, most commonly those related to impaired myocardial functioning, increased pulmonary congestion, and systemic venous congestion (Table 8.2).

There are four common defects that result in left-to-right shunt; each is described briefly below.

TABLE 8.2
Symptoms and Signs of Congestive Heart Failure

IMPAIRED MYOCARDIAL FUNCTIONING
- Increased heart rate even during sleep
- Sweating
- Fatigue
- Weakness
- Restlessness
- Loss of appetite
- Pale or cool hands and feet

INCREASED PULMONARY CONGESTION
- Increased respiratory rate
- Shortness of breath
- Decreased exercise tolerance
- Wheezing
- Coughing
- Hoarseness

SYSTEMIC VENOUS CONGESTION
- Weight gain
- Edema
- Distended neck and peripheral veins

Ventricular Septal Defects (VSDs)

Ventricular septal defects are abnormal communications (or "holes") between the left and right ventricles (Figure 8.1), which result in some of the previously oxygenated blood being shunted from the left ventricle into the right ventricle rather than into the aorta. As a result the blood, which is already rich in oxygen, is reoxygenated via the pulmonary circulation rather than traveling to the body tissues, where it would normally release the oxygen that is needed. The flow in the heart is always from left to right because the walls of the left side are thicker and more pressure is exerted on the left chamber and its contents. The increased amount of blood entering into the pulmonary circulation system causes more blood to return to the left atrium and ventricle, resulting, in some cases, in the thickening or enlargement of the left side of the heart, referred to as either **atrial** or **ventricular hypertrophy,** depending on the site of the enlargement.

The severity of VSD symptoms is related to the number and size of openings, the amount of blood that flows through the opening, the amount of resistance found in the pulmonary arteries, and the age of the child. Many newborns and young infants with VSD experience feeding difficulties that lead to a condition known as **failure to thrive,** in which growth is inadequate because of an inability to obtain and use calories. Frequent respiratory infections and increased fatigue are also common.

Many small septal defects close spontaneously during the first few years of life; others (both small and large) must be corrected surgically to treat shortness of breath. The surgery is usually performed between ages 1 and 4. Prognosis is variable, depending on the severity of the condition and the presence of additional cardiac disorders. If repair is completed before the left side of the heart becomes excessively enlarged, the long-term outlook is excellent. Unfortunately, in children with very large VSDs, advanced obstructive pulmonary vascular disease may develop.

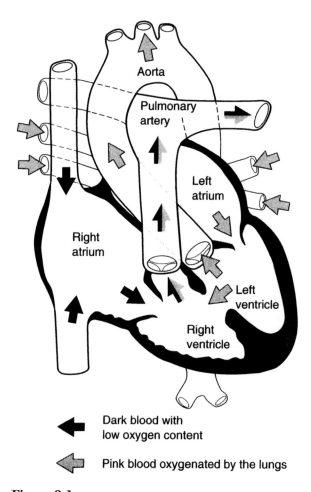

Figure 8.1
Ventricular Septal Defect
Source: Adapted from Bricker and McNamara, 1983, p. 225.

Known as **Eisenmenger's syndrome,** this irreversibly damages the pulmonary vessels. Such children may be candidates for a heart-lung transplant. VSDs are often found in association with other abnormalities, such as the transportation of the great arteries, coarctation of the aorta, and patent ductus arteriosus. VSDs are also commonly found in children with Down syndrome and those with fetal alcohol syndrome. VSDs occur in both sexes in equal numbers.

Patent Ductus Arteriosus (PDA)

Patent ductus arteriosus occurs when the normal muscular structures connecting the pulmonary artery and the descending aorta fail to close completely after birth (Figure 8.2). PDA is not really a "heart" defect, because there is no malformation of the heart. In children with PDA a blood vessel that would normally close shortly after birth remains open.[1] As a consequence of this condition, oxygenated blood from the aorta flows into the left pulmonary artery, resulting in an excessive volume of blood flowing through the lungs and into the left cardiac structures.

If the opening is small, the child with PDA may be asymptomatic. If the opening is large, respiratory infections are common and the child may show signs of congestive heart failure. Surgical correction is usually done between ages 1 and 2. The prognosis for children with PDA closure is excellent. PDAs are more common in premature babies but can also occur in full-term infants. This type of defect is more common in females than in males and in children whose mothers live at high altitudes. PDA is also seen in children whose mothers had rubella during their pregnancy and in children with Down syndrome.

Atrial Septal Defects (ASDs)

Atrial septal defects are abnormal holes in the atrial septum, the wall between the receiving chambers of the heart (Figure 8.3). Holes may occur in the central

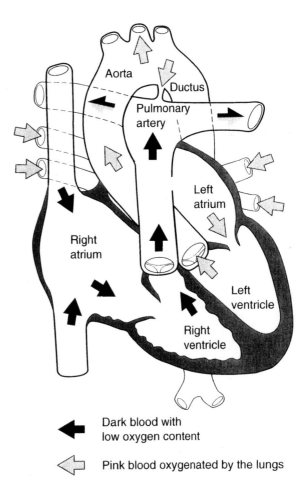

Figure 8.2
Patent Ductus Arteriosus
Source: Adapted from Bricker and McNamara, 1983, p. 225.

---

portion of the septum, lower down next to the mitral valve, or in the upper portion near the superior vena cava. **Ostium secundum defects,** those occurring in the central portion of the septum, are the most common form, accounting for approximately 8% of all cases of CHD. Regardless of the location of the ASD, oxygenated blood from the left atrium flows into the right atrium, resulting in an increased workload on the right side of the heart (i.e., right-side enlargement). Fatigue and shortness of breath are problematic. Exercise intolerance is common. More females than males are born with this condition. Many children with ASDs are asymptomatic

Some ASDs close spontaneously. Surgery, if required, is generally performed when the child is between ages 2 and 6 in order to prevent the development of congestive heart failure and pulmonary vascular disease. In more serious cases, repair may be

---

[1] Prior to being born, the developing fetus obtains its oxygen from its mother; consequently, it is not necessary for the blood to be transported to the lungs for oxygenation. However, at the time of birth, in order for the blood to be oxygenated, it must be transported to the lungs. Such a switch necessitates the closure of a blood vessel known as the **ductus arteriosus** that connects the pulmonary artery to the descending aorta. In most children this occurs within 8 to 72 hours after birth; however, in children with patent ductus arteriosus, the artery remains open (i.e., **patent**) and, as a result, the direction of the blood flow is altered.

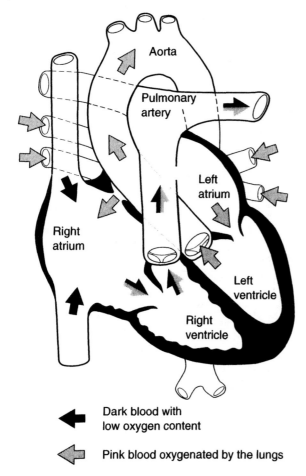

Dark blood with low oxygen content

Pink blood oxygenated by the lungs

Figure 8.3
Atrial Septal Defect
Source: Adapted from Bricker and McNamara, 1983, p. 225.

done at an earlier age. Even relatively minor atrial septal defects in females are usually corrected in order to prevent potential problems that might arise when they become pregnant. After closure, prognosis generally is excellent.

Atrioventricular Septal Defects (AVSDs)

Atrioventricular septal defects, also called **atrioventricular canal (AVC) defects** or **endocardial cushion defects,** are abnormalities of primitive structures of the heart known as the endocardial cushions. The **endocardial cushions** are a pair of tissue sections that develop during the third to fourth week of embryonic development. The cushions eventually merge to form the septum that divides into the various heart chambers and the mitral and tricuspid valves. If the development of the cushions is either arrested or abnormal, a large central hole may develop within the heart (Figure 8.4).

AVSDs are categorized as partial or complete on the basis of the extent of the fusion of the cushions. Alterations in blood flow depend on the size and location of the septal defects, the amount of pulmonary resistance, and the extent of the involvement of the atrioventricular valves. The greater the alteration, the more severe the symptoms. Children with moderate to severe AVSDs often show signs of cyanosis and congestive heart failure and experience recurrent pneumonia.

Surgical repair is often performed before the child reaches age two. Many of the children require continued cardiac follow-up, and some may require additional surgery later in life. Most children with AVSDs are able to live normal, active lives with proper treatment. AVSDs are often found in children with Down syndrome.

❧ Defects Characterized by Decreased Pulmonary Blood Flow

In CHDs that result in decreased pulmonary blood flow, some type of obstruction does not allow blood to exit the right side of the heart via the pulmonary artery and travel to the lungs. Because of the blockage, the pressure in the right side of the heart is greater than in the left side, thus allowing blood with an insufficient level of oxygen to travel from the right side to the left side (i.e., **right-to-left shunt**) and into the systemic circulatory system. Without adequate oxygenation, the body tissues become hypoxemic and cyanotic. The most common right-to-left abnormality is the tetralogy of Fallot.

Tetralogy of Fallot (TOF)

Tetralogy of Fallot involves four different cardiac abnormalities and is named after the French physician Etienne-Louis A. Fallot, who first identified these concurrent abnormalities (Figure 8.5).

The majority of the problems encountered by a person with TOF, sometimes called "tet," are caused by a narrowing at the entrance to the pulmonary artery, a condition known as **pulmonary stenosis.** The obstruction results in less blood being oxygenated and less oxygen being carried to the body tissues; therefore, the child becomes increasingly

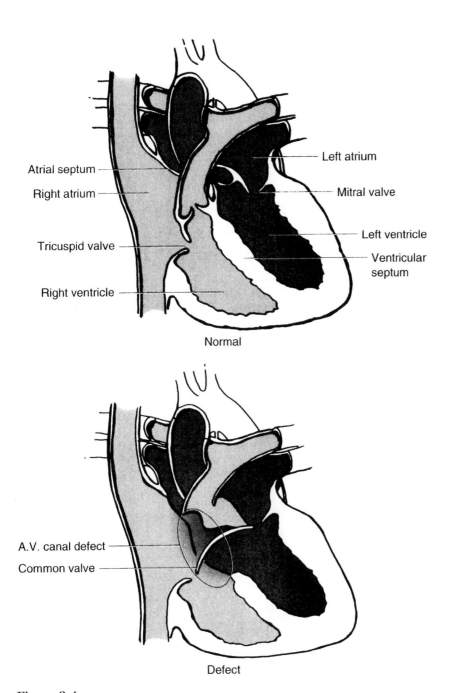

Figure 8.4
Atrioventricular Defects
Source: Adapted from American Heart Association, 1991, p. 26.

cyanotic with age. The other three defects that constitute TOF include (1) a ventricular septal defect, (2) a malpositioning of the aorta over the defect, and (3) an enlargement of the right ventricle muscle that results from overpumping caused by the stenosis. There is a great variety of symptoms among children with TOF. Some children, referred to as **"pink tets"** because of the lack of cyanosis, have little or no right-to-left shunt; others, with massive obstructions, referred to as **"blue tets,"** may be extremely cyanotic at birth and need immediate surgical intervention to correct the abnormality. Most

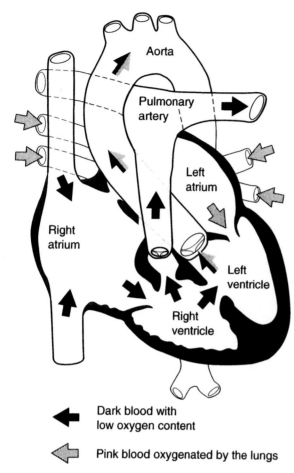

Figure 8.5
Tetralogy of Fallot
Source: Adapted from Bricker and McNamara, 1983, p. 226.

infants are mildly cyanotic and experience increased cyanosis (**"tet spells"**) only with crying or with some other type of physical exertion (e.g., a bowel movement).

Most cases of TOF are repaired within the first few years of life. Prognosis after surgical intervention has steadily improved over the years. Many children with TOF have excellent cardiovascular functioning through childhood and into adulthood.

Obstructive Disorders

Children with this disorder have some type of anatomic narrowing (i.e., stenosis), typically near a valve, that prevents the blood from exiting the heart in a normal manner. There are three major types of obstructive disorders, the most common being pulmonary stenosis, the others are coarctation of the aorta and aortic stenosis. Typically, the narrowing caused by the defect results in an increased pressure load on the ventricle, which in turn results in left ventricle enlargement and decreased cardiac output. Children with obstructive disorders often show signs of congestive heart failure; however, some children may be asymptomatic.

Pulmonary Stenosis (PS)

Pulmonary stenosis, as stated previously, refers to a narrowing at the entrance to the pulmonary artery, which results in less blood flowing to the lungs to be oxygenated (Figure 8.6). If a deformity of the valve is the reason for the narrowing, the condition is

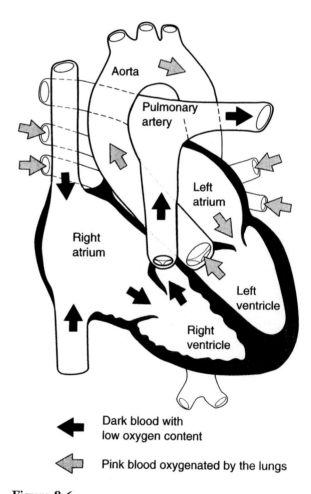

Figure 8.6
Pulmonary Stenosis
Source: Adapted from Bricker and McNamara, 1983, p. 229.

referred to as **pulmonary valve stenosis.** In extreme cases, no blood flows to the lungs at all.

As a result of the narrowing, the pressure in the right ventricle becomes elevated, and the ventricle hypertrophies and, in some cases, fails. Most children with PS typically experience shortness of breath, an increase in respiratory rate, and a rapid pulse. Fatigue, especially upon exertion, is often a major concern. Pulmonary stenosis is often associated with other cardiac abnormalities, such as tetralogy of Fallot, atrioventricular canal defects, and ventricular septal defects. PS is also found in children whose mothers contracted rubella during pregnancy.

Children with mild pulmonary stenosis may not need surgical intervention. Some, however, require an operation to open the obstruction. Many children with stenotic pulmonary arteries or valves can be treated successfully by a form of surgery that is less invasive than most conventional surgical procedures. The procedures are **balloon angioplasty** and **balloon valvuloplasty.** Rather than the heart being opened surgically, a **catheter** is inserted into a large vein and threaded carefully through the vessel until it reaches the heart. Once in the correct position, the "balloon" in the tip of the catheter is inflated to dilate the stenotic artery (angioplasty) or valve (valvuloplasty). In most cases, the prognosis is excellent. To be deemed successful there must be no significant incidence of restenosis or any significant backward flow of blood through the treated heart valve.

Coarctation of the Aorta (COA)

Coarctation of the aorta refers to a narrowing of the aorta, the main trunk of the systemic arterial circulation (Figure 8.7), ranging from a mild constriction to total occlusion. As a result of the blockage, blood flow to the lower part of the body is decreased, and the child may complain of weakness or cramping in the legs with exercise, or cold feet. As a result of the narrowing, the heart must work harder to pump blood through the vessel. The greater the narrowing, the greater the workload and possibility of serious cardiac complications.

Some children with mild constriction are asymptomatic, and the condition is detected only during routine physical examination in later childhood. Diagnosis of COA is usually based on the difference in blood pressure between the lower and the upper extremities and absent or diminished pulses in the legs and feet. Those with more acute symptoms may ex-

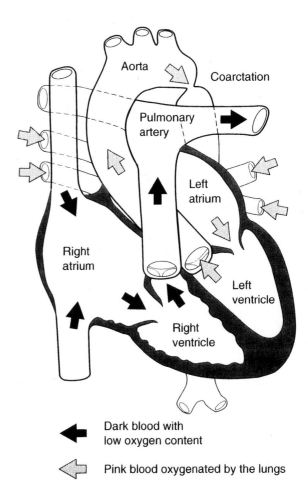

Figure 8.7
Coarctation of the Aorta
Source: Adapted from Bricker and McNamara, 1983, p. 229.

perience respiratory distress, increased heart rate, lack of weight gain, feeding problems, headaches, dizziness, and irritability. In some cases, this abnormality occurs in combination with other cardiovascular malformations. It occurs more frequently in males than in females. Surgery is usually performed between ages 2 and 5. If the situation is severe, surgery is performed sooner, often on an urgent basis.

Aortic Stenosis (AS)

Aortic stenosis refers to a narrowing of the aortic valve as a result of malformation during fetal development (Figure 8.8). The most common form is **aortic valve stenosis,** in which the child has a bicuspid rather than a tricuspid valve from the left

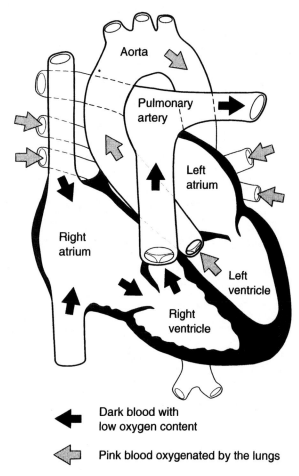

Figure 8.8
Aortic Stenosis
Source: Adapted from Bricker and McNamara, 1983, p. 228.

ventricle into the aorta. Depending on the degree of narrowing, the child may or may not show symptoms of cardiac distress. Children with a mild degree of stenosis may be asymptomatic; more severe forms are evidenced by fatigue and exercise intolerance.

Children with mild forms of AS need to be monitored carefully because the condition can be progressive; more severe cases need surgical correction. Success depends on the extent to which the reconstruction can be achieved; some children need more than one operation. A good quality of life is possible for many children after surgery; however, some may develop problems as adults. AS is found more commonly in males than in females. Not all forms of AS are congenital. The condition may develop in older children without CHD and adults who have no known heart defect as a result of rheumatic fever or

from progressive atherosclerotic disease, or "hardening of the arteries," a condition that is particularly common in people who have diabetes.

Defects That Result in Mixed Blood Flow

Mixed defects are those in which saturated and desaturated blood mix and can occur either in the heart or in the major coronary arteries.

Transposition of the Great Arteries (TGA)

In transposition of the great arteries, the most common mixed defect, the pulmonary artery exits from the left ventricle rather than the right and the aorta exits from the right ventricle rather than the left (Figure 8.9). As a result of this abnormality, the child has two independent and parallel circulatory systems, one in which oxygenated blood recirculates through the pulmonary system and one in which deoxygenated blood recirculates through the systemic system. For the child to survive, other defects that produce mixing of oxygenated and deoxygenated blood, such as septal defects or patent ductus arteriosus, must also be present. However, even with some mixing, a decreased amount of oxygen circulates to the tissues and the infant shows signs of cyanosis. The extent of the cyanosis depends on the degree of mixing between the two systems.

Surgical intervention is required in all cases of TGA or the child will die. Initial surgery often occurs within the first month of life; additional surgery may be needed before age one. Children with TGA require close cardiac follow-up throughout life.

Acquired Cardiac Disorders (ACDs)

Acquired cardiac disorders, also referred to collectively as **acquired heart disease (AHD),** may occur anytime during childhood or adulthood. Even though the exact incidence and prevalence figures are not available, AHD is less common in children than in adults (Bricker & McNamara, 1983). The factors that contribute to AHD occur individually or in combination and include infection, autoimmune

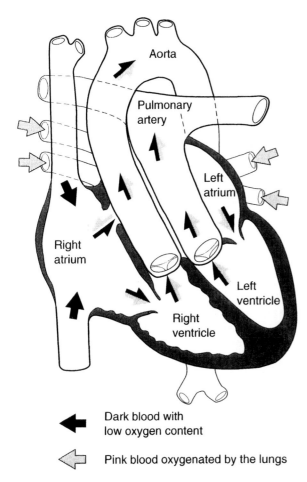

Figure 8.9
Transposition of the Great Arteries
Source: Adapted from Bricker and McNamara, 1983, p. 226.

responses, environmental factors, and familial tendencies (Whaley & Wong, 1995). The three most common causes of AHD in children are Kawasaki syndrome, rheumatic fever, and bacterial endocarditis.

Kawasaki Disease (KD)

Also known as **mucocutaneous lymph node syndrome (MLNS),** Kawasaki disease is reported to be the most common cause of AHD in young children, occurring at a rate of 6 to 8 per 1,000,000. Its incidence is believed to be on the rise (Lux, 1991). Kawasaki disease is most common in children of Japanese or Asian descent; however, it has been found in all racial groups. Males are more prone to KD than females, and it is more common in children

of higher socioeconomic backgrounds than lower. KD occurs most often in children under age 5, and it is rarely found in children over age 10.

Kawasaki disease is recognized as a combination of symptoms, including an unexplained fever, a rash on the trunk, bloodshot eyes, lymph node enlargement, changes to the mouth (e.g., "strawberry" tongue and dry, red, cracked lips), reddened palms or soles, and desquamation (peeling of skin) from the fingertips or toes. Approximately 10 days or more after the initial symptoms occur, acute systemic vasculitis may develop. The blood vessels of the body, both pulmonary and systemic arteries and veins, become inflamed in **vasculitis.** If the coronary arteries become inflamed, the heart muscles may be damaged from lack of blood supply; such complications occur in roughly 20% of cases.

The course of the KD is generally 6 to 8 weeks; it occurs more commonly in late winter and early spring. The cause is unknown; however, transmission is *not* from person to person. Treatment involves the administration of gamma globulin and aspirin to prevent an **aneurysm** (the dilation of a blood vessel wall).

Generally, the prognosis for Kawasaki disease is good, and most children recover fully. However, the long-term consequences of the heart disease are unknown because the disease has only been recognized since it was first described by Kawasaki in 1967. All children require continued follow-up because of the chance that cardiac problems may occur long after the acute phase of the disease. Parents and teachers should be vigilant for signs of cardiac complications, such as shortness of breath, cyanosis, chest pain, and periods of decreased activity level. As a result of the cardiac complications, children with Kawasaki disease may be at risk for **myocardial infarction.** Although this is rare, education staff should be trained in CPR.

Acute Rheumatic Fever (ARF)

Acute rheumatic fever is an inflammatory disease that usually develops as a result of a delayed reaction to an inadequately treated **group A beta-hemolytic streptococcal infection** of the upper respiratory tract, commonly referred to as "strep" throat. In some cases, the symptoms may be so mild as to go unnoticed, undiagnosed, and, consequently, untreated (Freund, Scacco-Neumann, Pisanelli, & Benchot, 1993).

ARF is considered to be the most common cause of AHD in the world, particularly for children living in underdeveloped countries where poor standards of living, overcrowding, poor hygiene, and malnutrition are all too common. Zabriskie (1985) has estimated that there are more than 5 million new cases of ARF worldwide annually. Interestingly, although in developed countries the incidence of ARF has been thought to be on the decline as a result of improved treatment and standards of living, small outbreaks of ARF in the United States occurring more often than usual have prompted the belief that there is a new virulent strain of streptococci. Many of the more recent cases have *not* been found exclusively in socioeconomically depressed populations; rather, many of the cases have been in white children living in suburban areas with parents who were employed and had adequate health insurance. The exact incidence of ARF in the United States is unknown; however, the commonly cited statistic of less than 1 case per 100,000 children may be an underestimate of its true occurrence (Freund et al., 1993). ARF is found most frequently in children between ages 6 and 15.

Cardiac complications develop in about 50% of children with rheumatic fever within 2 weeks of the onset of acute fever (Olson & Hazinski, 1990). Carditis is common. In some cases, permanent valve damage occurs and congestive heart failure (CHF) develops. Signs and symptoms of cardiac involvement include shortness of breath during periods of exertion; edema of the face, abdomen, or ankles; and pain in the chest wall in the area above the heart (Freund et al., 1993). Diagnosis is often made by detection of a heart murmur that results from the inability of the involved valves to close adequately. ARF not only affects the cardiovascular system but also can involve the joints, in particular the knees, elbows, hips, shoulders, and wrists; the central nervous system (e.g., brain); the skin; and connective tissues (e.g., cartilage). The most common presenting complaint is polyarticular arthritis, a condition that results in tenderness of the joints. Arthritis develops in about 75% of children with ARF (Freund et. al., 1993).

While ARF itself is not contagious, the underlying streptococcal infection that leads to ARF is. In places where there is close contact between people (e.g., classrooms), the likelihood of streptococcal disease increases. Teachers should be aware of how communicable diseases are spread and try to minimize exposure, particularly among those who have a history of strep conditions.

Rheumatic fever is treated with antibiotics and anti-inflammatory agents (e.g., aspirin, prednisone) and, during the acute phase, bed rest. Some children may be absent for only a few days; others may be at home for several weeks. In extreme cases, a child may be inactive for as long as 3 months. Unfortunately, with each recurrence of rheumatic fever the risk of cardiac sequelae increases. Children who have had ARF should, if possible, be protected from persons who might pass on the infection.

Bacterial Endocarditis (BE)

Also referred to as **infective endocarditis,** bacterial endocarditis is an infection of the endocardium or valves caused by bacteria, *Rickettsia* (a genus of microorganisms similar to bacteria), or fungi. Damage to the heart occurs as a result of the microorganism growing on the affected tissues.

BE occurs most often in children who have a history of a congenital or acquired heart lesion and become infected as a result of some type of invasive procedure. Surgery, dental work, urinary catheterization, and certain gynecologic procedures (e.g., implantation of an intrauterine device or a routine Pap smear) are all examples of invasive procedures that can introduce the microorganism. BE may also occur in children who do not have a heart defect.

Often children with bacterial endocarditis have nonspecific symptoms, such as a low-grade, intermittent fever; chills; loss of appetite and weight loss; lethargy and general malaise; headaches; myalgia (diffuse pain in the muscles); and arthralgia (pain in the joints such as knees, elbows and wrists). BE is more common in children over age 10. Treatment for BE consists primarily of the administration of antibiotics (e.g., penicillin, streptomycin) over 3 to 6 weeks. With early treatment the prognosis is generally good; however, if untreated, serious problems may occur. One complication is the development of a **thrombus** (pl. **thrombi**), or blood clot. If the thrombus travels through the circulatory system to the brain, lungs, or kidneys, serious tissue damage may occur.

❧ Acquired Cardiac Disorders of "Adulthood"

Every 33 seconds, in the United States alone, someone dies as a result of cardiovascular disease, making cardiovascular disease, particularly ACD, the leading cause of death. The effects of the disease are estimated to cost the nation $151 billion per year (Dowling, 1997). Two of the most common kinds of cardiovascular disease are systemic hypertension and hyperlipidemia. These two conditions, previously thought to be common only in the adult population, may actually have their early beginnings in childhood. Certain forms of these two conditions are potentially preventable if treated early by modifications to the diet.

Systemic Arterial Hypertension

Commonly referred to as high blood pressure, hypertension is believed to be common in 1 to 2% of children and 11 to 12% of adolescents (Olson & Hazinski, 1990). The African-American male adolescent is at greatest risk for the condition. In children, as in adults, there are two forms: primary and secondary.

Primary (or **essential**) **hypertension** refers to elevated blood pressure that is not attributable to any underlying condition or known cause. As in the case of adult hypertension, the exact cause of primary hypertension is unknown; however, heredity, race, and gender are believed to contribute to the incidence. A high intake of salt and calcium, stress, and obesity are believed to play a role in the development of hypertension. In children, lead poisoning and ingestion of large amounts of licorice may also contribute to the condition developing.

Secondary hypertension, the more commonly found form in infants and children, results from a structural anomaly of the cardiovascular system (e.g., coarctation of the aorta, large patent ductus arteriosus) or some other condition (e.g., a disease of the renal or endocrine system; the use of certain drugs, such as oral contraceptives, amphetamines, or corticosteroids). Typically, secondary hypertension decreases or even disappears when the underlying condition is treated.

Hypertension, the "silent killer," often goes unnoticed, particularly the primary form, because there generally are no symptoms. However, in more serious cases, blurred vision, headaches, dizziness, fatigue, irritability, pain in the abdomen or back, nausea, vomiting, and seizures may be experienced. If untreated, hypertension can result in heart failure, cerebrovascular accidents (i.e., strokes), or kidney failure.

Hypertension, depending on the severity of the condition, may be treated with drugs. However, a nonpharmacologic approach is preferred by many physicians. Encouraging the maintenance of a healthy lifestyle, which includes a regular exercise program and a diet that limits the intake of salt and decreases the likelihood of obesity, is a common way to prevent hypertension. Not smoking and avoiding sources of stress are also encouraged. For female adolescents, alternatives to oral contraceptives are often recommended. Most children with controlled hypertension are able to lead normal lives; however, long-term compliance with the medical regimen is required. As part of the health curriculum, teachers can instill in children the need for a healthy lifestyle to prevent later complications.

Hyperlipidemia

Hyperlipidemia, a general term used to describe excessive lipids (i.e., fat and fatlike substances) in the blood, and **hypercholesterolemia,** a specific term referring to the presence of excessive cholesterol (i.e., a fatlike steroid alcohol) in the blood, are known to contribute to the development of **atherosclerosis,** a condition in which fatty deposits accumulate on the walls of the arteries. Atherosclerosis eventually leads to the development of coronary heart disease. In recent years, research into the possibility that hyperlipidemia, common to adults, exists in children and that it may contribute to the condition developing in adulthood has been conducted. Although no studies have conclusively linked childhood hyperlipidemia and adult heart disease, the National Institutes of Health, the American Heart Association, and the American Academy of Pediatrics have all recommended that children over age 2 have a low-fat, low-cholesterol diet (Whaley & Wong, 1995). A diet which restricts the consumption of "junk" foods, which are typically high in saturated fats, and a program of regular physical exercise are recommended for all children.

🐦 Treatment of Congenital and Acquired Cardiovascular Disorders

Treatment approaches vary considerably from individual to individual based on the nature and severity of the condition. Surgical intervention, pharmacologic treatment, diet management, and prescribed exercise programs are common approaches to ameliorating the symptoms.

Surgical Intervention

Some children undergo simple procedures to correct a minor defect; others require more extensive surgery to correct defects that are more complex. Tong and Sparacino (1994) recently reported that approximately 20,000 open-heart surgeries per year are performed on children with CHD in the United States alone. The prognosis after surgery is, in most cases, excellent. Even though survival to adulthood is considered the norm, many children who have undergone surgical correction need continued follow-up to monitor the consequences of the underlying heart condition (Rosenthal, 1984). For a few individuals with defects that cannot be corrected by means of surgery, or who after the initial surgery continue to have severe residual cardiac disease, **transplantation** may be the only treatment that will result in continued life. Bernstein, Starnes, and Baum (1990), in discussing the increasing acceptance of cardiac transplantation for children as a form of treatment, reported that the quality of life for those who have received a transplant is, in most cases, excellent. For example, the researchers cited cases where the recipients of heart transplants had returned to school, held regular jobs after graduation, participated in noncompetitive and competitive sports or other age-appropriate activities with few restrictions, and on the whole, had adjusted well psychologically. The authors predicted that with improvements in diagnosis and treatment of rejection, the prospect of decades-long survival is possible.

Pharmacologic Treatment

For some children pharmacologic treatment is required either as an adjunct to surgery or alone to control the effects of the disorder or disease. Over the years, many drugs have been developed for the treatment of heart problems. The three major classes of cardiac drugs commonly used with children and adults with CHD and AHD are discussed briefly. The drugs are given either singly or in combination, depending on the underlying problem. School staff must know which heart drug(s) the child is receiving, the purpose for which they are given, and any potential side effects.

Drugs That Improve Cardiac Functioning By improving the force of the contraction of the heart, by decreasing the speed at which the heart beats, and by decreasing the buildup of fluid in the tissues by increasing the flow of blood through the kidneys, the first class of drugs improves the overall functioning of the heart. This group of drugs is often given to children who are prone to developing CHF and those who have irregular heart rates. Included in this group are the digitalis glycosides, such as digoxin (Lanoxin), and the newer angiotensin-converting enzyme inhibitors, or ACE inhibitors, such as captopril (Capoten) and enalapril (Vasotec).

Digoxin, from the plant *Digitalis purpurea*, is a cardiac drug that has been used with great success, both with children and with adults. However, it is a potentially dangerous drug, particularly if too much of the drug is given. Signs of digoxin toxicity include nausea, vomiting, loss of appetite, headaches, drowsiness, insomnia, dizziness, visual color distortions, and heart beat abnormalities (e.g., bradycardia). Teachers should be vigilant for signs of digitalis poisoning that may result from the administration of too much of the drug or from the cumulative effects of long-term administration.

ACE inhibitors function by dilating the blood vessels, so that there is less resistance in the systemic circulatory system. Children on ACE inhibitors must be monitored for signs of hypotension (e.g., periods of dizziness or faintness) and renal dysfunction (e.g., sluggishness, fatigue, decreased output of urine). Some children on this type of medication are prone to developing a nagging, noncommunicable cough.

Diuretics The second class of medications, used to decrease edema in the tissues and prevent reaccumulation of fluids, is known as diuretics. There are more than 50 diuretic drugs available, the most common ones used with children being furosemide (Lasix) and chlorothiazide (Diuril). Diuretics are often given in conjunction with drugs that improve cardiac function, particularly in children with CHF. Because diuretics cause increased excretion of urine, in some cases excessive excretion of potassium may occur and the child may need a potassium supplement or a diet that contain foods that are high in potassium (e.g., bananas, oranges, grapefruit, milk, carrots, potatoes). Children on diuretics should be observed for signs of **dehydration,** which is loss of water from the tissues of the body. Typical symptoms include flushed dry skin; dry, coated tongue; decreased urine output; and irritability. Children should be monitored for potential side effects of the drugs (e.g., nausea, vomiting, diarrhea, weakness).

Children on diuretics typically need to use the washroom more frequently than other children.

Vasodilators While the drugs mentioned above improve oxygenation of the body tissues, vasodilators increase the diameter of the blood vessels. By acting on the smooth muscle of the vascular system, these drugs increase cardiac outflow by decreasing the resistance in the systemic circulatory system. One common vasodilator is hydralazine (Apresoline). Teachers should be aware that this drug may cause drowsiness in the child. The most serious side effect of vasodilation is the development of hypotension.

Other Treatment Approaches

In addition to surgical and pharmacologic intervention, many children receive therapeutic **diet** and **exercise regimens.** Fluid restriction and a low-salt diet are two common approaches to decreasing the strain placed on the heart by disease and defect (Heller et al., 1996). Children with heart defects are encouraged to participate in physical activities that will strengthen the heart (American Heart Association, 1991), including swimming, bicycling, running, rope jumping, and tennis.

💘 Early Recognition of Cardiovascular Problems

Teachers who are cognizant of the various symptoms of heart disorders may recognize problems that have gone undetected in children and can provide a vital service by encouraging parents to seek medical evaluation and treatment before serious complications arise. For the child who has returned to school after treatment for a heart condition, an alert teacher may notice changes in the health status of the child either during the course of a day or over time. It is the teacher's duty to inform the child's parents of these observations.

The physical and behavioral changes that are of particular concern are shown in Table 8.3. The signs and symptoms of cardiac distress are child-specific; however, by reviewing the listed questions with the child's parents or physician, teachers will be better able to determine which behaviors and symptoms are abnormal for the child, and which signs, singly or in combination, may indicate a worsening status that requires immediate medical intervention.

💘 Educational Implications and Teaching Tips

Many, if not most, children with altered cardiovascular functioning encounter few problems in returning to school; others need a supportive staff to ensure that they participate to their maximum ability. The needs of the children will vary greatly; however, the following suggestions should be of assistance in planning for the successful re-entry of a child with altered cardiovascular functioning into the school program. The most important consideration for all children with chronic illnesses is to treat the child as normally as possible (i.e., setting consistent limits; maintaining normal standards of discipline) in order to foster independence, particularly since the educational goals and career plans for these children do not differ greatly from those of their peers (Bricker & McNamara, 1983). Overprotecting the child (e.g., excessively isolating the child from peers to prevent infection; preventing the child from engaging in play to avoid overexertion) does not benefit the child and will prevent the child from growing into a competent, healthy, secure adult. By encouraging the child to take responsibility for medical management, recognize the limits on activity level, and comply with prescribed dietary restrictions and medication regimens, parents and teachers can foster the development of independent behavior in the child (Kleinberg, 1982). If children with heart disease are seen as severely limited, handicapped children by those around them, these children may become unnecessarily dependent on others and develop a faulty self-image (Daberkow, 1989).

1 *One of the greatest concerns of teachers is the correct level of physical activity for a student with altered cardiovascular function.* Most educators automatically consider **recreational activities** (e.g., recess, lunch, and after school) and **sports** (i.e., in class and after school), but the daily **physical demands** of school attendance also must be examined (e.g., distance between classes, the number of stairs, physical demands of field trips).

If possible, the student's classes should be scheduled so that classrooms are in close proximity. If the school is not equipped with an elevator, the classroom may have to be located on the ground floor. Some students may need additional time to move

TABLE 8.3

Signs and Symptoms of Cardiac Distress: Questions to Determining Severity

1. **Rapid breathing**
   Is the child tachypneic (i.e., 20 to 40 breaths per minute above normal rate)?
   Is the child showing signs of dyspnea?
   When do the breathing difficulties occur: at rest, on exertion?
   How long do the breathing difficulties last: transient, prolonged?
   Does the tachypnea affect other activities: feeding, playing?

2. **Sweating**
   When does the child show signs of diaphoresis, or profuse perspiration: at rest, upon exertion?
   Is the temperature in the environment contributing to the diaphoresis?
   Does the child have too many clothes on?
   Where does the sweat occur: forehead; nose, upper lip; neck; trunk?
   How long does the sweating last: transient, prolonged?

3. **Behavioral changes**
   What changes have been noticed?
   During feeding, does the child eat or drink less? eat more slowly than usual? start eating well and then suddenly stop? act hungry but will not eat?
   During the waking hours, does the child appear to cry more than usual? want to sleep more than usual? avoid stimulation?
   Is the child listless? irritable? quieter than usual? tired all the time?
   During sleeping have there been changes in the sleeping pattern: more wakeful, sleeping longer than normal?

4. **Periorbital edema** (puffy eyelids)
   When does the edema occur: upon wakening, before medication?
   How long does the edema last: 1 to 2 hours, half the day, all day?
   Is there a decrease in urine output: less trips to the bathroom, fewer diapers to change?

5. **Hypoxia spells** (hypoxic "blue" attacks)
   Does the child assume a squatting position to relieve symptoms? How often? Under what circumstances?
   Is this behavior associated with other symptoms (e.g., cyanosis)?

6. **Cyanosis**
   What color are the skin and extremities? Is the child pale?
   Are the extremities cool to the touch? Do they appear mottled?
   How does the color compare to "normal" for the child?
   What color are the gums, lips, and tongue (pink, gray-pale, blue)?
   When do the cyanotic periods occur: at rest, upon exertion?

7. **Changes in heart rate**
   Is the heart rate unusual for child's age and current activity level?
   Is the child bradycardic or tachycardic?
   How does the child appear: pale, sweaty, or cyanotic?
   How long has the heart rate been irregular: few seconds, 30 minutes?
   How often does it occur: transient, more prolonged?
   If the child is on medication, is there a relationship between changes in heart rate and time medication was given? Was a dose missed? Is the child ready for the next dose?

8. **Other**
   Has the child vomited? Does the child have diarrhea?
   Is the child dehydrated?
   Can the child take prescribed medications?
   Does the child have an unexplained fever? Has the fever occurred after some type of invasive procedure: dental work, catheterization?

Sources: Clare (1985); Pitts-Wilhelm (1992)

from class to class to facilitate resting without excessive time constraints.

The student who has a lot of materials to carry from class to class should have a locker that is close to the homeroom to prevent having to carry a heavy load. Wheeled luggage carriers, small shopping carts, laundry baskets that have wheels attached, and even pieces of luggage that have wheels included in their design may allow the student greater independence. Some may be hesitant to use such devices. The advantage of not having to rely on someone to carry their belongings may outweigh the disadvantages (i.e., the visibility of the apparatus).

In addition to the physical demands of school programs, the number of hours of scheduled activity per day may be problematic. Some students may benefit from a shortened day (e.g., coming late or leaving early). Others may be able to tolerate a full day as long as they have regularly scheduled rest breaks. In some particularly severe cases, a student may require a home-based educational program, either on a temporary or permanent basis.

2 *In terms of recreational activities and sports, it is important to consider not only what the student should not do but to consider what the student can do* (Goldberg, 1990). Freed (1984) stressed the importance of making "recommendations that are neither too strict, so as not to eliminate those who could safely exercise if they were so inclined, nor too loose, so that children with heart disease but with an otherwise good prognosis will not be put in jeopardy" (p. 1310).

The greatest fear of school staff is that the student will have an acute episode of heart distress. **It should be remembered that even with overexertion, the worst consequences are usually fatigue and shortness of breath. Overexertion, except in extremely rare conditions, does not result in a heart attack** (Kleinberg, 1982). However, students with cardiovascular problems should *never* be pressured into participating in any physical activities beyond their capability nor should they be penalized for non-participation. Any alternatives that the student engages in as a substitute for physical activity should be viewed as a positive experience (Daberkow, 1989).

While chest pain is rare in those with cardiac problems, if students encounter any pain upon exertion, they should be allowed to sit down or lie down and rest. In cases where the pain is unexpected (e.g., a first time occurrence) the parents should be notified so that they can seek medical attention. If the pain is a common occurrence, lying down in the nurse's station for a brief period of time may be all that is needed. However, it is important to remember that any student experiencing chest pain should not be left alone in case he or she develops further difficulties. **If the pain worsens, or the student shows increasing signs of distress (e.g., difficulty breathing), call 911.**

3 *Most children and young adults are aware of their own physical limitations, based on how they feel, and generally stop the activity when fatigued.* However, teachers should be aware that certain students, particularly adolescent males, may engage in activities that are contraindicated to "keep up with the crowd" or prove that "everything is OK." In such cases, excessive and persistent activity may be a form of denial that should be carefully monitored (Rengucci, 1990) and reported to the student's parents.

In some students, particularly younger ones, a situation opposite to that mentioned above may occur. Teachers should be alert to those who "use" their heart condition to avoid participating in activities they want to avoid, even though they are capable of participating without any restrictions. Many individuals with heart problems may be afraid of engaging in physical activities, fearing pain or shortness of breath; however, staff should address such concerns.

4 *In 1986, the American Heart Association (AHA) revised its recommendations regarding sporting activities suitable for children and young adults with heart disease* (Gutgesell, Gessner, Vetter, Yabek, & Norton, 1986). Their recommendations are based on the type of lesion, the degree of severity, and the demands of the task. For further information, the reader is referred to that document, as well as the information that the American Academy of Pediatrics, Committee on Sports (AAP, 1995a, 1995b) has provided regarding physical activity levels of children with heartbeat irregularities or with mitral valve prolapse.

Freed (1984) has suggested that recreational and competitive activities should be divided into three categories: (1) **strenuous** (e.g., football, ice hockey, wrestling), (2) **moderately strenuous** (e.g., badminton, curling, golf), and (3) **nonstrenuous** (e.g., archery, bowling, riflery). Based on the degree of strenuousness and of heart disease (e.g., trivial, mild, moderate or severe), decisions should be made on a individual basis. As would be expected, as the degree of heart disease increases, the strenuousness of appropriate physical activity decreases.

Before a child resumes a program of physical activities, the teachers and coaches must discuss limitations with the parents and ask for a written list of acceptable and non-acceptable activities from the cardiologist. A sample form, developed for this purpose by the AHA (Gutgesell et al., 1986) for cardiologists, is found in Appendix D.

Even though the needs of a student with a cardiovascular problem differ significantly from the needs of a student with a respiratory problem, the reader may find some of the suggestions given in chapter 6 for students with asthma to be of assistance. For further detailed information on the cardiovascular response to exercise, exercise limitations for those with cardiovascular disease, and the assessment of activity and exercise tolerance, the reader is also referred to the works of Baas (1991), Goldberg (1990), and Rosenthal (1984).

5 *Children who have pacemakers implanted are a unique group.* Daberkow (1989) has suggested that they should avoid (a) activities that may result in a hard blow to the chest (e.g., wrestling, boxing, football, hockey), (b) movements that involve vigorous up-and-down motion (e.g., trampoline or bungee jumping), and (c) jumping from heights (e.g., trees, fences, obstacle courses). He suggests that vigorous sports (e.g., swimming, running, bicycle riding, baseball) may be allowed in place of contact sports. Additionally he has pointed out that students should be protected from exposure to ungrounded electrical current and from strong electromagnetic or radio waves (e.g., visits to a radio station, power plant) because exposure may result in changes to the pacemaker program and cause a malfunction.

Teachers of students with pacemakers should be aware of signs and symptoms of **pacemaker malfunction,** which include dizziness, fatigue, pallor, syncope (fainting), and a pulse rate of less than the minimum set rate (Daberkow, 1989). **In cases of malfunction, medical personnel should be contacted immediately.**

6 *When a child returns to school, staff may have concerns about health problems that may arise and may need guidance in determining when to contact the parents or medical staff.* O'Brien and Boisvert (1989) have provided a set of guidelines (Table 8.4) for parents that may be of assistance to school staff. The authors have recommended that it is better "to err on the side of caution" and to contact the physician sooner than later. The guidelines

TABLE 8.4
Signs and Symptoms of Illness in Children with Cardiovascular Problems

For children at risk for CHF:
Paler than usual
Increased respiratory rate
Poor feeding
Sweating with feedings
Signs of respiratory distress (such as retractions, grunting, and nasal flaring)
Sleeping more than usual
Listlessness when awake
Irritability
Cool, mottled extremities
For cyanotic children:
Increased cyanosis
Vomiting or diarrhea leading to dehydration
Irritability
Following surgery:
Signs of wound infection
Fever
Changes in color
Changes in activity level
Flu-like symptoms
Increased respiratory rate or respiratory distress
For all children:
Unexplained fever
Marked changes in activity, eating
Vomiting that prevents them from taking their medicine
Problems in giving medicines, resulting in missed doses
Any emergency

Source: O'Brien, P., & Boisvert, J. T. (1989). Discharge planning for children with heart disease. *Critical Care Nursing Clinics of North America, 1*(2), 297–305. Copyright 1989 by W. B. Saunders Company. Reprinted by permission.

should be examined along with the list of signs and symptoms of cardiac distress (Table 8.3).

7 *Many children with altered cardiovascular functioning require medication on a regular basis as part of their treatment regimen.* Teachers should be aware of the drugs the child is taking and their potential side effects. Most medications are given at home, usually at 8 AM and 8 PM, although with some children, doses of certain medications must be given during school hours, most commonly at noon.

For students who are not old enough to self-administer medications, school staff should make sure that the drugs are given on time. If a dose is required during school hours, staff should be aware of what to do if the drug is inadvertently missed. Staff must ensure that they have a sufficient supply (i.e., enough for at least three days) and that the medications are kept in a secured area to prevent accidental ingestion by other children in the class.

For students able to self-medicate, school staff should monitor administration so that a dose is not skipped inadvertently, particularly if the student is involved in some type of activity, such as eating or playing, and may forget to take the medication. Most children with cardiac problems comply with the required drug program; however, children should be allowed to take the medication privately if they are embarrassed about needing to take drugs in school. As noted earlier, those on diuretics may need additional opportunities to use the rest room.

8 *Some students with cardiovascular problems are on a modified diet; the most common is a sodium-restricted diet.* Those on such a diet should not have salt added to their food and should avoid foods that are high in salt (e.g., pretzels, potato chips). Students with hypercholesterolemia should not eat foods high in cholesterol and saturated fat, including dairy products (e.g., ice cream, certain cheeses, cream, butter, whole milk), processed meats (e.g., hot dogs, pepperoni), and meats high in fat (e.g., hamburger, spareribs, fried chicken, batter-fried fish).

All school staff should be informed of dietary restrictions of students with a heart problem and, if possible, monitor the consumption of "forbidden foods." School staff (e.g., administrative staff, school nurse) should inform the student's parents

of any obvious signs of noncompliance with the prescribed regimen. Kitchen staff at the school can assist by making foods that are suited for the diet available. Certain occasions, such as school parties, may be problematic; however, in such situations the student's doctor usually permits a small amount of cake and ice cream.

Because of restrictions in activity and side effects of certain medications, weight gain may become problematic over time. A dietitian may be of assistance in determining a satisfactory level of food intake. Often, hospital-based dietitians are available to consult with school staff to develop a food plan that is healthy for all students, not just those who have cardiovascular problems.

9 *The intake of fluids may also have to be restricted.* Each student should comply with the regimen, but school staff should be alert to any "violations." Drinking from a fountain is generally discouraged because it is difficult to monitor consumption; a glass should always be used (Heller et al., 1996).

For individuals with hypoxemia, rather than fluids being restricted, fluid intake is encouraged to decrease the possibility of a cerebrovascular accident occurring. Students may need to to take fluids throughout the day (e.g., supplemental fluids could be kept at their desk in a water bottle), if recommended by the physician. If the student appears not to be consuming enough fluids, a staff person should contact the parents to discuss the concern. Since fever, vomiting, and diarrhea affect fluid levels in the body, the student's doctor should be notified if dehydration occurs because of illness.

10 *For those with cardiac problems, the possibility of bacterial endocarditis is of particular concern.* Teachers should be alert to signs of potential infection (e.g., fever, weight loss, behavior changes) and report any observations to the child's parents. Parents should be informed of all outbreaks of communicable diseases (e.g., mumps, German measles) in the school because it may be prudent to prevent unnecessary exposure.

Good oral hygiene and the prevention of gingival and periodontal disease are important in preventing BE (Rosenthal, 1984). Teachers should reinforce the concepts of good dental practice (e.g., brushing, flossing, fluoride treatments) as part of the health curriculum. BE can develop at any time, so meticulous dental care, prompt treatment of infections, and the need to take prophylactic antibiotics are lifelong responsibilities (Higgins & Reid, 1994).

11 *Those with heart defects who have had natural cardiac valves replaced with prosthetic valves take* **anticoagulation drugs,** *such as warfarin sodium (Coumadin), to prevent the formation of blood clots.* These drugs, often referred to as **"blood thinners,"** ensure continuous blood flow through the circulatory system. Students who are receiving anticoagulants need to be carefully monitored for injury in the school and on the playground.

Normal cuts and scrapes should not bleed excessively; however, they may bleed longer than normal. Staff should be trained to apply pressure to minor cuts until the bleeding has stopped. The child should be transported to the nearest medical facility for immediate treatment if the injury is serious.

12 *All students who are taking medications to treat their cardiac problem should be encouraged to wear a Medic-Alert bracelet.* This particularly applies to those who are on anticoagulants or are taking some type of antiarrhythmic drug (i.e., a drug that corrects an irregular heart rhythm). Those who have pacemakers or heart transplants should also wear an identifying bracelet, particularly when they are older and are away from their parents (O'Brien & Boisvert, 1989).

13 *Although the teen years are a particularly difficult time for all, for the young adolescent who has a congenital heart disease this period can be even more troublesome.* During this time, physical appearance and body image are of extreme importance. For some with heart disease, the disease is "invisible" to others; however, for others the disease and its sequelae are very "visible" and can cause extreme self-consciousness of their "defective" body. For students who are chronically cyanotic, the blue color of their lips and fingers, their small stature and low weight, and the clubbing, thickening, or flattening of their fingers and toes may prevent "fitting in" with the crowd. Those who have had surgical intervention may have scars that cause embarrassment, particularly during physi-

cal education classes. At the time of discharge, the student who has had a heart transplant may experience hair loss, weight loss, and skin changes as a result of radiation treatments, all of which might result in psychological distress (Perez-Woods, Hedenkamp, Ulfig, Newman, & Fioravante, 1991). Teachers should be alert to teasing that occurs. Counseling and consultation with a dietitian and a beautician may be of assistance.

14 *One of the major tasks of adolescence is the determination and internalization of sexual identity and role* (Tong & Sparacino, 1994). However, a heart defect may lead to difficulties (e.g., frequent hospitalizations) in the ability to form relationships with individuals of the same or opposite gender and may lead to the development of fears (e.g., fear of rejection and self-consciousness about physical appearance; fear that sexual arousal may affect the heart and may lead to further complications and even death). A referral to the school counselor may be of assistance to some students.

15 *For the female adolescent with a heart problem, additional concerns include the safety of contraceptive methods, the effects of pregnancy, and the genetic risk of inherited cardiac problems.* For some individuals, pregnancy and genetic counseling that includes a frank discussion of the risks to the health of the mother and child may be beneficial. Generally such counseling is offered by the young adult's physician, cardiologist, or a geneticist. However, school counselors and nurses are often more accessible, and the child may turn to them to discuss issues that are of concern. Although school staff cannot replace physicians, they can assist the young adult in obtaining information.

16 *Even though adolescents want to be as independent as possible, the need to conform with the peer group is typically evident.* Peers may exert pressure to experiment with drugs, smoking, and alcohol. However, for the adolescent or young adult with a cardiovascular condition, experimentation may lead to more serious health consequences than for the adolescent without a chronic health problem. School staff should be on the outlook for signs that the adolescent is denying the presence of the heart condition or the severity of the illness.

17 As the child ages, occupational restrictions are also of concern. In the AHA recommendations regarding recreational participation (Gutgesell et al., 1984), guidelines regarding occupational activity in relationship to type and severity of heart condition are also given. Recommendations made by the student's cardiologist must be clearly communicated to vocational counselors. A form developed for this purpose by the AHA is contained in Appendix D.

18 McGrath and Truesdell (1994), in discussing employment and career counselling for adolescents and adults with CHD, stressed the importance of choosing an occupation in which persons with heart disease can continue if their level of ability deteriorates. They also cautioned that certain activities may result in an acceleration of disease and may even result in a life-threatening situation. The authors reviewed the federal regulations that are in force to protect the rights of individuals with disabilities and stated: "Patients with CHD need to know that they do not have to accept undesirable positions because of fear of losing health benefits or job security"(p. 326).

Summary

In this chapter, the most common congenital and acquired cardiovascular disorders in children and young adults were reviewed. Many students with altered cardiovascular functioning attend school without requiring any modifications or accommodations. Others need continuing assistance on a daily basis to gain full benefit from the opportunities that are offered. In order to ensure a safe return to school, teachers must be in close contact with the student's parents and willing to help monitor the student's medical condition so that treatment can begin early, if needed. School staff should not be hesitant to contact the student's physician for guidance in determining appropriate activity level and for suggestions on how to assist the student to return to a level of functioning that is appropriate physically and rewarding emotionally.

References

American Academy of Pediatrics, Committee on Sports Medicine and Fitness (1995a). Cardiac dysrhythmias and sports. *Pediatrics, 95,* 786–788.

American Academy of Pediatrics, Committee on Sports Medicine and Fitness (1995b). Mitral valve prolapse and athletic participation in children and adolescents. *Pediatrics, 95,* 789–790.

American Heart Association (1991). *If your child has a congenital heart defect: A guide for parents.* Dallas: Author.

Baas, L. S. (1991). Assessing and prescribing activity for the person with cardiac disease. In L. S. Baas (Ed.), *Essentials of cardiovascular nursing* (pp. 171–188). Gaithersburg, MD: Aspen.

Bernstein, D., Starnes, V. A., & Baum, D. (1990). Pediatric heart transplant. *Advances in Pediatrics, 37,* 413–439.

Bricker, J. T., & McNamara, D. G. (1983). Heart disorders. In J. Umbreit (Ed.), *Physical disabilities and health impairments: An introduction* (pp. 222–232). New York: Merrill.

Clare, M. D. (1985). Home care of infants and children with cardiac disease. *Heart & Lung, 14,* 218–222.

Daberkow, E. (1989). Nursing strategies: Altered cardiovascular function. In R. L. R. Foster, M. M. Hunsberger, & J. J. T. Anderson (Eds.) *Family-centered nursing care of children* (pp. 1271–1383). Philadelphia: J. B. Saunders.

Dowling, C. G. (1997, February). Body voyage. *Life,* 33–81.

Freed, M. D. (1984). Recreational and sports recommendations for the child with heart disease. *Pediatric Clinics of North America, 31,* 1307–1320.

Freund, B. D., Scacco-Neumann, A., Pisanelli, A. S., & Benchot, R. (1993). Acute rheumatic fever revisited. *Journal of Pediatric Nursing, 8,* 167–176.

Goldberg, B. (1990). Children, sports, and chronic disease. *The Physician and Sportsmedicine, 18,* 45–56.

Gutgesell, H. P., Gessner, I. H., Vetter, V. L., Yabek, S. M., & Norton Jr., J. B. (1986). Recreational and occupational recommendations for young patients with heart diseases: A statement for physicians by the Committee on Congenital Cardiac Defects of the Council on Cardiovascular Disease in the Young, American Heart Association. *Circulation, 74,* 1195A–1199A.

Heller, K. W., Alberto, P. A., Forney, P. E., & Schwartzman, M. N. (1996). *Understanding physical, sensory, and health impairments.* Pacific Grove, CA: Brooks/Cole.

Higgins, S. S., & Reid, A. (1994). Common congenital heart defects: Long-term follow-up. *Nursing Clinics of North America, 29,* 233–248.

Hoffman, J. I. E. (1990). Congenital heart disease: Incidence and inheritance. *Pediatric Clinics of North America, 37,* 25–43.

Jackson, D. B., & Saunders, R. B. (1993). *Child health nursing.* Philadelphia: J. B. Lippincott.

Kleinberg, S. B. (1982). *Educating the chronically ill child.* Rockville, MD: Aspen.

Lux, K. M. (1991). New hope for children with Kawasaki disease. *Journal of Pediatric Nursing, 6,* 159–165.

McGrath, K. A., & Truesdell, S. C. (1994). Employability and career counseling for adolescents and adults with congenital heart disease. *Nursing Clinics of North America, 29,* 319–330.

O'Brien, P., & Boisvert, J. T. (1989). Discharge planning for children with heart disease. *Critical Care Nursing Clinics of North America, 1*(2), 297–305.

Olson, J. M., & Hazinski, M. F. (1990). The cardiovascular system. In G. M. Scipien, M. A. Chard, J. Howe, & M. U. Barnard (Eds.), *Pediatric Nursing Care* (pp. 574–620). St. Louis: C. V. Mosby.

Perez-Woods, R., Hedenkamp, E. A., Ulfig, K., Newman, D., & Fioravante, V. L. (1991). Pediatric transplant recipients: Special nursing considerations and challenges. In B. A. H. Williams, K. L. Grady, & D. M. Sandiford-Guttenbeil (Eds.), *Organ transplantation: A manual for nurses* (pp. 249–274). New York: Springer.

Pitts-Wilhelm, P. L. (1992). Alterations in cardiovascular function. In P. T. Castiglia & R. E. Harbin (Eds.) *Child health care: Process and practice* (pp. 565–604). Philadelphia: J. B. Lippincott.

Rengucci, L. M. (1990). Circulation: Implications of abnormalities in structure and pressure. In S. R. Mott, S. R. James, & A. M. Sperhac (Eds.), *Nursing care of children and families* (2nd ed., pp. 1049–1136). Redwood City, CA: Addison-Wesley.

Rosenthal, A. (1984). Care of the postoperative child and adolescent with congenital heart disease. *Advances in Pediatrics, 30,* 131–167.

Roy, D. L., McIntyre, L., Human, D. G., Nanton, M. A., Sherman, G. J., Allen, L. M., & Finley, J. P. (1994). Trends in the prevalence of congenital heart disease: Comprehensive observations over a 24-year period in a defined region of Canada. *Canadian Journal of Cardiology, 10,* 821–826.

Tong, E., & Sparacino, P. S. A. (1994). Special management issues for adolescents and young adults with congenital heart disease. *Critical Care Nursing Clinics of North America, 6*(1), 199–214.

Whaley , L. F., & Wong, D. L. (1995). *Nursing care of infants and children* (5th ed.). St. Louis: Mosby.

Zabriskie, J. B. (1985). Rheumatic fever: A streptococcal induced autoimmune disease? *Pediatric Annals, 11,* 383, 386–389, 392–396.

Hematologic Disorders

There is wide variation in causes, severity, treatment, and prognosis of the various blood disorders found in children and young adults. In this chapter, disorders of the red and white blood cells and the platelets are discussed. Since the symptoms of blood disorders are often similar from person to person regardless of the type of cell involved (e.g., increased fatigue, increased susceptibility to infection), the accommodations needed to attend school are grouped together and addressed at the end of the chapter. Specific suggestions are also given for individual conditions, when appropriate.

Diagnosis of a blood disorder requires a number of tests. The most common test for hematologic function is the **complete blood cell (CBC) count,** which provides the physician with information on the hematologic status of an individual (e.g., number, size, shape of the various cells). For the CBC count, a small amount of blood is withdrawn and a smear of it is placed on a slide for examination under a microscope. Visually, any irregularities can be seen in the cells and, with the assistance of an **electronic counter,** the number of cells per cubic millimeter (mm^3) of blood can be tallied. The hemoglobin level can also be determined by means of a CBC count.

In addition to a CBC, some persons with a suspected blood disorder may also require a **bone marrow biopsy,** which involves the aspiration of a sample of bone marrow for examination. The red marrow is removed from specific sites by means of a large-gauge needle, most commonly the hip, the sternum (breast bone), or the tibia (the long bone in the leg). This test is used commonly in the diagnosis of leukemia, a cancer of the blood-forming tissues.[1]

🐾 Disorders of Red Blood Cell Function

Since red blood cells (RBCs) are required for the transport of oxygen to the body's cells, any disorder of the RBCs results in a decrease in concentration of oxygen in the blood and a decrease in oxygen supply to cells. There are several disorders of red cell function; in children and young adults, the most common are anemia and lead poisoning.

Anemia

Some types of anemia cause a decrease in the total number of RBCs; in others, the number of RBCs is adequate, but the concentration of hemoglobin in the RBCs is deficient. An example of the first type is the individual who loses a great deal of blood as a result of an acute hemorrhage. Anemia that results from hemorrhage is often referred to as **temporary anemia.** An example of the second type is a person who, perhaps as a result of insufficient intake of iron, does not synthesize hemoglobin at a normal rate, and consequently develops iron deficiency anemia, a form of **long-term anemia.** Anemia is believed to occur at a rate of 8.8 persons per 1,000 population (Newacheck & Taylor, 1992). It is the most common hematologic disorder found in children.

Anemia in itself is *not* a disease. Rather, anemia reflects some type of *alteration* in normal hematologic processes. The signs and symptoms that characterize anemia are related to the underlying disorder (e.g., loss of blood) and those that result from the anemia itself (e.g., loss of oxygen to the organs of the body). Some of the signs and symptoms are shown in Table 9.1; in addition to these, children with anemia are prone to developing infections.

There are several forms of anemia. The two most common in children and young adults are **iron deficiency anemia** and **sickle cell anemia.** In general, the more severe the anemia, the more severe the consequences. Management of anemia focuses on attempting to isolate and treat the underlying cause.

Iron Deficiency Anemia   Iron deficiency anemia typically results from an inadequate supply, intake, or absorption of **iron,** a common metallic element found in many foods. Foods that are high in iron include lean meat (e.g., organ meats and muscle meats), shell fish, poultry, whole grains, dried legumes (especially white beans), nuts (including peanut butter), dark green leafy vegetables (especially spinach), fortified cereals and enriched bread, molasses, egg yolks, and dried fruits, including raisins and apricots.

Without sufficient iron, the body's ability to synthesize hemoglobin is grossly altered. An estimated 10% to 30% of the population worldwide has a deficient supply of iron (Beck, 1990b). In the Western countries iron deficiency anemia is thought to be the most common nutritional deficiency in humans.

---

[1] For further information on leukemia and other malignancies of the body, please refer to chapter 22.

TABLE 9.1
Signs and Symptoms of Anemia

RELATED TO DECREASED OXYGEN TRANSPORT

- Headache
- Insomnia
- Fatigue; decreased spontaneous activity; lack of interest in events
- Syncope
- Dyspnea, especially on exertion
- Angina pectoris (i.e., chest pain)
- Widespread impairment of organ function (e.g., impairments of the organs of the gastrointestinal or genitourinary system, leading to anorexia or loss of appetite)
- Dizziness or confusion; irritability

THOSE RELATED TO DECREASED BLOOD VOLUME

- Pallor (of mucous membranes and skin)
- Postural hypotension (abnormally low blood pressure when standing, resulting in dizziness or faintness)

THOSE RELATED TO INCREASED CARDIAC OUTPUT

- Palpitations (i.e., pounding heart)
- Tachycardia
- Heart murmur
- Onset of congestive heart failure

Sources: Beck, 1990a; Turner, 1991.

Normal levels of iron are 60 to 190 micrograms per deciliter (μg/dl) of blood.

Although iron deficiency anemia can develop at any age, very young children, between ages 6 months and 3 years, and teenagers are particularly at risk. For both groups, two factors appear to contribute: (a) in general, neither age group prefers to eat foods that are high in iron; and (b) both age groups are experiencing rapid growth spurts. Adolescent girls are particularly at risk for anemia because of blood loss during menstruation.

Iron deficiency anemia is not recognized in many children because the symptoms tend to be rather vague and nonspecific. Similarly, because the anemia develops over time, rather than suddenly, the diagnosis is not made. Symptoms of iron deficiency anemia include irritability, listlessness, anorexia, reduced spontaneous activity, and dulled interest in the environment (Arkin, 1996). As the condition progresses, signs and symptoms related to severe anemia may develop (Table 9.1). Some individuals with iron deficiency anemia complain of **tinnitus** ("ringing" in

the ears) and some may describe a feeling of "pins and needles" in the extremities, a condition known as **paresthesia.** Children with long-term iron deficiency anemia may have some degree of growth retardation.

Many people assume that youngsters with iron deficiency anemia are thin. However, many are "chubby" as a result of excessive intake of foods that provide calories but not iron, such as milk and "junk" foods. Some children with iron deficiency anemia have an eating disorder known as **pica,** from the Latin word for magpie, in which the child develops a craving to ingest unusual substances that are not typically considered to be "food," such as ice, dirt, chalk, hair, glue, mud, starch, salt, and cigarette butts.

Treatment of iron deficiency anemia involves the oral administration of replacement iron (e.g., ferrous sulfate, gluconate, or fumarate). Therapy typically lasts for 2 to 4 months, during which time the level of iron in the blood is measured periodically. Typically, there are few side effects, and individuals respond rapidly; however, if too much iron supplement is given, nausea and abdominal cramps may develop. Iron toxicity can lead to liver damage.

Sickle Cell Anemia (SCA)   Sickle cell anemia, the second most common type, is so named because of the crescent shape of the red blood cells in persons with this condition. The deformity of the blood cells is the result of the production of an abnormal form of hemoglobin. As many as 1 in every 375 African American infants has SCA,[2] and in total, over 50,000 Americans, children and adults included, have this disorder (Selekman, 1993). In fact, SCA is the most commonly found genetic disorder in the United States (Turner, 1991).

Genetic transmission.   SCA is described as being a **co-dominant autosomal recessive condition.** To understand this description, each of the component parts of the term is outlined.

The term **"co-dominant"** is used to reflect the fact that the individual must inherit *two* abnormal genes, both of *equal* dominance (i.e., one gene does not have a greater effect than the other), one from the mother *and* one from the father, to have the disease. The abnormal gene is designated as **Hb S** (i.e., S for "sickled" hemoglobin, one of several abnormal forms of hemoglobin). Since persons with SCA must have two abnormal genes, they would be designated as **Hb SS** and would have sickle-shaped hemoglobin in their blood. In contrast, the gene for normal hemoglobin is designated as **Hb A** (i.e., A for adult hemoglobin, the normal form); persons who have only normal genes would be **Hb AA** and their blood would contain only normal hemoglobin. Persons who have two genes that are the same (either both abnormal or both normal) are described as being **homozygous.**

The term **"autosomal"** refers to the fact that the abnormal genes for the disease are located on an **au-**tosome as opposed to a **sex chromosome.**[3] In fact, in persons who have sickle cell anemia, the abnormal gene is located at the number 6 position of chromosome 11. Since the genes are not located on either of the sex chromosomes, i.e., it is *not* a sex-linked condition, either the mother *or* the father can pass on the defective gene to a son *or* daughter.

The term **"recessive"** refers to the fact that the effects of the gene may be hidden or masked if there is a normal gene (Hb A) on the other autosome. As stated above, for the person to have "full-blown" sickle cell anemia, the abnormal gene must appear on both autosomes (i.e., **homozygous** for the trait, or **Hb SS**). The abnormal gene on one autosome and the normal gene on the other indicates the individual is **heterozygous** for the condition (i.e., both the Hb A gene and the Hb S gene, or **Hb AS**). Such persons are said to have the **trait** for the condition, and are often referred to as being **"carriers"** (i.e., they can pass the gene to their offspring). In carriers, normal hemoglobin is partly replaced by a variant form; consequently, they would have a mixture of normal and abnormal hemoglobin in their red blood cells. Those with the trait may show symptoms of the disease under certain conditions (e.g., when at high altitude or when scuba diving), even though they have some normal hemoglobin; however, most carriers are asymptomatic.

Knowing that SCA is autosomal recessive explains the manner in which it is transmitted, because its transmission follows the basic principles of inheritance laid out by Gregor H. Mendel. If both parents have the disease, all of the children will have the disease; however, a complicating factor is that many persons who appear to be "normal" are in fact carriers and can pass on the defective gene to their offspring. Tests are available to determine carrier status; however, not all parents undergo screening before starting a family. If one parent has the trait and the other is normal, none of the children develop the disease (Figure 9.1); however, if both parents are carriers, one in four offspring may develop

---

[2] Another blood disorder that also results in anemia and affects African Americans, but to a lesser degree (0.5 percent of all children), is beta-thalassemia. It is also common in children of Mediterranean descent (e.g., Greek, Syrian, Italian). In the U. S., between 3% and 10% of Americans of Italian or Greek ancestry have the trait for this condition (Wofford, 1993). In beta-thalassemia, rather than the RBCs being sickle shaped, they are small and contain significantly less globin than normal cells. In the past, beta-thalassemia was commonly referred to as Cooley's anemia, after Dr. Thomas Cooley, one of the first physicians to recognize its signs and symptoms. For further information on this blood disorder, see Martin and Butler (1993).

---

[3] Human beings, regardless of sex, have 23 pairs of chromosomes in every cell. **Chromosomes** contain genetic material in genes. Each cell has 22 pairs of autosomes and one pair of sex chromosomes. **Autosomes** are chromosomes that are not involved in determining the sex of the individual, whereas **sex chromosomes** are those that determine gender. In humans, these are the **X** and **Y.** Females are XX and males are XY.

	Homozygous parent Hb AA (normal)	
Gametes	Hb A	Hb A
Hb A	Hb AA (normal)	Hb AA (normal)
Hb S	Hb AS (carrier)	Hb AS (carrier)

Heterozygous parent Hb AS (carrier)

Figure 9.1
Genetic Transfer of Sickle Cell Disease: Case #1. One parent has the sickle cell trait; one parent is normal. Two of the four children will have the trait. None of the children will have the disease.

	Heterozygous parent Hb AS (carrier)	
Gametes	Hb A	Hb S
Hb A	Hb AA (normal)	Hb AS (carrier)
Hb S	Hb AS (carrier)	Hb SS (affected)

Heterozygous parent Hb AS (carrier)

Figure 9.2
Genetic Transfer of Sickle Cell Disease: Case #2. Both parents have the trait. One in four offspring will have the disease. Two will have the trait and one will be normal.

half the offspring could have the disease and half could be carriers.

Characteristics. Even though individuals with SCA may have normal or increased numbers of RBCs because the sickled RBCs only live about 16 to 20 days (as opposed to the normal 120 days) and because they are less able to transport oxygen, those with this condition show the typical signs of anemia (Table 9.1). Some persons with SCA also show signs of **jaundice,** a condition in which the skin and the sclerae (the white parts of the eyes) have a yellowish cast that results from the build-up in the blood of bilirubin, a by-product of the metabolism of hemoglobin. Lesions of the skin (ulcers), particularly in the legs, are also common in adolescents and adults. Some children with the disease show signs of growth retardation in both height and weight, and some young adults show signs of delayed sexual maturity.

In most cases, children with SCA are asymptomatic for the first year of life; however, over time the deformed cells begin to "clump" together, making the blood increasingly viscous. In addition, the misshapen cells begin to adhere to the endothelial layer of the blood vessels, thereby "clogging" the circulatory system. As the rate of blood flow through the system is slowed down, organ damage, resulting from the decreased supply of oxygenated blood, begins to be evident. As the organs become dysfunctional, **necrosis,** or tissue death, results; the most vulnerable sites are the spleen, liver, kidneys, bones, central nervous system, and heart.

Sickle cell crisis. Many children and young adults with SCA have acute episodes that can also result in significant organ damage. These episodes, referred to as **sickle cell crises, sickling crises, painful crises,** or **vaso-occlusive crises (VOC),** also result from the inability of the misshapen red blood cells to travel successfully through the capillary network. Occurring very suddenly, RBCs occlude the vessels, resulting in decreased transport of oxygen to the tissues. Tissue injury and eventual necrosis of adjacent tissues are the final outcome.

Sickling crisis is often precipitated by some type of infection, such as an upper respiratory or gastrointestinal infection. Other causative factors include dehydration, strenuous exercise, ingestion of alcohol, and physical trauma. Exposure to extreme cold can also trigger a crisis. A crisis can last from 5 days to several weeks; however, frequency and severity vary from person to person (Gribbons, Zahr, &

the disease and two in four may be carriers (Figure 9.2). If either or both of the parents have the condition, the risk of having a son or daughter who is a carrier or has the disease increases. For example, if one parent has the disease and the other the trait,

Opas, 1995). During the episode, the individual typically shows signs of sudden severe pain. The location can vary from crisis to crisis; however, pain in the chest, abdomen, back, and joints is common. Chest pain may be the result of sickling in the lungs and is often accompanied by shortness of breath, rapid breathing, and in some cases, episodes of coughing. Pain in the abdomen may result from sickling in one or more of the abdominal organs; common sites are the liver, the spleen, and the pancreas. Pain in the lower back may indicate sickling in the kidneys, a condition that can result in permanent renal damage. If the bones or joints are involved, symptoms may include recurrent or constant pain and swelling of the soft tissues of the hands (fingers) and feet (toes), a condition known as **dactylitis,** or **hand-foot syndrome.** Some individuals having a sickling crisis may complain of headaches, dizziness, and disturbances in the auditory and visual system. These signs, along with loss of balance, weakness on one side of the body, and changes in academic performance that cannot be explained by other causes, may indicate a **cerebrovascular accident,** or **stroke.**

Even though the sickle cell crisis may cause great discomfort to the student, in most cases it is not life-threatening. During a mild crisis, children and young adults with SCA may be able to attend school if they are given medication for their pain, are provided with opportunity to rest, and are encouraged to drink plenty of fluids (Kim, Gaston, & Fithian, 1984). More fluids are required on days that are hot or humid or on days that the student is more active than usual.

Diagnosis and treatment. To determine whether or not a newborn has sickle cell anemia, several tests, such as the **sickle-turbidity test,** are available. In more than half of the United States, there are mandatory screening programs, and even though they are costly ($3,100 per identified child), knowing that a newborn has the condition allows the child's physician to initiate appropriate interventions to minimize potential complications and reduce mortality rates (Gribbons et al., 1995).

Although there is no "cure" for sickle cell anemia, with appropriate medical treatment (e.g., treating symptomatology present during sickling crises), many children and young adults with this disease are able to lead relatively normal lives. Many children with sickle cell disease used to die in infancy. Today there is an 85% chance that a person with SCA will live to age 20 (Selekman, 1993), and some individuals with this condition live into their thirties and forties.

Treatment of a severe sickle cell crisis generally includes the intravenous transfusion of normal packed red blood cells to decrease the anemia. Infusions of normal saline solute are also given to "thin" the blood and to hydrate the patient (i.e., provide increased amounts of water to the cellular tissues). In many cases, analgesics or narcotics are administered to treat the pain. If needed, oxygen is given. Bed rest may be required to regain strength; hospitalization may be required in events that are very painful.

Research is being focused on developing drugs that either prevent or reverse the sickling of RBCs; however, more clinical research is needed (Gribbons et al., 1995). A few children have been successfully treated by means of a bone marrow transplant; however, there is a 10% to 15% risk of death with this treatment, and transplant rejection is common. However, in discussing the use of bone marrow transplant to treat sickle cell disease, Gribbons and her colleagues made the following optimistic comment: "This treatment modality is very promising for the child with SCD who may one day be free from the multiple complications associated with the disease" (p. 238).

Lead Poisoning

Lead, a common metallic compound, does not serve any biologic function in the human body. Lead poisoning, also referred to as **plumbism,** unlike sickle cell disease, is an *acquired,* toxic condition that is essentially preventable.

Etiology Lead poisoning, caused by the concentrated or repeated inhalation, ingestion, or absorption through the skin of lead or lead compounds, can result in severe mental, emotional, and physical impairment in children. Lead poisoning is considered to be a disorder of the red blood cells because the lead accumulates predominantly in these cells. Potential sources of lead are shown in Table 9.2.

Characteristics The various signs and symptoms of lead poisoning are shown in Table 9.3. Because of the similarity of these symptoms to symptoms of other conditions (e.g., stomach flu), recognizing the condition is difficult. In the young child, decreased play activity is often one of the first symptoms. Interestingly, 90% of children with lead poisoning have a history of pica (Yoder, Burright, & Donovick, 1993), which may also be indicative of iron deficiency anemia.

TABLE 9.2
Potential Sources of Lead Exposure

INHALED

- Lead particles (e.g., industrial emissions from lead smelters, precious-metal refineries, battery recycling plants, radiator repair centers)
- Household dust
- Ambient air and airborne fumes (e.g., combustion of leaded gasoline; burning or sanding of painted wood; gasoline sniffing; welding, cutting or blasting of painted steel; incinerator ash)
- Dust from the improper removal of interior or exterior paint (e.g., during renovation of older homes; contaminated clothes)
- Airborne particles from the use of lead shot (e.g., target shooting)

INGESTED OR ABSORBED THROUGH THE SKIN

- Lead-contaminated food (e.g., wild birds killed with lead shot, especially liver and kidneys; soup made from bones)
- Food or drink contaminated by exposure to lead-soldered cans (usually imported from countries in which lead solder has not been prohibited), lead-glazed pottery, antique pewter, and other lead-containing cookware (e.g., lead crystal)
- Food stored in plastic bags printed with leaded paint
- Certain traditional folk medicines (e.g., Greta, Azarcon, Paylooah) and certain cosmetics (e.g., lead-containing eye cosmetics, in particular kohl)
- Soil or dust contaminated by lead sources (e.g., exterior paint, gas; soil contaminated by automobile gasoline vapors or gas leaks)
- Lead paint chips (e.g., from "gnawing" on old window sills, crib rails, old toys painted with lead-based paint, new toys imported from countries where lead-based paint is still used; art restoration)
- Lead chromate in plastics (e.g., chewing on coated electric wire)
- Water (i.e., lead leeched from pipes or solder in houses built before the late 1980s and in some newer or renovated buildings in which solder-containing lead has been used to connect copper pipes; water coolers soldered with lead)
- Handling or making lead shot, fish sinkers, certain objects (e.g., glazed pottery, metallic items), leaded (stained) glass, chewing on newspaper
- Gunshot wounds

Sources: American Academy of Pediatrics, 1987; Hanning, 1994; McCabe, 1991; Trachtenbarg, 1996.

Lead poisoning has a significant effect on a child's ability to reach his or her full potential. Teachers of children who have high lead levels report that they are "more distractible, less persistent, more dependent, less well-organized, less able to follow directions, and generally lower in overall functioning than students with lower levels of lead exposure" (Needleman, 1992, p. 36). Studies by Needleman and his colleagues have shown that children who had been exposed to lead early in life had a sevenfold increase in risk of failing to graduate from high school and a sixfold increase of risk for a reading disability (Needleman, 1992). Some children with lead poisoning are believed to be at risk for antisocial behavior, particularly aggressive behavior (Needleman, 1992). A recent study by Minder, Das-Smaal, Brand,

and Orlebeke (1994) found that students with relatively high concentrations of lead in their system showed a slower reaction time on certain tasks (e.g., the recognition of a certain visual stimulus) than those with lower amounts of lead. Similarly, students with high lead concentrations were significantly less flexible in changing their focus of attention, even with correction for reaction time, than those with lower levels. Other neurologic effects include delayed development of word-recognition abilities, speech impairments, impaired sense of equilibrium (e.g., clumsiness), and decreased fine motor coordination (Trachtenbarg, 1996). Visual problems (e.g., crossing of the eyes, damage to the visual cortex in the brain, decreased visuomotor control) as well as auditory problems (e.g.,

TABLE 9.3
Signs and Symptoms of Lead Poisoning

- Abdominal pain
- Anemia
- Anorexia
- Constipation or diarrhea
- Distractibility
- Headaches
- Hyperactivity
- Hyperirritability
- Impulsiveness
- Lethargy
- Listlessness
- Nausea
- Vomiting
- Weakness

degeneration of the auditory nerves) can also affect learning potential.

In severe cases, acute **encephalopathy** (damage to the structure or function of the brain) may occur from increased lead concentrations in the RBCs. Ataxia or impaired coordination, paralysis, blindness, altered consciousness, and seizures may also result. With extremely high blood levels of lead, the individual may become comatose and eventually die. The mortality rate from encephalopathy has been reported to be over 50% (Yoder et al., 1993). Eighty percent of children or young adults with encephalopathy have permanent or severe brain damage that affects their ability to learn (Olson & Anderson, 1990).

Incidence and Prevalence   With the introduction of lead-free paint and unleaded gasoline, the incidence of *overt* lead poisoning (i.e., lead poisoning that results in acute symptoms) has decreased over the past few decades (Piomelli, 1994). However, recent studies have shown that even low levels of lead in the blood, not previously recognized as being toxic, can result in serious sequelae (DeRienzo-DeVivio, 1992; Hanning, 1994; Piomelli, 1994). On average, a minimum of three months of exposure is required to produce the toxic effects (James, 1990); however, children can reportedly become severely poisoned by ingesting as little as 1 milligram (mg) of lead paint dust daily during their early years (Jezewski, 1992). This amount is equivalent in size to about three granules of sugar.

Although it was thought that only blood lead levels higher than 80 μg/dl were of concern, now a level of only 10 μg/dl is considered dangerous. Moel and Sachs (1992, cited in Trachtenberg, 1996) reported that blood levels of 10 to 30 μg/dl produced an IQ deficit of 4% to 5% by the time the children had reached age 7. Lead encephalopathy typically results when blood lead levels exceed 55 μg/dl.

As many as 16% of all children in the United States may have blood lead levels high enough to result in impaired neurobehavioral functioning; 8.9% of children nationally, ages 1 to 5, may have blood lead levels higher than 10 μg/dl; 2.7% may have blood lead levels of 15 μg/dl or higher; and between 3 and 4 million children in the United States between ages 6 months and 5 years are at risk for lead poisoning (De-Rienzo-DeVivio, 1992; Needleman, 1992; Trachtenberg, 1996). The incidence of lead poisoning is significantly lower in Canada than in the United States; however, above-average levels of lead exposure have been reported in the provinces of British Columbia, Quebec, and New Brunswick (Hanning, 1994).

Lead poisoning is more common in poor, inner-city African-American children than in rural white children (Olson & Anderson, 1990). However, it can affect youngsters of all social strata and of all races. Recent data from the Agency for Toxic Substances and Disease Registry have shown the occurrence rate of elevated blood lead levels to be approximately 7% for well-off white children, in comparison to 25% for poor whites and 55% for poor African-American children (Needleman, 1992). Certain factors are known to increase susceptibility to lead toxicity that are not necessarily related to socioeconomic status (American Academy of Pediatrics, 1987). They include nutritional deficiency of iron, calcium, or zinc; sickle cell anemia; young age; hand-to-mouth activity, including pica; and certain metabolic diseases.

Diagnosis and treatment   Lead poisoning is an acquired condition and can be detected by means of a blood test. The Centers for Disease Control and Prevention have recommended that all children be screened at about ages 1 and 2 (Arkin, 1996). With early diagnosis and treatment, prognosis is excellent.

Treatment consists of a diet low in fat and high in iron and **chelation therapy,** which involves the administration by intramuscular injection of chelating agents (i.e., substances that bind with the lead, such as calcium disodium edetate) for the purpose of removing the excess lead from the body. For children, chelation therapy is usually begun when blood lead levels reach 25 μg/dl; in adults, a level of 51 μg/dl is the common starting point.

Disorders of White Blood Cell Function

The major functions of leukocytes are protection from infection and disposal of the waste products of cellular breakdown. Consequently, any disorder in the production or function of white blood cells (WBCs) affects the individual's general health status and ability to fight infection. The most common WBC disorder is **leukemia,** a cancer of the blood-forming organs that results in a proliferation of leukocytes in the blood. Other diseases that affect leukocytes are far less common. Cancer, including leukemia, in children is discussed in detail in chapter 22. Chapter 22 deals with children who have altered immune function, and chapter 23 deals with communicable (i.e., infectious) diseases.

Disorders of Platelets and Coagulation Function

There are a number of conditions that can affect the platelets, in terms of number and of structure. **Thrombocytosis** is a condition in which there is an abnormal increase in the number of thrombocytes found in the blood. Persons with this condition, who may have as many as 1,000,000 platelets/mm^3, are likely to have thrombotic episodes, which are periods in which they develop blood clots within one or more blood vessels of the body. Children and young adults with Kawasaki disease, described in chapter 8, are prone to developing thrombocytosis. The opposite of thrombocytosis is **thrombocytopenia,** a condition in which there is an abnormal decrease in the number of platelets circulating in the blood. Thrombocytopenia is the most common cause of bleeding disorders in children and young adults and is common in those with leukemia.

Thrombocytopenia is not the only cause of bleeding. If the platelets, regardless of number, do not have certain coagulation factors, hemostasis does not occur. The most commonly known bleeding disorder, **hemophilia,** is a result of such a defect in the coagulation system.

Hemophilia

Hemophilia refers to a group of lifelong bleeding disorders that result from a deficiency in one of the 13 factors needed for the coagulation of the blood. Several forms of hemophilia are common in children and young adults, especially classic hemophilia and Christmas disease. **Classic hemophilia,** also referred to as **hemophilia A** or **factor VIII deficiency,** results from the lack of coagulation factor VIII. **Christmas disease,** also referred to as **hemophilia B** or **factor IX deficiency,** is a condition that is clinically similar to but less severe than the former. A small number of individuals, both male and female, are deficient in factor XI and have **hemophilia C,** a condition particularly prevalent in Jewish persons of Eastern European descent. Both hemophilia A and hemophilia B are sex-linked recessive disorders. Hemophilia C is an autosomal recessive condition.

Genetic Transmission   Classic hemophilia is an **X-linked (or sex-linked) recessive disorder.** The term "recessive" has already been described in the discussion on sickle cell anemia; the term "X-linked" or "sex-linked" refers to those conditions that result from the presence of one or more abnormal genes on the X chromosome. In an X-linked recessive condition, the defect becomes evident in males because they have only one X chromosome and, therefore, the action of the defective gene is not "masked" by the presence of the normal dominant gene on the other X chromosome, as is the case in females.

Women may inherit the abnormal gene (i.e., they can be a "carrier" of hemophilia); however, generally they are asymptomatic because of the presence of the normal, dominant gene on the second X chromosome. If they have the abnormal gene on both X chromosomes, rather than being carriers, they will have the condition. Such situations occur rarely, since for the woman to have both abnormal genes, she must inherit the recessive gene from both her mother (who would be a carrier) and her father (who would have the condition).

Typical patterns of inheritance of an X-linked recessive trait are shown in Figures 9.3, 9.4, and 9.5; the recessive gene is shown as X_o. The most common pattern of inheritance, shown in Figure 9.3, is between an unaffected (normal) father (XY) and a carrier mother (XX_o); however, as the prognosis for survival of persons with hemophilia has improved considerably with new medical treatments, the other two

	Carrier mother		
	Gametes	X	X_0
Normal father	X	XX (normal daughter)	XX_0 (carrier daughter)
	Y	XY (normal son)	X_0Y (affected son)

Figure 9.3
Genetic Transfer of X-Linked Recessive Hemophilia: Case #1.
The father is normal; the mother is a carrier of the trait. Half of
the daughters will be carriers. Half of the sons will be affected.

patterns, both involving an affected male (X_0Y) as father, are becoming more common. If an affected male mates with a carrier female, it is possible that half of the female offspring will have the disease. While hemophilia is more common in males, this is one manner in which females can inherit classic hemophilia.[4]

While the most common form of transmission of hemophilia A is by inheritance of the gene from one or more parents, in some cases **mutations,** unusual changes in genetic material that occur sponta-

neously, can result in the condition occurring unexpectedly. About one-third of all cases of hemophilia are thought to develop as a result of some type of mutation (Karayalcin, 1985). Mutations can result in the disease occurring in both sexes. Those with the mutant gene pass the defect on to subsequent generations in the typical X-linked recessive pattern.

Incidence and Prevalence The incidence rate of hemophilia A is approximately 1 in 10,000, making it the most common inherited coagulation disorder (Handin & Rosenberg, 1990). Other forms of hemophilia occur less often. Approximately 75% to 80% of all cases of hemophilia are of the classic form. The following text refers to this form of the disease.

---

[4] Since hemophilia C is not sex-linked (it is an autosomal recessive condition), it is possible for a female to inherit this form of disease; however, both parents would have to be carriers.

	Normal mother		
	Gametes	X	X
Affected father	X_0	XX_0 (carrier daughter)	XX_0 (carrier daughter)
	Y	XY (normal son)	XY (normal son)

Figure 9.4
Genetic Transfer of X-Linked Recessive Hemophilia: Case #2.
The mother is normal; the father has the disease. All daughters
will be carriers. Both sons will be normal.

Gametes	Carrier mother	
	X	X_0
Affected father X_0	XX_0 **(carrier daughter)**	X_0X_0 **(affected daughter)**
Y	XY **(normal son)**	X_0Y **(affected son)**

Figure 9.5

Genetic Transfer of X-Linked Recessive Hemophilia: Case #3. The father is affected with the disease; the mother carries the trait. There is a one in four chance of producing either an affected son or daughter, a carrier daughter, or a normal son.

However, the symptoms and treatment for all three forms of hemophilia are similar. About 12% to 15% of individuals with hemophilia have hemophilia B; the remaining 2% to 3% have hemophilia C.

Severity Scale Hemophilia is normally categorized by degree of severity of the condition. Between 60% and 70% of those with hemophilia A and 50% of those with hemophilia B have a severe form of the disease; the remainder have mild to moderate symptoms (Karayalcin, 1985).

Severe hemophilia. In severe forms of hemophilia, where there is little factor VIII or IX in the blood (<1% of normal), bleeding can occur spontaneously, i.e., with no known trauma, or as a result of minor trauma. For example, a bump against a piece of furniture or a slight fall that results in a superficial cut or scrape may result in a bleeding episode in a person who has a severe form of the disease.

Those with severe hemophilia often have as many as two or three bleeding episodes per week throughout their lifetime. Diagnosis of severe hemophilia usually occurs by the age of four, because at that point, joint and deep muscle bleeding begins to be problematic (Karayalcin, 1985). Blood in the urine (hematuria) and blood in the stools, which makes the feces look black and tarry, may be problems in persons with severe hemophilia.

Moderate hemophilia. In moderate hemophilia, where the level of factor VIII or IX is diminished to a lesser extent (1% to 5% of normal), bleeding typically occurs after some form of minor trauma. For example, a tumble from a bicycle or a fall from a swing may result in a bleeding episode. Occasionally those with moderate hemophilia have an episode of spontaneous bleeding; however, such occurrences are rare. A child or young adult with moderate hemophilia typically has only one or two bleeding episodes per year. Bleeding into the joint is less common in persons with moderate hemophilia, in comparison to those with a severe form of the disease.

Mild hemophilia. In mild hemophilia, the level of factor VIII or IX is between 5% and 50% of normal, and bleeding generally only results from moderate to severe trauma. A fall down the stairs or a car-pedestrian accident may result in a bleeding episode. Except in unusual circumstances, such as after surgery or dental work, many individuals with mild hemophilia have very few bleeding episodes. Joint and deep muscle bleeding are rare. Because of the lack of obvious symptoms, mild hemophilia may not be recognized until late childhood or even adulthood (Karayalcin, 1985).

Sites of "Bleeds" It is important to recognize that persons with hemophilia do not only bleed *externally*—many individuals will bleed *internally*. An example of an internal bleed is bleeding into the gastrointestinal tract. Because the blood is not evident to the eye, such bleeding episodes may go unrecognized.

Internal bleeding most often takes the form of **hemarthrosis,** the oozing of blood into a joint (Figure 9.6), the most common sites of which are the hinge-type joints, such as the knees, elbows, and

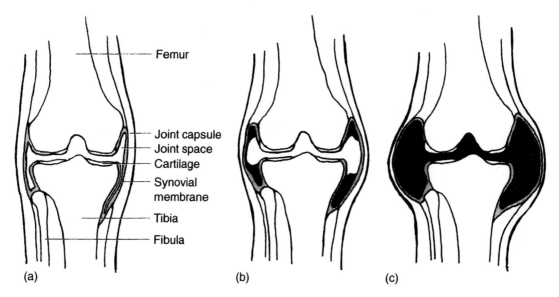

Figure 9.6
Hemarthrosis of the Knee: (a) a normal knee; (b) early hemarthrosis (bleeding into the knee joint); (c) acute hemarthrosis.

ankles. Socket-type joints, such as shoulders and hips, are less frequently involved. The wrist is the least likely spot of involvement. Hemarthrosis is typically evidenced at first by a tingling or prickling sensation in the joint, which may appear to be red, swollen, and warm to the touch. Stiffness and slight limitation of range of motion occur after an hour or more, followed within a few hours by pain, swelling, and more severe restriction of movement (Karayalcin, 1985). Over time, structural damage to the joint can occur.

The second most common site of internal bleeding is into the muscles, particularly the muscles found in the forearm and in the leg. Muscle "bleeds" are referred to as **muscle hematomas.** Pain, muscle spasm, and limitation of movement are typical signs of this type of bleeding.

While other sites of internal bleeding are rare, of particular concern is bleeding in the head region. Bleeding in the neck or mouth can lead to asphyxiation; bleeding in the cranium can result in death from the buildup of pressure. Early signs of intercranial bleeding are headaches and slurred speech.

Treatment and Prognosis The primary treatment of hemophilia is **factor replacement therapy,** in which the deficient factor is infused directly into a vein. In the case of a person with hemophilia A, for example, factor VIII concentrate from human plasma would be given in order to stop the bleeding. Usually one infusion is sufficient; however, in some cases a follow-up treatment may be required. The sooner the treatment is instigated, the sooner the bleeding is stopped.

Even though with proper treatment the bleeding may be stopped successfully in a student with hemophilia, the sequelae of the bleed may be noticeable for some time and may affect the student's ability to participate fully in school life. For example, a student who has residual swelling and tenderness in an elbow as a result of joint hemorrhage may find taking notes to be difficult. In such situations, the student should be encouraged to participate as much as possible by listening and taking part in any discussion (Gill & Butler, 1984). Photocopies of notes taken by a classmate ensure that the student has material for studying purposes. Carrying books and equipment may be problematic for those with pain in the elbows or shoulders or for those who are on crutches. Having a complete set of books at home and having books available in each of the student's classrooms will prevent the student from having to transport books to school and from room to room in school.

With early treatment, the risk of complications (e.g., damage to the joint, development of anemia) is lessened; however, replacement therapy is not without its own risks. Since almost all the substances used in the treatment of hemophilia are obtained from human blood, individuals with hemophilia have, particularly in the past, been at risk for contracting several communicable diseases, particularly hepatitis and acquired immune deficiency syndrome (AIDS). Between 1978 and 1985, about 80% to 90% of persons with hemophilia A and 50% of persons with hemophilia B were infected with the human immunodeficiency virus (HIV), the virus known to cause AIDS (Leonard, 1994). Data on the incidence of hepatitis are unavailable. Since the late 1980s, improved donor screening and improved processing of the replacement factor (e.g., heat treatment and pasteurization of the products) has decreased or eliminated the risk.

In addition to replacement therapy, treatment for hemophilia typically involves the administration of certain drugs, such as corticosteroids and narcotic and non-narcotic analgesics for reduction of inflammation of joints and decreasing of pain associated with the swelling. Restricting the movement of the joints (e.g., splinting, casting, use of elastic bandages) also has been found to assist the management of pain associated with internal bleeding.

Dealing with Bleeding Episodes   Even though hemophilia is a bleeding disorder, **individuals with hemophilia do not bleed to death. Persons with hemophilia do not bleed *faster* but they do bleed *longer* than those with a normal level of clotting factor.** Even in the case of a major wound, there is the same amount of time to transport the student to the hospital for treatment as there is for any other student (Gill & Butler, 1984). **All teachers and coaches, regardless of whether or not there is a student with a bleeding disorder in their classes or on their teams, should know basic first aid techniques.** Two resources, Eckert's manual for parents, *Your Child and Hemophilia* (1990), and the pamphlet by Carroll et al. (1990), *The Child with Hemophilia: First Aid in School,* will assist teachers in dealing with bleeding episodes. Even though the possibility of contracting hepatitis or AIDS is minimal during regular first aid procedures, before tending to a student who is bleeding, the caregiver should put on waterproof gloves. If blood gets on the caregiver's skin, the skin should be washed thoroughly with soap and water. Any blood that has spilled on the floor or countertops should be cleaned up with a solution of 10% bleach and 90% water or with rubbing alcohol. For further discussion of handling bodily fluids, the reader is referred to the section on Universal Precautions in chapter 24. **Hematologic disorders are typically invisible conditions. All students who have a hematologic disorder should be encouraged to wear a medical-alert bracelet at all times.**

For those with hemophilia, bleeding is a fact of life. Treatment with replacement factor generally takes only half an hour, so a student may treat a hemorrhage in the morning and still attend school the same day. If a bleeding episode occurs at school, the student's parents (or the student) can administer the factor in a private area and then return to class immediately after treatment. In comparing statistics for the period from 1975 to 1985, the National Hemophilia Foundation (1991) reported that, with the advent of self-infusion of clotting factor, the number of absences from work and school because of the illness dropped from an annual average of 14.5 days to 3.9 days.

Some parents of young children with severe hemophilia wear a beeper so that the school can contact them quickly if they are needed to provide replacement therapy. If the student's class is going on a field trip, special arrangements may have to be made. Often one of the parents will volunteer to go with the class so that treatment can be given if necessary. Pillow (1992) recommends that a "factor bag" that includes the following items accompany the student on all outings: cotton balls, adhesive bandages, acetaminophen, tourniquets, ace bandages, syringes, and factor.

School personnel should respect students' knowledge of their hemophilic condition. If students state they are bleeding or think they are bleeding, they should be believed, even if there are no outward signs of bleeding. In addition, teachers should rely on students to report what can and cannot be done on a given day, as limitations vary according to each student's condition (Gill & Butler, 1984). Unfortunately, not all students are as communicative with their teachers as would be ideal (Pillow, 1992), and as a result, misunderstandings can occur.

Educational Implications and Teaching Tips

In general, most blood disorders do not affect intellect but do affect physical endurance. Consequently, teachers should hold the same academic expectations for the students with hemophilia as they would for students without such a condition, provided the students are given extra support to cope with their frequent absences and their inability to participate fully in all school-based activities. It should be noted, however, that some conditions or the treatment regimen used to combat certain diseases may affect students' academic performance, and as a result, they may need extra assistance or remedial programs to reach their academic potential. The following suggestions may assist teachers in their ability to integrate students with hematologic disorders into the educational program. Even though some of the suggestions that follow are written with a specific type of blood disorder in mind, often the recommendations can be generalized from one condition to another, as the sequelae of the diseases are often similar.

1   *Teachers who have a student with a hematologic disease in their class must understand the student's condition, be comfortable with the condition, and be able to foster a sense of understanding and acceptance by the student's peers.* For example, teachers should recognize that students with certain hematologic conditions, such as sickle cell anemia, may show signs of growth retardation or retardation of sexual maturity. However, regardless of size and appearance, teachers must remember to treat the students the same as their chronological peers are treated and not as if they were considerably younger. If a student is conspicuously underweight or underdeveloped, having to undress in a public place (e.g., shower room) or to wear certain clothing (e.g., gym shorts, bathing suit) may cause embarrassment. Teachers should be aware of concerns such as these and discuss possible solutions with the student or the student's parents.

Gill and Butler (1984), in discussing the implications of differential treatment of children with hemophilia, emphasized the need for teachers to be good role models to discourage rejection by fellow classmates. These comments are equally appropriate for all students who have a blood disease:

> When the child with hemophilia has a good self-image, and parents and teachers have positive feelings about his abilities and treat him as a person rather than as a "sick person" or "hemophiliac," classmates will tend to be more understanding of the situation. Ideally, classmates should understand that hemophilia is a problem but that it is not the child's whole life. He has many concerns in common with other children,

and on most occasions, these will take precedence over the health problem as a focus for his life. Teachers can influence classmates' feeling toward the child by allowing him to compete with healthy children in a healthy way and by expecting him to follow the same rules as other children. (p. 178)

2   *Fatigue is a major problem with many students with altered hematologic functioning, as is the case with children and young adults who have cardiovascular disorders.* The suggestions given in chapter 8 should be reviewed, particularly those related to daily physical demands. All students with altered hematologic functioning should be encouraged to participate as much as possible in their school program, but they should never be pushed beyond their level of ability. Some individuals with a blood disorder may need one or more rest periods during the day. The availability of the nurse's office for brief periods of rest may offer the student some degree of privacy.

Activities that require less stamina, such as listening to music or taped books, painting, using a computer rather than a pen and paper to write a story, or playing chess or checkers, may be appropriate substitutes for more strenuous activities or may be alternated with activities that require more energy expenditure. Ideally, students should undertake such "energy conserving activities" with a peer or group of peers so that they do not feel isolated from their classmates. Because most individuals who have a blood disorder have greater strength in the morning, activities that require exertion should be scheduled early in the day, when the students are functioning at peak performance.

3   *Physical activities may need to be restricted for some students with altered hematologic functioning.* However, many are able to participate in most activities as long as they are allowed to rest when necessary and not pushed beyond their ability. Consultation with the student's physician is critical. Any restrictions should be clearly outlined and recorded. Several sample forms are offered in Appendix D.

Sickle Cell Anemia Activity Restrictions. Students with blood disorders, particularly those with sickle cell anemia, should be encouraged to drink plenty of fluids before and after engaging in an exercise program. Outdoor activities during bitterly cold spells may be contraindicated in those with sickle cell anemia because of the possibility that the peripheral vessels may constrict, thereby provoking a sickle cell crisis (Kim et al., 1984).

Hemophilia Activity Restrictions.   Teachers of students with hemophilia are often confused as to the extent to which they should participate in physical sports and recreational activities. The National Hemophilia Foundation, in conjunction with the American Red Cross, has prepared a comprehensive booklet, entitled *Hemophilia, Sports, and Exercise* (Wiedel et al., 1996), which groups sporting activities into three categories on the basis of risk. While the categories are applicable to most individuals with hemophilia, the authors caution that they may not be appropriate for all individuals and that the decision regarding any restrictions must be made by the child, the child's parents, and the child's physician (Table 9.4).

TABLE 9.4
Sport Activities for Students with Hemophilia: Risks and Recommendations

	Category 1	Category 2	Category 3
LEVEL OF RISK	Recommended sports in which most individuals with hemophilia can participate safely	Sports in which the physical, social, and psychologic benefits often outweigh the risks. For each individual, the risk/benefit ratio must be evaluated; but today, for most youngsters with hemophilia, these are reasonable activities.	Sports for which the risks outweigh the benefits for all hemophiliacs. The nature of these activities makes them dangerous even for those without hemophilia.
RECOMMENDED ACTIVITIES	Bicycling Fishing Frisbee Golf Hiking Martial arts (tai chi) Swimming Walking	Baseball Basketball Bowling Diving (recreational) Gymnastics Horseback riding Ice-skating Martial arts (karate, kung fu, tae kwon do) Mountain biking River rafting Roller-blading Roller-skating Rowing Running and jogging Skateboarding Skiing (downhill, cross country) Snowboarding Soccer Tennis Track and field Volleyball Waterskiing Weightlifting	Boxing Diving (competitive) Football Hockey (field, ice, street) Lacrosse Motorcycling Racquetball Rock climbing Rugby Wrestling

Adapted from Wiedel, J. D., Holtzman, T. S., Funk, S., Oldfield, D., Evans, D., Ward, R. S., & Low, M. (1996). *Hemophilia, sports, and exercise.* New York: National Hemophilia Foundation. Reprinted by permission.

Before any child with hemophilia participates in a sports program, a complete musculoskeletal examination by an orthopedic surgeon or a physical therapist must be undertaken to determine the level of joint motion, ligament stability, muscle strength, and flexibility (Gilbert et al., 1994). Recommendations, in the form of a letter from the student's physician, should be solicited to determine what activities should or should not be included in the educational program (Appendix D). The student's physician should also be asked to outline any specific treatment programs that may be necessary to control a bleeding episode. If there are changes in the student's status, this letter should be updated on a regular basis. Some physicians recommend that students have an infusion of the clotting factor before participating in a game or practice session; this should be discussed with the student's physician (Wiedel et al., 1996). Unlike other students with altered hematologic functioning, those with hemophilia usually do not necessarily suffer from extreme fatigue and do not need more rest than others (Gill & Butler, 1984). A trial-and-error approach to determining which activities can be undertaken successfully is recommended. Because there are no research data available to provide definitive guidelines suitable for each individual with hemophilia, it is only through participation that the likelihood of success can be determined for each student (Wiedel et al., 1996).

If students with a bleeding disorder have developed good self-discipline and a sense of responsibility, they are less likely to be injured while participating in various physical activities (Eoff, 1990). Students with bleeding disorders must learn to obey safety rules. Teachers should be alert to situations in which a student with hemophilia engages in risk-taking behavior in order to be "one of the group."

For children and young adults with hemophilia, a sensible, nutritional diet is recommended because excess weight can place excessive strain on the musculoskeletal system (Eoff, 1990). Those who are overweight are more likely to develop muscle and joint bleeds.

Wiedel et al. (1996) make the following statement in the closing section of the handbook. Even though the intended audience for these comments was parents, the sentiments expressed also apply to school staff:

It is strongly recommended that parents support children who wish to engage in sports while they are young. If parents adopt an attitude that allows them and their children to live an active life, both will reap the rewards. Although the child with hemophilia has a tendency to bleed, which is a considerable inconvenience, it is not necessarily an impediment to leading a normal and active life. (p. 22)

4   *While some hematologic conditions result in the student being absent from school for extended periods of time, school staff should be alert to excessive absenteeism and discuss any concerns with the student's parents and physician* (Berberich, 1982). In some cases, the loss of time from school may suggest a need to reevaluate the student's medical status. A change in treatment, such as increased replacement therapy, may result in increased school attendance and a decreased threat to academic achievement.

Similarly, as in the case of almost all students with a chronic disease, those with hematologic disorders should be observed for signs of "using" their condition to avoid disliked activities (e.g., homework or chores, physician-approved exercise).

5   *Some individuals with altered hematologic functioning, e.g., those with sickle cell anemia, have periods of intense pain.* However, even these students should be encouraged to return to school if at all possible. Rather than being alone at home, isolated and fearful, they will benefit from participating in school activities even if the degree of participation is limited and they need to take medication on a regular basis. Often by just being with peers, the student is distracted and is able to manage the painful episode more successfully.

Some children, particularly when young, have misconceptions about the consequences of reporting pain (Eoff, 1990). They may be reluctant to report any feeling of pain because they fear hospitalization, diagnostic procedures, and treatment. Teachers should be alert to signs of youngsters being in distress (e.g., facial grimacing, change in activity level).

6   *Students who have hematologic disorders do not, in most cases, require any major modification to their diet.* The exceptions are those with iron deficiency anemia and sickle cell disease.

Iron Deficiency Anemia.   Although iron deficiency anemia can be treated by giving the individual an iron supplement, both students and parents need to be educated about the significance of adequate nutrition and a balanced diet. Teachers can assist by providing all students with information regarding nutritional requirements for good health and by being a good role model (i.e., eating a well-balanced diet). School dietitians can assist by ensuring that foods high in iron are a part of the school's nutritional program. Teachers and dietitians should be on the lookout for students, particularly adolescent girls, who are engaging in "fad" diets in order to "improve" their physical appearance, as these girls are at particular risk for iron deficiency anemia. The school nurse and school dietitian may be able to provide dietary teaching for adolescent students that encourages proper nutrition while maintaining a steady weight loss (Eoff, 1990).

Sickle Cell Anemia.   Those with SCA do not require a "special" diet; however, they are required to increase their fluid intake to lessen blood viscosity and to prevent clot formation. Students should be encouraged to drink plenty of fluids and allowed to keep a water bottle at their desk or go to the drinking fountain on a regular basis. Because of the increased fluid intake, students with SCA need unlimited access to the bathroom. Teachers should be alert to any signs of dehydration (e.g., dry mucous membranes). Children and young adults with SCA may need to be excused from vigorous outdoor activities during the warmer months, since exercise during hot weather may cause an increased loss of body fluids. In cold weather, the students must be dressed appropriately so that they do not become overheated.

7 *Children and young adults with certain blood disorders (e.g., sickle cell anemia,[5] leukemia) are particularly susceptible to infection.* Students with a hematologic condition should be observed for signs of a fever (e.g., flushed face, warm forehead). More subtle signs include a change in temperament or a change in activity level. Headaches, vomiting, diarrhea, and bone pain are other cardinal features of

infection (Gribbons et al., 1995). Parents should be notified immediately so that appropriate medical treatment can be undertaken. Even though infection is a risk, it should be recognized that "overprotection can be equally as devastating emotionally as an infection is physically" (Whaley & Wong, 1995, p. 1584).

8 *Some students with hemotologic conditions encounter academic difficulties while in school.* This is especially true of those with SCA and those with lead poisoning.

Sickle Cell Anemia.   As many as 15% of children and young adults with SCA are believed to have neurologic symptoms that arise from either an overt or silent cerebrovascular accident (Gribbons et al., 1995). Strokes are more common in younger children than in older. Since strokes are one of the most serious complications that can occur in the classroom, the teacher should notify the parents or the student's physician immediately if any symptoms that indicate neurologic damage (e.g., headaches, dizziness, loss of balance, weakness on one side) are observed. Similarly, if a student with SCA has a seizure, the parents should be notified immediately.[6]

Teachers of students with SCA should also be on the lookout for any obvious symptoms of loss of visual or auditory acuity. All persons with SCA should have an annual eye examination to detect any changes in vision that may result from occlusion of blood vessels in the eye (Gribbons et al., 1995). Similarly, students with SCA should be referred for an audiologic assessment if there are any signs of hearing difficulty. About 12% of those with SCA have a unilateral or bilateral, mild, high-frequency, sensorineural hearing impairment (Friedman, Luban, Herer, & Williams, 1980).

Lead Poisoning.   If a school has a higher incidence of learning problems than is considered normal, lead poisoning may be a possible cause. Screening of students (Piomelli, 1994) and mandatory testing of suspect buildings are critical. Jezewski (1992) reported that there are 3 million tons of old lead on the walls and fixtures in 57 million private homes in the United States. Some of these may be buildings that children and young

---

[5] For children with SCA, infections caused by *Streptococcus pneumoniae, Haemophilus influenzae* type B and *Salmonella* are particularly problematic (Gribbons et al., 1995). For children with leukemia, exposure to any communicable disease is of concern.

---

[6] For more on neurocognitive aspects of pediatric SCA, see Brown, Armstrong, and Eckman (1993).

adults frequent on a regular basis (e.g., day care centers, after-school activity centers, museums).

All school personnel should be aware of potential sources of lead. Many schools, particularly those built before the 1960s, were painted with leaded paint and used lead pipe for the transportation of water. However, it is also important to recognize that schools that have been renovated and schools built in the 1970s, 1980s, and 1990s are not completely without risk. For example, in some renovated schools, although copper pipes were used to replace those made from lead, the solder that was used to form the proper connections has been found to contain lead. Some newer schools have been built in areas where the soil has been contaminated by lead; others have been built in high-risk areas (e.g., downwind from smelters or refineries).

Early childhood educators in particular must be familiar with the symptoms of lead toxicity so that young children with potential problems are identified as early as possible and obtain proper treatment. Early identification not only helps the affected children but may also help their siblings and other neighborhood children who are at risk for this condition (McCabe, 1991).

9 *In high school, as part of the science curriculum, students are routinely introduced to the concepts of genetic inheritance.* In discussing certain forms of transmission, SCA and hemophilia are often given as examples. Teachers should be aware that this material can be extremely distressing to the student with a blood disorder, particularly if the student does not have a thorough understanding of the condition and its mode of inheritance.

Before presenting information on genetic inheritance, the teacher should contact the parents to determine the student's knowledge level. Genetic counseling is usually available to the student through the hospital or treatment center. The student should receive genetic counseling from a trained counselor who is able to deal with the student's anxieties before the student learns about the consequences of the condition in a classroom full of peers.

10 *As part of the science or health curriculum, a field trip to the local community blood center or the hospital blood bank might be appropri-* *ate, particularly for a class which includes a student with a hematologic disorder.* There, the students can observe the procedures for collecting and processing blood products. If the students are old enough, they might be encouraged to donate a unit of blood. Teachers should check state or provincial regulations regarding minimum age requirements before scheduling such a visit.

11 *As the student matures, the hematologic disorder may affect future career goals.* For example, a student with anemia may require a job with few physical demands. Similarly, a student with a bleeding disorder may not be able to handle a job that requires heavy manual labor. Vocational guidance counselors should be aware of limitations that the student's health status may impose and explore a wide variety of appropriate vocational options with the student.

Since many vocational opportunities that are appropriate to individuals with a blood disorder require a strong academic background (e.g., clerical skills, managerial skills), education is particularly important for them (Corrigan & Damiano, 1983), and they should be encouraged to remain in school until graduation. Kleinberg (1982), in discussing the educational needs of those with hemophilia, suggested that "since job opportunities for non-high school graduates tend to rely heavily on manual labor, it seems that special efforts need to be made to provide the hemophiliac with the educational tools necessary to function in white-collar and technical jobs, which require fewer physical skills" (p. 110).

❧ Summary

Regardless of the prognosis of the hematologic illness, school should be a major focus of the child's or young adult's life, for he or she "needs to feel a part of the world and needs continuity in both academic and social experiences" (Kleinberg, 1982, p. 207). The tendency for parents (and school staff) to focus on the negative aspects of the student's illness often overshadow the rich, positive experiences that the student may experience by being with his or her peers even in time of poor or failing health. While new forms of treatment have had a significant impact by increasing the life expectancy of many who have a hematologic disorder, some children and young adults die as a result of their condition. For teachers of children whose life expectancy is shortened, the material contained in chapters 4 and 5 may be of assistance.

References

American Academy of Pediatrics (1987). Statement on childhood lead poisoning. *Pediatrics, 79,* 458–459.

Arkin, S. (1996). Anemia of iron deficiency. In F. D. Burg, J. R. Ingelfinger, E. W. Wald, & R. A. Polin (Eds.), *Gellis & Kagan's current pediatric therapy* (15th ed., pp. 275–277). Philadelphia: W. B. Saunders.

Beck, W. S. (1990a). Hematopoiesis and introduction to the anemias. In W. S. Beck (Ed.), *Hematology* (4th ed., pp. 1–23). Cambridge, MA: MIT Press.

Beck, W. S. (1990b). Hypochromic anemias I. Iron deficiency and excess. In W. S. Beck (Ed.), *Hematology* (4th ed., pp. 103–124). Cambridge, MA: MIT Press.

Berberich, F. R. (1982). Hemophilia. In E. E. Bleck & D. A. Nagel (Eds.), *Physically handicapped children: A medical atlas for teachers* (2nd ed., pp. 325–331): New York: Grune & Stratton.

Brown, R. T., Armstrong, F. D., & Eckman, J. R. (1993). Neurocognitive aspects of pediatric sickle cell disease. *Journal of Learning Disabilities, 26,* 33–45.

Carroll, B., Keyes, N., Bogner, D., Butler, R., Clements, M., & Augustyniak, L. (1990). *The child with hemophilia: First aid in school.* New York: National Hemophilia Foundation.

Corrigan, J. J., & Damiano, M. L. (1983). Blood diseases. In J. Umbreit (Ed.), *Physical disabilities and health impairments: An introduction* (pp. 167–174). New York: Merrill.

DeRienzo-DeVivio, S. (1992). Childhood lead poisoning: Shifting to primary prevention. *Pediatric Nursing, 18,* 565–567.

Eckert, E. F. (1990). *Your child and hemophilia.* New York: National Hemophilia Foundation.

Eoff, M. J. (1990). Hematologic composition: Implications of altered blood elements. In S. R. Mott, S. R. James, & A. M. Sperhac (Eds.), *Nursing care of children and families* (2nd ed., pp. 1282–1333). Redwood City, CA: Addison-Wesley.

Friedman, E. M., Luban, N. L. C., Herer, G. R., & Williams, I. (1980). Sickle cell anemia and hearing. *Annals of Otology, Rhinology, and Laryngology, 89,* 342–347.

Gill, F. M., & Butler, R. B. (1984). Hemophilia. In J. Fithian (Ed.), *Understanding the child with a chronic illness in the classroom* (pp. 165–179). Phoenix: Oryx Press.

Gribbons, D., Zahr, L. K., & Opas, S. R. (1995). Nursing management of children with sickle cell disease: An update. *Journal of Pediatric Nursing, 10,* 232–242.

Handin, R. I., & Rosenberg, R. D. (1990). Hemorrhagic disorders III: Disorders of primary and secondary hemostasis. In W. S. Beck (Ed.), *Hematology* (4th ed., pp. 457–473). Cambridge, MA: MIT Press.

Hanning, R. (1994, June). Lead toxicity: Yesterday's problem. *Contemporary Pediatrics,* 24–25.

James, S. R. (1990). Home care and emergency management of the child with a minor illness or injury. In S. R. Mott, S. R. James, & A. M. Sperhac (Eds.), *Nursing care of children and families* (2nd ed., pp. 761–811). Redwood City, CA: Addison-Wesley.

Jezewski, M. A. (1992). Alterations in neurological function. In P. T. Castiglia & R. E. Harbin (Eds.), *Child health care: Process and practice* (pp. 633–684). Philadelphia: J. B. Lippincott.

Karayalcin, G. (1985). Current concepts in the management of hemophilia, *Pediatric Annals, 14*(9), 640–659.

Kim, H. D., Gaston, G., & Fithian, J. (1984). Sickle cell anemia. In J. Fithian (Ed.), *Understanding the child with a chronic illness in the classroom* (pp. 180–197). Phoenix: Oryx Press.

Kleinberg, S. B. (1982). *Educating the chronically ill child.* Rockville, MD: Aspen.

Leonard, M. S. (1994). Altered hematologic function. In C. L. Betz, M. M. Hunsberger, & S. Wright (Eds.), *Family-centered nursing care of children* (2nd ed., pp. 1373–1412). Philadelphia: W. B. Saunders.

Martin, M. B., & Butler, R. B. (1993). Understanding the basics of β thalassemia major. *Pediatric Nursing, 19*(2) 143–145.

McCabe, P. P. (1991). Low level lead toxicity: The hidden challenge for educators. *Childhood Education, 68,* 88–92.

Minder, B., Das-Smaal, E. A., Brand, E. F. J. M., & Orlebeke, J. F. (1994). Exposure to lead and specific attentional problems in schoolchildren. *Journal of Learning Disabilities, 27,* 393–399.

National Hemophilia Foundation (1991). *What you should know about hemophilia.* New York: Author.

Needleman, H. L. (1992). Childhood exposure to lead: A common cause of school failure. *Phi Delta Kappan, 74*(1), 35–37.

Newacheck, P. W., & Taylor, W. R. (1992). Childhood chronic illness: Prevalence, severity, and impact. *American Journal of Public Health, 82,* 364–371.

Olson, J. M., & Anderson, K. M. (1990). The nervous system. In G. M. Scipien, M. A. Chard, J. Howe, & M. U. Barnard (Eds.), *Pediatric Nursing Care* (pp. 383–442). St. Louis: C. V. Mosby.

Pillow, S. K. (1992). Living with hemophilia: A world of changing needs for information. *HANDI-Quarterly, 3*(1), 1–2, 5.

Piomelli, S. (1994). Childhood lead poisoning in the '90s. *Pediatrics, 93,* 508–510.

Selekman, J. (1993). Update: New guidelines for the treatment of infants with sickle cell disease. *Pediatric Nursing, 19,* 600–605.

Trachtenbarg, D. E. (1996). Getting the lead out: When is treatment necessary? *Postgraduate Medicine, 99*(3), 201–218.

Turner, P. J. (1991). Care of the patient with a cardiovascular or blood disorder. In B. L. Christensen & E. D. Kockrow (Eds.), *Foundations of nursing* (pp. 702–765). St. Louis: Mosby.

Whaley, L. F., & Wong, D. L. (1995). *Nursing Care of infants and children* (5th ed.). St. Louis: Mosby.

Wiedel, J. D., Holtzman, T. S., Funk, S., Oldfield, D., Evans, D., Ward, R. S., & Low, M. (1996). *Hemophilia, sports, and exercise.* New York: National Hemophilia Foundation.

Wofford, L. G (1993). Nursing planning, intervention, and evaluation for altered hematologic function. In D. B. Jackson & R. B. Saunders (Eds.), *Child health nursing: A comprehensive approach to the care of children and their families* (pp. 1093–1138). Philadelphia: J. B. Lippincott.

Yoder, P. E., Burright, R. G., & Donovick, P. (1993). Lead: Still poisoning our children. *RN, 56*(2), 28–32.

Zabriskie, J. B. (1985). Rheumatic fever: A streptococcal induced autoimmune disease? *Pediatric Annals, 11,* 383, 386–389, 392–396.

PART IV

Innervation:

Children and Young Adults with Altered Neurologic Function

The nervous system is extremely complex, both in structure and function. Weighing less than most desktop computers, the human nervous system is the most complex computing device in existence (Waxman & deGroot, 1995). It is divided into two portions, the **central nervous system,** composed of the brain and the spinal cord, and the **peripheral nervous system,** composed of the nerves outside the brain and spinal cord. Since nerve cells and nerves are the basic units of the neurologic system, they are described first.

🍂 The Nervous System: Review of Structure and Function

The Nerve Cell

The nerve cell, or **neuron,** like all other cells, has a **cell body** (soma), containing the nucleus. However, unlike other cells, neurons have one or more processes, or extensions, known as axons and dendrites, that increase the relative size of the cell (Figure IV.1). **Axons** are long nerve fibers that conduct impulses away from the cell body; **dendrites** are shorter than axons and receive impulses and carry them towards the cell body. All neurons have at least one axon and one or more dendrites.

Some axons are bare; others are sheathed in **myelin,** a tissue composed mainly of fat that gives the fibers a whitish appearance. This protective covering functions as an "insulator," allowing the rapid conduction (in milliseconds) of nerve impulses along its length. In the peripheral nerves, the sheath is interrupted at irregular intervals by constrictions in the nerve fiber substance, known as **nodes of Ranvier.** It is believed that these nodes may assist in speeding the rate of transmission, because they allow for the impulse to "jump" from node to node (Schenk, 1991). Dendrites are not covered in the same manner.

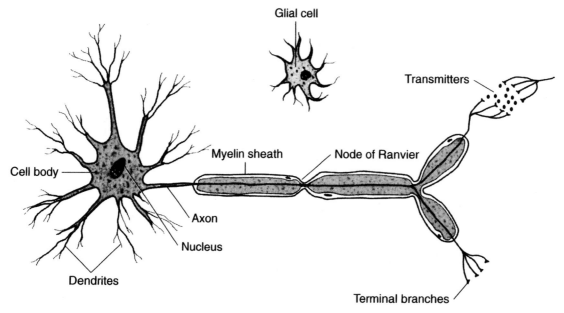

Figure IV.1
The Neuron
Source: Adapted from Umbreit, 1983, p. 17.

Even though some neurons are as much as several feet in length, in most cases a series of neurons, some as small as a micron, are required to carry the message from the brain to the rest of the body, and back. The space between two neurons is referred to as a **synapse.** For a neural impulse to be passed successfully from neuron to neuron, an electrochemical reaction must occur at the synapse, a process referred to as a **synaptic transmission,** illustrated in Figure IV.2. After an electrical impulse is generated in the cell body, it travels down the axon to its terminal end, where it encounters a **presynaptic membrane.** There, a **neurotransmitter,** which is a chemical such as dopamine or serotonin, is released from the synaptic vesicles into the **synaptic cleft,** or opening. After it diffuses across the gap, approximately a millionth of a inch in width, the neurotransmitter comes into contact with receptors in the adjacent dendrite or cell body. At the **postsynaptic membrane,** the chemical energy is transformed back into electrical energy, and the impulse travels to the next synapse, at which point the process is repeated.

At the area of contact between the nerve fiber and the muscle, referred to as the **motor end plate** or the **neuromuscular junction,** a **neuromyal transmission,** which is an electrochemical reaction similar to that described above, takes place if the final destination of the transmission is a muscle. The end result is some type of motor activity, such as the contraction of a muscle. If the final destination is a gland, some type of glandular material is excreted.

Nerves

Bundles of neurons that connect the brain and the spinal cord to the parts of the body and the skin are collectively referred to as **nerves.** Each nerve consists of several distinct parts. The outer covering, the **epineurium,** encloses the bundles of nerve fibers, referred to as the **fasciculi** (pl.). Each **fasciculus** (sing.) is also surrounded by its own sheath of connective tissue, known as the **perineurium.** Both types of covering sheaths, along with the **endoneurium,** which wraps around the myelinated sheath of the axon, provide sufficient insulation to

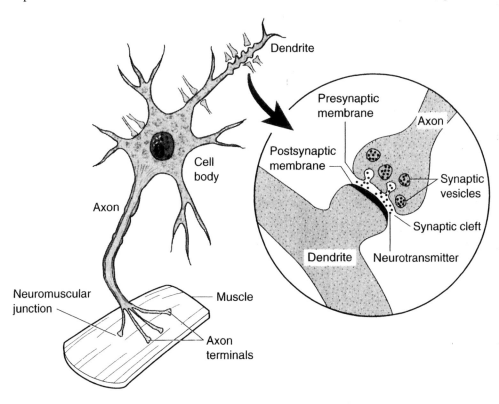

Figure IV.2
Central Nervous System Synapse: Site of Synaptic Transmission
Source: Adapted from Batshaw, 1997, p. 300.

facilitate the rapid transmission of impulses up or down the length of the nerve. It has been estimated that the body has about 45 miles of nerves, and impulses can travel as rapidly as 325 miles per hour (Dowling, 1997).

🐾 Central Nervous System (CNS)

The central nervous system (CNS), one of the two main divisions of the nervous system, includes the brain and the spinal cord. The brain is protected by bones that make up the **cranium,** commonly referred to as the **skull;** the spinal cord is protected by the bony or cartilaginous segments, known as **vertebrae,** that make up the **vertebral column,** commonly referred to as the **spine.** Figure IV.3 shows a cross section of the skull and spinal cord.

The Brain

Also known as the **encephalon,** the brain consists of four distinct parts: the cerebrum, the diencephalon, the brain stem, and the cerebellum. Together the four account for about 2% of the total body weight (approximately 3 lb in adults). The brain is composed of two different types of cells: neurons and **glial cells,** or **neuroglia,** that function to support, protect, and provide nourishment to the neuronal cells. The brain contains billions, if not a trillion, neurons and glial cells. Glial cells outnumber neurons by ten to one (Waxman & deGroot, 1995).

The Cerebrum   The largest part of the brain, the cerebrum, can be subdivided into several sections. From front to back, it is "split" into two halves, the left and right **cerebral hemispheres,** by a deep groove known as the **longitudinal fissure,** or **sulcus** (pl. **sulci**). The separation is not complete because the two hemispheres are joined together in the middle by a fibrous tissue known as the **corpus callosum.** Each hemisphere controls different areas of the body. The left cerebral hemisphere controls activities of the right side of the body; the right cerebral hemisphere controls the left side of the body. Consequently, for example, damage to the right hemisphere of the cerebrum would result in a contralateral impairment to the left side of the body (e.g., paralysis of the left arm or leg).

Each cerebral hemisphere is further subdivided, artificially, into several **lobes,** each named after the respective cranial bone that protects the underlying tissue. The sulci that "separate" the cerebrum into the various sections do not actually divide the cerebrum into distinct organs; rather, they are grooves on the surface that mark the division of the cerebrum into its recognizable parts. The divisions are as follows: (a) the **frontal lobe** is separated from the parietal lobe by the **central sulcus,** or fissure of Rolando; (b) the **occipital lobe** is separated from the parietal lobe by the **parieto-occipital sulcus,** also referred to as the occipitoparietal fissure; and (c) the **temporal lobe** is separated from the frontal and parietal lobes that lie above it by the **lateral fissure.**

The frontal lobe. As its name suggests, the frontal lobe, the largest of the cerebral lobes, is located in the anterior portion of the cranial cavity. This lobe, in particular the **motor area** of the lobe, located just in front of the central sulcus, has a major role in initiating voluntary movement and expressive language, both written and oral. The frontal lobe influences personality and behavior and higher mental activities, such as planning, judgment, conceptualizing, abstract thinking, and reasoning.

When the frontal lobe is examined in cross section at the **motor strip,** specific regions of the hemisphere are seen to be involved in the movement of specific body parts. At the lowest point are the areas that control the larynx, tongue, and lips, followed by areas that control the remainder of the head, the hands, arms, trunk, and finally, the legs. A comparatively large part of the motor cortex is involved with the use of the opposable thumb and the production of speech (Knight, 1992).

In addition to the part of the motor strip of the frontal lobe that is involved with speech, there is also an area, known as **Broca's area,** named after the French surgeon and anatomist Pierre Paul Broca, that is also involved in the production of sound. In almost all individuals who are right-handed, and 70% of those that are left-handed, Broca's area is located on the left side of the brain. In about 30% of those who are left-handed, the area is located on the opposite side. If a person is naturally left-handed and is forced to use the right hand, there is an increased probability that the individual will develop speech problems that result from interference with Broca's area (Knight, 1992).

If a person damages the frontal lobe, a variety of symptoms can result. Lack of tact and restraint, use of coarse language, and aggressive behavior are seen in some; apathy, indifference, lack of initiative, and

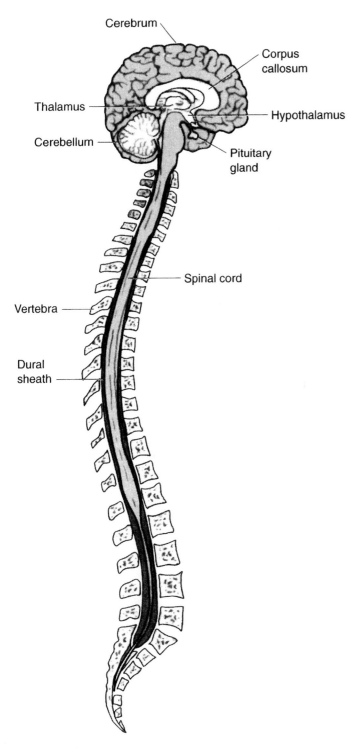

Figure IV.3
Cross Section of the Brain and Spinal Cord
Source: Adapted from *Mosby's,* 1994, p. 289.

lack of emotion in others. In addition, frontal lobe damage may cause difficulty learning new tasks that involve associations and organizing daily activities (Heller, Alberto, Forney, & Schwartzman, 1996). Some individuals experience motor or speech and language difficulties.

The parietal lobe. Located between the occipital and frontal lobes, the parietal lobe has an area similar to the motor area of the frontal lobe, directly behind the central sulcus, commonly referred to as the **sensory area,** where sensory input is received. Within this area are distinct locations for the processing of sight, hearing, touch, pressure, pain, smell, and temperature sensation that correspond to the adjacent areas in the motor area of the frontal lobe. A significant portion of the sensory area is devoted to the head, in particular the lips and tongue; less area is devoted to the hand.

The parietal lobe is also involved in a number of higher level cognitive functions, such as making simple calculations, understanding speech, navigating in the environment, and determining left from right, distances, shapes, and sizes as well as short-term memory function. If the parietal lobe is damaged,

difficulty interpreting and integrating sensory information is common; e.g., a person may not be able to recognize where his or her hand is without looking at it first (Heller et al., 1996).

The occipital lobe. Located at the back of the head, the occipital lobe is primarily concerned with vision. Incoming visual stimuli travel via the optic nerves, optic chiasm, and optic tract to the area of the occipital lobe commonly called the **visual cortex.** The visual pathway is shown in Figure IV.4. After the image is processed, it is then passed on to the temporal and parietal lobes to be integrated with information that has entered the body through the other senses, such as hearing and touch. The occipital lobe is involved in recognition and understanding of the written word and spatial orientation within the immediate environment. Damage to the occipital region can result in blindness.

The temporal lobe. Located on the lateral side of the cerebrum, the temporal lobe houses the center for the sense of smell; areas associated with long-term memory and learning, particularly visual and auditory memory and learning; and communication

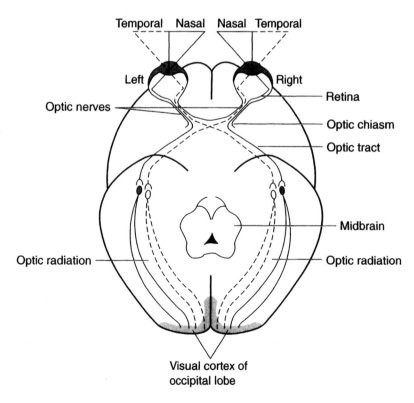

Figure IV.4
The Visual Pathway

186

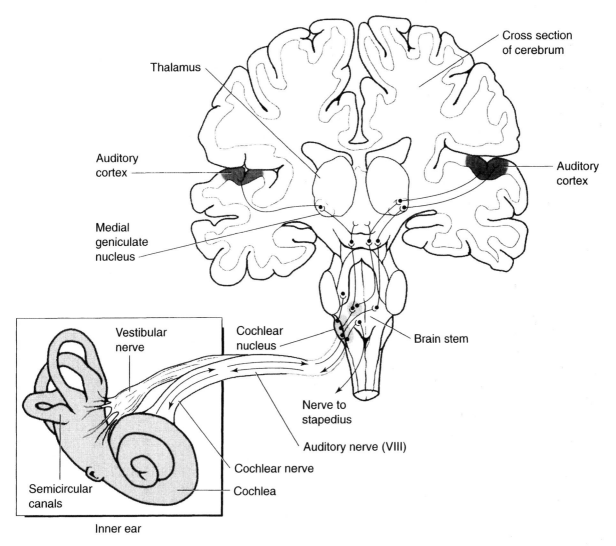

Figure IV.5
The Auditory Pathway
Source: Adapted from Seely, Stephens, & Tate, 1991.

(e.g., choice for expression of thoughts). The occipital lobe is primarily involved in the processing of visual information; the temporal lobe, which houses the auditory cortex, functions in an analogous manner by interpreting auditory information that enters via the ears. The auditory pathway is shown in Figure IV.5. A specific site for receiving and appreciating sound and for comprehending language is known as **Wernicke's area,** after the German neurologist Karl Wernicke. Like Broca's area, Wernicke's area is confined to one of the cerebral hemispheres, the left hemisphere in most individuals. Damage to the temporal area can result in deafness.

When the cerebrum is examined from top to bottom in cross section, the two hemispheres are seen to be made up of layers. Some of the anatomic divisions of the brain are illustrated in Figure IV.6.

Cerebral cortex. The outermost layer of the cerebral hemispheres, the **cerebral cortex,** is composed mainly of nerve cell bodies. Because of the gray color of the bodies, this layer is often referred to as **gray matter,** or **gray substance.** To maximize the surface area of the cerebral cortex, the surface is convoluted. Each convolution of the surface, caused by infolding of the cortex, is referred to as a **gyrus** (pl. **gyri**). The furrows that separate the gyri, similar to

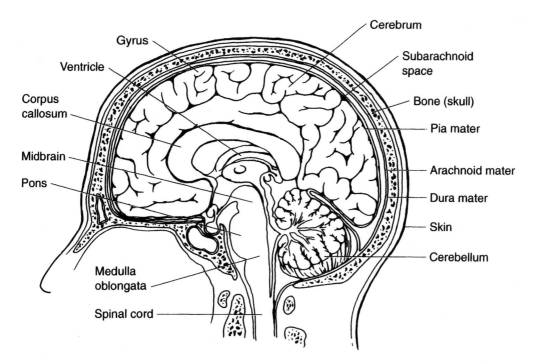

Figure IV.6
Cross Section of the Brain

those that separate the cerebral hemispheres and lobes, are also referred to as sulci. Below the gray matter lies a layer of axons, referred to as the **white matter,** or **white substance,** arranged in tracts, which connect the cerebral cortex to the brain stem and spinal cord. White matter is named for the whitish color of the myelin sheath covering the nerve fibers that form the layer.

Ventricular system. Within the white matter is located the **ventricular system.** The primary function of this system is the production of cerebrospinal fluid, a clear, watery liquid that resembles plasma. **Cerebrospinal fluid (CSF)** provides a protective cushion for the delicate cerebellar tissues. The fluid circulates through an area known as the **subarachnoid space,** located within the **meninges,** three membranes called the **dura mater,** the **arachnoid mater,** and the **pia mater** that cover the brain. The meninges not only cover the brain but also extend downward to encircle the spinal cord, thereby providing the spinal cord with additional protection. A person who develops an infection or inflammation of the meninges is said to have **meningitis.** If untreated, meningitis can lead to deafness, blindness, paralysis, and cognitive impairments. In addition to providing protection, the circulation of

CSF provides the adjacent tissues with nourishment and removes the waste products that have accumulated. The ventricular system consists primarily of the four collecting cavities, or ventricles, and their connecting channels, or ducts. The two uppermost cavities, the **lateral ventricles,** are located beside one another, one in each of the cerebral hemispheres. The **third ventricle** is located below the lateral ventricles in the diencephalon, and the **fourth ventricle** is located just above the brain stem.

Cerebrospinal fluid is constantly being secreted from the **choroid plexi** (sing., **plexus**), a network of capillaries located in the roof of the lateral and third ventricles. The fluid flows directly from the lateral ventricles into the third ventricle and then toward the fourth ventricle through a narrow tube, known as the **aqueduct.** Openings in the fourth ventricle allow the fluid to flow into the subarachnoid space around the brain and down the spinal cord. Newly produced fluid replaces that absorbed by the tissues on the surface of the brain. Absorption occurs in the **arachnoid villi** (sing., **villus**), a series of finger-like projections of fibrous tissues that extend from the arachnoid mater. An abnormal increase in the amount of CSF in the cranial cavity is called hydrocephaly, or hydrocephalus, commonly referred to as "water on the brain."

Basal ganglia. At the base of the white matter are "islands" of gray matter, referred to as the **basal ganglia** (sing., **ganglion**), located on either side of the midline. The most important ganglia are the **caudate nucleus,** the **globus pallicus,** and the **putamen.** The primary function of the ganglia is to integrate impulses coming from both sides of the cerebral cortex with the parts of the nervous system below the white matter (e.g., the spinal cord and the peripheral nerves), and vice versa, somewhat like a "sorting station." Damage to the basal ganglia can result in motor problems (e.g., spasticity, abnormal motor patterns).

Limbic system. Finally, underneath the gray and white matter layers are the structures that make up the **limbic system** (e.g., cingulate and hippocampal gyri). While the function of the limbic system is not completely understood, this portion of the brain is believed to produce expression of certain emotions and feelings, such as fear, pleasure, hate, sadness, and anger. The limbic system may also be involved in the sense of smell.

The Diencephalon The diencephalon is located directly beneath the cerebrum and above the brain stem. In this area, the **thalamus** and its related structures (i.e., the hypo-, meta-, and epithalamus) are located. The **thalamus** has various functions, a major one being the relaying of sensory impulses from the cerebrum and the spinal cord. This part of the brain is also believed to be involved in the arousal and reflex mechanisms of the body. The major function of the **hypothalamus** is to control the autonomic nervous system, or the involuntary nervous system, which is a subdivision of the peripheral nervous system. The hypothalamus assists, for example, in the maintenance of water balance throughout the body, the regulation of body temperature, and the control of secretions produced by the pituitary gland. In lower vertebrates, the diencephalon controls motor activity; however, in the human organism, this part of the brain functions primarily in modifying or altering impulses from the motor cortex located in the frontal lobe.

The Brain Stem Lying between the cerebral hemispheres, the brain stem consists of several areas, in particular the **medulla oblongata,** the **pons,** and the **midbrain,** also referred to as **mesencephalon.** The brain stem is the most critical portion of the entire brain, because it contains the cardiac, vasomotor,

and respiratory centers (in the medulla oblongata) that regulate the heartbeat, blood pressure, and breathing patterns. If these centers are damaged, e.g., through injury or disease, death may result from cardiac or respiratory distress. The medulla oblongata is also where certain fibers from the two cerebral hemispheres cross one another. The majority of the cranial nerves that control bodily functions originate from parts of the brain stem. One exception is the first cranial nerve, or olfactory nerve, which originates in the mucous membranes that cover the ethmoid bone located in the nasal cavity.

The Cerebellum Located at the back of the cranium is the cerebellum, a structure that is composed of two hemispheres joined together by a structure known as the **vermis.** The cerebellum, in turn, is linked to the brain stem by means of three pairs of "stem-like" connecting structures, or **peduncles.**

The cerebellum is the second largest part of the brain and functions to refine and coordinate voluntary muscular activity with the other parts of the brain to ensure that planned movements are executed smoothly and accurately and in a coordinated manner. The cerebellum is also involved in the reception of sensory information (e.g., hearing, sight, touch) and in maintaining posture, balance, equilibrium, and muscle tone. Damage to the cerebellum can result in significant motor problems.

The Spinal Cord

The spinal cord, an extension of the medulla oblongata, extends from the base of the skull to the pelvic region and conducts sensory and motor impulses up and down its length to and from the brain. Functioning as a conduit, the spinal cord allows for both voluntary and involuntary movement of the various structures and organs of the body. It is shown in cross section in Figure IV.7.

The spinal cord contains millions of nerve fibers, arranged into two distinct areas. Unlike in the brain, gray matter, rather than white matter, makes up the inner core. The gray matter, arranged in the form of a letter "H," consists mainly of nerve cells and is surrounded by white matter. The front part of the "H," known as the **anterior** or **ventral horn,** carries motor information (e.g., information to a muscle), and the back part of the "H," known as the **posterior** or **dorsal horn,** carries sensory information (i.e., information from a sensory receptor).

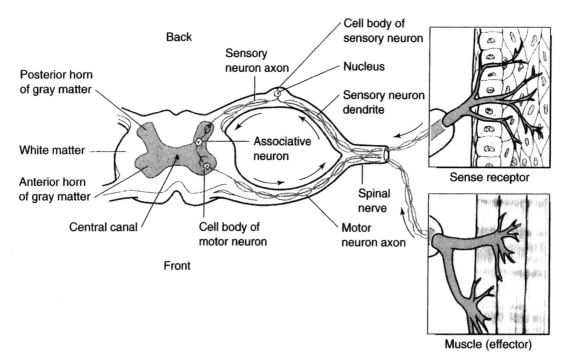

Figure IV.7
Cross Section of the Spinal Cord
Source: Adapted from Umbreit, 1983, p. 23.

The spinal cord is protected structurally by vertebrae, muscles, and ligaments. In addition, CSF adds supplementary protection, ensuring that the cord is not jarred excessively within its bony framework.

There are 7 **cervical,** 12 **thoracic,** 5 **lumbar,** 5 **sacral** and 4 **coccygeal vertebrae.** The cord is shorter than the bony column of vertebrae, ending at about the second lumbar vertebra.

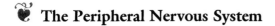 The Peripheral Nervous System

The peripheral nervous system is made up of the motor and sensory nerves and ganglia that are outside the brain and spinal cord. Specifically, it is composed of the following: (a) 12 pairs of **cranial nerves** that emerge from the base of the brain and travel through the opening in the skull to the disparate regions of the head; (b) 31 pairs of **spinal nerves** that emerge from the spinal cord and travel to the extremities; and, (c) numerous **ganglia** that control the actions of the smooth muscles of organs. The peripheral nervous system is composed of two subsystems, the somatic and autonomic nervous systems.

Cranial Nerves

The nerves that are primarily involved in carrying impulses to and from the sensory organs located in the head (e.g., eye, ear, tongue, nose) are known collectively as the cranial nerves. There are 12 nerves, designated by Roman numerals. It is important to remember that electrochemical information that travels from the left side of the body is processed in the right side of the brain and vice versa. For example, what is seen in the left eye travels via the optic nerve (cranial nerve II) to the brain, where it is processed in the right occipital cortex; what is heard in the right ear travels by means of the acoustic nerve (cranial nerve VIII) to the brain, where it is processed in the left temporal lobe.

Spinal Nerves

Like cranial nerves, the remaining peripheral nerves that extend from the spinal cord, shown in Figure IV.8, serve the right and left side of the body. As with the cranial nerves, there is a crossing over of impulses as they travel from the body to the brain for

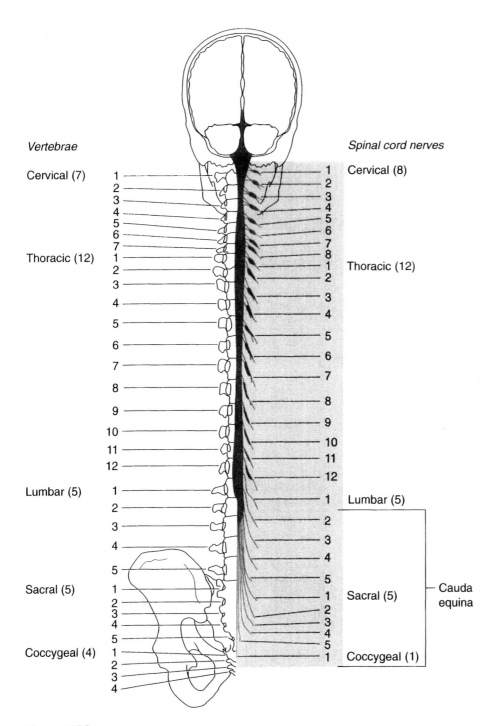

Figure IV.8

The Spinal Nerves

Source: Adapted from Heller, Alberto, Forney, & Schwartzman, 1996, p. 56.

processing. There are 31 pairs of spinal nerves: 8 pairs of **cervical nerves** (C1 to C8) serving the head, neck, upper limbs, scalp and back; 12 pairs of **thoracic nerves** (T1 to T12) serving primarily the thorax and abdomen; 5 pairs of **lumbar nerves** (L1 to L5) serving the lower extremities; 5 pairs of **sacral nerves** (S1 to S5) serving the pelvic region; and 1 pair of **coccygeal nerves** serving the end of the vertebral column, the coccyx. The 10 lowest spinal nerves, extending beyond the end of the cord, are known collectively as the **cauda equina,** or horse's tail, because of their appearance.

Each of the spinal nerves is made up of two sets of fibers, motor and sensory, and is attached to the spinal cord by an anterior and a posterior root. The **anterior root** transmits impulses *out* from the spinal cord via motor neurons, and the **posterior root** carries impulses *in* from the body via sensory neurons. The two roots combine to form a mixed nerve that travels to the skin, muscles, and joints located throughout the body.

In addition to *voluntary* movement (e.g., bending of elbow or knee), the spinal nerves are also involved in **reflex actions,** a form of *involuntary* body movement. Reflex movement differs from the other types of movement in that the neural impulse does not travel to the brain for processing; instead, the route, often called a **reflex arc,** is within a select area of the spinal cord. The individual may be aware of the movement, but the actual activity occurs without the individual's conscious assistance and, as a result, cannot be inhibited.

The **knee jerk response,** known more formally as the **patellar reflex,** is an example of a reflex action. To test this, the patellar tendon, which is located slightly below the kneecap, is tapped with a small hammer. Initially, the sensory information is transmitted by means of a sensory neuron to the spinal cord, where the information is interpreted by a central neuron in the cord. Then a motor neuron sends the message back to the quadriceps muscle, located above the kneecap, which results in a contraction of the muscle that extends the leg at the knee (the "jerk"). Even though the individual is aware of the movement, the action cannot be prevented. This test is commonly used by physicians to determine the integrity of the nervous system. In certain neurologic conditions, the response can be too strong; in others, it can be diminished or absent. An example of a reflex arc is shown in Figure IV.7.

Somatic Nervous System

The somatic nervous system is involved in transmitting impulses to and from the CNS and to and from the various structures of the body wall (i.e., striated muscles, skin, and mucous membranes). The somatic nervous system is composed of two types of fibers, which must function in tandem to produce smooth voluntary movements and to ensure proper muscle tone. In the peripheral nerves, the two types of nerve impulses often travel together in the same nerve along different axons; however, at the spinal cord level they separate into two (i.e., motor impulses travel to the anterior root of the cord; sensory impulses travel to the posterior root).

It is the **upper motor neurons** that carry the nerve impulse from the cortex, via the medulla, where the nerve tracts cross over, to the anterior horn cells in the spinal cord, whereas it is the **lower motor neurons** that travel to the muscle, ending at the neuromuscular junction. Upper and lower motor neurons are often referred to, collectively, as **efferent nerve cells** because they carry information away from the brain. The route they travel is known as the **pyramidal,** or **descending, tract.** At the end of their route the motor impulses activate either a muscle or a gland.

A different set of nerve fibers carries sensory information (e.g., visual, auditory, olfactory, gustatory, touch, temperature, painful, vibratory, positional, movement) from the skin, mucous membranes, and deeper structures via the posterior column of the spinal cord and through the thalamus to the cortical areas of the brain. Because these nerves carry sensory information to the brain, they are often referred to as **sensory** or **afferent nerves,** and their route is referred to as the **extrapyramidal, or ascending, tract.**

Autonomic Nervous System (ANS)

The autonomic nervous system transmits impulses to and from the CNS as well as to and from the smooth muscles of the body, including the cardiac muscle. Smooth muscles are made up of elongated cells arranged in thin sheets and are found throughout the body, e.g., in the intestines, stomach, bladder, and heart.

The ANS is primarily under the control of the hypothalamus. This system regulates the body's

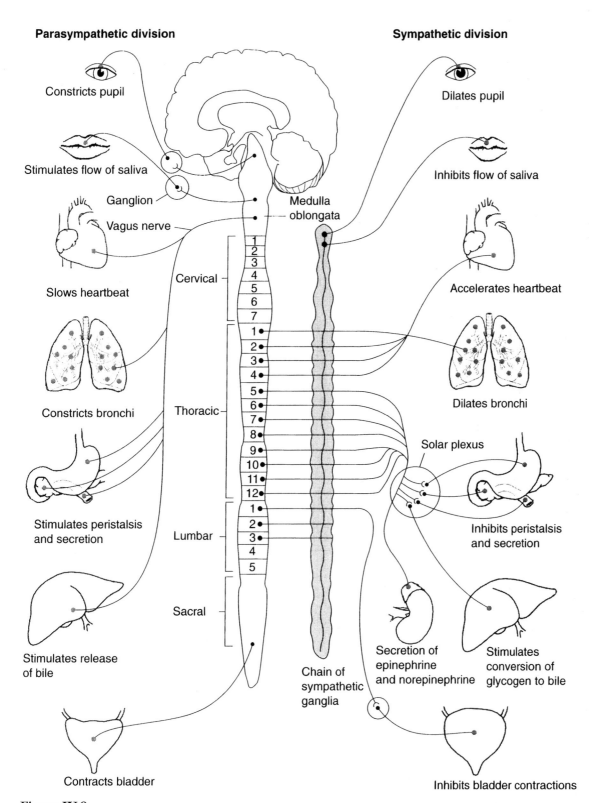

Parasympathetic division

Constricts pupil

Stimulates flow of saliva

Ganglion

Vagus nerve

Slows heartbeat

Constricts bronchi

Stimulates peristalsis and secretion

Stimulates release of bile

Contracts bladder

Sympathetic division

Dilates pupil

Inhibits flow of saliva

Accelerates heartbeat

Dilates bronchi

Solar plexus

Inhibits peristalsis and secretion

Secretion of epinephrine and norepinephrine

Stimulates conversion of glycogen to bile

Inhibits bladder contractions

Medulla oblongata

Cervical

Thoracic

Lumbar

Sacral

Chain of sympathetic ganglia

Figure IV.9
The Autonomic Nervous System
Source: Adapted from Deiner, 1983, p. 167.

193

internal environment (i.e., digestive, cardiovascular, respiratory, endocrine, urinary, and reproductive systems). A primary feature of the ANS is the clusters of neurons that are grouped in small bundles or "knot-like" masses, referred to as ganglia, which are shown in Figure IV.9.

The ANS is further divided into the sympathetic and parasympathetic nervous systems, which function simultaneously, with one dominating the other as the need arises (Schenk, 1991).

Sympathetic Nervous System   There are nearly two dozen ganglia in the sympathetic nervous system that serve as "cell stations" on the efferent pathway, just outside the spinal cord. The sympathetic nervous system acts on the various smooth muscles located throughout the body and helps to regulate glandular activity. For example, the action of the sympathetic system may result in the acceleration and strengthening of the heart rate; the dilation of the bronchi; increased secretion of sweat; or decreased secretion of digestive juices.

Parasympathetic Nervous System   Similar to the sympathetic system, the parasympathetic nervous system is also composed of a series of ganglia. Rather than being found close to the spinal cord, the parasympathetic ganglia are located near or in the walls of the organs that are to be innervated. The parasympathetic system functions in a somewhat contradictory, or antagonistic, manner to the sympathetic nervous system. For example, the parasympathetic system results in a slowing of heart rate and decrease in strength of the contraction and in the enlargement of the blood vessels leading to the digestive organs that results in increased production of gastric secretions. The parasympathetic nervous system also functions to constrict the pupils of the eye and bronchioles of the lungs, to increase the muscular contraction of the digestive system (i.e., increases intestinal peristalsis), and to induce the release of bile from the gall bladder and insulin from the pancreas.

❧ Voluntary Movement: The Sum of All the Parts

Up until this point, the parts of the nervous system have been described separately. In this section, the way the nervous system interacts with the body to produce purposeful movement is described. To do so, imagine that a young child sees a cookie that looks tempting to eat. The following events must occur for the child to reach the cookie. In each of the stages, the events occur almost simultaneously.

Sensory Input Stage

1(a). The neural cells of the retina of the child's eyes must be stimulated by light reflected off the cookie. The visual image is then conducted backwards, via the visual pathway, to the visual cortex located at the back of the brain in the occipital lobe, where it is interpreted by the visual association or reception areas.

1(b). At the same time, the child may receive olfactory sensations (i.e., the smell of the cookie) that travel via the olfactory nerve to the parietal and temporal lobes, or auditory stimuli (e.g., the sound of the cookie jar opening) that travel by means of the acoustic nerve to the receptive areas of the temporal lobe.

Cognitive Processing Stage

2(a). The visual information is then forwarded to the parietal lobes to join the olfactory and auditory information and to the frontal and temporal lobes, where the memory centers compare the incoming information with existing knowledge and determine whether what has actually been seen, smelled, and heard is worth pursuing.

2(b). At this point, the child must make the conscious decision to reach for the cookie. If the child is hungry (i.e., the feeding center in the hypothalamus is sending the message that it is time to eat), the child may decide to act; however, if the satiety center, also located within the hypothalamus, sends the message that the stomach is full, the child may decide to forgo eating.

Motor Stage

3(a). Neural impulses, originating in the motor area of the cerebral cortex, travel from the gray matter of the cerebrum through the basal ganglia, the diencephalon, and the brain stem, where they cross over in the medulla oblongata, to the spinal cord, where they travel down the anterior column to the anterior horn cells.

3(b). Additional information (e.g., to maintain appropriate muscle tone or posture) from the cerebellum that does not cross over in the medulla is also transmitted via the spinal cord, ensuring that the child is able to reach for the cookie with accuracy (i.e., the child does not overshoot and miss the target).

3(c). For the child to successfully reach the cookie, the spinal nerves that emerge from the spinal cord must extend to several muscles (e.g., the deltoids of the shoulder, the biceps of the upper arm, the extensors of the wrist and fingers) to instigate the appropriate actions (i.e., reach for and grasp the cookie). To ensure smooth movement, some of the muscles must be instructed to contract and others must be ordered simultaneously to relax.

3(d). The muscles, attached to the bones of the arm, cause the joints to flex, and the limb is raised towards the mouth. At this point a new set of instructions must be prepared, e.g., to order the mouth to open to receive the cookie and for the various glands to start producing secretions needed for digestion (e.g., saliva, digestive enzymes).

At any point along the way, both leaving and returning to the brain, a breakdown in the "relay" could result in either an inability to move or the production of a faulty movement. Some of these "breakdowns" are described in the following chapters.

References

Batshaw, M. L. (Ed.) (1997). *Children with disabilities* (4th ed.). Baltimore: Paul H. Brookes.

Deiner, P. L. (1983). *Resources for teaching young children with special needs.* New York: Harcourt Brace Jovanovich Inc.

Dowling, C. G. (1997, February). Body voyage. *Life,* 33–81.

Heller, K. W., Alberto, P. A., Forney, P. E., & Schwartzman, M. N. (1996). *Understanding physical, sensory, and health impairments: Characteristics and educational implications.* Pacific Grove, CA: Books/Cole.

Knight, B. (1992). *Discovering the human body: How pioneers of medicine solved the mysteries of the body's structure and function.* London: Bloomsbury.

Mosby's medical, nursing, and allied health dictionary (4th ed.). St. Louis: Mosby.

Schenk, E. (1991). Care of the patient with a neurological disorder. In B. L Christensen & E. O. Kockrow (Eds.), *Foundations of nursing* (pp. 1004–1053). St. Louis: Mosby.

Seely, R. R., Stephens, T. D., & Tate, P. P. (1991). *Essentials of anatomy and physiology.* St. Louis: Mosby-Year Book.

Umbreit, J. (Ed.) (1983). *Physical disabilities and health impairments: An introduction.* New York: Merrill.

Waxman, S. G., & deGroot, J. (1995). *Correlative neuroanatomy* (22nd ed.). Norwalk, CT: Appleton & Lange.

Cerebral Palsy

Cerebral palsy (CP) is a permanent, non-inherited, nonprogressive motor function disorder resulting from congenital or postnatal injury to the motor cortex, cerebellum, or basal ganglia of the brain. "Cerebral" refers to the involvement of the brain; "palsy" refers to the degree of paralysis that results from the brain insult. Congenital causes can be further differentiated into those that occur before birth **(prenatal)** and during delivery **(perinatal)**. Postnatal CP results from some type of injury, typically a traumatic event, that occurs during the early childhood years. If the injury that results in disordered motor function occurs after age 8 or 9 (i.e., after rapid growth and learning has ended), the child or young adult is usually said to have a traumatic brain injury rather than cerebral palsy (Sprague, 1992).

Etiology

The principal antecedent events, prenatal, perinatal, and postnatal, that result in an individual developing CP are shown in Table 10.1. The factors can occur singly or in combination.

The most common cause of cerebral palsy was once thought to be birth trauma, but now it is thought to be damage associated with **ischemia** (lack of oxygenated blood to the brain), **hypoxia** (inadequate oxygenation of the cells of the body), or **asphyxia** (lack of oxygen in the body) in either premature infants with a low birth weight or in fullterm infants who develop problems during the prenatal period (e.g., brain malformations, intrauterine infections). Pellegrino (1997), in discussing the changes in thought, made the following comments: "Although children with cerebral palsy are more likely to have had difficult deliveries, this appears to be more likely the result of preexisting brain abnormalities rather than the cause of it" (p. 500).

Incidence and Prevalence

Cerebral palsy is the most common cause of physical disability in children, occurring at a rate of between 1.5 and 5 new cases per 1,000 live births. Approximately 25,000 children with CP are born annually in the United States (Evans & Smith, 1993). The prevalence of CP has risen significantly in recent years in Western countries, in particular Australia,

England, and Ireland as a result of the decline in neonatal mortality (Menkes, 1995). CP is more commonly found in boys than in girls and in children who are white than those of color (Newacheck & Taylor, 1992). The incidence of CP in premature, low birth weight infants is higher than those of normal weight; 36% of all reported cases occur in infants who weigh less than 2500 g at birth (Dzienkowski, Smith, Dillow, & Yucha, 1996).

Classification Systems

Even though in the past cerebral palsy was known as **Little's disease,** after William John Little, an orthopedic surgeon who studied abnormal motor development in children, cerebral palsy is *not* a disease per se but rather a set of conditions that arise from an insult that results in development of a **lesion** (an abnormal change in structure of certain tissues) in the immature brain. There are a number of ways in which the different types or forms of CP have been classified. The most commonly used systems group persons with cerebral palsy on the basis of **anatomy** or **physiology** (the location of the insult and the effects of the insult on neuromotor functioning), **topography** (the effects of the insult on the limbs of the body), or **severity** (the effects of the insult on the ability of the individual to function independently).

Neuroanatomical and Physiological Classification

Grouped on the basis of the area of the brain that is damaged, there are four primary forms of CP: **spastic** (also known as pyramidal), **dyskinetic** (or extrapyramidal), **ataxic** (or cerebellar), and **mixed** type. Some of the regions of damage and resultant impairment are shown in Figure 10.1; each of the different forms is described in greater detail in Table 10.2. Because many children and young adults have "diffuse" brain damage, it is not uncommon for them to show characteristics of more than one or even of all types of CP. "Pure" cases of each type are rare (Jones, 1983), and it is customary to encounter a diagnosis such as "mixed spastic/athetoid quadriplegia, with an apparent underlying ataxic component" (Grove, Cusick, & Bigge, 1991, p. 5).

TABLE 10.1
Antecedents to Cerebral Palsy

PRENATAL FACTORS

Low birth weight (e.g., resulting from prematurity)

Intrauterine infection (e.g., rubella; toxoplasmosis; herpes simplex)

Maternal illness (e.g., anemia; toxemia of pregnancy; anoxia; metabolic diseases, such as maternal diabetes; infection; preeclampsia [i.e., acute hypertension after 24th week of pregnancy]; bleeding; drug abuse; seizures; nutritional deficits)

Intrauterine ischemic events and prenatal hypoxia (e.g., resulting from kinking, twisting, or knotting of the umbilical cord)

Congenital brain anomalies or malformations

Prenatal cerebral hemorrhage

Rh or ABO blood type incompatibility

Maternal irradiation

Genetic origin (e.g., genetic syndromes, such as Lesch-Nyhan syndrome; chromosomal abnormalities)

Maternal mental retardation

Unknown causes (e.g., environmental toxins, teratogens)

PERINATAL FACTORS

Prematurity (i.e., less than 32 weeks' gestation)

Anoxia, hypoxia, or asphyxia (e.g., as a result of anesthetic or analgesic drugs; prolonged labor; intrauterine ischemic events, such as placenta previa [malpositioning of placenta] or abruptio [separation of placenta before delivery of fetus], or asphyxia from umbilical cord around neck; respiratory obstruction)

Cerebral trauma during delivery (e.g., cerebral hemorrhage)

Complications of birth (e.g., from prematurity or precipitate delivery; breech presentation of fetus; hyperbilirubinemia [increased blood levels of bile pigment, bilirubin]; respiratory distress; CNS infection)

POSTNATAL FACTORS

Low birth weight (i.e., less than 2500 g)

Traumatic brain head trauma (e.g., from child abuse, vehicular accidents, falls)

CNS infection (e.g., neonatal meningitis, encephalitis, brain abscess)

Poisoning (e.g., lead, drugs, carbon monoxide)

Cerebral vascular accidents (e.g., brain hemorrhage)

Anoxia (e.g., from near-drowning, strangulation, cardiac arrest)

Neoplastic and late neurodevelopmental defects (e.g., brain tumors)

Neonatal seizures

Other

TABLE 10.2
Cerebral Palsy: Physiologic Type and Manifestations

Type of CP	Cause and Manifestations
SPASTIC PYRAMIDAL	**Etiology:** Damage to the anterior horn cells in the cerebral cortex (motor area) or neurons in the pyramidal tract that results in the reception of excessive impulses from the lower motor neurons. Quadriplegia results when the cerebral cortex is damaged extensively, hemiplegia occurs when damage is confined to one side of the cortex, and diplegia results from damage to the area that surrounds the lateral ventricles of the cortex; monoplegic, triplegic, and paraplegic spastic CP occur rarely.
	Characteristics: Exaggerated muscle tone (**hypertonia**) in selected muscle groups (typically the flexor muscles of the upper extremities and the extensor muscles of the lower extremities), which often results in the limb muscles being excessively tight; hyperactive deep tendon reflexes (e.g., knee jerk reflex too quick) may result in muscle contracting strongly (**spasm**) and repetitively (**clonus**).
	Limitations: Motor deficits range from mild to severe; mobility can be restricted as a result of sudden jerky, uncertain movements, as well as from contractures of affected joints (that result from the spastic muscle and associated ligaments becoming shorter) and the development of a curvature of the spine (e.g., scoliosis and/or kyphosis). Proximal joints, such as shoulders and hips, are the most likely to be contracted. Limitations that result from cognitive impairment vary widely; spasticity or rigidity may become more evident as child ages.
	Prevalence: Spastic CP is the most common form of CP, accounting for 50% to 60% of all cases.
Spastic Quadriplegia	**Characteristics:** Total body is affected with upper and lower limbs being affected equally (i.e., rigid in both flexion and extension); in some cases, legs are more affected than arms.
	Limitations: Degree of impact on motor development affects the attainment of normal milestones (e.g., reaching, sitting) proportionately; walking is often greatly hampered because of extreme tightness of the hip adductor muscles, resulting in the legs "scissoring," or crossing over; contractures of the joints (e.g., wrists, elbows, knees) are common; sitting is hampered by the inability to flex the knees or hips without triggering extensor spasticity; dislocation of the hips may occur, before or at adolescence; spinal curvature (e.g., kyphosis, lordosis, scoliosis) develops over time; hands often fisted; startle reflex often exaggerated.
	Many persons have oromotor difficulties because the musculature surrounding the mouth and cheeks is affected; feeding problems (e.g., difficulty swallowing, chewing, biting) are common; many drool as a result of an inability to swallow often enough; speech is often difficult to understand; facial expression may be "flat" because of muscle weakness or spasticity.
	Cognitive ability not directly related to degree of physical involvement (i.e., some with severe physical deficits may not show any cognitive impairment); visual problems (e.g., strabismus, the turning inward of one or both eyes) and seizures are common; 25% of cases are mildly affected and have minimal functional limitation, 50% moderately affected, and 25% severely affected, requiring almost total care; about 30% of those with spastic CP have quadriplegia.
	Prevalence: In 9% to 43% of all cases, spastic quadriplegia is the presenting manifestation.
Spastic Hemiplegia	**Characteristics:** One side of the body affected (right or left), with affected limbs (one arm and one leg) being underdeveloped.

Continued

TABLE 10.2
(Continued)

	Limitations: Motor involvement generally greater in arms than in legs; walking may be impaired; however, most children develop some degree of mobility (albeit they walk, with the affected foot inverted, the sole of the foot flexed, the knee flexed, and the leg adducted because of increased muscle tone in the calf, hamstring, and hip adductor muscles); hand use (e.g., fine motor tasks) is often limited because the affected arm is held inwards, close to the body, with the elbow and wrist bent, and the hands partially or completely fisted.
	If there is involvement of the parietal lobe, there may be impaired cortical sensory function (e.g., difficulty detecting size, shape, or texture of object held in affected hand, also termed cortical neglect or unawareness); some children may not attend visually to objects coming into the field of vision on the affected side.
	Prevalence: Hemiplegic involvement is a common form of spastic CP, accounting for about 45% of all cases. Spastic hemiplegia usually results in a milder impairment than other forms, particularly since there is less likelihood of concomitant cognitive deficits.
Spastic Diplegia	**Characteristics:** Legs are more affected than arms, with wide variation in degree of increased muscle tone or weakness in the legs. Some children have pronounced motor deficits to trunk and lower extremities.
	Limitations: Many children have difficulty walking (i.e., walking on their toes as a result of a tightened heel cord); sitting may be affected by increased extensor spasticity, abduction, and inward rotation of the legs and hips; upper extremities are generally only mildly affected, with subtle alterations in tone and reflexes, that may or may not affect ability to coordinate fine motor movements. Children may show signs of learning difficulties (e.g., reading). In some children, condition is not recognized until school entrance.
	Prevalence: Least common form of spastic CP, accounting for approximately 10% to 33% of all cases.
DYSKINETIC (EXTRAPYRAMIDAL)	**Etiology:** Results from lesions of the extrapyramidal tract and basal ganglia of the brain; **dyskinesia** refers to the inability to execute a voluntary movement (e.g., reach); condition may affect the tongue and mouth, making feeding and speaking difficult.
	Characteristics/limitations: In addition to motor difficulties, high frequency hearing loss and visual problems may occur, in particular, **conjugate upward gaze palsy,** in which the eyes are turned inward toward the midline and upward.
	Prevalence: About 20% of cases of CP involve dyskenetic movements, most commonly those with athetosis; rarer forms include hypotonia (atonia or dystonic), rigidity, and tremor. Dyskinetic CP occurs less often today due to the prevention of **kernicterus,** or bilirubin encephalopathy (elevated levels of bilirubin at birth that result in abnormal deposits and dysfunction of the basal ganglia).
Athetoid (Choreoathetoid)	**Characteristics/limitations:** Primary characteristic of children with athetoid CP is abnormal movements that increase with attempts at voluntary movement or when the individuals are stressed, anxious, or overexcited. Common is the rotary, twisting movement of the trunk, "wormlike" writhing, and flailing of extremities **(athetosis),** compounded by irregular involuntary, abrupt, jerky movements **(chorea)** of the hand, fingers, feet, and toes. Muscle tone often fluctuates from rigid tone to floppy tone as often as hour to hour or day to day. Abnormal movements disappear during sleep.
	Oromotor problems often evident (e.g., facial grimacing; dystonic movement of tongue, lips, and mouth; dysarthria).
	Spasticity is not common in purely athetoid form.

	Prevalence: Most common form of dyskinetic CP (accounting for approximately 15% of all cases).
Dystonic (Hypotonic or Atonic)	**Characteristics:** Most common feature is disordered tonicity of muscles **(dystonia),** which can range from decreased tone **(hypotonia)** to lack of physical tone **(atonia),** resulting in the child being limp and floppy. Those with dystonic CP often develop abnormal posturing that may develop into permanent deformities (contractures).
	Limitations: Often considered to be transient (i.e., atonia is replaced by spasticity, athetosis, or normal motor development).
	Prevalence: Accounts for 1% to 2% of all cases.
Rigid	**Characteristics:** Rigidity refers to the resistance of an individual to passive movement, either constantly ("lead-pipe" type) or intermittently ("cogwheel type"), that results from muscle tone being excessively increased and a loss of inhibition in both flexor and extensor muscles; usually all four limbs are affected.
	Limitations: Ability to instigate voluntary movement drastically reduced; skeletal deformities (e.g., contractures) are common.
	Prevalence: Very uncommon form of CP; rigidity, caused by trauma to the anterior horn cells of cortex, can occur in those with spastic CP and athetoid CP; prognosis is poor.
Tremor	**Characteristics:** Rhythmic, regular oscillations or tremors of the trunk or extremities occurring when the individual instigates some type of movement (i.e., intention tremor) are common; continuous tremor at rest is not common in children, as it is with adults with Parkinson's disease).
	Limitations: Musculoskeletal complications are rare; prognosis is good as motor accomplishments are favorable.
	Prevalence: Uncommon form of CP; however, tremor can be seen in those who have had a head injury.
ATAXIC (CEREBELLAR)	**Etiology:** A defect in the cerebellum or its pathways. **Ataxia** refers to the inability to coordinate voluntary movement. In about one-third of cases the disorder is autosomal recessive.
	Characteristics: Irregular muscular coordination, muscle weakness, tremor, irregular muscle action, hypoactive (diminished) reflexes, difficulty or inability in maintaining equilibrium (balance), and a lack of sense of position in space are common. Disorders in tone are common and can range from atonia to hypertonia.
	Limitations: Individuals often maintain a wide-based gait, with arms akimbo, to remain as steady as possible; however, gait is usually marked by high-stepping, stumbling, or lurching; disorder may be unilateral as evidenced by a child falling to one side only; reaching for objects is difficult because of "overshooting" the target; individuals have difficulty performing repetitive movements (e.g., placing pegs in container) quickly and are unable to execute movements such as touching nose with their finger; nystagmus (involuntary rapid movement of the eyes) is common.
	Development is slow and erratic during first 3 to 5 years of life; however, cerebellar coordination usually improves with age and the child may outgrow or learn to compensate; some children move quite stiffly if they overcompensate for their instability.
	Prevalence: Pure ataxia is rare (1% to 10% of cases); however, ataxia may be seen in combination with athetosis or spasticity.

Continued

TABLE 10.2
(Continued)

MIXED TYPE	**Characteristics:** A combination of the types of motor impairment is typical. Most common is spasticity of the lower extremities and athetosis of the upper extremities.
	Limitations: Clinical manifestations and subsequent limitations vary greatly from person to person. Individuals are often severely physically and cognitively impaired because the damage to the brain is extensive.
	Prevalence: Mixed CP occurs in about 15% to 40% of cases, often resulting from traumatic postnatal head injuries (e.g., from physical abuse, automobile accident).

Topographical Classification

Often the extent of CP is described in terms of the amount of paralysis of the limbs. The words used most often by the medical profession to describe the clinical manifestations of the condition are defined in Table 10.3. Many children and young adults with CP have differing degrees of motor involvement in different parts of the body (Dzienkowski et al., 1996). For example, if a student is described as having "spastic

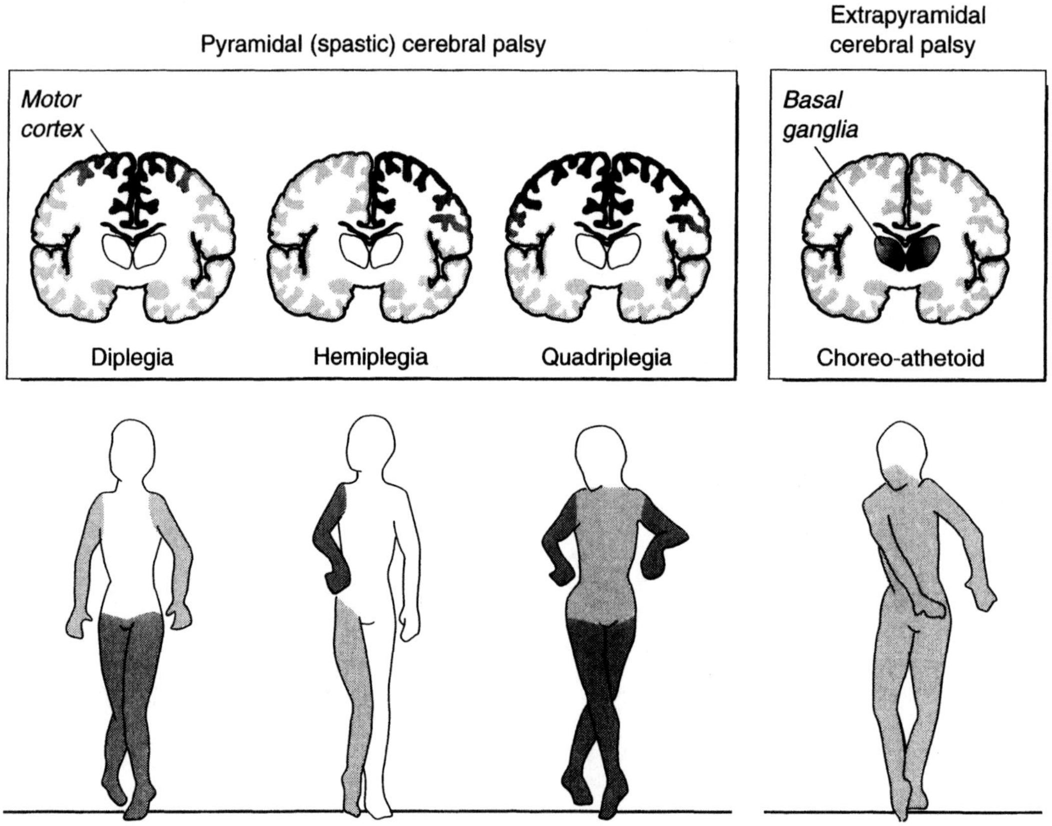

Figure 10.1
Regions of Brain Damage and Resultant Motor Impairment. The darker the shading, the more severe the impairment.
Source: Adapted from Batshaw & Perret, 1986, p.302.

TABLE 10.3
Limb Involvement in Cerebral Palsy

MONOPLEGIA	**One limb (upper or lower) involved;** seldom seen in children with CP, however, can occur as a result of injury at birth (e.g., brachial plexus trauma that results in paralysis in one arm).
HEMIPLEGIA	**Two limbs on same side involved;** arm usually more involved than the leg.
TRIPLEGIA	**Three limbs involved;** most common involvement is one arm and both legs.
QUADRIPLEGIA	**All four limbs involved** (also referred to as tetraplegia); face and trunk often also affected.
PARAPLEGIA	Involvement of the **lower limbs only.**
DIPLEGIA	**Primarily involvement of lower limbs;** upper limbs involved to a lesser extent.
DOUBLE HEMIPLEGIA	Primarily **involvement of upper limbs;** lower limbs involved to a lesser extent; often one side more affected than other.

quadriparesis with right hemiplegia,"[1] the individual in question has spasticity and slight paralysis to all of the extremities, but the right arm and leg are more severely involved than the left arm and leg. Hemiplegia (two limbs, same side), diplegia (primarily lower limbs as opposed to upper), and quadriplegia (all limbs) are the most common types of CP (Heller, Alberto, Forney, & Schwartzman, 1996).

Severity Classification

The degree of impairment in those with CP is often described as being **mild, moderate, severe,** or **profound,** and, even though such a classification system is shown in Table 10.4, "severity" or "prognosis" can be viewed in many ways. For example, one person observing a student who has great difficulty accessing the environment because of motor impairment and significant language problems may determine that the child or young adult is "severely" disabled. Another person, viewing the same student, may recognize that the child or young adult has normal or above normal cognitive ability, is able to travel fairly independently, and can "talk" to others by pointing to pictures. The second person may judge the same student to be only "mildly" im-

paired. This example highlights the different approaches used by medical and educational personnel in assessing those with cerebral palsy. Physicians have a tendency to look at the outwardly visible manifestations of the disease (e.g., the presence of abnormal motor patterns) that result in inability to travel with ease, whereas teachers tend to look at the functional implications of the condition (e.g., the student's ability to talk, walk, and perform activities of daily living) that result in the student having some degree of independence in day-to-day life activities.

 Characteristics

Typically, young children with very mild cerebral palsy have minimal difficulty in developing appropriate motor skills (e.g., walking, reaching). However, those that do have difficulty developing motorically (i.e., those with moderate to severe CP) do so because of the problems that arise predominantly from (a) the persistence or exaggeration of certain primitive reflexes, (b) the absence of or delay in the development of normal postural responses, and (c) the presence of "soft" or "hard" neurologic signs. While it is this triad of difficulties that contributes to the child's delay in or inability to acquire certain motor skills when age-appropriate, such a delay does not necessarily imply that the child's cognitive, social, emotional, and language abilities may be equally affected. In fact, it is the discrepancy between motor

---

[1] Both the combining suffixes -**plegia** or -**plegic** (complete or severe paralysis) and -**paresis** (partial paralysis) are used interchangeably; e.g. a child with both limbs on one side affected has either "hemiplegia" or "hemiparesis" or is "hemiplegic."

TABLE 10.4
Expanded Classification of Cerebral Palsy

Classification	Rate of Motor Development	Motor Signs	Associated Dysfunction
MINIMAL	Normal motor quotient (MQ 75-100); qualitative abnormalities only	Transient abnormalities of tone Persistence of some primitive reflexes to a mild degree Deviant postural development Mild neuro-developmental deficits in fine and gross motor abilities (i.e., clumsy)	Communicative disorder Specific learning disability Strauss syndrome[a]
MILD	2/3 normal (MQ 50-70); walks by 24 months	Several abnormalities of traditional neurological examination Unusual primitive reflex development Mildly delayed postural responses Moderate neurodevelopmental deficits in fine and gross motor abilities (i.e., tremor, synkinesis,[b] poor coordination)	Communicative disorder Specific learning disability Mental retardation Strauss syndrome[a]
MODERATE	1/2 normal (MQ 40-50); walks by age 3; may need bracing; usually does not require assistive devices or surgery	Many neurological findings Strong, persistent primitive reflexes with some obligates (those essential for survival) Delayed postural responses	Mental retardation Specific learning disability Communicative disorder Seizures Expanded Strauss syndrome[c]
SEVERE/PROFOUND	Less than 1/2 normal (MQ < 40); may not walk freely in the community; may need bracing, assistive devices, and orthopedic surgery	Traditional neurologic signs predominate Obligatory primitive reflexes Postural reactions absent or markedly delayed in appearance	Mental retardation Seizures Expanded Strauss syndrome[c] and others

[a] *Strauss syndrome:* hyperkinesis, attentional peculiarities (short attention span to perseveration), distractibility, easily frustrated, temper tantrums.
[b] *Synkinesis:* involuntary movement of a part of a body when another part is being moved voluntarily.
[c] *Expanded Strauss syndrome:* components of Strauss syndrome to a greater degree and includes repetitive stereotypic activities (e.g., rocking, head banging, flapping or spinning, and mild self-injurious behavior).
Source: Shapiro, B. K., Palmer, F. B., & Capute, A. J. (1987). Cerebral palsy: History and state of the art. In M. I. Gottlieb & J. E. Williams (Eds.), *Textbook of developmental pediatrics* (pp. 11–25). New York: Plenum. Copyright 1987 by Plenum Medical Book Company. Reprinted by permission.

and intellectual development in the early years that often provides the first significant "clue" to the existence of cerebral palsy, particularly if the discrepancy increases as the child ages (Pellegrino, 1997; Whaley & Wong, 1995).

Primitive Reflexes

Present in newborns, primitive reflexes are under the control of "primitive" regions of the neurologic system, such as the spinal cord, the labyrinths of the inner ear (the structures that help maintain equilibrium or balance), and the brain stem (Pellegrino, 1997), and are important for survival in infancy. Examples of such reflexes include the **grasp reflex** (i.e., if the palm of the hand is stroked or if an object is placed in the palm of the hand, the fingers flex to surround the object), the **sucking reflex** (i.e., if the child is stroked on the face near the mouth, he or she begins to suck), the **asymmetrical tonic neck reflex** (ATNR) (i.e., if the head is turned quickly to one side, the arm and leg on the side of the body to which the head is turned are extended and the opposite limbs are flexed, a position sometimes described as the "fencing" position, which prevents rolling over and suffocating), and the **positive support reflex** (PSR) (i.e., if the child is placed with the balls of the feet against a firm surface, the child extends his or her legs, thereby enabling support of the body weight while in an erect position).

Primitive reflexes generally disappear or become integrated into voluntary movement by the time the child is between 4 and 12 months of age, depending on the type of reflex; however, in the child with cerebral palsy, this is not always the case. If a reflex remains active, difficulties in motor development often occur. For example, if the ATNR persists beyond the normal developmental period, which is a common occurrence in children with cerebral palsy, the individual may have difficulty learning to roll over; similarly, if the PSR is too strong (or persists into later life), the knees of a person with CP can become "locked," which causes difficulty in learning to stand and walk in a normal manner.

Overly strong primitive reflexes can also contribute to feeding difficulties (Dzienkowski et al., 1996). Many children with cerebral palsy show signs of a **tonic bite reflex** (an involuntary reaction to stimulation of the oral cavity that results in a bite that is difficult to release) and a **hyperactive gag reflex** (a stronger than normal gag reaction elicited by touching the soft palate or the throat). These obstacles, in conjunction with a weak suck, poor coordination of the swallowing mechanism, tongue thrust, drooling, and possible aspiration, make feeding difficult. In addition, some children experience **gastroesophageal reflux** (a tendency for the stomach contents to be regurgitated upward) that results from muscle spasms or abnormal posturing.

Postural Responses

When the primitive reflexes normally disappear, children begin to develop appropriate postural responses, also referred to as **automatic movement reactions.** These responses allow for complex voluntary movement and better control of posture (Pellegrino, 1997). Also referred to by some as **postural reflexes,** these responses include, among others, the righting response and a variety of protective responses. In the **righting response,** the normally developing child is able to return to normal body position when it has been moved or has slipped from that position (e.g., a child who moves the head to an upright position and attempts to return to sitting posture when tilted slightly off balance). The **protective responses** (e.g., anterior, lateral, and posterior) ensure that the child is not injured by falling forward, sideways, or backwards (i.e., the child reaches out with his or her arms to "break" a fall). In children with cerebral palsy, these delayed (or absent) postural reactions are problematic, and consequently, they may have difficulty sitting, particularly sitting and using their hands simultaneously (e.g., to play with a toy) because they may need their hands to provide extra assistance to maintain their balance.

"Hard" vs. "Soft" Neurologic Signs

Many of the neurologic signs evident in those with CP have been outlined in Table 10.2 (e.g., hyperactive deep tendon reflexes, hypotonia or atonia, conjugate upward gaze palsy, seizure activity[2]). These obvious abnormalities are often referred to as **hard neurologic signs;** however, in the gray area between "normal" and "abnormal" are the more subtle **soft neurologic signs** that are difficult to detect and whose clinical significance is difficult to establish

---

[2] Between 35% and 50% of children with CP, in particular those who develop hemiplegic spastic CP before age 2, are diagnosed as having epilepsy (Dzienkowski et al., 1996).

(Whaley & Wong, 1995). Although "soft" signs are often considered to be normal in young children, particularly since they disappear with maturation, in those with CP the behaviors may persist or may become exaggerated and as a result may contribute to the functional limitation of the individual, particularly in those with a more severe form of the condition. Some of the soft neurologic signs that are evident in students with CP include poor coordination, poor sense of position in space, difficulty in right-left differentiation, impulsivity, inattention, distractibility, hyperactivity, and labile emotions. Because of the range of symptomatology (e.g., lack of hard signs, presence of vague soft signs) a definitive diagnosis of CP is often not made until the child is age 2 to 3, when some of the normal developmental milestones, typical for children at that stage in life (e.g., walking up and down steps), have not been reached.

 ## Associated Problems

In addition to motor difficulties, persons with CP often have other significant impairments. In one study of children with CP aged 4 to 16, it was reported that 18.6% of the subjects had one associated disability, 21.3% had two, and 42% had three or more (Lagergren, 1981). Although the initial lesion that causes the condition is nonprogressive, the physical deformities and functional impairments that result from the initial insult may be progressive.

Learning Problems

The intellectual impairments associated with CP may take the form of a **cognitive deficit** (i.e., lowered IQ) or a **learning disability** (e.g., difficulty in learning to read) and can be compounded by the existence of problems with attention and behavior (e.g., distractibility, hyperactivity), referred to in the medical literature as **Strauss syndrome** (see Table 10.4) and in the educational literature as **Attention Deficit Disorder.**

It has been estimated that one-third of children and young adults with CP have normal, or above normal, intellectual ability; one third have a mild cognitive impairment; and one third are moderately to severely cognitively disabled (Whaley & Wong, 1995). In the past, most, if not all, of those who had a moderate to profound motoric problem would

also be believed to have a serious cognitive deficit. However, in more recent years the intellectual ability of persons with CP, in some cases, has been seen to far surpass their motoric ability; the degree of cognitive deficit is more related to the type of cerebral palsy rather than to the extent of the motoric problem. On the whole, children and young adults with athetotic or ataxic CP have the greatest learning potential; those with spastic quadriplegia have the greatest deficit.

Sensory Impairments

Children and young adults with cerebral palsy may have difficulty processing visual, auditory, or tactile sensation. The most common visual problems include **oculomotor impairments** (e.g., strabismus, inability to track a moving object) and **defects in acuity** (e.g., nearsightedness or farsightedness). Children who were born prematurely may show signs of **retinopathy of prematurity,** a condition which can result in blindness. Oculomotor problems are most evident in those with spastic CP. In particular, individuals with hemiplegia may experience **hemianopia,** or loss of vision in half of the visual field. Visual problems occur in 50% of those with CP (Dzienkowski et al., 1996).

Approximately 5% to 15% of persons with CP have a hearing loss (Nehring & Steele, 1996). Some infants develop a sensorineural loss as a result of CNS infection at birth; others develop a conductive loss as a result of repeated middle ear infections. Sensorineural hearing loss is often found in those who have athetotic CP.

Some persons with CP are **hyposensitive,** which means they have a decreased sensitivity to touch. Some are **hypersensitive:** they have increased sensitivity to touch. In some, the hypersensitivity extends to the oral cavity. For these the touch of a toothbrush or a feeding utensil to the inner aspect of the cheeks or to the teeth may cause distress.

Perceptual Disorders

There are a variety of perceptual disorders common to those with CP. Most common are those related to **visual processing** (difficulty determining characteristics such as shape or depth visually) and **tactile discrimination** (the ability to discriminate objects on the basis of touch). In some children, loss of

proprioceptive sensation (difficulty in determining position of body parts or an object in space) is typical.

Diagnosis and Treatment

Unfortunately, in many cases CP is difficult to detect in newborns. Often the signs and symptoms are subtle, and it is not until the child is at least a year old that the presence of persistent primitive reflexes or postural responses, delays in motor development, and altered muscle tone alert the child's parents or physician to some type of problem. In some cases, feeding problems (e.g., inability to suck, sometimes accompanied by tongue thrust) are an indication that an infant may have CP. Other manifestations during infancy include the following: irritability; a weak cry; little interest in surroundings; abnormal resting position, either floppy (like a rag doll) or **opisthotonic** (arched and extended), which results from spasm of back muscles; and prolonged sleep patterns (Nehring & Steele, 1996).

Because no single test can be used to make a definitive diagnosis of CP, physicians base their findings on (a) a thorough history, (b) a physical examination, (c) a comprehensive neurologic assessment, and (d) the exclusion of differential diagnoses (Dzienkowski et al., 1996). It is not uncommon for the child to have to undergo repeated follow-up examinations to distinguish CP from other neurologic conditions, such as muscular dystrophy, brain tumors, and phenylketonuria.

Cerebral palsy is not a disease and it cannot be "cured." By means of an interdisciplinary team approach, children and young adults with CP are enabled to develop to their maximum potential. While the composition of the team varies according to the presenting difficulties, primary members include the student and family; one or more physicians (e.g., neurologists, ophthalmologists, orthopedists); physical, occupational, and speech therapists; the student's teachers; and one or more paraprofessionals (e.g., classroom, therapy, or personal assistance aide). In addition, the team may include a nurse, orthotist,[3] dietitian, audiologist, psychologist or psychiatrist, and social worker.

---

[3] **Orthotics** is a science devoted to providing appropriate support and bracing for weak or ineffective joints or muscles. The terms **orthosis** (pl., **orthoses**), **orthotic**, and **orthotic device** or **appliance** are commonly used to refer to braces specially designed to support affected body parts (*Webster's*, 1996).

Therapeutic Approaches

Early detection of CP is paramount so that appropriate sensorimotor experiences can be provided and necessary therapy can be implemented by team members. The major goals of therapy are: (a) to encourage the improvement of motor ability and the development of functional skills (e.g., locomotion, communication, self-help) or compensatory strategies; (b) to foster optimum appearance and integration of motor functions; (c) to prevent or correct associated defects or to mediate their long-term effects; (d) to provide educational and social opportunities adapted to the needs and capabilities of the child that support intellectual and emotional growth; (e) to provide the child and family with appropriate equipment (e.g., orthotics) to fit the individual needs of the child; and (f) to support the child and family, both emotionally (e.g., through counseling) and physically (e.g., by providing respite care), in their ability to cope with the effects of the condition (Dzienkowski et al., 1996; Evans & Smith; 1993; Whaley & Wong, 1995).

The main forms of intervention or treatment are **physical therapy, occupational therapy,** and **speech therapy.**[4] Typically, the physical therapist is involved in the development of motor skills (e.g., posture and ambulation). Specifically, the main goals of physical therapy are as follows: (a) for the child with spasticity, to develop good skeletal alignment; (b) for the child with dyskinetic CP, to provide training to enable purposeful movements, even in the presence of involuntary motion; and (c) for the child with ataxia, to develop maximum feelings of movement and position (i.e., proprioceptive sensation) (Whaley & Wong, 1995). These goals are accomplished by means of traditional therapeutic exercises (e.g., active and passive stretching of specific muscle groups or joints), which help to inhibit abnormal reflexes, facilitate normal reflex patterns and muscle tone, strengthen equilibrium, and prevent contractures (Maheady, 1992). In addition to traditional orthotic appliances (e.g., metal/plastic braces), supportive pressure garments (e.g., Jobst garments made of Lycra) are beneficial for promoting independence (Witoski, 1995).

Occupational therapy that focuses on training in manual skills (e.g., development of hand skills

---

[4] For review on how children respond to different forms of intervention, see the article by Parette, Hourcade, and Brimer (1996).

through handling and manipulating appropriate toys and specialized equipment) and activities of daily living (e.g., dressing, personal hygiene) is also an integral part of the student's total program. Occupational therapists are often involved in working to improve the student's oral-motor functioning. They may also be involved in adapting equipment and seating to promote better upper arm use and functional independence (Rosen, 1996).

Speech therapists are critical in enhancing the student's ability to communicate with others. Speech therapy, which focuses both on speech production (e.g., breath control, articulation of sound) and the understanding and use of language, should be started before speech problems develop. For the severely disabled student, alternatives to speech, such as the use of communication boards, sign language, or computerized speech, may need to be taught. In addition, speech therapists are often involved in the evaluation of oral motor coordination, chewing, and swallowing (Rosen, 1996).

Pharmacologic and Surgical Intervention

Pharmacologic intervention is also common in those with cerebral palsy. Medications may be prescribed, such as muscle relaxants (e.g., Dantrium, Lioresal, Valium), to inhibit the spasticity of the muscles or to decrease excessive motion and tension. Because such medication can lead to stomach upset, it is not uncommon for the child or young adult to be given adjunct medications, such as Tagamet or Zantac, to decrease stomach acidity and to promote gastric emptying (Dzienkowski et al., 1996). Those who have seizures are also given anticonvulsant medications. All of these drugs may result in increased drowsiness or lethargy, which in turn can affect the student's ability to concentrate on academic tasks.

In most cases, motoric problems are treated conservatively at first (e.g., by means of therapy or medication); however, in some instances, surgical intervention is required. Generally, surgery is performed to improve function, decrease discomfort, and correct or prevent deformity, as opposed to solely for cosmetic purposes (i.e., altering physical appearance). Specifically, orthopedic surgery is often considered to prevent or correct deformities that affect the development of motoric skills (e.g., contractures), to balance muscle power or muscle force that

is exerted on a particular joint, or to stabilize an uncontrollable joint (Sprague, 1992). One of the most common forms of surgical intervention, undertaken to enhance the individual's ability to walk, is the correction of deformities of the ankle and foot joints (i.e., equinus deformity). Many children and young adults with cerebral palsy have a "tight" Achilles tendon, or heel cord, which results in them walking on their tiptoes. By lengthening the tendon, they are able to stand flat-footed and walk with greater stability and control. Other joints that are often surgically corrected to improve range of motion include the hip, knee, wrist, and elbow. In cases of severe spinal curvature, surgical stabilization of the spine may be indicated.

A fairly new procedure, known as **selective posterior (or dorsal) rhizotomy,** in which sensory nerve rootlets located in the spine are isolated, divided, and cut, has been developed to reduce muscle tone, prevent contractures, and facilitate normal movement in those whose legs are spastic. Although initial results are promising, long-term outcomes are unknown at this time (Sprague, 1992). Performed in children as young as age 3, this procedure is hoped to someday replace more traditional orthopedic surgical procedures. However, more research is needed (Rosen, 1996).

Educational Implications and Teaching Tips

Children and young adults with cerebral palsy have the same educational, social, and emotional needs as their normally developing peers. Teachers must remember that "children with CP are like normal children in their need for love, independence, success, and acceptance by others; the only difference is that they cannot control their bodies with ease" (Olson & Anderson, 1990, p. 409). School staff need to maintain a positive attitude and accept working with such challenging students. While the students need an individualized approach, they also must be "approached with dignity and the expectation that they can achieve what is required of them" (Evans & Smith, 1993, p. 1423).

As mentioned previously, the severity of the student's motoric involvement does not necessarily reflect the ability to achieve, and it must not be assumed that a child or young adult with a severe motoric impairment has a correspondingly severe cognitive deficit. Teachers must use caution when interpreting test scores, particularly those that measure the intellectual potential of the student, given the difficulties that may arise during the testing situation. For example, if a young child with a severe language disorder is unable to answer a test item orally, even though he or she may know the correct answer, the test results will be questionable. It is not uncommon for a student with cerebral palsy to be classified, at one point in his or her life, as being profoundly retarded, only to be reclassified later as having near normal or even normal intelligence on further testing and evaluation when more appropriate testing materials or techniques are used.

1 *Most, if not all, students with CP should be educated in an integrated setting.* However, it is a grave injustice to place these children and young adults in general education classrooms and not give them the specialized educational assistance that they need. It is not uncommon to find severely impaired students with CP "integrated" physically with their able-bodied peers but academically "segregated" from their classmates for most learning activities. Placed at the back of the classroom, often under the care of an inadequately trained teacher's aide, and engaged in repetitive activities, they are frequently ignored by the teacher and the rest of the students. Given the extreme nature of the needs of some students, services from trained personnel (e.g., special education staff, occupational and physical therapists, speech therapists) are critical.

2 *Persons with CP typically do not need frequent hospitalization.* As a result, absenteeism is generally not a problem. However, if a student develops a severe respiratory infection (e.g., bronchitis, aspiration pneumonia) or requires surgery, school attendance may be affected.

Those with CP who have a curvature of the spine are particularly at risk for respiratory problems. Some require postural drainage and chest percussion to dislodge excessive secretions from the lungs (Smith & Woodring, 1990). This treatment may need to be carried out before meals and should be performed by an appropriately trained staff person in a private location (e.g., nurse's office).

Because of potential respiratory problems that result from inefficient musculature in the chest area, if at all possible, students with CP should not be in contact with others who have signs of a communicable condition (e.g., cold, flu). If there is an outbreak, school staff should notify the student's parents so that they can decide if any action needs to be taken.

3 *The degree to which each student will be able to participate in organized physical activities (e.g., sports, physical education classes) is individual-specific.* Staff should consult the student's physician or physical therapist for guidance in determining appropriate activities and the degree of support the student needs. The Recreational Activity Permission forms, found in Appendix D, may be of assistance in gathering information.

For students who are unable to benefit from the typical school-based physical education programs, an adaptive class that includes daily physical and occupational therapy may be more appropriate. An aide, working under the supervision of a qualified therapist, may be able to provide the student with a program of passive range of motion exercises and stretching activities that may assist in the prevention of deformities. For some, a swimming program (e.g., modified aquafit) may be beneficial. Arts and crafts activities may be an appropriate means to provide extra encouragement for developing fine motor skills.

As a result of increased caloric expenditure, many students with CP need frequent rest periods during the school day to conserve their strength. For further information regarding the impact of cerebral palsy on physical development and for descriptions of appropriate exercises that could be incorporated into the student's conditioning program, see Lockette and Keyes (1994).

4 *If the student is taking any medication, teachers should know the appropriate dosage, how often it should be given, what to do if a dose is missed, and the drug's potential side effects.* Many of the medications given to those with cerebral palsy to relax the muscles and to control spasticity, particularly if given in high doses, may cause the student to be drowsy in class.

5 *Nutritional management of those with CP is often of concern.* Some children and young adults need a high calorie diet as a result of the increased energy expenditure that results from muscle

TABLE 10.5
Feeding Techniques

- Proper positioning is critical to success in feeding. If the student is struggling to maintain balance, there will be difficulty attending fully to the eating process, and the ability to suck or chew will be compromised. A person with CP should not be positioned so that the head is tilted back, because this position may lead to choking, nor should sitting with a rounded back be allowed, because the student will have to compensate by lifting the chin, making it difficult to swallow. The student's head should not be supported from behind (e.g., by a caregiver's hand or a towel) because the child may hyperextend the body; instead, support should be from behind the neck. The individual's feet and arms should always be supported and not left dangling. To determine the most appropriate seating arrangements, consultation with a physical therapist is recommended.

- All students with feeding difficulties should undergo a thorough assessment to determine the types of adaptive equipment that may be beneficial (e.g., specially designed dishes or bowls, pliable plastic-rimmed glasses with a cut-out area for the mouth, utensils with built-up handles). Even something as simple as the shape of a spoon may exacerbate a feeding problem. A spoon that is too deep may result in the student having difficulty removing food from it; a spoon that is too long and pointed may cause the gag reflex to be stimulated. Consultation with an occupational therapist, who has expertise in managing feeding problems, is critical.

- Exercises may be beneficial in increasing muscle tone. However, those with poor jaw control may benefit from external assistance. In the technique known as *three-finger jaw control*, the person feeding the student positions the middle finger under the student's chin to apply light pressure upward to close the mouth; the index finger on the side of the cheek, just below the cheek bone, to ensure that the movement of the jaw from side to side is minimized; and the thumb on the chin just under the lower lip so as to help open and close the mouth. This technique has three purposes: promoting better movement of the jaw, maximizing closure of the lips, and developing better swallowing ability. The spoon should be placed on the tongue with firm downward pressure (minimizing the tongue thrust reflex). As the lips close, the spoon should be withdrawn so that the food is "scraped" off with the lips rather than the teeth.

- Some persons with CP are hypersensitive to touch in the oral cavity. By using good jaw control, it is less likely that the feeding utensil (e.g., spoon, straw) will inadvertently touch the inside of the cheeks or the teeth. Consultation with a speech and language therapist who has expertise in dealing with oromotor difficulties may be beneficial.

- Students who are overly sensitive to food texture and consistency (i.e., display oral tactile defensiveness) may benefit from a desensitization program. In the initial stages the student is given liquids and pureed foods that are readily accepted; foods that are rejected are slowly introduced in a predetermined schedule, starting typically with thickened, semisolid foods (applesauce), followed by soft solids (crackers, cheese), and solids (teething crackers). Acid-based foods, such as orange juice, should be avoided because they may increase saliva production. Consultation with a dietitian, who is knowledgeable about food preparation, is important.

- Mealtimes should always be pleasurable. The caretaker should be relaxed and supportive of the student's efforts. The students should only be fed when hungry. The room should be quiet and without disruptions.

Sources: Bigge, 1991; Finnie (1975, 1996).

tension and spasticity; others, who have reduced physical motion, may require a low calorie diet to prevent obesity.

As mentioned previously, many persons with CP have feeding problems. In Table 10.5, suggestions are offered that may be of assistance in developing a feeding program for the student.[5] Some individuals who have extreme feeding problems may have a nasogastric or gastrostomy tube to supplement or replace oral feedings. For further information on such equipment, see chapter 17.

Constipation, which results from decreased fluid and bulk intake, is also often a problem for those with CP (Ricci-Balich & Behm, 1996). School staff should be encouraged to follow through with the student's established bowel program (e.g., meeting the student's dietary and fluid intake needs, ensuring toileting at regular times, providing a scheduled exercise program, ensuring appropriate seating so as to relax muscle tone and facilitate elimination). In addition, due to immobilization, persons with CP

---

[5] For further information on feeding children with complex needs, see the classic texts by Nancie R. Finnie, entitled *Handling the Young Cerebral Palsied Child at Home* (1975), reissued in 1996 under the title *Handling the Young Child with Cerebral Palsy at Home,* and by June L. Bigge, *Teaching Individuals with Physical and Multiple Disabilities* (1991).

are prone to urinary infections and consequently need extra fluids (Evans & Smith, 1993). The student should be taught a way to communicate that he or she needs to use the facilities.

6 *A wide variety of orthotic devices (e.g., leg and hand splints, casts, orthopedic shoes, standing frames) is available to help prevent or reduce some of the deformities associated with cerebral palsy and to increase the energy efficiency of gait.* The student's teacher and aide should be aware of how the devices are applied and be alert to any potential problems, such as chafed skin from friction or pressure. Noncompliance with a bracing program should be discussed with the student's team of support staff. As can be seen in Figure 10.2, correct positioning is also important. Staff should be taught techniques that keep the student's body in correct alignment and that promote symmetry, comfort, and safety (Maheady, 1992). The student's teacher or aide should contact the physical therapist if there are any concerns related to proper positioning (e.g., for play, eating, sleeping).

Since bracing is a more conservative treatment than surgery, it is generally tried first; however, braces are also prescribed after surgery to maintain the improvement that has occurred from surgical intervention. It should be noted that many individuals with CP do not tolerate such equipment, and it is not uncommon for young children with good upper extremity functioning to remove their lower extremity braces when caregivers are not looking (Whaley & Wong, 1995).

7 *For students who are prone to falls or seizures, prevention of injury is a major concern.* A safe environment must be created (e.g., padding sharp corners of furniture, removing scatter rugs, avoiding highly polished floors) and normal safety procedures must be taught (e.g., a child should be taught not to walk while carrying a sharp object, such as a pair of scissors). Safety restraints (e.g., chest and shoulder restraints, seat belts, or harnesses) should be used, if necessary, to prevent the student from falling when in a sitting position. Proper head support is critical to prevent the head from slumping sideways or forward, because this can result in obstruction of the airway. The use of a protective helmet to prevent head injury may be appropriate in some cases.

8 *In the past, young children with CP whose mobility was greatly affected were provided with wheelchairs; more recently, these "antique mobilizing devices" have been "replaced by energy-efficient, creative, wheeled scooter boards and wheeled go-carts that provide mobility without restricting upper or lower extremity function"* (Evans & Smith, 1993, p. 1418). Young children (i.e., as young as 3 to 5), should be provided with such equipment: They will become more independent and more interested in their environment as a result of their increased ability to explore it with greater freedom (Jones, 1983).

Older children who are unable to travel independently on foot can often benefit from the use of motorized wheelchairs to access their environment. However, for those who are unable to control movement of their upper extremities, operating such equipment may be difficult. Some can learn to operate equipment by means of specialized switches (e.g., mouth switches). The student's teacher or aide should contact the physical therapist if they have any concerns regarding the equipment (e.g., appropriateness, safety concerns). For more information on wheelchair use, see part V.

9 *Students who spend long periods of time in one position (e.g., those in wheelchairs) should be repositioned on a regular basis (e.g., allowed periods of rest in a prone or supine position) to prevent pressure sores from developing.* Skin checks should be performed by staff at least twice daily. Older children and young adults should be encouraged to do the checks themselves (Ricci-Balich & Behm, 1996). The use of long-handled mirrors prevents the individual from having to rely on others. For information on how to position the student correctly to prevent skin breakdown, school staff should contact the physical therapist. Positioning is discussed in greater detail in chapter 16.

10 *A wide variety of **assistive devices**, also referred to as **technical aids**, is available that can assist students with CP to develop their maximum level of functioning, particularly in the area of daily living skills.* Some are considered "low-tech," others "high." Examples of **low-tech devices** include a spoon with a built-up handle that assists a young child to feed him or herself and a set of grab bars in the toilet area that allows the student to use the

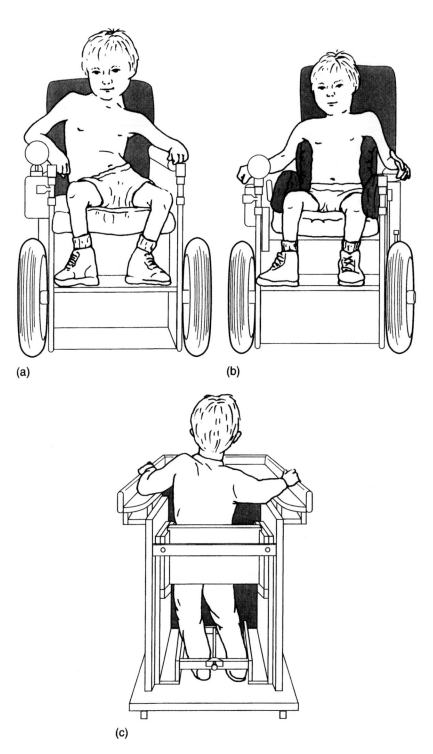

Figure 10.2
Examples of Positioning: (a) bad posture; (b) posture improved by pads
and cushions; (c) incorrect position in a standing table, resulting in student having to hold onto table due to inadequate support and stability.
Source: Adapted from Bigge, 1991, pp.135, 136.

bathroom independently. **High-tech devices** include specialized computers with adapted switches that allow the student to control the environment (e.g., answer the telephone, turn lights on or off) and to communicate with others (e.g., computers with programmable voice synthesizers that permit those with severe speech problems to "talk" to their friends and acquaintances). Occupational, physical, and speech and language therapists should be consulted to determine what types of equipment are appropriate for the student. It is important to recognize that the student's needs will change over time (e.g., as they move from school to the workplace), and periodic reevaluation (i.e., at least every 12 to 16 months) is critical.

11 *Because students with CP often have concomitant sensory problems, teachers should be alert to any vision or hearing problems.* The checklists in Appendix I may be of use in determining the extent of the student's visual or hearing loss or for making a referral to the appropriate specialist. Loss of hearing or vision may impact on the physical placement of the child in the classroom.

12 *Although some students with CP may have a hearing loss and need to communicate by means of sign language, for the majority of children with CP the difficulty is not receptive language (i.e., they hear) but expressive language (i.e., they are unable to talk or they talk with great difficulty).* For those who use an alternative form of communication, such as Blissymbolics, persons who communicate with them must be familiar with the system and be able to understand what is being said by means of pictures and symbols. Students *must* be given sufficient time to either speak (i.e., either in a conventional manner or by means of computerized speech) or to point out their thoughts on their communication board and not be either rushed or "cut off." Interaction can often be facilitated by questions that require either a simple short answer or a "yes" or "no" response (Betz, Hunsberger, & Wright, 1994).

13 *Adolescence is often considered a particularly difficult time for those with CP, as it is for all teenagers.* While not underestimating the problems that students encounter as they enter puberty, it has been reported that children with CP begin to regard themselves as being different from the "norm" as early as age 4 (Teplin, Howard, & O'Connor, 1981). In commenting on these findings, Teplin and his colleagues made the following statement: "However, these self-views and their potentially negative effects on self-esteem do not appear to crystalize until the children are in the primary grades at school" (p. 736).

As a result of poor speech and awkward movements, those with CP, regardless of age, may be shunned by their peer group because they are misunderstood and possibly feared. Older children and young adults, dependent on others for their physical care, may find that they are treated as if they were much younger than they actually are chronologically. Such frustrations may, over time, contribute to the development of poor self-esteem and resultant emotional problems (Smith & Woodring, 1990). However, the notion that adolescents with physical disabilities (including those with CP) automatically have lowered self-esteem or self-concept in comparison with their able-bodied peers has been challenged in a recently conducted study by King, Shultz, Steel, Gilpin, and Cathers (1993). The findings of this study reinforce the need to use an **individualized client-centered approach.** King and colleagues recommend that specific interventions be designed to address particular difficulties encountered by the students. For example, in regard to the students' perceptions of their romantic appeal, they suggest that students be encouraged to solve problems around practical issues (e.g., how to choose clothing that is "trendy"), to role play (e.g., how to ask someone for a date), to discuss societal attitudes and beliefs about physical attractiveness and sexuality (particularly with regard to those with disabilities), and to learn how to redefine attractiveness.

14 *The life-long needs of students with CP should be considered early on in the educational process, because most of them will live to adulthood, even though some (those with severe conditions) may have a shortened life expectancy as a result of respiratory and circulatory complications.* This includes training in the areas of daily living (e.g., cooking, dressing) that encourages independence, as well as appropriate vocational training that fosters employability. In addition, appropriate recreational activities should be included in the students' program, so that they learn ways in which to occupy their leisure hours when their schooling has ended.

Summary

Cerebral palsy is a condition that affects motor functioning. There are a number of antecedent events that can result in the condition developing; some occur prenatally and others perinatally or postnatally. More and more students with CP are receiving their education alongside their peers in general education classrooms. Many of them require only minor modifications or accommodations; others have more complex needs. For further information on the curricular and instructional needs of students with complex educational requirements and a description of teaching techniques and assistive technology that may be appropriate for this population, see the texts by Bigge (1991), Cipani and Spooner (1994), and Westling and Fox (1995).

References

Betz, C. L., Hunsberger, M. M., & Wright, S. (1994). Understanding altered development. In C. L. Betz, M. M. Hunsberger, & S. Wright (Eds.), *Family-centered nursing care of children* (2nd ed., pp. 953–1000). Philadelphia: W. B. Saunders.

Bigge, J. L. (1991). *Teaching individuals with physical and multiple disabilities* (3rd ed.). New York: Merrill.

Cipani, E. C., & Spooner, F. (1994). *Curricular and instructional approaches for persons with severe disabilities.* Needham Heights, MA: Allyn & Bacon.

Dzienkowski, R. C., Smith, K. K., Dillow, K. A., & Yucha, C. B. (1996). Cerebral palsy: A comprehensive review. *Nurse Practitioner, 21*(2), 45–59.

Evans, J. C., & Smith, J. (1993). Nursing planning, intervention, and evaluation for altered neurologic function. In D. B. Jackson & R. B. Saunders (Eds.), *Child health nursing: A comprehensive approach to the care of children and their families* (pp. 1353–1430). Philadelphia: J. B. Lippincott.

Finnie, N. R. (1975). *Handling the young cerebral palsied child at home* (2nd ed.). New York: E. P. Dutton.

Finnie, N. R. (1996). *Handling the young child with cerebral palsy at home* (3rd ed.). Oxford: Butterworth-Heinemann.

Grove, N., Cusick, B., & Bigge, J. L. (1991). Conditions resulting in physical disabilities. In J. L. Bigge, *Teaching individuals with physical and multiple disabilities* (3rd ed., pp. 1–15). New York: Macmillan.

Hagberg, B. (1979). Epidemiological and preventive aspects of cerebral palsy and severe mental retardation in Sweden. *European Journal of Pediatrics, 130,* 71–78.

Heller, K. W., Alberto, P. A., Forney, P. E., & Schwartzman, M. N. (1996). *Understanding physical, sensory, and health impairments: Characteristics and educational implications.* Pacific Grove, CA: Brooks/Cole.

Jones, M. H. (1983). Cerebral palsy. In J. Umbreit (Ed.), *Physical disabilities and health impairments: An introduction* (pp. 41–58). New York: Merrill.

Jones-Saete, C. (1986). The student with epilepsy. In G. Larson (Ed.), *Managing the school age child with a chronic health condition* (pp. 113–122). Wayzata, MN: DCI Publishing.

King, G. A., Shultz, I. Z., Steel, K., Gilpin, M., & Cathers, T. (1993). Self-evaluation and self-concept of adolescents with physical disabilities. *American Journal of Occupational Therapy, 47,* 132–140.

Lagergren, J. (1981). Children with motor handicaps. Epidemiological, medical and socio-paediatric aspects of motor handicapped children in a Swedish county. *Acta Paediatrica Scandinavia,* Suppl. 289.

Lockette, K. F., & Keyes, A. M. (1994). *Conditioning with physical disabilities.* Champaign, IL: Human Kinetics.

Maheady, D. C. (1992). Nursing care of children with disabling conditions. In P. T. Castiglia & R. E. Harbin (Eds.), *Child health care: Process and practice* (pp. 439–470). Philadelphia: J. B. Lippincott.

Menkes, J. H. (1995). *Textbook of child neurology* (5th ed.). Baltimore: Williams & Wilkins.

Nehring, W. M., & Steele, S. (1996). Cerebral palsy. In P. L. Jackson & J. A. Vessey (Eds.), *Primary care of the child with a chronic condition* (2nd ed., pp. 232–254). St. Louis: Mosby.

Newacheck, P. W., & Taylor, W. R. (1992). Childhood chronic illness: Prevalence, severity, and impact. *American Journal of Public Health, 82,* 364–371.

Olson, J. M., & Anderson, K. M. (1990). The nervous system. In G. M. Scipien, M. A. Chard, J. Howe, & M. U. Barnard (Eds.), *Pediatric nursing care* (pp. 383–442). St. Louis: C. V. Mosby.

Parette, H. P., Hourcade, J. J., & Brimer, R. W. (1996). Degree of involvement and young children with cerebral palsy. *Physical Disabilities: Education and Related Services, 14*(2), 33–59.

Pellegrino, L. (1997). Cerebral palsy. In M. L. Batshaw (Ed.), *Children with disabilities* (4th ed., pp. 499–528). Baltimore: Paul H. Brookes.

Ricci-Balich, J., & Behm, J. A. (1996). Pediatric rehabilitation nursing. In S. P. Hoeman (Ed.), *Rehabilitation nursing: Process and application* (pp. 660–682). St. Louis: Mosby.

Rosen, B. A. (1996). Cerebral palsy. In F. D. Burg, J. R. Ingelfinger, W. R. Wald, & R. A. Polin (Eds.), *Gellis &*

Kagan's current pediatric therapy (15th ed., pp. 79–82). Philadelphia: W. B. Saunders.

Shapiro, B. K., Palmer, F. B., & Capute, A. J. (1987). Cerebral palsy: History and state of the art. In M. I. Gottlieb & J. E. Williams (Eds.), *Textbook of developmental pediatrics* (p. 11–25). New York: Plenum.

Smith, M. P., & Woodring, B. C. (1990). Innervation and mobility: Implications of altered neurologic and neuromuscular function. In S. R. Mott, S. R. James, & A. M. Sperhac, *Nursing care of children and families* (2nd ed., pp. 1615–1730). Redwood City, CA: Addison-Wesley.

Sprague, J. B. (1992). Surgical management of cerebral palsy. *Orthopaedic Nursing, 11*(4), 11–18.

Teplin, S. W., Howard, J. A., & O'Connor, M. J. (1981). Self-concept in young children with cerebral palsy. *Developmental Medicine and Child Neurology, 23*, 730–738.

Webster's new complete medical dictionary (1996). New York: Smithmark.

Westling, D. L., & Fox, L. (1995). *Teaching persons with severe disabilities.* Columbus, OH: Merrill.

Whaley, L. F., & Wong, D. L. (1995). *Nursing care of infants and children* (5th ed.). St. Louis: Mosby.

Witoski, M. L. (1995). *The use of a pressure garment for a child having ataxic CP.* Unpublished master's thesis, University of Victoria, Victoria, British Columbia, Canada.

Defects of Neural Tube Closure

Alpha-fetoprotein

Amniocentesis

Hydrocephaly

Intercranial pressure

Latex alert

Myelodysplasia

Myelomeningocele

Neural tube defects

Neurulation

Shunt

Spina bifida cystica

Spina bifida occulta

In the normally developing fetus, within the first four weeks of gestation, the spinal column closes over the spinal cord to fully encase the developing nerves in a sheath composed of bone and meninges. This normal embryonic development is shown in Figure 11.1. In addition to this process, known as **neurulation,** the cranial bones develop for the purpose of enclosing the neural tissue of the brain to protect it from insult.

Neural Tube Defects

Neural tube defects (NTDs) are abnormalities of the spinal column or cranium that arise as a result of an embryologic developmental failure. The various types of NTDs are shown in Table 11.1. Defects of the spine are referred to generally as **spina bifida;** defects of the cranium are of two types and include **encephalocele,** a malformation of the skull that results in a section of the brain protruding through the skull, and **anencephaly,** an even more profound defect that is characterized by lack of tissue formation above the brain stem.

The level of disability associated with NTDs depends on several factors, primarily the extent of bony opening and resultant degree of the neural involvement and the location of the abnormality in the bony structure. If the closure is not complete (i.e., there is a **cleft** or opening), the resulting defect may range from mildly to severely disabling. Because defects of the spinal cord are more common than those that involve the cranium, they are the primary focus of this chapter.

Etiology

In about 90% to 95% of all cases of neural tube defects the condition is believed to be the result of an isolated malformation. In the remaining 5% to 10%,

TABLE 11.1
Common Neural Tube Defects or Myelodysplasia

SPINAL CORD DEFECTS
Spina bifida occulta
Spina bifida cystica (manifesta)
Meningocele
Myelocele
Myelomeningocele (or Meningomyelocele)
CRANIAL DEFECTS
Encephalocele
Anencephaly

genetic factors and environmental influences are believed to be the underlying cause. In terms of inheritance, although the spinal deformity is not the result of the presence of a specific gene on a specific chromosome, in some cases, the deformity may result from the interaction of several genes (i.e., the inheritance pattern is multifactorial or polygenic). Research data, which support the notion of some type of genetic predisposition to having a child with a neural tube defect, have suggested that for a woman who has one child with spina bifida, there is a 2% to 5% greater chance that subsequent offspring will also have the defect (Evans & Smith, 1993).

A number of environmental causes of NTDs, including maternal hyperthermia, malnutrition, and illness, have been suggested (Sandford, Kissling, & Joubert, 1992). To prevent **maternal hyperthermia,** a condition in which a pregnant woman's body temperature is higher than normal, women are advised not to use either a hot tub or a sauna during the early stages of pregnancy. Maternal malnutrition, specifically deficiencies in certain vitamins (e.g., A, C, and folic acid, a B complex vitamin found in leafy green vegetables, asparagus, lima beans, and certain

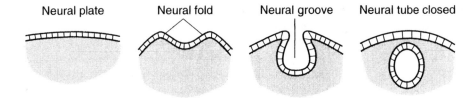

Figure 11.1
Normal Embryonic Development

nuts and whole-grain cereals) and certain minerals (e.g., calcium, zinc) are also thought to be contributing causes, particularly in high-risk mothers (e.g., teenagers, women of low socioeconomic status [SES]).[1] Maternal illness, such as maternal diabetes, and the need to take certain drugs, e.g., antiepileptic medications to control seizures, have also been proposed as risk factors.

Incidence and Prevalence

The prevalence of NTDs in the United States ranges from 1 in 10,000 births for encephalocele, to 2 in 10,000 for anencephaly, and to 6 in 10,000 for myelomeningocele (Liptak, 1997). The ratio of girls to boys with NTDs is significant—females are affected three to seven times as frequently as males (Liptak, 1997). Similarly, the rate of NTDs in Caucasian children is two to three times higher than that found in African American children (Greenberg, James, & Oakley, 1983).

The worldwide incidence of NTDs has dropped dramatically over time. In the 1970s in the United States, the incidence of NTDs was reported to be as high as 16 per 10,000 (Greenberg et al., 1983), more than double that reported today. Reasons for the decline include increased prenatal screening (and resultant termination of pregnancy), improved nutrition of pregnant mothers, and the availability of folic acid supplementation during pregnancy (Liptak, 1997).

Diagnosis

An elevated level of serum **alpha-fetoprotein (AFP)** in the blood of the pregnant mother or in the amniotic fluid, the liquid that surrounds the developing fetus, has been found to be indicative of a possible open NTD in the developing infant. In a normal child, AFP is not present in the amniotic fluid; however, if the fetus has a spinal cleft, AFP that is normally synthesized by the child leaks into the amniotic fluid, eventually entering the maternal bloodstream. The first diagnostic procedure is a blood test, and if the results indicate the presence of AFP,

further testing is scheduled. The second procedure typically involves the removal of a small sample of amniotic fluid by means of a needle inserted through the mother's abdomen, a test known as **amniocentesis.** In cases in which AFP is found, ultrasound examination is usually done to detect structural anomalies of the head or spine.

Spina Bifida (SB)

The term **bifida** comes from the adjective *bifid,* meaning divided into two parts. Spina bifida is a general term that refers to a separation of the posterior vertebral arch of the spine, and it is the most commonly found NTD. The term **myelodysplasia** is also used to refer to any type of abnormal development of the spinal cord during gestation. However, some physicians prefer to use this term only to describe those conditions that do not show any gross abnormality or defect, such as spina bifida occulta, described below. Spina bifida is also referred to as **spinal dysraphia** by some medical personnel. On the basis of severity, spina bifida is divided into two categories, spina bifida occulta and spina bifida cystica.

Spina Bifida Occulta

The mildest form of spina bifida is referred to as **spina bifida occulta.** The term **occulta** comes from the adjective *occult,* meaning hidden or difficult to observe. In this form of spina bifida, there is no protrusion or herniation of the spinal cord or the meninges beyond the vertebrae, and as a result, there usually are no neurologic sequelae (i.e., no paralysis, no loss of sensation). The failed fusion of the chord can result from the absence of a small portion of a particular vertebra or from the complete absence of bone (Farley & Dunleavy, 1996). This type of abnormality is shown in Figure 11.2. Spina bifida occulta is found in about 10% of the general population (Liptak, 1997).

Although spina bifida occulta is generally not visible externally (i.e., there is no "pouching"), in some cases, the condition is identified by the presence of tufts of hair or benign masses of fat cells, known as **lipomas,** in the area of the defect. In some individuals, there is a slight depression in the skin at the site of the incomplete closure. The depression looks like

---

[1] Findings such as these have given impetus to a new form of prevention, **nutritional supplementation,** specifically the administration of folic acid, to pregnant women.

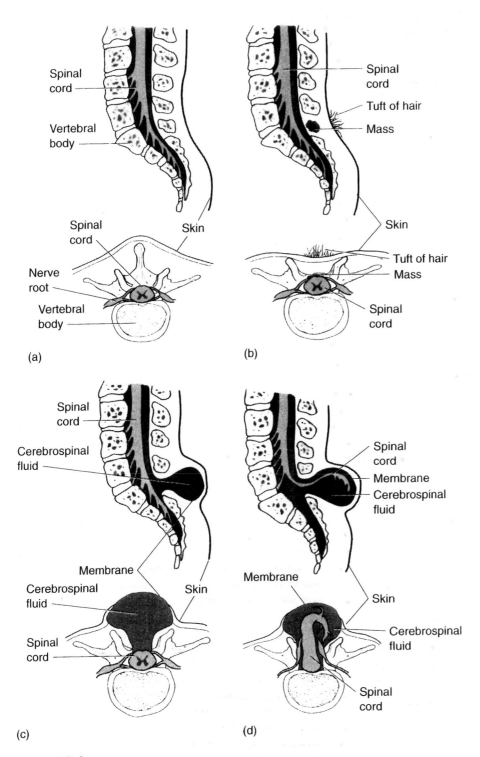

Figure 11.2
Defects of the Neural Tube: (a) normal; (b) spina bifida occulta; (c) meningocele; (d) myelomeningocele.

a dimple to the untrained eye. If the spinal cord adheres to the opening in the spine, a condition known as **tethered cord,** the individual may have difficulty walking as a result of lower extremity motor weakness or may have problems with bowel and bladder control. The first symptoms of tethered cord may occur after the growth spurt that occurs normally during adolescence.

Spina Bifida Cystica

In **spina bifida cystica,** the vertebra column is not completely closed over, and a **cyst** or sac, containing all or some of the contents of the spinal column, along with CSF that bathes the cord, protrudes outward through the opening in the midline of the spinal column. The protruding sac may be covered by either skin or a thin membrane, both of which are prone to tearing or rupture. This type of defect, which results in what is commonly referred to as an "open spine," occurs most often in the lumbosacral area. Rather than being hidden, this condition is *manifest,* or visible to the eye, and is often referred to as **spina bifida manifesta.**

If only the meninges protrude outward, which is a less common form of NTD, the condition is referred to as a **meningocele** (Figure 11.2). Because the spinal cord remains intact in this form, paralysis is rare. Similarly, there is generally no loss of sensation. However, if the spinal cord and its covering protrude outward, a condition referred to as a **myelocele,** there may be paralysis or loss of sensation, depending on the extent of damage to the neural tissue.

The most severe form of spina bifida cystica is known as a **myelomeningocele** or **meningomyelocele.** In this form both meninges and cord, including the spinal nerve root, are involved (Figure 11.2). Similarly, if the herniation involves both the brain and meninges, i.e., there is a defect in the skull through which a portion of the brain protrudes, the condition is called **encephalocele.** The most common site of this type of deformity is the occipital region of the brain, and the resulting sequelae include cognitive impairment, hydrocephalus, spastic diplegia, and seizures (Liptak, 1997). Encephalocele is relatively rare. Because myelomeningocele is the most common form of spina bifida, occurring four to five times more often than meningocele, the remainder of the chapter focuses on this form of NTD.

Myelomeningocele

The occurrence of myelomeningocele varies widely throughout the world. It has been reported to occur as often as 4 to 8 per 1,000 live births in the United Kingdom, Egypt, Pakistan, and India and as rarely as less than 0.5 per 1,000 live births in Japan, China, Israel, and Finland (Disabato & Wulf, 1994). The U.S. incidence is about 6 in 10,000 live births, resulting in at least 4,000 children annually with this condition (Rauen & Aubert, 1992). Worldwide variability in incidence is believed to be a reflection of the combination of genetic influences in certain ethnic groups and environmental factors. Meningomyelocele can be found in a number of genetic conditions, such as trisomy 13 and trisomy 18, as well as associated with other anomalies, such as cleft lip or palate and congenital heart disease (Brei, 1996).

Characteristics

In most cases, the defect involved in a myelomeningocele occurs in the lumbosacral area (85% of cases). However, it can occur in the upper thoracic or cervical regions (15% of cases) of the body. Typically, the higher on the spine the location of the defect, the greater the neural involvement and degree of impairment. For example, if the lesion occurs in the upper thoracic level, total paralysis of the trunk and lower limbs and an accompanying lack of sensation to pain, temperature, and touch are common, and the person requires a wheelchair to access the environment. However, if the lesion is in the lumbosacral area, the individual may have some degree of hip, knee, or ankle flexion that may permit walking, although in most cases the assistance of crutches, braces, or specially designed walkers is needed. In addition to difficulty in walking, there may be some loss of sensation in those who have lower spinal defects. The levels of paralysis are shown in Table 11.2.

Clinical manifestation of the condition may vary widely from person to person. Some show a minor degree of paralysis (e.g., muscle weakness); others are totally paralyzed below the site of the defect. Similarly, there may be a variation in the type of paralysis. Some persons are recognizable by their floppy muscle tone; others have a rigid form of paralysis. In addition, in a particular individual there can be a difference between the degree of paralysis and

TABLE 11.2

Motor Function Disability in Myelomeningocele

Location of Lesion	Disability
Above L2	Complete paralysis of lower extremities; weakened abdominal and trunk musculature in higher thoracic lesions; minimal ambulation with full orthoses and maximal support.
L2–L3	Paraplegia with some control of hip flexion; ambulation with long leg orthoses and crutches or walker.
L4–L5	Paralysis of lower legs and feet, with hip flexion, adduction, and knee extension present; ambulation with long or short leg orthoses and crutches or canes.
S1–S2	As above, with some control of foot and ankle movement; ambulation with minimal orthoses or other supports.
S3 and below	Normal lower extremity function; mild imbalance of foot muscular function possible; ambulation without support.

Source: Smith, M. P., & Woodring, B. C. (1990). Innervation and mobility: Implications of altered neurologic and neuromuscular function. In S. R. Mott, S. R. James, & A. M. Sperhac, *Nursing care of children and families* (2nd ed., pp. 1615–1730). Redwood City, CA: Addison-Wesley. Copyright 1990 by Addison-Wesley Nursing. Reprinted by permission.

corresponding sensation in the same area (e.g., little paralysis but high degree of sensation impairment), as well as differences between the left and right sides of the body (Mitchell, Fiewell, & Davy, 1983).

Although the person with myelomeningocele may appear to have only problems associated with mobility, the condition is complex and many of the body's systems are affected (Mitchell et al., 1983). The following manifestations are typical in children and young adults.

Skeletal Abnormalities   As a result of the muscle imbalance that occurs along with paralysis, bone deformities are common in those with myelomeningocele. Some infants are born with bilateral club feet or dislocated hips; others may develop spinal curvatures (e.g., scoliosis, kyphosis, lordosis) which, over time, may compromise respiratory and cardiovascular functioning. As many as 90% of individuals with a myelomeningocele above the sacral level may have a curvature or hump (Liptak, 1997). Contractures of the hip, knee, and ankle joints can also occur as a result of the muscle imbalance and, in some cases, because of improper positioning during childhood (e.g., poor seating arrangements).

Hydrocephaly   In approximately 80% to 95% of all cases of children with myelomeningocele, hydrocephaly may develop. The build-up of CSF in the

brain results from either overproduction of fluid or, more commonly, from an obstruction in the circulation mechanism (Pratt, 1984). Hydrocephaly, if untreated, can result in increased intercranial pressure that may culminate in damage to the cortical tissues, the development of a seizure disorder, and blindness.

The incidence of hydrocephalus depends on the location of the defect. Most, if not all, children with thoracic deformities develop hydrocephalus, but the occurrence rates for upper lumbar, lower lumbar, and sacral lesions are 70%, 50%, and 30%, respectively (Caldwell, Todaro & Gates, 1989). In some cases, the hydrocephaly is not evident at birth. Some children develop the symptoms within the first 2 to 3 weeks of life; others not until later. Interestingly, some children and young adults with hydrocephalus develop a condition known as **cocktail party syndrome** (Hurley, Dorman, Laatsch, Bell, & D'Avignon, 1990; cited in Heller, Alberto, Forney, & Schwartzman, 1997). Such individuals develop articulate speech and appear to function linguistically at a level higher than they in fact do. However, their speech is typically characterized by jargon and clichés and lacks relevance or depth.

Cerebral Malformations   In a vast majority of those with myelomeningocele above the sacral level, **Arnold-Chiari malformations (ACMs),** also known as **Chiari II malformations,** may be evident. This is a condition in which the accumulation of CSF causes a downward displacement of the cerebellum, parts of the brain stem, and the fourth ventricle into the upper cervical canal. Because of damage to the cranial nerves that originate in the medulla oblongata, ACMs can result in swallowing problems (e.g., excessive drooling, choking), breathing difficulties (e.g., apnea, breath holding, hoarseness), eye problems (e.g., strabismus), and oculomotor weaknesses (e.g., poor eye-hand coordination). In many with ACMs, the condition does not cause any major problems; in others, the symptoms include severe pain in the neck and head, stiffness in the arms, nausea, dizziness, opisthotonos, and loss of tongue movement and loss of sensation (Carpick, n.d.; Heller et al., 1996; Liptak, 1997). At least half of the children outgrow the symptoms, often by the time they reach age 5 (Caldwell et al., 1989). Children and young adults who have ACMs should be observed carefully for the onset of any of the symptoms listed above. Onset may be triggered by some type of trauma (e.g., fall from a bicycle). In such situations, immediate medical attention is needed (i.e., call 911). Surgical intervention may be required to relieve the pressure on the brain stem. However, 70% or more of persons with myelomeningocele have normal or above average intelligence (Brei, 1996). Those who have cognitive impairments typically have poorly controlled hydrocephalus, repeated episodes of shunt malfunction (blockage of the tube surgically implanted to relieve pressure in the cranium caused by the hydrocephalus) or infection, or a history of ventriculitis, an inflammation of the ventricles in the brain (Brie, 1996).

Seizure Disorder   Many individuals with myelomeningocele have additional problems as a result of the increased pressure within the cranial vault. For example, they are more likely to develop a seizure disorder than those who do not have the condition. In fact, epilepsy develops in as many as 15% of all persons with myelomeningocele (Liptak, 1997). The seizures are typically easy to control with medication (Brei, 1996).

Urinary Dysfunction   Because the defect usually occurs at a level above where the nerves that supply the bladder emerge from the spinal cord, lack of bladder control, i.e., urinary incontinence, is common in about 95% of all children. In some, there may be a constant dribbling of urine that results from an overly full bladder. Medications can be given to enhance storage of urine (Tofranil, Sudafed) and to lessen the contractions of the bladder walls (Ditropan). By combining the use of medications and a procedure where urine is removed by means of a tube inserted into the bladder (i.e., clean intermittent catheterization, or CIC), about 70% of children can achieve continence during their elementary school years (Liptak, 1997). If the bladder is not completely emptied on a regular basis, the retention of stagnant urine makes the student prone to urinary tract infections. Such infections can lead to permanent damage to the renal system (e.g., nephrosis), and if untreated, the urinary problems can result in renal failure and premature death.[2]

Bowel Dysfunction   Poor anal sphincter control, lack of rectal sensation, and uncoordinated propulsive actions of the intestines may result in bowel incontinence (Liptak, 1997). For some, constipation can be a major problem. In others, constipation interspersed with periods of diarrhea is typical. The use of medications (e.g., stool softeners, such as Colace) and biofeedback to improve rectal sensation have been successful. In some cases, surgical intervention is necessary to achieve satisfactory continence.

Diagnosis and Treatment

NTDs, including myelomeningoceles, can be detected prenatally. These days many physicians routinely check for AFP—particularly in high-risk mothers. However, if not detected prenatally, myelomeningocele is easily seen at birth, because the sac on the infant's back is very visible. Further testing to determine the extent of the deformity, such as the presence of Arnold-Chiari malformations, is performed as needed. X-rays and CAT scans are common diagnostic procedures. Less obvious conditions (e.g., spina bifida occulta) are more difficult to detect.

The overall goals of treatment include (a) maintaining health and preventing the occurrence of secondary disabilities, (b) maximizing the individual's potential to participate in society, and (c) fostering independence according to the individual's ability (Peterson, Rauen, Brown, & Cole, 1994).

Surgical Intervention   Primary treatment involves the early surgical closure of the spinal opening to

---

[2] For further information on CIC, see chapter 18.

minimize the possibility of infection and to prevent further damage to the neural tissues, particularly in cases where CSF is leaking. Although the surgery closes the spinal opening, the neural damage is not repairable. In addition to surgical repair of the cleft, if hydrocephalus develops in a person with a myelomeningocele, a **ventriculoperitoneal (VP) shunt** must be surgically implanted to correct the hydrocephalus and to relieve the pressure on the cranial tissues. In this operation, a catheter is inserted into the lateral ventricles of the brain and its connecting tubing is tunneled under the skin to the upper quadrant of the abdomen, thereby allowing excess CSF to drain from the brain to the peritoneum (abdominal cavity), where it is reabsorbed into the bloodstream. The position of the catheter in a VP shunt is shown in Figure 11.3. Because hydrocephaly does not necessarily develop when the child is born, individuals with a myelomeningocele must be watched carefully so that the operation can be performed before the cortical cells are damaged.

In addition to these types of surgery, in some cases orthopedic surgery is performed to prevent or treat the dislocation of the hip, to correct deformities of the feet, or to stabilize the vertebral column (Bleck, 1982).

Nonsurgical Intervention   Other forms of treatment include **orthotic management** (e.g., use of braces to treat curvatures of the spine), **physical and occupational therapy** (e.g., gait training, instruction in the use of technical aids), and **bladder and bowel training** (i.e., to promote urinary and fecal continence).

🦋 Educational Implications and Teaching Tips

Neural tube defects are congenital malformations, and for many, the consequences of the disability may have a profound impact throughout the individual's life. To achieve the goal of maximum independence, appropriate educational opportunities must be available to the child or young adult. Even though those with severe NTDs may have difficulty with mobility and may have a variety of health needs that extend throughout life, many persons with NTDs have normal or above normal intelligence and should be encouraged to develop to their maximum potential, within the limits of health and safety.

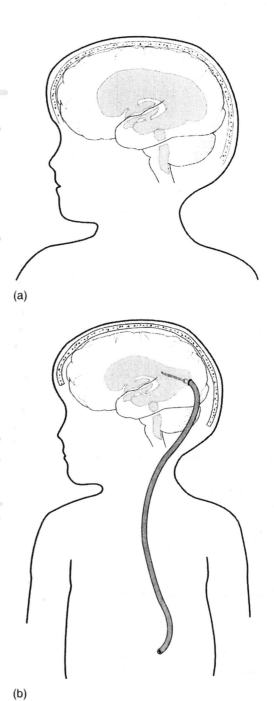

(a)

(b)

Figure 11.3
Hydrocephalus and Ventriculoperitoneal Shunt: (a) hydrocephalus with ventricles, very dilated; (b) ventricular-peritoneal shunt ending in the abdominal cavity.
Source: Adapted from Umbreit, 1983, pp. 120, 123.

Most important is to focus on the student's special qualities, uniqueness, and abilities rather than on the disabling condition; to set reasonable expectations for the student; to set appropriate limits; to encourage responsibility by assigning appropriate chores; and to encourage self-esteem by providing positive reinforcement and praising the student for a job well done (Ricci-Balich & Behm, 1996). The following suggestions are meant to assist teachers of students who have some form of NTD.

1 *Even though their intellectual potential may be normal or near normal, many children and young adults with myelomeningocele, particularly those who require shunts, have one or more specific learning disabilities.* Difficulties are common in the areas of visual-motor perception, determining a sense of direction and distance, spatial orientation and spatial judgment, motor planning and organization of motor skills, body image and body awareness, visual discrimination, and auditory discrimination, all of which may be compounded by difficulties in attending to tasks and impulsivity (Hallahan & Kauffman, 1994; Mitchell et al., 1983; Peterson et al., 1994). Particularly problematic is the development of mathematical reasoning, receptive and expressive language, prewriting and writing skills, and reading comprehension (Caldwell et al., 1989; Rauen & Aubert, 1992). Additionally, as a result of repeated hospitalizations, the stresses that arise in the presence of a chronic illness, and parental overprotectiveness, some students with NTDs are emotionally immature (Rauen & Aubert, 1992).

An individualized educational approach is necessary; however, in many cases, if not all, this can be achieved in the general educational classroom. However, some students with spina bifida lack motivation to work up to their potential; others may be easily distracted and be unable to concentrate in class (Pratt, 1984).

2 *Regular attendance at school is often problematic because of frequent hospitalizations (e.g., for surgery, to treat infections).* However, when the student returns to school, unlike some other children with chronic conditions, lack of stamina is not a major issue in most cases. A majority of students with NTDs are able to attend on a full-time basis (Hallahan & Kauffman, 1994). Because of the student's motoric difficulties, an aide may have to be employed to assist the student physically, e.g., during toileting procedures.

For some students with NTDs, in particular those who walk assisted by braces or crutches, traveling long distances may be problematic. For a young child, a belly board, similar to a large skateboard, or a scooter cart, a low-to-the-ground cart which the child propels by hand, may increase mobility, particularly when a great distance must be covered in a short period. For the older child or young adult, a wheelchair is more appropriate. If the decision is made to use a wheelchair for all or part of the school day, the student and the family and peers should not equate this decision with "failure" in ambulation (Rauen & Aubert, 1992; Smith & Woodring, 1990). For teenagers, learning to drive (with or without modified controls) may not only increase their opportunity to access their environment but may also increase their opportunity to socialize with their peers (Peterson et al., 1994).

3 *Ideally, by the time students with NTDs enter school, they have been trained to manage their bladder and bowel.* The student who has bladder problems should be able to perform CIC on a regularly scheduled basis, typically every 2 to 4 hours. The student who has bowel problems should have developed a schedule for daily bowel movements. However, accidents can and do happen, and they are embarrassing to the students. If such an accident occurs, it should be dealt with quickly and unemotionally.

It is important to be aware of the fact that some individuals with NTDs may become, over time, "desensitized" to the smell of urine or feces. Since a student may not know that there has been an accident (i.e., due to lack of sensitivity to smell or loss of sensation to wetness), the student should be taken aside by a caring teacher and told that cleanup is needed. A supply of wash cloths, towels, soap, and talcum powder should be kept in an accessible place (e.g., student's locker, nurse's office). Students who are prone to urinary or bowel incontinence should have a change of clothes at school. If the class is going on a school outing (e.g., field trip), clean clothes should accompany the student.

4 *For a student who either self-catheterizes or receives assistance from another person, privacy is important.* A wheelchair-accessible bathroom stall

or cot in the nurse's office should be available when needed. The student must have sufficient time, at least 20 minutes, to complete the procedure. Easy access to storage facilities must be available to house the necessary equipment.

5 *Bladder infections are common in those with NTDs.* Both the staff and the student should be alert to any signs of infection, such as a change in urine odor or color (e.g., cloudy or blood-tinged urine), increased frequency of urination with decreased volume, and the presence of a fever or chills. To prevent urinary infection (and also to promote bowel evacuation), diet is important. Students with NTDs should drink at least eight glasses of fluid a day. In addition, a diet with plenty of fiber also decreases the possibility of constipation. Staff should consult with the parents and the student's nutritionist regarding specific dietary needs.

6 *The degree to which a student with NTD can participate in physical activities is individual-specific.* Teachers should obtain guidance from the student's physician and physical therapist.[3] Many students with NTDs are at risk for fractures of lower-extremity bones; consequently, contact sports are often contraindicated. However, all students regardless of their disability should be encouraged to participate in some form of physical activity (e.g., adaptive physical education, aquafit program, wheelchair sports), because obesity compounds their physical problems by increasing the risk of deformities.

For those with good upper arm and shoulder strength, activities such as archery, weight lifting, horseshoes, and ball throwing might be appropriate. However, for some students, perceptual problems may affect their athletic performance. The reader is referred to the text by Lockette and Keyes (1994) for further information regarding developing an appropriate exercise program for students with an NTD.

7 *If the student has a shunt, the physician may recommend certain restrictions regarding participation in physical activities.* Typically, involve-

---

[3] See Appendix D for appropriate forms.

ment is not allowed in sports that might result in a neck, chest, or abdomen injury, such as gymnastics (e.g., headstands, forward and backward rolls) and contact sports (e.g., football, soccer, boxing). Sports that result in pressure to the head are also typically not permitted (e.g., deep sea diving).

Even if students are severely limited motorically, they should be encouraged to participate as much as possible in activities that involve peers to ensure social contact and promote the development of friendships. Being an umpire or referee is one role in which a motorically challenged student can still remain involved.

In some cases, the physical activity can be modified so that the student with an NTD can still participate, albeit in a more restricted manner. French, Keele, and Silliman-French (1997) have offered a number of modifications for the games of basketball (e.g., set a rule that the student with a shunt is allowed 3 feet of clearance to rebound), kickball (e.g., eliminate throwing at runners between the bases as an out), and volleyball (e.g., teach correct form for bumping, making sure the ball contacts a lower portion of arms and hands). Physical education staff should ensure that they discuss *all such* modifications with the student's physician, because each student has unique health care needs. Some physicians advocate that students with a shunt wear a helmet to prevent damage from a blow to the head (e.g., while playing on the playground; while riding a bicycle). Again, advice should be sought from the student's physician.

8 *Staff should be alert to the signs of the build-up of intercranial pressure that can result from untreated hydrocephalus or shunt failure.* If any of the signs or symptoms occur that are shown in Table 11.3, the student's family should be notified so that the student can be taken to the hospital for observation. It should be noted that these changes typically occur over a period of several days to several weeks. If the student becomes suddenly or violently ill, call 911.

Similarly, staff should be on the lookout for signs of spinal cord compression in those who have Arnold-Chiari malformations. The signs are very similar to those experienced by a student with shunt failure (e.g., severe headache, vomiting, paralysis, loss of sensation). If any of these signs develop suddenly, the student needs immediate medical

TABLE 11.3
Indications of Increased Intercranial Pressure

- Lethargy or generalized weakness or tiredness
- Difficult in waking or staying awake
- Dizziness or confusion
- Personality disturbances
- Increasing restlessness or irritability
- Lack of motivation or loss of interest in personal care
- Loss of appetite
- Vomiting (sometimes projectile)
- Fever
- Swelling or redness around the shunt path (side of neck or in abdomen)
- Recurrent headaches and back or neck pain or stiffness, particularly in the morning, that results from increased CSF pressure that occurs when the person is lying down asleep
- Enlargement of the head (in infants and toddlers)
- Visual disturbances (e.g., loss of vision; strabismus; blurred or double vision; pupil changes)
- A downward deviation of the eyes (in young infants)
- Increased sensitivity to noise
- Deteriorating school performance
- Development of spasticity in muscles that previously were normal
- Periods of total body rigidity
- Difficulties in maintaining balance
- Unsteady gait
- Ascending motor loss in lower extremities
- Tremors of the hands or eyelids
- Loss of upper extremity strength
- Deteriorating fine motor skills
- Increasing spinal curvature above the spinal defect
- Seizures
- Alterations in consciousness

attention (i.e., call 911) because they indicate a blockage in the flow of the cerebrospinal fluid.

While most students with spina bifida occulta have few motoric difficulties, staff (and students) should also be alert to signs of deteriorating ability (e.g., unsteady gait) or urologic changes (e.g., increasing bladder or bowel incontinence) that might result from a tethered cord, particularly in adolescents who are going through a growth spurt (Peterson et al., 1994).

9 *Because of the lack of sensation, students with NTDs may not experience any pain that warns them of an impending skin problem.* Skin abrasions

from a poorly fitting brace, blisters from shoes that are too tight, and pressure sores that come from sitting too long in one position are common. If not treated, they can result in infection and necrosis of tissue. To relieve pressure on the buttocks, some students may benefit from being positioned in a standing frame for certain periods in the day.

Individuals with NTDs should ensure that their feet are properly protected at all times. They should be discouraged from walking barefooted, particularly on rough surfaces, such as in a sandbox, not only because of the potential for injury, but also because of the possibility of developing a fungal infection (Rauen & Aubert, 1992). In the pool or at the beach, persons with an NTD should be encouraged to wear high-top aquasocks in order to prevent injury to the toes and ankles.

Burns can also be problematic. Students should be careful when out in the sun for long periods of time. Students should be taught to be extremely careful carrying hot foods or liquids, particularly in crowded situations (e.g., in school cafeteria). Hot water heaters at home and at school should be turned down to avoid scalding. In cold weather, students should be dressed warmly in order to prevent frostbite.

10 *Children must be taught, at an early age, to be responsible for keeping their skin clean and dry, inspecting their skin (aided by mirrors), and for ensuring that they reposition themselves frequently (e.g., by doing "pushups" in their wheelchairs).* As correct positioning is critical, the student's physical therapist should ensure that school staff are knowledgeable about how to prevent the occurrence of pressure sores. For further information on positioning, see part V.

11 *It has been reported in the medical literature that some individuals with spina bifida, particularly those with shunts, are at risk for an allergic reaction to products containing **latex** and that the risk increases as the student gets older* (Leger & Meeropol, 1992; Spina Bifida Association of America, 1993). The estimated incidence of allergy in those with NTDs is between 18% and 40%. Products containing latex that might be found in the school or community setting include the following: balloons, rubber balls, art supplies, "koosh" balls, beach toys, bottle nipples and pacifiers, and elastic on disposable diapers, around the waist and leg bands of pants and underpants, and in bras or girdles. Other potential sources of latex include surgical gloves, catheters, tourniquets, adhesive tapes, and elastic bandages. Alternatives, containing plastic, vinyl, or silicone, are available for most of these products.

The most common symptoms of latex allergy include watery eyes, sneezing, hives, nasal congestion, wheezing, rash on contact site, widespread rash, and cough. In some cases facial edema, "puffy eyes," itching, welts, swollen penis, and anaphylaxis (a life-threatening hypersensitivity reaction that may lead to respiratory distress and shock) are seen.[4] For those with a latex allergy, a number of practices, outlined in Table 11.4, should be followed.

12 *There has been a significant improvement in the life expectancy of those with NTDs.* In the 1950s, 90% of affected children died in infancy; in the 1990s, as many as 95% have a normal life expectancy, even though some may be severely disabled (Whaley & Wong, 1995). With increased longevity, planning for postschool opportunities becomes critical. Rauen and Aubert (1992) made the following points that should be recognized by all school staff:

> Career choices should be many. However, a long history of stigma and attitudes that conceptualize these individuals as being able to perform only limited jobs is difficult to break. Lack of adequate educational and vocational planning seems to be a greater challenge for these individuals than the physical problems that they face. (p. 22)

---

[4] For further information on allergies and allergic reactions, see chapter 22.

TABLE 11.4
Latex Allergies: Recommended Practices

- Place the student on "LATEX ALERT" (i.e., remove items that contain latex from the environment, thereby lessening the possibility of the allergic reaction).
- Teach the student to recognize latex products and to avoid them.
- Ensure that all caregivers (e.g., teachers, day care personnel, doctors, dentists, nurses) are aware of the potential or confirmed allergy.
- Require students to wear allergy alert (Medic-Alert) bracelets or necklaces.
- Ensure that emergency supplies, such as auto-injectable epinephrine (see chapter 22) and sterile non-latex gloves, are available.
- Educate adolescents about the potential risks of the use of latex condoms and diaphragms and offer guidance regarding alternative forms of birth control.

For children with myelomeningocele to successfully enter the world of adulthood, Rauen and Aubert stressed the importance of the development of leisure-time activities, the availability of counseling (including appropriate counseling in the area of sexuality) to assist adolescents to deal with the social and emotional challenges of their condition (e.g., altered body image), the training in acts of daily living that encourage independent living, the need for finding accessible housing, and the development of age-appropriate coping skills (e.g., assertiveness), which focus on ability, rather than disability.

13 *Unfortunately, during adolescence, compliance with established routines can be problematic.* Peterson et al. (1994) have suggested that the "adolescent's desire for complete independence can put him or her at high risk of neglecting health-care needs" (p. 238). Because the young adult may resist parental control, proper skin care, bowel and bladder programs, and hygiene routines may be ignored. Teachers and counselors should be alert to any signs that the student is neglecting his or her responsibilities.

While specialized counseling may not be available through the school system, school counselors may be able to assist the young adult to make contact with one of the various specialty clinics that have been developed to address the needs of those with NTDs (e.g., St. Michael Hospital Teen/Adult Focused Spina Bifida Multispeciality Center, in Milwaukee, WI). In addition, by contacting the local branch of agencies that support persons with spina bifida, it may be possible to connect young adolescents with older adults who can serve as role models.

♥ Summary

NTDs are congenital disorders in which there is improper closure of the spinal tube that results in a number of impairments. Many individuals born with neurologic defects were, in the past, "lucky" to survive infancy. Those who did live to school age were often denied an education. Those who were educated were, in most cases, placed in segregated classes away from their normally developing peers. Today, students with NTDs are attending public schools and are expecting not only to obtain an education commensurate with their needs but to receive their schooling in general education classrooms. In 1983, Mitchell and her colleagues made the following comments regarding the future for children with NTDs. Their comments are still appropriate 15 years later.

> Until the past few decades, schools and the general public have been unaware of congenital defects of the spinal cord and the vertebral column. . . . These birth defects are very common; yet, until good treatment evolved, they represented a private tragedy to affected families. . . . Modern medical and surgical care opened the door to effective treatment. . . . There has been a "quiet revolution" in interest, knowledge, quality of care, and realistic hope for persons born with spina bifida. (pp. 117–118)

The suggestions given in this chapter are intended to assist school staff develop appropriate educational programs. For further information on specific teaching techniques for students with spina bifida, the reader is referred to the texts by Bigge (1991), Rowley-Kelly and Teigel (1993), and Williamson (1987). An excellent source of information for teenagers with spina bifida is the manual by Susan Carpick, entitled *Yes You Can: A Kit for Teens,* available from the Spina Bifida Association of Canada.

References

Bigge, J. L. (1991). *Teaching individuals with physical and multiple disabilities* (3rd ed.). New York: Merrill.

Bleck, E. E. (1982). Myelomeningocele, meningocele, and spina bifida. In E. E. Bleck & D. A. Nagel (Eds.), *Physically handicapped children: A medical atlas for teachers* (2nd ed., pp. 345–362). New York: Grune & Stratton.

Brei, T. J. (1996). Meningomyelocele. In F. D. Burg, J. R. Ingelfinger, W. R. Wald, & R. A. Polin (Eds.), *Gellis & Kagan's current pediatric therapy* (15th ed., pp. 76–79). Philadelphia: W. B. Saunders

Caldwell, T. H., Todaro, A. W., & Gates, A. J. (1989). *Community provider's guide: An information outline for working with children with special health needs.* New Orleans, LA: Children's Hospital.

Carpick, S. (n.d.). *Yes you can: A kit for teens.* Winnipeg, MAN: Spina Bifida Association of Canada.

Disabato, J., & Wulf, J. (1994). Altered neurologic function. In C. L. Betz, M. M. Hunsberger, & S. Wright (Eds.), *Family-centered nursing care of children* (2nd ed., pp. 1717–1814). Philadelphia: W. B. Saunders.

Evans, J. C., & Smith, J. (1993). Nursing planning, intervention, and evaluation for altered neurologic function.

In D. B. Jackson & R. B. Saunders (Eds.), *Child health nursing: A comprehensive approach to the care of children and their families* (pp. 1353–1430). Philadelphia: J. B. Lippincott.

Farley, J. A., & Dunleavy, M. J. (1996). Myelodysplasia. In P. L. Jackson & J. A. Vessey (Eds.), *Primary care of the child with a chronic condition* (2nd ed., pp. 580–587). St. Louis: Mosby.

French, R., Keele, M., & Silliman-French, L. (1997). Students with shunts: Program considerations. *Journal of Physical Education, Recreation, & Dance, 68*(1), 54–56.

Greenberg, F., James, L. M., & Oakley, Jr., G. P. (1983). Estimates of birth prevalence rates of spina bifida in the United States from computer-generated maps. *American Journal of Obstetrics and Gynecology, 145,* 570–573.

Hallahan, D. P., & Kauffman, J. M. (1994). *Exceptional children: Introduction to special education* (6th ed.). Boston: Allyn & Bacon.

Heller, K. W., Alberto, P. A., Forney, P. E., & Schwartzman, M. N. (1996). *Understanding physical, sensory, and health impairments: Characteristics and educational implications.* Pacific Grove, CA: Brooks/Cole.

Leger, R. R., & Meeropol, E. (1992). Children at risk: Latex allergy and spina bifida. *Journal of Pediatric Nursing, 7,* 371–376.

Liptak, G. S. (1997). Neural tube defects. In M. L. Batshaw (Ed.), *Children with disabilities* (4th ed., pp. 529–552). Baltimore: Paul H. Brookes.

Lockette, K. F., & Keyes, A. M. (1994). *Conditioning with physical disabilities.* Champaign, IL: Human Kinetics.

Mitchell, D. C., Fiewell, E., & Davy, P. (1983). Spina bifida. In J. Umbreit (Ed.), *Physical disabilities and health impairments: An introduction* (pp. 117–131). New York: Merrill.

Peterson, P. M., Rauen, K. K., Brown, J., & Cole, J. (1994). Spina bifida: The transition into adulthood begins in infancy. *Rehabilitation Nursing, 19,* 229–238.

Pratt, L. (1984). Integrating the child with spina bifida into school. *Health Visitor, 57*(8), 242–243.

Rauen, K. K., & Aubert, E. J. (1992). A brighter future for adults who have myelomeningocele—one form of spina bifida. *Orthopaedic Nursing, 11*(3), 16–26.

Ricci-Balich, J., & Behm, J. A. (1996). Pediatric rehabilitation nursing. In S. P. Hoeman (Ed.), *Rehabilitation nursing: Process and application* (pp. 660–682). St. Louis: Mosby.

Rowley-Kelly, F. L., & Teigel, D. H. (1993). *Teaching the student with spina bifida.* Baltimore, MD: Paul H. Brookes.

Sandford, M. K., Kissling, G. E., & Joubert, P. E. (1992). Neural tube defect etiology: New evidence concerning maternal hyperthermia, health, and diet. *Developmental Medicine and Child Neurology, 34,* 661–675.

Smith, M. P., & Woodring, B. C. (1990). Innervation and mobility: Implications of altered neurologic and neuromuscular function. In S. R. Mott, S. R. James, & A. M. Sperhac, *Nursing care of children and families* (2nd ed., pp. 1615–1730). Redwood City, CA: Addison-Wesley.

Spina Bifida Association of America (1993). *Update: Latex allergy.* Washington, DC: Author.

Umbreit, J. (Ed.). (1983). *Physical disabilities and health impairments: An introduction.* New York: Merrill.

Whaley, L. F., & Wong, D. L. (1995). *Nursing care of infants and children* (5th ed.). St. Louis: Mosby.

Williamson, G. G. (1987). *Children with spina bifida.* Baltimore, MD: Paul H. Brookes.

Seizure Disorders

Regardless of whether an individual is awake or asleep, at any given moment, there is electrical activity occurring in the brain. Some groups of neurons of the brain are actively firing, some are firing but with less vigor, and others are inactive. In some individuals, for a variety of reasons, some known and others unknown, there can be, at certain times, a sudden, excessive, disorderly discharge of neuronal excitation in the brain, which may result in an involuntary, transient impairment of consciousness, sensation, memory, movement, behavior, or autonomic functioning in the human body. Some have likened the event, known as a **seizure,** to an engine misfiring or to a power surge in a computer. If the person has a tendency to have chronic, recurrent episodes, unaccompanied by fever or illness, the diagnosis is a **seizure disorder,** commonly referred to as **epilepsy.**[1] The primary focus of discussion in this chapter is on the chronic forms of the condition that may be evidenced in school-age children and young adults (i.e., those who have epilepsy), rather than on isolated "nonepileptic" seizures, which in most cases result from a specific medical problem, such as high fever,[2] alcohol withdrawal, imbalance of body chemicals or fluids, lack of oxygen to the brain, or severe allergic reactions (Jones-Saete, 1986). Emphasis is on how to ensure the safety of students with epilepsy during a seizure and how to support them in a manner that allows for maximum participation in the programs offered by the school.

Epilepsy

Epilepsy comes from the Greek word *epilepsia,* meaning "to seize upon" or a "taking hold of" and has, in the past, been referred to as the "falling sickness" or the "falling evil" (Adams & Victor, 1993). Regardless of the terminology, epilepsy is not a *disease* per se, nor is it a form of mental illness. Instead, the occurrence of repetitive seizures is a *symptom* of an underlying dysfunction of the brain. Seizures can occur for a variety of reasons, such as drug abuse, infection, and head trauma; however, a solitary seizure can occur to anyone under exceptional circumstances, such as when a person has a high fever. In the following sections some of these causes are examined in more detail. The discussion begins with a description of the various types of seizures—partial, generalized, and mixed.

Seizure Types

While it has been suggested that more than 30 types of seizures exist (Jones-Saete, 1986), there are two fundamentally different categories of seizures, those whose site of origin is localized to a specific group of neurons in a specific area of the brain **(partial seizures)** and those that involve a larger portion of the brain **(generalized seizures).** Some children have both types of seizures, a condition referred to as a **mixed-seizure disorder.**

Regardless of type, typically seizures can be divided into four general phases: (1) the **prodromal,** or **early warning, phase,** which is the period days or hours before the seizure begins, (2) the **preictal phase,** the period immediately before the seizure begins, (3) the **ictal phase,** the phase that begins with seizure activity and terminates when the seizure ends, and (4) the **postictal phase** or **recovery stage,** the period immediately after a seizure. The clinical manifestations of each of the stages differ depending on the type of seizure, and some stages are more evident in some types of seizures than in others. Each of the types and subtypes are listed in Table 12.1.

Partial Seizures   The discharge of electrical activity in a partial seizure is restricted, initially, to one or two areas within the same hemisphere (i.e., left *or* right) of the brain. Because the activity is localized in a specific area, referred to as the **epileptogenic focus,** and the effect on brain function is limited, or "focal," in nature, this type of seizure has been, in the past, referred to as a **focal seizure.**

Partial seizures usually occur as a result of some underlying condition that causes damage to a specific portion of the brain (i.e., they are secondary seizures, arising, e.g., from scar tissue that results from trauma or surgery), and while they originate most commonly in the frontal, temporal, or parietal lobes of the brain, they can occur anywhere within the cerebral cortex (Figure 12.1). As a partial seizure

---

[1] Some persons use the term **convulsion** rather than seizure and consequently refer to the chronic form as a **convulsive disorder;** however, others use the term to refer specifically to the muscle contractions that occur in certain types of motor seizures.

[2] Seizures that result from high fever (i.e., over 102°F, or 39°C) are referred to as **febrile seizures.** Common in children between 6 months and 5 years of age (peaking at 18 months), between 3% and 5% of all children have such a seizure in their early years (Nealis, 1983).

TABLE 12.1
Seizure Disorder: Classification by Type

PARTIAL SEIZURES
(local)

Simple partial (i.e., without impairment of consciousness)
With motor symptoms
With sensory or somatosensory symptoms
With autonomic symptoms
With psychic symptoms
Complex partial (i.e., with impairment of consciousness)
Partial seizures (simple or complex) with secondary generalization

GENERALIZED SEIZURES
(bilaterally symmetrical and not local)

Tonic-clonic seizures
Generalized tonic-clonic

Tonic

Clonic

Clonic-tonic-clonic

Absence seizures

Myoclonic

Infantile spasms

Atonic seizures

---

progresses, the abnormal electrical activity may extend to adjacent areas on the same side of the brain or, in some cases, may spread from one side of the brain to the other. When the electrical activity spreads in such a manner, a generalized seizure occurs.

Partial seizures are subdivided into two groups—**simple** and **complex.** The division is based on the degree to which consciousness is impaired during the event.

Simple partial seizure. In a simple partial seizure, an individual does *not* experience any loss of consciousness during the ictal phase. Generally, in this type of seizure, there is no forewarning that it is about to occur; i.e., there is no distinct preictal phase. Simple partial seizures differ from person to person; however, they tend to be stereotyped from episode to episode for each individual (Wyllie, Rothner, & Lüders, 1989). Symptoms can be primarily motoric (e.g., twitching of a body part), sensory (e.g., olfactory hallucination), autonomic (e.g., flushing, vomiting), or psychic and affective (e.g., feelings of fear or displeasure). However, the person does not lose awareness of his or her external environment. Because the child remains alert during a simple seizure, in most cases the activities that were engaged in before the episode can immediately be resumed. In some children, a simple seizure may

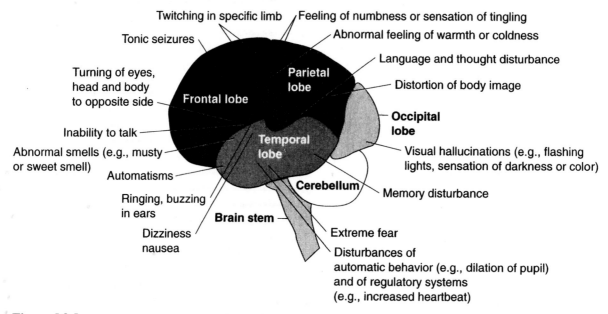

Figure 12.1
Origin of Symptoms and Signs in Focal (Partial) Seizures. The diagram shows the dominant hemisphere.

progress to a complex partial seizure or generalized seizure, a condition referred to as a simple seizure with secondary generalization.

Simple partial with motor symptoms—If the partial seizure originates in the motor areas of the frontal lobe, motor involvement during the ictal phase is typical. This is the most common form of simple partial seizure. Spasmodic twitching of a particular muscle group (e.g., a specific finger or toe) or contiguous groups of muscles (e.g., hand and arm or foot and leg) is typical. In some children, twitching of facial muscles is common. Children with spastic hemiplegic cerebral palsy commonly have this type of seizure.

If the motor area that controls the oromotor area is affected, the child may be seen to be making chewing, lip-smacking, and swallowing movements, and there may be evidence of profuse salivation (drooling). If the seizure begins in the section of the brain that controls eye movement, the child may turn the eyes or both head and eyes suddenly to one side. In some cases, at the same time as the eye movement, the child may extend an arm with fist clenched so that it appears as if the child is looking at his or her hand.

Depending on the site and spread of the electrical discharge, the motor pattern during a partial seizure typically varies from individual to individual. However, for a specific individual the pattern is often consistent from one episode to the next. For example, if only an isolated area on one side of the brain is involved, the symptoms occur, most commonly, in a defined spot on a contralateral side of the body. For example, if the site of the seizure is in an isolated spot in the right hemisphere, the left finger might begin to twitch, followed, possibly with the left hand and arm twitching as the burst of electrical energy progresses to the surrounding cells.

If the abnormal discharge of electrical activity in a partial motor seizure spreads to other areas within the same hemisphere, there may be **ipsilateral involvement;** that is, different limbs on the same side of the body begin to move. For example, in the case just described above, the muscle activity may spread so that not only the left hand and arm move but the left leg also begins to convulse. As long as the electrical discharge is isolated to one side of the brain, only one side of the body shows muscle stimulation. However, in some cases, the electrical discharge moves from an isolated spot on one of the hemispheres to other areas within the same hemisphere

and finally to the other hemisphere. Consequently the motoric activity pattern progresses from one limb to the second ipsilateral limb, and finally to the contralateral side, resulting in a generalized convulsion that may involve all four limbs. This pattern of progression has been referred to as **"march" epilepsy** or **jacksonian epilepsy,** after the British neurologist John Hughlings Jackson, who, in describing the various defects common to brain-damaged persons, proposed that there must be a specific area in the brain responsible for controlling motor activity (Knight, 1992). Even though a simple motor seizure usually lasts less than a minute, there may be a transient paralysis of the muscle groups that have been affected, known as **Todd's paralysis,** that can last for 24 hours or more (i.e., in the postictal phase).

Simple partial with sensory and somatosensory symptoms—If the partial seizure begins in the sensory areas of the parietal lobe, the first symptoms of the ictal phase may be either a feeling of numbness or a sensation of tingling or prickling, often described as being akin to "pins and needles" in a specific body part. Some individuals with partial sensory seizures may experience an abnormal feeling of warmth or burning or, conversely, coldness. Occasionally there are complaints of pain in a localized area. Some describe a particular limb as feeling "dead," whereas others may report the sense of movement in a specific limb. In most cases, the site of onset is the lips, fingers or toes, and quickly the sensations progress to adjacent parts of the body (e.g., face, hands, feet).

If the occipital lobe is affected, the individual may "see" flashing or flickering lights or spots before his or her eyes. In some cases, there may be a sensation of darkness; in others, the individual may report seeing colors, the most common being red, followed by blue, green, and yellow (Adams & Victor, 1993). If the temporal lobe is affected, the children may complain of ringing, roaring, or buzzing in the ears; however, as an initial manifestation of a seizure, auditory hallucinations are infrequent in children. In some cases, the children will experience an acrid, musty, or sweet smell, or an unpleasant taste. As in the case of motor seizures, the sensory pattern varies from person to person, but in most cases the symptoms experienced by the individual are consistent from seizure to seizure. For example, a child who frequently experiences visual hallucinations is unlikely to suddenly experience olfactory symptoms.

Sensory seizures are believed to occur more commonly in older children (i.e., over the age of 8) and in adults, compared to infants and young children. However, because this type of seizure does not result in abnormal body movements, as is the case with motor seizures, the episode may go unrecognized by others. Simple partial sensory seizures generally do not result in any long-term sequelae.

Simple partial with autonomic symptoms—Some simple partial seizures result in symptoms that are directly related to stimulation of the autonomic nervous system (e.g., increased heart beat, dilation of the pupil). Since autonomic symptoms are found more commonly in children who have complex partial seizures, they are described in greater detail in the following section.

Simple partial with psychic symptoms—In some cases, children who have simple partial seizures experience psychic symptoms (e.g., hallucinations, extreme fear). However, as in the case of autonomic symptoms, these types of symptoms are found more commonly in children who have complex partial seizures, so they are described later.

Complex partial seizure. In contrast to a simple partial seizure, during a complex partial seizure, a child loses consciousness for a period during the ictal phase. In most cases, a complex partial seizure lasts for up to several minutes (i.e., 5 to 10). However, in some cases, the period may be so brief, as little as 10 seconds,[3] that no one, except the child possibly, may be aware that a seizure has occurred. Children with this type of seizure have, in the past, been described as having **temporal lobe epilepsy** because the site of abnormal activity is usually the temporal lobe. However, because this type of seizure can originate in several areas of the brain, the term complex partial is preferred. In close to half of children with complex partial seizures, the seizure is preceded by a simple partial seizure; and in a manner similar to a simple partial seizure, a complex partial seizure may advance into a generalized seizure (a condition referred to as a complex seizure with secondary generalization).

Some children with complex partial seizures may be aware that a seizure is going to occur within the next few hours or within the next day or two. This subjective awareness is referred to as a **prodrome** and differs from an aura, described next, which is a memory of a specific part of a seizure. In the prodromal phase, the child may experience mood or behavioral changes (e.g., increasing irritation or anxiety, apathy, depression, or decreased concentration) that may be recognized by the child, or by adults who know the child well, as early warning symptoms. Sometimes the prodrome takes the form of a throbbing headache or other uncomfortable feelings of malaise (e.g., abdominal cramps, constipation). In a few cases, rather than feeling depressed, the child may become ecstatic and feel elated.

Immediately before the seizure begins, i.e., during the preictal phase, the child having a complex partial seizure may, just prior to losing consciousness, experience an **aura,** a specific sensation that is remembered on regaining consciousness. The aura marks the onset of a simple partial seizure that immediately precedes the complex partial seizure. Auras can also precede a generalized seizure and are experienced by between 50% and 60% of individuals with epilepsy (Pedley, Scheuer, & Walczak, 1995).

In most individuals, the aura is recognized by the presence of sensory or somatosensory symptoms. However, for some, the unusual sensations may be less specific and the symptoms more "psychic" in nature. For example, in some individuals, feelings of fear, excitement, déjà vu (an abnormal feeling that something is familiar, even though it is not), jamais vu (a feeling that something is unfamiliar, even though it is not), strangeness, anxiety, embarrassment, or light-headedness are common. Others may experience autonomic symptoms. For example, some children may complain of vague gastrointestinal pain that tends to rise upward to the throat region; others may just simply describe how they feel as being "yucky" or "funny" all over. The nature of the aura (e.g., sensory vs. psychic symptoms) can give a clue to the physician as to the area of origin of the abnormal electrical discharge. If the individual is able to recognize the aura, there may be enough time for the person to lie down. Because children have to learn to recognize this phase, in many cases the seizure, unfortunately, begins before any action can be taken. In some individuals, the aura may constitute an entire seizure; i.e., the seizure does not appear to progress.

During the ictal phase of a complex partial seizure, in many cases, it appears as if the individual

---

[3] Brief complex partial seizures are often mistaken for absence seizures; however, in most cases, complex partial seizures occur relatively infrequently (i.e., 1 to 2 times a day or week). Absence seizures often occur repetitively (e.g., 10 to 20 times a day).

is in a "dreamlike" state or trance, particularly if the person wanders in an aimless, purposeless manner; has a glassy look in the eyes; and when spoken to makes no response. Typically, a variety of stereotypic behaviors, referred to as **automatisms,** are observed. These involuntary motor movements, often described as being mechanical or repetitive in nature, appear to have no meaning. The following are common: lip chewing, spitting, gagging, choking, lip smacking, laughing, speaking (often incoherently), eye blinking, staring blankly, grimacing, waving, gesturing, clapping, scratching, skipping, walking, running, rubbing hands or legs, masturbating, and picking at clothing, or buttoning and unbuttoning clothing.

In a few cases, rather being in a dreamlike state, some have a look of fear in their eyes during a complex seizure and may run away from their caregiver. It is important to remember that if such an individual is restrained in any way, the response may be aggression (e.g., kicking, screaming, yelling, and crying). Others, rather than running away, may run towards the caregiver and clutch him or her tightly, refusing to let go voluntarily.

Complex partial seizures have in the past also been referred to as **psychomotor seizures** since the individual appears to be in an altered conscious state while at the same time being capable of carrying out, at an automatic level, complex, coordinated activities (e.g., eat, walk, and even talk, albeit incoherently in most cases). For this reason, this type of seizure is often mistaken for some type of emotional disturbance; however, the individual who experiences a complex partial seizure, or in fact any other type of seizure, is not, as was thought in the past, "possessed" by the devil or "consumed" by evil spirits.

Complex partial seizures may also be accompanied, during the ictal phase, by a variety of **autonomic symptoms,** including the following: vomiting, nausea, pallor, flushing, sweating, piloerection (i.e., erection of body hairs), increased or excessive salivation, dilated pupils, rapid pulse (tachycardia), abdominal pain, and bowel and bladder incontinence. Individuals who have complex partial seizures do not show all of these automatisms or autonomic symptoms, and the types of behaviors and symptoms differ from person to person. However, it is typical to see a child or young adult exhibiting the same pattern from one seizure to the next. For example, a person who is "dreamlike" during one episode is unlikely to become aggressive at a later time.

After a complex partial seizure, particularly one that lasts for a minute or more, the child is often confused and drowsy for minutes to hours. During the postictal phase all that the child may want to do is sleep; often there is no memory that a seizure has occurred, and the child may wonder why he or she is so tired.

Generalized Seizures The common characteristics of generalized seizures are that they involve both hemispheres of the brain and *always* involve a loss of consciousness. Some generalized seizures start from a localized site (i.e., a partial seizure) and then progress to affect the entire brain. However, in most cases, the onset is caused by bilateral brain involvement.

Tonic-clonic seizures. Formerly referred to as **grand mal seizures,** a French term that means "great illness," generalized tonic-clonic (GTC) seizures occur in approximately 75% to 80% of children with epilepsy. In some individuals, this form of seizure activity occurs alone; in others, it is typical to see GTC seizures in combination with other types (O'Donohoe, 1985). This type of seizure is not only the most common but also the most dramatic (and frightening to the observer), because the person experiences an almost immediate loss of consciousness with little or no warning. Before a seizure occurs, many individuals show distinctive prodromal symptoms or experience an aura.

The ictal phase of a tonic-clonic seizure is divided into the **tonic** (rigid) and the **clonic** (jerky) subphases. Each of the subphases is described in greater detail later. In some cases, the individual experiences only a tonic phase; in others, only a clonic phase. In a small number of individuals, a few clonic jerks may precede the tonic-clonic sequence; such persons are said to have **clonic-tonic-clonic epilepsy.** Similar to those who have had a complex partial seizure, the postictal phase in persons who have a tonic-clonic seizure is marked by drowsiness, lethargy, and confusion or disorientation. In general, duration of the seizure is correlated with the length of the postictal period (i.e., very brief seizure, few or no postictal symptoms; lengthy seizure, prolonged postictal period) although there may be some individual variation (Hirtz, 1989). Some individuals are extremely difficult to rouse after a GTC seizure and progress into a stupor-like, comatose state of deep sleep that may extend for a period lasting from 5 to 10 minutes to 3 to 4 hours. As the person resumes regular breathing, the cyanosis generally fades; however, in many cases the student remains pale for several hours. Upon awakening, when fully conscious, the individual's gross movements may be uncoordinated, and there may be difficulty with fine motor tasks because of limp muscles. In addition, speech may be slurred, and a pulsatile (pounding) headache or nausea may be present. As a result of excessive muscle fatigue, the child or young adult generally complains of feeling "achy" all over. Even though in most cases the individual has little or no recollection of the seizure, the mental confusion, anxiety, and fatigue can last for up to several days.

Tonic (rigid) phase—During the initial part of the tonic stage, the eyes may roll upward, the pupils may dilate, and the mouth may open; there is an immediate loss of consciousness. Persons who are standing may fall to the ground. Persons who are sitting may slump over or fall to the floor. Typically, the body becomes stiff (i.e., there is generalized contraction of all the skeletal muscles); the elbows, wrists, and hands are flexed; the legs, head, back, and neck are hyperextended; and the teeth are clenched. As a result of contraction of the muscles in the chest and mouth, the person may utter an eerie, piercing scream or cry as the air is forced passed the vocal cords. This cry is not indicative of pain; it is simply a physiologic response resulting from compression of the chest. The tonic phase generally lasts from 10 to 20 seconds, and during this time the individual may breathe very shallowly and the skin may become pale or dusky. If breathing stops for a few moments, the person may become cyanotic, evidenced by lips and fingernail beds turning blue. As a result of muscle spasm, the bladder may empty during this stage.

Clonic (jerking) phase—The rigid tonic phase is followed by the clonic phase, in which the muscles of the body begin to twitch, caused by opposing muscles alternately relaxing and contracting. Eventually, the twitching results in abnormal convulsion of some or all of the body. As the seizure progresses, the movements become less intense and less continuous until they cease altogether. The clonic phase can vary in terms of length, from as short as a few seconds to as long as 30 minutes; however, it usually lasts for less than 5 minutes. During this time, the child is able to breathe, although the respirations may be irregular or stertorous (labored and accompanied by a snoring sound), and there is often some degree of cyanosis. Some individuals exhibit increased salivation, and as a result of the inability to

swallow efficiently, they appear to be "frothing" at the mouth. If the jaws have clamped down on the tongue during the tonic phase, the tongue may be lacerated and the saliva may be mixed with blood. Urine or fecal incontinence, which typically occurs after the last clonic jerk as the sphincter muscles of the bladder and bowel relax, is common during the clonic phase. Because the episodes can be violent in nature, it is not uncommon for individuals to suffer an injury as they thrash about.

Absence seizures. Formerly referred to as **petit mal seizures,** or "little illness," absence seizures are seen in 2% to 5% of all individuals who have epilepsy (O'Donohoe, 1985). Absence seizures are notable for their brevity, typically lasting from 1 to 10 seconds, and their paucity of motor activity (Adams & Victor, 1993). Absence seizures may occur infrequently (1 to 20 times a day) or repetitively (as many as several hundred times within 24 hours). Rarely do the seizures last for more than 30 seconds. In cases where the absence seizure occurs frequently and the individual is never seizure-free, the condition is sometimes referred to as **pyknolepsy,** from the Greek word *pyknos,* meaning "close together" (Lockman, 1989).

Age of onset for absence seizures is typically between 5 and 12 years and, in approximately 50% of cases, the episodes cease with the onset of puberty. For the remaining adolescents, the absence seizures are replaced by tonic-clonic seizures (Lockman, 1989). Absence seizures are believed to be more common in girls than in boys and are often precipitated by hyperventilation. Absence seizures usually occur when the child is sitting quietly in the classroom, during periods of inattention, as opposed to periods of active participation in lessons (Adams & Victor, 1993).

Although the phases of an absence seizure are not as distinct as in the GTC seizure, they are still recognizable in some cases. Usually, the individual does not experience either a prodrome or an aura. During the seizure, the person momentarily ceases all activity and seems to stare blankly out into space. In some cases, the individual's eyes may roll upwards. Unlike a person who has a GTC seizure, the individual who has an absence seizure does not have a major loss of muscle tone; that is, generally the person does not fall to the floor or slump in the chair, and there is no bowel or bladder incontinence. In most cases, twitching is visible in the face, eyelids, hands, or fingers (i.e., there is a minor clonic phase).

Automatisms, such as lip smacking, chewing, and fumbling motions of the hands, are also common in absence seizures, particularly if the seizure lasts for more than several seconds. If there is loss of muscle tone, the person may drop whatever is in hand, such as a pencil or pen. During the seizure, the individual does not respond to verbal stimuli (e.g., a teacher admonishing the child to "pay attention"), as if he or she cannot hear; nor does the person respond to physical stimuli (e.g., a teacher shaking the child), as if he or she is paralyzed.

An example of what a person with an absence seizure may experience is illustrated in the following passage, which highlights how a student's academic progress can be greatly affected by absence seizures.

Class	get out your	and open
page	I want and	when	you
please	before you	home. Don't forget
tomorrow	and	now

When the seizure terminates, the person who had an absence seizure usually returns to the previous activities with no awareness that an episode has occurred. However, some may be confused and need to be reoriented to the task at hand. If the individual was talking when the episode occurred, the conversation may continue without any awareness that there has been a pause. Although there is no memory of the seizure, the person may be aware that there is a period of "lost" time that cannot, somehow, be accounted for.

Myoclonic seizures. More common in individuals who have severe cognitive deficits that result from diffuse brain damage, myoclonic seizures are characterized by brief, bilateral muscle spasms, or jerks, which may occur singly or repetitively, most often on awakening or going to sleep. Myoclonic seizures can also occur when the person is asleep. In the past, myoclonic seizures were often thought of as "minor motor" seizures. Severity of the spasms ranges from mild to profound.

During a mild seizure, the individual may drop whatever was in hand, whereas in a severe seizure, the person's head may drop suddenly, the arms may extend suddenly, and the trunk may flex, resulting in a sudden, forceful fall to the ground. There may be a brief loss of consciousness, but in many cases the jerk lasts only 1 to 2 seconds and the individual remains

alert. As a result of the sudden movement of the arms, whatever is in the person's hand may be thrown across the room, much to the surprise of the individual. No postictal drowsiness or confusion occurs after the seizure.

Infantile spasms. As the name suggests, infantile spasms occur in infants, usually between 3 and 12 months of age. In this type of seizure, believed to be an immature form of myoclonic seizure, there is often a brief flexion of the neck, trunk, and limbs followed by extension ("jackknife" movement) of the body. Infantile spasms often occur in clusters, as many as several hundred times per day. These spasms, also referred to as **salaam seizures,** are often associated with prenatal or perinatal brain abnormalities that result in several cognitive deficits, such as Down syndrome, Tay-Sachs disease, and phenylketonuria. They are usually replaced with other types of generalized seizures in later childhood. In some children, there is no underlying cause. Unfortunately, even though the spasms generally stop by the time the child is between ages 2 and 5 (in some cases without any form of intervention), up to 90% of children show signs of permanent cognitive impairment. More than 66% of children who have infantile seizures have a severe disability (Pedley et al., 1995).

Atonic seizures. Also referred to as **drop seizures** or **drop attacks,** this type of seizure occurs most commonly when the affected individual awakens in the morning or after a nap during the day. Atonic seizures are characterized by an abrupt loss of muscle tone, which results in head, upper body, or full body "drop." Typically, the person falls to the floor, somewhat like a rag doll being dropped, and since the individual is unable to "break" the fall, injury to the head, face, or shoulders is common.

Since there may not be any loss of consciousness during this type of seizure, the condition often goes unrecognized, and in the case of a child or young adult, the parents may attribute the falls to clumsiness or immaturity. In some cases, the atonic seizure is so momentary that the person is able to "catch" himself or herself before falling—observers may think that the individual has simply nodded off and consequently are not concerned until a pattern becomes well established. Onset of atonic seizures usually occurs when the child is between ages 3 and 12. If there is a loss of consciousness during the seizure, there may be some drowsiness during the postictal period. The longer the individual is unconscious, the greater the degree of drowsiness.

Etiology

Seizures, regardless of type, are often classified into two groups, **primary** and **secondary,** based on the underlying factor or factors that contribute to seizure activity.

Primary Seizures Also referred to as idiopathic, cryptogenic, genuine, essential, or genetic seizures, primary seizures are those that have *no* identifiable cause. Included in this group are those individuals who have a familial predisposition to seizure activity; however, the exact mechanism of transmission of epilepsy in such cases is unknown. It was once thought that epilepsy was, in some cases, an inherited disease[4]; today, most believe it more likely that it is a diminished **"seizure threshold"** passed from generation to generation.

It has been suggested that a person with a "low" seizure threshold requires less stimulation to "provoke" a seizure, whereas a person with a "high" seizure threshold may be more "resistant" to a seizure. For example, if two children both had an accident that resulted in brain injury, the child with a low threshold would be more likely to have a seizure disorder than the child with a higher threshold, even if the amount of damage to the children's brains was identical. It has also been suggested that many people who are highly susceptible to epilepsy as a result of inheriting a low threshold may in fact never have the condition, unless there is some circumstance, such as an illness or accident, that results in injury to the brain (Epilepsy Foundation of America, 1993).

Interestingly, research has shown that 9% of offspring of mothers with epilepsy have the condition by the time they are age 25, compared with 2.4% of sons or daughters of affected fathers. However, the reason for the increased risk of seizures in offspring of women with epilepsy is unknown at this time (Pedley et al., 1995). If both parents have the condition, the risk rises steeply to approximately 25% (O'Donohoe, 1985). As many as 60% of children with idiopathic seizures may eventually "outgrow" the condition (Nealis, 1983).

Secondary Seizures While the cause of epilepsy is unknown in approximately 70% of cases (Jones-Saete, 1986), in the remaining cases the causative

TABLE 12.2
Antecedents to the Development of a Seizure Disorder

- Alcohol or lead poisoning
- Brain hemorrhage
- Congenital cerebral malformations
- Drug abuse
- Fever
- Head trauma
- Hypoxia or anoxia
- Infections, such as meningitis and encephalitis
- Lesions, such as tumors or abscesses
- Metabolic disorders, such as hypoglycemia (too little glucose in the blood) and hypocalcemia (too little calcium in the blood)
- Sleep deprivation
- Strokes

factor is clearly identifiable. If a cause is known, the individual is said to experience a **secondary seizure,** also referred to as an acquired, symptomatic, or organic seizure. In general, the younger the child is when the initial secondary seizure occurs, the greater the likelihood the causative factor or factors can be identified (Disabato & Wulf, 1994).

There are at least 50 conditions known to result in secondary seizure activity (Evans & Smith, 1993). Some of the most common antecedents of seizure activity are shown in Table 12.2. For the condition to be recognized as epilepsy, the seizures must occur repetitively, regardless of whether the cause is primary or secondary. However, the period between seizures can range from minutes to weeks. In some cases, seizure activity may occur very sporadically (e.g., every year or two).

Other Contributory Factors Regardless of whether the cause of the seizure is primary or secondary in nature, there are a number of contributory factors that may "precipitate" a seizure in an individual who has a lowered seizure threshold. For example, time of day may be influential in some children or young adults because seizure activity tends to occur more often just as they are going to sleep or awaking. In others, excessive fatigue, lack of sleep, excitement, or emotional stress (e.g., fear, frustration, anxiety) has been implicated, along with illness, fever, alcohol consumption, and low blood

---

[4] As recently as 1971, there were laws in several states that required individuals with a seizure disorder to be sterilized (Heller, Alberto, Forney, & Schwartzman, 1996).

sugar. For some individuals, flickering lights (e.g., from the television when the vertical hold is poorly adjusted, video games, strobe lights, malfunctioning fluorescent lights, or the rays of the sun being intermittently blocked by branches of trees while driving) may result in seizure activity. For some persons with epilepsy, certain kinds of music, particularly those which are excessively loud and sharp or have a noticeable beat or buzz, may trigger an episode. Adolescent girls may experience more frequent seizures before or during their menstrual period; this increase is believed to occur as a result of fluid retention.

Incidence and Prevalence

Seizures are among the most commonly observed signs of neurologic dysfunction in children. As many as 8% of all children have had at least one seizure by the time they reach age 15 (Brown, 1997). Even though the exact prevalence of epilepsy is unknown, approximately 2% of individuals under the age of 20 are believed to have a chronic seizure disorder, compared with 1% of the total population, regardless of age (Jezewski, 1992). Seizures are more common in young infants and children up to age 2 as a result of the immaturity of the CNS (Smith & Woodring, 1990), and 90% of those who have the symptoms of epilepsy exhibit them before they reach age 20 (O'Donohoe, 1985). Epilepsy affects males 1.1 to 1.5 times more often than females (Pedley et al., 1995). The prevalence of epilepsy is substantially higher in children who are cognitively challenged, and there appears to be a positive correlation between the occurrence of seizures and increased severity of mental impairment. The incidence of epilepsy in those with mental retardation is 16%. Twenty-five percent of those with cerebral palsy and spina bifida are also prone to repeated seizure activity (Brown, 1997). The Epilepsy Foundation of America (EFA) (1993) has estimated that 50,000 children and adolescents develop a seizure disorder every year in the United States alone. In addition, 50,000 adults are believed to develop the condition annually. Cumulatively, 1% of the population (over 2 million people) have epilepsy (EFA, 1993). In Canada, approximately 280,000 individuals have this condition, and 24,000 new diagnoses are made yearly (Fisher, 1995).

The number of new cases of epilepsy per year has shown an increase in recent times (Epilepsy Canada, n.d.). Part of this increase may be attributable to the fact that children who, in the past, might have died are not only living but also living longer than would have been expected in previous times as a result of advances in medical and surgical care. Two notable groups are infants with prenatal or perinatal conditions that may result in seizure activity, e.g., premature infants with hypoxia, and young children who experience serious traumatic head injuries as a result of vehicular accidents, sports accidents, or gunshot wounds.

Diagnosis and Treatment

To determine the underlying cause of seizure activity, the child's neurologist relies on a detailed history provided by those in direct contact with the child on a regular basis, particularly those who have observed and recorded the behaviors exhibited during a seizure, such as a day care worker or a teacher. In addition to such reports, a variety of diagnostic tests, the most common being the **electroencephalogram** (EEG), are undertaken to assist in making a differential diagnosis (i.e., to rule out any other causative reasons for the seizures). During the EEG, electrodes are applied to the scalp to measure and record the electrical impulses of the brain. In addition, various imaging techniques, such as **computed tomography** (CT) or **magnetic resonance imaging,** (MRI), may also be used to determine any structural abnormalities of the brain that might be the underlying cause of the disorder. **Blood tests** may be done to see whether or not the seizure activity is caused by some form of chemical imbalance; similarly, CSF may be analyzed to check for infection.

Once a diagnosis of epilepsy is made, treatment is started. The goals of treatment are threefold: (1) to discover and correct the underlying cause, if and when possible; (2) to achieve the greatest degree of seizure control (i.e., to eliminate seizure activity entirely or, if that is not achievable, to reduce frequency to the maximum extent possible) to prevent or minimize secondary brain cell injury that may arise as a result of excessive neuronal discharge and hypoxia; and (3) to help the child live as normal a life as possible, with the fewest adverse side effects originating from the treatment plan (Smith & Woodring, 1990; Whaley & Wong, 1995).

Pharmacological Treatment   The primary form of treatment of a seizure disorder is pharmacologic. The most common **antiepileptic drugs** (AEDs), also known as anticonvulsant medications, used to decrease and, ideally, eliminate seizures from occurring, include Tegretol, Klonopin, Valium, Zarontin, Dilantin, Luminal, Mysoline, and Depakene. The choice of AED is determined primarily by the type of seizure, and in many cases, it takes a considerable amount of time to determine the correct drug and the appropriate dose. Holvoet and Helmstetteer (1989) have stressed that parents and teachers must be patient during the initial stages of pharmacologic therapy and recognize that a minimum of 2 months is needed to determine whether or not the drug regime is appropriate (i.e., controls the seizures without overmedicating the child).

The drugs are given daily, most often at bedtime. Some drugs need to be given two or three additional times throughout the day. In approximately half the children, seizures are controlled by means of one drug (**monotherapy**). Some children, particularly those children who have mixed forms of epilepsy, require a second drug. Rarely are more than two drugs given at the same time.

While AEDs are able to control seizures, either completely or partially, in approximately 60% to 70% of children with epilepsy, side effects attributable to the drug treatment are not uncommon (Pedley et al., 1995). Some side effects are acute; others are long-term and typically involve cognitive, behavioral, psychiatric, or somatic changes. Side effects that may affect a child's ability to function optimally in school are listed in Table 12.3. The most common side effect is drowsiness; however, rather than becoming lethargic, some children on anticonvulsant medications can become hyperactive and irritable. Three new drugs, vigabatrin, lamotrigine, and gabapentin, have shown to be effective in treating some individuals with epilepsy, with fewer side effects. However, these drugs are much more costly (more than $300 per month) than those that have been around for some time (Fisher, 1995). In discussing these and other new drugs, Brown (1997) commented: "It is too soon to know which of these drugs will eventually end in the first-line treatment of epilepsy and which in the epileptologist's armamentarium for drug-resistant seizures" (p. 580).

Surgical Intervention   While most drug effects are mild and dose-related (Pedley et al., 1995), Marshal and Cupoli (1986) have suggested that the "benefits of seizure control far outweigh adverse drug effects." In rare instances, e.g., if a person does

TABLE 12.3
Side Effects of AEDs

- Anemia
- Depression
- Double or blurred vision
- Drowsiness or decreased alertness; mental confusion
- Dry mouth
- Headaches
- Impaired memory and concentration
- Weight gain; increased appetite
- Indigestion; anorexia
- Lack of motor coordination; slurred speech; tremors
- Loss of stamina
- Mood changes (e.g., depression, irritability)
- Nausea or vomiting
- Skin rash; acne; body hair overgrowth
- Sleep disturbance
- Vertigo (dizziness); disturbed equilibrium

not respond to medication or has seizures caused by a tumor or progressive lesion, **surgical intervention** (removal of the part of the brain in which the seizures originate) may be necessary. Unfortunately, this approach may have negative outcomes, such as personality changes, depression, decreased cognitive ability, loss of vision, impaired language skills, and loss of memory (Spiegel, Cutler, & Yetter, 1996).

Dietary Management   For some children, particularly those with absence seizures, diet therapy may be beneficial. The diet, known as the **ketogenic diet,** requires that the child eat a diet of high-fat, low-carbohydrate, low-protein foods. In addition, the child's fluid intake is restricted significantly. Popular from the 1920s to 1970s, and regaining popularity in the 1990s (Brown, 1997), it is believed that this particular diet raises the seizure threshold in certain individuals. Unfortunately, a ketogenic diet is, to some children, unpalatable, and compliance may be problematic. Others tolerate it well (Brown, 1997). The diet is not without its risks. Some children have problems with weight loss; some become hypoglycemic (too little blood glucose[5]).

---

[5] See chapter 19.

Behavioral Management Research has shown that certain behavioral intervention techniques, such as relaxation, differential reinforcement, and competing response training, have been useful in decreasing seizure activities in children with epilepsy. Kuhn, Allen, and Shriver (1995) reported a case where a student went from a pre-treatment average of 25 seizures a day to a post-treatment average of 5 per day. Intervention involved teaching the student to induce relaxation through deep breathing and by invoking a pleasant image (her doll) that she had previously selected. Five months later, follow-up indicated that the seizures had dropped to less than 1 per day. While these researchers recognize that teaching the individual certain anticonvulsant coping behaviors may be beneficial to some, they do acknowledge that these techniques "are not meant to replace sound pharmacologic treatment, nor is it likely they could do so" (p.573).

Studies have shown that 60% to 70% of individuals with epilepsy become free of seizures for at least 5 years within 10 years of diagnosis (Pedley et al., 1995). Reviewing studies that have examined the prognosis of epilepsy in children, O'Donohoe (1985) suggested that the prognosis "worsens with long duration of illness, resistance to medication, association with neurological and intellectual deficits, the occurrence of different seizure types in the same individual and following the onset of one of the serious varieties of epilepsy [e.g., infantile spasms, myoclonic epilepsy] early in infancy and childhood" (p. 234). If children or young adults are able to remain seizure-free for a period of 2 to 3 years, they are often slowly weaned from the drugs to minimize the untoward effects of the anticonvulsant therapy. However, if individuals are weaned too quickly, there may be an increase in both the number and severity of the seizures. Sudden withdrawal of medication, e.g., a teenager who decides not to comply with the treatment regimen and, against the wishes of the physician and parents, stops taking the prescribed drugs, can lead to **status epilepticus,** a severe prolonged convulsion that may be potentially brain damaging and even life-threatening (O'Donohoe, 1985).

🐛 Educational Implications and Teaching Tips

The effects of epilepsy on learning vary widely from person to person. According to Marshall and Cupoli (1986), when those with epilepsy are examined as a group, several patterns emerge. They found that children with epilepsy could be divided into three obviously different groups, which they labeled I, II, and III.

Referred to as the "simple" group, group I consists of those children who have a good prognosis for normal intellectual functioning and generally do not encounter any major educational problems. The children in this group, on the whole, have uncomplicated epilepsy (e.g., they have only one seizure type), their seizures are well controlled by antiepileptic medication, and they do not experience any significant drug-related side effects. As many as 80% of all children with epilepsy, according to Marshall and Cupoli (1986), fall into this first group.

Referred to as the "devastated" group, group II consists of those children whose epilepsy is caused, in most cases, by degenerative brain disease or destructive brain lesions. In many cases, as a result of the diffuse damage to the brain, the children have mixed epilepsy that began early in life. Typically, regardless of the different types of medications tried, their seizures remain out of control. In terms of academic ability they are at the opposite end of the continuum from those in the first group. Many of the children in this group have severe cognitive deficits, and some have mild to severe cerebral palsy. More than 20% of children with epilepsy, according to Marshall and Cupoli (1986), fall into this category.

Even though the two groups described above should account for 100% of children with epilepsy, according to Marshall and Cupoli, between the two groups is a large group (group III) of children, referred to by them as the "compromised" group. These children, by and large, have well-controlled seizures and are free of serious mental or motor problems. However, they typically are experiencing "unsatisfactory school progress" as a result of significant social, emotional, and learning problems. The authors indicate that as many as 68% of all children with epilepsy may fall into this group. By examining seizure type, seizure frequency, and age of onset of the seizure disorder, certain characteristics that differentiate those who may do poorly from those who may not encounter any significant academic problems were discovered. Some of these differences are shown in Table 12.4.

Regardless of which group the child falls into, teachers perform a crucial role in normalizing the life of a student having epilepsy-related difficulties.

TABLE 12.4
Characteristics That Define and Qualify the Educational Impact of Epilepsy on Children

SEIZURE TYPE
- While no clear correlation between seizure type and overall IQ has been established, some studies have reported that students with generalized seizures are more likely to have a significant mental impairment (i.e., decreased scholastic aptitude) than those with partial epilepsy.
- Complex partial seizures typically affect learning more than simple partial seizures because the former interfere with consciousness.
- Generalized seizures that emanate from the brain's middle portions seem to affect attention, reaction time, and concentration, whereas temporal lobe seizures tend to affect memory functions.
- Left temporal lobe seizures correlate with disorders in reading, language, verbal memory, and verbal learning.
- Right temporal lobe seizures are typically related to impairments in visual-spatial skills.

SEIZURE FREQUENCY
- Most recent studies, contrary to earlier studies that included an overrepresentation of institutionalized individuals, have failed to find an equivocal relationship between seizure frequency and overall intelligence.
- While there is no clear relationship between seizure frequency and declines in cognitive functioning, there is evidence in adults that increased seizure control is related to better test performance.

AGE OF ONSET
- Early onset epilepsy is correlated with later test performance deficits and abnormal neurologic finding.
- Late onset is correlated with higher IQ scores and with less intellectual deterioration.

Adapted from Marshall, R. M., & Cupoli, J. M. (1986). Epilepsy and education: The pediatrician's expanding role. *Advances in Pediatrics, 33,* 159–180. St. Louis: Mosby-Year Book. Reprinted by permission.

The teacher should maintain a positive attitude towards the student, be understanding of the unique concerns of the student, and hold realistic expectations of the child's ability and the impact of epilepsy on the learning process (Yousef, 1985). It is the teacher's sensitivity and concern regarding the needs of the student and the teacher's knowledge of epilepsy that determine, from day to day, the quality of the student's program (Marshall & Cupoli, 1986). It is critical that teachers react appropriately to a student's seizures, because it is the reaction of the teacher to the seizure that dictates how the class reacts to the seizure and to the student. An excessive reaction may diminish self-esteem of the individual with epilepsy, raise anxiety levels of those in the immediate environment, and alter social interaction with classmates (Glaze, 1994; cited in Tyler & Colson, 1994).

With careful preparation and training, school staff and the student's peers can learn how to respond appropriately to the student with epilepsy, and with greater understanding of the nature of the condition, there can be greater acceptance of the student.

The first step is gaining as much information as possible about the type of seizure disorder the student has; the events that might trigger a seizure; typical behavior of the student before, during, and after a seizure; how the student reacts to a seizure; and information about the medication or the diet that the student may be on. This information can be obtained from either the student's parents or doctor. A sample Seizure Disorder Information Form is found in Appendix A. The following suggestions should be useful to prepare individuals to work with children and young adults who have a seizure disorder.

1. *A tonic-clonic seizure in someone who has epilepsy is not a medical emergency, even though it may look like one to a person who has never seen an individual having a convulsion.* In most cases, the episode ends after 2 to 3 minutes and the individual will be able, with time, to resume previous activities. Videos and films are available from the Epilepsy Foundation of America or Epilepsy Canada that demonstrate the typical stages of a generalized

seizure. Staff should be encouraged to view the materials at least once before contact with the student, so that they know what to expect, and should be given opportunities to discuss their concerns with persons who are knowledgeable about the condition.

2 *A seizure is not a crisis in a person who has a history of seizure activity, but all staff, including substitute teachers, should be trained to respond appropriately to a student during a seizure.* Although there is very little that can be done, except to ensure the safety of the student during the episode, staff can play a major role in modeling appropriate behavior and in reassuring both the student who has epilepsy and the other students in the class, who may be very distressed.

Overzealous first aid during a seizure episode, such as inserting objects in the person's mouth to prevent tongue biting, may cause more harm than good. Suggestions on how to respond when a student is having a seizure are given in Table 12.5. In most cases, there is little to be gained by summoning medical help, unless the student is injured as a result of the seizure (Spiegel et al., 1996), because by the time help arrives, the seizure will have ended.

3 *Very rarely, a "normal" seizure develops into a medical emergency; staff should be aware of the different types of emergencies and should be instructed to seek immediate medical assistance (i.e., call 911) if a crisis situation arises.* For further information, see Table 12.6.

4 *Teachers should be alert to signs of an impending seizure (i.e., the student's prodrome or aura).* If there is sufficient time, the student should be moved to an area where possibility of injury is minimized. Ideally, the location is away from the other students so that there is some privacy; however, because there is usually not sufficient time, privacy must take second place to safety.

Some students are able to recognize their prodrome or aura. They should be encouraged to tell a responsible adult that they "think" a seizure is about to occur so that action can be taken. Such communication is particularly important if the student is engaged in some type of activity in which injury may occur, such as conducting a scientific experiment with certain types of chemicals or with equipment that is hot (Spiegel et al., 1996).

5 *Although the student with epilepsy may be uncomfortable with friends knowing that he or she has a seizure disorder, classmates should be knowledgeable so that they will know how to respond.* The school nurse, the student's physician or parents, or the student's teacher or counselor should talk to the class, with the student's permission, about epilepsy, explaining what it is and what to do when the student has a seizure. The student may or may not want to participate in such discussions. There are a large number of books, films, videos, and pamphlets appropriate for children, both young and older, that can be used in the classroom setting. School staff can contact the Epilepsy Foundation of America or Epilepsy Canada for lists of appropriate materials.

6 *Teachers can be of great assistance in reporting on the nature of the seizures (e.g., frequency, type) that occur during school hours, because it is very rare for the student's doctor to have actually seen the student having a seizure in his or her office.* Sample copies of a Seizure Log and a Post-Seizure Report Form are contained in Appendix G. A full report should be filled out and logged every time a student has a seizure, no matter how "routine" it may be. Some parents may want a copy of the report. Regardless of whether or not they want a copy, the original, signed by the teacher, should be kept in the student's health file.

Teachers can also perform a vital role in carefully monitoring the performance level of those who are receiving AEDs and providing regular reports to the family that can be shared with the student's doctor. This role is particularly critical if, as Adams and Victor (1993) have suggested, it is "a common error [of physicians] to administer a drug to the point where the patient is so dull and stupefied that these toxic effects are more incapacitating than the seizures" (p. 293). While in some cases these "overdoses" may be an error in judgment, in others, the decision may be based on lack of information on how the student is responding. By being observant, school staff can assist the doctor in evaluation of the effectiveness of AEDs and determining whether or

TABLE 12.5
First Aid Strategies: Assisting the Student with a Seizure Disorder

---

GENERALIZED TONIC-CLONIC SEIZURE (GRAND MAL): ON LAND

During the Seizure:

- Remain calm and professional. If you become excitable, others in the room, particularly if they are very young, will become even more distressed. A level-headed approach will have a calming influence on others who are panicking. Do not leave the student alone.

- If the student indicates that a seizure is about to occur, if possible, move the student from his or her desk to a private area, such as a quiet area at the back of the classroom. Ideally the area should be carpeted and free of furniture so that the student will not be injured.

  Ease the student to the floor.
  If the student wears glasses, remove them and put them in a safe place.
  Remove any sharp, hard, or hot objects from the student's hands to prevent injury.
  If the student has food in his or her mouth, if possible, ask him or her to spit it out.

- If there is no time to move the student, and the student has fallen to the floor, move any objects (e.g., toys, furniture) that might be a potential risk. Do not move the student unless he or she is in a dangerous location (e.g., at the top of a flight of stairs).

- Get down on the floor with the student so that you are not standing over staring downward. Reassure the others in the area that the student having a seizure will be fine in a minute or two and that she or he is not in pain. Note the time that the seizure begins. Any seizure that is not resolved within 10 minutes is abnormal, and medical assistance should be obtained (i.e., call 911).

- Do not encourage the others to congregate around the student; suggest that they go back to doing whatever they were doing.

- Ideally the student should be placed on his or her side, with the neck hyperextended, to allow the drainage of saliva, to prevent the tongue from blocking the airway, and to ensure adequate breathing. With an older (larger) child or adult, it may be difficult to position the individual during the seizure; however, after the muscles relax, the individual should be moved into the side-lying position. In some cases, it may be easier to position the individual on his or her stomach; however, since breathing may be impaired and injury to the face may result, the individual should, if at all possible, be positioned on his or her side.

- Loosen any clothing that is tight and that might restrict the individual's breathing (e.g., ties, shirt collars, bra). Place a soft pillow, towel, blanket, or coat under the head (or any other part of the body that is hitting the floor) to cushion the impact.

- If there is nothing soft nearby to cushion the student, a caregiver can attempt to cradle the student's head in his or her lap or place a hand or arm under, or next to, the flailing limb to prevent injury. However, caregivers should weigh the possible injury to the student versus the potential injuries that might occur to themselves by attempting to "protect" the student from injury. If the caregiver cradles the individual's head, the caregiver should move with the head, rather than restrict the person's movement.

- Do not restrain or confine the student's movements in any way. It is impossible to "stop" a seizure, and the only appropriate action is to allow the seizure to take its course. Do not attempt to revive the student (e.g., do not slap the student's face, do not splash the student with water).

- Do not put anything in the student's mouth because the presence of any hard object can cause lacerations to the mouth or broken teeth. Even a padded tongue depressor can splinter and harm the person. Do not try to hold the student's tongue. The tongue cannot be swallowed.

After the Seizure:

- Do not expect the student to follow instructions during or immediately after a seizure.

- Do not give any fluids or food during or immediately after a seizure. If the student has a tendency to produce a great deal of saliva during a seizure, suctioning may be required (e.g., by means of a suction machine or a bulb syringe).

- If the student is not breathing (i.e., has not drawn a breath for a minute or more), artificial respiration should be started and an ambulance should be called.

- Upon the student's awakening, while reassuring him or her, check to see if there have been any injuries and whether he or she has been incontinent.

- By means of interaction with the student, determine the level of awareness. Let the student know that he or she has had a seizure, that everything is now all right, and that you or someone else will remain nearby.

- If the student has soiled him or herself, assistance should be given as unobtrusively as possible. All students with epilepsy should have a change of clothing at school for such situations.

- If the student has suffered any injury, it should be treated. If it is minor (e.g., a minor cut), standard first aid procedures should be followed; if it is major (e.g., a major laceration), the student should be taken to the emergency room for treatment.
- After a seizure, the student may be confused, disoriented, or drowsy and may want to sleep. When ready, help the student to his or her feet and move the student to a quiet area (e.g., nurse's station). The student should be placed on his or her side to prevent the aspiration of saliva or vomitus. The student should not be left alone, particularly if confused.
- Complete the Post-Seizure Report Form (see Appendix G).

GENERALIZED TONIC-CLONIC SEIZURE (GRAND MAL): IN WATER

- The student should be supported, with his or her head above the surface. If possible, the student's head should be tilted sideways to ease the flow of saliva.
- The student should be removed from the water as quickly as possible and positioned on the side as described previously.
- If the student is not breathing, artificial respiration should be started and an ambulance should be called.
- Even if there do not appear to be any major consequences when the student regains consciousness, his or her parents should be notified. Aspiration of water can damage the respiratory system, and the student should be seen by medical staff.

ABSENCE SEIZURES (PETIT MAL SEIZURE):

- Specific first aid is not required for a student who is having an absence seizure, unless the seizure progresses to a generalized convulsion; then aid should be given as described above.

PARTIAL SEIZURES (SIMPLE AND COMPLEX):

- In most cases, specific first aid is not required for a student who is having a partial seizure unless the seizure progresses to a generalized convulsion; then aid should be given as described previously.
- It is important to protect the student who is having a complex partial seizure from injury. Do not attempt to restrain the student (unless there is an impending danger) because the student may respond with terror and strike out, injuring the caregiver.
- Rather than pulling a student away from a set of stairs or from a hot stove, the caregiver should block the way by standing in front of the individual. In most instances, the student will move in another direction in an attempt to avoid physical contact with another person.
- Do not give the student anything to drink, even if conscious.
- Reassure the student by talking in a calming voice.

TABLE 12.6
Emergency Situations That May Arise During a Seizure Episode

PERSONS WITH EPILEPSY[a]

During a tonic-clonic seizure, medical assistance is generally not needed. However, call 911 immediately if:

(1) the child goes from one seizure to another repetitively without regaining consciousness, a condition referred to as **status epilepticus;**

(2) the seizure lasts for a **prolonged** period of time (i.e., more than 5 to 10 minutes);

(3) **consciousness does not return** after the convulsions have ended; or

(4) the child develops **extreme respiratory distress.**

Such complications occur very rarely.

---

[a]If the child has not been previously diagnosed as having epilepsy, the student should be seen by medical personnel to determine the cause of the seizure activity.

not the current drug regimen (i.e., drug choice, dosage, timing) is suitable for the academic needs of the student. While it is acknowledged that teachers can perform a vital role in reporting useful information, Chee (1984) has offered the following cautionary comments that should be heeded by school staff in general:

> Do *not* assume that every fall, temper tantrum, fainting spell, or daydreaming episode is a seizure or that all lethargy or lack of classroom preparation is due to the side effects of anticonvulsants. Other causes for this sort of behavior should be considered. All children may daydream if they are bored or fail to do class work if they are not motivated. *Erroneous reports of seizures from school personnel can provoke unwarranted alarm and lead to unnecessary changes in medication.* (p. 77, italics added)

7 *Some children need to take their antiepileptic drugs during school hours.* Forms that can be used to authorize and log the administration of medication are found in Appendix D. It is important that the medication be given at the same time each day, and if the child is away from school, e.g., on a field trip, that the medication accompany the child. To prevent the risk of running out of medication, the person responsible for administering the drug should ensure that the parents are informed when the supply is running out (i.e., when there is less than 3 days' supply).

Teachers should be aware of the major side effects of AEDs, shown previously in Table 12.3, and recognize that most students with epilepsy will be drowsy some or all of the day. The student should not be punished for not being able to stay awake in class. It is not uncommon for the student to "nod off," particularly while performing repetitive tasks or reading quietly. Since a student with epilepsy may not be able to concentrate for long periods of time, grades on a written test may be lower than expected.

Teachers should also be instructed on what to do if a dose is missed or if the student vomits the medication. Student-specific instructions on how to deal with a missed dose should be part of the emergency plan developed for the child with epilepsy (see Appendix C). In general, if a dose is missed, the medication is given as soon as the oversight is recognized; however, since it is generally best to allow 2 hours between doses, in some circumstances, physicians recommend that the missed dose not be administered if the next dose is about to be given. In such situations, the physician may suggest that the next regularly scheduled dose be given early (i.e., at the time that the oversight was recognized) and that the timing of the subsequent doses given that day be adjusted slightly (i.e., given earlier) until the regular schedule is resumed. If for some reason the student vomits the medication, readministering it immediately will generally produce the same result. Some physicians recommend waiting 1 to 2 hours and then trying to readminister the dose; however, advice specific to the student should be sought (from the parents or doctor). In all cases, the student's parents should be notified regarding the actions that were taken.

8 *Even in the case of well-controlled seizure disorders, the need to take drugs during school hours may draw unwelcome attention* (Bergen, 1991). Even though a student may, at times, need to be reminded to take his or her medication, the teacher should be discreet and ensure, perhaps by means of a secret signal, that the message gets to the student without classmates noticing. Students who need to take medication should be allowed to take it in private if they so desire (e.g., in the nurse's office). Even though older students are typically responsible for taking their own medication, teachers should be alert to any signs of noncompliance.

9 *All students with epilepsy should be encouraged to wear a Medic-Alert bracelet, because epilepsy is an invisible condition.* Older students who may be reluctant to wear a such a bracelet, because of its visibility, should be encouraged to carry a wallet card (Chee, 1984) or to wear a Medic-Alert necklace.

10 *Students with epilepsy are generally not absent from school for protracted periods of time as a result of the seizure disorder.* In fact, an episode should not be a reason to miss school, nor should the occurrence of a seizure be a reason for being sent home from school (Marshall & Cupoli, 1986). Nothing is gained by having the child miss school, and the less time spent out of the classroom the better (Killam, 1992).

It should be recognized that the person who has a seizure does not feel any pain during the seizure, even though it may appear the individual is in distress. While in some cases, the student may experience some abnormal sensations (such as abdominal uneasiness or nausea) before a seizure, such complaints are generally not sufficient to warrant any major concern. After a seizure, the student may feel tired all over; however, after resting, previous activities may often be resumed without difficulty.

11 *Parents should be notified that a seizure has occurred,* even though an uncomplicated seizure is a routine event in the life of a person with epilepsy. This can be done, in most cases, at the end of the day (i.e., by means of a copy of the Post-Seizure Report Form sent home with the child). If the parents are contacted by school staff at the time of the seizure, the seizure will have ended and the student will most likely be resting quietly by the time they arrive at school.

If a seizure is atypical (e.g., lasts longer than usual, but still within a normal length) or if the seizures are more frequent on a particular day than is typical, the parents should be notified immediately so that they can decide what course of action should be taken.

12 *Intelligence and epilepsy are not directly related.* IQ scores of individuals with epilepsy can span the whole range of intellectual ability, from gifted to severely cognitively impaired. Even though the student's learning potential may be in a normal or even above-normal range, a variety of learning problems may coexist (e.g., difficulty in attending), some of which may be related to medications taken to control the seizure activity, others to the fact that the student, during and immediately after a seizure, is "missing" out on learning experiences that are being offered to others. To determine any problem areas, a referral for diagnostic assessment may be appropriate, and based on the results, a remedial program may be appropriate.

13 *Teachers should not have lowered academic expectations solely on the basis of the diagnosis, because such an attitude can result in the student not working to maximum potential.* One study of teachers of 109 children with epilepsy found that about one quarter of the teachers seriously underestimated the intellectual ability of the students with

epilepsy (Bagley, 1970). In eight cases, children with an IQ of more than 120 were judged to be only of "average" intelligence.

Similarly, the same discipline standards should be applied to the student with epilepsy as to the rest of the class (O'Donohoe, 1985). It is not an uncommon experience for those with epilepsy to "use" their condition to gain favoritism or extra allowances (e.g., to get out of having to take a test, using the stress they are feeling as a form of "leverage" to gain the sympathy of an oversolicitous or overindulgent teacher).

14 *If the student's seizures are well controlled and there are no other neurologic problems, participation in most, if not all, activities both in and out of class should be possible.* This includes, in many cases, competitive individual or team sports. If any restrictions are imposed, written directives must be sought from the student's doctor (see Appendix D).

In some cases, physicians may recommend that the student with epilepsy not be involved in a swimming program because of the possibility of a seizure in the water. However, in many cases, if the student's seizures are well under control and the student is adequately supervised, most water sports, with the exception, perhaps, of scuba diving, may be possible. Other sports that may be contraindicated include boxing and football (i.e., due to the possibility of head injury); any sports in which there is a possibility of falling (e.g., rope climbing); specified gymnastic sports (e.g., use of high bar), and certain sports where seizures may result in injury (e.g., archery, riflery, and weight lifting) (American Academy of Pediatrics, 1994; see Appendix J).

Some medical practitioners have suggested that young children should be discouraged from using a bicycle on the street until seizures are well controlled because of the possibility of the student inadvertently cycling into the path of a vehicle (Killam, 1992). Similarly, students should be discouraged from skateboarding or rollerblading in the street. However, these activities may be permitted in a more appropriate setting (e.g., school yard, skateboard park). In all cases, the student should be required to wear a protective helmet. Today, helmets can be made quite attractive by means of "helmet hats," stylish hats (e.g., baseball cap) made to fit over a commercially available helmet.

15 *Rather than restricting physical activity, students should be encouraged to exercise.* Research has shown that exercise can actually raise the seizure threshold, thereby making the individual more "resistant" to seizure activity (O'Donohoe, 1985). If the student is exceedingly tired, a rest period may seem like a good idea; however, since seizures often occur just when going to sleep, a nap during school hours may not be advisable. If fatigue is problematic, the teacher (or the school nurse) should discuss the matter with the parents.

16 *The individual with epilepsy must maintain a wholesome diet, engage in a program of physical exercise, and get a good night's sleep.* Teachers should attempt to promote a healthy lifestyle by being good role models.

For students who have a seizure disorder, food should be given at regularly scheduled times, which may be problematic if the student is away from school on a field trip. Even if the student is unable to have a complete meal, something healthy should be eaten (e.g., an apple). Snacks that have a high sugar content should not be given (e.g., candies), because sweets have been implicated in seizure activity.

17 *Seizure episodes may increase when the person is ill.* The student's teacher should notify the parents if there is an outbreak of communicable disease in the school or if the student has been in direct contact with someone who has a contagious condition. If the student appears to be ill (e.g., has a fever), a school staff member should contact the parents to take the student home, where fever control measures can be implemented, if appropriate (e.g., giving the student cool, clear liquids; dressing the student in light clothing; giving tepid sponge baths).

18 *Teachers should be aware of the unique stresses that epilepsy places on the student.* Children and young adults may be reassured by the fact that, in many cases, individuals outgrow the condition. However, the teen years can be particularly hard for the adolescent with epilepsy, while waiting for the next seizure to happen. Wanting to be independent, these teenagers often feel insecure and inferior. They may be teased by their friends for

having to take "drugs" and, in extreme cases, may be rejected at a time when acceptance is so critical. At the same time, some students may be pressured to experiment with illicit drugs or alcohol.

The fear of having a seizure in front of friends can be overwhelming, and as a result, the teenager may withdraw from social situations with peers such as hanging out at the mall. For the young boy or girl who is starting to date, the dilemma of whether or not to inform the girlfriend or boyfriend can be very worrisome. Similarly, the recognition of the need to inform potential employers may be difficult to accept.

Getting a driver's license can also be problematic for the young adult with epilepsy. Many schools and state licensing boards will not allow a student to take driver's education or get a license until he or she has been seizure-free for at least a year. It is not uncommon for those who have been seizure-free for almost a year to have a seizure close to the anniversary date. Some persons argue that the underlying factor is stress, while others suggest that it is simply coincidence.

19 *Teachers should encourage the students to communicate the concerns they may have regarding their seizure disorders, even if the seizures occur infrequently.* Chee (1984) suggested that "the seizure itself is not as frightening as the concern about the care that will be given during the seizure and the reaction of those witnessing the episode" (p. 77). Students should be reassured that a responsible person will be nearby and that they will be treated with dignity and will be offered support, not ridicule. Peer support groups, arranged by the local chapter of the Epilepsy Foundation of America or Epilepsy Canada, may help the students and provide opportunities to work through their feelings of anger, frustration, and alienation.

20 *Discrimination in the workplace is a serious problem for many people with epilepsy.* In the past, the rate of unemployment among those with epilepsy has been shown to be much higher than the national average. However, employment records of people with epilepsy indicate, on average, less sick time taken and fewer accidents on the job than those of the general work force. One study, conducted by the Workman's Compensation Board of Canada, showed that 8.1 out of 1,000 accidents resulted from epileptic seizures, whereas 20.2 out of 1,000 resulted from coughing or sneezing in a "normal" person (Epilepsy Canada, n.d.).

While legislation prohibits discrimination on the basis of disability, it is unlikely that the negative attitudes and prejudices held by many will be changed. Consequently, some young adolescents and adults with epilepsy will be faced with unemployment or underemployment. The student must obtain realistic vocational counseling. If the seizures are under perfect control, the presence of epilepsy *should not* interfere with most career aspirations. However, the student who has recurrent seizures, even if they are very sporadic, should be discouraged from careers that may endanger the student or others (Chee, 1984).

If the student with epilepsy has a healthy mental outlook and has developed confidence in his or her abilities, epilepsy should not be a major factor in gaining appropriate employment. As stated earlier, it is often the stigma associated with epilepsy that is the greatest challenge to the student with a convulsive disorder. Nealis (1983), in describing some of the mistreatment that persons with epilepsy have had to suffer, made the following comments: "the epileptic is handicapped less by the disease than the superstitions surrounding it. Epilepsy can be less inhibiting than diabetes" (p. 75).

21 *Students who have generalized seizures are, in most cases, known to teachers before the beginning of the school year. Such is not necessarily the case in children who have absence seizures.* Nealis (1983) suggests that "thousands of children sit in classrooms quietly having petit mal spells day after day after day" (p. 75) and that, in many cases, these students go unnoticed until a later date, when they are referred to the school counselor as having behavior problems. Teachers can play an important role in recognizing students with absence seizures and reporting their concerns to the student's parents or to the school nurse.

Summary

Epilepsy is unlike most chronic illnesses because of its unpredictable nature. It is one of the most feared and misunderstood conditions; there is no other illness that has set individuals so far apart for so often

or so long (O'Donohoe, 1985). Lennox (1960; cited in Vining, 1989) described the condition in a very graphic nature in the following statement: "Epilepsy is not a continuously rough sea, but a recurrent tidal wave."

Teachers are typically apprehensive about having a student with epilepsy in their classrooms, fearing the worst. However, it is important to remember that even the child or young adult with a severe seizure disorder is "normal" most of the day and only at times "succumbs" to the condition (Nealis, 1983). While in most cases, epilepsy is not a truly disabling condition, it is the attitudes and prejudices of others that are the greatest handicap to those with epilepsy (Hampson, 1993). Schools, by providing others with education regarding conditions such as epilepsy, may be successful in changing the attitudes and prejudices that are so harmful to these children.

References

Adams, R. D., & Victor, M. (1993). *Principles of neurology* (5th ed.). New York: McGraw-Hill.

American Academy of Pediatrics (1994). Medical conditions affecting sports participation. *Pediatrics, 94,* 757–760.

Bagley, C. R. (1970). The educational performance of children with epilepsy. *British Journal of Educational Psychology, 40,* 82–83.

Bergen, D. (1991). The schoolchild with epilepsy: How do we respond? *PTA Today, 16*(3), 18.

Bergland, M., & Hoffbauer, D. (1996). New opportunities for students with traumatic brain injuries: Transition to postsecondary education. *Teaching Exceptional Children, 28,* 54–56.

Brown, L. W. (1997). Seizure disorders. In M. L. Batshaw (Ed.), *Children with disabilities* (4th ed., pp. 553–593). Baltimore: Paul H. Brookes.

Chee, C. M. (1984). Epilepsy. In J. Fithian (Ed.), *Understanding the child with a chronic illness in the classroom* (pp. 57–79). Phoenix: Oryx Press.

Disabato, J., & Wulf, J. (1994). Altered neurologic function. In C. L. Betz, M. M. Hunsberger, & S. Wright (Eds.), *Family-centered nursing care of children* (2nd ed., pp. 1717–1814). Philadelphia: W. B. Saunders.

Epilepsy Canada (n.d.). *Epilepsy—A fact sheet.* Montreal, PQ: Author.

Epilepsy Foundation of America (1993). *Q & A: Questions and answers about epilepsy.* Landover, MD: Author.

Evans, J. C., & Smith, J. (1993). Nursing planning, intervention, and evaluation for altered neurologic function.

In D. B. Jackson & R. B. Saunders (Eds.), *Child health nursing: A comprehensive approach to the care of children and their families* (pp. 1353–1430). Philadelphia: J. B. Lippincott.

Fisher, L. (1995). Prescription for hope: New drugs can help many epileptics lead normal lives. *Maclean's, 108*(28), 36.

Hampson, E. (1993). The special education teachers and epilepsy. *B.C. Journal of Special Education, 17,* 26–32.

Heller, K. W., Alberto, P. A., Forney, P. E., & Schwartzman, M. N. (1996). *Understanding physical, sensory, and health impairments: Characteristics and educational implications.* Pacific Grove, CA: Brooks/Cole.

Hirtz, D. G. (1989). Generalized tonic-clonic and febrile seizures. *Pediatric Clinics of North America, 36,* 365–382.

Holvoet, J. F., & Helmstetter, E. (1989). *Medical problems of students with special needs: A guide for educators.* Boston: Little, Brown.

Jan, J. E., Ziegler, R. G., & Erba, G. (1991). *Does your child have epilepsy?* (2nd ed.). Austin, TX: Pro-Ed.

Jezewski, M. A. (1992). Alterations in neurological function. In P. T. Castiglia & R. E. Harbin, *Child health care: Process and practice* (pp. 633-683). Philadelphia: J. B. Lippincott.

Jones-Saete, C. (1986). The student with epilepsy. In G. Larson (Ed.), *Managing the school age child with a chronic health condition* (pp. 113–122). Wayzata, MN: DCI Publishing.

Killam, P. (1992). Childhood epilepsy: Myth vs. reality. *American Journal of Nursing, 93*(3), 77–82.

Knight, B. (1992). *Discovering the human body: How pioneers of medicine solved the mysteries of the body's structure and function.* London: Bloomsbury.

Kuhn, B. R., Allen, K. D., & Shriver, M. D. (1995). Behavioral management of children's seizure activity: Intervention guidelines for primary-care providers. *Clinical Pediatrics, 34,* 570–575.

Lockman, L. A. (1989). Absence, myoclonic, and atonic seizures. *Pediatric Clinics of North America, 36,* 331–341.

Marshall, R. M., & Cupoli, J. M. (1986). Epilepsy and education: The pediatrician's expanding role. *Advances in Pediatrics, 33,* 159–180.

Nealis, J. G. T. (1983). Epilepsy. In J. Umbreit (Ed.), *Physical disabilities and health impairments: An introduction* (pp. 74–85). New York: Merrill.

O'Donohoe, N. V. (1985). *Epilepsies of childhood* (2nd ed.). London: Butterworth.

Pedley, T. A., Scheuer, M. L., & Walczak, T. S. (1995). Epilepsy. In L. P. Rowland (Ed.), *Merritt's textbook of neurology* (9th ed., pp. 845–868). Baltimore, MD: Williams & Wilkins.

Smith, M. P., & Woodring, B. C. (1990). Innervation and mobility: Implications of altered neurologic and neuromuscular function. In S. R. Mott, S. R. James, & A. M. Sperhac, *Nursing care of children and families* (2nd ed., pp. 1615–1730). Redwood City, CA: Addison-Wesley.

Spiegel, G. L., Cutler, S. K., & Yetter, C. E. (1996). What every teacher should know about epilepsy. *Intervention in School and Clinic, 32,* 34–38.

Tyler, J. S., & Colson, S. (1994). Common pediatric disabilities: Medical aspects and educational implications. *Focus on Exceptional Children, 27*(4), 1–16.

Vining, E. P. G. (1989). Educational, social, and life-long effects of epilepsy. *Pediatric Clinics of North America, 36,* 449–461.

Whaley, L. F., & Wong, D. L. (1995). *Nursing care of infants and children* (5th ed.). St. Louis: Mosby.

Wyllie, E., Rothner, A. D., & Lüders, H. (1989). Partial seizures in children: Clinical features, medical treatment, and surgical considerations. *Pediatric Clinics of North America, 36,* 343–364.

Yousef, J. M. (1985). Medical and educational aspects of epilepsy: A review. *Division of Physically Handicapped Journal, 8*(1), 3–15.

Head Injuries

Some of the commonly occurring injuries that affect the bones, muscles, and joints, including injuries to the spinal cord, are described in chapter 14. In most circumstances, a child or young adult who sustains such an injury, with time, makes full, or nearly full, recovery. This is not necessarily the case for many of those who sustain a **craniocerebral injury,** more commonly referred to as a **head** or **brain injury,** which is the subject of this chapter. Since most brain injuries result from an external physical force being exerted on the brain in a violent manner (e.g., as a result of vehicle accidents or physical abuse), the term **traumatic brain injury,** or **TBI,** is commonly used in both the educational and medical literature. However, brain injury can also occur from circumstances that do no not involve external force to the brain. For example, lack of oxygen to the brain that results from a person being choked or being submerged in water for too long or from occlusion of a blood vessel in the brain is a common cause of brain injury, as are certain illnesses, such as meningitis and encephalitis. These types of brain injuries are often grouped together and referred to by neurologists as **acquired brain injuries.**

Classification Systems

Head injuries are commonly classified on the basis of the **site of the damage** as well as on the **pathophysiology of the injury.** These classifications are shown in Table 13.1. In addition, all head injuries can be ranked on the basis of **severity** from minor to serious.

TABLE 13.1
Head Injuries: Classification by Site and by Pathophysiology

SITE
Scalp
Skull
Brain
PATHOPHYSIOLOGY
Primary vs. secondary
Localized vs. generalized
Open vs. closed
Coup vs. contrecoup

By Site of Damage

Craniocerebral injuries are divided into three groups on the basis of location. From the outside of the head inwards, the three groupings are scalp injuries, skull injuries, and brain injuries.

Scalp Injuries   Injuries that are confined to the skin covering the head, but excluding the face and ears, are referred to as scalp injuries and can range from mild to severe. Scalp injuries that are more pronounced may also involve damage to the underlying structures (i.e., the bony skull), as described later. The degree of severity of scalp injuries is generally dependent on the type of object that causes the injury (e.g., blunt object, such as a baseball bat, vs. sharp object, such as a knife) and the speed or force of the object as it makes contact with the head.

Scalp injuries, even minor abrasions, are often marked by a significant loss of blood caused by the dense vascularity of this region of the body. The amount of blood loss, however, is not always indicative of the damage to the underlying bone structure or neural tissue. Children with a minor scalp injury may have a serious brain injury; conversely, a major scalp injury, in some cases, may result in no permanent sequelae.

Skull Injuries   Injuries that are confined to the 8 bones that make up the cranium and the 14 bones of the face, referred to as skull injuries, can also range in severity from mild to profound. Skull injuries are also often referred to as **cranial vault injuries.** Traumas that result in the displacement of bone into neural tissue of the brain (e.g., a depressed fracture) are more likely to result in serious consequences than those that do not damage the underlying tissues (e.g., a simple or a linear fracture). The degree of severity of a skull injury depends on a number of factors, such as the weight of the object that has had contact with the head and the speed at which the skull was hit. For example, a low-velocity blow by a lightweight object (e.g., a blow to the head from the open hand of an assailant) may result in a linear fracture, whereas a high-velocity blow with a heavier or pointed object (e.g., a bullet) may result in a depressed or perforating fracture. Basilar fractures, i.e., those that occur at the base of the skull, often result from high-speed impact with a solid surface, such as the ground, a car windshield, or a wall, and usually result in a profound injury. In some cases, a minor skull injury can result in a serious brain injury.

Rarely, however, will a major skull injury result in minor neurologic consequences.

Brain Injuries   Injuries that involve the portion of the CNS contained within the skull, referred to as brain injuries, are the most serious form of craniocerebral injuries. In many cases, even those that appear to be extremely mild, there are long-term or permanent consequences. As stated previously, most brain injuries are a result of some form of trauma. Twenty years ago, 90% of people who sustained a head injury did not survive (Russo, 1991; cited in Turnbull, Turnbull, Shank, & Leal, 1995). Today, less than 10% succumb to their injuries (Johnson, 1988). Consequently, many children and young adults who have had a TBI are returning to school, albeit, in most cases, changed from their pretrauma state. These students are the focus of this chapter.

By the Pathophysiology of the Injury

The brain is basically a semisolid organ "floating" in the cranial vault, cushioned by surrounding CSF. In general, head injuries result because some type of force, too great to be absorbed by the skull and the supporting structures (e.g., bone, meninges), damages the intracranial contents. Situations in which either the stationary head is hit by a moving object or in which the moving head hits a stationary object cause the skull contents to shift within the skull. The impact can force the brain forward or backward in the skull or, in some cases, can cause the brain to shift and rotate within the cavity. The force may bruise the tissue directly at the site of impact or at the site opposite the initial site, particularly as the brain slams back and forth against the rough inner surface of the cranium. The impact can also cause the tearing, or shearing, of brain tissue (which may, over time, become the epileptogenic focus of seizure activity); the stretching of meningeal membranes; the rupturing of blood vessels within the cavity, which may result in a **hematoma,** or pool of blood, developing between the dura mater and the brain or between the skull and the dura; and the severing of cranial nerves (e.g., damage to cranial nerve VII, which results in facial paralysis).

Because the damage is often diffuse and not always visible by means of imaging techniques (e.g., X-ray, CT scan, MRI), the physician may have difficulty determining the prognosis, because posttraumatic sequelae depend on the damage incurred.

An individual who has sustained a TBI may become epileptic or hydrocephalic (which, if untreated, may be life-threatening) or may develop focal neurologic deficits, such as loss of vision or spasticity of specific limbs, similar to those seen in cerebral palsy. Some individuals with severe head injury become dependent on a ventilator to obtain oxygen.

Aside from the physiologic symptoms that may arise in children and young adults who have sustained an injury to the head, the educational implications that result in alterations in school performance (e.g., cognitive and behavioral changes) are of particular concern to teaching staff. These will be discussed later in this chapter.

While there are numerous ways in which head and brain injuries can be categorized, the patterns described below rarely occur in a "pure" form. It is more typical to see a mixture of different types of injuries. As noted previously, the visibility of the injury may have little or no relationship to the extent of the resulting deficit. It is common to categorize head injuries on the basis of pathophysiology as being primary or secondary, localized or generalized, open or closed, and coup or contrecoup. Closed head injuries are further subdivided into acceleration or deceleration injuries.

Primary vs. Secondary Head Injuries   Injuries that occur at the time of the trauma are referred to as **primary head injuries.** Fractures of one or more bones of the skull, **contusions** (bruising) of neural tissues, **concussions** (jolts or jarrings of the brain that result in a transient loss of consciousness), **lacerations** (tearing of cerebral tissue), and the development of an intracranial **hematoma** are all examples of common primary injuries.

Injuries that occur subsequent to the initial insult, i.e., they are the sequelae that may arise in the posttraumatic period, are referred to as **secondary injuries.** Damage to neural tissue that results from hypoxia, hemorrhage, infection, increased intracranial pressure, and edema are all examples of secondary complications. The rapidity with which a primary injury is treated often determines the extent to which these complications develop.

Localized vs. Generalized Head Injuries   Injuries in which the force exerted on the skull is restricted to a small area of the skull and its underlying brain tissue are referred to as **localized head injuries.** Localized head injuries are also often referred to as being **focal** in nature. Injuries in which the force is exerted on the entire skull, causing extensive damage to the neural tissue located within the brain (e.g., twisting of neuronal axons), are referred to as **generalized head injuries.** Generalized head injuries are often described as being **diffuse** in nature.

Both primary and secondary injuries can be either localized or generalized. Many traumatic accidents (e.g., vehicular accidents) result in concommitant localized and generalized injuries.

Open vs. Closed Head Injuries   Injuries in which the integrity of the bony skull is compromised and the brain is violated by a foreign object are referred to as **open head injuries.** Such injuries are also referred to as **missile injuries.** A gunshot wound, either self-inflicted or inflicted by another person, in which the skull is pierced by a projectile is an example of an open head injury. Since the injury is typically localized along the track of the missile, the effects of the injury are limited rather than generalized (e.g., a bullet that enters the motor strip of the right frontal lobe results in a motor impairment affecting only the left side of the body; the right side of the body is unaffected). Injuries in which the skull remains whole (i.e., the bones are not penetrated) but the tissues above or below the skull are traumatized are referred to as **closed head injuries.** Closed head injuries are also referred to as **nonpenetrating, blunt,** or **nonmissile injuries.** Closed head injuries are more common than open, and the most common closed form is a **concussion,** in which the brain is jarred against the skull.

Typically, in closed head injuries, since the injury is more generalized, the effects of the injury are often more diffuse. For example, closed head injury can lead to physical changes, such as paralysis; to cognitive changes, such as inability to attend or concentrate; and behavioral changes, such as increased depression and decreased motivation. In closed head injuries, the underlying mechanism of injury is either the rapid **acceleration** or **deceleration** of the brain, or in some cases a combination of the two.

Acceleration vs. Deceleration Injuries   Injuries that occur when the head is stationary and is hit by a moving object are referred to as **acceleration injuries.** A person who is hit over the head by a baseball bat would be described as having an acceleration injury. Injuries that occur when a moving head suddenly hits a stationary object are referred to as **deceleration injuries.** A person who is catapulted forward in a car and hits his or her head on the dashboard or windshield would be described as having a deceleration injury.

Coup vs. Contrecoup Injuries   Injuries in which the damage to the brain occurs at the site of the impact are referred to as **coup injuries.** For example, if a person falls and hits his or her forehead on the ground, the bruising of the tissue in the frontal lobe of the brain would be described as a coup injury. Rapid deceleration injuries, such as in the example given above, often cause the greatest injury at the impact site. Injuries that occur as a result of the brain rebounding off the side of the skull contralateral to the site of initial insult are referred to as **contrecoup injuries.** For example, if a person hit on the back of the head with a baseball bat sustains an injury to the frontal or temporal area that results from the brain moving forward in the cranial vault and coming into contact with the frontal bones, the injury would be described as a contrecoup injury.

Certain injuries, most notably injuries involving automobiles, typically involve both coup and contrecoup injuries, as a result of the brain being bounced back and forth in the skull. This combined type of damage is illustrated in Figure 13.1.

By Severity

Head injuries are also commonly classified on the basis of the seriousness of the insult. To describe the severity of a brain injury, Klonoff, Low, and Clark

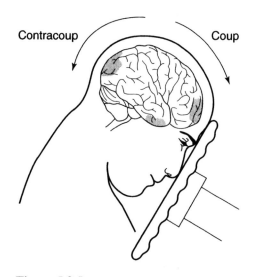

Figure 13.1
Coup and Contrecoup Injuries
Source: Adapted from Heller, Alberto, Forney, & Schwartzman, 1996, p. 59.

(1977) and also Johnson (1988) have proposed a ranking system that rates the condition from mild to severe. **Length of coma,** immediately after injury, is one of the major factors considered in such classification systems. Some of the typical characteristics of each level are shown in Table 13.2.

Although a "brain" injury, by definition, refers to some type of injury to the neural tissue located within the cerebrum, the diencephalon, the brain stem, or the cerebellum, a severe injury can also damage blood vessels, cranial nerves, and other cranial structures, such as the various ducts and meningeal membranes that contain CSF that are located within the skull cavity. If the brain stem, the area of the brain that controls many of the body's basic functions (e.g., breathing, swallowing, heart beat), is seriously damaged by the pulling or twisting motions of the brain as it is whipped back and forth rapidly within the skull, death may occur. Head injury in the pediatric population is one of the leading causes of death. Other children may be paralyzed from the neck down and be dependent on a ventilator for respiration.

TABLE 13.2
Ranking Severity of TBIs

Minor:	No loss of consciousness; head "bump" typically not seen by a physician.
Mild:	Transient loss of consciousness, if any; child may be lethargic and not be able to recall the injury; child may vomit (if more than three times, should be seen by emergency room staff).
Moderate:	Loss of consciousness is typically less than 5 minutes; on recovery, the child may be able to move spontaneously and purposefully; opens eyes in response to pain. Older children may be combative, telling others to "leave me alone."
Severe:	Loss of consciousness ranges from 5 to 30 minutes. Surgery may be needed if skull is fractured significantly; neurologic sequelae are common.
Serious:	Loss of consciousness more than 30 minutes; notable neurologic sequelae are typical.

Sources: Johnson, 1988; Klonoff, Low, & Clark, 1977.

 Etiology

When the incidence of head injury for children is examined in general, regardless of the age of the child, **motor vehicle–related accidents** are the leading cause of severe and fatal head injury. However, when age is considered more specifically, different incidence patterns become evident. For example, in neonates, **birth trauma** (e.g., from the use of forceps) is a major contributory factor to brain damage; in young children, particularly those under the age of 1, **physical abuse,** most often resulting from the child being shaken vigorously (often referred to as **whiplash syndrome,** or **shaken child syndrome**), is a common cause of severe head injury, as is **accidental dropping.** In the population under age 5, **falls from heights** (e.g., from the arms of a caregiver, furniture, windowsills, trees, or playground equipment) are the most frequent cause of TBI. Chorazy (1985) has suggested that the incidence of falls increases significantly as infants progress through the active toddler and preschool years "because judgment does not keep pace with developing motor skills" (pp. xix-xx). In addition, immature motor development makes toddlers clumsy, and as they run on unsteady legs, leaning forward precariously, they often run into things or trip over their own feet (Patterson, Brown, Salassi-Scotter, & Middaugh, 1992). In school-age children and adolescents, falls from bicycles and skateboards are typical.

In the elementary and middle school grades, **pedestrian–motor vehicle** and **bicycle–motor vehicle accidents** are common, as are motor vehicle accidents in which the child is a passenger. In older children, particularly in male children between the ages of 8 and 12, **impact injuries** from contact sports, such as football and soccer, occur with regularity. Such injuries continue to be prevalent through adolescence and into adulthood. Other recreational and sporting activities, such as skiing, skating, and horseback riding, are all often implicated in injuries of the older child and young adult.

In the adolescent population, **assault,** particularly among individuals who are members of a low socioeconomic group, is a cause of many head injuries (Chorazy, 1985). **Motor vehicle accidents** (i.e., accidents in which the injured person is the driver or a passenger) are a common cause, as are **sporting and recreational injuries,** both from competitive activities and from unsupervised activities (Chorazy,

1985). As would be expected in this population, head injuries occur most often in the spring and summer, on weekends, and in the late afternoon or early evening, as these are the times that young people are more likely to be outdoors engaging in physical activities that have a high degree of risk (Disabato & Wulf, 1994). Regardless of age, other factors that can contribute to the occurrence of a TBI include seizure disorders, gait instability, alcohol or drug ingestion, and cognitive delays, including poor judgment (Disabato & Wulf, 1994).

Incidence and Prevalence

One out of 30 students will sustain some type of significant head injury by the time they reach 15 years of age; 1 in 500 school-age children are hospitalized each year as a result of a head injury; and 1 in 10,000 children under the age of 14 die each year from head trauma (Kalsbeek, McLauren, Harris, & Miller, 1980; Whaley & Wong, 1995). These statistics,

however, are believed to be gross underestimations, since numerous head injuries, both minor and major, go unreported (Tyler & Colson, 1994). A classic example would be the parent who does not seek medical attention for his or her child when the trauma results from abuse. While exact statistics concerning incidence and prevalence are unknown, some estimates, as they pertain to the United States, are shown in Table 13.3.[1] Regardless of the actual incidence of brain injury, males sustain these injuries two to three times more frequently than females, in particular, males between the ages of 15 and 24 (Smith & Woodring, 1990).

---

[1] Over the past decade the incidence of TBI has increased dramatically, possibly because of use of motorized recreational vehicles that travel at high speeds and either do not require a license to operate or are frequently operated without a license (i.e., illegally) by children and young adults. Such vehicles include off-terrain vehicles, motorbikes, motorcycles, mopeds, snowmobiles, and skijets. Skateboards, inline rollerblades, and skiboards have also been implicated.

TABLE 13.3
Statistics Related to Incidence and Prevalence of TBI in the U.S.

- 1 million to 5 million head injuries occur every year in children alone.
- 4 people sustain a TBI every minute.
- 40% of all head injuries occur in children.
- 75,000 to 100,000 Americans die per year as a result of TBI; 1 person dies every 12 minutes.
- TBI is the leading cause of death related to trauma; since 1980, the death rate from TBI has exceeded total deaths from all wars during the past 200 years.
- 10 of every 100,000 children between infancy and age 14 die each year from head trauma; this rate is five times greater than death from leukemia, the second leading cause of mortality in children.
- 75% of people sustaining TBI are under the age of 34; TBI occurs most often in persons aged 15 to 24.
- 25,000 children are killed or permanently injured as a result of TBI annually.
- 166,000 children are hospitalized annually as a result of TBI; 16,000 to 20,000 children display moderate to severe symptoms of injury.
- 70,000 to 90,000 Americans suffer lifelong physical, intellectual, and psychological disabilities annually as a result of TBI.
- There are 5,000 new cases of epilepsy and 2,000 cases of persistent vegetative state per year resulting from TBI.
- Each severe head injury survivor requires between $4.1 and $9.0 million for a lifetime of care.
- In 1974, the total lifetime costs for survivors of acute TBI was estimated at $2.43 billion; by 1985, the costs had risen tenfold to $24 billion.

Sources: Accouloumre & Caldwell, 1991; Chorazy, 1985; Hilton, 1994; Jaffe et al., 1993; Johnson, 1988; McAllister, 1992; Michael & Finnegan, 1995; Mira & Tyler, 1991; Tucker & Colson, 1992.

Recently, Jaffe and his colleagues (1993) attempted to estimate the economic costs of TBI in children. Based on data from 96 pediatric patients with mild, moderate, and severe TBIs seen in two emergency departments in Seattle, Washington, between July 1987 and August 1988, they reported the following statistics: (a) acute care and rehabilitation median costs were $4,233 per child: $11,478 for hospitalized children and $230 for those only seen in the emergency department; (b) median costs for injuries due to motor vehicles, bicycles, and falls were $15,213, $6,311, and $792, respectively; and (c) median costs of mild, moderate, and severe traumatic brain injuries were $598, $12,022, and $53,332, respectively. In discussing the astronomical costs of TBIs, Chorazy (1985) suggested that not only are the dollar costs of head injuries "truly staggering," but that the costs, in terms of human suffering, are "overwhelming, not only to the patient, but also to family members and friends" (p. xxi).

🐾 Characteristics: Effects of Head Injury on Learning and Development

TBI has long been known to have a lifelong effect on learning and development; however, until passage of Public Law 101-476, the **Individuals with Disabilities Education Act (IDEA)** in 1990, students with TBIs were not recognized as a discrete group for educational purposes.[2] Before this time, if students who had sustained a head injury needed any services (e.g., physical therapy, speech therapy),

they had to be eligible under some other category, such as "other health impaired" or "specific learning disabled." With the recognition of students with TBI as part of a distinct group, there has been a corresponding increase in the number of students who have been classified in this manner, and it is expected that the numbers will continue to increase as state and local educational agencies identify and count these children and young adults as unique populations of students with disabilities. In 1991–92, the first year in which data were collected, 0.007% of the total special education population, ages 6 to 12, were students with head injuries (n = 330); one year later, in 1992-93, the percentage had increased to 0.1% (n = 3,903). The trend has continued. Figures for 1993-94 showed a 33.7% increase over the previous year (n = 5,295) (U.S. Department of Education, 1994, 1995).

Some educators have questioned the need for a distinct status under the law. Some have argued that the needs of those who have sustained a TBI are no different than others with a learning disability. Others have suggested that post-TBI learning problems are not the same as those found in individuals classified as learning disabled, and consequently, the learning needs (and possible placement options and instructional approaches) differ. The characteristics of students with learning disabilities are contrasted to those of students with TBI in Table 13.4.

The effects of TBI on learning and development are often subtle and therefore difficult to recognize, assess, and remediate. Typical physical, sensory, cognitive, social, emotional, behavioral, and personality changes are listed in Table 13.5. In addition, specific academic problems related to particular curricular domains (e.g., language arts vs. mathematics) are presented. For further detailed information on specific communication disorders in persons who are recovering from severe traumatic brain injuries, see the comprehensive article by Schwartz-Cowley & Stepanik (1989).

Students who have sustained a brain injury will not exhibit all of the changes listed in Table 13.5 because the sequelae depend on many factors. The site of the injury, the extent of the injury (e.g., the degree of axonal injury or brain stem dysfunction), the degree of severity of the injury, the length of time the individual was unconscious, the length of time since injury, the person's maturational stage when the injury occurred, and the presence of amnesia after the trauma must all be considered. However, between 80% and 100% of all individuals who sustain a mild head injury show

---

[2] Regulations contained in IDEA reflect the recognition that long-term sequelae of head injury can affect more than one area of performance. A traumatic brain injury, according to this specific legislation, is defined as follows:

Traumatic brain injury means an acquired injury to the brain caused by an external physical force, resulting in total or partial functional disability or psychosocial impairment, or both, that adversely affects a child's educational performance. The term applies to open or closed head injuries resulting in impairments in one or more areas, such as cognition; language; memory; attention; reasoning; abstract thinking; judgment; problem-solving; sensory, perceptual, and motor abilities; psychosocial behavior; physical functions; information processing; and speech. The term does not apply to brain injuries that are congenital or degenerative, or brain injuries induced by birth trauma.

TABLE 13.4

Comparison of Characteristics of Students with LD and Students with TBI

Learning Disability	Traumatic Brain Injury
• Congenital, perinatal, or early onset.	• Sudden onset.
• Cause may be unclear; often appears when new demands are introduced (e.g., school starts)	• Specific cause.
• Often manifests in only one area (e.g., mathematics).	• Resulting problems are strikingly complex.
• Status changes comparatively slowly.	• Status change ranges from irregular to remarkably rapid.
• Visual and auditory perceptual difficulties are often without specific organic damage.	• Visual and auditory perceptual difficulties are due to specific injury to the sensory system.

Source: Tucker, B. F. & Colson, S. E. (1992). Traumatic brain injury: An overview of school re-entry. *Intervention in School and Clinic, 27,* 198–206. Copyright 1992 by PRO-ED, Inc. Reprinted by permission.

signs of postconcussive syndrome within the first month after the injury (McAllister, 1992).

Postconcussive syndrome has been described by McAllister (1992) as a "constellation of symptoms" that include cognitive deficits (e.g., memory loss, decreased attention and concentration, disorganization of thinking), affective difficulties (e.g., mood swings, depression, irritability), and somatic problems (e.g., headache, dizziness, fatigue, sleep difficulties). While postconcussive sequelae typically decrease with time, it has been estimated that 100% of individuals with a severe injury, 67% of those with a moderate injury, and 10% of those with mild degrees of injury will show some type of long-term or permanent neurologic impairment. Whaley and Wong (1995) have suggested that the manifestations of postconcussive syndrome differ with age. Some of these differences are shown in Table 13.6. Structural complication can occur regardless of age.

Statistics such as those regarding postconcussive sequelae reported above, especially for those students who have sustained a mild head injury, have been questioned in the research literature. Fay and her colleagues (1993, 1994), in a series of studies that followed a cohort of 112 children between the ages of 6 and 15 who had sustained a head injury, found that three years after injury, students with mild head injuries were proficient in all neurocognitive academic and behavioral domains, including "intelligence, memory, adaptive problem solving, motor, psychomotor and academic skills," and that socialization, educational performance, and dysfunctional behavior showed "no important differences from controls" (1994, p. 740). They did acknowledge, however, that children with moderate and severe head injuries remained "at high risk to experience significant problems in the educational process" and that typically they "do not demonstrate long-term recovery from their injuries" (1994, p. 740).

First Aid for Head Injuries

Children who sustain a minor head injury (e.g., minor concussion) that does not result in any loss of consciousness generally do not need to be seen by a physician; however, the parents should be notified immediately that an accident has occurred. Appropriate first-aid procedures are outlined in Table 13.7 along with a list of symptoms that require immediate medical attention.

Children who show signs of a more severe injury (e.g., those that lose consciousness, those who experience a seizure) should be transported immediately to a medical facility for observation (i.e., call 911). All school staff should be trained to respond appropriately to a student with a head injury, particularly staff who are supervising students during activities in which head injuries are likely to occur (e.g., play group supervisors, physical education teachers, transportation staff).

Educational Implications and Teaching Tips

Not only are the academic and instructional needs of children who have sustained a TBI unique, the educational placement and service requirements are also unique. In a recent study, Donders (1994) examined the learning needs of 87 children who had a diagnosis of TBI with a documented loss of consciousness, who were between the ages of 6 years 6 months and 16 years 6 months at the time of initial assessment,

TABLE 13.5
Sequelae of Traumatic Brain Injury

PHYSICAL AND SENSORY CHANGES

- Chronic headaches; dizziness; light-headedness; nausea
- Vision impairments (e.g., double vision, visual-field defects, blurring, increased sensitivity to light)
- Auditory impairment (e.g., tinnitus, increased sensitivity to sound)
- Alterations in sense of taste, touch, and smell
- Growth problems
- Sleep problems (e.g., insomnia, day/night confusion)
- Stress-related disorders (e.g., depression)
- Flat emotional affect (e.g., no voice inflection, expressionless face, vacant eyes, rarely laughs or smiles appropriately)
- Impairment of sexual functioning (e.g., alteration in arousal levels)
- Poor body temperature regulation
- Recurrent seizure activity
- Poor coordination and balance
- Muscle weakness that results in lack of stamina; in extreme cases, may lead to debilitating fatigue
- Numbness and tingling in extremities; in severe cases, spasticity or paralysis, which can lead to difficulties in executing both gross and fine motor activities (e.g., running, writing)
- Reduced speed of motor performance and precision of movement

COGNITIVE CHANGES

- Slowness in processing information, particularly if the information is new or the person is fatigued or overstimulated (e.g., slowed processing speed may affect ability to read assignments, listen to directions)
- Slowed thinking and responses can lead to difficulty keeping up (e.g., in discussions, instructional presentations, assigned work in class, taking notes); the difficulty is particularly evident when the task is timed or if the material contains complex visual-spatial information
- Lack of ability to sustain the required degree of concentration or attention to the task at hand (i.e., distractible, confused, impulsive)
- Often complains of being bored
- Problems retrieving information from long- and short-term memory and difficulty interpreting or evaluating facts that are retrieved (e.g., difficulties with reasoning, judgment, problem solving, and decision-making; difficulty differentiating fact from opinion and with abstraction)
- Difficulty making transitions (e.g., home to school, class to class), including mental transitions within a specific subject (e.g., may have difficulty switching from fraction to decimal problems on same worksheet)
- Lack of insight or foresight
- Lack of self-awareness (i.e., lack of comprehension of their own cognitive or verbal deficits or the implications of these deficits)
- Inability to organize work and environment (e.g., may be unable to keep track of books, assignments, lunch boxes; may be unable to organize morning routine to get ready for school on time); may have problems planning, organizing, initiating, and pacing tasks or activities (e.g., may be unable to write an essay with a logical structure)
- Extremely sensitive to distraction (e.g., unable to take a test in a room with 20 other students)
- Difficulty with multi-tasking and sequencing (i.e., keeping track of two things at once)
- Tendency to perseverate; inflexible in thinking

Continued

TABLE 13.5
(*Continued*)

SPECIFIC ACADEMIC PROBLEMS

- Short- or long-term impairments in receptive oral language (e.g., difficulty following directions or instructions; misunderstanding what is said by others)
- Inability to perceive voice inflections or nonverbal cues
- Short- or long-term impairments in receptive written language (e.g., difficulties with higher level comprehension of the written word, which may be hidden by excellent decoding skills; difficulty in understanding the main idea or implied idea, making judgments, predicting outcomes, and sequencing events, particularly if materials are unfamiliar)
- Short- or long-term impairments in expressive oral or written language (e.g., aphasia, or inability to use language appropriately; anomia, or difficulty retrieving words; dysarthria, or poor articulation; slow speech; difficulty in punctuation and spelling), which may be evident as a reversion to more immature forms of communication; if the student has signs of gross or fine motor skill impairment, handwriting may be illegible)
- In mathematics, difficulty with abstraction (e.g., student may respond better at the concrete level at which manipulatives can assist in determining answers and results)
- May have difficulty in word math problems if there is an underlying reading problem

SOCIAL, EMOTIONAL, AND BEHAVIORAL PROBLEMS AND PERSONALITY CHANGES

- Chronically agitated, irritable, restless, or anxious
- Increased aggressiveness
- Impaired ability to self-manage; lowered impulse control (e.g., may interrupt conversation at inappropriate times; may be unable to wait for his or her turn); poor anger control
- Difficulty dealing with change (i.e., rigid); poor coping strategies
- Lowered self-esteem at the same time that the person is becoming egocentric or self-centered
- May overestimate own ability (often evidenced as "bragging")
- Decreased insight into self and others (i.e., reduced judgment)
- Difficulty following through with responsibilities at home, school, or work; lack of initiative (e.g., needs constant reminders to complete task at hand); lack of motivation
- Decreased frustration tolerance, easily angered, frequent temper outbursts, and overreaction to events
- May talk compulsively or excessively
- Shows signs of disinhibition (i.e., unable to inhibit inappropriate behavioral responses); may try to touch or hug everyone
- May fabricate experiences or situations (i.e., shows signs of confabulation)
- Inability to take cues from the environment (often leading to socially inappropriate behavior)
- Emotional lability (e.g., may cry for no apparent reason or laugh hysterically at inappropriate times)
- Social withdrawal
- Difficulty establishing and maintaining relationships; tendency for individual to become overly dependent on others (e.g., parents, spouse, other family members, attendant)

and who had been enrolled, before the injury, in a formal educational program (i.e., grades 1 through 12) for at least 6 months. After being in school for a minimum of 6 months after injury, only slightly more than half (51.7%) of the students with TBI were fully integrated into the mainstream and were receiving all of their academic instruction in the general education classroom without any assistance from special education staff. Slightly less than half (48.2%)

needed formal special education support. Of the students who needed special education services, the group was evenly split into two on the basis of time in the general education classroom. Half of these students (24.1% of the total sample) were spending 50% or more of their time in the general classroom, whereas the remainder (24.1% of the total sample) were spending less than 50% of their time in the general classroom. Both of these two groups were re-

TABLE 13.6
Clinical Manifestations of Posttraumatic
Postconcussion Syndrome

INFANTS
Pallor
Sweating
Irritability
Sleepiness
Possible vomiting

CHILDREN
Behavioral disturbances
  Aggressiveness
  Disobedience
  Withdrawal
  Regression
  Anxiety
Sleep disturbances
Phobias
Emotional lability
Irritability
Altered school performance
Seizures

ADOLESCENTS
Headache
Dizziness
Impaired concentration

STRUCTURAL COMPLICATIONS
Hydrocephalus
Focal deficits
  Optic atrophy [damage to optic nerve]
  Cranial nerve palsies
  Motor deficits
  Diabetes insipidus
  Aphasia [loss of speech]
Seizures

Source: Whaley, L. F., & Wong, D. L. (1995). *Nursing care of infants and children* (5th ed.). St. Louis: Mosby. Copyright 1995 by Mosby-Year Book, Inc. Reprinted by permission.

TABLE 13.7
Emergency Treatment: Head Injury

1. Assess child:
   A—airway
   B—bleeding
   C—circulation
2. Stablize neck and spine.
3. Clean any abrasions with soap and water. Apply clean dressing. If bleeding, apply ice for 1 hour to relieve pain and swelling.
4. Keep NPO [Latin for *non per os,* or nothing by mouth] or give only clear liquids until no vomiting for at least 6 hours.
5. Give no analgesics or sedatives.
6. Check pupil reaction every 4 hours (including twice during night) for 48 hours.
7. Awaken two times during night to check level of consciousness.
8. Seek medical attention if there is any of the following:

   Injury sustained
   • At high speed (e.g., auto)
   • Fall from a significant distance (e.g., roof, tree)
   • From great force (e.g., baseball bat)
   • Under suspicious circumstances
   Child less than 6 months of age
   Unconscious more than 5 seconds
   Discomfort (crying) more than 10 minutes after injury
   Headache that is severe, worsening, interferes with sleep
   Vomiting three or more times
   Swelling in front of or above earlobe or swelling that increases in size
   Confused or not behaving normally
   Difficult to rouse from sleep
   Difficulty with speaking
   Blurring of vision or seeing double
   Unsteady gait
   Difficulty using upper extremities
   Neck pain
   Pupils dilated or fixed
   Infant with bulging fontanel [space between the bones of an infant's skull]

Source: Whaley, L. F., & Wong, D. L. (1995). *Nursing care of infants and children* (5th ed.). St. Louis: Mosby. Copyright 1995 by Mosby-Year Book, Inc. Reprinted by permission.

ceiving instruction from special education personnel (e.g., resource room teacher, teacher consultant, tutor) in special education facilities (e.g., special class, resource room) when not integrated in the general education class.

By examining the data, the researchers attempted to isolate the most important factor in determining placement. The child's verbal IQ (VIQ) score after injury was critical (i.e., the lower the IQ score, the more likely special education services would be needed). The mean VIQ for those full time in general education classrooms was 100.29, compared to a VIQ of 90.76 for those who were in the regular classroom for at least half the time. For those who spent at least half the time in special education placements, the mean VIQ was 73.43. Performance IQ (PIQ) was also different among the three groups (PIQ of 95.60, 90.81, and 71.19, respectively), but its effect was determined to be less predictive of placement decisions. In addition, to a lesser degree, the length of time the child was in a coma and the type of cerebral lesion were associated with the need for special education support. Length of time in a coma for the three groups was 0.80, 3.59, and 8.83 days, respectively. For those in the general education classroom full time, 68.89% had diffuse lesions; for those in general education classroom for at least half the day, 90.48% had diffuse lesions; and for the last group, those who spent the majority of the day in the special education classroom, 95.24% had extensive damage. Regardless of these findings, the educational needs of all students with TBI must be evaluated individually, and particular test scores, length of time in a coma, and the type of cerebral lesion should never be the sole basis for placement decisions.

Because the needs of students with TBI vary widely from student to student, it is difficult to make recommendations that will be appropriate for all. However, the following suggestions should be useful for teachers as they face the challenges of working with students with head injuries returning to school.

1 *Successful reentry of a student who has sustained a traumatic head injury depends on collaboration among school, hospital, rehabilitation facility, family, community, and the student* (Funk, Bryde, Doelling, & Hough, 1996; Turnbull et al., 1994). While school reentry is often considered to be an "eagerly anticipated milestone along the

child's recovery continuum," all too often the "dream becomes a nightmare" as the "honeymoon period of sympathy and support ends when the student, friends, and teachers must struggle with the neurologically based problems" that are common to this population of students (Tucker & Colson, 1992, p. 202). Without proper reentry planning, there is the potential for disaster.

To provide appropriate programming that fosters academic and social success, Ylvisaker, Hartwick, and Stevens (1991) have suggested that professionals ensure that: (a) the strengths and needs of the student are recognized; (b) decisions about classification, placement, service mix, and modifications in services over time are made flexibly and creatively; (c) the academic and social support needed by the student is in place; (d) proper orientation and training are available to the significant people in the student's environment (e.g., parents, teachers, other school personnel, relevant community professionals, siblings, and peers); and (e) the student's program is monitored on a regular basis and modified as needed.

2 *Before the student reenters the school system, information regarding the student's status is critical (e.g., information on necessary assistive devices, physical limitations, expected behavior patterns).* Various forms that may be of use in gathering information can be found in appendices A to I.

The key assessment is a thorough psychometric evaluation—one that focuses not only on the cognitive weaknesses of the student but, more importantly, on the student's residual or reemerging strengths (Donders, 1994). The assessment of students who have had a head injury usually requires procedures that traditionally are not used by school psychologists or other educational specialists. Kazuk and Stewart (1993) have suggested that students with TBI be seen by a **neuropsychologist,** a person who has specific training in assessment of individuals who have altered neurologic functioning.

3 *The effects of TBI are often changeable.* One day a student with a TBI may function quite adequately; the next day the same student's performance level may be well below normal. It is not uncommon for students with a brain injury to continue to change neurologically for days, weeks, months, or even years after returning to school. Because of the changing needs, frequent assessment, with an emphasis on attempting to predict anticipated needs, is critical. Teachers should respond to the student's present strengths and weaknesses and *not* try to make the student conform to preinjury performance levels.

4 *Students who have had a TBI typically need an educational program quite dissimilar to that required by others with chronic health problems and other types of disabling conditions.* Kazuk and Stewart (1993) described the programming as one that requires "cross-disciplinary planning between educational and medical models" (p. 2). Specifically, the educational program should be highly structured and consistent from day to day. However, it also should be flexible so that modifications or alterations can be made from week to week or month to month (Steensma, 1992).

Individualized educational programs (IEPs) must be written for short periods to reflect the changing needs of the student (Savage, 1991), and reevaluation should occur as frequently as every 1 to 2 months, particularly in the early stages of recovery, rather than every 6 or 12 months, as is the usual practice in most schools (Kazuk & Stewart, 1993; Tyler & Colson, 1994; Ylvisaker et al., 1991). Szekeres and Meserve (1994) have suggested that students with TBI "often 'grow into' problems as academic and social demands outpace development of their cognitive-communicative and social skills" (p. 26) and that it is not uncommon for such difficulties to lead to grade failure. Consistent follow-up and monitoring are needed throughout the student's academic program.

5 *There is always the hope that those who have had a catastrophic injury will be able to return to their homes and schools as quickly as possible, but "many children return to school early in recovery disoriented, disinhibited, and totally unprepared to deal with the cognitive and behavioral demands of school."* As a result of being misunderstood and mismanaged, "the child is easily drawn into the downward spiral of failure, acting out, misinterpretation of the failure and acting out, and further behavioral deterioration" (Ylvisaker et al., 1991, p. 17).

6 *Transitioning from the biophysical environment of a hospital to the psychodynamic environ of a school is a critical step that must be carefully coordinated* (Kazuk & Stewart, 1993). Ideally, students who have sustained a head injury would enter a program specifically designed to meet their unique needs. A specialized classroom for students who have sustained a TBI, often referred to in the educational literature as a **transitional classroom** or a **reentry classroom,** is one that has a low teacher–student ratio and has minimal distractions (Steensma, 1992). A ratio of one specially trained teacher to three students is considered to be optimal, and maximum class size should be no more than six students. The goals of the transition and reentry class, according to Ylvisaker and colleagues (1991), would be as follows:

(1) to manage the behavioral, rehabilitative, and academic needs of children who may no longer be in need of intensive medical services but who are not yet ready to return to their community school; (2) to explore the child's functioning thoroughly so that there is a comprehensive, detailed, and tested plan available when the child returns to school; (3) to prepare the school for the child's return; and, (4) to promote successful reintegration of children into their school, family, and social life. (p. 17)

When the student is ready to move from the specialized classroom to the general education classroom, the shift should not occur too abruptly. Hours in the self-contained classroom should be reduced gradually, over time, as the student is reintroduced to the mainstream. Even when the student is fully reintegrated with his or her peers, the special education classroom can function as a resource room, particularly at times when the student simply cannot cope with being alongside others.

While this type of learning environment is ideal, there are few transitional classrooms in North America, even though many school districts have sufficient numbers of students with brain injuries to support such a program (Ylvisaker et al., 1991). As a result, students with a TBI are often placed in classrooms for other special needs students, specifically classrooms geared to meet the needs of those with cognitive impairments or emotional and behavioral disorders. Savage and Carter (1984) have warned against such practices, because "placement [of students with TBI] in such inappropriate environments will only inhibit cognitive remediation and the redevelopment of psycho-social skills" (p.29). Similarly, Funk and her colleagues (1996) have stressed the need for education professionals "to realize the importance of serving students with TBI where the goals and the objectives of the IEP can be met" and that "service delivery options that may not have been utilized traditionally, may be appropriate" (pp. 60–61).

For further information on the reentry process and educational planning for students with recent brain injuries, see the article by Doelling and Bryde (1995).

7 *Initially, if fatigue is a problem, a shortened school day may be required by some students; others may benefit from a daily rest period (e.g., at lunch, so that the student has more energy to make it through the afternoon period).* Some students who have sustained a TBI may benefit from an extended school year to prevent academic regression (Tyler & Colson, 1994).

8 *Typically, students with TBI need instructional accommodations rather than curricular modifications (e.g., teachers need to speak at a reduced speed and routinely repeat or rephrase directions and major points; teachers need to provide opportunity for repeated practice and to teach students compensatory strategies, such as mnemonic cueing and word association).* However, students who sustain a serious head injury, as a result of the severe memory problems, may also require alterations in the curriculum (e.g., specialized instruction on how to follow directions, structure events, or organize activities) to ensure that community, social skills, vocational, and leisure training needs are met (Bigge, 1991). In most cases, the student's course load should be reduced to include only those classes required for graduation.

Academic needs of students with TBI have been addressed extensively in the educational literature (cf. Cohen, Joyce, Rhoades, & Welks, 1985; Mira & Tyler, 1991; Savage & Carter, 1984; Steensma, 1992; Szekeres & Meserve, 1994; Tucker & Colson, 1992; and Turnbull et al., 1995). An indispensable resource is the book by Mark Ylvisaker (1985), entitled *Head Injury Rehabilitation: Children and Adolescents,* in particular the chapter by Cohen, Joyce, Rhoades, and Welks, entitled "Educational Programming for Head Injured Students." However, no one program or method is always ap-

propriate, because the needs of those recovering from a brain injury differ widely (Bigge, 1991).

9 *Adolescents who sustain a brain injury often have a very difficult time accepting the reality of the situation.* Savage (personal communication, cited in Turnbull et al., 1995) describes the difficulties encountered by this population:

> No matter how badly injured and what memory deficits teenagers have, they remember what they were like before. Their greatest loss is their sense of self, and it creates an extraordinary amount of anger and denial. They don't feel like the same person, and they have to redevelop who they are. (p. 669)

Accouloumre and Caldwell (1991) described the need for adolescents to reframe their lives:

> An adolescent who had established independence may suddenly be dependent on parents for basic needs such as feeding, dressing, and toileting. An excellent student with dreams of college and a career may no longer have the attention or the ability to learn new information. A high school athlete may experience physical difficulties, and a student who is a drama major may no longer be able to remember her lines or speak clearly. . . . These students need to set new, attainable goals such as remembering a friend's name, fixing lunch, walking two blocks, or working in a supported employment program. A major consideration of education must be to assist the student in developing new, meaningful and achievable goals. (p. 8)

Counseling opportunities must be made available, either through the school or from a community-based agency (e.g., local chapter of the state head-injury association). Role-playing activities may be useful in teaching or reteaching specific skills (e.g., asking a person for a date). For practical suggestions on how to counsel an adolescent with a head injury, see Barin, Hanchett, Jacob, and Scott (1985).

Counselors can also be of assistance in helping the student's peers to understand his or her needs. In an article written for parents of children with TBI, Savage and Carter (1984) made the following comments on the difficulties students with TBI face and how peers may react. This article may be of assistance for teachers of those with a TBI.

> It is not uncommon to find head injured adolescents returning to school and succeeding academically only to find their whole social life has fallen apart. Friends do not know how to react to your son or daughter; they begin to shy away from your child's strange

mannerisms; and your child becomes more frustrated since they judge their worth on how their peers "see them." Nothing you say as a parent can calm the anxiety storming within them.

The guidance counselor knows from experience that while high school students tend to avoid what they don't understand, they are also the first to volunteer huge amounts of energy and compassion in worthwhile human service. Your child's friends really want to help your son or daughter, but like many other community people, they tend to shy away when they do not know what to say or do. (p. 31)

10 *Flexibility is a major key to successful reentry.* Savage and Carter (1984) have suggested that flexibility is even more critical for high school students who are injured just before or during their senior year. The dilemma as they see it is described in the following passage:

A major problem lies in the fact that while it may seem, at the time, an important goal for the student to formally complete the high school degree, it may not be in the best interest of the student on a long term basis. Once a student has finished high school they are generally no longer eligible for additional high school courses. Hence, you have an 18-year-old young adult who needs head injury rehabilitation but the only places available are private or hospital institutions—places which may be beyond the family's financial capabilities. (p. 32)

To the authors, there is a simple solution. The student should participate in graduation ceremonies, since it is an important milestone both academically and personally, but the school should withhold the formal awarding of the diploma so that the student can return to school to receive the necessary services until he or she reaches the age when services no longer become available without cost, typically age 21.

11 *Many students with a TBI, in particular those with mild to moderate impairments, are able to pursue a postsecondary education.* However, before the transition, accessibility of the campus and the availability of certain academic programs and support services, including social and personal support systems and career and job placement services, should be addressed. For a comprehensive article on the transition of students with TBI from high school to community college or university, see Bergland and Hoffbauer (1996).

 **Summary**

The effects of a head injury can be significant. The damage to cerebral tissue may result in physical and sensory changes, cognitive changes, academic problems, social and emotional problems, behavioral difficulties, and personality changes. The magnitude of the problem is so great that the National Head Injury Foundation has referred to the number of children who sustain a TBI as being part of the "silent epidemic" of childhood, since many of the children are never recognized as even having a disability.

Even though the incidence keeps increasing, most head injuries are preventable. Schools can play a vital role in teaching students how to avoid injury, e.g., by providing instruction that stresses the importance of wearing seat belts in the car and the consequences of drinking and driving. In addition, schools can ensure that the school environment is as safe as possible, e.g., that there is sufficient supervision of students on the playground and that helmets are worn during certain sports, such as football, baseball, and hockey, in which the incidence of TBI is high.

References

Accouloumre, D. S., & Caldwell, T. H. (1991). Neurological conditions: Traumatic brain injury. In T. H. Caldwell, B. Sirvis, A. W. Todaro, & D. S. Accouloumre, *Special health care in the school* (pp. 5–13). Reston, VA: Council for Exceptional Children.

Barin, J. J., Hanchett, J. M., Jacob, W. L, & Scott, M. B. (1985). Counseling the head injured patient. In M. Ylvisaker (Ed.), *Head injury rehabilitation: Children and adolescents.* Austin, TX: Pro-Ed.

Bergland, M., & Hoffbauer, D. (1996). New opportunities for students with traumatic brain injuries: Transition to postsecondary education. *Teaching Exceptional Children, 28,* 54–56.

Bigge, J. L. (1991). *Teaching individuals with physical and multiple disabilities* (3rd ed.). New York: Merrill.

Chorazy, A. J. L. (1985). Introduction. In M. Ylvisaker (Ed.), *Head injury rehabilitation: Children and adolescents* (pp. xix–xxii). Austin, TX: Pro-Ed.

Cohen, S. B., Joyce, C. M., Rhoades, K. W., & Welks, D. M. (1985). Educational programming for head injured students. In M. Ylvisaker (Ed.), *Head injury rehabilitation: Children and adolescents* (pp. 383–409). Austin TX: Pro-Ed.

Disabato, J., & Wulf, J. (1994). Altered neurologic function. In C. L. Betz, M. M. Hunsberger, & S. Wright

(Eds.), *Family-centered nursing care of children* (2nd ed., pp. 1717–1814). Philadelphia: W. B. Saunders.

Doelling, J. E., & Bryde, S. (1995). School reentry and educational planning for the individual with traumatic brain injury. *Intervention in School and Clinic, 31*(2), 101–107.

Donders, J. (1994). Academic placement after traumatic brain injury. *Journal of School Psychology, 32*, 53–65.

Fay, G. C., Jaffe, K. M., Polissar, N. L., Liao, S., Martin, K. M., Shurtleff, H. A., Rivara, J'M. B., & Winn, H. R. (1993). Mild pediatric traumatic brain injury: A cohort study. *Archives of Physical Medicine and Rehabilitation, 74*, 895–901.

Fay, G. C., Jaffe, K. M., Polissar, N. L., Liao, S., Rivara, J'M. B., & Martin, K. M. (1994). Outcome of pediatric traumatic brain injury at three years: A cohort study. *Archives of Physical Medicine and Rehabilitation, 75*, 733–741.

Funk, P., Bryde, S., Doelling, J., & Hough, D. (1996). Serving students with traumatic brain injury: A study of educators' knowledge level and personnel preparation needs in Missouri. *Physical Disabilities: Education and Related Services, 15* (1), 49–64.

Heller, K. W., Alberto, P. A., Forney, P. E., & Schwartzman, M. N. (1996). *Understanding physical, sensory, and health impairments: Characteristics and educational implications.* Pacific Grove, CA: Brooks/Cole.

Hilton, G. (1994). Behavioral and cognitive sequelae of head trauma. *Orthopaedic Nursing, 13*(4), 25–32.

Jaffe, K. M., Massagli, T. L., Martin, K. M., Rivara, J'M. B., Fay, G. C., & Polissar, N. L. (1993). Pediatric traumatic brain injury: Acute and rehabilitation costs. *Archives of Physical and Medical Rehabilitation, 74*, 681–686.

Johnson, D. L. (1988). Head injury. In M. R. Eichelberger & G. L. Pratsch (Eds.), *Pediatric trauma care* (pp. 87–99). Rockville, MD: Aspen.

Kalsbeek, W. D., McLauren, R. L., Harris, B. S. H., & Miller, J. D. (1980). The national head and spinal cord injury survey: Major findings. *Journal of Neurosurgery,* Suppl. 53, 19–31.

Kazuk, E., & Stewart, D. (1993, August). Planning for traumatic brain injury (TBI): A new challenge for special education. *South Atlantic Regional Resource Center (SARRC) Reports,* 1–4.

Klonoff, H., Low, M. D., & Clark, C. (1977). Head injuries in children: A prospective five-year follow-up. *Journal of Neurology, Neurosurgery, and Psychiatry, 40*, 1211–1219.

McAllister, T. W. (1992). Neuropsychiatric sequelae of head injuries. *Psychiatric Clinics of North America, 15*, 395–413.

Michael, R. J., & Finnegan, T. (1995). Competencies for instructing students with traumatic brain injury. *Physical Disabilities: Education and Related Services, 13*(2), 7–16.

Mira, M. P., & Tyler, J. S. (1991). Students with traumatic brain injury: Making the transition from hospital to school. *Focus on Exceptional Children, 23*(5), 1–12.

Patterson, R. J., Brown, G. W., Salassi-Scotter, M., & Middaugh, D. (1992). Head injury in the conscious child. *American Journal of Nursing, 92*(8), 22–27.

Savage, R. C. (1991). Identification, classification, and placement issues for students with traumatic brain injuries. *Journal of Head Trauma and Rehabilitation, 6*(1), 1–9.

Savage, R. C., & Carter, R. (1984). Reentry: The head injured student returns to school. *Cognitive Rehabilitation, 2*(6), 28–33.

Schwartz-Cowley, R., & Stepanik, M. J. (1989). Communication disorders and treatment in the acute trauma center setting. *Topics in Language Disorders, 9*(2), 1–14.

Smith, M. P., & Woodring, B. C. (1990). Innervation and mobility: Implications of altered neurologic and neuromuscular function. In S. R. Mott, S. R. James, & A. M. Sperhac, *Nursing care of children and families* (2nd ed., pp. 1615-1730). Redwood City, CA: Addison-Wesley.

Steensma, M. (1992). Getting the student with head injuries back in school: Strategies for the classroom. *Intervention in School and Clinic, 27*(4), 207–210.

Szekeres, S. F., & Meserve, N. F. (1994). Collaborative intervention in schools after traumatic brain injury. *Topics in Language Disorders, 15*(1), 21–36.

Tucker, B. F., & Colson, S. E. (1992). Traumatic brain injury: An overview of school re-entry. *Intervention in School and Clinic, 27*, 198–206.

Turnbull, A. P., Turnbull III, H. R., Shank, M., & Leal, D. (1995). *Exceptional lives: Special education in today's schools.* Upper Saddle River, NJ: Prentice Hall/Merrill.

Tyler, J. S., & Colson, S. (1994). Common pediatric disabilities: Medical aspects and educational implications. *Focus on Exceptional Children, 27*(4), 1–16.

U.S. Dept. of Education (1994). *To assure the free appropriate public education of all children with disabilities: 16th Annual Report to Congress.* Washington: Author.

U.S. Dept. of Education (1995). *To assure the free appropriate public education of all children with disabilities: 17th Annual Report to Congress.* Washington: Author.

Whaley, L. F., & Wong, D. L. (1995). *Nursing care of infants and children* (5th ed.). St. Louis: Mosby.

Ylvisaker, M. (Ed.). (1985). *Head injury rehabilitation: Children and adolescents.* Austin, TX: Pro-Ed.

Ylvisaker, M., Hartwick, P., & Stevens, M. (1991). School reentry following head injury: Managing the transition from hospital to school. *Journal of Head Trauma Rehabilitation, 6*(1) 10–22.

PART V

Mobility:

Children and Young Adults with Altered Musculoskeletal Function

There are a number of disorders, many evident during childhood, that can affect a person's ability to move freely within his or her environment and to perform the activities of daily living. Although such conditions are often generally referred to as **physical disabilities** or, more specifically, as **orthopedic impairments,** disabling conditions that interfere with movement can also be classified by the part of the body most affected. Specifically, impaired mobility can result from diseases or defects in (a) the **supporting structures** (the bones and ligaments); (b) the **articulating structures** (the joints); and (c) the **movement-producing structures** (the muscles and tendons).

Although this classification system seems to make a clear distinction amongst the various groups, it does not. Some conditions may affect only the supporting structures (e.g., lordosis, a type of curvature of the spine), the articulating structures (e.g., arthritis), or the movement-producing structures (e.g., muscular dystrophy); however, others may involve more than one group (e.g., traumatic insult to the body). For this reason, two additional terms are often used to classify physical impairments. The term **musculoskeletal** is used to refer to impairments that involve both the muscles and the skeleton, and the term **neuromuscular** refers to those conditions that, as a result of a defect or disease of the nervous system, affect the muscles of the body.

In this part, chronic conditions that are musculoskeletal in origin and that result in difficulty in independent locomotion are described. We will begin with a brief overview of the anatomy and physiology of the supporting, articulating, and movement-producing structures of the human body.

The Supporting Structures: Review of Structure and Function

The supporting framework of the body, **the skeleton,** consists of 206 bones. At adulthood the skeleton accounts for about 14% of total body weight.

The skeleton is actually comprised of three distinct areas: the axial skeleton, the appendicular skeleton, and the ossicular chain. The major bones of the skeletal system, also referred to as the **bony framework,** are shown in Figure V.1.

The Human Skeleton

The **axial skeleton** includes the 74 bones that constitute the longitudinal fulcrum of the skeleton. The major bones of the axial skeleton are the 22 bones that make up the skull (8 cranial bones and 14 facial bones), the 33 vertebrae that form the spinal column (7 cervical, 12 thoracic, 5 lumbar, 5 sacral, and 4 coccygeal vertebrae), the 12 pairs of ribs of the thoracic cage, and the 3 bones that fuse to form the sternum (breastbone). The **appendicular skeleton** consists of the 126 bones that make up the free-moving appendages of the body (i.e., arms, hands, fingers; legs, feet, toes) and the **girdles** that attach the extremities to the axial skeleton (i.e., the pectoral or shoulder girdle that attaches the upper limbs to the upper torso; the pelvic girdle that attaches the lower limbs to the lower torso). While the 6 remaining bones of the body, 3 on each side, do not support it structurally, these tiny bones, known as **ossicles,** located in the middle ear (the malleus, the incus, and the stapes), referred to collectively as the **ossicular chain,** have an important function in the ability to process sound effectively.

Bones

The bones of the human body are composed of a hardened mass of living tissue. They not only function as a structure but also as an organ (Howe & Coffman, 1990; Jackson & Saunders, 1993; Spray, 1991). As a **structure,** bones provide a framework for the body (i.e., support) and serve a critical role in preventing injury to some of the vital organs of the body, such as the brain, spinal cord, heart, and lungs (i.e., protection). In conjunction with the muscles that are attached to them, bones also function

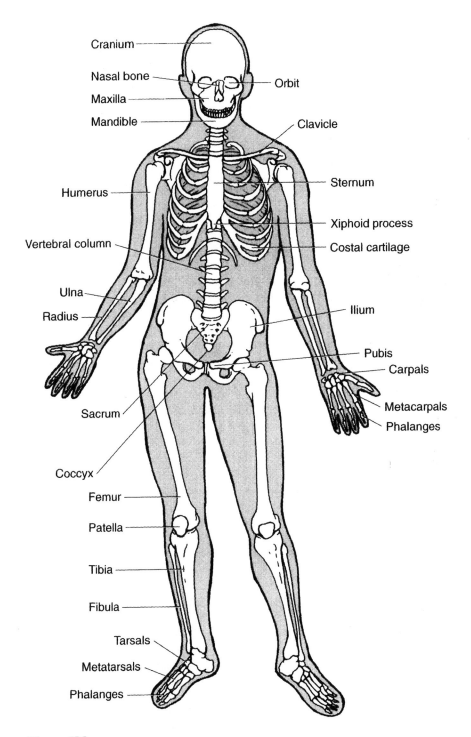

Figure V.1
Skeletal System: Anterior View

structurally as a leverage for movement (i.e., motion). As an **organ,** the bones of the body, particularly the sternum and the pelvis, contain tissues required for hematopoiesis (i.e., the production of blood cells). In addition, bones function as a reservoir of blood and as a repository for several essential minerals, especially calcium and phosphorus, which are necessary to support life (i.e., storage).

Types of Bones   The bones of the body are typically classified on the basis of length or shape. There are four different types of bones: long, short, flat, and irregular.

Long bones are located in the legs (e.g., tibia) and arms (e.g., humerus). They are characterized by their tubular shape and knobby ends. Not all long bones are actually "long." The shortest, the distal phalanx of the baby toe, is, at maturity, only 1/2 inch in length. The longest, the femur (thigh bone), can reach over 18 inches in length. Regardless of size, all "long" bones contribute to the overall length of a specific appendage. **Short bones,** those that permit the movement of the distal ends of the extremities, occur in clusters. They are found predominantly in the hands and wrists (e.g., metacarpals) and in the feet and ankles (e.g., metatarsals). Like long bones, many short bones are tubular in shape; however, some have a more irregular contour or are cube-shaped. In comparison to most long bones, short bones are, in fact, "short," some less than 1/2 inch in length.

Flat bones are shaped exactly as their name suggests. However, flat bones are often curved and, as a result, contribute to the rounded contours of the body's framework. Flat bones include the ribs, the shoulder bones, and some of the bones that make up the skull, such as the occipital and parietal bones. Some flat bones are small; others are relatively large. Bones that lack symmetry of form, referred to as **irregular bones,** are located throughout the body and vary widely in size. Included in this group are the vertebrae that make up the spine, the patella (kneecap), and certain bones in the head, such as the mandible (jaw bone), and the smallest bones in the body, the ossicles of the ear.

Bones are connected to each other by **ligaments,** which are bands of tough, fibrous, connective tissue that have a limited degree of elasticity. The key component of ligaments and other connective tissues, such as tendons, cartilage, and bursae, is **collagen,** an insoluble fibrous protein.

Anatomical Structure of Bones   Bones are composed of multiple layers. Each of the layers is served by one or more blood vessels that weave throughout the bone structure, ensuring that the various constituent parts receive adequate oxygen and nutrition necessary for growth.

The outer fibrous layer of a long bone, the **periosteum,** rich in blood supply and nerves, is a major site of bone growth (specifically growth in diameter), bone repair, and bone nutrition. The periosteum covers and protects the **diaphysis,** the shaft of the bone, which is composed of compact bone that provides strength and rigidity, without making the framework excessively heavy. Inside the diaphysis is the **medullary cavity,** containing fatty, yellow bone marrow. The ends of the long bone, known as the **epiphysis,** are composed of spongy, porous bone, whose lattice-like spaces are filled with red bone marrow.

The ends of long bones are covered by a thin layer of **articular cartilage,** which functions as a cushion against trauma, preventing the ends of the bone from being "ground down" with use. Cartilage is a translucent, nonvascular **connective tissue** that pervades, supports, or binds with other tissues or body parts and is composed of a variety of types of cells and fibers that make it durable and somewhat elastic. Between the epiphysis and the diaphysis there is an additional layer of cartilage, referred to as the **epiphysial plate.** The major role of the plate is to produce new bone cells that result in increased bone length—as opposed to bone width—during childhood. Long bones typically increase in length until skeletal maturity is achieved, usually around age 16 for girls and age 18 for boys.

Short, flat, and irregular bones, while also consisting of distinct layers, differ from long bones in that they consist primarily of spongy bone rather than compact bone. Each of these types of bones is also surrounded by a layer of denser bone that ensures firmness and relative inflexibility.

❧ The Articulating Structures: Review of Structure and Function

Every bone in the body except for the hyoid bone (a U-shaped bone that anchors the tongue in the mouth region) connects, or **articulates,** with at least one or more other bones (Spray, 1991). The point of articulation is commonly referred to as a **joint,** from the Latin word *jungere,* meaning to come together or to join.

Types of Joints

Typically, joints are classified on the basis of **structure** and **range of motion.** Range of motion, often abbreviated as ROM, refers to the degree of movability in a particular joint, which is measured in degrees of a circle (e.g., 45° flexion, 90° rotation). There are three basic types of joints in the human body: fibrous, cartilaginous, and synovial.

Fibrous joints, also known as **synarthrotic joints,** are immovable joints. They are so named because of the fibrous tissues that connect the bones together rigidly. An example of a fibrous joint would be the articulation between the bones of the cranium. On the other hand, **cartilaginous joints,** also known as **amphiarthrotic joints,** allow for slight movement. In this type of joint there is a disk of cartilage that unites the bony surfaces of two adjacent bones. The pubic bones of the hip are examples of cartilaginous joints.

In contrast to the two previous joints that are characterized by little or no movement, **synovial joints,** also referred to as **diarthrotic joints,** permit free movement between contiguous bones. In this type of joint, a fibrous capsule, filled with **synovial fluid,** which functions to lubricate the site, fits over the ends of the two bones, somewhat like a sleeve, encased by ligaments that are attached to the bones above and below the joint. Synovial joints are common throughout the body and are classified according to their structure. Common joints of this type include the **ball and socket joint,** in which a spherical end of one bone fits into the cup-shaped end of the other (e.g., the hip and shoulder joints); the **hinge joint,** in which two adjacent bones are able to move at a right angle to one another (e.g., elbow, knee); and the **gliding joint,** in which the bones are able to slide over each other (e.g., the intervertebral joints). Each of these types of joints is shown in Figure V.2.

❤ The Movement-Producing Structures: Review of Structure and Function

The ability to move from one place to another or from one position to another depends on a number of **movement-producing structures** found throughout the body. For locomotion to occur, the movement-producing structures, especially the muscles, must be innervated by the nervous system. Consequently, damage to the nervous system can also result in impaired mobility. Cerebral palsy is a good example of a condition that is neurologic in origin and which, in many cases, results in impaired movement. There are two different forms of movement: voluntary and involuntary. **Voluntary movement** occurs when muscles are consciously made to contract by the person. The movement of the extremities that occurs during walking is an example of voluntary action. **Involuntary movement** is not under the conscious control of the individual. Examples of involuntary movement are the beating of the heart and the churning of food that occurs during digestion.

Muscles and Tendons

A muscle is a particular type of tissue found in the human body that is composed of long cells known as **fibers.** Accounting for approximately 50% of a body's total weight, muscles share four principal characteristics (Spray, 1991). Not only are they **excitable** (able to respond to neural stimulation), muscles are able to **contract** (constrict to become shorter and thicker), to **stretch** (extend to become longer and thinner), and to return to their former shape after repeated contraction or extension, a characteristic referred to as **elasticity.** There are more than 600 muscles in the human body. Some of the major muscles of the body are shown in Figure V.3.

Whereas ligaments connect bone to bone, muscles are attached to bone by means of tendons. **Tendons,** like ligaments, are bands of fibrous, connective tissue that are extremely strong and flexible. However, unlike ligaments, they are inelastic. Tendons are found throughout the body and vary in terms of length and thickness. Between certain tendons and the bones beneath them, there are small sacs of fibrous connective tissue that are lined with a synovial membrane that secretes synovial fluid, similar to that found in synovial joints. These sacs are known as a **bursae** (sing., **bursa**). In a manner similar to that of the articular cartilage of the bones, bursae function as shock absorbers to cushion pressure from body movements and to permit opposing tissues to move smoothly over one another, without causing undue pain. Major bursae are found in the shoulder, elbow, hip, knee, and ankle joints.

Type of joint		Example	Description
Ball and socket	Shoulder		Freely movable; widest range of motion of all joints
Gliding	Intervertebral		Motion limited to gliding
Hinge	Elbow		Motion limited to flexion (bending) and extension (straightening) in a single plane

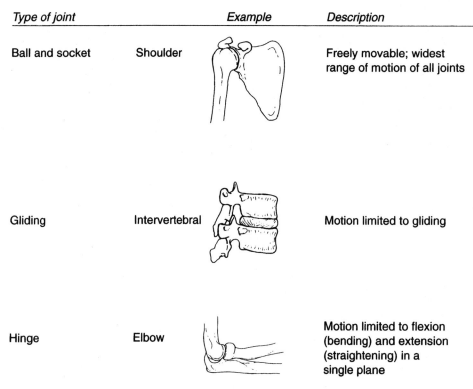

Figure V.2
Selected Joint Types

Types of Muscles There are three basic types of muscle tissue, each categorized by the structure of the muscle and the type of nervous system control needed to excite the muscle to action. The three muscle types include striated, smooth, and cardiac.

Striated muscles, so named because they appear to have stripes running the length of the tissue, are *long,* i.e., they have bundles of interwoven fibers that run parallel to one another, and are *voluntary.* Muscles that are attached to bones to produce voluntary movement, such as the skeletal muscles, are striated muscles. In contrast, **smooth muscles,** i.e., those that are not striated, are *short,* composed of small, spindle-shaped cells arranged in bundles, and are *involuntary.* The visceral muscles that serve the internal organs located within the abdominal cavity are smooth muscles. Contractions of the various smooth muscles of the body assist in **peristalsis** (waves of contractions passing along a tube, which help to move food through the digestive tract, bile through the bile duct, and urine through the ureters). The muscles found in the walls of large blood vessels throughout the body are also classified as smooth muscles. These muscles permit an increase or decrease in the diameter of the vessels, processes referred to, respectively, as **vasodilation** and **vasoconstriction.**

The myocardium, the layer of muscles that forms the bulk of the heart wall, is also made up of striated (i.e., *long*) muscles. However, unlike all other similarly structured muscles (i.e., *long* and *voluntary*), it is under *involuntary* control; i.e., it beats continuously without the individual making a conscious choice. For this reason, the myocardium is sometimes categorized as a third type of muscle, known simply as **cardiac muscle.**

Types of Movement When the muscles of the skeleton contract voluntarily, the tendons that connect the muscle to bone exert force on the joint. As a result of this force, the affected part of the skeleton moves in a particular direction. Given the structure of the joint and the positioning of the muscles, the various parts of the body (e.g., arms, legs, head) are able to move only in certain ways. Some of these movements (e.g., flexion vs. extension; adduction vs. abduction) are shown in Figure V.4.

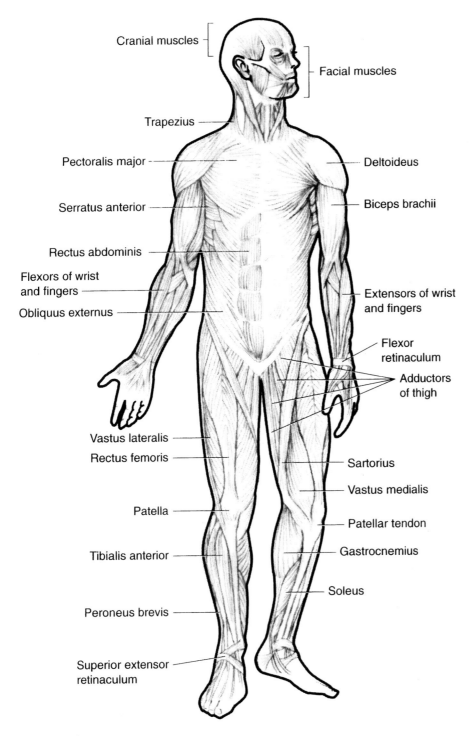

Cranial muscles

Facial muscles

Trapezius

Pectoralis major

Deltoideus

Serratus anterior

Biceps brachii

Rectus abdominis

Flexors of wrist
and fingers

Extensors of wrist
and fingers

Obliquus externus

Flexor
retinaculum

Adductors
of thigh

Vastus lateralis

Rectus femoris

Sartorius

Vastus medialis

Patella

Patellar tendon

Tibialis anterior

Gastrocnemius

Soleus

Peroneus brevis

Superior extensor
retinaculum

Figure V.3
Muscular System: Anterior View

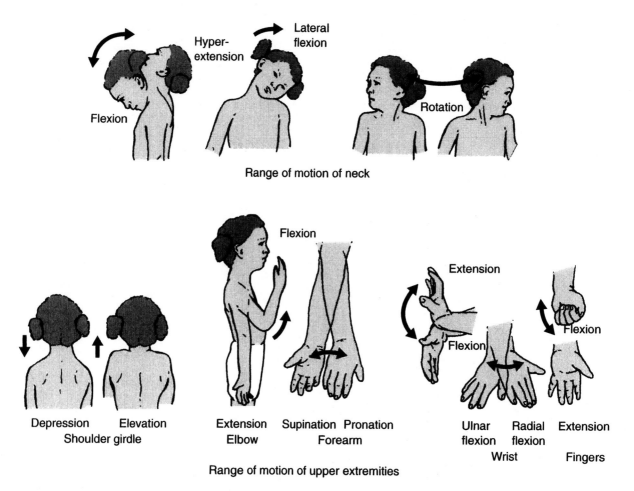

Figure V.4
Normal Range of Motion

Other Functions of Muscles In addition to supporting movement, muscles are integral to the maintenance of muscle tone and posture and the production of heat. **Muscle tone** refers to the partially contracted state of the muscles when not in use (i.e., at rest). An individual with too much muscle tone is referred to as being **rigid,** or **hypertonic,** whereas a person lacking adequate normal tone is described as being **floppy,** or **hypotonic.** Along with the maintenance of a certain degree of tone, the contraction of specific muscles, such as the muscles of the shoulder and back, allows for proper positioning (i.e., **posture**) while the individual is sitting, standing, or lying down. Extreme deviation of muscle tone adversely affects the individual's overall posture as well as the person's ability to execute certain types of movement.

Muscles are also the major **producer of heat** in the body. As a result of the release of **adenosine triphosphate** (ATP), a compound that serves to store energy in muscles, approximately 85% of the body's heat is generated by the voluntary contraction of muscles. In addition, when the individual is cold, involuntary, uncontrolled, rapid muscle activity, commonly referred to as **shivering,** results in the production of energy, which is retained by the body as heat. The heat produced prevents the development of **hypothermia,** a condition in which the body temperature drops significantly below normal.

To perform these additional functions, muscles need a constant supply of oxygen and nutrients, as well as a means to rid the tissues of waste products. Consequently, most of the muscles of the body are

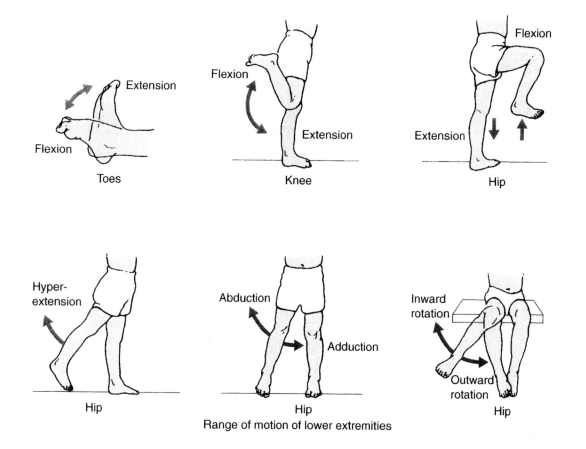

Range of motion of lower extremities

penetrated by one artery and one or two veins. In addition, at least one nerve must provide each muscle in the body with the necessary stimulus required to instigate a particular movement.

Musculoskeletal Difficulties in Children and Young Adults

This text cannot cover all the conditions that interfere with physical mobility, but some of the more common disorders of childhood and adolescence are presented in chapters 14 through 16. The common feature in many conditions is an interruption in the ability to navigate freely within the environment and to perform activities of daily living. A checklist to determine accessibility in the school setting is contained in Appendix A. Some devices used by persons with a physical disability are shown in Table V.1.

Regardless of the cause and course of the condition or the type or degree of medical supervision required to treat it, for those with musculoskeletal disorders, the condition itself (e.g., limb length discrepancy), the various forms of treatment (e.g., casting, splinting), and the concomitant difficulties in accessing the environment (e.g., use of braces or wheelchair) are often **visible** to curious onlookers and therefore create a unique set of challenges (and stressors) that greatly affect both the child or young adult and his or her family. For the student with a physical disability or deformity, the ability to develop normal relationships with peers and siblings is often as great a challenge as having to cope with the physical limitations imposed by the condition itself (Mason & Wright, 1994).

TABLE V.1

Assistive Devices Used by Persons with Physical Disabilities

MOBILITY DEVICES	PERSONAL AND LEISURE DEVICES
Accessibility equipment	**Feeding devices**
Ramps, lever door handles	Mechanical feeders
Environmental control systems	Sandwich holders
Wheelchair trays, slant boards	Plates with food guards
Handmade or commercial grips	Modified cups
Adapted keyboards	Utensils with built-up handles
Signature guides	Feeding tubes
Mobility aids	**Toileting devices**
Canes, crutches	Urinary collection devices
Scooter boards, walkers	Fecal collection devices
Helmets	Modified bathrooms
Wheelchairs (manual or power; racing)	(e.g., raised toilet seats, commodes)
Positioning aids	**Dressing aids**
Bolsters, cushions, wedges	Adapted clothing
Standing tables and frames	Button hooks
Sidelyers, prone boards	Velcro fastenings
Shoulder straps, pommels	**Leisure aids**
Orthotic and prosthetic devices	Computer games
Braces	Battery-operated toys
Splints	Paper and book holders
Artificial limbs	Page turners

References

Howe, J., & Coffman, C. P. (1990). The musculoskeletal system. In G. M. Scipien, M. A. Chard, J. Howe, & M. U. Barnard (Eds.), *Pediatric nursing care* (pp. 477–525). St. Louis: Mosby.

Jackson, D. B., & Saunders, R. B. (Eds.) (1993). *Child health nursing: A comprehensive approach to the care of children and their families.* Philadelphia: J. B. Lippincott.

Mason, K. J., & Wright, S. (1994). Altered musculoskeletal function. In C. L. Betz, M. M. Hunsberger, & S. Wright (Eds.), *Family-centered nursing care of children* (2nd ed., pp. 1815–1873). Philadelphia: W. B. Saunders.

Spray, M. E. (1991). Care of the patient with a musculoskeletal disorder. In B. L. Christensen & E. O. Kockrow (Eds.), *Foundation of nursing* (pp. 574–635). St. Louis: Mosby.

Disorders of the Supporting Structures

KEY WORDS

Accidental injury

Autosomal dominant

Autosomal recessive

Birth injury

Child abuse injury

Contractures

Decubitus ulcers

Fracture

Limb deficiency

Prosthetic device

Spinal cord injury

Spinal curvature

Sport injury

Trauma

Disorders of the supporting structures vary widely. Many of the conditions affect a specific part of the bony framework; others affect several bones at the same time. An example of the first type is a child who is born with a foot deformity, such as a clubfoot; an example of the second would be a child or young adult who develops skeletal tuberculosis as a result of having an active systemic infection, i.e., TB. In this chapter, some of the more commonly occurring conditions of the following types are discussed: those that have the potential of affecting all the bones of the body, those that are specific to just the upper or lower extremities, and those that affect only the spine. Educational implications and teaching tips are offered throughout the chapter as each condition is discussed.

🌱 Acute Conditions That Affect the Supporting Structures

Although *chronic* conditions affecting the supporting structures of the body, e.g., osteogenesis imperfecta, or brittle bone disease, are relatively rare, school staff frequently encounter students who have experienced some type of *acute* musculoskeletal condition, typically the result of some type of traumatic event, e.g., a sports injury or automobile accident.[1] Because such injuries often occur either at school or on the way to school, this chapter begins with a brief discussion of the different types of accidental injuries, with emphasis on how to deal with emergency situations that may arise in the school environment.[2] While each of these types of injuries is acute at the time of occurrence, for some children the effects of the trauma can last a lifetime.

The term **accidental injury**[3] is used to refer to a wide range of traumatic mishaps that often result from the everyday activities of childhood and adolescence (e.g., play) and normal characteristics of children and young adults (e.g., curiosity) that make them especially prone to injury. Accidental injuries are the leading cause of death in children over a year old, and more children die from injuries than from all diseases combined (Jones, 1992). Some recent statistics on the incidence of pediatric trauma are shown in Table 14.1.

"Accidental injury" primarily suggests accidents caused by motor vehicles, firearms, falls and jumps, drownings, poisonings, and fires and burns, because these are the most frequent mechanisms of injury that result in traumatic deaths (Committee on Trauma Research, 1985). However, many children and young adults are injured while participating in **sporting** and **recreation activities.** While these injuries are, in most cases, not life-threatening, they certainly may have a significant impact on the student and his or her family.

Bijur and her colleagues (1995) recently presented data on the number of children and young adults injured annually in the United States in sporting and recreational pursuits. Using data from the supplement to the 1988 National Health Interview Survey on 11,840 youngsters between the ages of 5 and 17, an injury rate of 4.3 million injuries per year was reported. This number represents an annual injury rate for approximately 10 episodes per 100 children and teens. This figure also represents approximately 36% of all injury episodes reported by respondents to the survey. In terms of gender and age, Bijur found that injuries were more frequent in boys than girls and increased with age in both sexes (Figure 14.1). For all age groups, except 10 to 11 years old, rates were higher for boys than girls. For both genders, there was a dramatic decline in the incidence of injuries after age 15. Approximately 1.3 million of the injuries were reported as serious.

In terms of specific sports, data from the National Youth Sports Foundation for the Prevention of Athletic Injuries (1991) have shown that contact or collision sports, such as ice hockey and football, have the highest injury rates. Noncontact sports, such as archery and table tennis, have significantly lower rates (Table 14.2).

Many sports injuries are preventable. They can be reduced significantly by competent coaching, adequate time for conditioning and skill development, the use of proper safety equipment, and the availability of safe playing surfaces. In addition,

---

[1] The most common traumatic injuries of the musculoskeletal system include (a) fractures of bones; (b) dislocations of joints; and (c) injuries of the muscles, ligaments, and tendons. See also chapters 15 and 16.

[2] Two other types of traumatic injury, **birth injuries** and **child abuse injuries,** can result in serious acute musculoskeletal injuries but are not covered here.

[3] For further information on head injuries, a specific type of accidental injury, see chapter 13.

TABLE 14.1
Epidemiology of Pediatric Trauma

- About 600,000 children are hospitalized annually as a result of injury; in addition, 16 million children are treated in emergency departments for traumatic injuries.
- About 23,000 children are killed each year in the United States; this rate is higher than in most other industrial nations in the world.
- It is far more likely that a child will die from an unintentional or preventable injury than a violent crime.
- Trauma is the leading cause of death in children over the age of 1; 22,000 children under the age of 19 died as a result of their injuries in 1988.
- For every child that dies as a result of a pediatric injury, 34 are admitted to hospital, and 1500 have some form of restricted activity after injury.
- About 20% to 30% of all children receiving acute care in a hospital are there as a result of some type of trauma.
- Motor vehicle accidents, including pedestrian-vehicle injuries, are the leading cause of pediatric injury. Burns and injury as a result of inhalation of smoke are the second leading cause of death. In some parts of the United States, drowning is close to second.
- Among the industrialized nations, teen homicide rates are highest in the United States.
- In 10% to 15% of all cases of pediatric trauma, one or more bones are fractured. In children who have been or who are suspected to have been abused, 30% have one or more fractured bones.
- As children mature, boys are more likely to suffer injury than girls; by adolescence the ratio is 2:1.
- Children who are from economically disadvantaged homes are 2.6 times more likely to die as a result of trauma than those from more affluent homes. Often the child is raised by a single parent (usually the mother), who is a teenager and who has not completed a high school education.
- Nearly 1 in 5 children seeks medical attention for an injury each year. The costs of medical care alone for treating accidental injuries is estimated at $5.1 to $7.5 billion annually.

Sources: Crawley, 1996; Losh, 1994; Pieper, 1994; Polhgeers & Ruddy, 1995.

limiting activities to those appropriate for the age and size of the child or adolescent decreases the risk of injury (Will, 1993). For further information on sports-related and recreational injuries and how to prevent their occurrence, see the articles by Jones (1992); McCoy, Dec, McKeag, and Honing (1995); and Ostrum (1993) and the text by Duff (1992), which is particularly useful as a reference book on how to treat common sports injuries.

Recreational injuries result from a wide variety of pursuits. For young children, injuries on the playground or from using playground equipment are of major concern. There are more than 200,000 playground injuries per year; approximately 25% of the accidents occur on school playgrounds (Jones, 1992). Falls from climbing equipment, seesaws, and swings are the most common accidents. Playground injuries can be reduced by the installation of energy-absorbing materials (e.g., wood chips, sand, grass, bare ground) under equipment rather than concrete and asphalt surfaces. In addition, injury reductions can occur as a result of providing workshops on play-

ground safety to school staff (Jones, 1992). If a student is injured at school, an Accident Report (Appendix C) must be filled out and submitted to the principal.

Fractures

A **fracture** refers to a situation in which the bone tissue becomes discontinuous as a result of excessive stress being placed on the bone. Fractures can result from trauma as well as from disease. Fractures are common in children because human bones do not reach their maximum level of strength, i.e., are not fully matured or **ossified,** until they are between the ages of 18 and 21. Fractures are also common in the elderly, because bones tend to lose their strength, primarily as a result of the loss of calcium, a process known as **decalcification,** which occurs with aging.

Fractures occurring in the young or the elderly often involve the upper extremities. This type of fracture is a result of the person extending his or her arm to break a fall. In this type of injury, the force travels

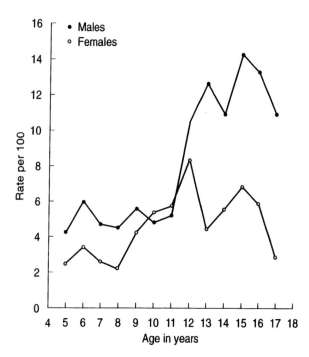

Figure 14.1
Rates of Sports and Recreational Injuries by Age and Gender
Source: Bijur et al., 1995.

TABLE 14.2
Sports Injury Statistics for Youths: Selected Sports (1991)

Sports	Estimated Number of Cases
CONTACT OR COLLISION	
Basketball	442,672
Football	236,806
Soccer	93,218
Wrestling	43,894
Ice hockey	31,145
Diving	14,838
Rugby	7,681
Boxing	5,536
LIMITED CONTACT OR IMPACT	
Bicycling	600,649
Baseball	282,413
Roller skating	113,150
Volleyball	91,156
Skateboarding	56,435
Ice skating	29,047
Gymnastics	23,965
Cheerleading	11,682
NONCONTACT SPORTS	
Strenuous	
Weight lifting	61,140
Swimming	34,738
Tennis	29,936
Moderately Strenuous	
Badminton	3,109
Table tennis	2,339
Nonstrenuous	
Golf	38,626
Archery	7,394

Note: Classification of sports by degree of contact is based on categories established by the American Academy of Pediatrics (Appendix D).
Source: Adapted from National Electronic Injury Surveillance System, U.S. Consumer Product Safety Commission, National Injury Information Clearinghouse (1991). *Statistics.*

upward, and it is common for the individual to injure one or more fingers, the wrist, the elbow, the shoulder, or the clavicle (part of the shoulder girdle). Also common in children and adolescents are fractures of the lower limbs (e.g., fractured tibia or fibula) that often result from falling off raised structures such as trees and skateboards. Hip injury is rare in youngsters compared with adults (Reff, 1988).

Another common cause of fractures in young children is being hit by a moving vehicle. These children typically display a triad of injuries (Figure 14.2): the femur is fractured as a result of the bumper of the car striking the child's upper leg; the ribs are damaged from the upper hood of the car striking the upper trunk; and the child sustains a head injury as a result of being thrown to the ground.

Basic Emergency Treatment   If a student breaks a bone, he or she must be transported to the hospital for assessment and treatment. However, to ease the pain and to minimize further injury, there are several steps that a caregiver can take (Table 14.3).

Long-Term Treatment of Fractures   Depending on the extent of the injury (e.g., tearing of muscle tissue vs. fracture of one or more bones), the student may be out of school for days or weeks. In many cases, the student is fitted with a **cast** to

Figure 14.2
Triad of Injuries Resulting from Pedestrian-Automobile Injuries

prevent movement of the limb during the healing process. Casts are made out of a variety of substances (e.g., plaster of Paris, fiberglass, polyurethane), and they extend above and below the site of injury. Although the extent of time the student is in a cast depends on the extent of the injury, bone healing is characteristically rapid in young children. For example, the approximate healing times for a broken femoral shaft can be as little as 2 to 4 weeks for a preschool child and as much as 8 to 12 weeks for an adolescent (Whaley & Wong, 1995). The same injury may, in an adult, take 10 to 16 weeks to heal.

TABLE 14.3
Emergency Treatment: Fractures

- Do not move the student unless absolutely necessary.
- Move the injured part as little as possible.
- Cover open wounds with sterile or clean dressing. Apply manual pressure or a pressure bandage (gauze pads wrapped with a gauze roll) (if there is bleeding) to minimize blood loss. Do not use elastic bandages, because further damage to the tissues can occur from the build-up of pressure.
- Do not attempt to reduce the fracture (i.e., do not manipulate the bone to restore it to its original position). Similarly, do not push any protruding bones under the skin.
- Immobilize the limb in the position in which it is found. Include the joints above and below the fracture site.
  Shoulder: Position arm in sling and swathe arm to chest.
  Upper or lower arm: Immobilize with a rigid support (e.g., rolled newspaper or magazine).
  Elbow or wrist: Immobilize with soft support (e.g., pillow, folded towel) in position in which found.
  Hips or back: DO NOT MOVE. Support body in position in which found (e.g., with pillow, sandbag) and call 911 for medical assistance. If absolutely necessary to move the student, place on a back board or similar device (e.g., a door).
  Upper or lower leg: Immobilize with rigid support (e.g., wooden plank). Uninjured leg can serve as a splint if no other material is available.
  Knee, ankle, or foot: Immobilize with soft support (e.g., pillow, folded towel) in position in which found.
- Elevate the injured limb if possible.
- Apply cold (e.g., ice pack, bag of frozen peas) to the injured area.
- Call 911 or transport to medical facility.

Sources: Reff, 1988; Whaley & Wong 1995.

There are four types of casts: (a) **upper extremity casts,** which immobilize the wrist (short arm casts), the elbow (arm cylinder casts), or both (long arm casts); (b) **lower extremity casts,** which immobilize the foot and ankle (bootie cast), ankle (short leg casts), the knee (leg cylinder casts), or all (long leg casts); (c) **spinal** or **cervical casts,** which immobilize the spine or neck; and (d) **spica casts,** which stabilize part or all of the trunk of the body (to waist level or chest level), the hip, and part or all of one or more extremities (one or more arms or legs). The term **body cast** is often used to describe any cast that extends from the neck or chest region to the groin (e.g., a spinal cast); however, since a spica cast can also immobilize part of the trunk, it is also referred to as a body cast by some.

🐾 Educational Implications and Teaching Tips: Students with Immobilizing Devices

While most routine cast care is carried out at home, there are several points that school staff should keep in mind when they have a student under their supervision who has been fitted with an immobilizing device:

1 *Staff should be alert to any sign of swelling or discoloration in the fingers or toes that may occur from the extremity being allowed to hang downward for too long or from the cast being too tight.* Usually, it is recommended that the student try to keep the injured extremity elevated as much as possible to prevent swelling. Standing in one place for long periods, such as in a cafeteria line, should be avoided for those with a lower limb or spinal injury. Students with a lower extremity cast or a body cast may find sitting for long periods of time to be painful. They should be allowed to get up and walk around periodically, if desired. The use of a chair pad may be helpful.

A student with a cast should try to avoid banging or hitting the cast on a hard surface, which unduly weakens it. If the edges of the cast become rough, masking tape over the area protects the underlying skin from breakdown.

2 *Teachers of very young children should ensure that the child and peers do not put any foreign objects, such as crumbs, stones, dirt, marbles and other small toys, inside the cast because this might* result in irritation or skin breakdown. Similarly, youngsters should be encouraged not to poke pencils, knitting needles, or any other long implements down the cast, no matter how "itchy" it is inside. Such objects cannot only injure the skin but can get "lost" inside, necessitating a premature cast change. Blowing cool air down the cast by means of a hair dryer can be helpful to minimize any unpleasant or annoying sensations (James, 1990). Some children are given an antihistamine (e.g., hydroxyzine) for the same purpose. However, many such drugs have a sedating effect that may impact the student's ability to function adequately in school.

3 *Casts, regardless of their composition, should be kept as dry as possible.* If the student is going to be in an environment where he or she may get the cast wet accidentally, such as on a field trip to the beach, the cast can be "waterproofed" by wrapping it in a plastic bag or plastic sheeting.

4 *The student with a lower limb cast may require crutches to access his or her environment, so it is wise to try to remove all obstacles in the student's path, such as toys, shoes, and books on the floor, which could be the cause of an accident.* If the student has to travel a great distance between classrooms, it might be helpful to excuse the student from class a few minutes early to avoid "fighting the crowds." Some students with a cast on one or both lower extremities, or one that covers the central body region, may require a wheelchair to move freely. If there is an elevator, the student should be allowed to use it. Backpacks or clothing with extra large pockets is useful for carrying needed supplies. A bicycle basket attached to the wheelchair may assist in carrying books and supplies.

5 *Most children and young adults respond well to having a cast.* In fact, for some, it is seen as a "badge of honor," which proves that they are "tough" (Whaley & Wong, 1995). For these students, returning to school is an "exciting" event. In contrast, some may fear being teased and being stared at by others and may be uncomfortable responding to the questions posed by curious individuals (James, 1990b). Such children need to be supported emotionally by others who recognize their concerns.

6 *While the cast is on, there may be certain restrictions in terms of physical activity, particularly if the cast is protecting one of the lower extremities or the torso.* While students should be encouraged to join in activities as much as possible, participation may have to be more sedentary (e.g., keeping score in a game or acting as a referee) than normal.

Spinal Cord Injuries (SCIs)

Spinal cord injuries that are traumatic in nature typically take one of two forms.[4] In the first instance, some type of **lesion** (wound or injury) to the cord results from a penetrating trauma (e.g., gunshot wound), from the stretching of the vertebral column (e.g., serious whiplash), from a fracture of one or more vertebral bones (e.g., person being hit by a car), or from the compression of the cord (e.g., diving accident). In the second instance, the cord **infarcts**, i.e., dies as a result of an interruption of blood supply. An infarct can also occur from the presence of an abnormal cell mass (tumor). Such cell growth can be either **benign** (noncancerous) or **malignant** (cancerous), and can be **intramedullary** (within the spinal medulla), **extramedullary** (outside the spinal medulla), or **extradural** (outside the dura mater of the spine). The focus in the following sections is traumatic injury that results in insult to the spinal column, the most common type of SCI.

Etiology The majority of SCIs are caused by vehicular accidents, sports injuries (particularly in teens), and interpersonal violence (particularly in preteens). Less common, particularly in comparison to incidence in adults, are SCIs that result from falling (Apple, Anson, Hunter, & Bell, 1995). If age is not considered, however, falls are the second most common cause of SCI (Gilgoff, 1983). Between 5% and 20% of those who experience a head injury also have an SCI.

Incidence and Prevalence Traumatic injuries to the spine occur in persons of all ages; however, in comparison to the incidence in the adult population, children are injured this way less often. The pediatric incidence has been reported to range from less than 1% to slightly more than 13% of spinal injuries in all age groups (Apple et al., 1995). Approximately 7,000 to 10,000 people in the United States experience a major SCI annually. The majority of those injured are between ages 15 and 25 (Laskowski-Jones, 1993). The incidence of SCI in males is five times greater than in females; however, as more women engage in hazardous sports and occupations, a change in the male-to-female ratio is predicted.

Characteristics SCIs typically occur in the area of greatest mobility—the cervical and lumbar areas (Laskowski-Jones, 1993). The degree of paralysis after injury depends on the location of the injury. If the damage is in the cervical region, paralysis from the neck down occurs; if the damage is in the lumbar area, the individual maintains some degree of upper extremity function. The critical area of demarcation is between the first and second thoracic vertebrae. Injuries below the first vertebra typically result in paraplegia; injuries above, in quadriplegia. In Table 14.4 the degree to which muscle functioning is affected by an SCI, in terms of the site of the injury, is outlined.

An SCI can also be classified as either complete or incomplete. A **complete SCI,** in which the cord is totally severed, results in permanent loss of sensory function (the feelings of touch, pressure, pain, and temperature), proprioception (the sense of position), and all voluntary motor activity below the level of damage. In an **incomplete SCI,** in which parts of the cord still remain intact, some sensory, proprioceptive, and motor impulses are still able to travel the length of the cord. The degree of sequelae for an incomplete SCI very much depends on the size and location of the lesion.

Diagnosis and Treatment After an SCI has been recognized, through observation, examination, x-ray, CT scan, or MRI, the primary need is **stabilization** of the affected area. This is often achieved through surgery (e.g., fusing of the vertebrae where the fracture has occurred; implantation of stabilizing rods) or casting, splinting, or traction. For those persons with a high cervical injury, the primary need is **ventilation.** Since the injury prevents the person from breathing independently, a **ventilator** is necessary to force air mixed with oxygen into the lungs. Since the paralysis that results from an SCI is irreversible, over time the main concern is to ensure that those muscles capable of functioning receive

---

[4] There are also a number of **nontraumatic conditions** that result in spinal cord dysfunction, such as spina bifida, a congenital disorder of the spinal column (chapter 11). In older adults, diseases such as **multiple sclerosis** and **amyotrophic lateral sclerosis (Lou Gehrig's disease)** can result in damage to the spinal cord. However, since such conditions are found relatively infrequently in children and young adults, they are not covered in this text.

TABLE 14.4
Functional Implications of Spinal Cord Lesion: By Site

Injury Site	MUSCLE FUNCTION		Functional Implications
	Retained	**Lost**	
C1–C3	None	All	• Lesions above C3 fatal unless CPR started immediately • Complete paralysis of all voluntary muscles (i.e., quadriplegia), including paralysis of bowel and bladder • May be able to use mouthstick or tongue to control computer • Continuous ventilatory assistance required
C4	None	All	• Quadriplegia • Paralysis of bowel and bladder; may be some control that results from reflex emptying • Individual probably will have a tracheostomy and require ventilatory assistance (intermittent or continuous) • Individual will be totally dependent for activities of daily living
C5	Neck Upper shoulder muscle	Arms Chest All below chest	• Quadriplegia; only movement possible is head and neck; head control permits better use of computer-assisted devices • May have weak abduction, flexion, and extension of forearm • Diaphragm partially paralyzed; remaining respiratory muscles (e.g., intercostal) paralyzed, poor respiratory reserve
C6–C8	Neck Some chest movement Some arm movement	Some arm Some finger movement Some chest All below chest	C6 Quadriplegia; adduction and medial rotation of arm; wrist extension and elbow flexion possible; some use of extremities for self-care and transferring; will need assistance a great deal of the time • Diaphragm paralyzed at time of injury, function typically returns to normal C7 Quadriplegia; grasp and release weak; lacks dexterity; self-feeding possible with adaptive equipment; may be able to drive with assistive devices; may be able to transfer from wheelchair to chair or wheelchair to bed without assistance

Sources: Jezewski, 1992; Schenk, 1991; Smith & Woodring, 1990; Whaley & Wong, 1995.

adequate stimulation to avoid muscle wasting (**atrophy**). Typically, this involves a combination of physical therapy and occupational therapy.

Another major focus of treatment is the prevention of further disability. In particular, the development of secondary contractures and of pressure sores is of concern. A **contracture** is an abnormal state of a joint, usually permanent in nature, caused by the shortening of muscle fibers from lack of use and atrophy or loss of the elasticity of the skin, which may, for example, result from formation of scar tissue over a joint (*Mosby's,* 1994). Typically, a contracture that results from an SCI is characterized by a combination of flexion (bending inward) and fixation of the affected joint. Contractures of joints in the upper extremities make it difficult for persons to use their arms to perform certain activities such as feeding themselves or using hand-held implements, such as a pen. Contractures of joints in the lower limbs may further impede the ability to move independently. Contractures of the spine may result in a deformity that compromises lung functioning. Through therapy (e.g., exercise

			• Diaphragm function normal; breathing affected by loss of function of abdominal and intercostal muscles
			C8 Quadriplegia; finger function impaired; movement is typically uncoordinated; can use hands voluntarily (e.g., eating, dressing, grooming, toileting)
			• Respiration only minimally affected
			• Loss of bowel and bladder control
THORACIC (T1-T12)	Neck	Trunk	**T 1–10**
			• Paraplegia; full use of upper extremities; no use of legs
	Arms (full)	All below chest	• Loss of bowel and bladder function; typically capable of bowel and bladder care
	Some chest		• Respiration typically not severely affected
			T 10–12
			• Paraplegia
			• Good trunk balance and good respiratory reserve
			• Sensory loss in sacral region, some degree of bowel and bladder dysfunction
LUMBO-SACRAL L1–S4	Neck Arms Chest Trunk	Legs	**L1–L2**
			• Paraplegia; may be able to ambulate with assistance of braces and crutches; distance may be restricted
			• Relatively independent in caring for self
			L3–L4
			• Paraplegia; partial loss of motor control in lower legs and feet; walking aided by orthotic devices
			L5–S1
			• May be able to walk without aids
			S4
			• Control of bladder and bowel function

programs) and the use of custom-made orthotic devices (e.g., splints, braces), contractures can often be avoided or minimized.

Pressure sores, also known as **decubitus ulcers,** or **decubiti,** from the Latin word *decumbere,* meaning to lie down, are areas in which, as a result of decreased circulation, the skin and underlying tissues are damaged to the point of tissue death (necrosis). Being in one position for too long (e.g., sitting in a wheelchair without adequate padding) and having some type of object push against the body for a long period (e.g., lying on bed linen that is wrinkled) are the most common causes of these ulcers. Decubiti that result from prolonged confinement to bed are often referred to as **bedsores.**

For some persons with SCI, **muscle spasms** (involuntary muscle contractions) are problematic. Pharmacologic treatment, such as the administration of antispastic agents (e.g., Lioresal) or muscle relaxants (e.g., Dantrium), may be of assistance. Both types of drugs may affect the student's ability to perform in school, because they can cause a state of drowsiness or confusion.

🌱 Educational Implications and Teaching Tips: Students with Spinal Cord Injuries

With advances in technology, the prognosis for survival after SCI has steadily improved. Today, it is not uncommon for youngsters to return to school after a period in the hospital. In fact, the goal of most rehabilitation programs is to have the child or young adult reintegrated as soon as possible after discharge so that he or she does not become socially isolated from peers and is not overprotected by parents (Graham, Weingarden, & Murphy, 1991).

In most cases, with proper planning and with the coordinated efforts of the medical-educational team, the reintegration process goes smoothly. However, without proper preparation, the degree of success may be limited. In a recent study by Graham and her colleagues (1991) that involved students who had experienced an SCI and who had returned to school after injury, a number of "good" and "bad" points were raised by the respondents. The majority of the positive comments were related to the positive and accepting attitudes of others. For example, students made the following comments: "Everyone was friendly and helpful, but I didn't need or want help"; "The teacher treated me like everybody else"; "The girls all wanted to help. They asked a lot questions, but I didn't mind"; "When the elevator broke down, the students carried me up the stairs." The negative comments were often related to problems with equipment or services. For example, students made the following comments: "I couldn't get a ramp, so I couldn't get the bus at the curb to go to school"; "I forgot to check my leg bag and it leaked"; "One teacher blamed me for being late even though I rode the bus"; "My school attendant was supposed to help me with note taking and things, but he was absent more than I was"; "If I wanted to stay for something after school, I had to arrange my own transportation home."

Even though most of the initial comments by the respondents in the Graham et al. study were positive and the students reported few, if any, problems, upon follow-up, 38% of the adolescents were found to have left school prematurely. Those who had left school, all victims of shootings, had dropped out in the 11th grade, before graduation. In reporting this finding, the authors speculated that the dropout rate was more related to problems that existed before on-set of the disability (e.g., drug usage) than to the injury.

A student with an SCI, on return to school, is not the same as before the injury, not only physically, but also emotionally. Having to adjust to the limitations imposed by the disability is difficult. Depression is not uncommon. A supportive teacher, who is aware of the student's emotional turmoil, is of great assistance. Teachers should be on the lookout for any signs of depression, such as loss of appetite, desire to sleep all the time, lack of energy, loss of interest in those around them, and withdrawal from social activities, and should ensure that the students receive the counseling they need. The following suggestions should be of assistance:

1 *A student with an SCI must have the ability to access the environment in a safe, reliable manner.* Not only will the student need a ramp to enter the school, he or she will need wheelchair-accessible transportation to get to and from school. If the school has more than one floor, an elevator will be needed. Some of the existing facilities may need to be retrofitted in order to be accessed by a student who has limited or no use of his or her hands or legs. Wheelchair-accessible bathrooms, with toilets that flush automatically and sinks that have automatic on/off water taps, are necessary, as are automatic door-opening devices that permit the student to enter or exit freely. All schools should be audited to determine the degree of physical access for those with motoric problems. An audit checklist is found in Appendix A.

It is helpful if the student's teacher is taught basic wheelchair maintenance by the physiotherapist, so that if problems arise simple repairs can be undertaken.

2 *An SCI not only affects mobility but can also affect significantly the ability to perform activities of daily living (e.g., eating, dressing, grooming).* Many students who return to school after injury, particularly in the early stages of rehabilitation, have a personal attendant available to assist them in these areas. There are a number of aids available (e.g., dressing aids, modified eating tools). Teachers should contact the student's occupational therapist to discuss what might be available for the classroom.

3 *Teachers who have a student in their class with an SCI should be aware of the importance of proper positioning and the need for the student to be repositioned on a regular basis.* Since the individual with an SCI has little or no sensation below the level of the injury, there is decreased sensation of pain or pressure. Pressure sores can develop in as little as 2 hours and, if untreated, can lead to serious infection. Guidelines for proper positioning of a student in a wheelchair are given in Table 14.5.

Students who are capable of using their arms should be taught to do chair **"push-ups."** By pushing down on the arms of the wheelchair, the individual is able to lift the buttocks off the chair for about 5 to 10 seconds, so that circulation can be restored to the tissues. By performing such a maneuver regularly, i.e., every 30 to 60 minutes, the

TABLE 14.5
Guidelines for Positioning in a Wheelchair

HEAD AND NECK

Midline position
Face forward (not pointed up or down)

Adaptations: **Headrest (maintain head alignment); head strap (to hold head back in headrest)**

SHOULDERS AND ARMS

Shoulders in midline and neutral position (not hunched over)
Elbows flexed about 90°

Adaptations: **Shoulder straps (to hold shoulders back); shoulder pommels [padded restraints that are on each side of the neck] (to hold shoulder back); wheelchair tray (to maintain alignment)**

TRUNK

Midline position
Maintain normal curve of spine

Adaptations: **H-strap (to bring shoulders back and keep trunk up); scoliosis pads and side pads (to align trunk)**

HIPS AND PELVIS

Midline position
Hips bent at 90°
Pelvis in back of seat
Pelvis not tilted to one side

Adaptations: **Seat belt across hips (to keep pelvis in back of seat)**

LEGS

Thighs slightly apart
Knees slightly apart
Knees bent at 90°
Feet directly below or slightly behind knees
Ankles bent 90° with feet on footrest
Feet facing forward
Ball and heel of foot flat on footrest

Adaptations: **Adductor pads (to keep knees aligned when knees are too far out); abductor pads (to keep knees aligned when knees are too close together); footrest straps.**

Source: Heller, K. W., Alberto, P. A., Forney, P. E., & Schwartzman, M. N. (1996). *Understanding physical, sensory, and health impairments.* Pacific Grove, CA: Brooks/Cole. Copyright 1996 by Brooks/Cole Publishing Company. Reprinted by permission of Wadsworth Publishing Co.

person may be able to prevent pressure sores. Those who are unable to perform a push-up independently may be able to shift their weight by bending either sideways or forward (Figure 14.3). Caregivers should also be taught how to lift the person in a safe manner—safe to both the student and the caregiver.

Pressure sores can also result from an object placing pressure directly on the skin, such as an ill-fitting brace or a shoe that is tied too tightly. Persons with SCI should be taught to inspect their body regularly, at least once a day, for any signs of redness. If the student is unable to perform the daily examination because of paralysis, a caregiver should assist the student. Mirrors may

be needed for a complete inspection. If a red area develops, the person should be positioned so that he or she is off the area until it returns to normal. A day in bed or a day without a splint or brace may prevent a 3-month hospitalization (Gilgoff, 1983).

4 *A person with an SCI generally has little or no control of bowel and bladder.* Consequently, a schedule must be maintained that ensures that accidents do not occur. Typically, by the judicious use of laxative suppositories and a carefully monitored diet, the bowel can be trained to evacuate in the evening while the student is at home. During the

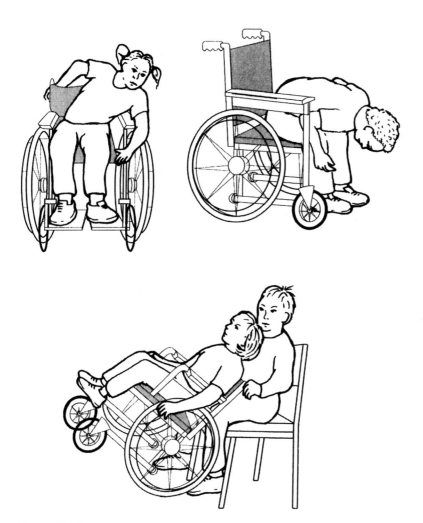

Figure 14.3
Weight Shifts
Source: Adapted from Hoeman, 1996, p. 295.

daytime, however, the bladder must be drained on a regular basis. For some students this is achieved by means of clean intermittent catheterization (CIC). Other students have an **indwelling catheter** (one that remains in place for an extended period) and a urine collection device (bag) that needs to be emptied on a regular basis to prevent overflow.[5] By ensuring that the bladder is emptied routinely, the likelihood of a bladder or kidney infection developing is minimized. School staff should be aware of the student's schedule. A change of clothing should be available at all times (e.g., at school, on a field trip), in case of an accident.

5 *For many persons with an SCI, particularly those with a high-level complete SCI, body temperature regulation can be a problem.* Because persons may be unaware of how hot or cold they are below the site of the injury, they may become either **hyperthermic** (body temperature is too high) or **hypothermic** (body temperature is too low). To decrease the possibility of such states occurring, the student should be dressed appropriately. Although it is the responsibility of the person's caregiver to ensure that the student arrives in school properly clothed, having an extra sweater, scarf, hat, and mittens on hand in cold weather can be extremely useful. The student should dress in "layers" to permit the removal of clothing in hot weather.

6 *Some students who have a high cervical injury, specifically those above T6 or T7, are prone to a condition known as **autonomic dysreflexia**, or **hyperreflexia**.* In such individuals, the sympathetic nervous system releases a compound known as catecholamine, in the presence of a noxious stimulus (e.g., overly full bladder, sitting too long without a change of position), which in turn results in a constriction of blood vessels, causing the blood pressure to increase suddenly. At the same time, to lower the blood pressure, the parasympathetic system attempts to release inhibitory signals. However, since the signals cannot traverse the spinal cord lesion, the patient begins to experience a number of "strange manifestations" above and below the lesion (Laskowski-Jones, 1993). **Above the injury,** the vasodilation results in the individual experienc-

ing flushing, increased sweating on the forehead, pupillary constriction, a severe headache, and nasal congestion. **Below the lesion,** the skin becomes cold to the touch and pale in appearance, and goose bumps may develop. If untreated, i.e., the noxious stimulus is not dealt with, the person may develop bradycardia, which can result in a myocardial infarction (heart attack), stroke, or hemorrhaging in the brain. Seizure activity is also possible.

Since autonomic dysreflexia can be life-threatening if untreated, assistance should be sought immediately (i.e., call 911). The key to reversing autonomic dysreflexia is finding and removing the offending stimulus immediately. Since bladder distention and bowel impaction are the most common causes, they should be suspected first and treated. Loosening tight clothing and having the individual sit upright also lessens the symptoms. The best treatment, however, is prevention. The condition should not be allowed to progress to the point that the student becomes distressed (e.g., catheterize regularly; monitor diet so constipation does not occur).

7 *For the student who is on a respirator,[6] the prevention of respiratory infections may be of concern.* However, with the administration of antibiotics, such problems are typically easy to manage. If the student is exposed to a peer who is ill, the parents of the student with an SCI should be informed so that precautionary measures can be taken. However, school staff and parents should not overreact to such situations. Gilgoff (1983) made the following comments, which should be heeded by teaching staff as well as medical practitioners:

> The fear of the respirator or the fear of possible infection is often more a threat to the patient than the infection itself. Careful medical management can correct pneumonia, but nothing can correct the isolation faced by patients forced to exist in sterile cages. (p. 142)

8 *The coordinated effort of the medical-educational team is critical to the reintegration of the student with an SCI.* School staff should not hesitate to contact medical support staff if they have any concerns. A physical therapist can assist greatly

---

[5] For further information on catheterization, see chapter 24.

[6] For further information on the use of assistive breathing devices in the classroom, see chapter 7.

in the areas of positioning and transfer; an occupational therapist can provide information on feeding problems and access devices (e.g., switches that can be used to activate computers or toys); a speech therapist can work with the student who is unable to talk to develop communicative competence by means of an augmentative communication system (e.g., symbol board); and a dietitian can help plan a diet that is appropriate for the student. For further information on teaching children and adolescents who have spinal injuries, see *Teaching Individuals with Physical and Multiple Disabilities,* by June Bigge (1991).

❦ Chronic Conditions That Affect the Supporting Structures of the Body

There are a number of chronic conditions that can affect some or all of the supporting structures of the body. In this section, osteogenesis imperfecta and limb deficiencies are described. In the first condition, typically all of the bones of the body are affected; in the second, the upper, lower, or both upper and lower limbs may be missing or misshapen.

Osteogenesis Imperfecta (OI)

Osteogenesis imperfecta, commonly known as **brittle bone disease,** is an inherited disorder that affects the production or structure of **collagen,** the protein necessary for the development of the inelastic fibers found in connective tissues. The major characteristics of the condition are excessive bone fragility and deformity resulting from the broken bones. Though the clinical manifestations vary widely from one student to another, the characteristics shown in Table 14.6 are the most common. There are four types of OI. Each varies in terms of the abnormalities seen, the degree of severity, and the prognosis (Bender, 1991).

OI is a genetic condition. The most common inheritance pattern is **autosomal dominant;** however, some forms of the disease appear to be **autosomal recessive.** In **autosomal dominant conditions,** the defective gene is found on 1 of the 22 pairs of

TABLE 14.6
Characteristics of Osteogenesis Imperfecta

- **Bones:** Long bones of the extremities, in particular, are often thin (decreased bone mass), slender, and brittle and are easily fractured and misshapen. Characteristics of a person with OI include mild to severe shortness of stature, bowing of the legs, flat feet, curvature of the spine, barrel-shaped chest, and deformities of the head (e.g., triangular face, disproportionally large skull).
- **Ligaments:** Excessively elastic in nature; consequently, the joints are often hypermobile or hyperextendable. Because the joints are "double-jointed," they are prone to dislocation.
- **Muscle Tone:** Decreased (i.e., the individual is "floppy")
- **Skin:** Thin and translucent, bruises easily, and is hyperelastic
- **Eyes:** The outer white membrane (sclera) of the eye is often abnormally colored, because the thinning and translucency of the scleral tissue allow the choroid layer of the eye to show through. The eyes can range in color from blue-white to robin's egg blue to blue-black. Visual problems as a result of cataract formation or macular bleeding (bleeding in the retina of the eye) may develop.
- **Ears:** Often abnormal. As a result of abnormal hardening of the cartilage contained in the bone of the middle ear (otosclerosis), abnormalities in structure of the ossicles, or pressure on the auditory nerve, there may be a loss of hearing when the person enters adolescence. This condition is known as **presenile deafness.** Tinnitus (ringing in the ears) or vertigo (dizziness) may also be present. Surgical intervention may decrease the hearing loss.
- **Teeth.** Typically poorly developed. Often break or chip easily and can be prone to cavity development. Teeth can be blue-gray or yellow-brown in color. This anomaly is known as **dentogenesis imperfecta.**

autosomes. On the corresponding chromosome, the individual typically has the normal gene. Since the gene is dominant, the characteristic is expressed with only a "single dose." Because the chromosome is not exclusively found in one sex, as is the case in sex-linked inheritance, either parent could potentially have the condition. Both male and female offspring can inherit the disease; the ratio of male to female is equal. The children who do not inherit the condition are not carriers of the disease and therefore will not pass the disease to their offspring. For a discussion of autosomal recessive conditions, see chapter 9.

The exact incidence of OI is unknown. Estimates have ranged from 1 per 5,000 live births (Byers & Steiner, 1992) to 1 per 20,000 live births (Bender, 1991). OI is believed to be the most common genetic bone disorder.

While there is no known cure for OI, the goals for treatment, according to Stoltz, Dietrich, and Marshall (1989), focus on attaining the highest level of mobility with minimal incidence of fracture, independence in activities of daily living, and social integration. Treatment is usually conservative, and "particular attention is paid to the social development of the growing child as well as to genetic counseling for parents" (p. 120). For most individuals with OI, the complete elimination of fractures is an unrealistic goal, as fractures are "sporadic, unpredictable, and inevitable" (Bender, 1991, p. 25). Many children and young adults with OI benefit from a program of physical therapy that emphasizes muscle stretching, strengthening, and ambulation (Bender, 1991). In some cases, surgery may be undertaken to correct or minimize skeletal deformities (e.g., curvature of the spine). Intermedullary rods are often implanted to provide additional strength and stabilization in the weight-bearing bones that fracture repeatedly. For further information on physical and occupational therapy for those with OI, see articles by Helga Binder and her colleagues (1984; 1993).

Educational Implications and Teaching Tips: Students with Osteogenesis Imperfecta

The greatest challenge in working with students who have OI is protecting the student from injury without inhibiting physical and psychosocial needs

(Boos, Janvier, McIlvain-Simpson, Sanford, & Wade, 1993). Although many adults are upset by the notion that a child's limbs can be repeatedly broken, fractures become an expected part of life as children with OI move through their early years, and consequently, in many cases, the children (and their parents) are not unduly alarmed if and when a fracture occurs (Bender, 1991). With some, however, the condition and its sequelae cannot be accepted. In such situations, as a result of repetitive fractures, the children become very fearful of participating in any type of physical activity, to the point that they may become social isolates. Teachers need to be extremely supportive and understanding of the needs of students with OI, and even though they may be anxious about the possibility of fractures occurring during school hours, they need to realize that the student's need to be part of the "crowd" and to participate in normal childhood activities is paramount for optimal development. In working with those who have OI, the following suggestions may be of assistance for school staff:

1 *Individuals with OI, even those with a serious physical impairment, are generally of normal intelligence and should be fully integrated into the general school program as much as possible to ensure academic progress at a rate commensurate with their peers.* Unfortunately, students with OI often miss a great deal of school as a result of frequent hospitalizations and the need for prolonged bed rest to promote healing, further restricting them in their ability to progress academically and to socialize with their peers. Such absences should be anticipated and "planned" for (e.g., assignments sent home for completion, classes videotaped, home tutors hired) so that the student is able to complete the academic year on schedule (Bender, 1991). Some students with more serious forms of OI may need the assistance of a personal aide, for example during toileting and while moving around the school building (e.g., someone to push a wheelchair).

2 *Students with brittle bone disease are able to participate in many of the activities that the local school program has to offer.* However, because of the progressive nature of this disease, they should be encouraged to develop interests in activities that involve fine motor, cognitive, and social skills (e.g., computer games, chess, musical instruments) rather

than activities that require the use of gross motor skills.

3   *Children and young adults with OI are often restricted from participating in certain physical activities, especially contact sports; however, some students with milder forms of the disease are, under the direction of their physician, allowed to participate in certain sports.* Teachers should ask for a detailed written list of acceptable and unacceptable activities from the student's orthopedist (Appendix D).

Water aerobics or distance swimming is often recommended to strengthen the muscles and thereby prevent further damage to the bony framework. Diving from a diving board is usually contraindicated. For some students, an exercise program, using well-padded mats, as part of the regular physical education program offered at school is beneficial. For others, wheelchair sports (e.g., wheelchair basketball) may be a means to encourage physical activity and social interaction (Bender, 1991). For further information on designing an exercise program for students with OI, see Lockette and Keyes (1994).

4   *With an increasingly sedentary lifestyle, some students with OI become obese.* The school dietitian, working with the student and family, may be able to provide nutritional counseling and ensure that the student is following a nutritious, balanced diet that does not result in excessive weight gain.

5   *Changes in body appearance (e.g., bowing of legs, curvature of the spine) can be very distressing, particularly to the adolescent who is already self-conscious of his or her developing body.* It is not only physical changes that can be worrisome. Students who are prescribed special seating supports, standing frames, or walkers to prevent further damage from excessive movement may also be embarrassed about having to use such aides. Counseling should be readily available, and students should be encouraged to join a support group for individuals with chronic health problems.

6   *Those with moderate to severe forms of the condition may need to use crutches or a wheelchair to access their physical environment; however, even those who are able to walk with or without crutches in the classroom may benefit from using a wheelchair for*

longer excursions (Grove, Cusick, & Bigge, 1991). Often, a motorized wheelchair is recommended because the student's arms may be too short to propel the wheelchair in a normal manner, or the act of pushing the chair with the arms may place too much stress on the brittle bones of the arm (Molnar, 1983). A referral should be made to the student's physical therapist if it appears that benefit could be gained from the use of any mobility aids.

7   *Many persons with brittle bone disease are prone to episodes of increased perspiration.* Consequently, the classroom temperature should be kept below 72°F (Bleck, 1982). Clothing should be layered so that the student can regulate his or her body temperature, and fresh changes should be available to replace clothes that have become damp from excessive sweat. Teachers should be aware of signs of dehydration (e.g., flushed dry skin, coated tongue, irritability) and of the need for maintaining adequate fluid intake. If these symptoms occur, the family should contact the physician or take the student to the nearest hospital.

8   *Injury is not always easy to recognize in those with OI.* In many cases, the fractures are incomplete (the bone is cracked rather than broken) and there is little soft tissue trauma (little or no swelling, bruising, or pain). Injuries are also often missed because if there is bruising, it does not always occur at the site of the injury (Paterson, 1990; cited in Bender, 1991). School staff should be alert to signs of an undiagnosed fracture (e.g., fever, irritability, refusal to eat) and should be taught how to immobilize the fracture site so that the student can be transported to the hospital without further injury. If the student shows changes in respiration, the underlying cause may be a fractured rib and damage to the lungs. Prompt medical treatment is needed.

9   *Teachers should be observant of signs of hearing or visual loss and should make the proper referral for testing and treatment.* All students with OI should be encouraged to have a yearly examination by their ophthalmologist or optometrist. The set of forms contained in Appendix I can be used to provide the doctor with important information regarding the student's auditory or visual status.

10 *Normal physical and psychological sexual interest and function are expected in those with OI.* Consequently, counseling that addresses topics such as sexuality, pregnancy, contraception, and genetic counseling should be made available, if needed (Bender, 1991). In addition, as the student matures, realistic occupational planning is critical.

11 *Teachers need to be aware of the stresses this particular condition places on the student and family.* Not only do parents have to come to grips with the "loss" of the perfect child, in many cases they are often falsely accused of child abuse when they take their son or daughter to the emergency room for treatment. As a result of such accusations, many parents have feelings of hostility towards medical professionals (James, 1990).

Congenital and Acquired Limb Deficiencies

The term **limb deficiency** is used to refer to skeletal anomalies in which one or more limbs (arms or legs) or limb parts (fingers or toes) are absent or malformed. Limb deficiencies can be evident at birth, or they can occur as a result of injury or disease. Deficiencies can be the result of the lack of development of a bone (e.g., the bone is missing) or can result from some type of alteration in prenatal growth (e.g., the bone may be shorter on one side of the body than on the other). Deficiencies can occur alone or in combination with other medical problems (i.e., as part of a syndrome).

The cause of congenital amputations is believed to be multifactorial. The deficiency may result from chromosomal aberrations (e.g., single-gene mutations), genetic disorders (e.g., trisomy 13 and trisomy 18), or environmental factors (e.g., excessively small uterine environments; the development of constricting bands of soft tissue that entangle fetal limbs during development). Certain drugs taken during pregnancy, the most notable being **thalidomide,** have also resulted in infants being born with abnormally formed or missing limbs. Other drugs that may be linked to limb deficiencies include antidepressants, antiemetics (drugs that relieve nausea and vomiting), anticoagulants, anticonvulsants, and quinine (a drug used to combat malaria) (Goldberg, 1981). Maternal consumption of alcohol during pregnancy has also been implicated.

The most common causes of acquired amputations are accidents involving trains, automobiles, motorcycles, or farm machinery; burns; and explosions (Brooks, 1983). In addition, tumors of the bone structure, either **benign** (noncancerous) or **malignant**[7] (cancerous), may result in a limb being surgically removed, as may loss of blood supply or long-standing, uncontrolled infections (Grove et al., 1991). The most common benign tumor found in young children is **osteochondroma,** a tumor composed primarily of bone and cartilage, that continues to grow until skeletal maturity is reached (Boos, et al., 1993). Other benign tumors include **osteoblastomas** (vascular tumors of the bone and fibrous tissues) and several types of **bone cysts** (tumor-like sacs filled with a semisolid or liquid material). In some cases, a limb or limb part may be removed surgically to modify an extremity that has some type of abnormality in order to promote better function or to permit the use of an artificial limb (Brooks, 1983).

Congenital deficiencies occur at the rate of approximately 1 in every 20,000 births (Setoguchi & Rosenfelder, 1982). Congenital deficiencies outnumber acquired amputations by a ratio of 3 to 2 (Ehrlich & Akelman, 1996). Boys have a higher incidence of amputations than do girls in both congenital and acquired losses, 1.2 and 2 times more prevalent, respectively (Krebs & Fishman, 1984).

Persons with a limb deficiency are often categorized according to limb parts that are absent or malformed. There are a number of terms used by the medical profession to describe the individual who is missing one or more skeletal parts. The terms are defined in Table 14.7 and examples are given in Figure 14.4. The terms are typically used in combination. For example, a child born without a lower leg and foot would be described as having a "terminal transverse below-knee limb deficiency," whereas a child missing the bone on the medial (little finger side) of the forearm would be described as having an "intercalary longitudinal limb deficiency," specifically a "longitudinal deficiency of the ulnar" or "ulnar hemimelia." The most common upper limb deficiencies are terminal transverse below-elbow

---

[7] The most commonly found childhood cancerous tumors of the bones include **osteosarcoma** (also known as **osteogenic sarcoma**) and **Ewing's sarcoma.** For further information on these and other malignancies common in childhood, see chapter 22.

TABLE 14.7
Limb Deficiencies: Classification by Types

1. **Classification by the PORTION of Limb Missing—top to bottom**
   - **Terminal limb deficiency:** the end portion of the limb is missing (e.g., a hand)
   - **Intercalary limb deficiency:** the middle section of the limb is missing (e.g., hand is connected to the elbow).

   Phocomelia: absence of the central portion of a limb that results in the feet or hands or both being attached to the trunk by means of short, irregularly shaped limbs or stumps, often referred to as "seal limbs" or "flippers." If the entire limb is missing, the term *complete phocomelia* is used; if a portion remains, it is *incomplete phocomelia.*

2. **Classification by the PORTION of Limb Missing—side to side**
   - **Transverse limb deficiency:** the defect occurs perpendicular to the long axis of the limb across the entire width of the limb (e.g., the lower part of the leg from the knee down).
   - **Longitudinal limb deficiency:** the defect occurs parallel to the long axis of the limb down the length of the limb (e.g., a complete leg in terms of length, but one of the major bones, such as the tibia, is missing). Also known as a **paraxial limb deficiency.**

3. **Classification by the NUMBER of Missing Limbs or Limb Parts**
   - **Amelia:** complete absence of one or more limbs

   Biamelia: absence of two limbs; if both arms or both legs are missing, the term "double amputee" is often used

   Triamelia: absence of three limbs

   Tetramelia (or *quadrimembral amelia*): absence of all four limbs
   - **Hemimelia:** absence of a major portion of a limb. The term **meromelia** is often used instead of hemimelia to refer to the absence of a part of a limb.
   - **Acheiria:** complete absence of the hands
   - **Apodia:** complete absence of the feet
   - **Adactylia:** one or more digits of the hand or foot missing

4. **Classification by LATERALITY (i.e., relationship of defect to midline)**
   - **Unilateral:** involving one side (i.e., left *or* right)
   - **Bilateral:** occurring on two sides (i.e., left *and* right)
   - **Trilateral:** involving three limbs
   - **Quadrilateral:** involving four limbs

5. **Classification by the LOCATION (i.e., relationship of defect to joint)**
   - **AK:** above the knee or through the knee joint
   - **BK:** below the knee, but above or through the ankle joint
   - **AE:** above the elbow or through the elbow joint
   - **BE:** below the elbow, but above or through the wrist joint

hemimelia (the absence of the hand and distal part of the arm) and longitudinal radial hemimelia (the total or partial absence of the major bone of the forearm that extends from the wrist to elbow, which results in a condition known as **radial clubhand**). The most common lower limb deficiency is longitu-dinal fibular hemimelia, which results in a markedly shortened lower leg. Foot abnormalities are also associated with this disorder.

Given the visible nature of this particular type of musculoskeletal problem, diagnosis is simple. Treatment, however, is more complex. The goal of

Terminal deficiencies
There are no unaffected parts distal to
and in line with the deficient portion.

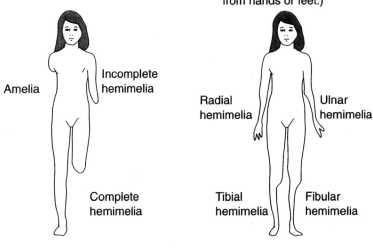

Transverse
Defect extends transversely
across the entire width of limb.
(Hand or foot is missing.)

Amelia

Incomplete
hemimelia

Complete
hemimelia

Longitudinal
Only a portion of the limb
is absent, extending to the
end of the limb. (Digits missing
from hands or feet.)

Radial
hemimelia

Ulnar
hemimelia

Tibial
hemimelia

Fibular
hemimelia

Intercalary deficiencies
Middle portion of limb is deficient, but
proximal and distal portions are present.

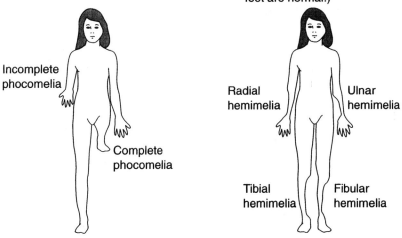

Transverse
Entire central portion of limb
is absent. (Hands and
feet are normal.)

Incomplete
phocomelia

Complete
phocomelia

Longitudinal
Segmental absence of part
of the limb—intact proximal
and distal. (Hands and
feet are normal.)

Radial
hemimelia

Ulnar
hemimelia

Tibial
hemimelia

Fibular
hemimelia

Figure 14.4
Types of Limb Deficiencies.
Source: Adapted from Heller, Alberto, Forney, & Schwartzman, 1996, p. 180.

treatment of those with missing limbs is to assist them to develop as normally as possible and to become as independent in their daily living activities as is feasible (Mason, 1991). To that end, children and young adults with missing limbs are often fitted with a **prosthetic device** (e.g., an artificial arm or leg) as early as possible. Although many will learn to use the device(s) with training and practice, it is not uncommon for those who have one or more partial limbs at birth (i.e., those who have meromelia, hemimelia, or phocomelia) to reject the use of prostheses and to rely on using their residual limb(s) as much as possible. In such cases, the children often develop a somewhat unique method to circumvent the physical limitation imposed by loss of the limb or limbs. For example, in the case of a student with missing arms, it would not be unusual for the student to use his or her feet to eat, to brush his or her teeth, and even to play the drums or the piano. Similarly, those with upper limb phocomelia often find that the digits of the deformed hand are very useful (e.g., to hold a spoon), and consequently, they reject having them "encased" in a prosthesis. Some children or young adults fitted with leg braces also reject them, as they tend to be heavy and awkward. They would often rather rely on a scooter board or wheelchair for mobility.

For those who lose a limb in later life, acceptance of prostheses typically occurs more readily because the individuals are replacing limbs that they have relied on up until the time that the limb was lost. Many of these children and young adults become very proficient in their use of the device(s), and at first glance, since so many prosthetic devices have developed to the point that they look "real," an observer may fail to recognize that the students are "different."

🍂 Educational Implications and Teaching Tips: Students with Limb Deficiencies

Children and young adults with limb deficiencies, both congenital and acquired, need the support of many persons to maximize their physical development. Typically, the medical-educational team includes physical and occupational therapists, prosthetists (persons who design and make artificial limbs), orthotists, and clothing designers, who can design and modify clothing that is not only attractive but also easy to don and doff. Even though the parents may be devastated by the loss of a limb in their son or daughter, they should be encouraged not to overprotect their children, because this may result in overdependency and maladjustment in later life (Whaley & Wong, 1995). Teachers can perform a vital role by accepting children and young adults with congenital limb deficiencies into their classrooms and by encouraging them to develop to their maximum potential, both physically and emotionally.

While both congenital and acquired situations result in an altered body structure, the needs of those with congenital disorders differ markedly from those who lose a limb later in life, after the normal developmental milestones have been reached. This is particularly true in cases of congenital limb deficiencies that involve more than one limb. In this section, the focus is on those born with a limb deficiency and who, consequently, have to learn to compensate for the loss of the limb or limbs at the same time as they are trying to master the typical fine and gross motor skills of childhood. For school staff, the following suggestions may be helpful:

1 *The mental abilities of those with limb deficiencies do not differ from those without (i.e., some are gifted, most are average, and some have cognitive deficits).* Regardless of cognitive level, many individuals with limb deficiencies are high achievers because they have to strive harder to accomplish many of the normal tasks of childhood (Brooks, 1983). For those with a positive self-image, school can be a positive experience; however, for those who are insecure, it can be a frightening encounter (Mason, 1991). Counseling should be made available to the student. Several organizations, such as the American Amputee Foundation and the War Amputations of Canada, have support groups that can be instrumental in helping the student accept the loss of a limb.

2 *In school, it is common for classmates to stare at the individual with a limb deficiency, particularly the student fitted with a prosthesis.* However, this behavior does not result from "revulsion," but from curiosity of what the "bionic" person can or cannot do. The student should be given the

opportunity to show his or her peers how the prosthesis works and to answer any questions that might arise. In most cases, the student is proud of the device and more than willing to show it off.

The teacher of a young child with a prosthesis should have a basic knowledge of the device to assist the student in responding to questions from peers (Setoguchi, 1983). In addition, the student's teacher should be aware of how the device is used so that if any concerns arise, e.g., the student appears to be having some type of problem with the device, the teacher can contact the student's parents or the medical team to discuss the difficulty.

3 *Because those with missing limbs have less surface area of skin and therefore have fewer sweat glands, they have a tendency to overheat quickly.* Individuals with prostheses may also have difficulty in regulating their body heat because some of their remaining body surface is covered by the prosthetic device. Teachers should be alert to signs of dehydration (e.g., flushed, dry skin; coated tongue; irritability) and should promote the use of layered lightweight clothing that can be easily taken off or put on so that the student can self-regulate body temperature (Mason & Wright, 1994). If the student perspires profusely, a change of underclothing may be necessary frequently during the day (Brooks, 1983). Extra clothing should be kept at school for this purpose.

4 *Those with missing limbs occasionally spike a fever as high as 105°F from a minor infection (e.g., a cold) and, consequently, need to be watched carefully for any adverse signs (e.g., lethargy).* Any concerns should be expressed promptly to the student's parents. If the student becomes suddenly ill, immediate medical assistance should be sought.

5 *A student who has a prosthetic device should be observed for blisters or abrasions that result from increased perspiration under the device, the accumulation of dirt or dried skin, and chafing of the skin by the prosthesis.* If the student complains of any soreness, the prosthesis should be removed for an inspection of the skin. Any redness that does not disappear within 20 to 30 minutes should be reported to the student's medical specialist.

As children grow, new prosthetic devices will be needed on a regular basis, usually every 12 to 18 months. Some devices, especially the newer myoelectric ones, i.e., electrically powered, can cost several thousand dollars. Some of the costs may be covered by governmental sources. However, in some cases, parents have to rely on assistance from non-profit organizations, such the Shriners' Hospitals for Crippled Children. Both the student with the device and the student's peers should treat it with care.

6 *The student with a limb deficiency may need additional pieces of adaptive equipment.* If there is a problem with mobility due to abnormalities of the lower extremities, a wheelchair may be of assistance, particularly if the distance to be covered is significant. Even though the student may not use such a device daily, having a chair may be invaluable on an outing. School staff should contact the student's physical therapist for information on availability and use.

If the deficiency involves the upper extremities, adaptive equipment such as specialized holders that can be used to grasp pencils, pens, or paint brushes may be of assistance. There are also a number of feeding aids that allow the student to be independent. School staff should contact the student's occupational therapist to discuss the types of aids that could be of assistance in the school setting.

7 *The degree to which a student with a limb deficiency can participate in physical activities is individual-specific.* Guidance should be obtained from the student's orthopedist and physical or occupational therapist. Forms that can be used for this purpose are found in Appendix D.

In general, the student should be encouraged to participate as much as possible in all activities offered in the school setting. However, participation in certain contact sports may be limited due to the possibility of damage to the prosthesis, possible injury to the student, and the potential risk of injury to others who inadvertently come in contact with the device (Setoguchi, 1983). For further information on developing an exercise program for individuals with missing limbs, see Lockette and Keyes (1994).

😌 Deformities or Disorders of the Lower Extremities

A variety of leg and foot deformities are found in children and young adults. Some are congenital (e.g., clubfoot), whereas some develop over time (e.g., leg-length inequality). In this section, a brief description of some of the more common leg and foot deformities is presented. Deformities of the hip joint are discussed in chapter 15.

Developmental Leg Deformities

Developmental leg deformities are those that develop as the child grows and the bones mature. There are two different types of developmental leg deformities: torsional and angular. In many cases, no treatment is required, i.e., the developmental deformity resolves itself without intervention; however, in some cases, there can be more serious consequences if the condition develops at the wrong time or if the deformity is severe (Mason & Wright, 1994). In such cases, surgical intervention, followed by casting, is common.

Torsional deformities are conditions in which one or more legs are rotated abnormally. "Torsional" comes from *torsus,* the past participle of the Latin verb *torquere,* meaning "to twist." Two common condi-tions are **internal** and **external tibial torsion** (e.g., in-toeing vs. out-toeing) (Table 14.8). Torsional de-formities are often caused by the positioning of the child (e.g., allowing the child to sit on top of malposi-tioned feet). These deformities generally disappear as the child matures. If spontaneous correction does not occur, treatment may be needed (e.g., physical ther-apy, wearing of orthotic shoes, surgery). Tibial tor-sion can also be secondary to myelomeningocele or cerebral palsy (Howe & Coffman, 1990).

Angular deformities are conditions in which the angle of the legs, at knee level, is altered (i.e., bowleg vs. knock-knee). There are two major types: genu varum and genu valgum (Table 14.8 and Figure 14.5). While "bowleggedness" occurs commonly in early childhood, it generally disappears after the child has been walking for about a year. In some cases, however, the condition may persist into middle childhood (Ma-son & Wright, 1994). Some children who are "knock-kneed" continue to display this angular deformity until they are approximately age 10, at which time the con-dition may improve. If angular deformities do not self-correct, bracing or surgery may be required.

Leg Length Inequality

A condition in which one leg is longer than the other may result from a variety of causes. Some of

TABLE 14.8
Developmental Deformities of the Lower Extremities

"Medical" Term	Description	"Lay" Term
Internal tibial torsion	• Inward turn of the tibia toward the midline of the body; results in the student's toes appearing to point inward toward the center of the body while the knee is facing forward. Appearance is similar to metatarsus varus.	• In-toeing
External tibial torsion	• Outward turning of tibia (i.e., opposite of internal tibial torsion). Similar in appearance to metatarsus valgus.	• Out-toeing
Genu varum	• One or both legs are curved outward at the knee.	• Bowlegged
Genu valgum	• Legs are curved inward, so that the knees are close together and the ankles are splayed.	• Knock-kneed

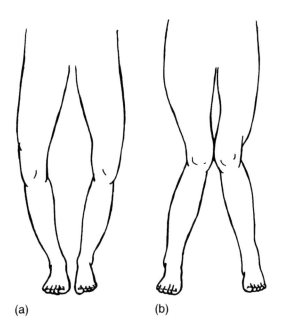

Figure 14.5
Developmental Angular Leg Deformities:
(a) bowlegs; (b) knock-knees.

the more common causes include: (a) overgrowth or deficient growth in the epiphyseal plates of the femur or tibia, which results from tumors that either stimulate or inhibit growth, (b) trauma to the cartilage cells of the plate; and (c) fracture of a long bone that results in increased circulation to the fracture site during the healing process, which, in turn, stimulates increased growth at the epiphysis (Mason & Wright, 1994). Other causes include: (a) congenital abnormalities that might result in a shortened or absent limb, (b) growth retardation that results from a bone infection, (c) damage to the hip joint as a result of a disease, or (d) one of a number of other neuromuscular diseases (James, 1990). Many children are born with a discrepancy, or one develops over time. In fact, 30% of the population may have a 1/2-inch (1.25 cm) or less difference in length between their legs (Ehrlich & Akelman, 1996). Typically, if the inequality is under 1/2 inch, it is not treated. If the discrepancy is between 1/2 and 1 inch, treatment involves the prescription of a **heel lift,** either inside the shoe (if minor) or outside the shoe (if major). Unfortunately, shoe orthoses are often considered unsightly by children, particularly adolescent children, so compliance may be a problem. In more se-

vere cases, surgery may be performed. If untreated, the child or young adult with a noticeable leg length discrepancy may develop a debilitating limp, a deformity of the spine, or degenerative arthritis of the hip.

Foot and Ankle Disorders

Anomalies that involve the feet and ankles are estimated to occur at a rate as frequent as 1 in every 700 infants (Boos et al., 1993). Foot and ankle disorders vary on the basis of the area affected and the degree of rigidity or flexibility in the joint. Some of the common disorders are shown in Figure 14.6. In some persons only one extremity is involved; in others, both feet and ankles show some degree of abnormality. In general, the earlier the treatment is started, the better the prognosis. In some cases, the deformity recurs and further surgical intervention is necessary (Boos et al., 1993).

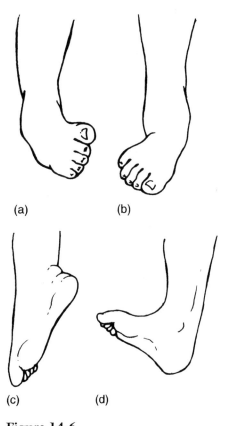

Figure 14.6
Common Foot and Ankle Disorders: (a) varus;
(b) valgus; (c) equinus; (d) calcaneus.

Foot and Ankle Deformities   Clubfoot, or **talipes,** a congenital disorder of the metatarsal bones of the forefoot and ankle joint, occurs at a rate of 1 to 1.4 per 1,000 births, making it the most common foot and ankle deformity (Mason & Wright, 1994). Approximately 9,000 infants are born each year in the United States with this type of disability alone (statistics cited in Lieber & Taub, 1988). There are several different types of talipes, classified on the position of the ankle (**tali**) and foot (**pes**) (Table 14.9). The various descriptors are often used in combination. Talipes equinovarus, talipes equinovalgus, talipes calcaneovarus, and talipes calcaneovulgus are terms used to describe those with clubfeet. **Talipes equinovarus** (foot and ankle are deviated inward and the plantar region of the forefoot is flexed) is the most severe and also the most common, accounting for approximately 95% of all cases of clubfoot.

The exact cause of talipes is unknown. However, both inherited (i.e., genetic) and environmental factors (e.g., positioning in utero; intrauterine compression; prenatal exposure to infection, drugs, or disease) are believed to contribute to its incidence (James, 1990). While it occurs more often in boys than girls, the reason for the higher incidence in males is unknown. There also appears to be a variation of incidence in different ethnic groups, with children of Chinese heritage showing a significantly lower incidence of clubfeet than those who are of Hawaiian or Polynesian descent (3:1,000 vs. 6 to 8:1,000, respectively) (Kyzer, 1991). In approximately 50% of all cases, both feet are involved (Kyzer, 1991). Clubfoot is often associated with other birth defects, such as spina bifida.

A clubfoot is also described as being either **flexible** or **rigid.** Treatment for the flexible condition typically involves repeated casting or splinting, a procedure known as **serial casting.** By "moving" the foot progressively into the correct position, and then immobilizing it in a fixed position by means of a cast, the deformity is treated without surgery. In many cases, correction is successful by the time the child is 6 to 8 weeks old, particularly if the cast is changed once a week (Scipien, 1991). Follow-up treatment may involve wearing specially designed corrective shoes. Cases that do not respond to this form of therapy may require surgery, which is usually performed between the ages of 4 months and 1 year (Kyzer, 1991). In most cases, rigid deformities require surgery, followed by casting.

With early treatment, particularly in cases of clubfoot that are not extremely severe or rigid, the prognosis is generally good. However, there may be some residual disability (e.g., underdeveloped musculature of the calf, smaller foot) that may affect the person's gross motor performance throughout his or her life span. In some cases the deformity may recur, necessitating further surgery. Unfortunately, with each successive surgery, the foot becomes less functional and increasingly painful (Kyzer, 1991).

Foot Deformities   While **talipes** refers to a deformity of the foot *and* the ankle, the term **pes** refers to an abnormality of the foot *alone*. In **pes cavus** (*cavus,* the Latin word for cavity) the foot has an excessively high arch. This condition is also known as clawfoot, gampsodactyly, or *griffe des orteils* (French for clawtoe). Some children are born with the condition; others may develop the condition later in life, e.g., as a result of a neuromuscular condition, such as Friedreich's ataxia. Pes cavus can occur in one or both feet. In mild cases, properly fitted insoles can

TABLE 14.9
Foot and Ankle Disorders: Clubfoot

"Medical" Term	Description	"Lay" Term
Equinus	• Foot is extended and the toes are lower than the heel.	• Tiptoe walking
Calcaneal or Calcaneas	• Foot is flexed and heel is lower than the toes.	• Heel walking
Varus	• Foot is turned inward (i.e., inverted).	• Toeing in
Valgus	• Foot is turned out (i.e., everted).	• Toeing out

alleviate the pain of the condition. In severe cases, surgery may be required to correct the abnormality.

The "opposite" of pes cavus is **pes planus,** a relatively common condition in both children and young adults. In this condition, there is a flattening out of the arch of the foot (either unilaterally or bilaterally), and the person is described as being **flat-footed.** Most often this condition can be treated successfully with shoe inserts. As in the case of pes cavus, pes planus can be congenital or adventitious.

Metatarsal Disorders   In addition to foot disorders, there are a number of disorders in which the bones that make up the toes, the metatarsal bones, are abnormally positioned. **Metatarsus varus** (also referred to as **metatarsus adductus**) differs from clubfoot in that the heel remains straight while the metatarsals of the forefoot rotate inward. Persons with this condition are often referred to as being **pigeon-toed.** It is the most commonly occurring congenital toe abnormality. In 85% of the cases, the condition resolves without treatment. If required, treatment involves gently stretching the forefoot towards the midline while keeping the heel stabilized in the forward position (Mason & Wright, 1994). In some cases, the child or young adult may need serial casting, splinting, or surgery. If the forepart of the foot rotates outward, a condition referred to as **metatarsus valgus,** the person is described as having a **duck walk.** Treatment for this condition is similar to that required for the vagus deformity.

Polydactylism and Syndactylism   The presence of more than the normal five toes per extremity at birth is referred to as **polydactylism,** or **polydactyly.** Typically, polydactylism causes no major physical problems; however, some young children may be embarrassed by the situation. In many cases, the extra digit is removed during early childhood for cosmetic purposes. The fusing of two or more toes together, also a congenital deformity, known as **syndactylism** or **syndactyly,** can range from an incomplete "webbing" of adjacent digits to a complete fusion, in which the bones and nails are united as one. Syndactylism generally does not cause any major disability to the child or young adult; however, teasing by peers may be a problem. In such cases, surgical separation of the digits may be possible, along with reconstruction of the foot so that it appears as close to normal as possible.

Deformities or Disorders of the Upper Extremities

In general, disorders of the upper extremities do not cause as great an impact, certainly in terms of mobility, on the individual as do those of the lower limbs. However, for the child born with a missing arm or arms, the deformity is extremely visible and may greatly affect social and emotional growth, as well as the ability to carry out some of the routine activities of daily living (e.g., eating, drinking, writing). For the deaf child, the loss of an upper limb may affect the ability to communicate by means of sign language. Some children, while not missing an upper limb, may have limited use of the upper limbs (e.g., paralysis of the arm). Congenital and acquired limb deficiencies have already been discussed. In this section, brachial plexus palsy is discussed, along with deformities of the hands and wrists.

Brachial Plexus Palsy

Also known as **Erb's palsy,** after the German neurologist Wilhelm H. Erb, **brachial plexus palsy** is caused by traumatic injury that occurs during a difficult or prolonged labor (e.g., breech presentation) or by injury that occurs in a delivery that necessitated the use of forceps. In this form of palsy, there is a paralysis of neck, shoulder, and arm muscles, which results from damage to the C5 or C6 spinal nerves. With treatment (e.g., exercises, splinting) there may be full recovery, particularly if the condition is mild. Those with a more serious case may never obtain normal functioning of the shoulder joint and may have limited range of motion of the affected limb.

Hand and Wrist Disorders

As in the case of the lower extremities, there are a number of congenital defects that involve the hands and arms. Not surprisingly, some of them are similar to those found in the feet (e.g., clubhand) and lower limbs (e.g., arm length inequality). It has been estimated that in 1 of every 626 live births there is some type of upper extremity anomaly; however, in only 10% of the cases does the abnormality result in either a significant cosmetic or functional deficit (Waters & Simmons, 1996). In the majority of the cases, the cause of the abnormality is unknown.

Polydactyly and Syndactyly Polydactyly (extra digits) of the hands usually involves either the thumb or fifth finger and is, in most cases, an autosomal dominant genetic condition. Thumb duplication occurs at a rate of 0.08 in 100,000 live births. Small-finger duplication occurs much more frequently. In the African American population, it can occur as commonly as 1 in 300; in whites, 1 in 3,000 (Waters & Simmons, 1996). In many cases the extra digit, which may be a complete finger or just a skin tag, is removed surgically, usually before the child enters school (Boos et al., 1993), and is often done solely for cosmetic purposes. Fusing of one or more fingers of the hands is one of the most common hand anomalies found in newborns. The digits most commonly fused are the ring and middle finger or the ring and little finger. **Syndactyly** occurs 1 in every 2,000 live births. In some cases, the condition is inherited (autosomal dominant). It is far more common in white persons than in African Americans (Waters & Simmons, 1996). As in the case of syndactyly of the toes, separation and reconstruction are often recommended to correct the condition.

🐾 Deformities of the Spine: Curvatures

Curvatures of the spine, the most common deformity of the spine, are found frequently in the pediatric population. These spinal problems do not normally result in significant sequelae (in contrast to spina bifida and spinal cord injuries); however, they are chronic conditions that can significantly affect the ability to move independently and, in severe cases, the ability to breathe.

There are three different types of spinal curvatures, referred to in the medical literature as **kyphosis, lordosis,** and **scoliosis** (Table 14.10 and Figure 14.7). The three can occur singly or in combination. For example, a person with a **kyphoscoliosis** would have a curvature that deviates both laterally *and* posteriorly. These terms are only anatomic or descriptive and do not refer specifically to any particular disease entity. In fact, all human beings, regardless of age, have a mild form of kyphosis and lordosis. However, any sideways curve greater than 10° is considered to be scoliotic (Mason & Wright, 1994).

Curvatures of the spine range from mild to severe. A mild condition would require little or no treatment.

A severe condition would necessitate more intensive treatment, which may last up to several years. Because scoliosis is the most common type of spinal curvature, it is described in greatest detail, after a brief description of the other two conditions.

Kyphosis

This hunchback curvature, known as a **kyphosis,** is considered pathological when the degree of deviation at the thoracic level exceeds 45°. Kyphosis, to a lesser degree, occurs in approximately 4% of all children (Boos et al., 1993). It is often postural in nature (i.e., the child sits with his or her shoulders "rounded over"); in such cases the condition can usually be self-corrected. In some children, however, kyphosis results from a primary condition, such as Scheuermann's disease, a condition of unknown cause that develops at puberty in both sexes. Children with significant kyphosis usually complain of back pain and excessive fatigue. Bracing or surgery may be required to treat such advanced conditions.

Lordosis

An exaggerated curve in the lumbar region of the spine, known as **lordosis,** is often described as a **swayback** or **saddleback.** A certain degree of postural lordosis is common in young children; however, it should disappear by the time the child is around 8 years old. In certain conditions, particularly those that are neuromuscular in origin, such as cerebral palsy and spina bifida, the condition can become so severe that the child encounters difficulty in sitting, standing, and even lying down (Rangaswamy, 1983). Bracing or surgery may be required to treat advanced conditions.

Scoliosis

When viewed from the back of the individual, **scoliosis** is a curvature that involves both a lateral deviation from the midline and a rotation of a series of vertebrae.

Classifications of Scoliotic Curves A scoliotic curvature can be characterized as being functional, nonstructural, or structural. The cause of scoliotic curvatures varies from person to person. In functional and nonstructural scoliosis, the cause is quite evident. Structural scoliosis may have a known cause; however, in many cases the cause is unknown.

TABLE 14.10
Curvatures of the Spine

"Medical" Term	Description	"Lay" Term
Kyphosis	• A posterior abnormality which, when examined from a side view, is characterized by a convex curve (i.e., the thoracic area of the spine curves outward).	• Hunchback or humpback
Lordosis	• An anterior abnormality which, when examined from a side view, is characterized by a concave curve (i.e., the small of the back curves inward)	• Swayback, saddle back, or hollow back
Scoliosis	• A lateral (sideways) abnormality which, when examined from the back view, is characterized by a long C- or S-shaped curve	(None)

Functional curvature. A scoliotic curve that is usually caused by chronic slouching or poor posture is referred to as a **functional** or **postural curvature.** A major characteristic of a functional scoliotic curvature is that it is not permanent; i.e., the individual can voluntarily correct the curve by "bending" to the opposite side so that the shoulders are "straight." This type of condition is generally mild, rather than moderate or severe, and is not painful to the student.

Nonstructural curvature. A curvature that is secondary to a known cause, such as a limb length discrepancy, is known as a **nonstructural curvature.** In such situations, the deformity can generally be corrected by treating the underlying cause rather than by treating the curvature itself (Rinsky, 1983). For example, the student with a length discrepancy could be fitted with specialized shoes to equalize the length of the legs and thereby "straighten" the spine. Nonstructural scoliosis is most often mild; however, in rare cases, this type of curvature can develop into a permanent deformity. There is also a **transient form** of a nonstructural curvature. This type of scoliosis arises from either pressure on a nerve root or inflammation in the spine (Whaley & Wong, 1995).

Structural curvature. A scoliotic curve that results in permanent changes to the bony structure of the spine, the soft tissues that surround the spine, or both and does not resolve without treatment is de-

scribed as a **structural curvature.** In 30% of the cases of structural scoliosis, there is a specific cause (e.g., a neuromuscular disorder, such as cerebral palsy, muscular dystrophy, polio, or spina bifida; a vertebral abnormality that develops in utero; an infection or tumor; trauma). In the remaining 70% of cases, the condition is said to be **idiopathic,** i.e., with no recognizable cause.

Occurring as frequently in 1 in every 10 persons, idiopathic scoliosis is a common condition (Brosnan, 1991). However, in most individuals, the curvature is usually less than 5°, and effects range in severity from mild to insignificant. In more severe cases, those in which the curvature exceeds 20°, the symptoms are more marked. However, the incidence of this degree of curvature drops to approximately 2 in 1,000 children. One child in 1,000 has a curvature greater than 40°.

Idiopathic scoliosis is found more often in girls than in boys, particularly in the case of adolescent onset scoliosis, where the ratio of females to males is 7 to 1 (Whaley & Wong, 1995). The age of onset of idiopathic scoliosis is variable, occurring any time from infancy through adolescence. In most cases, the condition arises when the individual is older than age 10 (i.e., during the "growth spurt"). In most cases, the individual is otherwise healthy.

"Idiopathic" scoliosis may in fact be "familial." It has been posited that scoliosis is transmitted as an

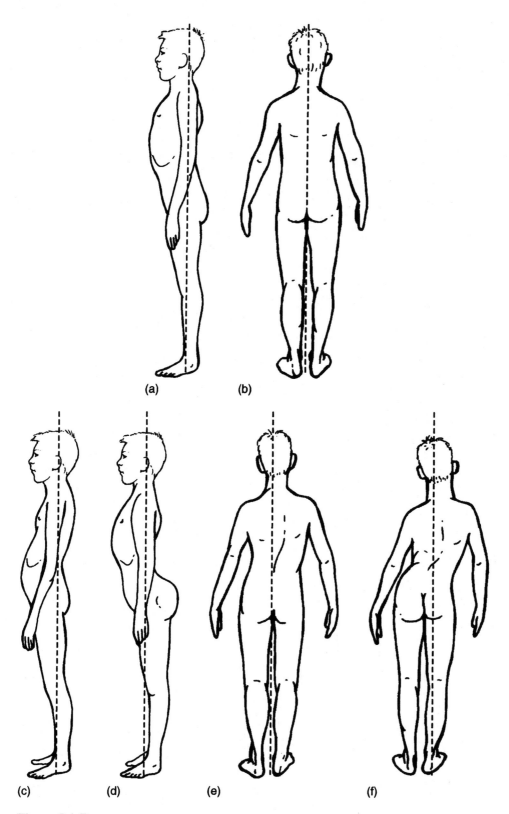

Figure 14.7
Curvatures of the Spine: (a) normal; (b) normal; (c) kyphosis; (d) lordosis; (e)
mild scoliosis; (f) severe scoliosis.

304

autosomal dominant trait or as an **X-linked dominant trait** (Mason & Wright, 1994; Whaley & Wong, 1995). An X-linked dominant trait is similar to autosomal dominant inheritance except that the dominant gene is found on the X chromosome rather than on one of the autosomes. Other researchers have suggested that the cause is multifactorial.

Diagnosis and Treatment Because scoliosis typically develops gradually, rarely does the individual experience any pain or discomfort until the deformity is well established (Whaley & Wong, 1995). Often, a scoliotic condition is recognized by parents, teachers, or school nurses by the "hump" that is noticeable in the student's back when bending over to touch his or her toes or to pick up something off the floor. In some cases, it is an uneven hemline in the student's clothing or pants that may alert a caregiver to the presence of the condition. In female adolescents, unequal breast size, due to differences in the underlying rib cage, may also be an indication of scoliosis (Rinsky, 1983). Some schools have a regularly scheduled screening program, targeting students between the ages of 11 and 15. For further information on screening students for scoliosis and a discussion of the pros (e.g., early diagnosis and less costly treatment) and cons (e.g., screening programs are not cost-effective), see the articles by Bunnell (1988) and Renshaw (1988).

Treatment for scoliosis, particularly postural scoliosis, typically involves an **exercise program** to strengthen the spinal musculature. However, if the curvature becomes marked (i.e., between 20° and 45°), **bracing** may be recommended to reduce the curve and to maintain the spine in the correct position. The brace, most commonly the **Milwaukee brace** (Figure 14.8), which extends from the neck to the pelvis, is individually fitted and must be worn 20 to 23 hours a day. The brace must be adjusted periodically, usually every 3 months. After x-rays show that the child's bones have matured, he or she is gradually weaned from the brace. Bracing may be required for several years until spinal growth has completed. Although bracing stops the curve from progressing, it does *not,* unfortunately, correct the condition (Mason & Wright, 1994).

As an alternative to bracing, some individuals with mild to moderate curvatures have been treated by **electrical stimulation** administered while they are asleep at night. In this form of treatment, which lasts for approximately 8 hours per night, electrical impulses from a battery-powered device are transmitted to the muscles on the opposite side of the curvature. The impulse is received by means of electrodes that are either taped to the skin surface or surgically implanted in the muscle tissue. The impulses cause the muscles to contract, thereby possibly straightening the spine. Several studies have reported this treatment to be ineffective, causing others to suggest that the approach not be recommended to parents (Sussman, 1996).

In some cases, in particular those with curvatures of 45° to 50°, **surgical correction** may be required to stabilize the vertebral column and to prevent progression of deformity. Surgery, which involves fusing or joining the vertebrae by means of rods, screws, or wires, is often considered if: (a) the student's pulmonary function is compromised or diminished by 50% or more; (b) the student has difficulty sitting (e.g., has to use upper extremities to maintain balance) or walking; (c) the student is noncompliant and rejects a bracing program (e.g., for cosmetic reasons) or is unable to tolerate a brace as a result of skin breakdown; (d) the student suffers from chronic pain or develops pressure sores from sitting on one buttock continuously; or (e) the condition affects the student's ability to function in social, educational, and vocational activities (Rangaswamy, 1983; Whaley & Wong, 1995). The decision to operate, however, must involve the consideration of the potential benefits and risks. In advanced cases, since the surgery does *not* result in a straight spine, the decision to operate depends on the degree of improvement in quality of life that can be realized (Rangaswamy, 1983). Those who require surgery usually are kept out of school for 3 to 4 weeks. After surgery, the student must wear a body cast or brace for several months.

Prognosis is best if the scoliotic curvature is mild and if the condition develops when the youngster is older and less growth remains to be done (Howe & Coffman, 1990). If left untreated, some cases, but not all, of scoliosis can result in a very severe deformity that is not only extremely painful but also life-threatening (i.e., the distortion of the rib cage can compromise cardiopulmonary function and lead to heart failure).

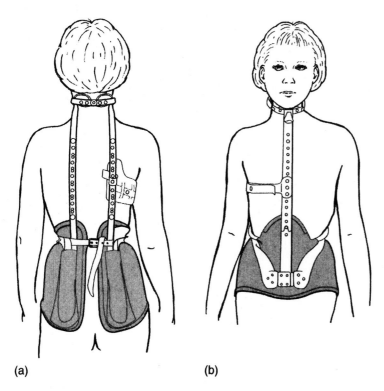

(a)   (b)

Figure 14.8
Milwaukee Brace: (a) posterior view; (b) anterior view.

🐾 Educational Implications and Teaching Tips: Students with Spinal Curvatures

The greatest problem encountered by those with spinal curvatures is body image, particularly in young adolescents who are extremely self-conscious about their evolving bodily changes. The following suggestions are given for school staff:

1 *Teachers should encourage all students to maintain good posture and to participate in an active program of exercise and sports that strengthens the musculature of the back and thereby prevents the development of a spinal curvature.* Teachers, as good role models, should maintain a healthy lifestyle, eat nutritionally balanced meals, participate in a regular program of exercise, and maintain good posture and appropriate body weight.

2 *Even though bracing is effective in about 85% of cases, noncompliance rates have been re-*

ported to be as high as 50% (Mason & Wright, 1994). School staff should be supportive and stress the importance of adhering to the treatment program as prescribed. The student's teacher or the school nurse can assist the student in coping with the stresses of immobilization by being an empathetic listener and by assisting the child or adolescent in developing good problem-solving skills (e.g., how to circumvent the problems caused by the brace). If the student reports that the brace is uncomfortable, his or her complaints should not go unheeded (Heller et al., 1996). Skin breakdown, resulting from the abrasion of the brace against the skin, is not uncommon and needs immediate treatment. The student with a curvature may need special seating equipment (e.g., cushions that relieve pressure on the buttocks). The student's physical therapist should be contacted to discuss specific needs.

3 *Feelings of vulnerability are not uncommon for young students, particularly adolescent girls who require surgery followed by casting.* They have to disrobe frequently during cast applications, are

restricted in terms of freedom of movement by the cast, may worry that the cast will prevent the growth of their breasts, and may even fear that their menstrual periods will come to a halt during the time that they are in a cast (Howe & Coffman, 1990). A supportive teacher can be of assistance. If the teacher thinks that counseling may be beneficial, this should be discussed with the student. Most teenage girls generally adjust to the treatment program fairly well over time because of their desire to improve their appearance.

4 *To minimize the visibility of the brace, the student should be encouraged to wear fashionable, loose, colorful shirts, sweaters, or sweatshirts* (James, 1990). Teaching the adolescent, in particular the female, teenager how to apply makeup and body fragrances and to style her hair in an attractive manner may assist in developing a positive self-image and may encourage compliance with a routine that lasts for several months or more.

5 *The degree to which a student can participate in a sports program is determined by his or her physician.* For students who are wearing a brace, activity may not be restricted as much as expected. Many children and young adults are allowed to ride a bike, run, jump, and participate in some school sports. Some are even allowed to participate in certain team sports. In some cases, the doctor may allow the student to remove his or her brace for a brief period to participate in strenuous activities, such as gymnastics or skiing (Springhouse Corporation, 1992). Students who wear a brace and are not permitted to take it off are usually prevented from activities such as horseback riding, skating, and gymnastics because of the possibility of injury. Forms that can be used to obtain information on any restrictions are found in Appendix D.

Brosnan (1991), in discussing permissible activities for students who wear a brace, made the following comments in relationship to a student who was an avid tennis player and a member of the school tennis team:

> Because we [the medical profession] are treating the whole person, it is more beneficial psychologically to permit time out for this important activity [tennis] to encourage social growth of the patient and, perhaps, better compliance with bracing. (p. 23)

6 *For those who have had surgery, any activities that require the individual to bend, twist, or stoop or to lift heavy objects are generally contraindicated.* Restrictions may be imposed for up to 2 years after surgery (Brosnan, 1991). However, after 3 to 4 months, many of the students are allowed to resume a majority of their favorite activities, such as cycling and swimming. Some may not be allowed to engage in competitive sports, ice skating, roller skating, skateboarding, skiing (water or snow), weight lifting, and other activities that might result in a jarring motion to the spine (e.g., horseback riding) or require extreme flexibility (e.g., gymnastics, ballet) for a protracted period.

❦ Summary

Disorders of the supporting structures can be either acute or chronic. Acute injuries often result from some type of accidental trauma; chronic conditions have a variety of causes, ranging from genetic abnormalities to infectious diseases. The major effect this type of disorder has is on the ability of the individual to access his or her environment and to perform routine activities, such as dressing, eating, and toileting. Students with disorders that affect the supporting structures typically attend school with their peer group. In some cases, the needs of the student are minimal; in others, major accommodations or adaptations are critical. The suggestions given in this chapter should be of assistance to those working with students who have a physical disability that results from some type of abnormality of the supporting structures of the body.

References

Apple, D. F., Anson, C. A., Hunter, J. D., & Bell, R. B. (1995). Spinal cord injury in youth. *Clinical Pediatrics, 34,* 90–95.

Bender, L. H. (1991). Osteogenesis imperfecta. *Orthopaedic Nursing, 10*(4), 23–31.

Bigge, J. (1991). *Teaching individuals with physical and multiple disabilities* (3rd ed.). New York: Merrill.

Bijur, P. E., Trumble, A., Harel, Y., Overpeck, M. D., Jones, D., & Scheidt, P. C. (1995). Sports and recreation injuries in US children and adolescents. *Archives of Pediatric and Adolescent Medicine, 149,* 1009–1016.

Binder, H., Conway, A., & Gerber, L. H. (1993) Rehabilitation approaches to children with osteogenesis imperfecta: A ten-year experience. *Archives of Physical and Medical Rehabilitation, 74,* 386–390.

Binder, H., Hawks, L., Graybill, G., Gerber, N. L., & Weintrob, J. C. (1984). Osteogenesis imperfecta: Rehabilitation approach with infants and young children. *Archives of Physical and Medical Rehabilitation, 65,* 537–541.

Bleck, E. E. (1982). Osteogenesis imperfecta. In E. E. Bleck & D. A. Nagel (Eds.), *Physically handicapped children: A medical atlas for teachers* (pp. 405–412). New York: Grune & Stratton.

Boos, M. L., Janvier K. W., McIlvain-Simpson, G. R., Sanford, C. C., & Wade, G. (1993). Nursing planning, intervention, and evaluation for altered musculoskeletal function. In D. B. Jackson & R. B. Saunders (Eds.), *Child health nursing: A comprehensive approach to the care of children and their families* (pp. 1679–1745). Philadelphia: J. B. Lippincott.

Brooks, M. B. (1983). Limb deficiencies. In J. Umbreit (Ed.), *Physical disabilities and health impairments: An introduction* (pp. 93–99). New York: Merrill.

Brosnan, H. (1991). Nursing management of the adolescent with idiopathic scoliosis. *Nursing Clinics of North America, 26,* 17–31.

Bunnell, W. P. (1988). The natural history of idiopathic scoliosis. *Clinical Orthopaedics and Related Research, 229,* 20–25.

Byers, P. H., & Steiner, R. D. (1992). Osteogenesis imperfecta. *Annual Review of Medicine, 43,* 269–282.

Committee on Trauma Research, Commission on Life Sciences, National Research Council, and the Institute of Medicine (1985). *Injury in America: A continuing public health problem.* Washington, DC: National Academy Press.

Crawley, T. (1996) Childhood injury: Significance and prevention strategies. *Journal of Pediatric Nursing, 11,* 225–232.

Duff, J. F. (1992) *Youth sports injuries.* New York: Collier.

Ehrlich, M. G., & Akelman, E. (1996). Orthopedic problems of the extremities. In F. D. Burg, J. R. Ingelfinger, E. R. Wald, & R. A. Polin (Eds.), *Gellis & Kagan's current pediatric therapy* (15th ed., pp. 479–483). Philadelphia: W. B. Saunders.

Frantz, C. H., & O'Rahilly, R. (1961). Congenital skeletal limb deficiencies. *Journal of Bone and Joint Surgery, 43A,* 1202–1205, 1224.

Gilgoff, I. S. (1983). Spinal cord injury. In J. Umbreit (Ed.), *Physical disabilities and health impairments: An introduction* (pp. 132–146). New York: Merrill.

Goldberg, M. J. (1981). The pediatric amputee: An epidemiologic survey. *Orthopedic Review, 10*(10), 49–54.

Graham, P., Weingarden, S., & Murphy, P. (1991). School reintegration: A rehabilitation goal for spinal cord injured adolescents. *Rehabilitation Nursing, 16,* 122–126.

Grove, N., Cusick, B., & Bigge, J. (1991). Conditions resulting in physical disabilities. In J. L. Bigge, *Teaching individuals with physical and multiple disabilities* (3rd ed., pp. 1–15). New York: Merrill.

Heller, K. W., Alberto, P. A., Forney, P. E., & Schwartzman, M. N. (1996). *Understanding physical, sensory, and health impairments.* Pacific Grove, CA: Brooks/Cole.

Hoeman, S.P. (1996). *Rehabilitation nursing: Process and application* (2nd ed.). St. Louis: Mosby.

Howe, J., & Coffman, C. P. (1990). The musculoskeletal system. In G. M. Scipien, M. A. Chard, J. Howe, & M. U. Barnard (Eds.), *Pediatric nursing care* (pp. 477–525). St. Louis: Mosby.

Hughes, R. B. Immune responses. In D. B. Jackson & R. B. Saunders (Eds.), *Child health nursing: A comprehensive approach to the care of children and their families* (pp. 619–639). Philadelphia: J. B. Lippincott.

James, S. R. (1990). Skeletal integrity and mobility: Implications of inflammation and structural abnormalities. In S. R. Mott, S. R. James, & A. M. Sperhac (Eds.), *Nursing care of children and families* (2nd ed., pp. 1553–1613). Redwood, CA: Addison-Wesley.

Jezewski, M. A. (1992). Alterations in neurological function. In P. T. Castiglia & R. E. Harbin (Eds.), *Child health care: Process and practice* (pp. 633–684). Philadelphia: J. B. Lippincott.

Jones, N. E. (1992). Prevention of childhood injuries. Part II: Recreational injuries. *Pediatric Nursing, 18,* 619–621.

Krebs, D. E., & Fishman, S. (1984). Characteristics of child amputee population. *Journal of Pediatric Orthopaedics, 4,* 89–95.

Kyzer, S. P. (1991). Congenital idiopathic clubfoot: Part 1. *Orthopaedic Nursing, 10*(4), 11–18.

Laskowski-Jones, L. (1993). Acute SCI: How to minimize the damage. *American Journal of Nursing, 93*(12), 23–31.

Lieber, M. T., & Taub, A. S. (1988). Common foot deformities and what they mean for parents. *MCN: Maternal and Child Nursing, 13*(1), 47–50.

Lockette, K. F., & Keyes, A. M. (1994). *Conditioning with physical disabilities.* Champaign, IL: Human Kinetics.

Losh, S. P. (1994). Injury prevention in children. *Primary Care, 21,* 733–746.

Mason, K. J. (1991). Congenital orthopedic anomalies and their impact on the family. *Nursing Clinics of North America, 26,* 1–16.

Mason, K. J., & Wright, S. (1994). Altered musculoskeletal function. In C. L. Betz, M. M. Hunsberger, & S. Wright (Eds.), *Family-centered nursing care of children* (2nd ed., pp. 1815–1873). Philadelphia: W. B. Saunders.

McCoy, R. L., Dec, K. L., McKeag, D. B., & Honing, E. W. (1995). Common injuries in the child or adolescent athlete. *Primary Care, 22,* 117–144.

Molnar, G. E. (1983). Musculoskeletal disorders. In J. Umbreit (Ed.), *Physical disabilities and health impairments: An introduction* (pp. 108–116). New York: Merrill.

Mosby's medical, nursing, and allied health dictionary (4th ed.) (1994). St. Louis: Mosby.

National Electronic Injury Surveillance System, U.S. Consumer Product Safety Commission, National Injury Information Clearinghouse (1991). *Statistics.* (Available from The National Injury Information Clearinghouse, U.S. Consumer Product Safety Commission, Washington, DC 20207).

Ostrum, G. A. (1993). Sports-related injuries in youths: Prevention is the key—and nurses can help! *Pediatric Nursing, 19,* 333–342.

Pieper, P. (1994). Pediatric trauma: An overview. *Nursing Clinics of North America, 29,* 563–584.

Polhgeers, A., & Ruddy, R. M. (1995). An update on pediatric trauma. *Emergency Medicine Clinics of North America, 13,* 267–289.

Rangaswamy, L. (1983). Curvatures of the spine. In J. Umbreit (Ed.), *Physical disabilities and health impairments: An introduction* (p. 59–73). New York: Merrill.

Reff, R. B. (1988). Musculoskeletal injury. In M. R. Eichelberger & G. L. Pratsch (Eds.), *Pediatric trauma care* (pp. 133–144). Rockville, MD: Aspen.

Renshaw, T. S. (1988). Screening school children for scoliosis. *Clinical Orthopaedics and Related Research, 229,* 26–30.

Rinsky, L. A. (1983). Scoliosis. In E. E. Bleck & D. A. Nagel (Eds.), *Physically handicapped children: A medical atlas for teachers* (pp. 433–443). New York: Grune & Stratton.

Schnek, E. (1991). Care of the patient with a neurological disorder. In B. L. Christensen & E. I. Kockrow (Eds.), *Foundations of nursing* (pp. 1004–1053). St. Louis: Mosby.

Scipien, G. M. (1991). Care of children with physical and emotional problems. In G. M. Scipien, M. A. Chard, J. Howe, & M. U. Barnard (Eds.), *Pediatric nursing care* (pp. 1218–1265). St. Louis: Mosby.

Setoguchi, Y. (1983) Amputations in children. In E. E. Bleck & D. A. Nagel (Eds.), *Physically handicapped children: A medical atlas for teachers* (pp. 17–26). New York: Grune & Stratton.

Setoguchi, Y., & Rosenfelder, R. (1982). *The limb deficient child.* Springfield, IL: Charles C. Thomas.

Smith, M. P., & Woodring, B. C. (1990). Innervation and mobility: Implications of altered neurologic and neuromuscular function. In S. R. Mott, S. R. James, A. M. Sperhac (Eds.), *Nursing care of children and families* (2nd ed., pp. 1615–1730). Redwood City, CA: Addison-Wesley.

Springhouse Corporation (1992). *Teaching patients with chronic conditions.* Springhouse, PA: Author.

Stoltz, M. R., Dietrich, S. L., & Marshall, G. J. (1989). Osteogenesis imperfecta: Perspectives. *Clinical Orthopaedics and Related Research, 242,* 120–136.

Sussman, M. D. (1996). Disorders of the spine and shoulder girdle. In F. D. Burg, J. R. Ingelfinger, E. R. Wald, & R. A. Polin (Eds.), *Gellis & Kagan's current pediatric therapy* (15th ed., pp. 475–479). Philadelphia: W. B. Saunders.

Waters, P. M., & Simmons, B. P. (1996). Congenital hand and upper limb deformities. In F. D. Burg, J. R. Ingelfinger, E. R. Wald, & R. A. Polin (Eds.), *Gellis & Kagan's current pediatric therapy* (15th ed., pp. 483–489). Philadelphia: W. B. Saunders.

Whaley, L. F., & Wong, D. L. (1995). *Nursing care of infants and children* (5th ed.). St. Louis: Mosby.

Will, S. I. S. (1993) IHP: Sports injury. In M. B. Hass (Ed.), *The school nurse's source book of individualized healthcare plans* (pp. 402–409). North Branch, MN: Sunrise River Press.

CHAPTER 15

Disorders of the Articulating Structures

Arthritis

Closed reduction

Dislocation

Dysplasia

Juvenile rheumatoid arthritis

NSAIDs

Open reduction

RICE

SAARDs and DMADs

Self-limited disease

Soft tissue injuries

Sprain

Articulating structures are the component parts that form the connection between two adjacent bones. They are more commonly referred to as **joints** and can be subdivided into those that are immovable (fibrous joints), those that allow a limited movement (cartilaginous joints), and those that permit free movement (synovial joints). In this chapter, conditions that affect a specific joint and those that are general to the entire body are described.

Conditions Affecting a Specific Joint

The joint capsule and the ligaments around the joint are stronger in children than in adults; consequently, children are *less* likely to experience joint damage than their adult counterparts (Ergin, 1996). However, even though such injuries occur less often, they do occur. Particularly at risk are those who engage in activities in which limbs are pushed, pulled, or twisted—activities such as gymnastics, wrestling, and football. Injuries that involve the articulating structures are often described as **soft tissue injuries** and can be divided into two different types: sprains and dislocations.[1] If the injury occurs at school, an accident report (Appendix C) should be filled out and sent to the principal by the person who cared for the injured student.

Traumatic Injuries: Sprains and Dislocations

An injury of a joint ligament that occurs when it is stretched, torn, or separated from the bone is known as a **sprain.** Sprains usually result from a sudden twisting or wrenching motion or from a forceful blow and are common in athletes who engage in contact or competitive sports, such as hockey, football, soccer, and baseball. The ligaments most susceptible to this type of injury are those found in the knees and elbows. Sprains can be mild, moderate, or severe. A mild sprain, also referred to as a **grade I sprain,** involves some overstretching of the ligament with possible microscopic tearing of the fibers; however, the ligament integrity remains essentially intact. In a

grade I strain, there is no change in the range of motion of the joint, nor is there any increase in joint laxity (looseness). In a moderate sprain, a **grade II sprain,** there is a partial tear of the ligament; however, the ligament is not completely discontinuous. Typically, in this degree of injury there is increased joint laxity and a concomitant loss of motion. In a severe sprain, a **grade III sprain,** the tear is complete and the ligament is severed. Joints with this degree of injury show clear-cut joint instability to stress (Ergin, 1996). When the ligaments are damaged, there is often a buildup of synovial fluid in the joint cavity. The accumulation results in the joint becoming swollen, tender, and painful, a condition known as **synovitis.** The joint most susceptible to synovitis is the kneecap.

Treatment of a sprain involves four components, which may be remembered by using the acronym **RICE: r**est, **i**ce, **c**ompression, and **e**levation. A typical treatment protocol is shown in Table 15.1.

TABLE 15.1
Treatment of Soft Tissue Injuries: RICE

Rest	The student should stop the activity to rest the affected body part, to relieve pain, and to prevent further damage. The affected joint should not be used for 2 to 3 days after the injury.
Ice	An ice pack, such as crushed ice in a towel or a bag of frozen peas, should be applied to the affected body part for at least 20 minutes two to four times daily for 2 to 3 days after injury. Cold packs cause vasoconstriction and result in decreased bleeding, inflammation, swelling, and pain.
Compression	The injured body part should be wrapped firmly in a wet elastic wrap to compress the joint. Compression aids in the control of edema.
Elevation	The affected body part should be elevated above the level of the heart to decrease swelling and promote return of venous blood.

---

[1] Soft tissue injuries that involve muscles (i.e., contusions and strains) are discussed in chapter 16.

Generally, treatment lasts 24 to 48 hours; however, duration depends on the extent of the injury. In some cases, the injury may require a complete cessation of activities for several days to a month or more so that the tissues are given sufficient time to heal.

The displacement or separation of a bone from its normal position within a joint is referred to as a **dislocation** or a **luxation.** A partial displacement, one in which there is incomplete separation, is called a **subluxation.** A dislocation is often accompanied by damage to the ligaments. In some cases, a fracture and a dislocation can occur at the same time (Reff, 1988). In very young children, the most common sites for dislocations are the fingers, wrist, and elbow. Such injuries are often the result of the child trying to twist away from the parent's tight grip on his or her hand. In older children and young adults, the type of sport the person engages in tends to determine the site of injury. For example, dislocations of the shoulder and knee are common in those who participate in gymnastics or who play football. Dislocation of the fingers occurs more frequently in those who play ball sports, such as basketball and volleyball. Dislocation of the jaw is often found in those who engage in combative sports, such as boxing and wrestling.

First-aid treatment for a dislocation is similar to that of a fracture. At the time of the injury, the joint must be immobilized so that the person can be transported to the hospital without further injuring the joint and surrounding tissues.

❦ Deformities or Disorders of the Hip Joint

The **hip joint,** also known as the **coxal articulation,** is one of the most flexible joints of the body. It is a true ball-and-socket joint and is formed by the articulation of the head of the thighbone, or **femur,** into the hip socket, or **acetabulum.** There are seven ligaments that secure the joint, making it, in most cases, not only a relatively strong joint but a joint that permits many different types of movement, including flexion, extension, adduction, abduction, circumduction, and rotation.

Even though the hip joint is built in a manner so as to be able to support the weight of the body, it is still a vulnerable joint. Hips can be either fractured or dislocated. Contrary to the norm mentioned previously (i.e., that children are less likely to experience joint damage than adults), dislocations occur *more* commonly than fractures in children and young adults. Less force is needed in children to dislocate the hip than is needed in the adult population (Ergin, 1996). Accidental injury is not the only cause of hip problems in children. In this section, two different hip problems, one that commonly occurs at birth and one that develops over time, are described in greater detail.

Developmental Dysplasia of the Hip

Formerly known as congenital hip dislocation, **developmental dysplasia of the hip (DDH)** refers to a variety of hip abnormalities in which the femoral head is prone to slide out of the hip socket. The change in nomenclature has resulted from an awareness that, for some children, the condition is not necessarily related to a neonatal abnormality (i.e., is not truly "congenital" and may arise in later life) and that in some cases, the condition does not result in "dislocation" but rather in an unstable hip joint (Shoppee, 1992). In DDH, the term "dysplasia," generally used by medical professionals to refer to any abnormal development of a tissue or organ, is used to refer to the shallowness of the acetabular cavity, the cavity being more vertical than normal, and the ossification of the femoral epiphysis perhaps being, for unknown reasons, delayed (Dyment, 1996). This condition can affect one or both hips. The positioning of the femur in relationship to the hip socket in a normal and a dislocated hip is illustrated in Figure 15.1.

Etiology   There is no one known cause for DDH; rather, the causative factors are believed to be many: Physiologic, mechanical, genetic, and even cultural factors have all been implicated. Because it is known that DDH occurs far more often in females than males, a number of theories have been proposed. In terms of **physiologic factors,** it has been hypothesized that the condition occurs more frequently in girls because the female fetus responds differently than the male fetus to certain maternal hormones, especially maternal estrogen. If this is true, it has further been posited that it is because the female fetal uterus secretes a chemical known as **relaxin,** in response to the maternal estrogen, that results in the infant's ligaments being more lax than those found in her male counterparts (Leck, 1994). In addition

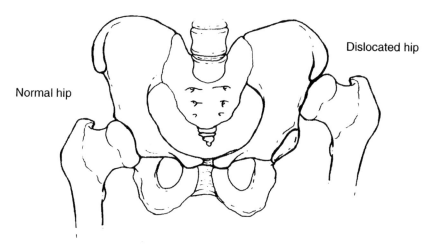

Figure 15.1
Congenital Dislocation of the Hip

to the hormone-induced joint laxity theory, certain **mechanical factors,** mostly related to space limitation in the uterus, are believed to contribute to dislocation in some children. Mechanical factors are not sex-related. The position of the fetus in utero (e.g., breech or feet-first presentation with one or both legs extended) and a small maternal uterus, often found in a woman's first pregnancy, may result in increased pressure on the fetus. Pressure may be further increased if the mother wears tight or heavy clothing during the late stages of her pregnancy. In addition, in some cases, a decrease in the amount of amniotic fluid **(oligohydramnios)** or a prolonged gestation period, which both can result in restricted fetal movement, may be contributing mechanical factors (Leck, 1994). These same mechanical factors can contribute to other physical anomalies, particularly congenital clubfoot, scoliosis, torticollis (wryneck), and lower jaw asymmetry (Leck, 1994).

However, not all children with a dislocated hip are born with the condition. In some, the condition develops postnatally, usually as a result of certain **cultural factors,** in particular certain positioning practices. For example, infants who are carried in a papoose or on a cradle board, such as Native American children, are often positioned so that their hips and legs are extended in a manner that predisposes the infant to dislocation. Similarly, infants who are tightly swaddled, for example certain European children, are more likely to show signs of hip dislocation as a result of hip extension than those who are not swaddled. In contrast, when infants are nursed in a position of flexion and abduction, for example in Africa and China, the incidence of DDH is dramatically decreased (Leck, 1994).

Older children and young adults, particularly those with cerebral palsy or spina bifida, may also have dislocated hips. In the case of those with CP, the condition is caused by unequal muscle pull that typically develops over time. As many as 25% of those with spastic CP have a subluxated hip, and between 50% and 75% of those with spastic quadriplegia, bedridden as a result of CP, have at least one dislocated hip (Nehring & Steele, 1996). In addition, individuals who have Down syndrome are also more prone to hip dislocation. In this case, the cause may be overall decreased muscle tone.

Incidence and Prevalence   DDH is believed to occur at an overall rate of 1 to 2 cases per 1,000 live births (Shoppee, 1992). As mentioned previously, the condition is far more likely to occur in females (1 in 300) than in males (1 in 2,000). Bennett and MacEwen (1989) have reported that the incidence rate of DDH is significantly higher (22 to 50 per 1,000 live births) for siblings of children who have the condition. This finding supports the hypothesis that some families may have a genetic predisposition for DDH.

Characteristics   While it would be expected that a dislocated hip in any newborn child would be detected by a formal evaluation of the stability of the hip joint (a procedure known as the **Ortolani test**), many children are not recognized as having the condition until later in infancy, when they become mobile. Limping and toe-walking to compensate for a shortened limb caused by the dislocation may be the first signs of a problem. Some children also acquire a curvature of the spine, usually a lordosis, as a result of the contraction of some of the muscles of the hip and the back of the leg.

Diagnosis and Treatment   All children who show signs of abnormal results on the Ortolani test, indicated by a "clunk" as the femoral head slides over the posterior rim of the hip socket when the physician abducts the child's leg, and all infants who are considered to be at high risk for developing DDH, even though their examination results may have been normal, should have x-ray films taken before they are 6 months of age (Dyment, 1996). Radiographs taken earlier may not be conclusive because absence of the ossification centers in the bones may make interpretation difficult. The earlier the condition is recognized, the earlier treatment can be started and, therefore, the better the outcome. For children under 6 months of age, treatment generally involves immobilizing the hip joints in the correct position (i.e., flexed and abducted) by means of a specially designed harness, known as a **Pavlik harness.** Typically, the infant wears the harness continuously for several weeks. Some children need to wear it for several months. Success rates with this type of harness are believed to be approximately 90% (Dyment, 1996). Without treatment, necrosis of the femoral head can occur.

Children older than 6 months generally cannot be treated successfully solely with the use of positioning devices. They require **traction,** a process that uses weights and pulleys to "stretch" the tissues of the joint so that at a later date, under anesthesia, the femur can be realigned (manually) with the acetabulum. This process is referred to as **closed reduction** and generally takes place after 2 to 3 weeks of traction. After surgery, the child is fitted with a spica cast that he or she must wear for 2 to 6 months to ensure that the hip remains in correct position. Full recovery, with no permanent sequelae, is typical in children who receive this form of treatment before age 3. However, if traction and reduction do not work, or if the child is diagnosed as having a dislocated hip after reaching 3 years of age, surgical intervention to correct the defect, referred to as **open reduction,** followed by casting, will be required.

However, even with surgery, there may be permanent sequelae (e.g., limited motion in the hip) that will affect the child's motoric capabilities as he or she matures (Katz, 1983). The older the child at the time of surgery, the poorer the prognosis. In adolescents and young adults, surgery is usually considered only if the individual is experiencing constant pain.

Legg-Calvé-Perthes Disease

Also referred to as Perthes disease, Legg-Perthes disease, osteochondritis deformans juvenilis, and coxa plana, **Legg-Calvé-Perthes disease (LCPD)** is a disorder of the proximal femoral head that occurs most often in male children between the ages of 4 and 8. This condition was named after three physicians: Arthur Legg from the United States, Jacques Calvé from France, and Georg Perthes from Germany, who simultaneously but independently described, in 1910, a specific hip condition that they thought was a form of arthritis (Heller, Alberto, Forney, & Schwartzman, 1996). More recently, it has been established that the condition is not, in fact, an arthritic condition but a circulatory problem.

Etiology   In this disease, the blood supply to the epiphysis of the upper thighbone is interrupted, resulting in fragmentation of the femoral head and necrosis of the bone tissues (Figure 15.2). However, the exact cause of the disruption is unknown. It is known that there is a familial predisposition to LCPD. Low birth weight (less than 5.5 pounds, or 2.5 kg) and retarded bone age (as evidenced by short stature for age) are also common to those who have the condition. It is more common in white children than in other racial groups (Dyment, 1996).

Incidence and Prevalence   The exact rate of occurrence of LCPD is unknown. Reported estimates range from 1 in 9,000 (Heller et al., 1996) to 1 in 20,000 (Dyment, 1996). The male-to-female ratio is 4:1, and peak incidence occurs at age 6 (Boos et al., 1993). In 86% of cases, only one hip is affected; however, the condition occurs bilaterally in 14% of all cases. The bilateral condition may occur concomitantly or serially.

Characteristics   The symptoms are usually insidious. In many cases, the child increasingly complains of pain in the hip, groin, thigh, or knee; has limited ability to move the hip joint; and develops a

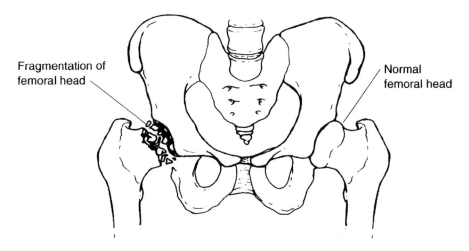

Fragmentation of femoral head

Normal femoral head

Figure 15.2
Fragmentation of the Femoral Head

noticeable limp. Some children, however, may limp without any complaint of pain. The symptoms result from the development of acute synovitis in the hip joint. Often, the swelling subsides and the pain in the joint disappears with rest.

Diagnosis and Treatment Legg-Calvé-Perthes disease is often suspected in children between the ages of 4 and 8, particularly in boys, when there is a history of pain in the hip or knee, or both, and there is evidence of an **antalgic gait** (i.e., the child takes a quick step to shorten the time of weight-bearing on the affected leg or hip). Other diagnostic signs include limited abduction of the leg away from the body, an inability to rotate the leg inward toward the body, atrophy of the thigh or calf muscles, and shortened leg length caused by the flattening of the femoral head (Dyment, 1996). However, diagnosis is not always easily accomplished because the presenting symptoms may be similar to a number of other conditions (e.g., a fracture). The condition is confirmed by a number of tests, including x-ray studies to examine the bone structure, analysis of synovial fluid to rule out any type of infectious condition that may result in similar symptoms, and blood tests to determine whether the cause could be hematologic.

Legg-Calvé-Perthes disease is considered a **self-limited** disease, which means that there is no known treatment to halt its progression and the condition resolves on its own after a limited period of time. Typ-ically, 2 to 4 years after onset, blood supply returns to the head of the femur and the dead tissue is replaced by living bone. In some cases, the disease may be present for up to 8 years before coming to an end (Howe & Coffman, 1990). Even though the condition is known to heal spontaneously, bed rest, with or without traction, is generally recommended in the early stages to decrease the swelling and alleviate the pain. After a week or more in bed, the child is usually fitted with a brace that, by means of a bar positioned at ankle or knee level, keeps the legs spread far apart. The purpose of the brace is to keep the femoral head in the hip socket in proper alignment until the dead bone is reabsorbed and new bone is formed. In this manner, the acetabulum acts as a "mold" for the femoral head. Without bracing, the new femoral head might grow flat and wide rather than round and small, as it had been originally before destruction (Katz, 1983). Typical braces are shown in Figure 15.3. Generally, the child must wear the device for 18 months to 2 years, removing it only for the purpose of bathing. In severe cases, the child may require surgery to insert pins to hold the bone in position, followed by casting or bracing. A second operation is then needed to remove the pins.

Prognosis is primarily dependent on the age of the child at the onset of the condition. Younger children often achieve complete recovery; older children may have some residual effects that remain throughout life. Osteoarthritis is very common in adults who had LCPD in their early years.

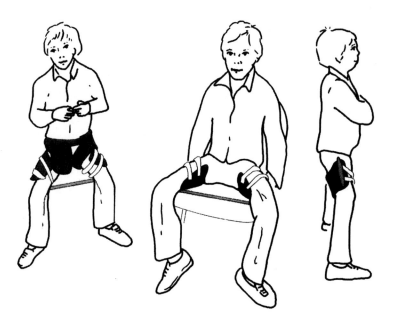

Figure 15.3
Braces Used to Treat Legg-Calvé-Perthes Disease

🍒 Educational Implications and Teaching Tips: Students with Hip Disorders

Many children with hip disorders have an excellent recovery, particularly if the problem is caught in its beginning stages and treatment is started without delay. In fact, it is not uncommon for many children with hip anomalies, in particular those with a congenital problem, to attend school without staff even knowing that there has been a problem in the past. However, since a number of hip problems can develop once the child has entered school, staff should be alert to any signs of a problem. In some cases, it will be teaching staff, especially physical education teachers, who may be the first to suspect a problem (e.g., notice the child limping). In other cases, it may be the school nurse who detects the impairment (e.g., the child turns to the nurse to discuss pain in the hip, thigh, or knee region). The child's parents must be contacted immediately so that the child can be seen by his or her physician.

1 *Resolution of hip problems takes time.* Many children will be out of school for weeks or even months. During that period, the student's educational program should be continued (through home tutoring) and the student should remain a participating member of the class (e.g., through e-mail, videotapes). Many students who are being treated for hip problems may experience some degree of pain when they return to school. Teachers should be aware that pain, and the medication that the student may be taking, may interfere with the student's ability to concentrate. If the pain seems to be too severe, i.e., not adequately resolved by rest or medication, staff should contact the family so that they can address proper pain management with the physician.

2 *Students with Legg-Calvé-Perthes disease return to school wearing a brace.* Even though the brace appears very awkward, most children learn to navigate around their environment with relative ease, in some cases with the assistance of crutches or a wheelchair. Stairs may pose a difficulty if the student's classroom is not on the main floor. Students should be permitted to use the elevator if necessary. Special attention may be required for outings away from the school, particularly since accessible transportation may be difficult to arrange. Because of the awkwardness of braces, the student may need assistance in toileting. However, for the rest of the day the child will probably not need much help, except, perhaps, when putting on pants or shoes.

Physical activities may need to be curtailed because running and jumping are impossible. The student should, however, be encouraged to continue to work his or her upper body (e.g., throwing darts, weight lifting). The student's physician should be contacted to determine what activities are appropriate during the treatment stage. Forms for this purpose are found in Appendix D.

3 *For the younger child, particularly the child who has been very active up until this point, the bracing program places major restrictions on life.* For such students, compliance may be problematic. It is not uncommon for children to remove the braces when not being closely supervised. Teachers are often asked to monitor the student and should be aware of how the brace is worn and the wearing schedule. By planning alternative activities that appeal to the student and that also keep the student occupied while others are engaging in physical activities, compliance may become less of an issue. If the student continues to be noncompliant, school staff should turn to the parents or the medical team for suggestions on how to deal with the problem.

❦ Generalized Disorders of the Articulating Structures

Inflammation of connective tissue of the joints, commonly referred to as **arthritis,** occurs very frequently in adults. In fact, an estimated 50 million people in the United States alone are affected by the condition, 4 million of them so seriously that they are dependent on others for their care (Spray, 1991). There are several different forms of arthritis found in adults, the most common being the following: (a) **rheumatoid arthritis,** a condition that not only can affect all of the joints of the body but also can involve many of the organ systems, including the lungs, heart, blood vessels, muscles, eyes, and skin; (b) **ankylosing spondylitis,** a condition in which certain bones of the body fuse together, occurring most often in the hip and spine, but also·in the neck, jaw, shoulders, and knees; (c) **osteoarthritis,** the form of arthritis believed to be related to aging, seen primarily in the hand, knee, hip, and cervical or lumbar vertebrae; and (d) **gouty arthritis,** a metabolic disease that results from the accumulation of uric acid in the blood and results in the formation of uric acid crystals in the synovial tissues of certain joints, most commonly the big toe. In the pediatric population, the most common inflammatory condition is **juvenile rheumatoid arthritis.**

Juvenile Rheumatoid Arthritis

Also referred to as juvenile chronic arthritis (JCA) or juvenile chronic polyarthritis (JCP), **juvenile rheumatoid arthritis (JRA)** is a chronic, idiopathic, inflammatory disease of the connective tissue that develops in children and young adults, typically before the age of 16. Because JRA differs in many aspects from the adult form of rheumatoid arthritis,[2] many in the medical profession, particularly in Europe, are now referring to the condition simply as **juvenile arthritis** (JA). However, the diagnostic term "juvenile rheumatoid arthritis" is the official term of the American College of Rheumatology and the one most widely used in the United States (McIlvain-Simpson, 1996).

The arthritic changes result from the inflammation of the synovial membranes and the joint capsule and the increased production of synovial fluids, which seep into the joint (i.e., joint effusion) (Figure 15.4). The chronic inflammation in the joints eventually leads to the destruction of the articular cartilage and the adjacent structures (Hartley & Fuller, 1997). Typically, the condition is marked by periods of remission and exacerbation. Even though, in comparison to adults, a longer period of inflammation is required in children before permanent damage occurs, up to one-third of all children are at risk for permanent disability and need aggressive medical intervention (Szer, 1996).

Etiology While there is disagreement in the medical literature as to the causative agent of JRA, in most cases the inciting agent is simply unknown (Whaley & Wong, 1991). Even though the condition occurs without a known cause (i.e., idiopathically), several mechanisms have been suggested, including infection by some type of unidentified

---

[2] The major difference is that in the adult form, an antibody known as **rheumatoid factor** is found in the blood of 70% or more of cases, but in children, it is only found in a few cases, most commonly those in whom the disease develops later in childhood.

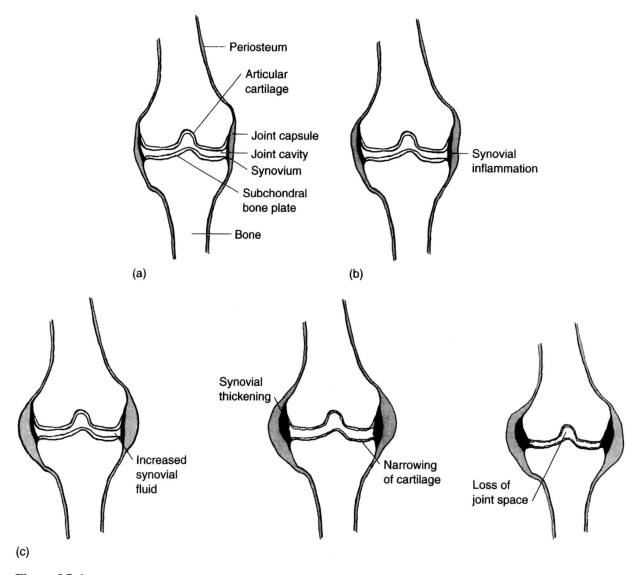

Figure 15.4
Arthritic Changes in Joint Structure in Juvenile Rheumatoid Arthritis: (a) normal diarthrodial joint; (b) early synovitis; (c) progressive destruction of inflamed joint.

microorganism, autoimmunity, genetic predisposition, stress, and trauma (McIlvain-Simpson, 1996).

Incidence and Prevalence   The exact incidence of JRA is also unknown. Singsen (1990) cited a number of studies in which the incidence rate ranged from 12 to 113 children per 100,000; however, more recently, Cassidy and Petty (1995) indicated that the incidence was less, from 9.2 to 13.9 children per 100,000. JRA is known to be more common in females than males and is slightly more common in white children than in Asian- or African-American

children, (Harkins, 1994). JRA accounts for 5% of all arthritis cases, young and old (Hughes, 1993). While it is rare to see the condition in more than one child in a family (Sanford, 1993), cases have been reported in the medical literature (cf. Hartley & Fuller, 1997).

Types and Characteristics   In children with JRA, the affected joints are stiff, swollen, and warm to the touch. In many cases, they are also tender and painful; however, in others, there is relatively little pain, particularly in the early stages of the disease.

Age at onset of JRA is usually between 2 and 12, with two peaks, i.e., between ages 2 and 5 and between ages 9 and 12 (Whaley & Wong, 1995). In some children, the onset is insidious and not recognized until the disease has progressed over time (e.g., the child begins to walk with a limp or to hold the arm in close to the body). In others, the onset may be marked by a sudden joint swelling, often mistaken for a traumatic injury (Harkins, 1994).

Many children with JRA show signs of growth retardation; however, the reason for their short stature is unknown. It has been hypothesized that the anorexia often associated with the disease may result in the child not growing at the same rate as his or her peers; other theories suggest that the inflammatory process may affect the epiphyses, resulting in either an overgrowth or undergrowth of certain limbs (Hartley & Fuller, 1997). If the child's jaw is underdeveloped, he or she is described as having **micrognathia.** Children with this condition experience pain and tenderness in the facial area. Between 20% and 30% of children with JRA develop feeding problems as a result of maldevelopment of the teeth, having difficulty swallowing, and being unable to open the mouth normally (McIlvain-Simpson, 1996).

In approximately 25% of all cases, the joints become permanently deformed as a result of a number of factors, including the overgrowth or undergrowth of the bones adjacent to the affected joint. In the remaining 75%, the overall prognosis is generally good; i.e., the children do not suffer permanent joint damage. In mild cases, the condition often appears to "burn itself out" after 2 to 3 years after the onset; in more severe cases, remission may occur 8 to 10 years after the initial symptoms are noticed (Whaley & Wong, 1995). While some children will continue to show signs of the disease into adulthood, in 70% to 90% of all cases, remission occurs with the onset of puberty (McIlvain-Simpson, 1996).

There are three different types of JRA: pauciarticular-onset, systemic-onset, and polyarticular-onset arthritis. The classification is determined by the manifestations of the condition during the first 6 months that the child has the obvious signs of the disease (Harkins, 1994). Each of the major types is described briefly below, in order of highest to lowest prevalence.

Pauciarticular-onset JRA. The most common form of JRA is pauciarticular-onset JRA, which accounts for as many as 40% to 50% of all cases. The prefix "pauci" refers to a paucity or limited number of joints involved; if less than five joints are involved when the condition is first recognized, the diagnosis of pauciarticular-onset JRA is made. Pauciarticular JRA is also known as **oligoarthritis,** the prefix "oligo" meaning "few" or "little."

In this form of JRA, the arthritic symptoms, on the whole, are mild and are confined to the joints alone; i.e., there are no systemic (generalized) symptoms (Sanford, 1993). The large joints of the lower extremities, such as the knees and ankles, are most frequently involved; however, in some cases the wrist or elbow joint may be affected. In many cases the distribution of joints is asymmetrical; e.g., a child may have swelling in the right knee and left ankle but not in the left knee or right ankle. In approximately 50% of the cases, only one joint is involved (Hughes, 1993). About 25% of children with pauciarticular-onset JRA will develop the condition in five or more joints and consequently will resemble children with polyarticular-onset JRA (Hanson, 1983). The most typical symptom is stiffness in the morning, which decreases in severity as the day progresses.

Pauciarticular-onset JRA can be further subdivided into two subgroups. The first type affects girls under the age of 4 (peak, age 2). In 75% to 85% of the females with this form of the disease, **antinuclear antibodies (ANA)** are present in the blood. Antinuclear antibodies react with nuclear material in the cells and are detected by means of immunofluorescent assay techniques. In this condition, primarily the large joints are affected (knees, ankles, elbows); however, in some cases, smaller joints (fingers, toes, jaw) can become inflamed. Children in this group are most likely to develop **iridocyclitis,** a chronic inflammatory condition of the iris and ciliary body of the eyes, also known as **uveitis.** The condition develops simultaneously in both eyes. Typical symptoms include loss of visual acuity, photosensitivity (increased sensitivity to light), and pain. Iridocyclitis may also contribute to the formation of cataracts (i.e., cloudiness in the lens) and the onset of glaucoma (i.e., a condition in which the pressure in the eye becomes elevated). Uveitis develops in between 2% and 20% of all children with JRA. In 15% to 30% of all cases, functional blindness occurs as a result of the eye involvement (McIlvain-Simpson, 1996).

Those in the second group are older. Peak age at onset is 8 years, and most of the cases are males. As in the first group, the large joints of the lower extremities, including the hip and girdle area, are most affected. The boys in this group have the **human leukocyte antigen B (HLA-B)**, in particular HLA-B27 on chromosome 6, which can be detected by testing white blood cells. This antigen is also found in those who have ankylosing spondylitis, and in fact, many boys with this form of JRA develop back problems, in particular a forward flexion of the spine (i.e.,"poker spine").

Both males and females with pauciarticular arthritis are predisposed to developing a sensorineural hearing loss. This type of loss is caused by problems in the inner ear or auditory nerve and results in the inability to hear sounds of certain frequencies, most often high-pitched sounds.

Systemic-onset JRA. The second most common type of JRA is systemic-onset JRA, evident in approximately 25% to 30% of individuals with JRA. In this form of the disease, also known as **Still disease** after the English pediatrician who first described it, joints located anywhere in the body, including the cervical spine, may be affected. The term "systemic" refers to the fact that the whole body is affected by the inflammatory condition, rather than just one or more joints. Common symptoms of systemic involvement include enlargement of the liver and spleen or involvement of the lymph nodes and lymph vessels and inflammation of the pleurae of the lungs or of the pericardium.

In systemic-onset JRA, the first symptom is often a recurrent high fever, over 104°F (40°C), which typically occurs once or twice a day, usually in the late afternoon or evening. During the fever, the child appears to be quite ill; when the temperature is back to normal or subnormal, e.g., in the morning, the child may appear to be quite healthy. Along with the fever, a salmon-colored nonpruritic (nonitchy) rash may develop on the trunk and the extremities. Usually the face does not show signs of outbreak. There may also be loss of appetite and subsequent weight loss in the early stages (James, 1990). The joint involvement may be evident right from the beginning; in some cases, however, the joints are normal for several months or even years, making diagnosis extremely difficult.

Systemic-onset JRA usually occurs when the child is around age 10 and is slightly more common in girls than boys. For many of the children the prognosis is good; however, polyarticular-onset arthritis may develop in approximately half of the children during the first few months of the disease (Howe &

Coffman, 1990; Miller, 1982). Half of these children recover with no major sequelae; half have intermittent exacerbations and will have joint deformities.

Polyarticular-onset JRA. The final type of arthritis, polyarticular-onset JRA, occurs less frequently than the other two types—approximately 20% to 30% of all cases. In polyarticular-onset JRA, five or more synovial joints of the body, usually in the wrists, hands, fingers, knees, ankles, elbows, neck, or feet, are involved simultaneously. Usually there is the same involvement on both sides of the body; e.g., the small joints of the fingers of both the right and left hand might be affected at the same time or both knees might be affected simultaneously (Grove, Cusick, & Bigge, 1991). It is rare to find the joints of the lumbodorsal spine affected (Howe & Coffman, 1990), and few systemic features are evident in the children (Sanford, 1993). Stiffness is generally worse after a night in bed or after sitting for long periods during the day, a characteristic that is often referred to as the **gel phenomenon** (James, 1990). Polyarticular-onset JRA tends to last longer, can be more painful, and may be more crippling than the other two forms; however, remission does occur in approximately 25% of the cases (Whaley & Wong, 1995). Onset is usually after age 10, and twice as many girls are affected as boys.

Diagnosis and Treatment As suggested above, diagnosis may be difficult in some cases, since not all who have JRA show the same characteristics. In many cases, it is difficult to determine whether it is arthritis or some other disease that is marked by joint problems, such as Legg-Calvé-Perthes disease, hemophilia, sickle cell anemia, or leukemia. Unfortunately, there is no one laboratory test that will confirm the presence of the inflammatory condition. However, the results of certain blood tests (e.g., elevated erythrocyte sedimentation rate, presence of ANA, presence of rheumatoid factor) may suggest that arthritis is the cause of the joint difficulties or may rule out other conditions. Other tests that may be used for diagnostic purposes include x-ray films and synovial fluid analysis.

Treatment of all forms of JRA is geared towards reducing the inflammatory process; maintaining or preserving joint position, function, and strength; preventing physical deformity; promoting normal growth and development; relieving the symptoms associated with the active disease; relieving stress (as the disease often is heightened in times of high stress); and supporting the child and family in their ability to cope with a chronic illness (Harkins, 1994; Hughes, 1993; Ludwig & Beam, 1992; Whaley & Wong, 1995). The most common form of treatment involves the administration of drugs to inhibit the inflammatory process and to provide relief from pain. The nature and the severity of the condition determine which drugs are administered (Szer, 1996). First-line agents are **nonsteroidal antiinflammatory drugs (NSAIDs),** such as ibuprofen (Advil, Motrin, Nuprin) and naproxen (Naprosyn Anaprox). In the past, children with JRA were given salicylates, such as acetylsalicylate acid (asprin); however, since this drug must be given more frequently than other NSAIDs and because it has been associated with Reye's syndrome, it is being prescribed less often (McIlvain-Simpson, 1996). If the child does not respond well to NSAIDs or is at risk for developing deformities, the second line of agents, **sloweracting antirheumatic drugs (SAARDs),** also known as **disease-modifying antirheumatic drugs (DMADs),** such as Azulfidine, Rheumatrex, or Plaquenil, and injectable gold salts (Myochrysine or Solganal) are administered. Third-line agents, **immunosuppressive drugs,** such as Leukeran and Imuran, are given to those children whose joints are severely damaged or who have been unresponsive to the first types of drugs. If the child experiences eye problems, medication is administered, in particular **ophthalmic corticosteroids,** such as Dexasporin. All of these drugs have specific side effects, the most common being gastrointestinal irritation, rashes, and abdominal pain; consequently, children need to be carefully monitored.

As long as the child is being treated with drugs, the arthritic condition is considered to be active. After a period of 12 months without any symptoms of active disease, the last 6 months of which must be after cessation of all medication, the disease is said to be in remission (McIlvain-Simpson, 1996). Approximately 75% of all children have remissions; however, in some cases, the condition returns to an active state in adulthood (Heller et al., 1996). Some of those in remission have residual problems, such as decreased range of motion due to contractures or decreased visual acuity resulting from cataracts.

In addition to pharmacologic therapy, physical therapy, often in conjunction with occupational therapy, is often prescribed to strengthen muscles, to decrease the immobilization of the joints and thereby increase the range of motion, to prevent or correct deformities of the joints, to control pain, and to improve the ability to perform activities of daily living, including ambulation (Harkins, 1994; Whaley & Wong, 1995). In some cases, splinting of the joints (e.g., knees, wrists, hands) is recommended in an attempt to prevent or reduce the development of contractures. Splints also function to minimize pain by supporting the joints in the correct alignment. In older children, after the child has reached skeletal maturity, joint replacement surgery may be undertaken to correct any obvious deformities.

Educational Implications and Teaching Tips: Students with Juvenile Rheumatoid Arthritis

Juvenile rheumatoid arthritis affects all aspects of the child's life. Tasks as simple as combing hair, brushing teeth, and cutting food may be painful for some and impossible for others. It has been reported in the medical literature that it is not uncommon to see a change in personality in children with JRA as well as the development of temporary or permanent maladaptive behaviors (e.g., hostility, irritability, uncommunicativeness) as the child struggles to come to grips with the condition (Whaley & Wong, 1991). However, other authors have suggested that "positive adaptation is more the rule than the exception and that, in fact, children with JRA are as emotionally healthy as their physically normal peers" (Hanson, 1983, p. 246).

School staff should focus on the child's abilities rather than on the limitations imposed by the condition and should encourage the child to participate as fully as possible (by assigning appropriate chores and responsibilities) so that a sense of normality, acceptance, and accomplishment is developed (Harkins, 1994). An understanding and caring teacher—one who recognizes the fluctuations in the disease, encourages a positive attitude, fosters understanding and acceptance by the student's peers, encourages the student to share thoughts and feelings about the disease, and advises the student to take each day as it comes—is extremely beneficial to the student who has to cope with the limitations of the condition. The same child does not benefit from being given preferential treatment inappropriately or from having a teacher who is overprotective or who has low expectations (Arthreya & Ingall, 1984; Spencer, Zanga, Passo, & Walker, 1986).

In a study published in 1987, Taylor, Passo, and Champion attempted to answer two questions: (1) What school-related problems do children with JRA, their parents, and their teachers perceive as occurring most frequently? and (2) To what extent do children, parents, and teachers view the resolution of these problems as the responsibility of the child's teachers? (p. 186). The areas that were rated as the responsibility of the child's teacher are shown in Table 15.2.

For the teacher of a student with juvenile rheumatoid arthritis, the following additional suggestions may be of assistance:

1 *Symptoms of JRA fluctuate widely from morning to afternoon, from day to day, week to week, and even month to month* (Hanson, 1983). However, all children and young adults with JRA should be encouraged to attend school as much as possible, even if they are in discomfort. It is not uncommon to hear a student complaining of pain and to observe his or her movements as being stiff and slow in the morning, and then to see that same student move about much more freely (even running) and with much less discomfort later in the day, without any form of intervention in between (Hanson, 1983). Teachers, however, should also be alert to those who "push" themselves too hard, especially students whose disease is in remission, to "keep up

TABLE 15.2
Areas Rated as the Responsibility of the Child's Teacher

Respondent Group	Teacher Responsibility[a]	Mean Rating[b]
CHILDREN	Serve as liaison between school and hospital	3.67
	Observe and assess progress in school	3.46
	Withhold information about diagnosis from other students	3.42
	Develop supportive relationship with student	3.33
	Develop supportive relationship with parents	3.29[c]
PARENTS	Help student develop a positive self-attitude	4.13[c]
	Have basic knowledge of JRA	4.08[c]
	Encourage student to continue peer interaction	3.96[c]
	Help student cope with teasing about arthritis	3.96[c]
TEACHERS	Encourage student to continue peer interaction	4.64[c]
	Help student develop a positive self-attitude	4.50[c]
	Develop supportive relationship with parents	4.43[c]
	Observe and assess progress in school	4.36
	Have basic knowledge of JRA	4.29[c]

[a] Five items with highest ratings by children and teachers with respect to the extent of the teacher's responsibility (taken from a list of 28 teacher responsibilities). Only four items are depicted for parents since four other items received the fifth highest mean rating.
[b] Possible range: 1–5
[c] Significant between-groups difference ($p < .05$).
Source: Taylor, J., Passo, M. H., & Champion, V. L. (1987). School problems and teacher responsibilities in juvenile rheumatoid arthritis. *Journal of School Health, 57,* 186–190. Copyright 1987 by the American School Health Association, Kent, Ohio. Reprinted by permission.

with the crowd," thereby neglecting the need for extra rest (Harkins, 1994).

2 *Some students may benefit from being allowed to come to school later in the day, thereby allowing them time at home during which they can gain maximum joint movement.* For example, a student could come to school midmorning, after taking a warm bath, having a hot pack applied to the painful joints, or doing limbering-up exercises. Others may benefit from a shortened school day, returning home in the afternoon to receive treatment. Generally, the best times for a person with JRA are from midmorning to early afternoon; consequently, the most demanding classes should be scheduled during this period and the less demanding classes at the beginning and end of the day (Arthreya & Ingall, 1984). For some, attendance can be facilitated by the use of a school bus or taxi to transport the students to and from school, provided that the bus ride is not excessive in length.

Fatigue can be a problem because children and young adults with active JRA often have periods of wakefulness in the night. Students should have access to a quiet place, such as the nurse's office, to lie down for a rest period, if required. Having an electric blanket to provide warmth may be beneficial.

3 *Those who have lower limb involvement often "stiffen up" after prolonged periods of sitting, e.g., in class or at scheduled events held in the auditorium.* They should be encouraged to stand up or move around every 20 to 30 minutes to loosen up the joints (Hanson, 1983). For some, being designated the class messenger or the person who hands out or collects papers for the teacher allows the student to get the needed exercise without attracting undue attention to the disability (Arthreya & Ingall, 1984). Students should be given ample time to move from class to class; however, if possible, the distances should not be too great.

Some students, particularly those with arthritis in the hip region, may benefit from being able to stand for short periods, as a change from sitting down, while doing their work. A drafting table that can be adjusted easily from a low to a high position is the perfect work station for such a student because his or her trunk is then extended rather than flexed (Scull, Dow, & Arthreya, 1986). Fifteen to

20 minutes of standing may be appropriate for some; others may not be able to work for that long in an upright position. Having a foot stool while sitting to allow for extension of the knees may be beneficial for some students (Hartley & Fuller, 1997).

Toileting may be a problem at school. Some students have difficulty transferring on or off the seat, managing toilet paper, and dressing and undressing (McIlvain-Simpson, 1996). Safety bars for transfer and elevated toilet seats may be of help; however, some students need the assistance of a staff person. School staff should contact the student's occupational or physical therapist for suggestions regarding possible aids and devices that may assist the performance of acts of daily living.

4 *For youngsters whose arms and hands are involved, having a locker close to the classroom may prevent them from having to carry their books great distances.* Book bags may be useful for some; others may find luggage carriers helpful if they have to carry excessive loads. If possible, students should be given two sets of texts, so that they do not have to carry books to and from school to complete their homework.

Similarly, at meal times, carrying heavy trays in the cafeteria may pose a problem. In some cases, the student may be able to carry food (if the load is not too heavy) by balancing the tray on the forearms and only using the hands to secure it from sliding. If this is not possible, a staff person may need to provide the extra assistance needed.

Students with hand or wrist involvement may be able to take notes if they have an extra large pencil, a "fat" felt marker, or a pen with a built-up area to hold onto. Some students are able to use a computer to take notes and to write tests; others may require someone else to take notes. The use of NCR paper (no carbon required) can provide the student with someone else's notes with no added work. Allowing the student to photocopy a classmate's notes, if a photocopier is available, is another option; however, tape-recording lectures is generally not a useful suggestion, because the student will need to review the tapes at a later date and still needs to take notes to study for examinations or tests. During examination periods, when the student is required to write for a prolonged time, the test could instead be given orally, or the child could dictate answers on a tape recorder or to a scribe. For those who are able to write their answers, giving them extra time to have the necessary rest breaks and to stretch their limbs and joints may be a suitable accommodation (Arthreya & Ingall, 1984). Students with upper arm involvement may also have difficulty raising their hands to answer a question, and some children may find writing on the blackboard laborious (Ludwig & Beam, 1992).

5 *Students should be allowed to take any medication that is prescribed for them during school hours, if needed.* Students who are old enough should be allowed to self-medicate. Young students will need assistance from school staff. Teachers should be aware of the types of medication the student takes, its side effects, and when and how it should be taken (e.g., with food or without food). School staff should ensure that the child's physician completes a Medication Authorization Form, found in Appendix D.

Students who are self-conscious about taking pills during school hours, or those who are teased by their peers for having to take medicine, should be allowed to leave the classroom if necessary. The teacher can assist by planning a way for the student to leave the room inconspicuously. Sending a child on an errand is an appropriate tactic (Arthreya & Ingall, 1984).

6 *Staff should be alert to any signs of medication side effects.* Ringing in the ears, headaches, nosebleeds, dizziness, confusion, drowsiness, and irritation of the stomach can occur with high dosages of NSAIDs. Photosensitive skin reactions may occur if the child is taking drugs such as Naprosyn, Rheumatrex, Azulfidine, or Plaquenil. Children on these drugs should wear a hypoallergenic sunscreen lotion with a minimum sun protection factor (SPF) of 15 (McIlvain-Simpson, 1996). Children who are on immunosuppressant drugs should be encouraged to wear a Medic-Alert bracelet.

7 *Teachers should be alert to any signs of vision or hearing loss and immediately report any concerns to the parents.* Children with iridocyclitis often use prescription eye drops. The drops, unfortunately, while helping to control the disease, further impair ability to read the blackboard or the fine print in books. Consultation with the teacher who works with children with visual problems may be appropriate; the student with JRA may benefit from books on tape or large-print materials. Similarly, if the student develops a hearing loss, the teacher should seek assistance from a teacher who works with those who are hearing-impaired for additional suggestions on how to accommodate a student with a hearing loss in the classroom.

8 *Even with the administration of pain relievers, most children with JRA suffer from chronic pain.* For some, the pain is continual and can even rob them of their required sleep, making them chronically fatigued. For others, the pain is intermittent, coming unexpectedly, often after they have "pushed" themselves too hard. Even with the tiredness, children with JRA should be encouraged to participate in a program of physical activity because prolonged sitting, e.g., while reading or watching TV, may result in a further weakening of the muscles and the development of contractures (Harkins, 1994).

9 *Diet is important to persons with JRA.* Some children and young adults become quite anorexic; however, at the same time, they need high-calorie meals to offset their increased metabolic needs. Some students benefit from being allowed appropriate snacks throughout the school day. Calorie-rich supplements, such as Boost or Ensure, may be enjoyed by the student. However, for some students, the high-calorie diet, in conjunction with a lifestye that is rather sedentary, may result in weight gain. In those with JRA, obesity can be a major problem, as the extra weight stresses the already inflamed joints, particularly those in the lower limbs (Whaley & Wong, 1995). If the student eats at school, the school dietitian can assist by providing appropriate foods. The school nurse may be able to provide nutritional counseling.

10 *A "formal exercise program that takes all areas of the body through maximum active range of motion is essential to maintain function"* (Harkins, 1994, p. 1597), *and teachers, both general classroom teachers and physical education teachers,* *working in conjunction with physical and occupational therapists, should attempt to develop such a program.* For the younger child, activities such as imitating the slow, controlled movements of birds and animals, kicking a balloon or soft beach ball, riding a tricycle or bicycle, playing with clay or Play-Dough, and noncompetitive swimming may be appropriate; for the older child or young adult, t'ai-chi has been found to be useful when joints are not inflamed or painful (Harkins, 1994). Swimming and ballet, which permit total body movement, are excellent forms of exercise for some individuals, whereas bicycling, which permits movement of the leg muscles, and catching soft balls, which develops strength in the arms, may be appropriate for others (Scull et al., 1986). Playing the piano is also an excellent exercise for the arms, wrists, and fingers.

11 *It is normally recommended that persons with arthritis avoid activities that involve a twisting or jarring motion that stresses the joints (e.g., jogging, jumping, lifting), because such activities may exacerbate or restart the inflammatory process* (Ludwig & Beam, 1992; Miller, 1982). During physical education classes, activities that stress maximum performance or endurance should, in general, be avoided. However, the degree of restriction depends on the current status of the illness and the specific joints involved. For example, a student with upper limb involvement should not participate in activities such as handstands, cartwheels, chin-ups, and push-ups, whereas students with lower limb involvement should be restricted from doing repeated knee-bends, running relay races, and playing dodge ball. Those with lower limb problems should also be discouraged from sitting cross-legged.

The student with JRA knows best what level of activity is appropriate, and school staff need to respect the student's signals regarding pain or fatigue (Scull et al., 1986). In periods of exacerbation, rather than participating in a particular game, it might be more appropriate for the student to keep score or to function as the timekeeper or as the umpire (Hanson, 1983). Takei and Hokonohara (1993) have developed an "exercise grid" (Table 15.3) that may be of assistance in determining exercises that are or are not appropriate. Input from the student's physician should also be obtained. Forms in Appendix D can be used for this purpose.

If, after exercise, the joints are swollen and painful, applying an ice pack to the muscles for 15 to 20 minutes may be therapeutic, particularly in situations in which the student's muscles are in spasm. Others may find heat to be more beneficial. Heating wet towels in the microwave for 15 to 30 seconds and then applying for 15 to 20 minutes may loosen a stiff muscle (Hartley & Fuller, 1997).

12 *Some children and young adults with JRA spike a mild fever and develop a rash when the inflammatory process is active.* However, the rise in temperature or nonitchy skin condition should not keep the student out of school, because such symptoms are not indicative of a contagious condition (Hanson, 1983). Most often the fever increases in the afternoon. During this time it is probably best that the student engage in activities that are not too physically demanding. Students should be dressed warmly if they are outside on a cold day, particularly if they have a fever.

13 *Even with good medical treatment, students with JRA miss, on average, 1.4 days of school per month* (Spencer et al., 1986). If the child misses more than 3 days at a time, the parents should contact the pediatrician (perhaps with encouragement from school staff) because the treatment program may need to be changed. School staff (and parents) should be alert to those students who "use" their condition to get increased attention, to gain control or to avoid difficult situations at school.

14 *Since many persons with JRA experience remission in adulthood, they should be encouraged to participate to the maximum extent possible in all school activities and to pursue academic and career goals that are commensurate with their intellectual ability.* It is tragic for children with JRA "to overcome a serious illness only to be faced with overcoming educational deficits that have accumulated during the years of illness" (Arthreya & Ingall, 1984, p. 102). If the students miss school during periods in which the illness is exacerbated, or if they only attend school on a part-time basis, they should be encouraged to keep up with the regular assignments at home so that they do not fall behind their classmates.

TABLE 15.3
Classification of Physical Education Exercise for Children with JRA

		UPPER LIMBS		
		Light Exercise	**Moderate Exercise**	**Heavy Exercise**
LOWER LIMBS	**Light Exercise**	Gymnastic exercise (upper body) Jungle gym Swedish bars Slide Seesaw Balance beam Rhythmic walking	Grabbing sticks Rolling a ball	Monkey bars Push-ups
	Moderate Exercise	Gymnastic exercise (lower body) Swing Tag Elastic rope jumping Kick ball Exercise using rings Walking in water pool	Various kinds of walking, running, and jumping Rope skipping Hurdle Track relay Picking up stones in water Dodgeball	Horizontal bar Mat exercise Pommel horse
	Heavy Exercise	Tag hopping on one leg Light jogging Soccer Jumping rope Rhythmic running or jumping	Fast running Distance race Track relay Water tag Portball	Complete body exercise Varied: rope skipping, horizontal bar, swimming, and pommel horse Pole climbing Sprinting Hurdle Softball Tennis Marathon Soccer Basketball Baseball Sumo wrestling

Source: Takei, S., & Hokonohara, M. (1993). Quality of life and daily management of children with rheumatic disease. *Acta Paediatrica Japonica, 35,* 454–463. Copyright 1993 by Blackwell Science Asia. Reprinted by permission.

The same standards should be imposed on students with JRA as are imposed on their classmates. Interestingly, Shear (1984, cited in Spencer et al., 1986) reported that a greater percentage of children with arthritis graduated from high school, college, and graduate school compared to the able-bodied peer group. Spencer and his colleagues have suggested that this finding resulted, in part, from the fact that the students with arthritis were unable to participate in some extracurricular activities (e.g., sports) and therefore may have given more of their energy to academic endeavors than social ones. Vocational counseling that is realistic and positive should be made available to students with JRA (Spencer et al., 1986) long before graduation.

🐾 Summary

Children and young adults who have problems with their body's articulating structure have difficulty primarily in accessing their environment. Children with joint problems often need assistance to continue with all the normal activities of daily living. Articulation problems can affect either a single joint or many joints throughout the body. Teachers of children who have joint problems can be of great assistance in helping them cope with their disease and in encouraging them to have a positive outlook. Most children and young adults with joint problems should be able to benefit from attending school alongside their peers and participating as much as possible within their own physical limitations.

References

Arthreya, B. H., & Ingall, C. G. (1984). Juvenile rheumatoid arthritis. In J. Fithian (Ed.), *Understanding the child with a chronic illness in the classroom* (pp. 93–104). Phoenix: Oryx Press.

Bennett, J. T., & MacEwen, G. D. (1989). Congenital dislocation of the hip: Recent advances and current problems. *Clinical Orthopaedics and Related Research, 247,* 15–21.

Boos, M. L., Janvier K. W., McIlvain-Simpson, G. R., Sanford, C. C., & Wade, G. (1993). Nursing planning, intervention, and evaluation for altered musculoskeletal function. In D. B. Jackson & R. B. Saunders (Eds.), *Child health nursing: A comprehensive approach to the care of children and their families* (pp. 1679–1748). Philadelphia: J. B. Lippincott.

Cassidy, J. T., & Petty, R. E. (1995). *Textbook of pediatric rheumatology* (3rd ed.). Philadelphia: W. B. Saunders.

Dyment, P. G. (1996). The hip. In F. D. Burg, J. R. Ingelfinger, E. R. Wald, & R. A. Polin (Eds.), *Gellis & Kagan's current pediatric therapy* (15th ed., pp. 489–491). Philadelphia: W. B. Saunders.

Ergin, T. M. (1996). Orthopedic trauma. In F. D. Burg, J. R. Ingelfinger, E. R. Wald, & R. A. Polin (Eds.), *Gellis & Kagan's current pediatric therapy* (15th ed., pp. 498–506). Philadelphia: W. B. Saunders.

Grove, N., Cusick, B., & Bigge, J.(1991). Conditions resulting in physical disabilities. In J. L. Bigge, *Teaching individuals with physical and multiple disabilities* (3rd ed., pp. 1–15). New York: Merrill.

Hanson, V. (1983). Juvenile rheumatoid arthritis. In J. Umbreit (Ed.), *Physical disabilities and health impairments: An introduction* (pp. 240–249). New York: Merrill.

Harkins, A. (1994). Altered immune function. In C. L. Betz, M. M. Hunsberger, & S. Wright (Eds.), *Family-centered nursing care of children* (2nd ed., pp. 1565–1647). Philadelphia: W. B. Saunders.

Hartley, B., & Fuller, C. C. (1997). Juvenile arthritis: A nursing perspective. *Journal of Pediatric Nursing, 12,* 100–109.

Heller, K. W., Alberto, P. A., Forney, P. E., & Schwartzman, M. N. (1996). *Understanding physical, sensory, and health impairments.* Pacific Grove, CA: Brooks/Cole.

Howe, J., & Coffman, C. P. (1990). The musculoskeletal system. In G. M. Scipien, M. A. Chard, J. Howe, & M. U. Barnard (Eds.), *Pediatric nursing care* (pp. 477–525). St. Louis: Mosby.

Hughes, R. B. (1993). Immune responses. In D. B. Jackson & R. B. Saunders (Eds.), *Child health nursing: A comprehensive approach to the care of children and their families* (pp. 619–639). Philadelphia: J. B. Lippincott.

James, S. R. (1990). Skeletal integrity and mobility: Implications of inflammation and structural abnormalities. In S. R. Mott, S. R. James, & A. M. Sperhac (Eds.), *Nursing care of children and families* (2nd ed., pp. 1553–1613). Redwood, CA: Addison-Wesley.

Katz, J. A. (1983). Hip conditions. In J. Umbreit (Ed.), *Physical disabilities and health impairments: An introduction* (pp. 86–92). New York: Merrill.

Leck, I. (1994). Structural birth defects. In I. B. Pless (Ed.), *The epidemiology of childhood disorders* (pp. 66–117). New York: Oxford University Press.

Ludwig, M. A., & Beam, T. (1992). Alterations in immune system function. In P. T. Castiglia & R. E. Harbin (Eds.), *Child health care: Process and practice* (pp. 685–728). Philadelphia: J. B. Lippincott.

McIlvain-Simpson, G. R. (1996). Juvenile rheumatoid arthritis. In P. L. Jackson & J. A. Vessey (Eds.), *Primary care of the child with a chronic condition* (2nd ed., pp. 530–552). St. Louis: Mosby.

Miller, J. J., III (1982). Juvenile rheumatoid arthritis. In E. E. Bleck & D. A. Nagel (Eds.), *Physically handicapped children: A medical atlas for teachers* (pp. 423–430). New York: Grune & Stratton.

Nehring, W. M., & Steele, S. (1996). Cerebral palsy. In P. L. Jackson & J. A. Vessey (Eds.), *Primary care of the child with a chronic condition* (2nd ed., pp. 232–254). St. Louis: Mosby.

Reff, R. B. (1988). Musculoskeletal injury. In M. R. Eichelberger & G. L. Pratsch (Eds.), *Pediatric trauma care* (pp. 133–144). Rockville, MD: Aspen.

Sanford, C. C. (1993). Nursing planning, intervention, and evaluation for altered musculoskeletal function. In D. B. Jackson & R. B. Saunders (Eds.), *Child health nursing: A comprehensive approach to the care of children and their families* (pp. 1679–1745). Philadelphia: J. B. Lippincott.

Scull, S. A., Dow, B. M., & Athreya, B. H. (1986). Physical and occupational therapy for children with rheumatic diseases. *Pediatric Clinics of North America, 33,* 1053–1077.

Shoppee, K. (1992). Developmental dysplasia of the hip. *Orthopaedic Nursing, 11*(5), 30–36.

Singsen, B. H. (1990). Rheumatic disease of childhood. *Rheumatic Disease Clinics of North America, 16,* 581–599.

Spencer, C. H., Zanga, J., Passo, M., & Walker, D. (1986). The child with arthritis in the school setting. *Pediatric Clinics of North America, 33,* 1251–1264.

Spray, M. E. (1991). Care of the patient with a musculoskeletal disorder. In B. L. Christensen & E. O. Kockrow (Eds.), *Foundation of nursing* (pp. 574–635). St. Louis: Mosby.

Szer, I. S. (1996). Juvenile rheumatoid arthritis and spondyloarthropathy syndromes. In F. D. Burg, J. R. Ingelfinger, E. R. Wald, & R. A. Polin (Eds.), *Gellis & Kagan's current pediatric therapy* (15th ed., pp. 383–386). Philadelphia: W. B. Saunders.

Takei, S. & Hokonohara, M. (1993). Quality of life and daily management of children with rheumatic disease. *Acta Paediatrica Japonica, 35,* 454–463.

Taylor, J., Passo, M. H., & Champion, V. L. (1987). School problems and teacher responsibilities in juvenile rheumatoid arthritis. *Journal of School Health, 57,* 186–190.

Whaley, L. F., & Wong, D. L. (1991). *Nursing care of infants and children* (4th ed.). St. Louis: Mosby.

Whaley, L. F., & Wong, D. L. (1995). *Nursing care of infants and children* (5th ed.). St. Louis: Mosby.

CHAPTER 16

Disorders of the Movement-Producing Structures

Chronic conditions of the movement-producing structures are relatively rare in children and young adults, but acute injuries that affect one or more muscles are very common. Often these injuries are caused accidentally, most often through play, whether on the playground or during an organized sporting event. Some of the injuries are very mild and, with time and rest, heal by themselves; others may be more serious, necessitating, in some cases, surgical intervention. Two common injuries, both muscle-specific, are **strains** and **contusions,** which are covered in this chapter. Chronic conditions that affect all the musculature of the body are also discussed.

❧ Conditions Affecting a Specific Muscle or Tendon

Children, particularly young children, by their very nature are accident-prone. Some children, even if they are not clumsy, in their zest to get somewhere quickly, constantly bump into objects. Others are known for falling off of objects, such as trees, or being hit by other objects or children, e.g., when "rough-housing" with their friends. In each of these situations, the youngster is quite likely to injure fibers that make up the muscles of the body (i.e., **soft tissue injuries**).

Not all conditions that affect a single muscle are traumatic in origin. One common condition, known as **torticollis,** or **wry neck,** results from a shortening of, or injury to, the sternocleidomastoid muscle. The sternocleidomastoid muscle is a thick muscle found on the side of the neck, arising from the sternum and connecting to the mastoid process at the bottom of the temporal bone just behind the jaw bone. This condition, which can be either congenital or adventitious, results in the individual holding the head to one side with the chin pointing toward the opposite side. In 20% of the cases that are congenital, other positional deformities, such as hip dysplasia, are common (Mier, 1996a). In such cases, the most common underlying cause is abnormal intrauterine positioning. Acquired torticollis typically results from minor soft tissue trauma or viral myositis (inflammation of the muscle tissue). Treatment typically involves stretching the affected muscles several times daily; sometimes surgery is required.

Contusions and Strains: Damage to Individual Muscles

An injury of the subcutaneous tissues (tissues located underneath the skin) or muscles, resulting from some type of force, such as a blow, being exerted on the body, is known as a **contusion.** Most people call the injury a **bruise.** Contusions of soft tissues surrounding bones and joints are seen in children and young adults who suffer from fractures or dislocations (chapters 14 and 15). Bruises are characterized by **ecchymosis,** the discoloration of the damaged tissues, as well as by swelling and pain, which generally can be alleviated by the application of cold compresses.

In contrast to bruises that result from pressure being "pushed" against the body or the body "pushing" against some type of rigid material, muscles can be damaged by actions that "pull" the body with force that is great enough to damage not only the skin but also the underlying muscle. The microscopic tears in the tissue of a muscle or group of muscles that occur, in most cases, from excessive physical effort over time, as opposed to a single traumatic episode, are referred to as a **strain.** As in the case of sprains of ligaments, strains are graded as being mild, moderate, or severe, depending on the extent of damage. Typically, if the strain occurs suddenly, the injury is likely to be more severe than injuries that have occurred gradually.

Tendonitis and Bursitis: Damage to Specific Tendons or Bursae

If a muscle is damaged by pulling, the tendons that attach the muscle to the bones are also vulnerable to injury. Because of their strength, **tendons** are relatively difficult to damage; however, they can become inflamed as a result of strain, a condition referred to as **tendonitis** or **tendinitis.** Bursae, the sacs that lie between the tendon and the bone, can also become inflamed, a condition referred to as **bursitis.** Bursitis often results from repetitive motions that cause a bone to rub against a tendon, producing irritation, as well as from arthritic conditions and from infection. Common forms of bursitis are **housemaid's knee, miner's elbow,** and **weaver's bottom** (*Mosby's,* 1994). Both tendonitis and bursitis can be extremely painful and may result in the joint becoming stiff and swollen. Treatment typically includes rest, injections of corticosteroids (a hormone that acts as an anti-inflammatory agent), and bandaging or immobilizing the limb or joint to support the appendage and decrease pain.

Generalized Disorders of the Movement-Producing Structures

Conditions that affect the movement-producing structures of the body can be described either as being musculoskeletal or neuromuscular. While the division is not always clear-cut, in this section, those common conditions that affect muscles that do not directly result from obvious neurologic impairments are discussed. Cerebral palsy, spina bifida, head injury, and spinal cord injuries are primarily neurologic in origin and have already been discussed. Other neurologic conditions typically found in the adult population, such as amyotrophic lateral sclerosis (Lou Gehrig's disease), myasthenia gravis, and multiple sclerosis, are not discussed here.

Congenital Muscular Defects

There are a number of congenital muscular defects, which may be categorized into two groups: those that result from an **embryologic absence** of a specific muscle or muscle groups and those that result from an **intrinsic abnormality** of muscle (Mier, 1996b). An example of the first group is **Poland's anomaly,** in which the child is born without the costal (rib) and sternal (breastbone) portions of the pectoralis major muscle of the chest, which "stretches" from the shoulder blade to the upper ribs. An example of the second group is **benign congenital hypotonia,** or "floppy baby syndrome," a disorder that affects all of the striated muscles of the body. Even though these children have extremely low muscle tone at or shortly after birth, they generally develop normally (Urion, 1996).

The most common congenital muscular disease is **Duchenne's muscular dystrophy (DMD),** named after the French neurologist Guillaume Benjamin-Amand Duchenne. Even though the child is born with the condition, the signs of the disorder are not evident for several years. In the following section, muscular dystrophies in general, and DMD in particular, are discussed. Muscular dystrophies are ex-

amples of intrinsic abnormalities of the muscle. In most cases, only the striated muscle is affected by this condition.

Muscular Dystrophy

The term **muscular dystrophy (MD)** actually refers to a group of diseases in children or adults that are marked by a gradual **atrophy,** or wasting, of muscle tissue without any evidence of neurologic tissue involvement or degeneration. In most cases, as a result of the atrophy, the affected individual has a shortened life expectancy. There are actually 13 different types of MD, each classified by the following criteria: (a) mode of inheritance, (b) age of onset, (c) muscles involved, and (d) severity and rapidity of the degeneration of muscular tissue (Sanford, 1993b). DMD is the most common. Of the six other types of MD seen in children, the most common are limb-girdle muscular dystrophy, also known as juvenile dystrophy of Erb or Erb's muscular dystrophy, and facioscapulohumeral muscular dystrophy, also known as Landouzy-Dejerine muscular dystrophy.

Etiology Muscular dystrophy is an inherited disease. Some types of MD are x-linked; others are either autosomal dominant or autosomal recessive. Each of the types is associated with a particular gene abnormality.

DMD, also referred to as pseudohypertrophic muscular dystrophy, is a sex-linked recessive condition found primarily in males. The location of the gene abnormality for this type of MD is on the Xp21 locus of the X chromosome. At this site a specific gene, the **dystrophin gene,** is either deleted or duplicated. As a result of the genetic abnormality, **dystrophin,** a protein product normally found in muscle tissue, is either absent or altered. In almost all cases, the defective gene is carried by the mother and is passed on only to sons. However, in a few cases, DMD can result from a spontaneous genetic mutation, and consequently, it can occur in a family with no history of the disease. Because of such unpredictability, it is possible to see DMD in females; however, such cases are rare. Daughters, however, may be carriers of the gene.

Limb-girdle muscular dystrophy is an autosomal recessive condition that results in atrophy of the pelvic and shoulder girdles. It typically arises in late childhood, adolescence, or adulthood. This form of muscular dystrophy has a relatively slow rate of progression that may result in minimal or incapacitating disability. The abnormal gene is found on either the 5q or 15q chromosome. Since it is a recessive condition, both the mother and the father must carry the gene in order to pass it on to their offspring. Autosomal recessive forms of muscular dystrophy can affect boys and girls equally. In these forms of the disease, dystrophin levels are normal; however, a dystrophin-related protein may be abnormal (Iannaccone, 1992).

Facioscapulohumeral muscular dystrophy is also a slowly progressing form of the disease, autosomal dominant in its mode of transmission, with onset during the second decade of life. It affects the face, shoulders, and upper arms, and generally does not shorten the life span. The defective gene in this particular form is believed to be on the 4q chromosome. Either the mother or the father can carry the defective gene, and either can pass it on to their son or daughter.

Rarer forms of MD include **Becker's muscular dystrophy,** a sex-linked recessive condition that is generally considered to be a milder form of DMD that may appear when the child is between 5 and 15 years of age and may result in a shortened life span, and **ocular myopathy,** a condition whose mode of inheritance is unclear (believed to be most likely autosomal dominant) that arises in childhood or adolescence and that affects primarily the extraocular muscles of the eye, particularly the muscles outside the eye that control the movement of the orb. In this particular form of dystrophy, cardiac problems may develop and may result in sudden death at any age. Because Duchenne's muscular dystrophy accounts for approximately 50% of all cases of muscular dystrophy, this form is described in greater detail in the following sections.

Incidence and Prevalence   The incidence of DMD is between 1 in 3,300 to 3,500 male births (Heydemann, 1996; Iannaccone, 1992). DMD is the second most common lethal genetic disorder in humans, second to cystic fibrosis.

Characteristics   During the infancy period, the young male child with DMD appears to be normal. However, about the time that he begins to walk (or at least by age 3) certain characteristic manifestations of the disease are noted. One of the early signs of DMD in approximately 85% to 90% of all cases by the time the child is age 5 is **pseudohypertrophy,** or

false enlargement of certain muscles. Most commonly the calf muscles are affected. In such cases, the lower legs appear to be large (hypertrophied) and muscular, as if the child had been strengthening them through an aggressive exercise program. In reality, the muscle enlargement is not due to increased muscle size, but rather to the fact that the normal muscle fibers of the lower legs are being replaced by abnormal fibrous tissue and by deposits of fatty material. Muscle pain is a common complaint in pseudohypertrophy. In some cases, the first symptoms of enlargement occur in the shoulder or hip region, rather than the calf area.

In addition to visible changes to the muscular structure of the body, the child's motoric skills begin simultaneously to show signs of deterioration. In its initial stages, DMD is usually characterized by a weakness in the voluntary muscles of the hip and pelvic region. Unfortunately, this weakness is often mistaken for clumsiness, and consequently, medical treatment is not sought (Iannaccone, 1992). Parents typically begin to become concerned when they recognize that their son is having difficulty getting up to a standing position from sitting on the floor. For the child to rise, he often assumes a kneeling position, gradually pushing his body in the upright position by "climbing" or "walking" his hands up his legs, a maneuver known as **Gowers' sign** (Figure 16.1), named after William Gowers, a physician who identified and described DMD.

Along with difficulty getting up, the child typically develops a wide-based, hip "waddling" gait, known as the **Trendelenburg gait,** often walking on his tiptoes. Such a gait develops as a means to compensate for the weakness in the anterior tibial muscles and quadriceps muscles of the legs and as a method to maintain balance (Howe & Coffman, 1990; Mason & Wright, 1994). Frequent falls are common and increase over time. Typically, the child also encounters difficulty in jumping, running, and riding a bicycle.

As the disease progresses, the student encounters problems getting up from a sitting to a standing position, in climbing stairs, and eventually even in walking on a flat, level surface. Crutches are generally not of assistance in stabilizing the young boy because of the shoulder girdle weakness common to the condition (Page-Goertz, 1992). However, for some, a standard, lightweight walker may be useful during prolonged periods of walking (Cusick, 1991).

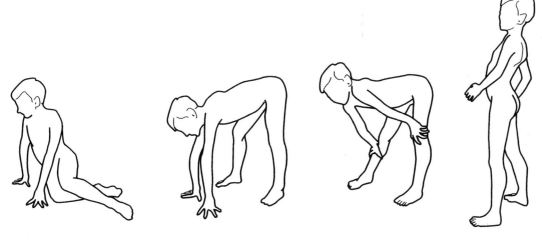

Figure 16.1
Gowers' Sign

As the ability to walk independently further deteriorates and the child stumbles and falls repeatedly, the child often needs to use a wheelchair. In many cases, particularly those in which there is upper limb involvement, an electric wheelchair is more appropriate than a manual chair. On average, children with DMD require a wheelchair by the time they are 11 years old (Iannaccone, 1992).

As the muscles of the spine become involved, usually within 3 to 5 years after onset, a pronounced lordosis develops and the student's abdomen begins to protrude noticeably. Gradually, hand movement becomes affected as the muscle weakness progresses and there is loss of shoulder and elbow stability, typically by age 10. At this stage, the young adolescent has difficulty raising his arms above the shoulder level (e.g., writing on a blackboard). As a result of lack of mobility, contractures of the elbows, feet, knees, and hips may develop. Once the child is in a wheelchair, a scoliotic or kyphoscoliotic curve often develops within about 2 years after walking has ceased (Mason & Wright, 1994). Eventually the spinal curvature affects the positioning of some of the vital organs, including the heart and lungs. At this time, the student begins to have difficulty holding up his head. Also, the boy's voice may take on a breathy, nasal quality (Heller, Alberto, Forney, & Schwartzman, 1996). Eventually the disease spreads to the involuntary muscles of the respiratory and cardiovascular system. Premature death typically results from a respiratory infection, such as pneumonia, or from heart failure. Death usually occurs 10 to 15 years after the initial onset of the disease. Boys with DMD rarely survive beyond the third decade of life (Mason & Wright, 1994): Most die when they are in their early 20s.

Diagnosis and Treatment   In most cases, the presence of the disease is confirmed by means of diagnostic tests that are usually performed when the child begins to show signs of the disease. Since it is known that the level of **creatine kinase (CK)** is markedly elevated in boys with DMD, a simple blood test can be used as a screening device. Serum CK can also be used to screen women at risk for being carriers (Iannaccone, 1992). A **muscle biopsy,** a procedure in which a small sample of muscle is obtained for analysis, is considered the single most important test, because this procedure provides a sample to measure the level of dystrophin. Muscle dystrophin must be altered or absent for the diagnosis of muscular dystrophy to be made (Iannaccone, 1992).

Treatment typically involves one or more therapeutic approaches, including pharmacologic intervention, physical and occupational therapy, and respiratory therapy. Treatment is geared towards the following aims: (1) maintaining function of unaffected muscles for as long as possible, thereby keeping the child or young adult as independent as possible; (2) facilitating ambulation; (3) managing respiratory or cardiac problems; (4) helping the child or young adult and family cope with the limitations that the disease imposes on both the individual and the family; and (5) providing emotional support and counseling to the child or young adult and his family during their times of emotional distress (Howe & Coffman, 1990; James, 1990; Sanford, 1993; Whaley & Wong, 1995). In many cases, boys with DMD are given prednisone (Liquid Pred, Deltasone) to slow the rate of muscle weakening and to prolong independent ambulation. Unfortunately, this corticosteroid has a number of side effects, one of the most serious being significant weight gain. Since the extra poundage may further affect the boy's ability to walk, this drug is usually only considered for selected young boys who are able to demonstrate an ability for weight control (Heydemann, 1996).

Along with pharmacologic intervention, boys with DMD are usually prescribed an exercise program (e.g., swimming classes, physiotherapy) that focuses on increasing (or maintaining) range of motion in the joints and in stretching the muscles to prevent, or at least minimize, the formation of contractures. Bracing and splinting are also common approaches to maintaining proper positioning of joints and to permit ambulation. Ankle-foot orthoses are often prescribed to keep the feet plantigrade (i.e., in correct alignment for walking); knee-ankle-foot orthoses are often prescribed to keep the knees locked when the child is walking (Heydemann, 1996). To maximize respiratory functioning, boys with DMD may be given breathing exercises, and to facilitate breathing and prevent infection in the lungs, they may receive chest physical therapy.

In some cases, surgical correction of deformities is considered; however, many factors must be considered first. For example, in the case of severe scoliosis (curvature greater than 35°), the timing of the surgery depends on overall health, the severity of the curve, respiratory status, and, most importantly, the risk of anesthesia. Since surgery has not "proven" to result in a longer life span for all students with DMD, not all physicians recommend this (Iannaccone, 1992).

There is at present no cure for this progressive disease. However, the techniques of gene transfer (inserting genetically altered genes into the body) are being explored. Heydemann (1996), in discussing the successes shown in animal research in which muscle degeneration has been prevented, made the following bold prediction: "Gene transfer therapy within the next decade seems within reach" (p. 511).

🍎 Educational Implications and Teaching Tips

As mentioned previously, isolated damage to a muscle or muscle group normally does not result in serious consequences. With time, the tissues heal and the student is able to resume all the normal activities of childhood. In severe cases, the student may be out of school for a time. For the student with muscular dystrophy, however, the effects of the condition are far more serious. Even though the life expectancy of a student with muscular dystrophy is typically shortened, "it would be a disservice to the child to lower teacher expectations or to abandon all future expectations, since individual symptoms are variable, and the disease progression may be slower than expected" (Kleinberg 1982, p. 193). This cautionary comment by Kleinberg is particularly true given the advances that are being made in medicine, both in terms of treatment and prevention, that may result in a much longer life than previously expected.

Teachers of boys with DMD often develop a unique relationship with them. In many cases, a young boy may feel more comfortable talking to his teacher than his parents about sensitive issues, such as his goals and aspirations and his life expectancy (Lyle & Obringer, 1983). There should be a good listener, such as a teacher, counselor, or administrator, readily available to respond to the student when he needs to talk. Chee and Packer (1984) made the following blunt but appropriate statement that should be kept in the forefront if the minds of all school staff: "If dystrophic children are to survive in the classroom, they cannot be ignored or 'shelved'" (p. 218). The following suggestions may be of assistance to teaching staff.

1 *Children and young adolescents with DMD should be encouraged to be as active as possible.* Such activity results in an extension of the period that the individual with DMD is able to travel independently without a wheelchair. It has been reported that prolonged bed rest and inactivity can result in a 3% loss of muscle strength per day spent in bed (Renshaw, 1986, cited in Sanford, 1993); those who walk less than 3 hours per day will, within months, lose the ability to walk without assistance (Lyle & Obringer, 1983); and a person who is capable of walking and who spends as little as 3 months sitting

in a wheelchair may never walk again (Hyde, 1984, cited in Grove et al., 1991). Teachers, in particular physical education teachers, should work together with the student's physical therapist and occupational therapist to encourage the student to participate as actively as is possible given the limitations of his condition. The student's physician should be contacted regarding which activities are permissible, forms for which are shown in Appendix D.

2 *The attitude of others is critical.* For example, Heller and her colleagues (1996) have suggested that when a student falls, he should be encouraged to get up without help unless help is really needed. The rationale behind this approach is simple—by ensuring that the student looks after himself, the student is forced to maintain a sense of independence and continue to hold a positive self-image in comparison to those around him. However, with this attitude in mind, the student must receive instruction on how to make falls as safe as possible, and the caregiver must be alert to any injury that may result and seek medical assistance if necessary. If assistance is needed to help the child get up, caregivers should never assist the student by simply pulling on his arm. Because the shoulder girdle is often weakened, it is easy to dislocate the student's shoulder, thereby causing a great deal of unnecessary pain. The student's physical therapist should be asked to show the staff correct lifting techniques.

Caregivers and teachers must establish realistic goals, and the "child's interests and genuine abilities should form the core of the curriculum, with emphasis on short-term goals, leisure pursuits such as literature, art, music, hand work (when possible), and practical, functional skills in areas like cooking, sewing, and budgeting" (Kleinberg, 1982, p. 193). The student should be encouraged to participate in as many school-based activities as possible (e.g., parties, movies, glee club).

Boys with DMD often become passive and withdrawn and, as the disease progresses, become socially isolated at a time when other teenagers are developing new interests and sexual relationships (Whaley & Wong, 1995). Continuation in a school program promotes social contact with friends and peers and minimizes the isolation of children with chronic degenerative diseases. However, in many cases, parents, in their attempt to shield and protect their child, opt to keep their son at home, particularly during the advanced stages of the disease (Kleinberg, 1982). By readily accepting the child in the school system and by fostering a positive attitude that emphasizes quality of life rather than quantity of life (Lyle & Obringer, 1983), staff can encourage parents to have their child remain in school rather than staying at home, spending an inordinate amount of time in front of the television, a pastime common to those who are homebound (Kleinberg, 1982).

It is important that all those in contact with the student with DMD (e.g., parents, teachers) foster independence and self-esteem by developing "a balance between limiting the child's activity because of muscular weakness and allowing the child to accomplish things alone"; however, it is often difficult to know when the student is seeking assistance "to get a little extra attention or because of overtired muscles" (Whaley & Wong, 1991, p. 1945). Gagliardi (1991) has suggested that programs such as computer game competitions in which boys with DMD can compete with those without the condition are beneficial, as are recreational activities and camping opportunities organized specifically for children with DMD.

3 *A number of assistive devices may be beneficial for the student with DMD (e.g., modified keyboards; tape recorders; pencil holders).* Some are low tech, others are high. School staff should work together with the student's occupational therapists to ensure that these devices are readily available. Computers may be appropriate tools for the student, particularly since they have a variety of means of access (e.g., switches vs. keyboard or mouse). Specially designed software allows students to use computers for drawing (e.g., art projects), leisure (e.g., games), jobs (e.g., word processing), and environmental control (e.g., turning appliances on and off) (Grove et al., 1991).

Self-help aids are also important. For example, an elevated toilet seat in the bathroom may permit the young boy some independence in toileting. In addition, clothing with Velcro fasteners so that the student can dress without assistance is critical.

4 *Proper positioning is important to minimize the development of contractures.* For the student in a wheelchair, the use of footrests to prevent foot drop and other foot deformities is often prescribed (Howe & Coffman, 1990). Children with leg braces may benefit from using a standing table to avoid the development of knee and ankle contractures and delay the onset of spinal curvature (Grove et al., 1991). School staff should communicate with the student's physical or occupational therapist to determine proper positioning, ensure that any orthotic devices that may assist the student are available, and be familiar with how the devices operate (e.g., how to lock the leg brace when the child is in a standing position). Equally important is the need for regular changes in position (e.g., every 2 hours) to avoid pressure sores. In repositioning the student, caregivers should be careful not to lift or pull children with DMD by the arms because it may result in dislocation of the shoulder. For further information on positioning a student in a wheelchair, see chapter 14.

5 *As the disease progresses, students with DMD will need the assistance of others to perform many routine activities (e.g., eating, toileting).* It is often suggested that a "meal buddy," a "bathroom buddy," a "hall buddy," a "playground buddy," a "locker buddy," and a "bus buddy" be "chosen" from the student's peers to assist him with complex physical needs. However, for the child with DMD, using a "buddy" makes the student dependent on one of his classmates, and consequently, such actions may undermine the already fragile self-esteem of the youngster and disrupt the normal relationships that develop between peers. Although some classmates will assume these "jobs" readily, as part of their normal friendship with the child, the needs of both the helper and the student with the condition must be considered. It is also important to acknowledge that many students may feel uncomfortable and shy around those who have disabling conditions, and for some, being "assigned" to assist the student may help in overcoming some of the feelings that they may have (Chee & Packer, 1984).

As a general rule, no student should be required to assist another with DMD if there is not sufficient interest or there are any "hard feelings" between the students that stem from the "job assignment." In such situations, other solutions, which may involve hiring a personal aide or arranging for a staff person or school volunteer to provide assistance, should be sought. For example, with advance planning, it is often possible to ensure that the student's food is cut up by the kitchen staff before he comes

to the cafeteria. Similarly, the lunchroom monitor can bring the boy's tray to the table and ensure that the necessary equipment, such as a flexible drinking straw, is available.

6 *Students with DMD must conserve as much energy as possible for the school day because they have a limited supply of energy.* If at all possible, they should attend neighborhood schools so that they do not have to expend energy sitting on a bus for a long period of time. Even students who live close to the school benefit from being allowed to travel by school bus (Chee & Packer, 1983). For the student in a wheelchair, a safe form of transportation (i.e., lift-equipped wheelchair van or taxi) must be available. For further information on the safe transportation of students, see chapter 3.

7 *The physical demands placed on the student with DMD in the school environment should be minimized and safety maximized.* If possible, the student's classroom should be on the ground floor as close to the entrance as possible. The student should be permitted to use an elevator to move from floor to floor, if there is one available. For students who are able to walk, albeit in some cases with crutches or other orthotic devices, it is critically important that the school environment be as hazard-free as possible (e.g., the floor of the classroom should not be littered with books, lunch boxes, and sneakers).

All schools should complete an audit of the facilities to determine which areas need to be improved to make the building accessible to those who have unique mobility needs (e.g., students, staff, and visitors). Just like other students in the school, the student with muscular dystrophy who is in a wheelchair needs to be able to reach objects within the school setting (e.g., blackboards, drinking fountains, lockers, telephones, school cafeteria counters). A checklist that can be used to determine the level of accessibility in buildings for persons with physical disabilities is found in Appendix A.

8 *As the disease progresses, fatigue always becomes a major limiting factor.* However, with adequate rest periods during the day or a shortened school day, many students with DMD are able to attend school even when severely debilitated by the disease and "should not be deprived of the feelings of accomplishment that come from meeting the challenges presented at school" (Chee & Packer, 1984, p. 218). The degree of restriction in physical activity is individual-specific, and school staff should consult with the boy's physician or physical therapist. For many students, a swimming program may be an excellent opportunity to get exercise and to maintain contact with friends and peers during or after school hours. Depending on the degree of disability, the student may need extra flotation equipment and trained personnel in attendance (Cusick, 1991). Some individuals, particularly those who have an increased number of fat cells (and a corresponding decreased number of muscle cells) are more buoyant in the pool than their able-bodied counterparts.

For the student who is more physically limited, sedentary activities, such as chess or other table games, may be more appropriate (Lyle & Obringer, 1983). However, it is only in the advanced stages of the disease that students should be excused from all normally scheduled physical education activities. Even if their participation is minimal, it should be encouraged. For suggestions regarding appropriate exercises with children and young adolescents with muscular dystrophy, see Lockette and Keyes (1994).

9 *Approximately 30% of boys with DMD show signs of cognitive deficit (i.e., IQ below 90), and many more have attention-deficit hyperactivity disorder (ADHD)* (Iannaccone, 1992). As a result of the combination of physical limitations and learning difficulties, the educational needs of these students are complex, and they need, in many cases, an individualized educational program. It is important for the teachers to remember that the learning problems seen in young boys with DMD are non-progressive and not proportional to the severity of the disease (Lyle & Obringer, 1983). Mental deterioration is not inherent in this disease, and in most cases, the cognitive abilities are within the normal to above-normal range (Heller et al., 1996).

In terms of classroom behavior, the same standards should be applied to the young boy with DMD as to any other student in the class. A consistent approach, i.e., one in which the student is not given special privileges unless required by the extreme nature of the disease, is best. While those who need assistance in activities of daily living (e.g.,

bathrooming procedures) benefit from the services of a personal aide, the aide should be trained to "assist" the student, not to "do for" the student.

10 *Boys with DMD, particularly those who are immobile and who use a wheelchair, are often prescribed a low-calorie diet, because they may have a tendency to become obese.* In some cases, it is boredom or depression that leads to excess eating; in others, it is lack of activity that results in fewer calories being used (Chee & Packer, 1984). The parents and the student should work together with the school's dietitian to establish a balanced diet that includes many of the foods that the boy likes, eats readily, and are nutritionally appropriate. School staff should attempt to monitor the student's caloric intake and discuss concerns that might arise regarding compliance with the parents. The student should be encouraged to drink a sufficient quantity of fluids to prevent urinary and renal difficulties, such as the pooling of urine (**urinary stasis**) that may result from immobility and can lead to a bladder infection.

Urinary or bowel incontinence is not part of this disease; however, students with DMD who have a severe motoric restriction may find using the toilet physically difficult. A hand-held urinal may be of assistance for emptying the bladder. In many cases, evacuation of the bowel can be "regulated" by maintaining an adequate diet and the judicious use of laxatives. With a proper program, bowel movements can be "scheduled" to occur either early in the morning or later in the day when the young boy is home from school. If a consistent schedule is not possible, the student may need assistance from an aide in getting on and off the toilet seat. The main consideration is that the student be comfortable with the person giving assistance and that he be assisted in a dignified, private, and supportive manner (Heller et al., 1996).

11 *Students in the advanced stage often have breathing problems.* Caregivers should be alert to signs of respiratory failure (e.g., presence of headaches, nightmares, difficulty sleeping, fatigue or daytime somnolence [drowsiness], difficulty chewing or swallowing, and weight loss). These signs generally occur insidiously rather than abruptly (Sanford, 1993). Other respiratory problems that should be noted are coughing, wheezing, or shallow breathing (Lyle & Obringer, 1983). In addition, staff should be alert to any signs of chest pain that may be indicative of heart failure. In such cases, the child should be transported to an emergency health center.

12 *Teachers should be aware that in-class discussions of genetic conditions can be distressing to students who have an inherited disease.* This is particularly true in the case of muscular dystrophy, in which material presented may include reference to the fact that this is a fatal condition and that many students with DMD do not live much beyond their teenage years. Teachers who plan to cover such material should contact the student's parents before the beginning of the term to determine the student's level of understanding of his condition and his level of comfort with the course content.

❧ Summary

The movement-producing structures of the body, the muscles and tendons, like other parts of the body that are involved in independent travel, are vulnerable to traumatic injury. In such cases, recovery is typically quick, and there are few if any sequelae. Such is not the case with those who have a systemic muscular condition, such as muscular dystrophy. However, students with generalized altered muscular function as a group are not homogeneous. In fact, when the dystrophies are examined, it is evident that the needs of affected persons vary considerably from person to person. In some cases, the disease progresses so slowly that major accommodations are not needed; in others, the disease progresses so rapidly that the teacher has to deal with the student having a terminal disease and the strong possibility that the student will not survive the academic year. Regardless of the prognosis, the most important consideration for the student with muscular dystrophy is a kind and understanding teacher who recognizes that the needs of the student change as the condition progresses. While some would question why a student who has only months to live would attend school, it should be remembered that school is a great normalizing factor for all children (Heller et al., 1996). The reader should benefit from suggestions given not only in this chapter but also in chapters 4 and 5, which address the needs of the student who has a terminal illness.

References

Chee, C. M., & Packer, R. J. (1984). The muscular dystrophies. In J. Fithian (Ed.), *Understanding the child with a chronic illness in the classroom* (pp. 198–221). Phoenix: Oryx Press.

Cusick, B. (1991). Therapeutic management of sensorimotor and physical disabilities. In J. L. Bigge, *Teaching individuals with physical and multiple disabilities* (3rd ed., pp. 16–49). New York: Merrill.

Gagliardi, B. A. (1991). The impact of Duchenne muscular dystrophy on families. *Orthopaedic Nursing, 10*(5), 41–49.

Grove, N., Cusick, B., & Bigge, J. Conditions resulting in physical disabilities. In J. L. Bigge, *Teaching individuals with physical and multiple disabilities* (3rd ed., pp. 1–15). New York: Merrill.

Heller, K. W., Alberto, P. A., Forney, P. E., & Schwartzman, M. N. (1996). *Understanding physical, sensory, and health impairments.* Pacific Grove, CA: Brooks/Cole.

Heydemann, P. T. (1996). Muscular dystrophy and related myopathies. In F. D. Burg, J. R. Ingelfinger, E. R. Wald, & R. A. Polin (Eds.), *Gellis & Kagan's current pediatric therapy* (15th ed., pp. 510–511). Philadelphia: W. B. Saunders.

Howe, J., & Coffman, C. P. (1990). The musculoskeletal system. In G. M. Scipien, M. A. Chard, J. Howe, & M. U. Barnard (Eds.), *Pediatric nursing care* (pp. 477–525). St. Louis: Mosby.

Iannaccone, S. T. (1992). Current status of Duchenne muscular dystrophy. *Pediatric Clinics of North America, 39,* 879–894.

James, S. R. (1990). Skeletal integrity and mobility: Implications of inflammation and structural abnormalities. In S. R. Mott, S. R. James, & A. M. Sperhac (Eds.), *Nursing care of children and families* (2nd ed., pp. 1553–1613). Redwood, CA: Addison-Wesley.

Kleinberg, S. B. (1982). *Educating the chronically ill child.* Rockville, MD: Aspen.

Lockette, K. F., & Keyes, A. M. (1994). *Conditioning with physical disabilities.* Champaign, IL: Human Kinetics.

Lyle, R. R., & Obringer, S. J. (1983). Muscular dystrophy. In J. Umbreit (Ed.), *Physical disabilities and health impairments: An introduction* (pp. 100–107). New York: Merrill.

Mason, K. J., & Wright, S. (1994). Altered musculoskeletal function. In C. L. Betz, M. M. Hunsberger, & S. Wright (Eds.), *Family-centered nursing care of children* (2nd ed., pp. 1815–1873). Philadelphia: W. B. Saunders.

Mier, R. J. (1996a). Torticollis. In F. D. Burg, J. R. Ingelfinger, E. R. Wald, & R. A. Polin (Eds.), *Gellis & Kagan's current pediatric therapy* (15th ed., pp. 507–508). Philadelphia: W. B. Saunders.

Mier, R. J. (1996b). Congenital muscular defects. In F. D. Burg, J. R. Ingelfinger, E. R. Wald, & R. A. Polin

(Eds.), *Gellis & Kagan's current pediatric therapy* (15th ed., p. 508). Philadelphia: W. B. Saunders.

Mosby's medical, nursing, & allied health dictionary (1994). (4th ed.). St. Louis: Mosby.

Page-Goertz, S. S. (1992). Alterations in musculoskeletal function. In P. T. Castiglia & R. E. Harbin (Eds.), *Child health care: Process and practice* (pp. 915–954). Philadelphia: J. B. Lippincott.

Sanford, C. C. (1993). Nursing planning, intervention, and evaluation for altered musculoskeletal function. In D. B. Jackson & R. B. Saunders (Eds.), *Child health*

nursing: A comprehensive approach to the care of children and their families (pp. 1679–1745). Philadelphia: J. B. Lippincott.

Urion, D. K. (1996). Benign congenital hypotonia. In F. D. Burg, J. R. Ingelfinger, E. R. Wald, & R. A. Polin (Eds.), *Gellis & Kagan's current pediatric therapy* (15th ed., pp. 508–510). Philadelphia: W. B. Saunders.

Whaley, L. F., & Wong, D. L. (1991). *Nursing care of infants and children* (4th ed.). St. Louis: Mosby.

Whaley, L. F., & Wong, D. L. (1995). *Nursing care of infants and children* (5th ed.). St. Louis: Mosby.

PART VI

Ingestion, Digestion, Absorption, and Elimination:

Children and Young Adults with Altered Gastrointestinal or Urinary Function

The **gastrointestinal (GI) tract** consists of the various organs, primarily the mouth, throat, stomach, and intestines, that are involved in the **ingestion, digestion,** and **absorption** of food substances necessary as a source of energy and for growth and repair of tissue. Part of the GI tract is also involved in the **elimination** of the waste products that result from breakdown of nutrients, specifically those that are not usable. Waste products that are expelled through the anal canal, the final segment of the large intestine, are referred to as **stools** or **feces** (from Latin, *faex,* meaning dregs). The GI tract is not the only part of the body that is involved in elimination. The **urinary system,** consisting of the kidneys, ureters, urinary bladder, and urethra, also plays a role in the elimination of body wastes. However, rather than being involved in the elimination of the by-products of the breakdown of solid food substances, the urinary system is the excretory system for fluids. Many of the fluids that the body excretes come from the breakdown of the various nutrients just mentioned; others result from the ingestion of liquids.

Since the GI and urinary systems both play a major role in the metabolism of foods, both solid and liquid, the two have been grouped together, even though they are quite separate. In this section, the structure and function of the two systems are examined. In addition, the functions of the **"accessory" digestive organs,** those that play a role in the digestive process but are not, in fact, part of the tract that leads from the mouth to the anal canal (e.g., the liver, the pancreas, the gallbladder), are discussed.

The Gastrointestinal System: Review of Structure and Function

The **GI tract,** also referred to as the **digestive tract,** the **alimentary canal,** or the **intestinal tube,** is approximately 30 feet (9 m) long at maturity. For study, it is divided into two parts, the **upper GI system,** which includes the mouth, pharynx, esophagus, and stomach, and the **lower GI system,** which includes the small and large intestines and the anus. The organs of the digestive system and some of the associated structures are shown in Figure VI.1.

The digestive tract, from the pharynx downward, is composed of several layers of specialized tissue. The innermost layer is referred to as the **mucosa,** or **mucous membrane layer.** The main purpose of this layer is to secrete **mucus,** a slippery fluid that helps ensure that food substances move through the tract with relative ease. The **submucosa layer,** lying beneath the mucosa, is rich in blood vessels and nerves, and at this level, nutrients from the breakdown of food sources are absorbed into the bloodstream to be transported to tissues that need nourishment. The third layer is composed primarily of circular and longitudinal muscles, which, when working in tandem, "push" the food along the passageway in the rhythmic contraction known as **peristalsis.** The fourth and fifth layers, the outermost pair, consist of a layer of fibrous connective tissue that gives the tract a degree of "toughness," lined by a relatively thin sheet of serous membrane, which functions to secrete **serum,** a watery fluid similar to mucus, that keeps the muscle fibers from becoming irritated from "rubbing" against each other as they contract and relax.

The process by which complex substances are reduced to simple nutrients that can be absorbed, known as **catabolism,** involves one or both of two different actions. The breaking down of food into smaller particles through chewing and the propelling of the food along the tract by means of peristalsis are primarily **mechanical actions,** whereas the conversion of carbohydrates, proteins, and fats, by specialized chemicals known as **enzymes,** into molecules that can be readily used or assimilated (specifically, simple sugars, amino acids, and fatty acids and glycerol, respectively) is primarily a **chemical action.** To enable understanding of the physiology of ingestion, digestion, absorption, and elimination, the complexities of digestion are described step by step, beginning

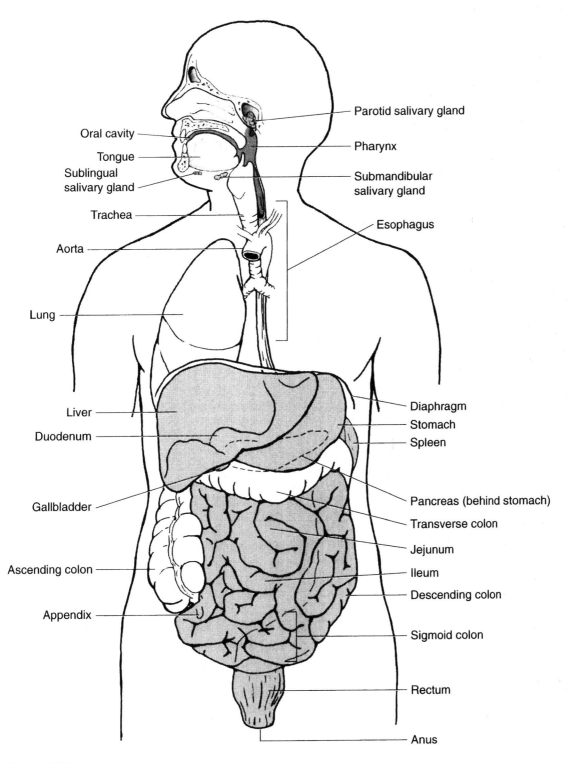

Parotid salivary gland

Oral cavity

Pharynx

Tongue

Sublingual
salivary gland

Submandibular
salivary gland

Trachea

Esophagus

Aorta

Lung

Diaphragm

Liver

Stomach

Duodenum

Spleen

Gallbladder

Pancreas (behind stomach)

Transverse colon

Jejunum

Ascending colon

Ileum

Descending colon

Appendix

Sigmoid colon

Rectum

Anus

Figure VI.1
The Digestive Tract

with the voluntary consumption of food via the mouth. However, it should be noted that there are alternative methods for obtaining nutrients needed for growth and development that bypass the oral cavity, and there are routes alternative to the anus for the evacuation of waste products. These are described in chapter 17.

Mouth and Salivary Glands

Food, either solid or liquid, usually enters the digestive system through the **oral** or **buccal cavity,** which is more commonly referred to as the **mouth.** Immediately upon ingestion, both mechanical and chemical digestion begin to occur. By means of chewing movements that involve both the tongue and teeth, the solids are shredded, ground, and mixed with **saliva,** a clear, viscous fluid secreted by the three pairs of salivary glands found within the mouth. Saliva consists of water, mucin (the chief ingredients of mucus), organic salts, and several enzymes. The major digestive enzyme of saliva is **amylase,** also referred to as ptyalin. Amylase initiates the digestion of complex carbohydrates (e.g., complex sugars, or polysaccharides) into simpler carbohydrates (e.g., double sugars, or disaccharides). In addition, saliva contains lysozyme, an enzyme that is capable of destroying bacteria. In this role, this particular enzyme, also found in sweat, breast milk, and tears, is able to protect the teeth from decay and to prevent the mucous membrane that lines the mouth from becoming infected. Once the food has been adequately chewed and mixed with saliva, the lump of semisolid food, referred to as a **bolus,** is ready to be passed along. Chewing is sometimes referred to as **mastication** and swallowing as **deglutition.**

Pharynx and Esophagus

The tongue propels the bolus backwards into the pharynx and downwards into the esophagus, and, aided by peristaltic movement, the bolus eventually enters the stomach. The **pharynx** is approximately 5 inches (12.7 cm) long; the **esophagus** is approximately 10 inches (25.4 cm) in length. To prevent the food from entering the nasopharynx or nasal cavity, the **soft palate** and the **uvula** are raised to form a barrier. In a similar manner, so that food does not enter the respiratory tract, the **epiglottis** closes over the larynx. No digestion takes place in the esophagus because the food moves through too quickly (approximately 5 to 6 seconds from start to finish). There is a ring of muscle fibers known as the **cardiac** or **lower esophageal sphincter** at the point where the esophagus joins the stomach. This band must be sufficiently "relaxed" in order to permit food to enter but, at the same time, be sufficiently "tight" to prevent the backward flow of gastric contents into the esophagus. If the gastric contents do travel in the wrong direction, a condition referred to as **gastroesophageal reflux,** the esophagus becomes irritated and the person complains of **heartburn.**

Stomach

The major organ of digestion is the **stomach.** By means of churning motions by the muscles that line the stomach, the ingested food is further mechanically mixed or "kneaded" in the stomach with the digestive enzymes produced by the glands that line the organ. Since the stomach is also known as the **gaster,** the digestive glands are called the **gastric glands.** The digestive enzymes are (a) **pepsin,** also called protease, which converts proteins to proteoses and peptones; (b) **rennin,** which converts caseinogen, found in milk, to casein; and (c) **lipase,** an enzyme that initiates the digestion of fats, changing the lipids to fatty acids and eventually to alcohol and glycerol. The digestive enzymes are mixed together with a combination of water, hydrochloric acid, and mucin. The **water** has a singular purpose, that of diluting the secretions so that they are not too caustic to delicate stomach tissues. However, the **hydrochloric acid** serves two major roles. First, it acts to soften the connective tissue that is found in meats, thereby allowing it to be "shredded"; second, it kills bacteria normally located within the stomach, which could, potentially, if allowed to flourish, cause an infection. The **mucin** functions to protect the lining of the stomach from being destroyed by the acidic contents, thereby preventing the formation of **ulcers,** which are crater-like lesions that result from the necrosis of a section of mucous membrane from overexposure to caustic agents, such as pepsin and hydrochloric acid. As the partially digested food, referred to as **chyme,** leaves the stomach, it must pass through the **pyloric sphincter,** or **valve,** a band of muscles similar to the cardiac sphincter that separates the **pylorus,** or bottom portion of the stomach, from the **duodenum,** or upper part of the small intestine. The primary role of the sphincter, is to "hold" the food in the stomach cavity until it is "ready" (i.e., sufficiently digested) to be passed on to the small intestine.

The holding or storage capacity of the stomach varies greatly by age. The stomach capacity of a newborn is only about 2 to 4 teaspoons (10 to 20 ml); by 3 weeks of age, its capacity has tripled in size. By the time the child is a month old, the capacity is five to ten times its original perinatal capacity (Whaley & Wong, 1995). The adult stomach, when filled, stretches to the size of a football, capable of holding approximately 4 to 8 cups (1 to 2 L) of food or liquid.

Small Intestine

Even though the small intestine is referred to as "small," it is the longest portion of the digestive tract. From pylorus to iliocecal junction, the small intestine at adulthood is, on average, 20 feet (6 m) in length. The small intestine is divided into three sections, the **duodenum,** the **jejunum,** and the **ileum.** The designation "small" refers to its girth in comparison to the large intestine, rather than its length. The inner lining of the small intestine, particularly the jejunum, contains many circular folds of tissue, referred to as **plicae** (sing., **plica**), that increase the surface area 600 to 700 times. As the food passes through, the assimilable nutrients are absorbed by the thousands of finger-like projections, known as **villi** (sing., **villus**), that cover these folds. Most of the food is absorbed before it even reaches the middle of the jejunum. The semiliquid chyme is further mixed with enzymes secreted by the **intestinal glands,** known as the **follicles of Lieberkühn.** These glands, like the gastric glands, produce a number of enzymes, which further assist to break the food sources down into usable nutrients. The intestinal secretions of the small intestine are composed primarily of (a) **peptidase,** a protein-splitting enzyme that converts peptides into amino acids; (b) **sucrase, maltase,** and **lactase,** enzymes that convert the disaccharides sucrose, maltose, and lactose into various simple sugars (or monosaccharides), specifically glucose, galactose, and fructose; and (c) **lipase,** an enzyme that acts on fats, mentioned above as a component of gastric juice. The intestinal juices also contain **enterokinase,** an enzyme that activates the enzyme **trypsin,** produced by the pancreas, and **amylase,** an enzyme that acts on carbohydrates, mentioned above as a component of saliva.

Accessory Digestive Organs

Secretions from the **liver** and the **pancreas** are added to the chyme in the small intestine. **Bile,** or **gall,** produced by the liver and stored in and concentrated by the **gallbladder,** is important in the digestion of fat. Bile consists primarily of cholesterol, phospholipids, bile salts, and bilirubin. Bile itself does not contain any enzymes, but bile acts to reduce the surface tension of fat so that an emulsion is formed that can be acted upon by lipase, produced by the pancreas. Bile, in particular the bile salts, also functions to increase the ability of the intestinal wall to absorb fatty acids, monoglycerides, cholesterol, and other lipids that result from digestion of ingested fats. The pancreatic secretions contain three primary enzymes. Two of the enzymes, **lipase** and **amylase,** have been described; the third is **trypsin,** an enzyme that breaks down the partially digested proteins into the final end product, amino acids. Another important substance in the pancreatic juice is **sodium bicarbonate,** an alkaline substance that helps to neutralize the acidity of the chyme as it moves through the small intestine, thereby preventing the formation of ulcers. The end products of carbohydrate and protein digestion are the monosaccharides and the amino acids, which pass directly from the villi into the circulatory system and travel to the liver via the portal vein, where they are either used for energy or stored for future use. The end products of fat digestion (i.e., fatty acids and glycerol) pass into the lymphatic system, which carries them to the venous circulatory system via the thoracic duct. In addition to food substances, the vitamins contained in food substances, along with some water and electrolytes, are absorbed in the small intestine.

Large Intestine and Anal Canal

After the food substances and vitamins are absorbed, the waste products, consisting mainly of indigestible residue and a small amount of undigested fat and protein, pass via the **ileocecal valve** into the **large intestine.** It usually takes approximately 6 hours for the chyme to pass through the small intestine and into the large intestine. The large intestine is also composed of three major sections: (1) the **cecum;** (2) the **colon,** consisting of the **ascending, transverse, descending,** and **sigmoid colons;** and (3) the **rectum.** At maturity, the large intestine is quite short, only 4 to 5 feet (1.2 to 1.5 m); however, it is relatively wide in comparison to the small intestine. As the wastes are passed through, the remaining water and electrolytes are absorbed, changing the waste material from liquid to semisolid. The fecal material is then evacuated via the **anal canal** and out the terminal opening, the **anus.** The elimination of feces is known as **defecation,** from the Latin word *defae-care,* meaning to clean. Because the intestine is often referred to as the **bowel,** from the diminutive of the Latin noun *botulus,* meaning sausage, the excretion of feces is also called a **bowel movement.**

🐾 The Urinary and Renal Systems: Review of Structure and Function

Excretion (and **retention**) of fluids begins at the cellular level. In the various cells of the body, waste products are continuously being emptied into the capillary system, by which they are transported to the appropriate excretory system. The main excretory system of the body for fluids is the **urinary system;** the main organ involved in the filtration of fluids and waste products contained in the fluids is the **kidney.** The Latin word for kidney is *ren,* and in English the term **renal** is used as an adjective referring to the kidney and its function. Consequently, the urinary system[1] is often referred to as the **renal system.** The major organs that make up the urinary system are shown in Figure VI.2.

Kidneys

While the ureters, urinary bladder, and urethra all play a role in the secretion and elimination of urine, it is the **kidneys,** two bean-shaped structures located in the back of the abdomen just above the waist, that are primarily involved in the formation of urine. Even though the human body has two kidneys, most individuals can live a normal life with only one. If one kidney is lost, through disease or injury for example, it is not uncommon for the other kidney, if it is not diseased in any way, to enlarge and do the work of two (Kidney Foundation of Canada, 1990).

In each kidney, about the size of a clenched fist at maturity, there are approximately 1.0 to 1.5 million filtering units, known as **nephrons** (from the Greek word *nephros,* meaning kidney) (Van Cleve & Baldwin, 1989). Blood that needs to be detoxified (i.e., "cleaned") enters the nephrons by means of the **re-**

---

[1] Often the urinary system and the genital system (i.e., the reproductive system) are considered together and are referred to as the **genitourinary** or **urogenital** system. Infectious diseases involving the reproductive system (sexually transmitted diseases) are discussed in chapter 23.

nal artery, which branches off from the abdominal aorta; blood that has been filtered (i.e., "cleansed") by the nephrons returns to the venous system through the **renal vein,** which enters the inferior vena cava. The various parts of the nephron are shown in Figure VI.3, and the function of each part (i.e., filtration, reabsorption, secretion) is described below, in a step-by-step manner.

In the first section of the nephron, known as the **glomerulus** (pl., glomeruli), the renal artery divides into approximately 50 capillary loops. As a result of the substantially high arterial pressure of the blood entering the narrow tubules, substances of small molecular weight, e.g., water and solutes, are filtered out of the blood into the lumen of the capsule that surrounds the glomerulus, known as **Bowman's capsule.** Those substances that are larger, such as blood cells and blood proteins, remain within the blood and leave via an **efferent arteriole,** which in turn branches into a series of capillaries that surround the remaining sections of the nephron. The substances that have been filtered out of the blood, known as the **filtrate,** then enter the **proximal convoluted tubule,** or **proximal tube.** As the filtrate enters the tubule, the volume is great, and if it were simply excreted from the body as urine, blood volume would rapidly become depleted to a level incompatible with life (Prosnitz, 1983). To prevent this, the filtrate passes through the various sections of the tubule, and a large percentage of the water, electrolytes, and other solutes necessary for life are reabsorbed by the capillaries that surround the tubule and are returned to the blood. Approximately 70% of the filtrate (including water, glucose, electrolytes, amino acids, and other necessary substances) is reabsorbed into the blood in the tubule, and 20% of the water, along with sodium and potassium, is reabsorbed in the next section of the nephron, the **distal convoluted tubule,** or **distal tube** (Luttrell, 1990). In addition to the filtration at the glomerulus, certain waste substances, such as hydrogen ions, some electrolytes, and ammonia, are removed from the blood by means of secretion from the capillaries surrounding the renal tubules. The amount of substances that are secreted is governed by the release of certain hormones, such as **aldosterone** and the **antidiuretic** hormone, from the adrenal glands located above each kidney. The secreted wastes are added to the filtrate as it passes through the system into the **collecting tubules** that join to form the **ureter.** The remaining wastes are

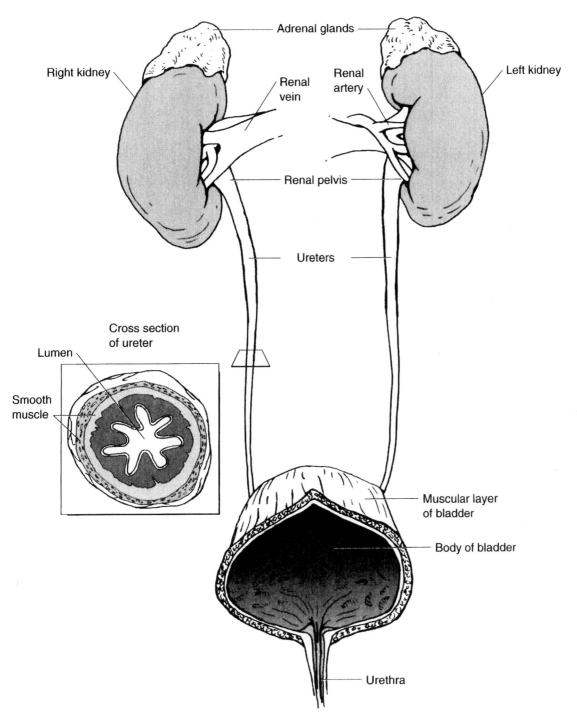

Figure VI.2
The Urinary System

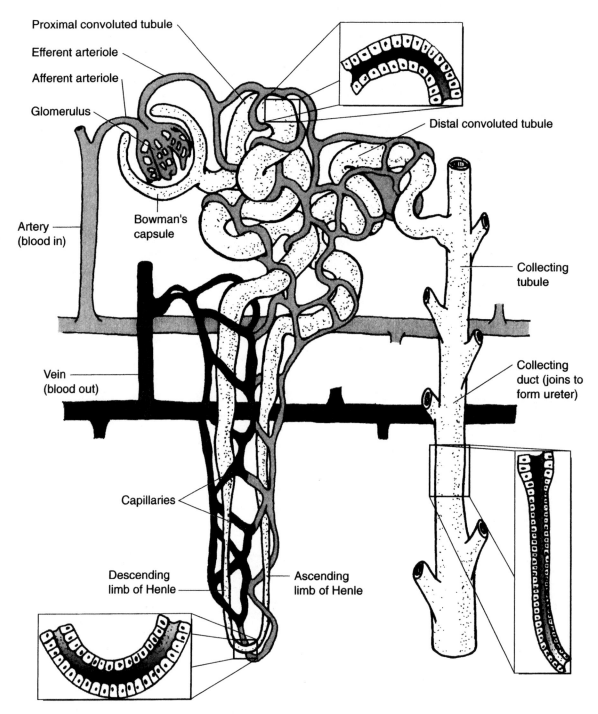

Proximal convoluted tubule

Efferent arteriole

Afferent arteriole

Glomerulus

**Artery
(blood in)**

**Bowman's
capsule**

Distal convoluted tubule

**Collecting
tubule**

**Vein
(blood out)**

**Collecting
duct (joins to
form ureter)**

Capillaries

**Descending
limb of Henle**

**Ascending
limb of Henle**

Figure VI.3
Detailed Structure of a Single Nephron with Blood Supply

excreted as **urine,** the composition of which is primarily water, urea, sodium and potassium chloride, phosphates, uric acid, organic salts, and the pigment urobilin.

Under normal conditions, the body is quite capable of adjusting the excretion of urine and solutes in response to its requirements for water and electrolytes. However, if ketones, protein, bacteria, blood, glucose, pus, certain casts (tiny structures formed by deposits of minerals or other substances), or crystals are found in the urine, their presence is indicative of some type of disease state. Similarly, if blood serum levels of sodium, potassium, chloride, phosphorus, urea nitrogen, creatinine (a waste product of muscle activity), glucose, and hemoglobin are abnormal, they may be indicative of a kidney that is not filtering out the waste products.

In addition to detoxifying the blood by means of elimination of waste products and regulating the volume and electrolyte concentration of fluids and acid-base balance in the body, the kidneys have several other functions that contribute to the maintenance of homeostasis in the body (Van Cleve & Baldwin, 1989). These functions include: (a) the regulation of blood pressure, by means of the release of renin and prostaglandins, and thus the rate of filtration; (b) the stimulation of new red blood cell production, as a result of the release of erythropoietin, a hormone discharged in response to anoxia; and (c) the regulation of calcium balance, through vitamin D metabolism. If the kidneys fail as a result of disease or injury, many other systems may be jeopardized.

Ureters

Multiple distal tubules empty into one single collecting tubule. Many collecting tubules coalesce to form the **ureter** (one for each kidney). From the kidneys, urine flows through the ureters to the urinary bladder, where it is collected and stored until the person urinates. The ureters are thick-walled tubes that vary both in length and in diameter. In adulthood, the average ureter is approximately 11 inches (30 cm) long and 0.05 inch (1 mm) to 0.5 inch (1 cm) in circumference. Urine travels down the ureters by means of peristaltic waves that result from the contraction of the smooth muscles that surround the tubes.

Urinary Bladder

The **bladder** is a hollow, muscular membranous sac that lies in the pelvis, behind the pelvic bones. The ureters enter the bladder, posteriorly, through an oblique tunnel that functions as a valve. The tunnel and its covering of bladder lining prevents the urine from flowing backwards (reflux) into the ureter when the bladder contracts (i.e., during voiding). When the bladder is approximately half full, the body senses an urge to void, as a result of stretch receptors being stimulated. However, urine does not flow from the bladder unless the sphincter muscle that surrounds the exit is relaxed, in most cases voluntarily, and the bladder contracts.

Urethra

The hollow tube that connects the bladder to the external opening, where urine is discharged from the body, is referred to as the **urethra.** The external opening is called the **urinary meatus.** In girls, the meatus is between the **labia,** the folds of skin that envelop the clitoris, meatus, and vaginal opening. In males, the meatus is in the tip of the penis, and the urethra is approximately 8 inches (20 cm) in length; in females, the urethra is 1 to 2 inches (approximately 3 to 5 cm) long. In both sexes, the urethra grows in length with age.

References

Kidney Foundation of Canada (1990). *Living with kidney disease.* Montreal, PQ: Author.

Luttrell, J. S. (1990). Genitourinary transport: Implications of inflammation, obstruction, and structural abnormalities. In S. R. Mott, S. R. James, & A. M. Sperhac (Eds.), *Nursing care of children and families* (2nd ed., pp. 1446–1498). Redwood City, CA: Addison-Wesley.

Prosnitz, E. H. (1983). Kidney disorders. In J. Umbreit (Ed.), *Physical disabilities and health impairments: An introduction* (pp. 250–256). New York: Merrill.

Van Cleve, S. N., & Baldwin, S. E. (1989). Nursing strategies: Altered genitourinary function. In R. L. R. Foster, M. M. Hunsberger, & J. J. T. Anderson (Eds.), *Family-centered nursing care of children* (pp. 1467–1523). Philadelphia: W. B. Saunders.

Whaley, L. F., & Wong, D. L. (1995). *Nursing care of infants and children* (5th ed.). St. Louis: Mosby.

CHAPTER 17

Altered Gastrointestinal Function

KEY WORDS

Anorexia

Atresia

Bulemia

Central venous access device

Cleft

Constipation

Diarrhea

Eating disorder

Elemental medical foods

Enteral feeding

Fistula

Malabsorptive disorders

Obesity

Ostomy

Parenteral feeding

Peristalsis

Projectile vomiting

Reflux

Problems related to the gastrointestinal (GI) tract are numerous in children and young adults. Common manifestations of GI dysfunction include the following: dysphagia (difficulty in sucking or swallowing); spitting up or regurgitation of food; heartburn; belching; vomiting and nausea; abnormalities of the stools, including diarrhea and constipation; distention of the abdomen that may or may not be accompanied by pain; abnormal bowel sounds that may or may not be accompanied by pain on defecation; and jaundice, a yellow discoloration of the skin and eyes. In cases of bleeding in the GI tract, there may be blood in the vomit or stool.

In some GI conditions, only one of the symptoms listed above may be observed; in others, there may be a constellation of signs and symptoms. Symptoms range in severity and may, in some cases, be life-threatening. Gastrointestinal difficulties can be divided into four subgroups. They are problems related to (a) ingestion, (b) digestion, (c) absorption, and (d) elimination. Some conditions are evident at birth; others develop later in life. Some of the most common GI difficulties in children and young adults are shown in Table 17.1. In this chapter, only conditions that are a direct result of either a congenital or acquired entity are discussed.[1]

---

[1] GI problems that result from a condition that is directly related to some other system of the body are covered in the sections dealing with that system.

TABLE 17.1
Commonly Occurring Gastrointestinal Difficulties in Children and Young Adults

Congenital Problems	Problems of Infancy, Childhood, or Adulthood
PROBLEMS OF INGESTION	
Cleft lip	Gastroesophageal reflux disease
• Without cleft palate	Ingestion of
• With cleft palate	• Foreign bodies
Cleft palate	• Corrosive substances
Esophageal atresia	• Drugs
• With tracheoesophageal fistula	
• Without tracheoesophageal fistula	
PROBLEMS OF DIGESTION	
Intestinal atresia	
Pyloric stenosis	
PROBLEMS OF ABSORPTION	
	Malabsorption syndromes
	• Celiac disease
	• Lactose intolerance
	• Cystic fibrosis
	Inflammatory bowel disease
	• Crohn's disease
	• Ulcerative colitis
PROBLEMS OF ELIMINATION	
Hirschsprung's disease	
Anorectal malformations	
OTHER COMMON GASTROINTESTINAL PROBLEMS	
	Hepatitis
	Intestinal parasites
	Peptic ulcers

The focus of this chapter is chronic GI problems, rather than acute. Even though many of the chronic conditions described can be corrected surgically or treated successfully by pharmacologic or dietary therapy, frequent hospitalizations and repeated surgical procedures can be very disruptive to the individual and his or her family. It is not uncommon for those with altered GI functioning to have to face a lifetime of adjustment (Cusson, 1994). Chronic GI dysfunction can affect an individual's growth and development, even with successful treatment. For example, certain conditions, such as malabsorption syndrome, can result in a child becoming malnourished and showing permanent signs of stunted growth.

♥ Problems with Ingestion

Individuals with ingestion problems have difficulty taking in food substances in a normal manner. Such problems are often referred to as "feeding problems." The most common causes of ingestion problems are congenital abnormalities of the facial structure, such as a cleft lip or cleft palate. Some children and young adults with neurologic problems also have feeding difficulties.

Cleft Lip and Palate

Referred to in the past as a **harelip**, a **cleft lip** is a condition that arises from incomplete fusion of the upper lip during the first trimester of fetal development. In a cleft lip, the lip is visibly interrupted, either unilaterally (on one side of the midline) or bilaterally (on both sides of the midline). The cleft can range in severity from minor, e.g., an indentation under one nostril, referred to as a **microform** cleft, to severe, e.g., a wide or deep fissure that extends from the lip into the nostril. In severe cases, various parts of the nose or teeth may be involved. The condition is described as being **complete** if the clefting extends into the nasal cavity and **incomplete** if only the lip tissue is affected. Children with a complete cleft in the lips often have either malformed or misplaced teeth.

A cleft lip may occur alone or in combination with a **cleft palate,** a condition in which there is incomplete fusion of the soft or hard palates, or both, that make up the roof of the mouth. As in the case of a cleft lip, a palatine cleft can range from minor to

severe; however, there is no standard classification system to describe the severity level (Curtin, 1996). Minor cases typically involve the soft palate and, in some cases, may even go unnoticed at delivery. Typically, however, a child with even a minor cleft has feeding problems because of the ineffective suck that results from an inability to create a tight seal on a nipple. In severe cases, the hard palate may be so completely open that the nasal and oral cavities become one. Persons with cleft palates have a higher incidence of middle-ear problems, in particular middle-ear infections, and many require ventilating tubes to prevent the buildup of fluid. Without proper treatment, some may experience a significant loss of hearing. Examples of cleft lips and palates are shown in Figure 17.1.

The incidence of cleft lip, with or without cleft palate, is approximately 1 in 1,000 births; the incidence of cleft palate is around 1 in 2,500 births (Chan, 1993). There is some racial variation. Cleft lips occur more often in Native Americans (3.6 in 1,000) and Asians (2 in 1,000) than Caucasians (1 in 1,000) or African Americans (0.3 to 0.4 in 1,000) (Curtin, 1996; Danek, 1990). For unknown reasons, cleft lip, with or without cleft palate, occurs more often in boys, whereas isolated cleft palate defects are more common in girls (Scipien & Kneut, 1990).

The cause of the anomaly is usually unknown; however, in most cases, it results from a multifactorial inheritance pattern. In some cases, prenatal exposure to teratogens (e.g., maternal consumption of the anticonvulsant drug Dilantin during pregnancy, maternal consumption of alcohol) is believed to be the underlying cause; in others, some type of chromosomal abnormality (e.g., trisomy 21 or Down syndrome) may also be present. Though not considered a genetic condition, in some cases a positive family history of clefting has been reported (Curtin, 1996).

Treatment is surgical. While one of the major goals is to achieve an optimal aesthetic repair so that the youngster develops a positive self-regard, achieving adequate airway function, good speech articulation, functional dental occlusion, and normal hearing are also critical (Curtin, 1996). Correction of the condition must occur before the child begins to speak, so that faulty speech patterns do not develop. In some cases, particularly cases in which feeding is problematic (e.g., difficulty sucking; leaking of fluid into the nose, causing gagging and choking),

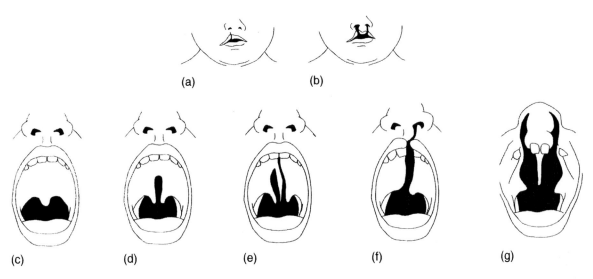

Figure 17.1
Cleft Lip and Palate: (a) unilateral cleft; (b) bilateral cleft; (c) normal palate and lip; (d) cleft of soft palate; (e) cleft of hard and soft palate; (f) complete unilateral cleft of lip and palate; (g) complete bilateral cleft of lip and palate.

surgery is undertaken at an earlier age. Until surgery takes place, there are a number of feeding devices, such as the Mead Johnson Cleft Lip and Palate Nurser, a compressible bottle with a longer and narrower nipple than normal to facilitate fluid consumption.

Even after surgical correction, the youngster's self-image may be affected, particularly if speech problems continue. Many children born with a cleft benefit greatly from the ongoing services of a speech and language pathologist. These children should be examined regularly by an audiologist to detect any signs of hearing loss. Counseling may also be appropriate.

Esophageal Atresia (EA)

While the term "cleft" refers to tissue that is divided, the term **atresia** is used to refer to the absence of a particular normal body opening, duct, or canal. **Esophageal atresia** refers to an abnormal esophagus that ends in either a blind pouch or a narrowing so severe that food cannot pass easily from the mouth to the stomach. This defect is believed to occur at a rate of approximately 1 in 3,500 live births (Lake & Buck, 1996). Esophageal atresia can occur with or without **tracheoesophageal fistula (TEF).** A **fistula** is an abnormal opening between two organs—a tracheoesophageal fistula is an open-

ing between the trachea and the esophagus that permits food to flow from the throat to the lung cavity. The three most common types of EA and TEF are shown in Figure 17.2.

The reasons why esophageal atresia occurs are unknown. Between 25% and 40% of affected children have associated anomalies, such as pulmonary, cardiovascular, intestinal, genitourinary, and neurologic defects (Chan, 1993; Danek, 1990). In as many as 50% of the cases, the mother had polyhydramnios during pregnancy (i.e., excessive amniotic fluid in the uterine cavity), and 40% of youngsters with this condition are born prematurely (Lake & Buck, 1996). Although atresias and fistulas can occur separately, it is more common to see a combination of the two.

Surgical correction is undertaken as soon as the condition is recognized. In most cases, the condition is recognized at the time the infant is first fed, by the resultant coughing, choking, and cyanosis. However, if the child has a tracheoesophageal fistula but does *not* have an esophageal atresia, it may be several months before the diagnosis is made. During this time, it is common for the infant to repeatedly aspirate food and have frequent coughing spells. The prognosis for complete recovery depends on a number of factors, including the nature and severity of the anomaly and the presence of additional abnormalities.

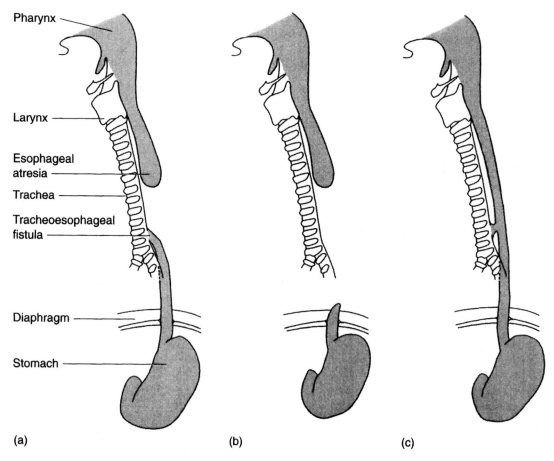

Figure 17.2

Esophageal Atresia and Tracheoesophageal Fistula: (a) esophageal atresia with distal fistula, in which the esophagus ends in a blind pouch and the trachea communicates by a fistula to the lower esophagus and stomach (80% to 90% of all cases); (b) atresia without fistula, in which both the upper and lower segments end in blind pouches (5% to 8% of all cases); (c) isolated tracheoesophageal fistula without esophageal atresia (also known as H-type), in which both the upper and lower segments of the esophagus communicate with the trachea (2% to 3% of all cases).

Gastroesophageal Reflux Disease

Ingestion problems can arise after birth, during infancy, or throughout the childhood years. One such condition is known as **gastroesophageal reflux disease (GERD).** In this condition, the contents of the stomach flow "backwards" into the esophagus as a result of failure of the cardiac sphincter to constrict to close off the passage. While most youngsters outgrow the condition by the time they are approximately 18 months of age, until that time GERD is typically evidenced by excessive nonforceful vomiting, failure to gain weight or failure to thrive, and repeated bouts of pneumonia that result from the aspi-

ration of stomach contents into the lungs. Between 5% and 30% of those with GERD continue to show symptoms beyond the age of 18 months. While GERD is believed to occur at a rate of approximately 1 in 500 children (Peck & Buzby, 1992), the causative mechanism of GERD is unknown. Many of these children have neurologic impairments (e.g., cerebral palsy or head injury) or other digestive problems (e.g., esophageal atresia, cystic fibrosis) that compound the situation.

Treatment is often pharmacologic. Typically, antacids (e.g., Maalox, or magnesium hydroxide), histamine H_2 receptor antagonists (e.g., Tagamet, or cimetidine), or motility modifiers (e.g., Reglan, or metoclopramide) are given to provide a protective barrier for the esophagus from gastric contents, to inhibit gastric acid production, and to accelerate gastric emptying, respectively. In severe cases, surgical intervention may be indicated. In some children, **esophagitis,** inflammation of the esophageal mucosa, results from the irritation of the mucosal lining of the esophagus by the acidic gastric juice. As the esophagitis may result in bleeding, the child may vomit bright red blood, a condition known as **hematemesis.** The most common symptoms of esophagitis are a burning sensation under the sternum and pain in the upper abdominal region.

Ingestion of Foreign Bodies and Corrosive Substances

Children, particularly infants and small children, are notorious for putting foreign objects, such as bottle tops, buttons, erasers, coins, and pins, into their mouths. In many cases, the object passes through the digestive system without any problem; however, in some cases, particularly if the object is long (e.g., needles, bobby pins), sharp (e.g., tacks, pull tabs on beverage cans), or large (e.g., buttons, coins), the object can cause an obstruction. In some cases, the object perforates the digestive tract. In children between the ages of 1 and 4, ingestion or aspiration of foreign objects is the fourth most common cause of accidental death (Chan, 1993).

Ingestion of corrosive substances (e.g., lye, drain cleaners) can result in severe burns to the mouth, esophagus, and stomach. Typically, acid ingestion results in oral and gastric burns, whereas alkali ingestion produces burns to the esophageal region. More than 500 ingestions of disc button batteries (i.e., those found in computer toys, games, watches, hearing aids, and calculators) are reported annually (First, 1996). Since these batteries contain potassium hydroxide, manganese dioxide, and either mercuric or silver oxide, leaking from the battery can cause significant damage to tissues.

🍃 Problems with Digestion

There are a number of digestive problems that are apparent at birth. In this section, difficulties that arise from congenital anatomic deformity, such as intestinal atresia or pyloric stenosis, are discussed. In-born errors of metabolism, which are conditions in which a child is unable to digest certain food because of an inherited defect of a single enzyme, are discussed in detail in Part VII.

Intestinal Atresia

If the bowel is completely obstructed, the individual is said to suffer from a condition known as an **intestinal atresia.** The incidence of this condition varies based on the location of the anomaly (Danek, 1990; Peck & Buzby, 1992). The most common are **duodenal atresias** (1 in 3,500 live births), **ileal atresias** (1 in 4,000), and **jejunal atresias** (1 in 5,000). Duodenal and ileal deformities are found more commonly in those who have cystic fibrosis (5% to 9%) or Down syndrome (1%). **Colonic atresias** are very rare, occurring at a rate of between 1 in 20,000 to 40,000 births. Evidenced at birth by vomitus containing bile, abdominal distention, and a failure to pass fecal material, colonic atresias require surgery to reconnect the two bowel segments. The cause of the defect, in most cases, is unknown.

Pyloric Stenosis

In pyloric stenosis, chyme is obstructed from flowing into the small intestine in a normal manner due to a narrowing of the pyloric sphincter caused by the overgrowth of the circular muscle of the pylorus. As a result of the obstruction, the infant vomits up quantities of partially digested food or milk. The term **projectile vomiting** is often used to refer to the force with which the contents of the stomach are expelled from the infant's body. In some cases, those that are most severe, the symptoms are evident at birth. In other cases, the first symptoms begin around 3 weeks of age.

Pyloric stenosis is more common in Caucasian male babies (1 in 150) than females (1 in 750), by a factor of 1:5. In addition, pyloric stenosis appears to be more common in first-born males than in any other group (Danek, 1990). Pyloric stenosis is less common in African American and Asian American children than in Caucasian infants, and it is less common in premature than full-term children (Whaley & Wong, 1995). The condition is treated surgically by means of a procedure referred to as a **pyloromyotomy.** In this operation, the pyloric muscle fibers are cut so that the tightness of the sphincter is released. Prognosis for full recovery is excellent.

❦ Problems with Absorption

For children to grow and develop, they require not only an adequate source of nutrition (i.e., a well-balanced diet with sufficient caloric intake) but also the ability to absorb the nutrients into their body as a source of energy. Problems with absorption are rare at birth; however, there are several conditions, often referred to as **malabsorptive disorders,** that can occur in infancy or childhood and may lead to serious consequences if unrecognized or left untreated. One of the most common malabsorptive disorders is **cystic fibrosis** (chapter 20). In this condition, affected individuals have difficulty digesting many foods because of thickening of the digestive secretions produced by the GI tract, the pancreas, and the liver.

Malabsorptive disorders lead to growth retardation. In most cases, weight is affected before height. Other signs and symptoms include chronic diarrhea, anorexia, abdominal distention, muscle cramps, and steatorrhea. Typically, the symptoms reflect the substances that are poorly absorbed (e.g., carbohydrate vs. fat malabsorption). It is also not uncommon to see a delay of the onset of puberty. Treatment varies depending on the cause of the condition. In some cases, manipulation of the diet may correct the problems. In other cases, rather than removing an offending food, a missing agent, such as an enzyme, is given to the individual. Two commonly occurring maladaptive disorders are discussed in this section: celiac disease and lactose intolerance.

Celiac Disease

Those with **celiac disease,** also referred to in the medical literature as **gluten-sensitive** or **gluten-induced enteropathy,** are unable to digest gluten, a protein constituent of certain grains, specifically wheat, rye, barley, and probably oats (Auricchio, Greco, & Troncone, 1988). Celiac disease is also known by laypersons as **celiac sprue,** or simply, **sprue.** If gluten is eaten, usually the person suffers from serious bouts of diarrhea, which can be life-threatening, particularly in young children, if not treated with haste. Many children with celiac disease are irritable, apathetic, and fretful and are often anorexic with significant eventual weight loss. As the subcutaneous fat disappears, the muscle begins to waste, the skin sags, and the abdomen becomes distended, resulting in a child or young adult who looks emaciated, pale, and weak. Symptoms of the disease most commonly appear at the time that gluten-containing foods are introduced (ages 6 to 8 months); however, in some, the symptoms may not be recognized for many years. The diagnosis is made by obtaining a biopsy specimen of the small bowel. A flattening of the villi or, in severe cases, absence of intestinal villi is a confirmatory symptom.

While the exact prevalence of this condition is unknown, celiac disease occurs more often in parts of Europe and Canada than in the United States (Cusson, 1994). The reported highest rate, 1 in 597, was found in Western Ireland by Silverman and Roy in 1983 (statistics cited in Cusson, 1994). On average worldwide, it occurs at a rate of approximately 1 in 1,000 live births (Auricchio et al., 1988). Peak age at onset is between 9 and 18 months, and it occurs more commonly in girls than boys.

Because gluten is a primary ingredient in many breads and cereals and is used as a thickener in many processed foods, such as gravy and puddings, the diet of a person with sprue needs to be altered radically. If the individual complies with the strict diet, one in which rice and maize, or corn, are used to substitute for the offending grains, improvement is noted within days. The diet is particularly difficult to follow for young adolescents, because they are unable to consume favorite foods such as spaghetti, hamburgers, hot dogs, and pizza. Individuals are also prohibited from drinking any fluids that are grain-based, such as beer and rye whiskey. Since the adolescent will not "outgrow" the condition, students must understand that the special diet must be followed for life. Some individuals with celiac sprue also show signs of lactose intolerance and may benefit from being on a milk-free diet.

Lactose Intolerance

The inability to digest lactose, a sugar contained in milk, is called **lactose intolerance.** This condition results from a deficiency in the production of the enzyme **lactase,** normally found in the small intestine, that breaks lactose down into glucose and galactose, which are absorbable by the body. Symptoms usually consist of severe watery diarrhea, abdominal distention and cramps, and flatulence (excessive air or gas in GI tract). Even though persons with lactose intolerance are born with the condition, rarely are the symptoms present from birth; it is more common to see a delayed onset. Many show the first signs during their preschool years.

Incidence varies by ethnic group. As many as 70% of African Americans have the condition; those of northern European ancestry generally are not affected (Danek, 1990). Between 50% and 90% of persons of Jewish, Indian, and Asian ancestry are also reported to be lactose intolerant (Gryboski & Walker, 1983, cited in Cusson, 1994).

Typically, treatment involves the removal of all milk and milk products containing lactose, such as ice cream, cheese, butter, puddings, cream soups, and certain salad dressings and sauces, from the diet and giving the individual only nondairy, lactose-free products, such as soy "milk" and soy "ice cream." Some individuals have found that they are able to eat milk products if they take the missing enzyme in either pill or liquid form (e.g., Lactaid, Lactrase) before the consumption of lactose. Without adequate treatment, in severe cases the person can become dehydrated and can develop serious health problems that may be life-threatening.

Chronic Inflammatory Bowel Disease (IBD)

Inflammatory bowel disease can take one of two forms: **ulcerative colitis (UC),** an inflammatory condition of the mucosal lining of the colon or rectum with diffuse ulcerations of the submucosal lining, or **Crohn's disease (CD),** an inflammatory condition that extends through all of the layers of the bowel wall, which can occur at any point in the GI tract from mouth to anus. While the two diseases are distinct entities, they are frequently discussed together because they share many of the same presenting signs and symptoms and are treated similarly (Pollack, 1996). For both conditions, the most common clinical features are diarrhea, blood in the stools or rectal bleeding, and abdominal pain. While IBD is considered a chronic disease, it should be noted that both UC and CD are episodic conditions in which there usually are periods of exacerbation followed by periods of remission.

Generally considered a disease of adulthood, IBD is known to occur in children as early as during the first few years of life. Age at peak onset is thought to be late adolescence (Hofley & Piccoli, 1994). Between 25% and 40% of adults with IBD experienced the first symptoms of the condition during their childhood or adolescent years (Kirschner,

1988). While the cause is unknown, research suggests that a combination of genes on chromosome 6 may be implicated in the susceptibility of individuals to IBD; however, no specific genetic pattern of transmission has been identified (Hofley & Piccoli, 1994).

The incidence of UC is believed to be approximately 7 to 10 per 10,000 (MacDonald, 1993). It is more common in Caucasians than in African Americans or Native Americans, and it is more prevalent in those of high socioeconomic status. UC occurs up to three to four times more often in the Jewish population than in the general population. CD is less common, believed to occur in 3 to 4 cases per 10,000 people (MacDonald, 1993), and like UC, Crohn's is less common in African Americans than in Caucasians. The Jewish population is affected three to six times more often with CD than the general population (Danek, 1990). The incidence of UC has remained relatively stable over time, but the incidence of CD appears to be on the rise (MacDonald, 1993). The reasons for the increase are unknown.

IBD does not just affect the intestinal tract (Pollack, 1996). At least one-fourth of those with IBD experience extraintestinal manifestations of the disease, the most common being a transient nondeforming inflammation of the large synovial joints of the lower extremities (arthritis), the pelvic bones (sacroileitis), and the spine (ankylosing spondylitis). Other manifestations of IBD include the following: growth failure; aphthus ulcers (ulcers of the oral mucosa); liver disease, including cirrhosis and pericholangitis (inflammation of the tissues surrounding the bile ducts); renal calculi (kidney stones); clubbing (enlargement of the fingertips); skin problems, including erythema nodosum (development of reddened, tender nodules, most often on the shins) and pyoderma gangrenosum (a skin infection that can lead to gangrene); blood clots (thromboembolic disease); and gallstones. Inflammatory conditions of the eye, most commonly uveitis (inflammation of the uveal tract), iritis (inflammation of the iris), and episcleritis (inflammation of the outer layers of the sclera), occur in some children. All children who display redness of the eye or complain of eye pain, blurred vision, or increased sensitivity to light should be referred to an ophthalmologist for follow-up. Significant GI complications or sequelae (e.g., massive bleeding, intestinal obstruction, perforation of the bowel, cancer of the colon) may also arise in severe cases of IBD, either during childhood or adulthood.

Many children with UC present a mild disease that can be successfully treated by drug therapy. The most common drug is the antibacterial Azulfidine. However, approximately 20% of children are unable to tolerate this drug because of significant side effects, which include nausea, vomiting, and headaches (Pollack, 1996). Children with moderate to severe disease are given corticosteroids (e.g., prednisone) in addition to Azulfidine. Unfortunately, prednisone is also known for its potential side effects, which include growth retardation, weight gain, mood swings, hypertension, and the development of cataracts. Those who have severe attacks often need to be hospitalized for treatment.

Children and young adults with CD do not respond as well to treatment as those with UC. The administration of corticosteroids is usually considered first-line therapy. In addition, some children are treated with the antibacterial Flagyl. Side effects of this drug include GI upset, urticaria (hives), metallic taste, furry tongue, and darkening of the urine (Pollack, 1996). Since as many as 50% of children who take this drug develop a peripheral neuropathy (inflammation of the peripheral nerves) or paresthesia, long-term use is generally contraindicated (Ramakrishna & Calenda, 1996).

Those with a more serious form of IBD may require surgical intervention (i.e., removal of the diseased portion), particularly if there are signs of massive uncontrollable bleeding, abscess, or perforation. As many as 70% of persons with CD require surgery. Since the inflammation often recurs in another section of the GI tract, repeated surgery is not uncommon. Approximately 20% to 30% of those with UC require surgery (Ramakrishna & Calenda, 1996).

In addition to pharmacologic and surgical therapy, nutritional intervention and stress management are important treatment approaches. Providing adequate caloric intake to meet the child's nutritional requirements for normal growth and development is important because the majority of children and young adults with IBD experience weight loss and growth failure. To prevent growth failure, many are given commercially available calorically dense nutritional supplements, such as Ensure and Boost. Some children with IBD are placed on a special diet in which they are given only commercially available **elemental medical foods (EMFs)** (i.e., formulas that provide total nutrition as well as nitrogen in the form of simple amino acids). While such a diet has been shown to

be useful in inducing remission in some who have CD, the diet is seldom well tolerated over the long term, nor is it believed to be useful in maintaining a remission (Ramakrishna & Calenda, 1996).

Since stress is believed to contribute to flare-ups of IBD, children and young adults are often given instructions on how to manage the stressors that may affect their well-being. Relaxation therapy, biofeedback, guided imagery, and controlled breathing techniques have been found to be useful therapeutic approaches for those with IBD. There are a number of support groups for persons with IBD that also may be helpful.

Chronic IBD should not be confused with **irritable bowel syndrome (IBS),** a common condition in childhood and adulthood characterized by abnormally increased motility of the intestines. Far less severe than IBD, IBS produces intermittent episodes of large, loose stools, which may or may not be accompanied by abdominal pain. Unlike IBD, however, IBS does not result in malabsorption syndrome or impaired growth.

In toddlers with IBS, increased passage of stools that become progressively watery throughout the day is typical. In many cases, the children are very thirsty, even though they may not show signs of dehydration. In school-age children with IBS, the most common symptom is recurrent abdominal pain. Constipation is common, along with headaches, dizziness, blurred vision, and dysuria. Treatment, regardless of age, is usually pharmacologic (i.e., antispasmodic drugs) or dietary (i.e., increased fiber).

A number of factors have been implicated in IBS, including the intake of fats, increased fluids, and artificial sweeteners (Cusson, 1994). Emotional factors, such as stress, have also been recognized as a possible cause. IBS is more common in adolescent girls than boys; in the younger age group, the incidence shows no gender difference (Cusson, 1994).

Problems with Elimination

The phrase "problems with elimination" generally evokes difficulty in passing stools, commonly referred to as **constipation.** This problem is found frequently both in children and adults and is often caused by inadequate fluid and fiber intake, in some cases in combination with uncoordinated muscle contractions and inadequate rectal sphincter control

(Eicher, 1997). Constipation can lead to a condition known as **encopresis,** a condition seen in as many as 1% to 3% of the pediatric population over the age of 4 (Chaney, 1995). Also known as **fecal incontinence,** encopresis is the involuntary passage of fecal material. The condition develops as follows. If the child withholds the bowel movement, perhaps to avoid painful defecation, the large stool mass stretches the walls of the colon and rectum and in turn puts pressure on the anal sphincter, causing it to relax. While the hard stool remains in the rectal cavity, the soft stool leaks out involuntarily, and the child soils his or her underwear. Levine (1982) listed the following factors that may contribute to the genesis of encopresis in school-age children: avoidance of school bathrooms; prolonged or acute gastroenteritis; attention deficit with task impersistence (i.e., they seldom finish the task at hand, leading to incomplete defecation); food intolerance or excess; frenetic lifestyle; and psychosocial stresses. Encopresis is believed to be as much as six times more common in males than females, and it "shows little or no preference for social class" (Levine, 1982).

The more common elimination problem in children is **diarrhea,** the opposite of constipation, defined as increased fluidity of fecal material and increased volume of stool or increased number of stools, typically caused by lack of dietary fiber, dumping (the abnormal rapid emptying of the stomach), overaggressive use of laxatives or enemas, or the passing of loose stool around a fecal impaction (Eicher, 1997).

Constipation and diarrhea are *not* diseases per se; rather, they are symptoms of some underlying condition. For example, constipation can be a problem for those with limited mobility, such as persons with a spinal cord injury or defect, and diarrhea is often associated with problems with absorption, such as celiac disease or lactose intolerance. In the pediatric population, there are three other problems that occur with some degree of frequency that can result in difficulty in eliminating solid waste material. They are Hirschsprung's disease, anorectal malformations, and intussusception.

Hirschsprung's Disease

Also known as **aganglionic magacolon** or **aganglionosis, Hirschsprung's disease** is a congenital condition that results from the absence of ganglion cells in the muscular wall of the intestine. The disease occurs at a rate of between 1 and 10 per 5,000 live births (Cusson, 1994; Peck & Buzby, 1992). The affected segment of the bowel of a child with this condition is in a contracted state, resulting in a functional obstruction that does not permit the passing of fecal material (i.e., inhibited peristalsis). The defect occurs upward from the anal area, and the normal portion of the bowel proximal to the constriction becomes dilated from the fecal material that has accumulated, resulting in the condition known as **megacolon.** In cases where the obstruction is not complete, the child is constipated and has a poor appetite. While there is no racial predilection, the ratio of males to females is 4 to 1 (Freeman & Adelson, 1996).

In most cases, the condition can be successfully treated surgically by the removal of the aganglionic segment and the surgical reconnection of the two remaining parts, a surgical procedure referred to as a **reanastomosis** of the intestine. Hirschsprung's disease may be associated with other types of congenital anomalies. Those with Down syndrome are ten times more likely to have Hirschsprung's disease than those without (Freeman & Adelson, 1996).

Anorectal Malformations

Anorectal malformations can range in severity from a mild narrowing of the anal canal (**anal stenosis**) to complete absence of the anal opening (**anal atresia**). The incidence for these malformations has been estimated to be between 1 in 3,000 and 1 in 5,000 live births (Cusson, 1994; Peck & Buzby, 1992). Anorectal malformation is more common in males than females. In 75% to 80% of the cases, the anus or rectum ends in a blind pouch, a condition known as **anal** or **rectal agenesis.** In cases where there is no anus, the infant often has a variety of other anomalies, a condition referred to as **VATER/VACTERL syndrome.** This acronym refers to vertebral abnormalities (**V**), anal atresia (**A**), tracheoesophageal fistula (**TE**), renal disorders (**R**), and cardiac (**C**) and limb (**L**) abnormalities. Surgical intervention is typically required to correct an anal anomaly to allow the fecal material to pass from the body with ease. In some cases, a series of surgeries may be needed before the defect is completely and adequately repaired.

Other Common Chronic Gastrointestinal Problems

Hepatitis, inflammation of the liver, is another chronic condition affecting GI function that is seen commonly in both children and young adults. In this population, the most common cause of this condition is a viral infection. For further information on infectious hepatitis, see chapter 23, where communicable diseases are addressed. Gastrointestinal upset that results from intestinal parasites, such as roundworms and tapeworms, is also covered in that chapter. In this section, ulcers, a condition normally associated with adults, are discussed.

Peptic Ulcer Disease

An ulcer is an erosion of the mucosa of the abdomen. **Peptic ulcers** are those found in the stomach (**gastric ulcer**) or duodenum and pylorus (**duodenal ulcer**) and are caused by an imbalance of acid and pepsin in the GI juices and a decreased ability of the GI mucosa to protect the underlying tissues from damage.

It is not uncommon for an ulcer to arise in an otherwise healthy youngster. Such an ulcer is referred to as a **primary** or **idiopathic ulcer.** The most common site in children is the duodenum, and typically only one ulcer develops at a time (Wenner & Piccoli, 1996). A **secondary ulcer** is one that arises as a result of some underlying systemic disorder (e.g., stress arising from a traumatic insult, such as a TBI or a severe burn) or as a result of taking certain types of medication (e.g., NSAIDs). It has been estimated that at least 50% of all cases of peptic ulcer disease result from *Helicobacter pylori* infection; some have suggested that as many as 100% are caused by this bacterium (Wenner & Piccoli, 1996). Boys tend to be more commonly affected than girls; the male-female ratio is 1.5 to 1 (Whaley & Wong, 1995).

The most common symptom of a peptic ulcer is abdominal pain either around or above the umbilicus. The pain can be steady or intermittent and may or may not be relieved by the consumption of food. Vomiting, nausea, dyspepsia (heartburn), and flatulence are other typical symptoms. Peptic ulcers are most commonly treated by over-the-counter (OTC) antacids (e.g., Maalox, Mylanta, Diovol) or by prescription drugs known as histamine H_2-receptor an-

tagonists, such as Tagamet, that inhibit the production of stomach acids. For ulcers that are believed to be caused by infection, antibiotics, such as Ampicin (ampicillin) or Amoxil (amoxycillin), may be prescribed in conjunction with the antacid Bismed (bismuth subsalicylate).

Dietary therapy may be of some assistance. It was once believed that a diet rich in milk and milk products would assist in "curing" ulcers; however, research has led physicians to believe that milk and milk products that are high in calcium may actually stimulate acid secretion and, consequently, result in a rebound effect that aggravates the condition. Generally, individuals who have ulcers are encouraged to refrain from consuming items that stimulate the production of acidic secretions (e.g., tea, coffee, carbonated beverages, alcohol, high-acid foods, and fried foods).

Educational Implications and Teaching Tips

Although the number of students with serious chronic digestive problems may not be great, for these children daily attendance at school may be difficult at best, given the very private nature of their problems, in particular those problems related to elimination (e.g., diarrhea, flatulence). For example, for the student with a colostomy, physical education classes, which may involve changing clothes in a public place, may be extremely stressful; for the student with CD, having to leave the classroom repeatedly throughout the day may be embarrassing. An understanding teacher can be invaluable to the student, as can membership in a support group. Some of the following suggestions may be of assistance to school staff in dealing with students with altered GI function.

1 *In many cases, students with a GI problem are able to attend school on a regular basis, as long as certain accommodations are permitted.* For example, the student who has chronic diarrhea needs unlimited access to washroom facilities and benefits from having a seat as close to the door of the classroom as possible, to slip out quickly and unobtrusively.

In some cases, however, particularly those situations in which there is an acute flare-up of the condition, such as celiac disease, the student may be absent for a period of time, often as little as a day or two, until the crisis situation is back under control. Students with IBD also often attend school sporadically. Some absences are the result of avoidance behavior, which has been attributed to a combination of embarrassment and a tendency of the symptoms to become worse under stress (Cusson, 1994).

2 *Many students who have altered GI functioning require a specialized diet.* If the student brings food from home, generally there are few problems; however, if the student eats in the school cafeteria, problems may arise. The school's dietitian and cook should meet with the student's parents or nutritionist to review which foods are acceptable so that a suitable selection may be made available.

Particularly problematic are those events in which food is served that is not prepared by persons who know the child's needs (e.g., off-campus outings). However, by working together with the student's parents, simple solutions can generally be found. In the case of special events at school (e.g., Halloween party), the students who have a special diet could bring in their own foods, such as gluten-free cakes and cookies, and share them with their friends.

3 *School staff should be alert to signs that the student has not been following the diet.* Typically, if the student has not been true to the diet that has been prescribed, there will be a noticeable increase of signs of the illness (e.g., frequent episodes of diarrhea, increased fatigue). If the student's teacher has any concerns, they should be raised with the student's parents or discussed with the school nurse or administrator, who can contact the student's family.

4 *In many cases, students with GI problems may not have sufficient energy to keep up with their peers.* For some, this may be a result of malnutrition; for others, the lack of stamina may be caused by the medication required to control the symptoms of the medical condition. If the prescribed drugs have a sedating effect, students may have difficulty concentrating on their work and may be drowsy. Some students may benefit from being able to have a nap if they are extremely tired. Work that

requires sustained concentration should be scheduled for immediately after the meal (e.g., first thing in the morning or afternoon). With this schedule, the drug, which is typically given with or shortly after meals, will only be beginning to take effect.

5 *Most students with a GI problem are typically not prohibited from participating in regular physical activities solely on the basis of the presenting condition.* Generally, if the student feels sufficiently rested, participation in permitted activities should be encouraged. Forms to use in contacting the student's physician regarding possible restrictions are found in Appendix D.

Those who have recently undergone abdominal surgery, such as the removal of a diseased section of the bowel, are generally not permitted to participate in most forms of sports (e.g., rough contact sports, such as football; weight lifting; gymnastics) and strenuous activities (e.g., long-distance running; bicycle riding) for at least a month or more after surgery or until the incision is well healed. Physical education instructors and coaches should make sure that the surgeon gives written clearance before the student returns to activities that were participated in before surgery.

Students with chronic IBD are generally advised to refrain from excessive physical activity during an exacerbation of the disease, to decrease intestinal mobility. Since they typically do not feel like participating as a result of general malaise and fatigue, compliance is generally not problematic.

A student who has a distended abdomen may find certain physical activities difficult because the enlargement may limit movement, put pressure on the lungs that causes shortness of breath, and result in increased pain. The student may benefit from pursuing more sedentary activities, such as photography, chess, and computer games (Danek, 1990).

6 *Individuals who have GI difficulties, in particular those with encopresis or IBD, have to live with the fear of fecal incontinence.* Classroom teachers must ensure that any incidents are handled with sensitivity and in a nonpunitive manner and that the student is able to retain as much control and dignity as possible (Chaney, 1995; Pollack, 1996). An extra change of clothes should be kept in the student's locker or in the nurse's or principal's office. A change of clothes should always accompany the student if a field trip is planned. If the student wears diapers, it is important that proper procedures for changing are used to ensure the safety of students and staff (see chapter 24, universal precautions).

7 *Safety should always be a concern for teachers.*
As mentioned previously, a frequent cause of morbidity and mortality in young children is the ingestion and inhalation of foreign objects, so all staff should attempt to make the learning environment as safe as possible. Extreme caution should be taken in day care centers and schools in which very young children are present. The safety procedures shown in Table 17.2 should be in place in all environments where young children are found.

Whaley and Wong (1995, p. 1455) have listed a number of procedures for caregivers to follow when a youngster ingests a foreign object. These guidelines (Table 17.3) may assist school staff in determining when to seek medical treatment. However,

TABLE 17.2
Ingestion and Inhalation of Foreign Objects: Basic Safety Precautions

- All corrosive substances must be put in a secure area (i.e., locked closets) to prevent accidental consumption.
- All medications must be placed in child-resistant containers and be placed in locked cupboards. It is not sufficient to "hide" the drugs by placing them on the top shelves of a medicine cabinet, as young children, who often equate pills with candy, typically are quite capable of getting into such hiding places.
- Caregivers must be alert to young children placing objects in their mouth, including pieces of food that have not been cut into an appropriate size. Very young children should not be given foods such as carrot chunks or cut-up hot dogs, because of the risk of asphyxiation. Other objects found in a school or day care center that pose a risk include erasers, paper clips, bottle tops, and small toys, such as marbles, jacks, and Legos.
- Young children should not be left alone to play with any piece of equipment that is powered by small batteries. All toys that contain disc button batteries should be carefully examined to ensure that the battery compartment is "childproof." Adults should be very careful in disposing of all used batteries.

TABLE 17.3
Emergency Treatment: Foreign Body Ingestion

1. Seek medical treatment immediately if:
   a. Any sharp or large object or a battery was ingested.
   b. There are signs that the object may have been aspirated (i.e., coughing, choking, inability to speak, or difficulty in breathing).
   c. There are signs of GI perforation (i.e., chest or abdominal pain, evidence of bleeding in vomitus, stool, hematocrit [measure of the ratio of RBC to volume of whole blood has been affected], or vital signs [e.g., hypotension].)
   d. There are signs that the object may be lodged in the pharynx (i.e., discomfort in the throat or chest—more likely with a fish or chicken bone or large piece of meat).
2. Seek medical advice even if the object is smooth and small (usually less than the size of a nickel).
3. If no treatment is required, check the stool for passage of the object; do not give laxatives.

Whaley, L. F., & Wong, D. L. (1995). *Nursing care of infants and children* (5th ed.). St. Louis: Mosby. Copyright 1995 by Mosby-Year Book, Inc. Reprinted by permission.

it is better to err on the side of safety and to ensure that the student is given medical attention if there is any risk of danger.

❧ Eating Disorders

The term **eating disorder** is used to refer to any severe disturbance in eating behavior (American Psychiatric Association [APA], 1994). In the U.S., it has been estimated that 700,000 children and young adults have an eating disorder (O'Neill, 1994). According to some researchers, eating disorders rank as the third most common chronic illness among adolescent females (Neumark-Sztainer, 1996).

Eating disorders are not new; they were documented as early as 1689 (Csapo, 1987; Kalb, 1993). In this section three different eating disorders are covered. The first, **anorexia nervosa**, results in excessive weight loss; in the second, **bulimia nervosa,** even though the condition is characterized by binge eating, weight gain does not occur because the individual uses inappropriate compensatory efforts, such as excessive exercise or vomiting after bingeing. The third, **morbid obesity,** is a condition of excessive weight gain. While all three eating disorders are distinct from each other in terms of cause, symptoms, and treatment, there are a number of characteristics, such as low self-esteem, that are common to all disease states (Kalb, 1993). It should be noted that some individuals have more than one eating disorder at one time. For example, a person can be obese *and* bulimic or be anorexic *and* bulimic.

Anorexia Nervosa (AN)

The term **anorexia,** from the Greek word *orexis,* meaning "not having an appetite," is a misnomer in the case of the condition known as **anorexia nervosa,** because rarely does the individual with this condition lose the desire to eat (Rock & Zerbe, 1995). Rather, with AN, the individual forces himself or herself not to eat (i.e., self-imposed starvation) and as a result is unable to maintain even a minimally normal body weight for age and height (APA, 1994). The condition is found almost exclusively in industrialized societies in which there is an abundance of food and where being "thin" is considered "attractive." The prevalence of AN is estimated at between 0.5% and 4%; the rate is thought to be on the increase (Connolly & Corbett-Dick, 1990). Sours (1980) has perhaps best described the paradox of AN: "Anorexia nervosa represents the oxymoronic ultimate in achievement, a conquest of the body by the self, whereby the self achieves the illusion of supreme glory" (p. 5).

Anorexia nervosa has an insidious beginning. Typically, the young adolescent, most likely female, believes that she is too fat and begins a diet in which there is a reduction in those foods that are highly caloric. Over time, the diet becomes more and more restrictive, to the point that the individual's food intake is limited to only a few select foods, such as rice cakes or celery sticks. One of the major manifestations of this condition is the intense fear expressed by the individual of gaining weight or becoming fat (APA, 1994). Oddly, in many cases, as the individual loses more and more weight, the concerns about weight gain increase exponentially. Aside from a dramatic loss of weight, other psychological signs and symptoms of AN include personality changes, depressed mood, apathy, social withdrawal, irritability, insomnia, bad dreams, preoccupation with thoughts of food, concerns about eating in public, feelings of ineffectiveness, a need to control one's environment, inflexible thinking, limited social spontaneity, and overly restrained initiative and emotional expression. Associated physical findings include constipation, abdominal pain, cold intolerance from the loss of subcutaneous fat, lethargy, excess energy, emaciation, hypotension, hypothermia, dry skin, scalp hair loss, brittle nails, growth of lanugo (a fine body hair on the trunk, similar to that found on newborns), heart irregularities (e.g., bradycardia), thinning of the bones and increased incidence of fractures, joint swelling, and yellowing of the skin (APA, 1993, 1994; Edwards, 1993; Maughan, 1991). In young women, amenorrhea (lack of menstrual cycles) is common; loss of sexual interest may also occur, particularly in young men. Individuals with AN often deny that they have any of these symptoms (Connolly & Corbett-Dick, 1990).

Persons with AN are typically high achievers, often with a perfectionist attitude combined with a tendency to be socially insecure and excessively dependent on others (Edwards, 1993). Although most individuals with AN consciously starve themselves, some have bulimic tendencies. Typically, those individuals who show both characteristics eat a copious amount of food, only to purge themselves of it (i.e., engage in self-induced vomiting); others eat only a minuscule amount of food and still purge themselves of it.

Treatment for AN, which commonly includes the use of support groups, psychotherapy (e.g., behavioral, cognitive, and family therapy), nutritional counseling, and psychopharmacology (e.g., administration of psychoactive drugs, such as the antidepressant fluoxetine hydrochloride, or Prozac), requires a multidisciplinary approach (Edwards, 1993). Ideally, physicians, psychiatrists, psychologists, family therapists, and nutritionists work together with the individual and his or her family. There is no "fast" cure or "magic bullet" that eradicates the condition; however, the younger the student when AN develops, the better the outlook for recovery. As many as 10% of those with AN die as a result of the illness. Mortality depends on the duration of the disorder, the time of initial intervention, the presence of depression, potential for suicide, the degree of food restriction, and whether or not the condition is complicated by purgation (Comerci, 1990).

Bulimia Nervosa (BN)

The eating disorder **bulimia nervosa** is often found in persons of normal weight. The term originated from the Greek words *bous,* ox, and *limos,* hunger. In this eating disorder, rather than self-imposed starvation, the individual has periods in which too much is eaten followed by periods in which the individual does something to prevent weight gain. The most common ways to eliminate the excess food from the body are to induce vomiting or to take laxatives or diuretics. Individuals who resort to such methods of losing weight are referred to as **purging bulimics**. Individuals who fast between binge periods to limit intake of calories or engage in excessive exercise to burn off the calories they have consumed are referred to as **nonpurging bulimics**. The prevalence of bulimia or bulimic behavior is significantly higher than that of AN, possibly as high as 15% to 30% of the population in Western society (Edwards, 1993), and like AN, bulimia occurs more often in women. However, those with bulimia tend to be somewhat older (i.e., between the ages of 17 and 25) than those with anorexia.

Typically, patients with BN have difficulty with impulse control. A high incidence of substance abuse, theft (e.g., shoplifting food, stealing money to buy food), and suicide is also common (Edwards, 1993). In comparison to those with anorexia, individuals with BN tend to be more flexible and more adaptive to their environment (Edwards, 1993). Psychiatric signs of BN include low self-esteem; mood disorders or borderline personality disorder; fear of social situations and of not being able to stop eating; and depression, guilt, or remorse after a binge. Physical signs and symptoms, typically quite subtle in nature and consequently difficult to detect, include tooth erosion, particularly of the front teeth, which results from recurrent vomiting; calloused knuckles (referred to as **Russell's sign**) caused by the backs of the hands coming in contact with the teeth as the individual attempts to stimulate the gag reflex; stomach lacerations; a chronically inflamed and sore throat, which has a tendency to bleed; esophageal infections from excessive vomiting; swollen salivary glands; puffy cheeks; abnormal heart rhythm; kidney and bladder infections that may result in kidney failure; and amenorrhea or menstrual irregularities (APA, 1993, 1994; Edwards, 1993; Maughan, 1991). Like those with AN, those with BN may fear gaining weight, desire to lose weight, and have a high degree of dissatisfaction with their bodies (APA, 1994). On the whole, those with BN are not as severely physically ill as those with AN.

Treatment options for individuals with bulimia are the same as those for anorexia. Although the complications of BN are typically not as severe as AN, in some cases, fluid and electrolyte disturbances caused from repetitive purging may be life-threatening. As in the case of AN, the number of individuals who, after treatment, can be considered completely cured is small. Comerci (1990), while acknowledging that there have been no truly long-term follow-up studies, has suggested that the success rate is somewhere between 40% and 50%.

Morbid Obesity

Defined as the excess accumulation of fat in the body, **obesity** has reached epidemic proportions in the United States (Atkinson, Callaway, St. Jeor, & Wolf-Novak, 1995). While in many cases obesity results from an excess intake of calories over the number of calories needed by the body, obesity may or may not be related to excess consumption of food. In some individuals, research has shown that genetic factors appear to play a significant role in determining body mass; in others, the presence of a specific disease, such as hypothyroidism, may be an underlying factor.

Obese children are at greater risk than their normal peers for conditions such as hypertension, respiratory disease, diabetes, and orthopedic problems such as Legg-Calvé-Perthes disease and genu valgum. They are also at risk for psychosocial dysfunction (Ryan, 1993). Obesity typically persists into adulthood; approximately 80% of overweight children become overweight adults (Huse, Branes, Colligan, Nelson, & Palumbo, 1982). In addition, if an older adolescent is obese, the chances are believed to be 28 to 1 that a normal body weight will not be achieved at a later date (Huse et al., 1982). The number of children between the ages of 6 and 11 who are considered obese rose by 54% from the mid-1960s to the late 1970s (Ryan, 1993). In children who have not reached puberty, the prevalence of obesity has been determined to be between 25% and 30%; in adolescents, the rate is between 18% and 25% (Whaley & Wong, 1995).

❧ The Educator's Role in Preventing Eating Disorders

There are obvious physical differences between those who lose a great amount of weight and those who gain a great deal. However, aside from the physical differences, the most critical difference is the person's emotional health. In most cases, individuals who become anorexic or bulimic have a severe psychiatric disorder; those who gain weight, in most cases, do not. However, some individuals who are morbidly obese use food as a means to reduce stress and anxiety and may show signs of serious emotional disturbance.

Although maintaining a healthy weight is lifelong work for those who are overweight and requires major lifestyle changes, obesity, in many cases, can be treated successfully. Teachers can assist students who have a weight problem by being supportive of their efforts to lose the extra pounds. However, prevention is the best approach for dealing with obesity because faulty eating patterns of early childhood are difficult to break once they have become well established. For those individuals who are obese, a combination of adhering to a well-balanced diet, engaging in structured physical activities, and applying behavioral techniques is believed to be the most efficacious treatment plan (Harbin, 1992). Teachers can not only provide their students with information on proper eating habits, they can also be effective role models.

Anorexia and bulimia are typically more difficult to treat than obesity. The following suggestions are given to help teachers not only deal with students who have an eating disorder that can lead to excessive weight loss, but also to assist in recognizing those individuals who have the potential to become anorexic or bulimic.

1 *School staff, especially school nurses, counselors, teachers (particularly physical education teachers), and athletic coaches and trainers can play a major role in recognizing those individuals who are at risk for developing an eating disorder that results in excess weight loss.* Connolly and Corbett-Dick (1990) listed the following risk factors to look for: (1) participation in body-conscious sports and activities such as wrestling, swimming, gymnastics, and dancing; (2) overachievement; (3) a perfectionistic or obsessional nature; (4) chaotic family systems; (5) a recent family crisis, such as death or divorce; (6) a friend or sibling with an eating disorder; (7) low self-esteem; and (8) impulsivity (p. 402).

2 *While recognizing that those with an eating disorder may be evasive or deny that a problem exists, it is best to confront the students in a way*

that is open, honest, and nonpunitive (Connolly & Corbett-Dick; 1990). Parents should be involved as soon as possible, particularly in light of the legal and ethical implications if the school chooses to ignore what could be a potential health problem (Connolly & Corbett-Dick; 1990). O'Neill (1994), whose daughter, a budding gymnast, developed an eating disorder, offers the following suggestions, which may be useful for school staff. Although these suggestions are given for the young girl who shows signs of an eating disorder, they are also appropriate for the male student:

- Don't make comments like "You're too thin!" Criticism will only fuel her obsession with her appearance and make her withdraw even further.
- Explain your suspicions, and describe the habits that aroused them. For example: "I noticed that you're skipping meals and losing lots of weight. I'm concerned for your health."
- Realize that she may respond to your overtures by becoming hostile. Try not to get discouraged by the rebuff. Remember, you're threatening to break through her denial, which is bound to frighten her.
- Make encouraging comments, like "I enjoy being around you." They'll make her feel safe and valued—and may help you get past her defenses.
- Forget about using scare tactics. They're out of line and aren't effective. Also refrain from constantly nagging, bribing, and manipulating her into eating.
- Recognize and rethink your attitudes toward your own body and dieting habits. Could you unwittingly be setting an unhealthy example? (p. 84)

3 *If school staff (e.g., teachers, school nurses) are going to provide instruction regarding eating disorders, the problems should not be glamorized.* Connolly and Corbett-Dick (1990) state that "if students view eating disorders as something that happens to smart, attractive, and popular students, the behavior may be emulated" (pp. 403–404). Csapo (1987) has suggested that curricula should include a thorough study of the influence of media, women's role in society, sexuality, and good nutrition. For further information on school-based programs to prevent eating disturbances, see the recent article by Neumark-Sztainer (1996).

4 *In the past, most individuals with an eating disorder were believed to be female, but the number of males with such disorders may be on the increase.* Those involved in certain sports where weight may be a factor in speed, such as swimming and track and field, are especially at risk. Connolly and Corbett-Dick (1990) have suggested that those who are involved in athletic programs "may" (perhaps should) be the first to recognize an eating disorder. They give three reasons to support this hypothesis: (a) physical endurance and performance are likely to suffer before academic performance declines or before other symptoms emerge; (b) it is hard to hide weight loss in skintight athletic gym clothes; and (c) to determine eligibility, students are often weighed before competition. Smith (1980) has suggested the following principles regarding weight levels of athletes:

1. The desired level of fatness that will be compatible with optimum health fitness and athletic performance must be precisely defined for each athlete.
2. A timetable of fatness reduction and muscle increase is established. This will project no more than a 2- to 3-lb. (0.9- to 1.3-kg) reduction in weight per week, making it mandatory that fatness reduction must be started well in advance of the competing season. Rapid "crash" programs cannot be compatible with good health and optimum athletic performance.
3. The negative energy balance required for reduction in body fat is created with a moderate increase in energy expenditure in training activities accompanied by a modest reduction in caloric intake. The diet should provide no less than 1,800 to 2,200 kcal for most young men or 1,600 to 2,000 kcal for most women athletes. A preseasoning conditioning workout of 90 minutes should expend 400 to 600 kcal or more. If a negative caloric balance of 1,000 kcal per day is achieved, there will be a loss of body fat of 2 lb. (0.9 kg) a week.
4. Some individual other than the coach should be responsible for supervising the weight control of athletes. A physician, school nurse, trainer, or assistance coach can serve in this role. (p. 141)

Other suggestions regarding the supervision and management of weight loss made by Smith (1980) include the weighing of all serious athletes on a weekly basis to ensure that the desired energy balance is being maintained and the medical referral of any student who shows a sudden loss or fluctuation in body weight.

❦ Alternative Methods of Ingestion

As mentioned previously, the most common (and ideal) way to consume food is by mouth. However, in some cases, an alternative method of delivering nutrition may be needed. The two different forms, **parenteral** and **enteral feeding,** can be either a replacement of the usual form of feeding or a supplement to the usual form of feeding.

Parenteral Feeding

The administration of nutrients directly into the vascular system, bypassing the digestive system completely, is known as **parenteral feeding.** The parenteral nutrition (PN) solution consists of various combinations of carbohydrates, proteins, fats, amino acids, electrolytes, vitamins, minerals, and trace elements, such as zinc and copper, dissolved in a saline solution. PN solution can be used to provide sufficient nutrition to meet the demands of the body for brief periods, such as immediately after surgery to restore adequate fluid and electrolyte balance that might have been diminished by blood loss, or for longer periods, such as when an individual is in a coma or when a person has short bowel syndrome, intractable diarrhea, or IBD. If parenteral feeding is the only means by which the person is obtaining nourishment, he or she is said to be receiving **total parenteral nutrition** (TPN). This method of obtaining nourishment is also referred to as **hyperalimentation.**

In the past, TPN was generally only administered in a hospital; however, it is now becoming more common to see youngsters returning home (and to school) receiving this form of nutritional therapy. This change has resulted from the development of **central venous access devices** (VADs) that can be surgically implanted for long-term use. By means of these devices, also known as **central lines, subcutaneous ports,** and **right atrial** or **central venous catheters,** nutrients (and medication, if needed) can be administered directly into the superior vena cava,

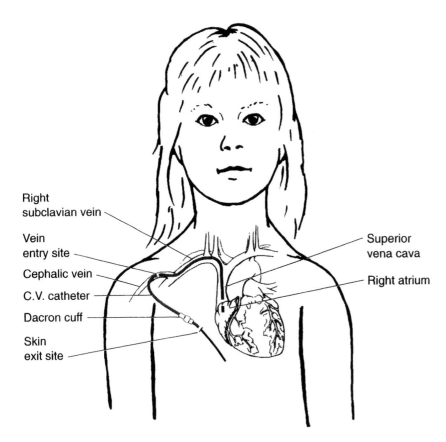

Right
subclavian vein

Vein
entry site

Cephalic vein

C.V. catheter

Dacron cuff

Skin
exit site

Superior
vena cava

Right atrium

Figure 17.3
Diagram of Long-Term Partially Implanted Device

the major vein leading into the right atrium of the heart.

Some VADs are **partially implanted (PIDs);** i.e., a catheter[2] protrudes outside the body (Figure 17.3). Others are **totally implanted (TIDs);** i.e., the device[3] is placed completely under the skin and access requires the piercing of the skin that covers it (Figure 17.4). Once in the heart, the PN solution circulates throughout the system, bringing nourishment where needed. This type of access allows individuals to receive nutrition without having to endure repeated needlesticks that occur with the standard intravenous route. Because a person's full nutritional

requirements can be met through TPN, it is possible for this alternative to be used indefinitely.[4]

The following points should be heeded by school staff:

1 *Staff working with students receiving parenteral feedings who have a venous access device surgically implanted should be provided with detailed*

---

[2] Catheters are often referred to by the name of the designer or the manufacurer. Common types include the Broviac, Cook, Groshong, Hickman, Leonard, and Quinton catheters.

[3] Different types of devices include the Port-a-Cath, Infus-A-Port, MediPort, and Norport SP.

---

[4] Students who have a VAD for the purposes of TPN, in many cases, are receiving nourishment continuously. For these students, the tubing that comes out of the chest and the intravenous equipment that holds the nutrient solution are very visible. However, for those who have a VAD to receive medication (e.g., a child with cystic fibrosis who is being given antibiotics on a regular basis or a child with cancer who is receiving chemotherapy intravenously), the venous catheter is most often capped during school hours and the tubing is covered by a sterile bandage, which in turn is hidden by the student's clothing. The VAD does not cause any discomfort if the tubing is properly secured (i.e., fastened to the chest wall with adhesive tape).

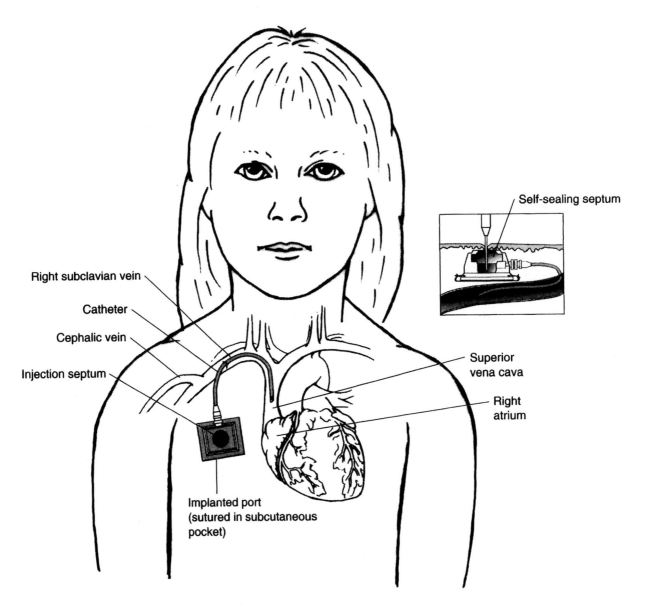

Figure 17.4
Venous Access Devices: Totally Implanted Device

information on what a VAD is, how it works, and the type of care that may be required. An emergency care plan must be developed (see Appendix C), and staff must be trained to know what to do if an emergency situation arises.

Even though the VAD should be secured with tape or clothing at all times, unintentional removal or displacement of the catheter can occur. In the case of implanted ports, young children have been known to "play" with the bulge under the skin, an activity that has been referred to in the medical lit-

erature as "twiddler's syndrome" (Marcoux, Fisher, & Wong, 1990). Signs of the catheter being displaced include swelling, pain, numbness, or tingling in the right side of the shoulder region. If a partially implanted device has been pulled out of the vein, the catheter may appear to be longer than normal (Marcoux et al., 1990). In either situation, the emergency plan should be activated immediately (i.e., the student should be taken to the hospital).

If the catheter is removed accidentally, pressure should be applied at the site where the catheter enters the right subclavian vein, just under the right shoulder blade, and not near the exit site (Figure 17.4). The student should be transported to a medical facility immediately.

If the catheter shows signs of leakage, the catheter should be clamped as close to the chest as possible and the student should be taken to the hospital for treatment. There should be an extra catheter clamp available near the student at all times (Meeske & Davidson, 1988).

2 *While in most cases the device operates without any difficulty, the student with a VAD should be carefully monitored for any signs of sepsis, which is an infection that arises from contamination of the indwelling catheter.* Visible symptoms include fever, chills, and decreased level of consciousness. Some students show signs of fatigue even without a fever (Marcoux et al., 1990).

Redness at the insertion and exit site may also be an indicator of infection. Even though the risk of infection can be significantly reduced if the caregiver is trained to provide meticulous catheter care, sepsis can occur even with proper care (Marcoux et al., 1990).

3 *If parenteral feeding occurs during school hours, the student would benefit from having access to a clean, private location, such as the nurse's office.* Therapy should not be given in front of a large number of people, heavy machinery, or other hazards (Wildblood & Strezo, 1987). All fluids should be properly stored in a secure storage area. Universal precautions should be taken in providing care (chapter 24).

4 *Students who have a VAD may have certain restrictions placed on them in terms of physical activity.* A Recreational Activity Permission Form (see Appendix D) should be used to obtain information from the student's doctor. As long as the tubing is properly covered or implanted device is protected as much as possible, students are generally permitted to participate in non-contact activities. While swimming may not be allowed if the student has a partially implanted device, if the device is totally implanted, swimming may be permitted after the suture line has shown signs of adequate healing (Marcoux et al., 1990).

Enteral Feeding

For those who can digest food but for some reason are unable to take food in the normal manner, that is, via the mouth, **enteral feeding,** more commonly referred to as **tube feeding,** may be a viable option. An example of a student who may need tube feeding would be a youngster who has a particular muscular disorder, such as cerebral palsy, that affects the ability to swallow. In such cases the student's problem is in getting the food from the mouth to the stomach, not from the stomach through the rest of the intestinal tract.

In enteral feeding, nutritionally balanced, liquefied "regular" food or commercially prepared formula (or a combination of both) is introduced into the body by means of a tube that is either passed through the nose and down the esophagus directly into the stomach (a **nasogastric,** or **NG, tube**) or surgically inserted into the stomach or the jejunum (a **gastrostomy tube,** or **G-tube;** or a **jejunostomy tube,** or **J-tube**). Nasogastric tubes are typically used for short periods, whereas G- or J-tubes are usually inserted for long-term access. Students who require a permanent placement may have a **gastrostomy button,** a device that is surgically implanted to which a tube is attached at the time of feeding.

Enteral feedings can occur intermittently or continuously. **Intermittent feeding** typically uses some kind of container (e.g., syringe, feeding bag) to hold the food or formula. At the time of feeding, the prescribed amount is placed in the container, which in turn is connected to the NG, G-, or J-tube. The rate of flow is regulated by the height of the container. **Continuous feeding,** as the name implies, involves continuous connection to some type of feeding bag (also known as a **kangaroo bag**), which is normally held aloft on either an intravenous stand (with or without a pump) or by some type of wall attachment (e.g., plant hook suspended from the ceiling). In systems that do not have a pump, the speed of flow is regulated by the height of the bag. In systems that have a pump, the flow rate is controlled mechanically.

The following pointers are for those working with students who are tube fed:

1 *During feeding, the student should remain stationary.* Quiet activities during the feeding time (e.g., listening to music, reading a book) are appropriate. For students receiving enteral feeding, privacy may be an issue. While being fed by a tube is a meal time just like it is for others, some students, particularly those who are older, appreciate being able to use the nurse's office.

2 *Persons involved in tube feedings must be properly trained.* Basic guidelines on how to tube feed a student are provided in Table 17.4. The suggestions given in this section are *not* sufficient for complete training. Caregivers should be trained by a qualified enterostomal therapist.

Caregivers should be alert to any signs of difficulty. If the student complains of being nauseated, the rate of feeding may be too fast. If cramps are a problem, the food, which should be at room temperature, may be too cold. If the student shows any signs of aspiration (e.g., changes in color, difficulty breathing, gagging, choking), the feeding should be stopped immediately. If the problem continues,

medical assistance should be sought immediately. All persons working with children who receive enteral feeding should be trained in CPR.

3 *Students who are receiving enteral feedings are typically allowed to participate in most physical activities.* However, during physical activities, care must be taken to ensure that the feeding tube is properly clamped so as to prevent leakage. The tube should also be adequately secured so that the likelihood of it being pulled out is minimized. However, if the tube is pulled out, the situation is *not* a medical emergency. In the case of a tube that is surgically inserted into the stomach, the opening should be covered with a dry bandage or Band-Aid, and the parents should be notified immediately. If the stomach contents leak, cover the opening with a diaper or some other cloth that is absorbent (Cusson, 1994).

TABLE 17.4
General Guidelines for Enteral Feeding

1. Gather and assemble equipment (e.g., food, syringe or feeding bag, tubing, intravenous pole or plant hook, plug or clamp, water, tape for securing tube). Wash hands thoroughly before preparing for a tube feeding. Gloves are not needed for this procedure.

2. Allow refrigerated formula or food to come to room temperature before serving (approximately 20 to 30 minutes). Heat food for those that need it slightly warm.
   Note: Never allow "regular" food to sit out of the refrigerator for more than 45 minutes. Never allow commercially prepared food to be left out for more than 4 hours. Check all cans of commercial formula to ensure that it has not expired. Top of the can should be carefully (a) washed with soap and water, (b) rinsed with clean water, and (c) dried before opening.

3. Position the child as instructed and check position of tube for placement and patency. Check for residual formula as instructed.

4. Follow procedure for tube feeding as instructed. Observe the student during feeding and note any abnormal reactions. If he or she appears agitated, the tube may be incorrectly positioned. Reposition as instructed. Stop feeding if student remains agitated.

5. Irrigate tube with water after feeding as instructed. Feed at rate that is appropriate or prescribed. If the food is flowing too slowly, raise the syringe or bag; if the rate is too fast, lower the syringe or bag.

6. At end of feeding, clamp tube as instructed. If any food or formula has leaked or spilled, clean up. Clean stoma as directed and if appropriate. Ensure tubing is secure (e.g., tucked inside clothing, taped to side of cheek). Disconnect the syringe or bag.

7. Wash all equipment in hot soapy water and rinse well. Label and date any unused formula or food and store in the refrigerator. Food should always be properly stored (i.e., covered). Leftover formula or blenderized food should not be kept more than 24 hours. Feeding equipment (e.g., syringe) should be stored in a clean, secure area.

8. Wash hands. Document procedure (e.g., amount, tolerance) in feeding log (Appendix G). Keep student elevated for prescribed period after a meal to prevent reflux.

Sources: Cusson (1994); Larson (1986); Porter, Haynie, Bierle, Caldwell, & Palfrey (1997)

The child should be taken to the hospital within 2 hours. The old tube should be taken along so that staff are able to determine the correct size. If the NG tube falls out, the parents should be notified; however, no other steps need to be taken.

🦋 Alternative Methods of Elimination

As described earlier, the normal way that an individual evacuates the various waste products from the body is via the anal canal. In some cases, however, a substitute method of elimination may be required. This is achieved surgically, and the procedure is referred to as an **ostomy.** The site of the surgery differentiates the type of ostomy. If the surgery involves the ileum, the person has an **ileostomy;** if the surgery is in the cecum, the person has a **cecostomy;** and if the opening was in the colon, the person has a **colostomy.** Regardless of the site, the procedure is basically the same; that is, the intestinal tube is brought to the surface of the body and an artificial anus, known as a **stoma,** is created. By means of a collection bag attached to the stoma, the fecal material is removed before it passes through the rectum.

Depending on where in the GI tract the ostomy is located, the fecal material differs in terms of consistency. For example, if the entire colon is removed, as in the case of an ileostomy, the fecal material is fairly watery in consistency because the colon is not there to absorb the water. If only part of the colon is removed the fecal material is more formed. For example, if the sigmoid colon (part of the descending colon) is removed, the discharge will not only be solid, it will be more likely to pass at a regular interval.

In some cases, such as when an individual has cancer of the bowel, the ostomy may be permanent; in others, such as when an ostomy is performed to treat an injury to the intestinal tract, the ostomy may be temporary. In short-term cases, the intestinal tract is surgically repaired so that its continuity is restored when it is deemed to be medically appropriate (in some cases as much as a year later).

The following suggestions are given for those who are working with students who have some type of ostomy:

1 *Most children who have a colostomy or an ileostomy are able to care for themselves by the time they are about age 10* (Danek, 1990). Younger children need the assistance of an adequately trained individual. Routine care involves primarily the emptying of the pouch of fecal material; however, if the pouch loosens or begins to leak, the

TABLE 17.5
General Guidelines for Ostomy Care

---

1. Gather and assemble equipment (e.g., soap and water, gauze pads, skin sealant, skin barrier, clean bag, disposable gloves).

2. Wash hands thoroughly and put on disposable gloves.

3. Empty contents of bag and flush fecal material down toilet. If able, the student should be positioned over the toilet when the bag is to be emptied. If not, the contents should be drained into a container (e.g., kidney basin). Rinse inside of pouch with warm water. Empty water into toilet or container. Dry outside of pouch with disposable towel. Apply deodorant, if needed. Ensure that the end of the pouch (known as the tail) is properly secured with either a clamp or rubber band.

   If bag needs to be changed, remove used bag (using adhesive remover or warm water) and dispose of the old pouch (wrap in a leakproof plastic bag and put in covered garbage pail). Clean stoma as instructed, inspecting skin for any signs of irritation or skin breakdown (redness, rash, bleeding, blistering). Dry skin by patting. Apply new bag as instructed.

   Note: Stomas should be dark pink in color and should be shiny or glistening. While they do not have any nerve endings (i.e., there is no sensation or pain), they are rich in blood vessels. Care should be taken not to injure the area inadvertently.

4. Remove gloves and thoroughly wash hands. Document procedure in daily log (Appendix G).

Sources: Cusson, 1994; Porter et al., 1997; Stever, 1986.

pouch may need to be changed. Adequate supplies should be kept at school and stored in a secure location. Basic guidelines for ostomy care are provided in Table 17.5.

2 *Regardless of the student's age, accidents can happen (e.g., leaks around the ostomy bag).* All children with ostomies should have a change of clothing at school and with them when they leave the school grounds (e.g., on a field trip). The child with as ostomy must have a place that offers privacy to perform the clean-up activities, including changing clothes, if necessary, as well as flushing the ostomy bag.

3 *Students who have an ostomy are not usually restricted from participating in physical activities.* However, it is a good practice to empty the ostomy bag before engaging in physical activity so that the risk of leakage is minimized.

Summary

There are many different types of GI disorders found in children that have a physical cause. Typically, they are grouped into four different types: problems of ingestion, digestion, absorption, and elimination. Many of the conditions are congenital; others are adventitious. Regardless of the type of problem and age at onset, growth may be affected, both physically and emotionally. For children with altered GI function to develop in a normal manner, they need the understanding of others around them. Teachers must be aware of the needs of these students and be as supportive as possible. Teachers should be particularly alert to any signs that a student may be developing an eating disorder such as anorexia, bulimia, or morbid obesity.

References

American Psychiatric Association (1993). *Let's talk: Facts about eating disorders.* [Brochure]. Washington, DC: Author.

American Psychiatric Association (1994). *Diagnostic and statistical manual of mental disorders (DSM IV)* (4th ed.). Washington, DC: Author.

Atkinson, R. L., Callaway, C. W., St. Jeor, S., & Wolf-Novak, L. (1995). A sane approach to weight loss. *Patient Care, 29*(18), 152–155.

Auricchio, S., Greco, L., & Troncone, R. (1988). Gluten-sensitive enteropathy in childhood. *Pediatric Clinics of North America, 35,* 157–187.

Castiglia, P. T. (1992). Neonatal growth, development, and health. In P. T. Castiglia and R. E. Harbin, *Child health care: Process and practice* (pp. 177–213). Philadelphia: J. B. Lippincott.

Chan, J. S. L. (1993). Nursing planning, intervention, and evaluation for altered head and neck function. In D. B. Jackson & R. B. Saunders (Eds.), *Child health nursing: A comprehensive approach to the care of children and their families* (pp. 813–867). Philadelphia: J. B. Lippincott.

Chaney, C. A. (1995). A collaborative protocol for encopresis management in school-aged children. *Journal of School Health, 65,* 360–364.

Christianson, D. (1994). Caring for a patient who has an implanted venous port. *American Journal of Nursing, 94*(11), 40–44.

Comerci, G. D. (1990). Medical complications of anorexia nervosa and bulimia nervosa. *Medical Clinics of North America, 74,* 1293–1310.

Connolly, C., & Corbett-Dick, P. (1990). Eating disorders: A framework for school nursing initiatives. *Journal of School Health, 60,* 401–405.

Csapo, M. (1987). Anorexia nervosa and bulimia. *B.C. Journal of Special Education, 11,* 251–288.

Curtin, G. (1996). Cleft lip and palate. In P. L. Jackson & J. A. Vesey (Eds.), *Primary care of the child with a chronic condition* (2nd ed., pp. 255–275). St. Louis: Mosby.

Cusson, R. M. (1994). Altered digestive function. In C. L. Betz, M. M. Hunsberger, & S. Wright (Eds.), *Family-centered nursing care of children* (2nd ed., pp. 1413–1505). Philadelphia: W. B. Saunders.

Danek, G.(1990). Ingestion, digestion, and elimination: Implications of obstruction and inflammation. In S. R. Mott, S. R. James, & A. M. Sperhac (Eds.), *Nursing care of children and families* (2nd ed., pp. 1334–1445). Redwood City, CA: Addison-Wesley.

Edwards, K. I. (1993). Obesity, anorexia, and bulimia. *Medical Clinics of North America, 77,* 899–909.

Eicher, P. S. (1997). Feeding. In M. L. Batshaw (Ed.), *Children with disabilities* (4th ed., pp. 621–641). Baltimore: Paul H. Brookes.

First, L. R. (1996). Foreign bodies in the gastrointestinal tract. In F. D. Burg, J. R. Ingelfinger, E. R. Wald, & R. A. Polin (Eds.), *Gellis & Kagan's current pediatric therapy* (15th ed., pp. 273–274). Philadelphia: W. B. Saunders.

Freeman, K. B., & Adelson, J. W. (1996). Hirschsprung's disease. In F. D. Burg, J. R. Ingelfinger, E. R. Wald, &

R. A. Polin (Eds.), *Gellis & Kagan's current pediatric therapy* (15th ed., pp. 212–213). Philadelphia: W. B. Saunders.

Harbin, R. E. (1992). Adolescent growth, development, and health. In P. T. Castiglia & R. E. Harbin, *Child health care: Process and practice* (pp. 329–362). Philadelphia: J. B. Lippincott.

Hofley, P. M., & Piccoli, D. A. (1994). Inflammatory bowel disease in children. *Medical Clinics of North America, 78,* 1281–1302.

Huse, D. M., Branes, L. A., Colligan, R. C., Nelson, R. A., & Palumbo, P. J. (1982). The challenge of obesity in childhood. I. Incidence, prevalence and staging. *Mayo Clinical Proceedings, 57,* 279–284.

Jackson, D. B., & Saunders, R. B (1990). Nursing assessment and diagnosis of renal function. In D. B. Jackson & R. B. Saunders (Eds.), *Child health nursing: A comprehensive approach to the care of children and their families* (pp. 1147–1159). Philadelphia: J. B. Lippincott.

Kalb, K. M. (1993). IHP: Eating disorders—anorexia, bulimia, morbid obesity. In M. B. Haas (Ed.), *The school nurse's source book of individualized healthcare plans* (pp. 249–261). North Branch, MN: Sunrise River Press.

Kidney Foundation of Canada (1990). *Living with kidney disease.* Montreal, PQ: Author.

Kirschner, B. S. (1988). Inflammatory bowel disease in children. *Pediatric Clinics of North America, 35,* 189–208.

Lake, A. M., & Buck, J. R. (1996). Disorders of the esophagus. In F. B. Burg, J. R. Ingelfinger, E. R. Wald, & R. A. Polin (Eds.), *Gellis & Kagan's current pediatric therapy* (15th ed., pp. 227–231). Philadelphia: W. B. Saunders.

Larson, G. (1986). Care for the student with a gastrostomy. In G. Larson (Ed.), *Managing the school age child with a chronic health condition* (pp. 153–163). Wayzata, MN: DCI Publishing.

Levine, M. D. (1982). Encopresis: Its potentiation, evaluation, and alleviation. *Pediatric Clinics of North America, 29,* 315–330.

MacDonald, M. J. (1993). Nursing planning, intervention, and evaluation for altered gastrointestinal function. In D. B. Jackson & R. B. Saunders (Eds.), *Child health nursing: A comprehensive approach to the care of children and their families* (pp. 1573–1652). Philadelphia: J. B. Lippincott.

Marcoux, C., Fisher, S., & Wong, D. (1990). Central venous access devices in children. *Pediatric Nursing, 16,* 123–133.

Maughan, K. K. (1991). Basic nutrition. In B. L. Christensen & E. O. Kockrow (Eds.), *Foundations of nursing* (pp. 376–397). St. Louis: Mosby.

Meeske, K., & Davidson, L. T. (1988). Teacher's reference on right atrial catheters. *Journal of Pediatric Nursing, 3,* 351–353.

Neumark-Sztainer, D. (1996). School-based programs for preventing eating disturbances. *Journal of School Health, 66,* 64–70.

O'Neill, K. (1994, November 1). Starving for success. *Woman's Day,* pp. 60, 84.

Peck, S. N., & Buzby, M. (1992). Alterations in gastrointestinal functioning. In P. T. Castiglia & R. E. Harbin (Eds.), *Child health care: Process and practice* (pp. 757–808). Philadelphia: J. B. Lippincott.

Pollack, V. P. (1996). Inflammatory bowel disease. In P. L. Jackson & J. A. Vessey (Eds.), *Primary care of the child with a chronic condition* (2nd ed., pp. 507–529). St. Louis: Mosby.

Porter, S., Haynie, M., Bierle, T., Caldwell, T. H., & Palfrey, J. S. (1997). *Children and youth assisted by medical technology in educational settings: Guidelines for care* (2nd ed.). Baltimore: Paul H. Brookes.

Ramakrishna, J., & Calenda, K. (1996). Inflammatory bowel disease. In F. D. Burg, J. R. Ingelfinger, E. R. Wald, & R. A. Polin (Eds.), *Gellis & Kagan's current pediatric therapy* (15th ed., pp. 243–246). Philadelphia: W. B. Saunders.

Rock, C. L., & Zerbe, K. J. (1995) Keeping eating disorders at bay. *Patient Care, 29*(18), 78–90.

Ryan, D. D. (1993). Health assessment, promotion, and maintenance for school age children. In D. B. Jackson & R. B. Saunders (Eds.), *Child health nursing: A comprehensive approach to the care of children and their families* (pp. 333–360). Philadelphia: J. B. Lippincott.

Scipien, G. M., & Kneut, C. M. (1990). The gastrointestinal system. In G. M. Scipien, M. A. Chard, J. Howe, & M. U. Barnard (Eds.), *Pediatric nursing care* (pp. 667–700). St. Louis: Mosby.

Smith, N. J. (1980). Excessive weight loss and food aversion in athletes simulating anorexia nervosa. *Pediatrics, 66,* 139–142.

Sours, J. (1980). *Starving to death in a sea of objects: The anorexia nervosa syndrome.* New York: Jason Aronson.

Stever, E. (1986). Stoma care for students with ostomies. In G. Larson (Ed.), *Managing the school age child with a chronic health condition* (pp. 199–206). Wayzata, MN: DCI Publishing.

Wenner, W. J., & Piccoli, D. A. (1996). Gastritis, duodenitis, and peptic ulcer disease. In F. D. Burg, J. R. Ingelfinger, E. R. Wald, & R. A. Polin (Eds.), *Gellis & Kagan's current pediatric therapy* (15th ed., pp. 233–236). Philadelphia: W. B. Saunders.

Whaley, L. F., & Wong, D. L. (1995). *Nursing care of infants and children* (5th ed.). St. Louis: Mosby.

Wildblood, R. A., & Strezo, P. L. (1987). The how-to's of home IV therapy. *Pediatric Nursing, 13,* 42–46, 68.

CHAPTER 18

Altered Urinary Function

KEY WORDS

Acid-base balance or imbalance

Clean intermittent catheterization

Dehydration

Diuretics

Edema

Electrolyte balance or imbalance

Fluid balance or imbalance

Glomerular filtration rate

Hemodialysis

Kidney transplantation

Peritoneal dialysis

Renal failure, acute and chronic

Renal replacement therapy

Renal reserve and failure

Voiding dysfunction

While there is a broad range of conditions that affect the urinary system, they all share one common characteristic—they focus attention on body parts and body functions that usually are considered to be personal and private (Vigneux & Hunsberger, 1994). More than 8 million Americans are estimated to have renal disease, and children and teenagers represent approximately 10% of this group (Taylor, 1996).

Although determining the cause of the renal condition is sometimes problematic, measuring the effects of the condition on the body is simplified by a number of laboratory tests, such as urinalysis and hematologic tests and radiologic tests, such as x-ray films and ultrasonography. For many youngsters with chronic renal conditions, these tests can be frightening, intrusive, painful, or uncomfortable (Vigneux & Hunsberger, 1994) and, in some cases, must be repeated on a regular basis, as often as once a day.

In this chapter, some of the more prevalent renal conditions, both congenital and adventitious, are described. Common symptoms, which are found in both types of disorders, are shown in Table 18.1. Since some individuals with altered urinary function require an alternative method of elimination, the procedure known as **CIC,** or **clean intermittent catheterization,** is described briefly. Tips for teachers of students who have altered urinary function are also presented.

The chapter begins with a brief overview of the importance of maintaining proper fluid balance in the body. It should be recognized that the kidneys are not the only organ involved in the excretion of fluids from the body, albeit they do produce the greatest volume of liquid in the course of a day.

Fluid Balance: Input vs. Output

The term **fluid balance** is used to refer to the state of equilibrium between the amount of fluid taken in by an individual and the amount of fluid excreted through urine and feces production, perspiration, and exhalation. For a variety of reasons the balance can become altered: input can exceed output *or* output can exceed input.

Under normal conditions, during a set period of time, e.g., 24 hours, the amount of urine produced by the kidneys and excreted through the urinary system equals the amount of fluid ingested, usually via the GI system, described previously. If the total output of fluid exceeds the input, the individual is described as being **dehydrated.** Although dehydration can occur as a result of insufficient intake of fluid, in young children in particular, it is more commonly the result of abnormal loss of fluids that may occur from excessive vomiting or diarrhea, or both, in either acute or chronic illnesses. Excessive fluid excretion, referred to as a **fluid volume deficit,** may also occur as a result of complications that arise from diabetes (i.e., ketoacidosis) or as a result of loss of fluid from extensive burns.

On the contrary, if the total input of fluid exceeds the output, i.e., the person drinks too many fluids without adequate elimination, the person is said to be in a state of **fluid volume excess.** Excess intake that results in excess volume of water in the body tissues is sometimes referred to as **water intoxication** or **water overload.** While extreme intake is a relatively uncommon occurrence, the retention of fluids in the body, i.e., insufficient output, is a common cause of the fluid volume excess. Known as **edema,** fluid retention can result from many conditions, including cardiac disorders and diseases of the urinary system.

Disturbances in the Fluid Balance in the Body

If the fluid balance is disturbed in some manner, there is a resultant imbalance in the concentration of **electrolytes** and in the **acid-base level** of the body's fluids that may potentially result in a situation extremely hazardous to the health of the individual.

Electrolyte Imbalance

Compounds that are dissolved in the body's fluids, such as blood plasma and other cellular fluids that enter the body by means of ingested fluids and foods, are known as **electrolytes.** The primary ones are sodium, critical for maintaining proper fluid balance within the body and for the transmission of nerve impulses and the contraction of muscles; calcium, necessary for adequate muscle functioning, cardiac functioning, and the coagulation of blood; and potassium, which plays a role in cell metabolism and in muscle contraction. Other important electrolytes include magnesium, chloride, bicarbonate, phosphate, and sulfate.

TABLE 18.1

Clinical Manifestations of Urinary Alterations

Clinical Manifestation	Clinical Significance
Headaches, irritability, visual disturbances, seizures	Indicative of hypertension, acidosis, or alkalosis
Paleness of conjunctivae (membrane lining inner surface of eye), skin, and mucous membranes (e.g., lining of mouth)	Indicative of anemia
Breath odor may be ammoniac or urine-like	Indicative of uremia (excessive amounts of urea and other nitrogenous waste products in the blood)
Heart murmur, arrhythmia, or pericardial friction rub (rubbing of the membranes of the pericardium)	Cardiovascular abnormalities may result from anemia, hypertension, or fluid overload
Tachypnea, rales (bubbling noises heard during inspiration), rhonchi (rumbling sound heard on expiration), Kussmaul breathing (abnormally deep, rapid respirations); infant may have nasal flaring, retractions	Respiratory alteration may indicate fluid overload, metabolic acidosis
Abnormal masses, abdominal or flank pain, palpation of enlarged kidneys	Indicative of hydronephrotic kidneys (distended kidney resulting from obstruction in the ureter), tumor, presence of infection
Urine color (e.g., tea- or cola-colored urine), odor, urinary stream (e.g., foaming urine), pain on urination, hematuria (blood in urine), frequency • In younger children: child may complain of abdominal pain, cry with urination • In older children: child may have enuresis (urinary incontinence, often occurring at night—"bed wetting"), complain of dysuria (painful urination)	Alteration may indicate presence of infection, obstruction, or dehydration
Skin color—pale, sallow, or jaundiced	Indicative of obstruction, anemia, or uremia
Edema, weight gain	Indicative of fluid retention
Growth retardation	Indicative of chronic infection or renal failure
Congenital anomalies: low-set ears, widely spaced nipples, absence of abdominal musculature (prune belly syndrome), spina bifida, abnormalities of the external genitalia	These anomalies are associated with genitourinary disorders

Source: Vigneux, A., & Hunsberger, M. (1994). Altered genitourinary/renal function. In C. L. Betz, M. M. Hunsberger, & S. Wright (Eds.), *Family-centered nursing care of children* (2nd ed., pp. 1506–1564). Philadelphia: W. B. Saunders. Copyright 1994 by W. B. Saunders Company. Reprinted by permission.

In a healthy individual, the electrolyte balance of the body fluids remains relatively stable. However, for a variety of reasons, including a fluid volume excess or deficit, the level of certain electrolytes may become deficient or excessive, resulting in a state often referred to as an **electrolyte imbalance.** Such an imbalance can result in serious illness. For example, as a result of certain kidney diseases, a depletion in sodium in the blood **(hyponatremia)** can result in dehydration, weakness, dizziness, nausea, abdominal cramps, and decreased blood pressure. The opposite, an excess of sodium **(hypernatremia),** can result in intense thirst, flushed skin, increased temperature, nausea, vomiting, and, in some cases, disorientation and convulsion (Whaley & Wong, 1995). The measure of electrolyte balance of a fluid is its specific gravity. The normal specific gravity of urine, for example, is 1.002 to 1.030, making it slightly more dense than water, which has a specific gravity of 1.000 (Luttrell, 1990).

Acid-Base Imbalance

All body fluids also have a specific **pH level** (or potential **h**ydrogen level), based on the number of hydrogen ions present in the fluid. If the fluid has a pH level of 7.0, it is said to be **neutral.** Any level below 7.0 is considered acidic; i.e., the fluid has the chemical characteristics of an **acid.** A level over 7.0 is considered to be alkaline, or having the chemical characteristics of a **base.** Urine is slightly acidic, with a pH level between 4.6 and 8.0.

The term **acid-base balance** refers to the state of equilibrium between the amount of acids or bases produced and the amount of acids or bases excreted. In a healthy individual, the acid-base balance remains relatively stable; however, in certain diseases, some involving the kidneys, the acid-base balance may become altered. **Acidosis** is an abnormal increase in the concentrations of hydrogen ions, whereas **alkalosis** is an abnormal decrease in the number of hydrogen ions. In either situation, the CNS can be affected. In acidosis, there is depression of the CNS, and as a result, the individual may become lethargic, have diminished mental capacity, and in severe cases, enter a comatose state. In alkalosis, the CNS becomes overstimulated, and as a result, the individual may become excitable and may experience a tingling sensation in the body. In severe cases of alkalosis, the individual may develop **tetany,** a condition characterized by cramps, twitching of the muscles, and, in some cases, convulsions.

Congenital Anomalies of the Urinary System

There are a number of abnormalities of the urinary system that can be evident at birth. Anomalies of **number** (the child with only one kidney or the child with more than two kidneys), of **position** (the child with an abnormally rotated kidney, which may result in obstruction), and of **structure** (the child with two ureters originating from the same kidney) are all possible. The nature of the problems experienced by the child depends on the extent of abnormality and the resulting inability of the system to produce and transport urine. Between 5% and 10% of all infants are born with some type of malformation of the urinary tract (Olson, Langner, & Phillips, 1990), but many abnormalities have little or no impact on the child's well-being; i.e., the abnormalities are either clinically unimportant or they are surgically correctable.

Adventitious Kidney Problems

Renal and Urinary Tract Trauma

Because the kidneys of youngsters are poorly protected as a result of undeveloped musculature, inadequate protection from the ribs, and lack of protective abdominal fat, traumatic injury that results in extensive damage is more likely to occur in children than in adults. In children who sustain multiple injuries, urinary tract trauma is second only to trauma involving the CNS (Livne & Gonzales, 1985). The most common cause of renal trauma in young children is automobile accidents. In older children, motorcycle accidents and sports injuries are more common causes (Luttrell, 1990). Other causes include blunt trauma (e.g., blows to the abdomen), penetrating injuries (e.g., knife or bullet wounds), and fractures of the ribs or pelvis (e.g., from a sport-related injury). Minor wounds may result in microscopic amounts of blood in the urine; major trauma may result in hemorrhage.

While many minor injuries heal after a period of bed rest, complications can occur for up to 2 years after injury, and careful follow-up is required (Luttrell, 1990). In serious trauma cases, the affected kidney may be removed surgically, a procedure referred to as a **nephrectomy.** If the remaining kidney is functional, the child may suffer no major consequences; however, any child with only one kidney needs to be monitored to ensure that damage does not occur to the remaining organ (Livne & Gonzales, 1985).

Nephrotic Syndrome (NS)

Nephrotic syndrome, also known as **nephrosis,** can be congenital, idiopathic (without any known cause), or secondary to some other disease condition. Congenital NS is often associated with toxemia of pregnancy, a condition occurring in 5% to 7% of all pregnancies, in which the mother develops acute hypertension. Some children born prematurely also show signs of nephrosis. One rare form of congenital nephrotic syndrome, transmitted by means of autosomal recessive genes, is found in children of Finnish extraction.

Nephrotic syndrome is also associated with sickle cell disease, diabetes, systemic lupus erythematosus, and AIDS, but in approximately 90% of cases the cause is unknown (Luttrell, 1990). In such cases, the condition is often suspected to result from some type of immunologic (or allergic) response.

In nephrosis, the glomerular membrane of the kidney becomes permeable to plasma proteins, especially albumin, and as a result, protein is lost through the urine—a condition known as **proteinuria.** Nephrotic syndrome is characterized by anorexia, general weakness and lethargy, generalized edema of all body tissues, and respiratory difficulties. Nephrotic syndrome is the most common disorder associated with injury to the glomerulus in children, occurring at a rate of 2 to 3 per 100,000. In children between the ages of 2 and 7, males are twice as likely to develop nephrotic syndrome as females. By adolescence, males and females are equally affected (Rosenblum, 1996).

Treatment includes bed rest, the administration of drugs (i.e., antibiotics, corticosteroids, or diuretics), and a diet high in protein and low in salt. While the prognosis is generally quite good, the condition is often marked by relapses. Ten percent to 15% of children with nephrotic syndrome go on to have chronic renal failure. Family and teachers should be alert to the signs of possible relapse (e.g., fever or edema).

Glomerulonephritis

Inflammation of the glomerulus is referred to as **glomerulonephritis.** Two forms of the condition occur. The first, known as **acute glomerulonephritis** **(AGN),** has a sudden onset and generally a short, self-limiting course. The other, **chronic glomerulonephritis,** has an insidious onset, which is followed by a prolonged, protracted course (Makker, 1996).

The most prevalent form of acute glomerulonephritis results from a group-A beta-hemolytic streptococcal infection of the upper respiratory tract (a cold) or of the skin (e.g., a case of impetigo). Such an infection is referred to as **poststreptococcal glomerulonephritis,** or **PSGN.** The average age of onset of PSGN is between 6 and 7 years, and like nephrotic syndrome, the occurrence in males outnumbers that in females two to one (Jackson & Saunders, 1993). Common symptoms include edema of the face, particularly evident around the eyes, and sudden onset of painless gross **hematuria** (blood in the urine that makes it tea-colored).

As the disease progresses, generalized edema, resulting in overall weight gain, is common, as are decreased urine output, abdominal pain, pallor, low-grade fever, loss of appetite, and, in some cases, hypertension and shortness of breath that is caused by pulmonary edema. AGN is treated by means of antibiotics, and in most cases the prognosis is excellent, with most children recovering within 2 weeks, if no serious complications occur. It does take, in most cases, a few months for the urine to become normal. In some cases, it may take up to 2 years (Makker, 1996).

Chronic glomerulonephritis actually includes a large number of diseases. In some cases the cause is known (e.g., congenital syphilis); however, in many others, the inciting agent is not known. In many cases the chronic form leads to chronic renal failure.

Renal Failure

There are two forms of renal failure, acute and chronic. **Acute renal failure (ARF)** is characterized by a sudden, rapid impairment of kidney function. **Azotemia,** excessive nitrogenous compounds in the urine, and **oliguria,** decreased urine output, are common in this form. ARF can be caused by certain disease states (e.g., gastroenteritis) or renal injuries (e.g. renal trauma). In some cases, chemotherapy is the inciting agent. ARF is a complex, life-threatening syndrome; however, not all cases are severe in nature (Heiliczer, 1996)

Chronic renal failure (CRF) refers to the progressive state in which an increasingly greater proportion of the nephrons become irreversibly damaged. In some cases, the condition develops relatively suddenly, e.g., over a period of months; in others, CRF develops over a period of several years. CRF can result from many different conditions. Approximately 40% of the cases are caused by glomerular disease, such as glomerulonephritis; 20% as a result of developmental anomalies of the kidneys and urinary tract, such as an obstruction; 15% as a result of hereditary renal disease, such as congenital nephrotic syndrome; 15% as a result of pyelonephritis, a bacterial infection of the kidneys; and 10% caused by other miscellaneous disorders of the kidney (Van Cleve & Baldwin, 1989). In preschool children, anatomic abnormalities of the renal or urinary tract are a major cause of CRF; in school-age children, glomerular diseases, such as chronic glomerulonephritis, and hereditary renal disorders are the most common causes (Jackson & Saunders, 1993).

Chronic renal failure is considered to be a relatively rare renal condition, with an incidence of 11 per million in the population less than 19 years of age. Males have a higher incidence of CRF than females. African Americans are at greater risk for developing CRF than Caucasians (Taylor, 1996). The progression of CRF is measured by the ability of the glomeruli to filter the blood. A person's **glomerular filtration rate,** or **GFR,** is calculated by determining the amount of certain substances in the blood, most notably creatinine and blood urea nitrogen.

There are four stages of CRF. In the first stage, referred to as the stage of **decreased** or **diminished renal reserve** (i.e., **early renal failure**), the person may not show any significant symptoms, or those that are shown are vague and nonspecific (e.g., general malaise, apathy, pallor, decreased appetite, inability to concentrate). At this stage the GFR is between 50% and 75% of normal. In the school-age population, headaches may be common, and students may become disinterested in school or play and have difficulty keeping up with their peers (Jackson & Saunders, 1993). When 60% or more of renal function is lost, the kidneys are no longer capable of balancing the composition of body fluids (Luttrell, 1990), and there may be elevated concentrations of nitrogenous waste within the blood (azotemia).

In the second stage, referred to as the stage of **chronic renal insufficiency (CRI),** the ability of the glomeruli to adequately filter the blood is severely compromised (i.e., GFR is 25% to 50% normal). By this point, the symptoms are generally quite noticeable and may include edema; high blood pressure and other signs of circulation overload; bone or joint pain

and muscle cramps; pale and sallow complexion with dry, itchy skin; ammoniac breath odor; and hematuria. Some individuals show emotional symptoms, including irritability, aggressiveness, and depression (Orrbine, 1987). As a result of the kidney's inability to produce usable vitamin D, the absorption of calcium in the GI tract is impaired, and uneven growth and demineralization of the bones, referred to as **renal osteodystrophy** (formerly referred to as "renal rickets") may also occur. Over the long period, growth of children with renal disorders may be delayed, and some may have spontaneous bone fractures.

In the third stage, known as **chronic renal failure (CRF),** the GFR is 10% to 25% of normal and the child shows increasing manifestations of renal failure. All of the symptoms found in the earlier stages are evident, generally in a heightened state. The fourth and final stage is referred to as **end-stage renal disease (ESRD).** At this point, the GFR is 10%, and as a result, oliguria and severe uremia (excessive amounts of urea and other nitrogenous waste products in the blood) develop. At this stage, **renal replacement therapy (RRT)** (i.e., hemodialysis or transplantation) is needed to sustain life. Symptoms at this stage may include vomiting, bloody diarrhea, bruising, visual disturbances, mental slowness, stupor, muscle twitching, and, in some severe cases, coma or seizures. Many individuals who experience kidney failure have anemia as a result of the failure of the kidneys to produce the hormone erythropoietin, which is necessary to stimulate the bone marrow to produce red blood cells.

🐾 Treatment of Kidney Disorders

Therapies to relieve the symptoms of kidney disease are varied; however, regardless of the treatment approach implemented, the ultimate goal is "to prevent deterioration in functioning and to restore the ability to pursue the maximum satisfaction that life can offer" (Klingenstein, 1986, p. 465). The most common treatment plans involve the use of pharmacologic, dietary, and surgical intervention to resolve the problem or prevent the development of sequelae. Each of these approaches is covered in this section, along with kidney transplantation, a procedure that has been available to children and adults, both young and old, since the early 1970s. In some cases, specific techniques (e.g., catheterization, dialysis) are used to replace normal body function of the urinary system. These alternative methods of elimination are described in the next section.

Pharmacologic Intervention

There are a number of drugs used to treat the symptoms of renal disease. In many cases, several of these drugs are given at the same time. **Immunosuppressive drugs,** such as corticosteroids, are administered to prevent the progression of glomerular closure, to decrease proteinuria, and to promote excretion of fluids. **Antihypertensive drugs,** such as vasodilators, are given to control symptoms of the hypertension. **Diuretics,** such as furosemide, are given to control hypertension and reduce edema. **Vitamin D analogs** (drugs that resemble vitamin D), **calcium supplements,** and **antacids** with aluminum are administered to treat or prevent renal bone diseases. If needed, **antibiotics** are given to treat or prevent urinary tract infection; and **folic acid** or **vitamin supplements** are typically administered to supplement a diet that may have to be restricted (Jackson & Saunders, 1993; Korsch & Fine, 1985). Children who have Wilms' tumor, a rare cancerous tumor (see chapter 22) that occurs in preschool children, may also require chemotherapy or radiation therapy after removal of the malignant tumor.

Dietary Intervention

For many children, dietary therapy is necessary to prevent the complications of kidney disease (Korsch & Fine, 1985). The most common restrictions include **sodium and fluid restriction,** to prevent hypertension and congestive heart failure; **potassium restriction,** to prevent excessive amounts of potassium in the blood (i.e., hyperkalemia), which can result in nausea, diarrhea, muscle weakness, and heart arrhythmias; **phosphorous restriction** or **calcium supplementation,** to treat and prevent bone disease; **caloric supplementation,** to encourage growth; and **protein restriction,** to limit symptoms of uremia. Although certain foods may need to be eliminated from the diet, the child with altered kidney function should be given a diet high in calories to combat anorexia and promote growth.

Surgical Intervention

Many children, particularly those with congenital anomalies, require surgery to correct the situation. For example, if the ureter is obstructed at birth, surgery is undertaken to relieve the symptoms that occur (e.g., lack of the flow of urine from the kidney). Similarly, if a child develops a renal **calculus** (kidney "stone"), removal of the stone may necessitate a surgical procedure. The child who injures a kidney as a result of some type of trauma may have to have the organ repaired or, in extreme cases, removed. Some conditions may also require a program of drug therapy in combination with surgical intervention; others may be treated by drugs alone. The ultimate surgery is a kidney transplant.

For children with end-stage renal disease, **kidney transplantation,** "with its potential ability to essentially normalize renal function," is often the treatment of choice (Hobbs & Sexson, 1993, p. 106). The transplant surgery involves placing the new kidney in the front part of the abdominal wall just above the bladder, close to the inferior vena cava and the aorta, to achieve satisfactory blood supply. In most cases, the failed kidneys are left in place, unless there is a specific reason to remove them, such as severe hypertension (Whaley & Wong, 1995).

The success rate for kidney transplants has improved dramatically as a result of several factors, including increased surgical experience, development of refined surgical techniques, improved assessment of immunologic aspects of tissue typing and histocompatibility, development of more effective immunosuppressant agents with fewer side effects, and more careful selection of transplant recipients (Hobbs & Sexson, 1993, p. 104). From 65% to 95% of recipients who have received their kidney from living relative donors (e.g., brother, sister, mother, or father) are alive 2 years after transplant. The comparable survival rate for recipients of kidneys from cadaver donors (i.e., genetically unrelated) is slightly lower, from 42% to 80% (Whaley & Wong, 1995).

While kidney transplantation may offer the person with ESRD an excellent opportunity for life and normal growth and development (Perez-Woods, Hedenkamp, Ulfig, Newman, & Fioravante, 1991), transplantation, although it increases survival, is not necessarily the ultimate cure. Hobbs and Sexson (1993), in discussing the medical considerations regarding transplantation, specifically renal and liver transplants, made the following comments:

> One would question whether transplantation represents an actual cure for the recipient, or the exchange of one chronic, imminently terminal illness for a longer term, chronic one. . . . The posttransplantation regimen . . . is complicated by the lifelong necessity of taking a number of medications, each of which

has its own list of unwelcome side effects. Transplant recipients must also continue to undergo blood testing and, in some cases, frequent surgical or instrumental interventions. Failure to comply with the complicated and often noxious regimen may result in organ loss and subsequent death. These multiple continued stresses, despite the improvement in physical status, may impinge on the transplant recipient's ability to resume normal activities at school or home. The relatively constant threat of transplant rejection and the realistic fear of infection may put the patient and his or her family in a situation of uncertainty similar to that described for cancer patients (Koocher & O'Malley, 1981). This situation has been referred to as the "Damocles syndrome"—patients and family members are constantly on edge, waiting for the sword of Damocles to fall (Reinhart & Kemph, 1988). This fear may lead the family to overprotect the patient, which may compromise his or her normal cognition, learning, and psychosocial functioning. (pp. 105–106)

Educational Implications and Teaching Tips

Because the needs of each student with chronic renal problems are unique, teachers should be aware of the individualized treatment plan and should attempt to facilitate compliance with the prescribed regimen. Teachers should monitor any potential side effects of the treatment and should ensure that they communicate with the student's parents on a regular basis, particularly if they have noted any particular changes in behavior (e.g., increased fatigue, irritability) or any signs of illness (e.g., fever, edema). Because some students with conditions that affect the urinary system may need to use the bathroom more frequently than others, they should be allowed unrestricted access to the facilities. The following suggestions may be of assistance to teachers who are working with students who have altered urinary system function:

1 *For many children and young adults, renal disease is a draining and emotional experience, both physiologically and emotionally* (Jackson & Saunders, 1993). As a result of lethargy and general malaise, the student may be unable to perform activities that are age-appropriate. Many students attending school have difficulty arising in the morning, particularly after a night in which their sleep was disturbed by having to get up repeatedly to void or to follow some type of treatment regimen, such as peritoneal dialysis. Some children and young adults with renal problems experience **enure-**

sis (bed wetting) and, consequently, may wake up as a result of contact with wet sheets or may be awakened by parents who want to change the soiled linen. In addition, several drugs used to treat renal problems result in hyperactivity, and even though the children may go to bed early enough to get a good night's sleep, they may have difficulty getting to sleep or remaining asleep throughout the night.

During the day, some students with urinary system dysfunction may need to have a nap to regain their strength. As a result, they may not be able to get together with their friends to participate in normal after-school activities. For the adolescent who needs to go to bed early, participation in social events that occur in the evening (e.g., going to a movie, hanging out at the mall) may not be possible. Regardless, students with chronic renal disorders should be encouraged to participate in as many activities as possible so that they do not become socially isolated from their friends. In some cases, substituting "quieter" activities for those that require greater energy expenditure may be a possible solution. For example, for the teenager who wants to go to a movie with friends, but is unable because of fatigue or treatment schedules, a teacher might encourage the students to have a movie party during school hours and assist by volunteering to rent a movie, to make popcorn, and to supply a variety of popular beverages.

2 *For students with altered urinary functioning, school attendance may be limited.* Those who are able to attend school may need to adhere to certain activity restrictions to protect their fragile renal function (Luttrell, 1990). Stair walking may be difficult, and students should be allowed to use an elevator if available.

Many students with chronic renal disease develop an aversion to school as a result of their awkward movements and their inability to keep up with their peers as a result of bone disease and growth retardation (Jackson & Saunders, 1993). School staff and parents should encourage the student to engage in activities that are offered in the school setting as much as is possible within the limits of tolerance and safety. Teachers should work closely with the student's family and physician to determine an acceptable level of participation and try to provide alternative activities that enhance normal growth and maturation and promote the development of self-respect and a positive self-concept. Even though students with renal disease may be small for their age, they must be treated in an age-appropriate manner.

3 *Some children with renal problems have to participate in treatment programs (e.g., hemodialysis, peritoneal dialysis) during or after school hours.* This is not only tiring but also takes time away from usual activities (Olson et al., 1990). If at all possible, treatment sessions should be scheduled so there is minimal disruption to the child's day.

4 *Many students with renal problems require a special diet.* For those students who eat in the school's cafeteria, as opposed to bringing their own food, the school's dietitian or cook should work with the parents and the student's renal dietitian to ensure foods that are suitable, such as foods cooked without salt or potassium, are available for the student. Unfortunately, many foods that are popular with school-age children and adolescents (e.g., chips, pizza, pretzels) are high in sodium, and it is not uncommon for them to sneak restricted foods and drinks while away from home. Peer pressure, particularly during the adolescent years, may affect choice of food, and school staff should be alert to signs of noncompliance with the prescribed regimen.

Many children with renal disease are anorexic. For these children, small, frequent meals may be more appealing, and the child should be allowed and encouraged to snack freely (e.g., during class) when hungry.

5 *Many children with renal problems require medications throughout the day.* Teachers should be cognizant of the type of medications, potential side effects, proper method of administration, what to do when a dosage is omitted, and recommended safety precautions. In many cases, as the kidney disease progresses, there are changes in medication and diet. Consequently, close communication between home and school is critical.

If the student complains of chest pain, numbness in the face or limbs, or generalized weakness, all of which may be indicative of excessive potassium in the blood; shortness of breath, which may be indicative of fluid in the lungs; or sudden onset of lo-

calized pain, which may be the result of bone fracture, the emergency plan that has been developed should be activated (e.g., the parents should be notified immediately, the child should be transported to the emergency room for treatment).

6 *It is often suggested that students with renal problems be protected from potential sources of infection; however, the benefits to the child or young adult of attending school must be weighed against the risks* (Olson et al., 1990). Parents of children who are taking corticosteroids (e.g., transplant recipients who are taking prednisone [e.g., Deltasone] or cyclosporine [e.g., Sandimmune] in order to prevent rejection) should be notified if their son or daughter has been in contact with individuals who have certain contagious diseases, especially chicken pox and measles. During outbreaks of such diseases, the student should remain at home to minimize the risk of becoming ill.

7 *Children who have had a kidney transplant must be carefully monitored.* Fever, unusual weight gain, malaise, edema, swelling and tenderness over the graft (the site of the transplant), pains in the arms or legs, decreased urine output, elevated blood pressure, and alterations in blood chemistry are all early warning signs of possible trouble (Jackson & Saunders, 1993). If any of these signs are present, the student's parents should be notified so that early treatment can be obtained.

8 *It is often believed that pre-adolescent children are not self-conscious about their bodies or inhibited about exposing themselves; however, this is not true.* For the youngster or teenager with a renal condition who has been poked and prodded repeatedly, it is particularly important he or she be treated with the same degree of respect that adults receive (Klingenstein, 1986). Many students with renal conditions are particularly self-conscious about their bodies as a result of the alteration from their previous physical appearance (e.g., edema, growth retardation, delay in sexual maturity, facial swelling). Those in contact with the student must understand his or her fears (e.g., fear of rejection or reaction by others) and concerns (e.g., inability to wear fashionable, "trendy" clothing as a result of the peritoneal catheter protruding from the abdomen) and should encourage the student to express in words, play, or pictures his or her emotions to ease adjustment (Luttrell, 1990; Vigneux & Hunsberger, 1994).

Teachers should be encouraged to discuss with qualified staff issues related to emotional problems that may be evident in their students. In some cases, students (and their families) will need ongoing counseling to deal with teasing they receive in their life outside the sheltered hospital setting and to handle their feelings regarding their disease.

9 *Children and young adults who have had a kidney transplant sometimes experience unique adjustment problems* (Whaley & Wong, 1995). If the kidney came from a cadaver (which in itself may be a disturbing notion to some), the student may speculate about the age, sex, personality, and physical characteristics of the donor. If the transplant came from an older person, the student may worry that the kidney will "wear out" before its time.

Some students are concerned that the donated organ might have come from someone of the opposite sex or from a different race and, consequently, may have difficulty accepting the transplant as part of themselves (Luttrell, 1990).

10 *In terms of activity restrictions, school staff should be in close contact with the student's physician to determine which are appropriate.* Children who have a solitary kidney, who have kidney anomalies, or who have had a kidney transplant are usually restricted from contact sports (e.g., football) to avoid injury (Livne & Gonzales, 1985).

Alternative Methods of Elimination

Some children and young adults who have conditions that affect the urinary system are unable to maintain adequate urinary drainage, even though the kidneys may be functioning normally. Such conditions are referred to as a **voiding dysfunctions**. Because it is important to reestablish urine flow to prevent the buildup of toxins in the bloodstream and to decrease the likelihood of bladder infection, a **urinary catheter** may be used either continuously or intermittently to ensure proper drainage (Sellers & Edwards, 1991). For those whose kidneys have failed, **dialysis** is an option for removing waste products. Both of these methods are described briefly.

Catheterization

The most common (and most similar to the natural) method by which urine is excreted from the body is by means of a **urethral catheter**, which drains fluids from the bladder via the urethra without requiring any form of surgery. Certain types of urethral catheters (e.g., Foley catheter) can be left in place for long periods of time, e.g., after surgery to the bladder, penis or vagina; others are used intermittently, a procedure known as **clean intermittent catheterization**, or **CIC**. Other types of catheters include a **nephrostomy tube**, inserted into the kidney; a **ureterostomy tube**, inserted into the ureter; a **suprapubic catheter**, inserted into the bladder; and a **perineal ureterostomy**, inserted into the middle portion of the ureter. These types of catheters are surgically implanted for the long term.

If there is need, e.g., in cases where the bladder is diseased or deformed, the bladder can be bypassed totally. Like ostomy surgery (chapter 17) that permits food to bypass all or some of the intestinal tract, a **urostomy** allows urine to come out of the body through a stoma created on the abdominal wall, where it is collected in a pouch known as a **urostomy bag**. Because the bladder is bypassed and therefore does not function to hold the urine until voiding time, there is a constant release of urine into the pouch. Care of a urostomy is similar to that for a colostomy. In the following section, CIC is described. This section is followed by a discussion on dialysis as a method of the removal of fluid wastes from the body.

In the hospital setting, it is not uncommon to see children who required an indwelling urethral catheter on a long-term, continuous basis (e.g., children who have had surgery; those who are critically ill). However, in the school setting, it is more common to see children who require catheterization on an intermittent, rather than steady, basis. In the procedure known as CIC, a catheter is inserted via the urethra into the bladder to remove the urine that has collected when needed (i.e., intermittently rather than continuously). CIC is usually performed every 3 to 4 hours to promote dryness and to enhance social acceptability (Taylor, 1990); however, frequency of catheterization is based on the type of dysfunction, the capacity of the bladder, the functional ability of the bladder sphincter to prevent urine leakage, and the amount of fluid intake (Vigneux & Hunsberger, 1994).

Many of the children or young adults who need CIC have a condition referred to as neurogenic bladder dysfunction that typically results from some type of CNS lesion (e.g., spina bifida). Those with neurogenic bladders typically are not only unaware of the sensation that occurs when the bladder fills to capacity but are also unable to empty the bladder voluntarily. In addition, some children do not perceive the sensation of wetness even when the bladder overflows or when they have voided involuntarily (Taylor, 1990).

The following suggestions are for teachers that have a student who requires CIC on a regular basis during school hours.

1 *Those providing CIC to students must be adequately trained and alert to possible signs of infection.* The procedure should be scheduled so there is minimal disruption to the student's activities, and the location in which the procedure takes place must be chosen to ensure privacy (e.g., nurse's office, washroom). General guidelines for CIC are shown in Table 18.2. The following suggestions are *not* sufficient for complete training. Child-specific training should be provided by qualified nurses or physicians.

2 *As the students with a voiding problem mature, in many (if not most) cases, they will be able to learn how to self-catheterize.* Children as young as 4 years of age have been taught to successfully carry out the procedure by themselves (Bigge, 1991); however, as a result of the Tatro case, discussed in chapter 2, CIC must be provided to all school-age children who require the procedure to access an educational program, regardless of their ability to catheterize themselves.

3 *Typically, CIC must be scheduled for every 3 to 4 hours.* If the student is going out on a field trip, the CIC should be scheduled before leaving the school, even though the normal amount of time may not have elapsed since the last voiding. For some, even with regularly scheduled CIC, there may be times in which the student experiences leakage (e.g., when the student laughs, sneezes, or coughs). Some students benefit from wearing

TABLE 18.2
Guidelines for Clean Intermittent Catheterization (CIC)

1. Assemble the necessary equipment (e.g., catheter, cleaning supplies, kidney basin, gloves).
2. Wash hands thoroughly with soap and water, as instructed, and put on disposable gloves.
3. Position the child, as instructed, and remove clothing as needed.
4. Cleanse the meatus with warm, soapy water, as instructed.
5. Lubricate the tip of the catheter (particularly for males, optional for females) and insert, as instructed, until there is an adequate flow of urine (typically 1 to 2 inches, or 2.54 to 5.1 cm) farther than the point at which urine begins to flow.
   If the child is sitting on the toilet, drain the urine directly into the basin. If the child is lying down, collect urine in a suitable container (e.g., large kidney basin) and dispose of it down the toilet. Before disposing of urine, measure volume, if required.
6. When the bladder is empty, pinch the catheter and slowly withdraw, tip up, as instructed. Wash the genitalia again to remove any urine that may have leaked.
7. Assist the child in dressing.
8. Wash catheter, rinse, dry, and put in a dry, clean bottle, plastic bag, or other small container. Store in secure storage area.
9. Remove gloves and wash hands thoroughly. Record procedure in procedure log (Appendix G). Replace catheter as directed (daily, weekly, or monthly).

Sources: Porter, Haynie, Bierle, Caldwell & Palfrey, 1997; Stever, 1986; Vigneux & Hunsberger, 1994.

specially designed underpants or absorbent liners under their normal underwear that can be changed easily in order to minimize embarrassment (Taylor, 1990). A clean change of clothing should be kept at school in case of accident.

Dialysis

Dialysis is based on the principle that small molecules, including undesirable solutes such as urea and potassium, in a volume of fluid (e.g., blood) diffuse through a semipermeable membrane from an area of higher concentration to one of lesser concentration (Olson et al., 1990). Larger molecules, such as blood cells, do not pass through the membrane because of their size and so remain in the original fluid, thereby ensuring a better composition.

There are two types of dialysis available to treat renal disease: **hemodialysis** and **peritoneal dialysis.** Dialysis, regardless of type, is a means of sustaining life, but it is not sufficient for replacing malfunctioning kidneys. Students on dialysis still need to monitor their diet and take a number of medications. In the long term, most of those on dialysis continue to look forward to the more permanent solution, kidney transplant.

Hemodialysis (HD) In this form of dialysis, blood is circulated outside the body into a machine, known as a **dialyzer** but often referred to as an **"artificial" kidney,** to be cleaned. This device filters the blood by passing it through a sheet of treated cellophane that functions as a semipermeable membrane before it is returned to the body (Figure 18.1).

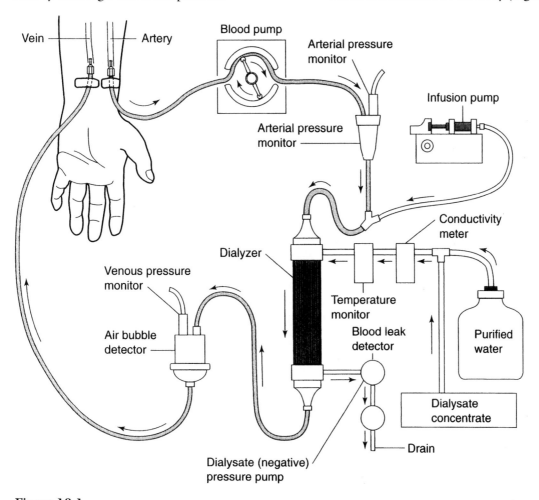

Figure 18.1
Hemodialysis
Source: Adapted from Thelan, Joseph, & Urden, 1990.

To have permanent access to the individual's bloodstream, an **arteriovenous shunt,** a tube that permits blood to flow from an artery to a vein, thereby bypassing the capillary system; a **fistula,** a surgical joining of an artery and a vein; or a **prosthesis,** a synthetic graft that connects an artery to a vein, must be created surgically, either external to the skin or subcutaneously (i.e., internal or under the skin). Common sites include the radial artery and the forearm vein in the lower arm (external) and brachial artery and brachiocephalic vein in the upper arm and neck region (internal).

Hemodialysis takes an average of 4 to 8 hours and must be performed 2 to 3 times weekly. It is either done in a dialysis unit in a hospital or, with the advent of smaller portable machines, in the home. Some children and young adults experience nausea or vomiting, headaches, muscle cramps, dizziness, or lightheadedness after the procedure. More serious complications include clotting, hemorrhage, infection of the access site, infection of the blood, and severe hypotension or hypertension. Seizure during or after hemodialysis is not uncommon, and as a result, parents of students on hemodialysis (and the children or young adults themselves) consider kidney transplantation as the preferred form of treatment in the long run (Whaley & Wong, 1995).

Peritoneal Dialysis (PD)   As an alternative to hemodialysis, **peritoneal dialysis** uses the abdominal cavity or peritoneum as the semipermeable membrane (Figure 18.2). Rather than blood being removed from the body, as in hemodialysis, fluid, referred to as a **dialysate,** is instilled into the body on a regular basis by means of a catheter surgically sutured into the abdomen below the umbilicus, or "belly button." The exchange of waste products occurs by means of osmosis and diffusion in the abdominal cavity. There are several types of peritoneal dialysis. Continuous ambulatory peritoneal dialysis and continuous cycling peritoneal dialysis are the most common.

Continuous ambulatory peritoneal dialysis (CAPD).   In this procedure, a dialysate with a specific concentration of electrolytes based on the homeostatic needs of the student is introduced by gravity into the abdomen. Once the solution has entered the abdominal cavity (approximately 5 to 10 minutes), the tubing is clamped, the tubing and bag are rolled up and placed in a pocket or secured to the body (at the abdomen or on the thigh), and the student is free to resume normal activities for a period of 4 to 6 hours. While the fluid is in the abdomen, referred to as the **dwell time,** the electrolytes that the body needs pass into the bloodstream from the dialysate, and the waste products not needed pass from the blood vessels into the dialysate by means of osmosis, diffusion, and filtration. After the exchange has occurred, the tube and bag are unrolled, the bag is positioned lower than the abdomen (e.g., on the floor), and the dialysate is allowed to drain from the cavity by means of gravity, taking approximately 10 to 15 minutes. While this takes place, the next bag of dialysate is prepared (i.e., warmed), and when the drainage is completed, a new bag of dialysate is connected and the infusion begins again.

On average, it takes approximately 20 to 30 minutes for the drainage and infusion. However, the time varies depending on the volume to be infused and the adequacy of inflow and outflow (Jackson & Saunders, 1993). In most cases, the procedure must be repeated four or five times a day, most often before school, around lunch time, after school and one or two times at night. A private room, such as the nurse's office, that is clean, quiet, and private should be available so that the student can undergo the procedure without being disturbed.

Continuous cycling peritoneal dialysis (CCPD). This procedure is a modification of CAPD. During the night, while resting in bed or asleep, the child or young adult is connected to a cycling machine that permits the dialysate to flow in and drain out on a scheduled basis, usually 6 to 10 times per night, over 10 hours. In the morning, the individual is disconnected from the machine and goes about regular activities until the procedure is repeated the following night. Fine, Salusky, and Ettenger (1987) have suggested that parents of school-age children and young adults often choose continuous cycling PD over continuous ambulatory PD because of "reduced parental tasks, the ability of the parent to maintain an active work schedule, and the reluctance of the patient [child] to undergo dialysate exchanges at school, thereby risking exposure to excessive peer scrutiny" (p. 796). However, although it may appear that CCPD would be more advantageous than CAPD, being hooked up to a machine nightly may result in decreased mobility and freedom. For example, the ability to participate in a "sleep over" at a friend's house may be extremely limited for the child with kidney disease who is on this form of treatment.

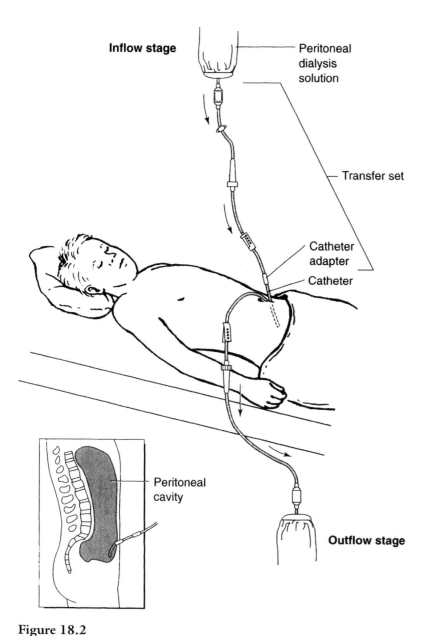

Inflow stage

Peritoneal
dialysis
solution

Transfer set

Catheter
adapter

Catheter

Peritoneal
cavity

Outflow stage

Figure 18.2
Peritoneal Dialysis
Source: Adapted from Mott, James, & Sperhac, 1990, p. 1487.

Because peritoneal dialysis is performed every day, as opposed to hemodialysis, which is performed every 2 to 3 days, the benefits of CAPD and CCPD include the allowance of a more liberal diet and increased fluid consumption. In addition, many individuals experience a decreased need for medications to treat the effects of kidney failure. In fact, many consider this newer form of treatment to have "revolutionized the approach to long-term care" and to be the "preferred method" for treating many children with end-stage renal disease (Jackson & Saunders, 1993). Generally, younger children need the assistance of a school nurse or trained aide; however, older children and adolescents can be trained to carry out the procedure themselves, thus providing them with some control over their condition and less dependency on others (Whaley & Wong, 1995). Unfortunately, peritoneal dialysis is not without risk.

Peritonitis, inflammation of the peritoneum as a result of bacterial or viral infection, is the most common complication, and parents and teachers should be alert to the warning signs (e.g., abdominal pain, fever, nausea, vomiting, and a cloudy appearing dialysate). Localized infection at the site of the catheter may also occur. Symptoms include edema, tenderness, and warmth along the catheter route. There may be discharge evident on the dressing used around the catheter site. Parents and teachers should also be aware of symptoms of complications related directly to the procedure (e.g., fluid overload, dehydration, abdominal or muscle cramps, dizziness) and those related to the catheter (e.g., obstruction due to blood, kink in the catheter) and should be properly trained to deal with such situations. Following are a few pointers for teachers of students who are undergoing dialysis.

1 *If the student is receiving dialysis, staff should be alert to the signs of potential problems and be properly trained to deal with emergency situations.* If the student receiving dialysis complains of abdominal pain, fever, nausea, or vomiting, the parents should be notified and the child taken to the hospital for treatment.

2 *The degree to which students on dialysis are permitted to engage in physical activity is student-specific.* Guidance should be obtained from the student's physician. Forms to be filled out by the student's physician are found in Appendix D.

If a student on hemodialysis has a shunt or fistula, care should be taken to protect the site from injury and infection; similarly, students on peritoneal dialysis should avoid situations in which their abdomen may be bumped or the tubing may be pulled out accidentally. Students on peritoneal dialysis are generally not permitted to swim, and it is recommended that they take showers rather than baths (Vigneux & Hunsberger, 1994).

🌱 Summary

There are a number of disorders common to children and young adults that affect the urinary system. Some of them are easily resolved by means of therapy; others progress to the point that the child's health is compromised. With the advent of new treatment, many children with kidney disease who in the past might not have been able to attend school are now doing so. In some cases, a number of accommodations, such as scheduling around treatment regimens, are necessary.

For a child or young adult to do well in school, one of the key players is an understanding teacher. Students, even those in end-stage renal failure, should be encouraged to attend school so that they can participate in the activities that school has to offer. Participation in extracurricular activities should be encouraged.

One of the greatest gifts a person can give at the time of his or her death is an organ. Sometimes it is knowing someone who needs a kidney transplant that prompts becoming an organ donor. Having a student with kidney disease in a particular school may give staff the impetus to sign an organ donor card. Remember that a severe shortage of organs and tissues prevents many transplants from being performed. Many persons needing a kidney die waiting for one.

References

Bigge, J. L. (1991). *Teaching individuals with physical and multiple disabilities.* New York: Merrill.

Fine, R. N., Salusky I. B., & Ettenger, R. B. (1987). The therapeutic approach to the infant, child, and adolescent with end-stage renal disease. *Pediatric Clinics of North America, 34,* 789–801.

Harbin, R. E., & Neft, M. W. (1992). Alterations in renal function. In P. T. Castiglia & R. E. Harbin (Eds.), *Child health care: Process and practice* (pp. 809–840). Philadelphia: J. B. Lippincott.

Heiliczer, J. D. (1996). Acute renal failure. In F. D. Burg, J. R. Ingelfinger, E. R. Wald, & R. A. Polin (Eds.), *Gellis & Kagan's current pediatric therapy* (15th ed., pp. 452–456). Philadelphia: W. B. Saunders.

Hobbs, S. A., & Sexson, S. B. (1993). Cognitive development and learning in the pediatric organ transplant recipient. *Journal of Learning Disabilities, 26,* 104–113.

Jackson, D. B., & Saunders, R. B. (1993). *Child health nursing: A comprehensive approach to the care of children and their families.* Philadelphia: J. B. Lippincott.

Klingenstein, J. A. (1986). Successful rehabilitation of the renal client. In C. J. Richard (Ed.), *Comprehensive nephrology nursing* (pp. 464–478). Boston: Little, Brown.

Korsch, B., & Fine, R. (1985). Chronic kidney disease. In N. Hobbs & J. M. Perrin (Eds.), *Issues in the care of children with chronic illness* (pp. 282–298). San Francisco: Jossey-Bass.

Livne, P. M., & Gonzales, E. T. (1985). Genitourinary trauma in children. *Urologic Clinics of North America, 12,* 53–65.

Luttrell, J. S. (1990). Genitourinary transport: Implications of inflammation, obstruction, and structural abnormalities. In S. R. Mott, S. R. James, & A. M. Sperhac (Eds.), *Nursing care of children and families* (2nd ed., pp. 1446–1498). Redwood City, CA: Addison-Wesley.

Makker, S. P. (1996). Acute and chronic glomerulonephritis. In F. D. Burg, J. R. Ingelfinger, E. R. Wald, & R. A. Polin (Eds.), *Gellis & Kagan's current pediatric therapy* (15th ed., pp. 441–446). Philadelphia: W. B. Saunders.

Mott, S. R., James, S. R., & Sperhac, A. M. (1990). *Nursing care of children and families* (2nd ed.). Redwood City, CA: Addison Wesley Nursing.

Olson, J. M., Langner, B. E., & Phillips, P. J. (1990). The urinary system. In G. M. Scipien, M. A. Chard, J. Howe, & M. U. Barnard (Eds.), *Pediatric nursing care* (pp. 667–700). St. Louis: Mosby.

Orrbine, E. (1987). *Understanding kidney failure: A handbook for parents.* Ottawa, ONT: Children's Hospital of Eastern Ontario Foundation.

Perez-Woods, R., Hedenkamp, E. A., Ulfig, K., Newman, D., & Fioravante, V. L. (1991). Pediatric transplant recipients: Special nursing considerations and challenges. In B. A. H. Williams, K. L. Grady, & D. M. Sandiford-Guttenbeil (Eds.), *Organ transplantation: A manual for nurses* (pp. 249–274). New York: Springer.

Porter, S., Haynie, M., Bierle, T., Caldwell, T. H., & Palfrey, J. S. (1997). *Children and youth assisted by medical technology in educational settings: Guidelines for care* (2nd ed.). Baltimore: Paul H. Brookes.

Rosenblum, N. D. (1996). The nephrotic syndrome. In F. D. Burg, J. R. Ingelfinger, E. R. Wald, & R. A. Polin (Eds.), *Gellis & Kagan's current pediatric therapy* (15th ed., pp. 446–448). Philadelphia: W. B. Saunders.

Sellers, A., & Edwards, C. S. (1991). Care of the patient with a urinary disorder. In B. L. Christensen, & E. O. Kockrow (Eds.), *Foundations of nursing* (pp. 770–819). St. Louis: Mosby.

Stever, E. (1986). Intermittent catheterization for urine. In G. Larson (Ed.), *Managing the school age child with a chronic health condition* (pp. 207–212). Wayzata, MN: DCI Publishing.

Taylor, J. H. (1996). Renal failure, chronic. In P. L. Jackson & J. A. Vessey (Eds.), *Primary care of the child with a chronic condition* (2nd ed., pp. 689–716). St. Louis: Mosby.

Thelan, L. A., Joseph, K. D., & Urden, L. D. (1990). *Textbook of critical care nursing: Diagnosis and management.* St. Louis: Mosby.

Van Cleve, S. N., & Baldwin, S. E. (1989). Nursing strategies: Altered genitourinary function. In R. L. R. Foster, M. M. Hunsberger, & J. J. T. Anderson (Eds.), *Family-centered nursing care of children* (pp. 1467–1523). Philadelphia: W. B. Saunders.

Vigneux, A., & Hunsberger, M. (1994). Altered genitourinary/renal function. In C. L. Betz, M. M. Hunsberger, & S. Wright (Eds.), *Family-centered nursing care of children* (2nd ed., pp. 1506–1564). Philadelphia: W. B. Saunders.

Whaley, L. F., & Wong, D. L. (1995). *Nursing care of infants and children* (5th ed.). St. Louis: Mosby.

PART VII

Metabolism:

Children and Young Adults with Altered Glandular Function

Throughout the body there are a number of glands whose purpose is to secrete or excrete chemicals that are used by the body to maintain homeostasis and ensure survival. The various glands work in an integrated manner with the nervous system, particularly the sympathetic and parasympathetic systems of the autonomic nervous systems, to coordinate the major body systems. The glands of the human body are organized into two distinct systems, the endocrine and the exocrine systems. The function of some of the major endocrine and exocrine glands is described briefly in this section, and the major problems that can occur in the body as a result of dysfunction are briefly outlined. Two specific conditions, **diabetes,** a disorder of the endocrine system, and **cystic fibrosis,** a disorder of the exocrine system, are presented in greater detail, and suggestions are given for teachers who may have students with these conditions in their classrooms. In addition, some of the conditions known as **inborn errors of metabolism,** genetic disorders that result in a person lacking a specific enzyme, are described briefly.

The Endocrine System: Review of Structure and Function

The **endocrine system** consists of a network of ductless glands that release their secretions directly into the circulatory system (**endo-** prefix meaning inward or within; **-crine,** from the Greek word *krinein,* meaning to secrete) so that they can be transported to nearby or distant sites, where they act to stimulate, regulate, catalyze, or serve as pacemaker substances for a number of metabolic processes, such as the regulation of the heartbeat, the maintenance of fluid and electrolyte balance, and the maturation of the reproductive system. The pituitary, the thyroid and parathyroid glands, the adrenal glands, the islands of Langerhans located in the pancreas, and the gonads are the major endocrine glands in the human body, and the glandular secretions they produce are known

as hormones. Often referred to as the chemical messengers of the body, **hormones** are complex chemical substances that exert a controlling or regulating effect on one of the body's other cells or groups of cells. If the body either overproduces or underproduces a particular hormone, the organs or tissues whose actions are "programmed" by that hormone react with some type of change in function. In some cases, if left untreated, the reaction can be life-threatening.

The system consists of three different parts: the **endocrine cell** that produces or synthesizes the hormone; the **target cells** or **end organ,** which receives the chemical messenger; and the **environment** through which the hormone travels. Endocrine glands are distributed throughout the body and are shown in Figure VII.1.

Pituitary Gland

Suspended beneath the brain, between the two frontal lobes, attached to the hypothalamus by the pituitary stalk, the **pituitary gland,** also known as the **hypophysis,** produces a number of hormones that initiate or regulate certain activities within the body. The pituitary gland, the size and shape of a pea, is actually composed of two glands, the anterior and the posterior glands.

The **anterior pituitary gland** (or **adenohypophysis**) is often thought of as the "master gland" because all of the other endocrine glands are under its direct influence. Two hormones produced by the anterior pituitary, among others, that have significant effects on normal growth and development and maturation of children and young adults include the somatotropin hormones and the gonadotropins. The **somatotropin hormones (STHs),** often referred to as the **growth hormones** of the body, act primarily on the bones, muscles, and organs. If deficient in these hormones, the child develops a condition known as **dwarfism,** characterized by deficient size and stature; if the hormones exist in excess, the child develops **gigantism,** characterized by excessive size and stature. **Gonadotropins** are hormones that

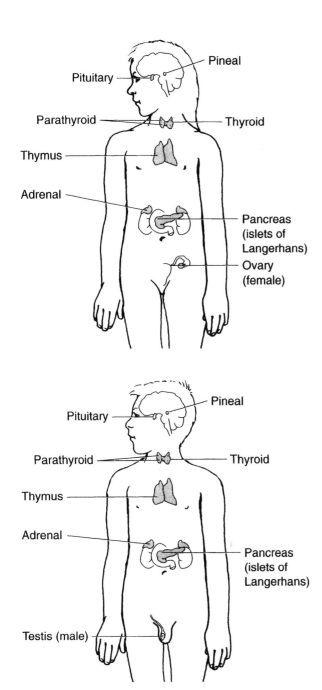

Figure VII.1
The Endocrine System

One of the primary hormones produced by the **posterior pituitary,** or the **neurohypophysis,** is the **antidiuretic hormone (ADH),** which acts on the distal tubules of the kidneys to enhance the reabsorption of water. If the body does not produce enough ADH, also known as **vasopressin,** diabetes insipidus may develop; if too much ADH is produced, edema and/or hyponatremia may develop, which if left untreated can lead to confusion, lethargy, convulsions, and coma.

The clinical manifestations of pituitary dysfunction are varied and depend on the hormone(s) involved. If there is overall diminished or deficient secretion of *all* of the pituitary hormones, the person is said to have **hypopituitarism,** or **panhypopituitarism.** The most typical complaint is delayed growth that results in short stature, which occurs, in many cases, along with absence of the development of secondary sex characteristics. If there is an excessive production of *all* of the various pituitary hormones, the person is said to have **hyperpituitarism,** marked by excessive growth during childhood. Individuals with hyperpituitarism are known to have reached a height of 8 feet or more. In many cases, however, it is only one hormone that is involved, such as is the case in diabetes insipidus.

Thyroid Gland

Consisting of two lobes on either side of the trachea and a connecting portion, known as the **isthmus,** the **thyroid gland** is located on the anterior aspect of the neck, just below the larynx and above the clavicle. The thyroid produces several hormones, including **triiodothyronine** (T_3), **thyroxine** (T_4), and **thyrocalcitonin,** which are all instrumental in regulating the basal metabolic rate of the body (e.g., regulating body heat production and dissipation; maintaining cardiac rate, force, and output) and in regulating the growth and development of the bones, teeth, and brain in children.

If an insufficient amount of the thyroid hormones is produced, the person will have a condition known as **hypothyroidism,** which can, depending on the age at which the deficiency occurs, result in a reduction in general growth. Also typical in hypothyroidism are skin changes, constipation, sleepiness, and mental decline. If too much hormone is produced, a situation known as **hyperthyroidism,** there may be accelerated linear growth, hyperactivity, weight loss, and insomnia.

stimulate the gonads to mature and to produce sex hormones. If deficient, a child does not show signs of reaching puberty; if in excess, a child becomes sexually mature significantly before his or her peers, a condition known as **precocious puberty.**

Parathyroid Glands

On the posterior side of the thyroid, there are 4 or 5 small round glands, known as **parathyroids.** These glands produce **parathyroid hormone (PTH),** which regulates the calcium levels in the blood. Too much PTH can result in **hypocalcemia** (too little calcium in the blood), which if untreated can lead to **tetany,** a condition characterized by muscle cramps and twitching, flexion of the wrist or ankle joints, and convulsions. Too little parathyroid hormone can result in **hypercalcemia** (too much calcium in the blood), which can lead to confusion, abdominal and muscle pain, weakness, and kidney failure that may be life-threatening if left untreated.

Adrenal Glands

Pyramidal in shape, the **adrenal glands** "sit" atop the kidneys, somewhat like a cap. They are made up of two distinct portions, the **cortex** (outer section) and the **medulla** (inner core). The cortex produces three major hormones: (a) **glucocorticoids,** steroid hormones that influence many body functions, such as the ability of skeletal muscle to contract without undue fatigue; (b) **mineralocorticoids,** hormones that assist to maintain normal blood fluid volume, promote the retention of sodium and water, and maintain appropriate levels of serum potassium by increasing excretion via the renal tubules; and (c) **sex steroids,** specifically androgens, estrogens, and progestins, which assist in the development of secondary sexual characteristics along with the sexual hormones produced by the gonads.

Addison's disease, more common in adults than in children, is a life-threatening condition caused by partial or complete failure of the adrenal glands to produce the various adrenal hormones. Signs of insufficiency include muscular weakness, mental fatigue, pigmentary changes of the skin, weight loss, and irritability. Addison's disease can be an autoimmune condition or can result from infection, a malignant tumor in the gland, or hemorrhage in the gland. **Cushing's syndrome** (or **hyperadrenocorticism**), also more common in adults than children, results from excessive production of the glucocorticoid **cortisol.** In children with Cushing's disease, the following characteristics are common: excessive hair growth; a rounded or "moon"-shaped face with overly red cheeks; fat pads on the neck or back, referred to as a "buffalo hump"; a distended, pendulous abdomen, marked by reddish purple abdominal striae (pl.; singular, stria), or "stretch marks," supported by thin extremities; excessive bruising and poor wound healing; and increased weight gain that results in part from increased appetite. If untreated, some of the physiologic disturbances, such as hypertension and susceptibility to infection, can be life-threatening. Cushing's syndrome can result from a pituitary tumor or from an increased growth of adrenal tissue.

The adrenal medulla secretes two hormones, **epinephrine** and **norepinephrine,** which, among other functions, increase cardiac activity, constrict the blood vessels (thereby elevating the blood pressure), dilate the bronchioles, increase muscular contraction, and heighten sensory awareness. Both of these hormones are also produced by stimulation of the sympathetic nervous system, and since one system can substitute for the other, decreased production of these hormones does not occur. Occasionally, however, hyperfunctioning of the medulla can result, and too much hormone is produced. The most frequent cause of this is the presence of some type of tumor. With surgical removal of the growth, the symptoms, which include high blood pressure, elevated blood and urine sugar levels, chronic diarrhea, persistent cough, abdominal distention, and sweating, disappear.

Pancreas

Located transversely across the posterior portion of the abdominal wall, behind the stomach, this fish-shaped organ secretes a number of substances that function primarily in the metabolism of food. Of particular interest are the 1 million clusters of endocrine cells, known as the **islands** or **islets of Langerhans,** located between the exocrine tissues of the organ, particularly in the tail end of the pancreas, that produce the hormone **insulin.** The primary role of insulin is to transport glucose to muscle and fat cells so that it can be used as a source of "fuel" or energy for the body. The chronic disorder that is characterized by the deficient production of the hormone insulin is **diabetes mellitus,** the most common metabolic disease that occurs in humans. The pancreas also produces **glucagon,** a hormone that triggers the liver to release stored glucose when the blood glucose level falls too low (i.e., glucagon and insulin are antagonists), and **somatostatin,** a hormone that functions to inhibit the secretion of certain other hormones, including insulin and glucagon, so that the appropriate amount of each is available as needed.

Gonads

In females, two almond-shaped glands, known as the **ovaries,** are located, one on each side of the uterus, attached to the uterus by means of a **fallopian tube.** The ovaries produce two major hormones, estrogen and progesterone. **Estrogen** has a variety of effects on the body, including promoting the development of the female secondary sex characteristics (e.g., the development of breasts) during puberty, stimulating the ripening and producing of eggs (**ova,** pl; **ovum,** sing.) for possible conception, and accelerating the growth of cells in the uterus that will become the source of nutrition for the fertilized embryo. **Progesterone** functions primarily to prepare the uterus for the reception and implantation of the fertilized egg. If there is too little hormone produced, the young female child may not develop sexually; if there is too much, the opposite, precocious puberty, may occur.

In males, the homologous counterpart to the female ovaries is the **testes.** These glands, oval in shape, are located in the scrotum. The primary hormone produced by the testes is testosterone. Similar to estrogen in females, **testosterone** plays a major part in promoting the development of the secondary sex characteristics in males. Too little testosterone results in delayed sexual development or **eunuchoidism** (a condition that is marked by lack of secondary sex characteristics, small testes, and abnormal tallness and which may result in sterility); too much results in precocious puberty.

The Exocrine System: Review of Structure and Function

The **exocrine system** consists of those glands that release their secretions through a duct to the outer surface of an organ or tissue (**exo-,** prefix meaning outside or outward) rather than into the circulatory system. Many of the various digestive glands located within the GI system, such as the salivary glands, gastric glands, intestinal glands, and liver, are exocrine glands. The pancreas, along with its endocrine tissues mentioned above, also contains exocrine tissues that produce digestive enzymes which are, in turn, transported by means of small ducts to the small intestine, where they act to break down food. Sweat glands, which produce perspiration, and sebaceous glands, which produce sebum, an oily secretion that lubricates the skin, are the most common exocrine glands in the human body. Exocrine glands can be **simple** (having one duct) or **compound** (having more than one duct).

Sweat Glands

The primary role of the **sweat glands,** also known as the **sudoriferous glands,** working in tandem with the circulatory system, in particular the blood vessels, is to regulate the body's heat. If the temperature in the blood vessels increases, the brain sends the message to the sweat glands to produce perspiration. The perspiration in turn flows to the surface of the skin through the sweat ducts, where it evaporates, thereby cooling the body. It has been estimated that there are 2 to 3 million sweat glands located throughout the body. The largest glands are located in the armpits and the groin.

Sebaceous Glands

The primary role of the sebaceous glands is to produce an oily substance, known as **sebum,** that "coats" the skin, keeping it supple and allowing it to retain its moisture. Sebum, when mixed with perspiration, makes sweat more difficult to evaporate, thereby preventing it from evaporating too rapidly (and cooling the body too fast). Sebaceous glands are found throughout the body, particularly in the scalp, face, genitals, anus, nose, mouth, and external ear. They do not occur on the palms or soles. Most of the sebaceous glands open into a hair follicle; however, some open directly onto the surface of the skin. The integumentary system (i.e., the skin, hair, nails, and sebaceous glands) is discussed in greater detail in part VIII.

Digestive Glands

In the body there are a number of glands that produce chemicals that are necessary to break down food into parts that can be absorbed by the bloodstream. Salivary glands, gastric glands, intestinal glands, the liver, and the pancreas are all digestive glands. Some of the different secretions include saliva, hydrochloric acid, bile, enzymes, and mucus.

Lymph Glands

The lymph glands, or lymph nodes, make up a small part of a much larger system that is located throughout the body, known as the **lymph system.** This system has a number of functions, the main one being fighting off infection (i.e., providing the body with immunity). The lymph system, which includes the tonsils, thymus, and spleen, is described in greater detail in part IX, which focuses on problems related to altered immune function.

❧ Inborn Errors of Metabolism (IEMs)

In part VI, the term **catabolism** was introduced to describe the destructive process by which complex substances, in that case, food substances, are reduced to simple, usable nutrients. During catabolism, energy is released and provides the cells with the strength required to carry out their designated tasks. In the constructive stage, referred to as **anabolism,** the energy is used by the body to convert certain simple substances into complex compounds of living matter, e.g., phospholipids, a component of cell membranes, which are anabolized from fatty acids. Together the two phases, catabolism and anabolism, make up the process known as **metabolism.**

A child who has an **inborn error of metabolism** (IEM) has an inherited defect in which the body is unable to perform the essential chemical tasks of catabolism or anabolism, or both, because of an absence of or defect in a particular substance essential for metabolism, most often an enzyme that is necessary for the biochemical reaction to take place. While not considered specifically a problem related to the GI system, inborn errors of metabolism are typically evidenced by an inability to break down certain food substances, referred to in the medical literature as **substrates** (i.e., proteins, carbohydrates, and fats). Inborn errors of metabolism can also affect the metabolism of certain minerals and vitamins.

Some of the more common inborn errors of metabolism are described in chapter 20, which deals with disorders of the exocrine system. Errors of metabolism are *not* exocrine disorders per se, for it is not the gland that produces the enzyme that is dysfunctional; rather, it is the genetic code of the individual that is altered. However, since all inborn errors of metabolism result in the body being unable to produce certain enzymes that normally are produced by the exocrine system, they have been placed in chapter 20 along with cystic fibrosis, which is a "true" exocrine disorder and also has a hereditary cause.

Altered Endocrine Function

Each of the organs of the endocrine system is vulnerable to specific diseases or disorders. Typically, one of two conditions occurs: either the individual produces *too much* of a particular hormone, such as is the case in *hyper*pituitarism, *hyper*thyroidism, and *hyper*calcemia, or the individual produces *too little* hormone, such as in the case of *hypo*pituitarism, *hypo*thyroidism, and *hypo*calcemia, described briefly in the introduction to this part. While each of these conditions can occur in childhood, none is as common as **diabetes,** the most prevalent endocrine disease of childhood and adolescence. Diabetes, in its most common form, is a condition that arises in people who have *hypo*insulinism, or too *little* **insulin,** a hormone normally produced by the beta cells located within the islets of Langerhans of the pancreas. Diabetes is the focus of this chapter.

❧ Diabetes

From the Greek word *diabainein,* meaning to pass or flow through or to siphon, **diabetes** is characterized by the secretion and excretion of copious amounts of urine. There are two different forms of diabetes, **diabetes insipidus** ("bland" urine diabetes) and **diabetes mellitus** ("sweet" urine diabetes). While both types of diabetes can occur in children and young adults, the more common is diabetes mellitus. Diabetes insipidus is described briefly, followed by a more in-depth look at diabetes mellitus, particularly type I diabetes mellitus, the type seen most commonly in the pediatric population.

❧ Diabetes Insipidus (DI)

Diabetes insipidus is a metabolic disorder that results from either a deficiency in the pituitary gland's ability to produce or secrete the antidiuretic hormone **vasopressin** or the inability of tubules of the kidneys to respond to the hormone that is produced. The first form of the disease is referred to as **neurogenic diabetes insipidus,** the second as **nephrogenic diabetes insipidus.** Neurogenic diabetes insipidus can result from a variety of causes, including the incomplete formation of the pituitary gland, the development of a tumor of the pituitary, and damage to the pituitary after traumatic head injury. In as many as 45% to 50% of cases, the cause is unknown (Whaley & Wong, 1995). Nephrogenic diabetes insipidus is a rare recessive X-linked genetic defect, found almost exclusively in males. Diabetes insipidus can also be self-induced by excessive water intake, a condition known as **psychogenic water drinking;** however, this type is extremely rare.

Typically, the child or young adult with diabetes insipidus, regardless of the type, shows some or all of the following characteristics: excretion of an abnormally large quantity of urine that is almost colorless, dehydration, insatiable thirst, anorexia, weight loss, vomiting, constipation, and irritability. Onset is typically abrupt and, if left untreated, can lead to shock. In some cases, children who have previously been toilet-trained develop night enuresis. Some may even become enuretic during the day.

Neurogenic diabetes insipidus can be resolved with hormone replacement therapy. Management of nephrogenic diabetes is primarily dietary (e.g., restriction in salt and protein; provision of adequate fluid to maintain normal molecular balance) or pharmacologic, or both.

❧ Diabetes Mellitus (DM)

Diabetes mellitus is a chronic disorder of carbohydrate and associated fat and protein metabolism that typically results from a lack of insulin. Less frequently, the condition results from a defect in the insulin receptors of cells located throughout the body. In such cases, insulin is produced by the pancreas, but the body cannot use it properly. While all forms of DM are characterized by variable and chronic **hyperglycemia** (increased glucose in the blood) and **glucosuria** (presence of glucose in the urine), there are several forms of the disease, the most common being type I and type II diabetes. The different forms of diabetes are shown in Table 19.1.

Idiopathic Diabetes Mellitus

Idiopathic conditions arise for no known cause; i.e., they are spontaneous conditions whose cause is unknown. There are three different types of idiopathic diabetes mellitus: type I diabetes, type II diabetes, and impaired glucose tolerance. While these forms are of unknown cause, after many years of research, scientists are slowly beginning to understand some of the causal and pathogenic mechanisms. Genetic and autoimmune factors have been a focus of much of the research.

TABLE 19.1
Diabetes Mellitus: Classification by Type

IDIOPATHIC DIABETES MELLITUS
Type I: Insulin-dependent diabetes mellitus (IDDM)
Type II: Non–insulin-dependent diabetes mellitus (NIDDM)
Impaired glucose tolerance (IGT)

NON-IDIOPATHIC DIABETES MELLITUS
Secondary Diabetes
Resulting from:
   Pancreatic trauma (e.g., blow to abdomen), disease or dysfunction (e.g., cystic fibrosis), or surgery (e.g., removal of pancreas)
   Endocrine disease (i.e., hormone-induced)
   Drug- or chemical-induced diabetes
   Genetic syndromes
   End-organ (insulin receptor) defects
   Malnutrition (malnutrition-related diabetes mellitus, or MRDM)
   Other
Gestational diabetes mellitus (GDM)
Secondary to pregnancy

- *Possible Genetic Factors:* While idiopathic diabetes is often referred to as **familial** or **genetic diabetes,** the exact mechanism for the inheritance of diabetes is still unknown. Certain combinations of genes, as many as five or six, located within the **human leukocyte antigen (HLA)** region of chromosome 6 may make the person susceptible to inheriting the disease. However, even with such a combination, without some type of event, typically a **viral infection,** the disease does not normally develop. This is not to say that a virus is the cause of the disease, but that the virus is a trigger that changes a person from being predisposed to the disease to actually having the disease. Viruses that have been implicated include the coxsackie B4, rubella, and mumps viruses. Other possible triggers include stress, injury or inflammation, drugs, chemical irritants, dietary proteins, and bacteria.
- *Possible Autoimmune Factors:* In addition to a causative genetic tendency, researchers have been examining the possibility that diabetes only develops in those individuals who have a predisposition to developing an autoimmune disease.[1] In such situations, as a result of one of the possible triggers mentioned above, it is theorized that the body, thinking that it is attacking foreign bodies, reacts by attacking and destroying the beta cells of the pancreas, which may have been altered in some way.
- *Other Factors:* Obesity, the aging process, diet, lifestyle, and ethnicity are all believed to contribute to the development of idiopathic diabetes mellitus.

Type I Diabetes   Formerly referred to as juvenile diabetes, juvenile-onset diabetes, youth-onset diabetes, unstable or brittle diabetes, or ketosis-prone diabetes, type I diabetes is the form usually seen in young people. Age at onset is typically less than 20 years; however, type I diabetes can occur at any age. Type I diabetes is also known as **insulin-dependent diabetes mellitus (IDDM).** Persons with IDDM, as the name suggests, depend on **exogenous insulin** (insulin manufactured from outside the body) to control the condition. The dependency is caused by the destruction of previously functioning beta cells that results in the eventual absolute lack of **endogenous insulin** (insulin manufactured within the body). Even though the progression of cellular damage is slow, the onset of symptoms in children is usually sudden.

Type II Diabetes   Formerly referred to as adult-onset diabetes, maturity-onset diabetes, stable

---

[1] For further information on autoimmune diseases, see Part IX.

diabetes, or ketosis-resistant diabetes, type II diabetes is more common in adults, typically those over the age of 30. However, type II, like type I, can occur at any age. When type II diabetes occurs in young children or adolescents, it is often referred to as **maturity-onset diabetes of the young (MODY)**, a condition that is believed to be inherited as an autosomal dominant trait (Lebovitz, 1984). Type II diabetes is also known as **non–insulin-dependent diabetes mellitus (NIDDM)**. In type II diabetes, the beta cells continue to produce endogenous insulin, albeit at a reduced rate compared with the rate of individuals without the condition. As a consequence, persons with NIDDM do not require exogenous insulin; rather, in most cases, the condition can be managed by controlling the amount of glucose added to the system (diet) in conjunction with regulating the amount of glucose needed by the system (exercise). In some circumstances, the individual with NIDDM may require exogenous insulin, for example, during stressful periods that result from illness, surgery, infection, or trauma. Typically, the onset of type II diabetes is gradual, and the condition often goes unrecognized unless the patient undergoes routine screening tests. MODY is usually seen in teenagers who are obese.

Glucose Intolerance In addition to type I and type II diabetes mellitus, there is a group of persons who have blood glucose levels that are higher than normal but lower than those found typically in persons with diabetes. These individuals are described as having **impaired glucose tolerance (IGT)**, a condition that in the past has been called asymptomatic diabetes, chemical diabetes, borderline diabetes, or latent diabetes. A person with IGT may not be aware that he or she has the condition because of lack of overt clinical symptoms; however, during periods of stress, the classic symptoms of diabetes may begin to show. In some individuals, IGT is a stage before they develop full-fledged diabetes; in others, the condition does not progress, and the blood glucose remains elevated but stationary. In a few, the raised blood glucose returns to normal levels, never to increase again.

Non-Idiopathic Diabetes Mellitus

There are two different forms of diabetes that result from some previous disease or condition; that is, rather than being idiopathic, they are non-idiopathic, or acquired. The two forms are secondary diabetes and gestational diabetes.

Secondary Diabetes In this form of diabetes, the condition is precipitated by one or more factors that are known or at least strongly suspected to be causative. The most common causes of secondary diabetes mellitus are listed in Table 19.1. In many cases of secondary diabetes mellitus, once the causative (primary) factor is isolated and the disorder is treated, the diabetes disappears; however, in some cases, the damage to the pancreas is irreversible (i.e., the person becomes diabetic).

Gestational Diabetes (GDM) This form of diabetes occurs in 1% to 2% of pregnant women, typically during the third trimester of pregnancy. Women in whom GDM develops typically have no previous history of the disease; however, during pregnancy they become unable to metabolize carbohydrates in the normal manner, possibly as a result of the influence of one or more other hormones, such as placental lactogen, on the islets of Langerhans. Although gestational diabetes does not usually affect the mother greatly, if left untreated, the developing fetus, who relies on maternal glucose as a primary source of energy, becomes overnourished and gains more weight than normal (Springhouse Corp., 1992). In some cases, perhaps as many as 50%, women who have a history of GDM develop type II diabetes mellitus within 10 years of the pregnancy (Lebovitz, 1984).

Prevalence and Incidence

Between 100 and 150 million individuals have the condition worldwide, and between 11 and 14 million persons in the United States are affected. This figure represents between 4% and 6% of the total population, making diabetes "one of the most prevalent, chronic, serious diseases in our society today" (Guthrie & Guthrie, 1991, p. 8). In the United States alone, between 123,000 and 150,000 children, adolescents, and young adults under the age of 20 have diabetes mellitus (American Diabetes Association, 1993; Castiglia, Kramer, Fong, & Lipman, 1992). More than 10,000 cases of type I diabetes are diagnosed in young people each year (Lloyd & Orchard, 1993). Although the prevalence and incidence of diabetes differ considerably when the different types of diabetes, the age of the individual at the time of diagnosis, and the person's ethnic background are examined, the vast majority have NIDDM.

Most children and young adults (approximately 95% of all new-onset cases) have classic type I diabetes. A smaller proportion (5%) have either MODY or secondary diabetes (Betschart, 1993). In children under 10, the prevalence rate is 0.6 per 1,000; however, for those over 10, the prevalence more than doubles to 1.5 per 1,000. In children and adolescents, diabetes is more common in whites (1.2 per 1,000) than in blacks (0.1 per 1,000). Diabetes occurs rarely in Native American, Hispanic, Eskimo, and Asian American children (Clark, Freezle, Gray, & Parker, 1993; Whaley & Wong, 1995).

Physiopathology and Resultant Characteristics

To understand how diabetes affects the lives of those with the condition, a basic understanding of the process by which the body obtains the energy it requires to run, think, play, and so on is necessary. All of the tissues of the body require glucose as a basic source of energy. **Glucose,** a simple sugar, comes primarily from the ingestion of carbohydrates. Sources of carbohydrates include cereals and grain products (e.g., alcohol); potatoes and other vegetables (e.g., beans and legumes); flour products, such as pasta; and all forms of sugar, including table sugar, sugar cane, beet sugar, milk sugar, and fruit sugar. The brain uses approximately 50% of the total supply of glucose, and since the energy stores of the brain are small, a constant source of glucose is needed (Guthrie & Guthrie, 1991).

In the individual who does *not* have diabetes, the process is as follows:

1. As the carbohydrates that the person has ingested are digested, the glucose is absorbed into the venous bloodstream, where it circulates freely throughout the body.
2. As the blood glucose level increases, the pancreas responds by producing insulin, which is also released into the bloodstream.
3. Via the bloodstream, the glucose and insulin travel to the specific organs or peripheral tissues that require energy. Here, as a result of the action exerted by the insulin, often described as being similar to a key that opens a lock, the glucose leaves the blood and enters the individual cells. As the glucose leaves the bloodstream the glu-

cose level "falls" back to normal. In children, the amount of glucose in the blood before meals is typically between 60 to 70 mg/dL and 110 to 120 mg/dL; 90 minutes after the meal has been completed, it is typically between 160 and 180 mg/dL.
4. If more glucose is taken in than is actually needed by the body at that particular time, the excess is converted to **glycogen,** a process known as **glycogenesis,** and is stored in the liver and, to a lesser extent, in muscle cells. Some glycogen is converted to **triglycerides** and stored in the fat cells of the body.
5. If the body has too little glucose, e.g., during a fast, the stored glycogen is then reconverted to glucose, a process known as **glycogenolysis,** and released into the circulation, to be used as needed. The triglycerides are metabolized into fatty acids, which are then converted into keto acids by the liver.

In the individual who has type I diabetes there are a number of consequences that result from the lack of insulin. The sequence of events is described below. The major consequences of diabetes are **polyuria** (increased urination), **polydipsia** (increased thirst), and **polyphagia** (increased hunger), often referred to as the "3 Ps" of diabetes.

1. Because of the lack of insulin in the blood, the glucose is not released to the cells as needed, and as the individual ingests more carbohydrates, the glucose level increases. Blood sugar levels can go as high as 1000 mg/dL or, in rare cases, even higher (Winter, 1983).
2. When the blood glucose level exceeds 160 to 180 mg/dL, the renal tubules, which normally reabsorb the glucose that is not needed by the body, are unable to handle the increased load; this causes the excess glucose, along with large amounts of electrolytes, particularly sodium and potassium, to "spill" into the urine. When glucose appears in the urine, the individual is said to have **glycosuria.** Since the loss of glucose is, in reality, a loss of potential energy, a person with glycosuria has the potential to become easily fatigued.
3. As the glucose is excreted in the urine, water is also removed, making the resultant urine less concentrated than normal. If water was not removed along with the glucose, the urine would become thick, like maple syrup, and difficult for

the individual to pass. As more and more water is excreted, more and more urine is produced. Polyuria is typically one of the first signs of diabetes.

4. Because of the loss of fluids that results from polyuria, the body becomes dehydrated, and the individual shows signs of **polydipsia**.

5. Because the glucose continues to circulate and does not enter the cells as needed, the body begins to behave as if the individual were fasting, turning to some of the stored foods, particularly fats and proteins located in the liver, fat cells, and muscles, as a source of energy.

   a. Although **fats** are able to provide energy to certain cells, the metabolism of fats causes a new set of potential difficulties. During catabolism, fats break down into fatty acids and glycerol, which in turn are converted into acids (known as **ketone bodies**) by the liver. The ketones do, in fact, function as an alternative source of fuel, but only a limited amount can be used at any one time; consequently, as the ketone bodies accumulate, a condition known as **ketosis,** they must be eliminated from the body. Some ketones, along with additional sodium and potassium, are filtered out by the kidneys into the urine, resulting in a condition known as **ketonuria** or **ketoaciduria,** and are eliminated as the person voids. Other ketones are eliminated via the lungs, resulting in breath odor, known as **acetone breath,** which is fruity and somewhat similar to the smell of overripe bananas. If the ketones are not adequately excreted by the body, the individual develops **diabetic ketoacidosis** (or **DKA**), a condition in which the acid-base balance of the blood is altered. The early stage of DKA is characterized by mental confusion, shortness of breath, abdominal pain, nausea, and vomiting. If untreated, DKA may lead to coma and death.

   b. If **proteins** are used as a source of energy, rather than solving the energy depletion problem, the hyperglycemic state is worsened. This occurs because as proteins are broken down in the liver, a process known as **gluconeogenesis** or **glucogenesis**, glucose is produced. The resultant glucose, added to the glucose that is already available from food sources, still cannot enter the body's cells because of the lack of insulin; consequently, the blood sugar level increases again.

6. Even though the metabolism of non-carbohydrate foods may meet the need for energy to a limited degree, eventually the body's fat and protein stores become depleted, and the hunger mechanism, located in the hypothalamus of the brain, becomes activated. The individual develops **polyphagia.** The resultant increase in food consumption, however, simply increases the problem further by elevating the blood glucose. Some individuals eat to the point of gluttony; however, typically, the person continues to (a) lose weight, due in part to the breakdown of the stored body fats, described above; (b) develop extremely dry skin, which is prone to infections that are slow in healing; and (c) become increasingly lethargic as a result of the continuing depletion of glucose in the cells. Some children and young adults develop anorexia rather than polyphagia.

Diagnosis and Treatment

Along with a complete history, the presence of diabetes is confirmed by blood and urine tests. If, after drinking a quantity of flavored glucose, the individual shows abnormally high levels of glucose in the blood and the urine, the diagnosis is established. Often it is the presence of the "3 Ps" that brings the child or young adult to the doctor in the first place.

For all persons with diabetes, the goal of treatment is to keep the blood and urine glucose levels as close to normal as possible so that there will be few (or at least fewer) long-term complications. Unfortunately, even with good control, it is "unusual" for an individual with IDDM to "achieve and maintain near metabolic normality for extended periods" (Drash & Arslanian, 1990, p. 1467). Control is achieved by a combination of insulin therapy, monitoring of food intake, and a program of regular exercise.

Insulin Therapy   There are various sources of exogenous insulin, the most common being "natural" insulin, which is extracted from the pancreas of cows or pigs. Recent research activities have led to the development of a newer form of insulin (e.g., Humulin, Novolin), which is often referred to as "human" insulin. Human insulins are not, in fact, extracted from humans, but are produced in a laboratory, using advanced recombinant DNA technology and chemical biosynthesis.

Insulin is manufactured in dosages that contain a specific number of units of insulin per milliliter of liquid, which is packaged in vials typically containing 40, 100, and 500 units/mL, labeled as U-40, U-100, and U-500, respectively. The number of units given per day is determined by such factors as the individual's height and weight, metabolic rate, physical maturity, blood glucose level, and expected food consumption and energy expenditure. By adding different chemicals to insulin, the producer can alter its "speed" of action, so that some is rapid-acting, some is intermediate-acting, and some is long-acting.

- *Rapid-Acting (Short-Acting) Insulins:* These insulins typically act between 30 minutes and 1 hour after injection. There are two different types: **regular insulin** (peaks in 2 to 4 hours; lasts 4 to 8 hours) and **semilente insulin** (peaks in 4 to 6 hours; lasts 12 to 16 hours). Because these act very quickly, they are typically given before each meal to ensure that the blood glucose level remains fairly stable after the ingestion of carbohydrates. Because of its rapidity of onset, this type of insulin can also be given in emergency situations to those individuals who develop ketoacidosis.
- *Intermediate-Acting Insulin:* These insulins typically act between 2 and 6 hours after administration. There are two different types: **neutral protamine Hagedorn,** more commonly referred to as **NPH insulin** (peaks in 4 to 14 hours; lasts 14 to 24 hours), and **lente insulin** (peaks in 4 to 14 hours; lasts 16 to 24 hours). Intermediate-acting insulins, because of their ability to act for long periods of time, are generally given to provide day-long control of the blood sugar level.
- *Long-Acting Insulin:* These insulins typically act 6 to 14 hours after administration. There are two types: **protamine zinc,** more commonly referred to as **PZI insulin** (peaks in 14 to 20 hours; lasts 24 to 36 hours or more), and **ultralente insulin** (peaks in 12 to 18 hours; lasts between 24 and 36 hours). Long-acting insulins are not used very often with children.

Children and young adults with IDDM are often given combinations of insulin to ensure that the peak level of action of the hormone coincides with their peak blood glucose level. If, for example, a particular individual were to get two doses of rapid-acting insulin per day, one at breakfast and one at supper, it would not be uncommon for the person to become hypoglycemic (i.e., show signs of decreased blood sugar level) approximately 2 hours after injection (between midmorning and lunch) or just before bed-

time, times when the action of the injected insulin peaks. If, however, instead of rapid-acting insulin, the same individual were to get two doses of intermediate-acting insulin (i.e., breakfast and supper), the periods from mid-afternoon until supper time could be problematic, as could the middle of the night. To prevent the blood sugar from dropping at *any* point during the day or night, a mixture of the two would likely be prescribed. Before breakfast, the person would receive one large dose of the mixture (i.e., two-thirds to three-fourths of the total daily dosage) that would cover the daytime meals, and before the evening meal, he or she would be given a second, smaller dose to obtain adequate nocturnal coverage. The control that is achieved by such a combination is depicted in Figure 19.1. This graph shows that, at all times of the day, one or more of the exogenous insulins would be exerting its effect.

Because insulin is a protein, it must be given by injection. If given orally, it would be destroyed by the body's digestive enzymes. In most cases, insulin is injected subcutaneously by means of a syringe and needle. Other methods of injection include automatic injectors (Injectease) and needle-free injectors (e.g., Medi-Jector EZ, Tender Touch), which deliver the insulin directly through the skin by means of high pressure. Regardless of the method of administration, the site chosen for the injection must be changed on a regular basis so that (a) the possibility of injury to the skin and underlying fatty tissue is reduced, (b) a buildup of scar tissue or swelling is prevented, and (c) the speed at which the insulin is absorbed is not altered as a result of the growth of fibrous tissue and decreased blood supply that occur with repeated injection at the same site (Springhouse Corp., 1992).

Some persons receive insulin by means of a **portable insulin pump** (e.g., MiniMed 507, Disetronic H-TRONplus). The process is known as **continuous subcutaneous insulin infusion,** or **CSII.** The battery-powered pump, about the size of a personal pager, weighing less than 4 ounces (113.4 grams), consists of a reservoir that stores the insulin, typically worn on a belt or in a pocket, and a thin 24- to 48-inch-long plastic catheter. At the end of the tube is a needle that is inserted into the subcutaneous tissue of the abdomen, thigh, hip, buttock, or upper arm. The pump is programmed to allow for continuous administration of fixed amounts of insulin (referred to as a **bolus**) throughout the day and at mealtimes (i.e., to mimic normal insulin delivery), based on the blood glucose level of the individual.

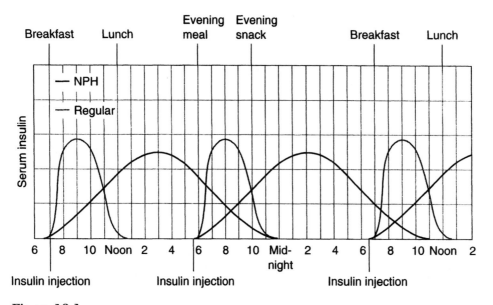

Figure 19.1

Two-Injection Regimen and Timing of Food Intake. In this example, a child receives insulin twice a day. At 6:30 AM and 5:30 PM, a combination of regular (rapid-acting) and NPH (intermediate-acting) insulin is given. Peak effect of the drugs occurs shortly after consumption of food.

Source: Strowig, S. (1995). Insulin therapy. Published in *RN, 58*(6). Copyright © 1995 Medical Economics, Montvale, N.J. Reprinted by permission.

While the pump may seem the best way to administer insulin, the pump is only as good as the person who programs it, because hypoglycemia or hyperglycemia can occur if too much or too little insulin is delivered. Typically, the pump is only considered for individuals who are 10 years of age or older.

While some may appreciate the ease of insulin administration by means of the pump, it may not be suitable for all persons. Many individuals, particularly adolescents, do not like its visibility; others, who participate in certain types of sports, such as contact sports or swimming, find it awkward to have to disconnect the pump and cap the catheter before each activity and before bathing. The fact that the pump cannot be disconnected for more than 1 hour at a time may be limiting to some. Other potential problems with the pump include blockages in the catheter, local infections, and abscesses at the needle site (Christman & Bennett, 1987), and because it runs on batteries, mechanical failure is possible.

Nutrition and Diet The nutritional needs of individuals with diabetes are the same as those who do not have diabetes. They do not require special foods or different amounts of vitamins or minerals (Wolfsdorf, Anderson, & Pasquarello, 1994). Simply put, they

need a good diet that (a) balances the energy expenditure of the individual (based on age, sex, height, weight, stage of sexual development, and level of physical activity) and (b) meets the normal requirements for age-related growth and development. Typically, it is recommended that children under age 7 have three well-spaced, nutritious meals a day, with snacks in between and at bedtime. Older children and young adults may not require a mid-morning snack; however, if they begin to experience hypoglycemic episodes that result from too little food or too much physical exercise during the morning recess period, the mid-morning snack should be reinstated. The total consumption of calories and the ratio of carbohydrate to protein and to fat in each meal or snack should be consistent from day to day (Wolfsdorf et al., 1994).

Exercise Exercise greatly improves the condition of individuals with NIDDM (i.e., lowers blood sugar concentration, results in better use of food, leads to a reduction in insulin requirements), but the benefits of exercise for individuals in those with IDDM are less clearly understood (Spelsberg & Manson, 1995). Although it is believed that the benefits are many (e.g., increased skeletal muscle sensitivity to insulin, which reduces insulin requirements;

decreased serum cholesterol and triglyceride levels; lower blood pressure) and that participation in virtually any sport is possible, including competitive sports, exercise for a person on insulin can be dangerous if certain precautions are not taken (American Diabetes Association, 1995; Christman & Bennett, 1987). Athletes with type I diabetes are most at risk for developing exercise-induced hypoglycemia or hyperglycemia and post-exercise hypoglycemia (Fahey, Stallkamp, & Kwatra, 1996).

Monitoring Glucose and Ketone Levels

Physicians typically recommend that blood glucose levels be measured several times a day, usually before each meal and before going to bed, particularly in the first months after the condition is diagnosed. The monitoring procedure involves pricking a finger to obtain a small sample of blood and then either putting a drop of blood on a blood glucose reagent strip or placing the blood sample in a **glucose meter,** an electronic device that calculates the level of blood glucose. There are several models and brands available, one of the more common being the **One Touch II.**

Once a stable pattern is established, the regimen may be relaxed. For example, in some situations the physician may agree to suspend the pre-noon glucose check, particularly if the testing is disruptive or if, in the case of a school-age individual, the student feels awkward having to leave the classroom; in others, the doctor may suggest that the individual only test his or her blood every second day. If the student's blood glucose level is not monitored every day, on the days that the blood testing is not performed, the child or young adult is usually instructed to test his or her urine for glucose by dipping a glucose testing reagent strip into a urine sample and visually examining the color reaction.

If at any time the student's blood glucose level exceeds 240 or 250 mg/dL or the urine glucose is 2% or more, the student is usually instructed to measure his or her urine for ketones, using a ketone testing reagent strip. In addition, the student should test for urinary ketones whenever feeling ill, such as when he or she has a cold, the flu, or an earache.

Prognosis and Sequelae

In the majority of cases, persons with diabetes are able to get the condition under control by means of diet, exercise, and administration of exogenous insulin. Unfortunately, however, they are not cured of the condition, for at this point in time, a readily available remedy has eluded researchers. The only known true "cure" is a pancreas transplant, a procedure that has been available since the late 1960s. While the success rate continues to improve, it has been cautioned that transplantation is unwarranted in children and adolescents because recipients "can hardly be considered normal, healthy individuals" since they "face a lifetime of immunosuppressive therapy" to prevent rejection (Drash & Arslanian, 1990, p. 1477). Research efforts are being directed towards the possibility of transplanting isolated beta cells from a donor into the body of a person with diabetes, and while this approach has been tried, to date the success rate has been described as "minimal" (Drash & Arslanian, 1990) and "disappointing" (Weir, 1995).

Persons with diabetes, in particular those with IDDM, often experience a number of long-term consequences (e.g., damage to large blood vessels that can result in coronary artery disease and impaired circulation to the extremities, in particular the feet; damage to small blood vessels that can lead to loss of vision and to kidney failure). Although the exact reasons for potentially negative sequelae are not completely understood, the thickening of the walls of the capillaries that supply blood and nutrients to certain organs (e.g., eyes) or systems (e.g., CNS) and the process known as **glycosylation,** in which blood proteins are deposited on the walls of the blood vessels, are believed to be major contributory factors.

Rarely do the chronic complications appear before puberty is reached, and in many cases, they do not begin to develop until at least 15 years after the initial diagnosis. However, in young children, alterations in normal growth and development, particularly in cases where there is less than optimal control of carbohydrate metabolism or persistent hyperglycemia, or both, are of particular concern. Children and adolescents with diabetes may also show signs of altered sexual maturation (e.g., delay in the onset of puberty). Some children and young adults with IDDM have limited joint mobility and stiffness of the hands and fingers.

Hypoglycemia, Euglycemia, and Hyperglycemia: A Continuum

It is not uncommon for children and adolescents, particularly in the early stages of the disease or during periods of growth, to have episodes in which their metabolic status fluctuates between periods of hypoglycemia and hyperglycemia, even though the goal of treatment is to maintain the glucose level within a normal range, a state known as **euglycemia** or **normoglycemia**. While hypoglycemia is the more common short-term problem, occurring in a mild form as frequently as two to three times per week (Clark et al., 1993), both conditions are described so that caregivers can be alert to the typical symptoms and be aware of how each of the conditions should be treated.

Hypoglycemia   Defined operationally as a level of blood glucose below normal (below 60 mg/dL), hypoglycemia is the most common complication of diabetes. It has been estimated that more than 90% of individuals with IDDM have periods of symptomatic hypoglycemia, and while it is less common in persons with NIDDM, those who are treated with insulin or oral hypoglycemic agents may show signs of this condition (Cryer & Gerich, 1985). Even though it is a common occurrence, hypoglycemia should *not* be dismissed as a trivial problem, because it is the cause of death in 4% of persons with diabetes under the age of 50 (Macheca, 1993). More importantly, in the young, severe hypoglycemic episodes have been shown to result in permanent impairment of intellectual function (Menon & Sperling, 1988).

Hypoglycemia is often referred to as an **insulin reaction** because it results from too much insulin in the system and typically occurs at the time that the action of the injected insulin peaks (e.g., 8 to 12 hours after NPH insulin is given; 14 to 20 hours after PZI insulin is given). Various reasons for the increased level of insulin in the body are shown in Figure 19.2. Frequently, the reaction is the result of too much exogenous insulin being administered in error. The symptoms of hypoglycemia by level (i.e., mild, moderate, and severe) are shown in Table 19.2.

Aside from too much insulin being given, hypoglycemia can also result from the correct dosage of insulin being absorbed too quickly. For example, if an individual injects the dose into his or her upper thigh, and then goes jogging, the insulin is absorbed more quickly than would normally be absorbed by the leg if it were at rest. If the individual compounds the situation by not eating some food before or during the run, the athlete's blood sugar may drop to a dangerous level. Hypoglycemia can occur up to 15 hours after strenuous exercise has stopped (Macheca, 1993).

Unplanned exercise can also lead to a hypoglycemic episode, as can "hidden" exercise. For example, if a student who takes his or her normal dose of insulin followed by a normal intake of food has the opportunity to participate in a spur-of-the-moment activity, hypoglycemia can result, particularly if the exercise is either prolonged or of increased intensity and there is no food available for the student to snack on. "Hidden" exercise refers to exercise that is not recognized as being physically demanding. For example, if a student who normally takes the bus to school decides to walk to school, he or she may not recognize that the walk is a form of exercise, and if the student did not alter his or her medication or food intake, hypoglycemia may result. Because children and young adults often participate in unplanned or hidden activities, they or their caregivers should always carry a source of fast-acting carbohydrate with them.

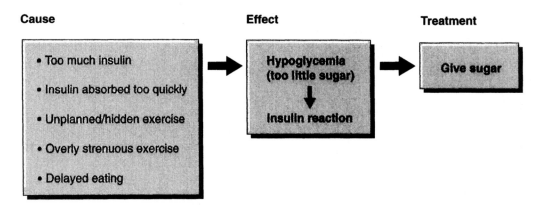

Figure 19.2
Hypoglycemia: Cause, Effect, and Treatment

TABLE 19.2

Signs and Symptoms of Hypoglycemia

MILD HYPOGLYCEMIA (BLOOD SUGAR LEVEL < 60 mg/dL):

One or more of the following symptoms, developing very rapidly:

Faintness
Dizziness
Headache
Excessive hunger
Pallor
Tremor
Shakiness
Nervousness
Irritability
Weakness
Tiredness
Increased heart rate (tachycardia)
Pounding heart (palpitation)
Sweatiness or increased perspiration (diaphoresis), a feeling of being "cold and clammy"
Cold hands and feet
Hair "standing on end" (piloerection)

MODERATE HYPOGLYCEMIA (BLOOD SUGAR LEVEL < 40 mg/dL)

One or more of the above symptoms, plus one or more of the following:

Headache (moderate to severe)
Lability of mood (i.e., mood changes)
Irritability
Inability to concentrate
Decreased attentiveness
Drowsiness
Fatigue
Mental confusion
Disorientation
Lightheadedness
Dizziness
Impaired judgment
Slurred, incoherent speech
Numbness, tingling, or pins and needles sensation (paresthesia), particularly of the lips and tongue
Staggering gait
Lack of coordination
Double vision (diplopia)
Blurred vision
Irrational behavior
Nocturnal hypoglycemia (symptoms include restlessness, nightmares, and night sweats)

SEVERE HYPOGLYCEMIA (BLOOD SUGAR LEVEL < 20 mg/dL)

Several or all of the following:

Extreme disorientation
Unresponsiveness
Convulsions
Seizures
Unconsciousness (coma)

TABLE 19.3
Typical Treatment of Hypoglycemia

MILD HYPOGLYCEMIA

1. The symptoms of mild hypoglycemia usually abate within 10–15 minutes of the administration of 10–15 grams of rapid-acting carbohydrates,[a] such as one of the following:

   2–3 glucose tablets
   6–8 Lifesavers candies
   6 jelly beans or gum drops
   1 fruit roll-up
   2–4 oz. grape juice
   4 oz. whole milk
   2–3 graham crackers
   Small tube of cake icing (Cake Mate)
   Single dose Monoject Insulin Reaction Gel
   1–2 hard candies (e.g., peppermints)
   2 T (small box) raisins
   4–5 pieces of dried fruit
   6 oz. regular (not diet) carbonated drinks
   6–8 oz. skim milk
   4 animal crackers

   While it may be distressing to both the caregiver and the student for the student to continue to experience the signs and symptoms of hypoglycemia, it is important **not to overtreat** hypoglycemia. After the first administration of an oral carbohydrate, it is important to wait between 15 and 30 minutes before the second blood glucose check is done.

2. After 15–30 minutes, blood sugar should be rechecked and the student observed for continuing symptoms. If blood sugar is still low, give a second amount of rapid-acting carbohydrate.

3. To prevent the blood sugar level from dropping again, once the student is feeling better, food or drinks with protein (e.g., cheese, meat, peanut butter) should be given. Protein typically is chosen because it metabolizes at a slower rate than carbohydrates.

If the student is known to have frequent, recurring hypoglycemia, treat as moderate hypoglycemia.

---

[a] Traditionally, hypoglycemia has been treated with a candy bar; however, this choice has been criticized by some because it may be misconstrued by the child as a "reward" for having a hypoglycemic episode (Betschart, 1993). In addition, the high fat content of a candy bar may retard the absorption of the needed sugars. The fact that a candy bar is also a rich source of cholesterol also mitigates against it being the first choice of treatment.

Finally, changes in dietary habits can contribute to the development of hypoglycemia. For example, if a student delays a meal or snack, skips a meal or snack, or does not consume the required number of calories per meal, the blood sugar level may drop to below normal. Young adolescents, girls in particular, need to be closely supervised to ensure that they maintain an adequate diet and are not jeopardizing their health by being influenced by their peers to "diet."

The symptoms of hypoglycemia can develop rapidly and progress at an alarming rate if the body is not given a source of sugar. To counteract the low blood sugar, the individual must be given a source of glucose. Typical treatment plans are shown in Table 19.3. School staff should contact the student's physician to ensure that any student-specific plans are known and implemented.

One of the major distinguishing signs of appropriate treatment is the rapidity with which the symptoms disappear. If, however, the individual does not respond and the symptoms become progressively alarming, immediate medical aid must be sought.

MODERATE HYPOGLYCEMIA

1. Give 1–3 teaspoons of honey or corn syrup or 2–3 teaspoons of sugar dissolved in water. Have the student hold food inside the cheek, if possible, to promote maximum absorption, then swallow.

2. After 10–15 minutes, give an additional snack of longer-acting carbohydrate, such as one of the following:

   8 oz. low-fat or skim milk and 3 graham cracker squares
   8 oz. low-fat skim milk and 6 saltines
   a slice of cheese and 5 or 6 crackers

3. After 10–15 minutes, check blood sugar and observe for continuing symptoms. If blood sugar is still low, readminister sugar and food.

4. When child is feeling better, give foods with protein, as described above.

If blood sugar does not rise after two or three sugar treatments, treat as severe hypoglycemia.

SEVERE HYPOGLYCEMIA

1. Squeeze a tube of glucagon gel between teeth and gums in buccal space or inject dose of glucagon intramuscularly or subcutaneously (dosage depends on age).

2. When the student regains consciousness and is able to take food by mouth, give honey or sugar as described above. Wait 10–15 minutes and give longer-acting carbohydrates (e.g., milk and cookies) as described above.

3. After 15–30 minutes, check blood sugar and observe for continuing symptoms. If blood sugar is still low, readminister glucagon, sugar, and food.

4. When child is feeling better, give foods with protein, as described above.

   Note: The rapid rise in blood glucose level after the administration of glucagon can result in the student becoming nauseated. It is not uncommon for a student to vomit the meal that has been given to sustain the blood glucose level. In such cases, the food should be given again.

If student does not improve within 10–20 minutes, call 911 or transport to the hospital so that the child can receive intravenous dextrose solution.

Hyperglycemia Defined operationally as too much sugar in the blood (250 mg/dL or more), hyperglycemia often results from having missed or forgotten a dose of insulin (in type I DM) or a dose of oral hypoglycemic agent (in type II DM). Some of the other causes, shown in Figure 19.3, include a diet that is too high in carbohydrates, particularly if the individual is also physically inactive. For example, if a man who typically does heavy labor at work takes a few days off and does not change his diet, he will be prone to hyperglycemia. In young children, a hyperglycemic reaction often is the result of overindulging in sweet foods (i.e., cakes, candies, chocolates), particularly during certain holidays (e.g., Hallowe'en) or special occasions (e.g., class or birthday parties). Severe hyperglycemia can also result from illness, infection, or emotional stress. Because hyperglycemia results from lack of insulin, the obvious treatment is the administration of insulin. However, in the early stages, the symptoms of hyperglycemia, shown in Table 19.4, can easily be mistaken for the symptoms of hypoglycemia. In such

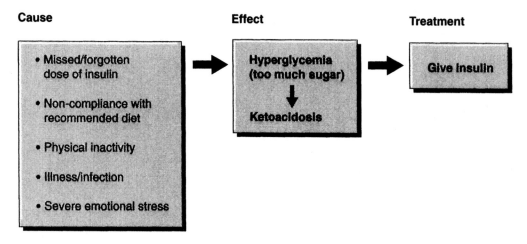

Figure 19.3
Hyperglycemia: Cause, Effect, and Treatment

TABLE 19.4
Signs and Symptoms of Hyperglycemia

EARLY-STAGE HYPERGLYCEMIA (BLOOD GLUCOSE LEVEL >250 mg/dL)

One or more of the following, which typically develop slowly over time:

Sugar in urine
Frequent urination (polyuria), often evident during the night (nocturia)
Increased thirst (polydipsia)
Increased appetite (polyphagia)
Dehydration (e.g., dry mouth, soft eyes)
Warm or hot, dry skin
Irritability

LATE-STAGE HYPERGLYCEMIA (BLOOD GLUCOSE LEVEL >300 mg/dL)

One or more of the following:

Ketones in urine
Acetone breath (sweet or fruity odor)
Weakness
Tiredness
Fatigue
Decreased appetite
Weight loss
Nausea
Vomiting
Abdominal pain or cramps (abdomen may be distended or tender)
Deep, rapid, labored breathing (i.e., Kussmaul respiration)
Headache
Mental changes
Drowsiness
Stupor
Decreased muscle tone and reflexes
Coma

situations, rather than being given insulin, the individual is given sugar. While this is the wrong treatment, the consequences are *not* immediately serious, because the progression from early to late stages of hyperglycemia is typically slow, occurring over hours or even days. If a person with hyperglycemia is given a single dose of rapid-acting carbohydrate in error, he or she will not show any signs of improvement after the normal 10 to 15 minutes. At that point, it should be recognized that the condition is not the result of missed food, but rather of missed insulin, and insulin should be given.

With the administration of insulin, the individual typically begins to show steady improvement; however, if he or she does not show improvement or begins to show signs of late-stage hyperglycemia, the person should be transported immediately to the hospital for proper treatment. Without treatment, hyperglycemia can progress to ketoacidosis and ketonuria.

🍎 Educational Implications and Teaching Tips

Yousef (1995) has suggested that teachers of students with diabetes have four major roles. They should be able to: (a) understand the condition and appraise the real limitations that diabetes imposes on the student, (b) encourage the student to develop self-sufficiency and autonomy, (c) maintain effective communication with the student's family, and (d) work as part of an interdisciplinary team. Lyen (1984) has also suggested that the teacher can fill an important role in providing career counseling to children and adolescents with diabetes. In addition, teachers should be able to recognize and respond to episodes of hypoglycemia or hyperglycemia, assist the student in making decisions about diet and exercise, understand when the student is ill, and know when to seek further medical aid if necessary (Jarrett, Hillam, Bartsch, & Lindsay, 1993). These skills are of particular importance when the student with diabetes is young and unable to care for himself or herself entirely. These skills, however, only result from education. Teachers are not the only ones who have training needs. In 1983, Winter made the following comment, which is probably quite appropriate today: "Diabetes is still a mysterious disease to most school personnel, including most school

nurses. As a result, there is a tremendous amount of anxiety and confusion surrounding the diabetic pupil" (p. 204).

One of the most important skills of school personnel is the ability to support and understand the student without being overly protective or reactive. Lyen (1984), in suggesting that a student with diabetes should not be unnecessarily restricted from participation in activities that occur during the school day, made the following comment that should be heeded by all school staff: "It is completely inappropriate for a child to be deprived of participating in a specific activity that is allowed by the physician and the family just because the teacher has particular fears about diabetes or does not have confidence in handling a situation such as hypoglycemia" (p. 50). To get basic information on the student's condition, the diabetes information form found in Appendix A may be of assistance.

The following suggestions are offered to assist staff who are in contact with students in the school system who have this condition.

1 *Even though the presence of diabetes affects the child or adolescent and the family in a profound way, there is little reason, on the basis of the condition alone, for* most *students with diabetes to require a special class placement, specific modifications to the curriculum, or a teacher trained to use special teaching methods* (Yousef, 1995). Typically, school performance of students with IDDM is comparable to that of those without a chronic health condition (Lloyd & Orchard, 1993). The students benefit from a teacher who treats them as they would treat other individuals in the class and who appreciates their specific health needs and the effect the condition has on their psychological well-being. However, even though learning ability is generally not affected by the condition, if the student with diabetes misses a great deal of school, his or her schoolwork may be affected.

2 *Even though most students with diabetes do not suffer major learning problems as a result of the condition, recently conducted research indicates that some will have neurocognitive sequelae that may, in fact, necessitate the provision of special education assistance.* Rovet, Ehrlich, Czuchta, and Akler (1993), in their review of the literature on the psychoeducational characteristics of children and adolescents with

IDDM, pointed out that while students who have diabetes, as a group, are not more intellectually impaired than those without diabetes, there are selective subgroups that are more likely to experience subtle, specific neuropsychological and educational dysfunction than others. In particular, the authors suggested that children who developed diabetes at a very early age (i.e., before the age of 5) are more likely to be intellectually compromised than those with later-onset diabetes and that children and adolescents with early-onset diabetes appear to be more vulnerable to difficulties in academic achievement than those with later-onset diabetes, particularly in the language arts area. In addition, the authors suggest that although both hypoglycemia and hyperglycemia have been implicated in the manifestation of specific neuropsychological deficits, the findings have not been consistent, suggesting the need for further research in this area.

3 *It is common for parents, school staff, and medical personnel to focus on the physical aspects of the disease; however, it is important that these persons recognize the delicate balance between the physical and the psychosocial factors that are components of diabetes.* Cerreto and Travis (1984) have suggested that "the child in good metabolic control who is also withdrawn, depressed, and socially isolated or aggressive, hostile, and resentful is *not* a healthy child" (p. 690). Conversely, they have pointed out that "*nor* is the child to be considered healthy who is functioning well at home, school, and with peers while demonstrating consistently high blood sugar concentrations" (italics added).

Acceptance by the peer group is as important for the student with IDDM as it is for a student who is in good health. Betschart (1993) has pointed out that the fear of showing symptoms of hyperglycemia and hypoglycemia in front of peers can have a tremendous effect on the student's already fragile self-esteem. Unfortunately, peers can also exert a great deal of pressure on the child or young adult with diabetes (Lyen, 1984). For example, it is not uncommon for a young child with diabetes to be coerced into giving away the candy that is carried in case of hypoglycemic reactions to a so-called "friend." Similarly, peers have been known to provoke adolescents with diabetes by encouraging them to eat foods that are restricted or by not allowing them to take a break and have something to

eat when it is time. Teachers should be alert to such situations and deal with them before they escalate.

4 *Teachers should be on the lookout for students who "use" their condition to avoid participating in certain activities.* Students have been known to pretend to be hypoglycemic, or even to omit eating so as to become hypoglycemic, to get out of having to participate in activities they dislike, such as having to write tests or exams. In discussing such behavior, Lyen (1984) made the following statement: "These actions amount to 'emotional blackmail' and are particularly difficult to manage, especially by teachers unfamiliar with the disease and who might be afraid of the life-threatening nature of these complications" (p. 51). In such situations, it is recommended that the teacher and the school nurse schedule a meeting with the student's parents or physician so that they can learn how to determine if the symptoms are genuine or if the student is malingering. In some cases, the parents may be unaware that a student is avoiding certain activities; however, in others, it may be that the parents are, in fact, the cause of the attendance problem (e.g., keeping the student home unnecessarily). If school absence is problematic, regardless of the cause, the student's teacher should contact the school nurse, who can discuss the situation with the parents.

5 *Although children and adolescents with diabetes are on a controlled diet, they do not need specially prepared foods; however, the "diet is the most difficult part of diabetes management" for many, especially adolescents* (Wolfsdorf et al., 1994). If a particular student is bringing food from home, the diet is obviously being monitored by the parents; however, if the student is eating at the school cafeteria, some supervision may be needed to ensure that the correct foods in the correct amounts are chosen. If possible, the school menu should be sent home with the student a few days in advance so that the student and parents can review the selections and determine which are the most suitable foods (Castiglia et al., 1992).

Regardless of the student's age, the diet should not be so restrictive that the individual feels "punished" for having the condition. If, for example, the class is going to have a birthday party and sweets are going to be served, by altering the daily insulin dose (with the physician's approval) or by altering the diet in a manner so that the sweets are a "trade-off" for an approved food, or both, the student, if given proper notice, in most cases, is able to share in the activity with his or her peers (although the student may be required to limit intake of sweets). Often parents of students with diabetes volunteer to prepare treats for the in-class party (e.g., birthday cake without icing, oatmeal cookies with raisins), so that they know exactly what their offspring is going to receive. In case of unforeseen circumstances, it is helpful if alternative foods, kept at school, perhaps in the school kitchen, are available for consumption.

Teachers can use the opportunity of having a student with IDDM in the classroom to provide the other students basic information regarding the importance of healthy eating. Chalmers (1994) has provided a two-part nutrition lesson, designed for use with students who have diabetes and are between the ages of 6 and 12, that can be easily adapted for use with students who have normal endocrine functioning. The lesson plan is developed so that teachers can provide a basic explanation of the various food groups and the important nutrients they provide and an explanation of good versus poor food choices in each food group. For further information, consult this resource.

6 *If the student has polydipsia, he or she should be allowed to drink as much as desired, because withholding fluids in the attempt to decrease the flow of urine has no effect (i.e., the individual will continue to show signs of polyuria).* Permitting the student to have a water bottle at his or her desk will prevent him or her from having to leave the class frequently to use the drinking fountain. Such an approach may also lessen the embarrassment the student has about having to drink so much water.

It is particularly important that the student with diabetes be given extra fluids during periods of increased physical activity. Similarly, if the individual is prone to increased perspiration, e.g., during field trips on hot, sunny days, extra water should be made available.

7 *If a student has polyuria, he or she should be given unlimited lavatory privileges.* Teachers should be alert, however, to the student who uses the facilities to an extreme. In most cases, more

than once every 1 to 2 hours would be considered to be excessive. In such cases, teachers should report their concerns to the school nurse or to the parents so that the issue of frequency can be raised with the student's physician.

8 *Children and young adults with IDDM do, even with good control, have episodes of hypoglycemia.* In fact, infrequent, mild, and brief symptomatic hypoglycemia is viewed by some as perhaps being "an inevitable consequence of good diabetic control" (Wolfsdorf et al., 1994, p. 540). While mild hypoglycemia can be a nuisance, it is important that moderate to severe episodes be prevented as much as possible because such episodes may be disabling to the student (e.g., affect school performance, make operating a car or dangerous machinery hazardous) and may result in permanent damage to the CNS.

Typically, each person with diabetes experiences different symptoms during episodes in which there is too little glucose in the blood. Teachers should be aware of the types of symptoms (Table 19.2) that are common to the specific student. In most individuals, there are two or three signals that occur more consistently than others (Balik, Haig, & Moynihan, 1986). In younger children, symptoms that are related to the CNS, specifically lack of sugar to the brain (e.g., drowsiness, confusion, lethargy, yawning, tremor, nervousness, headache) often occur in the initial stages (Guthrie & Guthrie, 1991). It is not uncommon for the child to be irritable, belligerent, or giddy. Sudden or marked mood swings are common, and often the child has periods of uncontrolled laughter or crying.

Hypoglycemia can occur at any time throughout the day, but typically it occurs just *before* meal or snack time. Teachers should be particularly vigilant at such times, especially if the student has a gym class right before lunch. It is advisable that teachers of young children with IDDM have a package of glucose tablets readily available, especially if their student is going to be away from school on a field trip. As the dosage can be easily calibrated, many feel that glucose tablets, each containing 5 grams of rapidly absorbable sugar, should be considered the treatment of choice, particularly since overtreatment is less likely than with other forms of food (Wolfsdorf et al., 1994). Other sources of rapidacting carbohydrates are listed in Table 19.3.

Older students should be allowed to keep a snack with them (e.g., at their desk), regardless of school policy regarding food consumption during class time. The consumption of "low noise" foods, such as dried fruits and cheese, should be encouraged because these draw less attention to the student (Balik et al., 1986).

Lyen (1984) has suggested that if a teacher observes that a student's work is uneven, it may be worthwhile for the teacher to examine whether or not the poor grades are occurring in subjects that are scheduled immediately before lunch time. If such is the case, it is possible that the student's low blood sugar may be resulting in loss of concentration or drowsiness that prevents maximum learning. The solution would be for the student to have a light snack just before the last class in order to stave off the hypoglycemia.

Since it is not uncommon for young children who are having a *mild* hypoglycemic reaction to not recognize it as such or for some children to confuse other feelings with those of hypoglycemia during periods in which they are, in fact, not hypoglycemic, it is best to confirm the condition by means of a blood glucose test. Once hypoglycemia is confirmed, the student should be given some food. However, if there is not a blood glucose monitoring device nearby, it is better to treat the condition by giving carbohydrates (i.e., **when in doubt, treat**) than to ignore it, because if left untreated, serious consequences (e.g., seizures, brain damage) can occur.

Students must *never* be left alone during a low-blood-sugar reaction (Clark et al., 1993). Even older students who recognize the symptoms may need assistance from a responsible adult. For example, the student who is having a *moderate* to *severe reaction* may be confused, have impaired judgment, and show signs of weakness or impaired coordination that may cause him or her to ignore the situation (Wolfsdorf et al., 1994). Although having a seizure as a result of low blood sugar is an exception rather than the rule, those that are in regular contact with the student should know how to respond in such situations.

Injectable glucagon should be available in the home and school for *severe* reactions, e.g., when the student is unresponsive or unable to swallow. Although the school nurse would be trained to give the medication, which is injected intramuscularly, the student's teacher or coach should be instructed in its use in emergency situations. A prepared kit, which includes glucagon (in powder form), a syringe prefilled with a diluent, and a source of concentrated carbohydrate (e.g., candy, glucose gel), is commercially available for emergency use. Such a kit should accompany the student when he or she is away from school (e.g., on a field trip), particularly if the student is going to be engaging in a great deal of physical activity (e.g., off-campus sporting event, such as a school basketball tournament). By injecting sugar, a trip to the emergency room can be avoided (Guthrie & Guthrie, 1991).

9 *While hypoglycemic episodes are more common than hyperglycemic, adults also need to be alert to signs that the student's blood sugar is increasing* (Table 19.4). Unlike hypoglycemia, hyperglycemia develops slowly over time, with the symptoms developing several hours after the blood sugar begins to rise. It is rare for persons with diabetes to progress to the point of a diabetic coma, unless there are other mitigating circumstances (e.g., illness).

Since a person with diabetes who is ill is more likely to develop hyperglycemia than one who is healthy, teachers should inform the student's parents if there are outbreaks of contagious illnesses (e.g., flu; colds; viral illnesses, such as mumps and rubella) in the class, so that they can try to lessen the chances that their son or daughter may develop the illness by keeping him or her home. Middle-ear infections are another common childhood complaint that can cause wide variations in blood glucose levels.

If the student is prone to having hyperglycemic episodes, a sufficient supply of insulin must be kept at school in a secure location. In addition, to lessen the effects of the dehydration that results from polyuria there should be a supply of sugar-free fluids. While water is readily available, the student may prefer a diet soda, such as ginger ale, that may assist in settling the nausea he or she may be feeling.

Just as it takes time for the symptoms of hyperglycemia to occur, it takes a comparable time for the symptoms to abate after treatment. If the student continues to feel really "off," he or she may need to be sent home or sent to the nurse's office to lie down. If it is determined that the student should be sent home because of illness, he or she must be accompanied by a responsible person who is able to monitor the student's status, and someone must be there to be stay with the student to ensure that the treatment is working and to provide any care that may be needed (Lyen, 1984).

If a student shows the following symptoms, the parents (or health care provider) should be contacted immediately: persistent vomiting (more than three or four episodes per hour); severe nausea and inability to take fluids; or persistent diarrhea (more than two or three stools per hour).

Adults in contact with a student who appears to have recurrent episodes of hyperglycemia leading to diabetic ketoacidosis (e.g., a student from an unstable home environment who may be under great emotional stress or who may not be taking insulin as prescribed) should not ignore the situation and should refer the student and his or her family to appropriate professionals for counseling or follow-up (Betschart, 1993).

10 *If the student needs insulin at lunch, a trained person (i.e., parent, school nurse) must be available to administer the drug unless the student is old enough to self-administer the medication.* The age at which a child is mature enough to be responsible for mixing and injecting insulin depends upon a number of factors (e.g., cognitive level, problem-solving ability). While supervision is still recommended for preadolescent and adolescent children, by age 12, most children are able to accurately mix the insulin dose and administer it safely. Savinetti-Rose (1994) has cautioned that "a careful assessment of the child's physical, emotional, and mental capabilities along with an understanding of family influence on the child's self-management is necessary before instructing diabetes management skills" (p. 14).

Regardless of whether the student administers the medication or it is given by a caregiver, privacy is important. The student should have access to a room that is suitable (i.e., has a sink for handwashing, is well lit for reading the blood glucose test results). Typically, the school nurse's office is used for this purpose; however, scheduling may be problematic. Other space, such as the principal's office, may be an alternative.

Blood-testing equipment (lancets, reagent strips), insulin, and hypodermic syringes and needles must be kept in a secure location, such as a locked filing cabinet. Vials of insulin that are opened do not need to be refrigerated; however, they should be protected from extreme temperatures, should not be exposed to direct sunlight, and should not be kept for more than a month. Unopened vials that are not going to be used for some time should be stored in a refrigerator. There must be a secure container in which the student can discard syringes and needles. School officials should check state and local laws regarding the disposal of biologic waste.

11 *The amount of insulin given depends on the individuals's blood glucose level.* Typically, fingersticks are taken 30 to 60 minutes before administration of the insulin, and the insulin is given 30 minutes before eating. For students who need insulin before lunch, these time requirements may mean that they need to be excused from the classroom twice between recess and lunch in order to carry out these tasks in private. While the following guidelines may be of assistance, staff should always check with the student's physician to ensure they are acting appropriately:

- If, for some reason, the student is late in getting his or her insulin (e.g., only 15 minutes before the beginning of the lunch period rather than 30), the student's physician will probably recommend that the student delay the start of his or her meal until 30 minutes have elapsed.
- If the student's blood glucose level is greater than 180 mg/dL, the student's physician will probably recommend that the meal time be delayed to allow extra time for the insulin to be absorbed into the circulatory system. The interval between injection and the meal, referred to as the "lag time," may, in most cases, be extended to 45 minutes without any complications.
- If the blood glucose level is less than 70 mg/dL, the student's physician will probably recommend that the student be given a rapidly absorbed carbohydrate (see treatment for mild hypoglycemia, Table 19.3), followed within 15 minutes by a regular meal.

12 *The site of the injection should be changed routinely to ensure adequate absorption of the insulin.* However, as Betschart (1993) has pointed out, "unfortunately, after living with diabetes for a while many children and teens consistently inject into a single spot owing to convenience, easy access, or comfort" (p. 37). Such a practice can lead to **lipohypertrophy,** a build-up of fat tissue at the site, which appears as a hard, egg-sized, thickened area. While these areas are not painful to inject into (in fact, they may be more comfortable than non-hypertrophied areas), the ability of the body to absorb the insulin is hampered in these areas, therefore making it difficult to achieve good glycemic control. Any school personnel noticing an abnormal swelling should bring this finding to the attention of the school nurse, who can discuss the situation with the student or parents. If a school nurse is supervising a young student who is self-administering insulin, the nurse should monitor the injection sites to make sure they are rotated.

13 *Although it is generally agreed that individuals with diabetes can participate in almost all forms of exercise, special considerations may be appropriate for those who have had IDDM for some time and are, therefore, more prone to showing the secondary complications that can arise as a result of the condition.* All individuals who have diabetes and who are about to undertake an unusual or particularly vigorous exercise program should have a thorough medical evaluation (Horton, 1988). If school staff are concerned about any restrictions, they should contact the student's physician to determine what activities are not permissible. Forms found in Appendix D may be of use.

- If a child or young adult is about to undertake a new activity or sport, it is recommended that blood glucose be checked before, during, and after the exercise program to plan food and insulin needs (Balik & Haig, 1986).
- If the student's diabetes is out of control (i.e., he or she has periods of pronounced hyperglycemia with ketonuria), regardless of the benefits of physical activity, the student should be cautioned from exercising until proper control has been restored (Wolfsdorf et al., 1994).
- Individuals with diabetes should ensure that they use proper footwear (i.e., well-fitting shoes, proper socks) and, if appropriate, other types of protective equipment (e.g., sports glasses while playing racket games, such as squash or tennis). They should make sure they inspect their feet after exercising for any signs of blistering and should avoid exercising in weather that is ex-

tremely hot or cold (American Diabetes Association, 1995).
- Persons with microvascular complications, such as damage to the retina of the eye (retinopathy) or to the kidneys (nephropathy), are typically not permitted to participate in high-intensity activities that cause the systolic blood pressure to increase to more than 180 to 200 mm Hg for substantial periods of time (Armstrong, 1991).
- Individuals with retinopathy should avoid any form of exercise that includes Valsalva-type maneuvers,[2] such as isometrics or heavy weight lifting, as retinal hemorrhage or detachment may result (Guthrie & Guthrie, 1991). Typically, it is also recommended that those with retinal problems do not participate in activities that include excessive jarring movements (e.g., football), as well as activities that include low head positions (e.g., gymnastics).
- Individuals who have damage to the peripheral nerves, particularly damage to the feet, should avoid traumatic, full weight–bearing exercise (Armstrong, 1991). Cycling, swimming, and rowing, for example, are far more suitable than activities that result in the pounding of the lower extremities, such as jogging or running sports (Horton, 1988).
- Individuals with diabetes should always make sure that when they exercise there is another person nearby (i.e., a buddy) so that if problems arise there is someone who can be of assistance. All individuals with diabetes should be encouraged to wear a medical alert bracelet or necklace.

14 *The student should develop strategies for avoiding exercise-related hypoglycemia or hyperglycemia.* While the American Academy of Pediatrics (1994) has advised that "all sports can be played [by persons with diabetes] with proper attention to diet, hydration, and insulin therapy," the Committee on Sports Medicine and Fitness has also cautioned that "particular attention is needed for activities that last 30 minutes or more" (p. 758).

All physical education teachers and coaches who work with students who have diabetes should be knowledgeable about the effects of diabetes on

---

[2] A Valsalva maneuver is one in which an individual holds his or her breath at the same time various muscles or muscle groups are being tightened.

physical activities. Articles by Armstrong (1991); Fahey et al. (1996); Horton (1988); and Petray, Freesemann, and Lavay (1997) should be consulted for further information.

On days that the student is planning to be particularly active (e.g., gym days, days with after-school sports), typically the physician recommends that extra food be given to ensure that the blood glucose level remains in a satisfactory range. A snack, such as a cracker with peanut butter, given before the activity begins provides the student with an ideal source of protein.

There are no hard-and-fast rules that govern how much food should be added to the diet in anticipation of exercise. Typically, by means of trial and error, the child or young adult and parents, with the advice of the physician, eventually determine how to make the necessary corrections.

Since an individual requires less insulin during increased physical activity, the physician may also recommend that the student administer a smaller dosage than usual before engaging in the exercise program. However, in children, particularly those who are very young, such measures may be difficult to implement because their level of activity typically varies not only from day to day, but also from hour to hour, and even more commonly from minute to minute. Rather than "load" the child with food or decrease the dosage of insulin (as you might in an older child or teenager, whom you know will have physical education class or organized competitive sport activity at a set time on a set day) in anticipation of being active, it generally is better to ensure that there are plenty of food snacks available, so that the student can have something immediately before or during the activity. Because many children and young adults are more active during the spring and summer months, it is not uncommon for physicians to recommend that less insulin be given during these times.

In addition, all students with diabetes should ensure that they have some type of snack with them when they exercise. To lower the risk of post-exercise, late-onset hypoglycemia, students should have a snack after completion, particularly if they exercise in the evening, after their last big meal of the day.

15 *Individuals with diabetes should be taught to keep careful records.* This was suggested by Callahan and Bradley (1988, p. 48), in describing the "juggling" of the "big three" (i.e., food,

medication, and exercise) that must occur while "keeping an eye on a fourth element, time." Ideally, in the log, information on the blood sugar levels (time and level), insulin (type, amount, time, and amount of last injection or bolus and amount), food intake (time and type of food consumed for meals or snacks), and physical activity (time, intensity, and duration) would be recorded daily (Petray et al., 1997). A sample log is found in Appendix G.

While Callahan and Bradley have suggested that this type of charting could be used for the individual's own personal information, undoubtedly, the information recorded by the student, teacher, and health aide would be invaluable for the parents, particularly in the early stages of treatment, when patterns or trends are being established.

Additionally, at the time that the student goes home each day, the teacher or health aide could use the journal to add any information that needed to be sent home with the student, such as a reminder to bring in new supplies or to warn the parents about serious illness in the class.

16 *Betschart (1993), in discussing the impact of diabetes on different developmental stages, made the following simple statement: "Adolescence is a difficult time to have diabetes"* (p. 42). Studies have consistently shown that metabolic control deteriorates during the teen years, regardless of whether or not the young adult adheres to the fairly strict regimen required to control the condition. The physiologic changes that are occurring at this time (e.g., rapid growth, hormonal changes) are compounded by the emotional stresses that puberty brings. The need to be part of the peer group is paramount, and if the treatment plan that students with diabetes must follow makes them stand out, it is not uncommon for teenagers to stop their self-care in an attempt to prove that they are, at least in their own eyes, "normal" (Wolfsdorf et al., 1994). While in the past they may have accepted the diagnosis of diabetes, with their increasing cognitive ability, the young adolescent, looking to his or her future, may now ask, "Why me?" The feelings of anger towards their parents (and any other authority figures, such as physicians and dietitians) may test the patience of those around them and lead to family conflicts that are not easily resolved.

A recent study of 144 adolescents treated at the Children's National Medical Center in Washington,

TABLE 19.5

Admitted Mismanagement of Diabetes Mellitus by Teenagers

Action	Percentage[a]
Ate inappropriate food	81%
Missed meals and snacks	56%
Took extra insulin to cover inappropriate food	34%
Made up blood test results because did not do test	29%
Made up blood test results because real ones were too high	29%
Missed insulin injection	25%
Missed injection and then took extra to cover	13%
Faked illness	13%
Changed test strip to give lower number	11%
Fixed blood glucose monitor to give lower number	10%

[a] The percentages add up to more than 100 because respondents were permitted to choose more than one behavior.
Source: Adapted from Weissberg-Benchell, J., Glasgow, A. M., Tynan, W. D., Wirtz, P., Turek J., & Ward, J. (1995). Adolescent diabetes management and mismanagement. *Diabetes Care, 18,* 77–82. Copyright 1995 by the American Diabetes Association. Reprinted by permission.

D.C. (Weissberg-Benchell et al., 1995) attempted to document the existence and prevalence of "mismanagement" behaviors of adolescents, particularly missing injections and making up results of missed blood tests. When adolescents were asked how many times they had, within the 10 days before the study, engaged in certain behaviors, the findings seemed to indicate that adolescents admitted to engaging in a wide variety of mismanagement behaviors, primarily around food, at least once in the specified time frame. Their admissions are shown in Table 19.5. In terms of missing shots or failing to perform the necessary blood tests, the most commonly reported reason was simply "forgetting." The reasons offered by the teenagers are shown in Table 19.6.

For the adolescent, the temptation to experiment with alcohol or drugs (e.g., cocaine, amphetamines) may be strong; however, such substances can result in hypoglycemia.

For the adolescent who wants to lose weight to have the "ideal" skinny body portrayed by the media, the rigidity of the imposed diet is difficult to accept, particularly if the young person's parents and physician overly stress the maintenance of "good control." It has been reported that many girls secretly begin to reduce their insulin, thereby "purging" calories in order to lose weight. This self-destructive cycle has been compared to bulimia nervosa; however, in the young adolescent with diabetes, this type of diabetes-specific "eating disorder" often results in repeated trips to the hospital to treat diabetic ketoacidosis (Wolfsdorf et al., 1994).

By gradually decreasing the caloric intake and, at the same time, increasing the amount of physical activity, the young girl, if she monitors her blood glucose level closely (and adjusts her insulin dosage accordingly), can safely lose weight; however, it is important that she work in close collaboration with her physician or dietitian. It has also been reported that some individuals who have an eating disorder have been known to deliberately overdose on their insulin to induce hypoglycemia before an eating binge (Macheca, 1993). Obviously, such a practice is not healthy, and those in contact with students with diabetes should be alert to students who abuse their bodies in this manner. For a complete discussion of eating disorders and IDDM, see the article by Butler and Wing (1994).

17 *Support groups may provide young adolescents with an opportunity to vent their feelings toward the disease.* Not only can the teenagers discuss their problems, but with the help of others who are also experiencing similar life events, the adolescent may be able to develop acceptable

TABLE 19.6
Reasons Offered for Missing Shots and Blood Tests

Shots	Percentage[a]
I just forgot	40%
I was away from home and forgot to bring it with me	24%
I didn't think the evening shot was necessary	12%
I didn't plan on eating, so I missed the shot	10%
I wanted to prevent a low reaction	8%
I wanted to see what would happen	6%
I wanted to lose weight	5%
I didn't want to give a shot in front of friends	5%
I wanted to get sick to get out of something	1%
I never miss my shots	41%
Blood Tests	
I just forgot	35%
Didn't test, wanted complete record, so made up	28%
I wanted to show good results to doctor	24%
I wanted to show good results to family	22%
I'm fussed at when high, so made up lower number	22%
I was away from home and forgot to bring it with me	20%
It hurts to test	6%
I didn't want to test in front of friends	3%
I never made up blood tests	22%

[a] The percentages add up to more than 100 because respondents were permitted to choose more than one reason.
Source: Weissberg-Benchell, J., Glasgow, A. M., Tynan, W. D., Wirtz, P., Turek J., & Ward, J. (1995). Adolescent diabetes management and mismanagement. *Diabetes Care, 18,* 77–82. Copyright 1995 by the American Diabetes Association. Reprinted by permission.

solutions. For some children and young adults with diabetes, the most rewarding experience is the opportunity to attend a summer camp specifically designed for persons with diabetes. A list of accredited camps is available free of charge from the American Diabetes Association.

18 *Although many of the long-term effects of diabetes may not be evident until 10 to 20 years after diagnosis, i.e., long after the student has left the school system, teachers should be alert to any abnormalities, such as visual problems, and report concerns to either the school nurse, who can contact the parents, or to the parents directly.* A checklist of indicators of vision problems is contained in Appendix I. In some cases, the child or young adult with diabetes (and possibly the parents) may not be aware

of the long-term consequences of diabetes (e.g., loss of vision, circulatory problems).

19 *Because of the potential complications of diabetes, persons with diabetes are often discouraged from pursuing certain occupations* (Lyen, 1984). While persons who have good metabolic control can perform commensurate with their peers, the reality is that they have been in the past and will continue in the future to be barred from piloting an aircraft, driving public service vehicles, working on high-rise construction sites, or being employed in the fire department, police force, merchant navy, or armed forces. Adolescents and young adults need career counseling from persons knowledgeable about the consequences of this disease. School staff should turn to counselors who are specifically trained.

🐦 Summary

Diabetes is an endocrine condition that results, in most cases, from lack of the hormone insulin. There are several forms of diabetes; the most common in the pediatric population is type I, insulin-dependent diabetes mellitus, in which control of the level of glucose in the blood is achieved by the administration of exogenous insulin. Diabetes can occur in persons of all ages. However, the presence of diabetes in the childhood years affects the life of the developing child and his or her family in a profound manner, every moment of the day and night. At the time of diagnosis, children and their parents are typically told that *if* the children (and until maturity, the parents) are responsible for the daily performance of the necessary health care behaviors, they will be able to lead a "reasonably 'normal' life" and can participate in most of the activities engaged in by peers. However, as Cerreto and Travis (1984) have so aptly stated, "this educational premise flies directly in the face of the fact that there is nothing 'reasonably normal' about multiple shots a day, constant monitoring of body systems, and a controlled diet" (p. 689). Furthermore, according to these authors, "the diabetic regime exposes the child during the most intimate of functions (for example, urine testing) as well as the most public and social (for example, administering injections, mealtimes)" (p. 689).

Often there is a tendency to see the person with diabetes, whether it be a patient or a student, in isolation and not as a person who has competing priorities and unique fears. Hoover (1991), a mother of a child with diabetes, in writing for physicians and nursing staff, makes the following points, which hopefully will make a teacher stop and take notice:

> Persons with diabetes do not only think about the medical aspects of their disease. They are concerned about the concept of themselves as whole and healthy individuals. They want to retain their independence. They wonder if they will be able to keep their jobs and support their families. They worry about the long-term financial costs of this disease and whether they can obtain adequate medical and life insurance. They dread social discrimination. They hope they can marry despite the disease and that love will continue even if they become chronically disabled. They wonder if they will be able to have children and if their children will inherit the disease. They fear becoming dependent on those they love or even on public assistance. . . . We hear a lot about the noncompliant patient, the patient who, for some unfathomable reason, refuses to follow instructions carefully and thus make good therapy impossible. We do not, however, hear much about the priorities of patients. *Diabetes is seldom the only thing that is going on in their lives.* Few people lead lives that are compatible with optimal diabetes management. They are bound to be caught in a traffic jam or be closing an important business deal just when they ought to be eating their lunches. They find that testing is awkward almost anywhere but at home, and troublesome and boring even there. They may not have enough money to see their physicians. *Life can be complicated by many things.* One young mother described her dilemma of experiencing an insulin reaction just as her toddler had escaped the yard and was running toward the street. What was her priority? (p. 319, 321, italics added)

Rather than being pessimistic, those with diabetes and their caregivers should recognize that the plight of the person with diabetes has changed dramatically since the discovery of insulin in 1921 by Banting and Best. Although a cure has not been achieved, research continues. Not only can teachers play an important role in recognizing that a student with diabetes may be having a hyperglycemic reaction, a vigilant teacher may be the first to recognize the signs of increased blood glucose in children or young adults who have diabetes that has not yet been diagnosed.

References

American Academy of Pediatrics, Committee on Sports Medicine and Fitness (1994). Medical conditions affecting sports participation. *Pediatrics, 94,* 757–760.

American Diabetes Association (1993). *Diabetes: 1993 vital statistics.* Alexandria, VA: Author.

American Diabetes Association (1995). Diabetes mellitus and exercise. *Diabetes Care, 18* (Suppl #1), 28.

Armstrong, J. J. (1991). A brief overview of diabetes mellitus and exercise. *The Diabetes Educator, 17*(3), 175–178.

Balik, B., & Haig, B. (1986). The student with diabetes. In G. Larson (Ed.), *Managing the school age child with a chronic health condition* (pp. 95–111). Wayzata, MN: DCI Publishing.

Balik, B., Haig, B., & Moynihan, P. M. (1986). Diabetes and the school-aged child. *Maternal and Child Nursing, 11,* 324–330.

Betschart, J. (1993). Children and adolescents with diabetes. *Nursing Clinics of North America, 28,* 35–44.

Butler, B. A., & Wing, R. R. (1994). Eating disorders and type 1 (insulin-dependent) diabetes. *Diabetes Annual, 8,* 437–458.

Callahan, M., & Bradley, D. J. (1988). Why you should teach your diabetic patients to chart. *Nursing 88, 18*(3), 48–49.

Castiglia, P. T., Kramer, D., Fong, C., & Lipman, T. H. (1992). Alterations in endocrine function. In P. T. Castiglia & R. E. Harbin, *Child health care: Process and practice* (pp. 871–913). Philadelphia: J. B. Lippincott.

Cerreto, M. C., & Travis, L. B. (1984). Implications of psychological and family factors in the treatment of diabetes. *Pediatric Clinics of North America, 31,* 689–711.

Chalmers, K. A. (1994). Tool chest: Nutrition basics for the pediatric patient with diabetes mellitus. *The Diabetes Educator, 20,* 429–430.

Christman, C., & Bennett, J. (1987). Diabetes: New names, new test, new diet. *Nursing 87, 17*(1), 34–41.

Clark, K. M., Freezle, L. St. D., Gray, D. L., & Parker, S. H. (1993). Nursing planning, intervention, and evaluation for altered endocrine function. In D. B. Jackson & R. B. Saunders (Eds.), *Child health nursing* (pp. 1459–1535). Philadelphia: J. B. Lippincott.

Cryer, P. E., & Gerich, J. E. (1985). Glucose counterregulation, hypoglycemia, and intensive insulin therapy in diabetes mellitus. *New England Journal of Medicine, 313,* 232–241.

Drash, A. L., & Arslanian, S. A. (1990). Can insulin-dependent diabetes mellitus be cured or prevented? *Pediatric Clinics of North America, 37,* 1467–1487.

Fahey, P. J., Stallkamp, E. T., & Kwatra, S. (1996). The athlete with type I diabetes: Managing insulin, diet and exercise. *American Family Physician, 53,* 1611–1617.

Guthrie, D. W., & Guthrie, R. A. (1991). *Nursing management of diabetes mellitus.* New York: Springer.

Hoover, J. (1991). Patient's perspective. In D. W. Guthrie & R. A. Guthrie (Eds.), *Nursing management of diabetes mellitus* (pp. 319–328). New York: Springer.

Horton, E. S. (1988). Role and management of exercise in diabetes mellitus. *Diabetes Care, 11,* 201–211.

Jarrett, L., Hillam, K., Bartsch, C., & Lindsay, R. (1993). The effectiveness of parents teaching elementary school teachers about diabetes mellitus. *The Diabetes Educator, 19,* 193–197.

Lebovitz, H. E. (1984). Etiology and pathogenesis of diabetes mellitus. *Pediatrics Clinics of North America, 31,* 521–530.

Lloyd, C., & Orchard, T. (1993). Insulin-dependent diabetes mellitus in young people: The epidemiology of physical and psychosocial complications. *Diabetes Annual, 7,* 211–244.

Lyen, K. R. (1984). Juvenile diabetes. In J. Fithian (Ed.), *Understanding the child with a chronic illness in the classroom* (pp. 40–56). Phoenix: Oryx Press.

Macheca, M. K. K. (1993). Diabetic hypoglycemia: How to keep the threat at bay. *American Journal of Nursing, 93*(4), 26–30.

Menon, R. K., & Sperling, M. A. (1988). Childhood diabetes. *Medical Clinics of North America, 72,* 1565–1576.

Petray, C., Freesemann, K., & Lavay, B. (1997). Understanding students with diabetes: Implications for the physical education professional. *JOPERD, 68*(1), 57–64.

Rovet, J. F., Ehrlich, R. M., Czuchta, D., & Akler, M. (1993). Psychoeducational characteristics of children and adolescents with insulin-dependent diabetes mellitus. *Journal of Learning Disabilities, 26,* 7–22.

Savinetti-Rose, B. (1994). Developmental issues in managing children with diabetes. *Pediatric Nursing, 20,* 11–15.

Spelsberg, A., & Manson, J. E. (1995). Physical activity in the treatment and prevention of diabetes. *Comprehensive Therapy, 21,* 559–564.

Springhouse Corporation (1992). *Teaching patients with chronic conditions.* Springhouse, PA: Author.

Strowig, S. (1995). Insulin therapy. *RN, 58* (6).

Weir, G. C. (1995). What lies ahead in diabetes care. *Patient Care, 29*(3), 75–93.

Weissberg-Benchell, J., Glasgow, A. M., Tynan, W. D., Wirtz, P., Turek, J., & Ward, J. (1995). Adolescent diabetes management and mismanagement. *Diabetes Care, 18,* 77–82.

Whaley, L. F., & Wong, D. L. (1995). *Nursing care of infants and children* (5th ed). St. Louis: Mosby.

Winter, R. J. (1983). Childhood diabetes mellitus. In J. Umbreit (Ed.), *Physical disabilities and health impairments: An introduction* (pp. 195–205). New York: Merrill.

Wolfsdorf, J. I., Anderson, B. J., & Pasquarello, C. (1994). Treatment of the child with diabetes. In C. R. Kahn & G. C. Weir (Eds.), *Joslin's diabetes mellitus* (13th ed., pp. 530–551). Philadelphia: Lea & Febiger.

Yousef, J. M. S. (1995). Insulin-dependent diabetes mellitus: Educational implications. *Physical Disabilities: Education and Related Services, 13*(2), 43–53.

CHAPTER 20

Altered Exocrine Function

KEY WORDS

Bronchiectasis

Chest physiotherapy

Cor pulmonale

Cystic fibrosis

Enzyme replacement therapy

Inborn errors of metabolism

Large and small molecule
disease

Salt depletion

Sweat test

Each type of exocrine gland is part of a larger system (e.g., the sweat glands are part of the integumentary system; the digestive glands are part of the digestive system; the lymph glands are part of the lymphatic system). In most situations, it is not the exocrine gland alone per se that is damaged or diseased; rather, it is either the total system (e.g., digestive system) or the specific organ in which the gland is located (e.g., liver) that is involved. However, there is one disease that affects all the glands that make up the exocrine system, regardless of their location. This condition, sometimes referred to as **mucoviscidosis** (**muco-**, referring to the mucus; **-viscidosis,** referring to the thick, viscid, or sticky nature of the secretions), is more commonly known as **cystic fibrosis.** This disorder is characterized not only by abnormally viscous secretions, but also by secretions that have an abnormal electrolyte composition.

While cystic fibrosis is a disease specific to the exocrine glands, a number of conditions exist in which a particular exocrine gland fails to produce a specific enzyme, and as a result of the lack, the person has difficulty digesting a particular type of food. These disorders are known collectively as **inborn errors in metabolism.** Crocker (1983) explained the choice of terminology as follows: "The term inborn refers to the inscrutable, constitutional nature of the variation, determined by the child's genetic makeup [whereas] the concept of an error of metabolism speaks to the fact that normal biochemical processes are altered, with varying degrees of significance" (p. 233). Since these conditions are fairly rare, they are only described briefly. The main topic of this chapter is cystic fibrosis.

Cystic Fibrosis

Cystic fibrosis (CF) is a multisystem multisymptom genetic disorder of the exocrine glands that results in the production of thick, gummy secretions. If the glandular secretions are allowed to accumulate in the duct of the glands, they eventually plug the passageway and damage the gland and tissues surrounding the gland. One of the organs most affected by CF is the pancreas; in fact, the term "cystic" was first coined to refer to the pancreas ducts' cyst-like appearance, which occurs as a result of dilation, and the term "fibrosis" to refer to the replacement of normal tissue in the pancreas by tissue that is fibrous. However, the pancreas is only one organ involved in

CF, and in some cases, pancreatic involvement is secondary to respiratory difficulties.

Etiology

Most cases of CF are caused by the mutation of a specific gene, the **cystic fibrosis transmembrane conductance regulator** (CFTR), located on the middle of the long arm of chromosome 7, specifically at position 7q31 (Wilmott & Fiedler, 1994). The mutation is termed **ΔF508;** Δ (delta) refers to a deletion of a substance, in this case, the amino acid phenylalanine, which is abbreviated as the single letter F, at position 508 on chromosome 7 (Beaudet, 1992). It has been estimated that the ΔF508 mutation is the cause of CF in 70% of persons with CF in North America (Beaudet, 1992; Tizzano & Buchwald, 1993). Individuals with CF who do not have this particular mutation must have one of the less commonly occurring mutations. It has been estimated that there may be as many as 300 possible alterations at position 7q31, of which at least 230 are associated with the presence of the disease (Tizzano & Buchwald, 1993).

Throughout the world, one person in every 20 to 25 is a carrier of the CF gene, making it the most common lethal gene in humans (Fulginiti & Lewy, 1993). Since it is a recessive trait, autosomal in nature (i.e., not sex-linked), the offspring must receive the defective gene from *both* parents to manifest the condition. If the parents are both asymptomatic carriers (i.e., have the defective gene but do not have the condition), a situation believed to occur as frequently as 1 in every 400 couples, there is a 1 in 4 chance that each offspring could have the condition; however, the incidence of the condition increases if one parent has the condition and the other parent is a carrier (i.e., 50% may be affected) or both of the parents have the condition (i.e., 100% will have the condition).

Even though it is possible that two persons with CF could have a child, such an occurrence is fairly unlikely, because in approximately 98% of all cases, men with CF are sterile. In addition, women with CF are less fertile than those without the condition. Fertility in women with CF is reduced to as low as 20% of that of healthy women (Cropp & Shames, 1994).

Incidence and Prevalence

It has been estimated that 30,000 persons in the United States and 2,800 in Canada have cystic fibrosis (Canadian Cystic Fibrosis Foundation, 1993;

TABLE 20.1

Cystic Fibrosis: Typical Progression of Symptoms in Various Age Groups

Developmental Stage	Common Presenting Symptoms
NEONATAL PERIOD	10%–15% of infants are born with meconium ileus (impaction of fecal material) and as a result may have difficulty in passing stools, show signs of abdominal distention, and have bouts of vomiting
	May experience jaundice
	Skin has a "salty" taste
EARLY INFANCY	Respiratory problems, including coughing, are common; typically the cough is a dry, hacking, nonproductive cough that sounds like whooping cough
	May be failure to gain weight and child may appear to be emaciated
	Fingers wrinkle in water more rapidly than normal
	Stools are soft, bulky, and greasy; the child may experience 3 or more bowel movements per day; abdominal cramps and excessive foul-smelling flatus are common
	May experience vomiting
LATE INFANCY	Digestive problems, including lack of substantial weight gain, abdominal distention, vomiting, stool abnormalities, protein deficiency, and salt loss typically continue, despite the child's voracious appetite
	Linear growth retardation may be evident
	Bronchitic involvement of respiratory tract may occur (e.g., may develop bronchiectasis); frequent respiratory infections are common
	Child may experience bouts of wheezing, similar to that seen in children with asthma; child may have a persistent runny nose
TODDLERHOOD	Similar to symptoms evident in late infancy
	May develop a "barrel" chest
CHILDHOOD	Respiratory problems continue to increase (i.e., airways become obstructed, there is increased

FitzSimmons, 1993). In addition, there are another 7 million Americans and 1 million Canadians who are asymptomatic carriers of the CF gene. Each year, in the United States, approximately 1,200 infants are born with the condition.

Cystic fibrosis is found predominantly in Caucasians. For various ethnic groups, the incidence has been estimated to be as follows: 1 in 3,500 live Caucasian births; 1 in 10,000 live Native American, Aleut, or Eskimo births; 1 in 11,500 live Hispanic births; 1 in 14,000 live African-American births; and 1 in 25,500 live Asian births (FitzSimmons, 1993).

For unknown reasons, the incidence of CF is quite rare in Asians living in Hawaii. For this particular group, there is 1 affected individual per 90,000 live births (Beaudet, 1992). The incidence of CF in male and female babies is equal, regardless of race.

Characteristics

While it is known that cystic fibrosis results from a genetic mutation of the CFTR, the exact cause of the condition remains unknown. However, it is believed that the problem originates at the cellular

	difficulty in the expectoration of mucus from the lungs, poor breathing pattern and cyanosis develop)
	Frequent chest or sinus infections are typical; may develop chronic secretory otitis media (middle-ear infection); may develop nasal polyps
	Finger or toe clubbing may occur
	Liver enlargement or insulin-dependent diabetes mellitus may develop
	Heat exhaustion can result from excessive salt loss
	Signs of cardiac failure (e.g., edema) may be evident; may develop cor pulmonale
ADOLESCENCE/ ADULTHOOD	Liver, lung, and heart dysfunction, intestinal blockage, duodenal ulcers, and diabetes may all develop or become more evident
	There may be a delay in the onset of puberty (i.e., secondary sexual characteristics may be slow in appearing)
	98% of males become sterile as a result of blockage of the vas deferens, a duct through which sperm travel during intercourse, or from aspermia (lack of formation of sperm)
	Most females remain fertile; however, conception may be difficult because vaginal and cervical mucus may be thick or sticky. In addition, women with CF may ovulate less frequently than normal and may experience irregular menstrual cycles, particularly if they have lung difficulties
ALL AGES (DATA FROM FITZSIMMONS, 1993)	75.7% of persons with CF show no medical complications; 8.3% may experience visible nasal polyps; 4.1%, Type I diabetes; 2.3%, intestinal obstruction; 1.4%, cirrhosis; 1.0%, massive hemoptysis; 0.7%, pneumothorax; 0.6%, gallbladder disease; and 0.4%, pancreatitis (inflammation of the pancreas)

level, resulting in abnormalities in the transmission of chloride and water in and out of the cell, which in turn result in an abnormal accumulation of thick, gummy mucus in the exocrine glands of the body. Even though individuals with CF are born with the condition, an accurate diagnosis may not be made until specific symptoms begin. FitzSimmons (1993) reported that in 70% of the cases, the typical age at diagnosis was in the first 12 months of life; 80% of cases were detected by age 4; and 90% by age 12.

The types of symptoms that occur and the severity of the condition can vary greatly from individual to individual. Some manifestations of cystic fibrosis, by developmental stage, are shown in Table 20.1; however, the clinical progression of this condition is highly variable.

Respiratory Involvement   One of the most serious complications of CF occurs when the "normally" produced mucus in the bronchioles of the lungs becomes "abnormal." In the human body, pulmonary mucus is produced for the purpose of removing bacteria and other foreign particles from the lungs, and when it becomes thick and tenacious, it becomes a breeding ground for infection, rather than preventing it (Chasnoff, Ellis, Fainman, & Mullen, 1993). *Pseudomonas aeruginosa* is the most common organism causing respiratory infection. Sixty percent of those with CF have a positive result on culture for this gram-negative bacillus; however, the rates vary by age. Approximately 20% of those with CF under the age of 1 year have positive test results compared to 80% in the population over the age of 26 (FitzSimmons, 1993). In addition to the abnormal mucus, there is abnormal ciliary clearance of the bronchioles, which can lead to obstruction of the small airways and to the development of **bronchiectasis,** a progressive condition in which the bronchi become stretched or dilated. The pathophysiology of cystic fibrosis lung disease is shown in Figure 20.1.

While all individuals with CF eventually show signs of respiratory problems, there is variation from individual to individual in terms of onset, duration, and severity of the condition (Heller, Alberto, Forney, & Schwartzman, 1996). FitzSimmons (1993)

reported that 66.7% of those with CF have mild pulmonary disease, 26.6% have moderate disease, and 6.7% have severe disease.

The respiratory condition is progressive, and as a result of breathing difficulties, the individual typically shows a decrease in exercise tolerance and an increased feeling of fatigue, which may be compounded by weight loss or poor appetite. In addition, a youngster with CF may develop infections of the nasal sinuses or nasal polyps that may compromise nasal breathing and may lead to headaches, facial pain, and fever (Wilmott, Burroughs, & Beele, 1984). Many individuals with CF experience dry mouth, resulting from blocked salivary glands, which can increase their susceptibility to oral infections (Whaley & Wong, 1995).

In the early stages of the disease, the impaired pulmonary function is similar in many ways to that found in children and adolescents with asthma; in fact, some are initially thought to have asthma before the correct diagnosis is made (Harvey, 1982). The major difference is that asthma is, in most cases,

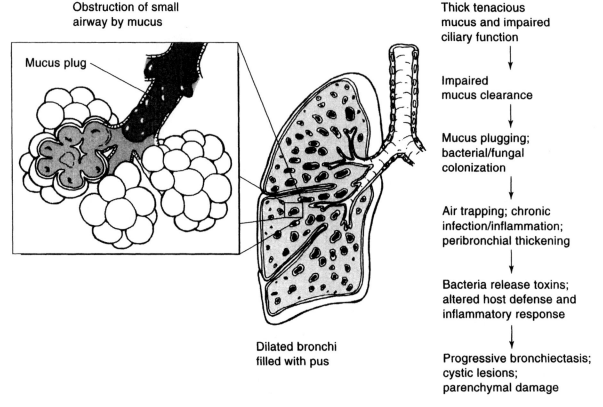

Figure 20.1
Pathophysiology of Cystic Fibrosis Lung Disease
Source: Adapted from Jackson & Vessey, 1996, p. 329.

a "reversible" condition, whereas, in the individual with CF, as the disease progresses, more serious respiratory sequelae are typically seen. Some individuals with CF, for example, cough up blood, a condition referred to as **hemoptysis;** others may experience a partial or total collapsed lung, a condition known as **atelectasis,** which results from an air leak into the pleural space from a ruptured area of lung tissue, a condition known as **pneumothorax.** For those with a rupture, the prognosis is more guarded because the recurrence rate for pneumothorax is high. It has been reported that 50% to 80% of those who suffer a rupture die within 3 years of the first episode (Cropp & Shames, 1994).

Cardiac Involvement The respiratory difficulties found in persons with CF are often compounded by the development of a heart condition known as **cor pulmonale,** an enlargement of the right ventricle that can lead to congestive heart failure. The steps by which this condition develops are as follows: (1) as the respiratory difficulties of an individual with CF increase over time, less oxygen enters the blood as a result of damage to the lungs; (2) to increase the oxygenation, the heart compensates by beating harder in an attempt to have more blood circulate through the lungs; (3) with the extra workload, the right side of the heart becomes thicker and larger. Wilmott and Fiedler (1994) have reported data that indicate as many as 95% of patients with CF eventually die from severe pulmonary hypertension complicated by cor pulmonale.

Pancreatic and Gastrointestinal Involvement Eighty percent to 85% of all persons with CF have digestive problems that result from the inability of the pancreatic enzymes to flow from the pancreatic glands into the intestines so that they can help metabolize food (Cunningham & Taussig, 1988). Those with pancreatic involvement are also at risk for developing IDDM. In such cases, the endocrine glands of the pancreas are damaged as a result of pressure exerted by the plugged exocrine glands. The incidence of diabetes is ten times more common in persons with CF than in the general population at the same age (Colten, 1996).

In addition to pancreatic involvement, the liver can also be affected. In such cases, the ducts that carry bile from the liver to the gallbladder for storage become obstructed, resulting in damage to the surrounding hepatic cells and a degenerative disease known as **cirrhosis.** Liver damage is more common

in older children and young adults than in young children. Some also experience gallbladder problems caused by blockage of the biliary system.

Because food is poorly digested and there is inadequate absorption of fats and proteins in the small intestine, youngsters with CF may show signs of inadequate growth (i.e., short stature) and malnutrition, even though they may have a voracious appetite and consume an adequate number of calories. To maintain an adequate nutritional status, the caloric needs of those with CF are 30% to 50% greater than those of the normal population (Colten, 1996).

As a result of faulty digestion, persons with CF may pass foul-smelling stools that have greater than normal amounts of fat (**steatorrhea**); they also may expel malodorous gas (**flatus**) that can be quite offensive to others. The inadequately digested food causes increased bulk, so the washroom may be needed more frequently than normal, in some cases as often as three to four times per day. Bowel movements may be accompanied by abdominal pain or discomfort arising from the stretching of the bowel. Approximately 25% of individuals with CF have **rectal prolapse,** a condition in which the mucus membrane of the lower part of the rectum protrudes out the anal opening (McMullen, 1996).

In addition to the digestive problems just described, some youngsters have difficulties in elimination. A small number (10% to 15%) of children with CF are born with a condition known as **meconium ileus.** Meconium is the medical term used to describe the thick, greenish-black stools of the newborn. In meconium ileus there is an obstruction caused by the impaction of the fecal material, which is abnormally thick, dry, and tenacious. If untreated, meconium ileus can lead to perforation of the intestinal tract. Meconium ileus may be the first indication that the newborn has CF.

While the fecal material, as mentioned above, may be bulky, children and young adults with CF may also produce a thick, sticky mucus that prevents food and wastes from passing through the intestinal passages in a normal manner. In such cases, constipation and abdominal distension are common. In extreme cases, a partial or complete blockage of the bowels may occur if the intestinal glands, located in the walls of the large and small intestine, produce too much of the defective secretion. Some individuals with CF suffer from chronic diarrhea rather than constipation.

Sweat Gland Involvement As stated previously, the mutant gene involved in CF results in altered transport of certain electrolytes, particularly sodium (Na^+) and chloride (Cl^-), through the cells. Typically, the sweat glands produce perspiration that has a higher salt (Na^+Cl^-) concentration than normal. In fact, it is the presence of a "salty" taste when a young infant is kissed that may prompt the parents to take their child to the doctor.

It has been estimated that 98% to 99% of all individuals with CF have elevated sodium and chloride levels (Hunsberger & Feenan, 1994). While the sweat of a person with CF is two to five times more salty than normal, the amount of sweat produced and the consistency of the fluid are normal.

Diagnosis and Treatment

To confirm the diagnosis of CF, the individual undergoes a procedure known as a **sweat test,** in which a gauze pad or piece of filter paper placed on the forearm or thigh collects sweat over 30 to 60 minutes and is sent to the laboratory for analysis. To ensure a sufficient amount of sweat is collected, the glands are stimulated chemically (i.e., by means of certain drugs) or by electric current (i.e., by means of electrodes placed directly on the skin). Chloride levels above 60 mEq/L (milliequivalent per liter, or one thousandth of a gram per liter of plasma) and sodium levels above 90 mEq/L are typically found in persons with CF. The diagnosis of CF is made when there is a positive sweat test in addition to either (a) clinical symptoms consistent with CF or (b) a family history of CF (McMullen, 1996). In addition to the sweat test, a number of other tests, such as stool analyses and chest x-rays, are often used to assist in the diagnosis.

In the past decade, there have been a number of major advances in the diagnosis and treatment of CF. Now that the CF gene has been isolated, carrier screening and prenatal diagnosis are both available. Not all CF mutations can be isolated, but specialized genetic laboratories in the United States are now able to screen for up to 32 of the most common CF mutations, which account for about 85% of the mutant CF genes found in ethnically diverse North Americans (McMullen, 1996).

Until a cure for CF is discovered, treatment is aimed at alleviating the symptoms of the condition.

Typically, treatment focuses on improving pulmonary function and on maintaining adequate nutritional status. Treatment has to be individualized, as no two individuals with CF show the same sequelae. Treatment typically involves one or more of the following: inhalation and chest therapy; enzyme replacement and nutritional therapy; and surgical therapy.

Inhalation and Chest Therapy The treatment of the respiratory conditions associated with CF generally consists of a combination of inhalation therapy and chest physiotherapy (Coe, 1989; Wilmott et al., 1984). **Inhalation therapy** involves the administration of medications, such as bronchodilators, by means of a fine mist for the purpose of (a) widening the bronchioles, (b) reducing the swelling of the airways, (c) thinning the mucus, and (d) loosening the secretion. **Chest physiotherapy** typically consists of (a) percussion or pummeling of the chest (i.e., a caregiver strikes, vibrates or squeezes the chest wall), (b) breathing exercises (e.g., blowing ping pong balls across a table), and (c) postural drainage, also referred to as bronchial drainage, a procedure that involves positioning the individual so that secretions from the lungs are drained by means of gravity (e.g., lying on a slant board with the head down) while a caregiver percusses (strikes the chest wall), vibrates, or squeezes the chest. These treatment options are very time-consuming. For example, the chest physiotherapy session may take as long as 20 minutes. Typically, therapy is performed twice a day, first thing in the morning and once during the evening; some young adults benefit from an additional midday session.

In addition, antibiotics are often prescribed to prevent a respiratory infection or to treat an existing condition. In severe cases, where respiratory function is severely compromised, oxygen therapy may be prescribed.

Enzyme Replacement and Nutritional Therapy The major form of treatment for the digestive problems of individuals with CF is the administration of **oral pancreatic enzyme replacement** to supplant the natural enzymes that do not reach the intestines. The supplements (e.g., Cotazyme, Pancrease) come in capsule or powder form and must be taken before each meal or snack. The amount taken depends upon a number of factors: (a) the individual's age and activity level, (b) the size of the meal or snack to be consumed, (c) the amount of fat to be digested, (d) the number of bowel movements per day and the type of stool, (e) the response of the person to the enzyme therapy, and (f) the philosophy of the individual's physician (Cunningham & Taussig, 1988; Hunsberger & Feenan, 1994; Whaley & Wong, 1995).

With the enzyme supplement and a well-balanced diet, most individuals with CF can do quite well; however, some may require an additional nutritional supplement (e.g., high-calorie drinks, such as Ensure, Boost, or Instant Breakfast) to maintain proper weight. If supplements do not result in weight gain, other forms of treatment may be prescribed, such as parenteral or enteral feeding. Because of the poor absorption of fats and the consequent inability to absorb the fat-soluble vitamins A, D, E and K, a vitamin supplement may be prescribed. Lack of these vitamins can result in bruising and inability of the skin to heal.

Surgical Therapy Most recently, some individuals with CF have been the successful recipients of heart-lung or bilateral lung transplants. Fiel (1993) reported that, as of December 1991, over 200 individuals with CF worldwide had received either a heart-lung or double-lung transplant; 72 had been performed in North America (Cropp & Shames, 1994). A 2-year survival rate of 50% to 60% has been reported (Wilmott & Fiedler, 1994).

Prognosis

In the past, cystic fibrosis was thought of as a terminal disease of *children;* however, as a result of new treatments that increase the longevity of individuals with CF, the disease is now being thought of as a chronic disease of *adults* (White, Munro, & Pickler, 1995). FitzSimmons (1993), after examining data from 17,657 patients from 114 CF centers in 1990, reported that while the majority of individuals with CF (61.7%) were younger than age 15, 7.3% of the patients were 31 years of age or older. The oldest individual with CF was age 67, a statistic that is quite amazing in itself when one considers that 50 years ago, half of those with CF died within the first 12 months of life! In terms of survival, in 1996 the medial survival time of all patients was 27.6 years, a rate that has improved, according to statisticians, by 1 year each year for the past decade.

In terms of treatment, not only is lung transplantation a viable option, but researchers are now looking at the benefits of gene therapy. The goal of this treatment is to insert coding for normal CFTR protein in airway epithelial cells. The first human trial occurred in 1993, and currently studies are in progress in a number of centers in North America that are attempting to investigate the safety and efficacy of this approach. (McMullen, 1996). Colten (1996), in discussing gene therapy, made the following optimistic comments:

> Gene therapy provides that promise of a definitive cure of CF lung disease. Early experimental data suggest that this will be clinically useful, but many problems remain. Progress has been rapid, however, and it is likely that these problems will be resolved. (p. 157)

❤ Educational Implications and Teaching Tips

The educational implications of having cystic fibrosis are student-specific. School staff must communicate regularly with the parents to discuss the disease and its progression and the student's ability to participate in school. It is important to recognize that CF is a disorder that affects primarily the lungs and the digestive system and not the CNS. Consequently, the learning potential of those with CF matches that of those without the condition—some have learning problems, others are gifted, most have normal potential. In one report (Mangos, 1983), the median IQ of a group of 27 patients with CF was found to be 124, compared with a median of 103 for a group of control patients who were matched on the basis of age, sex, and socioeconomic status. It was suggested that "CF patients may have high intelligence test scores because of their increased conversational and communication skills, which evolve and progress very early because of their close and frequent contact with adults as a result of their illness" (p. 208). In a similar manner, Harvey (1982), in discussing the impact of the condition on physical stamina and intellectual potential of students with CF, alluded to the learning characteristics of children with CF in the following comments: "Children with this disease are neither more nor less intelligent than their peers, although they may appear brighter because their orientation tends to be more intellectual than physical" (p. 263).

The student with CF should be treated in the same manner as any other student in the classroom. This includes setting limits. Because of the nature of the disease, many parents of children or young adults with CF are overindulgent or overprotective. Such behavior often leads to social or emotional problems later in life. The following suggestions are given to assist the teacher who may have a student with cystic fibrosis.

1 *Generally, in the early stages of the disease, school attendance may be near normal; however, as the disease progresses, attendance may not be ideal.* Children or young adults with CF may need frequent visits, usually every 2 to 3 months, to specialized cystic fibrosis clinics for reevaluation and alteration to the treatment plan, and while the appointments generally can be completed within a day, they may have to miss an additional day or two to travel to and from the clinic. Additionally, students with cystic fibrosis are hospitalized frequently (e.g., for the administration of intravenous antibiotics; to receive intensive respiratory care) and consequently may be absent from school for long periods (Wilmott et al., 1984). FitzSimmons (1993) reported that during the year 1989-1990, 37% of persons with CF were hospitalized one or more times and that the mean stay was 11.9 days.

It is important that the teacher keep in contact with hospital teaching staff (i.e., child life specialists) so that there is continuity of the educational program. Home tutoring should be made available to those students who return home but are still unable to attend school because of lack of stamina.

2 *The student's persistent cough may be distracting to the teacher and the class; however, it is not symptomatic of a communicable disease.* The cough is either dry and hacky or loose and productive, and it may be worsened by the exposure to airborne irritants. Some students may try to stop coughing out of embarrassment; this is not advisable because the mucus must be expelled. It is best that the teacher and other persons in the class try to ignore the sound; the student is more likely to feel free to cough as needed when less attention is paid. (Harvey, 1982).

If the student wants to leave the room during a particularly intense coughing paroxysm, this should be allowed as needed. For the student who travels from class to class, being permitted to arrive a few minutes late allows time to cough and expectorate mucus in private (Kleinberg, 1982). The student should be responsible for using a tissue to collect the mucus and for discarding it in an appropriate manner. The student who has a persistent cough should also be able to leave the room to get a drink of water when needed or be allowed to keep a water bottle at his or her desk.

Unfortunately, parents of the other students in the class often become alarmed when there is a student with a chronic cough in the same class as their own child. The teacher can use the opportunity to educate both students and their parents regarding the nature of this disease and to reinforce the fact that the cough is not infectious and that others cannot "catch" the disease. At the same time, the privacy of the student with CF and his or her family must be respected; the teacher should meet with them to explore how to best inform the other students and their parents of the child's condition.

3 *Individuals with CF are prone to respiratory infections, which generally come on gradually in the form of a flare-up of a smoldering infection* (Wilmott et al., 1984). However, if a student with CF develops a high fever or experiences chest pain, shortness of breath, or any other worrisome conditions (e.g., increased blood in the sputum), school staff should contact the student's parents immediately to arrange for prompt medical treatment. In many cases, however, school staff send students home unnecessarily. If the child or adolescent is feeling all right, despite a mild fever or other symptoms, there is probably no reason to remove the student from school. Guidance should be sought from the student's physician.

Teachers should inform the parents of the student with CF regarding outbreaks of communicable diseases (e.g., flu, colds) in the school. Because of the pulmonary involvement in CF, the development of an upper respiratory infection can be extremely detrimental.

4 *Physical exercise is particularly important for the youngster with CF because it may assist in strengthening the muscles involved in clearing mucus from the airways and therefore promote improved pulmonary functioning.* Good choices are running, swimming, and high-repetition, low-weight strength exercises. Physical training may also result in an improved self-image and better psychosocial development (Goldberg, 1990). In the early stages of the disease, children and adolescents may be able to participate in most physical activities quite freely; however, they may need supervision to ensure that they do not try to go beyond their limits in an attempt to hide the disease from their friends (Harvey, 1982). As the disease progresses, the student may need to be excused from physical education and sports, for unlike the youngster with asthma, the respiratory problems experienced by a student with CF are not transient, and the student will simply not be able to keep up with others the same age. Consequently, some individuals with CF feel uncomfortable exercising with their able-bodied peers (Loutzenhiser & Clark, 1993).

Even though exercise is important, fatigue is often a constant factor in the life of persons with CF. Because of their increased basal metabolic rate, the lack of sleep caused by nighttime coughing, the need to arise early for treatment sessions before school, and the energy expended in coughing spells, many students with CF come to school tired. When tired, they should be allowed to have a rest, either in the classroom or in the nurse's office. Some students benefit from a flexible schedule (e.g., half days; abbreviated course load).

5 *Some students with CF need treatment during school hours to relieve their pulmonary symptoms; however, in most cases, the student undergoes the program before school, immediately after school, and before going to bed.* If a parent, school nurse, or health aide must provide therapy during school hours, a private room (e.g., nurse's office) should be made available for this purpose. If a field trip is planned, the treatment schedule should be kept in mind (Kleinberg, 1982).

Aside from scheduled chest physiotherapy, certain activities that are "fun" can provide additional drainage during school hours. Hanging by the knees from a bar or low-hanging trapeze, turning somersaults, playing "wheelbarrow," and standing on the head are all beneficial (Whaley & Wong, 1995). After such activities, the student will need to cough up the mucus that has become loosened and should be provided with privacy if necessary. Additionally, as part of the physical education program, several play activities may encourage better breathing: blowing on pinwheel toys; moving small items, such as toy trucks or cars, by blowing through a straw; blowing cotton balls or Ping-Pong balls across a table or the gym floor; preventing a tissue

from falling by blowing it against a wall; and blowing up balloons (Whaley & Wong, 1995). In the music program, singing loudly, especially songs that have a lot of words between inspirations of air, encourages the student to take deep breaths. To prevent the development of poor posture (thereby further limiting pulmonary functioning), exercises that help maintain good posture (e.g., back extension and shoulder exercises) should be encouraged throughout the day.

6 *During hot weather, during or after strenuous exercise, or when the student has a fever, excessive salt loss can occur* (Cunningham & Taussig, 1988). Teachers should be aware of the signs and symptoms that are indicative of salt depletion (Table 20.2). If untreated, salt depletion can have serious consequences.

Because many individuals with CF often have a preference for salty foods (e.g., pretzels, potato chips), they are typically able to adjust their consumption of salt to match their needs (Whaley & Wong, 1995). However, salt tablets may be prescribed during the summer months or during periods of great physical activity to prevent excessive salt loss. When the salt intake has been increased, the student must also increase fluid consumption. It may be advisable to avoid situations where there is the potential for too much sweat loss (e.g., track meet under the hot, midday sun).

7 *Individuals with CF typically need a diet high in calories.* This is because: (1) an increased expenditure of calories results from coughing, from fighting off infection, and from breathing when short of breath; (2) an increased loss of calories results

TABLE 20.2
Indicators of Salt Depletion

- Fatigue
- Abdominal pain
- Weakness
- Vomiting
- Fever
- Heat prostration or heat stroke
- Muscle cramps
- Dehydration (e.g., flushed dry skin, poor skin turgor, coated tongue, decreased urine output, urine with strong odor)

from failure to absorb all the nutrients from foods; and (3) a reduced intake of calories results from not feeling up to par. Students should be encouraged to eat as much as they want so that they do not become malnourished. Sufficient time should be allowed to permit them to have second and third, or even fourth, helpings during a sitting. In addition, if the student is hungry between meals, snacking should be allowed. If privacy is an issue, the student should be allowed to use the nurse's office.

Teachers should be aware of the dietary habits of the student with CF and report any concerns they may have to the parents. Teachers should, in particular, be alert to teasing: the student with CF does not benefit from being called names, such as "Miss Piggy."

8 *Most individuals with CF have to take a large number of pills, as many as 20 per day.* Medications may include pancreatic enzymes, vitamin supplements, salt tablets, and antibiotics. Pancreatic enzymes, in particular, have to be taken at meals and snack times, and a student may be reluctant to take the pills in front of classmates. A private spot, such as the nurse's or principal's office, should be made available to the student. Generally, the best approach is to pay as little attention as possible to the student's self-medication so that embarrassment is minimized. Students with CF (or their teachers) must carry the pancreatic enzymes with them at all times so that whenever food is consumed (e.g., while out on a field trip), they are adequately prepared.

9 *Individuals with CF typically experience more bowel movements than normal.* Students should be allowed to use the bathroom as needed. The bowel movements and the student's flatus may be quite foul-smelling, and consequently, there may be ridicule from peers. If teasing occurs, it might be preferable to have the student use the washroom normally used by school staff. Room deodorizers, such as Niloder, may lessen the odor. Lighting a wooden sulfur match can also decrease the odor, but this should be done only by an adult or with adult supervision.

10 *Developing an infection is a major worry of all persons with CF.* Some children and young adults have an intravenous venous access device (VAD) inserted into the circulatory system to allow the intermittent administration of antibiotics in an attempt to decrease the number of hospital admissions for pharmacologic treatment. During the 1989–1990 year, FitzSimmons (1993) reported that 1,918 individuals with CF (12.3% of the study population) used some form of home intravenous therapy.

While a teacher or school nurse will not be giving medication through the VAD, staff should be aware that the student has the device and that certain precautions must be taken (i.e., the device must be protected so that the needle does not become dislodged accidentally). The student's physician should be contacted by the school to provide written information about the VAD, including its purpose, pertinent facts about any restrictions for the student, and directions related to the management of the device (Whaley & Wong, 1995). Physical education teachers and sport coaches should be informed about the VAD, which is not a deterrent to most activities. However, contact sports are generally prohibited because the catheter may be hit or pulled, and swimming may be limited to less than an hour or prohibited if the surgical site has not properly healed. Very young children should be closely supervised in their use of scissors to prevent the accidental cutting of the catheter. An eye bubble shield (available at most local pharmacies) taped over the site provides additional protection (Whaley & Wong, 1995).

11 *Individuals with CF, particularly those with severe respiratory conditions, may also be receiving oxygen therapy at home or school.* FitzSimmons (1993) reported that 1,490 individuals with CF (9.6% of his sample) in 1990 used oxygen while at home. Approximately 30% of those on oxygen needed it continuously; 40% needed it only during the night; and 5% required supplemental oxygen during periods of exercise. If oxygen is administered in school, staff must be adequately trained and proper safety procedures followed.

12 *As for all individuals with a chronic illness, adolescence is a difficult time, particularly for those young adults who are self-conscious about how they look.* It is not uncommon for children and young adults with CF, especially males, to be short in stature and excessively thin and to lack signs of sexual maturation until they are in their late teens (Hayward, 1988; Mangos, 1983). Often adolescent girls become amenorrheic (fail to menstruate), and some lack normal breast development (Whaley & Wong, 1995). In addition, although the student may have a large barrel chest or distended abdomen, the student may well appear emaciated with thin, underdeveloped buttocks, arms, and legs. In some children and young adults, the ends of the fingers and toes may become enlarged and thickened, a process known as **clubbing;** in others, there may be discoloration of the teeth from the administration of antibiotics.

The altered appearance, in combination with the chronic cough and the need for increased consumption of food and medicine, can result in loss of self-esteem. Involvement in a support group may allow the student to make new friends and obtain support from peers who understand what the student is going through. Specialized summer camps also provide an opportunity for socializing, as well as allowing time to be away from home (and from the day-to-day contact with parents!). However, while socializing with others with CF has many benefits, one of the "most poignant reminders of mortality" for the child or young adult with CF is seeing peers with CF die prematurely (Hayward, 1988). For an interesting look at the lives of children and young adults with CF, see the recently published article entitled "The Child's Eye: Memories of Growing Up with Cystic Fibrosis" by Christian and D'Auria (1997).

13 *In the past, many children and adolescents with cystic fibrosis died before reaching adulthood; however, survival rates have progressively improved over the past several decades.* In fact, individuals born in the 1990s with CF can expect to survive into their forties (FitzSimmons, 1993). The rate at which cystic fibrosis progresses in any given individual cannot be predicted. The large number of complications experienced by persons with CF makes it seem as if they are sick all of the time, but this is not usually true (O'Neill, 1990).

Because of potentially increased longevity, the adolescent or young adult should receive appropriate career guidance and counseling. Careers that are both of interest to the students and are within their current and projected physical capability must be selected (Wilmott et al., 1984). Although most persons with CF are not restricted in what they are capable of doing, very heavy physical work may not be appropriate for some. For others, the environ-

ment in which they work may need to be considered. Those with respiratory conditions may find, for example, certain environments (e.g., those that are extremely dusty) to be unsuitable.

14 *When school guidance counselors help students with CF explore vocational options, they must first confront their own feelings regarding students with terminal illness.* Wilmott et al. (1984), in stressing the need for future planning, gave the example of a student who "frittered away" his time until he was 26, at which point he was forced to plan a way for supporting himself. O'Neill (1990) perhaps best stated the philosophy that needs to be adopted by educators and counselors in dealing with children and young adults with cystic fibrosis:

> The underlying theme that should guide all therapeutic counseling of children with CF and their families should be that it is not the *quantity* of life but the *quality* put into life that really counts. Many children with CF have seen and accomplished more in their lives than some who have no medical problems. All of them cope with their illness and its resultant problems, and most come through with great sensitivity and maturity. (p. 135, italics added)

🐛 Inborn Errors of Metabolism

Inborn errors of metabolism (IEMs), as mentioned previously, are conditions in which a particular exocrine gland does not produce a specific enzyme, and as a result of the lack, the person has difficulty digesting an isolated type of food. IEMs are often grouped by the size of substrate that is affected (Crocker, 1983). Using this system, the conditions can be split into two groups: (1) **large molecule diseases,** or those that affect the metabolism of large molecules, such as lipids, glycoproteins, and mucopolysaccharides; and (2) **small molecule diseases,** those that affect the metabolism of the small molecules that make up amino acids or carbohydrates. IEMs can also be classified as (1) those that are "silent" (i.e., are not life-threatening) but if untreated can lead to brain damage and developmental disabilities; (2) those that produce acute toxicity (i.e., those that are typically life-threatening in infancy); and (3) those that cause progressive neurologic deterioration (i.e., those that destroy neurons in the brain) (Batshaw, 1997).

Almost all IEMs are autosomal recessive (Batshaw, 1997). Because the child must receive the defective gene from *both* the mother and the father, IEMs are generally rare; however, IEMs, when examined collectively, account for a significant proportion of health problems in children (Whaley & Wong, 1995). It has been estimated that 3 in 10,000 children are born with some type of deficiency in one of the regulatory enzymes (Batshaw, 1997). While it is beyond the scope of this text to describe the hundreds of IEMs, some of the more common conditions are described briefly. For a description of other IEMs, see Meyer (1997).

Large Molecule Inborn Errors of Metabolism

In individuals who have an IEM that affects large molecules, certain characteristics are common. Typically, there are changes in the structure of cells of the body that produce joint deformities and other dysmorphologic features (i.e., malformed body structures) that result from the accumulation of the molecules in the bones and connective tissues. In addition, there may be enlargement of certain organs (e.g., the liver and spleen) along with tissue damage in the brain that may result in severe cognitive dysfunction. Many children with this particular form of metabolic dysfunction have a limited life expectancy. Two of the most common small molecule IEMs include Hurler's syndrome and Tay-Sachs disease.

Hurler's Syndrome   In this condition, the metabolism of mucopolysaccharides is affected by a deficiency in the production of the enzyme iduronidase. Hurler's syndrome is an autosomal recessive condition that is sex-linked, affecting 1 in 144,000 children (Meyer, 1997). Symptoms, which typically begin to appear during the first year of life, include enlargement of the liver and spleen; facial disfigurement (e.g., enlarged head; low forehead; broad nose; thickened, full lips; enlarged, prominent tongue); clouding of the cornea that may impair vision; difficulties in hearing; skeletal abnormalities (e.g., barrel-shaped chest; short stature; short neck; short, broad hands and fingers; restricted joint mobility resulting in hips, knees, elbows, and fingers that are permanently flexed); and decreased mental ability. Often the skin of a person with Hurler's syndrome becomes thickened, and hirsutism (excessive body hair) is common. In many cases, the heart is affected.

Cardiac problems, compounded by respiratory difficulties resulting from pressure on the respiratory organs from the enlarged abdominal organs and from a thickening of the tissues in the upper airway, often cause premature death. Most children with Hurler's syndrome die before their 10th birthday; no treatment is available to halt the progression of the disease.

Hurler's syndrome is often referred to as **mucopolysaccharidosis I (MPS I or MPS I-H).** Less severe deficiencies of the same enzyme result in milder forms of the disease, known as **Scheie syndrome (MPS V or MPS I-S).** Several other conditions affect the metabolism of mucopolysaccharides. They are **Hunter's (MPS II), Sanfilippo (MPS III), Morquio (MPS IV), Maroteaux-Lamy (MPS VI)** and **Sly (MPS VII)** syndromes, each named after the person who discovered or first described the disease. Each condition is different because different enzymes are deficient; however, in general, they are similar to Hurler's syndrome.

Tay-Sachs Disease   A disorder of lipid metabolism caused by a deficiency of the enzyme hexosaminidase A, **Tay-Sachs** disease occurs most often in Ashkenazi Jews, who are originally from Eastern Europe. The disease was named after Warren Tay, an English ophthalmologist, and Bernard Sachs, an American neurologist.

In this particular condition, there is an ineffective breakdown of lipids found in the cell membranes of the nervous system. Large molecules of fat (i.e., sphingolipids) accumulate within the cells of the body, particularly in the head (e.g., brain, eye), resulting in head enlargement, blindness, neuromuscular deterioration, spasticity, seizures, and mental retardation.

In the first few months of life, the child may have an exaggerated startle response to sound, and by 6 months of age the obvious deterioration begins to occur. A distinctive cherry-red spot in the retina of the eye may be the first conclusive sign to confirm the diagnosis. No treatment is available to halt the disease progression, and death usually occurs before age 6.

Tay-Sachs disease is an autosomal recessive condition. The likelihood of having the Tay-Sachs gene for the disease is believed to be 1 in 300 for the population at large, 1 in 25 for the Ashkenazi Jewish population in general, and 1 in 16 in the ultra–Orthodox Ashkenazi Jewish population in New York City (Merz, 1987), but the incidence of the disease is 1 in 112,000 for the population as a whole, and 1 in

3,800 in the Ashkenazic population worldwide (Meyer, 1997). Carriers of the abnormal gene, located on the long arm of chromosome 15, can be determined by a simple blood test.

As a result of the efforts of an ultra–Orthodox Jewish rabbi in New York who had four of his children die from Tay-Sachs disease, a confidential screening program, known as the **Chevra Dor Yeshorim** (literally translated as "Association of an Upright Generation") has been available to Jewish persons in New York City since September 1983 (Merz, 1987). In this program, persons are assigned a number, and after the screening test, the number and the individual's status (i.e., carrier or noncarrier) are recorded. When a match of two individuals is proposed by a matchmaker, the matchmaker is able to contact the screening center to determine the "compatibility" of the match. If both members of the couple were carriers for the condition, and consequently, there was a one-in-four chance that their offspring would have the disease, the couple would be informed and the match would be broken. If only one was found to be a carrier and the other normal, the couple would not be informed and the marriage would proceed as planned. Between 1983 and 1987, over 4,000 adolescents and young adults were tested through this program, and six prospective matches between carriers have been identified. In each case, the marriage plans were terminated and the families looked for new matches. In this same time frame, *no* babies were born with Tay-Sachs disease from couples involved in the Chevra Dor Yeshorim program. Similar programs have since been developed in other locations where there is a high concentration of Jewish persons of Ashkenazic descent, including Israel, Montreal (Canada), Chicago, and Los Angeles (Merz, 1987).

Small Molecule Inborn Errors of Metabolism

In contrast to errors of metabolism that involve large molecules, small molecule diseases generally do not result in abnormal appearance. Described as being more dynamic, these conditions tend to predominantly affect blood vessels and brain cells (Crocker, 1983). While the infant's appearance may be normal, development may be affected, and in some cases, the condition results in a shortened life expectancy. Three of the more common small molecule diseases are phenylketonuria and maple syrup

urine disease, both of which involve the breakdown of amino acids, and galactosemia, a condition resulting from the inability to metabolize carbohydrates.

Phenylketonuria (PKU)   Perhaps the best known inborn error of metabolism is phenylketonuria, an autosomal recessive condition that results from the presence of the gene for PKU on chromosome 12. It is caused by the absence or reduction of the liver enzyme phenylalanine hydroxylase, required to convert the amino acid phenylalanine to tyrosine. One in 50 to 100 people is a carrier of this particular condition, but it is relatively rarely manifested and affects only 1 in 10,000 children (Davidson-Mundt, 1994; Giordano, 1990). PKU affects primarily Caucasian children; the highest incidence is in the United States and Northern Europe. The condition is seldom found in African, Jewish, or Japanese infants (Whaley & Wong, 1995).

At birth, the infant with PKU is normal; however, as the phenylalanine rises to toxic levels, damage to the gray and white matter of the brain occurs. Typically, PKU leads to severe mental retardation if untreated. Hanley, Linsao, and Netley (1971), after monitoring 94 individuals with PKU, reported that the earlier the diagnosis, the higher the ultimate IQ score of the child. In children recognized as having PKU between birth and 2 months of age and who are treated by means of dietary therapy, the mean IQ score was found to be 93.5 (n = 38) compared with those who were discovered to have PKU between 2 and 6 months of age and between 6 and 12 months of age, whose mean IQ scores were 71.6 (n = 6) and 54.5 (n = 11), respectively. In children whose diagnosis was delayed until between the ages of 1 and 2 years, the mean IQ score showed little change from those between the age of 6 and 12 months (i.e., IQ of 55.5); however, for those who were not treated until they were at least 2 years of age, the mean IQ score dropped dramatically to 40.8.

Even though the IQ may remain within the normal range in children whose disease has been discovered at a very young age, some children with PKU show signs of learning difficulties, such as visual and fine motor coordination problems and language difficulties, as they age (Crocker, 1983). Other characteristics of individuals with PKU include the following: blond hair, even though the child's siblings may be dark; blue eyes; light skin; eczema and other dermatologic problems, such as seborrhea (oily skin); and a distinctive, musty smell to their urine or skin, or both, that is often described as being "mousey." A youngster from a family with dark skin color may be either a redhead or brunette (Whaley & Wong, 1995).

Fortunately, physicians do not have to rely solely on observation of such characteristics. Since the 1960s, a screening test, known as the **Guthrie test,** has been widely available; it not only screens for this condition but for other metabolic diseases as well (e.g., galactosemia and maple syrup urine disease). In most developed countries, the test, which involves drawing a small amount of blood, is routinely administered within days or weeks of birth (i.e., after consumption of a certain amount of phenylalanine).

Because phenylalanine is an essential amino acid found in most animal and plant proteins, those with PKU must follow a restrictive diet (i.e., limited or no milk, cheese, meat, fish, legumes, and nuts). Special formula is needed for the young infant, and foods containing aspartame (Nutrasweet) must be avoided because aspartame is converted to phenylalanine in the digestive tract. Permitted foods include certain types of fruits, vegetables, and juices and some types of cereals, grains, breads, and starches. Small amounts of phenylalanine may be allowed because it is necessary for the growth of bone and tissue. In the past, the child with PKU was kept on the diet until between ages 5 and 8, at which time, more of the contraindicated foods were slowly reintroduced. As a result of research findings indicating that children did poorly off the diet (e.g., had difficulty concentrating, developed hyperactivity, did poorly in arithmetic, experienced visual-spatial problems), most physicians now recommend that the youngsters adhere to the regimen until their teen years or beyond (Davidson-Mundt, 1994; Whaley & Wong, 1995).

Maple Syrup Urine Disease (MSUD)   Like PKU, maple syrup urine disease is an autosomal recessive disorder that prevents the metabolism of certain amino acids. Maple syrup urine disease results from the absence of the enzyme needed to catalyze three particular acids: leucine, isoleucine, and valine. In the general population this condition is extremely rare, occurring at a rate of 1 in 220,000 (Meyer, 1997). It is more common in the Mennonite population, where the incidence is believed to be as high as 1 in 760 births (Davidson-Mundt, 1994).

The disease gets its name from the peculiar odor of the person's urine, sweat, and cerumen (ear wax). If untreated, the individual suffers severe neurologic symptoms (e.g., altered muscle tone, lethargy, ap-nea, seizures) that can lead to coma and death. As with PKU, treatment is dietary. A diet that is almost totally free of foods that contain branch-chain amino acids, such as milk and meat, is recommended. Typically, the youngster is allowed a small amount of milk or other foods containing the amino acids to ensure proper growth and development; however, the amount must be carefully controlled. There are a number of milk-substitute products available that can be given to the youngster, and fruits and vegetables are permitted in the diet. Without treatment, death typically occurs before the child is 1 month old. With early treatment (i.e., implemented before the child is 10 days old), the prognosis for normal growth is excellent.

Galactosemia   There are a number of disorders associated with faulty metabolism of carbohydrates; the most common is **galactosemia,** an autosomal recessive disorder that affects the metabolism of galactose, a simple sugar found in a number of carbohydrates, particularly milk (Davidson-Mundt, 1994; Whaley & Wong, 1995). The prevalence of galactosemia is estimated to be between 1 in 50,000 and 1 in 70,000 (Meyer, 1997). Resulting from a deficiency of the enzyme galactose-1-phosphate uridyl transferase, galactosemia is usually evident at birth because the infant is unable to digest milk (i.e., to convert galactose to glucose). Symptoms include failure to thrive, anorexia, weight loss, nausea, vomiting, and diarrhea. If untreated, the condition can lead to neurologic impairment that results in severe cognitive deficits. Liver damage (evidenced by jaundice) and eye problems (i.e., cataract formation) are also common.

Early recognition of galactosemia is important so that treatment can be started; however, even with strict adherence to a galactose-free diet (i.e., a diet that does not contain milk and milk products), the child may show mild speech difficulties, specific learning problems, and neurologic problems, such as tremors and ataxia. Typically, the child must maintain the diet until at least age 7 or 8; after that point, a less rigid diet may be tolerated (Whaley & Wong, 1995).

❧ Summary

The exocrine system consists of a number of glands that function to secrete chemical materials needed by the body for survival. The most common exocrine condition is cystic fibrosis, a condition that affects primarily the mucus-producing glands of the respiratory system and the enzyme-producing glands of the pancreas. While the CF gene is lethal, the life expectancy for those with the condition has increased dramatically over the past few decades. Most children and young adults not only continue through their elementary and secondary schooling, but many graduate from colleges and universities.

Unfortunately, the prognosis for those with inborn errors of metabolism is not always as optimistic. Inborn errors of metabolism are not diseases of the exocrine glands per se but are conditions in which the body, owing to genetic abnormalities, cannot produce certain enzymes that would normally be secreted or excreted by an exocrine gland.

References

Batshaw, M. L. (1997). PKU and other inborn errors of metabolism. In M. L. Batshaw (Ed.), *Children with disabilities* (4th ed., pp. 389–404). Baltimore: Paul H. Brookes.

Beaudet, A. L. (1992). Genetic testing for cystic fibrosis. *Pediatric Clinics of North America, 39,* 213–228.

Canadian Cystic Fibrosis Foundation (1993). *You were asking?* Toronto, ONT: Author.

Chasnoff, I. J., Ellis, J. W., Fainman, Z. S., & Mullen, P. B. (1993). *Family medical and prescription drug guide.* Lincolnwood, IL: Publications International.

Christian, B. J., & D'Auria, J. P. (1997). The child's eye: Memories of growing up with cystic fibrosis. *Journal of Pediatric Nursing, 12,* 3–12.

Coe, A. W. (1989). Cystic fibrosis: An introduction and the role of school personnel. *Education, 110,* 202–208.

Colten, H. R. (1996). Cystic fibrosis. In F. D. Burg, J. R. Ingelfinger, E. P Wald, & R. A. Polin (Eds.), *Gellis & Kagan's current pediatric therapy* (15th ed., pp. 155–157). Philadelphia: W. B. Saunders.

Crocker, A. C. (1983). Inborn errors of metabolism. In J. Umbreit (Ed.), *Physical disabilities and health impairments: An introduction* (pp. 233–239). New York: Merrill.

Cropp, G. J., & Shames, R. S. (1994). Respiratory and allergic diseases. In A. M. Rudolph & R. K. Kamei (Eds.), *Rudolph's fundamentals of pediatrics* (pp. 537–582). Norwalk, CT: Appleton & Lange.

Cunningham, J. C., & Taussig, L. M. (1988). *A guide to cystic fibrosis for parents and children.* Tucson, AZ: Tucson Cystic Fibrosis Center, University of Arizona Health Sciences Center.

Davidson-Mundt, A. (1994). Altered metabolic function. In C. L. Betz, M.M. Hunsberger, & S. Wright, *Family-centered nursing care of children* (2nd ed., pp. 2012–2041). Philadelphia: W. B. Saunders.

Fiel, S. B. (1993). Clinical management of pulmonary disease in cystic fibrosis. *The Lancet, 341,* 1070–1074.

FitzSimmons, S. C. (1993). The changing epidemiology of cystic fibrosis. *Journal of Pediatrics, 122,* 1–9.

Fulginiti, V. A., & Lewy, J. E. (1993). Pediatrics. *Journal of the American Medical Association, 270,* 246–248.

Giordano, B. P. (1990). Metabolism: Implications of altered hormonal regulation. In S. R. Mott, S. R. James, & A. M. Sperhac (Eds.), *Nursing care of children and families* (2nd ed., pp. 1499–1552). Redwood City, CA: Addison-Wesley.

Goldberg, B. (1990). Children, sports, and chronic disease. *The Physician and Sportsmedicine, 16*(1) 45–50, 53–56.

Hanley, W. B., Linsao, L. S., & Netley, C. (1971). The efficacy of dietary therapy for phenylketonuria. *Canadian Medical Association Journal, 104,* 1089–1091.

Harvey, B. (1982). Cystic fibrosis. In E. E. Bleck & D. A. Nagel (Eds.), *Physically handicapped children: A medical atlas for teachers* (2nd ed., pp. 255–263). New York: Grune & Stratton.

Hayward, J. (1988). Extending the good life. *Nursing Times, 84*(35), 55–58.

Heller, K. W., Alberto, P. A., Forney, P. E., & Schwartzman, M. N. (1996). *Understanding physical, sensory, and health impairments: Characteristics and educational implications.* Pacific Grove, CA: Brooks/Cole.

Hunsberger, M., & Feenan, L. (1994). Altered respiratory function. In C. L. Betz, M. M. Hunsberger, & S. Wright (Eds.), *Family-centered nursing care of children* (2nd ed., pp. 1167–1275). Philadelphia: W. B. Saunders.

Jackson, P. L., & Vessey, J. A. (Eds.). (1996). *Primary care of the child with a chronic condition.* St. Louis: Mosby.

Kleinberg, S. B. (1982). *Educating the chronically ill child.* Rockville, MD: Aspen.

Loutzenhiser, J. K., & Clark, R. (1993). Physical activity and exercise in children with cystic fibrosis. *Journal of Pediatric Nursing, 8,* 112–119.

Mangos, J. A. (1983). Cystic fibrosis. In J. Umbreit (Ed.), *Physical disabilities and health impairments: An introduction* (pp. 206–213). New York: Merrill.

McMullen, A. H. (1996). Cystic fibrosis. In P. L. Jackson & J. A. Vessey (Eds.), *Primary care of the child with a chronic condition* (pp. 324–349). St. Louis: Mosby.

Merz, B. (1987). Matchmaking scheme solves Tay-Sachs problem. *Journal of the American Medical Association, 258,* 2636–2637.

Meyer, G. (1997). Syndromes and inborn errors of metabolism. In M. L. Batshaw (Ed.), *Children with disabilities* (4th ed., pp. 813–834). Baltimore: Paul H. Brookes.

O'Neill, E. (1990). Cystic fibrosis. In D. L. Sexton (Ed.), *Nursing care of the respiratory patient* (pp. 109–136). Norwalk, CT: Appleton & Lange.

Tizzano, E. F., & Buchwald, M. (1993). Recent advances in cystic fibrosis research. *Journal of Pediatrics, 122,* 985–988.

Whaley, L. F., & Wong, D. L. (1995). *Nursing care of infants and children* (5th ed.). St. Louis: Mosby.

White, K. R., Munro, C. L., & Pickler, R. H. (1995). Therapeutic implications of recent advances in cystic fibrosis. *MCN: Maternal and Child Nursing, 20,* 304–308.

Wilmott, R., Burroughs, B. R., & Beele, D. (1984). Cystic fibrosis. In J. Fithian (Ed.) *Understanding the child with a chronic illness in the classroom* (pp. 114–133). Phoenix: Oryx Press.

Wilmott, R. W., & Fiedler, M. A. (1994). Recent advances in the treatment of cystic fibrosis. *Pediatric Clinics of North America, 41,* 431–455.

PART VIII

Protection:

Children and Young Adults with Altered Integumentary Function

CHAPTER **21**
Altered Integumentary Function

The skin performs several vital functions, in particular, sheltering the body against the "inhospitable environment" that surrounds it (Nicol & Hill, 1994). The skin offers protection from trauma, radiation, penetration of foreign bodies, moisture, and humidity, and it also forms a barrier against a variety of invading organisms, e.g., bacteria and viruses. Not often thought of as an organ, the skin is, in fact, the largest organ of the body, measuring, at maturity, approximately 18 square feet (1.7 m^2) and weighing between 7 and 9 pounds (3.2 to 4.1 kg).

There are a number of terms that are used in describing skin conditions. The prefixes **derma-, dermato-,** and **dermo-**[1] mean "pertaining to the skin," come from the Greek word *derma,* for skin, and are used frequently in referring to conditions that involve the outer covering of the body (e.g., **dermatosis,** any type of disorder affecting the skin; **dermatitis,** inflammation of the skin). A **dermatologist** is a physician who specializes in skin-related disorders, and **dermatology** refers to the study (e.g., anatomy, physiology, and pathology) of the skin (*Mosby's,* 1994).

In addition, *cutis,* from the Latin, means skin, and the prefix **cut-** is used to refer to the skin (e.g., **cutaneous,** meaning of or relating to the skin; **cuticle,** the epithelial cells that are located at the base of a fingernail). Finally, from the Latin word *integumentum,* meaning covering, the skin is also referred to as the **integument,** and the skin and its appendages (i.e., hair, nails, and glands) are referred to collectively as the **integumentary system.**

The Integumentary System: Review of Structure and Function

The Skin

Shown in Figure VIII.1, the **skin** is composed of three distinct layers, the **epidermis,** the **dermis,** and the **hypodermis.** Even though each layer is differ-

ent, the layers work in a coordinated manner, each layer relying on the others for regulation, modulation, and support (Rudy, 1993).

Epidermis The **epidermis,** the outermost layer, is actually composed of several distinct layers of avascular tissue. Each layer has a slightly different function; however, collectively, the major functions of the epidermis are to provide a protective barrier against microorganisms and macroorganisms attempting to enter the body and to prevent the loss of body contents, in particular, the dissipation of body fluid, thereby permitting humans to live in dry environments without dehydration. The epidermis varies in thickness from 0.0016 to 0.06 inch (0.04 to 1.5 mm) (Rudy, 1993).

The color of an individual's skin depends on the type and amount of pigment in the epidermal layers. Individuals with dark skin produce more of the pigment melanin than those who are lighter; however, some white persons have irregular patches of melanin, commonly known as **freckles.** Those of Asian descent have a yellowish hue to their skin due to the combination of two pigments, carotene and melanin.

Dermis Directly under the epidermis, the **dermis** (also known as the **corium**) is a tough, elastic layer that makes up the bulk of the skin. The dermis varies in thickness from 0.04 to 0.16 inch (1 to 4 mm) (Rudy, 1993). The dermis is thickest in the palms of the hands and the soles of the feet. The increased thickness provides maximum protection against minor injuries, such as cuts and splinters. Rich in blood vessels, the dermis also contains sweat glands, sebaceous glands, nerves, lymphatic vessels, and hair follicles.

The blood vessels in the dermal layer have two functions. In addition to providing the adjacent tissues with nutrients and oxygen, they assist the body in maintaining a satisfactory temperature (i.e., thermoregulation). When an individual has a fever, increased blood flow to the skin, recognized as the "flush" of a fever, results in the cooling of the blood;

---

[1] Similarly, the suffixes **-derma, -dermia,** and **-dermic** are also used in describing certain skin conditions (e.g., scleroderma).

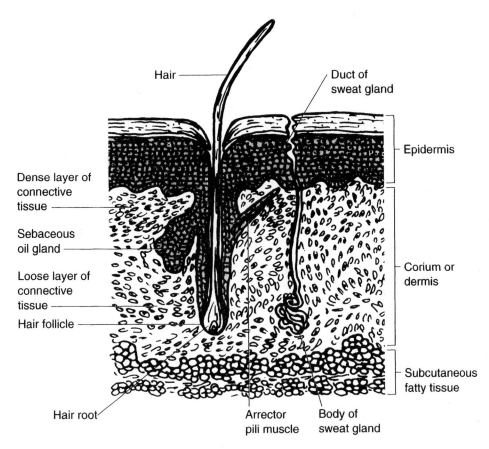

Figure VIII.1.
Structure of the Skin and the Subcutaneous Tissue

conversely, when an individual is exposed to the cold, diminished blood flow to the skin, recognized as the pallor associated with reduced body temperature, decreases the amount of heat that can be lost through the skin. The sweat glands also help to cool the body when it becomes overheated, and in conjunction with the sebaceous glands, the sweat glands assist in retaining heat when the body becomes too cool.

The nerves and nerve endings located in the dermal layer serve a protective function (e.g., providing the body with information regarding touch, pressure, temperature, and pain) as do the lymphatic glands (e.g., combating infections). In the past, when humans were living in caves, **body hair** provided extra protection from the cold and wet climate. Now, it serves primarily a decorative function. Body hair originates in the **follicles** located in the corium.

Hypodermis The innermost layer of tissue, made up predominantly of connective tissue and adipose (fatty) tissue, functions primarily as a form of insula-

tion protecting the body from cold. Known as the **subcutaneous layer, or hypodermis,** this layer also serves as a source of heat (i.e., from the metabolism of the fat cells) and as a shock absorber, padding the internal organs of the body against external forces. Located in this layer are blood vessels, nerves, some hair roots, and some sweat glands. Females have more subcutaneous tissue than males, and as a result, women typically have a more rounded, shapely figure than men.

Skin Appendages

Typically, one thinks of an arm or a leg when hearing the word "appendage." By definition, however, an appendage is an accessory structure attached to another part or organ (*Mosby's,* 1994). There are three accessory structures that are part of the integumentary system: the nails, the hair, and the glands located within the skin layers.

441

Nails Made of hardened skin cells, **nails,** both on the fingers and toes, function primarily to protect the soft tips of the extremities. Fingernails also are of assistance for grasping small objects, such as splinters. Each nail is made up of three parts: the **root,** which attaches the nail to the extremity; the **body,** the major portion of the structure; and the **free edge,** the section that overhangs the distal part of the toe or finger.

Hair Hair, a filament of keratin, consists of two parts: the **root,** the portion that develops in the hair follicle located in the hypodermal or dermal layer of the skin; and the **shaft,** the part that extends outward from the skin, which can grow as fast as 0.04 inch (1 mm) every 3 to 4 days. As mentioned previously, hair serves mainly a decorative function.

Glands The two major types of glands that are part of the integumentary system are the **sweat (sudoriferous) glands** and the **sebaceous glands.** Sweat glands produce sweat; sebaceous glands produce sebum. **Sweat** is composed primarily of water, with small concentrations of chloride, urea, ammonia, uric acid, and creatine. With a pH between 3.0 and 5.0, sweat is sufficiently acidic to prevent the growth of most disease-producing microorganisms (Rieg, Miller, & Ragiel, 1990). **Sebum** is composed primarily of keratin, a fibrous sulfur containing protein; fat; and cellular debris.

Sweat glands. There are two types of sweat glands, the eccrine glands and the apocrine glands. **Eccrine glands** are distributed over the entire body except for in a few areas such as the lip margins, the eardrums, and the nail beds. The eccrine glands fulfill the thermoregulatory function of the body. **Apocrine glands** are typically found in areas covered with hair, e.g., the anogenital area, armpits, eyelids, external ears, and around the nipples. The apocrine glands are not believed to have any major function, even though they do produce an odorless sweat, which in turn is acted upon by bacteria, resulting in a body aroma that can be strong in certain individuals. Typically, the apocrine glands do not become active until the onset of puberty.

Sebaceous glands. Typically found attached to the hair follicles, the primary purpose of the sebaceous glands is to produce sebum, which assists in keeping the skin lubricated while at the same time making the skin and hair water-repellent. It is also believed that the sebum, in conjunction with the slightly acidic sweat, inhibits the growth of bacteria and fungi on the skin.

References

Mosby's medical, nursing, and allied health dictionary (4th ed.).(1994). St. Louis: Mosby.

Nicol, N. H., & Hill, M. J. (1994). Altered skin integrity. In C. L. Betz, M. M. Hunsberger, & S. Wright (Eds.), *Family-centered nursing care of children* (2nd ed., pp. 1648–1677). Philadelphia: W. B. Saunders.

Rieg, L. S., Miller, M., & Ragiel, C. R. (1990) Protection: Implications of inflammation and altered skin integrity. In S. R. Mott, S. R. James, & A. M. Sperhac (Eds.), *Nursing care of children and families* (2nd ed., pp. 1137–1225). Redwood City, CA: Addison-Wesley.

Rudy, S. J. (1993). Anatomy and physiology of the integumentary system. In D. B. Jackson & R. B. Saunders (Eds.), *Child health nursing: A comprehensive approach to the care of children and their families* (pp. 1749–1759). Philadelphia: J. B. Lippincott.

Altered Integumentary Function

While most skin conditions are not particularly serious, i.e., not life-threatening, they should not be considered as trivial. Rieg, Miller, and Ragiel (1990) aptly described the skin as "the visual presentation each individual gives to society" (p. 1140), and a student with an obvious skin condition, e.g., a young child who has extensive burns to the body, may be the brunt of unmerciful teasing by peers. In some cases, such as an adolescent who has a severe case of acne, the student may even be totally rejected by classmates, who may falsely believe that the skin problem is the result of uncleanliness or ungodliness. Such rejection undoubtedly harms the child or young adult psychologically and has a negative impact on his or her fragile self-esteem.

There are more than 2,000 recognized skin disorders (Rudy, 1993), so it is probable that most teachers will have students in their classroom who are experiencing or who have experienced some type of skin disorder. In this chapter, some of the more common integumentary problems are described briefly. Those conditions that are **noninfectious** (i.e., those that do not spread from one person to another) are described first, followed by a discussion of those conditions that are either (a) **infectious,** in and of themselves, or (b) result from an infectious process. Conditions that are generalized to the whole body (i.e., systemic) are covered, as well as those that are localized to a specific site.

🍎 Noninfectious Skin Conditions

Noninfectious skin conditions, even though they may look unpleasant, are *not* communicable per se. Teachers and students should not be fearful of "catching" the condition, even if they are in direct physical contact with the individual's skin. However, noninfectious skin conditions *can* become infected by bacteria, viruses, or fungi. Infectious conditions *are* communicable, and proper precautions should be taken in such situations.

Some of the noninfectious skin conditions experienced by children and young adults are age-dependent. For example, infants are prone to diaper rash, whereas both infants and young children often have eczema. Adolescents and young adults are particularly susceptible to acne. Bites, stings, lacerations, or burns can occur at any time during life. Noninfectious dermatologic conditions can be further subdivided into two groups: (a) those that are

systemic (affecting the whole body); and (b) those that are a result of specific injury (i.e., localized).

Noninfectious Systemic Skin Conditions

Atopic Dermatitis More commonly known as **eczema, atopic dermatitis** is an intensely itchy, chronic skin condition that is usually found in allergy-prone (i.e., atopic) individuals. Triggers include food (most often milk, peanuts, soy, wheat, or eggs) and contact with specific allergens, such as hair, wool (lanolin), harsh detergents, feathers, and second-hand smoke. In older children and adults, stress can lead to the development of eczema. Children with eczema often also have asthma and hay fever.

It has been estimated that between 10% and 15% of children up to age 14 will, at some point in their childhood, have atopic dermatitis. In 95% of the cases, the condition is apparent before the child reaches age 5 (Guzzo, 1996). Half of those with eczema in childhood continue to have a persistent form of the disease during their adult years (Guzzo, 1996). Eczema is believed to be more common in girls than boys.

The most common characteristic of atopic dermatitis is the lesions that occur on the body. Typical sites include the chest, cheeks, forehead, scalp, neck, and the inside surface of the elbows and knees. In the early stages, **papulovesicles** (pimple-like skin lesions), which tend to ooze, are common. In the later stages, the skin becomes crusty and scaly. Atopic dermatitis can range in severity from mild to severe. Periods of exacerbation followed by periods of remission are not uncommon. Treatment typically involves the administration of topical medications (e.g., corticosteroids, tar compounds). During flare-ups, it is particularly important to control for infection. It has been reported that 95% of atopic children are infected with the bacterium *Staphylococcus aureus* (Guzzo, 1996).

Allergic Contact Dermatitis Allergic contact dermatitis (ACD) arises when a person is in direct contact with some type of agent, either natural or manufactured, that triggers an allergic response. The most common **natural agents** are poisonous plants and trees, such as poison ivy, sumac, or oak. In most cases, the skin reaction is the result of direct contact (i.e., touch) with the offending substance. In cases in which the individual is hypersensitive to the allergen, indirect contact, such as patting a dog that may have small amounts of the plant sap on its coat, can result in a reaction. Examples of **manufactured items** that may cause a reaction include certain metallic substances (e.g., nickel, commonly found in the backs of watches), cosmetics, topical medications, dyes, turpentine, paint remover, gasoline, soaps, bleaches, detergents, and fabrics.

The typical reaction in ACD is the development of a rash a few hours after exposure. In most cases, the rash improves without any specific treatment. In some cases, the rash can last as long as 2 to 4 weeks. Scarring is rarely a problem. As the rash is extremely itchy, often a soothing ointment is prescribed, such as calamine. In more serious cases, topical corticosteroids or antihistamines may be used. In extreme cases, the individual may need to take an oral corticosteroid.

Psoriasis   Psoriasis is a chronic, recurrent, inflammatory skin condition that results from the excessive development of epithelial cells in the epidermal layer of the skin. The condition, which can develop in infancy but occurs more commonly in adolescence or adulthood, is characterized by reddened patches of skin that are covered with thick, grayish or silvery-white scales of dry skin that can occur anywhere on the body. In some cases, the patches can be very itchy, whereas in others, the pruritus is mild. Common sites are the tops of the knees and bony prominences of the elbows. Psoriasis can also develop on the scalp and ears, and in 25% to 50% of cases, nail involvement (pitting) can occur (Rudy, 1993). Three percent of the population are estimated to have some form of psoriasis during their lifetime (Fine & Guest, 1996).

Typically, the cause of psoriasis is unknown; however, in 35% of cases, there is a familial history of the condition (Nicol & Hill, 1994). It is believed that in some cases psoriasis may be triggered by stress (Whaley & Wong, 1995). Treatment typically involves the application of coal tar preparations or topical corticosteroids. Some individuals appear to benefit from exposure to ultraviolet light (either natural or artificial). This type of therapy is referred to as **phototherapy** and is often prescribed in conjunction with pharmacologic therapy. Special shampoos are available for those who have the condition on their scalp.

Disorders of Pigmentation   Skin pigment is critical for protecting the skin and underlying structures from excessive ultraviolet radiation; however, some individuals experience conditions in which there is either (a) a change in the amount of pigment or (b) a change in the manner in which the pigment is dispersed in the skin (Eichenfield, 1996). Pigmentary disorders are very common and can range in severity from mild (i.e., primarily a cosmetic effect, as is the case of freckles) to serious (e.g., a systemic disorder, such as neurofibromatosis, an autosomal dominant condition that can result in developmental delay, seizures, speech defects, and scoliosis).

Disorders of pigmentation can be further subdivided into two groups: **hypopigmentation** (too little pigment) disorders and **hyperpigmentation** (too much pigment) disorders. Both types of disorders can have an adverse effect on a person's psychosocial development and self-image (Eichenfield, 1996).

Hypopigmentation disorders.   Occurring either congenitally or adventitiously, hypopigmentation disorders range from mild to severe. Regardless of the cause of the loss of pigment, individuals who do not have a normal amount of melanin in their skin are vulnerable to sunburn. Wearing adequate protection (e.g., sunscreen, wide-brimmed hats) is critical.

Persons born with a condition that makes them unable to produce melanin are said to have **albinism**. Such persons often have fair skin and hair. Those who also have **ocular albinism** (lacking pigment in the colored portion, or iris, of the eye) may have reduced visual acuity and are, in most cases, extremely photosensitive (sensitive to light).

Albinism is believed to occur at a rate of between 1 in 15,000 and 1 in 40,000 worldwide (Castiglia, 1992). However, it is known to affect as many as 1 in 200 individuals belonging to certain tribes of Native Americans, such as the Hopi, Zuni, and Jemez of the Southwest (McClellan & Moran, 1992). Some persons with albinism have a number of other systemic abnormalities, such as deafness and coagulation disorders (Rasmussen, 1996). The method of transmission of albinism, in most cases, is autosomal recessive.

Similar to albinism, **vitiligo** is a hypopigmentary condition in which a person experiences a loss of pigment **(depigmentation);** however, in this condition, only patches of the skin are affected. Vitiligo occurs in approximately 1% to 4% of persons in the United States. While it is not a congenital condition, it is common in children. Half of those that develop vitiligo do so before their 18th birthday (Rudy, 1993). The cause of vitiligo is unknown. It is believed to be an autoimmune disease (Eichenfield, 1996).

Hyperpigmentation disorders. Also either congenital or adventitious, hyperpigmentation disorders are characterized by lesions that occur, most frequently, in the form of spots (regular, round areas) or splotches (irregularly shaped areas). **Café au lait spots,** lesions that are the color of coffee with milk in it, are found in 10% to 20% of all children. Some can be more than 8 inches (20 cm) in size, and they can occur anywhere on the body. Most commonly the spots occur singly; however, if they are found in multiples (i.e., six or more spots greater than 0.02 inch [0.5 mm] in diameter), their presence may be indicative of **neurofibromatosis type 1 (von Recklinghausen disease),** an autosomal dominant condition that is characterized by numerous fibrous tumors of the nerves. Prevalence of this condition is believed to be 1 in 3,500 (Meyer, 1997). Café au lait spots can also develop during childhood or adolescence.

The most common form of benign hyperpigmentary lesion, developing during infancy or early childhood, is the **freckle.** Freckles are usually between 0.08 and 0.16 inch (2 to 4 mm) in diameter and range in color from light tan to brown. Freckles result from exposure of the skin to sunlight. In some individuals, the freckles are so numerous, the child or young adult has a mottled appearance.

In addition to the types of spots described above, some children are born with benign congenital tumors or tumor-like malformations, known as **congenital nevi** (pl.; **nevus,** sing.). These abnormally pigmented splotches, more commonly referred to as **birthmarks,** are differentiated on the basis of color and pattern. The most commonly occurring nevi are **salmon patches;** pale pink to red in color, these lesions, most commonly found at the nape of the neck, redden on crying. They occur in approximately 45% of all newborns and do not grow. Typically, they resolve within the first year of life, and no treatment is needed (Johnson, 1996). **Port-wine stains** (nevi flammeus) are flat reddish-purple patches that may increase in size as the child grows. Found most commonly on the face, they are one of the more obvious type of nevi. Laser treatment, while successful in many cases, can be extremely painful. **Acquired nevi,** those that occur any time after birth, are commonly referred to as **moles.** Approximately 90% of people have one or more acquired nevi; however, the incidence is less in pigmented races (Johnson, 1996).

All abnormally pigmented spots, especially acquired nevi, should be watched carefully for changes because a significant alteration may indicate a cancerous condition. The **ABCD system** of identifying changes, shown in Table 21.1, may be of assistance in monitoring the growth of a suspicious lesion. If any of the changes listed are noticed, the individual should be examined by a doctor (Rudy, 1993). **Malignant melanoma** (MM), a cancer of the cells that produce melanin, is rare in young children; however, it does occur frequently in adolescents and adults. It is more common in females than males, especially girls with fair skin. A family history of MM is a strong risk factor for the condition developing in childhood (Rudy, 1993). Without surgical treatment, the condition can be fatal.

Noninfectious Skin Disorders Resulting from Injury

Abrasions, Lacerations, and Punctures One of the most common injuries of early childhood is the scraping or rubbing off of skin that results from some type of friction. Referred to as **abrasions,** skinned knees and skinned elbows are part of growing up. Other types of integumentary injuries include **lacerations** (torn, jagged wounds) and **punctures** (wounds made by piercing). First-aid procedures for individuals who have had injuries to the epidermis are shown in Table 21.2.

Thermal Injuries Exposure of the skin to heat can result in a **thermal injury,** more commonly referred to as a **burn.** It has been estimated that 2 million

TABLE 21.1
The ABCD System of Identifying Changes in Nevi and Nevoid Tumors

A = Asymmetry	The two halves of the lesion become unequal in size or shape
B = Borders	The edges of the lesion become irregular in contour; indentations or notches develop
C = Color	A haphazard pattern of pigmentation occurs
D = Diameter	The lesion increases in size

TABLE 21.2
First Aid for Minor Abrasions, Lacerations, and Puncture Wounds

1. **Reassure the student.** Remember that some young children are terrified by the sight of blood. It is important to get the wound assessed, cleaned, and covered as quickly as possible.

2. **Examine the injury.**

   Abrasions: If minor, cleanse as directed below. If more than 15% of the body is involved, medical attention should be sought.

   Lacerations: If the cut is less than 1 inch (2.54 cm) long and less than 1/4 inch (6 mm) in depth, suturing will probably not be required. If the wound is straight and has a clean edge, it can probably be held together with tape rather than sutures. If the cut is more extensive or jagged, apply pressure to stem the bleeding, elevate the cut above the level of the heart (unless a fracture is suspected), and transport to a medical care facility.

   Punctures: If minor, remove puncturing object (e.g., remove splinter with tweezers) and cleanse as directed below. If major (e.g., knife wound to the head, chest, or abdomen), leave the puncturing object in place, secure with a donut-shaped dressing, and transport to a medical care facility.

   Note: Regardless of size, location, or type of injury, if the wound bleeds persistently, suturing will probably be required. Apply a pressure dressing to stem the bleeding and transport to a medical care facility. If the wound is contaminated with dirt and bacteria, the student may need a tetanus booster if he or she has not received one in the previous 5 years. With a cut to the face, stitches may be needed to prevent scarring.

3. **Cleanse the wound.**

   a. Wash your hands thoroughly.

   b. Wash the wound, scrubbing vigorously but gently with plain, warm, soapy running water for at least 5 minutes to remove all gravel and dirt and to prevent the debris from "tattooing" the skin permanently when it heals. If necessary, remove foreign matter with clean tweezers. Puncture wounds, once the puncturing object has been removed, should be soaked in warm, soapy water for 15 minutes.

   c. Rinse thoroughly with warm, running water. Dry the skin with cotton swabs. Always swab away from the wound.

4. **Dress the wound.**

   a. If the wound is in an area that will probably get dirty, cover the wound with a clean gauze pad or a Band-Aid. However, if possible, the wound should be left open to the air for faster healing.

   b. Do not apply any sprays, ointments, alcohol, or antiseptic preparations.

5. **If there is bruising, apply ice for 20–30 minutes.**

6. **Report the injury to the student's parents.**

   Note: If the student experiences pain, analgesics, such as acetaminophen, could be given if permission is obtained from the parents.

persons require medical treatment for burns annually in the United States; 100,000 of them require hospitalization. Between 30% and 40% of the patients are under the age of 15; the average age is 32 months (Antoon, 1996).

In addition to resulting from dry heat sources (e.g., fire, flame, hot objects), burns can result from exposure to corrosive chemical agents (e.g., cleaning agents, gasoline, paint removers, certain gases), electricity (e.g., a youngster biting an electrical cord), and ultraviolet rays (i.e., direct sunlight). Burns can also result from friction (e.g., skin being rubbed by a moving wheel or rope). **Scalds** are caused by moist heat (e.g., boiling liquids, steam, hot tar).

Since the effects of burns and scalds are similar, for the purpose of simplicity, injuries of this nature are simply referred to as burns.

Severity of a burn is often described in terms of (1) **depth** of injury and (2) **amount of body surface area (BSA)** affected. In general, the deeper the burn, the greater the degree of damage. However, it is difficult to determine depth visually, and all major burns should be seen by medical staff. Similarly, the greater the BSA affected, the more significant the burn. However, some areas of the body are not only more susceptible to damage (e.g., eyes, lungs), but the damage that can occur can be far more serious in the long run than damage to other parts of the body.

Depth of burns. Burns, classified on the basis of depth, are rated as first-, second-, third-, or fourth-degree burns.

A first-degree burn involves only the epidermis. This type of burn is also referred to as a **partial-**

thickness burn. Typically, in a first-degree burn, the skin becomes reddened (**erythematous**) and there may be swelling (edema). Even though the area may be painful, in this type of burn there is no blistering. There may be **desquamation** (peeling) that typically heals without any scarring. Healing time is typically 2 to 5 days.

A second-degree burn is also a partial-thickness burn; however, the damage extends into the dermis and blistering occurs. The skin becomes edematous and the individual experiences considerable pain. Usually there is little or no scarring after the skin heals. Healing time is typically 5 to 21 days. If the burn becomes infected, the amount of time for proper healing to occur increases considerably.

A third-degree burn is a full-thickness burn and by definition involves all of the skin layers. Third-degree burns can range from white to cherry-red in color. In some cases, the skin appears to be dry and leathery. Because of the damage to nerve endings, a person experiencing a third-degree burn may experience little or no pain. Skin that has been destroyed to this degree is not able to regenerate; consequently, skin grafts are required for healing to occur. Scarring is typical. The individual is usually hospitalized for a long time.

A fourth-degree burn is the most severe type of burn. It extends beyond the skin and affects muscles, tendons, or bones. This type of burn is similar to a third-degree burn in appearance and also requires grafting. Hospitalization is always lengthy.

Amount of body surface. The area of skin that is affected can range from a small localized burn to one that affects a major portion or all of the body. There have been a number of approaches to describing the extent of a thermal injury; the most common approach is the **rule of nines.** In this method, each part of the body, except for the region between the legs (the perineum), is designated to be 9% or a multiple of 9% of the total surface. For the older child the head is 9%, each arm is 9%, each leg is 18%, and the anterior and posterior trunk are each 18%. The perineal area is 1% of the body surface. While these areas are easy to calculate, the proportional areas of a young infant are dissimilar to those of an older child or adult (i.e., the infant has a larger head and smaller limbs compared to an older child), and consequently, the system is not very accurate. In the young child, the head is considered to be 18% of the total body surface area, whereas each leg is approximately 14%. Some have recommended that the rule

of nines be used only in those over age 14 (Antoon, 1996).

Overall severity of burns. The extent of a burn is often described as being either mild or major. In determining the severity, the depth of the burn *and* the amount of body surface are considered simultaneously.

In terms of partial-thickness burns, a burn is classified as minor if less than 10% of the body is affected. In terms of full-thickness burns, a burn is minor if it involves less than 2% of the total body surface (Whaley & Wong, 1995). The classification of minor is also made if (a) the burn does not include the hands, face, feet, or perineum; (b) the injury is not circumferential, i.e., does not completely encircle the neck, chest, or extremities; (c) the burn is not caused by an electrical source; (d) there are no significant concurrent injuries; and (e) there is no history of chronic or severe illness. A burn is also considered minor if, in addition to the above, the individual is over the age of 4 (Archambeau-Jones, Simmons, & Feller, 1994).

A partial-thickness burn that covers more than 25% of the body and a full-thickness burn that involves more than 10% of the total body surface would be considered major (Whaley & Wong, 1995). In addition, a burn is classified as major if it (a) involves the face, hands, feet, or perineum; (b) is circumferential; (c) is caused by high-tension electrical sources; or (d) is caused by inhalation of fumes. These types of burns are all considered major, regardless of BSA affected (Antoon, 1996). Burns that result from child abuse or neglect are always considered to be major, as are burns in which the child is less than 4 years of age (Archambeau-Jones et al., 1994).

Treatment. First-aid treatment for minor and major burns is shown in Table 21.3. Typically, minor burns heal without any major sequelae in a relatively short time; however, in the case of major burns, it is not uncommon for the individual to spend weeks or months in the hospital undergoing prolonged, painful treatments. Whaley and Wong (1991), in discussing the restrictive hospitalization of burn victims, suggested that many children "emerge from the experience with scars to both body and personality that profoundly affect their social and emotional development" (p. 1298).

The primary long-term goals of therapy for a person with a major burn are for him or her to (a) remain free of infection, thereby permitting the skin to

TABLE 21.3
First Aid for Burns

MINOR BURNS

1. **Stop the burning process.** Apply cool water to burn (e.g., cool water compresses) or hold burned area under cool running water. In cases in which the injury results from a corrosive chemical, flood the part (e.g., hand, eye) continuously with running water for at least 5–10 minutes. *Do not use ice.*

2. **Reassure the student.**

3. **Leave small burns exposed to air.** Do not apply any lotions or ointments to wound. Do not apply butter or any oil dressings.

4. **Cover loosely with dry, nonstick dressing if risk of damage or contamination.**

5. **Observe for signs of infection.** Do not prick any blisters that form.

6. **Notify parents of injury.**

MAJOR BURNS

1. **Stop the burning process.**

   Fire: Lay the student down and wrap with blanket or similar nonflammable object (e.g., coat) to stop combustion. Avoid covering head. Direct smoke away from the student's head. All preschool children should be taught to "stop, drop, and roll" if their clothing catches on fire.

   Electrical: Disconnect power source or break contact by moving wires away from the student with a nonmetal object (e.g., broom handle, wooden oar).

   Chemical/Smoke Fumes: Remove source of fumes (e.g., smother chemicals) or remove the student from source. Call for help even if there are no signs of a burn. Damage to lungs, if not treated immediately, can be fatal.

2. **Assess for adequate airway and breathing.** If not breathing, begin mouth-to-mouth resuscitation.

3. **Do not try to cool burned area,** as large burn areas result in a decreased body temperature and put the student at greater risk. **If burn is caused by corrosive chemical, burn site should be flushed with water** (e.g., place student in shower). Clothing should be removed from involved areas.

3. **Remove burned clothing or clothing saturated with hot liquids if not sticking to skin.** Remove constrictive objects (e.g., rings, bracelets, shoes) before swelling occurs. Remove all objects that continue to retain heat (e.g., buckles, shoes). Raise limbs to reduce swelling.

4. **Cover wound with clean, nonstick cloth** (e.g., sheet, pillow case). Keep the student warm. Do not give any fluids or food by mouth.

5. **Call 911, or transport to medical facility immediately.**

---

heal without further complications, (b) encourage growth or regrowth of skin tissue, and (c) regain functional use of the burned areas. In addition to medical and surgical procedures (e.g., removal of necrotic tissue; skin grafts), proper positioning and splinting techniques, along with intensive physiotherapy focusing on full range of motion of affected joints, are the main approaches to minimizing scar formation and avoiding the development of contractures. In addition, a person who has suffered a major burn usually is fitted with a pressure (elasticized) garment as soon as the wounds are sufficiently healed, which is worn for 23 hours a day for up to 18 months after injury to discourage the formation of scar tissue. These specialized garments can be custom-made to fit virtually any part of the body (e.g., gloves for the hands, socks for the feet); specialized appliances (e.g., face masks) have been instrumental in decreasing the amount of scar tissue that forms.

The following points are important to remember:

1 *Students who have suffered a burn may be out of school for several months.* Those with severe burns may have to return to the hospital on a regular basis for reconstructive or plastic surgery.

2 *When the student returns to school, he or she will most likely be wearing some type of compression garment to prevent the formation of excess scar tissue.* During physical activity, these garments can make the individual exceedingly warm. Some students may need to be excused from full participation. Students

recovering from serious burns are typically advised not to participate in contact sports until the scar tissue is mature enough to stand a certain degree of pressure.

3 *Rehabilitation is not easy.* Whaley and Wong (1991) perhaps best summarized some of the issues faced by burn patients in the following quotation:

> Life becomes a struggle for children after burn trauma. They are puzzled, confused, and bombarded by a new way of life in a frightening world of strange people, things, and language. They wonder why this has happened to *them*—what they have done that they should be punished so. Past experiences cannot serve them in this crisis. They do not understand the "ugliness" and disfigurement they see as their bodies. They wonder, "Am I going to die?" (p. 1321)

4 *Students who are recovering from burns may not be able to tolerate extremes of temperature* (Falvo, 1991). Lack of fat insulation and increased sensitivity of skin grafts necessitate extra care when the student is outside.

5 *Education is a major key to preventing burns.* All children should be taught the hazards of fire and what to do if their clothing catches on fire (i.e., stop, drop, and roll) or a fire breaks out at school or home (e.g., crawl to safety). Routine fire drills should be held at school; staff from the local fire station often offer educational programs that are extremely valuable.

Cold Injuries Exposure to extreme cold can also result in an integumentary injury. Particularly vulnerable are the nose, ears, fingers, and toes. If the dermal tissues are *not* actually frozen, the term **chilblain** or **pernio** is used to describe the redness and swelling of the exposed flesh that may occur after exposure to cold. If the cellular water in the flesh becomes frozen, the term **frostbite** is used to describe the condition.

Depth of frostbite. Like thermal burns, the terms first-, second-, third- and fourth-degree are used to describe the depth of damage.

First-degree frostbite, also referred to as **"frost nip,"** involves mild freezing of the epidermis. Upon rewarming, blisters do not form.

Second-degree frostbite involves the epidermis and part of the dermis (i.e., partial-thickness frostbite) and is white in color. To the touch, the skin may feel hard and the youngster may complain that the area feels numb. In partial-thickness frostbite, as the affected part is rewarmed, it is typical for the person to complain of pain, burning, and itching. The skin, as it warms, becomes red and inflamed, and in some cases, it may become edematous. Typically, the area is extra sensitive to the cold for several weeks after the injury.

Third-degree or full-thickness frostbite involves all of the epidermis and the dermis, though it may not differ significantly from partial-thickness frostbite in appearance. However, in full-thickness frostbite, the symptoms typically are more severe (e.g., severe swelling) and it is common for blistering to occur 24 to 48 hours after injury. The extent of the freezing determines the amount of necrosis (death) of the skin and the degree of sensation. While the tissues are frozen, there may be no pain; however, upon rewarming, the pain may be intense.

Fourth-degree frostbite occurs when the epidermis, dermis, and hypodermis are frozen. Complete necrosis with gangrene is common, and amputation of the affected areas (i.e., toes, fingers, nose) may be required.

Treatment. First aid for frostbite is shown in Table 21.4. Frostbite damage can be more severe if the affected area is rewarmed and then refrozen (Rieg et al., 1990). In cases where continuous warmth is not available, it is better to wait before rewarming.

The following points should be heeded by school staff:

1 *To prevent frostbite, children and young adults should be encouraged to dress appropriately (i.e., several layers of light clothing under waterproof outerwear) and to not play outside when it is excessively cold.*

2 *If hands or feet begin to "sting," children and young adults should be instructed to warm their extremities (e.g., by placing their hands in their armpits). Rubbing frozen areas should be discouraged because tissue damage may result.*

Insect Bites and Stings Many insects obtain nourishment by biting human skin. In most cases, a bite or sting is inconsequential; however, the consequences

TABLE 21.4
First Aid for Frostbite

PARTIAL-THICKNESS FROSTBITE:

1. Move the student to a warm environment.
2. Remove any clothing that is wet.
3. Wrap the student loosely in a blanket.
4. Handle all frostbitten areas with care to minimize the possibility of further trauma.
5. If the student experiences pain, analgesics, such as acetaminophen, could be given if permission is obtained from the parents.
6. Rewarm the affected body part by immersing in warm, agitated water (104°F to 110°F, or 40°C to 43°C).
7. Elevate the affected body part(s) to minimize edema.

FULL-THICKNESS FROSTBITE:

1. Transport to the emergency room (**CALL 911**), as the student may need a variety of warming techniques (e.g., gastric lavages or enemas) and will need fluid volume replacement (e.g., intravenous therapy).

---

can sometimes be serious, specifically when the individual is hypersensitive.[1] Stings from insects of the order *Hymenoptera* (honeybees, wasps, hornets, yellow jackets, fire ants), as well as bites by arthropods, especially arachnids (scorpions, tarantulas, brown spiders, black widow spiders), result in approximately 50 deaths per year in the United States. While only 1 to 2 deaths occur in children per year, it is estimated that nearly 3% of children are allergic to insect stings (Friday, 1996). First aid for individuals who have been bitten is shown in Table 21.5.

1 *All students should be taught how to prevent being bitten or stung by insects.* Suggestions are given in Table 21.6. If schools are located in areas where flying insects are a major problem, windows should be covered with screens. In addition, all damp areas should be drained, all insect nests removed from school property, and all garbage properly stored in covered containers to prevent attracting insects, as well as rodents. (Gold, Sussman, Loubser, & Binkley, 1996).

2 *All students should be taught to recognize the various plants and trees that can result in an allergic response (e.g., poison ivy, oak, sumac).* School

---

[1] For further information on hypersensitivity reactions and anaphylactic shock, see chapter 22.

staff should ensure that poisonous plants are not permitted to grow in areas adjacent to the school yard.

Noninfectious Conditions Affecting the Skin Appendages

Disorders of the Nails A number of conditions can affect the human nail. Some conditions are congenital (e.g., **nail dystrophy** or **onychodystrophy,** a condition that occurs at birth in which the nail plate is malformed); others are adventitious (e.g., **ingrown toenail,** a condition in which the margin of the toenail grows into the skin of the toe, often caused by ill-fitting shoes). Some nail disorders are indicative of other types of health problems. For example, **clubbing,** a condition in which the nail plate is curved downward, is associated with certain cardiovascular, pulmonary, and gastrointestinal diseases, whereas the opposite, **koilonychia,** more commonly referred to as "spoon nails," a condition in which the nail curves outward, may be indicative of iron deficiency anemia. Nail disorders are generally not severe; however, children and young adults with abnormal nails, like those with skin problems or hair disorders, may be teased by their peers and suffer socially and emotionally from their condition.

Disorders of the Hair Disorders of the hair can be either congenital or acquired. Two conditions often seen in children and young adults are (a) premature

TABLE 21.5
First Aid for Bites and Stings

FIRST AID FOR INSECT BITES (FLIES, GNATS, MOSQUITOES, ETC.)

1. Treat with antipruritic agents (e.g., calamine lotion) or other household products (e.g., lemon juice; paste made with aspirin or baking soda or meat tenderizer). Cool compresses or a cool bath may alleviate some of the swelling and pain.

2. If the student continues to show discomfort, with the permission of the student's parents, an oral antihistamine may be given to bring relief.

3. Try to prevent the student from scratching the bites. Once the skin is broken, the risk of a secondary infection is greater.

FIRST AID FOR STINGS (BEE, WASP, ANT, ETC.)

1. Remove stinger[a] by gently scraping horizontally with your fingernail, a plastic credit card, or a clean, dull knife. *Do not pull out. Do not squeeze.* Squeezing or using a pair of tweezers or your fingers to remove stinger may result in more venom being released. Stinger can sometimes also be removed by covering the bite with transparent adhesive tape and then peeling the tape off.

2. Cleanse with soap and water.

3. Apply a cold compress to relieve pain. *Do not use ice directly on skin.* Apply antipruritic agents (see above).

4. Elevate extremity to reduce swelling.

5. Administer antihistamines (if needed and permitted). Discourage the student from scratching. Typically the reaction subsides in a few hours.

6. Observe for any further reaction (e.g., muscle spasms, vomiting, severe pain). Transport to medical care facility if student appears ill.

IN CASE OF SEVERE ALLERGIC REACTION

Defined as swelling around eyes or mouth; difficulty breathing; frothing at the mouth; presence of hives; severe nausea; and vomiting.

1. Administer epinephrine[b] (e.g., EpiPen) if available, or call 911.

2. Perform CPR if the person stops breathing.

---

[a] Note: Bees may leave a stinger. Other insects do not.
[b] See chapter 22 for further information on the use of an EpiPen.

loss of hair (alopecia) and (b) development of excess hair (hypertrichosis).

Alopecia. A person has approximately 100,000 hair follicles on his or her body (McClellan & Moran, 1992). If a child or young adult loses hair prematurely (e.g., due to an endocrine disorder, a drug reaction, a reaction to a specific hair preparation, a skin disease or infection, or an anticancer treatment), he or she is said to have **alopecia**. Alopecia can be partial (e.g., **alopecia areata**, characterized by round or oval bald patches on the scalp or other hairy parts of the body) or total (i.e., **alopecia universalis**). If a person loses all the hair on his or her head, but does not lose the hair from the rest of the body, the person has **alopecia totalis**. In some cases the alopecia results from the actions of the person with the condition. For example, in **traumatic alopecia,** hair is lost around the margins of the scalp as a result of the hair being pulled to form braids,

ponytails, or corn rows. If an individual pulls his or her hair to the extent that there is a significant loss, the person suffers from **trichotillomania,** a psychiatric condition often seen in individuals who are mentally challenged. In many cases the cause of the alopecia is unknown. Alopecia is usually not permanent, unless the hair loss is a result of aging.

Hypertrichosis. Excessive growth of hair in a masculine distribution pattern, known as **hypertrichosis** or **hirsutism,** is a relatively uncommon disorder. In most cases, the cause is hormone dysfunction. However, it can result from the administration of certain types of drugs. In some cases, there is a familial tendency to develop excessive body hair. By treating the underlying cause, in many cases the growth can be halted; in some cases, the excessive hair must be removed (e.g., by means of electrolysis, chemical depilation, shaving, plucking, rubbing with pumice).

TABLE 21.6
Preventing Insect Bites and Stings

When outdoors, students should be encouraged to:

1. Wear insect repellent containing DEET (diethyltoluamide). Reapply regularly, especially after sweating, swimming, or exposure to rain. Note that some individuals have an adverse reaction (i.e., seizures) to certain repellents; therefore caution should be taken (e.g., the repellent could be applied to the clothes, not the skin).

2. Wear long pants and a long-sleeved shirt. Tuck pants into socks and tuck shirt into pants. Avoid loose-fitting garments, because insects can become trapped inside. Wear shoes or sneakers and socks at all times.

3. Avoid wearing brightly colored clothing (especially blue or yellow clothing), dark clothing, or flowery prints.

4. Avoid wearing shiny jewelry.

5. Avoid using perfumes, scented cosmetics or soaps, and scented hair spray.

6. Avoid places where the insects may be contacted (e.g., tall grass; underbrush; woodpiles; swamps; flower beds). Stay indoors for recess and lunch during bee or wasp season. Keep automobile windows closed at all times when driving. Leave the room if a stinging insect flies in.

7. Avoid eating food or drinking sweet drinks outdoors. If drinking outdoors, always pour drink into a cup and dispose of cans or bottles in covered container.

Note: **Students who have a known hypersensitivity to insect bites should wear a Medic-Alert bracelet and carry an emergency anaphylaxis kit (e.g., EpiPen) with them at all times.**[a]

[a] For further information on hypersensitivity disorders, see chapter 22.

Disorders of the Glands As mentioned in the introduction, the sebaceous glands secrete sebum, a greasy material that lubricates both the skin and the hair. Acne and seborrheic dermatitis are common disorders of the sebaceous glands.

Acne. From the Greek work *akme,* meaning point, **acne** is a chronic inflammatory skin condition that typically occurs either in or near a sebaceous gland. Two groups of individuals are particularly susceptible to developing acne: newborn infants **(acne neonatorum)** and adolescents and young adults **(acne vulgaris).** In persons between the ages of 12 and 25, it has been estimated that 85% have acne vulgaris (Nicol & Hill, 1994). Acne vulgaris can occur in children as young as age 8 (Gellis, 1996).

In both infants and teenagers, **comedones** (pl.; **comedo,** sing.), commonly referred to as **blackheads,** typically form on the nose, cheeks, and forehead. In older children and adults, comedones are also often found on the neck or upper trunk. In older children, **papules** (small, raised, solid skin lesions), **pustules** (fluid-containing lesions), or **abscesses** (pus-filled cavities) may also occur. Treatment typically involves the administration of topical antibiotics or oral antibiotics. In severe cases, corticosteroid injections directly into the nodule may be prescribed. Persons with acne should be encouraged not to pick or squeeze the lesions because this may lead to tissue damage or secondary infection.

Seborrheic dermatitis. Common in children under the age of 6 months and in adolescents, **seborrheic dermatitis** is believed to result from the increased production and accumulation of sebum; however, its exact cause is unknown. Increased hormone levels found in children in these age groups may contribute to the development of seborrhea. Characterized by greasy scales, which are either dry or moist, and yellowish crusts, seborrhea is found most often in areas of the body that are naturally hairy (e.g., scalp, eyelids, and groin). Special shampoos (e.g., tar shampoo) and prescription ointments (e.g., topical antibiotics) are commonly applied to prevent the development of scales. Scaly tissue can be removed with a comb or brush.

In young infants, seborrheic dermatitis is often referred to as **cradle cap.** In older children and young adults, seborrheic dermatitis of the scalp is commonly referred to as **dandruff.** If the eyelids develop seborrhea, the lash follicles and sebaceous glands of the eyelids can become swollen and red. This condition is known as **seborrheic blepharitis** and is more common in adolescents than in young children.

TABLE 21.7

Common Bacterial Skin Infections Found in Children and Young Adults

Condition	Symptoms and Educational Implications
IMPETIGO *Agent:* Streptococcal or staphylococcal *Source of Transmission:* Weeping lesions *Mode of Transmission:* Direct physical contact; vehicle-borne by fomites. In many cases, the portal of entry is an insect bite or a cut; in others, impetigo is secondary to an infection of the respiratory tract.	*Symptoms:* Infection of the superficial skin layers, often recognized by the moist, honey-colored or brown, crusty areas. Common sites for the lesions, which range in size from small to large, include the face, forearms, and lower parts of the legs. Often multiple lesions are evident. Those whose impetigo is caused by beta-hemolytic streptococci, particularly those under the age of 6, may develop acute glomerulonephritis after the lesions have healed. Puffiness around the eyes and blood in the urine are signs of this complication. **Students with impetigo should not attend school or day care until they have been taking antibiotics for a minimum of 48 hours and/or until the lesions are completely dry** (Nicol & Hill, 1994).
FURUNCLES CARBUNCLES *Agent:* Staphylococcal bacteria *Source of Transmission:* Weeping lesions *Mode of Transmission:* Direct physical contact; indirect vehicle-borne (e.g., infected washcloth).	A furuncle is a localized abscess of the skin or subcutaneous tissue caused by the obstruction of a sebaceous gland or the ingrowth of a hair follicle, also known as a boil. A carbuncle is a more severe abscess than a furuncle. *Symptoms:* Abscess can occur anywhere in the body; the most common spots are the neck, back, buttocks, and thighs. **Students with furuncles and carbuncles, even if they are draining, should be allowed to attend school as long as the abscesses are properly covered. If the student is in severe pain, school attendance may be inappropriate** (Nicol & HIll, 1994).
HORDEOLUM (STY OR STYE) *Agent:* Staphylococcal bacteria *Source of Transmission:* Discharge from eyes *Mode of Transmission:* Direct physical contact; indirect vehicle-borne via fomites.	A hordeolum is actually a furuncle that originates in the sebaceous gland of an eyelash. *Symptoms:* In most cases, an individual complains of pain, and the eye appears red and swollen. **Typically, a stye will last 4 or 5 days. Students need not be kept out of school. Students should wash their hands frequently to avoid spread.** Some persons have styes repeatedly. They should be encouraged to have their vision checked because they may have a refractive error; i.e., they may be either near- or farsighted and, consequently, rub their eyes more frequently than normal. It is the rubbing, *not* the refractive error, that results in the development of hordeola. To prevent spread, young adolescent girls should be encouraged not to share eye makeup. They should also be encouraged to throw out their eye makeup at least every 3 months.

❦ Infectious Skin Conditions

Diseases of the skin that are infectious are typically caused by **bacteria, viruses,** or **fungi.** Some conditions result from the infestation of some type of **parasite,** such as a louse or a mite.[2] In most situations, a break in the skin allows the pathogenetic microorganism to invade the body. The cause of the infection is commonly determined by examining the skin lesion and by taking a culture of the lesion to establish the origin of the condition. Treatment depends on the type of infectious agent (e.g., antibiotics for bacterial infections; antiviral agents for viral infections).

The conditions described in this section are **contagious,** and the individual may transmit the infection to other people that he or she is in contact with. The most common form of spread for integumentary conditions is either by (a) **direct transmission** (e.g., physical or sexual contact; airborne "spray") or (b) **indirect transmission** (e.g., vehicle-borne, or as a result of contact with infected items, referred to as **fomites;** vector-borne, or by means of insects or animal bites). For further information on modes of transmission, see the introduction to part IX. In this section, infectious conditions that affect only the skin are covered.[3]

In terms of schooling, students with contagious conditions (e.g., boils, herpes simplex, scabies, molluscum contagiosum) typically are able to participate in a regular school program. However, they are usually prevented from participating in certain activities, such as gymnastics with mats, martial arts, wrestling, or other collision, contact, or limited contact sports, while they are contagious (American Academy of Pediatrics, 1994).

Common Bacterial Infections

Bacterial skin infections are very common in children; the most common is impetigo. Other common conditions include furuncles, carbuncles, and hordeola. They are described briefly in Table 21.7.

---

[2] For further information on bacteria, viruses, fungi, and parasites, see chapter 23.

[3] Systemic conditions (i.e., those that involve the whole body rather that a localized area), which also may have some type of integumentary manifestation, are covered in chapter 23. For further information on how to handle contaminated body fluids, see chapter 24.

Common Viral Infections

While there are more than 200 known pathogenic viruses, not all result in cutaneous involvement. Some of the more common integumentary conditions include cold sores, warts, and a common condition with an uncommon name, molluscum contagiosum. They are shown in Table 21.8.

Common Fungal Infections

The most common fungal infections in children and young adults are dermatophytosis and candidiasis (Table 21.9). Fungal infections generally are not life-threatening; however, to an individual whose immune system is compromised (e.g., a child with a transplanted organ, an adolescent with AIDS), they can be fatal. Not only can skin be infected by fungus, but so can the nail structures. Both in children and in adults, fungal infection of the nail **(onychomycosis)** is common. A typical symptom is **onycholysis,** the separation of the nail plate from the nail bed.

Common Parasitic Infestations

The most common parasitic infections that affect the integumentary system in children and young adults are lice and scabies (Table 21.10). Other parasitic infections include roundworms, tapeworms, and pinworms. These types of infestation occur within the body (specifically in the GI tract) and are described in greater detail in chapter 23.

❦ Educational Implications and Teaching Tips

Regardless of the type of skin disorder, a common characteristic of many integumentary conditions is **pruritus,** or itchiness. Aside from it being a nuisance, pruritus can be potentially serious because it often leads to scratching, which in turn results in the epidermis being damaged to the extent that the body becomes vulnerable to the invasion of potentially more serious pathogenic organisms.

1   *Even though it is difficult to stop youngsters from scratching, they can be taught to apply pressure to the itchy surface, rather than scratching it, to obtain some relief.* Gently rubbing the opposite

TABLE 21.8

Common Viral Skin Infections Found in Children and Young Adults

---

HERPES SIMPLEX

Agent: Herpes simplex virus I or II

Source of Transmission: Weeping blisters

Mode of Transmission: Direct physical or sexual contact

Symptoms: An infection of the skin or mucous membranes by **type I herpes simplex virus (HSV-I)** is more commonly known as a **cold sore** or **fever blister.** The most frequent site of infection is the area around the mouth, both inside and outside, and the nose; however, lesions can occur anywhere on the body. Herpes infections that occur in the genital area are typically caused by the **type II herpes simplex virus (HSV II).**[a]

Students with type I herpes simplex virus do not need to be isolated from their peers. However, they do need to be taught how to control the spread of the condition.

WARTS (or VERRUCA)

Agent: Human papillomavirus (HPV)

Source of Transmission: Lesion of infected person

Mode of Transmission: Direct physical or sexual contact; spread from one part of the body to another (i.e., autoinnoculation) is also common.

In the case of plantar warts, transmitted by means of indirect vehicle-borne contact (e.g., from the locker room floor)

Symptoms: There are a number of types of warts, the most common being the **common wart** or **verruca vulgaris,** found in most cases on the fingers. Two other common types are **anogenital warts,** found on or around the mucous membranes of the vagina, rectum or urethra, and **plantar warts,** found on the soles of the feet.

Students with warts do not need to be kept out of school. However, they do need to be taught how to control the spread of the condition.

Teachers should be alert to teasing that may occur and report incidents to the student's parents.

MOLLUSCUM CONTAGIOSUM

Agent: Member of the poxvirus group

Source of Transmission: Lesion of infected persons

Mode of Transmission: Direct physical or sexual contact

Symptoms: Translucent, flesh-toned pearly white papules, 0.08 to 0.6 inch (2 to 15 mm) in diameter, occurring either singularly or in multiple groups on the trunk, face, and extremities of young children and in the anogenital region of sexually active adolescents and young adults.

Students with molluscum contagiosum do not need to be kept out of school. However, they do need to be taught how to control the spread of the condition.

---

[a] See chapter 23.

limb in the corresponding spot may also lessen the itch (Nicol & Hill, 1994). Since young children cannot be watched at all times, their fingernails should be kept short, and if all else fails, they should be given mitts or gloves to wear, particularly when asleep or not being closely supervised by a caregiver. A major form of treatment for itchiness is the administration of specific antipruritic agents (e.g., topical anesthetics, corticosteroids, or antihis-tamines) in the form of a gel, cream, or ointment. In addition, some are given oral antihistamines to reduce the itch; however, these drugs may cause drowsiness, which may, in turn, lead to poor academic performance.

If a student is being treated for a skin condition, school staff should monitor compliance. Some treatment protocols require that a student apply a lotion or gel periodically throughout the day. In

TABLE 21.9
Common Fungal Skin Infections Found in Children and Young Adults

---

DERMATOPHYTOSIS (RINGWORM or TINEA)

Agent: Dermatophyte fungus

Source of Transmission: Weeping lesions

Mode of Transmission: Indirect vehicle-borne via infected fomites (e.g., comb, hat, towel); in some cases, direct physical contact from person to person; can also be transmitted by certain animals (i.e., vector-borne), such as the person's cat or dog.

Symptoms: Red, scaly, raised skin lesions that spread outward to form circular, ring-shaped lesions with a clear central portion. In younger children, the most common forms are **tinea capitis** (infection of the scalp and hair, characterized by dandruff, followed by patchy hair loss) and **tinea corporis** (infection of the non-hairy skin of the body). Athlete's foot, or **tinea pedis,** is common in adolescents and adults. Other common sites include the face (**tinea faciei),** the groin area (**tinea cruris,** or **jock itch**), the hands (**tinea manum),** and the nailbeds (**tinea unguium**). In most cases, ringworm is very itchy, and in some cases, the lesions can become quite painful.

Students with ringworm do not need to be kept out of school. However, they do need to be taught how to control the spread of the condition.

CANDIDIASIS

Agent: Yeast, *Candida albicans*

Source of Transmission: Weeping lesions

Mode of Transmission: Direct physical or sexual contact

Symptoms: Three different types with different symptoms: (a) candidiasis of the mucous membranes, in particular the mucous membranes of the mouth and vaginal area; (b) candidiasis of the skin and nails, or cutaneous candidiasis; and (c) mucocutaneous candidiasis, a combination of the two.

Candida infection of the mouth is commonly referred to as **thrush** and is characterized by whitish, cheesy looking patches on the tongue that when scraped off reveal a raw and inflamed underlying surface. Cutaneous candidiasis, typically evidenced as patches of deep red, oozing skin, is commonly found in skin folds (e.g., diaper area, neck area).

Students with candida do not need to be removed from school while being treated. However, since the infection can be spread from person to person, items that may be contaminated (e.g., clothing, combs, pillows) must not be shared.

---

most cases, treatment is completed at home; however, if the student needs to treat the condition during school hours, a private room should be made available.

2 *Disorders of the integumentary system can be devastating to children and young adults.* Rudy (1993) stated the following:

> The skin is more than a simple, flexible, passive covering for the body's internal organs. Instead, it is a dynamic, complex organ with many protective, metabolic, immunologic, and interactive tasks of its own. The skin is the outer self we present to the world. When it is healthy and attractive, it boosts morale and self-confidence. However, when it is marred by lesions or trauma, it can become a physical, social, and emotional handicap. (p. 1845)

Similarly, Falvo (1991) made the following comments:

> The skin, exposed and readily observable, determines to a great extent an individual's appearance to others, and it is through personal appearance that others build an image about an individual. The individual, in turn, observes the reactions of others and incorporates it into his or her own self-image. Consequently, conditions that affect the skin can have a considerable impact on an individual's perception and attitudes. (p. 271)

Teachers should be sensitive to the student's need to be accepted by others and be particularly alert to situations in which teasing or ridiculing occurs. Teachers should avoid designing activities that may place the student in an awkward situation, such as a game that may involve the students coming in direct contact with one another, e.g., holding hands.

TABLE 21.10
Common Parasitic Skin Infections Found in Children and Young Adults

LICE

Agent: Wingless insect of the order *Anoplura*

Source of Transmission: Blood

Mode of Transmission: Direct or indirect contact

Symptoms: Typically found on the head, the body, or the pubic region. If a person is infested with lice, he or she is said to have **pediculosis**.

Head Lice. Referred to colloquially as a "cootie," known medically as the *pediculus humanus capitis,* head lice can live for 40 to 50 days on a host. If the louse becomes separated, i.e., it loses its ability to feed on the person's blood, survival is limited to between 6 and 20 hours (Rudy, 1993). Head lice need to obtain nourishment from their human host at least five times a day. Head lice multiply rapidly. Each female is capable of laying eggs, which in turn are "glued" to the individual's hair shafts until they mature, roughly 7 to 10 days later. Head lice can easily be passed from individual to individual if there is sharing of contaminated combs, brushes, headgear (e.g., hats, headbands), and headsets.

Pubic Lice. *Phthirus pubis,* the louse found in the groin area, often referred to as the "crab louse," lays eggs, which attach to the pubic hair or any other accessible hairs (e.g., beard, hair in the armpits, eyelashes, scalp). The life span of a crab louse is similar to that of a head louse, and like the head louse, pubic lice reproduce rapidly. While it is generally thought that crab lice can only be spread by means of sexual intercourse, such is not the case. Crab lice can also live independently from their hosts for short periods of time, and consequently, the infestation can be spread by means of sharing bed linen, towels, and clothing.

Body Lice. *Pediculus humanus corporis,* the body louse, has a slightly shorter life span than the head louse, between 30 and 40 days, and like head or pubic lice, it is able to live separate from the human host. In fact, body lice prefer living separate, typically in the seams of clothing, bedding, and mattresses and only "jump" onto a host to obtain nourishment. Body lice are spread by direct contact (e.g., through the sharing of infected clothes).

Students with lice are typically not required to keep away from school, even though some individuals and groups (e.g., the National Pediculosis Association) have recommended that students be prevented from attending school until they are completely free of nits (Whaley & Wong, 1991). Students should be allowed to return to school 24 hours after the application of an effective pediculicide (Cordell, Solomon, & Hale, 1996). Because of the possibility that nits will be missed, it is important that the students be treated at least twice, with 10–14 days elapsing between treatments.

SCABIES

Agent: Mite, *Sarcoptes scabiei*

Source of Transmission: Eggs, larvae, or fecal material produced by the adult mite

Mode of Transmission: Direct (physical contact); indirect (vector-borne); commonly transmitted by the sharing of bed linens and bed clothing (i.e., vehicle-borne)

Symptoms: The female mite, after copulation, enters the skin for the purpose of laying her eggs. In infants and young children, the webs of the fingers are the most common site of infestation; other areas include the wrists, thighs, buttocks, soles and medial aspects of the feet, and the neck. In some cases the burrows can be seen as grayish-brown, wavy threadlike lesions, and the mite as a black dot at the end of the tunnel; however, since the lesions and the animal are so minute, they are often missed. Typically, there is a delay between the infestation and the beginning of the intense itching that is common in the condition. The incubation period can be as little as 2 weeks or as much as 4 months. The itch often becomes more severe at night and often results in the infected person being kept awake for long periods.

As scabies is most commonly transmitted by the sharing of bed linens and bed clothing, it is generally *not* thought that the likelihood of the disease being spread from student-to-student or student-to-adult in the school setting is great.

Students with scabies do not need to be isolated from school. However, it is recommended that all persons who have close contact with the affected student be treated.

Staff persons in direct contact (i.e., touching, holding an affected student) should wash his or her hands carefully after contact (Whaley & Wong, 1991).

3 *Particularly distressing to a student with an integumentary disorder is facial disfigurement.*
Falvo (1991) described the reactions of others to this type of injury in the following passage:

> Visible disabilities provoke greater discrimination and social stigma than do invisible disabilities. Skin disorders, especially if they involve the face, evoke even more profound responses from others. People may feel uneasy in the presence of individuals with a disfigurement or deformity and uncertain what to do or say. In a social setting, individuals . . . may encounter staring, feelings of pity, or repulsion. These reactions may cause individuals with a skin condition to limit or avoid social activities or to restrict their social interactions with others. (pp. 273–274)

School staff should recognize that the "disfigurement" does not have to be extensive. Teenagers with acne that might be described by a physician as "mild" are often teased and taunted—in some cases even shunned. Counseling may be helpful; membership in a support group may give students an avenue to express their feelings of despair.

4 *Students with impaired integumentary function are usually not absent from school for long periods, nor are they restricted in terms of physical activity.* However, in some cases, there may be some protracted periods of absenteeism or restrictions. Advice should be sought from the student's physician. Forms for soliciting information from the student's physician are found in Appendix D.

5 *Good hygiene is the best form of prevention in halting the spread of infectious conditions.* Of special concern is the spread of infectious conditions to those who are particularly vulnerable, such as infants, children with congenital immune deficiency disorders, those on immunosuppressive therapy, those with generalized cancer such as leukemia or lymphoma, and those with other debilitating conditions (Whaley and Wong, 1995). For these children, a minor skin disorder may result in serious sequelae.

The child or young adult with an infectious condition should be encouraged not to touch the infected area and to wash his or her hands if contact is made with the lesions. Students with infectious skin conditions should have their own towel and face cloth for washing up.

Handwashing is the primary means of preventing spread. Caregivers in direct contact with a person with an infectious skin condition should carefully wash their hands with soapy water after contact to prevent the spread of the disease to themselves and others. For detailed instructions on proper handwashing procedures, see chapter 24.

Any materials that may be soiled by drainage (e.g., dressings, bandages) should be secured in a closed container and disposed of properly. For detailed instructions on how to dispose of contaminated waste (i.e., universal precautions), refer to chapter 24. Students should be taught not to share utensils, such as drinking glasses, or to share the same soda bottle or juice box.

To reduce the spread of lice, the following suggestions are given:

a. Students should be assigned individual coat hooks in the coat closet. Each student should be responsible for placing his or her hat in the pocket of his or her coat. If a student shares a locker with a student who develops pediculosis, the locker and its contents should be treated.

b. Students need to be reminded continuously not to share items that may be contaminated (e.g., hats, headgear, hair accessories). Drama teachers and teachers who encourage thespian activities (e.g., provide dress-up clothes) may have to limit the use of hats, wigs, and other headgear.

c. All contaminated objects must be treated. Clothes (e.g., hats, caps, scarves, coats), towels, and bed linens must be washed in hot water and dried at high heat in a clothes dryer for a minimum of 20 minutes, or dry cleaned. Those objects that cannot be washed and dried at high heat (e.g., synthetic wigs, pillows, soft toys) should be sealed in a plastic bag for 10 to 14 days. Hair combs, brushes, and hair accessories (e.g., barrettes) should be treated with a pediculicide or soaked in a 2% Lysol solution for a minimum of 1 hour. If a contaminated article is made of metal (e.g., hair scissors, hair comb) it is ideal to boil it for at least 10 minutes.

d. All floors, rugs, stuffed animals, mattresses, couches, pillows, chairs, and chair seats should be vacuumed thoroughly to remove all infested hair and then sprayed with an approved insecticide spray. Vacuuming also assists in getting rid of any nits that have been shed by the affected individual. After cleaning, the vacuum bag should be disposed of carefully.

To reduce the spread of fungal diseases, the following suggestions are given by the National Skin Centre (1995):

a. Children and young adults should be taught to keep the space between the toes, the skin folds in the groin, and the armpits dry at all times, since fungus grows in areas that are warm and moist.

b. Children and young adults should be taught not to walk barefoot in areas where the floor is wet (e.g., bathrooms, lavatories, swimming pools).

c. Children and young adults should be encouraged to wear cotton socks or open-toed sandals if their feet sweat profusely. Nylon socks and covered shoes should not be worn because they tend to make the feet sweat.

6 *Excessive exposure to the sun should be a concern to all classroom teachers.* Teachers need to educate students about the hazards of ultraviolet rays. Staff should be good role models and wear sunscreen and protective clothing when outdoors (e.g., on playground supervision, taking students on an outing). All students should be encouraged to apply sunscreen on a regular basis and to wear sunglasses to protect their eyes.

Children and young adults with hypopigmentation disorders must be protected from the sun. They must wear long sleeves and long pants and wear a hat to protect their face. Similarly, it is important for those who are recovering from thermal burns that the burned areas be protected from sunlight.

7 *School staff can be instrumental in recognizing that a student has a skin condition.* In cases where there are outbreaks of lice and scabies, for example, teachers may be the first to notice that the students are scratching more than normal.

8 *Typically, skin disorders do not have a major implication in terms of career or vocational choices.* However, individuals whose skin condition is either exacerbated or precipitated by some type of allergic substance may have to consider their health needs (Falvo, 1991). Those who cannot tolerate sun exposure should look for indoor employment.

❦ Summary

School staff are very likely to encounter students with skin alterations because they are one of the most common health problems seen in children and adolescents. Disorders of the integumentary system can be major or minor; congenital or acquired; acute or chronic; self-limiting or requiring treatment. Some conditions are seen in some age groups and not in others; some conditions are caused by internal factors, such as genetic factors, whereas others are due to external factors, such as bacteria.

Regardless of the characteristics or cause, skin disorders may be very traumatic to the child or young adult. Some may be able to cope with the skin disorder; others may respond in a negative behavioral fashion. Students with altered integumentary function need supportive persons in their environment. Teachers can be very supportive if they are educated to understand the nature of the child's specific condition.

References

Antoon, A. (1996). Burns. In F. D. Burg, J. R. Ingelfinger, E. R. Wald, & R. A. Polin (Eds.), *Gellis & Kagan's current pediatric therapy* (15th ed., pp. 740–744). Philadelphia: W. B. Saunders.

Archambeau-Jones, C., Simmons, F., & Feller, I. (1994). The child with burns. In C. L Betz, M. M. Hunsberger, & S. Wright (Eds.), *Family-centered nursing care of children* (2nd ed., pp. 2127–2165.). Philadelphia: W. B. Saunders.

Castiglia, P. T. (1992). Neonatal growth, development, and health. In P. T. Castiglia & R. E. Harbin (Eds.), *Child health care: Process and practice* (pp. 177–213). Philadelphia: J. B. Lippincott.

Cordell, R. L., Solomon, S. L., & Hale, C. M. (1996). Exclusion of mildly ill children from out-of-home child care facilities. *Journal of Infectious Medicine, 13*(1), 41, 45–58.

Eichenfield, L. F. (1996). Disorders of pigmentation. In F. D. Burg, J. R. Ingelfinger, E. R. Wald, & R. A. Polin (Eds.), *Gellis & Kagan's current pediatric therapy* (15th ed., pp. 531–534). Philadelphia: W. B. Saunders.

Falvo, D. R. (1991). *Medical and psychosocial aspects of chronic illness and disability.* Gaithersburg, MD: Aspen.

Fine, J-D., & Guest, P. J. (1996). Papulosquamous disorders. In F. D. Burg, J. R. Ingelfinger, E. R. Wald, & R. A. Polin (Eds.), *Gellis & Kagan's current pediatric therapy* (15th ed., pp. 521–524). Philadelphia: W. B. Saunders.

Friday, G. A. (1996). Insect stings. In F. D. Burg, J. R. Ingelfinger, E. R. Wald, & R. A. Polin (Eds.), *Gellis & Kagan's current pediatric therapy* (15th ed., pp. 734–735). Philadelphia: W. B. Saunders.

Gellis, S. E. (1996). Disorders of the sebaceous glands and sweat glands. In F. D. Burg, J. R. Ingelfinger, E. R. Wald, & R. A. Polin (Eds.), *Gellis & Kagan's current pediatric therapy* (15th ed., pp. 544–545). Philadelphia: W. B. Saunders.

Gold, M., Sussman, G., Loubser, M., & Binkley, K. (1996). Anaphylaxis in schools and other child care settings. *Canadian Journal of Allergy and Clinical Immunology, 1,* 4–11.

Guzzo, C. (1996). Atopic dermatitis. In F. D. Burg, J. R. Ingelfinger, E. R. Wald, & R. A. Polin (Eds.), *Gellis & Kagan's current pediatric therapy* (15th ed., pp. 516–517). Philadelphia: W. B. Saunders.

Johnson, B. L. (1996). Nevi and nevoid tumors. In F. D. Burg, J. R. Ingelfinger, E. R. Wald, & R. A. Polin (Eds.), *Gellis & Kagan's current pediatric therapy* (15th ed., pp. 535–538). Philadelphia: W. B. Saunders.

McClellan, M. A., & Moran, M. (1992). Alterations in integumentary function. In P. T. Castiglia & R. E. Harbin (Eds.), *Child health care: Process and practice* (pp. 955–990). Philadelphia: J. B. Lippincott.

Meyer, G. (1997). Syndromes and inborn errors of metabolism. In M. L. Batshaw (Ed.), *Children with disabilities* (4th ed., pp. 813–834). Baltimore: Paul H. Brookes.

National Skin Centre. (1995). *Fungal infections of the skin.* Singapore: National Skin Centre [on-line-medical education material].

Nicol, N. H., & Hill, M. J. (1994). Altered skin integrity. In C. L Betz, M. M. Hunsberger, & S. Wright (Eds.), *Family-centered nursing care of children* (2nd ed., pp. 1648–1677). Philadelphia: W. B. Saunders.

Rasmussen, J. E. (1996). Genodermatosis. In F. D. Burg, J. R. Ingelfinger, E. R. Wald, & R. A. Polin (Eds.), *Gellis & Kagan's current pediatric therapy* (15th ed., pp. 539–542). Philadelphia: W. B. Saunders.

Rieg, L. S., Miller, M., & Ragiel, C. R. (1990) Protection: Implications of inflammation and altered skin integrity. In S. R. Mott, S. R. James, & A. M. Sperhac (Eds.), *Nursing care of children and families* (2nd ed., pp. 1137–1225). Redwood City, CA: Addison-Wesley.

Rudy, S. J. (1993). Nursing planning, intervention, and evaluation for altered integumentary function. In D. B. Jackson & R. B. Saunders (Eds.), *Child health nursing: A comprehensive approach to the care of children and their families* (pp. 1777–1847). Philadelphia: J. B. Lippincott.

Whaley, L. F., & Wong, D. L. (1991). *Nursing care of infants and children* (4th ed.). St. Louis: Mosby.

Whaley, L. F., & Wong, D. L. (1995). *Nursing care of infants and children* (5th ed.). St. Louis: Mosby.

Defense:

Children and Young Adults with Altered Immune Function

The **immune system,** a collection of organs, glands, cells, and proteins located throughout the human body, serves primarily a protective function, guarding the body from the invasion of disease-producing microorganisms (e.g., bacteria and viruses), referred to as **pathogens,** or foreign bodies (e.g., dust, smoke). In simple terms, the immune system's main function is to recognize **"self"** from **"non-self"** and to eliminate from the body all foreign substances, referred to collectively as **antigens,** that may be harmful (Whaley & Wong, 1995). The word "immune," meaning to be protected from infectious or allergic disease, comes from the Latin word *immunis,* meaning "free from" or "freedom." The immune system also protects the body from an overaccumulation of cellular wastes or cells that no longer have any usefulness, such as dead or damaged cells, as well as from the development, growth, and dissemination of abnormal cells, which can be either cancerous or noncancerous and serve no function.

The noun **immunity** is used to refer to the body's ability to defend itself against foreign substances. A person is described, for example, as "being immune" or "having immunity" to a particular disease when he or she is resistant to the organism that causes the disease. While a person who is unaffected by pollen could be described as being "immune," since most people are unaffected by pollen, the term "allergic" is used to describe those who do react, while those who do not have a response are described as being "normal."

Immunity to diseases can occur **naturally,** at birth, or it can be **acquired,** during infancy or childhood. If a person has **natural immunity,** he or she is born resistant to the particular disease as a result of the transmission, in utero, of the mother's disease-specific antibodies. **Antibodies** are proteins known as **immunoglobulins** (Ig) that are produced in response to specific antigens for the purpose of "counteracting" the effects of the antigens (e.g., agglutinating a specific bacteria).

Acquired immunity can be either natural or artificial. **Natural acquired immunity** is a result of contact with a particular disease so that the individual produces antibodies that prevent the disease a second time or a result of obtaining the mother's antibodies by consuming colostrum, the fluid secreted by the breast the first days after birth and before the production of breast milk. **Artificially acquired immunity** is achieved by means of **vaccination.**

The immune system is extremely complex. In the section that follows, there is a simplified description of some of the major component parts of the immune system. In chapter 22, a more in-depth examination of some of the types of problems that can affect the immune system of children and young adults is presented.

❦ The Immune System: Review of Structure and Function

The major organs and tissues of the immune system are shown in Figure IX.1. Typically, the system is divided into two parts, the primary and secondary organs. **Primary organs,** also referred to as the **central organs,** consist of the thymus, liver, and bone marrow. In the primary organs, lymphocytes (i.e., T-cells and B-cells) are developed. **Secondary organs,** or **peripheral organs,** include the lymph nodes and nodules (e.g., tonsils), lymphatic vessels, skin-associated lymphoid tissue (SALT), bronchus-associated lymphoid tissue (BALT), gut-associated lymphoid tissue (GALT), spleen, and the blood. In the secondary organs, the lymphocytes reside in their mature form. Since pathogens typically enter the body through breaks in the skin, by being breathed in by the lungs during inhalation, or by means of ingestion via the GI tract, it is appropriate that some of the major defense organs against the invasion of disease-producing organisms, i.e., the SALT, BALT, and GALT, respectively, are located where infection is most likely to occur. In addition to the various organs, the immune system includes a variety of "immune cells" (e.g., monocytes), which

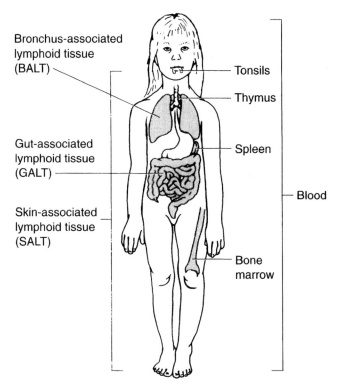

Bronchus-associated lymphoid tissue (BALT)

Gut-associated lymphoid tissue (GALT)

Skin-associated lymphoid tissue (SALT)

Tonsils

Thymus

Spleen

Blood

Bone marrow

Figure IX.1
Organs and Tissues of the Immune System

travel throughout the body via the lymph and circulatory system, searching out and destroying those substances believed to be "foreign" but avoiding those regarded as "self" (Hughes, 1993).

First Defensive Reaction: Nonspecific Immune Defense

The body's first line of defense includes the outer coverings of the body (i.e., the skin and the mucous membranes lining the vagina, bladder, lungs, intestines, nose, and mouth) and certain body secretions, such as saliva, sweat, tears, and gastric acids, that contain chemicals that can kill specific antigens. However, if this line of defense is ineffective, e.g., if the skin is abraded, burned, or cut, pathogens may be able to enter the host. If invasion does occur, the first defensive reaction that occurs is **phagocytosis,** the term given to describe the body's attempt to ingest and digest the foreign substance. Both the prefix **phago-** and suffix **-phage** come from the Greek word *phagein*, meaning to eat. Since at this point the body is only capable of establishing that the organism or foreign body is "non-self," the first reaction is referred to as a **nonspecific immune defense.**

The primary agents of phagocytosis are the phagocytic white blood cells, in particular the neutrophils and the monocytes. **Neutrophils,** which constitute between 55% and 70% of the circulating white blood cells, travel throughout the blood system until they are needed. With invasion of some type of microorganism, such as the virus that causes the common cold, neutrophils migrate rapidly to the site of the infection, in this case the lungs. In an attempt to fight off the invading pathogen, the neutrophils surround the foreign body and, by producing toxic enzymes, destroy it. After destruction, the lysosomes of the neutrophil digest the phagocytosed material. If more neutrophils are needed to attack the foreign material than are available at the time, the bone marrow is stimulated to increase production. **Monocytes,** accounting for 2% to 8% of white blood cells, are relatively large compared to their smaller counterparts, the neutrophils. Their major function is also to devour foreign material, particularly material larger in size than that which can be consumed by neutrophils. Monocytes typically circulate in the blood system for a brief time, after which they migrate to certain lymphatic organs, such as the liver, spleen, and lymph nodes, where they are transformed into **macrophages.** Macrophages are called into action when needed, in response to the production of a chemical known as the **macrophage migration inhibiting factor** by the **lymphocytes,** another type of white blood cell, and are capable of destroying unwanted bacteria, excess body cells, neoplastic cells (those that result in abnormal growth), and antigen-antibody complexes.

Second Defensive Reaction: Specific Immune Defense

If the body is able to recognize the antigen, it is able to respond more selectively. This process is known as the **specific immune response.** Two types of specific response lead to immunity: **humoral immunity** and **cellular immunity.** Both types involve a third type of white blood cell known as a lymphocyte. **Lymphocytes** are small, round cells that account for approximately 20% to 40% of all circulating white cells. The two major forms of lymphocytes involved in the immune system are **B-lymphocytes,** or **B-cells,** and **T-lymphocytes,** or **T-cells.**

Humoral Immune System   If the antigen is present *outside* the cell, e.g., on a cell surface or in a specific body fluid, the **humoral immune system**[1] is activated. B-lymphocytes, believed to originate in the bone marrow and stored in the spleen, gut, bronchi, and skin, are produced and begin to secrete large quantities of immunoglobulins specific to the particular antigen. Produced at a rate of as many as 2,000 per second, five classes of immunoglobulins, A, E, D, G, and M, have been recognized, each serving a specific function. For example, the production of IgM, the largest of the immunoglobulins, which occurs within the first 2 to 3 days of invasion, triggers the production of IgG, an antibody which is particularly effective in fighting off bacteria, fungi, and viruses.

As the various antibodies are produced, it is believed that they bind to the surface of the antigen, creating an **antigen-antibody complex cell,** which is either weakened or killed. If the cell's strength is diminished, i.e., the microorganism is "slowed down" by the increased weight of the antibodies that are adhering to its surface, it is easier for the various phagocytes to attack. The process by which bacteria are rendered more susceptible to phagocytosis is referred to as **opsonization,** or **opsonification,** from the Greek word *opsonein,* meaning "to supply food."

Cell-Mediated Immune System   If the antigen is present *inside* the cell, e.g., a specific virus, fungus, protozoan, or bacterium has entered a particular cell, the **cell-mediated immune system** is activated. T-lymphocytes, which originate in the thymus and are stored in the various lymph nodes and spleen, begin to act directly on the foreign microorganism. There are two types of T-cells, the **effector T-cells,** which are able to destroy the antigen directly, i.e., without the aid of an antibody, and **regulator T-cells,** which regulate the actions of the B-cells.

The Lymph System

The immune system is extremely complex, and while it is beyond the realm of this text to describe each component part in detail, brief mention must be

---

[1] The Latin word *humor* means liquid. The English noun "humor" is used to refer to any fluid or semifluid specific to the body (e.g., blood; lymph; and aqueous humor and vitreous humor, found in the eye).

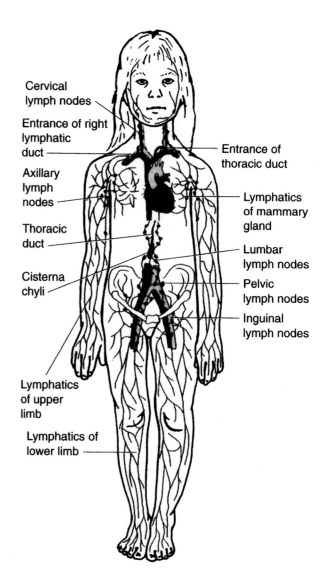

Figure IX.2
Lymphatic System

made of the **lymph system** (Figure IX.2), which is often referred to as the body's "drainage" system.

One of the primary purposes of the lymphatic system is to produce **lymph,** a fluid made up predominantly of chyme, erythrocytes, and leukocytes, particularly lymphocytes. Lymph travels throughout the body by means of a complex network of vessels, referred to as **lymphatics.** Lymphatic channels are found in all parts of the body except the cornea and the CNS. Clustered in certain areas of the body (e.g., mouth, neck, armpit, breast, and groin), like beads on a string, are **lymph glands,** also referred to as **lymph nodes,** small oval structures that range in size from a pinhead to a lima bean. Each node is composed of, in part, closely packed lymphocytes, some of which are capable of acting directly on invading microorganisms. The primary purpose of the glands is to filter the lymph as it circulates. Through this filtration process, the body is typically able to protect itself from the invasion of various pathogens. The lymphatic system also includes a number of organs. The most well-known are the tonsils and adenoids, the thymus, and the spleen.

Tonsils and Adenoids   Tonsils are small, rounded masses of tissue, primarily lymphoid tissue, located in the intestine (**intestinal tonsils,** also known as **Peyer's patches**) and the mouth region (**palatine tonsils** on either side of the throat; **lingual tonsils** located at the base of the tongue). If the palatine tonsils become infected by either a bacteria or a virus, a condition known as **tonsillitis,** the child may have a sore throat, a hoarse voice, and a productive cough. The child may also complain of pain in the ears. Fever, headache, and general malaise often accompany the sore throat, and if the child has a tendency to have recurrent episodes, a **tonsillectomy** (the surgical removal of the inflamed tissue) may be considered.

Typically, at the same time that the tonsils are removed, the child will also have an **adenoidectomy.** In this procedure, the **adenoids,** also made up of lymphoid tissue, located in the uppermost region of the throat behind the nose, are removed to prevent possible problems at a later date. In the past, tonsillectomy and adenoidectomy (**T & A**) were common surgical procedures; today, the operation is carried out less frequently because of the recognition of the important role these specific lymphoid tissues play in the body's line of defense against infection.

Thymus   The **thymus gland,** located just below the thyroid behind the sternum, is a central gland of the lymph system. In the thymus, the T-cells of the cell-mediated immune response develop. During infancy and early childhood, the thymus gland is relatively large; however, after puberty, it shrinks and is replaced by fatty tissue.

Spleen   Located on the left side of the abdomen, between the stomach and the diaphragm, the **spleen** has a number of functions. The spleen is responsible for producing specific types of white blood cells, such as monocytes, as well as being responsible for filtering blood and lymph. The spleen is considered part of the lymph system since it contains lymphatic nodules within its sinuses (cavities), in which macrophages reside. The spleen is critical in screening out foreign particles and organisms, as well as "worn-out" blood cells, which are devoured by the macrophages. If the spleen is injured or diseased, the person has an increased risk of infection.

Chain of Infection: Etiologic Agent, Host, and Means

The terms "communicable," "contagious," and "infectious," when used to describe certain diseases, are used synonymously to refer to those conditions that are transmittable from one person or animal to another. The series of events or conditions that lead to the development of a particular communicable disease is often referred to as the "chain of infection" (Clark, 1992). The primary "links" include the **etiologic agent,** the pathogen that causes the condition; the **source of the agent,** often referred to as the **host;** and the **means** by which the causative agent is transmitted from an infected host to an uninfected person. The manner by which the infectious agent is transmitted is referred to as the **mode of transmission.**

Communicable diseases are caused by **microorganisms,** tiny microscopic entities, such as **bacteria, viruses,** or **fungi,** that are not visible to the naked eye. While not all microorganisms are pathogenic, i.e., do not have the potential to cause a disease, each communicable disease is a result of the actions of a specific agent. For the agent to pass from the "old" host to a "new" host, the causative agent must leave the first host (via the agent's **portal of exit**), travel to the second host and, on arrival at the second host, find a means to enter the susceptible new host (via the agent's **portal of entry**). Typically, the first host is either a human being (e.g., a person with measles) or an animal (e.g., a rabid cat); however, in some cases the causative agents can be found in nonanimal hosts (e.g., fungi found in garden soil or dust).

The manner in which a disease is transmitted from one host to another can be either direct or indirect. **Direct transmission** refers to the spread of the disease from one host to another without any type of intermediary carrier, whereas in **indirect transmission,** either an inanimate object (often referred to as a **fomite**) or some other type of vector (e.g., an arthropod) is involved. Some of the more common modes of transmission, both direct and indirect, are shown in Table IX.1.

Transmission can be either **vertical** (i.e., from mother to child via the placenta) or **horizontal** (i.e., across a group of people, such as the members of a school class). While chapters 22 and 23 focus primarily on horizontal spread of infectious conditions, commonly referred to as **acquired infections,** several agents can cause serious damage in a developing fetus if the pregnant mother becomes infected in the early stages of pregnancy (i.e., first or second trimester) and passes the infection on to her developing fetus. These agents are often referred to as the **TORCH,** or **STORCH, agents. TORCH** stands for **t**oxoplasmosis, **o**ther viruses (e.g., hepatitis B, coxsackievirus, mumps, poliovirus, varicella, gonorrhea), **r**ubella virus, **c**ytomegalovirus, and **h**erpes simplex type II virus. Some use the acronym **STORCH** and include **s**yphilis in the group along with the other agents. Each of these causative agents is covered in greater detail in chapter 23. In the category "other," it is generally believed that hepatitis B offers the greatest danger to the unborn child

TABLE IX.1
Modes of Transmission of Communicable Diseases

Mode of Transmission	Diseases Transmitted	Portal of Entry	Portal of Exit
A. DIRECT TRANSMISSION			
1. **Airborne:** coughing, spitting, sneezing, singing, talking; urine spray	Measles, rubella, mumps, chicken pox, strep throat, poliomyelitis, influenza, tuberculosis, pneumonia, scarlet fever, pertussis, diphtheria	Mouth Nose	Mouth Nose
2. **Fecal-oral:** via the hand or other object; by means of sexual contact	Hepatitis A, polio, typhoid, shigellosis, salmonellosis	Mouth	Anus
3. **Physical contact:** involving skin to skin or mucous membrane discharge to skin via touching; kissing or saliva-oral	Impetigo, lice, scabies, ringworm, infectious mononucleosis, conjunctivitis	Skin Mucous membranes Eye	Skin Mucous membranes Eye
4. **Sexual contact:** sexual intercourse, oral-genital intercourse, anal intercourse	Various sexually transmitted diseases (STDs)	Skin Mouth Urethra Vagina Anus	Skin Mouth Urethra Vagina Anus
5. **Direct inoculation**	Syphilis, hepatitis B, HIV infection	Placenta Bloodstream	Blood
B. INDIRECT TRANSMISSION			
1. **Vehicle-borne:** via fomites, such as toys, toothbrushes, toilets, bed linens, eating utensils, hairbrushes, currency, stethoscope, thermometer, soil	Scabies; lice; various bacterial, viral, and parasitic diseases	Mouth Skin	Mouth Urethra Anus
2. **Vector-borne:** insect or animal bite	Scabies, lice, malaria, plague, rabies, Rocky Mountain spotted fever	Skin	Blood Saliva
3. **Fecal-oral:** via contaminated food or water	Hepatitis A	Mouth	Feces
4. **Other:** soil, dust	Tetanus	Wound in skin	

Sources: Clark, 1992; Dash, 1993.

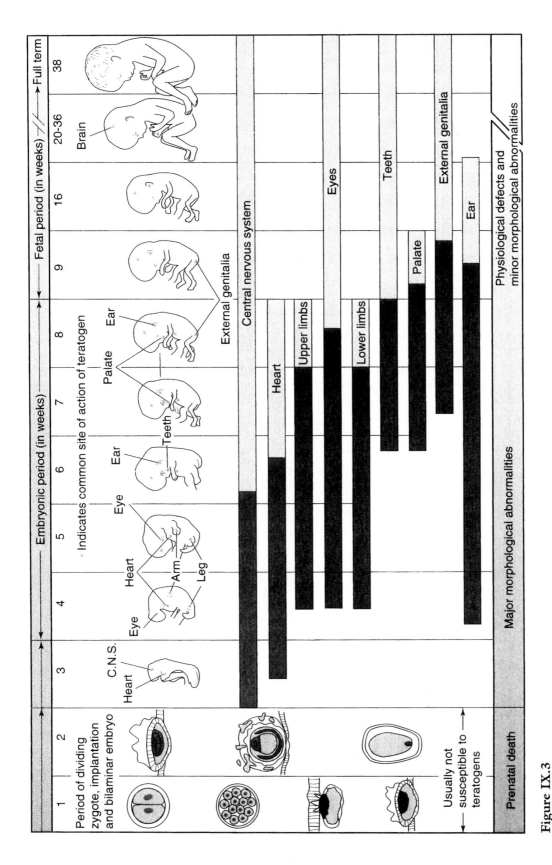

Figure IX.3

Critical Periods of Human Development. Dark gray bars denote highly sensitive periods; light gray bars indicate stages that are less sensitive to teratogens. Note that each organ or structure has a critical period during which its development may be deranged, and that physiologic defects, functional disturbances, and minor morphologic changes are likely to result from disturbances during the fetal period. Severe mental retardation may result from exposure of the developing human to high levels of radiation during the 8- to 16-week period.

Source: Moore, K. L., and Persaud, T. V. N.: *Before we are born: Basic embryology and birth defects* (4th ed.). Copyright 1993 by W. B. Saunders Co. Reprinted by permission.

(Castiglia, 1992). Frequently found impairments that result from such infections include visual impairments, auditory impairments, anemia, encephalitis, jaundice, liver or spleen enlargement, low birth weight, low platelet count, microcephaly (abnormally small head), seizures, and skin rash (Heller & Kennedy, 1994). During the first three months of pregnancy, the organs of the child are being formed and the undeveloped fetus is at greatest risk. As can be seen in Figure IX.3, during the first 9 weeks, the major organs, including the eyes, ears, heart, and brain, are being developed, along with the upper and lower limbs. Consequently, damage can result in a number of serious consequences, including blindness, deafness, cardiac abnormalities, and cognitive and motoric impairments.

The period of time between contact with the specific agent and the first signs of the disease (i.e., the onset of symptoms) is referred to as the **incubation period.** For some conditions, during this period the individual is capable of passing the disease to others; in other conditions, the individual is able to pass on the disease only when the symptoms have become evident. The period in which the individual is able to transmit the condition is often referred to as the **communicability period.** The amount of time that children should be kept at home varies by disease. In the following chapters, some of the more common communicable diseases are described, and although guidelines are given regarding the amount of time the child should be isolated, each State and Provincial Board of Health has specific regulations that must be followed. The school nurse and the administrative staff of the school must know the applicable public health laws.

References

Castiglia, P. T. (1992). Caring for children with infectious diseases. In P. T. Castiglia & R. E. Harbin (Eds.), *Child health care: Process and practice* (pp. 415–437). Philadelphia: J. B. Lippincott.

Clark, M. J. (1992). Communicable disease. In M. J. Clark, *Nursing in the community* (pp. 730–807). Norwalk, CT: Appleton & Lange.

Dash, D. (1993). Communicable disease. In J. M. Swanson & M. Albrecht, *Community health nursing: Promoting the health of aggregates* (pp. 533–565). Philadelphia: W. B. Saunders.

Heller, K. W., & Kennedy, C. (1994). *Etiologies and characteristics of deaf-blindness.* Monmouth, OR: Teaching Research Publications.

Hughes, R. B. (1993). Immune responses. In D. B. Jackson & R. B. Saunders (Eds.), *Child health nursing: A comprehensive approach to the care of children and their families* (pp. 619–639). Philadelphia: J. B. Lippincott.

Moore, K. L. (1993) *Before we are born: Basic embryology and birth defects* (2nd ed.). Philadelphia: W. B. Saunders.

Whaley, L. F., & Wong, D. L. (1995). *Nursing care of infants and children* (5th ed.). St. Louis: Mosby.

CHAPTER 22

Altered Immunity

KEY WORDS

Anaphylaxis

Autoimmune diseases

Benign cells

Cardinal signs

EpiPen

Graft-versus-host disease

Hypersensitivity disorder

Hyposensitivity disorder

Immediate and delayed hypersensitivity conditions

Immunodeficiency disorder

Localized and systemic allergic
reactions

Malignant cells

Like any other system of the human body, the immune system can malfunction, resulting in a variety of conditions quite harmful to the individual (Harkins, 1994). Most failures of the immune system are believed to result from genetic factors, developmental defects, infection, malignancy, injury, drugs, and altered metabolic states (Mueller, 1991). The most common physiologic alterations of the immune system occurring in children and young adults are hypersensitivity disorders, immunodeficiency disorders, autoimmune diseases, and cancer. While most children do not experience one of these types of immune disorders, a majority of children do experience, at some point in their lives, one or more diseases that result from the body's inability to completely prevent the invasion of certain pathogens. Such conditions are referred to as **communicable** or **contagious diseases,** and since they are so common

in childhood, the most frequently occurring communicable diseases (e.g., mumps, German measles, sexually transmitted diseases) are examined in chapter 23.

 Hypersensitivity Disorders

If the immune elements that are involved in defending the body against invading organisms or foreign bodies overreact, the person may show signs of hypersensitivity to certain stimuli. The stimuli are called **allergens,** and the condition is commonly referred to as an **allergy.** The most common allergic condition found in children and young adults is **asthma.** Other allergies common to this population include reactions to certain drugs, skin products, and foods. Rejection, which can occur after transplantation of

TABLE 22.1

Typical Localized and Systemic Symptoms of an Allergic Reaction

LOCALIZED ALLERGIC REACTIONS	
Symptom	**Description**
INTEGUMENTARY SYSTEM	
Urticaria (hives)	Transient, pale pink, raised wheals that vary in both size and shape. Can occur anywhere on the body. Most common sites are skin, mouth, and larynx. Often occurs after consumption of certain foods (e.g., strawberries, nuts, tomatoes, shellfish) or food colorings. Often intensely itchy.
Eczema	Inflammation of the skin, typically on knee or at bend in arm or on the face. In early stages, characterized by an oozing, itchy, red rash. Later, skin becomes crusted, scaly, hardened, and thickened.
MUCOUS MEMBRANES	
Rhinitis	Inflammation of the mucous membranes of nose, accompanied by swelling (nasal stuffiness) and discharge (runny nose). Often, nose is itchy, and the youngster is seen to rub it with the palm of his or her hand, an action referred to as the **allergy salute.** If acute, mouth breathing is common.
Conjunctivitis	Inflammation of the conjunctiva of eyes, resulting in itching, tearing, and redness. May have persistent black discoloration under the eyes, a condition referred to as **allergic shiner.**
Otitis Media	Inflammation of middle ear, resulting in the accumulation of fluid that may produce an intermittent loss of hearing. Feeling of fullness in the ears and hearing popping or cracking noises are common.

certain organs or tissues, is also a type of hypersensitivity disorder, one in which the body responds in a negative manner to material that has been surgically implanted into the recipient. This particular condition is known as **graft-versus-host disease** and is especially common in bone marrow transplants. It is also referred to as **homologous disease.**

Incidence

It has been estimated that between 20% and 25% of all children and young adults in the United States experience some form of immunologic allergic reaction (McLoughlin & Nall, 1994) and that as many as 1.5 million school days are lost per year as a result of this condition (Trzcinski, 1993). Between 1% and 5% of the general population may be prone to having a severe generalized allergic reaction that can lead to rapid death if left untreated (Minister of Supply and Services Canada, 1996).

Types of Allergic Responses

There are two different types of allergic responses, immediate and delayed. As would be expected, time is a major factor in differentiating the two.

Immediate Hypersensitivity Reactions In this type of allergy, the individual shows an almost instantaneous response to the allergen. A child or young adult who begins to sneeze, cough, and tear immediately upon exposure to pollen would be described as having immediate hypersensitivity. Immediate hypersensitivity disorders result from a genetic defect that allows for the increased production of immunoglobulin E (IgE) in the system.

SYSTEMIC ALLERGIC REACTIONS	
Symptom	**Description**
RESPIRATORY SYSTEM	
Dyspnea	Difficulty breathing (e.g., shortness of breath).
Bronchospasm	Contraction of the smooth muscle of bronchi, resulting in coughing, particularly after exertion; wheezing; and shortness of breath. Throat tightness or closing may occur in extreme cases.
GI SYSTEM	
Diarrhea	Loose, watery stools; may be accompanied by abdominal pain or cramps, nausea, or vomiting.
VASCULAR SYSTEM	
Migraine Headaches	Dilation of blood vessels in the brain, resulting in intense pain, often accompanied by nausea, vomiting, and increased sensitivity to light. Often occurs after ingestion of certain foods (e.g., chocolate, cheese, citrus fruits) or beverages (e.g., hard liquor, red wine).
MULTISYSTEM	
Anaphylaxis	Generalized, life-threatening hypersensitivity reaction to an offending allergen. Can occur within seconds or minutes of exposure. **The more sudden the symptoms, the more serious the reaction.** Can include all symptoms described above, as well as swelling of body parts (lips, face, tongue, throat), difficulty swallowing, dizziness, change of color, and fainting or loss of consciousness. If CNS is involved, seizures can occur. Cardiovascular symptoms can include tachycardia, dysrhythmia, and hypotension.

Delayed Hypersensitivity Reactions In this type of allergy, there is a lag between exposure and symptoms. A person who touches poison ivy, oak, or sumac and develops a rash several hours later would be said to have delayed hypersensitivity. Delayed reactions typically occur from 24 to 72 hours after exposure, the average being 36 hours after contact. Delayed hypersensitivity reactions are believed to be controlled by specifically sensitized T-cell and do not involve the production of antibodies.

Characteristics of Allergic Responses

Because school staff may be the first to recognize that a student has an allergy, they should be aware of the typical symptoms. Regardless of the speed of response, it is important to remember that the reaction can be either **localized** (specific to a particular site) or **systemic** (found throughout the whole body). Typical symptoms, found in localized and systemic responses, are shown in Table 22.1.

Severity of Response

The **degree** or **severity** of an allergic response is the result of a number of factors. For example, typically, the more sensitive the individual, the greater the amount of allergen the individual is exposed to, and the longer the individual is exposed, the greater the response (Mueller, 1991). In some cases, the allergic reaction is so severe that the individual develops respiratory congestion, experiences a swelling of the airways that can lead to suffocation, and even loses consciousness. This reaction is referred to as **anaphylaxis,** a generalized allergic reaction, and in severe cases can be life-threatening (Table 22.1). The most common triggers of a severe anaphylactic reaction include certain **insect venoms**[1] (e.g., from wasps, yellow jackets, hornets, and honeybees), **drugs** (e.g., penicillin, sulfonamides, certain vaccines, anesthetic agents), and **foods** (e.g., tree nuts, such as hazelnuts, walnuts, almonds, and cashews; fish and shellfish; eggs; peanuts; sesame seeds; cow's milk; wheat; soy). Most children who have an allergy to milk, soy, eggs, or wheat outgrow their allergy by the time they are of school age; however, reactions to the other foods typically persist through childhood and adulthood (Gold, Sussman, Loubser, & Binkley, 1996). **Latex,** a rubber that is common in balloons, certain toys, and rubber gloves, can also be the cause of an anaphylactic reaction.[2]

Educational Implications and Teaching Tips: Students with Allergies

Many researchers have attempted to investigate the relationship between allergies and problems with learning. In the past, it was believed that allergies were a major contributing factor that resulted in poor school performance. While allergies do contribute to absenteeism, after a thorough review of the literature, McLoughlin and Nall (1994) came to the following conclusions:

> Overall, research results suggesting a relationship between allergies and academic underachievement and conduct problems is tenuous at best, especially in terms of actual learning and behavioral disabilities. An allergy may make a student tired, listless, nauseated, and even irritable. But are they ill enough to be excused from doing their school work and behaving themselves? The answer is, probably not, given suitable support and understanding from educators and parents. The absenteeism that plagues many of these students is also preventable with proper medication, supportive environmental controls, attention to coping strategies, and family education. (p. 201)

The following points might be of assistance to the classroom teacher:

1 *Although there is no "cure" for an allergy, it is important to try and control the symptoms as much as possible* (McLoughlin & Nall, 1994). Chronic allergies, such as asthma and hay fever, are typically treated primarily pharmacologically. The most common medications are **antihistamines,** drugs which inhibit or reduce the effects of the histamine released by the cells in an allergic reaction. The most common negative side effect of this class of medication is drowsiness; however, in some youngsters, antihistamines can have an opposite reaction, resulting in them becoming overly excited, dizzy, nervous, and unable to sleep. Teachers should know about the medication the student is

---

[1] For further information on insect bites and stings, and how to prevent exposure, see chapter 21.

[2] For further information on latex allergies, see chapter 11.

on and report to the parents any adverse reactions that they note in school.

2 *In addition to medication to control the symptoms, teachers should try to remove all the offending allergens from the student's environment to prevent a reaction in the first place.* Many suggestions on achieving this in the classroom are given in chapter 6.

While it is relatively easy to ensure that a classroom is free of allergens such as animal dander and fumes from felt-tip pens, making a school "peanut-free" is more difficult. However, for those who react to the breath of someone who has eaten peanuts, drastic steps are required to prevent a tragic incident. Recently the Canadian School Boards Association, with support of Health Canada, put together a comprehensive document entitled *Anaphylaxis: A Handbook for School Boards* (Minister of Supply and Services Canada, 1996) that attempts to "provide information, advice, and guidelines to school boards on the complex issue of managing anaphylaxis in schools" (p. iv). In this document, the division of responsibilities is clearly laid out to ensure the safety of anaphylactic students. The responsibilities of the parents of the student with an allergy and the parents of the student's classmates, the school principal, classroom teacher, and nurse, as well as those of the anaphylactic student and the other students in the class, are listed in Table 22.2. For further information, see this very valuable resource.

3 *All school personnel must be knowledgeable about anaphylaxis so that they are able to better respond to a student who may have a severe allergic reaction* (Hay, Harper, & Courson, 1994). All staff need to be trained on how and when to administer **epinephrine,** an adrenal hormone that is given to treat the symptoms. Any student who has a history of severe reaction to any allergen should have on hand, at all times, an emergency self-treatment kit that contains an **auto-injector device,** which contains a premeasured dose of this drug. The most commonly available device is the **EpiPen,** a spring-loaded, self-injectable system with a concealed needle, available by prescription. The **Ana-Kit,** a similar device, consists of a preloaded syringe that can deliver two doses of epinephrine; however, given the ease and simplicity of administration of the EpiPen, this type of device is typically recommended by physicians (Gold

et al., 1996). Instructions on how to use an EpiPen are shown in Table 22.3.

The symptoms of anaphylaxis can develop in individuals with extreme hypersensitivity very quickly (i.e., within seconds). More commonly, the reaction occurs within 15 to 30 minutes after exposure. **If it appears that a child is having an anaphylactic reaction (e.g., the child is upset, restless, anxious, red in the face, develops hives, has difficulty breathing, or is sneezing) or the child complains of any symptoms that could be the signal of an impending reaction, medical treatment should be begun immediately.** There is no danger in starting treatment immediately; however, the student could be in grave danger if those around him or her react too slowly (Minister of Supply and Services Canada, 1996). Similarly, accidental administration of the medication is not a cause for concern. **Rather than wait, caregivers should not hesitate to administer the epinephrine if there is any reason for suspecting a reaction is about to occur** (Minister of Supply and Services Canada, 1996).

It is critical that every school have an emergency plan developed to ensure the safety of students who are anaphylactic. The anaphylaxis handbook published by the Minister of Supply and Services Canada recommends that the school's emergency plan include procedures to:

- Communicate the emergency rapidly to a staff person who is trained in the use of the auto-injector.
- Administer the auto-injector. (*Note:* Although most anaphylactic children learn to administer their own medication by about age 8, individuals of any age may require help during a reaction because of the rapid progression of symptoms, or because of the stress of the situation. **Adult supervision is required.**)
- Telephone 911 or an ambulance. (Inform the emergency operator that a child is having an anaphylactic reaction; in some areas, hospitals will send a physician on the ambulance to begin emergency treatment at once.)
- Transport the child to hospital at once, if no ambulance service is available. (School boards should ensure that their insurance policies cover such an emergency situation.)
- Telephone the hospital to inform them that a child having an anaphylactic reaction is en route.

TABLE 22.2
Division of Responsibilities: Children with Severe Allergies in the School Setting

Ensuring the safety of anaphylactic children in a school setting depends on the cooperation of the entire school community. To minimize risk of exposure and to ensure rapid response to emergency, parents, students, and school personnel must all understand and fulfill their responsibilities.

RESPONSIBILITIES OF THE PARENTS OF AN ANAPHYLACTIC CHILD
- Inform the school of their child's allergies.
- Provide a medic alert bracelet for their child.
- Provide the school with physician's instructions for administering medication.
- Provide the school with up-to-date injection kits, and keep them current.
- Provide the school with an auto-injector trainer.
- Provide support to school and teachers as requested.
- Provide in-service for staff, if requested.
- Participate in parent advisory/support groups.
- Assist in school communication plans.
- Review the school action plan with school personnel.
- Supply information for school publications:
  - recipes
  - foods to avoid
  - alternate snack suggestions
  - resources
- Be willing to provide safe foods for special occasions.
- Teach their child:
  - to recognize the first symptoms of an anaphylactic reaction
  - to know where medication is kept, and who can get it
  - to communicate clearly when he or she feels a reaction starting
  - to carry his/her own auto-injector in a fanny-pack
  - not to share snacks, lunches, or drinks
  - to understand the importance of hand-washing
  - to cope with teasing and being left out
  - to report bullying and threats to an adult in authority
  - to take as much responsibility as possible for his/her own safety
- Welcome other parents' calls with questions about safe foods.

RESPONSIBILITIES OF THE SCHOOL PRINCIPAL
- Work as closely as possible with the parents of an anaphylactic child.
- Ensure that the parents have completed all the necessary forms.
- Ensure that instructions from the child's physician are on file.
- Notify the school community of the anaphylactic child, the allergens, and the treatment.
- Post allergy-alert forms in the staffroom and office.
- Maintain up-to-date emergency contacts and telephone numbers.
- Ensure that all staff and volunteers have received instruction with the auto-injector.

- Ensure that all substitute teachers are informed of the presence of an anaphylactic child and have been adequately trained to deal with an emergency.
- Inform all parents that a child with life-threatening allergies is attending the school and ask for their support.
- Arrange for annual in-service.
- Develop an emergency protocol for each anaphylactic child.
- Store auto-injectors in easily accessible locations.
- Establish safe procedures for field trips and extra-curricular activities.
- Develop a school policy (or implement the board policy) for reducing risk in classrooms and common areas.
- Establish a disciplinary procedure for dealing with bullying and threats.

RESPONSIBILITIES OF THE CLASSROOM TEACHER
- Display a photo-poster in the classroom, with parental approval.
- Discuss anaphylaxis with the class, in age-appropriate terms.
- Encourage students not to share lunches or trade snacks.
- Choose allergy-free foods for classroom events.
- Establish procedures to ensure that the anaphylactic child eats only what he/she brings from home.
- Reinforce hand-washing before and after eating.
- Facilitate communication with other parents.
- Follow the school policies for reducing risk in classrooms and common areas.
- Enforce school rules about bullying and threats.
- Leave information in an organized, prominent, and accessible format for substitute teachers.
- Ensure that auto-injectors are taken on field trips.

RESPONSIBILITIES OF PUBLIC HEALTH/SCHOOL NURSE
- Consult with and provide information to parents, students, and school personnel.
- Participate in planning school policy.
- Participate in in-service and auto-injector training.
- Assist in developing emergency response plans.
- Refer known cases of anaphylaxis to the school principal.

RESPONSIBILITIES OF ANAPHYLACTIC STUDENTS
- Take as much responsibility as possible for avoiding allergens.
- **Eat only foods brought from home.**
- Take responsibility for checking labels and monitoring intake (older students).
- Wash hands before eating.
- Learn to recognize symptoms of an anaphylactic reaction.
- Promptly inform an adult as soon as accidental exposure occurs or symptoms appear.
- Keep an auto-injector handy at all times.
- Know how to use the auto-injector.

Continued

TABLE 22.2
(Continued)

RESPONSIBILITIES OF ALL PARENTS

- Respond cooperatively to requests from school to eliminate allergens from packed lunches and snacks.
- Participate in parent information sessions.
- Encourage children to respect anaphylactic child and school policies.

RESPONSIBILITIES OF ALL STUDENTS

- Learn to recognize symptoms of anaphylactic reaction.
- Avoid sharing food, especially with anaphylactic children.
- Follow school rules about keeping allergens out of the classroom and washing hands.
- Refrain from "bullying" or "testing" a child with a food allergy.

Source: From *Anaphylaxis: A Handbook for School Boards,* Health Canada, 1996. Reproduced with permission of the Minister of Public Works and Government Services Canada, 1998.

- Notify the police and provide them with a description of the vehicle and license number if transportation is by car.
- Telephone the parents of the child.
- Re-administer epinephrine every 1 to 15 minutes while waiting for the ambulance and en route to the hospital, if breathing does not improve or if symptoms reoccur.
- Assign a staff person to take extra auto-injectors, accompany (or follow, if necessary) the child to the hospital, and stay with him or her until a parent or guardian arrives. (p. 28)

5 *The school should develop a policy regarding the location of auto-injectors.* The following guidelines are suggested:

- Auto-injectors should be kept in a covered and secure area, but unlocked for quick access. Although epinephrine is not a dangerous drug, the sharp needle of the self-injector can cause injury, especially if injected into the fingertip.
- As soon as they are old enough, students should carry their own auto-injectors. Many young children carry an injection kit in a fanny pack around their waist at all times.
- An **up-to-date** supply of auto-injectors, provided by the parents, should be available in an easily accessible, unlocked area of the child's classroom and/or in a central area of the school (office or staff room). *Note:* Auto-injectors are expensive. If families have difficulty supplying the school with an adequate supply, the school board should consider seeking financial assistance to ensure that medication is

TABLE 22.3
Administering Epinephrine by Means of an EpiPen

---

1. Remove the gray safety cap (this prepares the injector to be triggered).
2. Place the black tip on outer mid-thigh at right angle to the leg. Jab (i.e., press hard) the black tip of the pen into the leg until mechanism activates. The student's clothing does not need to be removed before administration.
3. Hold the EpiPen in place for 10 to 15 seconds to ensure the fluid enters the body (counting "one thousand and one, one thousand and two," etc.). Do not release pressure when device "clicks"—keep pressure firm for the designated amount of time.
4. Massage the area for 10 seconds to increase speed of absorption.
5. Discard the unit in a safe manner.
6. If breathing remains labored, administer a second dose within 5 to 10 minutes.
7. Epinephrine should be administered immediately and repeated at 10- to 15-minute intervals until medical assistance has been obtained.
8. The student should be kept warm, and nonalcoholic beverages should be given if the student is conscious.

Note: If the anaphylaxis is a result of an insect bite, a tourniquet should be applied just above the site of the sting (i.e., between the sting and the heart), if possible. The tourniquet should be tight, but not so tight that circulation is obstructed.

---

available, whenever and wherever it is required. It is important that the expiration date of the device be checked periodically to ensure that the medication is still acceptable.

- All staff should know the location of the auto-injectors. Classmates should be aware of the location of the auto-injector in the classroom. (Minister of Supply and Services Canada, 1996, pp. 28–29)

In addition, it is important that the student have an adequate supply of auto-injectors when traveling to and from school or away from the school on a field trip. Back-up devices should also be available in areas frequented by the student, such as the gym, assembly room, cafeteria, school yard, and, most importantly, the school bus (Gold et al., 1996).

6 *While it is important that teachers attempt to "protect" the student from the offending allergens, "extraordinary" measures taken to ward off a reaction have been known to provoke the opposite* (Dedyna, 1995). In one school jurisdiction, a teacher warned the other boys and girls about a particular student's extreme reaction to peanuts; however, other pupils in the class, as a prank, decided to put peanuts in the allergic child's sandwich. Fortunately, the child looked inside and did not eat it.

Teachers should be alert to any signs of teasing or taunting by classmates and ensure that students do not share food (either intentionally or unintentionally) with the child who has a known allergy.

7 *Teachers should be alert to the possible allergens presented in everyday curricular materials.* Materials such as Playdough and bean bags may cause a reaction in some children (Minister of Supply and Services Canada, 1996).

8 *While it is the responsibility of the parents to ensure that the school is equipped with an epinephrine injection device and that the medication has not expired, it is the responsibility of school personnel to be accepting of students with hypersensitivity disease.* Hay and her colleagues (1994) made the following comments, specifically in regard to food allergies, but they may be applied to all types of life-threatening allergies and should be heeded by all school personnel:

When contemplating the seriousness of potential life-threatening food allergic reactions in school children, [the] attitude of school personnel may be the single most important factor for ensuring fair and proper

treatment of these children. School personnel must listen carefully to parents of children with severe food allergies and obtain the necessary medical information. If school personnel are open, knowledgeable, and understanding, they can successfully respond to emergency life-threatening food reactions. (p. 121)

9 *All persons who have an anaphylactic reaction should be taken to the hospital for medical attention, even if the epinephrine has been administered and the individual appears to be recovering.* Since symptoms have been reported to occur as long as 8 hours after the initial exposure to the allergen, further treatment may be required. In fact, it has been suggested that treatment should be continued for a minimum of 48 hours after contact (Cavales-Oftadeh & Heiner, 1996).

10 *To be prepared, schools should occasionally simulate an anaphylactic emergency.* Such a drill ensures that all elements of the emergency plan are in place. All students with extreme allergies should be encouraged to wear a Medic-Alert bracelet.

Hyposensitivity or Immunodeficiency Disorders

If the system underreacts (i.e., is **hyposensitive**), the body may be unable to defend itself against disease-producing organisms, such as bacteria, viruses, and fungi. A person with extreme hyposensitivity is said to be **immunodeficient** and to have an **immunodeficiency disorder**.

In contrast to a person who has a health condition that results from a disorder of the immune system, there are some persons who become immunodeficient as a result of some type of action. For example, the administration of specific pharmacologic agents can inhibit both cellular and humoral immunity. In such cases, the person is said to be **immunosuppressed.** Immunosuppression can also result from exposure to roentgen rays (i.e., irradiation). In some cases, immunosuppression is deliberate; in others, the state is incidental. An example of the first would be a case in which a child is given megadoses of radiation before organ transplantation (e.g., kidney transplant) in an attempt to prevent rejection of the donor organ. An example of the second would be a case in which a child becomes immunosuppressed as a result of treatment (e.g., chemotherapy) to suppress the growth of a cancerous tumor. In either case, the individual becomes unable to fight off infection.

The most publicized immunodeficiency disorder is **acquired immunodeficiency syndrome (AIDS).** This condition results from the invasion of the body by the retrovirus known as the **human immunodeficiency virus (HIV).** Other conditions in which the body is unable to react to invading pathogens include **severe combined immunodeficiency disease** and **Wiskott-Aldrich syndrome,** both of which occur relatively infrequently.

Acquired Immunodeficiency Syndrome

More than 15 years after the first reported cases of an "unusual illness" in gay men, the worldwide pandemic of HIV infection "rages on" (Ungvarski, 1997). It has been estimated that 20 million people worldwide are infected with the virus and that 100,000 people become infected every day (Ungvarski, 1997). There are a number of ways in which a person can come into contact with HIV. The most common ways are by exposure to contaminated blood or blood products or by exposure to other bodily fluids of infected persons (e.g., semen, cervical secretions, breast milk). Children can also contact the disease from their mothers in utero or during delivery.

In those who are infected with HIV by means of **direct contact** with blood or blood products or bodily fluids (predominantly adolescents, young adults, and mature adults), most often through illicit intravenous drug use, blood transfusion, or through intimate sexual contact (anal, oral, or vaginal) (i.e., **horizontal transmission**), there is, typically, a slow reduction in the number of a specific type of T-cells, known as **helper T-cells, T4 lymphocytes,** or CD4+ T lymphocytes. The function of helper T-cells is to help stimulate the production of antibodies by B-cells, in contrast to suppressor T-cells, which suppress B-cell activity. The reduction in numbers of T4 lymphocytes is caused by HIV invading the T4 cells and replicating within the cells to the point that the cell "bursts." After the T4 cell is destroyed, each of the replicated viruses is then free to enter another T-cell, where again the virus replicates to the point of destruction, and the cycle begins again.

The normal level of T4 lymphocytes is approximately $1,000/mm^3$ of blood; AIDS is currently defined as less than $200/mm^3$.

Since helper T-cells have a role in destroying or neutralizing non-self substances, with the gradual decrease in number, the individual's immune defenses are damaged and **opportunistic infections** occur with greater regularity. It is common for persons with AIDS to experience one or more infectious conditions, the most common being *Pneumocystis carinii* pneumonia, meningitis, and encephalitis. The greater the drop in T4 cells, the more likely the individual will become seriously ill.

In children who contract the disease from their mothers in utero, during delivery, or as a result of breast feeding (i.e., **vertical transmission**) (Rutstein, Conlon, & Batshaw, 1997), abnormal B-cell function, rather than T-cell function, is more common. As a result of the action of HIV on the B-lymphocytes, there are deficiencies in both the cellular and humoral systems, and like those who contract the virus via blood, there is an increased risk for infections. Common are bacterial infections, such as strep throat; viral infections, such as cytomegalovirus; and parasitic infections, such as toxoplasmosis. Children can also contract HIV through drug use or through sexual intercourse.

In both children and adults, HIV can also invade the body's macrophages, and since these cells are capable of crossing the blood-brain barrier, the virus can spread to the brain, resulting in extensive brain damage. In younger children, the neurologic disorder is referred to as **progressive encephalopathy,** a condition that typically results in developmental delay or loss of specific skills (e.g., cognitive, motor, linguistic, psychosocial, and sensory or perceptual skills). In older children and adults, the CNS disorder takes the form of **AIDS-dementia complex (ADC).** Early symptoms include impaired concentration and forgetfulness; however, typically, there is eventual confusion, disorientation, and psychosis. Neurologic signs of ADC include weakness in the legs that results in an unsteady gait, tremor in the arms and hands, and spasticity. Children with progressive encephalopathy may also show signs of a movement disorder (e.g., spasticity, ataxia). It is believed that 10% of all children with AIDS show signs of progressive encephalopathy (Rivera-Hernandez & Scott, 1996). To monitor the progress of students with CNS involvement, a full assessment should be undertaken on a regular basis, no less frequently than every 6 months.

Educational Implications and Teaching Tips: Students with Immune Diseases Students who are immunodeficient or immunosuppressed are at risk for infection. Unlike the same infections in the student who has a normally functioning immune system, the infections in an HIV-infected student may have dire consequences. For example, a minor illness, such as measles, can be life-threatening to a student who is extremely immunosuppressed. The following suggestions are for teachers working with children and young adults who have an immunodeficiency disorder:

1 *Parents of a student who has an immune disease must be informed immediately that their son or daughter may have been exposed to a communicable disease (i.e., other children in the school who have diseases that are contagious).* Of particular concern are infectious chicken pox, cytomegalovirus, herpes simplex, measles, toxoplasmosis, and tuberculosis. The parents, once informed, can determine the degree of risk for their child and seek out medical assistance.

2 *Because it may be unknown that a particular child has a hyposensitivity disorder, such as AIDS, all staff should use universal precautions in dealing with blood and bodily fluids (e.g., tending a student with a bleeding nose).* For further information on communicable diseases (including AIDS) and suggestions on how to prevent transmission, including details on precautions to take, the reader is referred to chapter 24.

3 *Although there have been no reported cases of transmission of HIV in schools or child care settings, it is not uncommon for infected children and their families to face prejudice and isolation.* For a thorough discussion of some of the legal issues facing children with AIDS and their families, see the recent article by Gross and Larkin (1996).

Autoimmune Diseases

If the immune elements that are involved in the destruction of cellular wastes and nonfunctional cells malfunction and begin to destroy healthy tissues, the individual is said to be **autosensitive** (i.e., hypersensitive to internal cells located within the body), and the person so affected is referred to as having an **autoimmune disease.** The most common diseases that occur in children and adolescents that are thought to be autoimmune diseases (either totally or in part) are rheumatic fever (chapter 8), juvenile rheumatoid arthritis (chapter 15), glomerulonephritis (chapter 18), and juvenile-onset, insulin-dependent diabetes (chapter 19). Multiple sclerosis, a neurologic disease; myasthenia gravis, a neuromuscular disease, and systemic lupus erythematosus, a multisystem inflammatory illness, are also believed to be autoimmune diseases; however, since they are found more commonly in the adult population, these diseases are not addressed here.[3]

Malignant Tumors

If the immune elements that are involved in monitoring the growth of abnormal cells fail to dispose of mutant cells, the body is more susceptible to **malignant disease,** commonly known as **cancer,** a condition in which certain types of abnormal cells, referred to as **anaplastic,** or **undifferentiated, cells,** grow and multiply in a disorderly way in some organ or tissue of the body, thereby replacing or killing the normal cells by robbing the healthy cells of nutrients and blood supply. The terms **neoplasm** ("new growth") and **tumor** are used interchangeably to refer to abnormal cell masses. Since cells that have lost their differentiation are no longer able to perform their intended function, the stage is set for chaos within the organ or the body. It is unknown why some people develop cancer and others do not. Environmental, genetic, and viral factors have all been implicated as causative agents.

The role of the immune system in preventing the development and spread of abnormal cells is not fully understood; however, it has been hypothesized that if the immune elements that are involved in monitoring the growth of abnormal cells fail to dispose of mutant cells in the normal manner, the individual has the potential to develop a cancerous growth. Because

---

[3] In about 20% of all cases of systemic lupus erythematosus, the age of onset is between 8 and 16 years of age (Baumeister & Nicol, 1994). For further information see recently published articles by Baumeister & Nicol (1994), Fuller & Hartley (1991), Halverson & Holmes (1992), and Kuper & Failla (1994).

cancer is more likely to occur in the elderly, it has also been hypothesized that the immune system may be weakened by the aging process. However, cancerous growths are not only found in the adult population. There are approximately 6,500 new cases of cancer per year in children under age 15 in the United States alone, compared to 985,000 new adult cases (Mooney & Field, 1990). One in 600 youngsters is at risk for cancer before the age of 15, with cancer being slightly more common in Caucasians than in African Americans (1.25:1) and in boys than girls (1.07:1) (Robison, Mertens, & Neglia, 1991).

Not all growths are cancerous. Most neoplasms are **benign,** i.e, non–life-threatening. A benign growth typically poses little threat to the individual; however, in some cases, since the tumor, as it grows, can crowd normal tissue, it may require surgical removal. This would be true in the case of a benign brain tumor, which, if allowed to grow, could result in damage to the surrounding tissues from the increased intracranial pressure. Since benign cells are typically **encapsulated,** i.e., enclosed within a fibrous capsule, most noncancerous tumors are localized, making surgical removal relatively easy. In most cases, a benign growth does not recur after removal. Malignant cells that make up life-threatening neoplasms, however, are often *not* encapsulated, and consequently, the likelihood of spread is greater. The invasion can occur in healthy tissue that is adjacent to the primary tumor, or if cells of the tumor "break off," migration can occur so that the malignancy develops at one or more sites distant from the original or primary tumor. The term **metastasis** is used to describe the process by which the cells escape the primary tumor and travel via the blood or lymph system to a new, secondary location.

Once a growth has been located, there are a number of procedures available for the purpose of determining the size of the tumor, whether or not it is malignant, the type of malignancy, and whether the growth has metastasized to surrounding tissues (Heller, Alberto, Forney, & Schwartzman, 1996). Common procedures include physical examination (e.g., palpitation of lumps), blood tests (e.g., CBC count), x-rays films or nuclear medicine scans, and biopsies. A **biopsy** is a surgical procedure in which a small amount of tissue or the entire tumor is removed for further analysis. In children, early detection is mostly accidental (Fernbach & Vietti, 1991). For this reason, teachers should be alert to signs that

a student may be ill and report any symptoms they note to the student's parents.

Because of the potential for spread, treatment for cancer often involves more than simply the surgical removal of the tumor. By using the combination of **radiation therapy** (treatment that involves the use of roentgen rays or gamma rays) and **chemotherapy** (treatment involving chemical agents, known as cytotoxic agents or anticancer drugs), as well as **surgical intervention,** the abnormal cells located throughout the body are removed or destroyed in an attempt to prevent them from continuing to multiply and spread.

Cancer is no longer thought of as an inevitably *fatal* disease; advances in treatment have resulted in cancer being viewed by many to be a *chronic* disease of childhood (Mooney & Field, 1990). In 1960, the 5-year survival rate for cancer in youngsters under age 15 ranged from 3% to 52%, depending on the type and site of the cancer. On average, 28% of children with cancer (all sites included) did not have a relapse within 5 years (Parker, Tong, Bolden, & Wingo, 1997). In contrast, in 1992, the 5-year survival rate[4] was 71% when all types of cancers were examined, and for individual types, the rates ranged from a low of 33% to a high of 93%. The trends in cancer survival for children under age 15 are shown in Table 22.4. It has been estimated that by the year 2000, 1 out of every 900 young adults will be a survivor of some form of childhood cancer (Schwenn, 1996). It is statistics such as these that prompted Fernbach and Vietti (1991) to make the following statement: "The treatment of children with cancer has become increasingly precise. . . . The assault on cancer in children is no longer limited to achieving remission but is directed toward the eradication of tumors to produce cures and to include total rehabilitation" (p. 8).

Unfortunately, however, even with treatment breakthroughs, approximately 1,600 children still die per year as a result of malignancy, making cancer the second most common cause of death in children between the ages of 1 and 14, second only to accidents, which result in approximately 6,000 deaths per year (Parker et al., 1997).

There is no one disease that is known as "cancer"; rather there are more than 100 diseases in which

---

[4] Five years is the period of time that conventionally is believed to be indicative of a "cure" (Tuffrey, Muir, Coad, & Walker, 1993).

TABLE 22.4
Trends in Cancer Survival for Children Under Age 15, United States, 1960–1992

| | FIVE-YEAR RELATIVE SURVIVAL RATES % | | | | | | |
| | YEAR OF DIAGNOSIS | | | | | | |
Site	1960–1963	1970–1973	1974–1976	1977–1979	1980–1982	1983–1985	1986–1992
ALL SITES*	28	45	56	61	65	68	71[†]
Acute lymphocytic leukemia	4	34	53	67	70	70	79[†]
Acute myeloid leukemia	3	5	14	26[‡]	21[‡]	32[‡]	33[†]
Bones and joints	20[‡]	30[‡]	54[‡]	52[‡]	54[‡]	58[‡]	65[†]
Brain and other CNS	35	45	54	57	55	62	61[†]
Hodgkin's disease	52[‡]	90	79	83	91	91	92[†]
Neuroblastoma	25	40	52	53	53	54	63[†]
Non–Hodgkin's lymphoma	18	26	45	51	62	70	71[†]
Soft tissue	38[‡]	60[‡]	60	69	65	78	72[†]
Wilms' tumor	33[‡]	70[‡]	74	77	86	86	93[†]

* Excludes basal and squamous cell skin cancer and in situ carcinomas, except bladder.
[†] The difference in rates between 1974–1976 and 1986–1992 is statistically significant ($p < 0.005$).
[‡] The standard error of the survival rate is between 5 and 10 percentage points.
Source: Parker, S. L., Tong, T., Bolden, S., & Wingo, P. A. (1996). Cancer statistics, 1997. *CA—A Cancer Journal for Clinicians, 47,* 5–27. Copyright 1997 by the American Cancer Society, Ltd. Reprinted by permission.

cells can grow out of control. Children and teens typically have cancers that are known as **sarcomas,** i.e., cancers that are derived from rapidly growing connective or supporting tissue (e.g., bone, cartilage, nerve, muscle, fat), whereas adults typically develop **carcinomas,** i.e., cancers that are derived from epithelial tissues (e.g., skin, large intestine, lungs, stomach, prostate gland, cervix, and breast). In adults, it is prolonged exposure to carcinogens, agents believed to be the cause of cancer, such as smoke, asbestos, and radiation, that appears to be the primary cause of most carcinomas. While exposure to certain carcinogens may be the causative factor in certain cancers in children and teenagers (e.g., exposure to radiation that is linked to certain leukemias), in most cases, it is unknown why some develop sarcomas while the majority do not.

Most adults are aware of the cardinal signs of cancer; the early warning signs of cancer in children differ somewhat (Fernbach, 1985; Fernbach & Vietti, 1991). The differences are primarily a result of the divergent types of cancers that are found in each group. Most cancers in adults involve organs (e.g., breast, lung, colon, prostate gland, uterus), whereas those in children involve tissues (e.g., hematopoi-

etic, lymphatic, CNS, sympathetic nervous system, muscle, bone). The cardinal signs for both groups are shown in Table 22.5.

Some of the most common malignancies found in children are described briefly in the following pages. They are presented in order of highest to lowest frequency. Leukemia, the most common cancer in children, is covered in greater depth than the others.

Leukemia: Cancer of the Hematopoietic System

Leukemia is a malignant disease of the hematopoietic, or blood-making, system of the body (e.g., bone marrow, lymphatic system) that results in normal bone marrow elements being replaced by abnormal, poorly differentiated, immature white blood cells. Leukemia accounts for approximately 30% of all pediatric cancers.

Etiology　Why leukemia occurs is unknown; however, it is known that environmental factors such as exposure to radiation or certain chemicals may contribute to the disease appearing both in children and

TABLE 22.5
Cardinal Warning Signals of Cancer in Children and Adults

Children	Adults
• Persistent fever (increased temperature of unknown origin or caused by infection secondary to the malignancy is often unresponsive to treatment)	• Recurrent fever; weight loss
• Unusual mass or swelling (e.g., abdominal mass; enlargement of lymph node)	• A sore that does not heal; obvious changes in the appearance of a mole or wart
• Development of a bleeding disorder (e.g., sudden tendency to bruise; increased incidence of nose bleeds; collection of blood beneath skin)	• Change in bowel or bladder habits (including bleeding)
• Persistent, localized pain (e.g., pain in lower extremity; severe headache, often with vomiting)	• Unusual bleeding or discharge
• Unexplained paleness and loss of energy; excessive, rapid weight loss; general malaise	• Persistent, nagging cough; hoarseness of voice
• Sudden changes in eye (e.g., yellow-white reflection seen through pupil; swelling of the orbit; crossing of the eye)	• Dyspepsia (indigestion); epigastric distress (pain in the pit of the stomach); difficulty swallowing
• Neurologic abnormalities (e.g., disturbances of balance, gait, or personality; seizures)	• Thickening or lump in breast or anywhere else

adults. Several genetically determined diseases, such as Down syndrome, are also known to be associated with an increased incidence of leukemia.

Different Types of Leukemia   There are several types of leukemia. The two most common forms are acute lymphoid leukemia and acute nonlymphoid leukemia.[5]

Acute lymphoid leukemia. In children, **acute lymphoid leukemia (ALL)** is the most common type of leukemia, occurring in approximately 80% of the cases of this childhood disease (Harmon, 1990). The prefix **lympho-** refers to the involvement of the **lymphatic system** (i.e., lymph nodes, thymus, spleen, tonsils). ALL is also referred to as lymphatic, lymphocytic, lymphoblastic, lymphoblastoid, stem cell, or blast cell leukemia.

Acute nonlymphoid leukemia. The second most frequent type of leukemia, **acute nonlym-**
phoid leukemia (ANLL), accounts for approximately 20% of childhood leukemia (Harmon, 1990). In ANLL, the origin of the disease is the **bone marrow** rather than the lymph system. ANLL is also referred to as granulocytic, myeloid, myelocytic, monocytic, myelogenous, monoblastic, monomyeloblastic, splenomedullary, and splenomyelogenous leukemia.

Incidence and Prevalence   The incidence of leukemia in children and adolescents under the age of 15 is believed to be approximately 43.7 per million and 25.2 per million for white and black children, respectively. In terms of cumulative probability, it is estimated that leukemia will be found in 1 out of every 1,610 white children and 1 out of every 2,730 black children (Robison et al., 1991). Leukemia is found more commonly in boys than in girls, regardless of race. Few children develop leukemia before their first birthday. The incidence peaks between the ages of 2 and 6.

There are approximately 2,000 new cases of ALL each year in children and adolescents under the age of

---

[5] Two forms of leukemia found in children, **basophilic leukemia** and **eosinophilic leukemia**, each named for the specific type of white blood cell involved, are not covered, because they are very rare.

15, accounting for approximately 23% of all new cancers. One case of ALL is diagnosed out of every 2,160 white children and 4,670 black children (Robison et al., 1991). Approximately 350 new cases of ANLL are recognized per year, accounting for approximately 5% of all new cancers in those less than 15 years of age. One case of ANLL is found in every 11,110 white children, and one is found in every 12,500 black children (Robison et al., 1991). The incidence of nonlymphoid leukemia increases with age, making it the most common form of leukemia found in adults.

Characteristics   Regardless of the type of leukemia and the age of the individual, the disease is characterized by an unrestricted proliferation of immature white blood cells, known as **lymphoblasts, or blast cells.** The increased number of blasts infiltrate the bone marrow, crowding out the normal cells. As a result, there are decreased numbers of RBCs, WBCs, and platelets produced by the hemopoietic organs. The consequences of the reduction in number of these normal blood cells are, respectively, **anemia** (as evidenced by fatigue, pallor, dizziness, headache, and insomnia), **infection** (of any organ, including the skin), and **hemorrhage** (as evidenced by bruising of the skin, often without any obvious cause; increased incidence of nose bleeds and bleeding gums; and the development of petechiae, tiny purple or red hemorrhages on the skin). The presence of infection is typically characterized by an increase in body temperature.

Leukemia is also characterized by a number of systemic problems. One potential problem is organ failure, which results from the migration to infiltration of the organ by immature blasts. The spleen, liver, and lymph nodes are common sites of such damage. Not only do the organs become enlarged, but they also eventually develop **fibrosis,** a serious condition in which smooth muscle is replaced by fibrous connective tissue. In some individuals, there may be CNS involvement, resulting in **leukemic meningitis,** which contributes to increased pressure in the cranium. Symptoms include headaches, pain and stiffness in the neck and back, vomiting, irritability, and lethargy. Invasion of immature lymphocytes into the bones and into the membranes covering the bones (i.e., the periosteum) can result in the bones becoming thin and weak, leaving the individual prone to fractures. Severe bone and joint pain is common, accompanied in some cases by swelling of the tissues. Some youngsters with leukemia have a noticeable limp when walking or running. Finally, as a result of the metabolic needs of the increased number of immature WBCs, the other "normal" cells throughout the body suffer. Muscle wasting, weight loss, fatigue, and loss of appetite are typical symptoms in the person with leukemia.

Diagnosis and Treatment   Many children or young adults with leukemia are brought initially to their physician as a result of parents' concerns about their general malaise or weight loss. Because the presenting symptoms are often nonspecific, at first, some other condition, such as an undefined viral syndrome, rheumatoid arthritis, or aplastic anemia (a form of anemia that often results from neoplastic disease, toxic chemicals, radiation, or long-term usage of certain medications), may be suspected (Breitfeld, 1996). A number of laboratory tests (e.g., CBC count, chest x-ray films) confirm the presence of the condition.

Pharmacologic therapy. Treatment for both ALL and ANLL involves the use of a variety of chemotherapeutic agents that are administered orally, intravenously, intramuscularly, or intrathecally (i.e., directly into the spinal cord). These drugs are sometimes given in combination with radiation therapy of the CNS. In many cases, a long-term indwelling central venous access device is inserted to minimize the trauma of frequent needle sticks and vein irritation from the chemotherapy (Dragone, 1996). Treatment typically consists of three or four of the following stages:

1. *The Induction Phase or Remission Induction Phase:* In this initial phase, by means of vigorous treatment with a combination of drugs, typically given orally or by means of intravenous infusion, an attempt is made to reduce the number of leukemic cells to the point that there is no evidence of the disease. Drugs that prevent the proliferation of malignant cells, known as **antineoplastics,** are one of the main classes of drugs given during this stage. Approximately 90% to 98% of youngsters with ALL achieve remission after initial treatment (Steinherz, 1987). Induction therapy can last as long as 4 to 6 weeks.

2. *Central Nervous System Prophylaxis or Sanctuary Therapy:* After remission is achieved, the youngster may undergo further treatment to prevent any possibilities of leukemic infiltration of the CNS. This stage is also referred to as the

intensification-consolidation stage. In the past, the treatment typically involved radiation of the cranium or, in some cases, the cranium and the spine; however, due to the adverse side effects of this particular form of treatment, it is now more common to see children and young adults taking additional antineoplastic drugs on a weekly schedule. The drugs during this stage of treatment are administered directly into the CSF by means of a lumbar puncture. Sanctuary therapy usually begins 6 to 8 weeks after the first phase and generally lasts for about a month.

3. *Maintenance Therapy:* Once remission of the disease occurs, maintenance therapy, usually involving cycles of 3 to 4 weeks of more antineoplastic drugs, may continue for as long as 2 to 3 years to ensure the elimination of any residual leukemic cells that might result in a relapse.

   Maintenance therapy typically has a positive outcome. Poplack (1989), in discussing the research studies that have investigated the optimal lengths of maintenance therapy, reported that after 2.5 years of therapy, approximately 80% of those with ALL were disease-free. During the second, third, and fourth year, the risk of recurrence was 2% to 3% per year, and in most cases, 4 to 6 years after the cessation of therapy, recurrence of the leukemia was uncommon.

4. *Reinduction Phase:* If relapse does occur, a second remission induction phase of treatment may be started. Unfortunately, each time a relapse occurs, the long-term prognosis becomes more guarded; consequently, once the individual achieves remission the second time, a bone marrow transplant, once considered to be an experimental procedure, may be considered to prevent further complications.

Transplantation therapy. The purpose of a **bone marrow transplant (BMT)** is to provide the individual with healthy bone marrow that produces healthy, functioning blood cells. Before the transplant, the child or adult undergoes chemotherapy and total-body irradiation, a process referred to as **conditioning.** There are three purposes for conditioning. The first is to create sufficient space in the bone marrow for the donated cells to produce healthy formed elements; the second, to suppress the person's immune system so that rejection will not occur; and the third, to eradicate the remaining leukemic cells (Vega, Franco, Abdel-Mageed, & Ragab, 1987). During the

transplant, donated bone marrow, along with packed red blood cells and platelets, is transfused intravenously into the blood system. Marrow can come from a genetically dissimilar donor of the same species **(allogenic BMT),** from an identical twin **(syngeneic BMT),** or from the individual's own previously harvested marrow **(autologous BMT).**

A serious complication of bone marrow transplant is **graft-versus-host disease (GVHD).** In GVHD, the person rejects the donated marrow. Rejection typically occurs within weeks or months of the transplant. If the reaction occurs within the first 100 days after transplant, the GVHD is considered acute. If the rejection occurs after 100 days, the condition is considered chronic (August, 1996).

The first sign of GVHD is a rash which first appears on the palms of the hands and soles of the feet, later spreading to the rest of the body. In addition, there may be liver involvement (increase in the level of bilirubin) as well as GI tract upset (diarrhea, abdominal pain). On average, approximately 10% to 25% of children under the age of 10 develop GVHD after an autologous BMT. In youngsters over the age of 10, the incidence of GVHD is higher, typically between 25% and 40%. In BMTs using alternate donors, the percentages can be as high as 60% to 90% (August, 1996).

Side Effects of Treatment   While the various drugs given to fight leukemia are very effective, they have a number of side effects. **Alopecia** (loss of hair) and the development of **oral ulcerations** are the most common side effects, both of which are extremely distressing to the individual. Of greater importance in terms of life expectancy are the potent effects the drugs have on the immune system. Many antineoplastic drugs result in a state of immunosuppression.

Prognosis   In the past, the prognosis of a child or young adult with leukemia was extremely guarded. Before the introduction of antileukemic agents in the late 1940s, most children died within 2 to 3 months of diagnosis; however, Steinherz (1987) reported that the rate of long-term, disease-free survival of children with ALL had increased from less than 1% in 1968 to approximately 60% by the late 1980s. Today the cure rate is approximately 65% to 70% (Breitfeld, 1996). These are the youngsters who are able to come off therapy and continue without a relapse for prolonged periods. Unfortunately, there has not been a corresponding increase in remission rates for individuals with ANLL. For those with this form of leukemia, the prognosis is generally poor and the outcome less favorable. Only 35% to 40% of those with ANLL survive (Breitfeld, 1996).

Cancer of the Central Nervous System

Approximately 19% of all childhood cancers involve the central nervous system (e.g., brain, spinal cord). Tumors of the CNS are the most common solid tumors of childhood. Incidence is reported to be 24.1 per million youngsters under 15 years of age. Approximately 1,100 new cases are diagnosed yearly in the United States (Robison et al., 1991).

Approximately two-thirds of all brain tumors are located in the bottom of the cerebellum or in the brain stem (i.e., in the posterior third of the brain); the remaining third are located above the cerebellum, most commonly in the anterior two-thirds of the brain. Symptoms depend on the anatomic area of the brain affected; however, regardless of the location, in most cases the tumor results in increased intracranial pressure. Headaches (particularly in the morning), general malaise, sleepiness, irritability, changes in personality and behavior, impaired vision, and projectile vomiting (unaccompanied by nausea) are all typical of cranial tumors, along with disturbance in gait and balance, visual field disturbances, and nystagmus (involuntary movement of the eyes). For childhood brain tumors, the peak age of incidence is between 5 and 10 years of age (Hockenberry-Eaton, 1993).

If the CNS tumor is lower in the spine, there may be motoric impairments (e.g., difficulty walking, reaching), bowel or bladder dysfunction, and sensory impairment. In advanced cases, paralysis can occur. Seizures, common in adults with brain tumors, are seen less often in childhood tumors.

Treatment of CNS tumors typically involves surgical removal of the offending mass; however, since not all growths can be removed safely, i.e., without increasing the risk of further damage, radiation or chemotherapy is a common option. Survival rates vary widely. Regardless of the tumor type, the degree of malignancy, and location of the tumor, in approximately 50% of all cases, the prognosis for survival is good.

Cancer of the Lymph System

Neoplasms of the lymphoid tissues, referred to as **lymphomas,** are the third most common form of childhood malignancy. There are a number of kinds of lymphomas, each differing on the basis of degree of cellular differentiation. The most commonly known lymphomas are known as **Hodgkin's disease.** Others are referred to as **non–Hodgkin's lymphomas,** or **lymphosarcomas.** Tumors of the lymph system account for approximately 12% of all childhood cancers.

Hodgkin's Disease Found more commonly in those who are between the ages of 15 and 34, Hodgkin's disease, characterized in its early stage by abnormal cellular proliferation in a single lymph node, can be found in children as young as 5 years of age. It occurs in the United States at a rate of 6.5 cases per million white males, 5.9 per million white females, 7.5 per million black males, and 1.9 per million black females in the population under 15 years of age (Robison et al., 1991).

Hodgkin's disease is usually first evidenced in the neck region, just above the collarbone, with the disease later spreading to the armpit area. As the disease progresses, the cancer typically metastasizes to one or more extranodal organs, such as the spleen, lung, liver, and bone. Symptoms of this particular form of cancer include anorexia, weight loss, malaise, fever, and night sweats. Typically, the individual does not complain of pain in the region around the affected node(s).

Treatment usually involves radiation therapy or chemotherapy or both. Survival rates are between 80% and 90%, depending on the extent of the disease. Unfortunately, those with Hodgkin's disease are at increased risk for developing a second malignancy, the most common one being acute nonlymphocytic leukemia.

Non–Hodgkin's Lymphomas A disease of lymphoid tissues, non-Hodgkin's lymphoma can occur throughout the body. It is found primarily in the abdomen, the chest, the head, and the neck region. Unlike Hodgkin's disease, the lymphoma is rarely localized to one or more nodes. Occurring at a rate of 6.9 cases per million white males, 2.8 per million white females, 3.9 per million black males, and 1.5 per million black females, the incidence increases with age. Annual rates are 6, 9, and 10 per million for children age 4 and younger, ages 5 to 9, and ages 10 to 14, respectively (Robison et al., 1991).

Symptoms of non-Hodgkin's lymphoma depend on the site of the disease. Those with abdominal involvement may experience diarrhea, abdominal distention, vomiting, and colicky pain. Those with tumors in the thorax may have episodes of coughing, wheezing, and shortness of breath. Head and neck disease may be recognized by enlarged lymph nodes, tonsillar masses, nasal congestion, rhinorrhea (nasal discharge), nose bleeds, and loosening of the teeth (Waskerwitz, 1994).

As in the case of Hodgkin's lymphoma, non-Hodgkin's tumors are treated by means of chemotherapy or radiotherapy or both. Prognosis depends on the extent of the disease at the time of diagnosis. Those who have a limited form of the disease in most cases survive. Unfortunately, between 25% and 50% of those with extensive disease succumb to the condition. Individuals with AIDS are at increased risk for non-Hodgkin's lymphoma.

Cancer of the Musculoskeletal System

If considered together, the cancers that involve the musculoskeletal system account for approximately 11% of all pediatric cancers. Cancer of the striated muscle cells (**rhabdomyosarcoma**) accounts for 6% of all cases, whereas bone cancer, the most common being **osteogenic sarcoma,** accounts for 5% of cases. In the United States, the annual incidence of muscle cancer is 4.4 cases per million white children and 1.3 per million black children, whereas for bone cancers, the rates per million are 5.5 for whites and 4.3 for blacks (Robison et al., 1991). Peak incidence of osteogenic sarcoma in adolescents is 11 cases per million population.

Rhabdomyosarcoma   Slightly more common in males than females (1.17:1), rhabdomyosarcoma is usually detected in early childhood or late adolescence. Rhabdomyosarcoma occurs most commonly in the head and neck. Other sites include the genitourinary system, extremities, trunk, and the GI tract. The most common symptom is a hard, nontender mass. Treatment is primarily surgical.

Osteogenic Sarcoma   Also called osteosarcoma, this type of cancer occurs with greatest frequency in persons between 10 and 20 years of age (i.e., during the pubertal growth spurt). Eighty percent of cases are found in children between the ages of 10 and 14, with slightly more girls than boys being affected (1.3:1). The tumor most commonly occurs in the epiphysis region of the long bones but may occur in the diaphysis region. Approximately 80% of all tumors occur around the knee and shoulder, the most common site being the distal femur.

The most common symptom of osteosarcoma is pain over the area of the tumor, unrelated to physical activity. A tender, swollen area or palpable mass is also typical, and the area around the cancer may be warm to the touch. Surgery is the usual form of treatment, and in some cases, depending on the size and location of the tumor, surgery may result in limb amputation. At the time of diagnosis, it is not uncommon for the cancer to have already spread to the lungs; as a result, survival after treatment is lower than that for other forms of cancer (i.e., approximately 60%).

Ewing's Sarcoma   A rarer form of bone cancer, found more commonly in adults than children, Ewing's sarcoma affects primarily the midshaft of the long bones or the various flat bones of the body, such as the pelvis, scapulae, or ribs. The symptoms (i.e., pain, swelling) are similar to those of osteosarcoma. Thirty percent of all bone tumors in children are of this type. The male-to-female incidence ratio is 1.6 to 1.0, and, for no known reason, Ewing's sarcoma is found very infrequently in blacks (2.4 per million incidence for whites, 0.4 for blacks) (Robison et al., 1991).

Cancer of the Sympathetic Nervous System

The fifth most common cancer in children and young adults is tumors of the sympathetic nervous system, referred to as **neuroblastomas.** The most common site is the adrenal medulla; however, other sites include ganglia located within the chest, neck, or head. Approximately 8% of all childhood cancers involve the sympathetic nervous system. This particular type of tumor occurs more frequently in white children than black (12.5 vs. 10.2 per million, respectively), and in 88% of all cases, diagnosis is made before the child reaches age 5. The median age at diagnosis is between the ages of 1 and 2 (Hockenberry-Eaton, 1993).

Symptoms of neuroblastomas depend on the location; however, abdominal pain, loss of appetite, and bowel or urinary problems are typical. Chest pain is common in those tumors that arise in the chest region. Eye problems (e.g., drooping of the eyelid, constriction of the pupil) are common in those whose tumors occur in the head. Surgery and chemotherapy are common forms of treatment. Prognosis varies widely. The younger the child at time of treatment, the better the prognosis. If there is metastasis, survival rate can be as low as 5% or 10%.

Cancer of the Urinary System

Approximately 6% of all pediatric cancers involve the renal system. The most common kidney tumor is **Wilms' tumor,** a mass which develops in the nephrons. In more than 75% of all cases, the diagnosis is made before the child has reached the age of 5. Incidence, which varies on the basis of race, is higher in blacks (11.1 per million) than in whites (8.9) (Robison et al., 1991). Wilms' tumor is also found more commonly in girls than boys (1.00:0.92 for a unilateral tumor and 1.00:0.60 for bilateral tumors) (Green et al., 1996). Approximately 15% of children with Wilms' tumor are born with other anomalies, such as genitourinary malformations and aniridia (iris absent in the eye). Many show signs of cognitive retardation. When the signs are evident at birth, it is believed that the cause is autosomal dominant.

In most cases of Wilms' tumor, a large, firm, non-tender abdominal mass can be easily seen and felt; however, aside from the abdominal enlargement, the youngsters often appear to be otherwise healthy and active (Mooney & Field, 1990). Additional signs of the presence of a tumor may include hypertension, pain, blood in the urine, general malaise, fever, and loss of appetite. The tumor typically is found in only one kidney. If treatment is not initiated, the cancer can metastasize into the lymph system and the respiratory system. Surgery, combined with radiotherapy and chemotherapy, is a typical form of treatment. With early treatment, long-term survival rates approach 90%.

Cancer of the Visual System

Retinoblastomas, tumors that arise in the retina of the eye, account for 3% of all pediatric cancers. The incidence is slightly higher in black children (5.1 per million) compared with white (4.0) (Robison et al., 1991); similarly, the incidence is higher in girls (12.1 per million) than in boys (9.9). This particular cancer is a disease of younger children—almost all cases are discovered before age 5. In approximately 20% of cases, the condition is transmitted as an autosomal dominant trait. As this particular tumor is one that grows rapidly, spreading readily to the brain and other distant sites in the body, surgical removal of

the affected eye(s) is critical. Enucleation (removal) is typically followed by radiation or chemotherapy, or both.

Educational Implications and Teaching Tips

There are a number of resources available for teachers of children and young adults who have some form of cancer. One of the best is a publication entitled *Students with Cancer: A Resource for the Educator,* produced by the National Cancer Institute (National Institutes of Health, 1990). In this publication, it is suggested that the teacher contact the student's parents to obtain the following information before the student returns to school:

- Specific type of cancer and how it is being treated
- Treatment the student is taking, when it is administered, what potential side effects are, and effects on appearance and behavior
- Approximate schedule of upcoming treatment, procedures, or tests that may result in the student's absence from the classroom
- Limitations, if any, on the student's activities (with periodic updates)
- What the student knows about the illness
- For younger students, what the family would like classmates and school staff members to know
- For adolescents, whether the student wishes to talk directly with teachers about any of the above points (p. 6)

It is very important that school staff be knowledgeable about the student's illness. Ross (1984a) made the following comments:

> Uninformed school personnel can hinder the patient's reintegration to school. A lack of knowledge of childhood cancer, negative personal experiences, and changes in the child's appearance or stamina may lead teachers and other school staff to think the worst. Even though the disease is responding to treatment, the child may be perceived as near death, resulting in isolation, overreaction to ordinary complaints, or favoritism. (p. 84)

Peckham (1993), in an article entitled "Children with Cancer in the Classroom," also stressed the importance of teachers being in contact, not only with the student's family, but also with the student. By meeting with the child or young adult, concerns such as the following can be addressed: "Will others stare at me because I look funny?" "Will I still be included, or be dropped from my group?" "Is the teacher mad at me because I missed so much school?" "Will the principal not let me pass the year because I am sick?" "Will I be dumber than the other kids?" "Will I know what to wear?" "Will I be 'out of it'?" (p. 31). A sample lesson plan on childhood cancer is also found in this article. Appropriate for children in grades 1 to 6, recommended questions that can be posed to the class to encourage interaction and discussion include the following: How many of you know someone who has cancer? Did you know that childhood cancer is different from adult cancer? Did you know that there are different kinds of childhood cancers? Does anyone know what cancer is? Do you know how kids get cancer? Can you get cancer by sitting next to or playing with someone with cancer? Do you know how cancer is treated? How do you think the doctors know when the cancer has gone away? Do you know what side effects are? Sample answers are offered, along with a multitude of suggestions that may facilitate the child's reentry to school.

Another useful publication, produced by the Canadian Cancer Society (1993), is *Talking with Your Child about Cancer*. Although written for parents, it has many suggestions that are appropriate for educators. Since it is important that teachers maintain open communication with the student's parents, the following suggestions from this publication (pp. 14–15) may be useful, particularly if the parents turn to school staff for advice:

- Tell your child that they did not do something to get cancer. They are not being punished.
- Be honest about what really happens, and what your child will feel during treatments.
- Say "I do not know" instead of making up answers, which could prove wrong.
- Ask your child what they think, feel, or want to know.
- Let your child express sadness and fear by crying or saying so.
- Let your child express feelings during play. Drawing feelings, or role playing with puppets or dolls, helps children talk.
- Maintain limits on usual rules. Bending rules too far creates anxiety.
- Keep your child in touch with friends. They can help your child feel normal.
- Keep your school-age child in touch with school. Doing homework and going back to class help your child feel normal.

- Let your child have some control over making decisions. They can decide many things if they do not interfere with their health or treatment.
- Get the whole family to talk together about the illness and treatments. They can support each other.
- Do not forget that your child will have good days and bad days.
- Take time every day to love and support each other.
- Get support from others when you need it.

In the preceding section, each of the most common types of cancer in childhood and adolescence has been described briefly. The following suggestions are applicable to most youngsters who have cancer; however, it may be advisable for the reader to review the suggestions given in previous chapters as they relate to specific body systems. For example, a teacher with a student who has leukemia may benefit from reading chapter 9, in which the hematologic system is described in detail and in which specific suggestions are given regarding students who have symptoms typical of a blood disorder. Similarly, the teacher of a student who has osteosarcoma may find useful information in chapter 14, which covers disorders of the supporting structures in general and such topics as limb amputation.

1 *Children and young adults with cancer should return to school as soon as possible after discharge from the hospital, because "returning to school and rejoining classmates are psychologically therapeutic for the sick child"* (Fernbach, 1985, p. 267). Research has shown that those who delay reentry have more problems with reintegration than those who return early (Ellerton & Turner, 1992). Katz, Varni, Rubenstein, Blew, and Hubert (1992), in discussing the importance of resuming pre-illness activities and environments as soon as medically feasible, made the following comments:

> For the child with cancer, continuation of his/her social and academic activities provides an important opportunity to normalize as much as possible a very difficult and ongoing stressful experience. The child who is denied continued school participation is, in effect, being denied a major opportunity to engage in age-appropriate, goal-oriented behavior. Such interference with normal activities of daily living may lead to a sense of learned helplessness, reinforcing feelings of hopelessness and despair, thus obstructing the child's ability to cope with his/her illness and rehabilitation process. (p. 69)

In a similar manner, Ross (1984a) suggested that "returning to school is particularly significant because of the symbolic message that the child is better" (p. 84). It is her position that "academic success helps the child maintain a degree of control over his/her life and the changes wrought by the disease." In another article, Ross (1984b) made the following comment: "School is a focal point of achievement for all children, but for the child experiencing a life-threatening illness, school symbolizes the possibility of a future. . . . At school, expectations are placed and connections are maintained with regard to aspects of life that are separate from illness"(p. 152).

Chekryn, Deegan, and Reid (1986), after interviewing students with cancer on the experience of returning to school after treatment, made the following comments regarding the importance of school as part of the "usual business of living":

> The children perceived school as a normalizing environment in and of itself. Since school is the work of children, the return to the classroom signaled the resumption of the child's usual routines of life. School symbolized normalcy: "I got better and I wanted to do the things I used to do. So, I went back to school." (p. 20)

Link (1982), in discussing the impact of treatment on children with cancer, stressed the importance of classmates and daily routine of classes "for the child for whom other measures of normalcy no longer exist" (p. 56). He suggested that it is desirable for children with cancer to "progress in school along with their classmates, so that the years of therapy can be remembered as a difficult period in their lives—not as lost years."

2 *Returning to school is not without problems.* Tuffrey and her colleagues (1993), in a study of 33 students who had been diagnosed with cancer and who had returned to school—22 at the primary and 11 at the secondary level—found that the students experienced a number of physical and psychological problems. The major obstacles that were reported by teachers are shown in Table 22.6.

3 *In many cases, the student who has cancer will continue to receive treatment on an out-patient basis after returning to school.* Students are more likely to cooperate with their treatment regimen if it does not interfere significantly with their normal daily routine. School staff, medical staff, and parents, working together, can often prevent excessive absenteeism by means of careful planning. Ideally,

TABLE 22.6
Reintegration Problems Experienced by Children with Cancer

Physical Problems	No. of Children
Fatigue and physical weakness	22
Skin problems and hair loss	4
Pain	2
Neurologic problems	6
Tendency to infection	1
Dressings to be changed	1
Psychological and Behavioral Problems	**No. of Children**
Embarrassment	3
Anxiety and depression	8
Reluctance to return to school	2
Poor relationship with peers	8
Uncooperative with staff	1

Source: Tuffrey, C., Muir, K. R., Coad, N. A. G., & Walker, D. A. (1993). Return to school in children treated with cancer. *Journal of Cancer Care, 2,* 194–200. Reprinted by permission of the publisher, Churchill Livingstone.

treatments should be scheduled so that there are as few disruptions to the student's life as possible. In some cases, however, regardless of careful planning, assignment deadlines may need to be extended, and times for tests and examinations may need to be rescheduled to fit the student's scheduled appointments.

4 *Some students with cancer, particularly leukemia, may develop academic difficulties as a result of treatment.* Impairments in visual-motor integration, problem-solving, and short-term memory, along with decreased intelligence scores, have been reported in youngsters who have undergone radiation treatments (Brown & Madan-Swain, 1993). However, as more and more pediatric oncologists (cancer specialists) are becoming aware of the potential academic problems of those who have received radiation, treatment protocols are changing so that long-term CNS sequelae are either avoided or minimized (Poplack, 1989). For further discussion of the cognitive, neuropsychological, and academic sequelae in children with leukemia, see the in-depth article by Brown and Madan-Swain (1993).

In children whose academic performance is affected, the student should have a complete psychoeducational assessment upon return to school, and remediation should be made available if necessary. In addition, teachers should be aware that the external psychological stresses related to the trauma of illness, to painful diagnostic procedures, and to subsequent hospitalization, along with depression related to the diagnosis and uncertainty about the future, may interfere with optimal performance in the classroom (Link, 1982; Mahaney, 1992).

5 *Persons with certain types of cancers, particularly leukemia and lymphoma, become immunosuppressed as a result of the disease or its treatment.* Consequently, they are extremely susceptible to infections. **The student's family must be contacted if it appears that the student has a temperature higher than 101°F and if any of the following symptoms occur: cough, rapid breathing, congestion, diarrhea, stomachache, headache, lesions or sores, earache, sore throat, or pain around the rectum** (Hockenberry-Eaton, 1993). Good handwashing practices should be used by all to prevent the spread of infection. Typically, the student's physician will determine that the student is able to return to school if the absolute neutrophil count is above $500/mm^3$ blood (Whaley & Wong, 1995). However, if the count falls below this level, the student should probably be isolated at home to prevent illness.

It is critical that students who are immunosuppressed not be exposed to certain communicable diseases, particularly shingles (herpes zoster), chicken pox (varicella), and measles (rubeola). Outbreaks of any of these conditions should be reported to the student's parents, along with any actual or suspected exposure to one of these diseases, so that the student can be given appropriate treatment (National Institutes of Health, 1990). Students who are immunosuppressed should be kept home from school in times of moderate or severe risk (Mooney & Field, 1990).

6 *Students with cancer who have a low platelet count may develop a bleeding disorder.* **All bleeding episodes, including blood in the sputum, vomit, or feces, no matter how minor, must be reported to the parents.** Typically, blood in sputum or vomit is bright red. Bleeds that occur in the upper GI tract are recognized by the presence of dark, tarry-appearing stools; lower GI bleeds are recognized by fresh blood in the stool. If the student has a nose bleed, pressure should be applied below the bridge of the nose (by pinching the nostrils) for a minimum of 10 to 15 minutes.

Students with cancer should also be monitored for the appearance of **petechiae** (purple or red spots on the skin that range from pinpoint to pinhead in size), **ecchymosis** (discoloration of an area of skin, also known as a bruise), and **hematomas** (collection of blood under the skin, also known as a blood blister), because these are all additional signs of bleeding.

7 *Students with cancer who are encountering pain may appreciate a shortened day.* Since pain on arising is common in certain types of cancer, the student may be better off being in school from mid-morning to mid-afternoon, thereby having a chance to feel better before coming to school, and to leave early if fatigue sets in.

8 *Children and young adults typically know their own limits—they should be encouraged to do as much as they feel like doing, but they should never be pushed beyond their limit.* Some days they may be able to participate in certain physical activities; on others they may simply be too tired. Teachers should be alert to any students who "push their limits." Such behavior is more common in adolescents who want desperately to be "part of the crowd."

Students with cancer who have bleeding tendencies should be prevented from participating in contact sports and activities that might place them at risk for injury, particularly head injury. Students with low platelet counts (below $100,000/mm^3$) should take extra precautions to prevent falling and running into objects. Climbing, bicycling, skateboarding, roller skating, and "roughhousing" activities may need to be postponed until the count rises (i.e., after the student receives a blood transfusion).

Students with cancer who have low hemoglobin levels and develop anemia that results from either the cancer or the treatment tire easily. Other symptoms of anemia include shortness of breath on exertion, general weakness, and headaches. Some may complain of being dizzy. Students who suffer from fatigue may benefit from having a rest period during school hours; others may benefit from reduced attendance at school (e.g., half-days) until the count rises. Physical activities may need to be curtailed.

9 *Students who have been treated for cancer may develop a disturbance in personal identity that comes from an altered body image and decreased self-esteem.* Loss of hair, development of cushingoid features (e.g., a moon-shaped face), and amputation scars are all realities of the world of those who have undergone surgery, chemotherapy, or radiation therapy. The teacher should be alert to the emotional state of the student and ensure that teasing by classmates does not occur. Referral for counseling may be appropriate.

10 *School staff can play a very supportive role in working with students who have cancer.* Laurie Bildfell (1995),[6] who at the age of 40 received a diagnosis of cancer, wrote an article entitled "When a Friend Has Cancer." The following pointers, written in the first person, are from that article:

- **Be there.** Don't suddenly drop off the face of the Earth just because I have cancer. I'm easily pleased: a post card, a two-dollar violet, a phone call. Don't procrastinate—I need your friendship and support now.
- **Don't treat me differently.** I am the same person. Some cells are running wild in my body, but I still like to laugh, go to movies, swim at the Y. Life goes on.
- **Please do ask me how I am.** I may not always want to talk about my illness or my treatment, and I probably won't, but if you don't even ask "How are you?" a central fact of my life suddenly becomes shuttered, forbidden and unacknowledged, a deep black hole that we tiptoe carefully around, pretending it's not there.
- **Listen to me.** I get tired of being strong all the time. It's great to hear about your cousin in Montreal who had exactly the same cancer and is doing fine, but there are days when I really don't feel things are going well. I'd like to be able to talk about it. Please don't silence me with bouncy optimism. Every cancer patient knows we don't all make it. I need to be able to acknowledge that.
- **Do unto others.** Perish the thought, but you may be here one day too. Think about how you would like to be treated. Then do it.

The following letters, one written by Amy Louise Timmons (1975)[7] a month before she died and the second by her attending physician, shortly after her death, reinforce the importance of positive outlook, taking each moment as it comes, and living life to the fullest.

Letter by Amy Louise Timmons

I have acute lymphoblastic leukemia. But please don't feel sorry for me. I live a perfectly wonderful life.

I go to parties, play games, swing on swings, and, for the most part, I am able to do whatever I want. I think that this is an important part of life which some parents of children who have leukemia overlook, and I think they should not! I think that children who have leukemia should be able to play when they feel up to it, unless they have a cold or have just had a shot that makes them sick. . . .

Even though you have leukemia and can still have fun, it's not all fun and games. There are some disadvantages and pain along with having fun. But aren't there disadvantages and pain in every life?

There are more chances of living with leukemia now than there ever were before. But not many people realize this. They still think it's an awful disease and almost everyone who has it dies. Not so! The doctor told me that I would probably live only for another year. But look what happened! I have lived for four years, and I am still living to write this article. So instead of feeling sorry for people with leukemia, just say to yourself, look how much medicine has accomplished.

Also you must think of people with leukemia as people with feelings, and you must treat them as people with feelings, not as pitied objects. Is it really so awful?

Letter from Amy's Doctor

Amy Timmons wrote this in May 1974, and died one month later, on June 14. In spite of her illness, she was an honor student, president of her class, and active in the Girl Scouts. She left the hospital to attend her sixth-grade graduation, and to go on a four-day vacation with her family. The day before she died she had enjoyed swimming and playing on the beach, and that night, she had stayed up until 11 p.m., playing games with her family. Amy died in a coma the day she was to return to the hospital. (p. 988)

🐾 Summary

Disorders of the immune system take on a number of forms. Some children and young adults are hyper-

---

[6] Bildfell, L. (1995, November). When a friend has cancer. *Chatelaine, 68*(11), 208. Reprinted by permission.

[7] Timmons, A. L. (1975). Is it so awful? *American Journal of Nursing, 75,* 988. The American Nurses Association. Copyright © 1975 by Lippencott-Raven Publishers, Philadelphia, PA. Reprinted by permission.

sensitive to specific stimuli; others are hyposensitive. In some cases, the stimuli that the individual is sensitive to are a part of his or her own body; in other cases, the child or young adult is not sufficiently sensitive to part of his or her own body that is growing abnormally. Each type of disorder has a different effect on the individual's growth and development. Some of the disorders are relatively easy to treat; others are fatal.

Children and adolescents who have altered immunity often return to school during periods of relative good health. Having an understanding teacher is critical in helping the student to adjust to the major life changes that must be faced. Some of the suggestions given in this chapter should be of use to school staff who are working with these students on a daily basis.

References

August, C. S. (1996). Bone marrow transplantation. In F. D. Burg, J. R. Ingelfinger, E. R. Wald, & R. A. Polin (Eds.), *Gellis & Kagan's current pediatric therapy* (15th ed., pp. 315–318). Philadelphia: W. B. Saunders.

Baumeister, L. L., & Nicol, N. H. (1994). Pediatric lupus and the role of sun protection, *Pediatric Nursing, 20,* 371–375.

Bildfell, L. (1995, November). When a friend has cancer. *Chatelaine, 68*(11), 208.

Breitfeld, P. P. (1996) Acute leukemia. In F. D. Burg, J. R. Ingelfinger, E. R. Wald, & R. A. Polin (Eds.), *Gellis & Kagan's current pediatric therapy* (15th ed., pp. 303–306). Philadelphia: W. B. Saunders.

Brown, R. T., & Madan-Swain, A. (1993). Cognitive, neuropsychological and academic sequelae in children with leukemia. *Journal of Learning Disabilities, 26,* 74–90.

Canadian Cancer Society (1993). *Talking with your child about cancer.* Toronto, ONT: Author.

Cavales-Oftadeh, L., & Heiner, D. C. (1996). Anaphylaxis. In F. D. Burg, J. R. Ingelfinger, E. R. Wald, & R. A. Polin (Eds.), *Gellis & Kagan's current pediatric therapy* (15th ed., pp. 713–715). Philadelphia: W. B. Saunders.

Chekryn, J., Deegan, M., & Reid, J. (1986). Normalizing the return to school of the child with cancer. *Journal of the Association of Pediatric Oncology Nursing, 3,* 20–24, 34.

Dedyna, K. (1995, January 17). Extreme reactions. *The Times Colonist, C,* 1.

Dragone, M. A. (1996). Cancer. In P. L. Jackson & J. A. Vessey (Eds.), *Primary care of the child with a chronic condition* (2nd ed., pp. 193–231). St. Louis: Mosby.

Ellerton, M.-L., & Turner, C. (1992). "Back to school"— An evaluation of a re-entry program for school-aged children with cancer. *Canadian Oncology Nursing Journal, 2*(1), 8–11.

Fernbach, D. J. (1985). The role of the family physician in the care of the child with cancer. *CA—A Cancer Journal for Clinicians, 35*(5), 258–270.

Fernbach, D. J., & Vietti, T. J. (1991). General aspects of childhood cancer. In D. J. Fernbach & T. J. Vietti, *Clinical pediatric oncology* (pp. 1–10). St. Louis: Mosby.

Fuller, C., & Hartley, B. (1991). Systemic lupus erythematosus in adolescents. *Journal of Pediatric Nursing, 6,* 251–257.

Gold, M., Sussman, G., Loubser, M., & Binkley, K. (1996). Anaphylaxis in schools and other child care settings. *Canadian Journal of Allergy and Clinical Immunology, 1,* 4–11.

Green, D. M., D'Angio, G. J., Beckwith, J. B., Breslow, N. E., Grundy, P. E., Ritchey, M. L., & Thomas, P. R. M. (1996) Wilms' tumor. *CA—A Cancer Journal for Clinicians, 46,* 46–63.

Gross, E. J., & Larkin, M. H. (1996). The child with HIV in day care and school. *Nursing Clinics of North America, 31,* 231–241.

Halverson, P. B., & Holmes, S. B., (1992). Systemic lupus erythematosus: Medical and nursing treatments. *Orthopaedic Nursing, 11*(6), 17–24.

Harkins, A. (1994). Altered immune function. In C. L. Betz, M. M. Hunsberger, & S. Wright (Eds.), *Family-centered nursing care of children* (2nd ed., pp. 1565–1647). Philadelphia: W. B. Saunders.

Harmon, D. C. (1990). The leukemias. In W. S. Beck (Ed.), *Hematology* (4th ed., pp. 323–337). Cambridge, MA: MIT Press.

Hay, G. H., Harper III, T. B., & Courson, F. H. (1994). Preparing school personnel to assist students with life-threatening food allergies. *Journal of School Health, 64,* 19–121.

Heller, K. W., Alberto, P. A., Forney, P. E., & Schwartzman, M. N. (1996). *Understanding physical, sensory, and health impairments: Characteristics and educational implications.* Pacific Grove, CA: Brooks/Cole.

Hockenberry-Eaton, M. (1993). Children with cancer. In D. B. Jackson & R. B. Saunders (Eds.), *Child health nursing: A comprehensive approach to the care of children and their families* (pp. 731–759). Philadelphia: J. B. Lippincott.

Katz, E. R., Varni, J. W., Rubenstein, C. L., Blew, A., & Hubert, N. (1992). Teacher, parent, and child evaluative rating of a school reintegration intervention for children with newly diagnosed cancer. *Children's Health Care, 21*(2), 69–75.

Kuper, B. C., & Failla, S. (1994). Shedding new light on lupus. *American Journal of Nursing, 94*(11), 26–32.

Link, M. P. (1982). Cancer in childhood. In E. E. Bleck & D. A. Nagel (Eds.), *Physically handicapped children: A medical atlas for teachers* (2nd ed., pp. 43–58). New York: Grune & Stratton.

Mahaney, F. X., Jr. (1992). Late effects of childhood cancer treatment can be life-threatening. *Journal of the National Cancer Institute, 84*(5), 42K–42L.

McLoughlin, J. A., & Nall, M. (1994). Allergies and learning/behavioral disorders. *Intervention in School and Clinic, 29,* 198–207.

Minister of Supply and Services Canada (1996). *Anaphylaxis: A handbook for school boards.* Ottawa, ONT: Author. [Available from Canadian School Boards Association, 130 Slater St., Suite 350, Ottawa, Ontario I1P 6E2.]

Mooney, K. H., & Field, R. B. (1990). Aberrant cellular growth: Implications for the child and family. In S. R. Mott, S. R. James, & A. M. Sperhac (Eds.), *Nursing care of children and families* (2nd ed., pp. 1781–1843). Redwood City, CA: Addison-Wesley.

Mueller, I. L. (1991). Care of the patient with an immune disorder. In B. L. Christensen & E. O. Kockrow (Eds.), *Foundations of nursing* (pp. 1054–1069). St. Louis: Mosby.

National Institutes of Health (1990). *Students with cancer: A resource for the educator* (NIH Publication No. 91–2086). Bethesda, MD: National Cancer Institute. [Available from NCI, 1-800-4-CANCER]

Parker, S. L., Tong, T., Bolden, S., & Wingo, P. A. (1997). Cancer statistics, 1997. *CA—A Cancer Journal for Clinicians, 47,* 5–27.

Peckham, V. C. (1993). Children with cancer in the classroom. *Teaching Exceptional Children, 26*(1), 27–32.

Poplack, D. G. (1989). Acute lymphoblastic leukemia. In P. A. Pizzo & D. G. Poplack (Eds.), *Principles and practice of pediatric oncology* (pp. 323–366). Philadelphia: J. B. Lippincott.

Rivera-Hernandez, D. M., & Scott, G. B. (1996). HIV infection. In F. D. Burg, J. R. Ingelfinger, E. R. Wald, & R. A. Polin (Eds.), *Gellis & Kagan's current pediatric therapy* (15th ed., pp. 645–651). Philadelphia: W. B. Saunders.

Robison, L. L., Mertens, A., & Neglia, J. P. (1991). Epidemiology and etiology of childhood cancer. In D. J. Fernbach & T. J. Vietti (Eds.), *Clinical pediatric oncology* (4th ed., pp. 11–28). St. Louis: Mosby.

Ross, J. W. (1984a). Resolving nonmedical obstacles to successful school reentry for children with cancer. *Journal of School Health, 54*(2), 84–86.

Ross, J. W. (1984b). The child with cancer in school. In J. Fithian (Ed.), *Understanding the child with a chronic illness in the classroom* (pp. 152–163). Phoenix: Oryx Press.

Rutstein, R. M., Conlon, C. J., & Batshaw, M. L. (1997). HIV and AIDS. In M. L. Batshaw (Ed.), *Children with disabilities* (4th ed., pp. 163–181). Baltimore, MD: Paul H. Brookes.

Schwenn, M. R. (1996). The child cured of cancer. In F. D. Burg, J. R. Ingelfinger, E. R. Wald, & R. A. Polin (Eds.), *Gellis & Kagan's current pediatric therapy* (15th ed., pp. 306–307). Philadelphia: W. B. Saunders.

Steinherz, P. G. (1987). Acute lymphoblastic leukemia of childhood. *Hematology and Oncology Clinics of North America, 1*(4), 549–566.

Timmons, A. L. (1975). Is it so awful? *American Journal of Nursing, 75,* 988.

Trzcinski, K. M. (1993). Update on common allergic diseases. *Pediatric Nursing, 19,* 410–414.

Tuffrey, C., Muir, K. R., Coad, N. A. G., & Walker, D. A. (1993). Return to school in children treated with cancer. *Journal of Cancer Care, 2,* 194–200.

Ungvarski, P. J. (1997). Update on HIV infection. *American Journal of Nursing, 97,* 44–51.

Vega, R. A., Franco, C. M., Abdel-Mageed, A. M. S., & Ragab, A. H. (1987). Bone marrow transplantation in the treatment of children with cancer: Current status. *Hematology and Oncology Clinics of North America, 1*(4), 777–800.

Waskerwitz, M. J. (1994). Neoplasms/cancer. In C. L. Betz, M. M. Hunsberger, & W. Wright (Eds.), *Family-centered nursing care of children* (2nd ed., pp. 1874–1937). Philadelphia: W. B. Saunders.

Whaley, L. F., & Wong, D. L. (1995). *Nursing care of infants and children* (5th ed.). St. Louis: Mosby.

CHAPTER 23

Communicable Diseases

KEY WORDS

Antifungals or fungicides

Antiparasitic agents

Antivirals or virucides

Bacteria

Bactericidal antibiotics

Fungi

Parasites

Sexually transmitted diseases (STDs)

Viruses

It has been estimated that 60% of all youngsters who go to their doctor with a specific health problem are diagnosed as having some form of infectious disease—the most common being the flu, the common cold, or a sore throat (Harrington, 1992). While some infectious conditions, such as poliomyelitis, have been almost entirely eliminated in developed nations, there are others, such as AIDS and hepatitis, that are reaching epidemic proportions both in developed and undeveloped countries. It is the increased numbers of persons with these conditions that have changed the world as we know it today. Gostin (1990), in discussing the various court cases that have involved persons with AIDS, made the following comments:

> Discrimination based on an infectious condition is just as inequitable as discrimination based on race, gender, or handicap. In each case, people are treated inequitably not because they lack inherent ability, but solely because of a status over which they have no control. Complex and often pernicious mythologies develop about the nature, cause, and transmission of disease. As the Supreme Court [of the United States] has recognized, "society's accumulated myths and fears about disability and disease are just as handicapping as are the physical limitations that flow from actual impairment. Few aspects of handicap give rise to the same level of public fear and misapprehension as contagiousness." (p. 2086)

Communicable diseases are the result of the invasion of pathogenic agents (i.e., bacteria, viruses, fungi, parasites) into the body. Some conditions, such as conjunctivitis, may have more than one causative agent; others, such as mumps, are caused by a specific agent. Many of the more common communicable diseases found in young children, such as impetigo, affect primarily the integumentary system; others, such as measles, may involve several systems at the same time. While it is beyond the scope of this text to discuss all of the communicable diseases in detail, information regarding some of the more common conditions is given, along with the information regarding the educational implications of the disease. While many consider infectious diseases a part of childhood, in some cases complications can arise that are life-threatening. In Table 23.1, some of the complications from selected childhood diseases for which immunizations are available (i.e., preventable diseases) are shown.

Common Bacterial Infections

Bacteria (pl.; **bacterium,** sing.) are unicellular microorganisms, of which there are many different types. The major distinguishing features are the shape, size, and number. If the bacterium is round or egg-shaped, the suffix **-coccus** (sing.; **-cocci,** pl.) is used (e.g., *Staphylococcus,* a genus of bacteria commonly found on the skin and in the mouth and throat). Cocci can occur singly, in pairs, in chains, or in irregular bunches. Rod-shaped bacteria are referred to as **bacilli** (pl.; **bacillus,** sing.) (e.g., *Bacillus anthracis,* a species of bacteria that can cause anthrax, a disease that affects the respiratory and the integumentary systems). Spiral-shaped bacteria are referred to as **spirochetes** (e.g., *Spirochaeta pallida,* the causative agent of syphilis), and those that are shaped like a comma are known as **vibrios** (e.g., *Vibrio cholerae,* the agent implicated in cholera, a disease of the small intestine). Some bacteria are able to live in the presence of air (**aerobic** bacteria), whereas others cannot (**anaerobic** bacteria).

The primary treatment of bacterial infections is pharmacologic. There are a number of **bactericidal antibiotics,** drugs that kill bacteria, the most common being penicillin and erythromycin. Antibiotics are available in many different forms (e.g., pills, ointments, eye drops), and the choice depends primarily on the site of the infection.

It is normal for the human body to harbor a variety of bacteria. In most cases, however, there is little risk of disease, unless the bacteria invade the body, take up residence, and multiply to the point that illness occurs. For example, it is normal for the human body to have bacteria in the mouth; however, in some individuals, particularly those who do not floss their teeth on a regular basis, the bacteria may become mixed with mucin (a secretion of the salivary glands) and adhere to the surface of the teeth and between the teeth and the gums (gingiva), resulting in the development of dental cavities and infections of the gingival tissue. The development of this film, often referred to as dental plaque, is typically not considered to be life-threatening; however, if as a result of periodontal disease (disease of the gingival tissues that surround the teeth at the gum line) or as a result of the tissue being cut during dental work or when the individual flosses, the bacteria enter the blood system and travel to the heart, a condition known as bacterial endocarditis may occur (chapter 8). Without treatment, this condition can be fatal,

TABLE 23.1

Some Complications from Selected Childhood Diseases for Which Immunizations Are Available

Complication	DISEASE						
	Mumps	Rubeola	Rubella	Polio	Tetanus	Pertussis	Diphtheria
Cognitive impairment		X	X			X	
Brain damage		X	X			X	
Meningoencephalitis	X	X	X				
Paralysis				X			X
Blindness		X	X				
Deafness	X	X	X				X
Pancreatitis	X						
Juvenile-type diabetes	X						
Orchitis[a] (postpubertal)	X						
Oophoritis[b] (postpubertal)	X						
Sterility (males)	X						
Pneumonia	X	X			X	X	X
Heart damage/pericarditis	X						X
Polyarthritis			X				
Hepatitis	X						
Nephritis	X						X
Cerebral hemorrhage						X	
Muscle spasm					X		
Death	X	X	X	X	X	X	X

Source: Clemen-Stone, S., Eigsti, D. G., & McGuire, S. L. (1995). *Comprehensive family and community health nursing* (4th ed.). St. Louis: Mosby. Copyright 1995 by Mosby-Year Book, Inc. Reprinted by permission.

[a] Inflammation of the testes
[b] Inflammation of the ovaries

particularly in cases where an individual has some type of unresolved cardiac difficulty.

Some of the most common bacterial infections seen in children and young adults are described in Table 23.2.

🦠 Common Viral Infections

Viruses are ultramicroscopic parasitic organisms, smaller than bacteria, that are capable of growing and replicating within a living cell. There are more than 200 viruses that can cause disease in humans, including the **adenoviruses**, implicated in certain types of conjunctivitis, upper respiratory infections, and infections of the GI tract; the **enteroviruses**, which cause, among other conditions, pericarditis and meningitis; the **rhinoviruses**, which are the causative agent of many types of respiratory infec-

tions, including the common cold; and the **myxoviruses**, a class of viruses that includes the influenza viruses, the causative agents of what is often referred to as the "grippe" or the "flu."[1]

As in the case of bacterial infections, treatment for viral infections typically involves the administration of drugs, specifically **antivirals**, or **virucides**, drugs that are capable of destroying a virus or making it inactive, such as Zovirax, used in the treatment of genital herpes simplex.

In Table 23.3 some of the more common viral diseases of childhood and adolescence are shown. Two conditions, **poliomyelitis**, more commonly referred to as **polio**, and **smallpox**, have virtually been

---

[1] Viral infections that are transmitted by means of sexual contact (e.g., AIDS, genital herpes) are described in the section on sexually transmitted disease.

TABLE 23.2
Common Bacterial Infections in Children and Young Adults

Condition	Symptoms/Educational Implications
CONJUNCTIVITIS ("Pinkeye") *Agent:* Bacterial or viral; allergy or environmental factor *Source of Transmission:* Tears of infected person *Mode of Transmission:* Direct contact from infected person; can also spread indirectly by fomites	*Symptoms:* Swollen eyelids, inflamed conjunctiva (inner lining of eye), excessive tearing (particularly in viral conjunctivitis), production of a thick discharge that typically makes the eyelids sticky, particularly upon awakening **Bacterial and viral conjunctivitis are highly contagious. Students with bacterial or viral conjunctivitis should remain out of school until the acute symptoms subside, typically 24 hours after the start of antibiotic treatment** (Cordell, Solomon, & Hale, 1996). **They should be encouraged not to rub their eyes and to wash their hands after touching their face. Caregivers and other students should try to avoid touching the face of an affected individual. If contact is made, the person should be particularly careful not to touch his or her own eyes and be sure to wash his or her hands immediately.**
PERSUSSIS ("Whooping Cough") *Agent:* Coccobacillus, *Bordetella pertussis* *Source of Transmission:* Discharge from respiratory tract of infected persons *Mode of Transmission:* Direct contact or droplet spread; can also spread indirectly by means of fomites (e.g., washclothes, handkerchiefs)	*Symptoms:* Characterized by attacks of severe coughing, known as **paroxysms,** which end in a loud "whooping" inspiration as the individual gasps for air. Cough can trigger gag reflex (i.e., person will vomit). Can result in severe complications (e.g., pneumonia, convulsions, hemorrhage, asphyxia); children under 1 year of age are particularly at risk. Symptoms can last for at least 6 to 8 weeks. **Students with whooping cough should remain out of school until at least 5 to 7 days of antibiotic therapy have been completed** (Cordell et al., 1996). **Students can return to school while still having a cough, but they should be sufficiently recovered before reentry. Students who have no evidence of immunity should remain out of school for at least 14 days after last exposure, or until they have completed 5 to 7 days of antibiotic treatment** (Cordell et al., 1996).
PNEUMONIA *Agent:* Streptococcal or staphylococcal bacteria; virus (e.g., rhinovirus); or mycoplasma (ultramicroscopic organism similar to a virus) *Source of Transmission:* Discharges from mucous membranes of nose and nasopharynx *Mode of Transmission:* Direct contact; droplet spread; fomites	*Symptoms:* Severe chills, high fever, headache, productive cough, and pain in the chest area **A student with pneumonia typically is kept home for at least 48 hours after the initiation of antibiotics or until sufficiently recovered and capable of benefiting from being in school** (Clark, 1992).

Continued

TABLE 23.2
(Continued)

Condition	Symptoms/Educational Implications
SCARLET FEVER ("Scarlatina") *Agent:* Group A beta-hemolytic streptococcal bacteria *Source of Transmission:* Nasopharyngeal secretions of infected person *Mode of Transmission:* Direct contact; droplet spread; fomites; or ingestion of contaminated milk or food	*Symptoms:* Fever, vomiting, sore throat, headache, chills, abdominal pain, irritability, and general malaise. Within 12 to 72 hours after onset, a rash appears. Most common sites are the base of the neck, the armpits, the groin, and the trunk. Typically, the rash spreads so that the entire body, except the face, is covered. In the early stages, the tongue looks like it has a white furry coat. After 4 or 5 days, the white coat peels off and the individual is left with a reddened tongue, often referred to as a **strawberry tongue.** Early treatment is important because acute complications, in particular glomerulonephritis and rheumatic fever, can occur. **Because scarlet fever, or at least the streptococcal pharyngitis that causes it, is highly contagious, isolation is mandatory. An infected student should not be allowed to return to school until the fever has disappeared and antibiotics have been taken for at least 24 hours** (Castiglia, 1992).
DIPHTHERIA *Agent:* Bacterium, *Corynebacterium diphtheriae* *Source of Transmission:* Mucous membrane discharge (nasopharynx, skin, other lesions) *Mode of Transmission:* Direct contact; fomites	*Symptoms:* Characterized by the production of a toxin that is damaging to the heart, respiratory system, and circulatory system. If untreated, can be fatal. **Students with diphtheria must stay at home until cultures of the nose and throat are negative (i.e., there is no evidence of the bacteria in the respiratory system)** (Clark, 1992).
LYME DISEASE *Agent:* Spirochete bacterium, *Borrelia burgdorferi.* *Source of Transmission:* Blood of infected person *Mode of Transmission:* Bite of a tick; mammalian host is commonly either the white-tailed deer or the white-footed mouse	*Symptoms:* Recognized by the development of a particular type of skin lesion, an **erythema chronicum migrans** (ECM). Starting as a small papule, which spreads outwards, it enlarges in size, taking on the appearance of a doughnut. Lesions can be as large as a small plate. Other symptoms include fever, headache, malaise, fatigue, anorexia, stiff neck, muscle and joint pain, sore throat, abdominal pain, and cough. Some individuals develop meningitis, facial palsy, or heart abnormalities 2 to 11 weeks after the initial bite. Approximately 50% develop arthritis, typically in the large joints (e.g., knee). **Person-to-person spread does not occur in tick-borne diseases. Isolation is not necessary. However, the student should remain at home until sufficiently recovered.**
MENINGITIS/ENCEPHALITIS *Agent:* Bacterial meningitis usually caused by *Streptococcus pneumoniae*, *Neisseria meningitidis*, or *Haemophilus influenzae;* can also be caused by viruses, yeasts, and fungi. Encephalitis can be caused by anarbovirus	*Symptoms:* Severe headaches, irritability, and general malaise; may be marked stiffness of the neck. If not treated early, deafness, blindness, paralysis, or cognitive impairment can result. **Students with meningococcal meningitis should remain out of school for at least 24 hours after drug therapy has been initiated or until the student is sufficiently recovered** (Clark, 1992).

(arthropod-borne virus) transmitted by an infected mosquito.

Source of Transmission: Discharges from mucous membranes of nose and nasopharynx

Mode of Transmission: Direct contact; droplet spread; fomites. Can gain entry by means of penetrating wound, spinal cord anomaly (e.g., spina bifida), or surgical procedures (e.g., lumbar puncture).

Students with bacterial encephalitis should remain out of school for at least 24 hours after drug therapy has been initiated or until the student is sufficiently recovered (Clark, 1992).

OTITIS MEDIA (Middle-Ear Infection)

Agent: Bacterium, most commonly *Haemophilus influenzae* or *Streptococcus pneumoniae;* can also be viral

Source of Transmission: Nasopharyngeal secretions of infected person

Mode of Transmission: Causative agent travels via the eustachian tube from the throat region into the middle ear

Symptoms: Sensation of "fullness" in the ear. Earaches, fever, headache, and general malaise are common. Typically, one ear is involved at a time, and often, in the case of the child who has repeated ear infections, the same ear tends to be involved. May show signs of hearing loss.

In severe cases, surgical intervention may be required. Under general anesthesia, **tympanotomy tubes** are inserted into the eardrum so that fluid can drain from the middle ear to the outer ear and air can enter the middle ear from the outer ear. While most children with tubes in are allowed to swim, albeit with earplugs in, it is important that they do not engage in activities that permit excessive amounts of water to enter the ears (e.g., diving from a board, scuba diving, jumping into the water) or permit contaminated water to enter (e.g., wash their hair in water from the bathtub, swim in contaminated water from a lake or river).

While otitis media is not considered an infectious condition per se, the upper respiratory infection that causes the condition can easily be spread. In the early stages of the "cold" the student should remain at home until the acute symptoms subside. Those with lingering symptoms or a mild respiratory tract infection can return to school if they feel sufficiently recovered.

ROCKY MOUNTAIN SPOTTED FEVER

Agent: Rickettsial bacteria, *Rickettsia rickettsii*

Source of Transmission: Blood of infected person

Mode of Transmission: Bite from an infected tick; mammalian sources include a variety of wild rodents (e.g., ground squirrels, wood rats, chipmunks, weasels) and dogs

Symptoms: General malaise, fatigue, fever (which can last for 2-3 weeks), chills, severe headache, deep muscle and joint ache, photophobia (increased sensitivity to light), anorexia, nausea, abdominal distention, and mental confusion. Symptoms may not occur for 3 to 12 days after the bite (CDC, 1995a). Skin involvement starts as a red rash that appears on the ankles and wrists. Typically spreads quickly so that the entire body, including the palms of the hands and soles of the feet, is covered. Gangrene may develop in vulnerable sites, such as the terminal parts of bodies (e.g., toes, earlobes, scrotum). If not treated, the condition can be fatal.

Person-to-person spread does not occur in tick-borne diseases. Students with Rocky Mountain spotted fever do not need to be isolated. However, a student with this condition should remain at home until sufficiently recovered.

TABLE 23.3
Common Viral Infections in Children and Young Adults

VARICELLA ("Chicken Pox")

Agent: Varicella zoster virus

Source of Transmission: Respiratory tract secretions; fluid from skin lesions

Mode of Transmission: Direct contact; droplet spread; fomites

Symptoms: Low-grade fever, anorexia, general malaise, or listlessness. Skin rash involves lesions that appear in crops, first on the trunk, followed by areas on the scalp, face and extremities. Lesions typically progress rapidly from a **macule** (small, flat blemish) to a **papule** (raised skin lesion) to a **vesicle** (a blister containing fluid). Within 8 hours from the initial eruption, vesicles rupture and crust appears. Scabs fall off in 5 to 20 days after they appear.

Chicken pox can be fatal to those who have a suppressed immune system.

Students with chicken pox should be kept home and should remain there until no longer contagious (i.e., all vesicles are dried and the scabs are well formed/crusted). In most cases they can return to school approximately 5 to 6 days after the onset of the rash, barring any complications (Cordell et al., 1996). In some cases, a student continues to have weeping lesions for as long as a week to 10 days, and during that time he or she should stay out of school (Puzas, 1994).

RUBELLA (German Measles or 3-Day Measles)

Agent: Rubella virus

Source of Transmission: Nasopharyngeal secretions; blood, stool, and urine of infected person

Mode of Transmission: Direct contact; airborne droplets; fomites

Symptoms: Stiffness and soreness of the neck area that result from the enlargement of the lymph nodes; diffuse, fine, red rash, which first appears on the face and later spreads, within 12 to 24 hours, until the entire body is covered; general malaise, arthralgia, loss of appetite, low-grade fever, headache, conjunctivitis, rhinitis (inflammation of the mucous membranes of the nose); symptoms usually only last for 2 to 3 days.

Isolating the student while the rubella rash is present will help stop the spread of the disease. However, since the student is communicable before and after the outbreak, it is impossible to prevent the disease from spreading. It is generally recommended that the student remain home for at least 6 to 7 days after the rash appears (Cordell et al., 1996). If at all possible, a student with rubella should not have direct contact with women who are in the first trimester of pregnancy.

If a student has no evidence of immunity to rubella, he or she should not attend day care or school for 3 weeks after the onset of a rash in the last case or until all susceptible students have been immunized (Cordell et al., 1996).

Children who are born with rubella are considered to be contagious for 1 year after their birth unless cultures of their urine or nasal secretions are negative after 3 months of age (Bale & Murph, 1992).

RUBEOLA (Red Measles or Regular Measles)

Agent: Rubeola virus

Source of Transmission: Respiratory tract secretions; blood and urine of infected person

Mode of Transmission: Direct contact with airborne droplets

Symptoms: Early stages often mistaken for a severe cold because the primary symptoms include a fever, general malaise, nasal congestion, coughing and sneezing. Conjunctivitis is also common; 3 days after onset, symptoms worsen, and by the 4th day, a rash that starts around the hairline of the neck, ears, and forehead is obvious; as the rash spreads downwards, the symptoms tend to increase in severity and the individual is most uncomfortable; 7 to 8 days after onset, temperature begins to return to normal, the cold-like symptoms lessen, and the rash fades.

Students with measles should remain isolated at home for at least 4 to 6 days after the rash appears.

If a student has no evidence of immunity to measles, he or she should not attend day care or school for 2 weeks after the onset of a rash in the last case or until all susceptible students have been immunized (Cordell et al., 1996).

PAROTITIS (Mumps)

Agent: Paramyxovirus

Source of Transmission: Saliva

Mode of Transmission: Direct contact; droplet spread; can be spread by kissing

Symptoms: Swelling of one or both **parotid glands** (salivary glands located just below and in front of the ear); anorexia, fever, headache, earache, and pain on eating or drinking. Complications can include inflammation of the brain, heart, pancreas, testes, ovaries, kidneys, and liver. Deafness can also occur, as can arthritis.

Mumps is highly communicable; unfortunately, the condition is most contagious 2 to 3 days before the symptoms appear, so it is difficult to isolate the student to prevent the spread. Since the student remains communicable while there is swelling, he or she should remain home for a period of no less than 9 days after onset of swelling (Clark, 1992).

If a student has no evidence of immunity to mumps, he or she should not attend day care or school for 3 weeks after the onset of a rash in the last case or until all susceptible students have been immunized (Cordell et al., 1996).

INFECTIOUS MONONUCLEOSIS ("Mono" or "Kissing Disease")

Agent: Epstein-Barr virus, a herpes virus; also believed to be associated with other agents (e.g., rubella virus, hepatitis A virus, cytomegalovirus)

Source of Transmission: Saliva

Mode of Transmission: Direct contact; kissing

Symptoms: Extreme fatigue, lethargy, fever, sore throat, swollen lymph glands, and enlargement of the spleen and liver. "Mono" is a self-limiting condition and typically resolves in several weeks; relapses are not uncommon. Some develop acute ulcerative gingivitis (infection of the gum tissues). As a result of this condition, the breath may take on a fetid odor.

Students who have infectious mononucleosis should remain out of school until after acute symptoms subside. If the student has shown signs of spleen involvement, there should be a delay in resumption of strenuous physical activity until spleen is nonpalpable (i.e., cannot be perceived by touch). The student should not engage in any contact sports until permission is received from the physician (Clark, 1992; James, 1990a).

ERYTHEMA INFECTIOSUM (Fifth Disease)

Agent: Parvovirus B_{19}

Source of Transmission: Infected persons; possibly respiratory secretions

Mode of Transmission: Unknown; probably airborne droplets; possibly blood

Symptoms: Initially, the child may feel feverish and complain of a headache and general malaise; 1 to 4 days later, rash develops on the cheeks, later spreading to the arms, thighs, trunk, and buttocks. Typically lasts for up to 10 days; however, for a variable period of time after that, the rash may reappear if the individual is exposed to heat, cold, or sunlight or the skin is irritated; some youngsters develop a transient form of arthritis and arthralgia.

When the cheeks are fiery red (in the later stage of the disease), the condition is no longer contagious, so there is no reason for isolation; however, since the red cheeks are occasionally mistaken for signs of child abuse, the parents may opt to keep their son or daughter inside. In the medical literature, erythema infectiosum is sometimes described as **"slapped cheek syndrome."**

Continued

TABLE 23.3
(Continued)

Although erythema infectiosum is highly contagious, isolation is not necessary with this condition because it is considered a mild disease. Students do not need to stay home from school unless they are feeling poorly (Cordell et al., 1996). Students with this condition should be kept away from women who are pregnant because there is an increased risk for fetal abnormalities and anemia.

CYTOMEGALIC INCLUSION DISEASE (CID)

Agent: Cytomegalovirus (CMV), a herpes-type virus

Source of Transmission: Saliva, vaginal secretions

Mode of Transmission: Direct contact; sexual activity

Symptoms: Often mistaken for the flu, because symptoms include general malaise, low-grade fever, and anorexia.

In persons who are immunosuppressed, CMV can cause retinal infections that can lead to blindness as well as GI and respiratory infections that can be severely debilitating.

CMV infection is not considered to be highly contagious. Isolation is not required under normal circumstances (Cordell et al., 1996).

It is important that staff, particularly female staff who are pregnant, be alert to the potential spread of the disease and use precautions, such as proper hand-washing techniques and diapering procedures, to avoid contracting the condition.

Children who are born with CID are considered to be communicable and may be capable of spreading the condition for as many as 8 years after birth (Heller, Alberto, Forney, & Schwartzman, 1996). Spread is the result of the virus being present in the urine, saliva, blood, tears, stool, cervical secretions, and semen.

HEPATITIS A & B

Agent: Hepatotropic virus (e.g., hepatitis A virus, hepatitis B virus)

Source of Transmission: Hepatitis A: Fecal material, contaminated food or water; Hepatitis B: Blood and other bodily fluids; fecal material

Mode of Transmission: Differs depending on type—Hepatitis A: mainly by means of fecal-oral transmission; Hepatitis B: often arises from contact with contaminated needles, equipment, and blood and through sexual intercourse

Symptoms: Often mistaken for the flu, typical symptoms include loss of appetite and gastric discomfort (e.g., nausea and vomiting); fever, jaundice, clay-colored stools, tea-colored urine, and pain in the area over the liver (upper right quadrant of the abdominal cavity) are common. Typically, hepatitis A has a rapid, acute onset, whereas hepatitis B has a slower, insidious progression. Those with hepatitis B are at increased risk for developing cirrhosis of the liver and primary liver cancer.

Students with hepatitis A should remain out of school until at least 1 week has elapsed since the onset of the illness or the development of jaundice (Cordell et al., 1996). Even though the student may remain jaundiced beyond a week, he or she is no longer communicable, and if he or she feels well enough to benefit from being at school, the student's doctor will most likely permit the student's return.

Students with hepatitis B should be managed in a case-by-case manner. Typically, students with chronic hepatitis B virus infection do not need to be excluded from school (Cordell et al., 1996).

eradicated in North America as a result of widespread vaccination programs. Polio does still occur sporadically in developed countries and, with greater frequency, in undeveloped countries. No cases of smallpox have been reported in the United States since 1949.

❦ Common Fungal Infections

Fungi are plants that lack chlorophyll. Included in this classification are the various types of **molds, rusts, mildews, smuts, mushrooms,** and **yeasts** that are common in our environment. In the world there are over 100,000 known species of fungi; over 100 species are found in human beings (*Mosby's,* 1994).

In most cases, fungi cause little or no problems; however, ten different types are known to be pathogenic to humans. The most common site of a fungal infection is the skin; however, several fungi are known to invade other organs. For example, in aspergillosis, a fungal infection caused by the genus *Aspergillus,* the ears and the lungs are vulnerable sites. In histoplasmosis, an infection caused by inhaling spores of the fungus *Histoplasma capsulatum,* the mouth, nose, spleen, lymph nodes, and lungs can be affected. However, systemic fungal infections such as these are relatively uncommon in children and young adults. Common fungal infections in this population include dermatophytosis and pityriasis versicolor. Candidiasis is a common yeast infection. These three conditions are described in chapter 21. Treatment of fungal infections is typically pharmacologic. Administration of an **antifungal,** or **fungicide,** a drug that kills a fungus, such as Fungizone or Nizoral, is routine.

❦ Common Parasitic Infestations

A **parasite** is not a specific organism; rather, a parasite is an organism that obtains nourishment from another organism (the host). In this group are such organisms as tapeworms, pinworms, lice, and mites. Parasites are classified into two groups: **facultative parasites,** those that live on a host but are capable of living independently, and **obligate parasites,** those whose survival depends on the host. Treatment involves the administration of an **antiparasitic agent.**

The choice of drug is linked to the type of parasite. For example, an anthelmintic is given to destroy parasitic worms, such as tapeworms and roundworms, whereas a pediculicide is given to treat lice.

While most people are disturbed by the thought of children or adolescents being infected by parasitic animals, such infestations have plagued the human race throughout its existence. Parasitic infestations can affect the young and the old, the rich and the poor, and can occur in both males and females. While parasitic infections are more common in undeveloped countries because of poor sanitation and suspect hygiene practices, many North American children, particularly preschool children, become infected as a result of participating in certain activities that put them at risk (Feroli, 1994). The three major activities include: (1) engaging in spontaneous hand-to-mouth activities without hand washing; (2) playing on the ground and investigating dirt with their hands, mouth, and feet; and (3) going barefoot. Several parasites that affect the integumentary system, in particular lice and scabies, were introduced in chapter 21. Three additional parasitic diseases are described in Table 23.4.

❦ Educational Implications and Teaching Tips: Students with Communicable Diseases

In most cases, students who have a communicable disease are kept at home until they are no longer able to transmit the condition to another person; most students will be out of school for only a few days. Typically, the educational program does not suffer, and the child or young adult returns capable of resuming a full schedule of activities. In contrast, the special educational needs of children who have one of the congenital STORCH infections can be quite intense, particularly if they have the dual impairment of blindness and deafness. While it is beyond the scope of this text to attempt to cover the topics of curriculum options and academic instruction, the reader may consult the text by June Bigge (1991) entitled *Teaching Individuals with Physical and Multiple Disabilities.* In this section, suggestions are given that primarily relate to efforts that should be undertaken to decrease the likelihood of spread of a communicable disease.

TABLE 23.4
Common Parasitic Diseases in Children and Young Adults

ASCARIASIS (Roundworm)

Agent: Roundworm, *ascaris lumbricoides.*

Source of Transmission: Eggs of roundworm found in contaminated soil or the feces of a child who is infected

Mode of Transmission: Oral-fecal; consumption of contaminated food

Symptoms: In many cases, the young child will be asymptomatic; however, in some cases, complaints of mild abdominal discomfort are typical. Condition is first recognized by the presence of eggs in the feces. In cases where the worm grows to a large size (e.g., 15 to 35 cm by 3 to 4 mm), intestinal obstruction can occur. Symptoms of this complication may include nausea, vomiting, pain, and, in some cases, abdominal distention.

After ingestion, the eggs develop into larvae in the intestine, and over time, the larvae migrate, via the lymphatic and circulatory system, to the lungs. First signs of a parasitic infestation may be early respiratory symptoms (e.g., coughing, wheezing, fever), which are sometimes mistaken for pneumonia. As the child coughs, the larvae are expelled upward into the throat region, at which point they are swallowed. The larvae then travel to the jejunum, where they take up residence. At maturity, eggs are produced that either are expelled in the feces or develop into larvae, and so the cycle begins again.

Students are not typically removed from school. Treatment, repeated until the student is free of all eggs or larvae, must be implemented as soon as the condition is recognized.

It is important that all those in direct contact with the student (e.g., family members, particularly young siblings) be treated simultaneously. The development of good hygiene practices is critical to keep the condition from spreading further.

1   *The development and widespread use of vaccines in developed countries has led to a significant reduction in the incidence of many communicable diseases that were, in the past, quite common.* Currently, immunizations are available for measles, mumps, pertussis, polio, rabies (available on a limited basis), rubella, tetanus, diphtheria, hepatitis B, influenza, and tuberculosis (not commonly used because only moderately effective). Researchers are actively working on the development of vaccines against chicken pox, cytomegalovirus, herpes, and HIV (Matocha, 1995).

Even with these medical breakthroughs, there are a number of children and young adults in developed countries, such as the United States, who are not vaccinated. Even though it has been reported

that toddler immunizations are at an all-time high (i.e., 75% of all 2-year-olds have received their full series of recommended shots), it has been estimated that more than 1 million American children still need one or more doses of a vaccine (Stenson, 1996).

The following factors may contribute to some children not being immunized before they enter school (Clark, 1992; Clemen-Stone et al., 1991; James, 1990a; Stenson, 1996):

- Financial hardship of the parents
- Religious beliefs of the parents
- Media coverage of adverse reactions to immunizations, resulting in some parents fearing the consequences of having their child immunized

---

ENTEROBIASIS or OXYURIASIS (Pinworm, seatworm, threadworm)

Agent: Nematode, *Enterobiasis vermicularis*

Source of Transmission: Several animals are hosts for the pinworm, including the domestic dog and cat

Mode of Transmission: Fecal-oral route (e.g., ingestion of traces of cat/dog feces after playing in a sandbox); can be spread through the inhalation of eggs (e.g., if contaminated underwear or bedclothes are shaken, the eggs can become airborne)

Symptoms: Intense anal itching (the worms themselves cause little discomfort; it is the depositing of the eggs in the rectal and vaginal areas by the female worm that results in severe itching); fatigue (which results from difficulty sleeping because of the itch). Since the eggs can adhere under the fingernails, it is important that the child's nails be kept short and that the child's hands be washed regularly (e.g., after toileting, before eating, before preparing food). Children with pinworms should be discouraged from sucking their thumbs and from biting their nails.

Students are typically not restricted from being in school.

Rarely do parents inform the school that their child has the condition, so staff must be careful to ensure that they do not inadvertently become infected. The best preventative measure is good hygiene (e.g., scrupulous hand washing).

TOXOPLASMOSIS

Agent: Protozoan parasite, *Toxoplasma gondii*

Source of Transmission: Common in cats, which acquire the protozoan by consuming infected birds and mice; pigs and cattle can also be hosts

Mode of Transmission: Handling cat feces; eating inadequately cooked meat that contains toxoplasmosis cysts

Symptoms: Low-grade fever, sore throat, general malaise, and rash; in most cases, symptoms are very mild and, in some cases, virtually nonexistent; complications can include the development of an inflammation of the heart muscle and lungs.

It is extremely difficult to isolate students with toxoplasmosis because in many cases parents would be unaware that their son or daughter is harboring this parasite.

Pregnant women and immunosuppressed individuals should routinely be screened for the condition so that they can be treated. This can be a very serious condition in those who are immunosuppressed.

To prevent spread, all sandboxes on the school grounds should be covered when not in use. If impossible to cover, sand pits should be raked daily to ensure that all cat feces are removed.

- Lack of understanding of the complicated vaccine schedule
- Mistaken belief of parents that children do not need to be vaccinated until they enter school
- The increased mobility of families, leading to fragmented health care
- Lack of consumer awareness, understanding, and responsibility
- Inadequate funding for immunization research at the federal level
- Resistance by public school systems to compliance with state immunization requirements
- Apathy because the evidence of childhood disease is no longer obvious

Cases of communicable disease must be reported to the Centers for Disease Control and Prevention.

As can be seen in Tables 23.5a and 23.5b, while there has been great success in decreasing the number of cases of some diseases (e.g., mumps, rubella), there has also been a resurgence in the incidence of some of the others (e.g., gonorrhea, tuberculosis). The numbers in Table 23.5a are for all age groups, and even though all of the conditions are referred to as "reportable diseases," some conditions are very much underreported. One such disease is hepatitis. In 1992, the CDC suggested that approximately 300,000 people were infected with hepatitis and that only 22,000 cases were reported to the authorities.

If possible, school personnel should encourage parents to have their children vaccinated before they enter school because, in most cases, the risk of serious illness and even death are far greater than the risks from vaccination. The recommended

TABLE 23.5A
Notifiable Diseases, Summary of Reported Cases by Year, United States, 1950–1990

Disease	NUMBER OF REPORTED CASES BY YEAR				
	1950	1960	1970	1980	1990
AIDS	NA	NA	NA	NA	41,595
Encephalitis, primary infection	1,135	2,341	1,580	1,362	1,341
Encephalitis, postinfection	NA	NA	370	40	105
Gonorrhea	286,746	258,933	600,072	1,004,029	690,169
Hepatitis A	2,820	NA	56,797	29,087	31,441
Hepatitis B[a]	NA	NA	8,310	19,015	21,102
Measles (rubeola)[b]	319,124	441,703	47,351	13,506	27,786
Mumps[c]	NA	NA	104,953	8,576	5,292
Pertussis (whopping cough)[d]	120,718	14,809	4,249	1,730	4,570
Poliomyelitis (paralytic)[e]	NA	2,525	31	8	6
Rubella (German measles)[f]	NA	NA	56,552	3,904	1,125
Syphilis (all stages)	217,558	122,538	91,382	68,832	134,255
Tuberculosis (new-active)	NA	55,494	37,137	27,749	25,701
Varicella (chicken pox)*	NA	NA	346	510	173,099

NA = not available (i.e., at that time, the disease did not need to be reported)
[a] Hepatitis B vaccine licensed 1982
[b] Measles vaccine licensed 1963
[c] Mumps vaccine licensed 1967
[d] Pertussis vaccine licensed 1949
[e] Poliomyelitis vaccine licensed 1955; oral vaccine licensed 1961
[f] Rubella vaccine licensed 1969
* Varicella is only reportable in 25 states. Approximately 3.7 million cases occur annually; of these, an estimated 4% to 5% are reported.
Source: Centers for Disease Control and Prevention. (1994). Summary of notifiable diseases, United States, 1994. *MMWR, 43,* 71–79.

schedule is widely available in public health, pediatric, and general practice offices.

Not only should there be concern about children not being immunized, there should be particular concern for the young females who grow up into mature young adults capable of producing children. However, the young males who are not immunized are also capable of spreading the disease, so immunization efforts should not be directed solely towards female adolescents.

2 *Hepatitis B can be an "occupational hazard" for those who are working with special needs children, particularly children who have previously been in segregated institutions for the disabled (e.g., mental hospitals, segregated schools for the mentally retarded)* (Bauer & Shea, 1986). Those who have limited contact with persons who have hepatitis B (e.g., in corridors, assemblies, or cafeterias) are *not* at risk. **Only those who have had prolonged, close contact with the carrier or with fomites are likely to become infected.**

There is a vaccination that offers protection from hepatitis B virus (HBV), and all staff working with individuals who are infected with HBV should be inoculated as a condition of employment. However, even with inoculation, extra care should be taken when in contact with potentially contaminated blood or other body fluids.[2] If an unvaccinated staff person is exposed to HBV, **hepatitis B immune globulin (HBIG)** can be administered prophylactically in an attempt to prevent the spread of the disease. For further information on the prevention of HBV infection in school settings, see the published guidelines offered by the American Academy of Pediatrics (1993).

[2] For further information on universal precautions, see chapter 24.

TABLE 23.5B
Notifiable Diseases, Summary of Reported Cases by Age Group, United States, 1994

	NUMBER OF REPORTED CASES BY AGE GROUP				
Disease	**Under 1**	**1–4**	**5–9**	**10–14**	**15–19**
AIDS	318	418	148	146	324
Encephalitis (primary infection)	54	71	86	72	42
Encephalitis (postinfection)	7	17	31	11	8
Gonorrhea	—	—	—	8,508	123,079
Hepatitis A	130	1,911	4,076	2,492	2,036
Hepatitis B	55	73	82	165	807
Lyme disease	27	650	1,142	831	632
Measles (rubeola)	72	174	95	128	255
Mumps	13	237	473	271	128
Pertussis (whooping cough)	1,640	837	496	548	301
Rocky Mountain spotted fever	3	29	51	24	34
Rubella (German measles)	11	17	13	4	11
Syphilis (all stages)	—	—	—	118	2,234
Tuberculosis	164	860	399	272	544
Varicella (chicken pox)	227	2,772	4,119	771	256

Source: Centers for Disease Control and Prevention. (1994). Summary of notifiable diseases, United States, 1994. *MMWR, 43,* 10.

3 *Since children with congenital rubella are known to harbor the virus for several years after their birth, staff working with young children who are infected should be tested to determine their level of immunity.* Those who are not immune should be vaccinated.

4 *To prevent the spread of communicable diseases, if appropriate, the infected student be kept at home until he or she is no longer able to spread the disease to others.* However, in many cases, parents are not aware of the signs and symptoms of the disease and may not be aware of the recommended period of isolation. Schools can and should take an active role in educating parents in how to recognize the condition and what to do if they suspect that their child has become ill. Parents should be informed if there has been an outbreak of a particular condition in their child's school, so they can be alert to the condition possibly occurring in their child.

5 *If a student cannot produce evidence of immunity to vaccine-preventable diseases (e.g., has not been immunized or does not have a history of*

physician-diagnosed illness), it is typically recommended, and often mandated by the public health authority, that the student be removed from the day care center or school if there is an outbreak of certain diseases, in particular, measles, mumps, pertussis, and rubella (Cordell et al., 1996). For further information, staff should contact their local public health nurse.

6 *Parents of students who are immunosuppressed (e.g., receiving corticosteroid therapy) or have some form of immune deficiency (e.g., have leukemia or are HIV-positive) must be informed immediately if their child has been exposed to any communicable disease.* Of particular concern are chicken pox, cytomegalovirus, herpes simplex, measles, toxoplasmosis, and tuberculosis, because the consequences of these conditions may be fatal if the child does not get immediate medical treatment. However, since all communicable diseases pose some degree of risk, early notification is critical for all outbreaks.

7 *The spread of many communicable diseases can be decreased by practicing proper hygiene measures.* Not only can teachers function as proper role models, they can also teach children the standards of good hygiene.

Hand washing is undoubtedly the most important preventative measure for most communicable diseases. The three main objectives of proper hand washing are (a) to remove disease-causing organisms from the hands, (b) to prevent the spread of microorganisms from person to person, and (c) to prevent the spread of microorganisms to the caregiver's body, e.g., through a break in the skin or by mouth through food (Silkworth, 1986). The recommended procedures for proper hand washing are found in chapter 24.

Silkworth (1986) has listed the following situations in which caregivers should be sure that they wash their hands:

- Before and after caring for any student
- After contact with any contaminated equipment, urine collection bags, toilets, dressings, and sinks
- Before and after assisting with a special procedure, such as tracheostomy suctioning or catheterization
- Before eating, drinking, or smoking
- Before administering medication
- Before handling any clean or sterile equipment or utensils
- Before and after handling students' food or dishes
- After handling soiled diapers, garments, or equipment
- Before and after going to the bathroom

Silkworth (1986) has also listed the following situations in which students should wash their hands:

- Before eating
- After going to the bathroom
- After hands have come in contact with any infected material, e.g., bandages, respiratory or nasal secretions, or body fluids from their own or others' bodies
- Before and after a self-care procedure, such as catheterization

8 *Not only is hand washing important, ensuring that food and drink are not contaminated is also critical.* The following suggestions address these areas of concern.

a. Proper food preparation (i.e., fastidious cleaning of all equipment, such as cutting boards and knives) and storage (e.g., foods are properly covered to prevent contamination by flying insects) are essential, as are a proper waste disposal system and a safe water supply. Foods that are to be eaten hot must be kept hot, and foods that are to be eaten cold must remain cold.

b. All food preparation areas should be kept as dry as possible, and areas that have been in contact with potentially contaminated materials (e.g., meat, fish) should be wiped down with some type of disinfectant at least once a day. To reduce the risk of infection, meats, especially poultry, should be cooked adequately. All dishes and glasses should be washed and dried in a dishwasher. Items washed by hand need to be washed with soap and hot water.

c. While away from the school (e.g., on field trips, outdoor camping adventures), students should be taught never to drink water from streams or lakes. All water that might be suspect must be properly treated.

d. All fruits and vegetables should be washed before serving. Food that has fallen on the floor should be washed before eating or be thrown out if it is impossible to ensure that washing will remove all dirt.

9 *Two diseases, Lyme disease and Rocky Mountain spotted fever, are transmitted by means of ticks.* Since ticks typically inhabit trees and long grasses, children who are in wooded or grassy areas for any amount of time (e.g., out playing, participating in a nature hike) are particularly vulnerable. Suggestions on how to prevent insect bites in general were presented in chapter 21. The following points should be noted:

a. Caregivers should check the child's clothing and skin for the presence of ticks often (i.e., every 2 to 3 hours). The most frequent sites of infestation are the child's head and around the waist.

b. If a tick is found, it should be removed immediately. However, in order for tick-borne conditions to be transmitted, the infected tick must be embedded in the child for a considerable amount of time, at least 6 to 8 hours (James, 1990b). The proper method to remove a tick is given in Table 23.6.

TABLE 23.6
Correct Procedure for Removing a Tick

1. Ticks should be removed as soon as they are noticed. Ideally, they should be removed with a pair of tweezers or forceps; however, if none is available, ticks can be removed by hand. However, to prevent contamination of the skin, fingers should be covered with tissue paper, or a pair of rubber or latex gloves should be worn.

   Do not attempt to remove the tick with petroleum jelly, nail polish, or any hot objects, such as a hot paper clip, a lit match, or a burning cigarette or by means of any other home remedies; such procedures may actually increase the chance of contamination.

2. Gently grasp the tick as close as possible to the skin.

3. Slowly pull the tick with a firm, steady pressure until it separates from the body. It is important not to squeeze, crush, or puncture the body of the tick because this may result in the organisms the tick is harboring being released into the skin of the student or onto caregiver's hands.

4. After removal, wash the area around the tick bite carefully with soap and water and disinfect with isopropyl alcohol or other disinfectant (e.g., tincture of iodine).

5. Dispose of the tick by flushing down the toilet or by burning it in a wood stove.

6. Carefully wash your hands with soap and water to ensure that the tick's blood or feces are completely removed from your skin.

7. If the tick is not completely removed, the student should be seen by a doctor.

 ## Sexually Transmitted Diseases

Sexually transmitted diseases, or **STDs,** are those diseases that are transmitted primarily by means of sexual intercourse or direct genital contact. STDs are the second most prevalent infections found in humans; the first is the common cold (Dash, 1993). Referred to as **venereal diseases** in the past, STDs are caused by a variety of bacteria, viruses, fungi, and other organisms. There are at least 20 organisms that are sexually transmitted. The most common STDs are described in Table 23.7.

The data shown in Table 23.8, gathered from a variety of current medical publications, demonstrate the extent of the problem worldwide. All of the figures cited are probably, at best, an estimation because many cases go unreported. In fact, it is probable that more cases go unreported than are reported.

Aside from causing a variety of symptoms, sexually transmitted diseases can have devastating sequelae, including sterility, miscarriage, birth defects (blindness, developmental delay, neurologic impairment), and cervical and genital cancers. Greco (1996) stated it bluntly: "STDs can be uncomfortable or painful, inconvenient, embarrassing, anxiety

producing, or fatal to a large percentage of those infected" (p. 620). Unfortunately, in many cases, the person with a sexually transmitted disease is asymptomatic, and as a result, those who need treatment do not recognize the urgency.

Educational Implications and Teaching Tips: Students with Sexually Transmitted Diseases

Most adolescents believe wholeheartedly that they are indestructible and that, consequently, it would be impossible for them to develop an STD. Coupled with this belief is the lack of recognition that what they do now may have future consequences (Miller, 1993). The articles by Greco (1996) and Lerro (1994), written for young adults who are sexually active, may be useful as a basis for discussions. School staff may also find the following suggestions to be of assistance:

1 *Adolescents must be taught to recognize the signs of STDs.* The most common symptoms include discharge (from the vagina or penis), itching

TABLE 23.7
Sexually Transmitted Diseases: Agent and Symptoms

Agent	Usual Symptoms and Possible Complications
BACTERIAL STDs	
Neisseria gonorrhoeae Causative agent for **gonorrhea**, also known on the street as the clap, dose, or drip	• **Males and Females:** Sore throat, pain on defecating, arthritis, meningitis, endocarditis. Note: 80%–90% of females and 10%–20% of males are asymptomatic. • **Females:** Copious pus-like vaginal discharge, urethritis (inflammation of the urethra that can lead to pain and frequency of urination), cervicitis (inflammation of the cervix, which may result in bleeding during intercourse), PID (pelvic inflammatory disease, which may result in chronic pelvic pain, infertility, and ectopic pregnancy, which is a pregnancy in which the fertilized egg develops outside the uterine cavity), and even death. • **Males:** Milky, yellowish discharge from penis, prostatitis (inflammation of the prostate gland), epididymitis (inflammation of the sperm ducts). Men may become sterile.
Chlamydia trachomatis Causative agent for **chlamydia**, also known on the street as chlam, pronounced "clam"	• **Males and Females:** conjunctivitis, lymphogranuloma venereum (ulcerative lesions located in the genital area). Symptoms often mild; 70% of females are asymptomatic. • **Females:** Slight white or clear discharge, urethritis, cervicitis, PID. • **Males:** Urethritis, epididymitis, prostatitis.
Treponema pallidum Causative agent for **syphilis**, also known on the street as syph, lues, pox, and bad blood	• **Males and Females:** Primary stage (infectious): painless pustule/chancre at site of infection (typically anogenital area; may be hidden in vagina, rectum, or mouth). Heals spontaneously in 2–3 weeks. Secondary stage (very infectious): nonpruritic rash, fever, headaches, sore throat, general malaise, anorexia, nausea, bone and joint pain, loss of hair. Third stage, or early latent stage (may be infectious): no symptoms, can last for 10–20 years. Fourth stage or late latent stage (blood infectious): development of gummas (tumors that can grow anywhere on the body as well as in the eyes, liver, lungs, stomach or reproductive organs); CNS involvement can lead to blindness, deafness, motor weakness, and insanity (syphilitic dementia); cardiovascular involvement can lead to aortic insufficiency or aneurysm.
VIRAL STDs	
Human immunodeficiency virus (HIV) Causative agent for AIDS	• **Males and Females** (both children and adults): Incubation period as long as 10 years. Immediately after infection, symptoms similar to infectious mononucleosis; however, in many cases persons may be asymptomatic for years. At some point, symptoms of immunocompromise develop (i.e., AIDS), including the development of **opportunistic infections**. Individuals can have more than one infection at the same time or in succession. Common infections include the following:

Toxoplasmosis of the brain that may lead to an altered mental state and result in convulsive seizures
Candidiasis of the esophagus, trachea, bronchi, or lungs, resulting in sore, burning mouth and throat and difficulty eating
Cytomegalovirus infection, can result in retinitis (loss of vision) and colitis (severe diarrhea)
Herpes simplex virus infection, causing bronchitis, pneumonitis (inflammation of the lungs), or esophagitis (shortness of breath, cough, and chest pain)

- **Adults:** Kaposi's sarcoma, a type of skin cancer, common in adults and rare in children; *Pneumocystis carinii* pneumonia often causes death.

- **Children:** Bacterial infections such as bacterial meningitis (fever, headache, and stiff neck), bacterial gastroenteritis (diarrhea, abdominal cramping, and dehydration), ear infections (loss of hearing) and bacterial pneumonia (breathing difficulties). Thrush, a fungal infection of the mouth, is common in children.

Herpes simplex virus, type II
Causative agent for genital herpes

- **Males and Females:**
Symptomatic stage (contagious): minor itching or extensive rash in genital area; formation of blister-like lesions at site of infection (e.g., lips and nose of face; inner/outer vaginal labia; rectum; buttocks), which develop into ulcers; painful urination; fever; malaise.

Dormant phase: individual asymptomatic, but symptoms may reappear with emotional or physical stress. Recurrent episodes generally lessen in frequency and severity over time.

- **Females:** increased vaginal discharge, painful urination and intercourse.

Human papillomavirus (HPV)
Causative agent for anogenital warts

- See chapter 21.

FUNGAL STDs

Candida albicans or *Candida tropicalis*
Causative agents for **candidiasis,** a yeast infection involving the skin or mucous membranes (e.g., in a woman's vagina; on a man's penis)

- **Males and Females:** 40% of females and 95%–100% of males are asymptomatic.
- **Females:** Flare-ups typically occur during pregnancy, while taking antibiotics, or during periods of emotional stress. Use of oral contraceptives and corticosteroid therapy can increase the possibility of infection. Candidiasis is more common in those with diabetes mellitus. Intense, intolerable vaginal itching; profuse discharge, usually thick and cottage cheese–like.
- **Males:** Dermatitis on penis.

PROTOZOAL STDs

Trichomonas vaginalis

- **Males and Females:** 95%–100% of men and 25% of women are asymptomatic.
- **Females:** Vaginitis (inflammation of the vagina that causes itching and burning), yellowish-green or gray discharge with foul odor, pain on urinating, erosion of the cervix.
- **Males:** May have slight, clear discharge from penis; may have itching after urination.

TABLE 23.8

Facts and Figures Regarding Sexually Transmitted Diseases (STDs)

FACTS:

In the United States:

- An estimated 78% of adolescent girls and 86% of adolescent boys have engaged in sexual intercourse by age 20.
- STDs affect almost 12 million persons each year, 86% of whom are age 15 through 29.
- Every 13 seconds, a teenager contracts an STD.
- About one fifth of all young people, by the time they reach 21, have needed treatment for an STD.
- 1 in 10 persons is infected with chlamydia, gonorrhea, syphilis, genital warts, or genital herpes.

FIGURES:

Gonorrhea

- It has been estimated that 250 million people contract gonorrhea annually around the world. In the United States, the incidence is estimated at 300 cases per 100,000 people. In the age group 15 through 19, the incidence is believed to be as high as 1,125 per 100,000.
- For every case of gonorrhea reported, two cases go unreported.
- Gonorrhea is 10 times more frequent among nonwhites than in whites.
- The incidence of antibiotic-resistant strains of *Neisseria gonorrhoeae* has risen steadily over the past decade.

Chlamydia

- Every year, approximately 3 to 4 million women in North America contract chlamydia.
- Over 1 million women in the United States per year are diagnosed as having pelvic inflammatory disease (PID), the most common complication of chlamydia infection. Approximately one-third of these cases occur in sexually active teenagers between the ages of 15 and 19. Up to $3 million is spent annually on treating PID.
- 15% to 37% of pregnant adolescents are infected with chlamydia; 50% of their newborns contract conjunctivitis from delivery.

Syphilis

- Infection rates for syphilis in 15- to 19-year-olds have risen from 15 per 100,000 in 1985 to 30 per 100,000 in 1990. There are 45,000 new cases per year in the United States and as many as 50 million worldwide.
- In North America, congenital syphilis is a factor in 1 of every 10,000 pregnancies. In 1990, nearly 3,000 cases of congenital syphilis were reported in the U.S. alone.

(around the genitalia or anus), soreness and swelling (around the genitalia or lymph nodes), pain (on intercourse, in joints, in the abdomen, or of the genitalia), rash (anywhere on the body), odor (particularly from the genitalia), the presence of organisms that are visible to the naked eye, and fever or fatigue (Feroli, 1994). All teenagers who are sexually active, especially those that are not in a mutually exclusive relationship or who have recently changed partners, should be tested for STDs as part of their annual medical examination (Greco, 1996).

2   *Nurses, health teachers, or counselors are often involved in the teaching of reproductive health,* *both formally (through structured lessons) and informally (during counseling sessions). While many people would like to stop all adolescents from being sexually active, thereby decreasing the likelihood that they will contract an STD or become pregnant, it is unlikely such suggestions will be heeded.*

Students who are not yet sexually active should be given explicit education on how to make responsible sexual decisions, how to avoid being sexually exploited, how to engage in safer sex practices, and how to prevent pregnancy.

Students who are sexually active and have an STD should be treated in a manner that is sensitive and nonaccusatory. Emphasis at first should be placed on explaining how STDs occur and the rea-

HIV/AIDS
- By the year 2000 there will be between 30 and 40 million individuals with HIV worldwide. By the year 2000, there will be between 5 and 10 million infants born with HIV worldwide.
- Approximately 1 in 250 people in the U.S. is infected with HIV—1 in every 100 males and 1 in every 800 females.
- In the United States, every day there are 90 new cases of HIV identified and 60 people die from AIDS.
- As of July 1996, in the United States, a total of 548,102 AIDS cases had been reported; 540,806 in adults and adolescents; 7,296 in children. Of these, 201,975 adults and adolescents and 3,127 children were alive. It is believed that 650,000 to 900,000 people are infected with HIV but have not been diagnosed as having AIDS.
- The number of children infected with HIV is 2 to 10 times greater than the number who have AIDS. As many as 20,000 children with HIV are attending school.
- In 83% of the cases of AIDS in children, the infection results from the transmission of the virus from an infected mother. Most of the children with AIDS are from minority populations: 75% are either black or Hispanic.
- In the years 1989 to 1992, an estimated 7,000 HIV-infected women delivered infants in the United States each year. Assuming a perinatal transmission rate of 15% to 30%, approximately 1,000 to 2,000 HIV-infected infants were born annually during these years.
- AIDS has become one of the top 10 causes of death for children under age 5. It is predicted to rank in the top five by the year 2000.

Herpes Simplex Type II
- 20 million Americans are infected with the herpes simplex virus Type II.
- Genital herpes is the most common cause of genital ulcers in the Western world. There are as many as 700,000 new herpes simplex infections per year in the United States.
- From 1966 to 1984, the incidence of HSV Type II infection increased almost ninefold. The greatest increase was among middle-class and upper-class individuals.
- Among sexually active teens, between 3% and 12% have positive cultures for herpes simplex Type II.

Human Papillomavirus (HPV)
- 3 million cases of anogenital warts are seen each year, making this the most common viral STD in the United States.
- The number of physician-patient consultations regarding anogenital warts increased sevenfold from 1966 to 1984.
- Between 1% and 3% of all Pap smears intimate infection. In the adolescent, the majority of (if not all) abnormal Pap smears are related to HPV infection.

sons for complying with the treatment protocol, followed by a frank discussion on the need for prevention of STDs and the use of appropriate contraceptive methods.

For those students who have not used illicit drugs, programs should encourage students to remain drug-free; those students who are using drugs should be encouraged to seek treatment for their habits and be encouraged not to share needles or other injection equipment.

3 *The number of children and young adults who are HIV-infected is increasing.* As a result of better medical treatment, they are not only remaining symptom-free longer, but those that are born with the infection are surviving longer and entering school alongside their healthy peers, in many cases without staff even knowing that they have the virus. In the past, and even to this day, teachers have been very concerned about the possibility of the condition being spread to the other children in the classroom and to themselves. Conclusive proof that the condition *cannot* be spread through casual contact has helped to lessen their fears; however, many are still misinformed, and fear is still rampant. Gross and Larkin (1996), in their opening remarks in a recently published article entitled "The Child with HIV in Day Care and School," stated:

Fifteen years after the start of the HIV epidemic, people continue to debate the advisability of infected children attending school. . . . Although there are no re-ported cases of transmission of HIV in school or child care settings, infected children and their families still face prejudice and isolation. As a result, many families keep their children's HIV status private, and confidentiality[3] continues to be a sensitive topic in communities, schools, and day care centers. (p. 231)

Fost (1991), in a discussion of ethical issues in pediatric AIDS, made the following comments which should be heeded by school personnel:

The chance of dying at school from bus or automobile accidents, contact sports, other infectious diseases, or schoolmates or strangers using lethal weapons is already higher than the chance of dying from HIV infection. Some efforts to reduce those risks are reasonable, but the cost of reducing them to zero would virtually require closing the schools. If particular families or personnel are especially risk-averse regarding HIV infection—empirically a zero risk at present—there are ways they can reduce that risk, by working in communities where the virus is uncommon, or by forming private schools where HIV screening might be a condition of entry. There is no particular duty for an HIV-positive child to bear the burden by exclusion or segregation. (p. 601)

The Council for Exceptional Children, a professional body of teachers of children with special needs, adopted a set of policy statements on the management of students with communicable diseases in April 1986. The wording was very emphatic and blunt:

The Council for Exceptional Children believes that in developing appropriate policies for managing communicable diseases, schools and public health agencies should assure that any such policies and procedures:

1. Do not exclude the affected child from the receipt of an appropriate education even when circumstances require the temporary removal of the child from contact with other children.
2. Provide that determination of a non-temporary alteration of a child's educational placement should be done on an individual basis, utilizing an interdisciplinary/interagency approach including the child's physician, public health personnel, the child's parents, and appropriate educational personnel.

The American Academy of Pediatrics has developed a number of documents that provide staff of day-care centers and schools with guidelines to assist in planning educational programs for children who are infected with the HIV virus or who have developed AIDS. Some of these guidelines are found in chapter 24.

4 *In the past, it was generally believed that those born with congenital AIDS would succumb to the disease in infancy; while still an incurable disease, the advent of certain antiviral drugs, in particular azidothymidine, more commonly known as AZT, has resulted in many children living longer than originally expected.* Unfortunately, in many cases, the children, while enjoying relatively good health, may show signs of one or more impairments, including immunologic, physical, developmental, neurologic, sensory, social, behavioral, and educational impairments (Cohen & Diamond, 1992). Of particular concern to teachers are the neurologic sequelae that may result in serious educational consequences.

While many of the children with neurologic impairment resemble children with cerebral palsy (CP), many display the learning needs of those with mild to severe cognitive deficits. Reports of a cohort of children with HIV infection seen in one American University Affiliated Program, cited by Diamond and Cohen (1992), provide the following prevalence statistics: 29% of the children had signs of spastic quadriplegic type CP with associated mental retardation; 50% of children had conductive and 5% had severe-to-profound sensorineural hearing loss; 38% had either borderline intellectual functioning or mild mental retardation; 10% had attention deficit disorder; and 10% had developmental language disorder. The symptoms of developmental delay may be compounded by a number of psychosocial factors, including prolonged hospitalization, poor nutrition, environmental deprivation, and depression or grief that results from the separation or loss of the parent(s) or caregiver(s) (Rosen & Granger, 1992).

Critical to the success of designing educational programs for children with AIDS is the need for a thorough assessment. Additionally, children with AIDS need a multidisciplinary approach to programming, which typically involves a combination of services, including regular and special education, physical therapy, speech therapy, occupational ther-

---

[3] For further information regarding the legal rights of children with HIV/AIDS to access educational programs and the issues regarding confidentiality and public policy, see the articles by Hanlon (1991) and Harvey (1994), respectively.

apy, health and medication monitoring by a nurse, counseling, behavior management, and social work (Seidel, 1992). For further information on the learning needs of children with HIV infection, the reader is referred to the recent articles by Armstrong, Seidel, and Swales (1993); Caldwell, Sirvis, Todaro, and Accouloumre (1991); LeRoy, Powell, and Kelker (1994); Prater, Serna, Sileo, and Katz (1995); and Seidel (1992).

Many children with a disabling condition (e.g., children with cognitive impairments or learning difficulties) may be at greater risk for HIV/AIDS as a result of not having the critical thinking skills needed to make safe and effective decisions. Colson and Carlson (1993) have developed a comprehensive "AIDS 101" curriculum that includes a list of eight specific skill areas that must be addressed. The skills include: (a) general knowledge, (b) affective development, (c) sexuality and physical growth, (d) positive self-esteem, (e) personal relationships, (f) sexual abuse, (g) drug abuse, and (h) sexual responsibility and safer sex practices and are broken down into four levels of learning: (a) readiness, (b) beginning, (c) intermediate, and (d) advanced. For further information, consult this source.

According to Millicent Kellogg, a public health nurse who has been a pioneer in AIDS services (cited in Stiggall, 1988), the basic message that must be taught to all children, regardless of their mental ability, is as follows:

- AIDS is dangerous.
- It can happen to you.
- A person can have AIDS and not know it.
- You can prevent AIDS.

 **Summary**

Communicable diseases, i.e., those that are easily transmitted from person-to-person, are, for the most part, preventable. With proper education, children and young adults can be taught how to lessen the chances of becoming infected; however, if infected, they can also be taught how to lessen the chances of infecting those around them. In this chapter, some of the more common bacterial, viral, fungal and parasitic infections have been discussed, along with the common sexually transmitted diseases.

References

American Academy of Pediatrics. (1993). Prevention of hepatitis B virus infection in school settings. *Pediatrics, 91,* 848–850.

Armstrong, F. D., Seidel, J. F., & Swales, T. P. (1993). Pediatric HIV infection: A neuropsychological and educational challenge. *Journal of Learning Disabilities, 26,* 92–103.

Bale, J. F., & Murph, J. R. (1992). Congenital infections and the nervous system. *Pediatric Clinics of North America, 39,* 669–690.

Bauer, A. M., & Shea, T. M. (1986). Hepatitis B: An occupational hazard for special educators. *Journal of the Association for Persons with Severe Handicaps, 11,* 171–175.

Bigge, J. L. (1991). *Teaching individuals with physical and multiple disabilities* (3rd ed.). New York: Merrill.

Caldwell, T. H., Sirvis, B., Todaro, A. W., & Accouloumre, D. S. (1991). *Special health care in the school.* Reston, VA: Council for Exceptional Children.

Castiglia, P. T. (1992). Caring for children with infectious diseases. In P. T. Castiglia & R. E. Harbin (Eds.), *Child health care: Process and practice* (pp. 415–437). Philadelphia: J. B. Lippincott.

Centers for Disease Control and Prevention (CDC). (1992). Important information about hepatitis B, hepatitis B vaccine, and hepatitis B globulin. In *Hepatitis B: 5/27/92.* Washington, DC: CDC, U. S. Department of Health and Human Services.

Centers for Disease Control and Prevention (CDC). (1994). Summary of notifiable diseases, United States, 1994. *Morbidity and Mortality Weekly Report, 43,* 10.

Clark, M. J. (1992). Communicable disease. In M. J. Clark, *Nursing in the community* (pp. 730–807). Norwalk, CT: Appleton & Lange.

Clemen-Stone, S., Eigsti, D. G., & McGuire, S. L. (1995). *Comprehensive family and community health nursing* (4th ed.). St. Louis: Mosby.

Cohen, H. J., & Diamond, G. W. (1992). Developmental assessment of children with HIV infection. In A. C. Crocker, H. J. Cohen, & T. A. Kastner (Eds.), *HIV infection and developmental disabilities: A resource for service providers* (pp. 53–61). Baltimore: Paul H. Brookes.

Colson, S. E., & Carlson, J. K. (1993). HIV/AIDS education for students with special needs. *Intervention in School and Clinic, 28,* 262–274.

Cordell, R. L., Solomon, S. L., & Hale, C. M. (1996). Exclusion of mildly ill children from out-of-home child care facilities. *Journal of Infectious Medicine, 13*(1), 41, 45–48.

Council for Exceptional Children: Governmental Relations Committee. (1986). *Report of the Council for Exceptional Children's task force on policy issues relating to the management of students with communicable diseases.* Reston, VA: Author.

Dash, D. (1993). Communicable disease. In J. M. Swanson & M. Albrecht, *Community health nursing: Promoting the health of aggregates* (pp. 533–565). Philadelphia: W. B. Saunders.

Feroli, K. L. (1994). Infectious disease. In C. L. Betz, M. Hunsberger, & S. Wright (Eds.), *Family-centered nursing care of children* (2nd ed., pp. 1678–1716). Philadelphia: W. B. Saunders.

Fost, N. (1991). Ethical issues in pediatric AIDS. In P. A. Pizzo & C. M. Wilfert (Eds.), *Pediatric AIDS: The challenge of HIV infection in infants, children, and adolescents* (pp. 599–604). Baltimore, MD: Williams & Wilkins.

Gostin, L. O. (1990). The AIDS litigation project: A national review of court and human rights commission decisions, Part II: Discrimination. *Journal of the American Medical Association, 263,* 2086–2093.

Greco, S. B., (1996). Sexuality education and counseling. In S. P. Hoeman (Ed.), *Rehabilitation nursing: Process and application* (pp. 594–627). St. Louis: Mosby.

Gross, E. J., & Larkin, M. H. (1996). The child with HIV in day care and school. *Nursing Clinics of North America, 31,* 231–241.

Hanlon, S. F. (1991). School and day care issues: The legal perspective. In P. A. Pizzo & C. M. Wilfert (Eds.), *Pediatric AIDS: The challenge of HIV infection in infants, children, and adolescents* (pp. 693–703). Baltimore: Williams & Wilkins.

Harrington, R. G. (1992). Children and communicable disease. In National Association of School Psychologists (NASP), *Helping children grow up in the 90s: A resource book for parents and teachers.* Silver Spring, MD: NASP.

Harvey, D. C. (1994). Confidentiality and public policy regarding children with HIV infection. *Journal of School Health, 64,* 18–20.

Heller, K. W., Alberto, P. A., Forney, P. E., & Schwartzman, M. N. (1996). *Understanding physical, sensory, and health impairments. Characteristics and educational implications.* Pacific Grove, CA: Brooks/Cole.

James, S. R. (1990a). Defense: Implications of impaired immunity. In S. R. Mott, S. R. James, & A. M. Sperhac (Eds.), *Nursing care of children and families* (2nd ed., pp. 1226–1281). Redwood City, CA: Addison-Wesley.

James, S. R. (1990b). Home care and emergency management of the child with a minor illness or injury. In S. R. Mott, S. R. James, & A. M. Sperhac (Eds.), *Nursing*

care of children and families (2nd ed., pp. 761–811). Redwood City, CA: Addison-Wesley.

LeRoy, C. H., Powell, T. H., & Kelker, P. H. (1994). Children with disabilities and AIDS: Meeting of responsibilities in special education. *Teaching Exceptional Children, 26*(4), 37–44.

Lerro, M. (1994). Teaching adolescents about AIDS. *Teaching Exceptional Children, 26*(4), 49–51.

Matocha, L. K. (1995). Communicable diseases. In C. M. Smith & F. A. Maurer, *Community health nursing: Theory and practice* (pp. 473–516). Philadelphia: W. B. Saunders.

Miller, K. (1993). Nursing planning, intervention, and evaluation of altered reproductive function. In D. B. Jackson & R. B. Saunders (Eds.), *Child health nursing: A comprehensive approach to the care of children and their families* (pp. 1851–1911). Philadelphia: J. B. Lippincott.

Mosby's medical, nursing, & allied health dictionary (4th ed.). St. Louis: Mosby.

Prater, M. A., Serna, L. A., Sileo, T. W., & Katz, A. R. (1995). HIV disease: Implications for special educators. *Remedial and Special Education, 16*(2), 68–78.

Puzas, M. I. (1994). Chicken pox (Varicella). In M. Gulanick, M. K. Puzas, & D. Gradishar (Eds.), *Ambulatory pediatric nursing: Plans of care for specialty practice* (pp. 90–93). Albany, NY: Delmar.

Rosen, S., & Granger, M. (1992). Early intervention and school programs. In A. C. Crocker, H. J. Cohen, & T. A. Kastner (Eds.), *HIV infection and developmental disabilities: A resource for service providers* (pp. 75–84). Baltimore: Paul H. Brookes.

Seidel, J. F. (1992). Children with HIV-related developmental difficulties. *Phi Delta Kappan, 74*(1), 38–40, 56.

Silkworth, C. S. (1986). Hand washing techniques. In G. Larson (Ed.), *Managing the school-age child with a chronic health condition: A practical guide for schools, families, and organizations* (pp. 141–145). Wayzata, MN: DCI Publishing.

Stenson, J. (1996). Toddler immunizations at all-time high. *Medical Tribune News Service* [on-line medical news].

Stiggall, L. (1988). AIDS education for individuals with developmental, learning, or mental disabilities. In M. Quackenbush & M. Nelson (Eds.), *The AIDS challenge: Prevention education for young people* (pp. 405–417). Santa Cruz, CA: Network Publications.

Policies and Procedures

Throughout this text, suggestions have been given to ensure the safety of students in the school setting. Many of the suggestions have related to providing respondent care to students who have been injured while at school as well as to students who have a known medical problem. Other suggestions have attempted to educate staff on how to recognize potentially serious health problems in those who are believed to be in good health. While it is hoped that these suggestions have been, or will be, of assistance to those in the school system, even more important is the development of a well-formulated set of policies that govern some of the day-to-day occurrences that are a part of the lives of these children. In this final chapter, some of the more controversial areas, such as the administration of medications, the management of "Do Not Resuscitate" orders, and the prevention of communicable diseases, are examined and policies that have been developed by various bodies, such as the American Academy of Pediatrics and the National Association of School Nurses, are presented. These policies may be of assistance to district administrators, school officials, and staff who are responsible for developing such statements.

In order to ensure that all children and young adults with special physical and health care needs are served adequately and consistently in the school system, a set of policies, i.e., principles that govern the actions of others, must be written to guide staff at both the local and district levels. In Part I, the issue of qualifications of staff was introduced. As more and more children with unique needs are integrated into neighborhood schools, the need for adequate training remains paramount. It seems fitting that the final chapter of this text begins with an examination of some of the problems related to the delegation of school health services.

CHAPTER 24

Policies and Procedures: Planning for the Unforeseen

KEY WORDS

"Do Not Resuscitate" Orders

Confidentiality and FERPA

Legal liability

Medication prescribed by physician, parent, or self

Delegation

Supervision

Universal precautions

🍂 Delegation of School Health Services: A Matter of Qualifications

In 1990, the Joint Task Force for the Management of Children with Special Health Care Needs attempted to provide guidance in how to deal with some of the responsibility issues regarding the provision of care to those with special health care needs in the general education classrooms of the United States. Over a two-year period, representatives from the American Federation of Teachers (AFT), the Council for Exceptional Children (CEC), the National Association of School Nurses (NASN), and the National Education Association (NEA) reviewed 66 special health care procedures (e.g., catheterization, administration of medications) that students with chronic conditions may require while attending school. The resultant matrix, contained in Table 24.1, delineates who is qualified to perform the procedure, who should ideally perform the procedure, and the circumstances under which these persons would be deemed to be qualified. In preparing the document, members of the Task Force were guided by the principles shown in Table 24.2.

Even though it would appear that the Task Force has recommended that selected "medical" procedures can be safely carried out by nonmedically trained personnel subsequent to receiving appropriate training, several controversial issues remain outstanding. The first is related to the supervision of those who might be asked to perform specific medical procedures. This concern is particularly evident in schools where there is no nurse on staff, a situation that is not uncommon. It has been reported that the National Association of School Nurses estimated that in 1995 there were approximately 30,000 full-time nurses serving approximately 85,000 American schools, or approximately 1 nurse for every 3 schools (Weiss, 1997). Recent data from a study conducted in Texas indicated that each school nurse served, on average, 1.5 schools (Koenning et al., 1995). DiCroce (1990), referring to the lack of school-based nursing staff, made the following comment: "Under such circumstances, each nurse's scope of responsibility makes adequate monitoring of children with special needs unlikely" (p. 82).

The second issue, related in part to the first, revolves around the delegation of responsibility and the issue of legal liability. While it may appear reasonable to train nonmedical personnel to provide certain services, in many states and provinces, the Nurse Practice Act actually prevents non–medically trained personnel from performing such duties. The underlying reason for such a provision is related to the liability of the person delegating the responsibility, as well as that of the person carrying out the procedure. The American Federation of Teachers, in a recent publication entitled *The Medically Fragile Child in the School Setting* (1997), in a section entitled "What's Legal? Who's Liable?" raised the following points:

> All nursing procedures ultimately are the legal responsibility of the health professional/school nurse assigned to a facility. State laws . . . usually require that nursing procedures be performed only by a person educated and licensed to practice as a registered nurse, unless he or she has trained another person and is confident of that person's ability. In this case, the nurse may delegate a task to an individual, but the nurse retains full responsibility and liability should any problems arise. Not all procedures can be delegated, however, and each state's board of nursing makes these determinations. Unfortunately, many school personnel are not aware of these facts. (pp. 10–11)

Interestingly, in a recent survey by the National Association of School Nurses (1993), an association that at that time had approximately 700 members, it was reported that one-third of the respondents felt pressured by their administrators to delegate nursing care to unlicensed assistive personnel. Eighty-five percent of the respondents also stated that the nurse-to-pupil ratio[1] was the major area of concern, particularly in light of the complexity of student problems.

Of even greater concern to some are the liability issues surrounding the provision of health care services by those who are employed to provide *educational* services as opposed to *medical* services. In recent years, several research studies have shown that certain forms of health care are being provided by

---

[1] While recognizing that it is not realistic or feasible to have a nurse in every school in the nation, there have been attempts to determine the adequate nurse-to-child ratio. The figure most commonly cited, 1 nurse to 750 general school-age children, has been promoted by the National Association of School Nurses (1995a). For districts with children with special health care needs who are mainstreamed, it has been recommended that the ratio be reduced to 1 to 225 and that for students who have severe or profound needs because of chronic illness or developmental disability, the ratio should be 1 to 125.

TABLE 24.1

Guidelines for the Delineation of Roles and Responsibilities for the Safe Delivery of Specialized Health Care in the Educational Setting†

Procedure	Physician Order Required	Registered Nurse (RN)	Licensed Practical Nurse (LPN)	Certified Teaching Personnel	Related Services Personnel[1]	Para-Professionals[2]	Others[3]
1.0 ACTIVITIES OF DAILY LIVING							
1.1 Toileting/Diapering		A	A	A	A	Ⓐ	A
1.2 Bowel/Bladder Training (Toilet Training)		A	A	Ⓐ	A	S	S
1.3 Dental Hygiene		A	A	A	A	S	S
1.4 Oral Hygiene		A	A	Ⓐ	A	S	S
1.5 Lifting/Positioning		A	A	Ⓐ	A	S	S
1.6 Feeding							
1.6.1 Nutrition Assessment		A	X	X	N	X	X
1.6.2 Oral-Motor Assessment		X	X	X	Ⓢ̲P̲/̲T̲H̲	X	X
1.6.3 Oral Feeding		A	A	A	A	Ⓢ	S
1.6.4 Naso-Gastric Feeding	*	Ⓐ	Ⓢ	X	X	Ⓢ/HA	X
1.6.5 Monitoring of Naso-Gastric Feeding		A	S	S	S	S	X
1.6.6 Gastrostomy Feeding	*	Ⓐ	Ⓢ	X	X	Ⓢ/HA	X
1.6.7 Monitoring of Gastrostomy Feeding		A	S	S	S	S	X
1.6.8 Jejunostomy Tube Feeding	*	Ⓐ	Ⓢ	X	X	X	X
1.6.9 Total Parenteral Feeding (Intravenous)	*	Ⓐ	Ⓢ	X	X	X	X
1.6.10 Monitoring of Parenteral Feeding		A	S	S	S	S	X
1.6.11 Naso-Gastric Tube Insertion	*	Ⓐ	Ⓢ	X	X	X	X
1.6.12 Naso-Gastric Tube Removal	*	Ⓐ	Ⓢ	EM	EM	EM/HA	X
1.6.13 Gastrostomy Tube Reinsertion	*	Ⓐ	Ⓢ	X	X	X	X

Continued

DEFINITIONS OF SYMBOLS

A   Qualified to perform task, not in conflict with professional standards

S   Qualified to perform task with RN supervision and inservice education

EM   In emergencies, if properly trained, and if designated professional is not available

X   Should not perform

N   Nutritionist only

TH   Occupational or physical therapist only

SP   Speech/language pathologist only

HA   Health aide only

○   Person who should be designated to perform task

[1] Related Services include N, TH, and SP.

[2] Paraprofessionals include teacher aides, health aides, uncertified teaching personnel.

[3] Others include secretaries, bus drivers, cafeteria workers, custodians.

†DELINEATION OF RESPONSIBILITIES MUST ADHERE TO EACH STATE NURSE PRACTICE ACT.

TABLE 24.1
(*Continued*)

Procedure	Physician Order Required	Registered Nurse (RN)	Licensed Practical Nurse (LPN)	Certified Teaching Personnel	Related Services Personnel[1]	Para-Professionals[2]	Others[3]
2.0 CATHETERIZATION							
2.1 Clean Intermittent Catheterization	*	(A)	(S)	X	X	S/HA	X
2.2 Sterile Catheterization	*	(A)	(S)	X	X	X	X
2.3 Crede	*	A	S	S	S	S/HA	S
2.4 External Catheter	*	(A)	(A)	S	S	S/HA	X
2.5 Care of Indwelling Catheter (Not Irrigation)	*	(A)	(S)	S	S	S/HA	X
3.0 MEDICAL SUPPORT SYSTEMS							
3.1 Ventricular Peritoneal Shunt							
3.1.1 Pumping	*	(EM)	(EM)	X	X	X	X
3.1.2 Monitoring	*	(A)	S	S	S	S	X
3.2 Mechanical Ventilator							
3.2.1 Monitoring	*	(A)	(S)	EM	EM	S/HA	X
3.2.2 Adjustment of Ventilator	*	X	X	X	X	X	X
3.2.3 Equipment Failure	*	(A)	(S)	EM	EM	EM	EM
3.3 Oxygen							
3.3.1 Intermittent	*	(A)	(S)	EM	EM	EM	X
3.3.2 Continuous (Monitoring)	*	A	S	S	S	S	S
3.4 Hickman/Broviac/IVAC/IMED	*	(A)	(S)	X	X	X	X
3.5 Peritoneal Dialysis	*	(A)	(S)	X	X	X	X
3.6 Apnea Monitor	*	A	S	S	S	S/HA	X

4.0 MEDICATIONS

Medications may be given by LPN's and Health Aides only where the Nurse Practice Act of the individual state allows such practice, and under the specific guidelines of that Nurse Practice Act.

4.1 Oral	*	(A)	(S)	X	X	S/HA	X
4.2 Injection	*	(A)	(S)	X	X	X	X
4.3 Epi-Pen Allergy Kit	*	(A)	(S)	EM	EM	EM	EM
4.4 Inhalation	*	(A)	(S)	EM	EM	EM/HA	EM
4.5 Rectal	*	(A)	(S)	X	X	X	X
4.6 Bladder Installation	*	(A)	(S)	X	X	S/HA	X
4.7 Eye/Ear Drops	*	(A)	(S)	X	X	S/HA	X
4.8 Topical	*	(A)	(S)	X	X	S/HA	X
4.9 Per Nasogastric Tube	*	(A)	(S)	X	X	S/HA	X
4.10 Per Gastrostomy Tube	*	(A)	(S)	X	X	S/HA	X
4.11 Intravenous	*	(A)	(S)	X	X	X	X
4.12 Spirometer	*	(A)	(S)	X	X	S/HA	X
5.0 OSTOMIES							
5.1 Ostomy Care	*	(A)	(S)	EM	EM	EM	X
5.2 Ostomy Irrigation	*	(A)	(S)	X	X	X	X
6.0 RESPIRATORY ASSISTANCE							
6.1 Postural Drainage	*	(A)	(S)	S	S	S/HA	S
6.2 Percussion	*	(A)	(S)	S	TH	S/HA	S
6.3 Suctioning							
6.3.1 Pharyngeal	*	(A)	(S)	S	S	S/HA	X
6.3.2 Tracheostomy	*	(A)	(S)	S	S	S/HA	X
6.4 Tracheostomy Tube Replacement	*	(EM)	(EM)	EM	EM	EM	EM
6.5 Tracheostomy Care (Cleaning)	*	(A)	(S)	X	X	X	X

DEFINITIONS OF SYMBOLS
A Qualified to perform task, not in conflict with professional standards
S Qualified to perform task with RN supervision and inservice education
EM In emergencies, if properly trained, and if designated professional is not available
X Should not perform
N Nutritionist only   HA Health aide only
TH Occupational or physical therapist only
SP Speech/language pathologist only
○ Person who should be designated to perform task
[1]Related Services include N, TH, and SP.
[2]Paraprofessionals include teacher aides, health aides, uncertified teaching personnel.
[3]Others include secretaries, bus drivers, cafeteria workers, custodians.

Continued

TABLE 24.1
(Continued)

Procedure	Physician Order Required	Registered Nurse (RN)	Licensed Practical Nurse (LPN)	Certified Teaching Personnel	Related Services Personnel[1]	Para-Professionals[2]	Others[3]
7.0 SCREENINGS							
7.1 Growth		(A)	(S)	S	S	S	X
7.2 Vital Signs		(A)	(S)	X	X	S/HA	X
7.3 Hearing		(A)	(S)	X	(SP)	S/HA	X
7.4 Vision		(A)	(S)	X	X	S/HA	X
7.5 Scoliosis		(A)	(S)	S	TH	S/HA	X
8.0 SPECIMEN COLLECTING/TESTING							
8.1 Blood Glucose	*	(A)	(S)	X	X	S/HA	X
8.2 Urine Glucose	*	(A)	(S)	X	X	S/HA	X
9.0 OTHER HEALTH CARE PROCEDURES							
9.1 Seizure Procedures		A	A	A	A	A	A
9.2 Soaks	*	(A)	(S)	X	TH	S/HA	X
9.3 Dressings, Sterile	*	(A)	S	X	X	X	X
10.0 DEVELOPMENT OF PROTOCOLS			(WITH PHYSICIAN CONSULTATION)				
10.1 Health Care Procedures		(A)	X	X	X	A	X
10.2 Emergency Protocols	*	(A)	X	X	X	X	
10.3 Individual Education Plan Health Objectives		(A)	X	X	X	X	X
10.4 Nursing Care Plan		(A)	X	X	X	X	X

DEFINITIONS OF SYMBOLS

A Qualified to perform task, not in conflict with professional standards
S Qualified to perform task with RN supervision and inservice education
EM In emergencies, if properly trained, and if designated professional is not available
X Should not perform

N Nutritionist only
TH Occupational or physical therapist only
SP Speech/language pathologist only
○ Person who should be designated to perform task

HA Health aide only

[1]Related Services include N, TH, and SP.
[2]Paraprofessionals include teacher aides, health aides, uncertified teaching personnel.
[3]Others include secretaries, bus drivers, cafeteria workers, custodians.

Source: Joint Task Force for the Management of Children with Special Health Care Needs of the AFT, CEC, NASN, and NEA (1990). *Guidelines for the delineation of the roles and responsibilities for the safe delivery of specialized health care in the educational setting.* Copyright 1990 by The Council for Exceptional Children. Reprinted by permission.

TABLE 24.2

Principles to Be Followed in Determining the Management of Children with Special Health Care Needs

- Every student is entitled to a free, appropriate public education in the least restrictive environment.
- The family is the constant in the child's life and should be an integral part of decision making regarding the provision of healthcare in school.
- The provision of special healthcare procedures should promote developmentally appropriate student independence.
- A multidisciplinary meeting that includes the family and student, where appropriate, should be conducted for every child with special healthcare needs for the purposes of reviewing the special health needs and the delineation of roles for services delivery.
- Every child who has a special healthcare need requiring nursing care, intervention, or supervision should have a nursing care plan written by a nurse.
- To the degree possible, the delivery of any healthcare procedures should not significantly disrupt or have a negative impact on the educational process of the individual student.
- To the degree possible, the delivery of any healthcare procedures should not significantly disrupt or have a negative impact on the educational process of other students.
- Personnel who are responsible for the education and care of children with specialized healthcare needs should receive training from persons who are qualified to provide such training and certified or licensed to perform the procedure being taught.
- Specialized healthcare procedures should be performed by qualified personnel who have received child-specific training as defined by the child's principal healthcare providers and the child's family.
- Appropriate resources and environmental conditions should be available to the personnel who are providing school health procedures before the child's placement in the classroom.

Source: Joint Task Force for the Management of Children with Special Health Care Needs of the AFT, CEC, NASN, and NEA (1990). *Guidelines for the delineation of the roles and responsibilities for the safe delivery of specialized health care in the educational setting.* Copyright 1990 by The Council for Exceptional Children. Reprinted by permission.

educators and their assistants (Johnson & Asay, 1993; Johnson, Lubker, & Fowler, 1988; Krier, 1993). One study (Krier, 1993) found that educational staff were being asked to perform health care procedures such as administering medication during school hours (35%), tube feeding (12%), ostomy care (5%), catheter care (2%), and tracheostomy care (1%). Similarly, Johnson and Asay (1993) reported that teachers and teacher aides were responsible 44% of the time for performing a number of health-related procedures, such as monitoring vital signs, administering gastrostomy feedings, administering oxygen and non-oral medications, and providing tracheostomy care, whereas registered nurses, licensed practical nurses, and parents performed the procedures 20%, 6%, and 8% of the time, respectively. As mentioned previously, the involvement of

teaching staff in such practices raises a number of points related to legality and liability of staff, as well as the time that may be taken away from educational activities when teachers perform health-related activities. The AFT (1997) has made the following points regarding the legality and liability of teaching staff in providing medical care to students:

Teachers and paraprofessionals often are designated to perform nursing procedures by their school principal or another supervisor. This is clearly in violation of most state Nurse Practice Acts. Generally, only the nurse assigned to a particular school can delegate nursing duties, and the person to whom the task has been delegated must be properly trained and under the supervision of a licensed nurse. If a mistake is made and a child injured, under most state Nurse Practice Acts, it is the nurse who is legally liable. (p. 11)

The final issue relates to legal requirements versus practical reality. While many have advocated a transdisciplinary approach to serving children with severe medical and physical challenges (cf. Orelove & Sobsey, 1992), the guidelines of the Task Force raise some concerns regarding such an approach. Sobsey and Cox (1991), referring specifically to the recommendations of the CEC Task Force, made the following comments:

> While the guidelines recommended are consistent with law in most states, they prohibit many transdisciplinary practices that frequently are carried out in schools. For example, teachers would not be permitted to administer oral medication, feed a child with a gastrostomy or nasogastric tube, or perform clean intermittent catheterization. To conform to these guidelines would require a massive influx of healthcare personnel into the schools, or the clustering of students with disabilities into segregated settings, or both. (p. 158)

Recently, Weiss (1997), in discussing the position of the National Education Association, made the following comments:

> In an ideal world, every school would have licensed, certified healthcare personnel on the premises who would ensure the safety and well-being of our students by attending to their special healthcare needs. The National Education Association fully supports this position: At the 1995 convention, the NEA adopted a new business item opposing "any law, policy, or regulation that supports, permits, or requires any educational personnel who are not medically certified or licensed to perform any medical services or invasive procedures."
>
> But this isn't an ideal world. In reality, more students with special healthcare needs are attending schools at a time when school district resources in many communities are level or declining, and when school nurse positions are often among the first to be pared back. . . . In this environment of increasing demands, educational support personnel (ESP) are often asked, expected, or ordered by their supervisor to provide care and assistance to students with special healthcare needs. (p. 2)

While some may not agree to having teachers or teacher aides, regardless of their training and background, performing medical procedures in the classroom because of their responsibility to the other students, in reality, the likelihood of an increase in number of health care personnel is remote, and consequently, such practices may be financially driven. The AFT (1997) made the following recommendation regarding the hiring of staff:

> Schools should be employing more, not fewer, school nurses to address the health care needs of students with serious health impairments. Court decisions have mandated that schools provide these services but often do not designate who is to perform them. Ironically, school nurses are often among the first let go when layoffs occur, and many of these nurses have overseen several facilities. (p. 10)

These issues, and others, must be addressed by school districts, particularly as the number of children with special health care needs who are entering or reentering the school system increases (Johnson & Asay, 1993). The AFT (1997) has published the following position statement for its membership:

> The AFT believes that medically fragile children in conventional school settings should be placed in a safe and healthy environment where their health needs are attended to by professionals and trained support personnel. We recommend that the nurse and health care aide, respectively, have the primary responsibility for providing health care services to medically fragile children. Teachers, paraprofessionals, and other school personnel should not be the primary service providers. School districts and state legislatures must ensure that there are adequate numbers of nurses and support personnel to provide health-related services to children who need them. (p. 11)

While it would seem that the recommendations put forward by the Joint Task Force for the Management of Children with Special Health Care Needs would make it clear who can do what when, the issue of delegation still is of concern in the school system (cf. Francis, Hemmat, Treloar, & Yarandi, 1996; Fryer & Igoe, 1996; Heller, Fredrick, & Rithmire, 1997). School nurse consultants have raised concerns about the safety of the students who are receiving medical care during the school day. In a recent position paper adopted by their organization in July of 1995, the National Association of State School Nurse Consultants (NASSNC, 1996), stated that the delegation[2] of nursing activities to unlicensed assistive personnel (UAPs)[3] was deemed to be permissible only when:

- it is not otherwise prohibited by state statute of regulations, legal interpretations, or agency policies;
- the activity does not require the exercising of nursing judgment; and

---

[2] Delegation is defined as "the transfer of responsibility for the performance of an activity from one individual to another with the former retaining accountability for the outcome" (NASSNC, 1996, p. 72).

[3] UAPs are defined as "individuals who are trained to function in an assistive role to the registered professional nurse in the provision of student care activities as delegated by and under the supervision of the registered professional nurse" (NASSNC, 1996, p. 72).

■ it is delegated and supervised by a registered nurse. (p. 73)[4]

In the position paper the need for a case-by-case determination is highlighted. It is suggested that the following steps must occur before a decision is made:

1. The registered nurse (RN) validates the necessary physician orders (including emergency orders), parent/guardian authorization, and any other legal documentation necessary for implementing the nursing care.
2. The RN conducts an initial nursing assessment.
3. Consistent with the state's nursing practice act and the RN's assessment of the student, the RN determines what level of care is required: registered professional nursing, licensed practical or vocational nursing, other professional services, or care by unlicensed assistive personnel (UAP).
4. Consistent with the state board of nursing regulations, the RN determines the amount of training required for the UAP. If the individual to whom the nurse will delegate care has not completed standardized training, the RN must ensure that the UAP obtains training in addition to receiving child-specific training.
5. Prior to delegation, the nurse evaluates the competence of the individual to safely perform the task.
6. The RN provides a written care plan to be followed by the unlicensed staff member.
7. The RN indicates, within the written care plan, when RN notification, reassessment, and intervention are warranted, due to change in the student's conditions, the performance of the procedure, or other circumstance.
8. The RN determines the amount and type of RN supervision necessary.
9. The RN determines the frequency and type of student health reassessment necessary for ongoing safety and efficacy.
10. The RN trains the UAP to document the delegated care according to the standards and requirements of the state's board of nursing and agency procedures.
11. The RN documents activities appropriate to each of the nursing actions listed above. (p. 73)

If the school nurse determines that the needs of a student cannot be met safely by means of the UAP,

the policy recommends that the following steps be taken:

1. The RN should write a memorandum to his/her immediate supervisor explaining the situation in specific detail, including:
   a. Recommendation for safe provision of care in the school; or,
   b. The reason the care or procedure should not be performed in school and a rationale to support this.
2. The RN should maintain a copy of the memo for the RN's personnel file.
3. The RN should allow the supervisor a reasonable period of time to initiate action to safeguard the student.
4. If such action does not occur, the RN should forward a copy of the memo to the following as indicated: the state board of nursing, the district superintendent, the state school nurse consultant, and the division of special education, department of education.
5. The RN should regularly notify his/her supervisor and others, as appropriate, that the unsafe situation continues to exist until such time as the issue is resolved. (p. 74)

One of the procedures routinely delegated to an unlicensed staff person is the administration of medications. School districts need to develop policies that address not only this issue but also a myriad of other issues related to the dispensing of pharmaceuticals, such as a student's right to self-medicate, to ensure not only the safety of the student but the safety of others in the educational facility. Guidelines are offered for the safe handling and administration of medications in the next section.

❦ Handling and Administration of Medication

In a recent survey by Francis and her colleagues (1996), it was found that during a 1-week period, in 36 public schools and 6 private schools in one Florida county, out of a population of 28,134 students, a total of 1,010 students (3.6%) received 5,411 total doses of medication during school hours. Medications ranged from over-the-counter drug formulations to narcotic analgesics, the most common being methylphenidate hydrochloride (Ritalin). While information is not given on precisely who administered these drugs, in discussing the implications of the finding, the authors made the following statements that seem to indicate that the

---

[4] National Association of State School Nurse Consultants (NASSNC) (1996). Delegation of school health services to unlicensed assistive personnel: A position paper of the National Association of State School Nurse Consultants. *Journal of School Health, 66,* 72–74. Copyright 1996 by NASSNC. Reprinted by permission.

pharmaceuticals were being given out by untrained, unlicensed staff persons:

> It was clear that the individuals giving the drugs did not know what they were giving to the student . . . . the individuals giving the drugs had no knowledge of the medications or their side effects. (p. 357)

In another recent study, there was an attempt to determine who exactly was involved in the provision of health-related procedures, including, among others, the administration of medications. Fryer and Igoe (1996), by means of a systematic random sample of all school districts in the United States, were able to determine that in 396 (82.15%) out of 482 school districts surveyed, school nurses were directly involved in the administration of medication, whereas school health assistants, clerks, or paraprofessionals were involved in the administration of drugs in 240 (49.8%) school districts. These figures are strikingly similar to those found by Heller and her colleagues in the state of Georgia (1997); in this study, it was reported that in 49% of the 147 school districts that responded, "anyone but the nurse" was providing medications to students. In breaking down the numbers in terms of unlicensed personnel performing health care procedures, it was found that in 6% of the districts teachers alone were dispensing medications, compared with 3% for paraprofessionals. Twenty-five percent of the time, "others" (i.e., principals, clinic workers, secretaries, or clerical staff) were reported to be giving out medications.

Several organizations and persons have attempted to provide guidelines to ensure the safe handing and administration of medications that might assist a particular district or school. The following guidelines are from the Committee on School Health of the American Academy of Pediatrics (AAP, 1993).[5] In addition to heeding the recommendations given here, school districts are advised to seek counsel regarding liability coverage for staff persons involved in the administration of the medication. For further information, see materials by Silkworth (1986a, 1993).

---

[5] American Academy of Pediatrics, Committee on School Health (1993). Guidelines for the administration of medication in school. *Pediatrics, 92,* 499–500. Copyright 1993 by the American Academy of Pediatrics. Reprinted by permission.

Physician-Prescribed Medications

1. The school should require a written statement from the physician that provides the name of the drug, the dose, the times when the medication is to be taken, and the diagnosis or reason the medicine is needed, unless the reason should remain confidential.
2. The physician should alert the school when a student might experience a serious reaction while receiving prescribed medication. The school may facilitate this communication by having a check-off space on its medication form to highlight this possibility.
3. The physician also should alert the school when the medication prescribed may cause a severe reaction even when administered properly. Any necessary emergency response should be outlined by the physician, either directly on the form or as an attachment describing the appropriate treatment.
4. The physician should state whether the child is qualified and able to self-administer the medication.
5. The parent or guardian should provide a written request that the school district comply with the physician's order. This may be a preprinted statement as a separate form, or the parent or guardian may indicate approval by signing on the same medication form used by the physician.

Parent- or Self-Prescribed Medications

1. Schools should consider developing guidelines for allowing children with minor illnesses into the classroom, with appropriate attention to recognized contagious disease policies and to pertinent state codes.
2. Students (especially older ones) should be allowed to self-medicate at school with over-the-counter medications when the parent has provided an appropriate note to the school specifying the medication, the amount to be given, the time it may be taken, and the reason for its administration.
3. The parent's note should include a statement relieving the school of any responsibility for the benefits or consequences of the medication when it is parent-prescribed and self-administered and acknowledging that the school bears no responsibility for ensuring that the medication is taken.

4. The school should retain the note for at least the duration of time the medication is used at school. It is preferable that the note remain a permanent part of the student's school health record.
5. The school should reserve the right to limit the duration of parent-prescribed medications and/or to require a physician statement for continued use of any medication beyond a specified time period.
6. The school also should restrict the availability of the medication from other students, with immediate confiscation of the medication and loss of privileges if medication policies are abused or ignored.
7. Special consideration may need to be given to adolescents for self-prescribing medications without parental request. Depending on the school's size and need for security regarding drug use, the school may require the same policy as required for younger children.

Security and Storage of Medication

1. All prescription medications brought to school should be in a container appropriately labeled by the pharmacist or the physician. All over-the-counter medications should be in their original container.
2. The school should make secure storage available for all medications, especially when administered by school personnel. The storage of self-administered medications is important when the school determines that the nature of the medication or the school environment requires greater security or when the student is too young or unreliable to personally maintain safe use.
3. The parent or physician should request that medications be secured by the school when this is appropriate. Some medications require refrigeration.
4. All parenteral medications and all drugs controlled by the Drug Enforcement Agency must be appropriately secured by the school.
5. A student may be allowed to carry his or her own medication when it does not require either refrigeration or security as determined by the school and when the school has granted permission for the student to take the medication.
6. The school may require that a student demonstrate the capability for self-administration and for responsible behavior. The school may need to

develop a "medication pass" that the student can show to any inquiring school personnel to verify that he or she has school permission for carrying and taking medication.
7. For selected medications or circumstances, the school should consider the convenience of administering a medication when the treatment may have an impact on the medical outcome. Prepared syringes of epinephrine for treating serious allergic reactions are one example. Answers to questions, such as when the medication will be stored, who is responsible for the medication, and who will carry the medication for field trips, should be defined in advance to maintain medication security and safety while ensuring timely treatment.

In discussing these policies, the Committee on School Health concluded with the following comments:

> As policies and related procedures are determined, school administrators and physicians must be aware of the variations among states regarding legal requirements and constraints on who can legally administer medications in schools. Protection of the safety of the child (including immediate access to life-sustaining medications, e.g., epinephrine for severe insect bite allergies) and the legal rights of school personnel who dispense medications must share equal concern. The rights of children to take ever-increasing responsibility for their own health should be strongly considered. When state codes or statutes prohibit such self-administration of medication or a child's or parent's right to participate in other health procedures, advocacy efforts by the school on behalf of the child are indicated and should be strongly considered. We recommend that advice of knowledgeable school medical consultants and legal counsel experienced in school health affairs be sought as these policies, procedures, and monitoring guidelines are determined.

Provision of Specialized Health Care Procedures

School districts must also ensure that they have clear policies regarding the provision of **specialized health care procedures** (e.g., chest physiotherapy, administration of oxygen, catheterization). School staff should view the provision of health care procedures with the same degree of vigilance as they would the administration of medications. The child's physician should be requested to submit information on the nature of the procedure, the frequency or time schedule of the procedure, and any precautions that should be taken during the procedure. In performing any health care procedures, the safety of the staff from communicable diseases, such as AIDS and hepatitis B, is of prime concern. In the following section, information on how to safely handle blood and other body fluids is discussed.

❦ Contact with Body Fluids: Universal Precautions

Throughout this book suggestions have been given on how to care for children and young adults with physical and medical challenges in the school system. Some of the care that has been outlined is what would be referred to by many as "basic first aid." In the past, if an individual saw a person who appeared to be injured, in most cases, the first person would rush to the assistance of the second, without much thought to his or her own safety. Today, however, with the fear of catching AIDS and other communicable diseases, such as hepatitis B, people may be responding a little more cautiously.

Since school staff may not be aware that a particular student in their school has a bloodborne pathogen, it is best that they respond as if *all* students are infected. To this end, the Centers for Disease Control and Prevention (CDC) use the term **universal precautions** to describe the techniques, outlined below, that should be applied to *all*, not just those with a communicable disease, to attempt to prevent the spread of infection. The CDC has issued the following blunt warning to medical personnel that also applies to those in nonmedical settings (1988): "Under universal precautions, blood and certain body fluids of *all* patients are *considered potentially infectious* for human immunodeficiency virus (HIV), hepatitis B virus (HBV), and other bloodborne pathogens" (p. 377, italics added).

Those fluids to which universal precautions apply are shown in Table 24.3. In dealing with those fluids, which are in the "apply" column (i.e., those fluids which can be the source of a life-threatening infection), the use of **personal protective equipment** (also referred to in the medical literature as a **barrier**), such as gloves, gowns, lab coats, masks, and protective eyewear, is critical. For those fluids that are in the "do not apply" column, caregivers are

TABLE 24.3
Body Fluids to Which Universal Precautions Apply or Do Not Apply

BODY FLUIDS	
Precautions Apply	**Precautions Do Not Apply***
Blood and serous drainage from scrapes and cuts	Feces
Semen	Nasal secretions
Vaginal secretions (fluids produced by the mucous membrane of the vagina)	Sputum
	Saliva
Cerebrospinal fluid (fluid that circulates through brain and spinal cord)	Sweat
Synovial fluid (fluid found in joints, bursae, and tendons)	Tears
	Urine
Pleural fluid (fluid found between the various layers of the lungs)	Vomitus
	Breast milk
Peritoneal fluid (fluid found in the abdominal cavity)	***Note:**
Pericardial fluid (fluid found in the sac that surrounds the heart)	1. Universal precautions would apply to these body fluids if they contained visible blood.
Amniotic fluid (fluid that surrounds the developing fetus)	2. Even though universal precautions do not apply, you are advised to wash your hands after contact.

Source: Centers for Disease Control (1987, 1988).

urged to routinely wash their hands after exposure to these fluids, as they can be sources of less serious infections, such as GI or respiratory infections, but the need for additional protective equipment is not warranted unless the fluids contain blood.

Porter, Haynie, Bierle, Caldwell, and Palfrey (1997) have suggested that gloves be worn at the following times:

- When having contact with blood, other potentially infectious material, mucous membranes, and non-intact skin
- When changing diapers or assisting the student with cleansing after toileting or catheterization
- When changing dressings or bandages and sanitary napkins or tampons
- When providing mouth, nose, or tracheostomy care
- When the caregiver has broken skin on the hands or around the fingernails
- When cleaning up spills of secretions, blood, or other potentially infectious material
- When touching or cleaning items contaminated with secretions, blood, or other potentially infectious material (p. 76)[6]

All schools should have an adequate supply of disposable gloves, in all sizes, in readily accessible locations (Utah State Office of Education, 1995). Disposable gloves should not be used more than once, and care should be taken when removing the gloves to prevent contaminating your skin. The first glove should be removed by grasping the glove at the wrist and pulling downward while at the same time turning the glove inside out. To remove the second glove, while holding the first glove in the second-gloved hand, one should slip the fingers of the un-gloved hand under the second glove at the wrist and pull it down and inside out, sealing the first glove inside the second. All gloves should be disposed of in a covered, child-proof waste receptacle with a disposable plastic liner.

As mentioned in chapter 23, proper hand washing is the most important step in preventing the spread of disease. Suggestions for proper handwashing techniques are given in Table 24.4. All schools should be equipped with dispensable soap and disposable paper towels. A waterless skin antiseptic

should be used when soap and water are not available; however, an antiseptic should not be considered a substitute for the recommended handwashing procedure (Porter et al., 1997). Even if gloves are used, hands should be washed thoroughly after disposing of the gloves.

To minimize risk of contagion, the following precautions should be heeded by all school staff. For further information, school staff are encouraged to contact their regional branch of the United States Department of Labor, Occupational Safety and Health Administration (OSHA).

Provision of First Aid (Contact with Bodily Fluid)

1. Care should be taken when tending to a student who is bleeding (e.g., from a nose bleed or cut). All bleeding episodes should be managed in a manner that minimizes direct contact of the caregiver with blood. Water-impervious, disposable gloves (latex or vinyl) should be made available so that individuals who wish to further reduce the minute risk for contamination may opt for their use. However, under no circumstance should the urgent care of a bleeding individual be delayed because gloves are not immediately available (AAP, 1988).

2. Skin of the caregiver exposed to blood or other body fluids visibly contaminated with blood should be cleaned as promptly as is practical, preferably with soap and warm water. Skin antiseptics (e.g., alcohol) or moist, germicidal towelettes may be used if soap and water are not available (AAP, 1991a). If gloves have been worn by a caregiver, hands should be washed as soon as the gloves are removed. Gloves should be placed in a plastic bag or a lined trash can, secured, and disposed of daily (Brainerd, 1986).

3. Students who are old enough should be taught to wash their own cuts and to apply pressure to stop the bleeding. All open wounds (e.g., abrasions, cuts) should be covered with some type of bandage (e.g., a Band-Aid). If a student sees another person bleeding, he or she should be taught to seek the assistance of an adult rather than tend to the injured individual.

4. If, during a sporting event (e.g., hockey game), a bleeding wound occurs, the individual's participation should be interrupted until the bleeding

---

[6] Porter, S., Haynie, M., Bierle, T., Caldwell, T. H., & Palfrey, J. S. (1997). *Children and youth assisted by medical technology in educational settings: Guidelines for care* (2nd ed.). Baltimore: Paul H. Brookes. Copyright 1997 by Paul H. Brookes Publishing Co., Inc. Reprinted by permission.

TABLE 24.4
Handwashing Techniques to Minimize Transmission of Infections

1. Inspect your hands for any visible soiling, breaks, or cuts in the skin or cuticles.

2. Remove any jewelry.* If you have a watch on, push it up your arm as high as possible. Also push up the sleeves of your blouse or jacket so that they are well above the wrist.

3. Turn on the water and adjust water flow and temperature to ensure that it is not too hot or has too much flow. Warm water is needed to ensure proper action of the soap. Use cold water only if warm water is not available. Water that is too hot will remove the protective oils of the skin and will dry the skin, making it vulnerable to damage. Water that comes out of the tap with too much force is more likely to splash onto the floors and walls, possibly spreading the microorganisms.

4. With the water running, wet your hands and wrists. Ensure that your hands are lower than your elbows so that the water flows from the least contaminated areas (i.e., the wrists) to the most contaminated areas (i.e., the hands). Lather hands with soap. Liquid soap is preferable to bar soap, which can be a reservoir for bacteria. Use bar soap only when dispensed soap is not available.

5. Wash thoroughly for at least 30 seconds. If you have just handled a contaminated object (e.g., a dirty glass), wash for 1 minute. If you have been in direct contact with any type of bodily fluid (e.g., you have just changed a diaper), you should wash for up to 2 minutes. Use a firm, circular motion and friction and ensure that you wash the back of hands, palms, and wrists. Wash each finger individually, making sure that you wash between fingers and knuckles (i.e., interlace fingers and thumbs and move hands back and forth) as well as around the cuticles. Do not use too much pressure, as this may result in the skin being damaged.

6. Rinse thoroughly with warm water. Use a fingernail file or orange stick and clean under each fingernail while the water is still running. If a file or stick is not available use the fingernails of the opposite hand.

7. Shake hands to remove excess water. Dry your hands thoroughly using a paper towel, working upward from fingertips, to hands, to wrists, and finally to forearms. When drying, rather than rub vigorously, it is best to pat the skin. It is important that the hands be dried well to prevent chapping.

8. Turn off the taps using the paper towel you used to dry your hands. Use the paper towel to wipe the surfaces surrounding the sink. Dispose of the paper towel in a covered, child-proof receptacle with a disposable plastic liner.

9. Apply lotion, if desired, to keep skin soft, to reduce the risk of chapping, and to act as a barrier for invasion of microorganisms.

*Since microorganisms can lodge in the settings or stones of rings, it is recommended by some that staff working with students who need physical care do not wear *any* jewelry (Silkworth, 1986b); others have suggested that it is permissible to leave on a plain wedding band (Sitler, 1991).
Sources: Silkworth (1998b); Sitler (1991); Utah State Office of Education (1995).

has been stopped and the wound has been cleansed with an antiseptic and covered securely or occluded (AAP, 1991a). Similarly, if an open skin lesion is observed, it should be cleaned and covered. If a student's wound is infected with another student's fresh blood, gently bleed the wound, wash thoroughly with soap and water, apply a disinfectant, and call the student's doctor for further advice. If an injury occurs and no gloves are readily available (e.g., on the football field), a bulky towel should be used to cover the wound until an off-the-field location is reached where gloves can be used for a more definitive treatment (AAP, 1991a).

5. Students with oozing wounds (e.g., those with impetigo or herpes) should be taught not to touch the sore and then touch another individual; likewise, students who do not have an infectious condition should be encouraged not to be in direct contact with a peer who has an obvious disease. For example, students should be discouraged from placing their own fingers in the

mouths of others and vice versa. Individuals with respiratory or GI infections should be taught to never share food or drinks.

6. To prevent the spread of droplets, students should be taught to cover their mouths and noses when coughing or sneezing and use Kleenex tissues or handkerchiefs to blow their noses. Contaminated tissues should be properly disposed of (e.g., flushed down the toilet or placed in a covered garbage pail with a disposable plastic liner). Handkerchiefs should be washed in very hot water. All items that are contaminated by nasal secretions (e.g., from sneezing) or saliva (e.g., from drooling) should be cleaned with a mixture of bleach and water.

7. If a person is accidentally exposed to blood or body fluids, he or she should wash the contaminated area immediately with warm, soapy water. If the eyes or mouth is splashed, the person should irrigate the area thoroughly with warm, running water. A person cut or stuck with a needle should wash the area thoroughly and contact his or her physician for treatment. The incident should be documented and reported to the person's supervisor.

Other Safeguards

1. Teach children not to touch syringes or other sharp objects, particularly those that are of unknown origin. Transmission of communicable diseases is more likely to occur from contact with infected body fluids of unrecognized carriers than from contact from known carriers (Brainerd, 1986).

2. Proper diapering procedures must be followed. Guidelines are shown in Table 24.5. Toilet seats and diaper changing areas should be disinfected regularly using a fresh mixture of bleach and water.

3. Clothing and other nondisposable items, such as cloth diapers, that are soaked through with body fluids, such as urine, should be rinsed and placed in leak-proof plastic bags for transport home. Any persons handling such items are advised to wear disposable gloves (Brainerd, 1986). Contaminated clothing should be washed in hot water. A 1/2 cup of bleach should be added to the wash cycle.

4. Females need to be taught how to properly dispose of pads and tampons used during their menstrual period (i.e., place in plastic bag and seal with a knot). Cleaning staff who may be in con-

tact with pads or tampons should wear disposable gloves. If contact is made without any form of protection, the person should wash his or her hands immediately.

5. While saliva does not transmit HIV, because of potential fear on the part of those providing cardiopulmonary resuscitation, breathing (Ambu) bags and oral airways for use during cardiopulmonary resuscitation should be available in athletic settings for those who prefer not to give mouth-to-mouth resuscitation (AAP, 1991a).

Safe School-Cleaning Practices

1. All soiled surfaces (e.g. table tops, sinks, wrestling mats, toilet seats) should be promptly cleaned with a suitable disinfectant. A dilution of 1:10 to 1:100 bleach to water is the perfect disinfectant and should be prepared daily for use in the school. Other disinfectants include ethyl or isopropyl alcohol (70% U.S.P.) and various types of commercially available germicidal detergent; however, bleach is preferred, particularly for cleaning objects that may be put in the mouth (Brainerd, 1986).

2. Disposable towels or tissues should be used whenever possible and should be disposed of properly (in sealed plastic bag). Nondisposable cleaning utensils (e.g., mops, sponges, dust pans, buckets) should be rinsed in disinfectant.

3. Most schools have in place guidelines for the disposal of body fluids such as vomitus (e.g., covering spills with absorbent agents before vacuuming up). Cleaning staff should review these procedures to determine whether appropriate disinfection steps have been included (Brainerd, 1986). Vacuum bags should be disposed of properly, and cleaning utensils (broom, dustpan) should be disinfected.

In addition to ensuring that all staff are aware of proper procedures in dealing with body fluids, the American Federation of Teachers (1997), in the resource guide entitled *The Medically Fragile Child in the School Setting*, has made the following recommendations regarding the development of a

---

[7] American Federation of Teachers, AFL-CIO (1997). *The medically fragile child in the school setting* (2nd ed.). Washington, DC: Author. Copyright 1997 American Federation of Teachers, AFL-CIO. Reprinted by permission.

TABLE 24.5
Proper Diapering Procedures

1. Ensure that you have all the necessary equipment ready and that there is adequate privacy. Wash hands.

2. Cover the changing table or diapering surface with a disposable paper liner. Put on disposable gloves

3. Place the individual on the change table. **Do not leave the child alone for any reason.**

4. Remove the child's clothing and the soiled diaper, ensuring that the diaper does not touch your clothing. Fold inward so that the diaper is "wrapped" in its own plastic liner. If the child's clothing is soiled, place in a leak-proof plastic bag that can be properly secured and labeled. Do not reuse plastic grocery shopping bags because they are not leak-proof. Place diaper in a child-proof container, double-bagged with a leak-proof bag.

5. Cleanse the child's perineal area and buttocks with a premoistened disposable germicidal towelette, being careful to move from front to back, thereby decreasing the risk of urinary tract infection. Give particular attention to skin creases. Dispose of towelette by placing in container with soiled diaper. Dispose of paper underneath child in same manner. If the child's bottom is very dirty, use soap and water and a paper towel to thoroughly cleanse the area. Ensure that all traces of soap are removed by wiping with a clean, damp paper towel. Dispose of towels properly.

6. Ensure that the child's skin is dry before putting on a clean diaper. Do not put on any ointments or powders unless instructed by parents (who are responsible for supplying any such materials). If an ointment is requested, use a disposable spatula to remove from jar if it is not in a squeezable tube or bottle. Dispose of spatula along with towels.

7. Replace clothing or put on clean clothes. Make sure that any soiled clothes are sent home with the child at the end of the day.

8. Remove gloves and dispose of them safely.

9. Thoroughly wash the child's hands (or wipe with germicidal towelette if water is not available) before returning the student to the classroom.

10. Clean and disinfect (1:10 to 1:100 solution of bleach to water) the diapering area as well as any equipment and supplies that might have become contaminated. Thoroughly wash your hands.

11. Report any abnormal conditions (e.g., stool that contains blood, mucus, or pus; stool that is watery or liquid; stool that is abnormally hard; stool that is abnormally colored; stool that has an unusual odor; any breaks in skin, skin rashes, or bruises) to the appropriate person(s), (e.g., child's parent or guardian or your supervisor).

12. If the child appears to be having frequent bowel movements, record number and report to the appropriate person.

Sources: Heller, Alberto, Forney, & Schwarzman (1996); Silkworth (1986c); Utah State Office of Education (1995).

comprehensive communicable disease policy.[7] It is recommended by this body that the policy should at a minimum provide:

1. Training and updating of school staff on their risk as well as the risk to their children of communicable diseases and preventive measures that should be taken.

2. A comprehensive immunization program for staff and students; for instance, influenza vaccine should be offered to staff to reduce the number of respiratory illnesses during the year and hence improve attendance rates.

3. Treatment for infected staff and payment through worker's compensation (there should be a presumption that staff infections are work-related).

4. A plan to deal with outbreaks of infectious diseases that keeps staff informed of procedures which should be taken during the duration.

5. Information for pregnant school staff that explains how to safeguard the fetus against harmful expo-

sure and protection that provides medical removal with full pay and benefits in the event that a pregnant employee must leave the school setting.

6. Written information sent to parents on the appropriate measures to take at home with a child who is infected or infested. (p. 42)

🔹 Confidentiality: Protecting the Privacy of Student Educational Records

It is critical for schools to be aware that if the parents or guardians disclose information regarding their son's or daughter's medical condition, either orally or in writing, that information must be treated confidentially. This means that school staff cannot, in turn, disclose any information regarding the student to others, including other staff or the student's classmates (or their parents) without the written permission of the parents. School staff must recognize that all school records, including medical and health records that the school either creates or collects and maintains, are protected by the Family Educational Rights and Privacy Act of 1974, often referred to as FERPA, also known as the Buckley Amendment (Policy Studies Associates, Inc., 1997). Staff must also recognize that some states have laws that go beyond FERPA. Staff are wise to familiarize themselves with such policies.

In a recently published document by the Utah State Office of Education (1995, pp. 57–58), a policy on confidentiality of student records, which incorporates FERPA regulations, was presented.[8] The policy, which could be used as a model for other states, is as follows:

Each school district and educational agency maintaining student records must:

1. Formulate and adopt institutional policy and procedures concerning student records (FERPA, Reg. 99.5).
2. Annually notify parent and student in attendance or eligible students (attained 18 years of age and in attendance) of their rights pertaining to student records (FERPA, Reg. 99.6).
3. Maintain separate special education records.
4. Establish written procedures for the destruction of confidential records.

5. Maintain a record of each request and each disclosure of personally identifiable information from the education records of a student (FERPA, Reg. 99.32).
6. Provide public notice that directory information is to be developed (FERPA, Reg. 99.37).
7. Permit the parent of a student or an eligible student to inspect and review the education records of the student. Must comply with request within a reasonable time, but in no case more than 45 days after the request has been made (FERPA, Reg. 99.11).
8. Amend the education records of a student upon an approved request by parent or eligible student. The request is authorized when parent or eligible student believes the information is inaccurate or misleading or violates the privacy or other rights of the student. When a decision is made not to amend records, the parent or eligible student must be informed of their right to a hearing (FERPA, Reg. 99.20).
9. Establish procedures for and conduct a hearing as required when parent or eligible student appeals the denial to amend a student's educational records (FERPA, Reg. 99.22).
10. Also must be informed of their right to place in the record a statement commenting on the information or setting forth any reasons for disagreeing with the decision of the agency.

These confidentiality requirements can be breached only in emergency situations when knowledge of information is necessary to protect the health or safety of the student or other individuals (FERPA, Reg. 99.36).

Confidentiality is a controversial issue when it comes to disclosure of a student's being infected with HIV. A number of documents have addressed some of the issues; most have been proposed by the American Academy of Pediatrics. The Task Force on Pediatric AIDS, in a publication entitled "Education of Children with Human Immunodeficiency Virus Infection" (AAP, 1991b), made the following comments regarding confidentiality that should be heeded by all medical (and educational) personnel[9]:

1. As long as the presence of AIDS or HIV infection stigmatizes the patient and his family, confidentiality will continue to be an important issue in which the need to safeguard the rights of the patient must be balanced by the school's request for

---

[8] Utah State Office of Education (1995). *Utah guidelines and procedures for serving students with special health care needs.* Salt Lake City: Author. Reprinted by permission.

[9] American Academy of Pediatrics, Task Force on Pediatric AIDS (1991b). Education of children with human immunodeficiency virus infection. *Pediatrics, 88,* 645–648. Copyright 1991 by the American Academy of Pediatrics. Reprinted by permission.

information. The primary responsibility of the pediatrician is to serve the patient and the family. Because of the possible occurrence of fear and hysteria in the school, it is particularly important that disclosure of the child's HIV status to anyone in the school be done only with the informed consent of the parent and age-appropriate assent of the child.

2. Some parents may be unwilling to agree to even limited disclosure. This should not prevent the child from attending school.

3. HIV-infected children may need medication administered during the school day. . . . Because the nature of the medication may identify a child as previously HIV-infected, only those who are involved immediately with the medication decisions in school need to be informed. In most circumstances, only the school medical advisor and school nurse will need such information. The decision for this limited disclosure should be made by the child's physician and the parents.

In addition, the AAP has issued a policy regarding participation of students infected with HIV in athletic settings. The following five points are contained in this document (AAP, 1991a)[10]:

1. Athletes infected with HIV should be allowed to participate in all competitive sports. This advice must be reconsidered if transmission of HIV is found to occur in the sports setting.

2. A physician counseling a known HIV-infected athlete in a sport involving blood exposure, such as wrestling or football, should inform him [her] of the theoretical risk of contagion to others and strongly encourage him [her] to consider another sport.

3. The physician should respect an HIV-infected athlete's right to confidentiality. This includes not disclosing the patient's status of infection to the participants or the staff of athletic programs.

4. All athletes should be aware that the athletic program is operating under the policies in recommendations 1 and 3.

5. Routine testing of athletes for HIV infection is not indicated.

In addition, the Task Force on Pediatric AIDS (AAP, 1991b) has issued a set of guidelines regarding the education of children with HIV infection.[11] They are as follows:

1. All children with HIV infection should receive an appropriate education that is adapted to their evolving special needs. The spectrum of needs differs with the stage of the disease.

2. HIV infection should be treated like other chronic illnesses that require special education and other related services.

3. Continuity of education must be assured whether at school or at home.

4. Because of the stigmatization that still exists with this disease, it is essential that confidentiality be maintained by limiting disclosures and disclosing information only with the informed consent of the parents or legal guardians and age-appropriate assent of the student.

😈 Do Not Resuscitate (DNR) Orders

In chapter 3, the issue of DNR orders was introduced. Since the number of children with complex medical problems entering or reentering the school system is increasing, all school boards must develop a policy that provides staff with direction on how to respond to DNR requests by parents. Most policies that have been developed to date state that school staff *will* provide life-sustaining emergency care until such time that medical personnel are able to take over; however, recently the National Education Association (NEA, 1994) has developed a set of guidelines that specify the conditions that must be established before following a DNR order. The main points of the policy follow. In the preamble the following *caveat* is made:

> The . . . policy does not take a position on whether school districts *should*, as a matter of public policy, honor DNR orders; that is an issue that should be resolved at the state and/or local level. However, in considering a request to honor a DNR order, the school district should consult with counsel to

---

[10] American Academy of Pediatrics, Committee on Sports Medicine and Fitness (1991a). Human immunodeficiency virus [acquired immunodeficiency syndrome (AIDS) virus] in the athletic setting. *Pediatrics, 88,* 640–641. Copyright 1991 by the American Academy of Pediatrics. Reprinted by permission.

[11] American Academy of Pediatrics, Task Force on Pediatric AIDS (1991b). Education of children with human immunodeficiency virus infection. *Pediatrics, 88,* 645–648. Copyright 1991 by the American Academy of Pediatrics. Reprinted by permission.

determine what legal rights and responsibilities it has, including the applicability of a collective bargaining agreement.

This statement is similar to that adopted by the National Association of School Nurses (1995b), which states:

> It is the position of the National Association of School Nurses that DO NOT RESUSCITATE orders for medically fragile students must be evaluated on an individual basis at the local level, according to state and local laws. The local Board of Education should refer this matter to school district legal counsel for guidance.

NEA Policy on DNR Orders[12]

While requests to honor DNR orders must be handled on a case-by-case basis, NEA recommends that no request be granted unless the following minimum conditions are met:

1. The parents' or guardians' request is submitted in writing and accompanied by a written DNR order signed by the student's primary licensed physician.
2. The school district establishes a "team" consisting of the parents/guardians, student's physician, school nurse, student's teacher(s), appropriate support staff, and school superintendent or designee to consider the request. The team first considers all available alternatives. If no other option is acceptable to the parents/guardians, then the team develops a "medical emergency plan," which includes the following essential elements:
   a. The plan specifies what actions the student's teacher or other school employee should take in the event that the student suffers a cardiac arrest or other life-threatening emergency, e.g., telephone the local emergency medical service, apply emergency procedures as determined by the team, contact the parents/guardians, evacuate other students from the classroom, etc.
   b. All school employees who have supervision of the student during the school day are fully briefed on the procedures to follow in the event of a medical emergency involving the student.
   c. The student wears an ID bracelet while at school indicating that he/she is subject to a DNR order and a medical emergency plan.
   d. The parents execute a contract with the local emergency medical service providing that the service will honor the DNR order; a copy of the contract is made available to the superintendent/designee.
   e. The team agrees to review the plan and the student's health condition at least on an annual basis.
3. School staff receives the necessary training and counseling, and educational death and dying programs are provided for students. In the event that the student subject to a DNR order dies, appropriate counseling will be provided to staff and students.

For persons who want a more thorough discussion of the ethical and legal issues surrounding DNR orders and the school system, see the recent article entitled "To Honor and Obey—DNR Orders and the School" by Rushton, Will, and Murray (1995).

❦ Disagreement with Physician's Orders

Finally, there may be situations in which school staff may disagree with one of the orders given by a particular student's physician. School districts should develop a policy that deals with such situations (e.g., the use of a second independent physician, reimbursement of cost).

❦ Summary

As more and more children with special health care needs are entering or reentering the general education classrooms of the nation, school staff must be aware of some of the controversial areas, and school administrators must ensure that a set of policy guidelines that can assist staff in carrying out their day-to-day duties has been developed. In this chapter, some controversial issues have been addressed—delegation of school health services, handling and administration of medications, contact with bodily fluids, confidentiality, do not resuscitate (DNR) orders, and, finally, issues related to disagreement with physician's orders. The material included in this chapter should assist administrators in their endeavors to develop policies that are fair and equitable to all concerned—in particular, children with special health care needs, their families, and friends.

---

[12] National Education Association. (1994, June). *NEA policy on "do not resuscitate" orders.* Washington, DC: Author. Copyright 1994 by the National Education Association. Reprinted by permission.

References

American Academy of Pediatrics, Committee on Sports Medicine and Fitness. (1991a). Human immunodeficiency virus [acquired immunodeficiency syndrome (AIDS) virus] in the athletic setting. *Pediatrics, 88,* 640–641.

American Academy of Pediatrics, Task Force on Pediatric AIDS. (1991b). Education of children with human immunodeficiency virus infection. *Pediatrics, 88,* 645–648.

American Academy of Pediatrics, Committee on School Health. (1993). Guidelines for the administration of medication in school. *Pediatrics, 92,* 499–500.

American Federation of Teachers, AFL-CIO. (1997). *The medically fragile child in the school setting* (2nd ed.). Washington, DC: Author.

Brainerd, E. (1986). Guidelines for handling body fluids in schools. In G. Larson (Ed.), *Managing the school age child with a chronic health condition* (pp. 213–217). Wayzata, MN: DCI Publishing.

Centers for Disease Control and Prevention. (1987). Recommendations for prevention of HIV transmission in health-care settings. *Morbidity and Mortality Weekly Report, 36,* (suppl. no. 2S).

Centers for Disease Control and Prevention. (1988). Update: Universal precautions for prevention of transmission of human immunodeficiency virus, hepatitis B virus, and other bloodborne pathogens in health-care settings. *Morbidity and Mortality Weekly Report, 37,* 377–87.

DiCroce, H. R. (1990). Stop the world, they want to get on. *Health Progress, 71*(3), 80–92.

Francis, E. E., Hemmat, J. P., Treloar, D. M., and Yarandi, H. (1996). Who dispenses pharmaceuticals to children at school? *Journal of School Health, 66,* 355–358.

Fryer, G. E., & Igoe, J. B. (1996). Function of school nurses and health assistants in U.S. school health programs. *Journal of School Health, 66,* 55–58.

Heller, K. W., Alberto, P. A., Forney, P. E., & Schwartzman, M. N. (1996). *Understanding physical, sensory, and health impairments.* Pacific Grove, CA: Brooks/Cole.

Heller, K. W., Fredrick, L., & Rithmire, N. M. (1997). Special health care procedures in the schools. *Physical Disabilities: Education and Related Services, 15*(2), 5–22.

Johnson, M. P., & Asay, M. (1993). Who meets the special health care needs of North Carolina schoolchildren? *Journal of School Health, 63,* 417–420.

Johnson, M. P., Lubker, B. B., & Fowler, M. G. (1988). Teacher needs assessment for the educational management of children with chronic illnesses. *Journal of School Health, 58,* 232–235.

Joint Task Force for the Management of Children with Special Health Care Needs of the AFT, CEC, NASN, and NEA. (1990). *Guidelines for the delineation of the roles and responsibilities for the safe delivery of specialized health care in the educational setting.* Reston, VA: Council for Exceptional Children.

Koenning, G. M., Todaro, A. W., Benjamin, J. E., Curry, M. R., Spraul, G. E., & Mayer, M. C. (1995). Health services delivery to students with special health care needs in Texas public schools. *Journal of School Health, 65,* 119–123.

Krier, J. J. (1993). Involvement of educational staff in the health care of medically fragile children. *Pediatric Nursing, 19,* 251–254.

National Association of School Nurses. (1993). *Membership survey: Executive summary.* Scarborough, ME: Author.

National Association of School Nurses. (1995a). *Resolution and policy statements.* Scarborough, ME: Author.

National Association of School Nurses. (1995b). *DO NOT RESUSCITATE position statement.* Scarborough, ME: Author.

National Association of State School Nurse Consultants. (1996). Delegation of school health services to unlicensed assistive personnel: A position paper of the National Association of State School Nurse Consultants. *Journal of School Health, 66,* 72–74.

National Education Association. (1994, June). *NEA policy on "do not resuscitate" orders.* Washington, D.C.: Author.

Orelove, F. P., & Sobsey, D. (1991). *Educating children with multiple disabilities: A transdisciplinary approach* (2nd ed.). Baltimore: Paul H. Brookes.

Policy Studies Associates, Inc. (1997). Protecting the privacy of student education records. *Journal of School Health, 67,* 139–140.

Porter, S., Haynie, M., Bierle, T., Caldwell, T. H., & Palfrey, J. S. (1997). *Children and youth: Assisted by medical technology in educational settings: Guidelines for care* (2nd ed.). Baltimore: Paul H. Brookes.

Rushton, C. H., Will, J. C., & Murray, M. G. (1994). To honor and obey—DNR orders and the school. *Pediatric Nursing, 20,* 581–585.

Silkworth, C. S. (1986a). Administering medication. In G. Larson (Ed.), *Managing the school-age child with a chronic health condition: A practical guide for schools, families, and organizations* (pp. 147–152). Wayzata, MN: DCI Publishing.

Silkworth, C. S. (1986b). Handwashing techniques. In G. Larson (Ed.), *Managing the school-age child with a chronic health condition: A practical guide for schools, families, and organizations* (pp. 141–145). Wayzata, MN: DCI Publishing.

Silkworth, C. S. (1986c). Guidelines for diapering. In G. Larson (Ed.), *Managing the school-age child with a chronic health condition: A practical guide for schools, families, and organizations* (pp. 195–197). Wayzata, MN: DCI Publishing.

Silkworth, C. S. (1993). Supplement B. Medication procedure that allows self-medication—Sample. In M. B. Haas (Ed.), *The school nurse's source book of individualized healthcare plans* (pp. 143–144). North Branch, MN: Sunrise River Press.

Sitler, A. (1991). Medical asepsis. In B. L . Christensen & E. O. Kockrow (Eds.), *Foundations of nursing* (pp. 212–239). St. Louis: Mosby.

Sobsey, D., & Cox, A. W. (1991). Integrating health care and educational programs. In F. P. Orelove & D. Sobsey, *Educating children with multiple disabilities: A transdisciplinary approach* (2nd ed., pp. 155–185). Baltimore: Paul H. Brookes.

Utah State Office of Education. (1995). *Utah guidelines and procedures for serving students with special health care needs.* Salt Lake City: Author.

Weiss, J. (1997). *Providing safe health care: The role of educational support personnel.* [on-line]. Available at http://nea.org.

Sample Forms

Student Information Checklists

Student Information Checklist

Student's Name _____

Student's Teacher _____ School _____

Grade _____ School Year _____

Hospital Health Care Coordinator _____ Phone _____

School Health Care Coordinator _____ Phone _____

Education Coordinator _____ Phone _____

INFORMATION REQUIRED	PERSON RESPONSIBLE	INFORMATION REQUESTED (DATE)	INFORMATION OBTAINED (√ OR X)
1. MEDICAL Health History			
Present Physical Status			
Motor Skills			
Sensory Skills			
Specific Treatments			
Related Services			
Specialized Equipment			
Need for Activity Restrictions			
Other:			
2. ACADEMIC Cognitive/Academic Ability			
Communication Skills			
Adaptive Behavior/Self-Care			
Social/Emotional Development			
Need for Academic Accommodations			
Other:			

Additional Information Needed _____

_____

_____

Seizure Disorder Information Form

Student's Name _____

Student's Teacher _____ School _____

Grade _____ School Year _____

Physician's Name _____

Address _____ Telephone Number _____

Parents/Guardians _____ Home Phone _____

Work Phone (Mother) _____ Emergency Phone _____

Work Phone (Father) _____ Emergency Phone _____

Work Phone (Guardian) _____ Emergency Phone _____

1. What type of seizure disorder does your child have? _____

2. Is your child on any medication? ❏ Yes ❏ No If yes, please tell me about the medication (its name) and how it affects your child _____

   _____

   Have there been any recent changes in your child's medication? ❏ Yes ❏ No If yes, please describe the changes _____

   _____

3. Is your child on a specific diet? ❏ Yes ❏ No If yes, please tell me about the diet and how it affects your child _____

   _____

   Have there been any recent changes in your child's diet? ❏ Yes ❏ No If yes, please describe the changes _____

   _____

4. Is there any particular event(s) that causes the seizure to occur? (Please describe) _____

   _____

5. Does your child appear to sense that he or she is about to have a seizure? ❏ Yes ❏ No (Please describe)

   _____

   _____

   Does your child do or say anything to indicate that a seizure may occur? ❏ Yes ❏ No (Please describe)

   _____

   _____

6. Describe the kinds of behaviors that may occur during a seizure _____

   _____

Does your child's body stiffen? ❏ Yes ❏ No (Please describe) _____

Does your child's body shake? ❏ Yes ❏ No (Please describe) _____

Which parts of the body are most commonly affected? _____

_____

Does your child engage in repetitive, purposeless movements during a seizure? If yes, please describe _____

_____

7. Does your child often have difficulty breathing: (add comments)

before a seizure? ❏ Yes ❏ No _____

during a seizure? ❏ Yes ❏ No _____

after a seizure? ❏ Yes ❏ No _____

8. Does your child wet or soil often during a seizure? (add comments)

urine ❏ Yes ❏ No _____

feces ❏ Yes ❏ No _____

9. Does your child vomit often during a seizure? (add comments)

❏ Yes ❏ No _____

10. Is there often a change in color of your child's: (add comments)

lips? ❏ Yes ❏ No _____

nailbeds? ❏ Yes ❏ No _____

skin? ❏ Yes ❏ No _____

11. How long does your child's seizure typically last? _____

12. What types of behaviors do you see most commonly after a seizure? (Please describe) _____

Is your child usually drowsy? ❏ Yes ❏ No

For how long? _____

Is your child usually confused? ❏ Yes ❏ No

For how long? _____

13. Describe what you would like school staff to do when your child has a seizure _____

_____

14. Who do you want a staff member to call? _____

Signature _____   Date _____

Signature _____   Date _____

Diabetes Information Form

Student's Name _____

Student's Teacher _____ School _____

Grade _____ School Year _____

Physician's Name _____

Address _____ Telephone Number _____

Parents/Guardians _____ Home Phone _____

Work Phone (Mother) _____ Emergency Phone _____

Work Phone (Father) _____ Emergency Phone _____

Work Phone (Guardian) _____ Emergency Phone _____

1. What type of diabetes does your child have? _____

2. What type of insulin is your child taking? _____

   Is your child able to administer his or her insulin independently? _____

   _____

   Have there been any recent changes in your child's medication? ❑ Yes ❑ No If yes, please describe the

   changes _____

   _____

3. Is your child on a specific diet? ❑ Yes ❑ No If yes, please tell me about the diet (e.g., acceptable and

   unacceptable foods; quantities) _____

   List what he or she should have as a snack in the morning _____

   in the afternoon _____

   What do you suggest for in-school "treats" (e.g., parties)? _____

   Would you prefer to provide homemade "treats"? ❑ Yes ❑ No What kind? _____

   _____

   Have there been any recent changes in your child's diet? ❑ Yes ❑ No If yes, please describe the

   changes _____

   _____

4. What types of symptoms does your child experience during an **insulin reaction** (i.e., hypoglycemic reaction that

   results from too little sugar)? _____

   _____

   At what time of day is an insulin reaction most likely to occur? _____

   _____

5. What is the best source of sugar to treat the hypoglycemia? _____

_____

    How much should be given? _____

6. What types of symptoms does your child experience if she or he becomes **hyperglycemic** (i.e., too much sugar in the blood)? _____

_____

7. How much insulin should be administered if your child has a hyperglycemic reaction? _____

8. Who do you want a staff member to call in an emergency? _____

_____

9. Additional comments/special instructions _____

_____

_____

_____

_____

_____

Signature _____   Date _____

Signature _____   Date _____

School Accessibility Checklist

INDIVIDUALS WITH PHYSICAL DISABILITIES

PARKING	YES	NO	N/A
1. Accessible parking spaces clearly identified.	❏	❏	❏
2. Ten percent of spaces accessible.	❏	❏	❏
3. Accessible spaces located shortest possible accessible route to accessible building entrance.	❏	❏	❏
4. Accessible spaces are 12′ (3.7 m) wide and 8′ (2.4 m) high.	❏	❏	❏
5. Passenger drop-off zone with curb cuts near accessible entrance.	❏	❏	❏
6. Parking lot surface is smooth and hard.	❏	❏	❏

WALKWAYS AND RAMPS			
1. Walkways are 5′ (1.5 m) wide.	❏	❏	❏
2. Ramps are 3′ (.9 m) wide.	❏	❏	❏
3. Surfaces are hard, smooth, and non-slip.	❏	❏	❏
4. Surfaces are continuing and uninterrupted by steps or abrupt changes in level.	❏	❏	❏
5. Walkways are free of gratings or have openings maximum $\frac{1}{2}$″ (1.25 cm).	❏	❏	❏
6. Maximum gradient (slope) of all walkways and ramps is 5% (1:1).	❏	❏	❏
7. Walkways and ramps have 5′ × 5′ (1.5 m × 1.5 m) level platforms at top, bottom, and direction change and at 30′ (9 m) intervals.	❏	❏	❏
8. Handrails on both sides when slope is more than 1:20.	❏	❏	❏
9. Handrails mounted 32″ (81.3 cm) above ramp surface on both sides, 1 $\frac{1}{2}$″ (3.8 cm) from wall, and extend 12″ (30 cm) beyond top and bottom.	❏	❏	❏
10. Walkways and ramps free of obstructions, including vegetation and signs.	❏	❏	❏
11. Temporary ramps anchored securely.	❏	❏	❏
12. Night lighting throughout length of walkways or ramps.	❏	❏	❏

ENTRANCES, CORRIDORS, AND STAIRS			
1. Clearly marked routes from accessible parking to accessible entrances.	❏	❏	❏
2. Doorways minimum 3′ (.9 m) wide.	❏	❏	❏
3. Doors are easy to open (require maximum 8.5 lbs [3.8 Kg] for push or pull and 5 lbs [2.2 Kg] for sliding doors).	❏	❏	❏
4. Doormats stationary, flat or recessed, and maximum $\frac{1}{2}$″ (1.25 cm) thick.	❏	❏	❏
5. Door hardware on accessible doors can be easily grasped.	❏	❏	❏
6. Thresholds of exterior doors flush with floor to maximum height of $\frac{1}{2}$″ (1.25 cm).	❏	❏	❏
7. All stairs have closed risers.	❏	❏	❏
8. All stairs have risers of uniform height.	❏	❏	❏
9. Tread width at least 11″ (28 cm).	❏	❏	❏
10. Tread nosings project maximum 1 $\frac{1}{2}$″ (3.8 cm).	❏	❏	❏
11. Handrails on both sides of stairs.	❏	❏	❏

Source: Adapted from BC Ministry of Education & Ministry Responsible for Multiculturalism and Human Rights (1992). *Access to Conferences, Institutes and Meetings.* [Document RB0024]. Victoria, BC: Author. Reprinted by permission of the British Columbia Ministry of Education. Unauthorized duplication of this form is prohibited.

12. Handrails extend 12″ (30.5 cm) beyond top riser and beyond the bottom tread. ❏ ❏ ❏

13. Handrails are $1\frac{1}{4}$″ to $1\frac{1}{2}$″ (3.3 cm to 3.8 cm) in diameter and easy to grasp. ❏ ❏ ❏

14. Handrails are $1\frac{1}{2}$″ (3.8 cm) from the walk. ❏ ❏ ❏

15. Entrances, corridors, and stairs clear of protruding objects. ❏ ❏ ❏

16. Emergency evacuation equipment at top of stairs. ❏ ❏ ❏

PUBLIC WASHROOMS

1. Accessible washrooms clearly identified. ❏ ❏ ❏

2. Washroom entrances minimum 36″ (.9 m) wide. ❏ ❏ ❏

3. Mirror mounted to floor or down to backsplash (if mounted over sink, should be top-angled out from wall). ❏ ❏ ❏

4. Toilet seat raised 19″ (48 cm) from floor. ❏ ❏ ❏

5. Protective covering on hand basin hot water pipes to prevent burns. ❏ ❏ ❏

6. Accessible cubicle 5′ × 5′ (1.5 m × 1.5 m) [entrance minimum 36″ (.9 m) wide]. ❏ ❏ ❏

7. Temperature control on hot water faucet. ❏ ❏ ❏

8. Blade-type or push-button faucet controls. ❏ ❏ ❏

9. Accessible dispensers and hand dryers. ❏ ❏ ❏

10. Handle inside cubicle. ❏ ❏ ❏

11. Coat hook and shelf inside cubicle. ❏ ❏ ❏

12. Grab bars on both sides of cubicle from wall, 33″ to 36″ (84 cm to 90 cm) from floor. ❏ ❏ ❏

13. Non-slip, non-glare floor surface. ❏ ❏ ❏

PUBLIC TELEPHONES

1. Accessible telephones clearly identified. ❏ ❏ ❏

2. At least one telephone in any "bank" accessible with clear approach of 32″ (81 cm). ❏ ❏ ❏

3. At least one telephone in any "bank" has dial and coin slot 39″ (1 m) from ground with a cord minimum 29″ (74 cm) long. ❏ ❏ ❏

4. At least one telephone in any "bank" has amplification control. ❏ ❏ ❏

5. Telephone directories usable from wheelchair. ❏ ❏ ❏

6. TDD (Telecommunication Device for the Deaf) available. ❏ ❏ ❏

DRINKING FOUNTAINS

1. Upper edges of drinking fountain basins maximum 3′ (.9 m) above floor. ❏ ❏ ❏

2. Lever or push-button control located in front. ❏ ❏ ❏

3. If set in recessed area, recess maximum 3′ (.9 m) wide. ❏ ❏ ❏

MEETING ROOMS AND CLASSROOMS

1. Meeting rooms/classrooms centrally located. ❏ ❏ ❏

2. Route to meeting rooms/classrooms accessible. ❏ ❏ ❏

3. Meeting room/classroom doors 36″ (.9 m) wide. ❏ ❏ ❏

4. Thresholds of interior doors have maximum edge of $\frac{1}{2}$″ (1.25 cm). ❏ ❏ ❏

5. Floor surface level, non-slip, and non-glare. ❏ ❏ ❏

6. Adequate space provided for wheelchairs. ❏ ❏ ❏

7. Tables have 30″ (76 cm) clearance, floor to undersurface. ❑ ❑ ❑

8. Space between tables 42″ (107 cm). ❑ ❑ ❑

9. Stable temporary ramp available for podium or head table. ❑ ❑ ❑

10. Microphones accessible and flexible. ❑ ❑ ❑

11. FM systems available. ❑ ❑ ❑

12. Good lighting on speaker. ❑ ❑ ❑

13. Good lighting on interpreter. ❑ ❑ ❑

RESTAURANTS, CAFETERIAS, AND LOUNGES

1. Direct access available. ❑ ❑ ❑

2. Accessible tables 30″ (76 cm) floor to undersurface. ❑ ❑ ❑

3. Minimum width between tables 66″ (1.7 m). ❑ ❑ ❑

4. Cafeteria aisles between control railings and tray slides 34″ (86 cm). ❑ ❑ ❑

5. Cafeteria rail heights maximum 34″ (86 cm). ❑ ❑ ❑

6. Cafeteria cutlery and food display racks visible to individuals in wheelchairs. ❑ ❑ ❑

7. Cafeteria cutlery and food display racks within reach of individuals in wheelchairs. ❑ ❑ ❑

ELEVATORS

1. Elevator access to all facility levels. ❑ ❑ ❑

2. Accessible elevator controls, maximum 42″ (1 m) from floor. ❑ ❑ ❑

3. Cab dimensions at least 5′ × 5 ′ (1.5 m × 1.5 m). ❑ ❑ ❑

4. Clear door opening of 3′ (.9 m). ❑ ❑ ❑

5. Elevator stops within $\frac{1}{2}$″ (1.25 cm) of floors on each level. ❑ ❑ ❑

6. Space between floor and elevator platform maximum $1\frac{1}{4}$″ (3.3 cm). ❑ ❑ ❑

7. Elevator doors have an automatic safety system. ❑ ❑ ❑

8. Handrail mounted 3′ (.9 m) above floor. ❑ ❑ ❑

HAZARDS AND EMERGENCY PROCEDURES

1. Facility staff have received instructions about needs of individuals with disabilities, particularly emergency procedures. ❑ ❑ ❑

2. Emergency exits clearly marked. ❑ ❑ ❑

3. Emergency exits equipped with crash bars. ❑ ❑ ❑

INDIVIDUALS WITH VISUAL IMPAIRMENTS

WALKWAYS AND RAMPS

1. Surfaces are hard, smooth, and non-slip. ❑ ❑ ❑

2. Ramps have tactile warning surface. ❑ ❑ ❑

3. Handrails on both sides when slope is more than 1:20. ❑ ❑ ❑

4. Handrails mounted 32″ (81.3 cm) above ramp surface on both sides, $1\frac{1}{2}$″ (3.8 cm) from wall, and extend 12″ (30 cm) beyond top and bottom. ❑ ❑ ❑

5. Ramps and walkways free of obstructions, including vegetation and signs. ❑ ❑ ❑

ENTRANCES, CORRIDORS, AND STAIRS

	YES	NO	N/A
1. Doormats stationary, flat or recessed, and less than $\frac{1}{2}''$ (1.25 cm) thick.	❑	❑	❑
2. All stair risers of uniform height.	❑	❑	❑
3. Tread nosings do not project more than $1\frac{1}{2}''$ (3.8 cm).	❑	❑	❑
4. Handrails on both sides of stairs.	❑	❑	❑
5. Suspended stairs provided with sufficient warning devices, e.g., planters or railing.	❑	❑	❑
6. Entrances, corridors, and stairs clear of protruding objects.	❑	❑	❑

PUBLIC WASHROOMS

1. Accessible washrooms clearly identified.	❑	❑	❑
2. Non-slip, non-glare floor surface.	❑	❑	❑

MEETING ROOMS AND CLASSROOMS

1. Meeting rooms/classrooms centrally located.	❑	❑	❑
2. Floor surface level, non-slip, and non-glare.	❑	❑	❑
3. Lighting system non-glare, non-reflecting, and non-blinking.	❑	❑	❑

RESTAURANTS, CAFETERIAS, AND LOUNGES

1. Menus in braille and large print.	❑	❑	❑

ELEVATORS

1. Braille controls.	❑	❑	❑
2. Elevator stops within $\frac{1}{2}''$ (1.25 cm) of floors on each level.	❑	❑	❑
3. Elevator doors have automatic safety system.	❑	❑	❑

HAZARDS AND EMERGENCY PROCEDURES

1. Facility staff have received specific instructions about needs of individuals with disabilities; particularly emergency procedures.	❑	❑	❑
2. Boundary between pedestrian and vehicle area has tactile warning.	❑	❑	❑
3. Tactile warning present for hazards, e.g., floors, stairs, pools, and doors.	❑	❑	❑
4. Emergency exits clearly marked.	❑	❑	❑
5. Audible signals.	❑	❑	❑
6. Doors leading to dangerous areas have textured surface on handle, knob, or pull.	❑	❑	❑

INDIVIDUALS WITH HEARING IMPAIRMENTS

PUBLIC TELEPHONES

1. Accessible telephones clearly identified.	❑	❑	❑
2. At least one telephone in any "bank" has amplification control.	❑	❑	❑
3. TDD (Telecommunications Device for the Deaf) available.	❑	❑	❑

MEETING ROOMS AND CLASSROOMS

1. Lighting system non-glare, non-reflecting, and non-blinking.	❑	❑	❑
2. Meeting room/classroom has FM system.	❑	❑	❑

ELEVATORS

	YES	NO	N/A
1. Visual signals.	❏	❏	❏

HAZARDS AND EMERGENCY PROCEDURES

	YES	NO	N/A
1. Facility staff have received specific instructions about needs of individuals with disabilities, particularly emergency procedures.	❏	❏	❏
2. Emergency exits clearly marked.	❏	❏	❏
3. Emergency exits equipped with crash bars.	❏	❏	❏
4. Visual signals.	❏	❏	❏

Sample Individualized Health Care Plan (IHCP)

Student Individualized Health Care Plan

☐ 504

☐ Special Education

Student's Name _____ Birth Date _____

Student's Teacher _____ School _____

Grade _____ School Year _____

Physician's Name _____

Address _____ Telephone Number _____

Parents/Guardians _____ Home Phone _____

Work Phone (Mother) _____ Emergency Phone _____

Work Phone (Father) _____ Emergency Phone _____

Work Phone (Guardian) _____ Emergency Phone _____

Hospital Health Care Coordinator _____ Phone _____

School Health Care Coordinator _____ Phone _____

Education Coordinator _____ Phone _____

MEDICAL OVERVIEW

Brief Medical History _____

_____

_____

_____

Known Allergies _____

_____

_____

Medications _____

_____

Medication Authorization Form Attached for Each Medication ☐ Yes ☐ No

Specific Health Care Needs _____

_____

_____

Procedure Authorization Form Attached for Each Procedure ☐ Yes ☐ No

ADDITIONAL NEEDS/PLANS

Emergency Plan Attached ☐ Yes ☐ No

Recreational Activity Permission Form Attached ☐ Yes ☐ No

Transportation Plan Attached ❏ Yes ❏ No

Personnel Training Plan Attached ❏ Yes ❏ No

Entry/Reentry Checklist Completed ❏ Yes ❏ No

Other: _____

ADDITIONAL INFORMATION

Special Diet _____

_____

_____

Additional Information Attached ❏ Yes ❏ No

Special Safety Measures _____

_____

_____

Additional Information Attached ❏ Yes ❏ No

Special Equipment _____

_____

_____

Additional Information Attached ❏ Yes ❏ No

Other: _____

_____

_____

Additional Information Attached ❏ Yes ❏ No

PARENT/GUARDIAN AUTHORIZATION

We (I) _____ hereby request and approve this Individualized Health Care
               (name)

Plan for our (my) child _____ as prescribed by our (my) child's physician
                                    (name)

_____ .
          (name)

We (I) will notify the school immediately if there is any change to or cancellation of these orders. We (I)

release school personnel from liability should reactions result from any treatments given.

Signature _____ Date _____

Signature _____ Date _____

Next IHCP Review Date _____

Emergency Care Plan Forms

Emergency Care Plan (Generic)

Asthma Action Plan

Emergency Telephone Procedure

Accident Report

Emergency Care Plan

Student's Name _____

Address _____

School _____

Student's Teacher _____ Grade _____

School Nurse _____

Telephone Number _____

PLACE
PHOTO
HERE

PARENTS/GUARDIANS

NAME	TELEPHONE NUMBER		
	HOME	WORK	EMERGENCY
Mother:			
Father:			
Guardian:			

EMERGENCY TELEPHONE NUMBERS (IF APPLICABLE)

NAME	TELEPHONE NUMBER
Primary Physician: _____	_____
Specialist(s): _____	_____
_____	_____
_____	_____
EMT: _____	_____
Fire: _____	_____
Electrical Co.: _____	_____
Police: _____	_____
Gas Co.: _____	_____
Medical Supplier: _____	_____

TO BE FILLED OUT BY THE STUDENT'S PHYSICIAN

In my opinion, the following emergency procedures are medically appropriate for the above-named student and should be administered at school if necessary:

SIGNS/SYMPTOMS OF DISTRESS	ACTIONS TO BE TAKEN
_____	_____
_____	_____
_____	_____
_____	_____
_____	_____
_____	_____
_____	_____

Physician's Name _____   Signature _____

Address _____

Telephone Number _____   Date _____

PARENT/GUARDIAN AUTHORIZATION

We (I) _____ hereby request and authorize that the assistance listed above
(name)
be given to our (my) child _____ as prescribed by our (my) child's physician
(name)
_____ in the case of an emergency.
(name)
We (I) will notify the school immediately if there is any change to or cancellation of this emergency care

plan. We (I) release school personnel from liability should reactions result from this assistance.

Signature _____   Date _____

Signature _____   Date _____

The following staff persons are trained to deal with the child-specific emergencies listed above:

_____   _____

_____   _____

Asthma Action Plan

Student's Name _____

Student's Teacher _____ School Nurse _____

TO BE FILLED OUT BY THE STUDENT'S PHYSICIAN

In my opinion, the following actions are medically appropriate for the above-named student and should be administered at school if necessary:

If **peak flow meter reading** is between **90% and 100% of normal** or if the following symptoms are noted _____

_____

the following actions are to be taken:

MEDICINE	DOSAGE	FREQUENCY AND TIME	RESTRICTED ACTIVITIES
1.			
2.			
3.			
4.			

If **peak flow meter reading** is between **50% and 90% of normal** or if the following symptoms are noted _____

_____

the following actions are to be taken:

MEDICINE	DOSAGE	FREQUENCY AND TIME	RESTRICTED ACTIVITIES
1.			
2.			
3.			
4.			

If **peak flow meter reading** is less than **50% of normal** or if the child is showing signs of **respiratory distress, call the parents or doctor immediately. At the same time the following actions are to be taken:**

MEDICINE	DOSAGE	FREQUENCY AND TIME	RESTRICTED ACTIVITIES
1.			
2.			
3.			
4.			

If the student does not respond to the treatment prescribed and/or shows signs of acute respiratory distress (i.e., is struggling to breathe, develops blue/gray-colored lips or nail beds, becomes tired from the amount of energy required to breathe, is unable to talk or walk, or is not fully alert),

CALL 911 IMMEDIATELY

Physician's Name _____ Signature _____

Address _____

Telephone Number _____ Date _____

PARENT/GUARDIAN AUTHORIZATION

We (I) _____ hereby request and authorize that the assistance listed above
(name)
be given to our (my) child _____ as prescribed by our (my) child's physician
(name)
_____ in the case of an asthma episode.
(name)
We (I) will notify the school immediately if there is any change to or cancellation of this asthma action

plan. We (I) release school personnel from liability should reactions result from this assistance.

Signature _____ Date _____

Signature _____ Date _____

The following staff persons are trained to deal with the child-specific emergencies listed above:

_____   _____

_____   _____

EMERGENCY TELEPHONE PROCEDURE
To Be Posted by Every Telephone in the School

IF A LIFE-THREATENING EMERGENCY OCCURS:

1. **Be calm.** Take charge and act decisively.

2. **Stay with the student** or designate another adult to stay with the student. Reassure the student that help is being sought.

3. **DIAL 911 OR DESIGNATED AMBULANCE COMPANY.**

4. State **who** you are (teacher, nurse, paraprofessional).

    State **where** you are (name of school, address, city).

    State **what** is wrong with the student (signs and symptoms of distress).

    State **what measures** have been taken so far.

5. **Give specific directions to your location** (e.g., specific classroom) and how to get there (e.g., closest entrance).

6. **Do not hang up** until response team has indicated that they have all the necessary information.

7. **Notify or designate an adult to notify the school principal** or designated person (e.g., school nurse) that an emergency has occurred. State what actions have been taken.

The principal (or designee) is responsible for calling the parents or guardians and any other necessary persons (e.g., child's physician).

A school staff person (ideally someone who knows the child well) should accompany the child to the hospital in the ambulance.

Accident Report

To be filled out at the time of the accident by the person caring for an injured student who is referred to a doctor

Student's Name _____ Phone _____

Address _____ Age _____ Sex _____

Date _____ Time _____ Insurance _____

Grade _____ Teacher _____ School _____

Location of accident _____

Person in attendance _____

NATURE OF ACCIDENT (CIRCLE ALL THAT APPLY)		PART OF BODY INJURED (CIRCLE ALL THAT APPLY)		
Abrasion	Head injury	Abdomen	Eye*	Head
Bruise/bump	Fracture	Ankle*	Face	Knee*
Burn	Laceration	Arm*	Finger*	Leg*
Cut	Puncture	Back	Foot*	Teeth
Convulsion	Shock	Chest	Hand*	Wrist*
Dislocation	Sprain	Elbow*		
Other:		Other:		

*State left, right, or both

How did it happen? _____

_____

_____

Were parents notified?   Yes ❏   No ❏

Treatment and disposition _____

_____

Follow-up _____

Amount of time lost from school _____

Signature (principal, teacher, or nurse) _____

Source: *Implementation Guide for the Standards of School Nursing Practice*, 1993. American School Health Association, Kent, OH. Reprinted with permission. Unauthorized duplication of this form is prohibited.

Treatment Plan and Activity Restriction Forms

Medication Authorization Form

Student's Name _____

Student's Teacher _____ School _____

Grade _____ School Year _____

Parents/Guardians _____ Home Phone _____

Work Phone (Mother) _____ Emergency Phone _____

Work Phone (Father) _____ Emergency Phone _____

Work Phone (Guardian) _____ Emergency Phone _____

PHYSICIAN'S ORDER

Please complete one form for each medication.

Name of Medication _____ Dosage _____

Route _____ Time/Frequency _____

Reason for Medication _____

Possible Side Effects _____

_____ Termination Date _____

❑ Child is knowledgeable about this medication.   ❑ Child may self-administer medication.

If a dose is delayed or missed or if the child vomits up the medication, the following actions should be taken _____

_____

Physician's Name _____ Signature _____

Address _____

Telephone Number _____ Date _____

PARENT/GUARDIAN AUTHORIZATION

We (I) _____ hereby request and authorize that _____ be
      (name)   *(medication & dose)*

given to our (my) child _____ as prescribed by our (my) child's physician
                              (name)

_____ .
   (name)

Our (my) child may self-administer this medication.   ❑ Yes   ❑ No

We (I) will notify the school immediately if there is any change to or cancellation of this prescription. We (I) understand that we (I) will be responsible for supplying the prescription in a container appropriately labeled by the pharmacist or the physician. We (I) release school personnel from liability should reactions result from this drug.

Signature _____ Date _____

Signature _____ Date _____

Medication Administration Log (Part 1)

Student's Name _____

Student's Teacher _____ School _____

Grade _____ School Year _____

MEDICATIONS

1. Name of Medication _____ Dosage _____

   Route _____ Time/Frequency _____

   Possible Side Effects _____

2. Name of Medication _____ Dosage _____

   Route _____ Time/Frequency _____

   Possible Side Effects _____

3. Name of Medication _____ Dosage _____

   Route _____ Time/Frequency _____

   Possible Side Effects _____

I have been trained and understand how to administer the medications listed above.

Employee's Name _____ Initials _____ Date _____

Employee's Name _____ Initials _____ Date _____

Employee's Name _____ Initials _____ Date _____

PARENT/GUARDIAN AUTHORIZATION

We (I) hereby give permission for these personnel to administer the medications named above to our
(my) son or daughter _____ , prescribed by Dr. _____ , as or-
                              (name)   *(name)*
dered on the Medication Authorization Form, dated _____ , on file in the principal's/nurse's office.

Signature _____ Date _____

Signature _____ Date _____

Medication Administration Log (Part 2)

Student _____ Month/Year _____

KEY: √ = Medication taken	A = Student absent	X = School not in session

EMPLOYEES AUTHORIZED TO ADMINISTER MEDICATIONS

Name _____ Initial _____

Name _____ Initial _____

Name _____ Initial _____

WEEK OF _____ TO _____		Initial (After Administration)				
MEDICATION	TIME(S)	MON	TUE	WED	THUR	FRI
1.						
2.						
3.						

WEEK OF _____ TO _____		Initial (After Administration)				
MEDICATION	TIME(S)	MON	TUE	WED	THUR	FRI
1.						
2.						
3.						

WEEK OF _____ TO _____		Initial (After Administration)				
MEDICATION	TIME(S)	MON	TUE	WED	THUR	FRI
1.						
2.						
3.						

Health Care Procedure Authorization Form

Student's Name _____

Student's Teacher _____ School _____

Grade _____ School Year _____

Parents/Guardians _____ Home Phone _____

Work Phone (Mother) _____ Emergency Phone _____

Work Phone (Father) _____ Emergency Phone _____

Work Phone (Guardian) _____ Emergency Phone _____

PHYSICIAN'S ORDER FOR HEALTH CARE PROCEDURE

Please complete one form for each procedure.

Physical condition for which procedure is required _____

Procedure to be performed _____

Frequency/time schedule for procedure _____

Ability of student to assist or perform _____

Suggested setting _____

Precautions and possible adverse reactions _____

Procedures should be continued until (date) _____

Physician's Name _____ Signature _____

Address _____ Telephone Number _____

Date _____

PARENT/GUARDIAN AUTHORIZATION

We (I) _____ hereby request and authorize that the health care procedure listed
          (name)

on this form _____ be administered to our (my) child _____
          (name)   *(name)*

as prescribed by our (my) child's physician _____ .
                         (name)

We (I) will notify the school immediately if there is any change to or cancellation of this order. We (I) release school personnel from liability should reactions result from this treatment.

Signature _____ Date _____

Signature _____ Date _____

Health Care Procedure Log (Part 1)

Student's Name _____

Student's Teacher _____ School _____

Grade _____ School Year _____

PROCEDURE

Physical condition for which procedure is required _____

Procedure _____

Frequency/time schedule _____ Setting _____

Ability of student to assist or perform _____

Possible adverse effects _____

I have been trained and understand how to perform the procedure listed above.

Employee's Name _____ Initials _____ Date _____

Employee's Name _____ Initials _____ Date _____

Employee's Name _____ Initials _____ Date _____

PARENT/GUARDIAN AUTHORIZATION

We (I) _____ hereby give permission for these personnel to perform the
        (name)
procedure named above to our (my) son or daughter _____ , prescribed by
                                                          (name)
Dr. _____ , as ordered on the Health Care Procedure Authorization Form,
     (name)
dated _____ , on file in the principal's/ nurse's office.

Signature _____ Date _____

Signature _____ Date _____

Health Care Procedure Log (Part 2)

Student _____   Month/Year _____

EMPLOYEES AUTHORIZED TO PERFORM PROCEDURE

Name _____   Initial _____

Name _____   Initial _____

Name _____   Initial _____

DATE/TIME	PROCEDURE NOTES	INITIALS
Monday		
Tuesday		
Wednesday		
Thursday		
Friday		

DATE/TIME	PROCEDURE NOTES	INITIALS
Monday		
Tuesday		
Wednesday		
Thursday		
Friday		

Recreational Activity Permission Form

Staff at _____ School need assistance in determining what activities are appropriate for your

patient _____ , D.O.B. _____ . Please indicate with a √ those sports that you

think are **appropriate** based on _____ 's medical condition. The sports have been grouped

on the basis of degree of **contact.**

CONTACT/COLLISION	LIMITED CONTACT	NON-CONTACT
❑ Basketball	❑ Baseball	❑ Archery
❑ Boxing	❑ Bicycling	❑ Badminton
❑ Diving	❑ Cheerleading	❑ Body building
❑ Field hockey	❑ Canoeing/kayaking (whitewater)	❑ Bowling
❑ Football, touch	❑ Fencing	❑ Canoeing/kayaking
❑ Football, tackle	❑ Field, high jump	(flat water)
❑ Ice hockey	❑ Field, pole vault	❑ Crew/rowing
❑ Lacrosse	❑ Floor hockey	❑ Curling
❑ Martial arts	❑ Gymnastics	❑ Dancing
❑ Rodeo	❑ Handball	❑ Field, discus
❑ Rugby	❑ Horseback riding	❑ Field, javelin
❑ Ski jumping	❑ Racquetball	❑ Field, shot put
❑ Soccer	❑ Skating, ice	❑ Golf
❑ Team handball	❑ Skating, inline	❑ Orienteering
❑ Water polo	❑ Skating, roller	❑ Power lifting
❑ Wrestling	❑ Skiing, cross-country	❑ Race walking
❑ _____	❑ Skiing, downhill	❑ Riflery
❑ _____	❑ Skiing, water	❑ Rope jumping
❑ _____	❑ Softball	❑ Running
❑ _____	❑ Squash	❑ Sailing
❑ _____	❑ Ultimate Frisbee	❑ Scuba diving
	❑ Volleyball	❑ Strength training
	❑ Windsurfing/surfing	❑ Swimming
	❑ _____	❑ Table tennis
	❑ _____	❑ Track
	❑ _____	❑ Weight lifting
		❑ _____
		❑ _____
		❑ _____

Additional Comments/Qualifications _____

_____

Physician's Name _____ Signature _____

Address _____ Telephone Number _____

Parent/Guardian Name _____ Date _____

Recreational Activity Permission Form

Staff at _____ School need assistance in determining what activities are appropriate for your patient _____ , D.O.B. _____ . Please indicate with a √ those sports that you think are **appropriate** based on _____ 's medical condition. The sports have been grouped on the basis of degree of **strenuousness.**

HIGH TO MODERATE INTENSITY		
HIGH TO MODERATE DYNAMIC AND STATIC DEMANDS	HIGH TO MODERATE DYNAMIC AND LOW STATIC DEMANDS	HIGH TO MODERATE STATIC AND LOW DYNAMIC DEMANDS
❑ Boxing ❑ Crew/rowing ❑ Cross-country skiing ❑ Cycling ❑ Downhill skiing ❑ Fencing ❑ Football ❑ Ice hockey ❑ Rugby ❑ Running (sprint) ❑ Speed skating ❑ Water polo ❑ Wrestling ❑ _____ ❑ _____ ❑ _____ ❑ _____	❑ Badminton ❑ Baseball ❑ Basketball ❑ Field hockey ❑ Lacrosse ❑ Orienteering ❑ Table tennis ❑ Race walking ❑ Racquetball ❑ Soccer ❑ Squash ❑ Swimming ❑ Tennis ❑ Volleyball ❑ _____ ❑ _____ ❑ _____	❑ Archery ❑ Auto racing ❑ Diving ❑ Equestrian ❑ Field events (jumping) ❑ Field events (throwing) ❑ Gymnastics ❑ Karate or judo ❑ Motorcycling ❑ Rodeoing ❑ Sailing ❑ Ski jumping ❑ Water skiing ❑ Weight lifting ❑ _____ ❑ _____ ❑ _____
LOW INTENSITY (LOW DYNAMIC AND LOW STATIC DEMANDS)		
❑ Bowling ❑ Cricket	❑ Curling ❑ Riflery	❑ Golf ❑ _____

Additional Comments/Qualifications _____

_____

_____

Physician's Name _____ Signature _____

Address _____ Telephone Number _____

Parent/Guardian Name _____ Date _____

Recreational Activity Permission Form for Students with Altered Cardiovascular Function

Student's Name _____

Student's Teacher _____ School _____

Grade _____ School Year _____

Parents/Guardians _____ Home Phone _____

Work Phone (Mother) _____ Emergency Phone _____

Work Phone (Father) _____ Emergency Phone _____

Work Phone (Guardian) _____ Emergency Phone _____

PHYSICIAN'S RECOMMENDATION FOR RECREATIONAL ACTIVITY

Please check one box.

❏ Category I	*No Restrictions* Activities may include endurance training, interscholastic athletic competition, contact sports.
❏ Category II	*Moderate Exercise* Activities include regular physical education classes, tennis, baseball.
❏ Category III	*Light Exercise* Activities include nonstrenuous team games, recreational swimming, jogging, cycling, golf.
❏ Category IV	*Moderate Limitation* Activities include attending school, but no participation in physical education classes.
❏ Category V	*Extreme Limitation* Activities include homebound or wheelchair activities only.

Additional Comments/Qualifications _____

_____

Physician's Name _____ Signature _____

Address _____ Telephone Number _____

_____ Date _____

Occupational Activity Restriction Form for Students with Altered Cardiovascular Function

Student's Name _____

Student's Teacher _____ School _____

Grade _____ School Year _____

Parents/Guardians _____ Home Phone _____

Work Phone (Mother) _____ Emergency Phone _____

Work Phone (Father) _____ Emergency Phone _____

Work Phone (Guardian) _____ Emergency Phone _____

PHYSICIAN'S RECOMMENDATION FOR OCCUPATIONAL ACTIVITY

Please check one box.

❏ Category I	*Very Heavy Work* Peak load of 7.6 cal/min and above. Involves lifting objects in excess of 100 lb, with frequent lifting or carrying of objects weighing 50 lb or more.
❏ Category II	*Heavy Work* Peak load of 7.6 cal/min and above. Involves lifting 100 lb maximum, with frequent lifting or carrying of objects weighing up to 50 lb.
❏ Category III	*Medium Work* Peak load of 5.0 to 7.5 cal/min. Involves lifting 50 lb maximum, with frequent lifting or carrying of objects weighing up to 25 lb.
❏ Category IV	*Light Work* Peak load of 2.6 to 4.9 cal/min. Involves lifting 20 lb maximum, with frequent lifting or carrying of objects weighing up to 10 lb. Even though the weight may be negligible, a job is also in this category if it requires considerable walking or standing, or if it involves sitting most of the time with some pushing and pulling of arm or leg controls.
❏ Category V	*Sedentary Work* Peak load of 2.5 cal/min and below. Involves lifting 10 lb maximum and occasionally lifting or carrying such articles as dockets, ledgers, and small tools. Although a sedentary job is defined as one that involves sitting, a certain amount of walking and standing is often necessary. Jobs are sedentary if walking and standing are required only occasionally and other sedentary criteria are met.

Additional Comments _____

_____

Physician's Name _____ Signature _____

Address _____ Telephone Number _____

_____ Date _____

Recreational Activity Permission Form for Students with Altered Hematologic Function

Student's Name _____

Student's Teacher _____ School _____

Grade _____ School Year _____

Parents/Guardians _____ Home Phone _____

Work Phone (Mother) _____ Emergency Phone _____

Work Phone (Father) _____ Emergency Phone _____

Work Phone (Guardian) _____ Emergency Phone _____

PHYSICIAN'S RECOMMENDATION FOR RECREATIONAL ACTIVITY

Please indicate with a √ those sports you think are appropriate.

Category I Sports in which most individuals with hemophilia can participate	❏ Bicycling ❏ Fishing ❏ Frisbee ❏ Golf	❏ Hiking ❏ Martial arts: tai chi ❏ Swimming	❏ Walking ❏ _____ ❏ _____ ❏ _____

Category II
Sports in which the physical, social, and psychological benefits often outweigh the risks
	❏ Baseball
	❏ Basketball
	❏ Bowling
	❏ Diving, recreational
	❏ Gymnastics
	❏ Horseback riding
	❏ Ice-skating
	❏ Martial arts:
	   karate, kung fu,
	   tae kwon do
		❏ Mountain biking
		❏ River rafting
		❏ Roller-blading
		❏ Roller-skating
		❏ Rowing
		❏ Running and jogging
		❏ Skateboarding
		❏ Skiing, downhill
		❏ Skiing, cross-
		   country
		❏ Snowboarding
			❏ Soccer
			❏ Tennis
			❏ Track and field
			❏ Volleyball
			❏ Water-skiing
			❏ Weight lifting
			❏ _____
			❏ _____
			❏ _____
			❏ _____
			❏ _____

Category III Sports for which the risks outweigh the benefits for all hemophiliacs	❏ Boxing ❏ Diving, competetive ❏ Football ❏ Hockey: field, ice, street	❏ Lacrosse ❏ Motorcycling ❏ Racquetball ❏ Rock climbing ❏ Rugby	❏ Wrestling ❏ _____ ❏ _____ ❏ _____ ❏ _____

Additional Comments _____

_____

Physician's Name _____ Signature _____

Address _____ Telephone Number _____

_____ Date _____

Source: Adapted from Wiedel, J. D., Holtzman, T. S., Funk, S., Oldfield, D., Evans, D., Ward, R. S., & Low, M. (1996). *Hemophilia, sports, and exercise.* New York: National Hemophilia Foundation. Reprinted by permission.

APPENDIX ***E***

Transportation Plan

Transportation Plan for Students with Special Health Care Needs

STUDENT
PICTURE
HERE

Student's Name	
Address	Home Phone
School	Grade/Teacher
Parent/Guardian	Work Phone (Father)
	Work Phone (Mother)
Receives Medications ❏ Yes ❏ No	Possible Side Effects
Method of Mobility	Method of Communication
Childcare Provider	Emergency Drop-Off Site
Address	Phone

I. ADAPTATIONS/ACCOMMODATIONS REQUIRED

❏ None required   ❏ Chest harness

❏ Bus lift   ❏ Booster seat

❏ Seat belt   ❏ Other _____

❏ Wheelchair tie-downs   Walks to and from bus ❏ Yes ❏ No

                         Walks up and down stairs ❏ Yes ❏ No

Identify equipment that must be transported on bus and method of securing (including oxygen, life-sustaining equipment, wheelchair equipment, or communication device)

Source: Utah State Office of Education (1995). *Utah guidelines for serving students with special health care needs.* Salt Lake City: Author. Reprinted by permission. Unauthorized duplication of this form is prohibited.

II. POSITIONING OR HANDLING REQUIREMENTS

Describe

III. BEHAVIOR CONSIDERATIONS

Describe

IV. TRANSPORTATION STAFF TRAINING

Describe training

NAME OF INDIVIDUAL TRAINED	SIGNATURE	DATE

V. STUDENT-SPECIFIC EMERGENCY PROCEDURE
A copy of student's emergency information and emergency plan must be attached.

Personnel Training Plan

Personnel Training Plan

Student's Name _____

Student's Teacher _____ School _____

Grade _____ School Year _____

GENERAL TRAINING PLAN

DESCRIPTION OF TRAINING NEEDED	PERSON(S) NEEDING TRAINING	POTENTIAL TRAINER(S)	DATE OF TRAINING	TRAINING COMPLETE (√ OR X)
1.				
2.				
3.				
4.				

Recommendations for follow-up review _____

_____

_____

_____ Date of review _____

CHILD-/STUDENT-SPECIFIC TRAINING PLAN

DESCRIPTION OF TRAINING NEEDED	PERSON(S) NEEDING TRAINING	POTENTIAL TRAINER(S)	DATE OF TRAINING	TRAINING COMPLETE (√ OR X)
1.				
2.				
3.				
4.				

Recommendations for follow-up review _____

_____

_____

_____ Date of review _____

Staff person(s) in charge of training plan _____

_____

Communication Logs

Home–School Communication Log

Date _____

Notes from School _____

_____

_____

_____

_____

_____ Teacher _____

Notes from Home _____

_____

_____

_____

_____

_____ Parent _____

Date _____

Notes from School _____

_____

_____

_____

_____

_____ Teacher _____

Notes from Home _____

_____

_____

_____

_____

_____ Parent _____

Asthma Diary

Name _____

WEEK OF _____ TO _____

SYMPTOM	RATING	M	T	W	TH	F	COMMENTS
Wheeze	None . . . . 0 Little . . . . 1 Moderately bad . . . . 2 Severe 3						
Cough	None . . . . 0 Little . . . . 1 Moderately bad . . . . 2 Severe 3						
Sputum Volume Color: Yellow (Y) Green (G) Clear (C)	None . . . . 0 A few small blobs . . 1 Large amount . . . . . 2 Record color						
Activity Level Today	Quite normal . . . . . . 0 Can only run short distance. . . . . 1 Can only walk . . . . . 2 Too breathless to walk 3						
Asthma Attack(s)	Number of attacks Time of attack(s)						
Severity of Attack(s) Shortness of Breath	Mild . . . . 0 Mild to moderate . . . 1 Moderate . . . . 2 Moderate to severe . 3 Severe 4						
Length of Attack(s)	Record in minutes						
Possible Triggers	Indicate triggers if known or suspected						
Treatment	Drug(s) taken Number of doses						
Response to Treatment	Number of minutes before improvement was seen						
Other:							

Ventilator Checklist

Student's Name _____

Student's Teacher _____ School _____

Grade _____ School Year _____

Oxygen delivery days _____

Can student breathe on his or her own? ❑ Yes ❑ No

WEEK OF _____ TO _____

KEY: √ = checked, X = not checked, * = refer to notes						
1. EQUIPMENT	DAY/TIME	M	T	W	TH	F
Power source checked						
Oxygen source checked (record pressure or weight)						
Oxygen recorded (record percentage)						
Alarm checked						
Inspiratory pressure (record setting)						
High-pressure alarm checked						
Tidal volume setting checked						
Humidifier/water level checked						
Temperature (record if appropriate)						
Tubing water checked						
Respiratory rate (record bpm)						
Resuscitation bag checked						
2. STUDENT						
Tracheostomy care						
Respiratory treatments						
Breath sounds checked						
Suctioning						
Tubing changed						
PERSON RESPONSIBLE (initials)						

Additional comments _____

_____

_____

Source: Carroll, P. F. (1987). Home care for the ventilator patient: A checklist you can use. Adapted with permission from *Nursing87* 17(10):82–83, © Springhouse Corporation. All rights reserved. Unauthorized duplication of this form is prohibited.

Seizure Log

Student's Name _____

DATE	LOCATION	TIME	INTENSITY / LENGTH 1 (MILD) TO 10 (GRAND MAL)	CIRCUMSTANCES
4/3/97	In gym	2:58 PM	2/approx. 45 seconds each	Sitting, watching basketball game

Post-Seizure Report

Student's Name _____

Student's Teacher _____ School _____

Grade _____ School Year _____

1. BEHAVIORS BEFORE SEIZURE

   Student's location _____

   Student's activity _____

   Significant behavior (aura) noted before seizure (describe) _____

   _____

2. INITIAL BEHAVIOR DURING SEIZURE

   Significant behavior noted during initial stages of the seizure (describe) _____

   _____

   _____

3. BEHAVIORS DURING THE SEIZURE

   Time of the seizure _____ Approximate duration of seizure _____

   Did the student fall? ❑ Yes ❑ No Any apparent injury? ❑ Yes ❑ No

   Describe injury _____

   Was the student aware of his or her environment? _____

   Did the student's body: (1) stiffen? ❑ Yes ❑ No

                        (2) shake? ❑ Yes ❑ No

   Part(s) of the body involved? _____

   Color of: skin? _____ lips? _____ nails? _____

   Did the student wet or soil? urine ❑ Yes ❑ No

                            feces ❑ Yes ❑ No

   Did the student have difficulty breathing? ❑ Yes ❑ No _____

   Other behaviors: _____

   Who observed the seizure? _____

   _____

Source: Adapted from Kuhn, B. R., Allen, K. D., & Shriver, M. D. (1995). Behavioral management of children's seizure activity: Intervention guidelines for primary-care providers. *Clinical Pediatrics, 34,* 570–575. Copyright 1995 by Westminster Publications. Reprinted by permission. Unauthorized duplication of this form is prohibited.

4. BEHAVIORS AFTER THE SEIZURE

Was the student confused? ❏ Yes ❏ No _____

Was the student upset? ❏ Yes ❏ No _____

Was the student drowsy? ❏ Yes ❏ No _____

Did the student sleep? ❏ Yes ❏ No How long? _____

How was the student after sleeping? Did she or he resume normal activities? _____

_____

5. FIRST AID GIVEN

What type of first aid was given? _____

_____

By whom? _____

Was emergency response team called (911)? ❏ Yes ❏ No

If yes, why? _____

_____

6. FOLLOW-UP

Were the parents notified? ❏ Yes ❏ No

How? _____

By whom? _____

Additional comments _____

_____

_____

_____

Reported by _____ Reported to _____

Date _____

Feeding Log

Student's Name: _____

Prescribed amount of food (amount per feeding) _____ water _____

Temperature of food ❑ room temperature ❑ warmed to _____ degrees

Prescribed number of feedings per day _____

Prescribed medications per feeding _____

DAY	DATE AND TIME	AMOUNT OF FOOD	AMOUNT OF WATER	ADDITIONAL COMMENTS	INITIALS
Mon.					
Tues.					
Wed.					
Thurs.					
Fri.					

DAY	DATE AND TIME	AMOUNT OF FOOD	AMOUNT OF WATER	ADDITIONAL COMMENTS	INITIALS
Mon.					
Tues.					
Wed.					
Thurs.					
Fri.					

Ostomy Care Log

Student's Name _____ Month/Year _____

DAY AND DATE	TIME	POUCH EMPTIED	POUCH CHANGED	COMMENTS (stoma appearance, consistency)	INITIALS
	AM PM				
	AM PM				
	AM PM				
	AM PM				
	AM PM				
	AM PM				
	AM PM				
	AM PM				
	AM PM				
	AM PM				
	AM PM				
	AM PM				
	AM PM				
	AM PM				
	AM PM				
	AM PM				

Catheterization Care Log

Student's Name _____ Month/Year _____

DAY AND DATE	TIME	AMOUNT	COMMENTS (appearance, odor)	INITIALS
	AM PM			
	AM PM			
	AM PM			
	AM PM			
	AM PM			
	AM PM			
	AM PM			
	AM PM			
	AM PM			
	AM PM			
	AM PM			
	AM PM			
	AM PM			
	AM PM			
	AM PM			
	AM PM			

Diabetes Care Log

Student's Name _____

Date _____ Signature _____

BLOOD GLUCOSE LEVEL		INSULIN INTAKE (INJECTION OR BOLUS)			FOOD (MEAL OR SNACK)		PHYSICAL ACTIVITY		
Time	mg/dl	Time	Type	Units	Time	Contents of Food	Time	Intensity	Duration

Date _____ Signature _____

BLOOD GLUCOSE LEVEL		INSULIN INTAKE (INJECTION OR BOLUS)			FOOD (MEAL OR SNACK)		PHYSICAL ACTIVITY		
Time	mg/dl	Time	Type	Units	Time	Contents of Food	Time	Intensity	Duration

Source: Petray, C., Freesemann, K., & Lavay, B. (1997). Understanding students with diabetes: Implications for the physical education professional. Reprinted with permission from the *Journal of Physical Education, Recreation & Dance, 68*(1), 57–64. *JOPERD* is a publication of the American Alliance for Health, Physical Education, Recreation and Dance, 1900 Association Drive, Reston, VA 20191. Unauthorized duplication of this form is prohibited.

Entry/Reentry Checklist

Entry/Reentry Checklist

Student's Name _____

Student's Teacher _____ School _____

Grade _____ School Year _____

Please √ box when completed. If not applicable, mark with an X.

	DATE	PERSON RESPONSIBLE	√ OR X
REFERRAL RECEIVED			
Hospital Health Care Coordinator assigned	_____	_____	☐
School Coordinator assigned	_____	_____	☐
Education Coordinator assigned	_____	_____	☐
HEALTH TEAM ESTABLISHED			
Initial meeting held	_____	_____	☐
Additional meetings scheduled	_____	_____	☐
ASSESSMENT AND PLANNING			
Medical and educational information obtained	_____	_____	☐
Assessment data reviewed	_____	_____	☐
HEALTH CARE PLAN (HCP) DEVELOPED			
Orders (medication and procedures) obtained from physician	_____	_____	☐
HCP integrated into child's IEP	_____	_____	☐
Placement options reviewed	_____	_____	☐
Placement determined	_____	_____	☐
Personnel training plans developed	_____	_____	☐
Emergency care plans (plus backup) developed	_____	_____	☐
Transportation plan developed	_____	_____	☐
Equipment ordered and obtained	_____	_____	☐
Supplies ordered and obtained	_____	_____	☐
TRAINING OF STAFF AND STUDENTS			
Training schedule determined	_____	_____	☐
General training (staff and students)	_____	_____	☐
Child-specific training	_____	_____	☐
Training of child	_____	_____	☐
Follow-up inservice schedule determined	_____	_____	☐
Training of back-up personnel arranged	_____	_____	☐

ENTRY/REENTRY			
Ongoing communication process developed	_____	_____	☐
Final authorization obtained (HCP signed)	_____	_____	☐
Final review of preceding steps	_____	_____	☐
FOLLOW-UP AND EVALUATION			
Periodic reevaluation meetings scheduled	_____	_____	☐
Follow-up inservice conducted (as needed)	_____	_____	☐

Case Manager _____   Date _____

Sensory Impairment Checklists

ABCs of Vision: Indicators of Possible Vision Loss

ABCs of Hearing: Indicators of Possible Hearing Loss

ABCs of Vision: Indicators of Possible Vision Loss

Student's Name _____

Student's Teacher _____ School _____

Grade _____ School Year _____

Please indicate with a √ any signs of vision loss observed.

A = APPEARANCE

❏ Eyes deviate: One or both eyes turn ❏ in ❏ out ❏ up ❏ down

❏ One eye appears to be higher in relation to other

❏ Eyes do not track adequately in all directions of gaze (i.e., they do not move smoothly and in unison when following a moving object)

❏ Eyes are red-rimmed and ❏ lids are encrusted and swollen

❏ Eyes are inflamed (bloodshot) or ❏ watery (excessive tearing)

❏ Hordeola (styes) occur frequently on eyelids

❏ Nystagmus (involuntary, rhythmic movement of the eyes) is present, often rapid, and from side to side

❏ Irregular-shaped pupils; ❏ pupils uneven in size

❏ Opacities of the lens located behind the pupil

❏ Clouding of the iris (the colored part of the eye that circles the pupil)

❏ Enlargement of the eyeball

B = BEHAVIORS

❏ Rubs eyes excessively or ❏ pushes eyeballs with fingers or knuckles

❏ Blinks repetitively or constantly

❏ Shuts one eye when reading (e.g., leans on elbow or hand, covering eye to read)

❏ Tilts head or thrusts head forward

❏ Holds head at awkward angle when using eyes

❏ Holds reading material either very close or at arm's length

❏ Colors or writes with head resting on table

❏ Experiences difficulty with reading or other close-up work (e.g., makes many errors, such as confusing similar-shaped letters and misaligning horizontal and vertical series of numbers)

  ❏ Reads slowly; often skips lines

  ❏ Loses place frequently

  ❏ Needs frequent rest breaks

  ❏ Uses finger as a marker when reading

  ❏ Obvious head movement, side to side, when reading

❏ Avoids doing close-up work

- ❏ Irritable when required to perform close-up tasks

- ❏ Handwriting is immature

- ❏ Pages of notebooks poorly organized

- ❏ Unable to read print at distance (signs, blackboard); has to approach the blackboard in order to read

- ❏ "Tunes out" when required to read information on the chalkboard

- ❏ Student appears bored or disinterested in activities that are occurring at a distance (classroom demonstrations, assembly hall activities on stage)

- ❏ Squints or frowns when focusing at a distance; ❏ often does not acknowledge presence of others at a distance

- ❏ Clumsy: ❏ frequently trips or stumbles; ❏ difficulty recognizing drop-offs (curbs); ❏ walks cautiously and hesitantly; ❏ hesitant to run freely or to walk down stairs; ❏ frequently bumps into objects

- ❏ Fails to see objects that are not directly in line of vision (e.g., off to one side)

- ❏ Has difficulty judging distances (e.g., under- or over-shoots when picking up an object)

- ❏ Frequently asks, "What's going on?"

- ❏ Unable to see things at certain times of the day (e.g., at dusk, when dark)

- ❏ Doesn't remember what has been seen

C = COMPLAINTS

- ❏ Pain in the eyes

- ❏ Frequent headaches; ❏ "eyestrain"; ❏ periods of dizziness or ❏ nausea, particularly after close-up activities

- ❏ Itchy, burning, scratchy feeling in the eyes or eyelids

- ❏ Cannot see clearly (e.g., complains of blurred or fuzzy vision)

- ❏ Experiences double vision

- ❏ Color vision may be deficient (e.g., difficulty discriminating between certain colors, in particular red and green)

- ❏ Photophobia (increased sensitivity to light); ❏ cannot cope with glare

- ❏ Difficulty adjusting from near to far vision and back again (i.e., difficulty accommodating objects at different distances)

- ❏ Difficulty adapting to changes in lighting conditions (e.g., adaptation to light changes may be very slow when student goes from a brightly lit area to a dark one, and vice versa)

- ❏ Complains of seeing halos around lights

Additional comments _____

_____

_____

_____

_____

Observed by _____   Date _____

ABCs of Hearing: Indicators of Possible Hearing Loss

Student's Name _____

Student's Teacher _____ School _____

Grade _____ School Year _____

Please indicate with a √ any signs of hearing loss observed.

A = APPEARANCE

❏   Ear discharge

❏   Excessively heavy buildup of cerumen (earwax)

❏   Frequent upper respiratory tract infections (e.g., complains of cough, runny nose, sore throat)

❏   Fever

❏   Frequent use of cotton in the ears

❏   Breathing through the mouth

❏   Tired, strained expression, even early in the day after a good night's sleep

❏   Unusual concentration on speaker's face or mouth;   ❏   appears to "hear" better when facing the speaker (i.e., using lip reading to augment hearing)

❏   Cocks head or turns body towards speaker in order to hear;   ❏   "cups" ear with hand in order to direct sound

B = BEHAVIORS

❏   May appear to be bored or inattentive;   ❏   often appears to be "in a world of his/her own" or in his/her own "dream world"

❏   May be unresponsive to loud sounds (e.g., environmental sounds, such as thunder)

❏   Unwilling to mingle with others;   ❏   shy, timid, or withdrawn, preferring to play alone

❏   Reluctant to participate in oral activities

❏   Fails to follow spoken instructions and directions, especially in group settings

❏   Appears disoriented or confused when noise levels are high

❏   Frequently requests repetition of spoken words, particularly questions

❏   Says "Huh?" when unable to make an acceptable response

❏   Inconsistent or inappropriate responses to verbal requests (e.g., has trouble following directions; gives incorrect answers to simple questions)

❏   Responds more to facial expression and gestures than verbal explanation

❏   Works better in small-group or one-on-one situations

❏   Uses gestures to express desires rather than verbalization

❏   Relies on classmates for directions and assignments

❏   Frequently mimics behavior of peers

❏   Has poor articulation; in particular, misses some of the consonant sounds

- ❏ Voice is monotonal

- ❏ Vocalizations are too loud for the setting (e.g., sings and talks loudly)

- ❏ May yell or screech to express pleasure, annoyance, or need

- ❏ Talks too much, appearing to not want to relinquish control of the conversation

- ❏ When listening to radio or TV, etc., turns volume so loud that others complain

- ❏ Discrepancy between academic potential and performance

- ❏ May develop behavior problems (e.g., stubborn behavior) as a result of lack of comprehension

- ❏ Irritable when not understood

C = COMPLAINTS

- ❏ Earache or ear pain

- ❏ Sores in ears

- ❏ Sense of fullness or stuffiness in ears (ears feel "plugged")

- ❏ Tinnitus (ringing or buzzing in ears)

- ❏ Head noise

- ❏ Diminished hearing

Additional comments _____

_____

_____

_____

_____

Observed by _____   Date _____

Medical Conditions and Sports Participation

Medical Conditions and Sports Participation[*]

CONDITION	PARTICIPATE?
Bleeding disorder Explanation: Athlete needs evaluation.	Qualified yes
Cardiovascular diseases *Carditis* (inflammation of the heart) Explanation: Carditis may result in sudden death with exertion. *Hypertension* (high blood pressure) Explanation: Those with significant essential (unexplained) hypertension should avoid weight and power lifting, body building, and strength training. Those with secondary hypertension (hypertension caused by a previously identified disease) or severe essential hypertension need evaluation. *Congenital heart disease* (structural heart defects present at birth) Explanation: Those with mild forms may participate fully; those with moderate or severe forms, or who have undergone surgery, need evaluation. *Dysrhythmia* (irregular heart rhythm) Explanation: Athlete needs evaluation because some types require therapy or make certain sports dangerous, or both. *Mitral valve prolapse* (abnormal heart valves) Explanation: Those with symptoms (chest pain, symptoms of possible dysrhythmia) or evidence of mitral regurgitation (leaking) on physical examination need evaluation. All others may participate fully. *Heart murmur* Explanation: If the murmur is innocent (does not indicate heart disease), full participation is permitted. Otherwise the athlete needs evaluation (see congenital heart disease and mitral valve prolapse above).	No Qualified yes Qualified yes Qualified yes Qualified yes
Cerebral palsy Explanation: Athlete needs evaluation.	Qualified yes
Diabetes mellitus Explanation: All sports can be played with proper attention to diet, hydration, and insulin therapy. Particular attention is needed for activities that last 30 minutes or more.	Yes
Diarrhea Explanation: Unless disease is mild, no participation is permitted, because diarrhea may increase the risk of dehydration and heat illness. See "Fever" below.	Qualified no
Eating disorders: anorexia nervosa, bulimia nervosa Explanation: These patients need both medical and psychiatric assessment before participation.	Qualified yes

*For classification of sports by degree of contact or degree of strenuousness, please refer to listings in Appendix D.

Source: Adapted from the American Academy of Pediatrics, Committee on Sports Medicine & Fitness. (1994). Medical conditions affecting sports participation. *Pediatrics, 94,* 757–760. Copyright 1994 by the American Academy of Pediatrics. Used with permission of the American Academy of Pediatrics.

601

CONDITION	PARTICIPATE?
Eyes: functionally one-eyed athlete, loss of an eye, detached retina, previous eye surgery, serious eye injury Explanation: A functionally one-eyed athlete has a best corrected visual acuity of <20/40 in the worse eye. These athletes would suffer significant disability if the better eye was seriously injured as would those with loss of an eye. Some athletes who have previously undergone eye surgery or had a serious eye injury may have an increased risk of injury because of weakened eye tissue. Availability of eye guards approved by the American Society for Testing Materials (ASTM) and other protective equipment may allow participation in most sports, but this must be judged on an individual basis.	Qualified yes
Fever Explanation: Fever can increase cardiopulmonary effort, reduce maximum exercise capacity, make heat illness more likely, and increase orthostatic hypotension (low blood pressure caused by erect posture) during exercise. Fever may, rarely, accompany myocarditis or other infections that may make exercise dangerous.	No
Heat illness, history of Explanation: Because of the increased likelihood of recurrence, the athlete needs individual assessment to determine the presence of predisposing conditions and to arrange a prevention strategy.	Qualified yes
HIV infection Explanation: Because of the apparent minimal risk to others, all sports may be played that the state of health allows. In all athletes, skin lesions should be properly covered, and athletic personnel should use universal precautions when handling blood or body fluids with visible blood.	Yes
Kidney, absence of one Explanation: Athlete needs individual assessment for contact, collision, and limited contact sports.	Qualified yes
Liver, enlarged Explanation: If the liver is acutely enlarged, participation should be avoided because of risk of rupture. If the liver is chronically enlarged, individual assessment is needed before collision, contact, or limited contact sports are played.	Qualified yes
Malignancy Explanation: Athlete needs individual assessment.	Qualified yes
Musculoskeletal disorders Explanation: Athlete needs individual assessment.	Qualified yes
Neurologic disorders *History of serious head or spine trauma, severe or repeated concussions, or craniotomy* (surgical opening of the skull) Explanation: Athlete needs individual assessment for collision, contact, or limited contact sports, and also for noncontact sports if there are deficits in judgment or cognition.	Qualified yes
Convulsive disorder, well-controlled Explanation: Risk of convulsion during participation is minimal.	Yes
Convulsive disorder, poorly controlled Explanation: Athlete needs individual assessment for collision, contact, or limited contact sports. Avoid the following noncontact sports: archery, riflery, swimming, weight or power lifting, strength training, or sports involving heights. In these sports, occurrence of a convulsion may be a risk to self or others.	Qualified yes

CONDITION	PARTICIPATE?
Obesity Explanation: Because of the risk of heat illness, obese persons need careful acclimatization and hydration.	Qualified yes
Organ transplant recipient Explanation: Athlete needs individual assessment.	Qualified yes
Respiratory problems *Pulmonary compromise including cystic fibrosis* Explanation: Athlete needs individual assessment, but generally all sports may be played if oxygenation remains satisfactory during a graded exercise test. Patients with cystic fibrosis need acclimatization and good hydration to reduce the risk of heat illness.	Qualified yes
Asthma Explanation: With proper medication and education, only athletes with the most severe asthma have to modify their participation.	Yes
Acute respiratory infection Explanation: Upper respiratory obstruction may affect pulmonary function. Athlete needs individual assessment for all but mild disease. See "Fever" above.	Qualified yes
Sickle cell disease Explanation: Athlete needs individual assessment. In general, if status of the illness permits, all but high exertion, collision or contact sports may be played. Overheating, dehydration, and chilling must be avoided.	Qualified yes
Sickle cell trait Explanation: It is unlikely that individuals with sickle cell trait have an increased risk of sudden death or other medical problems during athletic participation except under the most extreme conditions of heat, humidity, and possibly increased altitude. These individuals, like all athletes, should be carefully conditioned, acclimatized, and hydrated to reduce any possible risk.	Yes
Skin: Boils, herpes simplex, impetigo, scabies, molluscum contagiosum Explanation: While the patient is contagious, participation in gymnastics with mats, martial arts, wrestling, or other collision, contact, or limited contact sports is not allowed. Herpes simplex virus probably is not transmitted via mats.	Qualified yes
Spleen, enlarged Explanation: Patients with acutely enlarged spleens should avoid all sports because of risk of rupture. Those with chronically enlarged spleens need individual assessment before playing collision, contact, or limited contact sports.	Qualified yes

Resources

Listings of Information and Referral Sites on the Internet

Medical/Pediatric Links

http://healthweb.org/index.html
http://med-www.stanford.edu/healthlib
http://pegasus.cc.ucf.edu/~wink/home.html
http://rdz.stjohns.edu/athenaeum//support/our-kids/Disweb/diswebtoc.html
http://sis.nlm.nih.gov/hotlines
http://www.aap.org
http://www.arcade.uiowa.edu/hardin-www/md.html
http://www.cc.emory.edu/WHSCL/medweb.html
http://www.childmedlib.org
http://www.chronicillnet.org
http://www.cmrg.com
http://www.geocities.com/HotSprings/1505/guide.html
http://www.healthfinder.gov
http://www.healthy.net/index.html
http://www.icondata.com/health/pedbase/pedlynx.htm
http://www.intelihealth.com
http://www.internetdatabase.com/med.htm
http://www.ktv-i.com
http://www.kumc.edu/gec/support/groups.html
http://www.med.jhu.edu/peds/pedspage.html
http://www.medhelp.org
http://www.medicinenet.com
http://www.medscape.com
http://www.ohsu.edu/cliniweb
http://www.pslgroup.com/docguide.htm
http://www.slackinc.com/child/pednet-x.htm
http://www.uab.edu/pedinfo/index.html
http://www.webcom.com/rusleepy/welcome.html

Special Education Links

http://ksc.geo.ukans.edu/seik.html
http://primes6.rehab.uiuc.edu/pursuit/pursuit-info/intro.html
http://specialed.miningco.com
http://unr.edu/homepage/maddux
http://www.acs.ucalgary.ca/~jross/Sped.html
http://www.blue.net/~goose/#add/adhd
http://www.dssc.org/frc/frc1.htm
http://www.edc.org/FSC/NCIP/links.html
http://www.edlaw.net
http://www.geocities.com/SunsetStripStudio/4436/links.html
http://www.hood.edu/seri/serihome.htm
http://www.ldonline.org/index.html
http://www.mcrel.org/connect/sped.html
http://www.mts.net/~jgreenco/jerdeb.html#Main Index
http://www.pitsco.com/pitsco/specialed.html

http://www.schoolnet.ca/sne/index2.html
http://www.sped.ukans.edu/disabilities
http://www.yahoo.com/text/Education/Special_Education

Disability Links

http://disability.com
http://home.earthlink.net/~dawwn
http://hyped.com/planetnews/planetnews/disabled/homepage.htm
http://nac.adopt.org/me8.html
http://TheArc.org/misc/dislnkin.html
http://www.abilityinfo.com
http://www.cais.com/naric/search
http://www.clark.net/pub/pwalker/Health_and_Human_Services
http://www.disabilityresource.com
http://www.disserv.stu.umn.edu/disability
http://www.dreamms.org/index.html
http://www.eskimo.com/~jlubin/disabled.html
http://www.gate.net/~fnd/index.html
http://www.icdi.wvu.edu/Others.htm#g11
http://www.igc.apc.org/pwd
http://www.indie.ca
http://www.irsc.org/index.htm
http://www.naotd.org/links.htm
http://www.nchrtm.okstate.edu/index_3.html#World
http://www.nichcy.org
http://www.radix.net/~ccd/welcome.html
http://www.tnet.com/cool
http://www.valleyweb.com/krrc/resource.html#5
http://www.yuri.org/webable
www.disabilityresources.org, or http://www.geocities.com/~drm

Websites for a Specific Illness or Disability

http://crossroads.gower.net/gtubehome.html (Gastrostomy Feeding)
http://toma.axess.com (Burns)
http://users.southeast.net/~bbaughn/childamp.htm (Amputation)
http://www.childrenwithdiabetes.com (Diabetes)
http://www.parentsplace.com/readroom/lead/index.html (Lead Poisoning)
http://www.tchin.org (Congenital Heart Disease)

Parents Links

http://familyeducation.com/directory.asp
http://homepage.usr.com/p/pex/4008.shtml
http://www.accessunlimited.com/children.html
http://www.coast-resources.com
http://www.coin.missouri.edu/community/soc-services/family-net/page1.html
http://www.familyvillage.wisc.edu
http://www.gate.net/~fnd/index.html
http://www.kidsource.com
http://www.npnd.org
http://www.parentsplace.com/genobject.cgi/welcome.html

http://www.php.com
http://www.specialchild.com/welc.html

Kids Links

http://cancernet.nci.nih.gov/occdocs/KidsHome.html
http://funrsc.fairfield.edu/~jfleitas/sitemap.html
http://thinkquest.phillynews.com/tq1997/11799/index.html
http://toma.axess.com
http://www.chmc.org/departmt/sibsupp
http://www.geocities.com/~drm//KIDS.html
http://www.harwich.edu/bear
http://www.maniax.com
http://www.wowusa.com/wowintro.html

Self-Help/Support Groups Links

http://kidshelp.sympatico.ca/links.html
http://www-med.stanford.edu/touchstone
http://www.cmhc.com/selfhelp.htm
http://www.metronet.com/~tlc/index.htm
http://www.support-group.com/index.htm

Listservs (Websites)

http://comeunity.com/special_needs/speclists.html
http://www.chmc.org/departmt/sibsupp/sibkids1.htm
http://www.inform.umd.edu/EdRes/Topic/Disability/InternetRes/Listserv
http://www.liszt.com

Listservs (Subscription Addresses)

http://www.familyvillage.wisc.edu/master.html
http://www.webcom.com/impulse/list.html
http://www.vicnet.net.au/vicnet/Adrian/dislist.htm
http://www.edlaw.net/public/listserv.htm

Sources of Free Information: Organizations Serving Individuals with Physical and Health Care Needs

http://www.ir-net.com

This directory, maintained by the Information and Referral Resource Network, lists agencies throughout the United States that provide services to the public. A wide variety of services are represented, including information and referral, social service, case management, health care, counseling, mental health, day care, education, employment, domestic violence, recreation, substance abuse, and welfare programs.

http://www.pacer.org/natl/yellowna.htm

Maintained by the Parent Advocacy Coalition for Educational Rights (PACER), this web site provides the addresses and phone numbers of national disability organizations and agencies. Links to other WWW sites are found at http://www.pacer.org/natl/wwwlinks.htm.

Other Sources

Other sources of information can be found at the following sites:
http://www.idealist.org
http://www.nichcy.org
http://sis.nlm.nih.gov/hotlines
http://nhic-nt.health.org/Scripts/Tollfree.cfm
http://infonet.welch.jhu.edu/advocacy.html
http://vtprojects.elps.vt.edu/FACT/tollfree/tollfree.html

Disease Condition	Phone Number	Website
AIDS		
CDC National AIDS Clearinghouse	(800) 458-5231	http://www.cdcnac.org
CDC National AIDS Hotline	(800) 342-2437	
HIV/AIDS Treatment Information Service	(800) 448-0440	http://www.hivatis.org
National Center for HIV, STD, and TB Prevention (NCHSTP)		http://www.cdc.gov/nchstp/od/nchstp.html
National Pediatric HIV Resource Center	(800) 362-0071	
Allergy/Asthma		
Allergy and Asthma Network/Mothers of Asthmatics	(800) 878-4403	http://www.podi.com/health/aanma
American Academy of Asthma, Allergy, and Immunology	(800) 822-2762	http://www.aaaai.org
American Lung Association (ALA)	(800) 586-4872	www.lungusa.org
Asthma and Allergy Foundation of America	(800) 727-8462	http://www.aafa.org
Asthma Society of Canada	(800) 787-3880	
Food Allergy Network	(800) 929-4040	
National Jewish Center for Immunology and Respiratory Medicine	(800) 222-5864	http://www.nationaljewish.org

Disease Condition	Phone Number	Website
Arthritis		
Arthritis Foundation	(800) 283-7800	http://www.arthritis.org
The Arthritis Society (Canada)	(800) 321-1433	
Birth Defects		
Association of Birth Defect Children	(800) 313-2223	http://www.birthdefects.org
March of Dimes Birth Defects Foundation	(888) 663-4637	http://www.modimes.org
National Easter Seal Society	(800) 221-6827	http://www.seals.com
Burns		
American Burn Association	(800) 548-2876	
Shriners Hospital Referral Line	(800) 237-5055	
The Phoenix Society	(800) 888-2876	
Cancer		
AMC Cancer Information and Counseling Line	(800) 525-3777	
American Cancer Society	(800) 227-2345	http://www.cancer.org
Canadian Cancer Society/Cancer Information Service	(888) 939-3333	
Candlelighters Childhood Cancer Foundation	(800) 366-2223	http://www.candlelighters.org
National Cancer Institute/Cancer Information Service	(800) 422-6237	http://www.nci.nih.gov/hpage/cis.htm
National Children's Cancer Society	(800) 532-6459	http://webusers.anet-stl.com/~nccs
Cerebral Palsy		
United Cerebral Palsy Associations, Inc.	(800) 872-5827	http://www.ucpa.org
Cleft Palate		
American Cleft Palate-Craniofacial Association	(800) 242-5338	http://www.cleft.com
Cooley's Anemia		
Cooley's Anemia Foundation	(800) 522-7222	http://www.thalassemia.org
Crohn's Disease		
Crohn's and Colitis Foundation of America	(800) 932-2423	http://www.ccfa.org
Cystic Fibrosis		
Canadian Cystic Fibrosis Foundation	(800) 378-2233	http://www.ccff.ca/~cfwww
Cystic Fibrosis Foundation (U.S.)	(800) 344-4823	http://www.cff.org
Diabetes		
American Diabetes Association	(800) 232-3472	http://www.diabetes.org
Juvenile Diabetes Foundation Canada	(800) 668-0274	
Juvenile Diabetes Foundation International	(800) 223-1138	http://www.jdfcure.com
Digestive Diseases		
National Digestive Diseases Information Clearinghouse	(800) 891-5389	http://www.niddk.nih.gov/Brochures/NDDIC
Disabilities (Nonspecific)		
Disabilities Information Access Line (DIAL)	(800) 922-3425	
National Clearinghouse on Post-Secondary Education for Individuals with Disabilities	(800) 544-3284	
National Information Center for Children and Youth with Disabilities	(800) 695-0285	
National Information Clearinghouse for Infants with Disabilities and Life-Threatening Conditions	(800) 922-9234	

Disease Condition	Phone Number	Website
Eating Disorders		
Eating Disorders Awareness and Prevention, Inc.		http://members.aol.com/edapinc
Epilepsy		
Epilepsy Foundation of America	(800) 332-1000	http://www.efa.org
Epilepsy Information Service	(800) 642-0500	
Genetic Diseases		
Alliance of Genetic Support Groups	(800) 336-4363	http://medhelp.org/www/agsg.htm
Head Injuries		
Brain Injury Association	(800) 444-6443	
National Institute of Neurological Disorders and Stroke	(800) 352-9424	http://www.ninds.nih.gov
Heart Disease		
American Heart Association	(800) 242-8721	http://www.amhrt.org
CHASER (Congenital Heart Anomalies—Support, Education, Resource)		http://www.csun.edu/~hfmth006/sheri/heart.html
Heart Information Service	(800) 292-2221	http://www.tmc.edu/thi/his.html
National Heart, Lung, and Blood Institute	(800) 575-9355	http://www.nhlbi.nih.gov/nhlbi/nhlbi.htm
Hemophilia		
Hemophilia and AIDS/HIV Network for the Dissemination of Information (HANDI)	(800) 424-2634	http://www.hemophilia.org
National Hemophilia Foundation	(888) 463-6643	http://www.infonhf.org
World Federation of Hemophilia		http://www.wfh.org
Hepatitis/Liver Disease		
American Liver Foundation	(800) 223-0179	http://sadico.ucsf.edu/alf/alfinal/homepagealf.html
Canadian Liver Foundation	(800) 563-5483	http://www.liver.ca
Hepatitis Foundation International	(800) 891-0707	http://www.hepfi.com
Hydrocephalus		
Guardians of Hydrocephalus Research Foundation	(800) 458-8655	
National Hydrocephalus Foundation	(800) 431-8093	
Immunodeficiency		
Immune Deficiency Foundation	(800) 296-4433	http://www.clark.net.net/pub/idf
Incontinence		
National Association for Continence (NAFC)	(800) 252-3337	http://www.nafc.org
Kidney Disease		
American Association of Kidney Patients	(800) 749-2257	http://www.aakp.org
National Kidney Foundation	(800) 622-9010	http://www.kidney.org
Lead Poisoning		
Alliance To End Childhood Lead Poisoning		http://www.aeclp.org
National Lead Information Center	(800) 424-5323	http://www.nsc.org/ehc/lead.htm
Leukemia		
Leukemia Society of America	(800) 955-4572	http://www.leukemia.org
National Children's Leukemia Foundation	(800) 448-3467	http://www.nclf.com
Muscular Dystrophy		
Muscular Dystrophy Association	(800) 572-1717	http://www.mdausa.org
Muscular Dystrophy Association of Canada	(800) 567-2873	

Disease Condition	Phone Number	Website
Osteogenesis Imperfecta		
Osteogenesis Imperfecta Foundation	(800) 981-2663	http://www.oif.org
Ostomy		
United Ostomy Association	(800) 826-0826	http://www.uoa.org
Pediculosis		
National Pediculosis Association	(800) 446-4672	http://www.headlice.org
Psoriasis		
National Psoriasis Foundation	(800) 248-0886	http://www.psorias.org
Rare Diseases		
National Organization for Rare Disorders	(800) 999-6673	http://www.pcnet.com/~orphan
Scoliosis		
National Scoliosis Foundation, Inc.	(800) 673-6922	
Scoliosis Association	(800) 800-0669	http://www.spine-surgery.com/Assoc/scoliosis
Sexually Transmitted Diseases		
CDC National STD Hotline	(800) 227-8922	
Herpes Resource Center	(800) 230-6039	
Sickle Cell Disease		
Sickle Cell Disease Association of America, Inc.	(800) 421-8453	http://SickleCellDisease.org
Skin Conditions		
American Academy of Dermatology	(888) 462-3376	http://www.aad.org
Spina Bifida		
Spina Bifida Association of America	(800) 621-3141	http://www.sbaa.org
Spina Bifida Association of Canada	(800) 565-9488	
Spinal Cord Injury		
National Spinal Cord Injury Association	(800) 962-9629	http://www.spinalcord.org
Spinal Cord Injury Hotline	(800) 526-3456	
Tay-Sachs Disease		
National Tay-Sachs and Allied Diseases Association	(800) 906-8723	
Miscellaneous		
American Association on Mental Retardation	(800) 424-3688	http://www.aamr.org
Association for the Care of Children's Health	(800) 808-2224	http://www.acch.org
Council for Exceptional Children	(888) 232-7733	http://www.cec.sped.org
Make a Wish Foundation	(800) 722-9474	http://www.wish.org/index.html

Author Index

Subject Index